FYFFES DICTIONARY OF IRISH SPORTING GREATS

JOHN GLEESON

Foreword by

JIMMY MAGEE

Published in Ireland by
Etta Place Publishers
75, Lucan Road
Chapelizod
Dublin 20.

ISBN 0 9521827 0 X

Typeset by Typeform Repro
Designed and Printed by Colorprint

Cover Photographs
Front, Left to Right: Paul McGrath, Dave McAuley, Nicky English and Sonia O'Sullivan
Back: Left to Right: Ollie Campbell, Philip Orr, Willie Duggan: Christy O'Connor Sen and Colm O'Rourke

FYFFES DICTIONARY OF IRISH SPORTING GREATS

JOHN GLEESON

ETTA PLACE PUBLISHERS

Dedicated To :

All sports administrators, coaches, and the sporting press.
All men and women who can sing in the morning.
The Artman, the Doctor, their Wifes and their Children.
Ballina R.F.C..
Aimee, Rachel, Justin, Mark and Jane.
Ballybunion Golf Club (heaven on earth).
Ballyclare R.F.C..
Bob Beamon.
Fintan Buckley.
Maurice Bembridge.
George Best.
Aubrey, Oliver and Mary Bourke.
Castleknock College.
Eugene Cawley (and all other 2nd row partners).
Christy Centro.
Colaiste Mhuire, Parnell Square.
David Coleman.
John Deacon and John Shackelton.
John Egan.
Nicky English.
Enniscrone Golf Club.
Jim Flynn.
Mike Gibson (simply the best).
David, Mark and Judy Gleeson.
Hermitage Golf Club.
Harry Hughes.
Kerry.
The Lark and the Boxcar.
Longford R.F.C..
John Patrick McEnroe.
Ronan McGivney.
Paul Maher and the Maher girls.
Oggie Moran.
Terry Mullen.
D'other Murphy.
Jack Nicklaus (the greatest).
Lester Piggott.
Bernie and Mary Quinn.
Pat and Sheelagh Richardson.
Mick Rowe (and all fast cars).
Charles Tanqueray.
Derek Turner (and all dummy sellers).
University College Dublin.
Wanderers R.F.C.
and to
All those Irish sporting greats who, through my ignorance
of their deeds, have been excluded from this book.

Foreword by JIMMY MAGEE

If love of sport can be obsessional, John Gleeson may be obsessed. How else can be explained the volume of work that he undertook to assemble the data for this remarkable tome. To contemplate such a dictionary is praiseworthy, to set about attaining it's publication is an achievemnet that makes it's compiler a man apart.

It takes remarkable enthusiasm for a person to author a dictionary ..... it takes courage for a sponsor to become involved in it's publication. This offering deserves to be gratefully received. It will stand as a reference work of considerable substance, protecting the sporting greats, whose deeds are recorded, against the ravages of time, their achievements at the instant recall of the curious.

In this spectacular first in the library of Irish sport, setting criteria may have been John Gleeson's biggest headache. Who merited inclusion and why? Assessing international fame against domestic success. It cannot have been easy, but I am happy with the book's final file of more than 2,500 names. Not all of them are famous in general terms, but each is renowned and revered in his or her own sport.

Kris Kristofferson once said 'the great thing about sports players is, they have a great sense of their own importance. They know the first thing that goes is your legs, the next thing that goes is your reflexes, the next thing to go are your friends". I would like to think that the people honoured in this book have and will continue to have millions of friends.

The names jump off the page: Eddie Boyle, a prince of gaelic football full-backs ...... Paddy Neville, a gentle giant who played hockey, soccer and cricket to the highest level ..... Michael Carruth to whom 'thanks' for the Barcelona memories ...... Stephen Roche with his never-to-be-forgotten triple-crown ..... Eamonn Coghlan, our first ever world athletics champion ..... Ronnie Delany whose Olympic track gold still sounds and stands supreme ..... Sean Kelly the indestructible ...... George Best of the fantastic skills ...... Liam Brady of the football class and culture ..... John Giles, perhaps the best of them all ..... Pat Jennings the greatest goalkeeper ..... Barry McGuigan, a wonderful fighting featherweight who raised the spirits on many a sweat-stained night.

All my special national heroes are there in John Gleeson's precious pages ..... the majestic Christy Ring... the artistic Eddie Keher ..... the Rackard brothers ..... Matt Connor, a genius in football boots ..... the Tipperary Doyles, John and Jimmy ..... Down's unforgettable triumvirate, O'Neill, McCartan and Doherty ..... Kerry's football legends and the Dubs who gave them so many great runs for their money.

Sport has always been a large patch on the fabric of Irish society. We enjoy and are proud of our sports heroes. We talk about them as though they were school pals ..... we argue about their values and vulnerabilities, setting ourselves up as experts as we bask in their reflected glory.

In Ireland there are more discussions and debates about sport than even politics: teams are chosen, players are dropped, reputations are gnarled. Hours are spent on the subject. Bill Shankly, the legendary Liverpool manager once said "sport isn't a matter of life and death, it's more important than that". Outrageous. Of course. Although in Ireland sometimes one wonders if Shankly wasn't right.

Imagine, for a moment, the amount of work that it has taken to get this book between the covers. Printed detail is easy to read and maybe even easy to digest but we are inclined to be unaware of the effort it takes to procure the information. Aim at the impossible and get the unusual, this is what John Gleeson may have done. His FYFFES Dictionary of Irish Sporting Greats will answer many a question and no doubt pose more than a few in clubs and pubs, hotels and households in years to come.

The man who tried his best and failed is superior to the man who never tried at all. The people in this book tried their best and succeeded, making them truly superior. Of course, every day someone new is attaining their goal, at world, Olympic, All-Ireland level. When they've met the criteria demanded by John Gleeson, then he'll include them in the next edition of the FYFFES Dictionary of Irish Sporting Greats.

In the meantime, marvel at his labour of love. He sought and he gleaned enough data to drive the average man or woman 'bananas'. John Gleeson did the next best thing ...... he went to bananas ..... to Fyffes who were so impressed that they agreed to sponsor the book. I am sure that every sports person honoured on the following pages will or would have deemed their inclusion to be an important acknowledgement of their place in the society of Irish sporting heroes.

When last seen John Gleeson was on his way to the human 'battery-charger', there to re-charge and repose before plunging into his next project. I believe that I was right in that opening paragraph, he is obsessed by the irresistible attraction of the world's only unrehearsed drama ..... sport.

Jimmy Magee.

Dublin, June 1993.

A WORD FROM THE PROMOTER **FYFFES plc**

We are delighted to be associated with the publication of this most exhaustive record of sports personalities from our island. It has given us particular pleasure to facilitate the bringing of this very professional work to the point where it can be accessed by the general public. Our small population can often mean that the sales outlook for such works cannot justify their production. Fyffes have been the catalyst in overcoming these obstacles in this case.

Fyffes are famed for their bananas, and in recent times the nutritional values of Fyffes bananas, widely recognised as the energy fruit, have become known to all involved with sports and an active life-style. Our involvement with this work therefore, is appropriate as:

- *our bananas are the ideal snack to take before, during and after exercise to maintain energy levels; sound nutritional reasons for this exist;*
- *the brand Fyffes was introduced in 1929. This makes it the oldest banana brand in the world showing that it has stamina, a property which our fruit can impart to all competitors!*

We wish John Gleeson untold success with this his first substantial publication. We applaud his tenacity and dedication to accuracy, and we commend this work to all interested in sport and sports personalities.

Neil V McCann
Chairman

GLEESON, JOHN.

Sportsman, sports fan, writer and publisher. Born in Tralee, Co Kerry, 20th December 1953. A product of Colaiste Mhuire of Parnell Square (where he played gaelic football badly) and Castleknock College (where he was a winning captain in basketball and swimming, and won billiards and snooker titles); he won a bronze medal at the Leinster Schools intermediate high jump in 1970, and played for the Castleknock College rugby side the the Leinster Schools Senior Cup in 1971. He later played rugby for Wanderers, U.C.D., Ballina (winning Connacht Junior Cup and League medals in 1977 and 1978) and Longford RFCs. He played rugby for the Connacht 'B' side 3 times in 1978 (and claims to be the only Munster-born Leinster-man to win an away match in Ulster while playing for Connacht). Latterly taking to golf, he is a former member of Enniscrone GC, and is a member of Hermitage Golf Club. His brothers David and Mark have played senior club rugby, and his uncle Der Gleeson was an Irish rugby selector 1969-1972. This is his 2nd published work.

Introduction

This book began out of a sense of frustration. I was researching another project, and found that I wanted specific information about various Irish sportspersons. I found this very hard to come by, annoyingly so as there is a multitude of Irish sports books available. So on the spur of the moment I decided (wisely?) to do something about this anomaly.

The problems I began to face were enormous. Being born in 1953, my first real comprehension of the joy of sporting greatness I think started with Bob Beamon's jump into immortality at the Mexico Olympics of 1968. Therefore no matter how much a sports fan I was, and no matter how eager, it was a major task to try to comprehend what had happened in Irish sport before 1968. I had never seen Christy Ring play (not even on television); I only knew Jackie Kyle by reputation; T.G. McVeagh might well have been a British Cabinet Secretary; I had never heard of Mabel Cahill, or Lory Meagher, or Denis Horgan, or Bertie Peacock, or John Pius Boland; or ..... What's more I only knew about Christy Ring by word-of-mouth. I did not know exactly what he had achieved, apart from the fact that he had won 8 All-Ireland Senior Hurling Championship medals with Cork. So unless I could find a book to give me this information (in fact a fine biography does exist for this genius, as does also for a few other of our sporting heroes), my ignorance would remain.

So, modelling myself on the format of a mixture of a dictionary of biography and a Who's Who, I decided to jump headlong into this project that you find on the following pages. My first conclusion, on completion of a 5 year task, try as best as I could to be objective, to include the cream of all sports, to include all the most important details about each individual, is that I have failed to live up to my intention. I know that there must be at least a few hundred other sportspersons who probably deserve to be included in a dictionary such as this. I also know that there are probably thousands of Irish sportspersons who think they have a unique reason to warrant inclusion. I would like to think, also, that there are many thousand who have played (or who still are playing their sports) who would aspire to being included in such a work. This may sound pompous from a sportsman whose pinnacle of sports achievement would not warrant inclusion in a book containing 50,000 Irish sportspersons, but I see this book as a neccessary first step, a watershed, and that hopefully it's 2nd edition will, down the road, 'get it right'.

I have avoided including sports administrators, managers and coaches (unless a certain level of achievement in their sport is obvious) not because they do not deserve recognition, but because it would have made the book imbalanced, much longer, and much more difficult for me to research (I have plans, as a future project, to cover these worthy people in some detail). No, this was to be a book of performers.

Let me say from the outset that I take full responsibilty for each entry, it's accuracy, and it's relevance, but in my defence let me add that many obstacles came my way. Irish sports books are very common, but when trying to find out specific information about the deeds of any individual, it was often extremely difficult. In some sports there are enough books written to make my task of researching their great players comparatively easy (soccer, golf and rugby are good examples). Other sports are not so good, and G.A.A., for all the good books written about it, suffers from lack of the type of detail that I required. Some of our minority sports associations have very limited facilities, and it is to their eternal credit that I have come up with some fine entries from their adminstrators (I mention here only two of the many, who were typical of some of the wonderful voluntary help given to me: Harry Havelin on motor cycling and Michael Johnston on rowing).

Because of the distinct lack of research material available on some of our minority sports, and difficlty on my part in extracting from those connected with the sport that I contacted anything solid enough to use, some minority sports persons may be disappointed with the quality of their contribution to this work. This I regret, but would only be too glad to cure this problem in the next up-dated edition, if someone is willing to assist me in upgrading their particular sport's input.

In all sports some criteria have been set to warrant inclusion, in a lot of cases with consultation with their relevant associations. For example, in both soccer and rugby, one of the criteria used for each sport was that any player who accumulated 10 international caps is automatically included. Obviously, as international matches are far more frequent now that say back in the 1920's or 1930's, a balance may be lost, but if this gives a slight bias towards modern sportspersons, I have no defence. In gaelic games one criteria used is that every player to win an All-Star award is included (these are regarded in the sport as a top honour), and that by doing so I may again favour modern players. I know somebody will come up with many more players who, in their opinion, would have won copious All-Stars in the pre All-Star period. My only answer to that is : HELP !

Basically what I am saying is that if this first edition helps to create enough debate and controversy (as I hope it does), then the revised edition, planned for 3 or 4 years hence, will be vastly improved. If any sports associations, county or provincial secretary, any club official, any relation of a past sportsperson ignored in this book, or even any entrant himself or herself, feel that something is lacking, or that an entry can be improved, I beg them to write to me care of the publishers.

Please accept this work as a first step in my quest to ensuring that the deeds of our best sportspersons are remembered in the future.

JOHN GLEESON

September 1993.

Acknowledgements

My 2 main acknowlegements go to my father Des Gleeson and to Paul Maher, both of whom know how much help they have given me, and enough to say that without their help this project would never have been completed. Philip Halpenny from Fyffes was the catalyst by which our happy arrangement came about, and to him much thanks is due. My thanks also to Sean and Declan Walshe of Colorprint and to John Shackleton. The cover was designed by the very capable Tony Cerasi. The colour photos have been supplied by Inpho (thanks especially to Billy Stickland); the black and whites have been supplied by Danny Thornton of Independent Newspapers (and thanks to him). The 'golden oldies' photos are from a collection supplied by Paul Harris of Dublin Public Libraries (Paul gave other hints etc which I found invaluable).

Great help was given to me at individual sports level by (amongst others) the following:

— In Camogie, Sheila Wallace, Joe Golden, and especially Mary Moran (P.R.O.), all of the Cumann Camogaiochta na nGael.

— In golf, Pat Turvey of the I.L.G.U.: Bill Menton, Phil Coonagh, Barry O'Connor.

— In Rugby, Edmund Van Esbeck of the Irish Times: my father, Des Gleeson.

— In Mens Hockey, R David Balbirnie, Keith Morrow. In ladies hockey, Anita Manning.

— In badminton, Audrey Kinkead of the B.U.I., Frank Peard.

— In boxing, George Peters, Pam Kelly of the I.A.B.A..

— In croquet, Jane Shorten of the C.A.I..

— In Equestrian Sports, Michael Stone, Secretary General of the Equestrian Federation of Ireland: Michael Slavin of R.T.E., Donal Corry.

— In Gymnastics, Richard Farrell of the I.A.G.A.

— In Motor Cycling, Harry Havelin.

— In Motor Rallying, Alex Sinclair of the R.I.A.C..

— In Netball, Maura Butler of the R.I.N.A..

— In Pitch and Putt, Michael Hayes of the P.P.U.I.

— In Rowing, Micheal Johnston, former President of the I.A.R.U..

— In Table Tennis, Tony Martin, Hon Secretary of the I.T.T.A. (Irish Table Tennis Association).

— In Squash, Maura Doyle and Shirley O'Regan of the Irish Women's Squash Rackets Association, and Brendan Ryan of the Irish Squash Rackets Association.

— In Ladies Gaelic Football, to Christy Byrne and Brendan Dardis of the I.L.G.F.A.

— In Fencing, to Shirley Armstrong Duffy.

— Many other people who have helped me in my research: many individual sportspersons, to whom I am eternally grateful; Mary Murray of Kenmare Library; Fiona Tobin of Carrick-on-Suir; Paul Kelly, etc.

— Library staff in many Irish libraries have been of enormous help (especially those in the ILAC Centre and Trinity College), and even some in the U.S.A. and Australia.

".... and if I can
remember
what you had
I'll die a happy man."

WILLIAM GOLDMAN (1969)

A

ADAIR, RHONA (later became MRS CUTHELL).

Amateur international golfer. Club: Portrush (where she won 3 of her major titles). Born in 1878, she died in 1961. She won the prestigious British Ladies Championship twice at the turn of the century, in both 1900 and 1903, being runner-up in 1901. She also won the Irish Ladies Championship 4 times in succession, in 1900, 1901, 1902, and 1903, and played in a Home International match in 1905. A rival and contemporary of the Hezlett sisters (cv), she had the distinction of once defeating the famous 'Old' Tom Morris off level terms. In 1930 she became President of the I.L.G.U.

ADAMS, CHARLES.

Rugby international forward. Born in December 1883, he died in Malahide in 1965. Club: Old Wesley, and the Barbarians. Ten times a Leinster interprovincial 1908-1913, he won 16 rugby international caps for Ireland between 1908 and 1914 in the years leading up to World War One, scoring one international try, and playing in the sharing of the International Championship of 1912. He toured South Africa with the British team in 1910. A civil servant, he was a member of the Barbarians Committee.

ADAMS, RONNIE J.

Rally car driver. An Ulsterman, he won many Irish rallies, and in 1955 he was placed 8th in the highly prestigious Monte Carlo Rally. The following year, in 1956, he became the first Irish driver to actually win the Monte Carlo Rally (the only other being Paddy Hopkirk cv), when along with Frank Bigger and Derek Johnston, he won the race in a Mark VII Jaguar.

AGAR, ROBERT Dunlop (BOB).

Rugby international 2nd row, flanker and No 8 forward. Born in Fenagh Co Carlow, 29th February 1920. Club: Malone. A product of Mountjoy School and Kilkenny College, he won 10 senior rugby international caps for Ireland between 1947 and 1950, including playing in some of the games of the Grand Slam/Triple Crown years of 1948 and 1949. A policeman, he was also a Barbarians player.

AHEARNE, DANIEL (DAN).

Triple Jump athlete. Born in Limerick. When he broke the world record for the triple jump in 1910 at 15.52 metres (50'1"), he made 2 landmarks: he was the first man to break the 'barrier' of 15 metres for the discipline: and by breaking the record of his brother Tim (cv), he ensured that they became only the 2nd of 3 (and 2nd Irish) set of brothers to break individual world records. He finished 6th in the triple jump in the 1920 Olympic Games in Antwerp, representing the U.S.A., with a jump of 46'2".

AHEARNE, Leslie FERGUS Patrick (GUS).

Rugby international scrum-half. Born in Cork, 16th March 1963. Clubs: U.C.C. (captaining them to win the Munster Senior League title in 1984-1985), Dolphin, and Lansdowne (winning a Leinster Senior Cup medal in 1991). An Irish Universities representative, he won the first of his 15 international caps (to date) against England in 1988 before winning any other representative honours, and has scored one international try. He has toured with Ireland to France in 1988, to North America in 1989, to Namibia in 1991, and to New Zealand in 1992. A member of the World Cup squad in the 1991 World Cup, his father Gerald played rugby for Munster.

AHEARNE, MICHAEL ('GAH').

G.A.A. hurling forward, Cork. Club: Blackrock. He won 4 All-Ireland Senior Hurling Championship medals with Cork, in 1926, 1928 (scoring a Liam McCarthy Cup final record score of 5 goals and 4 points, 19 points, in the final against

Galway), 1929 and in 1931, and played on the losing All-Ireland S.H.C. final team of 1927. He was also a member of the Cork side which won the first ever National Hurling League final in 1926, and of the side which won this accolade again in 1930. A great score getter, he won his only Railway Cup winner's medal in 1929, after being on the Munster side beaten in the inaugural final of 1927. He is a younger brother of Paddy 'Balty' Ahearne (cv).

AHEARNE, TIMOTHY J (TIM).

Triple jump and long jump athlete. Born in Athea, Co Limerick, 2nd April 1888 (or 18th August 1885?), he died in 1968. He won a gold medal in the triple jump at the 1908 Olympic Games in London (and became the only sportsman representing Great Britain to win Olympic gold in the field events until Lynn Davies won the long jump 56 years later in 1964). He finished 8th in the long jump in the same Games, and also competed in the standing long jump and the high hurdles (at which he became Irish champion). Later in that year of 1908 he jumped 24'11" in the long jump (only 2 inches short of Peter O'Connor's cv world record). In 1909 he jumped a disallowed world long jump best of 25'3" in his home town of Athea, and in the same year also won the A.A.A. title at the triple jump. He and his brother Dan (cv) were the 2nd set of only 3 sets of brothers in athletics history (see Tom and Pat Davin) to both break world records, Tim breaking the triple jump record in 1908 with a jump of 14.91, achieved in the Olympic final (this was also an Olympic record), and which was achieved on his last jump. His brother Dan beat his world record 2 years later, but the Tim's Olympic record lasted 16 years, until 1924.

AHEARNE, PADDY ('BALTY').

G.A.A. hurling forward, Cork. Club: Blackrock. He was the first Blackrock club player to win 5 All-Ireland Senior Hurling Championship winner's medals, achieving them in 3 different decades, the first player in either code to do so. His wins came in 1919, 1926, 1928, 1929 and in 1931. He also played on Cork sides which lost 2 All-Ireland S.H.C. finals, in 1920 and 1927. He won a Railway Cup medal in 1931 with Munster, and also won 2 National Hurling League medals with Cork, in 1926 (the inaugural year of the competition), and 1930. An older brother of Michael 'Gah' Ahearne (cv).

ALDRIDGE, JOHN W ('ALDO').

Soccer international full-forward. Born in Liverpool, 18th September 1958. His earlier clubs included South Liverpool, Newport County (scoring 69 league goals in 170 games, including 32 in the final season, and helping them to win promotion from Division 4, and to a Welsh Cup success in 1980), and Oxford United (scoring a club all-time record tally of 90 goals in 141 matches, winning promotion from Division 3 in 1984, and from Division 2 when becoming champions the following year, also winning a League Cup medal in 1986), from where he won his first cap against Wales in 1986. Joining Liverpool for £750,000 in 1987, his stature increased (becoming the First Division's top scorer with 26 goals in the 1987-88 season), gaining an F.A.I. Cup winner's medal in 1989 (having the previous year been the first man to miss a penalty in an F.A. Cup final), and a League Championship medal in 1988, and scoring 31 goals in the 1988-89 season. Then joining Real Sociedad for £1.1 million, he just failed to win the 'Golden Boot' award for the leading goalscorer in the league in the 1990-91 season. He then joined Tranmere Rovers, and kept up his goal-scoring record (scoring 23 goals in his first 23 games with them, with 40 in all in his first season there, a joint club record, and the best tally in all divisions of the league that season). A scorer of over 240 league goals in Britain (2nd in all-time list of current league players in 1992), he has been a prominent member of the Irish side since 1986, being one of the heroes of the June 1988 European Championship efforts. He scored his first international goal when gaining his 20th cap, in October 1988 against Tunisia, and 2 more in Ireland's final match to ensure qualification for the World Cup finals in 1990, against Malta in November 1989. His 50th cap was reached in November 1992 (with 11 international goals), when he was also named as that year's Opel 'Player of the Year'.

ALEXANDER, Conel HUGH O'Donel.

Chess master. Born in Cork, 19th April 1909, he died in 1974. Soon moving to Birmingham, he won the British Boys in 1926. Becoming an international master in 1950, he also won the British Championship in both 1938 and in 1956. He became a household name in British chess, and won enormous acclaim for his win over Russian Grandmaster David Bronstein in Hastings in 1953. A part-time chess-player, he also scored wins over 2 world champions (Botvinnik and Euwe). His big tournament wins included 1947 and 1953 wins at Hastings. Representing Great Britain at 5 chess Olympiads (1933, 1935, 1937, 1954 and 1958), he later became chess correspondent with the 'Sunday Times' and 'The Spectator'. A mathematics professor, he was awarded the O.B.E., the C.B.E. and the C.M.B.

ALEXANDER, ROBERT (BOB).

Rugby international flanker, and cricketer. Born in Belfast on September 24th 1910, he was killed in action in Burma while serving there as a captain in the Royal Eniskillen Fusilliers in 1943, at the age of 33. Rugby club: N.I.F.C. (winning an Ulster Senior Cup medal in 1935), R.U.C. and Police Union. Winning 11 international rugby caps for Ireland between 1936 and 1939, he was a dynamic flanker, skilled at dribbling and in defence. He played 14 times (including all 3 Test matches) for the 1938 British and Irish Lion's in South Africa, scoring 6 tries on tour (the most for a forward). He also played cricket for Ireland, when as a right hand batsman and bowler, he played in a first class match in 1932, scoring 29 runs and taking no wickets for 55 runs.

ALLEN, DENIS (DINNY).

G.A.A. footballer and hurler, Cork, and soccer player. Born in 1952. In 1973, while playing soccer with Cork Hibernians, he won an F.A.I. Cup medal (later while at Cork Celtic he was approached by Brian Clough to sign for Nottingham Forest). In 1974 his ability as a hurler enabled him to win a Munster Senior Hurling Championship medal with Cork. In football, as a member of Nemo Rangers (with whom he won 3 All-Ireland Club Championship winner's medals, in 1979, 1982, and 1984), he first played senior championship football with Cork in 1972, and after many years he captained the Cork side to their 1989 All-Ireland Senior Football Championship success over Mayo, having played on the Cork side beaten by Meath in the 1988 final. He also captained Cork to win the 1989 National League, winning a previous League medal in 1980. He became one of very few players to win an All-Ireland S.F.C. and an F.A.I. Cup medal (see Val Harris, cv), accomplishing the feat with a 16 year gap. He has won one All-Star award, in 1980 at centre half forward. In 1984 he was voted on the 'Team of the Century' for those never to win an All-Ireland S.F.C. medal, therefore becoming the only man in either code to subsequently go on to do so.

ALLEN, Charles ELLIOT ('ELLIE').

Rugby international prop forward. Born in Gibraltar in 1880, he died in Canada in 1966. Clubs: Derry, Liverpool. He won 21 rugby caps for Ireland between 1900 and 1907, scoring one international try. He captained Ireland in 10 of his caps, including the famous 1906 Irish team which beat the Triple-Crown seeking Welsh 8-3, in a game described then as 'the greatest of all wins in international or any rugby', thus giving Ireland a share in the International Championship that year. His older brother Glynn Allen (born in 1874), a half-back, was capped for Ireland 9 times from 1896 to 1899, being in the side for all 3 matches when Ireland won the International Championship in 1896, and scoring a try against England in the first of the 3 matches in the 1899 season which secured Ireland's second Triple Crown.

ALLEN, SAMMY.

Bowls player. Born in Ballymena on 6th July 1938. Becoming an international bowls player in 1977, he won the British Isles Singles in 1980. He won a Commonwealth Games bronze medal for Northern Ireland in the Four's in Edinburgh in 1986, and followed it with a silver (again in Four's) in the Games at Auckland in 1990. In 1984 he shared in the World Championship Triples victory for Ireland, and in 1988 in New Zealand he shared the success in Ireland's World Championship Fours win.

ALLEN, TOMMY J.

Hockey international goalkeeper. Club: Monkstown. He won 28 outdoor caps for Ireland between 1974 and 1981, playing in the Intercontinental Cup, the World Cup in Buenos Aires, and the European Cup. In 1988 he was joint record holder as the most capped Irish indoor player, with 60 caps gained from 1976 to 1987 as a goalkeeper (including 49 in succession).

ALLISON, Dr JOSEPH JAMES BARNETT.

Rugby international centre three-quarter. Born in 1880. Clubs: Queen's College Belfast and Edinburgh University. He was capped 12 times for Ireland between 1899 and 1903, dropping one goal for his country (doing so against England in 1900, when it was Ireland's only score in that entire season, and thus becoming the first to score for Ireland in the 20th century). His first cap was gained at the age of 18, while he was still at Campbell College school, and as Ireland went on to win the Triple Crown that season, he remains, to this day, the youngest Irishman to participate in a Triple Crown success (he in fact missed the final match against Wales, suffering from the mumps). He died at the age of 26, in 1907.

ALLISTER, COLIN B.

Hockey international right wing. Club: Banbridge H.C. (winning 2 Irish Senior Cup medals, in 1982 and 1984). He has been capped 59 times at international hockey for Ireland from 1978 up to 1987, mostly on the right wing. His father Aubrey A Allister, also a Banbridge right wing (who won an Irish Senior Cup medal in 1956), played in 24 international matches for Ireland in hockey between 1951 and 1961.

ALLMAN-SMITH, EDWARD PERCEVAL.

Hockey international player. Club: Dublin University. Although only gaining 4 international caps for Ireland, they were all gained in the Olympic year of 1908, and he was to share in Ireland's successful silver medal winning side, his last cap being gained in the 8-1 final loss to England.

AMBROSE, PADDY.

Soccer international forward. From Clontarf, he was born in Dublin, 17th October, 1929. A great Shamrock Rovers stalwart, in the 15 years with them between 1949 and 1964, he scored 109 league goals, therefore becoming the Hoops highest aggregate scorer ever in the League of Ireland. With Rovers he won 4 League of Ireland Championship medals, in 1954 (when he was their leading scorer), 1957, 1959 and in 1964. He also won 4 F.A.I. Cup medals with them, in 1955, 1956, 1962 (scoring 2 of the 4 goals in the final), and in 1964. He won Inter-League honours, and also won 5 international caps for the Republic of Ireland, 2 in 1955, and after a gap of 9 years, 3 more in 1964, scoring one international goal.

ANDERSON, Dr FREDERICK Edmund ('FUZZY').

Rugby international prop forward. Born in Belfast 29th August 1929. Clubs: Q.U.B. (winning an Ulster Senior Cup medal in 1951), N.I.F.C. (winning Ulster League and Cup double medals in 1955). A Barbarian, he won 13 international caps for Ireland between 1953 and 1955, only 3 of which Ireland won. A doctor, he emigrated to Australia.

ANDERSON, HENRY James.

Rugby international wing threequarter. Clubs: Queen's College Galway, Old Wesley, Blackheath, Bedford. A product of Galway Grammar School, he was capped for Ireland 4 times, twice in each of 1903 and 1906 (when Ireland shared the International Championship), thereby becoming the first Connachtman to be play for Ireland (although he actually was capped by Leinster 4 times from 1901 to 1905). Also a Barbarian, he played for both Blackheath and Bedford against the All-Blacks in 1905. A dentist, he was a stalwart in the forwarding of Connacht rugby, became a member of the I.R.F.U. executive in 1937, and in 1945-1946 he was President of the I.R.F.U.

ANDERSON, IVAN John.

Cricket international right hand batsman and off-break bowler. Born in Armagh, 13th August 1944. A product of Royal School, Armagh, he played 86 international cricket matches for Ireland between 1966 and 1985, making him the country's third most capped cricketer up to 1992. In that period he scored more runs than any other Irish cricketer in international match history, his 3,777 runs coming in 141 innings, with a commendable average of 32.56 runs per innings, and by doing so he compiled more international centuries (7) than any other Irish cricketer, while also scoring thirteen 50's. Regarded as Ireland's top batsman of the post War era, his best innings was (an Irish record) 198 runs against a Canadian XI in 1973; in a match versus Scotland in Glasgow in 1976, he scored 147 in the first innings and 103 in the 2nd, making him the only Irishman to score centuries in 2 innings in the same match. His best bowling for Ireland was 5 for 21 against Scotland in 1974.

ANDERSON, JOHN.

Soccer international defender. Born in Dublin, 7th November 1959. Apprenticed to W.B.A. in 1977, before playing with Preston North End, he later played over 220 league games since joining Newacastle United in 1983, scoring at least 8 goals. He has been capped for the Republic of Ireland 16 times from 1980 to 1988, 4 of these as a substitute.

ANDERSON, Dr NEIL H.

Amateur international golfer. Club: Shandon Park (winning a Senior Cup medal in 1991). He has won 3 championship events, the South of Ireland in 1984, and both the 1988 and 1989 North of Ireland Championship titles. An interprovincial for Ulster, he played Home international golf from 1984 to 1990 (gaining 39 points out of a possible 80), and was on the Triple Crown winning sides of 1987 and 1990. He has also played 19 European Team matches for Ireland 1985-93. In 1988 he was one of 3 Irishmen on the winning St Andrews Trophy side. In 1993 he reached the semi-final of the British Amateur Championship (held at Portrush), beaten at the 22nd by the eventual winner, and regained his place in the Irish side after an absence of 3 years.

ANDERSON, TREVOR.

Soccer international forward. Born in Belfast 3rd March 1951. Moving from Portadown to Manchester United in 1971, he played 13 league games with them in 2 years. In 128 league appearences for Swindon 1974-77, he scored 34 goals. In one season with Peterborough, 1977-78 he scored 6 goals. He won 22 senior international caps for Northern Ireland between 1973 and 1979, scoring 4 international goals.

ANDERSON, WILLIE Andrew ('TAM').

Rugby international 2nd row and No 8 forward. Born in Sixmilebridge, Co Tyrone, 3rd April 1955. Club: Dungannon (captaining them to their Ulster Senior Cup triumph in 1993). A product of Stranmillis College, Belfast, he captained Ulster in 1985 and 1986, and played a B international game in 1982. First capped in 1984, he was a constant member of the 1985 Triple Crown-winning side, and he gained his 27th and last cap in 1990 against Scotland. Having toured Japan with Ireland in 1985, he captained, with success, Ireland's 1988 tour of France and the 1989 Irish tour of Canada and the U.S., before captaining his country 3 times in the 1989-1990 season, including against the All Black's in 1989. He later became an I.R.F.U. Regional Technical Officer, helping in the coaching of the international XV, having previously been a schoolteacher.

ANDREWS, WILLIE.

Soccer international half-back. Born in Kansas City, U.S.A. Clubs: Glentoran and Grimsby Town. In 1908, while playing for Glentoran, he became the first ever (and only for many years) non British-born player to play in the Home International Championship series, togging out for Northern Ireland against Scotland. His total international cap tally came to three, between 1908 and 1913.

ANTHONY, ALGERNON (ALGY).

National Hunt jockey and trainer. For years he was an assistant to the great H.E. Linde (cv) at the Curragh, and later took charge of this stable. He trained the winner of 2 Aintree Grand Nationals, in 1900 (when he trained and rode Ambush for the Prince of Wales), and in 1920 when he trained the brilliant Troytown (which also won the 1919 Grand Steeplechase de Paris for him). His relation, J Anthony, rode Troytown, and also rode 2 other Grand National winners, in 1911 with Glenside, and in 1915 with Ally Sloper.

ARIGHO, JOHN Edward (JACK or 'JOXER'').

Rugby international wing three-quarter. Born in Dublin, 10th July 1907. Club: Lansdowne (being a member of the 5-in-a-row Leinster Senior Cup winning side, 1927-1931). A product of Castleknock and Blackrock Colleges, he played 9 times for Leinster in the interprovincial championship, and was capped 16 times for Ireland between 1928 and 1931, scoring 2 tries on his interntional debut against France. In that 1927-28 international championship season, he scored 5 tries for Ireland (with two against France, one against England, and 2 more against Wales), an Irish record that still stands, even though he missed the Scottish match due to injury. His total try tally for Ireland was 6. A journalist and businessman, in 1989 he was presented with the Irish Rugby-writers Hall of Fame award.

ARMSTRONG, DOROTHY.

Squash international player. Born in Portstewart, Northern Ireland, 17th October 1946. Club: Windsor L.T.C. She was capped 64 times for Ireland from 1974, and won the Irish National (Close) title in 1974 and 1978, having previously won the Irish International title in 1972. A member of the Irish side in the first Women's World Championships in 1976 in Brisbane, she was also in the team also for both the 1st and 2nd World Team Championships in Birmingham in 1979 and Toronto in 1981 respectively. She was on the Irish Ladies team which finished 2nd in the European Championships in 1979, and was also an accomplished tennis player (playing the sport for Ulster in 1966, 1967 and 1970-74 inclusively). Later she was Ulster Ladies Squash Veteran Champion in 1987, 1988 and 1989, and in Denmark in 1989 won the World Masters (Over 40) Championship.

ARMSTRONG, GERRY.

Soccer international forward. Born in Belfast, 23rd May 1954. His clubs have included Bangor, Tottenham Hotspur (19 goals in 65 appearances), Watford, Real Mallorca, W.B.A., and Chesterfield. His 21 caps gained while at Watford was a club record until surpassed by England's John Barnes. He held, jointly with Joe Bambrick and Billy Gillespie (until surpassed by Colin Clarke in 1992), the record for scoring most international goals for Northern Ireland (twelve), in a 10 year international career from 1977 to 1986, during which he gained 63 international caps. He won the Texaco Soccer Sportstar of the Year award in 1982 for his achievements with Northern Ireland in their memorable World Cup finals run, in which he scored 3 goals in his 5 appearances, including his famous winner against the host nation, Spain. He was also in the Northern Ireland panel in the 1986 World Cip finals, coming on as a sub in the Brazil match.

ARMSTRONG, KEVIN ('ARMY').

G.A.A. hurler and footballer, Antrim. Born in 1922. Club: O'Donovan-Rossa, Belfast (football), and O'Connell's, Belfast (winning 5 county hurling championship medals). A high class dual player, he won Ulster Senior Football Championship medals with Antrim in both 1946 (the county's first such title in 33 years) and 1951. In a football career that lasted from 1937 to 1957, he was also a member of the first Ulster football team to win the Railway Cup, when he played at right half-forward in the 1942 decider (winning 3 other medals, in 1943 and 1950, and in 1947 when he became the first man from the Six Counties to captain a winning side). As a hurler in the dominant Antrim side, he won 21 successive Ulster S.H.C. titles from 1940 to 1961. He was a member of the first Ulster hurling side to compete in the Railway Cup in 1944, and of the side which reached the final in 1945. Selected in 1984 at left half-forward on the hurling 'Team of the Century' for players never to win an All-Ireland medal, he was to make his only appearence in an All-Ireland S.H.C. final when beaten by Cork in the 1943 hurling final. In 1988 he was awarded the All-Time Football All-Star. His son Donal, also an O'Donovan-Rossa clubman, was at right corner forward on the Antrim S.H.C. side in 1989 which reached it's first All-Ireland final since the side of his father's in 1943.

ARMSTRONG, REG.

Motor cycle road racer. Born in Dublin circa 1929. Machines: A.J.S., Norton, Gilera and N.S.U. He started racing at age 17 and retired at the age of 28. He was 5 times runner-up in the World Road Racing Championships (twice in 500cc in 1953 and 1955, being never out of the top 6 from 1951 to 1956; twice in 350cc in 1949 and 1952; and once at 250cc in 1953). His total of 7 World Championship Grand Prix victories between 1952 and 1956 place him (after Ralph Bryans cv) second in the list of Irishmen in such victories since the War (and therefore as southern Ireland's most successful post-war road racer). They include the Ulster and Czech G.P.'s in 1953 at 250cc; a 1953 win at 250cc in the Swiss G.P.; and 4 victories at 500cc, in 1952 at the Senior Isle of Man Senior T.T. and in West Germany, in 1953 in the English, and the 1956 West German. His other Isle of Man T.T. results include two 2nd's and two 3rd's, and he also finished in a 4th and 5th place in the Manx Grand Prix. In his last year of racing, 1956, he set one of the fastest ever average speeds, in a 500cc event in Berlin, at 126.88 m.p.h. He later took up car racing, and in 1961 (with an average speed of 102.40) he was the first Irishman to finish in the International Formula Junior Scratch in the Phoenix Park, in 4th place. Running a successful motor assembly business at Ringsend in Dublin, he was killed in a car accident in 1979.

ARRIGAN, TOM.

Soccer international player. Clubs: Bohemians, Glentoran and Waterford. He won 2 I.F.A. Cup medals with Glentoran (in 1933 and as captain in 1935), and followed up with an F.A.I. Cup medal as captain with Waterford in 1937. He was capped once for the Irish Free State, in 1938 against Norway.

AUSTIN, LIAM.

G.A.A. midfielder, Down. Born in 1958. He made his senior inter-county debut for Down in 1976, and played at midfield for the county right up to 1991, when he was a playing sub for the county's All-Ireland Senior Football Championship win. He had previously won Ulster S.F.C. medals with the county in both 1978 and 1981. Many times an Ulster player, he has won 5 Railway Cup medals, including in 1979, 1980, 1983 and 1984. He won an All-Star award in 1983 in midfield.

B

BAGOT, Dr JOHN CHRISTOPHER.

Rugby international back. He lived from 1859 to 1935. Clubs: Dublin University and Lansdowne. He played 3 interprovincial matches for Leinster. Although he was capped for Ireland only 5 times from 1879 to 1881, his contribution to Irish rugby, because of one drop goal, was immeasurable. It was during the last match in which he was capped, that the goal he kicked against Scotland in the dying moments in 1881 enabled Ireland to win their first ever international match, after 10 straight defeats.

BAILEY, AIDAN Hilary.

Rugby international centre three-quarter. Born in Dublin on New Year's Day 1916. Clubs: U.C.D., Lansdowne (winning a Leinster Senior Cup medal in 1933). He was just 18, and still at school at Presentation College Bray, when he won the first of his 13 rugby international caps in 1934, and he had contributed 22 points (including 4 international tries in all) up his last cap in 1938. He played 10 interprovincial matches for Leinster. His brother J J Bailey, also a U.C.D. and Lansdowne player, played 3 times for Leinster. His nephew Niall Bailey, a Northampton player, won one international cap for Ireland in the centre against England in 1952.

BAILHAM, EDDIE.

Soccer international forward. Club: Shamrock Rovers, being the club's (and the League of Ireland's) leading league goal scorer twice, in 1961-62 with 22 goals, and in 1963-64 when his 18 goals helped the club to the Grand Slam success of F.A.I. Cup, League of Ireland, Leinster Shield, and Charity Cup. He also won an F.A.I. Cup medal in 1962. He was capped once for the Republic of Ireland, in 1964 against England, and scored 4 Inter-League goals for the League of Ireland XI, one of them in the famous match when they beat the English League for the first time in 1963.

BAKER, JIM.

Bowls player. Born in Belfast, 18th February 1958. Clubs: Cliftonville (outdoor), and County Antrim (indoors). He has won 3 Irish Singles titles, and won the British Isles Singles title in 1984. He skipped the winning World Championship Three's Irish side of 1984, and also won the prestigious U.K. singles title in 1985. His greatest feat to date was winning the 1984 Embassy World Indoor Singles title, beating England's Nigel Smith in the final. He won a gold medal in the 1988 World Championship Four's championship. He was Texaco Bowls Sportstar of the Year in 1984. His cousin Cecil Worthington is also a fine bowls player.

BAKER, ROY.

Kick boxer. Born in Dublin in 1965. Club: Bushido, Palmerstown. He won the Irish light heavy discipline for 6 consecutive years, 1986, 1987, 1988,

1989, 1990 and 1991, and was unbeaten in Ireland in any discipline for 4 years up to 1991. He won a bronze medal in the world men's light heavy section in Austrian in 1989, and went on to gain silver in the same discipline in Berlin in 1991.

BALLINGALL, FRED, HARRY M, W and J.B.

Golfing family. Fred won the South of Irleand 3 times (the first to do so, until John Burke cv repeated the feat in 1930), twice (in 1897 and 1898) when he beat his brother Harry in the final, and again in 1900. Two other members of the family won the 'South', W in 1902, and J.B. in the following year.

BAMBRICK, JAMES (JOE, or 'HEAD, HEEL OR TOE').

Soccer international centre-forward. Born in Belfast, 3rd November 1905, he died in 1983. Clubs, Rockville, Ulster Rangers, Bridgemount, Glentoran, Linfield (scoring all 4 goals in the clubs 4-3 I.F.A. Cup final win in 1930), Chelsea (scoring 33 goals for them in only 59 games), Walsall. On 1st February 1930 at Celtic Park, he scored a record 6 goals in a home international match against Wales (it made him the first British player to score a double hat-trick in a full international match), and his international 12 goals in all (out of a total of 11 caps won between 1929 and 1938), shared him the record total for his country, until surpassed by Colin Clarke (cv) in 1992. His 9 goals for the Irish League against all opposition is also a record. In the 1929/1930 season with Linfield he scored a phenomenal total of 94 first-class goals (50 of them in the Irish League), only 2 short of Fred Robert's Irish League all-time record. An extremely popular player, his career tally in the years 1925 to 1940 is said to approach 1,000 first class goals.

BAMFORD, J.L. (IAN).

Amateur international golfer. Club: Royal Portrush and Warrenpoint. He has won 3 important championships in Irish amateur golf: the Irish Amateur Open Championship in 1957, and the North of Ireland title twice, in 1954 and 1972 (a gap of 18 years, making it the longest period between 2 'North' wins). Also winning the Boyd Quaich at St Andrew's in both 1953 and 1956, he played in the Home international series from 1954 to 1956, winning 3 of his 10 matches played. He was an Ulster interprovincial twice, in 1957 and in 1972, and he became President of the G.U.I. in 1993.

BANNON, SEAMUS.

G.A.A. hurling midfielder and corner full-forward, Tipperary. He gained 3 All-Ireland Senior Hurling Championship winner's medals with the great 3-in-a-row Tipperary side, in 1949, 1950 and 1951 (when he scored 2 goals in the final). A brilliant goal in the 1948 Munster final was disallowed. In the Munster final of 1951 he was opponent to Christy Ring in the midfield in Ring's finest hour. He won National League medals with Tipperary in 1949, 1950, 1952, 1954 and 1955. In the Railway Cup he won 4 medals with Munster, in 1950, 1951, 1952, and 1953, while in the final of 1954 he partnered Ring in one of the great midfield partnerships. He died in March 1990.

BARBER, ERIC.

Soccer international centre-forward. Born in Dublin 18th January 1942. Clubs: St Finbarr's, Shelbourne (winning an F.A.I Youth Cup medal in 1959, he was the club's leading league scorer 9 times, in 1960-61, 1961-62 when his 15 goals helped the club to League of Ireland success, 1962-63, 1963-64, 1964-65, 1965-66, 1972-73, 1973-74, and 1974-75; he also scored in every round of Shel's 1960 F.A.I. Cup win, and won a 2nd medal in 1963, while winning a runner-up medal in 1962), Birmingham City, Chicago (finishing 3rd highest scorer in the N.A.S.L. in 1967-68, and 2nd highest in 1968-89), Kansas, Shamrock Rovers, and Wiener Sportsclub (Austria). He is the scorer of 142 League of Ireland goals, 126 of them for

Shelbourne (a club record) between 1958-66 and 1971-75, placing him 6th on the League's all-time goalscorers. He was capped twice for the Republic of Ireland in 1966, and played for the League of Ireland 3 times.

BARLOW, M .

Rugby international forward. Clubs: Wanderers, New South Wales. He won only one international cap for Ireland, in the country's inaugural (losing) game against England in 1875. Later emigrating to Australia, he went on to play for New South Wales in their tour of New Zealand, playing in all 7 games, and thereby becoming the first Irish player to tour New Zealand. He had played 2 interprovincial matches with Leinster in 1875 and 1876.

BARNES, ROBERT JAMES.

Cricket international left hand batsman and slow left arm bowler, and rugby international centre threequarter. Born in Armagh, 25th April 1911. As a member of Waringstown, he played for Ireland in cricket 8 times in 1st class matches between 1928 and 1949 (and won 14 caps in all), his best figures being 48 runs v Scotland in 1946 (his batting tally was 433 runs to an average of 19.68), and 4 for 18 as a bowler. He also won one international cap for Ireland in rugby, gained in the centre against Wales in 1933, while at Trinity, and scored a try in Ireland's win. A clerk of the Holy Orders, his younger brother J.H. (born in Armagh, 14th November 1916), a right hand bat, played one 1st class cricket match for Ireland in 1937.

BARNIVILLE, GERALDINE.

Squash and tennis international player. Born on 7th of November 1942 in Birr, Co Offaly. A member of many squash clubs, she won provincial titles in Leinster (her own province), Munster, Connacht and Ulster and also won the Surrey Open, all between 1973 and 1983. She won the Irish National (Close) Squash title in 1977 and 1981, having won the Irish Internatational (Open) title in 1973. In 1976 she was a member of the Irish team in the first Women's World Championship, and was also in the side in 1978, 1981, and 1983 (when Ireland finished 3rd, 5th, and 4th, in that order), also being a member of the side which had finished 2nd in the European Championships. She represented Ireland 71 times at international level, and was until surpassed by Marjorie Croke (cv), the world's most capped womans squash player. She was also a tennis international between 1963 and 1977, and won the Irish Open Ladies Doubles title in 1966 with the great Australian, Margaret Court. A hockey player also of some ability, she was a Leinster interprovincial from 1962 to 1964.

BARNVILLE, HENRY Thomas (HARRY).

Tennis player. Born on 20th January 1927. Club: Fitzwiliam L.T.C. (being club tennis champion 5 times, in 1956, 1960, 1961, 1963 and 1975). He was capped 5 times for Ireland in tennis between 1956 and 1962, being Leinster Open Singles Champion in 1959 and 1967. He also played for represented Leinster in bridge, and played rugby for Leinster at Junior interprovincial level, playing for U.C.D. in the final of the Leinster Senior Cup in 1946. He became a consultant physician with the Mater Hospital in Dublin.

BARR, AINSWORTH.

Rugby international half-back. Club: Methodist College. 1875-1934. A product of Methodist College, he won 4 international caps for Ireland between 1898 and 1901 (one of these in the win over Scotland during the Triple Crown-winning year of 1899). A solicitor and stockbrocker, he went on the become President of the I.R.F.U. 1908-1909.

BARR, CIARAN.

G.A.A. hurling centre-half and full forward, Antrim and Dublin, and international water-polo player. Club: O'Donovan Rossa, Belfast (with whom he reached the All-Ireland Club

Championship final in 1989). Born in Belfast in 1964, he is a product of St Mary's C.B.S. in Andersonstown, playing for Ireland in the World Student Games at waterpolo in Zagreb in 1987, and winning 10 international caps in all. An Antrim minor and Under 21 player, he first played senior county hurling in 1984, and later captained Antrim to their historic win over Offaly in the All-Ireland Senior Hurling Championship semi-final in 1989, allowing his county to reach the final for the first time since 1943. He also played for Antrim in the All-Ireland S.H.C. semi-final in 1991. In 1988 he became the first Ulster hurler since the inception of the All-Stars in 1971 to win an award, being selected at centre-forward. An accountant, he declared for Dublin in 1993.

BARR, HUGH H.

Soccer international centre-forward. Born in Ballymena, May 1935. Clubs: Linfield, Coventry. He scored 15 goals in 47 league appearences for Coventry in 1962-63. He won 3 international caps for Northern Ireland in 1962-1963, scoring one international goal (in his debut against England in Belfast in 1962).

BARR, KEITH.

G.A.A. football centre half-back, Dublin. Born in 1968. Club: Erin's Isle. A product of Beneavin in Finglas, he made his senior inter-county debut in 1989, was a member of the Dublin side which won the National Football League in both 1991 and 1993, and of the side which lost the famous 4-match Leinster S.F.C. 1st round clash with Meath in 1991. He won Leinster S.F.C. medals in 1989, 1992 (when Dublin were defeated in the All-Ireland final) and 1993. He has won one All-Star award, in 1991 at centre half-back. Going on the Compromise Rules tour of Australia in 1989, he played soccer with Gillingham briefly. His brother Johnny joined him as a sub in the county's Dublin Leinster S.F.C. winning side of 1993.

BARRETT, EDMOND or EDWARD (NED).

G.A.A. hurler, London, Tug-of-War participant, field athlete, and wrestler. Born the youngest son of a large family in Rahela, Ballyduff, near Listowel Co Kerry, 3rd November 1880. Emigrating to London in 1900, in 1901 he was a member of the only London side to win an All-Ireland Senior Hurling Championship, when the City of London Police Selection beat Cork side of Redmonds in the decider by the margin of 1-5 to 0-4. Seven years later, in the 1908 Olympic Games in London, he was a member of the Great Britain side represented by the London City Poilce which beat their Liverpool colleagues to win the gold medal in the Tug-of-War event. This made him the only Olympic Gold Medal winner to win an All-Ireland Senior Hurling Championship winner's medal. In the same Olympic Games he won a bronze medal in his specialist sport, the heavyweight freestyle wrestling division. To prove his versatility he also represented G.B. in the 1908 games in 4 other events, the shot-putt in which he finished 5th, the discus throw, the javelin, and the Greco-Roman wrestling (in which he also competed in 1912). As a wrestler he won the British heavyweight free-style championship in 1908 and 1911. His brother James won the Irish shot-putt title 7 times (1903, 1906, 1907, 1908, 1909, 1910 and 1911), won the British A.A.A. shot-putt title in both 1911 and 1923, and represented Great Britain in this event at the 1908 Olympics, failing to qualify. Another brother John was a fine wrestler.

BARRETT, Capt FREDERICK Whitefield ('RATTLE').

Polo player. Born in Co Cork, 20th June 1875, he died in Wiltshire in 1949. He captained the British team which won the prestigious Westchester Cup in 1914. He later won 2 Olympic medals with the Great Britian polo side, a gold in the 1920 games at Antwerp, when Spain were beaten by 13-11 in the final, and also winning a bronze medal 4 years later in Paris. Also a steeplechase rider, he later trained horses for 3 English kings, and put out Annandale to win the 1931 Scottish Grand National.

BARRETT, JOE.

G.A.A. football full-back, Kerry. Club: Rock Street (in 1929, as well as captaining the county side to National League and All-Ireland success, he captained his club to the Kerry Championship success). He was twice captain of the Kerry side when they won the All-Ireland Senior Football Championship title, in 1929 when they beat Kildare by 1-8 to 1-5 (the first time Kerry won the Sam Maguire Cup), and in 1932 when Mayo were beaten by 2-7 to 2-4. In all he won 6 All-Ireland S.F.C. medals with Kerry, being also on the victorious Kingdom sides of 1924, 1926, 1930, and 1931. He played in 8 All-Ireland finals in the 10 year period from 1923 to 1932, being on the losing Kerry sides in 1923 and 1927. Regarded as one of the games great full-backs, he won 2 Railway Cup medals with Munster, in the inaugural year of 1927, and on the occasion of Munster's 2nd win in 1931, when he became the 2nd Kerryman to captain a victorious side.

BARRINGTON, JONAH.

Squash international player. Born 29th April 1944 in Cornwall, he played squash for Ireland because of his father's birthright. Educated in Trinity College, he was capped 18 times for Ireland between 1966 and 1981. His influence on the world of squash was enormous, causing the boom in Ireland and elsewhere. He won 4 Irish Open titles, in 1966, 1967, 1969, and 1979, also being runner-up to Geoff Hunt in both 1972 and 1976. A colourful figure, he won the prestigious British Open title 6 times (then the unofficial world title), in 1967, 1968, 1970, 1971, 1972, and 1973, having previously won 3 British Amateur titles in succession, 1966, 1967, and 1968. He also won the Australian Open in 1970, the Egyptian and South African Opens in 1968, the Irish Open in 1980, and also the Pakistan Open in 1970. Later he won the British Closed title in 1980 and 1981, and won the 1984 Over 35 British Open title. His brother Nick won 2 caps for Ireland in squash (and 3 times as a veteran), although not with Jonah in the side.

BARRINGTON, MANLIFF.

Motor cycle racer. Born in Dublin c 1913. In a career spanning pre and post World War II, he competed in different branches of the motor cycle sport, and was also a competant car racing driver (finishing 3rd in the 1926 Leinster Trophy). He won the 1937 Dublin "100" race in the Phoenix Park (500cc class), and in 1938 set a lap record of 86.50 for the Park. His career highlight were two World Championship Grand Prix race wins at 250cc on Moto Guzzi machines in the Isle of Man, in the 1947 and 1949 T.T.'s (finishing 2nd in the 1949 World Championship at 250cc).

BARRON, DECLAN.

G.A.A. football centre half-forward, Cork. A Bantryman, he won an All-Ireland M.F.C. medal with Cork minors at full-forward in 1969, and in the following 2 years won All-Ireland Under 21 Championship winner's medals. He was on the 40 for Cork's All-Ireland Senior Football Championship win of 1973. A brilliant fielder of the ball, he has won 2 All-Star football awards, in 1974 (when he was the only Corkman selected) and 1978, both at centre-half forward.

BARRON, JOHN.

G.A.A. hurling full-back, Waterford. Club: De La Salle. Born in 1935. He played senior inter-county hurling for Waterford from 1954 to 1964, and after the disappointment of losing the All-Ireland Senior Hurling Championship final of 1957 to Kilkenny, won his sole Liam McCarthy Cup medal against the same opposition in 1959 (he later won his 3rd Leinster S.H.C. medal in 1963). He won a National Hurling League medal (the county's only success in this competition) in 1963, and won an Oireachtais medal in 1962. He also won 4 successive Railway Cup medals with Munster in 1958, 1959, 1960 and 1961.

BARRY, DAVE

G.A.A. footballer and soccer player, Cork. Born September 16th 1961. Clubs: St Finbarr's, (G.A.A., with whom he won an All-Ireland Club medal in 1981), and Cork City (Soccer). In gaelic football he was a member of the Cork Under 21 side which won the All-Ireland football title in 1981. He was later a member of the Cork side which were beaten by Meath in the 1988 All-Ireland S.F.C. final, and which won the 1989 and 1990 All-Ireland Senior Football Championship finals. He was on the team which won the Home final of the 1989 National Football League, and he won an All-Star award that year at right half-forward. He is also an accomplished soccer player, playing for Everton in Cork before his League of Ireland debut with Cork City in 1984. He played for Cork City in 2 losing F.A.I. Cup finals, in 1989 and 1992, having been the club's leading scorer in the League of Ireland in 1986-87, and helped them to win the Prremier League of Ireland Championship in 1992-93. He won All-Star League of Ireland awards in both 1991 and 1992. A plumber, his great grandfather, Harry Buckle, won an F.A.I. Cup medal in 1925 with Fordson's, while his grandfather, Bobby Buckle, won an F.A.I. Cup medal with Cork in 1934. His is the nephew of Dave Creedon (cv), who won 3 All-Ireland S.H.C. medals with Cork in succession, 1952, 1953 and 1954. Dave retired from gaelic games in 1991.

BARRY, JOHN JOE ('THE BALLINCURRA HARE').

Middle-distance Athlete. Born in Joilet, Illinois, U.S.A., 5th October 1924, his family moved to Ballincurra, Co Tipperary when he was 2. Attending Villanova University, he was the first Irish miler to gain a U.S. sponsorship. He broke the Irish record over 3 miles, 2 miles, and I mile (in 1949 he ran 4:16.2, breaking the record by more than 2 seconds). He was also Irish champion over the 1 mile, 2 mile and 3 mile distance. In 1949 he won the British A.A.A. title over 3 miles, and also won the U.S. Championship over the One Mile distance. He broke the world record for the 2 miles, and represented Ireland at both 1,500m and 5,000m at the 1948 Olympic Games in London. One of the great charismatic athletes of his time, he wrote an autobiography called 'The Ballincurra Hare'.

BARRY, MARINA.

G.A.A. footballer, Kerry, and soccer international. In G.A.A., as a member of the Austin Stacks club, she won 2 All-Ireland M.H.C. medals with Kerry in 1980 and 1981. She was in the half forward line on the Kerry side which won the All-Ireland woman's final for the 8th year in succesion in 1989, captaining the winning side against Wexford in 1983, and being player-of-the-match for their 1986 win. She has also won 9 National League medals, 2 International Championship medals, and has been an All-Star twice. She is also a soccer international.

BARRY, MICK.

Champion road bowlplayer. Born in Barryroe, Co Cork on 10th January 1919. Regarded as the greatest exponent of 'bowles' this country has known, so far was he ahead of his contemporaries that attempts were made to have him excluded from competition. First starting competitions in 1937, he had what it took, a natural skill, strength, a good length of arm and a full swing. Mainly because of World War II, it was after reaching the age of 35 that he won all his major titles, including 13 Munster championships. Equally adept with both the 16 or 28 ounce ball, he also won 11 All-Ireland 'Bowles' championships (including singles wins in 1955, 1959, 1962, 1965, 1966 and 1967), more than any other player in the games history. He also played many international matches, including against Germany, Holland and Northern Ireland. A legend in his own sport, in autumn 1991 he won the Over 60 Irish title, at the ripe old age of 72. He is also reputedly the first bowler to 'loft' a ball over the famous Chetwynd Viaduct on the Cork-Bandon road. His brothers Ned and John were also fine bowlplayers.

BARRY, PADDY.

G.A.A. hurling goalkeeper, Cork. Club: St Vincent's. A product of North Monastery, he was captain of the winning Cork side in the 1970 All-Ireland Senior Hurling Championship 6-21 to 5-10 win over Wexford (making him the first man to recieve the Liam McCarthy Cup after a 60 minute final, and the only Cork skipper to captain a Liam McCarthy Cup triumph from goals), having also been in goals for Cork's win of 1966 (playing a major role with some brilliant saves), and been on losing All-Ireland S.H.C. final sides in both 1969 and 1972. Although never winning a Railway Cup medal, he was also on 3 National League-winning Cork sides, in 1970, 1972, and 1974.

BARRY, PADDY.

G.A.A. hurling left-full forward, Cork. Club: Sarsfields. He was captain of the winning Cork side in the 1952 All-Ireland Senior Hurling Championship title (when Dublin were beaten by 2-14 to 0-7), the first of a 3-in-a-row sequence which included 1953 and 1954, in all of which he played at left corner forward. He also played in the famous loss to Wexford in the 1954 All-Ireland S.H.C. final. He won 4 Railway Cup medals with Munster, in 1953, 1957, 1958, and 1960.

BARRY, RON E ('THE BIG FELLOW').

National Hunt jockey. Born in Limerick, 28th February 1943. Among his retainers were Gordon Richards (at Greystoke). Serving a 5 year apprenticeship in Ireland with T Shaw, he rode his first winner in 1964, and moved to Britain that year. Having finished 4th in the table in 1970-71, he went on the become the leading National Hunt Jockey in Britain in 2 successive seasons, 1972-1973 (125 winners from only 430 rides, breaking the then 3-year-old record for one N.H. season) and 1973-1974 (94 winners). He also rode over 50 winners in Britain in 3 others seasons, 1970-1971 (65 winners), 1971-72 (66 winners), and in the 1974-1975 season (63 winners), while his overall tally of winners from 1964 to 1983 was 823 winners, which placed him 8th on the all-time list in British N.H. racing. His major wins include the 1973 Cheltenham Gold Cup on the Dickler (he was just pipped for the Champion Hurdle in the same year on Easby Abbey), 3 Whitbread Gold Cups (1971 on Titus Oates, 1973 on Charlie Potheen, and 1974 on the Dikler), the 1976 Schweppes Gold Cup on Irish Fashion, the 1979 Mackeson Gold Cup on Man Alive, 2 Massey Ferguson Chases, a Scottish Grand National on Playlord, and 2 Colonial Cup wins in Camden, South Carolina on Grand Canyon. He was selected as Horse Racing Texaco Sportstar of the Year on 1973.

BARRY, Dr WILLIAM J M ('JUMBO').

Hammer thrower and shot putter. A Corkman, he was born on 23rd September 1863. He won 8 British A.A.A. field events over an 11 year period in the late 19th century: 5 at the hammer throwing discipline (1885, 1889, 1892 with 40.62 metres, his best in these championships, 1894 and in 1895 at the age of 32), and three titles putting the shot (tieing in 1889, and winning outright in 1891 and 1892).

BARRY-MURPHY, DINNY.

G.A.A. hurling right half-back, Cork. From Farranferris. Club's: Cloughduv and Erie Og (captaining them to the county championship in 1928). He won 3 All-Ireland Senior Hurling Championship winner's medals with Cork, in 1926, 1929 (when he was captain of the side which beat Galway by 4-9 to 1-3 at Birr), and 1931, being on the losing All-Ireland final side in 1927. He played for Munster in the Railway Cup for seven successive seasons from 1928, captaining the winning side in 1930, and winning medals also in 1928, 1929, 1931 and 1934, for a tally of 5. He was later a selector for Cork sides.

BARRY-MURPHY, JIMMY.

G.A.A. hurling and football dual player, Cork. Born on August 22nd 1954. Club: St Finbarr's (being a member of the 'Barrs' side which won the All-Ireland H.C. club title in 1975 and 1978; uniquely he also won 2 All-Ireland Club F.C. medals with Finbarr's, in 1980 and 1981, and with the club he won in total 5 county medals in football 1976-1985, as well as six at hurling SHC medals 1974-1984). One of Gaelic Games's great all-rounders, as a minor he won an All-Ireland M.H.C. medal in 1971, and an All-Ireland M.F.C. medal in 1972. He then won an Under 21 All-Ireland hurling medal in 1973. Like Jack Lynch (cv), he won one All-Ireland Senior Football and five All-Ireland Senior Hurling medals. He was in the Cork team which beat Galway to win the 1973 Sam Maguire Cup. Later he was a star player on 5 victorious Cork All-Ireland Senior Hurling Championship sides that won that won the Liam McCarthy Cup, in 1976, 1977, 1978, 1984 and 1986, while he was also captain of the losing All-Ireland sides in 1982 and 1983 (making him the most recent of only 3 men to captain 2 losing Liam McCarthy Cup finals). He won 3 National League medals with Cork, two in hurling (1980 and 1981) and one in football (in 1980), and won 4 Railway Cup medals. He is a winner of 7 All-Star awards, twice winning in football at right full-forward in both 1973 and 1974, and then winning 5 awards at hurling, at left-half forward in 1976, centre half-forward in 1977, right half-forward in 1978, and at full forward in both 1983 and 1986. He later became a hurling analyst for R.T.E.

BEAMISH, CHARLES E StJ.

Rugby international prop forward and hooker. Born in Cork 23rd June 1908, he died in Templemore, Co Tipperary in 1984. Clubs: R.A.F. and Leicester. An Ulster player and a Barbarian, he was capped 12 times for Ireland between 1933 and 1938, and was the first Irish player to score a try against the All-Blacks, in the 17-9 loss in 1935. He is a younger brother of George Beamish (cv), with whom he played in his first 2 international caps.

BEAMISH, Sir GEORGE Robert.

Rugby international No 8 forward. Born 29th April 1905, he died in Castlerock in 1967. Clubs: R.A.F., Leicester, and Midland Counties. Rated as the finest forward in the game at his peak, he was capped 25 times at rugby for Ireland between 1925 (when he was only 19) and 1933, captaining the side in the 1931/1932 season, his cap tally making him Ireland's most capped No 8 for almost 50 years. He captained Ireland when they shared the International Championship in 1931, and when Ireland won at Cardiff for the last time for 31 years to come. He toured with the British and Irish Lion's in Australia and New Zealand in 1930 (playing the most games on the tour by any player, 21), winning 5 test caps, 2 on winning sides. He captained the Midland Counties in their famous 30-21 victory over the touring Springboks of 1931, inflicting on them the most points ever scored against them in this, the only loss of their tour. He was awarded the C.B.E. in 1942, and the K.C.B. in 1955. He was the older brother of Charles Beamish (cv).

BEARY, MICHAEL.

Flat jockey, and trainer. Born in Co Tipperary in 1895. Riding his first winner in 1913, he was Irish Champion Jockey in 1920. Although mainly riding in England, (his best tally there was 81 winners in 1949, at the age of 53) he accumulated winning rides in 8 Irish Classics from 1919. They were: 2 Irish Derby winners

(1927 on Knight of the Grail and 1932 on Dastur); 4 Irish Oaks winners (the first three in succession, with 1919 on Snow Maiden, 1920 on Palace Royale and The Kiwi in 1921, then scoring again with Theresina in 1930); and 2 Irish St Leger winners (in 1921 with Kilcubbin and in 1929 with Trigo). He also won 4 English Classic races: the Epsom Derby on Mid-day Sun in 1937; the 1932 Oaks on Udaipur; and 2 Doncaster St Leger's (on Trigo in 1929 and on Ridge Wood in 1949, when aged 53). He later as a trainer won the English 2,000 Guineas in 1951 with Ki Ming. He died in 1956.

BEASLEY, Henry ROBERT (BOBBY).

National Hunt Jockey. Born in 1936. A grandson of Harry Beasley (cv), he is one a select few jockeys to ride the winner of the 'Big Three' in National Hunt racing, winning the Aintree Grand National in 1961 on Nicolaus Silver, the Champion Hurdle in 1960 on Another Flash, and riding the winner of the Cheltenham Gold Cup twice, in 1959 on Roddy Owen and in 1974 on Captain Christy (on whom he also won the Irish Sweeps Hurdle). He rode with great success in Britain (winning the Mackeson Gold Cup in 1963 on Richard of Bordeaux), and he was also champion jockey in Ireland in 1960.

BEASLEY, H. H. (HARRY),

National Hunt jockey. Born 1850. A Kildareman, he won the Aintree Grand National once, in 1891 on Come Away, and was runner-up twice. He also won the Irish Grand National on 2 occasions, and the Grand Steeple in Auteuil twice. He won 6 Sefton Chases at Liverpool, 2 Grand Steeplechases de Paris, and also won 6 Conyngham Cup races, the last of these being in 1905 at the age of 56 on his own horse Lively Lad. In 1923, at the age of 71, he won a race, and on 10th June 1935, he rode his last race at Baldoyle Racecourse, Dublin, when he was 85 years old, making him the oldest jockey in racing history. He died 4 years later. His son H H Beasley (Harry) was also a successful jockey, riding the winners of the Newmarket 2,000 Guineas in 1929 on Mr Jinks, and the Irish Derby in 1918 (King John), having his best tally in Britain in 1930 with 56 winners. Another son, P T ('Rufus') rode the 1936 winner of the Doncaster St Leger with Boswell. He is a younger brother of Tommy Beasley (cv), and is the grandfather of H R (Bobby) Beasley (cv).

BEASLEY, TOMMY.

National Hunt jockey, amateur. Died in 1905. The eldest and most successful of 4 jockey sons of a Kildareman, Joseph Lapham Beasley. As a teenager in 1876 he rode the winner of the Irish Grand National, the Conyngham Cup and the Galway Plate in the same season. He rode the winner of 3 Aintree Grand Nationals, Empress in 1880, Woodbrook in 1881, and in 1889 on Frigate (he was 2nd in this race both 1878 and 1882). He also won the Grand Prix of Paris. He won 2 Irish Grand Nationals, in 1876 on Grand National, and in 1877 on Thiggin Thur. He also won 3 Conyngham Cup races, and had 3 Galway Plate winners, and to show his versatility also won the Irish Derby on 2 occasions, in 1889 on Tragedy (thus becoming the only jockey in history to win the Aintree Grand National and the Irish Derby in the same season, and both as an amateur) and in 1891 on Narraghmore. His other brothers were Harry (cv), Johnnie (who won the Irish Grand National in 1878 and the Conyngham Cup in 1877), and Willie (who won the Conyngham Cup in 1891). In 1879 all four Beasley brothers rode in the same Aintree Grand National, with Tommy finishing 2nd on Martha.

BEATTIE, PHILIP Garth (PHIL).

400 metres hurdling athlete. Born in Belfast, 8th September 1963. Club: Wolverhampton and Bilston. He won the U.K. Championship at 400 metres Hurdles in both 1983 and 1985, and reached the semi-final of the Commonwealth Games in 1982. His career peaked in the 1986

Commonwealth Games 400 metres hurdles event in Edinburgh, when he won Northern Ireland's first ever men's track gold medal, when finishing 0.17 of a second clear of England's Max Robertson in a time of 49.60 seconds. He represented Great Britain at the Olympic Games in 1984, finishing 8th in his first round heat. His brothers Paul, Colin and Clive have all represented Northern Ireland at athletics.

BECK, DOROTHY (nee PIM) ('BABA').

Amateur international golfer, and hockey international player. Dorothy, or 'Baba', was born on 1st July 1901 in Cabinteely, Co Dublin. In golf, she was Irish Ladies Champion in 1938, and runner-up in 1949. She was Veteran's Ladies Champion in 1952, 1955, 1956, and 1959. She was non-playing captain of the Curtis Cup in 1954, thereby completing a unique family double, as her husband John Beck had captained the Walker Cup side of 1938, while Baba was actually winning her Irish title. In 1961 she reached the semi-final of the British Ladies, at the age of 59. She played in the Home International series 20 times for Ireland over a period of 31 years from 1930 to 1961. She was also capped for Ireland as an hockey international player in 1920.

BECKER, VINCENT A (VINNY).

Rugby and athletics international. Born in Dublin, 9th October 1947. A flying redhead, he was a product of Gonzaga and Mungret Colleges. In rugby, having played interprovincial level for Leinster 11 times betwen 1968 and 1974, he won 2 international caps at wing three-quarter for Ireland, while playing for Lansdowne (with whom he won a Leinster Senior Cup medal in 1972 and a Leinster Senior League medal in 1973-74), against France and Wales in 1974. As an athlete he became Irish 100 metres champion.

BECKETT, BARBARA.

Badminton international player. She won the Irish National badminton ladies singles title 8 times in the 12 years between 1973 and 1984, her wins coming in 1973, 1974, 1975, 1976, 1977, 1979, 1980 and in 1984. She won 12 other Irish Close titles, 6 at ladies doubles (1974, 1975, 1976, 1977, 1980 and 1984), and 6 at mixed doubles (1973, 1974, 1975, 1976, 1979 and 1980). She won the Irish Open Ladies title twice (1973 and 1976), winning the mixed doubles twice also, in both 1973 and 1976. Between 1971 and 1985, she has made a then record 68 international appearences for Ireland, surpassing the previous total of 57 caps held by Yvonne Kelly (cv).

BECKETT, DERRY.

G.A.A. dual hurler and footballer, Cork. Hurling club: Sarsfields. He was at left corner forward on the Cork side which won the 1942 Senior Hurling Champinship title (scoring a goal in the final), and went on to win an All-Ireland Senior Football Championship winner's medal in 1945, also at left full-forward, thereby joining the exclusive band of dual players to win All-Ireland medals in both disciplines.

BECKETT, J.C. (JIM).

Water-polo player, swimmer and all-round sportsman. An uncle of the writer Sam Beckett, he was one of Ireland's finest water polo players, winning 23 international caps between 1902 and 1926, captaining the side on many occasions, including the Irish team which competed in the Olympic Games in 1924 in Paris. But for the dominance of George Dockrell (cv), he would have won many more than the 11 Irish National Swimming titles that he captured. A very versatile sportsman, he also was capped at interprovincial level for Leinster twice in rugby while at Old Wesley (in 1905 and in 1911), won an inter-provincial medal for high-diving, and boxed for Trinity College. He spent over 30 years of his life building up Pembroke S.C. to be one of the country's finest swimming club's. He is the father of Margo Magan (cv).

BEGGS, ROBERT (BOBBY).

G.A.A. football half-forward, half-back and full-back, Dublin and Galway. Originally a fisherman from Skerries, he was born in 1911. Clubs: Skerries Harps (winning a Dublin junior championship medal in 1943), St Joseph's, Galway Gaels and Wolfe Tones (winning 2 county championship medals in 1936 and 1941). In the 1934 All-Ireland Senior Championship Football final, he played in the half-forward line on the Dublin side beaten by Galway. Four years later in 1938 he was in the half-back line on the winning Galway side in the All-Ireland Senior Football Championship replay final, when they beat Kerry; he was also on the Galway sides beaten in the successive finals of 1940 and 1941. Then in 1942 he played again for Dublin (at right corner back), this time on the side which beat Galway for the Sam Maguire Cup (the first Dublin side to win this trophy), thus being among the select few to win All-Ireland Senior titles for 2 different counties (from a total of 6 All-Ireland S.F.C. final games played). Winning a National Hurling League medal with Galway in 1940, he also won 2 Railway Cup medals with Connacht in 1936 and 1937, having already won one with Leinster in 1935. His son Brian and 2 of his grandsons also played football for Dublin. He died, aged 82, in 1993.

BEGGY, DAVID.

G.A.A. footballing right half-forward, Meath, and rugby player. Born September 8th 1966. Club: Navan O'Mahony's (winning 4 county champinships). Making his senior inter-county debut in 1986, he was a prominent member of the Meath side which won 5 Leinster S.F.C. titles (1986, 1987, 1988, 1990, and 1991), and 2 All-Ireland Senior Football Championship winner's medals in 1987 and 1988: he was on the losing Meath team in both the 1990 and 1991 All-Ireland S.F.C. finals. Also helping the Royal County to National Football League medals in 1988 and 1990, he has won two All-Star awards, in 1987 and 1990, both in the right half-forward position. An all-round sportsman, he has played rugby for Currie, Wanderers and Blackrock, representing the Irish Exiles rugby XV on the right-wing in 1991, and helped the Wolfhounds side to win the prestigious Melrose Sevens in the same year. His brothers Paul and Gerry have won Provincial Towns Rugby Cup medals with Navan in 1990 and 1991.

BEGLIN, JIM.

Soccer international full-back. Born in Dublin, 29th July 1963. Clubs: Shamrock Rovers, Liverpool (establishing himself as one of the English League's best defenders, and winning the English First Division/F.A. Cup double in 1986, having been on the side beaten in the final of the 1985 European Cup at the Heysel Stadium), Leeds United (helping them to a Division 2 Championship winner's medal in 1989-90 in the No 3 shirt). A quality defender, he has been capped for Ireland 15 times from 1984 to 1987, when injury kept him out of the side which played in the European Championships in Germany in 1988, and out of the game altogether for more than 2 years. He retired through injury in 1991, and has done some journalistism/radio work.

BEHAN, BILLY.

Wheelchair athlete. Born in Dublin. Prior to an accident which left him paralyzed from the waist down, he excelled at 3 different sports; he played in goals for Shamrock Rovers for 2 seasons, played senior level cricket for Malahide, and also played senior hockey for St Ita's. Since then he has reached a fine standard in Lawn Bowling, and at his first Paralymic Games, in Seoul in 1988, he won a silver medal in the pairs event. He now lives in England.

BEHAN, KEVIN.

G.A.A. football midfielder and right wing-forward, Louth. A young member of the Louth side which won the Leinster S.F.C. in 1953 (and which were beaten by Kerry in the All-Ireland semi-final), he was a star member of the Louth Senior Football Championship side which won the last of the county's 3 All-Ireland titles in 1956, scoring the winning goal. Later playing on 2 Louth sides beaten in Leinster S.F.C. finals in 1958 and 1960, he won his only Railway Cup medal with Leinster in 1961.

BEHAN, LILIAN.

Amateur and professional golfer. Born in Co Kildare, 12th January 1965, one of 16 children. In 1984, not long after taking up the game, she won the Leinster Championship and reached the quarter-final of the Irish Close. She first played for the Irish Home International side in 1984, and played in both following years. In 1985, at the age of just 20, and as only a comparative novice at this level, she achieved a feat only 5 other Irish lady golfers had achieved before her (and none since), when winning the prestigious British Women's Open Amateur Championship, defeating the British Stroke Play Champion, Claire Waite, in a close final. An enormous hitter, her play ensured her a place as a member of the Curtis Cup side in 1986, which became the first ever to win on American soil, with Lilian winning 3 of her 4 matches. She turned professional soon after, and after years of comparative failure, applied in 1992 to re-instate her amateur status.

BELL, ARTIE.

Motorcycle racer. Born in Belfast circa 1915. Known as a motorcycle sprinter, a grasstrack rider, a hill-climber and as a car rallyer (he competed in the Circuit of Ireland Rally), he was best known as a post-War road racer, being a member of the Norton factory team. He won 2 Isle of Man T.T. races, the 1948 Senior T.T., and the 1950 Junior T.T., both on Nortons. He also won 3 European Grand Prix races on Nortons, the 1947 and 1948 Dutch T.T.'s at 500cc, and the 1948 Swiss G.P. He finished 5th in the 1949 500cc World Championship, and 4th in the 1950 350cc World Championship. In the 1950 Belgian G.P. he had a serious accident, forcing him to give up racing. He died in 1972.

BELL, COLIN.

Ten pin international bowler. Born in Dublin in 1960. Scoring his first 'perfect' score of 300 in 1984, he has represented Ireland at both junior and senior level. First capped in 1986, he won a bronze medal for Ireland at the European Junior Championships in Holland in 1975. He won the Irish National Championship in 1987.

BELL, EILEEN.

Bowls player. Born in 1938. Clubs: Belfast BC (outdoors) and Shaw's Bridge (indoors). An outdoor specialist, she has won 3 British Isles Singles title as well as many Irish titles. At indoors she won many National titles at Singles, Triples and Four's, and reached 6 semi-finals (and 3 finals) in British Isles championships at that code. In the 1980's in Canada, she skipped, when partnered by Nan Allely, the Pairs combination representing Ireland to win a gold medal in the World Championship outdoor bowls, a career peak performance.

BELL, RICHARD J.

Rugby international half-back. Club: N.I.F.C. He played only twice for Ireland, on losing sides against England twice in 1875 (the first of these was the first match Ireland ever played in the international arena), and he captained the side in the second match, making him Ireland's second ever rugby interntional captain. He later umpired the 1877 Irish/Scotland match.

BELL, Sir William EWART K.C.B.

Rugby international flanker. Born in Belfast, 13th November 1924. Club:

Collegians (winning Ulster Senior Cup and League medals in 1952). He was capped 4 times for Ireland in the 1953 Championship season, when Ireland lost only one match. He was an Irish selector 1966-67 and 1969-70, President of the Ulster Branch of the I.R.F.U. in 1974-75, and was President of the I.R.F.U. itself in 1986-1987. He was one of Ireland's representatives on rugby's International Board from 1987 to 1993, being made supremo of the 1995 World Cup. He became Head of the Northern Ireland Irish Civil Service.

BENNETT, ALEC.

Motorcycle racer. Born at Craigantlet, Co Down, April 1897. He rode dirt track in Canada, then as a road tester for Sunbeam. In the 1920's he was among the world's top motorcyclists, when although riding in only 29 top events, he won 11 of them. He won 7 European Grand Prix events, the French G.P. five times (in 1921, 1922, 1923, 1924 and 1926), and the Belgian G.P. twice, in 1924 and 1925. He also won 5 Isle of Man T.T. races: the 1922 Senior race on a Sunbeam, the 1924 Senior race on a Norton, the 1926 Junior race on a ona Velocette, the 1927 Senior Race on a Norton, and the 1928 Junior race on a Velocette. He also won a Gold Medal in the 1923 International Six Days Trial. He ran a successful motorcycle business in Hampshire up to his death in 1973, aged 75.

BENNETT, BILL ('BENNETT THE BOWLER').

Champion road bowlplayer. The first great champion of road bowles, he was born in Killeady, Co Cork in 1877, and died in 1967. He was champion bowlplayer in Ireland on-and-off until his 50th year, winning a famous 'score' against Timmy Crowley (mentioned in the song 'On the banks of my own lovely Lee'), in 1912. He lost very few scores, among them being to Michael McCarthy-Quirke, and 2 to Mike Deasy. Also a fine athlete, he was Irish champion at shot putt, high jump, the 56lb over the bar, and held an Irish record at the standing long jump. While stationed in South Africa, he also won 4 Cape Colony Championships on the same day (in the long jump, high jump, shot and hurdles). On return from Africa, he became the undisputed bowlplaying champion of Ireland. His sons George and Ossie were also fine bowlplayers.

BENNIS, RICHIE.

G.A.A. hurling midfielder, Limerick. Club: Patrickswell (he shared a Limerick championship county medal, the club's first, with 5 of his brothers in 1966, Gerry, Pat, Peter, Phil and Tom, while another older Sean also won a county championship winner's medal with Ballybrown). He played in midfield alongside the captain Eamonn Grimes on the famous Limerick side which won its first All-Ireland Senior Hurling Championship title for 43 years in 1973 (scoring a vital '70' in the provincial final's dying moments against Tipperary), also playing on the side which lost the final in 1974. In the 1973 season, he scored 9 goals and 87 points (114 points) to become a 'ton-up' player, and make a Limerick scoring record. He has won one All-Star award, in 1973 at mid-field. His brother Phil was at right half-back on the side which won the All-Ireland S.H.C. in 1973 (and subbed in the 1974 final), and trained Limerick to All-Ireland success in minor and Under 21 hurling championships in 1984 and 1987 respectively, and to the National Hurling League win in 1992. Another brother Peter also played for Limerick.

BERESFORD, Captain the Hon JOHN GEORGE. Polo player.

Born in Ireland, 10th June 1847. A member of the Hurlingham Club, and attached to the 7th Hussars, he played in one game, as a replacement in the semi-final, for the Foxhunters-Hurlingham polo team which won the 1900 Olympic gold medal in Paris for Great Britain. He also played in the prestigious Westchester Cup 3 weeks later when the Americans were beaten by 8 goals to 2. He died in Ireland in 1925.

BERGIN, STANLEY Francis.

Cricket international left hand batsman. Born in Dublin, 18th December 1926, he died at the age of 42 in 1969. His international career with Ireland extended from 1949 to 1965, during which his 1st class record at the bat was 27-52-5-1,610-137(v Scotland in 1959)-34.5-2. His tally of 1st class cricket runs for Ireland (of which over 1,000 were against Scotland, unique for an Irishman) is 1,601 runs, a national record. His total runs for Ireland in all matches was 2,524 (a record at the time of his death, and still third of all time up to the end of 1992) in 53 matches, with an average of 27.73. His older brother, Bernard F Bergin (born 20th September 1913), also played cricket for Ireland, in 1937.

BERKERY, PATRTCK Joseph (PADDY).

Rugby international full-back. Born in Clonmel, 3rd February 1929. Clubs: Lansdowne (winning a Leinster Senior Cup medal in 1953), and Garryowen. He was capped 11 times for Ireland between 1954 and 1958, including against Australia in 1958, which was Ireland's first ever victory over a touring side. Also a Barbarians player, he scored 5 points for Ireland.

BERMINGHAM, JIMMY.

G.A.A. footballer and soccer player. As a soccer player he won F.A.I. Cup, Leinster Senior Cup, League of Ireland and League of Ireland shield medals, and played with Bohemians in their record breaking 1927-1928 season, being capped once for the Irish Free State in 1929 against Belgium. As a gaelic footballer he won an All-Ireland medal with Dublin and played for Kerry in the 1924 Munster S.F.C. championship run.

BERMINGHAM, MICK.

G.A.A. hurling left full-forward, Dublin. Club: Kilmacud Crokes. Regarded as one of the great players never to win an All-Ireland medal (and selected on the 'Team of the Century' for players in this category), he holds the hurling scoring record for a Dublin player in a full programme, when he scored 90 points in 1971. He is the only Dublin hurler to win 5 Railway Cup medals with Leinster, playing in 1964, 1965, 1971, 1972 (as a sub), and in 1973. In 1971, the inaugural All-Star year, he became the first Dublin player of either code to be honoured, being selected at right full-forward, although Dublin had not reached the Leinster S.H.C. final since 1964.

BERMINGHAM, PATRICK (PADDY).

Discus throwing athlete. He won 5 British A.A.A. titles in the discus over an eleven year period from 1924 to 1934. His winning years were 1924 (41.18 metres), 1925 (42.24 metres), 1926 (43.38 metres, his best in this championship), 1932 (42.44 metres), and again in 1934 (with 41.28 metres). He represented Ireland in the 1924 Olympic Games in Paris, finishing in 11th place with a throw of 40.42 metres.

BERRY, FRANCIS (FRANK).

Jump jockey. Born in 1952. As an 18-year-old apprentice with Mick Hurley at the Curragh, he won the 1968 Irish St Leger on Giolla Mear. His many fine winners included 6 winners at the National Hunt Meeting at Cheltenham, while the most prestigious win of his career came when he rode the winner of the 1972 Cheltenham Gold Cup, Glencarraig Lady. He was Ireland's leading National Hunt jockey ten times in a 20 year career between 1968 and 1988, the winning years include: 1975 (sharing the title with Tommy Carberry), 1980 (with 50 winners), 1981 (42 winners), 1982 (68 winners), 1983 (49 winners), 1984 (50 winners), 1986 (51 winners) and 1987 (55 winners). A fine stylist and a great finisher, he retired from the saddle in December 1988.

BEST, GEORGE ('GEORGIE').

Soccer international midfielder and forward. Born at the Royal Maternity Hospital in Belfast, 22nd May 1946. He joined Manchester United as a junior in 1961, and in 10 glorious years in the first team there from 1964, he won 2 English League Championship medals (in 1964-65 and 1966-67), a Fairs Cup medal in 1964-65, and most notably a European Cup medal on the great side of 1968. He scored 137 league goals in 361 league appearences for United, and was joint top scorer in Division One in 1968. In 1970, by scoring 6 goals in an F.A. Cup tie versus Northampton Town, he became a joint record holder for goalscoring in such a game. His other clubs included Stockport County (playing 3 games), Los Angeles Aztecs, the Fort Lauderdale Strikers, Fulham (scoring 8 goals in 42 league matches), Cork Hibernians, the San Jose Earthquakes, Golden Bay and Bournemouth. He was capped 37 times for Northern Ireland between 1964 (when playing alongside fellow debutante Pat Jennings in the 2-1 win over Wales), and 1977, scoring 9 international goals. He has scored 11 goals in European club competitions. He was Texaco Soccer Sportstar of the Year in 1967, and in 1968 (when he was at his peak) he became the 3rd of only 4 Irishmen to be named as the F.W.A.'s Footballer of the Year; also in 1968 becoming the only Irishman (North or South) to date to be named as European Footballer of the Year. Arguably the most talented footballer ever to come from the island of Ireland, or even the British Isles, he mesmerised a generation of soccer followers like nobody before or since. In 1991 he published his autobiography 'The Good, the Bad and the Bubbly'.

BINGHAM, WILLIAM P ('BILLY').

Soccer international outside-right, winger and manager. Born in Belfast, 5th May 1931. After leaving Glentoran at 19, he played for Sunderland 1950-57, scoring 45 league goals for them. He then spent 2 seasons with Luton (scoring 27 league goals, and winning an F.A. Cup runner-up medal in 1959); two more seasons with Everton (scoring 25 league goals and winning a League Championship winners medal in 1962-63); and later played with Port Vale. His tally of goals in 419 Eglish league matches was 102. He played 56 times for Northern Ireland as the first choice outside-right between 1951 and 1964, scoring 10 international goals, during which time he had an enormous influence on his country's game. Later became the manager of Southport, Plymouth, Linfield, Everton and Mansfield. He is the most successful manager of the Northern Ireland soccer team, guiding them to World Cup qualifying in both 1982 and 1986, and being in charge of the team for 118 matches up to the end of 1993. He was Texaco Soccer Sportstar of the Year in 1981, a year in which, for his achievement with Northern Ireland in the World Cup, he was also voted Texaco Supreme Sportstar of the Year. He also managed the Greek national side in 1971-73. He was awarded the M.B.E. in 1981.

BLACK, KINGSTON.

Soccer international midfielder. Born in Luton, 22nd june 1968. Joining Luton Town as a schoolboy, he won a League Cup winner's and runner's-up medal in 1988 and 1989 respectively, and played in 125 league matches for them before moving to Nottingham Forest. He has been capped 27 times for Northern Ireland from 1988 up to mid 1993, mostly in the No 11 shirt.

BLACKMORE, KEN W.

Hockey international right half-back. Club: Dublin Y.M.C.A. (winning Irish Senior Cup medals in 1954, 1957 and 1965). A masterful right half-back, he was capped for Ireland 43 times at hockey (then an Irish record) over a 13 year period between 1954 and 1967, captaining the Irish international side 9 times in the period 1962-1966. He later coached Leinster.

BLAIR, RON.

Soccer international midfielder. Born in Coleraine, 26th September 1949. His clubs included Coleraine, Oldham, Rochdale, and another 8 seasons at Oldham, scoring 23 league goals in a total of over 350 appearences for the Boundary Park Club. He won 5 international soccer caps for Northern Ireland between 1975 and 1976.

BLAIR-WHITE, MRS A (PHOEBE).

Ladies international tennis player. Born in 1895, she died at age 96 in 1991. She won the Monkstown L.T.C. tournament 3 times, in 1919, 1920 and 1921. She won the Ladies Singles Championship at the prestigious Boat Club Tournament in Belfast in 3 successive years, 1923, 1924 and 1925, and competed for Ireland in the 1924 Olympic Games in Paris in both singles and mixed doubles. She went on to win 2 Irish Ladies Lawn Tennis Singles Championships, in 1928 and 1931, winning the Doubles also in 1928. One of the outstanding ladies tennis players in Ireland of her time, she played in Wimbledon in 1929, and played for Ireland in many matches against England and Australia.

BLAKE, Colonel ARTHUR J.

Horse trainer, flat. Based at The Heath, Maryborough (Portlaoise), he sent out the winner of a then record 17 Irish Classic races, placing him now in 3rd place on the all-time list for these races. The winners were: 5 Irish 2,000 Guineas triumphs (1929 with Salisbury, 1930 with Glannarg, 1932 with Lindley, 1940 with his own horse Teasel, and in 1945 with Stalino); 6 Irish 1,000 Guineas winners (1925 with Flying Dinah, 1929 with Soloptic, 1931 with Spiral, 1937 with Sol Speranza, 1940 with Gainsworth, and in 1941 with Milady Rose); 2 Irish Derbys (Rosewell in 1938 and Sol Oriens in 1941); 2 Irish Oaks (1929 with Soloptic and 1937 with Sol Speranza); and 2 Irish St Legers (in 1930 with Sole de Terre and in 1938 with Ochiltree). He was also leading trainer in Ireland 3 times, in 1930, 1931 and 1938.

BLAKE, Mr EDMUND.

Steeplechaser. In 1729, he raced a fellow huntsman, Mr O'Callaghan, over a distance of 4 miles between the steeples of Buttevant church and that of St Mary's in Doneraile (it's tower was called the St Leger) in County Limerick. As this was the first recorded 'Steeplechase', they are regarded as the founders of this sport.

BLANCHFLOWER,, Robert DENIS (DANNY or 'DANNY BOY' or 'THE PRINCE OF BLARNEY').

Soccer international half-back or wing-half. Born in Belfast, 10th May 1925. After a spell with Glentoran, he signed for £6,500 with Barnsley, staying there for 2 seasons and 68 league games 1949-51, leaving for £15,000 for 3 seasons (1951-54) and 148 games with Aston Villa; he then joined Tottenham Hotspur in December 1954 for £30,000. In ten years with Spurs, he played 337 league matches, scoring 15 league goals, and skippered them in their wonderful double-winning F.A. Cup/English League campaign of 1960/61, and to the F.A. Cup triumph again the following year, while in 1963 he was a member of the Spurs side which became the first British club to win a major European trophy, i.e. the Cup Winners Cup. His total tally of English League matches comes to 553 from 1949 to 1964. He played for Northern Ireland 56 times (scoring 2 international goals), captaining them into the last eight of the 1958 World Cup, an achievement not previously attained by them, while between 1952 and 1962 he played in a record 33 successive Home International games. He also represented the Irish League and the Football League in Inter-League matches. Having a natural ability to run a game, he was voted as the F.W.A.'s Footballer of the Year in 1958 and 1961 (making him the only Irishman to be honoured twice). He managed the Northern Ireland soccer squad from 1976 to 1979, later turning to journalism. He was selected as Texaco Soccer Sportstar of the Year for 1962, and in 1987 became the 4th soccer player to be elevated in to the Texaco Hall of Fame. An older brother of Jackie (cv).

BLANCHFLOWER, JACKIE ('TWIGGY').

Soccer international centre-half. Born in Belfast, 7th March 1933. Joining Manchester United as a junior, he debuted in 1951-52. Winning a League Championship medal in 1955-56, and recieving a runners-up medal in the F.A. Cup final of 1957 (in which he took over in goal for the injured Ray Wood), he was in the party in the Munich air crash in February 1958 (receiving the last rites). Unable to continue his career (having played 116 games for 'United', scoring 27 goals for them), he had up to this point won 12 caps for Northern Ireland. A younger brother of Danny Blanchflower (cv).

BLANEY, GREG.

G.A.A. football centre half-forward, Down. From Kircubbin, he was born in 1963. Club: Ballycran. A product of St Colman's College, Newry, he was playing inter-county football and hurling at the age of 19, won a Sigerson Cupo medal at Queen's, and won an Ulster S.F.C. medal with Down in 1981. He was one of 2 the Downmen who helped the county to win the 1983 National Football League to win an All-Star award in that year, being selected at left half forward (he won his 2nd All-Star in 1991 at centre forward). He played in the first 4 series of Tests in the Compromise Rules against the Australians, in 1984, 1986, 1987 and in 1990. After years of championship failures, he became in 1991 an influential member of the Down side which captured it's first All-Ireland Senior Football Championship title in 23 years, when they beat Meath in the final (he only missed Down's attempt to win the Ulster S.H.C. final in 1991 through suspension). His father played football for Armagh. A dentist.

BLANEY, JOHN JOSEPH.

Rugby international centre-three-quarter. Born in Dublin, 13th March 1925. Clubs: University College Dublin and Wanderers. Playing for Leinster 3 times in the interprovincial champinship of 1949/50, he won only one international cap for Ireland, in the 1950 season against Scotland, scoring a try in the game. A barrister, he became a Supreme Court judge in 1992.

BOLAND, JOHN Mary PIUS.

Tennis player. Born at 135 Capel Street, Dublin on 16th September 1870. While a student at Christ's College, Oxford in 1896, he was a spectator at the inaugural Olympic Games in Athens, when a Greek friend on the organising committee entered him for the tennis Men's Singles. He went on to win the title on 30th March 1896 (only 4 entered the competition), defeating the Greek Demis Kasdaglis in the final by 7-5, 6-4, 6-1, thus becoming the first Irish-born person to win an Olympic gold medal. He also went on to win the Doubles title at the same games, in partnership with the German Fritz Traun, and insisted that the officials change the Union Jack flag to an Irish flag on the pole of honour. A father of the playwright Bridget Boland (best known for her play 'The Prisoner'), he later became a barrister, author, and politician (he was a Nationalist M.P. for South Kerry 1900-1918), and died in London on St Patrick's Day 1958.

BOLGER, JAMES (JIM).

Horse trainer, flat and National Hunt. Born Christmas Day 1941 into a farming background in Co Wexford. Based at Glebe House, Coolcullen, Co Kilkenny, his quality horses have included Give Thanks (winner of the Irish Oaks in 1983), Flame of Tara (winning the Coronation Stakes), Polonia (winner of the Prix de l'Abbaye), Park Appeal, Park Express, Jet Ski Lady and St Jovite. Taking his licence in 1975, he saddled his first winner in

1976 and since 1977 he has been constantly in the top six of winners produced by Irish stables. In 1990, by saddling his 100th winner for the year in September, he became only the third Irish-based trainer (after Parkinson and Dermot Weld) to achieve this feat, and later set a new Irish flat season number of winners, with 134 (surpassing the 1923 record of Parkinson cv), and a record combined total of 148 (beaten the following year by Dermot Weld cv). In 1991, after saddling Star of Gdansk to finish 3rd in the Epsom Derby, he sent out Jet Sky Lady, at odds of 50/1, to win the Epsom Oaks. In 1992 he won 2 Italian classics, the 1,000 Guineas with Treasure Hope, and the Oaks with Ivyanna, and saddled his 1,000th winner in June. Also in 1992 his St Jovite, having finished 2nd in the Epsom Derby, won the Irish Derby (in record time and by a record 10 length's), and the King George VI. In 1993 another of his charge's (Blue Judge) finished 2nd in the Epsom Derby. On money's earned he was leading trainer in Ireland in 1990, 1991 and 1992 (when he also lead the winners with 119). In both 1990 and 1991 he was selected as Texaco Sportstar of the Year for Horse Racing.

BOLTON, Mrs S. M.

Ladies amateur international golfer. She won the Ulster Senior Ladies Championship a record 7 times, 4-in-a-row after W.W.II, in 1947, 1948, 1949 and 1950; and again in 1955, 1956 and 1960 (she was runner-up in 1959, 1963 and 1964). She was an Ulster interprovincial, and represented Ireland.

BOLTON, WILFRED NASH.

Rugby international, England. Born in Dublin, Bolton won 11 international caps for England between 1882 and 1887. In 1884 he became the first Irishman to share in a Triple Crown triumph, when he was omni-present in the conquering England side of that season, scoring a try against his native country, converting a try in the Welsh victory, and contributing to the try which ensured the win over Scotland in the same year.

BONNAR, CORMAC, COLM and CONAL,

G.A.A. hurling brothers, Tipperary. Club: Cashel King Cormac's (helping the club to win it's first ever Tipperary senior county hurling title in 1991). All three were born in Cashel, to a family of 13 children of Donegal parent's. Colm, a product of Templemore C.B.S., was a member of the Tiperary side which won the Munster S.H.C. title in 1987, and who lost to Galway in the All-Ireland S.H.C. final of 1988 (he was selected as an All-Star centrefield in 1988). His 2 brothers, the older Cormac (a full-forward born in 1959, who also played senior football for Tipp, and who won an All-Ireland Under 21 Championship winners medal with Tipp in 1980, and Fitzgibbon Cup medals with U.C.D. in 1977 and 1978) and the younger Conal (a right half-back), both also from the Cashel club, were with him on the Tipperary side which won the All-Ireland Senior Hurling Champinship final in 1989 (making them the third set of 3 brothers to win senior hurling All-Ireland medals on the same day), and again in 1991. Both Conal and Cormac won All-Star awards in both 1989 and 1991, at right half back and centre forward respectively, making it a rare treble for three brothers to be so honoured. Cormac having retired, Colm and Conal won Munster S.H.C. medals again in 1993. A sister, Triona, was on the beaten Tipperary side in the final of the All-Ireland Senior Camogie Championship in 1984, while their father Pierce played football for Donegal.

BONNER, PACKIE.

Soccer international goalkeeper. Born in the Rosses area of Co Donegal, 25th May 1960, he is a native of Burtonport. He was a gaelic footballer of some worth, playing for Donegal at all levels, including the senior county team at midfield at the age of 18. Clubs: Keadue Rovers, and Glasgow Celtic (for whom he has played over 400 games since his first team debut at 18, winning 4 Scottish Premier League Championship medals, and 3 Scottish Cup medals). First capped against Poland in 1981, having previously won Under 21 caps, he has been the Republic of Ireland's No 1 choice goalie since 1987. In 1988, for his outstanding performances in that year's European Championship finals in West Germany, he was named as Texaco's Soccer Sportstar of the Year. In 1990, for his heroic display in Ireland's run to the quarter-finals of the World Cup in Italy in which he saved the vital penalty in the shoot-out with Romanina (thus becoming a household name), he was again nominated as Texaco Soccer Sportstar of the Year. Capped in all 66 times for the Republic of Ireland up to September 1993, he had 36 clean sheets in these games (and also played in an Irish record 22 consecutive World Cup matches). His younger brother Denis (born in Dungloe, 24th May 1960) has played League of Ireland football for Galway United, Finn Harps and Sligo Rovers, winning a 'player of the month' award in 1991.

BONNER, SEAMUS.

G.A.A. football, Donegal. Born in 1951. Clubs: Clann na NGael (Donegal), Garda and Civil Service (winning one Dublin SFC medal). Playing minors, under 21 and seniors for Donegal in an inter-county career that stretched from 1969 to 1983, he won 3 Ulster Senior Football Champinship winner's medals, in 1972, 1974 and 1983. Also a winner of 2 McKenna Cup medals, he was a replacement All-Star on the 1975 side, and became a Donegal selector from 1989.

BOOKMAN, LOUIS O.

Soccer international outside-left, and cricket international. Soccer clubs: Bradford City, West Bromwich Albion, Luton Town. He was capped at soccer 4 times for Ireland between 1914 and 1922, spanning the gap of the First World War years. He was then the only Jewish player to play soccer for any of the Home International nations. An all-round sportsman, he also played cricket 14 times for Ireland between 1920 and 1930, scoring 573 runs (including four 50's) for a commendable average per innings of 22.92.

BOTHWELL, A W.

Soccer international No 7. Club: Ards (he is the clubs most capped player). He won 5 soccer international caps for Northern Ireland, in 1925 and 1926, all while at the Ards club. He was in the No 7 jersey when his club Ards won the first of the club's I.F.A. Cup successes, in 1926-27.

BOUCHER, JAMES Chrisotum (JIMMY).

Cricket international, right hand batsman and off break bowler. Born in Dublin, 22nd December 1910. For many years he was regarded as Ireland's finest cricketer (he twice topped the English first-class bowling figures in the 1930's); in 28 first class matches for Ireland over a 25 year period between 1930 and 1954, his record was: 28-51-5-625-85(against M.C.C. in 1936)-13.58-2359- 168-14.04. His total caps for Ireland were 60 from 1929-1954, during which he took 307 wickets (2nd in the all-time tally for an Irishman) for a fine average of 15.25 runs per wicket (the best average for any Irish bowler to play in over 30 matches). His best international bowling figures, 7 for 13, remarkably came in a match that Ireland lost, against New Zealand in 1937. Third in all-time catches taken for Ireland (42 in total), he was a cricket commentator for many years, and was Hon Sec of the Irish Cricket Union for 20 years from 1954 to 1973.

BOUCHIER-HAYES, JOHN.

Fencing champion. A disciple of Paddy Duffy (cv), he was the major force in Irish fencing for many years, winning many Irish Men's epee, sabre, foil and All-Weapon titles in the 1960's and 1970's. He is one of a very small group of Irish sportspersons (and the only Irish fencer) to compete in 3 different celebrations of the Olympic Games. In the 1964 games in Tokyo he went in both the foil and sabre along with the epee events; in the 1968 games in Mexico he represented Ireland only in the foil, the team foil, the sabre and the team sabre events; and in 1972 he represented Ireland in the foil and epee events. He advanced to the third round of the World Championships twice, in Tokyp and Vienna (1971). His brother Timothy also was an internantional class fencer, winning many Irish National titles in the various disciplines.

BOWDEN, JOHN (JACK).

Hockey international forward, and cricket international slow-left-arm bowler. Hockey club: Lisnagarvey (winning Irish Senior Cup medals in 1945, 1946, 1951 and 1952). He won 19 hockey international caps for Ireland between 1938 and 1950, scoring many vital goals. He was a member of the Irish hockey side which captured 4 Triple Crown's, in 1938, 1939, 1947, and in the country's last such success at Londonbridge Road in Dublin in 1949. His brother Joseph had previously won one international cap in hockey for Ireland in 1934. A dual international, Jack played cricket 18 times for Ireland between 1946 and 1955, 6 of these being in first class games. A bowler of some skill, his best international figures were 6 for 23 against Scotland in 1949, while his tally for Ireland was 41 wickets for an average of 22.36. He died in 1988 at the age of 72.

BOWEN, Daniel St JAMES (JIMMY).

Rugby international wing-threequarter. Born in Cork, 11th February 1957. A product of 'Pres' Cork, he is one a select few to represent his country at all levels of international rugby, i.e. Full, 'B', Under 23, and Schools (Pres. Cork). He played for Ireland's full international side 3 times in 1977 (all on losing sides), and was also a member of the Munster side that beat the All-Blacks in 1978.

BOWLES, JOHNNY J. Handballer.

Born at Thomondgate, Co Limerick in 1879. He won his first Cork Tournament (regarded then as the equivalent of the All-Ireland title) in 1902, at the age of 23. He won it again in 1905, and from that period until 1920, he was the games most dominant figure. He was Irish Professional Champion for the periods of 1905-10 and 1912-1920. His last Irish title was in the 1926, when at the age of 47, he took the Senior Hardball Doubles, winning with Stephen Gleeson of Fedamore, Co Limerick. He died in 1949.

BOYD, DOROTHY.

Squash international player. Born in Belfast, 15th October 1931. Club: Crawfordstown Belfast Boat Club, Lisburn. An Ulster inter-provincial squash player, she was first capped for Ireland in 1954, going on to win 26 caps in all, and captaining the international side 12 times. She was Irish Open Ladies squash champion in 1964, 1966 and in 1968, and won the Ulster championships 1958-1963. Also an inter-provincial tennis player, she won numerous Ulster titles in singles, ladies doubles and mixed doubles.

BOYD-ROCHFORD, CECIL.

Horse trainer. Born in Middlepark, Co Westmeath, 16th April 1887, he died in 1983. Setting up stables in England, he was best known as a royal trainer to both King George VI and Queen Elizabeth II. He was leading trainer in Britain 5 times (firstly in 1937), and he trained a total of 1,169 winners. His horses won 13 English classic races: the Epsom Derby in 1959 with Parthyr; six St Legers (1936 vwith Boswell, 1941 with Sun Castle, 1948 with Black Tarquin, 1953 with Premonition, 1955 with Meld and in 1958 with Alcide); the 2,000 Guineas in 1958 with Pall Mall; three 1,000 Guineas (1933 with Brown Betty, 1946 with Hyperium and 1955 with Meld); and two Epsom Oaks (1944 with Hycilla and in 1955 with Meld). He also won 6 Irish classic races: four Oaks (1927 with

Amethystine, 1927 with Cinc A Sept, 1934 with Foxcroft and in 1939 with Superbe); and two Irish St Legers (1949 with Brown River and 1952 with Judicate). Among his many other big race wins were the Ascot Gold Cup 3 times (he trained the runner-up in this race 7 times), 4 Eclipse Stakes and 6 Goodwood Stakes.

BOYLE, EDDIE.

G.A.A. football full-back, Louth. Clubs: Cooley Kickhams (winning Louth S.F.C. medals in 1935 and 1937), and Dublin's Sean MacDermotts (winning a Dublin S.F.C. medal in 1947). In 1934 he was a member of the Louth Junior's which reached the All-Ireland final, and was given a winner's medal although he was promoted to the senior side before the county won the final. A member of the Louth side which won the Leinster Senior Football Championship for the first time in 31 years in 1943, he is the only Louthman to have won 5 Railway Cup winner's medals with Leinster in either code, his medals being gained in 1935, 1939, 1940, 1944 and in 1945. One of the games greatest full-backs, he was selected on the 'Team of the Century' of 1984 for players never to win an All-Ireland medal, and was elected in the Texaco Hall of Fame in 1990.

BOYLE, CHARLES VESEY.

Rugby international left wing three-quarter. Club: Dublin Uniersity. He won 9 international rugby caps for Ireland between 1935 and 1939, scoring one international try, and may have won more only for the interference of World War One. He won 3 British and Irish Lion's Test caps on the 1938 South Africa tour, and scored 6 tries on the tour. He played 6 interprovincial matches for Leinster between 1935 and 1938, 3 of them along side his brother Cyril, a Lansdowne and Trinity player who played for the province 8 times in all over the same period. Vesey won the Distinguished Flying Cross in W.W.II. Cyril's son Peter, in the 1983-1984 season, became the yougest ever President of the Leinster Branch of the I.R.F.U, at 29 years of age.

BOYLE, JANET Margaret.

High jump athlete. Born in Belfast, 25th July 1963. She captured the U.K. high jump title in 1985 and 1989. She won the the Women's Indoor A.A.A. in 1987, and the British W.A.A.A. in 1989. She won a bronze medal (at 1.90 metres) for Northern Ireland in the Commonwealth Games in Edinburgh in 1986, and went to win a silver medal in the high jump in the Auckland Games 4 years later, after a titanic play off with the local girl, Tania Murray, having cleared 1.88 metres. Also qualifying for the Olympic final in the Seoul Games in 1988, she finished in 12th place. A schoolteacher, she represented Great Britain 13 times at the high jump between 1983 and 1989, her best height being 1.92 metres. Her brother Simon has cleared 2.12 metres in the high jump.

BOYLE, HUGH.

Professional golfer. Born in Omeath, Co Louth, 28th January 1936, his family moved to Birmingham when he was 2. As a professional his victories included the 1966 Daks Tournament, the Yomiuri Open in Japan in 1966 (becoming the first player from the British Isles to win a Japanese tournament), the 1967 Blaxnit tournament, the Irish Professional Championship of 1967, the Irish Dunlop in 1970, and the Midland Professional in 1975. He played for Ireland in the World Cup side of 1967. In 1965, on the Dalmahoy East course he shot the (then) 2nd lowest tournament round by a British or Irish player, a 61. He became a Ryder Cup player in 1967, losing his foursomes and fourball matches to combinations which included Arnold Palmer, and failing to Gay Brewer in the singles by 5 and 4.

BOYLE, MANUS.

G.A.A. football left-full forward, Donegal. Born 3rd September 1966.

Club: Killybegs (helping them to win county championship titles, including in 1992). Winning an All-Ireland Vocational Schools medal in 1984, he was a member of the Donegal side which won the All-Ireland Under 21 football title in 1987. Winning an Ulster S.F.C. medal in 1990, he went on to become man-of-the-match in the historic All-Ireland Senior Football Championship final win over Dublin in 1992, the county's first such success, when his 9 points was half his side's total that day.

BOYLE, TONY.

G.A.A. football full-forward, Donegal. He was a member of the Donegal side which won the county's first ever All-Ireland Senior Football Championship in 1992. He won an All-Star award in 1992 in the right corner-forward position.

BRABAZON, AUBREY.

National Hunt jockey. Born 7th January 1920. He was Ireland's Champion jockey in 1945 and 1949. Most associated with Vincent O'Brien's (cv) steeplechasing days, he won 3 successive Cheltenham Gold Cup races, all on the great Cottage Rake, in 1948, 1949 and 1950. He also won the Cheltenham Champion Hurdle twice, in 1949 (thus completing the vaunted Cheltenham Double) and 1950, both on Hatton's Grace. His other big race successes include the 1948 King George VI race on Cottage Rake. Also a flat jockey of some ability, he won 2 successive Irish Oaks, in 1947 on Desert Drive and in 1948 on Masaka (completing the remarkable double of this race and the Champion Hurdle in the same season), and was third in the Irish Derby in 1955 on Ann's Kuda (he also won the Irish Lincoln and Irish Cesarawitch). He later trained winners of the Ulster Derby (1966) and the Ulster Grand National (1967). In 1979 he was elevated into the Texaco Hall of Fame in 1979. His father Cecil Brabazon trained the winner of the Galway Plate in 1941, St Martin, ridden by Aubrey (who won it 3 times in all).

BRACK, SOPHIE.

G.A.A. camogie full-forward, Dublin. Clubs: C.I.E., and Austin Stacks. A prolific goalscorer, and a fine distributor of the ball, she is the holder of 8 All-Ireland Senior Championship medal with Dublin, won in the successive years of 1948, 1949, 1950, 1951, 1952, 1953, 1954, and 1955, being captain of the side on six of these occasions. Later she took up a prominent role in the administration of the game.

BRADLEY, BRENDAN.

Soccer inside and full-forward, Born in Derry, 7th June 1949. His total of 235 League of Ireland goals (scored over 17 years from 1969 to 1986) marks him out as the greatest goalscorer in that league's history. It was achieved for various clubs, principally Finn Harps (with 181 league goals, and 2 goals in the F.A.I. Cup final of 1974, his only major medal), but also Athlone Town, Sligo Rovers (scoring 43 league goals in 3 seasons) and Derry City. He also scored 12 goals in 31 appearences with Lincoln City in 1972. He was the League of Ireland's leading scorer 4 times (a joint record), in 1969-70 with 18 goals, 1970-71 with 20 goals, 1974-75 with 21 goals, and 1975-76 (with his seasonal best of 29 goals), and was his clubs' leading scorer in the league 11 times in all.

BRADLEY, MICHAEL James (MICK).

Rugby international prop and lock forwrd. 1898-1951. Club: Dolphin (winning a Munster Senior Cup medal in 1921 as vice captain, the club's first success). He was capped 19 times in the pack for Ireland between 1920 and 1927, twice being on sides which shared the international championship, in 1926 and 1927). He toured with the 1924 British and Irish Lions to South Africa, although he did not play in the Tests.

BRADLEY, MICHAEL Timothy (MICK, 'BRAD').

Rugby international scrum-half. Born in Cork, 17th November 1962. Club:

Cork Constitution (winning Munster Senior Cup medals in 1983, 1985 and as captain in 1989, and in 1990-91 he captained the 'Con' side which won the inaugural running of the All-Ireland League Division One, defeating Garryowen in the decider in Limerick). A product of P.B.C. Cork (winning a Munster Senior Schools medal in 1981, and with whom he won 4 Irish School's caps, 2 as captain, touring Australia in 1980), he was a sub for Ireland 4 times before playing for Munster, and also playing 'B' internatioanal rugby before being first capped in in the senior side 1984 against Australia. He played a vital role in Ireland's 1985 Triple Crown success, and was voted Irish Player of the Year for the 1986-1987 season. He played in the 1987 World Cup, and has toured with Ireland to Japan in 1985, to North America in 1989, and to New Zealand in 1992 (where he captained the tourists in some matches). Captaining the Irish side in 1993, he won his 29th cap (his first 22 had been consecutive) in that season (in the watershed 17-3 win over England), thus overtaking Mark Sugden (cv) as Ireland's most capped scrum-half, while he has scored 4 international tries. His father Austin was also a fine rugby player, and played amateur international soccer for Ireland.

BRADSHAW, ELAINE.

Amateur international golfer. Born in Dublin in 1941. Club: Clontarf. She won the Irish Ladies Close Amateur Championship 3 times, in 1966, 1968, and 1971 (being runner-up in 1975), and won the Leinster Ladies title in both 1968 and 1969. She played in 12 Home International series for Ireland from 1964 to 1981, captaining the side in the famous win at Cruden Bay in 1980. She played in the Vagliano Trophy twice (in 1969 and 1971), and was in the Irish side in the European Team Championships in 1967, 1969, 1971 and 1975. In 1968 she became the Texaco Golf Sportstar of the Year.

BRADSHAW, GEORGE.

Rugby and lacrosse dual international. From Methodist College, as a Collegians winger he played interntaional rugby once for Ireland, in a losing match against Wales in 1903. He also played to international level for Ireland at lacrosse.

BRADSHAW, HARRY ('THE BRAD').

Professional golfer. Born in Delgany, Co Wicklow, on 9th October 1913. Turning professional in 1934, he had periods as club professional at Kilcroney and Portmarnock (where he became an institution for 40 years). One of Ireland's truly great professional golfers, he won the Irish Professional title 10 times over a 16 year period, in 1941, 1942, 1943, 1944, 1947, 1950, 1951, 1953, 1954, and 1957. He won the Irish Open twice, in 1947 and 1949, the Irish Dunlop once (in 1950) and the British Dunlop Masters twice, in 1953 and 1955. He won the P.G.A. Close and tied the Penfold Swallow tournaments in 1958. In the 1949 British Open, he lost a play-off to Bobby Locke (by 12 shots) after his drive finished in a bottle at the 5th hole in the second round at Sandwich, costing him a 77 (his four rounds were 68, 77, 68 and 70). He played in the Ryder Cup 3 times, 1953 (when he and Fred Daly were the only 'home' foursomes winners), 1955, and in the famous winning side at Lindrick in 1957. He represented Ireland in the country's first 6 years in the Canada Cup (World Cup), from 1954 to 1959, peaking with the famous win with Christy O'Connor Snr (cv) in 1958 in Mexico, when he lost the individual title only in a play-off to Spain's A. Miguel, after both had finished on 286. He won the Moran Cup a record 13 times between 1940 and 1959. He died in 1990 aged 77.

BRADSHAW, PADDY.

Soccer international centre-forward. Born in North Wall, Dublin in 1912. Clubs: B & I, Hospitals Trust, St James Gate, Shelbourne. A great goal-getter, in four seasons with St James Gate he scored a club record 68 league goals, being the League of Ireland's top goal-scorer twice, scoring 22 goals in 1938-39, and scoring 29 (a club record) in the 1939-40 season when helping the 'Gate' to win the League. He was capped 5 times for Ireland, all in the pre-war year of 1939, scoring 4 international goals (being the last Irishman to score a goal before World War Two, ironically against the Germans), and also was on the mark 4 times in many appearences for the League of Ireland sides.

BRADY, Dr AIDAN.

G.A.A. football goalkeeper, Roscommon. From Elphin, he was born in 1928. He won an All-Ireland College's medal in 1947 with St Jarlath's in Tuam, and played minors for his county in 1948. He went on to win 4 Connacht S.F.C. medals with Roscommon, in 1952, 1953, 1961 and in 1962 when the side went on to lose to Dublin in the All-Ireland Senior Football Championship final. A quality goalkeeper during lean times for his county, he won 2 Railway Cup medals with Connacht, in 1957 as a sub, and in 1958, being on losing Railway Cup final teams in 1954 and 1955. Against hot opposition, he was picked in the goalkeeper's jersey on the 'Team of the Century' in 1984 for players who never won an All-Ireland medal. A horticulurist, he was a director of the Boitanic Gardens in Glasnevin, Dublin, becoming known for his gardening expertise on R.T.E. He died at age 64 in 1993.

BRADY, JAMES R.

Rugby international second-row forward. Born in Belfast, 11th, February 1931. Club: C.I.Y.M.S. (winning an Ulster Senior Cup medal with them in 1953). A product of Belfast HS, he was capped 12 times for Ireland between 1951 and 1957, when Ireland lost only 4 of his games. Also a Barbarian player, he helped Ireland to share in the International Championship of 1951.

BRADY, LIAM ('CHIPPY').

Soccer international mid-fielder. Born in Dublin, 13th February 1956. He joined Arsenal in 1973, and in a distinguished carreer at Highbury, won an F.A. Cup medal in their 1979 win (his influence in this game is now legendary), and runners-up medals in 1978 and 1980, as well as in the 1980 Cup-Winners Cup (when he missed a vital penalty shoot-out effort), scoring 43 goals in 225 games for the Gunners. In 1979 he was voted Player of the Year by 3 different bodies. His later clubs included a 7-year stint in Italy (the longest by a British-based player); with Juventus (who bought him for a fixed fee of £600,000) whom he helped win the 1981 and 1982 Italian Championship titles, scoring 13 times in 57 games, including the vital penalty to win the 1982 title, Sampdoria (6 goals in 57 games), Internationale Milan (who paid £1.2 million for his services, and with whom he reached the semi-final of the UEFA Cup twice), and Ascoli, before returning to West Ham in 1987. First capped as an 18 year-old against the U.S.S.R. in the famous 1975 3-0 win, he has been the architect of many fine Irish performances since then, none more so in helping Ireland to finally qualify for a major competition in 1987-88, the European Champinship, although he was injured for the finals. His cap tally on his retirement in 1990 reached 71, making him the Republic of Ireland's most capped international, scoring 9 international goals. He has scored 10 goals in European club competitions. He wrote an autobiographical book 'So Far So Good'. He was voted Texaco Soccer Sportstar of the Year 3 times, in 1976, 1979, and 1987. He was appointed manager of Glasgow Celtic in 1991. A younger brother of Ray Brady (cv), his grand uncle Frank Brady was an Irish soccer international in the 1920's, playing against Italy in both 1926 and 1927 while a member of Fordsons F.C.

BRADY, MICK and PETER

G.A.A. football father and son, Offaly. Mick was a wing-back turned centre-half on the Offaly side which won the Leinster S.F.C. in 1960 (the county's first such title), and on the side which went on to be beaten in the All-Ireland Senior Football Championship final in 1961. He also won a Railway Cup medal with Leinster in 1961. His son Peter, a forward, was a member of the Offaly Under 21's beaten in the All-Ireland final in 1986, being also a classy regular on the Offaly side in the late 1980's and early 1990's. Peter's older brother, Michael Og also played senior football for Offaly.

BRADY, OLLIE.

G.A.A. footballing centre back, Cavan. Club: Redhill's. A senior inter-county stalwart for many years, he came on as a sub in Cavan's All-Ireland Senior Football Championship semi-final loss to Offaly in 1969. He won an All-Star award in 1978, at centre half-back, making him the first (and only to date) Cavan player to win such an award, being a member of the Cavan side beaten by Down in the Ulster S.F.C. final that year.

BRADY, PHIL ('THE GUNNER').

G.A.A. football midfielder and full-back, Cavan. Clubs: Mullahoran (winning Cavan SFC medals with them in 1945, 1947, 1948, 1949 and 1950), and Garda (Cork). He is a winner of 3 All-Ireland Senior Championship medals with Cavan, playing in midfield in the wins of 1947 at the Polo Grounds and in 1948, while he played at full-back in the 1952 replay win over Cork. A household name in Cavan football, he won a National Football League medal in the county's first ever win of 1948, and won a Railway Cup medal in 1950, both from the midfield position.

BRADY, T RAYMOND (RAY).

Soccer international centre-half. Born in Dublin, 3rd June 1937. He joined Millwall from Home Farm in 1957, and after 166 league games in 5 years there he went to Q.P.R. for 2 seasons. He played 6 international matches for Ireland, all in 1964. His older brother Pat, born in Dublin on 11th March 1936, a full-back, followed the same career path, from Home Farm to Millwall (for whom he played 145 league games, many alongside Ray) and Q.P.R., but was not capped for Ireland. He is an older brother (by 19 years) of Liam Brady (cv), his other brother Frank winning an F.A.I. Cup medal with Shamrock Rovers in 1968.

BRAITHWAITE, ROBERT S.

Soccer international winger. Born in Belfast 24th February 1937. He played for Linfield initially, and later for Middlesborough, 1963-1966. He was capped 10 times at senior international level in soccer for Northern Ireland between 1962 and 1965.

BRAND, Thomas NORMAN.

Rugby international forward. Born in 1899. Club: N.I.F.C. As an uncapped player, he (after helping Ulster to win the interprovincial series of that year, and failing to convince in the Final Trial) was selected on the 1924 Lions tour to South Africa, winning 2 Test places while there. He subsequently played only one game for Ireland, on a losing side against New Zealand in 1924 (this makes him the only Irish player to be capped for the Lions before going on to be capped for Ireland). He accidently drowned in 1938 at Poole in Dorset, at the age of 39.

BRANIGAN, DECLAN.

Amateur international golfer. Born in Drogheda, 22nd July 1948. Club: Laytown and Bettystown. Capturing the Irish Youths in 1969, in 1976 he won both the Irish Close Championship and the West of Ireland, and in 1981 he completed the unique treble by capturing the Close, West and East titles. He is the only Irish amateur golfer to win 3 Willie Gill awards for the most consistent player of a season in the amateur 'majors', in 1976 (the inaugural year), 1981, and in 1985. He has played

84 interprovincial matches for Leinster 1972-90, winning 45; he has played 37 Home international matches for Ireland in 7 series, 1975, 1976, 1977, 1980, 1981, 1982 and 1986, winning 11; and has played 10 European Team Championship matches in 1977 and 1981, winning 7.

BREEN, BARRY.

G.A.A. football midfielder, Down. Club: Downpatrick (winning a county champinship medal in 1991). He was an influential midfielder on the Down side which captured, for the first time in 23 years, the All-Ireland Senior Football Championship in 1991. He won an All-Star in 1991 at midfield.

BREEN, TOM.

Soccer international goalkeeper. Born in Drogheda (or Belfast ?), 27th April 1917. Clubs: Drogheda United, Newry Town, Belfast Celtic (twice), Manchester United (playing 72 games for them 1936-1939), Shamrock Rovers (winning inter-League honours while there), and Linfield. He was capped 9 times for Northern Ireland between 1935 and 1939, and 5 times for the Irish Free State, twice in 1937 and 3 more times ten years later, in 1947.

BRENNAN, ANTHONY (TONY).

G.A.A. hurling full-forward and full-back, Tipperary. He won 4 All-Ireland Senior Hurling Championship medals with Tipperary, in 1945 (at full-forward), and three-in-a-row at full-back, in 1949, 1950 and 1951. He also won National Hurling League medals in 1949 and 1950 with Tipp.

BRENNAN, BARRY.

G.A.A. footballer, Galway. He was a member of the Galway side which won the Connacht S.F.C. title in 1982, 1983, and 1984, playing at right half-forward on the side beaten by Dublin in the 1983 All-Ireland final. In 1981, he was one of 2 Galwaymen to be selected on the All-Star side, along with Seamus McHugh, being picked at right half-forward.

BRENNAN, J .

G.A.A. footballer, Dublin. He won 4 All-Ireland Senior Football Championship winner medals with Dublin, playing for the Bray Emmets side in their 1902 win, for the Kickhams in the wins of both 1906 and 1907, and playing for the Geraldines selection in their win of 1908.

BRENNAN, J.J.

G.A.A. hurler, Kilkenny. He won 4 All-Ireland Senior Hurling Championship winner's medals with Kilkenny, in 1905 with the Erin's Hope, in successive wins in 1911 and 1912 with the Tullaroan selection, and lastly in 1913 with Mooncoin.

BRENNAN, KIERAN.

G.A.A. hurling half-forward, Kilkenny. He was on the Kilkenny minors beaten in the All-Ireland M.H.C. final in 1974, and came on as a sub in the All-Ireland Under 21 Championship final win in 1977. He played at left half-forward in Kilkenny's 1982 All-Ireland Senior Hurling Championship victory, and moved into the centre of the half forward line for the win of 1983. He was also a member of the Kilkenny side which was beaten in the All-Ireland final of 1987. He won one All-Star award, in 1984 at centre half forward.

BRENNAN, MARTIN ('GOGGY') and JAMSIE ('SHINER').

G.A.A. hurling father and son, Kilkenny. Martin ('Goggy'), won 2 All-Ireland Senior Hurling Championship medals in the full forward line with Kilkenny, in 1967 and 1969. His son Jamsie (born in 1970), a member of the Erin's Own club, was captain of the Kilkenny side which won the All-Ireland Under 21 Championship in 1990, and won a Liam McCarthy Cup medal in the full-forward line in 1992 when Kilkenny won the title after a 9-year-gap, and won a 2nd medal as as sub in the final of 1993.

BRENNAN, MICK.

G.A.A. hurling right corner forward, Kilkenny. He has won 3 All-Ireland

Senior Hurling Champinship winners medals with Kilkenny, all at right corner forward (in 1974, 1975 and 1979), playing twice on the losing side in 1973 (at left full forward), and 1978, thus playing in 5 Liam McCarthy Cup finals in a 7 year period. He has won 3 All-Star awards, in 1975, 1976 and 1979, all at right full-forward.

BRENNAN, ROBERT A.

Soccer international inside-forward. Born in Belfast, 14th March 1925. Clubs: Distillery, Luton Town, Birmingham City, Fulham, and Norwich City. He scored a total of 86 English League goals, 44 of them in 6 years at Fulham. He was capped 5 times for Northern Ireland betwen 1949 and 1951, scoring one international goal, in a losing 9-2 match versus England in 1949.

BRENNAN, SEAMUS (SHAY, 'THE BOMBER').

Soccer international full-back. Born in Manchester, 6th May 1937. He joined Manchester United as a junior in 1955, and played with the side in 289 league matches from 1957 to 1969, during which time he helped the club to win the European Cup in 1968 (the first English side to achieve this prestigious goal), and the English League Division One in 1966-67. He was capped 19 times for the Republic of Ireland from 1965 to 1971, being the first to play for the Republic under the later much-used parentage rule.

BRESNIHAN, Dr FINBARR Patrick K (BARRY).

Rugby international centre three-quarter. Born in Waterford, 13th March 1944. Clubs: U.C.D., Lansdowne, London Irish and Barbarians. A product of Gonzaga School and U.C.D., he was capped 25 times for Irleand between 1966 and 1971 (only 8 of these games were lost), scoring 5 international tries. A fine centre, he went on 2 British and Irish Lion's tours, to Australia and New Zealand in 1966, and to South Africa in 1968, where he played in 3 test matches, and when (on the first tour match) he became the first replacement in representative rugby history. He is a brother-in-law of Con Feighery (cv).

BRIGGS, W RONNIE.

Soccer international goalkeeper. Born in Belfast, 29th March 1943. Clubs: Manchester United (1960-62, playing just 2 matches for them), Swansea City (1964-65), and Bristol Rovers (1965-68). Apprenticed to Manchester United, he played for their League side before his 18th birthday. He was capped twice for Northern Ireland, first in 1962 (in a 4-0 defeat by Wales), before his 20th birthday, and again in 1965, in a 2-1 win over Holland.

BRITTON, W. T.

Hammer throwing athlete. Clubs: Ballinamore and Cavan. He won 2 British A.A.A. titles in the hammer event, in 1928 and 1929. He was Ulster Champion for his discipline for 8 successive years from 1928 to 1935, and was Irish National Champion 6 times, in 1923, 1924, 1925, 1926, 1929 and in 1933. His feats were completely overshadowed by Pat O'Callaghan's (cv) 2 gold medals in the same event in the Olympic Games of the same era.

BRODERICK, PADDY.

Jump jockey. Born in Mullingar in 1939. Apprenticed to Cyril Bryce Smith, he rode his first winner in 1953, and moved to work in Britain in 1961, attaining his best season's tally of 50 winners in 1966-67. He is associated mainly with the brilliant Night Nurse, on whom he won 2 Champion Hurdles in 1976 and 1977; 2 Welsh Champion Hurdles in 1976 and 1977; an Irish Sweeps Hurdle in 1975; and a Scottish Champion Hurdle in 1976. He also rode the 1966 winner of the Mackeson Gold Cup (Pawnbroker), and the 1964 winner of the Scotish Grand National, Rainbow Battle. His career of over 500 winners in the saddle finished in an accident on Boxing Day 1977.

BROGAN, J BARRY.

Jump jockey. Born in Cork on 18th April 1947. He was leading Irish Amateur rider in 1964-65, and moved to Britain. He won the 1971 King George VI Chase in 1971 on the Dikler; the 1972 Hennessy Gold Cup on Charlie Potheen; the 1970 Scottish Grand National on the Spaniard; and the 1970 Benson and Hedges Gold Cup on Even Keel. He acheived 4 high placings in the British jump jockey's championship: 6th place in 1967-68 with 57 winners; 4th in 1968-69 with 46 winners; 3rd in 1970-71 with 67 winners; and 4th in 1971-72 with 70 winners. His father, Jimmy Brogan, was a professional jockey and trainer.

BROGAN, BERNARD.

G.A.A. football midfielder, Dublin. Club: Oliver Plunkett's. He has won 2 All-Ireland Senior Football Championship winner's medals with Dublin, in 1976 and 1977, both in a dynamic midfield partnership with Brian Mullins (cv), and he was also on the Dublin side defeated by Kerry in the finals of 1978 and 1979. He won one All-Star award, in 1979 at centre field. A fine all-round athlete, he represented Ireland in the World Superstars competition in the Bahamas in 1980, finishing 6th, having previously twice come 2nd and once winning the Irish Superstars title in the late 70's.

BROHAN, JIMMY.

G.A.A. hurling right full-back, Cork. Club: Blackrock (helping them to win their first county championship title in 25 years in 1956). One of his county's finest cornerbacks, he was at his peak when Cork's fortunes in terms of major titles was at a low ebb. His only All-Ireland Senior Hurling Championship final appearance was in 1956, when Cork lost the famous 'Art Foley final' to Wexford. He did however win 5 Railway Cup medals with Munster, in 1957, 1959, 1960, 1961 and 1963. A brother-in-law of Mick Cashman (cv).

BROPHY, NIALL Henry.

Rugby international wing three-quarter. Born in Dublin, 19th November 1935. Clubs: Blackrock College (winning Leinster Senior Cup medals in 1957 and 1961), U.C.D., London Irish. For Leinster he played in 14 interprovincial matches between 1955 and 1967. He was capped 20 times on the wing for Ireland over an 11 year period from 1957 to 1967, scoring 4 international tries, including one in his debut against France. He toured Australia and New Zealand with the 1959 British and Irish Lions (only to be injured 3 minutes into his first match), and later won two test caps while playing 7 matches on the 1962 Lions tour of South Africa. He was an Irish selector 1975-78. His brother Bobby Brophy was President of the Leinster Branch of the I.R.F.U. in 1988-1989.

BROSNAN, CON.

G.A.A. footballer, Kerry. He won 6 All-Ireland Senior Football Championship winner's medals with the Kingdom, in 1924, 1926, and in the 4-in-a-row years of 1929, 1930, 1931 (when he captained the side which beat Kildare by 1-11 to 0-8) and 1932. He played on a losing Kerry S.F.C. All-Ireland final in 1923, thus playing in 7 finals. He won his sole Railway Cup medal with Munster in the competition's inaugural year of 1927.

BROSNAN, PADDY 'BAWN'.

G.A.A. left wing forward and full-back, Kerry. Born in Dingle on 16th November 1917. Club: Dingle (winning 6 county Championship medals). First playing senior inter-county football with the 'Kingdom' in 1936, he went on to win 3 All-Ireland Senior Football Championship medals, in 1940 (as a sub in the final), 1941 and 1946, while he also played on losing Kerry S.F.C. sides in 3 All-Ireland finals, in 1938, 1944 (when captain of the side), and the Polo Ground game of 1947. Winning a tally of 12 Munster S.F.C. medals in all, he also won 3 Railway Cup medals, in 1941, 1948 and 1949, before retiring in 1952.

BROSNAN, SEAN.

G.A.A. football, Kerry. Born in Dingle in December 1916. He won 3 All-Ireland Senior Football Championship winner's medals, in 1937, 1940 and 1941. He was on the losing Kerry All-Ireland S.F.C. side in 1938 and 1944. He won his solitary Railway Cup medal in Munster's win of 1941. Credited in some quarters with introducing the one arm catch, he became a Fianna Fail T.D. for Cork North East 1969-82.

BROTHERSTON, NOEL.

Soccer international midfielder. Born in Belfast, 18th November 1956. Apprenticed to Tottenham Hotspur, he later joined Blackburn Rovers, staying there from 1977 up till 1984. Having won an Under 21 cap, he was capped for the senior side 27 times for Northern Ireland between 1980 and 1984, 6 times as a sub, and scored 3 international goals (all in 1980).

BROWN, HENRY Joseph.

Hockey international full-back. Clubs: Three Rock Rovers and Roscommon. He won 22 caps (15 of these as captain) for Ireland between 1908 and 1923 (making him by far and away the most capped Connacht hockey player). He was a member of the Irish side which beat Wales 3-1 before losing 8-1 to England in the final of the inaugural Olympic Games hockey tournament, so winning an Olympic silver medal.

BROWN, JOHN.

Soccer international outside-right. Born in Belfast 8th November 1914. He played for Belfast City, Wolves, Coventry, and Ipswich, playing League football until the age of 36. He was capped 10 times for Northern Ireland between 1935 and 1939, and twice for the Republic of Ireland in 1937.

BROWN, JOSEPH C (JOE).

Amateur international golfer. Clubs: Tramore and Waterford. His tally of 6 Irish championship wins places him in 6th place in the all-time list for these events. After winning the Irish Close Championship in 1934, he won the Irish Amateur Open Championship in 1936, having been runner-up in 1932. He also won the South of Ireland title 3 times, in 1932, 1933 and 1958, and was runner-up in 1930. He was the runner-up in the Irish Close title in 1952, when he also captured the West of Ireland title. He played senior interprovincial golf for Munster in 1961, being one of only 5 players to play in both the old series (in 1938 and 1939), and the new series which stated in 1957). He played 52 Home international matches in 9 series for Ireland between 1933 and 1952, winning 19, halving 3, and losing 30 of his matches.

BROWNE, COLM.

G.A.A. footballer, Laois. He was a star member of the Laois team which won the county's 2nd ever National Football League, in 1986 (they had won the first one in the inaugural year of the competition, 1926-27). He won an All-Star award in 1986, at right half back, one of 2 Laois players to be so awarded that year, making them the only 2 Laois players up to date to win selection.

BROWNE, JIMMY.

G.A.A. football right full-back, Mayo. Born 1960. Club: Ballina Stephenites (captaining them to county Under 21 title in 1980, and to senior county championship in 1985, winning a 2nd medal in 1987). He was captain of the Mayo side which reached their first All-Ireland Senior Football Championship final for 38 years in 1989. He won an All-Star award in 1989 at right full-back.

BROWNE, LIAM.

Horse Trainer. Born April 3rd 1937. As a jockey he was a champion apprentice while with Paddy Prendergast in the 1950's, and won the Lincoln Handicap. Based at Maddenstown Lodge, the Curragh, Co Kildare, he has trained over 550 winners since getting his first licence in 1971, his big wins including the Irish 2,000 Guineas of 1982 on Dara Monarch (saddling the third in the same race, Red Sunset), the Gallinule Stakes on Carlingford Castle (which finished 2nd in the 1983 Epsom Derby), the Sun Alliance Hurdle of 1978 with Mr Kildare, the 1980 Waterford Crystal Supreme Novice Hurdle with Slaney Idol, and the 1983 Phoenix Stakes with King Persian. His is the father of both Dermot Browne (born 29th October 1961), who has been champion amateur rider in Britain twice, and who while attached to the Michale Dickonson stable, rode Brown's Gazette to win the Waterford Crystal Hurdle, and Martin Browne, who is a professional flat jockey.

BROWNE, ROBERT J (BOBBY).

Soccer international wing half. Born in Londonderry, 9th February 1912. Clubs: Malevan, Clooney Rangers, Derry City (where he twice represented the Irish League), Leeds United (making 110 league appearences 1935-1947), York City, Thorne Colliery (as player-manager). He was capped 6 times (while at Leeds) for Northern Ireland in the 4 years before World War Two. He later had a brief period as both coach and manager of Halifax Town. An Army PT Staff Sergeant.

BROWNE, WILLIE.

Soccer international player. Club: Bohemians. A League of Ireland stalwart for many years, he won 3 senior international caps for the Republic of Ireland, all in 1964. He was voted Texaco Soccer Sportstar of the Year in 1963, also being a winner of the S.W.A.I. Personality of the year for the same season

BROWNE, WILLIAM FRASER ('HORSEY').

Rugby international forward. Born in 1903. Clubs: United Services and Army. A captain of Campbell College, and initially a rugby threequarter, he was capped in the pack 12 times for Ireland between 1925 and 1928. A renowned tackler, he is one of Ireland's most respected forwards. He died from leukhaemia at the young age of 28.

BRUEN, JAMES (JIMMY).

Amateur international golfer. Born in Belfast in May 1920, he was nevertheless a Corkman. Clubs: Muskerry and Cork (winning Barton Shield in 1937 and 1938, and the Senior Cup in 1939). He easily won the 1936 British boys by 11 and 9 at Royal Birkdale at the age of 16. He won the Irish Close Championship in 1937 and 1938 (and was later beaten in a classic match in the semi-final of 1963 by Joe Carr cv), and was the Irish Amateur Open winner in 1938. At the age of 17, he made a huge impact on his first visit to the British Amateur Championship. In 1938, at St Andrew's, at the age of 18 years and 25 days, he became the youngest player to play in the Walker Cup (a record he held until beaten by Ronan Rafferty cv in 1981), and crowned it when the home side won the trophy for the first time. In 1939, at the age of 19, he led the qualifiers for the British Open (and if the qualifying rounds had counted, he would have won it outright !), being the leading amateur that year. In 1946, after being deprived of championship golf during W.W.II., he beat the 1937 British Amateur Champion Robert Sweeny, at Royal Birkdale to take the British Amateur Championship for the only time, and played in it regularly up to 1960. He won 2 further Walker Cup places, in 1949 and 1951. He was leading amateur 3 years in succession in the Irish Open (1937, 1938, 1939), and he played 24 Home International matches in 4 series for Ireland between 1937 and 1950, winning 12 and halving 5. His famous loop style makes his standard of achievement even more remarkable. He was an international selector 1959-62, and was captain and president of Cork G.C. (whose scratch cup he won 4 times in succession 1938-41). He died of a heart attack in 1972, at the age of 52.

BRUTON, NIALL.

Middle-distance athlete. Club: Clonliffe Harriers. Born in 1972, he did a scholarship in the University of Arkansas. In the 1991 Student Games in Sheffield, he won the 1,500 metres title, one of 3 Irish gold medals in these games. He won the B.L.E. Irish National 1,500m title in 1993. A burgeoning talent, he participated in the 1,500 metres at the World Athletic Championships in Stuttgart in 1993, reaching the semi-final.

BRYAN, MARY (nee O'SULLIVAN).

Badminton player. In a 21 year period at the top of Irish ladies badminton, she was capped 53 times between the years of 1955 and 1975. Regarded as one of Ireland's finest ever ladies badminton players, she won many singles titles, being a particularily good match player. A winner of 23 Irish National titles (including 10 singles successes, in 1959, 1960, 1962, 1963, 1964, 1966, 1968, 1969, 1971 and 1972), she and Yvonne Kelly (cv), a regular doubles partner, won 16 out of 17 consecutive Irish Singles titles between them from 1955 to 1972. A winner of 10 Open titles and several International Championship events in both singles and doubles, she became a coach after her playing days, and was National Squad coach from 1986 to 1988.

BRYAN, WILLIE.

G.A.A. football centre-fielder. Born in 1947. He was a member of the first Offaly minors to capture the All-Ireland M.F.C. in 1964. Having played on the unsuccessful Offaly side in the 1969 All-Ireland S.F.C. final, he was captain of Offaly's first ever All-Ireland Senior Football Championship winning side in 1971, when the beat Galway 1-14 to 2-8. He also played a leading role in Offaly's victory in the replayed final of 1972 over Kerry. He won 2 All-Star awards, in 1971 and 1972, both at centre-field. In 1972 he became the 2nd of only 3 Offalymen to be nominated as Texaco Footballer of the Year.

BRYANS, RALPH.

Motor Cyclist. Born in Northern Ireland in 1941. Machines: Bultoco and Honda. His total of 10 Grand Prix victories between 1964 and 1967 place him as top post-war Irishman in number of victories. He won a total of 7 G.P. wins at 50cc (namely the West German in 1964 and 1965, the Dutch in 1964 and 1965, the Belgian and French in 1964, and the T.T. in 1966, his only Isle of Man success, setting a long-held lap record of 86.49 m.p.h), 2 at 250cc (the West German and Japanese in 1967), and one win at 350cc (in Italy in 1967). He won the World Championship at 50 cc in 1965 on a Honda with 36 points when winning it in the last race in Japan, gaining the distinction of being the first Irishman to win such a title in motorcycling (he was 2nd in 1964 and 3rd in 1966). He was also placed 3rd in the World Championship at 125cc (1966) and 350cc (1967), and 4th at 25cc in 1967. He scored wins in many non-championship races in Italy, and won the North-West 200 3 times. He retired at age 28 in 1970. He later lived in Scotland.

BUCHANAN, CATHY.

International rower. Clubs: Queen's University, and Belfast Rowing Club. She holds a unique record in Irish rowing; she has won Irish titles in all the elite championships open to her: coxed four, coxless pair and single sculls. Her tally of titles come to 8 in all. She sculled lightweight for Ireland in the World Championships of 1987, and she rowed in the Northern Ireland coxed and coxless fours at the Commonwealth Games Regatta at Stathclyde in 1986.

BUCKLE, HARRY R.

Soccer international player. Clubs: Sunderland, Bristol Rovers, Coventry, Fordsons (winning an F.A.I. Cup medal in 1925), and Belfast Celtic. He was capped twice for the I.F.A., against England in 1904 and against Wales in 1908. His son Bobby won an F.A.I. Cup medal with Cork in 1934.

BUCKLEY, CONNIE.

G.A.A. hurling centre half-forward, Cork. He captained the Cork side which won the first of its famous 4-in-a-row, in 1941 when they beat Dublin by 5-11 to 0-6 in the final (although they were in fact beaten comprehensively by Tipperary in the Munster final that year). He had played on the Cork side beaten in the All-Ireland S.H.C final in 1939. He won National Hurling League medals with Cork in both 1940 and 1941.

BUCKLEY, DIN JOE.

G.A.A. hurling half-back and left full-back, Cork. Club: Glen Rovers. He won an All-Ireland M.F.C. medal with Cork in 1937. He was a member of the famous Cork 4-in-a-row team which appeared in 6 All-Ireland Senior Hurling Championship finals in the seven years from 1941 to 1947, winning Liam McCarthy medals in 1941, 1942, 1943, 1944 and in 1946, and on the losing side in the 1947 final. He won National Hurling League medals with Cork in 1940 and 1941.

BUCKLEY, KITTY.

G.A.A. camogie player, Cork. Clubs: U.C.C. and Old Aloysians. A fine quality player, she won 4 All-Ireland medals, in 1936, 1939, 1940, and as captain of the winning Cork side in 1941 in the 7-5 to 1-2 win over Dublin (her 6 goals in this final still stands as a record individual in an All-Ireland final). A fine ball player, she also achieved inter-provincial level in tennis for Munster.

BUCKLEY, MICK.

G.A.A. footballer, Kildare. Club: Caragh (captaining them to Kildare JFC in 1917 and Kildare SFC in 1918, 1919 and 1926). He captained the winning Kildare side in the 1927 All-Ireland Senior Football Championship. Playing also in the victory the following year (1928), and also playing in the county's earlier win in 1919, he joins Paul Doyle (cv) in being the only 2 Kildaremen to win 3 All-Ireland S.F.C. medals.

BUCKLEY, P J .

G.A.A. football left half-back, Dublin. Born in 1955. Club: Erin's Isle. A member of the Dublin side which won the All-Ireland Senior Football Championship title in 1983, he was also a member of the side beaten by Kerry in the 1984 and 1985 finals. Playing for Dublin on and off up till 1986, he won one All-Star, in 1984 at left-half back.

BUGGY, NED.

G.A.A. hurling midfielder, Wexford. A winner of an All-Ireland M.H.C. medal with the Wexford minors in 1966, in 1969 he was a member of the county side beaten in the All-Ireland Under 21 Championship final. He was a member of the last 2 Wexford sides to win the Leinster Senior Hurling Championship, in 1976 and 1977, when they went on to lose the successive All-Ireland S.H.C. finals. He won Railway Cup medals with Leinster in 1977 and 1979, and a National League medal with Wexford in 1973. A stalwart in the Wexford side for many years, he won one All-Star award, in 1979 at right full-forward.

BUGGY, PADDY.

G.A.A. hurling right half-back, Kilkenny, and administrator. Club: Slieverue (winning one county championship medal, the club's sole success). Winner of a Railway Cup medal in 1954, he won an All-Ireland Senior Hurling Championship medal with Kilkenny in the 1957 win over Waterford, and won five Leinster S.H.C. medals in all, 1950, 1953, 1957, 1958 and 1959 (when he played in his only other All-Ireland S.H.C. final). Also winning 2 Oireachtais medals, he went on to become the 28th President of the G.A.A., serving during the centenary year of 1984.

BULGER, D.D.

Sprint athlete. Club: Trinity College. In the 1890's, he was the dominant Irish sprint athlete, winning the Irish 100 yards title six times, the 220 yards four times, and the 120 yards hurdles four times, while he also won the Irish long jump championship 4 times. He also won the British A.A.A. championship at both the long jump and the 120 yards hurdles.

BULGER, LAWRENCE Quinlivan (LARRY or 'FAT CUPID').

Rugby and athletics international. Born 5th July 1875, he died in 1928. Rugby clubs: Dublin University, Lansdowne. He was capped 8 times as a wing three-quarter for Ireland between 1896 and 1898, scoring 20 points (including 2 tries), He played 4 test matches for the British Lions in their 1896 South African Tour (on this tour he became the first Irish player to score a test try for the Lions and the first to score a try against South Africa), and his tally of 20 tries on the whole tour stood as an Irish record until surpassed by Tony O'Reilly (and consisted of 30% of all points scored by the visitors on tour). His older brother Michael J Bulger, played 4 interprovincial matches for Leinster 1886-1889, won one international cap in 1888, and won a Leinster Senior Cup medal with Lansdowne. Both brothers represented Ireland in athletics.

BULL, MICHAEL Anthony (MIKE)

Pole vault and decathlon athlete. Born 11th September 1946. He won a record 13 British pole vault titles (representing Northern Ireland), winning eight indoor titles (1967, 1968, 1969, 1970, 1971, 1972, 1974 and 1977, also a record), and five outdoor titles at R.A.F. Cosford (1966 at 4.57 metres, 1967, 1969, 1971, and 1972 at a National record of 5.21 metres, the first 17 foot vault in championship history). Representing Great Britain in the Olympic Games of both 1968 and 1972, he won 4 Commonwealth Games medals (a Northern Ireland record for a male athlete), 3 in the pole vault (silver in Kingston in 1966, gold in Edinburgh in 1970 at 5.10 metre, and silver in Christhurch in 1974), and a gold in the decathlon (with 7417 points) in the 1974 New Zealand Games. He first broke the British record in 1966, and broke his own record 10 times until 1972, and in September 1968 he became the first Briton to clear 5.00 metres in the pole vault. His 69 international caps for Great Britain (23 indoors) from 1965 to 1977 was a record at the time. He was voted Texaco Athletics Sportstar of the Year in 1966.

BURKE, FLORRIE.

Soccer international centre back. Clubs: Cork Athletic (helping them to win 2 successive League of Ireland titles, in 1950 and in 1951 when they also won the double by capturing the F.A.I. Cup; he won a 2nd F.A.I. Cup medal in 1953). Born in Cork, he played hurling for the Blackrock club before concentrating on soccer. In a 14-year career in Cork soccer he became one of the finest centre backs the League of Ireland has witnessed. Winning only one international cap for Ireland, against West Germany in 1952, he was honoured the S.W.A.I. in 1993.

BURKE, FRANK.

G.A.A. hurler and footballer, Dublin. A native of Kildare, he was born in 1895. Clubs: Collegians (winning 4 Dublin county championships), Carbury. In an inter-county career from 1917 to 1923, he played in 9 All-Ireland senior finals, 5 of his football appearances being successive (1920-1924), and 3 of his hurling finals also were in sequence (1919-1921). He shares with Pierce Grace (cv), a fellow Dublinman, the distinction of having won more than one All-Ireland title at each code, when he won two All-Ireland Senior Hurling Championship medals with Dublin in 1917 and 1920, and then went on to win three All-Ireland Football Championship titles, also with Dublin, in 1921 (making him the first of only 3 players to win All-Ireland medals in 2 codes in successive years, the others being Jack Lynch and Martin Currams), 1922 and 1923 (during 5 months in this year he played in 3 All-Ireland senior finals, winning 2 of them). He has the unique double of losing a All-Ireland senior football final and winning a hurling final in the same year (1920), and to then do the opposite in the following year, when in 1921 he won a football medal and lost the All-Ireland S.H.C. final.

BURKE, FRANK.

G.A.A. hurling centre-half forward, Galway. He was at centre-field on the Galway side which captured the All-Ireland Under 21 title in 1972. He went on to play in 2 All-Ireland Senior Hurling Championship finals with Galway in 1975 and 1979 before capturing a Liam McCarthy Cup medal (the county's first All-Ireland S.H.C. win in 57 years) in the fine side of 1980, being again on the losing side in the final of 1981 (as a playing sub). He won one All-Star award, in 1979 at centre half-forward.

BURKE, ITA (MRS EDDIE BUTLER).

Amateur international golfer. Born in Nenagh. Club: Nenagh (also honorary member at Elm Park, Killarney and Woodbrook). She was 3 times runners-up in the Irish Ladies Championship title between 1972 and 1978, and was Leinster Ladies Champion 3 times. She won selection on the 1966 Curtis Cup, winning 2 of her 3 matches (being the only British and Irish player to win any match outright in this clash), and in the same year won World Amateur Team honours. In 1966 she also won World Cup selection, and played Home International series matches 13 times for Ireland over an 18 year period between 1962 (when she was Leinster Champion) and 1979. She also played European Championship for Ireland in 1967, and Vagliano Trophy in 1965. She was later non-playing captain of the Irish team, capturing the Home International Championships in 1986.

BURKE, JOHN ('TIPP').

Soccer international player. Clubs: Cahir Park, Shamrock Rovers (winning 5 F.A.I. Cup medals in succession with them in 1929, 1930, 1931, 1932 and in 1933, and helping the club to the League/Cup double in 1931-32). He was capped once for the Irish Free State, in the 1929 match against Belgium. His son Mickey, a right-back who played to Inter-League standard, won 2 F.A.I. Cup medals with the 'Coad's Colts' Shamrock Rovers side in 1955 and 1956.

BURKE, JOHN Martin.

National Hunt jockey. Born in 1953. A good point-to-point and amateur jockey with Fred Rimmell, he turned pro in 1974. In 1976 he became only the 5th jockey ever to ride the winner of the Cheltenham Gold Cup and the Aintree Grand National in the same season, when winning on Royal Frolic and Rag Trade respectively. In the same season he also won the Welsh Grand National on Rag Trade. In 1977 he won the Whitbread Gold Cup on Andy Pandy. He was voted Texaco Sportstar of the Year in 1976 (Horse Racing).

BURKE, JOHN (SEAN).

Amateur international golfer. Club: Lahinch. Born in Lahinch, Co Clare in 1900. He has won a record number of South of Ireland titles, with an astonishing 11 wins over a 19 year period, in a 4-in-a-row of 1928, 1929, 1930 and 1931; again in 1939; and then for 6-in-a-row in 1941, 1942, 1943, 1944, 1945 and 1946. He has also won Ireland's premier amateur event, the Irish Close Championship, a record 8 times, being victorious in 1930, 1931, 1932, 1933 (giving him 4-in-a-row), 1936, 1940, 1946 and 1947, while he was runner-up twice, in 1935 and 1937. He also won the West of Ireland Championship 6 times, in 1933, 1934, 1936, 1938, 1940 and 1941. He won the Irish Open Amateur title once, in 1947, beating the young Joe Carr. He won a Walker Cup place at Brookline, Mass in 1932, becoming the first Irish-based player to be so honoured, and halved his singles with Jack Westland. A great amateur, he was Ireland's most consistent player for a 21 year period including the 30's and 40's. Having played 8 individual matches against the other 'Home' countries from 1929, he went on to play 58 Home International matches in 10 series for Ireland (placing him joint 4th on the all-time Irish list) between the inaugural year of 1932 and 1945 with a gap for the war, winning 23 and halving 9. In 1962, he was the first golfer to be elevated into the Texaco Hall of Fame. He developed spinal problems in his forties, and died in 1972.

BURKE, TOM.

G.A.A. football goalkeeper, Mayo. He played in goals on the Mayo side which won it's first ever Sam Maguire Cup in 1936, having previouusly played on the losing All-Ireland Senior Football Championship side of 1932. He shares the Mayo record of having won 4 Railway Cup medals with Connacht, in 1934, 1936, 1937 and 1938. A sound goalkeeper, he also won National Football League medals with Mayo in 1935, 1936, 1938, 1939 and 1940.

BURNS, BOBBY.

G.A.A. footballer, Longford. One of his county's best players, in 1966 he was a star member of the only Longford senior side to win a national senior title, when the county beat Galway by 9-8 in the final of the National League in football. Part of a county side which reached 4 Leinster S.F.C. semi-finals in 6 years up to 1970, in 1968 he was a member of the only Longford team to win the Leinster Senior Football Championship (beating Laois by 3-9 to 1-4 in the final, before going on to lose to Kerry by 2 points in the All-Ireland semi-final), having been also in the side which reached it's first ever Leinster S.F.C. final in 1965.

BURNS, DECLAN.

K2 canoeist. Born in Enniskillen in 1954. Club: Eniskillen Canoe Club. Canoeing since 1971, he has represented Ireland at 3 Olympic Games (one of a select number of Irish sportspersons to do so), in 1976 at Montreal in both the K2 and K4 events (finishing 19th overall in both disciplines), 1980 at Moscow (when although breaking the K1 Irish record by 2.7 seconds, failed to qualify for the 2nd round), and 1988 at Seoul (in the K2 1,000 metres event, finishing 4th in a semi-final). He became Irish Superstar Champion in 1980, and in 1981 became runner-up in the World Superstars contest, the highest placing attained by an Irishman.

BURNS, MIKE.

G.A.A. hurling half-back. Tipperary. He won an All-Ireland M.F.C. medal with Tipperary minors in 1955, being also on the team beaten in the previous years final. He has won 4 All-Ireland Senior Hurling Championship winner's medals with Tipperary in the space of 5 years, in 1961, 1962, 1964, and in 1965, while he was also on 3 Tipp sides beaten in the final for the Liam McCarthy Cup, in 1960, 1967, and 1968, thus playing in 7 out of a possible 9 successive All-Ireland S.H.C. deciders. He also won 5 National Hurling League medals with Tipp, in 1959-60, 1960-61, 1963-64, 1964-65, and in 1967-68.

BURNS, MARK.

Hockey international forward. Clubs: Cookstown, Hollywood 87, Mossley, Belfast Y.M.C.A. He has won 86 caps for Ireland from 1979 up to 1988, and was also capped 12 times in the indoor game from 1984 up to 1988. He was capped for Great Britain twice in 1988. His brother Harold was capped 15 times at outdoor in the late 1970's (and 3 times in the indoor code in 1980) .

BURNS, MICHAEL.

Amateur international golfer. Club: Tramore (winning Barton Shield and Irish Senior Cup medal in 1992, the club's first success either competition). He was runner-up in the 'South' in 1983. He has played 75 interprovincial matches for Munster between 1972 and 1988 (making him that provinces most capped interprovincial player since 1956), winning 41 and halving 6 (giving him a success percentage of just less than 60%); he has played 12 Home international matches in 3 series 1973-83, winning 4.

BURNS, RAYMOND.

Amateur international golfer. Born in October 1973. Club: Banbridge. In 3 years 1989-1991 at junior international level for Ireland, he picked up a possible 17 points out of 20 for his country, a record. He helped the Irish side to win the Home international championship in both 1991 and 1992, and in 1991 he was runner-up in both the Irish Boys and Irish Youths. Showing precocious talent at a young age, in 1992 he became the youngest ever player to win the East of Ireland Championship (aged 18 years and 8 months), and also set a lowest aggregate record for the tournament at 279 shots; he won the East again the following year with a new record aggregate score of 278. He played Walker Cup golf for Britain and Ireland in 1993 in the U.S.A., winning one of his 2 matches. He was picked for the Britain and Ireland side in 1992 for the successful St Andrew's Trophy win, and was also picked for the Eisenhower Cup. He turned pro in late 1993.

BURNS, TOMMY ('THE SCOTSMAN').

Flat jockey. Born in Scotland of Irish descent on February 14th 1899, he did most of his racing in Ireland from 1914. His first ride in Ireland was a winner, and he was leading professional jockey in Ireland in 1916, and became Champion Jockey in 1932. Riding for such trainers as Michael Dawson, Jack Rogers and Senator Parkinson, he had 21 wins in Irish Classic races, putting him 2nd on the all-time list of winners for an Irish jockey. They are: 5 Irish 2,000 Giuneas winners (1921 on Soldemis in the race's first running, 1923 on Soldemino, 1939 on Cornfield, 1947 on Grand Weather and 1948 on Beau Sabreur); 5 Irish 1,000 Guineas winners (1927 on West Indies, 1930 on Star of Egypt, 1933 on Spy-Ann, 1934 on Kyloe and 1953 on Northern Gleam); one Irish Derby winner, in 1936 on Raeburn; 4 Irish Oaks winners (1916 on on Captive Princess, 1917 on Golden Maid, 1926 on Resplendent and 1941 on Uvira), and 6 Irish St Leger's (in the first running of the race in 1916 on Captive Princess, 1917 on Golden Maid, 1919 on Cheap Popularity, 1931 on Beaudelaire, 1940 on Harvest Feast, and in 1948 on Beau Sabreur). Riding his last of over 2,000 winners of a 41 year career in the saddle in 1954, he later also trained with some success, saddling the winner of the Irish St Leger in 1961, Vimadee. His sons, T.P. (cv), Jimmy and John, were all in the racing game. He died in 1991 aged 92.

BURNS, THOMAS PASCAL. ('T.P.').

Flat and hurdle jockey. A son of 'The Scotsman' Burns cv. Riding his first winner at the Curragh in 1938, he became Irish Champion jockey 3 times, in 1954, 1955 and in 1957. He was also an accomplished National Hunt jockey, winning 7 divisions of Cheltenham's Gloucester Hurdle. He has won 7 Irish Classic races; 2 Irish 2,000 Guineas winners (in 1959 on El Toro and in 1966 on Paveh); 2 Irish 1,000 Guineas winners, Northern Gleam in 1953 (beating his father by a neck) Shandon Belle in 1962; one Irish Derby (in 1957 on Ballymoss), and 2 Irish St Legers (in 1961 on a horse trained by his father, Vimadee, and 1972 in on Pidget). After riding over 1,000 winners in a 37 year career in the saddle up to 1975, he later became an assistant trainer with Vincent O'Brien (cv) and Dermot Weld (cv). His brother Jimmy, also a jockey, was killed while racing.

BURTON, LOWRY.

Motorcycle side-car racer. From Carrickfergus, Co Antrim, he is, without doubt, Ireland's most successful sidecar racer of all-time. After a brief initial foray as a solo rider, he turned to sidecar racing and was the Isle of Man Southern 100 Champion 4 times in all, in 1980, 1981, 1983 and in 1988. He won 2 Isle of Man T.T. races, the 1986 'A' race, and the 1987 'B' race (this made him, at 49 years of age, the oldest ever winner of a

T.T. race), before retiring after the 1988 season.

BUTLER, TOMMY.

G.A.A. hurling left full-forward, Tipperary. He was a member of the Tipperary side which won the 1978-79 National Hurling League. In 1978 he won a Railway Cup medal with Munster, and in the same year he became the first Tipperary player to win an All-Star award in 4 years, when he was selected in the left corner-forward position.

BUTTIMER, PAUL.

Amateur international boxer. Born in 1966. Club: Sunnyside BC, Cork. A Corkman, he has won four Irish National Senior Championship titles, 3 at the flyweight division (in 1987, 1990 and 1992), and one at bantamweight in 1993. A regular international boxer, he represented Ireland at the Barcelona Olympics in 1992 at flyweight.

BYRNE, ANTHONY (TONY, 'SOCKS').

Amateur featherweight and lightweight boxer. Club: Tredagh B.C.(Drogheda). He was born in Drogheda in 1929. Winning an Irish Junior title in 1950, he won his first of 3 Irish National Senior Championship titles in 1951 at featherweight, before winning in both 1952 and 1956 at lightweight. Captaining the Irish boxing squad to it's most successful haul (in terms of number of medals won) in any Olympic Games in 1956, he himself won a bronze medal for Ireland at those games at Melbourne, Australia, beating a Czech and an American before losing to the German Harry Kurschat in the semi-final. The following year he beat the gold medal winner from those games, Tony McTaggart (G.B.) in a bout.

BYRNE, ANTHONY (TONY).

Soccer international defender. Born in Rathdowny, 2nd February 1946. Clubs: Millwall, Southampton, Hereford and Hereford. He played 216 league matches in English League football from 1966 to 1978, playing with Southampton in the European Fairs Cup in 1969-70, and in the U.E.F.A. Cup of 1971-72. He was capped 14 times for the Republic of Ireland between 1970 and 1974.

BYRNE, DAVID ('BABBY').

Soccer international forward. Born in Ringsend, Dublin, 28th April 1905. He was the first player in the League of Ireland to score 100 league goals, which he achieved in only 7 seasons, scoring 119 league goals in all (to place him in the top 20 on the all-time list). He played for many clubs, including Bradford and Shelbourne (winning a League of Ireland medal as the club's top scorer in 1928-29). With Shamrock Rovers he was the joint top scorer in their League of Ireland success of 1926-27 with 17 goals; he also won another League of Ireland medal with Rovers in 1931-32, and won 4 successive F.A.I. Cup medals with them in 1930 (when he scored the winning goal), 1931, 1932 and in 1933 when again scored a goal in the final. His other clubs included Manchester United; Coleraine; Larne; Hammond Lane. He won 3 international caps for the Ireland between 1929 and 1934.

BYRNE, EDWARD M J ('NED').

Rugby international prop forward and G.A.A. hurler. Born in Kilkenny, 14th September 1948. A product of St Canices, playing both G.A.A. football and hurling, he also won the All-Ireland Schools Senior shot putt and hammer championships in 1964, and represented Irish Schools in 3 atheltics internationals. Then as a hurler with the James Stephens club (winning county championship medals in 1969 and 1975), he won an All-Ireland Senior Hurling Championship winner's medal with his native Kilkenny when playing at left full forward in the 1972 side. He then went on to play 6 rugby interprovincial matches for Leinster when a member of Blackrock College (with whom he won Leinster Senior League medals in 1975, 1976 and 1983, and Leinster Senior Cup medals in 1983 and 1986). He was capped as a prop for

Ireland on 6 occasions in 1977 and 1978 (each time on the losing side), and toured Australia with his country. This places him in the rare position of winning the highest honours in both Gaelic Games and Rugby. A cousin of Willie Duggan (cv), his uncles Eddie and Podge Byrne both won All-Ireland S.H.C. winners medals with Kilkenny in the 1930's.

BYRNE, JOHN .

Soccer international striker. Born in Manchester, 1st February 1961. Clubs: York City (scoring 55 league goals in 175 games), Queen's Park Rangers, Le Havre, Sunderland (scoring a goal in each round up to the losing F.A. Cup final of 1992), Brighton and Hove Albion. First capped in 1985, he has been capped 23 times for the Republic of Ireland (up to mid 1993), many as a substitute, and has scored 4 international goals.

BYRNE, JAMES.

G.A.A. footballer, Wexford. He captained the Wexford side which won the last of their 4-in-a-row of All-Ireland Senior Football Championship wins, in 1918 (when the county's Blues and Whites side beat the Fethard selection of Tipperary by 0-5 to 0-4), having played in each of the 1915, 1916 and 1917 wins, making him one of 9 Wexford players to play in each of these triumphs.

BYRNE, MICKEY ('THE RATTLER').

G.A.A. hurling right full-back, Tipperary. He was a prominent member of the 3-in-a-row Tipperary side which won the 1949, 1950, and 1951 All-Ireland Senior Hurling Championships, and won a 4th Liam McCarthy medal in 1958. He won National Hurling League medals with Tipp in 1949, 1950, 1952, 1954, 1955 and 1957.

BYRNE, PAT.

Soccer international midfielder. Born in Dublin, 15th June 1956. Clubs: Rangers (of Dublin), Shelbourne, Bohemians (winning an F.A.I. Cup medal in 1976, and winning League of Ireland Championship medal in 1977-78), Philadelphia Furies, Leicester City (helping them to win the Division 2 Championship in 1979-80), Heart of Midlothian (helping them to win the Scottish Division 1 in 1979-80), Shamrock Rovers (winning 4 League of Ireland Champinship medals in succession, in 1983-84, 1984-85, 1985-86 and 1986-87, and completing the League-and-F.A.I. Cup double in the latter 3 years), and Shelbourne again (initially as a player/manager, eventually leading them in 1992 to win their first League of Ireland Championship success since 1962, and in 1993 to their first F.A.I. Cup win in 30 years). He was capped 8 times for the Republic of Ireland between 1984 and 1986, the last 3 as a sub. In 1985 he was voted S.W.A.I. Personality of the Year, and he received this award again in 1992.

BYRNE, PHIL.

G.A.A. hurler, Tipperary. He won 4 All-Ireland Senior Hurling Championship winner's medals with Tipperary over a 5 year period at the end of the last century, in 1895, 1896, 1898 (all three of these being with the Tubberadora selection), and in 1899 with the Moycarkey side.

BYRNE, Dr SEAMUS J.

Rugby international winger. Born in Dublin, 7th Jume 1931. Clubs: U.C.D., Lansdowne (winning a Leinster Senior Cup medal in 1953). Although capped for Ireland on only three occasions, his scoring of 3 tries in his international debut, against Scotland in 1953, is not only unique in all international rugby, but until 1991 equalled the most by any Irish player in any international game. He moved to live in the U.S.A. His younger brother, Noel F Byrne (born in the Curragh, 18th December 1938), a winger with U.C.D., won one international rugby cap for Ireland, against France in 1962, having played 3 interprovincial matches for Leinster.

BYRNE, TOMMY.

Car racing driver. Born in Dundalk in 1959. In 1980 he won 2 British Formula Ford 1,600 Championships, the R.A.C. and the P&O Ferries, both in a Van Dieman car. The following year he went on to win the Formula Ford 2,000 Pace British Championship, again in a Van Dieman car. In 1981 he was awarded the Texaco Motorsport Sportstar of the Year Award.

BYRON, WILLIAM G (BILLY).

Rugby international forward. Club: N.I.F.C. (winning many Ulster Senior Cup medals with them up to 1899). A product of Edinburgh University, he was capped 11 times in the pack for Ireland between 1896 and 1899, including being one of only 5 players to play in all matches in Ireland's 2nd Triple Crown success in 1899. He died in 1961.

C

CADDELL, Dr ERNEST Duncan (TOMMY).

Rugby international scrum-half. 1881-1942. Clubs: Dublin University and Wanderers. Capped 4 times for Leinster between 1904 and 1906, he was capped 13 times in all for Ireland between 1904 and 1908, including being on the famous side that beat the Triple Crown-seeking Welsh side in 1906 (and which shared the International Championship that year), and he scored 2 international tries. He served in World War One, and was awarded the Military Cross.

CAGNEY, STEPHEN J.

Rugby international prop-forward. Club: London Irish. He won 13 international caps for Ireland between 1925 and 1929, nine of these matches being won (Ireland shared the International Championship in both 1926 and 1927). He also played for Leinster 4 times in the interprovincial series in the 1920's. A bank official, he died in 1961.

CAFFREY, (nee STAPLETON) SIOBHAN.

International basketball player. Born in Dublin in 1960. Clubs: Killester Kittens and Meteors. With her school, St Mary's Faith, Killester, she won a gold medal at Under 16 in the F.I.S.E.C. final in Zaragosa, and played with success at Under 16 and Under 19 for Ireland. With Meteors she won 4 National League titles, 3 National Cup titles, 3 Top Four championships, and several Dublin league titles. Playing for Ireland in 3 Pre-Olympic tournaments, she also played in 5 European Championships. She captained Ireland to win the quadrangular Four Nation competition 3 times, also captaining Ireland to 3 American tours, and won 107 caps in all. She won M.V.P. in the National Cup in 1986, and was an Independent Sportstar of the Month in 1986.

CAFFREY, TOMMY.

Table-tennis international player. Born in Balbriggan in 1943. Club: Balbriggan. First capped for the Irish senior side at the age of 13, he retired in 1982, having won 151 caps for Ireland in that 25 year period, making him arguably then Ireland's most capped sportsman. A winner in 1957 of all 4 titles available to male competitor's at the Irish Close (the Boy's singles and Doubles, and the Men's sinles and doubles), his total tally of Irish Senior Table-tennis Close titles reached 9 in the 1950's, 1960' and 1970's. He also became the first Irishman to win the Irish Open title, capturing it both in 1963 in Balbriggan, and in 1965 in Cork. He represented Ireland at 2 World Championships, in Dortmund in 1959 and in Munich in 1967. He also took part in 6 European Championships between 1959 and 1968. A jeweller and watchmaker in Balbriggan, he has also played veteran's table tennis.

CAHALANE, NIALL.

G.A.A. football half-back and corner-back, Cork. Club: Castlehaven. A member of the Cork minors which captured the All-Ireland M.F.C. in 1981, he was captain of the Cork side which won the All-Ireland Under 21 Football Championship in 1984. He was a star player on Cork's 2 successive defeats in All-Ireland Senior Football Championship finals by Meath in 1987 and 1988, and went on to win Liam McCarthy Cup medals in 1989 (in an injury-laden year) and 1990. He has won All-Star recognition, including in 1987. He was also a member of the Cork side which won the Munster S.F.C. again in 1993, when they again reached the All-Ireland final losing to Derry.

CAHILL, HAROLD Alexander (HARRY).

Hockey international goalkeeper. Born on 9th June 1930. Clubs: Pembroke Wanderers, Belfast Y.M.C.A., Tamworth and Coventry & North. Over a 20 year period between 1953 and 1973 he was Ireland's leading hockey goalkeeper (and rated by many as the best in the world for some time), being capped for a then record 72 times (being in the side which won the Home International title for the first time in 19 years in 1968, and also in the side which achieved the famous win in Santander in 1972). He also played in Ireland's first venture into the European Cup, and toured South Africa. He was capped 53 times for Great Britain between 1959 and 1968, and played with the G.B. team in 3 successive Olympic Games, in 1960 at Rome (when the side finished in 4th place), 1964 at Tokyo, and in Mexico 1968. One of the truly great hockey goalkeepers the world game has known.

CAHILL, MABEL E.

Tennis player. Born in Ballyragget in Co Kilkenny, 2nd April 1863. Moving to New York in 1889, she won the 1891 United States Ladies Tennis Singles title (by beating E.C. Roosevelt in the final), and also captured the doubles. In 1892 she became the first player in U.S. tennis history to capture the Triple Crown of titles, winning the Singles (beating the 15-year-old Bessie Moore in the final), the Mixed Doubles with Adeline McKinnan, and completing the hat-trick by winning the Women's Doubles in partnership with Clarence Herbert. In 1893, after defaulting the U.S. Women's Singles final, she won the New York State Singles final, which proved to be her last win of any importance, as she then stopped competitive tennis. In 1976 she was placed in the Tennis International Hall of Fame, and still remains the only Irish-born person to win any U.S. Championship Grand Slam tennis title.

CAIRNES, H M .

Amateur international golfer. Club: Portmarnock (winning 7 Senior Cup medals in 1904, 1906, 1907, 1913, 1919, 1930 and 1932; and 2 Barton Shield medals in 1920, and 1932)). He played 14 international matches for Ireland between 1901 and 1927. An administrator of note, he won the Irish Close Championship title in 1907 at Portrush, and was beaten finalist on three occasions in the same event, in 1906, 1925 and 1927. He was also beaten finalist in the Irish Amateur Open in 1908.

CALDWELL, JOHNNY.

Bantamweight boxer, amateur and professional. Born in Belfast, 7th May 1938. As an amateur member of the Immaculatta club in Belfast (and losing only 7 out of 250 amateur bouts), he won the Irish National Senior Championship at bantamweight in both 1956 and 1957. He won a bronze medal at that weight at the Melbourne Olympic Games in 1956, beating a Burmese and an Australian before losing his semi-final bout to the Romanian Mircea Dobrescu. Being only 18 years and 209 days old when doing so, he became, and remains, Ireland's youngest ever Olympic medal winner. Turning professional in 1958, inside 2 years he had won his first 21 pro fights (12 inside the distance), including the British flyweight crown (in a k.o. in 3 rounds over Frankie Jones at the Kings Hall). He then went on to win the vacant world bantamweight crown by defeating the Frenchman, Alphonse Halimi in May 1961, before beating the same opponent, again on points, in October of the same year, both fights being at Wembley. Losing his world title (in a bid for the undisputed crown) in January 1962 to Eder Jofre of Brazil in Sao Paulo, he then lost to Freddie Gilroy in the famous Belfast fight for the British and Commonwealth titles in October of the same year. He went on to recapture the British and Commonwealth crowns in 1964 by beating George Bowes over 7 rounds. He lost them to Alan Rudkin in 1965, and retired that year after only one more bout, fighting 35 pro fights in all.

CALLAN, COLM Patrick.

Rugby international lock-forward. Born in Port, Co Louth, 6th January 1923. Club: Lansdowne. A product of Castleknock College, he played in the 4 Victory internationals during W.W.II., before going on to be capped 10 times for Ireland between 1947 and 1949. He was one of the 9 players to play in all 4 of the games when Ireland won it's only Grand Slam title in 1948. Also a Leinster interpro, he played Barbarians rugby as well.

CALLINAN, JOHN JOE.

G.A.A. hurling forward, Tipperary. He captained Tipperary to their All-Ireland Senior Hurling Championship success of 1930 (scoring 1-1 in the 2-7 to 1-3 win over Dublin). He won a Railway Cup medal with Munster in 1928, the province's first win in this sphere.

CALLINAN, JOHNNY.

G.A.A. hurling right half-forward, Clare. Born in 1955. Club: Clarecastle. First playing senior inter-county hurling at the age of 18 in 1973, he won 2 National Hurling League winner's medals with Clare, in 1977 and 1978, and was on 3 Clare sides beaten in N.H.L. finals, in 1975, 1976 and 1985. A member of Clare S.H.C. sides beaten in 4 Munster finals (1974, 1977, 1978 and 1981), he also played Railway Cup for both the Combined Universities and Munster (winning medals in 1976, 1978 and 1981). He won 2 All-Star awards, in 1979 and 1981, both as a right-half forward.

CAMERON, ANTHONY (TONY).

Equestrian rider. In the Rome Olympic Games in 1960, on Black Salmon, he was on the Irish side in the Team 3-Day Event which finished in 6th place, and 4 years later he was the leading Irish rider on the side which finished in 4th place in Tokyo of 1964. In the 1964 Olympic Individual Three Day Event, he finished in 5th place on his mount Black Salmon (the best ever individual performance in an Olympic Games by an Irish rider), finishing less than 3 points off a bronze medal.

CAMPBELL, ALBERT C.

Soccer international defender. Club: Crusaders (he was a member of the only 2 Crusaders sides to win I.F.A. Cups, in both 1967 and 1968). Although he won only 2 senior caps for Northern Ireland, in 1963 against Wales and in 1965 against Sweden, these make him the Crusaders club's most capped player. He was voted Ulster Footballer of the Year in 1961.

CAMPBELL, ALAN.

Soccer international forward. Clubs: Shamrock Rovers (with whom he was leading scorer in the League of Ireland twice, in 1979-80 with 22 goals and in 1983-84 with 24 goals which helped the club to win the League of Ireland), Santander, a Belgian league side, and Dundee. He won 3 international caps for the Republic of Ireland in 1985 while with Santander, one as a substitute.

CAMPBELL, DAVID A (DAVY).

Soccer international midfielder. Born in Eglington, 2nd June 1965. Clubs: Oxford BC, Nottingham Forest, Notts County (on loan) and Charlton Athletic. He has been capped 10 times in the midfield for Northern Ireland from 1986 up to 1988, 4 of these as a sub.

CAMPBELL, EDWARD F.

Rugby international threequarter. Club: Monkstown. He was capped only 4 times for Ireland, but his first two were in Ireland's 2nd Triple Crown success in 1899, when he scored one of Ireland's 3 tries in the 9-3 win over Scotland. He played interprovincial rugby for Leinster twice in 1899.

CAMPBELL, Charles ERIC.

Rugby international 2nd row forward. Born in Tullow, Co Carlow, 12th December 1942. Club: Old Wesley. A product of Wesley College, he played for Leinster 13 times in the interprovincial series over a twelve year period from 1964 to 1975, and played 8 matches for Dublin against French sides in the 1960's. His only full international match was against South Africa in the 8-8 draw of 1970.

CAMPBELL, J .

Soccer international midfielder. Club: Cliftonville (winning Irish Cup medals in 1897, 1900, 1901, and 1907) and Distillery (winning an Irish Cup medal in 1896). He was capped 15 times in all for Ireland between in the formative soccer years of 1896 and 1904, scoring one international goal.

CAMPBELL, JOHN P (JOHNNY).

Soccer international outside-left. Born in Belfast, 28th March 1923, he died in 1968. Clubs: Belfast Celtic and Fulham. Once an Ulster 100 and 200 yards sprint champion, he, while on a tour of America with Belfast Celtic in 1949, scored both goals when the club beat the full Scottish national XI in New York. An Irish League representative, he was capped twice for Northern Ireland, in 1951.

CAMPBELL, NOEL.

Soccer international forward. Clubs: St Patrick's Athletic (being the club's leading league scorer in 1968-69 and 1969-70) and Fortuna (Cologne). He was capped 11 times at soccer for the Republic of Ireland side between 1971 and 1977, three times as a sub.

CAMPBELL, ROBERT M (BOBBY).

Soccer international forward. Born in Belfast, 13th September 1956. Clubs: Aston Villa, Halifax (twice), Huddersfield (twice), Sheffield, Brisbane City, Bradford City (in his two periods with the club, from 1981-84 and 1984-86, he scored a club record most league goals in aggregate, with 121 goals; and also he helped the club to win the Division 3 Championship in 1984-85). He was capped twice for Northern Ireland in 1982.

CAMPBELL, Dr SAMUEL BURNSIDE BOYD.

Rugby international forward. 1889-1971. Clubs: Edinburgh University, and Derry. He assisted his country to win 7 wins in his 12 international caps for Ireland between 1911 and 1913, helping Ireland to share the International Championship in 1912. He won a Military Cross in World War One.

CAMPBELL, Seamus OLIVER (OLLIE).

Rugby international out-half, and centre. Born in Dublin, 3rd March 1954. Club: Old Belvedere. A product of Belvedere College (winning a Leinster Senior Schools medal in 1971), he won 22 international caps for Ireland between 1976 and 1984 (failing to score in only 2 games). A great all-round outhalf, he was also a brilliant placekicker. He was a vital cog in Ireland's 1982 Triple Crown success, scoring all 21 points in the final match against Scotland. He toured twice with the British and Irish Lions sides: to South Africa in 1980, being the highest scorer on tour (60 points), with a record 19 penalties; and to New Zealand in 1983, being again, with 124 points, the tours highest scorer, and winning a total of 5 Test caps (his 12 points in the first test gives him the record high of most points for British Lions in a test when all points are scored). Among his outstanding Irish scoring achievements are: scoring a then world record-equalling 6 penalty goals in the 1982 Scotland game: most points in an international championship season by an individual (46 in 1979-80, equalled in 1982, succeeded by 52 in 1982-83); most penalties (14) in an international championship season; most points (60) for Ireland on an overseas tour (Australia 1979), most points in a tour match (19 v Australia,1979), most points in an international match (21 versus Scotland in 1982): most successive international points for Ireland (38 in 1982 to 1983); and most drop goals for Ireland (7). He is Ireland's 2nd highest record points scorer in internationals, with 217 (passing Tom Kiernan's record of 158 points in 1980), consisting of 1 try, 15 conversions, 7 drop goals, and 54 penalties (a record), along with his total of 26 international points for the Lions giving a total of 243 international points. For his prodigious feats of 1982, he was voted Texaco Sportstar of the Year for rugby, and also as Supreme Sportstar for that year, the 3rd rugby player to be so voted.

CAMPBELL, WILLIAM G.

Soccer international forward. Born in Belfast, 2nd July 1944. Clubs: Distillery (helping tem to an Irish League triumph in 1962-63), Sunderland, Dundee. He was capped 6 times for Northern Ireland between 1968 and 1970, having also been capped 3 times at Under-23 level.

CAMPBELL, William THOMAS ('TOMMIE').

Golfer. Born 24th July 1927. A member of Foxrock Golf Club. In July 1964, at the age 37 he set the still-held world record long drive (in an officially regulated contest over level terrain), when, at Dun Laoghaire GC, he hit the ball 392 yards (358 metres) off the last drive of his round on the 18th fairway.

CAMPBELL, WALTER Islay Hamilton.

Hockey international player. Born on 14th October 1886. Club: Dublin University. He was a member of the Irish hockey team which won a silver medal in the inaugural hockey tournament in the 1908 London Olympic games, a side which beat Wales 3-1 in the semi-final before being beaten 8-1 by England in the final (this match was the last of his 2 international caps for Ireland).

CANAVAN, PAT.

G.A.A. football half-back, Dublin. Club: St Vincent's (a member of the side beaten in the All-Ireland Club Championship final in 1985). He was on the Dublin minors beaten in the All-Ireland M.F.C. final of 1978. He was at right half back on the Dublin side which won the All-Ireland Senior Football Cfinal in 1983, playing in that position also on the sides beaten by Kerry in the 2 All-Ireland S.F.C. finals that followed. He won a Railway Cup medal with Leinster in 1985. He won one All-Star award, in 1983, at right half back.

CANNIFFE, DONAL Martin.

Rugby international scrum-half. Born in Mullingar, 14th August 1949. Clubs; Cork Constitution (winning Munster Senior Cup medals with them in 1970, 1972 and 1973), and Lansdowne (winning Leinster Senior Cup medals in 1979, 1980 and 1981, and Leinster Senior League medals in 1977 and 1981). A product of P.B.C. Cork, with whom he won a Munster Senior Schools Cup medal in 1966, he captained the first Ireland 'B' XV against France in 1975. He played for Ireland twice while at Lansdowne, against Wales and England in 1976. He toured New Zealand and Fiji with Ireland in 1976. On 31st October 1978, he was captain of 'The Munster Team That Beat The All Blacks', which ensures his place in rugby history.

CANTILLON, CHRISTY.

Munster and Ireland 'B' rugby wing-forward. Clubs: U.C.C. (winning a Munster Senior Cup medal in 1976), and Cork Constitution (captaining the side to the Munster Senior Cup win of 1983). A member of the C.B.C. Cork schools side which won the Munster Senior Schools Cup in 1972, he won his only 'B' international cap against England in 1982. It is for scoring the only try in the momentous 12-0 Munster win over the New Zealand All Blacks in 1978, that he will be remembered forever in the proud history of Munster rugby. In Munster's 15-6 win over the touring Australian side of 1981 he was one of 5 remaining players left from that famous day of 1978. He toured Australia with Ireland in 1979.

CANTRELL, JOHN Leo (JOHNNY).

Rugby international hooker. Born in Limerick, 10th January 1954. Clubs: U.C.D. and Blackrock College. He played 15 senior Interprovincial matches for Leinster betwen 1974 and 1978. Winning a B cap in 1975, he was capped at hooker 9 times for Ireland between 1976 and 1981, being on the losing side 8 times. He went on the Irish tours of New Zealand and Fiji in 1976 and South Africa in 1981 (when he played in both tests).

CANTWELL, NOEL Euchuria Cornelius.

Soccer international full-back, and international cricketer. Born in Cork 28th February 1932. At the age of 20, he joined West Ham from Cork Athletic (playing with the Hammers from 1952 to 1960 in 245 league matches, and playing a vital role in their promotion from Division 2 in 1962). He then transfered to Manchester United for 6 seasons, playing 123 league matches, winning an F.A. Cup medal as captain in 1963, and a League Championship medal in 1966/67 (as club captain, although only playing 4 games). He was capped 36 times for the Republic of Ireland between 1954 and 1967, scoring 10 international goals (making him then the Republic's leading goalscorer). He scored Ireland's first penalty in the European Championship in 1958 versus Czechoslovakia. He was voted in 1958, the inaugural year, as Texaco's Soccer Sportstar of the Year. He later managed Coventry City, Peterborough United, and briefly the Republic of Ireland XI. In cricket, as left hand batsman and right hand medium paced bowler, and a member of the Cork Bohemians club, he played 5 times for Ireland between 1956 and 1959

CANTY, JOE.

Flat jockey. Born in Knocklong, Co Limerick in 1895, he died in 1971. He was champion jockey in Ireland for a total of 7 times, starting in 1919, and in the year of 1925 he rode a total of 117 winners over flat and fences, a record for one year not equalled by an Irish jockey for a long time. Attached to the Michael Dawson stable initially (and marrying his daughter), he is placed third (and leading Irish-born) jockey in the all-time winner's of Irish Classics tally, with 15. They are: 3 Irish 2,000 Guineas (1934 with Cariff, 1936 with Hocus Pocus and 1943 with The Phoenix); 5 Irish 1,000 Guineas winners (1939 with Serpent Star, 1942 with Majideh, 1944 with Annetta, 1946 with Ella Retford and, at the age of 53, in 1948 with Morning Wings); 4 Irish Derby's (a dead heat with Haine in 1924, with Sea Serpent in 1931, in 1939 with Mandragon, and with his favourite horse The Phoenix in 1943); 2 Irish Oaks winners (1942 with Majideh and 1943 with Suntop); and 2 Irish St Leger's (1941 with Etoille de Lyond and 1944 with Water Street. An accomplished jockey, he also won 7 National Stakes, 7 Railway Stakes, even 4 Galway Hurdles, as he was also a capable jockey over jumps (also winning 2 Leopardstown Chases). His brother James trained (and Joe rode) the winners of 2 Irish Classics in 1939, Mondrogon in the Irish Derby and Serpent Star in the Irish 1,000 Guineas. James's son, Phil Canty, trained the winner of the 1950 Irish St Leger, Morning Madam; another son, John, trained in California.

CARBERRY, TOMMY.

Natinal hunt jockey. Born in 1941. Associated mainly with Tom Dreaper and his son Jim (ccvv), he married Tom's daughter Pamela. One of Ireland's finest modern National Hunt jockeys, he has ridden the winner of the prestigious Cheltenham Gold Cup 3 times, in 1970 and 1971 with L'Escargot (with whom he was also 3rd in 1973 and 2nd in 1974), in 1975 with Ten up, also coming home first in 1980 with the subsequently disqualified Tied Cottage. He has had twelve Cheltenham National Hunt Festival winners in all. He won the Grand National at Liverpool on L'Escargot in 1975, in a famous race in which Red Rum was 2nd. Many time champions jockey in Ireland, he won the Irish Grand National twice on Brown Lad, in 1975 and 1976. His son Paul Carberry has emerged in the early 1990's as one of the finest of prospect's over jumps.

CAREW, TOMMY.

G.A.A. footballer and hurler, Kildare. Born in 1945. Clubs: Clane (football, winning 4 Kildare SFC medals)) and Coill Dubh (winning one Kildare SHC medal). Playing minor hurling for the county, and Under 21 at both codes for Kildare, he played senior county hurling and football over a 15 year period between 1965 and 1980. In football he won an All-Ireland Under 21 medal in 1965 (along with 2 other Leinster medals), and played in 6 Kildare sides beaten in the Leinster Senior Football Championship final, in 1966, 1969, 1971, 1972, 1975 and 1978. He played on the Kildare side beaten in the National Football League final in 1968, and also played Railway Cup for Leinster. In hurling (his favourite code) he won an All-Ireland JHC medal in 1962, and 2 All-Ireland 'B' SHC medals. He was a replacement All-Star for both codes in 1975 and for football in 1978. Later becoming a full-time G.A.A. coach for Kildare schools, he was a Kildare senior football selector in 1991-92.

CAREY, CIARAN.

G.A.A. hurling centre half-back, Limerick. As a comparative new-comer to senior inter-county hurling, he was a star member of the Limerick side which captured the National League in hurling in 1991-92. In 1992 he became one of only 2 Limerick hurlers to win All-Star awards, gaining his spot at centre half-back.

CAREY, DENIS JOSEPH (D.J., 'DODGER').

G.A.A. hurling forward, Kilkenny, and handballer. Club: Young Irelanders (of Gowran). Born in 1971, he is a product of St Kieran's College (winning one minor and 2 senior All-Ireland school's medals with them). He won an All-Ireland M.H.C. medal with Kilkenny in 1988, and 2 years later helped the county to win the All-Ireland Under 21 Championship of 1990. First playing senior inter-county hurling in 1989, he then played with Kilkenny in 3 successive All-Ireland Senior Hurling Championship finals, in 1991 (scoring 9 points in the final loss to Tipperary), 1992 (when his 3-23 made him the championship's biggest scorer, helping the county to win the Liam McCarty Cup), and also in the in 1993 win (when he scored over 40 points in the championship). He won a National Hurling League medal with the 'Cats' in 1990 (scoring 10 points in the final). A richly talented hurler, he is the grand-nephew of Paddy Phelan (cv), the Kilkenny left half-back in the 1930's. He has won 2 All-Star awards, in both 1991 and 1992, both at left corner-forward. He has also won 12 All-Ireland medals at handball, and won a U.S. Junior championship medal in 1988.

CAREY, JOHN J (JACKIE, 'GENTELMAN JOHN').

Soccer international right full-back and utility player. Born in Dublin, 23rd February 1919. Moving to Old Trafford for £250 from St James Gate, his period at Manchester United stretched from 1936 to 1953, during which he scored 15 goals in 306 games. At that club he had enormous influence in many positions, and he captained them to win the F.A. Cup in 1948 (the club's first success in the cup for 40 years), and won an English League 1st Division winner's medal with them in 1951-52. He was a fine captain, both at club (being United's longest serving captain) and international level, and was capped 29 times for the Republic of Ireland from 1938 (when aged 19) to 1953 (spanning 3 decades and scoring 3 international goals). He was capped a further 7 times for Northern Ireland in 1946-49. In the space of 2 days in September 1946 (28th and 30th) he played for the 2 different Ireland sides against England. He also captained the Rest of Europe against Great Britain in the 1947 game. In 1948-49 he became the first (and thus far only) player from the Republic of Ireland to win the prestigious Football Writer's Association Award of Footballer of the Year. Retiring gracefully at the end of the 1952-53 season, he went on to manage Blackburn Rovers, Everton, Leyton Orient and Nottingham Forest.

CAREY, SUE

Handball champion. Born in Aughrim Street in Dublin. Clubs: St Aughrim, (from 1979) Na Fianna, Naoimh Mhuire. As a youngster she won all the under-age national handball titles, and has won 8 National Senior titles at singles and doubles. In 1986 she reached her peak when becoming the first Irishwoman to capture a world singles title, which she achieved in Vancouver, and also (by partnering Liz Hall) won the world doubles title, beating the local favourite combination of Canadians in the final. In the 1988 world championships she reached the semi-finals in the singles, and in her day has beaten all the world's best players.

CARMODY, TOMMY.

Natinal Hunt jockey. In 1978, on his first rides at the Cheltenham Festival, he had wins on Mr Kildare and Hilly Way, and later had wins at the festival with Slaney Idol, Buck House and Galmoy. He was champion National Hunt jockey in Ireland twice, in 1985 and 1988. He had a 3 year spell in England with the successful Michael Dickinson, and was twice runner-up in the British jockey's championship, winning the King George VI Chase 3 years in a row (in 1978 on Gay Spartan, and in 1979 and 1980 on Silver Buck). After a long successful career, he retired, at the age of 35 in 1992, through injury.

CARNEY, MARTIN.

G.A.A. football forward, Donegal. Club: St Joseph's, Bundoran-Ballyshannon (winning county championship medals with them). He won Ulster Senior Championship medals with Donegal in 1972 and 1974. He also helped Donegal to win the 1975 Dr McKenna Cup. He won a Railway Cup medal with the Combined Universities in 1973 at right half-forward, and won again with Ulster in 1975. He was the county's top scorer in each year from 1975 to 1978.

CAROLAN, GUS.

Pitch and putt player. Club: Glenane P.P.C. He has won 3 Irish national titles in pitch and putt, beginning in 1968 when he won the National Gents Matchplay Championship. Then by winning the 1974 National Strokeplay Championship, he became the first player to win both of the sport's Mens national premier titles. By winning the National Strokeplay Champiponship again in 1975, he became the most recent player to win this title back to back. Now a golfer with Beech Park.

CARR, CAROL.

Blind Athlete. Club: Dublin City Harriers. In the European Games for the Blind of 1981 she won a silver medal in the 1,500 metres, and went on 2 years later to win gold medals in the same games at 2 disciplines, the 400 and 1,500 metres (and both in world record times). In the 1984 Olympics for the disabled at Uniondale, New York, she won a gold medal in the 400 metres B2 final in a time of 65.5 seconds. In the 1985 World Championships for the Blind, she won silver in the 800 metres and gold in the 400 metres.

CARR, DECLAN.

G.A.A. hurling midfielder, Tipperary. Club: Holycross-Ballycahill (captaining them to their first SHC in Tipperary for 38 years in 1990). Born in Dublin in 1965, he won an All-Ireland Senior Hurling Championship medal with Tipperary in 1989, and won an All-Star place at midfield in the 1989 line-up. He was captain of the Tipperary side which won the 1991 Liam McCarthy Cup (his 2nd medal), defeating Kilkenny in the final by 1-16 to 0-15. He is a younger brother of Tommy Carr (cv) with whom he played inter-county football.

CARR, JOSEPH Benedict (JOE or 'J.B.').

Amateur golfer. Born in Dublin, 18th February 1922. Club: Sutton (winning 3 Barton Shields and 6 Senior Cups). Ireland's greatest amateur golfer, he won the Irish Amateur Open 4 times, in 1946, 1950, 1954, and 1956 (and was runner-up in 1947, 1948, 1951, and 1958). He won the prestigious British Amateur Championship 3 times, in 1953, 1958 and 1960 (he was also runner-up in the event in 1968 at the age of 46, and was 3 times a beaten semi-finalist). He won the Irish Close Championship 6 times, in 1954, 1957, 1963, 1964, 1965 and 1967 (and was runner-up in 1951 and 1959). He was leading amateur in the British Open in 1956, 1957 and 1958. He won the East of Ireland Championship a record 12 times, in 1941 (the inaugural year, when he was 19), 1943, 1945, 1946, 1948, 1956, 1957, 1958, 1960, 1961, 1964 and 1969 (he was runner-up in 1944 and 1966). He also won the 'West' a record 12 times, in 1946, 1947, 1948, 1951, 1953, 1954, 1956, 1958, 1960, 1961, 1962 and 1966 (and was never beaten in a final); and he won the 'South' 3 times, in 1948, 1966 and 1969, having been runner-up in 1946. His tally of 40 championship wins puts him 14 ahead of the 2nd place Irishman in this tally, John Burke (cv). He was on the Walker Cup side a record 10 times, 1947, 1949, 1951, 1953, 1955, 1957, 1959, 1961, 1963, 1965 as non-playing captain when the sides drew, and as playing captain in 1967, his record being 5 wins in 20 matches. He played in an Irish record of 138 Home international matches in 23 successive series from 1947 to 1969, winning 78 and halving 10, and was on the first Irish side to win the series outright in 1955: and he played in the European Amateur Team championship winning sides of 1965 and 1967. The father of Roddy Carr (cv), the swashbuckling Joe was the first amateur golfer to win the Golf Writers Association trophy in 1953, and in 1961 he won the Bobby Jones Award for Distinguished Sportsmanship in Golf. In 1960 he was the first amateur golfer to win the Texaco Golf Sportstar of the Year, and in 1978 became the 2nd golfer to be elevated into the Texaco Hall of Fame. He was a Walker Cup selector 1979-86, and was captain of the R.&A. in 1992.

CARR, NIGEL John.

Rugby international wing-forward. Born in Belfast, 27th July 1959. Clubs: Queens University Belfast, and Ards (the 2nd player from that club to be capped for Ireland). A product of R.B.A., he was first capped for Ireland at 'B' level, his 4 caps (one each in 1979, 1980, 1982, and 1984), making him Ireland's most capped B international. A fine open-side wing forward, he was deprived of many caps due to injury in a 1987 bomb explosion, and after a valiant effort to get back to international fitness, retired from the game in 1988, having won only 11 senior caps for his country, between 1985 and 1987. An outstanding member of the 1985 Triple Crown-winning Ireland back-row with Philip Matthews, and Brian Spillane, in 1986 he was awarded full Lions honours as being one of 6 Irishmen selected in a squad of 21 to play against the Rest of the World.

CARR, RODDY.

Amateur and professional golfer. Born in Sutton Co Dublin, 27th October 1950. He won the 1970 East of Ireland title, and in the same year won the Turnberry Foursomes with Jimmy Martin (also finishing runner-up in the North of Ireland). He won the West of Ireland title in 1971. At the age of 20 he was a key player in only Britain and Ireland's second victory ever in the Walker Cup series, in 1971 at St Andrew's, when he halved his singles match with Bill Hyndnman, and won one of the crucial victories on the 2nd day, against Jim Simons. His Walker Cup record is 87.5% in four matches, winning 3 out of a possible 4 points (his 3 wins all coming on the last green), this making the first of only 2 Irishmen unbeaten in the Walker Cup matches. He was voted as Texaco Golf Sportstar of the Year in 1971, following on from his father's selection in 1960. He turned pro in late 1971, with little success, and later joined the Mark McCormack team of golf consultants. He now runs Camcorp in Ireland. The 2nd son of the great Joe Carr (cv), they are the only father and son to play Walker Cup golf. His younger brother John was also an Irish international golfer 1981-83, reached the semi-final of the British Amateur Championship in 1981, and was in the Irish side which won the European Team title in 1983.

CARR, ROSS.

G.A.A. football right half-forward, Down. Born in 1965. Club: Clonduff. Normally a back, he was the county's biggest scorer in the championship when he scored 30 points in the 6 games during the run-up to Down's All-Ireland Senior Football Champoionship win of 1991. He won an All-Star award in 1991 at right half-forward.

CARR, TOMMY.

G.A.A. football right half-back and left full-back, Dublin. Born in Dublin, in 1963. Club: Ballymun-Kickhams. A product of King's Hospital, he has won 3 Leinster Senior Football Championship medals with Dublin, in 1989 and 1992, and previously when coming on as a sub in Dublin's defeat at the hands of Kerry in the All-Ireland S.F.C. final of 1985 (he missed the 1993 win through suspension). He captained the victorious Dubs side in their 1991 National Football League final triumph over Kildare, in their epic losing 4-match battle against Meath in the Leinster S.F.C. 1st round in 1991, and to their All-Ireland S.F.C. defeat in 1992 against Donegal. He won a 2nd National League medal in 1993 (being sent-off in the 5th minute of the replayed final). A brother of Declan Carr (cv), he won an All-Star award in 1991, at right half-back.

CARROLL, ANN.

G.A.A. camogie full-back and full-forward, Tipperary and Kilkenny. Clubs; St Patricks (Glencoole-Ballingarry, Tipperary), U.C.C., and St Pauls (Kilkenny). Born in London, she won 2 All-Ireland Club Championship medals with her St Patricks (Glencoole) side from Tipperary in 1965 and 1966, also winning 3 Gael Linn medals with Munster in 1963, 1965, and 1966. She later played for St Pauls in Kilkenny, winning All-Ireland Club Championship medals with them in the late 60's and early 70's (becoming the first camogie player to win All-Ireland club championship medals with 2 different clubs from 2 different counties), and winning 3 Gael Linn medals with Leinster. She won 2 All-Ireland Senior Championship medals with Kilkenny in the 1970's, the first while in the full-back position, and also at full-forward. She later became a national coach.

CARROLL, JAMES P (JIMMY).

Amateur international golfer. Club: Sutton (winning Senior Cup medals in 1948, 1949, 1950, 1958 and 1962). He won 4 championship titles, highlighted by the Irish Close Championship in 1949 in Galway, a year in which he also won the 'South' (he was runner-up in 1948). He also twice won the East of Ireland title, in 1950 and 1953, being runner-up in 1948. He played 28 matches for Ireland in the Home International Championship from 1948 to 1956, winning 14. His grandson, Sean Dollman (born in South Africa, 6th December 1968), a member of Leevale AC, won the U.S. National collegiate cross country in 1991, the U.S. Collegiate 10,000 metres in 1992, and represented Ireland in the 10,000 metres at the Barcelona Olympics in 1992.

CARROLL, MICHELE (nee WALSHE).

Sprint international athlete. Club: Crusaders. Born in 1961 in Dublin. Dominating the Irish domestic sprinting scene for over 16 years, by winning the B.L.E. National sprint titles at 100 metres and 200 metres in 1993, her tally of B.L.E. National Championships had reached the remarkable (and unlikely-to-be-equalled) total of 28 titles (14 titles at 100m, 11 at 200 metres, and 3 at 400m). Since her first B.L.E. title success in 1977, she had by 1993 accomplished the 'double' of Irish 100m and 200m titles eleven times. She held the Irish record at 100 metres and 200 metres for many years. Married to athlete Ronnie Carroll, she was never selected to represent Ireland in either Olympic or World Championship celebrations.

CARROLL, NOEL.

Middle-distance international athlete. Born in the village of Annagassan, Co Louth, 7th April 1941. Attending Villanova University, he became the world's fastest 18 and 19-year-old over the half mile and 800 metres distances, and was a member of the All-American Athletics team in 1963 and 1965. He won a total of 14 Irish Championship titles, at 440 yards and 880 yards. He also won three British A.A.A. 880 yards titles, in 1963 in 1.50.3, in 1966 in 1.48, and in 1968, in 1.50.0 (he finished 2nd in 1964, 1967 and 1969). He won the first 3 European Indoor Championships at 800 metres, in 1966 at Dortmund, 1967 at Prague, and in 1968 at Madrid. He competed in 2 Olympic Games (over 800m in 1964 in Tokyo, and over both 400m and 800m in 1968 in Mexico) and 3 European Championships. He set a world record at the 4x880 yards relay with Villanova in 1964 (becoming the first Irish athlete to recieve a 'World-Record Holder' plaque), and set a European record at 880 yards in 1963. In 1972 he was appointed P.R.O. to Dublin Corporation, a post he still holds. Still an active runner in international veteran events, he was twice voted as Texaco's Athletics Sportstar of the Year, in 1961 and 1967. He is married to the harpist and singer Deirdre O'Callaghan.

CARROLL, JACK.

Hockey international goalkeeper. Clubs: Belfast Y.M.C.A., and Banbridge. He won 15 international hockey caps for Ireland in the Golden days, and with 14 wins and one draw in that period between 1937 and 1948 (with a break for World War II), he conceded only one goal in the nine matches 3-in-a-row success of 1937, 1938, and 1939, and was also on the Triple Crown winning sides of 1946 and 1947.

CARROLL, PAT .

G.A.A. hurling forward, Offaly. He was at right full-forward on the Offaly side which won the Liam McCarthy Cup for the first time in 1982, being also a member of the side beaten by Cork in the 1984 All-Ireland Senior Hurling Championship decider. He won 2 All-Star awards, in 1980 at right half-forward, and in 1981 at left full-forward. He died in 1986 after a long illness.

CARROLL, TED.

G.A.A. hurling centre-back and right full-back, Kilkenny. Born in 1939. Club: Lisdowney. He won an All-Ireland Colleges medal with St Kieran's Kilkenny in 1957. As a minor he was on 2 successive Kilkenny M.F.C. sides beaten in the All-Ireland final, in 1956 and 1957. Later, in a senior inter-county career that went for 1961 to 1971, he won 3 All-Ireland Senior Hurling Championship medals with Kilkenny, in 1963 at centre back, in 1967 at right corner back, and 1969, again at right corner back. He was also on 3 Kilkenny sides defeated in 3

All-Ireland finals, in 1964, 1966, and as a sub in 1971. He won one Railway Cup medal with Leinster in 1965. He won a National Hurling League medal in 1966 and 3 Oireachtas medals (in 1966, 1967 and 1969). In 1969 he was nominated as Texaco's Hurling Sportstar of the Year, the 3rd Kilkennyman to be so honoured.

CARROLL, TOM.

Soccer international full-back. Born in Dublin, 18th August 1942. He played at Cambridge City, Ipswich (playing 115 league games for them 1966-1971, helping them to capture the Division 2 Championship in 1967-68), and Birmingham City. He won 17 senior international soccer caps in the full-back line for the Republic of Ireland between 1968 and 1973.

CARROLL, WILLIE (Sen) and WILLIE (Jun).

Father and son boxers. Willie Senior was a sportsman of many talents at the turn of the century. A boxer of class, he once fought against a Charlie Burgess (later to become the patriot Cathal Brugha). As a gymnast, and member of the City of Dublin G.C., he won the title of 'International Gymnastic' and 'The Moore Street Athletic Wonder', and represented Ireland in a huge sports tournament held in Rome in 1908. As a rope-climber he won a major international event, and broke the world record by many seconds. He was also an accomplished diver, winning many championships. He was, in 1911, a co-founder of the Irish Amateur Boxing Association, and was later a trainer, promoter, judge and referee. His son Willie Junior helped him to found the famous St Andrew's B.C. of York Street, Dublin, and Willie Junior won the Irish National Senior Championship at Flyweight in 1923.

CARRUTH, MICHAEL.

Lightweight, light-welterweight and welterweight amateur international boxer. Born on 9th July 1967 in Dublin, he hails from the Greenhills area. Club: Drimnagh BC. A winner of many Dublin and Leinster titles and 3 Irish juvenile titles (as well as Under-18 and junior titles), he has won 4 Irish National Senior Championship titles, in 1987 and 1988 as a lightweight, in 1990 as a light welterweight, and as a welterweight in 1992. He represented Ireland at the 1987 Europeans at Turin, the 1988 Seoul Olympics (losing to a Swede, George Cramme, in his 2nd bout at light-welterweight), and the 1989 Europeans. Winning 40 out of his first 50 international bouts for Ireland, in 1989, by gaining a bronze by beating the American Skipper Kelp in the quarter-final of the World Championships in Moscow, he had won Ireland's only 2nd medal at this level (he was beaten for the silver by an East German, Andreas Otto). He was selected on a European boxing team in 1990 for a match against the U.S.A. He reached his career pinnacle in 1992 when he won the gold medal in the welterweight division at the Barcelona Olympic Games (beating 4 opponents, in order: Maselino Tifao by 11-2, Andreas Otto on a count-back on 6-6, Arkom Chenglai from Thailand by 11-4, and in the memorable final he beat the world champion Cuban, Juan Hernandez by 13-10). He thus became the first Irish Olympic Games gold medal winner since Ronnie Delaney 36 years before, and only the fifth ever Irish sportsperson to win a gold for his country (and the first boxer). His triplet brothers Martin (an Irish international welterweight) and William, both also boxed for the Drimnagh BC, and his father Austin is a boxing coach (playing his part with the Irish team in Barcelona in 1992). His uncle Michael Humpston was the first Irish National Senior Champion at light-middleweigth in 1951.

CARSON, ALVIN.

Hockey international goalkeeper. Clubs: Antrim and Belfast Y.M.C.A. He was capped for Ireland 90 times between 1970 and 1983 (making him Ireland's most capped hockey goalkeeper), playing a major role in Ireland's 4th place finish in the 1981 Interncontinental Cup in Rome. He also won 10 international caps for Great Britain betwen 1972 and 1976. He also won 3 indoor caps for Ireland in 1976.

CARTON, PAUL.

Hockey international right wing. Club: Dublin University, and Three Rock Rovers. One of the pioneers of Irish international hockey, he played in Ireland's first eleven matches between 1895 and 1903, and captained the side on 3 occasions, making him on retirement Ireland's then most capped player and the most often to be captain.

CASCARINO, TONY ('CAS').

Soccer international forward. Born at St Paul's Cray, Kent, to an Italian father and Irish mother, 1st September 1962. Clubs: Crockenhill (in the Kent League), Gillingham, Millwall, Aston Villa, Glasgow Celtic and Chelsea. He scored 78 league goals in 219 appearences for Gillingham, being their leading scorer 4 times, in 1983 (18 goals), 1985 (20), 1986 (20), and 1987 (30), before joining Millwall in 1987, for a club record of £200,000. His 23 goals in the 1988/89 season helped Milwall to gain promotion to the First Division. He had a short stint in Aston Villa before joining Glasgow Celtic in 1991 for £1,000,000, and later going to Stamford Bridge. He has won (up to September 1993) 44 caps for Ireland (the 3 caps he gained while at Gillingham made him the club's most capped player), being one of the stars of the Irish side which qualified for the World Cup finals in 1990, and he has scored 11 international goals.

CASE, R. N. (RITCHIE).

Swimmer. Club: Clontarf S.C. Regarded by many as the most stylish Irish swimming champion ever, he dominated Irish national swimming events in the 1930's. He won 21 Irish titles in the period from 1929 to 1938, at 3 different strokes, freestyle, breast-stroke and backstroke. He also won both the Liffey Swim and the Dun Laoghaire Swims 4 times each, and at one stage held every Irish swimming record from 100 yards up to 1 mile. He also played water-polo, winning many club and interprovincial titles over a 15 year period, and was capped for Ireland at the sport on many occasions, captaining the side in 1938. His father Harry was a champion cyclist and swimmer, while both of his brothers, Harry and Wilie, won many Irish swimming titles in the 1920's and 1930's.

CASEY, BILL.

G.A.A. footballer, Dublin, and international basketball player. Born in Dublin in 1943. G.A.A. club: Na Fianna (winning Dublin senior championship medals in 1969 and 1979, at 36). A product of St Vincents CBS, Glasnevin, he won county championship medals at Under 15 hurling and minor football and handball, and for 2 succesive seasons played for Dublin at inter-county level at 4 sports; football, hurling, handball and basketball (at age 18 he was selected at senior level for Dublin in both football and basketball, and once played at inter-provincial level in both sports in the same weekend). A winner of a Leinster M.F.C. medal in 1961, he went on to win an All-Ireland Senior Football Championship medal with Dublin in 1963. As a basketball playing member of the St Vincent's club (from 1962), he won 6 Roy Curtis trophies and 3 All-Ireland inter-county medals, and having at played youth international basketball for Ireland in 1960 and 1961, he then played at senior level between 1962 and 1970, coaching the side occasionally during this period. A major force in basketball coaching, he played in his 34th year of competitive play in the Dublin Leagues in 1992. He is a nephew of the noted Westmeath footballer of the 1920's, Larry McEvoy.

CASEY, CATHAL.

G.A.A. hurling left half-back and midfielder, Cork. From Ballynoe on the Cork/Waterford border, he was born on 4th September 1967. Club: St Catherines. A product of St Colman's Fermoy, he won an All-Ireland M.H.C. medal with Cork in 1985 and an All-Ireland Under 21 Championship medal in 1988. He has also won 4 Fitzgibbon Cup medals with U.C.C. He was a non-playing sub on the Cork Senior Hurling Championship wins of 1986 and 1990. He won a Munster S.H.C. medal in 1992, when the Rebel County were defeated in the All-Ireland S.H.C. final, and won a National Hurling League medal in 1992-93. Winner of an All-Star award in 1991 at left half-back, he is a U.C.C. lecturer.

CASEY, EOIN.

Tennis international player. Born in Glasnevin, Dublin in 1969. Clubs: Riversdale, Charleville and Riverview. A 4-year tennis and marketing scholarship at both Anderson and Clemson universities in the U.S.A. helped develop his skills. A Davis Cup player for Ireland from 1988, he turned pro in 1990. A regular winner of sattelite leg events in both doubles and singles, he has held many national titles. In 1991 he won the Irish Indoor Championships, won a satelite event in Israel, and also reduced his world ranking from 845th to 379th on the A.T.P. ratings. Becoming No 1 ranked player in Ireland, in 1992 his ranking reached into the world's top 300. He represented Ireland in 2 Olympic Games, in Seoul in 1988 at doubles, and in 1992 in Barcelona in doubles and singles.

CASEY, STEVE 'THE CRUSHER', MICK, TOM, PADDY, JIM, JACK and DAN. ('THE TOUGHEST FAMILY ON EARTH').

Wrestling, rowing and tug-of-war brothers. From Ballough, Sneem Co Kerry. Steve, the most illustrious of the family, was nicknamed 'The Crusher', and was World Heavyweight All-In Wrestling Champion from 1939, holding off many contenders until 1946 when he was defeated by Frank Sexton. Among those he defeated in 201 European professional triumphs was the famous 'Danno' O'Mahony (cv), whom he beat in the 12th round of a 26 round bout. He introduced the 'Killarney Flip' to the sport, and in 1936 reached the semi-final of the the Olympic Games, representing Great Britain. Along with 3 of his brothers, Paddy, Mick and Jim, he won the Henley Fours event in rowing, and they won the celebrated Salter Challenge Cup in 1931, 1932 and 1933. Unbeaten in 38 races with the Ace Rowing Club, they were favourites for the 1936 Olympic Games gold medal, but were deemed professional and did not compete (the club's 2nd string side were just pipped for the title). In a famous match rowing against the American champion, Cussen Codman in Boston in 1940, Jim (who had been a British wrestling champion) came first, Steve 2nd and Tom third, all ahead of Codman. In tug-of-war, they were also very successful, becoming All-Irleand Champions. Jack's son, Michael Noel Casey, was coach to the British Rowing squad in the 1984 Olympic Games, while his daughters Bernie and Caroline were All-Ireland champion rowers in 1984 and won the Henley Sculls and Pairs.

CASEY, JAMES C ('TER').

Rugby international hooker. Born in Limerick. Club: Young Munster (helping them to Munster League vicories in both 1930 and 1932, to Munster Senior Cup wins in 1928 and 1930, and the famous Bateman Cup success). He was the first 'Munsters' player to be capped for Ireland, playing against Scotland in 1930 and against England in 1932. A carter by trade.

CASEY, NOEL.

G.A.A. hurling half-forward, Clare. With Clare he won 2 National Hurling League titles in succesive seasons, in 1976-77 and in 1977-78. He was also a member of the Clare side which as beaten by Cork in the Munster S.H.C. finals of 1977 and 1978. He won one All-Star award in 1978, when he was selected at centre half-forward.

CASEY, PATRICK Joseph (PAT or 'CASO').

Rugby international wing three-quarter. Born in Dublin, 4th August 1941. Clubs: U.C.D. (winning Leinster Senior Cup medals in 1963 and 1964) and Lansdowne. Playing 10 times for Leinster in the interprovincial series from 1962 to 1965, he was capped for Ireland 12 times between 1963 and 1965, scoring 3 international tries from the right wing, among them one of Ireland's great tries in the 1964 England match. He also played at out-half and in the centre.

CASEY, PHIL,

Handballer. Born in Mountrath in 1841. His family emigrated to the U.S. when he was 15, and he soon continued his passion for handball. He won his first U.S. title at the age of 35, beating the Swinford-born Barney McQuaide in 1876. From that day on he was undefeated in singles competition. In 1887 he beat John Lawlor for the title of Champion of the World. A great doubles player as well, his span of wins in the American two-hand title stretched over 26 years, from 1871 to 1897 (when he was 56 years old). He died in 1904.

CASEY, TOM.

Soccer international wing-half. Born in Camber, Bangor, 11th March 1930. Clubs: Belfast YMCA, East Belfast, Bangor (winning a Youth cap in 1948), Leeds United, Bournemouth, Newcastle (winning an F.A. Cup medal in 1955), Portsmouth, and Bristol City. This 'iron man' from Comber won 12 international caps for Northern Ireland between 1955 and 1959, playing twice in the vaunted World Cup finals side in 1958 (in the 2-2 draw against West Germany and in the 0-4 defeat by the French), and scoring 2 international goals. He later managed Gloucester City, Distillery and Grimsby amongst other jobs in the game, and also managed the Northern Ireland youth team.

CASEY, WILIAM (BILLY).

G.A.A. football centre half-back, Kerry. He won 4 All-Irelands Senior Football Championship medals at centre-back with the Kingdom, in the 3-in-a-row of 1939, 1940 and 1941, and again in 1946, being on the losing side in the All-Ireland S.F.C. finals of 1938 and the Polo Ground final of 1947. He won a solitary Railway Cup winners medal with Munster in the replay win of 1941.

CASEY, WILLIE.

G.A.A. football right full-back, Mayo. A winner of a Connacht Senior Football Championship medal with Mayo in 1955, he also won a National League medal with the county in 1953-54. His Railway Cup successes for Connacht came in 1958 and 1959. A quality player, he was selected in the right corner-back position in 1984 on the 'Team of the Century' for players never to win an All-Ireland senior medal.

CASKEY, WILLIAM (BILLY).

Soccer international forward and midfielder. Born in Belfast, 12th October 1953. Clubs: Glentoran, Derby County, Tulsa Roughnecks and Glentoran again (winning 5 Irish Cup winner's medals, 4-in-a-row of 1985, 1986, 1987, 1988, and in 1990, and an Irish League medal in 1987-88). He won 7 international caps for Northern Ireland betwen 1979 and 1982 (3 as a substitute), and scored one international goal. He has also played for the Irish League, scoring one goal for them. Having been the N.I.P.F.A. most promising newcomer in 1975, he was N.I.F.W. Player of the Year in 1977.

CASHMAN, JIM.

G.A.A. hurling centre half-back, Cork. Club: Blackrock. A son of Mick Cashman, he won an All-Ireland Senior Hurling Championship medal in midfield in 1986, when his brother Tom (cv) was captain, and later went on to collect his 2nd Liam McCarthy medal in Cork's winning

All-Ireland S.H.C. final in 1990 against Galway. He was also a member of the Cork side beaten in the All-Ireland S.H.C. final of 1992, and won a National Hurling League medal in 1992-93. He won 2 successive All-Star awards at centre-half back, in both 1990 and 1991.

CASHMAN, MICK.

G.A.A. hurling goalkeeper, Cork. Born in 1931. Club: Blackrock (leading them to victory, after a gap of 25 years, in the Cork SHC in 1956). He was Cork's goalkeeper during a lean period in medal terms, his only All-Ireland S.H.C. final appearence was in the 1956 Cork side beaten by Wexford, while he captained the side which lost the Munster S.H.C. final to Waterfod in 1957. Also in 1957 he became the 10th Corkman to captain a Railway Cup winning side in hurling for Munster, and won 5 other interprovincial medals, in 1958, 1959, 1960, 1961, and in 1963 (his tally of 6 being a record for a goal-keeper). He also played outfield on occasions, being at centre-back in the 1954 Munster S.H.C. final. He is the father of both Tom (cv) and Jim Cashman (cv), and is a brother-in-law of Jimmy Brohan (cv).

CASHMAN, SUE.

G.A.A. camogie player, Antrim. Club: Deirdre. She first played senior inter-county camogie with Antrim at the tender age of 13, and by the age of 17, in 1967, she was captaining the Antrim side to their 5th All-Ireland Senior Championship title, when the county won the O'Duffy Cup in a replay against a Dublin side seeking their 11th sucessive title. Her bubbling enthusiasm, speed and energy in that classic 3-9 to 4-2 win meant that she was voted as only the 2nd Camogie player to win a Texaco Sportstar of the Year award, in 1967. She was a member of the first Ulster side to win a Gael Linn Senior Interporvincial title, also in 1967.

CASHMAN, TOM.

G.A.A. hurling centrefield, and right half-back, Cork. Born in 1958. Club: Blackrock (winning an All-Ireland Club Championship medal in 1977). Having won an All-Ireland M.H.C. medal with Cork in 1974 (he performed the 'double' that year, also being on the Cork minor footballers who captured the All-Ireland M.F.C.), he also won an Under 21 hurling championship medal in 1976. Making his senior hurling inter-county debut in 1976, he later won 4 All-Ireland Senior Hurling Championship winner's medals with Cork, at midfield in the triumphs of 1977 and 1978 (at this stage in his career he had won 5 All-Ireland medals at the age of 21); at right half-back in 1984; and as captain from the right half-back position in the 1986 triumph over Galway by 4-13- 2-15. Also playing on Cork sides beaten in All-Irleand S.H.C. finals in 1982 and 1983, he gained 3 All-Star awards, being honoured in 1977 and 1978 at centre-field, and in 1983 at left half-back. He is an older brother of Jim Cashman (cv), and a son of Mick Cashman (cv).

CASSELLS, JOE.

G.A.A. midfielder and centre half-forward football, Meath. Club: Navan O'Mahony's (winning many county championships from 1973, captaining them to the title in 1989). Born October 10th 1954. He won the All-Ireland Under 14 Cross Country Championship in 1968. Having won a Leinster M.F.C. medal with Meath in 1974, he was introduced into the senior inter-county side (winning an O'Byrne Cup medal in 1974). He played a major role at midfield on the Meath side which won the National League final in 1975. Having captained Meath to win the Centenary Cup in 1984, he captained the county side in the replayed 1988 All-Ireland Senior Football Championship final win over Cork (by 0-13 to 0-12), thus becoming the first holder of the new Sam Maguire Cup. He was also the eldest member of the team. He had won another medal the previous year when he was substituted in the final against Cork; he also came on as a sub in

Meath's losing All-Ireland final of 1990 against Cork. He won a Railway Cup medal in 1985 with Leinster. His uncle Eamonn played football for Meath, and his brother Oliver played hurling for the county. Another brother, Peter, is General Secretary of the I.C.T.U.

CASSIDY, TOMMY.

Soccer international midfielder. Born in Belfast, 18th January 1950. Clubs: Coleraine, Newcastle (scoring 22 goals in 170 league matches for them in the 1970's), Burnley. He was capped 24 times for Northern Ireland over a 12 year period between 1971 and 1982 (coming on as a sub in his last international match, the famous 1-0 win over Spain in the 1982 World Cup finals match), and scoring one goal for his country.

CAUL, PADDY.

Amateur international golfer. Club: The Island (where he was the club greenkeeper, winning Barton Shield medals in 1971, 1978 and 1982 and a Senior Cup medal in 1965). He won the East of Ireland Championship at Baltray twice, in 1968 and 1980. He was capped for Leinster in 62 interprovincial matches betwen 1965 and 1977, winning 38 and halving 6 of these: he was capped for Ireland in 7 Home International series betwen 1968 and 1975, winning 19 and halving 4 matches of his 39 matches. He died in 1992.

CHAMBERS, J .

Soccer international forward. Clubs: Distillery, Bury and Nottingham Forest. He won 12 soccer international caps for Northern Ireland between 1921 and 1931, scoring 3 goals at international level for his country.

CHAMBERS, SIR JOSEPH K.C.B. C.M.B.

Rugby international forward. Lived 1864-1935. Club: Trinity College, Dublin. He played in 5 internationals for Ireland between 1886 and 1887. He later became a renowned referee, was President of the I.R.F.U. 1887-1888, and reached the rank of Surgeon Vice Admiral in the Royal Navy.

CHASE, JACK.

Amateur international boxer. Club: Garda. Born in 1905. He was the first Irish amateur boxer to capture 7 Irish National Senior Championship titles, doing so in succession in the middleweight division in 1926, 1927, 1928, 1929, 1930, 1931 and 1932. He was European Police Champion 3 times, and in 1928 reached the last 8 in the Olympic Games at Antwerp. One of those to establish the name of Irish amateur boxing, he lost only 8 of the 60 international bouts for Ireland in the green singlet. He died in 1991.

CHRISTLE, TERRY, MEL and JOE.

Amateur international boxing brothers. Clubs: Trinity College (all 3 brother winning 'pinks' in 1978), and Crumlin. Enormously popular in their time, these three brothers won a total of 7 Irish senior titles between them in the late 1970's. Terry, a middleweight, won 3 successive Irish National Senior Championship titles, in 1978, 1979, and 1980. In 1979 he also won the middleweight championship of France. His brother Mel won an Irish Senior National Championship title at light heavyweight in 1977, and won at super-heavyweight in 1980 (the first boxer to win the national crown at this new discipline). Another brother, Joe, won the Irish heavyweight title in both 1979 and 1980. In 1980 the 3 brothers each won an Irish National Senior Championship on the same night, Terry at middle, Joe at heavy and Mel at super-heavy, an unique record in Irish boxing. Terry was voted as Texaco's Boxing Sportstar of the Year in 1979. Their uncle, Jim Christle, who boxed for Ireland at light-heavyweight in the 1940's (and who was also an accomplished cyclist), coached the 3 brothers for a time.

CLANCY, CARRIE.

G.A.A. camogie player, Limerick. Club: Ahane. One of Limerick's finest camogie players, her career in the county colours spanned over 20 years. She captained Limerick to win the All-Ireland Junior Championship title in their 2-7 to 3-1 win over Wexford in 1977. She played for Munster in many Gael Linn campaigns, and was a member of the only Limerick side to reach and All-Ireland Senior Championship final (when they were beaten by Cork in a replay in 1980).

CLANCY, SEAMUS.

G.A.A. football corner-back, Clare. From Corofin, he was born in 1965. Playing senior football with Clare from 1983, he was a member of the famous side which captured the Munster Senior Football Championship in 1992 when beating Kerry in the final (their first such win since 1917), playing alongside his brother Colm in the side. He was named player of the month for his display in that final, and won an All-Star award also in 1992 as full-back.

CLANCY, THOMAS Patrick John (TOM).

Rugby international prop-forward. Born in Dublin, 16th March 1963. Clubs: Old Belvedere, Landsdowne (helping them to Leinster Senior League wins in 1986 and 1987, and Leinster Senior Cup win s in 1986 and 1991), London Irish. Capped at under 25 level, he has won 9 senior caps for Ireland since 1988. He toured New Zealand with Ireland in 1992.

CLARKE, AUSTIN.

Handballer. Born in 1918 in Dublin. He won Ireland's most coveted title, the Harty Cup for the Irish Senior Hardball Singles title, six times (repeating the feat of his fellow Dublinman Tom Soye cv), in 1944, 1948, 1949, 1951, 1954, and 1955. He also won the Irish Senior Hardball Doubles title in 1942 (with his brother) and 1950. He died at the age of 45, in 1963.

CLARKE, CIARAN Paul.

Rugby international full-back. Born in Dublin, 8th March 1969. Club: Terenure College (appearing in 2 Leinster Senior Cup finals). A product of Terenure College, he first played for Leinster in the 1992-1993 season, gaining his first cap in that season, contributing a drop goal to Ireland's landmark win over Wales in Cardiff (their first win in 11 Home International matches).

CLARKE, COLIN J.

Soccer international forward. Born in Newry, 30th October 1962. Clubs; Ipswich (as an apprentice), Peterborough, Gillingham, Tranmere Rovers (scoring 22 league goals in 45 games), Bournemouth (scoring 26 league goals in 46 matches), Southampton (scoring at a rate of almost one for every 2 games), Portsmouth. First capped while at Bournemouth in 1986 (the 6 caps gained while at the club make him that clubs most capped player), in 1992 he broke the Northern Ireland record for most goals scored in internationals, when scoring his 13th goal in a World Cup qualifying match against Albania.

CLARKE, DARREN.

Amateur and professional golfer. Born 14th August 1968. Club : Dungannon. First capped for Ulster in the interprovincial series in 1988, he played in the Home International series from 1987. He won the 1989 East of Ireland Champinship title and the Mullingar Scratch Cup (by 7 shots). In 1990 he became only the 3rd Irishman to win the Spanish Amateur Championship, and completed a dominant season by capturing the South of Ireland, the 'North' and Irish Close Championships (becoming the first Irish amateur to win successive Willie Gill awards). He then turned professional in September 1990, and has shown steady progress, with some top ten finishes on the European pro circuit.

CLARKE, EDEL.

G.A.A. ladies football left half-forward, Westmeath. Club: Rochfortsbridge (winning 7 county championship, and 2 All-Ireland club runners-up medals in 1981 and 1983). She is a versatile player, and was on the Westmeath team beaten by Kerry in the 1987 All-Ireland Senior Championship final.

CLARKE, Father IGNATIUS (IGGY).

G.A.A. hurling left half-back and midfielder, Galway. Born in 1954. Clubs: Mullagh and Maynooth (winning 2 Fitzgibbon Cup medals). He captained the Galway Under 21 side which captured the county's first All-Ireland Under 21 hurling title in 1972, being previously a member of the minors beaten by Cork in the All-Ireland M.H.C. final of 1970. He was on the Galway side defeated in the All-Ireland Senior Hurling Championship finals of 1975, 1979 and 1981, missing out on the breakthrough Liam McCarthy win of 1980. He won a National Hurling League medal in 1975. He won 3 Railway Cup medals with Connacht, in 1980, 1982, and 1983. A fine player, he attained 4 All-Star awards, in 1975, 1979 and 1980 (at left half-back), and in 1978 at midfield,

CLARKE, JACK.

Rugby international wing-threequarter. Club: Dolphin. A product of Rockwell College, he represented Ireland at schools international level in both rugby and athletics (javelin). He went on to play rugby for Ireland at under-21, under 23, and 'B' levels, before gaining his first cap against Wales in 1991, and it was he who set up Gordon Hamilton in the famous try against Australia in the 1991 World Cup quarter-final. He toured New Zealand with Ireland in 1992. His brother Gearoid, an Athlone scrum-half, played for Connacht from 1991.

CLARKE, JAMES Michael (JIM).

Tug-of-War competitor. From Bohola in Co Mayo, he was born on the 6th October 1874. In the 1908 Olympic Games in London, he was on the much-fancied runners-up Liverpool Police-selected United Kingdom squad, which lost out in the final of the tug-of-war to the London Police squad, which contained Ned Barrett (cv). So a Bohola-man won a silver medal in the Olympics, to add to the many won by his cousin, Martin Sheridan (cv). He died in 1929.

CLARKE, JOSEPH A B (JOE).

Rugby international scrum-half. Club: Bective Rangers (winning Leinster Senior Cup medals in 1923 and 1925). He won 7 international caps for Ireland betwen 1922 and 1924 (scoring his only international try on his debut), including Ireland's first win on Welsh soil in 25 years, in 1922. A dentist, he played interprovincial rugby for Leinster 7 times between 1920 and 1923.

CLARKE, PAUL.

G.A.A. football midfielder, Dublin. Born in 1966. Club: Whitehall Colmcille. He captained the Dublin minors which won the All-Ireland M.F.C. in 1984, and made his senior debut in 1985. A member of Dublin teams beaten in Leinster S.F.C. finals in 1986, 1987 and 1990, he won 2 Leinster championship medals, in 1989 and 1992 (when the Dubs were beaten in the All-Ireland S.F.C. final by Donegal). An airport policeman, he won 2 National League medals, in 1991 and 1993.

CLEARY, CHARLES.

Versatile sportsman. A fitness-fanatic army-man from Dublin, as a gymnast he led the Command team to win the Irish Senior Shield, the country's premier award, for 10 years in succession from 1930 to 1939. As a weight-lifter he became the first Irishman to 'clean and jerk' a barbell weighing more than twice his own bodyweight, held the Irish 'Olympic three' featherweight weightlifting championship each year from 1943 to 1947, and was Irish individual gymnastic champion for 7 years. Also a winner of titles in amateur wrestling, pole-vaulting and long-jumping. In 1948 he won the Irish steel strandpulling championships, and a month later set a world record to become the Irish best-all-round champion. One of the founders of the Irish Amateur Weightlifting Association, he also excelled at boxing, swimming, diving, football, hurling and handball.

CLEARY, EAMON.

G.A.A. hurling full-back, Wexford. He was a member of the Wexford minors beaten in the All-Ireland M.H.C. final by Tipperary in 1980. A stalwart of Wexford sides which saw few successes in the late 1980's, he was on Wexford sides beaten in the twice replayed National Hurling League final of 1992-93. In 1989 he was the sole Wexfordman to win an All-Star award, being nominated in the full-back position.

CLEARY, MICHAEL.

G.A.A. hurling half-forward, Tipperary. Born 16th August 1966. Club: Eire Og, Nenagh. He won an All-Ireland B Colleges medal with Nenagh, and played minors and Under 21 for Tipp. After being on the bench for the losing final of 1988, he was a member of the Tipperary side which in 1989 won their first All-Ireland Senior Hurling Championship in 18 years, having won a Munster S.H.C. medal in 1988. He won a National Hurling League medal with Tipp in 1990. With an outstanding display in the semi-final against Antrim, and the decisive goal in the final, he was a king-pin on the Tipperary S.H.C. side which won the 1991 All-Ireland final (scoring his sides biggest tally in the game of 1-6). In 1990 he was the only Tipperary forward to win an All-Star award, at right-half forward (he won a 2nd award in the same position a year later), and recieved his 3rd successive award in 1992, this time at right corner-forward.

CLEARY, TOM.

Amateur international golfer. Club: Fermoy and Cork (winning a Barton Shield medal in 1990, and a Senior Cup medal in 1989). He won the East of Ireland title in 1977 and 1989, and was runner-up in the 'South' in 1979, and in the 'West' in 1976. He played in 8 Home International series for Ireland between 1976 and 1986, winning 16 and halving 8 of his 41 matches; he played 69 interprovincial matches for Munster between 1976 and 1987, winning 37 and halving 3. He also played on the winning Irish side in the 1983 European Team Championship.

CLEMENTS, DAVE.

Soccer international wing-half and full-back. Born in Larne, 15th September 1945. He left Portadown to join Wolves, and played league football for Coventry City (from 1964 to 1971, helping them to win promotion for the first time to Division One in 1967), Sheffield Wednesday, and Everton. He was capped 48 times for Northern Irealnd between 1965 and 1976, having won honours at junior levels (the 21 caps won while at Highfield Road make him Coventry City's most capped player). A valuable left foot player, he later played for the New York Cosmos.

CLERE, SEAMUS.

G.A.A. hurling right half-back, Kilkenny. Club: Bennetsbridge. He captained Kilkenny to their 1963 All-Ireland Senior Hurling Championship win over Waterford, by 4-17 to 6-8, and in the same year became the first Kilkennyman to win the Texaco Hurler of the Year award. Having been on county sides beaten in All-Ireland S.H.C. finals in 1964 and 1966, he again won a Liam McCarthy Cup medal in 1967. He won National Hurling League medals in 1962 and 1966. One of the games great stylists, in 1964 he became the 7th Kilkennyman to captain a winning Leinster side in Railway Cup hurling.

CLIFFORD, BASIL.

Middle-distance athlete. A winner of many middle distance Irish national titles, he ran for Ireland in the Tokyo Olympic Gamess in the 1,500 metres discipline in 1964, finishing 8th in his heat in 3-54.9. He was voted Texaco's Athletics Sportstar of the Year in 1964. He died in an explosion in Birmingham in1973.

CLIFFORD, Jeremiah THOMAS (TOM).

Rugby international prop forward. Born near Ballyporeen in Co Tipperary, 15th November 1923. Club: Young Munster (winning Munster Senior League and Limerick Charity Cup medals). A soccer player who played to League of Ireland standard with Limerick, he developed into a great loose and tight Munster prop forward, also playing for the Barbarians. He played international rugby for Ireland 14 times between the Championship and Triple Crown winning year of 1949, and 1952, scoring one try in the famous 9-8 win over France in 1951 (when Ireland again won the international championship). He toured with Karl Mullen's 1950 British and Irish Lions to Australia and New Zealand (becoming the first Limerickman and Young Munster player to gain Lions recognition), winning 5 Test caps, and playing in 19 matches on the tour. An aircraft refueller, he was one of Irish rugby's great characters. He died in 1990, aged 66, and the Young Munster's ground at Greenfields has been re-named 'Tom Clifford Park'.

CLINCH, Dr ANDREW Daniel ('COO').

Rugby international wing-forward. Born 28th November 1867, he died in 1937. Clubs: Dublin University, Wanderers (winning a Leinster Senior Cup medal in 1894). The first pupil of Belvedere College to be capped for Ireland, he played 10 times between 1892 and 1897, playing in all the Championship-winning side's matches in 1896. Selected for the British and Irish Lions tour of South Africa in 1896, he played in all four Test matches. He played interprovincial rugby for Leinster 12 times between 1891 and 1896. He was President of the I.R.F.U. 1904-05, was Ireland's representative on the International Board 1928-1936, and was an Irish international selector 1903-13. He is the father of the great 'Jammie' Clinch (cv), and together they remain the only Irish father and son to play for the Lions. His grandson and great-grandson both won colours for Trinity, making it, uniquely, 4 generations to do so.

CLINCH, Dr JAMES Daniel ('JAMMIE').

Rugby international wing-forward. Born in Clondalkin, Co Dublin, 28th September 1901, he died in 1981. Clubs: Dublin University (winning Leinster Senior Cup medals in 1920 and 1921), R.C.S.I., Wanderers, and Barbarians. Playing 20 times for Leinster in the interprovincial series between 1922 and 1932, he was capped for Ireland 30 times between 1923 and 1931 (16 of these matches were won), and was a fun-loving gregarious character. One of Ireland's greatest forwards in the period between the wars, he toured South Africa with the 1924 British and Irish Lions, playing once as an emergency full-back (although not gaining a test place), and ensuring a record of being the younger part of the only Irish father and son to represent the Lions on tour. He later practiced medicine in Gwent in Wales. He is the son of Andrew Clinch (cv).

CLOHESSY, DAVE.

G.A.A. hurling full-forward, Limerick. A great goal-scorer, he won 2 All-Ireland Senior Hurling Championship winner's medals with Limerick, in 1934 (scoring 2-2 in the drawn final game, and getting 4 goals in the replay, the highest individual score in any Liam McCarthy Cup final in the 1930's), and in 1936 (scoring 2 goals in the final). He also played in 2 Munster S.H.C. winning sides in 1933 and 1935, when the county was beaten in the All-Ireland S.H.C. final each year. He also won National League medals with the county.

CLOHESY, PEADAR (PADDY).

G.A.A. hurling centre half-back, Limerick. He won 3 All-Ireland Senior Hurling Chamnpionship winner's medals with Limerick in their great era, in 1934, 1936, and 1940, and was on losing All-Ireland S.H.C. final sides in both 1933 and 1935. He was a member of the squad which won National League medals for Limerick in 5 successive years from 1934 to 1938, and he also won 6 Railway Cup medals with Munster, in 1934, 1935, 1937, 1938, 1939, and 1940.

CLOHESSY, PETER Martin.

Rugby international prop-forward. Born in Limerick, 22nd March 1966. Club: Young Munster (helping them, under the captaincy of his older brother, Ger, a wing forward, to win the All-Ireland League in 1992-93). Capped for Ireland at, Under 25 and 'B' levels in 1989, he assisted Munster to beat the touring Wallabies in 1992. He won his first cap for Ireland against France in February 1992.

CLOHESEY, SEAN.

G.A.A. hurling left full-forward, Kilkenny. Club: Tullaroan (winning a county title with them in 1958, their first in 10 years). A prolific scoree-getter (he was Kilkenny's first ever Ton-Up scorer, and he led the county's scoring in 1955 and 1956), he won 2 Liam McCarthy Cup medals with Kilkenny, in 1957, and 1963, and captained the losing Kilkenny side in the 1959 All-Ireland S.H.C. final. A beautiful stylist, he won a National League medal with Kilkenny in 1962, although he never won a Railway Cup medal.

CLOSE, RAY.

Super-middleweight professional boxer. Born in Belfast in 1969. He won the European super-middleweight title in 1993 when defeating the Italian Vincenzo Nardiello. In May 1993 he drew on points with Chris Eubank for the W.B.O. World Super-Middleweight crown in Glasgow, and gained a W.B.O. number two ranking as a result. He relinquished his European tilte in August 1993 to concentrate on a world title shot.

COAD, PADDY.

Soccer international wing-half, inside forward, midfielder half-back and coach. Born in Waterford in 1920. Playing for 2 years with Glenavon and then for his home town club, he moved from Waterford (where he gained junior international honours) to Shamrock Rovers in 1941, and in 18 years service there (becoming coach in 1949), he helped them to win 3 League of Ireland Championships, in 1954, 1957 and 1959. He scored 126 League of Ireland goals in all (placing him 11th on the all-time list, being joint leading scorer in 1946-47), and was renowned for his passing and his football brain, which he put to use to fashion 'Coad's Colts', the great Rovers team of the 50's, as player-coach from 1954 to 1960. He holds the record, unlikely to be equalled, of scoring 41 F.A.I. Cup goals, and won 4 winner's medals with the Hoops in 1944, 1945, 1948 and 1956 (he also won 4 runner-up medals). He won 6 Shield medals with the Hoops, including 4-in-a-row from 1955 to 1958. He captained the Hoops against Manchester United in the European Cup in 1957. Regarded by many as the best League of Ireland player to be capped for the Republic of Ireland (and therefore the most skilful never to try cross-channel soccer), his midfield prowess won him 11 caps between 1947 and 1951, scoring 3 international goals. He also won many Inter-League honours, and later managed and coached Waterford for a period, helping them to win their first League of Ireland title in 1966. In 1981 he became the 3rd soccer player to be voted onto the Texaco Hall of Fame, and in 1991 became one of the 3 inaugural members of the League of Ireland Hall of Fame. He died in 1992.

COBURN, JOE.

Prize-fighting boxer. Born in Middletown, Co Armagh, 29th July 1835, he died in New York at the age of 55 in 1890. Having moved to America, he fought a draw against Ned Price in Boston in 1856, and won over 70 minutes against Mike McCoole in 1863. He twice fought for the world title against Jem Mace, in 1864 when the police interrupted the bout after 77 minutes, and again 6 months later against the 40-year-old Englishman, when they again fought out a draw, this time over 12 rounds.

COCHRANE, DAVID (DAVY).

Soccer international outside-right. Born in Portadown 14th August 1920. He played for Portadown (turning pro just after his 16th birthday, scoring 14 goals in 13 games for them), Leeds United (scoring 28 league goals in 175 appearences), Linfield and Shamrock Rovers. Only 5'4" in height, he won 12 caps for Northern Ireland between 1939 and 1950 (being the first Leeds United winger to gain full international honours, when just over 18 years old), the Second World War interferring in both his club and international ambitions. Enormously talented with blinding pace and fine ball control, in the war years he played for Portadown, Shamrock Rovers (appearing 4 times for the League of Ireland), and Linfield (winning an I.F.A. Cup medal in 1945, and playing 8 times for the Northern Ireland Regional League).

COCHRANE, RAYMOND (RAY) .

Flat jockey. Born in the Dromore area of Co Down, 18th June 1957. Achieving his first winner at Stratford in 1974 during his apprenticeship with Barry Hills, he has won many major British races, including the 1984 July Cup on Chief Singer (on whom he also won the 1983 Coventry Stakes and the 1985 St James Palace Stakes). He has won 3 English Classics, the 1986 1,000 Guineas and Epsom Oaks on Midway Lady, and the 1988 Epsom Derby on Kayashi (on whom he also won the 1988 Irish Derby). His other Irish Classic winner was the 1989 Irish 1,000 with Ensconce, while he has also won 2 Phoenix Stakes. Since having 51 winners in 1986 he has averaged over 100 winners each year since, up to the early 1990's, having 120 winners in both 1988 and 1989. Retained now by Luca Cumani, he has also ridden under National Hunt rules, achieving 8 winners over hurdles.

COCHRANE, TERRY.

Soccer international midfielder. Born in Killyleagh, 23rd January 1953. Clubs: Coleraine, Burnley, Middlesborough, Gillingham. Between 1976 and 1984 he won 26 international caps for Northern Ireland, 11 of them as a substitute, scoring one international goal. His 2 last 2 caps, gained while he was at Gillingham in 1984, made him that club's most capped player until passed out by Tony Cascarino (cv).

CODD, MARTIN.

G.A.A. hurling centre-half forward, Wexford. Born in 1929, Club: Rathnure (winning 3 county championship medals). In a senior inter-county career which lasted on and off for 16 years from 1949 to 1965, he won one All-Ireland Senior Hurling Championship winner's medal in 1956 (scoring 2 points), and was also in the side beaten in the final of 1965 (scoring 3 points). He won one National Hurling League medal in 1958, and 2 Oireachtas medals.

CODY, BRIAN.

G.A.A. hurling full-back, Kilkenny. Born in July 1955. Club: James Stephen's (winning 2 All-Irleand Club Championship winners medals, in 1976 and 1982). Winning an All-Ireland Colleges medal with St Kieran's in 1971, he was captain of the winning All-Ireland M.F.C. side in 1972, and was a member of the Kilkenny side which won both the 1974 and 1975 Under 21 All-Ireland Championships. He has won 4

All-Ireland Senior Hurling Championship winner's medals with Kilkenny, in 1974 as a sub, in 1975 at left corner-back in a masterly display, in 1982 (captaining the side which defeated Cork by 3-18 to 1-13, becoming the first James Stephen's clubman to lift the Liam McCarthy Cup) and 1983, both at full-back. He was on the losing All-Ireland S.H.C. side in both 1973 and 1978. He won 3 National Hurling League medals, in 1975-76, 1981-82 (as captain), and 1982-83). He has been honoured with 2 All-Star awards, in 1975 at left corner back, and again in 1982 at full-back. His father Bill was the club chairman of James Stephens from 1969 to 1987.

CODY, KATHLEEN.

G.A.A. camogie player, Dublin. Clubs: Optimists, Celtic, and C.I.E. She won 7 All-Ireland Camogie Senior Championship medals with Dublin. A fine, individual natural player, she perfected the aerial part of the game. She is a cousin of the great Kilkenny hurler Jimmy Langton (cv).

COFFEY, JOHN J ('JACK').

Rugby international second row forward. Lived 1877-1945. Club: Lansdowne (winning 2 Leinster Senior Cup medals, in 1901, and in 1904 as captain). Playing 14 interprovincial matches for Leinster between 1899 and 1906, he won 19 international caps over an 11 year period for Ireland between 1900 and 1910 (including all 3 of the Championship- winning side of 1906), the last one after he had officially retired. He was President of the I.R.F.U. 1924-25. He is the father of Jack Coffey, who was President of the I.R.F.U. in 1977-78 (one of only 2 father and sons to be so honoured), and who was manager of the successful Irish tour of Australia in 1979.

COFFEY, MOSES.

G.A.A. footballing midfielder, Wicklow. Born in 1949. Club: St Earnan's of Rathnew (winning 2 Wicklow SFC medals including 1970, and 2 Wicklow MFC medals). A star Wicklow player for many years (minors 1965-66, Under 21 1969-70, juniors 1969, and senior from 1969 to 1982), his only medals at senior level county level include 1981 Special League Final win, and promotion from Division 3 and 2 of the National League. When he was called on to the 1982 All-Stars as a replacement, he became the first Wicklow player to win such an honour. He also won an All-Irleand J.F.C. 'home' medal in 1969, and played Railway Cup for Leinster. His sons Darren and Ronan have both played football for Wicklow.

COGHLAN, EAMONN.

Middle-distance athlete. Born in Dublin 21st November 1952. Clubs: Celtic Athletic and Metro. A schoolboy champion, trained by Gerry Farnan, he attended Villanova University, under the wing of coach Jumbo Elliot. The Crumlin man won 11 Irish National titles between 1974 and 1983, 5 at 800 metres, 5 at 1,500m, and one at 5,000m, and also held 14 national outdoor records. He finished fourth in 1976 Olympics 1,500 metres final behind John Walker. He was winner of the 1979 European indoor 1,500 metres title, and runner-up in the 1978 European Championships 1,500 metres behind Steve Ovett. He won the 1977 1,500 metres A.A.A. title, and the 1979 and 1981 5,000 metres A.A.A. titles. He finished again fourth in an Olympic final in 1980 (at 5,000 metres) behind Miruts Yifter. He then won the 1981 World Cup 5,000 metres. His career highlight was his win in the inaugural World Championship 5,000 metres title in magnificent style at Helsinki in 1983, beating Rusian Dmitry Dmitriev with consumate ease. Missing the L.A. Olympics, he reached the semi-final of the 5,000 metres in Seoul in 1988. In indoor running he had few peers, winning 7 prestigious Wannamaker Mile's in Madison Square Garden between 1977 and 1987 (also winning 7 Melrose Miles), his 52 wins in 70 races over a 14 year period between

1974 and 1987 earning him the title of 'Chairman of the Boards'. He broke the World indoor 1,500 metres and one mile records in 1981 at 3.35.6 and 3.52.6 seconds, respectively. He again broke the world indoor mile record in 1983, at East Rutherford, in a time of 3.49,78, and also the world indoor 2,000 metres (broken in 1987 in Inglewood, California, at 4.54.07). In 1993 he twice broke the Over 40's world record for the mile. He was a member of the 4 x 1 mile world record-setting Irish team in 1985. He was the first sportsman to win 6 Texaco Sportstar of the Year awards, placing 2nd only to Sean Kelly in total awards, winning in Athletics in 1975, 1976, 1977, 1980, 1981, and 1983 (when he also became the 2nd athlete to be selected as Supreme Sportstar of the Year). In 1991 he was appointed briefly as C.E.O. of B.L.E.

COHEN, MARK Francis.

Cricket international right hand batsman. Club: Carlisle. Born in Cork, 22nd March 1961. In 1981 he joined Middlesex, but did not play for the county. He made his Irish debut in 1980, and up to the end of the 1993 international season had played 67 times for Ireland, with a tally of 2,440 runs, for an average-per-innings of 28.37. One of Ireland's finest modern-day batsmen, he is 4th on the all-time runs for his country, including scoring 2 centuries and 16 other 50's.

COLE, JONATHAN.

Hockey international midfielder. Clubs: Dublin University, Dublin Y.M.C.A., and Avoca. A fine goal-scorer, he was capped 66 times for Ireland (including 58 in succession) between 1977 and 1983, captaining his country 28 times. He was outstanding at the European Cup at Hanover in 1978, and also toured Australia. He also played in Kuala Lumper (as captain) and Amstleveen with Irish sides. He also won 20 indoor international caps between 1977 and 1983. His uncle G F M Cole was Hon Treasurer of the Leinster Branch of the I.H.U.

COLEMAN, BILLY.

Rally driver. From Millstreet, Co Cork. He is the only Irish rally driver since Paddy Hopkirk (cv) to win more than one Circuit of Ireland Rally, winning three times in all: for 2 years in succession, 1975 (co-driven by Phelan) and 1976 (co-driven by O'Sulivan), both in a Ford Escort RS; and again in 1984 (when co-driven by Morgan), when racing in an Opel Manta 400. Winning and being placed in many other rallies in Ireland and abroad, he was regarded as a fine natural talent, while his 14 international rally successes (including a joint record 3 Donegal Rally wins) places him ahead of other Irish rally drivers in such attainments. He was selected as Motorsport's Texaco Sportstar of the Year in 1974.

COLEMAN, EAMONN.

G.A.A. football left half-forward, Derry. Born in Ballymaughan (helping the local side to win it's only county championship when he was only 14). He was a member of the Derry minors which captured the All-Irleand M.F.C. for the first time in the county's history in 1965, and 3 years later he was a member of the Derry side which won the county's first ever All-Ireland Under 21 Championship. He played senior football for Derry from 1966 to 1973, and won an Ulster S.F.C. medal in 1970. He also won Westmeath senior county championship medals twice. He managed the Derry minors to All-Ireland success in 1983, and trained the senior side to win the All-Ireland S.F.C. title in 1993. His son Gary was in the half-back line on that 1993 Derry side which reached the All-Ireland S.F.C. final for the first time since 1958, when they won their first Sam Maguire Cup.

COLEMAN, MICHAEL.

G.A.A. hurling midfielder and centre-back, Galway. Born in 1964. Club: Abbeyknockmoy. Having won an All-Ireland Under 21 Championship medal with the county in 1983, he made his senior championship debut in 1988, when he became a member of the Galway side which won All-Ireland Senior Hurling Championship that year. He was also on losing All-Ireland S.H.C. final side in 1990 (when he became one of the rare bunch of hurlers to be nominated as a unanimous choice for one of the mid-field berths on the All-Star XV), and again in 1993. He also won an All-Star in 1988, again in midfield. He won a National Hurling League medal in 1987. His older brother Mattie played football for Galway for many years, winning an All-Ireland M.F.C. medal in 1976, and being on the side beaten in the All-Ireland S.F.C. final in 1983 by Dublin.

COLHOUN, OSMOND David.

Cricket international right hand batsman and wicketkeeper. Born in Sion Mills, Co Tyrone, 6th June 1939. Clubs: Sion Mills and Royal Ulster Constabulary. Primarily a wicketkeeper, as a batsman in 28 first class matches for Ireland between 1959 and 1979, his highest score in his 35 innings was 9 runs. However, as a wicketkeeper he is unrivalled in Irish cricket, taking a record 46 1st class dismissals (44 catches and 2 stumpings) in that period. His total dismissals as a wicket-keeper for all matches for Ireland in the 87 matches (a then Irish record cap tally) he played between 1959 and 1979 was 190 (a record unlikely to be matched), from 158 catches and 42 stumpings. His total runs for Ireland in all matches is 296 from 89 innings, for an average of 6.88 runs.

COLLERAN, ENDA.

G.A.A. football right full-back, Galway. From Moylough, between Tuam and Ballinasloe. He was at right half-back on the Galway minors which took the 1960 All-Ireland M.F.C. title. He captained the Galway side to victory in 2 successive All-Ireland Senior Football Championship finals, the 1965 win over Kerry by 0-12 to 0-7, and the 1966 win over Meath by 1-10 to 0-7, having also played in the 1964 final of the 3-in-a-row sequence. Winning a National League medal with Galway in 1965, in 1967 he became the 4th Galwayman to captain a winning Railway Cup football side, his only interprovincial medal. He was selected at right corner back on the Sunday Independent 'Team of the Century' in 1984. His brothers Seamus, Gerry and Gabriel were all quality players (Seamus being a non-playing sub in the All-Ireland S.F.C. final of 1956).

COLLERAN, PADDY.

G.A.A. footballer, Sligo (and 6 other counties: Mayo, Galway, Cavan, Cork, Waterford and Tipperary). He won county championship medals in 3 of the 7 counties for whom he played, in Sligo (with St Mary's), Waterford and Cavan (he also won a Sigerson Cup medal with U.C.C.). He was a member of the first Sligo senior football side to capture the Connacht Championship in 1928. In 1927 he was at right full forward on the Connacht side beaten in the final of the inaugural Railway Cup series by Munster, and won a place in the Tailteann Games of 1928. He was the most famous of 7 footballing brothers from Corry in Sligo, 5 of whom played on the same Sligo S.F. team, and 6 of whom played on teams which reached All-Ireland semi-finals at various grades between 1923 and 1934. One of these brothers, Luke, also played in the 1928 Tailteann Games of 1928, making them the only 2 brothers to achieve this honour.

COLLIER, PAT ('RED').

G.A.A. footballing right half back, Meath. Born in 1942. Club: St Patrick's (Stamullen and Julianstown, winning a Meath J.F.C. and a I.F.C. medal). He played county football at minor level in 1959-60, and at Under 21 level for Meath in 1960. A skilful and popular wing back, he played senior inter-county football for Meath from 1961 to 1969, and was a star member of the Meath side which, by defeating Cork in the 1967

All-Ireland S.F.C. final, won the Sam Maguire Cup for the Royal County for the first time in 13 years. He also won Leinster S.F.C. medals with Meath in 1964, and in 1966 at right wing half when Galway beat them in the All-Ireland Senior Football Championship final. He played Railway Cup football with Leinster, and won 3 All-Army medals with the Air Corps, and a Leinster J.F.C. medal with Meath. A winner of 2 Green Jersey awards (an equivalent to the All-Star award), he toured the U.S. with Meath in 1966 and to Australia in 1968.

COLLINS, EOIN.

Tennis international player. From Sutton in Dublin, he was born in 1969. Club: Sutton LTC. A left handed player, he has won the Irish Close singles title 4 times up to and including 1993, the first of these at the age of only 15. He has played Davis Cup for Ireland from 1987, and assisted Ireland to qualify for Group 1 status in the European Zone in 1989. He has represented Ireland at 2 Olympic Games as a doubles partner to Owen Casey (cv), in 1988 and 1992 (when he became ranked 507th in the world doubles rankings). He is a coach in the U.S.A.

COLLINS, JOE ('DANCING MASTER', 'THE PRIDE OF ENGINE STREET').

Amateur and professional boxer. Born in 1924, he hails from Engine Alley in Dublin's Meath Street. Club: Avona. A boxer from age 12, he was a winner of a tally of 17 amateur and professional titles, in 1943 he became the first Irish boxer to hold four Irish titles at the same time, including the Irish National Senior Championship at flyweight. Turning pro later in the same year, he retired at 28 in 1952.

COLLINS, MICHAEL C and CON.

Father and son flat trainers. Michael, born in Mallow, Co Cork, was the leading Irish trainer 4 years in succession, 1941, 1942, 1943 and 1945. Associated early in his career with the horses of Joseph McGrath, and invariably using the skills of Morny Wing (cv), he trained the winners of 5 Irish Classic races (including an Irish Triple Crown winner in Windsor Slipper). these wins being: 2 Irish 2,000 Guineas winners (Windsor Slipper in 1942 and Solonaway in 1949), the Irish Derby in 1942 on Windsor Slipper again, one Irish 1,000 winner (Panastrid in 1945), and one Irish St Leger (Windsor Slipper in 1942). He was succeeded at his Conyngham Lodge stables at the Curragh by his son Con, who trained the winner of the 1984 Irish Oaks, Princess Pati.

COLLINS, PADDY ('FOX').

G.A.A. hurling full-back, Cork. Born in 1903. Club: Glen Rovers (winning 7 county championships with them, including the club's first such win in 1934). In a senior inter-county playing career which lasted from 1929 to 1938, he won 2 All-Ireland Senior Hurling Championship winner's medals with Cork, in 1929 and 1931, and won a National Hurling League medal in 1930. He won a Railway Cup medal with Munster in 1931. He was a major influence and an able administrator with the great 'Glens' club.

COLLINS, STEVEN.

Middleweight boxer. Born in Cabra, Dublin, 21st July 1964. As an amateur he won Irish Junior Heavyweight, Light-heavyweight and Middleweight titles. Turning profesional at the middleweight discipline in Massachussetts in 1986, he won the Irish middleweight title against Sam Storey in Boston in 1988. He later beat the world No 5 Kevin Watts, and won 16 straight pro fights before being outpointed by Mike McCallum over 12 rounds in a world W.B.A. middleweight title fight in Boston in February 1990. In April 1992 he was again beaten on points for the W.B.A. middleweight championship of the world, this time by Reggie Johnson, in Meadowlands, New Jersey. Also losing the E.B.U. decider to Sumbu

Kalumbay, in 1993 he won the W.B.C. Penta Continental title in a fight against Gerhald Botes of South Afirca, thus giving him (up to June 1993) a pro-career record of 24 wins in 27 fights.

COLLIS, Dr William ROBERT Fitzgearald (BOB), and WILLIAM STUART.

Father and son rugby internationals. William Stuart, a Wanderers forward, was capped once against Wales in 1884, while his son, Dr William Robert, a Cambridge Blue 1919-20, and a K.C.F., Harlequins and Surrey hooker, won 7 caps for Ireland between 1924 and 1926, when only 2 matches were lost. He also played 7 interprovincial rugby matches for Leinster in 1991-25.

COLLOPY, S RICHARD (DICK).

Rugby international lock/prop. Club: Bective Rangers (winning Leinster Senior Cup medals in 1923 and 1925). He won 13 international caps for Ireland between 1923 and 1925. He played alongside his older brother, Billy Collopy (cv), 7 times in an Irish jersey (once, in the 1924 win over Wales, three sets of 2 brothers played for the national side), and is the son of George Collopy, a Bective Rangers forward who won 2 caps in 1891 and 1892. He later played rugby league with Huddersfield.

COLLOPY, WILLIAM P (BILLY).

Rugby international hooker/prop. 1894-1972. Club: Bective Rangers (winning Leinster Senior Cup medals with the club in 1914, 1923 and 1925). He was capped 19 times for Ireland over an 11 year period between 1914 and 1924 (becoming one of only 8 Irish players to span the First World War), captaining the Irish team once in 1924. He was an outstanding and durable player, one of the 1920's finest forwards in the green jersey. He is the brother of Dick (cv), playing with him twice for Leinster, and is a son of a former international, George Collopy.

COMMINS, JOHN.

G.A.A. hurling goalkeper, Galway. Club: Gort (playing when the club were losing finalists in the All-Ireland Club Championship of 1984). A winner of an All-Ireland Under 21 Championship medal with Galway in 1986, he had 3 years earlier won an All-Ireland M.H.C. medal with the county. He played on Galway's All-Ireland Senior Hurling Championship winning sides of 1987 and 1988, being also in goals for their final defeats of both 1986 and 1990. A winner of a Railway Cup medal in 1987 on the all-Galway Connacht side, he won his first All-Star award in 1988, one of 7 Galwaymen to win awards that year, and won his place in this line-up again in 1989. A single-handicap golfer.

CONDON, SEAN.

G.A.A. hurling half-forward, Cork. Club: St Finbarrs. He won an All-Ireland M.H.C. medal with Cork minors in 1941. Gaining promotion to the senior side the following year, he won 3 All-Ireland Senior Hurling Championship winner's medals with the Rebel County, in 1942 (his first year at this level), 1943 and 1944 (when he captained the side which completed the 4-in-a-row by beating Dublin by 2-13 to 1-2). He became the 5th Corkman to captain a winning Munster Raliway Cup side in 1944.

CONDON, T.

G.A.A. hurler, Tipperary. He captained the Tipperary side of Moycarkey which won the 1899 All-Ireland Senior Hurling Championship, the middle of a county run of 3-in-a-row, when they beat the Blackwater Selection from Wexford by 3-12 to 1-4. He had won 2 previous All-Ireland S.H.C. medals, in 1896 and 1898.

CONNELL, DAVEY.

Amateur international boxer. Club: Avoca. A Dublinman, he won 4 Irish National Senior Championship titles over a period of 6 years in 3 different weight divisions: winning at flyweight in 1946; at bantamweight in both 1947 and 1948; and finally at lightweight in 1951. He represented Ireland at the Olympic Games in Helsinki in 1952.

CONNELLON, GERRY.

G.A.A. footballer, Roscommon. Club: Kilmore. He was at right half back on the Roscommon side which beat the much-vaunted Kerry side in the 1978 Under 21 All-Ireland final. In 1980 he was one of only 3 of the Roscommon side (which had then won 4 successive Connacht S.F.C. titles) who were beaten in the All-Ireland S.F.C. final by Kerry to receive an All-Star award, being selected at left corner back.

CONNOLLY, JOE.

G.A.A. hurling half-forward, Galway. Club: Castlegar. He captained the Galway side to their win over Limerick in the 1980 All-Ireland Senior Hurling Championship final, also being a member of the sides beaten in the finals of both 1979 and 1981. He also led Galway to the National League title in 1980, and was only the 2nd Galwayman to captain a winning Connacht Railway Cup side in 1980. He won an All-Star award in 1980 at left-half forward, becoming the first Connachtman to score more that 100 points in county games that season. A brother of John Connolly (cv), his other brother Michael was also on the winning All-Ireland S.H.C. side of 1980, later captained the Galway side beaten in the All-Ireland final of 1985, and led the Castlegar club to victory, along with Joe and John (cv) and 4 other brothers, in the All-Ireland Club final in 1980.

CONNOLLY, JOHN.

G.A.A. hurling midfielder and forward, Galway. Born in Leitir Moir, Connemara in 1948. Club: Castlegar (winning 6 county championships, highlighting in 1980 when he and all of his six younger brothers won All-Ireland Club championship medals with the club: Padraic, Michael as captain, Joe cv, Jerry, Tom and Murth). He was captain of the Galway side defeated in the final of the 1975 All-Ireland S.H.C., also being on the losing side in 1979 and 1981. He won his only All-Ireland Senior Hurling Championship winner's medal as a centre forward in the 1980 win over Limerick, when he played alongside his brothers Joe (cv) and Michael (Padraic was a sub), making them the 2nd of only 3 sets of three brothers to win Liam McCarthy Cup medals on the same day. He captained Galway to win the 1975 National League. He won an All-Star award in the inaugural Carrolls year of 1971 at midfield, and again in 1979 in the inaugural year of the Bank of Ireland sponsored All-Stars, also in the same position. In 1980 he became the first Galway player to be honoured as Texaco Hurler of the Year. He was also a useful footballer, playing Galway at minor, under 21 and senior level, and even won a Connacht junior light-welterweight championship in boxing in 1965.

CONNOLLY, JOHN.

Flat jockey. He was the most outstanding Irish jockey of his period, being the first to ride the winning horse in 4 Irish Derbys. They were in 1879 on Soulouque, in 1883 on Sylph, in 1884 on Theologian, and in 1886 in on Theodemir. A brilliant rider at the Curragh, he rode the brilliant Barcaldine to an unbeaten career in Ireland and England. He died in 1896. His uncle Pat Connolly was a champion jockey in Ireland for many years, and later rode, and won in, all the English Classics, including the Epsom Derby twice, in 1834 on Plenipotentiary and in 1841 on Coronation.

CONNOLLY, PATRICK ('PA').

G.A.A. footballer, Kildare. Club: Clane. He played on Kildare teams which lost National League finals 10 years apart, at left full back against Dublin in 1958, and later as captain and full forward in the 1968 decider, when the Lily-Whites were beaten by Down. He also represented Leinster in Railway Cup football.

CONNOLLY, Corporal PADDY.

International amateur fly-weight boxer. Club: Army (he won 6 successive Army titles 1932 to 1937). He won the Irish National Senior Championship flyweight title 3 times, in 1933, 1936 and 1938. In an international career lasting 7 years he only lost 8 bouts, thus ranking as one of Ireland's best amateur fly-weights (among those he defeated were a European champion, a reigning Olympic champion and a Golden Gloves champion).

CONNOR, LIAM and TOMAS.

G.A.A. footballing brothers, Offaly. Both were members (Liam at full-back and Tomas at mid-field) of the Offaly side beaten in the All-Ireland S.H.C. final by Kerry in 1981, and both went on to win an All-Ireland Senior Football Championship winner's medal in the 'Seamus Darby' final of 1982. Liam won an All-Star award in 1982 at full-back. They are cousins of Matt (cv) and Ritchie (cv) Connor.

CONNOR, MATT.

G.A.A. football forward, Offaly. Born on 9th July 1959. Club: Walsh Island (with whom he won 6 consecutive Offaly senior county championship medals, in 1978, 1979, 1980, 1981, 1982, and 1983). Making his senior inter-county debut in 1978, he won one All-Ireland Senior Football Championship medal at full-forward with Offaly, in the 1982 side which stopped Kerry's bid for 5-in-a-row, having previously won Leinster S.F.C. medals both in 1980 and 1981. A brilliant free-taker for Offaly, he was the country's top scorer nationally for a record 5 successive years, in 1980 (his 201 points in 29 games is a G.A.A. record for a season, and his tally of 46 points being a record for a championship season), in 1981 with 188 points, in 1982 with 133 points, in 1983 with 145 points, and in 1984 with 150 points. His final tally for Offaly in the 161 county games he played in was 906 points (from 82 goals and 660 points). Although he failed to win Railway Cup or National League honours, he won 3 All-Star awards, in 1980 at right corner forward, in 1982 at left-half forward, and in 1983 at centre-half forward. A motor accident in 1984 ended his classy career prematurely, and he remains as one of the game of football's greatest stylists. He is a brother of Ritchie Connor (cv).

CONNOR, MAURICE.

Soccer international right-wing or inside left. Born of Irish parents in Dundee, Scotland in july 1877. Clubs: Glentoran, West Bromwich Albion, Walsall (scoring 15 goals in 52 games), Bristol City, Arsenal, Brentford (becoming the club's first ever capped player), Fulham, Blackpool, Glentoran (again) and Treharms. A talented, wanderlust player, he scored a goal in his international debut for Ireland in 1903, and also played on the winning side against Wales in the same season, when helping his country to it's first ever shared winning of the Home International series. He won his third and last cap in 1904. He died in 1957.

CONNOR, RICHIE.

G.A.A. footballing full-back and centre-half back, Offaly. From Monevane, Walsh Island, Co Offaly, he was born in 1956. Club: Walsh Island (winning 6 consecutive Offaly county championship titles, in 1978, 1979, 1980, 1981, 1982 and 1983). A product of St Mary's Primary school, he captained the Offaly side (at centre half-forward) which won the 1982 All-Ireland Senior Football Championship title, when they beat Kerry with the classic late goal by Seamus Darby, to win by 1-15 to 0-17. He had also been captain of the county team the previous year when Kerry beat them in the All-Ireland final, having also won a Leinster S.F.C. medal in 1980. In 1981 he won his only All-Star, at centre half-back. Later he became team manager of neighbouring Laois.

CONRAN, JOHN.

G.A.A. hurling left half-back, Wexford. Club: Rathnure (with whom he won 5 county championships, and 3 Leinster titles). A product of St Peter's, he played all grades for Wexford, and was on 4 Wexford sides beaten in Leinster Senior Hurling Championship finals, in 1979, 1981, 1984, and 1988, and which lost National League finals in 1982 and 1984. He won an All-Star award in 1987 at left half-back,

CONROY, GERARD A (TERRY).

Soccer international forward. Born in Dublin, 2nd October 1946. Clubs: Glentoran, Stoke City (with whom he scored 49 league goals in 11 years service, 1967-1978, winning a Football League Cup medal in 1971), Hong Kong, and Crewe Alexander. He won 27 senior international caps for the Republic of Ireland between 1970 and 1977. scoring 2 international goals.

CONROY, TOMMY.

G.A.A. football centre-half forward, Dublin. Club: St Vincent's (being on the side beaten in the All-Ireland Club Championship final of 1985 by Castleisland Desmond's). He was a member of the Dublin side which won the 1983 All-Ireland Senior Football Championship final against Galway, and lost the S.F.C. finals of 1984 and 1985. He won an All-Star award in 1985, at centre half-forward. He won Railway Cup medals with Leinster in 1985 and 1986.

CONSIDINE, JOHN.

G.A.A. hurling right full-back, Cork. He was a member of the Cork side which won the Liam McCarthy Cup in 1990. He won a National Hurling League medal with the Rebel County in the three-match 1992-93 National Hurling League final. He won an All-Star award in 1990, at right corner-back.

CONSIDINE, BRENDAN.

G.A.A. hurler, Clare and Dublin. Born in 1897. In a senior inter-county career which lasted from 1914 to 1930, he played with Clare, Cork, Waterford, and Dublin. He won 2 All-Ireland Senior Hurling Championship winner's medals with different counties, in 1914 with Clare (playing alongside his brother Willie 'Dodger' Considine), and then 3 years later when playing for Dublin in the decider of 1917 (being also in the Dublin team which was defeated in the 1919 final). An older brother of 'Tull' Consideine (cv).

CONSIDINE, TURLOUGH ('TULL').

G.A.A. hurling left full-forward, Clare. A stalwart member of the Clare side for many years, he was a star left full forward on the last Clare Senior Hurling Championship side to win the Munster Championship, in 1932, when he scored 6 goals in last quarter of the All-Ireland semi-final match to turn a 15 point second half deficit into a famous 9-4 to 4-14 win over Galway. Clare thus reached the All-Ireland S.H.C. final (in which he scored 2-1), only to be beaten by Kilkenny. He was the first Clareman to win 4 Railway Cup medals, being on each of Munster's 4 initial triumphs, in the successive years 1928, 1929, 1930 and 1931.

CONWAY, CONNIE.

G.A.A. ladies football full-back, Laois. Club: Crettyard (winning 3 Leinster County Championship medals). A member of the Laois side beaten by Kerry in 2 All-Ireland Senior Championship finals, in 1985 and 1988, she has won 3 All-Star awards, and has won 2 Interprovincial Championship medals with Leinster. She has been prominent in the county's ladies football administration.

CONWAY, JAMES P (JIMMY).

Soccer international forward. Born in Dublin, 10th August 1946. Clubs: Bohemians, Fulham (with whom he scored 67 league goals in 311 appearences 1966-1975, helping them gain promotion to Division 2 in 1971, and winning a runners-up medal in the F.A. Cup final of 1975), and Manchester City. A former amateur international soccer player, he won 20 senior international caps for Ireland between 1967 and 1977, scoring 3 international goals.

CONWAY, PHILIP (PHIL).

Shot Putt athlete. Born in Dublin 1948. A product of Rockwell (playing schools interprovincial rugby with Munster in 1964 and 1965, and winning a Munster Senior Schools medal in 1964), he won All-Ireland senior schools titles in both shot and discus in 1964 and 1965. In 1967 he broke the 3-year-old Irish shot putt record, and the 28-year-old discus record of Ned Tobin. In 1969 he won Irish National titles in 3 events, (shot putt, hammer and discus). He represented Ireland in the shot putt at the Munich Olympics in 1972. He later became a physical fitness expert, working in Belvedere College, and was physical fitness coach for the winning Tipperary S.H.C. side of 1989.

COOGAN, MARTIN.

G.A.A. hurling left half-back, Kilkenny. He won 4 All-Ireland Senior Hurling Championship winner's medals with Kilkenny, in 1963, 1967, 1969, and 1972 (as as sub), playing also on 3 beaten All-Ireland S.H.C final sides, in 1964, 1966 and 1971, so playing in 7 finals in a ten year period. He won 3 Railway Cup medals with Leinster, in 1964 (as a sub), 1967 and 1972, and won National Hurling League medals in 1962 and 1966. He won an All-Star award in the initial year of the scheme, in 1971 at left half-back.

COOK, C W ('BUNTER').

Hockey international inside forward. Clubs: Kingston G.S., and The Army. He was capped for Ireland on 25 occasions betwen 1927 and 1935, captaining the side in 1934. He scored the winning goal in Ireland's 4th Triple Crown success, in 1930, and also was a member of the Triple Crown-winning side of 1933.

COOK, H G.

Rugby international forward. Club: Lansdowne. Although he was only capped once for Ireland (in a losing match against Wales in 1884), he is one of only 5 Irish rugby players to captain his country on this his international debut. Also an international referee in 1886, he was Hon Sec of the I.R.F.U. from 1882 to 1886.

COOK, JOHN GILBERT.

English international rugby player, and Irish cricketer. Born in Bedfordshire in 1911. As a member of the Bedford club, he won one international rugby cap for England on St Patrick's Day of 1938, in the win against Scotland. However, as a member of the North of Ireland C.C. (and also of Bedfordshire C.C.C.) he played 2 first class matches for Ireland, in 1935 against the M.C.C., and in 1936 against India. He died in 1979.

COONAN, ROBERT (BOBBY).

Champion jump jockey. Born in Ballymore Eustace, he served his time in England. Associated mainly with Paddy Sleator of Grangecon, the best horse he rode was Captain Christy, on whom he won the King George in 1975. Highly successful, he was champion jump jockey of Ireland seven times in all, including 6 times in succession, 1968, 1969, 1970, 1971, 1972 and 1973. He rode Sweet Dreams to win the 1969 Irish Grand National. His nephew A R Coonan is an amateur jockey.

COONEY, JIMMY.

G.A.A. hurling back, Galway. Club: Sarfield's. From Bullaun near Loughrea, he was a member of the Galway side which won the county's first All-Ireland Senior Hurling Championship for 57 years in 1980, and also played in the losing final team of the 1981. He won an All-Star award in 1980 at left corner back. An older brother of Joe Cooney (cv), he won a county championship medal in 1989 with Joe and 4 other brothers, and was a sub on the Sarsfield's side which won the All-Ireland Club Championship in 1993.

COONEY, JOE.

G.A.A. hurling half-forward, Galway. Born St Patrick's Day 1964. Club:

Sarfields (with whom, along with 4 of his brothers, Brendan, Packie, Michael, and Peter, he won Galway SHC medals in 1989 and 1992, and won the All-Ireland Club Championship final in 1993 when Pakie was captain). A native of Bullaun, near Loughrea, he won an All-Ireland M.H.C. medal with Galway in 1983, and an Under 21 All-Ireland winner's medal in 1986. Having been a member of the Galway side beaten in the All-Ireland S.H.C. finals of 1985 and 1986, he was a key member of the team which captured the Liam McCarthy trophy in both 1987 and 1988. He was captain of the Galway side beaten in the 1990 All-Ireland final, in which he completely dominated the first half, and was again on the losing final side in 1993, his 6th appearance in the final. He has also won 2 National League winner's medals, and has won Railway Cup medals with Connacht twice. One of the game's great half-forwards, he has won 5 All-Star awards, in 1985 and 1986 at left half forward, and in 1987, 1989 and 1990 at centre-half forward. In 1987 he became the 2nd Galway player to be nominated as Texaco Hurler of the Year. His brothers Brendan and Michael were on Galway S.H.C. squads, while Jimmy Cooney (cv) is also an older brother. His sister Angela played camogie for Galway.

COONEY, JOHNNY.

G.A.A. football right wing-forward, Offaly. A member of the county side which was beaten in the final of the 1969 All-Ireland S.F.C., he went on to help Offaly to win the All-Ireland Senior Football Championship in both 1971 and 1972. He won 2 All-Star awards in succession, in 1972 and 1973 (when he won another Leinster S.F.C. medal), both at right half-forward. He won a Railway Cup medal with Leinster in 1974.

COOTE, NINA.

Croquet international player. Born in 1884. Probably Ireland's greatest ever woman croquet player, she went over to win the British Women's Open Championship in 1903. Then in 1908, in the last time women were allowed to compete in the event, she captured the prestigious Men's Gold Medal. A close rival to the dominating Lily Gower of that era, she died at the age of 61 in 1945.

CORBALLY, CYRIL.

Croquet player. Lived 1881-1946. One of 3 Irish male croquet players who dominated the British scene in the early part of the century, he had a short career. He entered the English Open Croquet Singles Championship seven times between 1902 and 1913, winning it 5 times (the first person to achieve this feat, which was not passed until 1950), in 1902 (at his first attempt), 1903, 1906, 1908, and 1913 (this still places him 4th in the all-time list of winner's of this prestigious title). He also won the British Closed Men's Championship once in 1926, and the mixed doubles twice. He also won the President's Cup (then known as the Champions Cup) three times between 1909 and 1920. Regarded by many as the best player of his generation, his brother Herbert Corbally was also a noted croquet player, being twice a Champions Cup player, and was always to the fore in the Irish Championships and the Gold Medals.

CORBITT, DENNIS.

G.A.A. footballer, Limerick. He captained the 21-a-side Limerick Commercials side, representing Limerick, to win the inaugural All-Ireland Senior Football Championship final of 1887 (the game was actually played on 29th April 1888 in Clonskeagh, Dublin), against Young Irelands of Louth, by a score of 1-4 to 0-3.

CORCORAN, BRIAN.

G.A.A. hurling right full-back and utility player, Cork. From Glounthane, he was born in late 1973. Club: Erin's Own (scoring 10 points in the final when the young club won it's first Cork SHC in 1992). A dual player, he won an All-Ireland minor medal in football in 1991 (and was on 2 minor hurling final losing sides in both 1988 and 1990).

Making his senior inter-county hurling debut in 1992, he was brilliant in Cork's failed bid for the All-Ireland Senior Hurling Championship final, winning the G.A.A. Personality of the Month for June. He captained the Cork side which won (after a 2nd replay of the final against Wexford) the 1992-93 National Hurling League. A phenomenon at the age of 19, he became only the 4th hurler in the history of the awards to win an automatic All-Star award in 1992, placed at right corner-back, while in the same year was also voted as Texaco's Hurling Sportstar of the Year. Also a Red Belt at Tae-kwon-do, his grandfather Bill Corcoran was a fine athlete in the 1920's, becoming Irish champion in the Mile. Brian won a Munster S.F.C. medal with Cork footballers in 1993, playing in the All-Ireland final loss against Derry.

CORCORAN, JAMES Crothmans (JIMMY).

Rugby international prop forward. Born in Cork, 14th July, 1922. Club: U.C.C. (winning a Munster Senior Cup medal in 1941), and Sundays Well (winning a Munster Senior Cup medal in 1949). Playing for Ireland in a match against the British Army in 1944 and in 2 Victory internationals in 1946, he won only 2 full caps for Ireland, against Australia in 1947 and against France in the 'Grand Slam' year of 1948.

CORCORAN, JOE.

G.A.A. footballer, Mayo, and interprovincial golfer. G.A.A. club: Ardnaree (Ballina). A member of the Mayo minors beaten in the All-Ireland M.F.C. final of 1958 (when he scored a record 4 goals and 19 points in 3 games), he was at left half-forward on the most recent Mayo side to win a National Football League title, when they beat Down in 1970, being also on the team beaten in the 1972 final. He won Connacht S.F.C. medals with the county in both 1967 and 1969, and won 2 Railway Cup medals with Connacht in 1967 and 1969. As a scratch golfer, and a member of Ballina and Enniscrone GC's, he played 23 senior interprovincial matches for Connacht between 1978 and 1984, winning 7 times. His immediate family have won 7 All-Ireland medals at various levels of golf.

CORCORAN, MIKE.

Slalom canoeist. From Glasnevin in Dublin, he was born in 1965. Club: Wild Water Kayak Club. He has won the Irish National C1 title 6 years in succession, 1988, 1989, 1990, 1991, 1992 and 1993. Studying in (and later moving to) the U.S.A., he became a world-ranked slalom canoeist (whose deeds were outshone initially by Ian Wiley cv). In 1991 he was placed 11th in the Pre-Olympic trial and finished 9th in the World Cup series, In 1992 he finished 7th in the Pre-World Championship event, and finished 12th overall in the C1 event at the Barcelona Olympics.

CORCORAN, PETER.

Bareknuckle boxer. Born in Athy. Having won many fights at home, he left Ireland in haste after slaying a man in a love tussle, and became a prize-fighter in England, under the 'guidance' of a Colonel O'Kelly. He became England's first ever Irish-born heavyweight bareknuckle champion, when beating Bill Darts (reputedly 'bought' by O'Kelly in what was termed a 'cross') in a bout that lasted less than a minute in May 1771. He held on to the title for 5 years, with suspect wins over Ned Turner and Sam Peters, before being beaten by Harry Sellers in Staines, Middlesex in 1776.

CORK, M H.

Hockey international inside forward, and centre half. Clubs: Royal Hibernians, and Aldershot. He was capped for Ireland 17 times over a 20 year period between 1913 and 1933. He played on the Triple Crown winning sides of 1920 and 1924, then after a 9 year absence from the national side, went on to captain the Triple Crown winning side of 1933, accomplishing this feat with Ireland's first ever away win against England.

CORKERY, COLIN.

G.A.A. football right corner-forward, Cork. Born in 1960. Club: Nemo Rangers. A member of 2 Cork minor sides beaten in Munster M.F.C. finals by a point by Kerry in 1988 and 1989, he was also on the Colaiste Chriost Ri side beaten in the All-Ireland Colleges final. He was a member of the Cork side which won an All-Ireland Under 21 Championship in 1989 while he was still a minor. Having spent 15 months in Australia playing 'Footie' for Carlton (and playing for Ireland on the Compromise Rules tour of 1990), he made the Cork senior inter-county panel in 1991. In his debut year in the team itself, he was the All-Ireland Senior Football Championship season's leading scorer in the 1993 season, scoring a tally of 3-26 (35 points) in the 4 games up to Cork's appearence in the final, which they lost to Derry.

CORKHILL, DAVID S ('THE PINK PANTHER').

Bowls player, outdoor and indoor. Clubs: Sandown (1971-77), and Knock (1977-date). Born in Belfast, 15th February 1960. A product of Dundonald High School, he was a short mat champion at the age of 14. He has won 7 Irish National titles, and 9 Private Green League titles. Since 1978 (up to Feb 1989) he has won a total of 55 outdoor and indoor caps (including World Championships in Australia, New Zealand, and Hong Kong), and had won 5 British Isles titles (being one of only 2 players to win such titles in both outdoor and indoor codees). With his distinctive bowling style (aptly described in his nickname), he has won twice won the prestigious Granada Television 'Superbowl' Singles titles, in 1986 (beating fellow Irishman Jim Baker in the final), and in 1988, when he beat another Irish bowls player, Maggie Johnston (cv), in the final. He was losing finalist in 1989.

CORLETT, SIMON C.

Cricket right hand batsman and right hand medium fast bowler. Born in Blantyre, Nyasaland, 18th January 1950. Club: Northern Ireland Cricket Club (winning All-Ireland Scweppes Cup winner's medal in 1981, and runner-up medals in 1983 and 1991). He played 18 first class matches for Oxford University in 1970-1972, winning Blues in 1971 and 1972. A brilliant pace bowler against all class opposition, he was capped for Ireland 73 times from 1974 to 1987. He is 3rd in the all-time Irish figures for most international wickets, with 233 wickets taken in 114 innings, for an average of 23.12 per innings. One of Ireland's outstanding all-round cricketers, he has made the 2nd highest tally of catches in Irish international history, with 48. To round off his cricket skills, he also scored over a 1,000 international runs in his career.

CORLEY, HENRY HAGARTY.

Rugby international half-back and centre, and international cricketer. In rugby, while playing for Dublin University and Wanderers, he won 9 caps for Ireland between 1902 and 1904, his first 3 caps as captain, and scoring 5 points for his country. As a right hand bat cricketer he played 4 first class international matches for Ireland between 1907 and 1909, scoring 50 runs for the Gentlemen of Ireland.

CORMICAN, GRETTA.

Ladies road bowlplaying champion. Born in Bandon, Co Cork, 29th October 1963. She is Ireland's most outstanding ladies road-bowlplayer, winning 5 All-Ireland Championships, in 1982, 1983, 1985, 1987 and 1989. In 1988, when ladies first took part in international competition, she won the gold medal (and finished 6th overall in the 1988 international match).

CORR, KAREN.

Snooker professional. Born in Northern Ireland, 10th November 1969, she is based in Peterborough. Having won Northern Ireland and All-Ireland titles (both without losing a frame), she reached a world ranking of number 4. In

November 1990, she won the Trust House Forte World Women's Snooker Championship in London, when beating the then 4-time world champion Alison Fisher in the semi-final by 5-2 (on her 21st birthday), and the world No 1 Stacy Hilliard 7-4 in the final, to become the first Irishwoman to win this prize (a record £10,000). Later in that season she also captured the first ever Sky World Masters ladies title.

CORR, TOMMY.

Amateur light-middleweight boxer. Club: Clonoe. He won 2 Irish National Championship titles at light-middleweight, in 1982 and 1983. He is Ireland's first (of only 3) amateur to win a World Championship medal, gaining a bronze at middleweight at the Munich games of 1982. He boxed at middleweight at the 1984 Olympic Games at Los Angeles, losing in his 2nd bout. He also played gaelic football for Tyrone.

CORRIGAN, COLMAN.

G.A.A. football full-back, Cork. In 1981 he was a half-back member of the Cork Under 21 side which won the All-Ireland Championship at that grade. He was in the full-back position for Cork in the 2 All-Ireland Senior Football Championship finals they lost in succession in 1987 and 1988. He has won one All-Star award, in 1987 at full-back.

CORRIGAN, MARK.

G.A.A. hurling left half-forward, Offaly. Born in 1960. Club: Kinnity (winning 5 county championship medals). Debuting for the senior county team in 1980, he went on to play on 11 successive Offaly sides in Leinster S.H.C. finals between 1980 and 1990, being on the winning side in 1980, 1981, 1984, 1985, 1988, and in 1989 (when captain, scoring 3-7 in the Leinster final), and being the county's leading marksman in that decade. He was a member of the Offaly side which won the All-Ireland Senior Hurling Championship in both 1981 and 1985, also playing on the losing final side of 1984. He won a National League medal in 1991. He has won one All-Star award, in 1981 at left half-forward, and was an All-Star replacement at least five times. His younger brother Paddy (born in January 1962, also a member of Kinnity club) played as a wing forward for Offaly, and was the county's (and the country's) leading marksman in 1985, winning a Liam McCarthy medal alongside Mark in that year.

CORRY, Colonel DAN.

Showjumping equestrian rider. Born in Loughrea, Co Galway, on 31st October 1902. In 1926 he joined the Army Equitation School on it's foundation, being one of it's first riders. His successes in many competitions in Europe and the United States gave him a wide international reputation, ranging from Lucerne, Rome, Toronto, New York and Mexico. He was part (mainly on his best horse Red Hugh) of 7 Irish Aga Khan Cup winning sides (most often with Lewis Ahern, Cyril Harty and Jed O'Dwyer) before and after World War Two (in 1928, 1935, 1936, 1937, 1938, 1946 and in 1949 when he was nearly 47 years old), and was also part of Irish sides which were deemed almost unbeatable, winning 23 Nations Cup competitions before the War. He spent all of his career with the school, except during World War Two, and but for clashes with the Dublin Horse Show, may have won Olympic medals (he actually competed in only one games, in 1948). Retiring in 1958, he was later an instructor, and and was an active judge at international eqiune events including the Royal Horse Show at the R.D.S. In 1973 he became the first Equestrian eventer to be elevated into the Texaco Hall of Fame. Also having a keen interest in horse racing, he owned the great Hatton's Grace when it won it's bumper in Bellewstown.

COSGRAVE, JACK.

G.A.A. football full-back, Galway. A stalwart member of the Galway team which won 4 Connacht Senior Football Championship titles, in 1970 and 1971 (when they were beaten by Offaly in the All-Ireland S.F.C. final), 1973 (beaten in final by Cork), and in 1974 when their bogey team was Dublin, making it 3 losing All-Ireland finals in 4 years. He won an All-Star award in the inaugural All-Star awards in 1971, at full-back.

COSTELLO, PADDY.

Rugby international forward. Born in Dublin, 18th March 1931. Club: Bective Rangers (winning Leinster Senior Cup medals in 1955, 1956 and 1962). He was capped for Leinster 7 times in the interprovincial series betwen 1956 and 1960. He was capped once for Ireland, against France in a 23-6 loss in Paris in 1960. His son Victor (born 23rd October 1970), an outstanding No 8 with Blackrock College in schools rugby (winning a Leinster Senior Schools Cup medal in 1989), has represented Ireland at schools and Under 21 level. He won the National B.L.E. shot putt championship 4 times, the first at a record young age of 16, and again in 1989, 1990 and 1991. In 1992 he broke the Irish record (with a throw of 19.93 metres), and represented Ireland at the Olympic Games in Barcelona. An older sister of Victor's, Suzanne, has represented Ireland in the sprinting events of athletics.

COSTINE, MARIE.

G.A.A. camogie full-back, Cork. Clubs: Youghal, Cloyne, and Killeagh (with whom she won an All-Ireland Club Championship medal in 1980). A holder of 4 O'Duffy Cup medals for the All-Ireland Senior Championship with Cork, won in 1970, 1971, 1972, and 1973 (when she captained the only Cork side to achieve a 4-in-a-row, by beating Antrim by 2-5 to 1-4). One of the game's most accomplished full-backs, she was strong and tall, and had superb ball-control.

COUGHLAN, DENIS.

G.A.A. dual footballer and hurler, Cork. Born in 1945. Clubs: St Nicholas (football, winning 2 Cork SFC medals and one Munster club SFC medal), and Glen Rovers (hurling, winning 5 Cork SHC medals and 2 All-Ireland Club Hurling medals, in 1973 and 1977). Having played on a losing All-Ireland Under 21 football final Cork side in 1965, he captained the losing Cork side from centre half-back in the losing 1967 Sam Maguire Cup final, and 6 years later he won an All-Ireland Senior Football Championship medal in Cork's win of 1973 over Galway. His tally of Munster S.F.C. medals with Cork (in a senior career from 1964 to 1974) was five, the other 3 wins coming in 1966, 1971 and 1974. In 1971, in 15 inter-county games, he scored 6-74 (92 points), still a Cork football record. He also won a Railway Cup medal in football in 1972. Winning a Liam McCarthy medal as a non-playing sub in 1970, he went on to join the ranks of dual code All-Ireland winner's when Cork won the S.H.C. title in 1976, also gaining 2 more medals in 1977 and 1978, all at half-back. As a hurler he also won 3 other Munster S.H.C. medals (in a senior career from 1965 to 1980) in 1969, 1972 and 1979, giving him a tally of seven. He also won 4 National Hurling League medals, in 1970, 1972, 1974 and 1980. An All-Star hurler, he won 4 awards, in 1972 at centre-field, and in 1976, 1977, and 1978, all at left-half back. In 1977 he became the 4th Corkman to be honoured as Texaco Hurler of the Year. He later trained the Cork senior football team.

COUGHLAN, EUGENE ('EUDIE' or 'HUDIE').

G.A.A. hurling half-forward, Cork. Born in 1900. Club: Blackrock (winning 7 county championships). A non-playing sub in Cork's title win in 1919, 12 years later he captained the Cork side which won the 1931 All-Ireland Senior Hurling Championship final against Kilkenny, after 2 replays, when his brother John was goalkeeper in the side. His tally of

Liam McCarthy Cup medals is 4, as he had previously won All-Ireland winner's medals in 1926 (John was also in this side), 1928, and 1929, while he was on the losing Cork side in the All-Ireland S.H.C. final of 1927. He was a member also of the first side ever to win the National Hurling League, when Cork triumphed in 1926 (and won a 2nd medal in 1930). He won Railway Cup medals with Munster in 1928 and 1929. Although he retired from inter-county hurling after the 1931 All-Ireland win, he went on to win his last medal for hurling in 1954, in an inter-firm competition, at the age of 54. One of Cork's truly great hurlers, in 1985 he joined Jack Lynch as the first 2 Corkmen to recieve All-time All-Star awards for hurling. His father Patrick 'Parson' Coughlan won All-Ireland S.H.C. medals with Cork in 1893 and 1894; and his 4 uncles also won All-Ireland senior medals, Dan in 1892 and 1894, Denis in 1902, Tom in 1902 and 1903, and Jer in 1903.

COUGHLAN, EUGENE.

G.A.A. hurling full-back, Offaly. Born in November 1956. Club: Seir Kieran's of Clareen (captaining the club to it's first ever county championship in 1988). Making his senior inter-county debut in the League in 1976, he played in all eleven successive Leinster S.H.C. finals which Offaly competed in between 1980 and 1991, being on the winning side 7 times, in 1980, 1981, 1984, 1985, 1988, 1989 and 1990. He was an outstanding full-back in Offaly's only 2 All-Ireland Senior Hurling Champinship title wins, in 1981 and 1985, also playing in the beaten All-Ireland S.H.C. side of 1984. He has won 2 All-Star awards, in 1984 and 1985, both at full-back. In 1985 he became the 2nd and most recent Offaly player to be nominated as Texaco Hurler of the Year.

COUGHLAN, GER.

G.A.A. hurling left half-back, Offaly. Born in 1956. Club: Kinnity (winning many county championship medals with them). He was a pillar at left half-back for Offaly in their All-Ireland Senior Hurling Championship wins of 1981 and 1985, playing also in the 1984 final, when Cork defeated them. He was a member of the Offaly line-up which won 6 out ten successive appearences in the Leinster S.H.C. final 1980-1989. He won 2 All-Star awards, in 1981 and 1985, both at left half-back. His brother, Seamus Coughlan, who played senior football for Offaly, was killed in a boating accident in 1989.

COULSON, Major DENIS J.

Hockey international half-back. Clubs: Dublin University (being a member of the side which for 3 years went without losing any match), Three Rock Rovers (being club President in 1974-77), and the British Army. One of the British Isles finest half-backs of the 1930's, he was capped 21 times for Ireland between 1933 (while still at Avoca School) and the start of the second World War, and played in all 9 matches in the Golden period for Irish hockey, when the Triple Crown was won 3 years in succession, 1937, 1938, and 1939, and he reputedly played in 100 consecutive hockey matches without losing in that period. Noted for his fitness and his fine stickwork, in 1935-36 he captained both Trinity and Ireland. He later became an international secretary. Regarded by some as Ireland's greatest hockey player, his daughter Jane was also a hockey international. He died in 1992 aged 79.

COULTER, JACKIE.

Soccer international winger and outside-left. Clubs: Belfast Celtic (winning an Irish League medal in 1932-33), Everton (who paid £2,750 for him), Grimsby Town, and Chelmsford City. He was capped 11 times for Northern Ireland between 1934 and 1939, including the famous victory over Scotland in 1934, and scored one international goal. A brilliant winger, a leg fracture cut short his international career. He was also a roller skating Champion of Ireland.

COUNIHAN, CONOR.

G.A.A. football centre-half half-back, Cork. Club: Aghada (winning the Cork junior county championship in 1989). Winning an All-Ireland Under 21 medal with Cork in 1980, he was on the Cork Senior Football Championship which were beaten in 2 successive All-Ireland finals in 1987 (as captain of the side beaten by Meath), and 1988, before winning a Sam Maguire medal with the winning side of 1989, repeating the win again in 1990. He came on as a sub in Cork's S.F.C. Final loss of 1993. He won 2 successive All-Star awards in 1989 and 1990, both in the centre half-back position.

COURTNEY, A C.

Middle-distance athlete. At the College Races in Trinity College Dublin in 1873, he ran the 1,000 yards in a time of 2 minutes and 23.4 seconds, setting the first world record made by an Irishman in a flat race. This feat was also recognised to be the first ever world record for a race.

COURTNEY, PAT.

Soccer left full-back. Clubs: Mulvey Celtic, Shamrock Rovers. In a period with Shamrock Rovers from 1959 to 1971, when he retired, he won 7 F.A.I. Cup medals with the Hoops being the only player to participate in all 33 campaign games in the famous six-in-a-row wins of 1964 (when he helped the club to win the League-Cup double), 1965, 1966, 1967, 1968 and 1969, having also won a medal in the 1962 victory. He shares with Sacky Glen (cv) the record of having won 7 F.A.I. Cup medals with the same club. Uncapped as a professional, he did gain amateur international caps and Inter-League honours.

COYLE, ROBERT (ROY).

Soccer international inside forward. Born in Belfast, 31st January 1948. Clubs: Glentoran, Sheffield Wednesday, Grimsby. He was capped 5 times for Northern Ireland between 1973 and 1974, the last 4 of these as a substitute. He later became an enormously successful manager at Linfield, helping to bring 13 major trophies to Windsor Park, with 10 Irish League titles (in 1978, 1979, 1980, then to a record 6-in-a-row in 1982, 1983, 1984, 1985, 1986 and 1987, and to a 10th title in 1989), and 3 Irish Cup successes, in 1978, 1980 and 1982. Moving to manage Derry City in 1991, he was voted Manager of the Year in Northern soccer 6 times.

COYNE, TOMMY.

Soccer international forward. Born in Glasgow, 14th November 1962. Clubs: Hillwood B.C., Clydebank (scoring 37 goals in 80 league games for them 1981-83), Dundee United (1983-86), Dundee (1986-89, scoring 33 goals in 43 league games in 1987-88), and Glasgow Celtic (1989-1993), Tranmere Rovers. He won his first cap for the Republic of Ireland in 1992, scoring a goal on his debut, and had gained 9 caps up to June 1993, with 3 international goals.

CRADDOCK, TOM.

Amateur international golfer. Born in Malahide, Co Dublin, 16th December 1931. Clubs: I.A.G.A. and Malahide (winning Senior Cup and Barton Shield medals, including with 2 brothers in 1982). He won the last Irish Open Amateur title in 1958. He was a winner of the East of Ireland title 3 times, in 1959, 1965 and 1966, and was runner-up in 1960 and 1963, being also runner-up in the 'West' in 1960. He won the Irish Close Championship in 1959, beating Joe Carr at the 38th hole, and was runner-up in 1965. He won the prestigious Lytham Trophy in 1969. He was twice honoured at Walker Cup level, in 1967 and 1969, winning 2 points out of a possible 6. He played in 82 interprovincial matches for Leinster (2nd in tally of matches only to Brian Malone cv) between 1956 and 1971, winning 44 and halving 10. He is Ireland's 4th most capped Home International player, having played 67 matches over 10 series between 1955 (becoming the first member of the Artisans to play at international level, when Ireland won the series for the first time) and 1970, winning 29; and he has played in an Irish record (up to 1987) of 22 European Team Championship matches, winning 16 (being a member of winning sides in 1965 and 1967). A plus 3 handicapper at his lowest, in 1965 he became Texaco's Golf Sportstar of the Year. His 3 brothers, Joe (a professional at Clontarf), Mick (who played 27 interprovincial matches for Leinster in 1956-70, and was an Irish selector) and Paddy, were all fine golfers.

CRAIG, DAVID J.

Soccer international defender. Born in Belfast 8th June 1944. Clubs: Newcastle. In 14 seasons with Newcastle United between 1963 and 1977 he played in 347 league matches, scoring 8 league goals (and gaining a League Cup runners-up medal in 1976). He played senior international soccer for Northern Ireland 25 times between 1967 and 1975, twice as a substitute.

CRAIG, J K.

Hockey international player. Club: Dublin University. He played 15 times for Ireland between 1935 and 1939, and was a member of the 3-in-a-row Triple Crown winning side of 1937, 1938 and 1939, playing in all nine games.

CRANWELL, BEN.

Squash international. Born in New Zealand, 26th October 1947. Club: Leinster C C (being a member of the All-Ireland club championship winning side of 1976). He was capped 76 times for Ireland in squash between 1974 and 1981. He was runner-up 4 times in the Irish National (Close) Championship (in 1972, 1975, 1978 and 1980). He also won the Leinster Open in 1975, the Old Belvedere Open in 1975 and 1977, the Munster Open in 1976, the Ulster Open in 1974.

CRAWFORD, NORMAN G.

Hockey international player. Club: Belfast Y.M.C.A. He won 39 caps for Ireland between 1974 and 1981. He played in the Irish squads in Hanover and Kuala Lumpur. He also has won 60 indoor hockey caps, making him Ireland's joint holder of most indoor caps at the end of 1988, captaining the side a number of occasions.

CRAWFORD, William ERNEST (ERNIE).

Rugby international full-back. Born in Belfast, 17th November 1891. Clubs: Malone, Lansdowne (winning 4 Leinster Senior Cup medals, in 1922 as captain, and in 1927, 1928 and 1929), Cardiff, Barbarians. He won the first of his 30 caps at the age of 28 in 1920, and was a constant presence until 1927, captaining the side with distinction on 15 occasions, and scoring 18 points with his boot. One of Ireland's greatest full-backs, he was a great tackler, and had a fine pair of hands. He invented the word 'alickadoo', saying to a fellow player who preferred to read an oriental book rather than join in a game of poker, "You and your bloody Ali Khadu!". He became an Irish rugby selector, and was President of the I.R.F.U. 1957-58. He was also a handy soccer player, playing for both Bohemians and Cliftonville. He is the father-in-law of the twice capped flanker of 1956, Jim Ritchie, who captained Ireland on his first cap.

CREAN, Dr THOMAS Joseph (TOMMY).

Rugby international forward. Born at Northbrook Road, Dublin 1873. Club: Wanderers (winning a Leinster Senior Cup medal in 1894). He was capped 9 times for Ireland between 1894 (being ever present in Ireland's first ever Triple Crown victory) and 1896, scoring 2 tries. He was on the first ever British and Irish Lions tour to South Africa in 1896, and played in all 14 tour matches and all 4 Test matches (scoring a try in the 2nd test), and became the first Irishman to captain the Lions in a test match when leading the 1st and 3rd test wins. He won a Victoria Cross (one of only 3 Irish rugby internationals, all Wanderers players, to be so honoured) while serving in December 1901 as a Surgeon Captain in the Boer War. He later won a D.S.O. in W.W.I.

CREEDON, DAVE.

G.A.A. hurling goalkeeper, Cork. Born in 1919. Club: Glen Rovers (winning 9 county championship medals between 1940 and 1954). After being in an out (mostly out) of the Cork side from 1938, he was made first choice goalie only in 1952. He was then to become a member of the 3-in-a-row Cork side which won the All-Ireland Senior Hurling Championship in 1952, 1953, and 1954, conceding only 1 goal in all between the 3 finals. He won a National League medal with Cork in the 1952/53 final. An uncle of Dave Barry (cv).

CREGAN, EAMONN ('BLONDIE').

G.A.A. hurling half-back and left corner-forward, Limerick. Born in 1946. Club: Claughaun. A product of Limerick C.B.S. (winning Dr Harty Cup and All-Ireland Colleges winner's medals in 1964). Making his debut in All-Ireland senior ranks in 1964, he won a National Hurling League medal in 1971. He moved to centre half-back with great effect for Limerick's great triumph in the 1973 All-Ireland Senior Hurling Championship win over Kilkenny, also playing in the All-Ireland final losses of both 1974 and 1980 (when scoring 2-7 in the final). He was placed at No 1 on the scorers list for the country's annual programme in both 1980 and 1981, scoring 108 points each year. He has won 3 Railway Cup medals with Munster, in 1968, 1969, and 1981. He has won 3 All-Star awards, in 1971 and 1972 at left full forward, and again in 1980 in the same position. His father Ned Cregan of Monagea won an All-Ireland S.H.C. medal with Limerick in 1940. His brother Mick was also a member of the National Hurling League winning side of 1971, when he also captained Craughan to the Limerick county championship, with Eamonn and another brother Conor in the side, and trained the Limerick All-Ireland success in 1973.

CREGAN, JOHN FRANCIS.

800 metre athlete. Birthplace and birthdate unknown. Said to be Irish, he won the American 800 metres title in 1897. In the Paris Olympic Games of 1900, he (while representing the U.S.A.) won a silver medal in the 800 metres event, finishing almost 2 seconds behind the Briton, Alfred Tysoe. His Irish credentials are not confirmed.

CREGAN, PETER.

G.A.A. hurling half-back, Limerick. Born in 1917. Club: Croom (winning 7 West Limerick championships and 2 county championships, both won against the mighty Ahane, in 1940 and 1941, when he marked Mick Mackey). Playing senior inter-county hurling for 11 years from 1937 to 1947, he won an All-Ireland S.H.C. medal with Limerick in 1940. He was a member of the Limerick side which won the first Oireachtas final in 1939, and won a National Hurling League medal in 1938. He won 4 successive Railway Cup medals with Munster, in 1942, 1943, 1944 and 1945.

CREITH, DICK.

Motor Cyclist. A farmer from Bushmills, Co Antrim. In 1962 he won the Mid Antrim 150; in 1963 he won the Temple 100; in 1964 he won the North-West 200 race for 500cc, and finished 2nd in the Ulster Grand Prix 500cc race, both on Norton machines. In 1965, apart from winning both the North-West 200 and Skerries 100 races on 500cc machines, he reached a career high when he won the Ulster Grand Prix race at 500cc on a Norton machine, when he shocked many world class riders on the rain swept Dunrod track. He retired at the end of the 1965 season, never having ventured abroad to show off his skills. His son John has become a motorcycling racer of some promise.

CRICHTON, Dr ROBERT YOUNG ('JOHN WILLY').

Rugby international 2nd row and prop forward. 1987-1940. Clubs: Dublin University (winning Leinster Senior Cup medals in 1920, 1921 and 1926), Barbarians. He was capped for Ireland 15 times betweeen 1920 and 1925 (only 3 of these matches were won), and at 18 stone in weight, ranks as one of Ireland's heaviest ever players. He played 10 times for Leinster between 1919 and 1923.

CRINIGAN, OLLIE.

G.A.A. footballing goalkeeper, Kildare. A native of Carrick, he was born in 1947. Club: Carbury (for whom he played over 600 senior matches in a 20 year career, playing in 13 Kildare SFC finals, winning 7 medals, including 1965, 1966, 1969, 1971, 1972, and 1974). Playing minor, Under 21 and Senior football for Kildare in the same year of 1965, he won an All-Ireland Under 21 medal that year, winning Leinster medals again in 1966 and 1967. He was the first (and until Martin Lynch in 1991, only) Kildare footballer to win an All-Star award since their inception in 1972, getting the goalkeepers spot on the 1978 team. He was a member of the Kildare side which was beaten in 6 Leinster S.F.C. finals between 1966 and 1978 (the years being in 1966, 1968, 1971, 1972, 1975 and 1978), and played in total 143 times for Kildare seniors up to 1986. He also played Railway Cup for Leinster, and won a National League Division 2 medal. A maintenance fitter, he also won a New York SFC medal with the Sligo team.

CROFTON, JOHN.

G.A.A. football full-back, Kildare. Born in 1958. He was a member of the Kildare Under 21 side beaten in the All-Ireland final of 1975. He debuted for the county's senior side later that year. After 15 successive seasons with Kildare, he played in his only national final in 1991 when Kildare lost the National Football League final to Dublin. Apart from a few O'Byrne Cup medals and tournament plaques, his only major recognition was as a replacement for the 1985 All-Star tour to New York.

CROKE, MARJORIE (nee BURKE).

Squash international player. Born in Ballina, Co Mayo, 31st May 1961. First capped for Ireland in 1981, she has reached a total of 108 international caps by the end of the 1992/93 season, and has been the world's most capped women's squash player. In 1984, she became the first Irish lady's squash player to beat an English player, when she beat A Cummings in the European Championships in Dublin. In 1985 she beat the World No 9 ranked player, Carin Clonda of Australia. A pharmacist, she lives in Galway with her husband, a Connacht interprovincial squash player.

CROMEY, GEORGE Ernest.

Rugby international fly-half. Born in Ahogil, Ballymena, 8th May 1913. Club: Queen's University, Belfast (winning Ulster Senior Cup medals in 1936 and 1937). A minister, he was capped 9 times for Ireland between 1937 and 1939, scoring 2 international tries, and was selected on the British and Irish Lions tour of South Africa in 1938, winning a place in the winning 3rd Test.

CRONE, CALEB.

G.A.A. football left full-back, Dublin and Cork. Three years apart he won All-Ireland Senior Football Championship winner's medals for different counties, being at left full-back on the Dublin side which won in 1942, and again in the left corner-back position on the Cork side which won the Sam Maguire Cup in 1945. He won Railway Cup medals for 2 different provinces also, one each for Leinster (in 1944) and for Munster (in 1946).

CRONE, W.

Soccer international defender. Club: Distillery (winning 4 Irish Cup medals, in 1884, 1885, 1886 and 1889). He was capped 12 times for Northern Ireland between 1882 and 1890 (all gained while at Distillery, making him that club's most capped player), scoring one international goal (against England in 1888). His brother, R Crone, a Distillery defender who won a I.F.A. Cup medal also in 1889, was capped 4 times in 1889 and 1890.

CRONIN, JIMMY.

G.A.A. football full-forward, Cork. He was a member of the Cork side which won the All-Ireland Senior Football Championship in 1945. A quality full-forward, he won 3 Railway Cup medals with Munster, in 1946, 1948 and 1949, sharing with P A 'Weeshie' Murphy the honour of being the first Cork footballer to do so.

CROSBIE, GEORGE F.

Amateur international golfer and yachtsman. Born in Cork, 10th February 1926. As a golfer out of Cork GC at Little Island, he played 24 Home International matches in 4 series between 1953 and 1957, winning 7, and played 40 interprovincial matches for Munster 1956-64, winning 16 and halving 11. He was beaten in 3 successive Irish Close Championship finals, 1955, 1956 and 1957. He has also been an international yachtsman for Ireland, winning 2 Irish Open Dragon Championships, and one Irish Dragon Championship. A director of the Cork Examiner, he captained the Irish amateur golf side which won the Home International 'triple crown' in 1990. His father, Commandant George Crosbie, was the first Munster-based holder of the office of President of the G.U.I., in 1938-1942.

CROSSAN, KEITH Derek ('GREMLIN').

Rugby international wing three-quarter. Born in Belfast, 29th December 1959. Club: Instonians. A product of Belfast R.A., he was first capped against Scotland in 1982, in the deciding Triple Crown match, and he was a constant member of the Triple Crown and Championship winning side of 1985, scoring a valuable try against Wales. He has toured Japan with Ireland, and was in the side for the World Cup in Australia in 1987, and again in the 1991 World Cup. He was the first Irish international to score 3 tries in a match at Lansdowne Road, against the Romanians in 1986, a then joint Irish record. His is the country's most capped wing three-quarter, with 41 international caps up to 1992. He has played 70 times for a successful Ulster side, first playing senior interprovincial rugby at the age of only 18. A flying winger, in 1986 he was nominated as Texaco's Rugby Sportstar of the Year. A bank official, he is a nephew of the former Irish captain, Deryk Monteith (cv). He retired in 1992.

CROSSAN, JOHNNY A.

Soccer international inside-forward. Born in Londonderry, 29th November 1938. In a career that went from 1958 to 1970, his clubs included Derry City, Rotterdam Sparta, Standard Liege, Sunderland (scoring 36 goals in 82 games in the years 1962 and 1963, and helping them to gain promotion to Division One in 1963), Manchester City (helping them to win the 2nd Division title in 1965-1966), Middlesborough and Tongren (Belgium). In his 7 years in English league football, he scored 72 league goals. He was capped 23 times for Northern Ireland between 1960 and 1968, scoring 10 international goals. He was banned by Irish and English leagues in 1959 for a time because of a tranfer scandal. His older brother Eddie (also born in Derry, 17th November 1925), also an inside forward, played for Blackburn (scoring 73 league goals for them) and Tranmere Rovers, and won 3 caps for Northern Ireland between 1950 and 1955, scoring one international goal.

CROTTY, MICK.

G.A.A. hurling half-forward, Kilkenny. Born in 1947. Club: James Stephens (with whom he won 4 Kilkenny SHC medals, and 2 All-Ireland Club Championship medals in 1976 and 1982). A county minor in 1963-64, he played senior inter-county hurling from 1970 to 1980, and won 4 All-Ireland Senior Hurling Championship winner's medals with Kilkenny in the seventies, in 1972, 1974, 1975 (all at right half-forward), and in 1979 at left half-forward. He was on losing All-Ireland S.H.C. final sides in both 1973 and 1978, his tally of Leinster S.H.C. medals coming to 6. He won National Hurling League medals with Kilkenny in 1976 and 1977, and won one All-Star award, at left half-forward in 1974.

CROTTY, PETER ('THE IRON-MAN FROM CLONMEL').

Amateur interntional welterweight boxer. Club: Clonmel. He was the first boxer to win 4 successive Irish National Senior Championships at welterweight, winning in 1949, 1950, 1951 and 1952. He represented Ireland at the Helsinki Olympic Games in 1952.

CROWE, Dr LOUIS.

Rugby wing three-quarter and athletics international. Club: Old Belvedere (winning Leinster Senior Cup winner's medals in 1951 and 1952). He was capped 3 times on the wing for Ireland in 1950 while playing for Old Belvedere, scoring one international try. He played interprovincial rugby for Leinster 7 times between 1949 and 1951, and was also an international athlete.

CROWE, Dr MORGAN Patrick.

Rugby international centre three-quarter. Born in Dublin, 5th March 1907. Club: Lansdowne (winning 4 Leinster Senior Cup medals with them in 1928, 1929, 1931 and 1933) and Leicester. Ten times a Leinster interpro, he was capped 13 times for Ireland between 1929 and 1934, scoring 2 international tries. His younger brother, Philip Martin Crowe, a Blackrock RFC centre and full-back, was 4 times a Leinster player, and was capped twice for Ireland, in 1935 and 1938 (scoring 2 conversions); and his son James Fintan ('Jaimsie' or 'Golly') Crowe, a U.C.D. (and later of Lansdowne) centre-threequarter, was capped once for Ireland in 1974, against New Zealand (and played 6 times for Leinster).

CROWLEY, D J ('DINJO').

G.A.A. football midfielder, Kerry. Club: Rathmore. Having played at left full-forward on the Kerry S.F.C. side beaten in the All-Ireland final in 1968, he went on to play in midfield alongside Mick O'Connell in the All-Ireland Senior Football Championship winning sides of both 1969 (when he was the man-of-the-match) and 1970.

CROWLEY, JOHN.

G.A.A. hurling half-back, Cork. A winner of All-Ireland medals at all 3 principal levels, he won an All-Ireland M.H.C. medal with Cork in 1974, and an All-Ireland Under 21 Championship medal in 1976. He also won 5 All-Ireland Senior Hurling Championship medals with Cork, 3-in-a-row in 1976, 1977 and 1978 (all at centre half-back), in 1984 also at centre back (when he played a 'stormer'), and in 1986 at left corner back. He was also on Cork sides beaten in 2 All-Ireland S.H.C. finals, in 1982 and 1983. He won one All-Star award, in 1984 at centre half-back.

CROWLEY, TIM.

G.A.A. hurling midfielder, Cork. Born in 1952. Club: Newcestown. Winning Harty Cup and All-Ireland College's medals with St Finbarr's, he won 2 successive All-Ireland M.H.C. medals with Cork minors, 1969 and 1970. He won an All-Ireland Under 21 Championship medal with Cork in 1973. In a ten-year career with the senior county side (1976-1985), he won 3 All-Ireland Senior Hurling Championship medals with Cork in 3 different positions, in 1977 at centrefield, in 1978 at left half-forward, in 1984 at centre half-forward. He was twice on losing All-Ireland S.H.C. sides, in 1982 and 1983, and won 2 other Munster S.H.C. medals, in 1979 and 1985, bringing his tally of Munster senior medals to 7. Also winning 2 Cork J.H.C. medals, he won a National Hurling League medal in 1981, and won a Railway Cup medal with Munster in 1981 as a sub. He won one All-Star award, in 1982 at centre-field with Kilkenny's Frank Cummins.

CROWLEY, TADGH.

G.A.A. football centre half-back, Cork. Club: Clonakilty (with whom he won 7 county championships 1939, 1942, 1943, 1944, 1946, 1947 and 1952). A player of dual ability, he won an All-Ireland hurling minor medal with Cork in 1939. He captained Cork to their 1945 All-Ireland Senior Football Championship final win over Cavan by 2-5 to 0-7, the first win for Cork since 1911 and tha last before 1973. He also won 3 further provincial S.F.C. medals with Cork. He won two Railway Cup medals with Munster, in 1946 and 1948. He later became a referee of note.

CRYAN, FRANCES.

International sculler. Club: Carrick-On-Shannon Rowing Club. In 1976 she won the inaugural Irish women's sculling championship; she then proceded to dominate this event for over a decade, winning the title 11 times in all, and all consecutively, in 1976, 1977, 1978, 1979, 1980, 1981, 1982, 1983, 1984, 1985, and finally in 1986. She sculled for Ireland in both World Championship and Olympic regattas, her best result being in the Single Sculls in the Olympic Regatta in Moscow in 1980, when she finished 7th over the 1,000 metre course.

CUDMORE, HAROLD.

Yachting helmsman. Born in Cork, 1944. The youngest member to be elected to the Cork Cruising club, he came to the top through experience at Enterprises, 505's, and Flying Dutchman (in which he represented Ireland in the 1972 Kiel Olympic Games (finishing 17th in that class), in which year he was also Ireland's Champion of Champions. In 1976 he won the World Half Ton Championship (and was 2nd in 1977), and won the One Ton World title in 1981 in 'Justine III', and also won a pair of Two Ton World Cup titles. As a match racer he is Britain and Ireland's top performer, winning the noted Lymington Cup a record 6 times (including 4 in a row in the early 80's), and has won the prestige U.K. Congressional Cup a record 6 times also, in 1978, 1980, 1981, 1982, 1984, and 1985 (and the U.S. version in 1986). In 1981 he was voted as Texaco's Yachting Sportstar of the Year. He was overall skipper of the 1987 British challenger in the America's Cup race, 'White Crusader'. His Admiral's Cup record is also admirable, being in the top individual boat outright twice and once in the winning team, and he managed the successful British team win in the event in 1989. In 1991 he captained the Ireland team to win this country's first ever Southern Cross Cup in Australia, and also, in the same series, skippering Atara to win the prestigious classic, the Sydney to Hobart race.

CUDDY, MICK ('The CUD').

Rugby inter-provincial prop-forward. Born in Dublin in 1932. Club: Bective Rangers (winning 3 Leinster Senior Cup medals, in 1955, 1956 and 1962). A product of Castleknock College, he played senior inter-provincial rugby for Leinster 9 times in 1959-1961, and won 3 final trial places, although remaining uncapped. He was an Irish selector 1980-84 and became President of the I.R.F.U. in 1993-94.

CULL, EDMUND (EDDIE).

Marine species fisherman. He is currently holder of 4 species weight records in Irish Marine waters, a record. In 1980 he caught a record Painted Ray (14.37 pounds) at Garryvoe Co Cork. In 1982 he caught a record Plaice (8.23 lbs) at Ballycotton Pier, Cork. In 1983 he captured, at Cork Harbour, a record 8.28 pounds Homelyn Ray. His fourth record marine species catch took place in 1986 at Ballycotton, when he caught an Irish record for Black Sole (6.32 lbs).

CULL, STEVEN.

Motorcycle rider. From Bangor, Co Down, he raced from the mid-1970's. In 1980 he was 3rd in the British 250cc title and 2nd in the Motocourse/B.P. championship. In 1988, on a 500cc Honda, he set a new absolute lap record of 119.08 m.p.h. in the Isle of Man, having the previous year been the first rider to lap a circuit in southern Ireland at over 100 m.p.h, at Skerries. He has 2 Isle of Man T.T. wins to his credit, the 1984 350cc Historic T.T., and the 1986 Junior T.T. He won 6 North-West 200 races between 1980 and 1988, and won the 600cc class at the 1990 Ulster Grand Prix. His fine career was prematurely halted in 1991.

CULLEN, PADDY.

G.A.A. footballing goalkeeper, Dublin. Club: O'Connell Boys (a junior club). Born 18th October 1944. From playing junior soccer in the mid-sixties, this ex-pupil of O'Connells C.B.S. became a prominent member of the famous 'Heffo's Army' of the 1970's, winning 3 All-Ireland Senior Football Championship finals with Dublin, in 1974 against Galway, 1976 against Kerry, and in 1977 against Armagh, and was three times on the losing side in the final, all against Kerry, in 1975, 1978 (when the infamous 5 goals were scored against him in the final), and 1979. Without a win in Railway Cup, he won National League medals with the Dubs in both 1976 and 1978. He won a tally of 4 All-Star awards as a goalkeeper (a joint football record for the position with Martin Furlong), in 1974, 1976, 1977 and 1979. A publican, he was appointed Dublin's football mamager 1990-92, helping them to win the National Football League in 1991, and to reach the All-Ireland S.F.C. final in 1992.

CULLEN, WILLIE.

G.A.A. footballing forward, Carlow. Club: Palatine. Playing for the county in lean times, he is one of Carlow's most consistent scorers in county football history, he finished in the top 5 national scorers in 1962. Sixteen years later, in 1978, he became the only Carlow player to head the annual programme scorers record, when in 15 games he scored 92 points, finishing one point ahead of the winner for the previous 3 years, Jimmy Keaveny of Dublin (cv).

CULLITON, M GERRY.

Rugby international second row and No 8 forward. Born in Clonaslee, Co Laois, 15th June 1936. Club: Wanderers (winning 2 Leinster Senior Cup medals, in 1959 and in 1973 when the club became the first to win the Leinster Senior League and Cup double). He played interprovincial rugby for Leinster 25 times over a 10 year period between 1958 and 1967. He was capped 19 times for Ireland between 1959 and 1964, many times alongside Bill Mulcahy (cv), scoring one international try for his country. In that period, Ireland won only 4 matches. He toured South Africa with Ireland in 1961. A farmer, his 2 sons, prop Brian and 2nd row Ronnie, were members of the Wanderers side which won the Leinster League and Cup double in 1990.

CULLOTY, JOHNNY.

G.A.A. football goalkeeper and forward, Kerry. Born in 1938. Club: Killarney Region (winning 4 Kerry SFC medals with Kerry East and one Kerry SHC with Killarney). He played at centre half-forward on the Kerry football minors beaten in the final of the All-Ireland M.F.C. in 1954. In a 16-year-career with Kerry seniors (1955-1971), he captained the county to win their 1969 All-Ireland Senior Football Championship final victory by 0-10 to 0-7 over Offaly, winning 4 other Sam Maguire Cup medals, in 1955 (at right corner-forward), 1959, 1962 and 1970, bringing his tally to 5, the last 4 all while playing as a goalkeeper. He played in 9 All-Ireland S.F.C. finals with Kerry in the 11 year period from 1955 and 1970, as he was goalkeeper on 4 Kerry teams which were beaten in Senior All-Ireland football finals (1960, 1964, 1965 and 1968). He also won 4 National Football League medals with the 'Kingdom', in 1959, 1961, 1963 and 1969. Also a useful hurler, he played Kerry minors 1951-1954, and played senior inter-county hurling for Kerry over a 17 year period from 1954 to 1971.

CUMMINS, EDDIE.

Hockey international left midfielder. Club: Catholic Institute, Limerick. A fine international hockey midfielder, he was capped 67 times (at least 62 of which were in succession, an Irish record) for Ireland between 1978 and 1985.

CUMMINS, GEORGE R.

Soccer international inside forward. Born in Dublin, 12th March 1931. Joined Everton from St Patricks in 1950. He also played for Luton (playing in 186 league matches for them 1953-1960, helping them to finish 2nd in Division 2 in 1954-55, and to their first ever F.A. Cup final appearence in 1969) and Hull City. He was capped 19 times for the Republic of Ireland between 1954 and 1961, scoring 5 international goals.

CUMMINS, FRANK.

G.A.A. hurling midfielder, Kilkenny. Club: Cork's Blackrock (winning 3 All-Ireland Club Championship winner's medals in 1972, 1974 and 1979). He won 8 All-Ireland Senior Hurling Championship medals with Kilkenny (the most by any Blackrock player), 7 of these on the field of play (in 1969, 1972, 1974, 1975, 1979, 1982, and 1983), all in the midfield position, having previously won a medal as non-playing sub in 1967. He played in 10 All-Ireland S.H.C. finals in a 15 year period from 1969 to 1983, being on 3 losing sides with Kilkenny, in 1971, 1973 and 1978, and thus won 11 Leinster S.H.C. medals in all. He also won 6 Railway Cup winner's medals with Leinster (in 1971, 1972, 1973, 1974, 1975 and 1977), and was also on 3 National League-winning sides, in 1976, 1982 and 1983. He has won 4 All-Star awards over a 12 year period, in 1971, 1972, 1982, and 1983, all in the midfield. In 1983 he became the 9th Kilkenny player to be nominated as Texaco Hurler of the Year.

CUMMINS, MICK.

G.A.A. hurler, Wexford. He was a member of the first Wexford Senior Hurling side to win the All-Ireland Championship in 1910, when 21 played on each team. One of the county's stars of the 1910-1920 decade, he later captained the county when th 15-a-side team were beaten at the All-Ireland S.H.C. final stage by Limerick in 1918.

CUMMINS, RAY.

G.A.A. hurling full-forward, and football full-forward, Cork. Born in 1949. Club: Blackrock (winning 3 All-Ireland Hurling Club Championship medals in 1972, 1974 and 1979). A member of the Cork hurling minors beaten by Wexford in the final of the All-Ireland M.H.C. of 1966, he won 2 All-Ireland Under 21 Championship hurling medals in 1968 and 1969. By winning an All-Ireland Senior Football Championship medal with Cork in 1973, to add to the All-Ireland S.H.C. medal he won in 1970 (one year after his senior inter-county debut), he became the first player in 28 years to win All-Ireland's in both codes. He captained Cork to their All-Ireland S.H.C. title of 1976 (the first Blackrock club-man to do so since Eudie Coughlan cv in 1931) in their 2-21 to 4-11 win over Wexford; he won 2 more Liam McCarthy Cup medals in 1977 and 1978 (and played in losing All-Ireland S.H.C. final sides in 1969 and 1972). He was also the first player ever to win Railway Cup medals for both codes along with All-Ireland titles, achieving this when Munster won the football Railway Cup for the first time since 1949 in 1972;. he won his hurling medals in 1970 and 1976. An 5-time All-Star, he won, uniquely to these awards, in both codes in the initial year of 1971 (full-forward in hurling, and centre half-forward in football), and went on to win again for hurling in 1972, for football in 1973, and again for hurling in 1977, all at full-forward. His younger brother Brendan was also in the Cork side during the 1976 S.H.C. All-Ireland win (doing so on his 26th birthday, September 5th), being also in the right corner-back spot in the wins of 1977 and 1978 (and on the losing All-Ireland sides of 1972, 1982 and 1983).

CUNNINGHAM, BERTIE.

G.A.A. football centre half-back, Meath. A member of the Meath team defeated in the All-Ireland Senior Football final in 1966 by Galway, he was a starring centre half-back in Meath's fine win over Cork in 1967, the county's first success in 13 years in the Sam Maguire Cup. He was later at left corner-back on the Meath side beaten in the All-Ireland final by Kerry in 1970. In 1967 he became the first Meath man to be honoured as Texaco Footballer of the Year.

CUNNINGHAM, GER.

G.A.A. hurling goalkeeper, Cork. Born in late August 1961. Club: St Finbarrs. Winning an F.A.I. Youths Cup medal in 1980 with Tramore Athletic, in hurling he was an automatic choice for Cork at all levels as a goalkeeper from the age of 15. He was on the Cork minors which captured 2 successive All-Ireland M.H.C. triumphs in 1978 and 1979, and won an All-Ireland Under 21 Championship winner's medal in 1982, all in goals. He has won 3 All-Ireland Senior Hurling Championship winner's medals with Cork, in the Centenary final of 1984, in 1986 and 1990, and has three times been on the losing side in All-Ireland S.H.C. finals (1982, 1983 and 1992), and captained the side in their All-Irleand S.H.C. semi-final defeat of 1985. He was the 16th Corkman to captain a Munster side to a Railway Cup success in 1985, winning 2 other medals, and won a National Hurling League medal in 1992-93. He won the Poc Fada competition in the Cooley Mountains for seven years in succession, in 1984, 1985, 1986, 1987, 1988, 1989, and 1990 (and holds the record of only 53 pucks for the 3 mile course over the Cooley Mountains). He won 3 successive All-Star awards as goalkeeper, in 1984, 1985, and 1986, and won his 4th award in 1990. In 1986 he became the 7th Cork man to be honoured as Texaco Hurler of the Year. His younger brother Brian, a forward, was on the Cork side beaten in the All-Ireland M.H.C. final of 1986.

CUNNINGHAM, MARTIN John ('MARNEY').

Rugby international flanker. Born in Cork, 23rd June 1933. Clubs: U.C.C. (winning a Munster Senior Cup medal in 1955), Cork Constitution, Barbarians. A product of 'Pres' Cork, he was capped 7 times on the flank for Ireland in 1955 and 1956, scoring one international try, against Wales in his last cap. He became a priest.

CUNNINGHAM, MICHAEL.

Horse trainer, flat and National Hunt. Born 15th May 1942. His best horses include Cairn Rouge (winner of the Irish 1,000 Guineas, Coronation and Champion stakes in 1980); For Auction (winner of 1982 Champion Hurdle), Greaswpaint (2nd in Aintree Grand National in 1982 and 1983). In 1980 he was voted as Texaco's Horse Racing Sportstar of the Year. Trains at Gormanstown Stables, Kildalkey, Navan, Co Meath.

CUNNINGHAM, MICHAEL.

Wheelchair athlete. Born in Tipperary. A versatile all-round sportsman, his fields vary from Track and Field, on to Basketball and Table-tennis. He has competed for Ireland in 5 Paralympic Games, in 1972, 1976, 1980, 1984, and 1988, winning one medal. He is rated as one of the top ten wheelchair table tennis players in Europe, and excels in able-bodied tournaments also. He also won the inaugural wheelchair section section on the Dublin City Marathon, and broke the world record for Javelin, three years after winning the Gold Medal in the

Canada Games of 1976. Now living in Dublin.

CUNNINGHAM, VINCENT John Gerald (VINNIE).

Rugby international centre and out-half. Born in Dublin, 14th March 1967. Club: St Mary's (being on the side which won the Leinster Senior Cup in 1993, soon after being defeated for the top spot in that season's All-Ireland League). A schoolboy international at both cricket and rugby, he has played rugby for Leinster, Ireland Under 25 and Ireland 'B' sides. First capped in 1988, his international cap tally reached 14 up to March 1993, with 3 international tries scored. With Ireland he toured France in 1988, Namibia in 1990, and New Zealand in 1992. He went (as a replacement) on the British and Irish Lions tour of New Zealand in 1993.

CUNNINGHAM, WILLIAM A (BILL or WILLY).

Rugby international scrum-half and full-back. (1900-1959). Club: Lansdowne (winning a Leinster Senior Cup medal in 1922). He won 8 international caps for Ireland between 1920 and 1923, scoring one try. After emigrating to Johannesburg in 1923, he was unexpectedly called up by the touring 1924 Lion's team to South Africa, who were plagued with injuries, and played in the drawn 3rd test (scoring a try in his debut and only test match). So without being either selected to go on tour, or as a replacement, he gained the honour of playing for the British Isles.

CUNNINGHAM, WILLIAM E ('WILLY').

Soccer international full-back. Born in Mallusk, 20th February 1930. Joined St Mirren, from where he transferred at a big fee to Leicester City in 1954, winning the second division championship with them. A strongly built ball-playing full-back, he was capped 30 times for Northern Ireland, including playing in the No 5 jersey in all five games the successful 1958 World Cup campaign.

CUPPAIDGE, JOHN LOFTUS.

Rugby international forward. Born in 1858. Clubs: Dublin University, Wanderers. Six times a Leinster player between 1875 and 1880, he won 3 international caps for Ireland in 1879 and 1880, and although Ireland lost all 3 games, he has the distinction of having, on January 30th 1880, in a match against England, scored Ireland's first ever try in international rugby. He spent most of his later life as a doctor in Australia, dying there in 1934, at the age of 76.

CURLEY, CATHAL (C.B.).

Rally driver. Born in Irivinestown, Co Fermnanagh, 5th February 1941. In his 12 year career in rallying he won many rallys, triumphing in the Donegal Rally 3 years in succession, 1972, 1973 and 1974. His best year was in 1974 when he won 5 international rallys (Cork, Galway, Donegal, the Circuit of Ireland and the Manx International). His 1974 win of Ireland's premier event makes him the last Ulster driver to win the Circuit of Ireland rally. He has also finished 2nd 8 times in the Manx rally (to add to his win in 1974, and this was in only 10 attempts at the race). He also became the first U.K. driver to drive the works Lancia Stratus in the mid 1970's. A brother of Barney Curley, the horse trainer and gambler, Cathal had a hit song by the Bay City Rollers pop group of the 1970's named after him (titled 'Hey C.B.'), through his association and friendship with Phil Coulter. He owns his own motor business in Derry.

CURRAMS, LIAM.

G.A.A. dual hurler and footballer, Offaly. From Kilcormac, he was born 26th January 1961. A dual player of note, in 1981 he became (at the age of 20) the first man to play in both codes All-Ireland finals in the same year since 1956, winning a All-Ireland Senior Hurling Championship medal in the final with Offaly against Galway, but losing out in his bid to do the 'double' in the one season, when the county were beaten by

Kerry in the Sam Maguire Cup final a few weeks later. In 1982, while playing a vital role at left half-back on the Offaly S.F.C. side which deprived Kerry of their 5-in-a-row, he joined the select band of players to win senior All-Ireland medals at both codes. He has also won All-Star awards at both codes, in 1981 in hurling (his favoured code) at midfield, and in 1982 at football, at left-half back.

CURRAN, KATHLEEN.

G.A.A. ladies gaelic footballing goalkeeper, Kerry. Club: Beaufort. A former Dublin goalkeeper (winning 2 All-Stars while playing for them), she has won 5 consecutive All-Ireland Ladies Senior Football Championship medals with Kerry, in 1986, 1987, 1988, 1989 (when she captained the side that beat Wexford) and 1990, also winning 4 National League medals in that time, and has won 4 interprovincial Championship medals. A winner of 4 All-Star awards, she is also a raquetball player of note and in 1988 she won European gold medal honours with the Irish team in Paris.

CURRAN, MARY JO and PHIL.

G.A.A. ladies gaelic footballing sisters, Kerry. Mary Jo, a half forward from the Beaufort club, has won 2 All-Ireland Minor medals with Kerry (1980 and 1981), and 9 consecutive All-Ireland Senior medals, 1982, 1983, 1984, 1985, 1986, 1987, 1988, 1989 and 1990 (making her one of only 4 players to win 11 successive All-Ireland titles), and has also won 9 National League and 7 Interprovincial medals. One of the games finest exponents, she has won an All-Star each year from its inception in 1981 up to 1989, a total of 9 times. Mary Jo is also a basketball international. Phil, her sister, a Beaufort full back, has won 8 successive All-Ireland Senior medals, 8 National Leagues, 2 Interprovincial medals, and has won one All-Star award.

CURRAN, MATT ('NUTTY').

Heavyweight boxer. Born in Lisdeen, Ennis, Co Clare in November 1882, he died in Sydney Australia in 1938. He was British Empire Heavyweight champion for a period in 1911, having won on a disqualification when his opponent, Australian Bill Lang, struck him while he was on the canvas. He lost 23 of his 83 professional fights, winning 45 bouts.

CURRAN, NOEL and PAUL.

G.A.A. football father and son. Noel (born in 1943), a full-forward from the Dunshaughlin club (winning Meath I.F.C. and J.F.C. medals), was a member of the Meath team which won the All-Ireland Senior Football Championship in 1967, also playing on the side which lost the previous year's All-Ireland S.F.C final. A minor in 1961, who played senior inter-county in 1964 to 1971, he also played Railway Cup with Leinster. His son Paul (born in 1969), a product of Tallaght CS and a Thomas Davis clubman (winning 3 successive Dublin county championship medals in 1989, 1990, and in 1991 when the Leinster championship was also won, and with whom he was on the losing end of the 1992 All-Ireland Club Championship final), first played for Dublin senior's in championship football in 1989 at 19, having played 2 years on the minors. He has won 3 Leinster S.F.C. medals with Dublin in 1989, 1992 (when they were beaten in the All-Ireland final) and 1993, and has also won 2 National Football League medals in 1991 and 1993. He won an All-Star award in 1992 in the centre half-back position.

CURRAN, SAMMY.

Soccer international forward. Clubs: Belfast Celtic (with whom he scored a club record of 56 goals in his first season, and won an Irish League and Cup double success in 1925 and 1926). He won 3 international caps for Northern Ireland between 1926 and 1928.

CURRIVAN, BARRY.

Lightweight international rower. Club: Neptune R.C. Ireland's outstanding lightweight rower (almost matching that of the heavyweight sculler, Sean Drea cv), he has eight times (in 3 different classes of boat: double scull, coxless four and eight) represented his country in World Lightweight Championships. He made the Grand Finals in 3 of these events, finishing 4th in the coxless fours in 1982, 4th in the eights in 1984, and 6th in the coxless fours in 1987. He has won a total of 6 Irish Senior Championships in 4 of the 5 classes open to him: coxed four (1981), coxless pairs (1982), double sculls (1979), and 3 titles in 'eights' (1980, 1984 and 1989), having also competed in single sculls.

CURTIS, Arthur BRIAN, and Michael DAVID.

Rugby international father and son. Brian, a Shanghai-born (27th March 1924) flanker with Oxford University R.F.C. (winning a Blue in 1949), won 3 caps for Ireland (all lost) in the back-row in the 1950 international Championship season, against France, England and Scotland, before emigrating as a headmaster to South Africa in 1954. He won a Distinguished Flying Cross in 1945. His son David (born in Zimbabwe 10th April 1965, and who won a Blue for Oxford in both rugby and cricket), having played for South Africa at Under 19 level, and for Connacht and Ireland B, was first capped as a London Irish centre-threequarter for Ireland in the 1991 season, when he also a member of Ireland's brave World Cup performance. His cap tally upon retiring in 1992 was 13, with one international try. He toured Namibia with Ireland in 1991.

CURTIS, DERMOT.

Soccer international centre-forward. Born in Dublin, 26th August 1932. He left Shelbourne in 1956, and in 12 years of English League football, with Bristol City, Ipswich Town, Exeter City (2 spells, scoring 33 league goals in 162 appearences), Torquay United, he scored 67 league goals in all. He was capped 17 times for Ireland, scoring 8 international goals. His one cap obtained while he was based at St James Park in 1963 makes him Exeter City's only (and therefore most) capped player.

CURTIS, RICHARD (DICK).

G.A.A. footballer, Dublin. The first player to win 4 All-Ireland Senior Football Championship winner's medals, he played on the Dublin sides which 4 won championships in the 1890's. His first 3 successes, in 1891, 1892 and 1894 were with Young Ireland's, while he was later on the Kickham's team which won in 1897. An all-round sportsman, he also was All-Ireland wrestling champion for several years in the 1890's.

CUSACK, NEIL.

Long-distance runner. Born 30th December 1951. Club: Limerick A.C. He won the American Collegiate cross-country title in 1972 (the only Irishman to do so), and was disqualified after winning the A.A.U. title a week later. In 1974 he became the only Irishman to win the prestigious Boston Marathon, in a time of 2 hours, 13 minutes and 39 seconds, then an Irish record. He won the 2nd Dublin City Marathon in 1981 in a time of 2 hours, 13 minutes and 46 seconds. A veteran of 2 Olympic Games (1972 over 10,000m and 1976 when he finished 55th in the marathon) and a European Champinship in Rome in 1974 (finishing 8th in the marathon), he has run in the World Cross-Country Champinships 13 times. He also set a European record indoor for 3 miles at 13-10.8. In 1974 he was voted as Texaco's Athletics Sportstar of the Year.

CUSH, WILBUR W.

Soccer international half-back, inside-forward and wing-half. Born in Lurgan, 10th June 1928. His playing clubs included Shankhill YMCA, Glenavon (1947-57, eight of his caps were gained while he was at this club, making him the club's most capped player; he helped them to their first ever wins in the Irish League in 1952 and 1957, and to their debut I.F.A. Cup success in 1957; also winning 2 Irish Gold Cup wins in 1954 and 1956), Leeds

United (signing him for £7,000 as Ulster's Player of the Year, and scoring 9 league goals in 87 matches 1957-59), and Portadown (his 3 caps gained here make him also this club's most capped player). He was capped 26 times for Northern Ireland, scoring 5 international goals, and was a member of the World Cup squad in 1958, playing in all 5 matches (and scoring the historic winning goal against Czechoslovakia). He also played for the Irish League, scoring 2 goals for the side. He died aged 53 in 1981.

CUSSEN, DENIS John.

Rugby international wing three-quarter and athlete. Born in Newcastle West, Co Limerick, 19th July 1901, he died in 1980. Clubs: Dublin University (winning Leinster Senior Cup medals in 1920, 1921 and 1926), St Mary's Hospital, Barbarians. He was capped 15 times for Ireland in the 1920's, between 1921 and 1927, and scored 5 international tries. His speed and hard-as-nails thrusting runs made him a fearful opponent and a darling of Irish crowds. He also played interprovincial rugby for Leinster 12 times from 1920 to 1926. He was also a sprint champion, being the first Irishman to break 10 seconds, and holding the Irish 100 yards record at 9.8 seconds for many years (he represented Ireland in the 100 metres in the 1928 Olympic Games in Amsterdam, reaching the 2nd round). A doctor, he later practiced in England, and became official medical officer to the British Olympic team.

D

DAGG, T S C.

Hockey international. Club: Dublin University. He was capped for Ireland only twice, once in 1903 and again 1911. He became the first former international hockey player to become President of the I.H.U. in 1920 to 1924, and again held that post in 1930-31. He was among the first group to be given the Merit Badge of the Union, and he wrote the definitive book on the early history of Irish hockey, 'Hockey in Ireland'.

DALTON, W.

Soccer international. Clubs: Y.M.C.A., and Linfield. In the formative years of international soccer between 1888 and 1894, he played 11 times for his country, scoring 8 international goals for the I.F.A. side (Northern Ireland). He also helped Linfield to 2 Irish Cup successes, in 1891 and in 1892.

DALY, BILL.

Champion road bowlplayer. From Leap, near Skibereen Co Cork, he was born in 1958. As a youngster he won West Cork under 14 and under 18 titles, and went on the win the Senior title in 1979. He won the first ever World Road-Bowling Championship title (using a 28 ounce 'ball' over a 2,750 metre 'score', and winning a prize of £2,000) in 1985 in Cork, and retained the title in 1987 at Whitechurch when he beat off opposition from Germany, Holland, County Armagh and of course Co Cork. A Garda.

DALY, DEREK.

Motor Racing Driver. Born in Dundrum, Co Dublin, 11th March 1953. Early in his career he raced Formula 2 and Formula 3 cars, along with Formula Ford 1600. In 1977 he won the British Formula 3 Championship (becoming the first Irishman to do this), having the previous year won the Formula Ford Festival. In 1978 he finished 3rd in the European Formula 2 Championships, winning 2 Grand Prix in Chevron Hart B42. Between 1978 and 1982 he raced in 49 Formula One World Championship Grand Prix races, attaining a total of 15 World Championship race points (mostly for the Candy Tyrrell team), surviving huge crashes at Monaco and at Zandvoort. In 8 years in the U.S.A. Indycar racing scene in the United States, his best finish has been a 3rd place. In 1988 he finished 3rd in the Le Mans 24 Hour Race, and led the event for a time in 1989. He was selected as Texaco's Motor racing Sportstar of the Year in both 1977 and 1978. His wife Beth was placed 5th in the world finals of the ski jet championships in 1989.

DALY, DENIS St George.

Polo player. Born in Co Galway, 5th September 1862, he died in Oxford in 1942. As a member of the Foxhunters-Hurlingham polo team representing Great Britain/U.S.A., he won a gold medal in the Olympic Games of 1900 in Paris, when they defeated the Club Rugby side by 3-1 in the deciding game. A quality player, he did not however ever win a Westchester Cup. An army major later on, he was the son of an Irish Peer, Lord Dunsandle, and was also a handy huntsman, becoming Master of the Heythrop.

DALY, FRED.

Professsional golfer. Born in Portrush, 11th October 1911. After spells at other clubs, he was appointed pro at Balmoral in 1944 and was attached there until his death at 79 in 1990. He won the Irish Open in 1946, becoming the first home winner of the title. To date is the only Irishman to win the British Open Golf Championship, which he did at Hoylake in 1947, with rounds of 73, 70, 78 and 72, for a one shot victory over Reg W Horne and the amateur Frank R Straqnahan, securing the win by holing a 13 yard putt on the final green. In the same year he also won the British Professional Matchplay title (this double had not been achieved since 1905), also capturing this title in 1948 and 1952 (when a third round match went to a record 12th tie-hole). His other outstanding high-placing British Open finishes include 8th place in 1946, 2nd in 1948, 3rd in 1950, 4th at his home club of Portrush in 1951, and 3rd in 1952. He attained Ryder Cup honours 3 times, in 1947, 1949, and 1953 (in his 8 Ryder Cup matches his record was 43.75%, winning 3, halving one, and losing 4 matches). He also won the Ulster Professional title eleven times (1936, 1940, 1941, 1942, 1943, 1946, 1951, 1955, 1956, 1957 and 1958), and won the Irish Professional Championship 3 times (1940, 1946 and 1952). Other tournament wins included both the Dunlop Southport and Penfold events in 1948, the Lotus tournament of 1950 and the Daks tournament in 1952. Playing World Cup for Ireland in 1954 and 1955, he won the Miss Tooting Bec Cup in both 1950 and 1952. Made an M.B.E. in 1983, in 1984 he became the 3rd golfer to join the Texaco Hall of Fame, and because he is the only Irish professional golfer to win a 'major', he must rank among the country's greatest ever professionals.

DALY, JOHN CHRISTOPHER ('J.C.' or CHRIS).

Rugby international prop-forward. Born in Cobh Co Cork, 12th December 1912, he hailed from 'The Holy Ground' area of Cork (of song fame). Clubs: London Irish, Barbarians. He played international rugby 7 times for Ireland in 1947 and 1948. His only score for Ireland was the try that won the Triple Crown for Ireland against Wales in Belfast in March 1948, thereby bridging a gap of 49 years. On his way off the pitch his jersey was stripped off his back by souvenir hunters. He never played for Ireland again, as he joined the professional ranks of Rugby league with Huddersfield in 1948, where he distinguished himself. He died in 1987.

DALY, JOHN Joseph.

Middle-distance and steeplechasing athlete. Born in Ballyglunin, Co Galway, 22nd February 1880. He won Irish titles from 1902 at the mile, 4 miles and cross country. Representing Ireland in the Olympic Games of 1904, held in St Louis, Missouri, he won a silver medal in the steeplechasing event, running the 2,590 metres distance in 7 minutes and 40.6 seconds, being passed out close to home by the American James Lightbody, who won by a second. He ran in the marathon of the Intercalated Games in Athens in 1906, withdrawing after 18 miles (and also ran in the 5 miles race, in which he finished in 3rd place, but was deprived of a bronze by disqualification). Settling in America, he later won their championships at 5 miles (in record time) and 10 miles, and won the Canadian title at 3 miles in record time. Although he entered for 4 events in the 1908 Games, he did not compete.

DALY, GERRY.

Soccer international midfielder. Born in Dublin, 30th April 1954. Clubs: Bohemians (sold to old Trafford for £20,000), Manchester United (scoring 32 goals in 137 matches, 1973-1976 with a penalty success rate of 16 out of 17, helping them to gain promotion to Division One in 1975), Derby County (scoring 31 league goals in 111 league matches 1977-1981), New England Teamen, Coventry City (1981-84, and for a time on loan to Leicester), Birmingham City (1984-85), Shrewsbury Town (1985-87), Stoke City (1987-89), and Doncaster Rovers (1989-). He was capped 47 times for the Republic of Ireland in a distinguished 15-year career for his country between 1973 and 1987, scoring 13 international goals, and placing him 4th in the Republic's all-time scorer's tally.

DALY, Dr TOMMY.

G.A.A. hurling goalkeeper, Dublin. He won 4 All-Ireland Senior Hurling Championship winner's medals with Dublin, in 1917, 1920, 1924, and in 1927, and was on losing All-Ireland S.H.C. sides in 1919 and 1921. He was the goalkeeper on the Leinster side which won the inaugural Railway Cup hurling contest on St Patrick's Day 1927. One of hurling's masters between the posts, a ballad was composed about him, such was his reputation.

DALY, VAL.

G.A.A. football centre-half forward, Galway. A member of the Galway Under 21 side beaten in the All-Ireland Under 21 final in 1981, he is the winner of 5 Connacht S.F.C. medals with Galway (in 1982, 1983, 1984, 1986 and 1987). He played in one All-Ireland Senior Football Championship final, when the Tribesmen lost in the ill-tempered decider to Dublin in 1983. He has won 2 All-Star awards, in 1987 at right corner-forward, and in 1990 at centre-half forward.

DALY, WILLIE JOHN.

G.A.A. hurling half-forward and centre-back, Cork. Born in 1925. Club: Carrigtohill. He played senior inter-county hurling for Cork over an eleven year period from 1947 to 1957, winning 3 successive Liam McCarthy Cup medals in 1952, 1953 (palying a fine game in the final) and 1954. He was a member also of the Cork side beaten in the All-Ireland S.H.C. final of 1956. He also won 2 National League medals with the Rebel County, in both 1948 and 1953, and won Railway Cup medals with Munster in both 1953 and 1955. He later trained the Cork senior hurlers from 1973 to 1976.

DANAHER, PHILIP Paul Anthony.

Rugby international full-back and centre three-quarter. Born in Abbeyfeale, Co Kerry, 5th October 1965. Clubs: Lansdowne (winning Leinster Senior Cup medals in 1986, 1987 and 1988), Garryowen (captaining them when runners-up in the 1990-91 inaugural All-Ireland League, again captain when they won that competition in 1991-92; and winning a Munster Senior Cup medal in 1993). A product of St Munchin's, he was an outhalf on the side which captured the Munster Senior Schools Cup in 1982, and won 2 Irish School's caps at out-half in 1983. His first 6 international caps were at full-back, and then after coming on as a substitute on the wing against the All-Blacks in 1989, he gained a further international cap as a centre against France in 1990, thereby being among the select band to play in 3 positions for Irleand. He went on the Irish tour of North America in 1989, and captained the Irish senior squad on their tour of New Zealand in 1992 (having earlier captained the Ireland Under 25 side against U.S.A. in 1990). In 1991 he played one game in the World Cup 91, and became only the 2nd Irish rugby international since the 'Ban' was removed to play senior championship football, when he lined out for Limerick in the Munster S.F.C. final against Kerry. His cap tally came to 16 by March 1993.

DANIELS, MICK.

G.A.A. hurling half-back, Dublin. Born in 1905 in Carrickmore, Co Tipperary. Club: Army Metro (winning 3 county championships). Having been a member of the Dublin side beaten by Limerick after a replay in 1934, he captained the Dublin side which won the 1938 All-Ireland Senior Hurling Championship final against Waterford by 2-5 to 1-6, the last time Dublin captured this title. He also won a National Hurling League medal in 1939, and won a Railway Cup medal with Leinster in 1936. His senior inter-county career with the Dubs stretched from 1930 to 1939.

DARBY, PETER.

G.A.A. footballing left corner back, Meath. He captained the Meath side which won the 1967 All-Ireland Senior Football Championship final for the first time since 1954, when they beat Cork by 1-9 to 0-9. He was also at left back in the Meath side beaten in the All-Ireland final the previous year by Galway, and he captained the successful Meath tour of Australia in 1968.

DARBY, SEAMAS.

G.A.A. footballer, Offaly. He was a member of the Offaly S.F.C. side which won the Sam Maguire Cup in 1972. Being in and out of the inter-county side for more than a decade, he will be forever remembered as the scorer, after coming on as a substitute, of the highly controversial late goal which not only gained Offaly their 3rd All-Ireland Senior Football Championship title in 1982 (and his 2nd medal), but also deprived the great Kerry side which were in line for an unprecedented 5-in-a-row Sam Maguire medals (this game will forever be known as the 'Seamas Darby final'). His brother Stephen came on as a sub in the same final in 1982.

DARCY, EAMONN.

Professional golfer. Born in Delgany, 7th August 1952, he turned pro in 1969, winning the Assistants Championship that season. He has won 13 tournaments, his victories include the World Under 25 Championship in 1976, the Greater Manchester Open in 1977, the West Lakes and Air New Zealand Open in 1981, the Spanish Open in 1983, the Lawrence Batley in 1983, the Mulifira Open in 1984, the Belgian Open in 1987, and the 1990 Desert Classic in Dubai (thereby becoming the 2nd Irishman to win major tour events in 3 different decades). He has won Ryder Cup honours on 4 occasions, in 1975, 1977, 1981, and in the victorious side of 1987, when in the crunch match against Ben Crenshaw in the final day's singles at Muirfield Village, Ohio, he sank a difficult putt on the home green to win the vital point for the European side, ensuring their first ever win on American soil (this was his only win in 11 matches, although he halved 2). His best Order of Merit placings include 3rd in 1975, and 2nd in 1976. He was captain of the victorious Irish team which made Irish golfing history by winning the 4th Dunhill Cup, a medal matchplay tournament, at St Andrew's in October 1988 (when they beat Canada, England and Australia in that order). His Irish wins include the 1976 Irish Dunlop, the 1981 Irish Matchplay, and the Irish Professional Championship in both 1988 and 1992. He was chosen as Texaco's Golf Sportstar of the Year twice, in 1976 and 1987.

DARGAN, MICHAEL James.

Rugby international flank forward and cricket international batsman. Born in Dublin, 9th October 1928. A product of Belvedere and Clongowes Colleges, he was capped for Ireland in rugby 3 times in 1952 on the flank, while playing for Old Belvedere (with whom he won Leinster Senior Cup winners medals in 1951 and 1952), also playing 5 times for Leinster, and was also on the Irish tour of Argentina in 1952. As a right hand batsman and member of Phoenix, he also won international honours once at cricket, playing in the first class match against the M.C.C. in 1954, scoring 7 runs.

DARLING, JOHNNY.

Soccer international No 4. Club: Linfield. He was capped 21 times for Northern Ireland over a 15 year span between 1897 and 1912, scoring one international goal. He helped Linfield to win 5 Irish Cup titles, in 1898, 1899, 1902, 1904, and 1913.

DARRAGH, PAUL.

International show jumper. Born 28th April 1953. As a junior he won 4 medals in the European Junior title, silver in 1969, bronze in 1970, and silver again in 1970 (when he helped Ireland win the gold in the team event). Among the many national and international wins he achieved was the Hickstead Derby in 1975. He has ridden over 36 Nation's Cup events since 1972. With Heather Honey he finished 7th in the World Cup Preliminary event in Dublin in 1979. On Carrolls Young Diamond, he has had a 2nd, a 3rd, and 2 5ths in World Cup Preliminary Events in 1980 to 1984. He has helped Irish teams to Aga Khan Cup successes and has represented Ireland at 2 Olympic Games, in 1988 in Seoul and in 1992 at Barcelona, and has won the Irish National Championship.

DAVIDSON, IAN G R.

Rugby international wing three-quarter. Club: N.I.F.C. He played international rugby for Ireland 9 times between 1899 (the Triple Crown year in which he was in the side which beat England) and 1902, scoring 2 tries. Touring with an Irish team to Canada in 1899, he was also selected on the British and Irish Lions tour of South Africa in 1903.

DAVIDSON, JAMES Charles (JIMMY).

Rugby international wing-forward and coach. Born in Armagh, 23rd October 1942. Club: Dungannon. He played international rugby for Ireland on 6 occasions, against the four home countries in 1976, and twice against New Zealand, in 1973 and in 1976 when he joined the Irish tour of that country in place of Shay Deering (cv). He became a successful coach for Queen's University, the Combined Universities, and particularily Ulster in the 1980's, and was appointed coach to the Irish squad in 1987-1990, when Ireland won 3 out of 12 International Championship matches played.

DAVIN, MAURICE, TOM and PAT.

Field event athletics brothers. From Carrick-on-Suir. Tom, the eldest of the 3, set a world record height for the high jump of 1.78 metres in 1873. When Pat (1857-1849), the youngest of the three, went on to set a new mark of 1.93 in 1880, they became the first of only 3 sets of 2 brothers (see Dan and Tim Ahearne) to break individual world records in athletics history. Pat, who also set the first recognised British record of 23' 2" in the long jump at Monasterevan in 1883, won the British A.A.A. titles at both High Jump and Long Jump in 1881. He was the first man to jump over 6 feet in the high jump, and at one stage held 6 world records (including the 100 yards in 10 seconds, the hurdles in 16 seconds, the high jump at 6'2, and 23' 2" for the broad jump off grass). At the same British A.A.A. championships in 1881, the third brother Maurice (1841-1927, who at 39 years of age was the oldest man to compete at the games) won the Shot Putt and the Hammer events.

Maurice was adept at many other sports, including rowing, running, jumping and swimming, and won the Irish All-Round Championship in 1888 at the age of 47. Maurice was also the first President of the Gaelic Athletic Association.

DAVIS, EUGENE ('POOCH').

Soccer forward. Born in Dublin, 17th October 1953. A product of St Joseph's club in Sallynoggin, he won youth's caps with the Republic of Ireland. A prolific League of Ireland goalscorer, up to the end of the 1986-87 season he had scored 123 League goals. He was leading scorer in the 1980-81 league season when his 23 goals with Athlone Town (a club record) helped them to win the League. His other clubs include St Patrick's Athletic, Bohemians, U.C.D. and Bray Wanderers.

DAVIS, TONY.

G.A.A. football left half-back, Cork. Club: O'Donovan Rossa (helping them to win the county championship for the first time in 1992, and to win the subsequent All-Ireland club final in 1993). He won an All-Ireland M.F.C. medal with Cork in 1981, and 2 All-Ireland Under 21 football medals, in 1984 and as captain in 1985. Having played left full back in Cork's 1987 All-Ireland defeat by Meath, he moved to the left half-back position in the 1988 loss in the same position, and was one of the outstanding team which won the All-Ireland Senior Football Championship in 1989. In 1989 All Stars, for his first award, he joined a select band of players to be the only one nominated for his position, left half back. In 1993 he won another Munster S.F.C. medal, being sent off in the losing All-Ireland Final against Derry, a match in which his brother Don also played.

DAVY, EUGENE O'Donnell.

Rugby international out-half and centre. Born in Dublin, 16th July 1904. Clubs: U.C.D., Lansdowne (winning 6 Leinster Senior Cup medals, in 1927, 1928, 1929 and 1930 as captain, and in 1931 and 1933). He played 20 times for Leinster over a ten year period between 1924 and 1933. This complete player, a strong fast runner and noted tackler, was one of Ireland's greatest out-halves, and was capped 34 times between 1925 and 1934 (making him Belvedere College's most capped player), captaining the side in the 1932-33 season. In 1930, in Murrayfield, he scored 3 tries against Scotland, an Irish record he shared until 1991. His total scoring tally for Ireland is 8 tries and 3 drop goals. He was President of the I.R.F.U. 1967-68, and was manager of the Irish party for the Australian tour of 1967. A stockbroker.

DAWSON, Alfred RONALD (RONNIE).

Rugby international hooker and administrator. Born in Dublin, 5th June 1932. Club: Wanderers (winning Leinster Senior Cup medals in 1954 and 1959). Playing 24 times for Leinster over a ten year period from 1955 to 1964, he was capped for Ireland 27 times between 1958 and 1964, captaining the side 11 times, and scored one international try (in his debut against Australia in 1958, thus sharing in the first Irish victory over a visiting side). Also a Barbarian (captaining them to beat the Springboks in 1960), he captained the Irish touring party to South Africa in 1961, losing only the international. He became the 5th Irishman to captain the British and Irish Lions, on the 1959 tour of Australia, New Zealand and Canada, playing in all 6 Test matches, a record for Lion's captaincy, winning a joint-Lions captain's record three of these test matches. The tour record was 33 played, 27 won, 6 lost, 824 points for (a record) and 353 points against, with a record Lion's tour try tally of 165. He later became Assistant Manager-cum-Coach to the 1968 Lions tour of South Africa. He was an Irish selector 1969-72, coaching the side during that time, being the first to be appointed to the post. He has been an Irish representative on the International Board since 1975, and has been a member of the Barbarians committee. He was President of the I.R.F.U. in the 1989-1990 season. An architect.

DAWSON, MICHAEL

Flat jockey and horse trainer. As a jockey he rode the winner of the Irish Derby in 3 out of 4 years: Kentish Fire in 1890, Roy Neill in 1892 and Bowline in 1893. He was later leading Trainer in Ireland for nine years in succession, in 1906, 1907 (winning 61 races and £9,221), 1908, 1909, 1910, 1911, 1912, 1913 and 1914. As a trainer at Rathbride Manor in the Curragh, he won 6 Irish Classic races, including 4 Irish Derby's (St Brendan, the best horse he trained, in 1902, Royal Arch in 1904, Killeagh in 1906 and Bachelor's Double in 1908), and 2 Irish Oaks (Marievaale in 1902 and Tullynacree in 1911). Ireland's leading trainer in the first half of the century, his son Michael Junior trained the winner of the 1958 Irish Derby, Sindon.

DAWSON, RICHARD Cecil (DICK).

Horse trainer, Natinal Hunt and flat. Born in Ireland in 1865, winning the Galway Plate for the first time in 1896 with Castle Warden. He won the Aintree Grand National in 1898 with Drogheda, having recently moved from the Curragh to England to train. Changing to the flat, he went on to win the unofficial Epsom Derby and Oaks in 1916 with Finfinella, and the real thing in 1929 with Trigo and the following year with Blenheim (making him the 2nd trainer to win both an Aintree Grand National and an Epsom Derby, and most recent until his feat was equalled by Vincent O'Brien cv). Champion trainer in England in 1919, 1924 and 1929, his other English Classic winners included Diophon in the 2,000 Guineas of 1924, a St Leger win in the same year with Salmon Trout, and an Oaks triumph in 1923 with Brownhylda. One of Ireland's finest trainers, he also won 8 Irish Classic races: 3 Irish Derby's (Zionist in 1925, Harinero in 1933 and with the dead-heating Primero in 1934); 2 Irish Oaks (Theresina in 1930 and his own horse Salar in 1933); and 3 Irish St Leger's (Trigo in 1929, Harinero in 1933 and Primero in 1934). Another great horse of his was Blandford, who has sired the winners of 6 Irish Classics.

DEACY, EAMONN.

Soccer international midfielder. Born in Galway, 1st October 1958. Clubs: Galway Rovers, Aston Villa, Galway United (gaining a runner-up medal in the 1985 F.A.I. Cup). He was capped 4 times for the Republic of Ireland in 1982. He was Galway United's manager when they won the 1991 F.A.I. Cup.

DEAN, PAUL Michael.

Rugby international out-half and centre. Born in Dublin, 28th June 1960. Club: St Mary's (winning Leinster Senior League medals with them in 1979 and 1989). A product of St Mary's School in Dublin, he was capped 5 times at school international level. Playing 'B' international level in 1980, he was first capped on the senior Irish side against South Africa in 1981. He was an integral part of both of Ireland's 1982 (as a centre) and 1985 (as a stand off) Triple Crown winning teams, playing in all 8 matches in those 2 memorable years (and one of only 6 players to play in all 6 Triple Crown matches). A gifted runner and defensive player, he also played for Ireland in the inaugural World Cup in 1987, having previously toured with Ireland in 1981 to South Africa and in 1985 to Japan. A member of the British and Irish Lions team which toured Australia in 1989, he was injured in his first match and came home early, and he retired in 1989 with a tally of 32 international caps for Ireland, and scorer 4 international tries. He is a low-handicap golfer.

DEEGAN, CONOR.

G.A.A. football full-back, Down. Born in 1969. Club: Downpatrick (winning a county championship medal in 1991). He was a pillar in the defence of the Down side which captured the All-Ireland Senior Football Championship for the first time in 23 years in 1991. He won an All-Star award as full-back in 1991, having been nominated the previous year.

DEEGAN, MICK.

G.A.A. right full-back, Dublin. Club: Erin's Isle. Born in 1966. A product of St Kevin's CBS, he won an All-Ireland M.F.C. medal in 1982, and 2 Leinster S.F.C. medals with the Dubs, in 1989 and in 1992 when the Dubs were beaten in the All-Ireland Senior Football Championship final. He has also won 2 National Football League medals with Dublin (in 1991 and 1993), and played a fine role in their dour 4-match struggle with Meath in the 1991 1st round of the Leinster S.F.C. Missing the Dubs Leinster S.F.C. win in 1993 through injury, he won his first All-Star in 1991 at right corner-back.

DEENIHAN, JIMMY.

G.A.A. football right full-back, Kerry. Born in Listowel, Co Kerry, 11th September 1953. Club: Finuge. Having played in an All-Ireland M.F.C. final with Kerry in 1970, and later winning an All-Ireland Under-21 medal in 1973, he went on to win 5 All-Ireland Senior Football Championship winner's medals with the Kingdom, in 1975, and then being ever-present in the 4-in-a-row of 1978, 1979, 1980, and in 1981 when he captained the side which defeated Offaly 1-15 to 0-17. He played in one losing All-Ireland S.F.C. final, against Dublin in 1976. He was made an All-Star in 1981 at right corner back. He won 3 Railway Cup winning medals with Munster, in 1975, 1976, and 1981. Retiring through injury in 1982, he was a Senator 1982-1987, and became a F.G. T.D. for Kerry North in 1987.

DEERING, SEAMUS J.

Rugby international prop and 2nd Row forward. Born in Dunlavin, Co Wicklow, 1906. Club: Bective Rangers (with whom he won 2 Leinster Senior Cup medals, in 1934 and 1935). Seven times a Leinster interprovincial, he was capped 9 times for Ireland between 1935 and 1939, being on the Irish side which won the International Championship title in 1935. His older brother Mark, also a Bective Rangers forward and twice a Leinster player, was capped once for Ireland in rugby in 1929, in a drawn match agaist Wales. Seamus is the father of Shay Deering (c.v.)

DEERING, SEAMUS Mary ('SHAY').

Rugby international wing-forward. Born in Dublin, 5th August 1948, he died aged only 40, in 1988. Clubs: U.C.D. (winning a Leinster Senior Cup medal in 1970), Garryowen (winning Munster Senior Cup medals with them in 1974 and 1975) and St Mary's College. He was capped 8 times for Ireland between 1974 and 1978, captaining Ireland for his last cap (against New Zealand), and would have gained more if not for injury and selectorial indifference. He played for Leinster over 10 times. He is the son of Seamus Deering (cv).

DEIGNAN, SIMON.

G.A.A. football half-back, Cavan. He was a member of 2 Cavan sides beaten in All-Ireland S.F.C. finals in the forties, in the replayed final of 1943 and again in 1946. He was then, in 1947, a member of the famous Cavan side which won the 'Polo Ground Final' in 1947, when Kerry were beaten, and again won an All-Ireland Senior Football Championship medal in the following year of 1948, in the defeat of Mayo. He was on his 3rd losing All-Ireland S.F.C. final in 1949. He won 3 Railway Cup medals with Ulster, in 1942, 1943 and 1947. He was later to referee 3 All-Ireland S.F.C. finals in the space of 11 years.

De LACY, HUGH.

Rugby international scrum-half. Clubs: Trinity College Dublin, Harlequins, and Barbarians. Although he won only 2 international rugby caps for Ireland, both of these came during the Grand Slam season of 1948 (picked in place of Ernie Strathdee cv), when he was on the sides that beat both England and Scotland. He died in 1979. He is a brother of Stan de Lacy (cv).

De LACY, STAN.

Hockey international right winger. Born in 1915. Club: Limerick P.Y.M.A. (sharing the Irish Senior Cup win in 1941). He was capped for Ireland 37 times between 1937 and 1954 (then a record tally for an Irish hockey player) during it's golden era, and went through his first 20 international caps without being on a losing side. In that time he was part of 5 Irish Triple Crown-winning sides, in 1937, 1938, 1939, and after a break for the war, again in 1947 (when he captained the side) and 1949 (also playing in the only drawn game of that period, in the 1948 game against England), making him the only player to perform in each of these historic 18 games. Scoring a goal in the 3-2 win against England in 1949 (the last time Ireland has beaten that opposition in men's hockey), he retired in 1954 aged 39. Probably Ireland's fastest ever hockey winger, he gained his speed from his athletic prowess, as he was Irish 100 yards champion in 1937 under N.A.C.A. jurisdiction, and won the A.A.U. version in 1938. He is a brother of Hugh de Lacy.

DELANEY, BILL.

G.A.A. football midfielder and forward, Laois. Club: Stradbally (with whom he won 7 Laois County Championship medals). He was a member of the Laois minors which lost the All-Ireland M.F.C. final in 1932. He won 4 Leinster Senior Football Championship medals with Laois, in 1936 (when he and his 3 brothers, Jack, Tom and Matt all played on the side beaten by Mayo in the All-Ireland S.F.C. final), 1937, 1938, and the county's most recent success, 1946. He is the only Laoisman to captain a winning Leinster Railway Cup football side (in 1939), also winning medals in 1935, 1940, 1944, and 1945. A brother of Jack Delaney (cv), he later refereed some All-Ireland S.F.C finals.

DELANEY, JOHN (JACK Jnr).

G.A.A. footballer, Laois. Club: Stradbally (with whom he won 8 Laois County Championship medals). A member of the Laois side which won the inaugural National Football League competition in 1926, he was selected for Ireland in the 1932 Tailteann Games. He won 3 Leinster Senior Football Championship medals, in successive years of 1936, 1937, and 1938. He was the first footballer ever to win 7 Railway Cup medals, winning in 1928 (as a sub), 1929, 1930, 1932, 1933, 1935, and 1939 (again as a sub). One of 17 children, his brother Matt also was on the Laois side which was victorious in the National Football League win, and won 2 Railway Cup medals, bringing the family tally to a record 19 winner's medals. His sons Noel, Paschal and Brian all played for Laois, and his daughter Mary married the Dublin footballer John Timmons.

DELANEY, PAT.

G.A.A. hurling centre and right half-back, Offaly. Club: Kinnity (with whom he has won 2 Offaly S.H.C. medals in 1978 and 1979). Having helped Offaly to win their first Leinster S.H.C. title in 1980, he was a constant member of the side which went on to play in 10 succesive Leinster S.H.C. finals up to 1989, winning in 1980, 1981, 1984, 1985, 1988 and 1989. The Gracefield-man has won 2 All-Ireland Senior Hurling Championship medals with Offaly on the only 2 occasions the county has captured that title, in 1981 and 1985, both at centre half-back, also playing on the losing All-Ireland side of 1984. He was made an All-Star in 1985 at centre-half back. In 1981 he became the first of only 2 Offalymen to be honoured as Texaco Hurler of the Year.

DELANEY, PAT.

G.A.A. hurling half-forward, Kilkenny. He has won 4 All-Ireland Senior Hurling Championship medals with Kilkenny, in 1969, 1972, 1974, and 1975, all at centre-half forward, and played on losing sides in Liam McCarthy Cup finals in 1971 and 1973 (when he captained the side beaten by Limerick), making it 6 appearences in All-Ireland finals from 1969 to 1975, the last 5 being successive. He won 5 successive Railway Cup medals with Leinster, in 1971, 1972, 1973 (when he became the 11th Kilkenny player to captain a winning side), 1974, and 1975. He was made an All-Star in 1973 at centre-half forward. His son P J Delaney (born in July 1973), who has won national medals with St Kieran's College, and won 2 All-Ireland M.H.C. medals with the county minors in 1990 and 1991, scored the crucial late goal in the All-Ireland S.H.C. final win for the county in 1993 (when he was the youngest player on the pitch).

DELANEY, PAUL.

G.A.A. hurling right full-back, Tipperary. A member of the Tipperary side which won the 1991 All-Irleand Senior Hurling Championship, he was denied a medal in 1989 due to suspension. He also played on the Tipp side which won the Munster S.H.C. in 1987, 1988 (losing the All-Ireland final that year), and again in 1993. He won an All-Star award in 1991 at right-corner back.

DELANY, RONNIE.

Middle-distance runner. Born in Arklow Co Wicklow, 6th March 1935. A BSc graduate from Villanova University, where he was coached by the great Jim 'Jumbo' Elliot. Bursting on to the scene in 1952, at the age of 18 in 1954 he reached the final of the European Championship 1,500 metres. In early 1956 at Campton, California he became the 7th man in history to beat the 4 minute mile barrier. However after a disappointing mid-season when he ran only 4:20 in a mile race at home, and was beaten comprehensively twice by Brian Hewson, he only just got into Ireland's Olympic team for the Melbourne Olympics. He qualified for the 1,500 metres final in third place, and was unfancied and placed tenth at the bell, but in a last lap of 53.8 seconds (and a last 100 metres of 12.9 seconds), he overcame the whole field to beat West Germany's Klaus Richtzenhain by almost 4 metres in the Olympic record time of 3;41.2 (only 0.6 seconds outside the world record), making him, at 21 years and 171 days old, the Republic of Ireland's youngest gold medal winner. In 1957 he ran 3:58.8 for the mile to finish 2nd behind the 3:57.2 world record set by Derek Ibbotson at White City, and then in the greatest mile race ever seen in Ireland, he reduced his best to 3:57.2 when finishing third behind his great rival John Landy, who shattered the world record at 3:54.5. He won (in a championship equalling time of 1:49.6) the British A.A.A. 880 yards title in 1957. In 1958 he finished 3rd in the European 1,500 metres Championship. In the 5 years from 1955 to 1959, he won 40 consecutive indoor races in the U.S.A., and broke the world indoor mile record on 3 occasions, finally at 4:01.4, before an Achilles tendon finished his career at the age of 27 in 1962. But it is for his great Olympic gold, one of only five won by the Republic of Ireland, that has made him a legend of Irish sport. Having won a Texaco Sportstar of the Year award in 1959, in 1982 he became the 3rd athlete to be elevated to the Texaco Hall of Fame, and is also a member of the Helms Hall of Fame and the Madison Square Garden Hall of Fame. His older brother Joe was a fine Irish high jumper.

DELEA, PADDY.

G.A.A. hurling forward, Cork. Club: Blackrock. He won 4 All-Ireland Senior Hurling Championship winner's medals, in 1926, 1928, 1929 (scoring 2 goals in the final), and 1931, while he also played in the Leesiders losing effort in the 1927 All-Ireland S.H.C. final. He was a member of the Cork side which won the National Hurling League in 1930.

DEMPSEY, JACK ('NONPAREIL').

Middleweight professional boxer. Born as John Kelly in Clane, Co Kildare, on 15th December 1862, he changed his name to hide his boxing career from his family. He became World Middleweight Champion boxer from 1884-1891. In his professional career, he lost only 3 of his 68 bouts, winning 50. After only one years pro boxing (and 14 bouts), he won the world crown at Great Kills, New York, when in the first ever world middleweight title fight, he knocked out George Fulljames of Canada after 22 rounds on 30th July 1884. He had five successful title defences (against Jack Fogarty; George La Blanche; Johnny Reagan; a re-match against Le Blanche, a bout which he actually lost, but was later awarded it because of his opponents use of the illegal backhand 'pivot' blow; and the Australian Bill McCarthy). He was eventually surprisingly knocked out in 15 rounds by Bob Fitsimmons in New Orleans on January 14th 1891, after a reign of 5 years. Called 'Nonpareil' because nobody could be found to beat him, he gave his Christian name to William Harrison Dempsey, who took it in respect of Nonpareil's genius, and went on to become world heavyweight champion 1919-1926 as the great Jack Dempsey. Died in Portland, Oregon, 1895, at the age of 32.

DEMPSEY, JOHN Thomas.

Soccer international centre-half. Born in Hampstead, 15th March 1946. Apprenticed to Fulham at 18, he left in 1968, after playing over 150 games, to join Chelsea, with whom he played over 170 games over 7 of the Stamford Bridge club's most successful seasons (winning an F.A. Cup medal in 1970, and a European Cup Winner's Cup medal in 1971). Later playing with the Philadelphia Furies, he was capped 19 times at senior international level for the Republic of Ireland between 1967 and 1972.

DEMPSEY, J .

G.A.A. footballer, Dublin. He captained the Dublin (Bray Emmetts) side which won the 1902 All-Ireland Senior Football Championship, when they beat London (Hibernians) by 2-8 to 0-4. He went on to win 2 more All-Ireland S.F.C. medals with Dublin, in 1906 and 1907, and played in the losing All-Ireland final of 1904.

DENNEHY, (nee MAGUIRE) ITA.

International basketball player. Born in Dublin. Going unbeaten in schools competition with St Louis High School Rathmines, she captained the side which won the F.I.S.E.C. games in Avignon in 1971. Then joining the Meteor club, she helped them to win 9 National League titles (including the famous 4-in-a-row in the mid-1980's); also to win the inaugural National Cup in 1984-85, and also to win the 1989 Top Four Championship (scoring the winning 3-pointer). Selected to play for the 1st Irish Ladies Senior basketball side in 1973, she captained the Irish side in the Olympic qualifying tournament in Poland in 1974, and played in all internationals up to 1980, and for a few more in 1984. Later she got involved in basketball coaching.

DENNEHY, MIAH.

Soccer international forward. Born in Cork, 29th March, 1950. Clubs: Cork Hibernians (winning a League of Ireland winner's medal in 1970-71, and F.A.I. Cup medals in both 1972 and 1973, being the first person to score a hat-trick in a F.A.I. Cup final), Nottingham Forest, Walsall (scoring 22 goals in 123 league matches 1975-77), Bristol Rovers, Cardiff City. Between 1972 and 1977 he was capped 11 times for the Republic of Ireland, seven of these as a substitute.

DENNISON, ROBERT (ROBBIE).

Soccer international midfielder. Born in Banbridge, 30th April 1963. Clubs: Glenavon, West Bromwich Albion, Wolverhampton Wanderers (with whom he has played over 250 league matches, scoring over 30 goals). First capped in the midfield for Northern Ireland in 1988, his cap tally up to June 1993 has come to fifteen.

DENNISON, SEAMUS Patrick.

Rugby international wing three-quarter. Born in Abbeyfeale, Co Limerick, 26th January 1950. Clubs: U.C.G., U.C.C., and Garryowen. He was capped 4 times for Ireland between 1973 and 1975, being dropped after scoring a try in his last international. He was a member of the famous Munster team that beat the All-Blacks by 12-0 in 1978, and won 3 Munster Senior Cup medals with Garryowen, in 1971, 1974 and 1975.

DERMODY, DOROTHY ('TOMMY').

All-round sportswoman. A candidate for Ireland's best ever all-round sportswoman, she represented Ireland at international level at 4 different sports. Her forte was fencing, becoming Irish Ladies Fencing Champion 7 times, in 1940, 1942, 1944, 1946, 1947, 1949 and 1950. Also winning the Scottish Open title in 1950, she was a member of numerous Irish fencing teams, and represented Ireland at the 1948 Olympic Games in London in the foil event. She was also Irish Ladies Diving Champion, taking the title 6 times, in 1936, 1938, 1940, 1941, 1942 and in 1944. A physical education teacher, she also played both squash and lacrosse for Ireland.

DERMODY, JIM.

G.A.A. hurling goalkeeper, Kilkenny. He won 2 All-Ireland Senior Hurling Championship medals with Kilkenny, in 1932 and 1933, having previously played on the side beaten in the decider of 1931. In 1932 he became the 2nd Kilkennyman to captain Leinster in their 2nd Railway Cup win, winning another provincial medal in 1933.

DESMOND, PETER.

Soccer international inside-forward. Born in Cork, 23rd November 1926. Clubs: Waterford, Shelbourne (being on the side beaten in the 1948-49 F.A.I. Cup final), Middlesborough, Southport, York City and Hartlepool. He was capped 4 times for the Republic of Ireland in the 1949-1950 season, including being on the side which beat England at Goodison Park (by him being brought down in the penalty area resulting in a penalty goal, in what was to be England's first defeat by a 'foreign' side at home). He died in 1990.

DEVANEY, LIAM.

G.A.A. hurling forward and versatility player, Tipperary. Born in 1935. Club: Borrisoleigh (winning one county championship medal, at age 19, in 1953). He won 2 All-Ireland M.H.C. medals with Tipperary minors in 1952 and 1953, both at right half-forward. With his county senior hurling side from 1955 to 1968, he has won 5 All-Ireland Senior Hurling Championship winners medals with Tipp, in 1958 at full-forward, 1961 at left half-forward, 1962 as centre-field, 1964 (coming on as a sub in the final), and 1965 at left half-forward. He was on losing All-Ireland S.H.C. Tipperary sides in the finals of 1960 as centre-forward, 1967 as left half-forward, and in 1968 as left-full forward, thereby playing in 8 finals in an eleven year period. In all he played in 14 different positions for Tipp, all except full-back. He won 3 Railway Cup medals with Munster, in 1961, 1963, and 1966. He also won 8 National Hurling League winner's medals with Tipp, 1954-55, 1956-57, 1958-59, 1959-60, 1960-61, 1963-64, 1964-65, and in 1967-68; he also won 6 Oireatchtas medals. In 1961 he became the 2nd Tipperaryman to be awarded the title of Texaco Hurler of the Year.

DEVINE, JOHN ('JOKER').

Soccer international defender. Born in Dublin, 11th November 1958. Clubs: Arsenal (to whom he was apprenticed at 17, playing in 108 first team games, playing in the losing F.A. Cup final of

1980, and in the final of a European Cup Winners Cup), Norwich (winning a League Cup medal in 1985), Stoke City, IKF Start (Norway), India (various clubs), and Shamrock Rovers. In a career which included 3 broken legs and a wrecked knee-cap, he was capped 12 times for the Republic of Ireland between 1980 and 1985.

DEVLIN, J FRANK.

Badminton player. Born in Dublin, 19th January 1900. Although losing half a heal at an early age due to osteomyelitis, he went on to represent Ireland in badminton 14 times between 1919 and 1931. Regarded as the first 'modern' player, between the years of 1922 and 1931 he dominated the badminton world, winning a total of 18 All-England titles, consisting of: 6 singles wins in 1925, 1926, 1927, 1928, 1929 and 1931 (this record tally of single's titles held until 1967); he won 5 mixed doubles wins, in 1924 and 1925 with Kitty McKane, in 1926 and 1927 with E.G. Peterson, and in 1929 with Mrs R J Horsely; and 7 mens doubles titles, the first with G A Sauter in 1922, and the other 6 with 'Curly' Mack (cv), in 1923, 1926, 1927, 1929, 1930, and 1931 (in the 3 years of 1926, 1927 and 1929 he won all 3 titles open to him). Playing most of his badminton in England, he turned professional in 1931, and later coached the Winnipeg Winter club, and eventually settled in Baltimore, becoming an authority and writer on the game. Regarded as one of the sport's all-time greats, he was responsible for much of badminton's developement outside Europe. He died in Ireland in 1988. His daughter Judy Hashman (born in Winnipeg, 22 October 1935), represented both U.S.A. and England in badminton, and won 3 Uber Cup titles in badminton (also winning a record 10 All-England Singles titles from 1954 to 1967, and 7 in Doubles), for the U.S.; she also played for the U.S. Junior Wightman Cup team in tennis, and was an All-American Lacrosse player. Another daughter, Susan, played with her sister Judy in 6 of her All-England Doubles wins, and married the prominent Irish badminton player, Frank Peard (cv) .

DICK, Dr CHARLES JOHN (IAN) and Dr JAMES.

International rugby playing brothers. Both born in Ballymena. Ian, a Ballymena 2nd row and No 8 forward (with whom he won an Ulster Senior Cup medal in 1963), won 8 international caps for Ireland between 1961 and 1963, being on only one winning side (his last cap). His younger brother, Ian, a Queen's hooker, was capped once for Ireland (not with his brother), on a losing Irish side against England in 1962.

DICKSON, DES.

Soccer international forward. Clubs: Coleraine (winning I.F.A. Cup medals in 1972, 1975 and 1977, and was a member of the only Coleraine side to win the Irish League, in 1973-74; he is the club's leading goalscorer in European competitions, with 7 (placing him 3rd in all-time scorers in Europe from Northern Ireland). He was capped 4 times for Northern Ireland between 1970 and 1973, all while at the Showgrounds, making him Coleraine's joint most capped player with Felix Healy. He was N.I.P.F.A. Player of the Year in 1970.

DICKSON, H D L.

Hockey international right back. Club: Cliftonville. He was capped 32 times for Ireland between 1924 and 1939 (a record at the time), and captained the side on 9 occasions. He played in 2 of the nine 3-time Triple Crown wins of the 1937-1939, and scoring the winning goal against England at Warwickshire C.C.G. in the fine win of 1939.

DICKSON, WILLIAM (BILLY).

Soccer international wing-half. Born in Lurgan, 15th April 1923. Clubs: Notts County, Chelsea (playing over 100 league games for them 1947-1952), Arsenal (playing 31 games) and

Mansfield. An attacking half-back, he was capped 12 times for Northern Ireland between 1951 and 1955.

DILLON, BILL.

G.A.A. football left-half back, Kerry. Having won an All-Ireland M.F.C. winner's medal with the Kingdom in 1933, he went on to win 4 All-Ireland Senior Football Championship medals with Kerry, in 1937, 1939, 1940, and in 1941 as captain (when they beat Galway by 1-8 to 0-7). He was also on 2 Kerry sides beaten in All-Ireland S.F.C. finals, in 1938 and 1944.

DINES, JAMES.

Flat jockey. He rode the winning horse in 4 Irish Classic races: the Irish Oaks in 1922 with Miss Hazelwood; the Irish 2,000 Guineas in 25 with St Donagh; and 2 Irish St Leger wins (in 1926 on Sunny View and in 1928 on Law Suit).

DIXON, BILLY.

Soccer wing-half. Born in Dublin, 12th February 1941. He played for Home Farm, Waterford, Drumcondra (winning a League of Ireland medal in 1964-65), Shamrock Rovers (winning an F.A.I. Cup medal in 1967, scoring the winning goal), and Boston (in the N.A.S.L.). He scored 34 League of Ireland goals in total, and played for the League of Ireland. Although never capped for the Republic of Ireland, his 6 goals in European competition (which include 2 against the mighty Bayern Munich) is a record for a home-based League of Ireland player.

DIXON, Thomas ROBIN Valerian.

Bobsled brakesman champion. A son of Lord Glentoran (with a family seat in Dooagh, Co Antrim), he was born on 21st April 1935. An Eton graduate, he and his partner Anthony Nash finished 3rd in the World Championships at Igls, near Innsbruck in 1963. In 1964, while representing Northern Ireland, he (a brakesman in partnership with the driver Anthony Nash), won an Olympic gold medal at Innsbruck in the Winter Olympics, competing in the Two-Man Bobsled. They completed the 4 runs in a combined time of 4'21.90", less than one second ahead of the silver-medal winning pair from Italy. This also gave them the World Championship for that year, and they retained their World Championship in 1965. In the 1968 Winter games the same pair finished 5th in the bobsled event at Grenoble-Aple d'Huez. A heir of Lord Glentoran, he was awarded an M.B.E. for his Olympic deeds.

DIXON, T H.

Cricket international bowler. Although he only played 17 international cricket matches for Ireland (between 1927 and 1932), his bowling average of 16.92 runs per wicket (79 wickets from 1339 runs) places him high up on such averages for his country. He also scored 372 runs for Ireland in 28 innings, for a fairly modest average of 15.50 runs per innings.

DOCKEREL, GEORGE Shannon.

Swimmer and water-polo player. Born in Dublin. Club: Trinity College. He became prominent in Irish swimming circles in the early years of the 20th century, and eventually dominated the sport in Ireland for many years from 1904, when he won the Irish 100 and 440 yards championships. A member of the Dublin Swimming Club, he tried his luck in the U.S.A., and came 3rd in the 1905 American Championships at both 440 and 880 yards. Introducing the 'American Crawl' to Ireland on his return in 1906, he went on to dominate Irish swimming for 6 years, winning 20 of the 27 championships he entered for, and holding Irish records at 3 of the 4 record events. He competed at 100 yards in the Olympic Games for Great Britain in London in 1908, reaching the semi-final, and the following year reached his peak, when capturing the world championship title at 100 metres in Paris. He also won 7 international caps at water-polo. His brother H.M. Dockrell was also a swimming champion, and H.M.'s daughter, Marguerite Dockrell won 9 Irish championship swimming titles from 1926 to 1933, swimming in the Olympics 100m for Ireland in 1928.

DOHENY, CIARA.

International badminton player. From Killiney, Co Dublin, she was born in 1965. At 17 she won the Leinster Open and beat the prominent English international Barbara Sutton. After a U.C.D. scholarship and training in Kuala Lumpar (where she guested for the Malaysian international squad), she went to England to train under Barbara Beckett (cv), and in 1990 played on the Hertfordshire team which won the English Inter County League. She won the Irish Ladies Singles Championship 6 times in succession, in 1986, 1987, 1988, 1989, 1990, and 1991. In 1990, despite injury, she finished 9th in the European Championships.

DOHERTY, ALAN E.

Rugby international centre-threequarter. Club: Old Wesley. He played interprovincial rugby for Leinster 4 times between 1973 and 1975. In 1974, by coming on as a substitute in the centenary match Ireland were playing against the President's XV, he became the only Irish player to win his only full international cap while not playing against one of the major rugby countries. His brother Dave, an Old Wesley flanker, played for Leinster against Fiji in 1973, alongside Alan.

DOHERTY, DAVE.

Squash and badminton international. He was capped 9 times for Ireland in squash in 1978 and the following year. He also represented Ireland in badminton (making him the only Irishman to be capped in both these sports), and won the Irish Men's Doubles badminton titles 3 year-in-a-row, in 1972, 1973 and 1974.

DOHERTY, KENNETH Joseph (KEN).

Snooker amateur and professional. Born in Dublin in 1969. Club: Jason's, Ranelagh. A product of Westland Row C.B.S., he was runner-up in the the Irish Amateur Championship in 1985; then he won it twice, in 1987 (to become Ireland's youngest ever champion), and again in 1989. In 1988 he won the prestigious Pro-Am at Pontins in Prestatyn, beating world ranking professionals in the process. In 1989, having early in the year become World Junior Champion in Iceland, he became the first Irishman to become World Amateur Snooker Champion, when he beat the No 1 seed, Britain's John Birch, by the fine score of 11-2 in the final in Singapore (he lost only 13 frames in the entire tournament). Based at Ilford, he turned professional, making steady initial progress (reaching a world ranking of 51 in his first year), and won his first tournament in 1991, the Benson and Hedges championship in Glasgow, when beating Darren Morgan in the final by 9-3. In 1992 he was runner-up in the Benson and Hedges Irish Masters, beaten 9-6 in the final by Stephen Hendry, and was runner-up also in the highly prestigious Rothman's Grand Prix, losing the final to Jimmy White by 10-9. In 1993 he won his first ranking tournament, the Welsh Open, beating Alan McManus in the final in Newport by 9-7 (and the following week was beaten finalist in the Strachan Challenge), reaching No 11 rank in the world, and captured the Irish Professional title, becoming the first Southerner to do so. In September 1993, he won the £45,000 first prize in the Scottish Masters at Motherwell. He has twice been voted as snooker's Texaco Sportstar of the Year, in 1989 and in 1992.

DOHERTY, JOHN.

Middle distance athlete. Born in Leeds of Irish parents, 22nd July 1961, he represented England at youth levels athletics, but switched to Irish colours in 1986. He qualified for the final of the

1988 Olympic 5,000 metres, finishing 9th, and also ran in the Olympic Games of 1992 in Barcelona. He finished a highly creditable 2nd (behind Said Aouita) in the final of the prestigious 1989 World Cup 5,000 metres Championship, in which year he was ranked as World No 1 in this event. Ranked as Irish all-time No 2 at both 5K and 10K, he is based in Providence, Rhode Island, and is a member of Leeds AC.

DOHERTY, PADDY.

G.A.A. football left-half forward. Down. Having won 2 All-Ireland M.F.C. medals with Down's minors in 1961 and 1962 (as captain), he later went on to win 3 All-Ireland Senior Football Championship winner's medals with the county: in 1960 (when scoring a vital penalty) and in 1961 (when he was captain in the victory over Offaly by 3-6 to 2-8), both years in a formidable half-forward line (regarded as one of the best in the game's history) with Jim McCartan (cv) and Sean O'Neill (cv); and winning his 3rd Sam Maguire medal in 1968. Also winning Ulster S.F.C. medal in 1963 and 1965, he won 5 Railway Cup medals with Ulster, in 1960, and then in the famous 4-in-a-row wins of 1963, 1964 (as captain), 1965 and 1966, when he was the only Ulster player to play in all 8 games of this run, a record he shares with Ollie Freaney and Stephen White from the Leinster 4-in-a-row of 1952 to 1955.

DOHERTY, PETER Dermont ('PETER THE GREAT').

Soccer international inside-forward. Born in Magherafelt, Co Derry,5th June 1913. He joined Blackpool from Glentoran (winning an Irish Senior Cup medal in 1933), and scored 18 goals in 83 appearances 1933-36, before going on to win a League Championship medal with Manchester City in 1936-1937 when his 30 goals contributed greatly to the success (he scored 76 goals in all for them 1936-45). He later won an F.A. Cup medal with Derby County (playing in harmony with the great Raich Carter) in 1946. He became a player manager at Huddesfield Town (scoring 33 goals in 83 league games 1946-49) and Doncaster Rovers (scoring 55 goals in 106 league games 1949-53), and helped both of them in relegation/promotion battles; and later of Bristol City (he was also Alan Ball's assistant manager at Preston North End for a time). Arguably Northern Ireland's finest ever inside forward, he played 16 matches for them between 1936 and 1951, with a gap for World War II, and scored 3 international goals, including a brilliant equaliser against England in 1947. After a playing career from 1933 to 1953, he became (in 1971) the 2nd soccer player to be elevated in to the Texaco Hall of Fame. He was Northern Ireland's first international team manager, holding the post form 1951 to 1962, and led the country to it's finest hour in international football, when they qualified for the World Cup finals in 1958 in Sweden, and won through, against all the odds, to the quarter finals.

DOHERTY, R .

G.A.A. hurler, Kilkenny. He won 5 All-Ireland Senior Hurling Championship winner's medals with Kilkenny sides, in 1907 and 1909 with the Mooncoin Selection, in the awarded final of 1911, with Tullaroan in 1912, and again with Mooncoin in 1913.

DOHERTY, SEAN ('THE DOC').

G.A.A. football full-back, Dublin. Clubs: Ballyboden St Edna's, St Annes and Ballyboden Wanderers. Winning Dublin JFC, JHC, IFC and IHC medals, he played junior football for the county in 1966-67. A product of Wicklow Town CBS, he played senior inter-county football from 1968 to 1980. He won 3 All-Ireland Senior Football Championship winner's medals with Dublin, being captain of the great 'Heffo's Army' side which beat Galway by 0-14 to 1-6 to win the 1974 final, also winning S.F.C. medals in 1976 and 1977. He was on the

Dublin sides beaten by Kerry in the 1975 and 1978 All-Ireland S.F.C. finals, and won a 6th Leinster S.F.C. medal in 1979. He won 2 National Football League medals with the 'Dubs' in 1976 and in 1978. A tough, resilient full-back, he won his only All-Star award in 1974 at full-back.

DOLAN, BRENDAN.

International oarsman. Born in 1967. Club: Neptune Rowing Club. A lightweight sculler, in 1991 he won both the Irish National Championship at both elite sculls and lightweight sculls. In 1992 he won the Heads at Limerick, Newry, New Ross (beating Niall O'Toole cv), Galway and the Neptune regatta, while winning at Ghent and Ratxeburg on the continent. Also in 1992 he won a bronze medal in Mexico, reached the final of the Lucerne International, and won the Irish National Championship at lightweight sculls.

DOLAN, EUNAN.

International oarsman. Club: Neptune Rowing Club (helping them through their most successful period in their history, when he won 7 Irish Senior Eights Championships, 1980, 1984, 1985, 1986, 1987, 1989 and 1990). He also won 6 Irish Senior Fours Championships, in 1981, 1985, 1986, 1987, 1988 and 1991, his tally of 13 placing him 2nd only to Frank Moore's record total of 14 Irish Championships won. He was twice a member of winning crews at Henley, the Britannia Cup for coxed fours in 1982 and the Ladies Plate for eights in 1986. He represented Ireland at the World Championships in 1987 in coxed fours.

DONAGHY, MAL.

Soccer international full-back or central defender. Born in Belfast, 13th Septeber 1957. He moved from Larne to Luton Town in 1978 and played 410 league matches for them as a local hero up to 1989, winning a Littlewoods Cup medal in 1987-88, and helping the club to win the Division 2 crown in 1981-82 (and to their highest ever placing in Division One, 7th in 1986-87). Later with Manchester United he played 89 league matches, and won a Rumbelows Cup medal in 1992, and a European Cup-Winners Cup medal in 1991. He has latterly played with Chelsea. First capped in 1980, in April 1992 he became Northern Ireland's 3rd most capped player of all-time, winning his 75th cap against Lithuania in a World Cup match, while his tally up to mid 1993 reached 84 caps. He played an important role (4 of the five matches) in Northern Ireland's successful run in the 1982 World Cup in Spain, and also played in the No 3 jersey for all three matches in which his country were involved in the the World Cup of 1986 in Mexico. He is Luton Town's most capped player, gaining 58 caps while at Kennilworth Road.

DONAGHY, PLUNKETT.

G.A.A. football midfielder, Tyrone. Club: Moy. Born in 1962. Playing his first senior championship game in 1984, he won an Ulster S.F.C. title with Tyrone that year. He was selected at midfield for the 1986 All-Stars, being a key player in the Tyrone side which won the Ulster title that year, and went on to be defeated by Kerry in the All-Ireland final. He later captained the winning Tyrone side in the their 1989 Ulster S.F.C. win. His older brother Colm played alongside him many times for Tyrone, and his father Pat was a member of the Tyrone senior team in the late 1950's.

DONALDSON, DOROTHY (DORRIE).

Badminton and hockey international player. In badminton, she was capped 9 times for Ireland between 1950 and 1957, and won 3 National doubles titles with Jean Lawless (Sharkey), and also won 5 National Mixed Doubles titles with Frank Peard (cv). She also won a National Singles title. A dual international, she was also capped for Ireland at hockey.

DONLEAVY, KATHLEEN.

Netball international player. Born c 1961. Club: St Anne's (Dublin). Ireland's most illustrious and capped netball player, she captained her country at Under 18, Under 21 and at senior level, gaining over 60 senior international caps up to 1992. While still a junior player, she was a member of the Ireland team which competed in the 5th World Championships in Trinidad in 1979. She captained the Irish senior squad to both the 7th and 8th World Championships in Scotland and Australia respetively in 1987 and 1991. In 1992 she became player/coach to the Irish senior squad, helping them to record the country's first ever international defeat of Scotland. Her sister Mary played netball at Under 21 level for Ireland.

DONLON, SEAN.

G.A.A. football, Longford. He was a member of the Longford side which captured the 1966 National Football League (beating Galway by 9-8 in the final), the county's only national honour at senior level. He was also on the Longford S.F.C. side which reached 4 Leinster S.F.C. semi-finals in the mid and late 1960's, and which captured the county's only Leinster Senior Football Championship title, in 1968, when they beat Laois by 3-9 to 1-4.

DONNELLAN, JOHN.

G.A.A. football right-half back, Galway. Born at Cloonmorre, Dunmore, Tuam, Co Galway in March 1937. He won 3 All-Ireland Senior Football Championship winner's medals for Galway in their 3-in-a-row of 1964, 1965 (being sent off in this game, making him the only T.D. ever to be sent off in an All-Ireland final), and 1966 (coming on as a sub). He captained the side in the 1964 final win over Kerry by 0-15 to 0-10. A charismatic player, he also won a National Football League with Galway in 1965 and a Railway Cup medal with Connacht in 1967. He was a Fine Gael T.D. in Galway West from 1964 to 1989, and is a former Minister of State. His brother Pat was on the winning All-Ireland S.F.C. final sides alongside John in both 1965 and 1966, playing both games at centre-field (both brothers also played in the losing Galway team in their All-Ireland S.F.C. final in 1963). Their father, Mick Donnellan, a fine player, was captain of the Galway side beaten in the All-Ireland S.F.C. final in 1933, winning a Railway Cup medal in 1934 with Connacht (and was a Clann na Talmhan T.D. for Galway East 1943-64, later dying on the day his son captained the winning All-Ireland side in 1964).

DONNELLY, BERTIE.

Cyclist. Born in Arran Quay, Dublin. Club: Harp Cycling Club. Between 1915 and 1941 he won an astonishing 61 Irish Senior Championship titles, including G.A.A., N.C.A., and N.A.C.A., and in 1931 and 1932 he won all 5 Irish National Championships. He also won 3 Tailteann Games titles, in 1924, 1928 and 1932, as well as 4 Irish Army championships. His other big wins include the 1935 British 5 Mile Open title at Bristol, and 3 successive prestigious Hospital Cup wins (over 5 miles), in 1932, 1933 and 1934. He represented Ireland in the 1,000 sprint at the 1928 Olympics. Later as an administrator with the National Cycling Association, of which he was a founder member, he was also an Hon Secretary and Hon Treasurer, as well as a track cycle secretary. Ireland's finest cyclist in his time, he was elevated into Texaco's Hall of Fame in 1968, the only cyclist to be thus far nominated.

DONNELLY, BRAIN, DESSIE, EDDIE and KEVIN.

G.A.A. hurling brothers, Antrim. Club: Ballycastle McQuillans (whom they assisted to win 4 Antrim county championships in the 1980s). Brian, a right half-forward (born in 1962), and Dessie (who made his inter-county debut in 1977), a left full-back born in 1960, both played in the Antrim side which reached the All-Ireland Senior Hurlong Champinship final in 1989 for the first time in 46 years for the county. Dessie won an All-Star award in 1989 as a left corner back, one of only 2 Antrim to be honoured that year. Their older brother Eddie won a record 8 Antrim SHC medals with Ballycastle, and in 1970 won both a National League (Division 2) medal and an All-Ireland I.H.C. He also played in 2 shinty internationals and went to the U.S.A. as a replacement All-Star in both 1975 and 1977. Another brother Kevin also played for Antrim hurlers.

DONNELLY, DAN.

Prize ring fighter. Born in Dublin in 1788. He was the first Irish champion bare-knuckle fighter, and is the only bareknuckle boxer to be knighted. In a famous fight attended by 40,000 in 1814 he beat an English pugilist named Hall, and a year later in a natural amphitheatre at the Curragh (later to be known as 'Donnelly's Hollow'), he beat the English Champion George Cooper in 11 rounds. He later gave sparring exhibitions in England, became a publican, and died aged 32 in 1820. One of his huge arms is preserved in a pub in Kilcullen.

DONNELLY, DONAL.

G.A.A. football forward, Tyrone. He won an All-Ireland Minor Football Championship medal with Tyrone in 1948 at right corner-back, having been a sub in the victory of the previous year. He won 2 Ulster Senior Football Championship medals with Tyrone, in 1956 at right half-forward, and in 1957 at right corner-forward. In 1972 and 1973 he was coach to Tyrone minors in All-Ireland M.F.C. finals, losing to Cork, and beating Kildare respectively. He coached the Tyrone S.F.C. side which won the Ulster title in 1989.

DONNELLY, FRANKIE.

G.A.A. football left full-forward, Tyrone. Club: Carrickmore (with whom he won 4 county championship medals betwen 1949 and 1969). In 1950 he played minor, junior, and first played Senior football for Tyrone. A member of the first Tyrone side to win an Ulster S.F.C title in 1956, winning again in 1957 (during which season he was a member of the first Tyrone side to win a Dr McKenna Cup). He was the country's leading scorer 2 years in succession, in 1956 (scoring 106 points), and in 1957 (scoring 117 points from 5 goals and 102 points in 22 games, a Tyrone record). He won a Railway Cup medal with Ulster in 1964, and a 2nd as a substitute. He later won an All-Ireland J.F.C. medal with Tyrone in Tyrone's first win in 1968. He was honoured at left full forward on the Ireland Selection in 1957.

DONNELLY, J J (JIMMY).

Bowls player. Club: Falls, Belfast. Born in Belfast, 11 April 1928. He won the British Isles and I.B.A. fours title in 1968, and became a bronze medallist in the 1970 pairs event at the Commonwealth Games at Edinburgh. An Irish international bowls player.

DONNELLY, JOEY.

Soccer international inside-forward. Born in Dundalk, 1st October 1910. Clubs: Dundalk (debuting with them in 1929 and winning an F.A.I. Cup medal in 1942), and Belfast Celtic (winning an Irish League medal with them in 1932-33). He is Dundalk's leading goalscorer in the League of Ireland, with 69 goals scored 1929-32 and 1934-43. He was capped 10 times for Ireland between 1934 and 1938, scoring 4 international goals (one against Hungary on his debut in 1934, and 2 more in the 5-2 win over Germany in 1935). In 1963 he was manager of Dundalk when they became the first League of Ireland club to win an away fixture in European competition, beating Zurich 2-1. In 1991 he was one of 3 inaugural entrants into the League of Ireland Hall of Fame.

DONNELLY, MARTIN.

Motor Racing driver. From West Belfast, he was born in 1964. He won the Irish Formula Ford 2000 Championship in 1982, and in 1985 finished 2nd in the British and 3rd in the European Formula Ford 2000 Championships. In 1987 he won the 'Most Promising Driver' in Formula 3 racing. His Formula Ford 3000 Championship record in 1989 included 2 wins (and a retiring while leading a race), and 2 second places, this success earning him his first Formula One race in late 1989, finishing 12th place in an Arrows at the French event at Paul Ricard. In 1990 he became No 2 driver for the Camel Team Lotus to Britain's Derek Warwick, but a horrific injury curtailed his career.

DONNELLY, TONY.

G.A.A. fooballer, Meath. A member of the Meath Senior Football Championship side which won the 1939 provincial title for the first time since 1895, and which was beaten by Kerry in the All-Ireland final, he won a 2nd Leinster S.F.C. medal the following year. Regarded by his Meath peers as among the best to play for the county, he won 3 Railway Cup medals with Leinster (the first Meathman to do so), in 1935, 1939 and 1940.

DONOVAN, DONAL.

Soccer international full-back. Born in Cork, 23rd December 1929. He joined Everton from Dalymount Rovers in 1949, and played 178 league matches for Everton up to 1957, when he joined Grimsby, playing 236 league matches for them in a 5 year period. He was capped 5 times for the Republic of Ireland between 1955 and 1957. His son Terry (born in Liverpool 27th February 1958), a forward whose clubs included Louth United, Grimsby (scoring 23 goals for them in 52 league games in 1976-78) and Aston Villa, was capped for Ireland at Under 23 level, and won a solitary senior international against Czechoslovakia in 1980. They are one of only 6 sets of fathers and sons to play soccer for the Republic of Irleand.

DONOVAN, PAUL.

Middle-distance athlete. Born 11th July 1963. He has represented Ireland in 2 Olympic Games, both at 1,500m, in 1984 in Los Angeles, and in 1992 in Barcelona. He won a silver medal in the inaugural World Indoor Track and Field Championships 3,000 metres event, in Indianapolis in 1987, finishing 2nd behind fellow-Irishman Frank O'Meara. His career since has been injury-laden.

DOOLIN, PAUL.

Soccer midfielder. Born in Dublin, 26th March 1963. Clubs: Shamrock Rovers (winning the 'Double' twice i.e. the League of Ireland and F.A.I. Cup in both 1986 and 1987), Derry City (winning the League of Ireland and F.A.I. Cup double again, in 1989), Portadown (helping them to the Irish League and Irish Cup 'Double' in the 1990-1991 season), Shamrock Rovers again, and Shelbourne (winning an F.A.I. Cup medal in 1993, the club's first in 30 years). Thus he has won the 'double' in both the North and South, a rare achievement for a player, and has accumulated 4 'doubles' in Irish soccer. He is also the only player to win the Players' Player of the Year award twice, capturing this honour in both 1986 and 1989.

DORAN, COLM.

G.A.A. hurling half-back, Wexford. Club: Buffers Alley (winning many Wexford county championship winners medals). A younger brother of Tony Doran (cv), he played in the All-Ireland Senior Hurling Championship losing finals of 1976 and 1977 alongside Tony. He won 4 Railway Cup medals, in 1974, 1975 (as a sub), 1977 and 1979. Tony and Colm both won National Hurling League medals with Wexford in 1973. In 1984 Colm was selected in the half-back line on the 'Team of the Century' for those who never won an All-Ireland senior medal.

DORAN, GERALD PERCY ('BLUCHER').

Rugby international wing three-quarter. 1877-1943. Club: Lansdowne (winning 3 Leinster Senior Cup medals, in 1901, 1903 and 1904). While capped only 8 times for Ireland at rugby between 1899 and 1904, it was he who scored the winning try in Ireland's first ever Triple-Crown victory in 1899 against Wales, and he was one of only 3 Irishmen to be selected on the first British and Irish Lion's team, to Australia in the same year. Two of his brothers, both Lansdowne players, also played for Ireland: Bertie (a centre who won 8 international caps 1900-1902, scoring a try in 1901, making the Dorans the only brothers to score international tries in different centuries) and Eddie (2 international caps in 1890). Both Bertie and Eddie also won Leinster Senior Cup medals with their club, Bertie captaining the side in the 1901 win. Between them the 3 brothers played 23 times for Leinster at interprovincial level.

DORAN, JACK F.

Soccer international centre-forward. Clubs: Brighton & Hove Albion. He is the only player in English League history since World War One to twice score more than half of his team's Football League goals in a completed season: doing so for Brighton in 1920-21 in Division 3 South when scoring 22 out of 42, and in the following season, again for Brighton, when scoring 23 out of 45. He won his only 3 caps for Northern Ireland while at Brighton, in 1921 and 1922.

DORAN, TONY.

G.A.A. hurling full-forward, Wexford. Born in 1946. Club: Buffer's Alley (winning 11 Wexford county championship medals, 2 Leinster Club titles, and at the age of 42, helping them to win their first All-Ireland Club Championship title in 1989). A sturdy full forward, he won an All-Ireland M.H.C. medal in 1963, an All-Ireland Under 21 medal in 1965, and completed his collection with a coveted Senior Hurling Championship medal in 1968 (scoring 2-1 in a fine display in the final). In a senior inter-county career that spanned 20 years from 1965 to 1984, he was also on 3 All-Ireland losing S.H.C. final teams, in 1970, 1976, and 1977 (the last 2 as captain, thus being one of only 3 captains to lose 2 McCarthy Cup finals), gaining in all 4 Leinster S.H.C. winners medals. Winning National Hurling League medals with Wexford in 1967 and 1973, he won 7 Railway Cup medals with Leinster, in 1971, 1972, 1973, 1974, 1975, 1977, and 1979 (captaining the winning side in 1971 and 1977, the most recent Wexfordman to do so). He won an All-Star award in 1976 at full-forward, and in the same year he became the 3rd (and most recent) Wexfordman to win nomination as Texaco Hurler of the Year.

DOUGAN, DEREK ('DOUGIE' or 'THE DOOG').

Soccer international centre-forward. Born in Belfast, 20th January 1938. His clubs have included Distillery, Portsmouth (moving there at 19, scoring 9 goals in one season), Blackburn Rovers (scoring 25 league goals in 2 seasons 1958-60, and winning an F.A. Cup runners-up medal in 1960), Aston Villa (scoring 19 goals in 1960-62), Peterborough (38 goals in 77 games), Leicester City (35 goals in 2 seasons, 1965-66, winning a League Cup medal in 1964), and most prominently Wolverhampton Wanderers (for whom he scored 93 league goals in 244 matches betwee 1967 and 1974, helping them to gain promotion in 1967, while also winning a League Cup medal in 1974 and getting a U.E.F.A. Cup runners-up medal in 1972). A great extrovert and natural goal snatcher, he won 43 caps for Northern Ireland between 1958 and 1973, scoring 8 international goals. His 12 goals in European club competitions is a record for a Northern Ireland player. He was Chairman of the Proffessional Footballers Association (P.F.A.) from 1970-1978.

DOUGLAS, ARTHUR COATES.

Rugby and cricket international. Born on 16th August 1902, he died aged 35 in 1937. He won 5 rugby caps on the wing for Ireland between 1923 and 1928 (all on losing sides), while playing for Instonians (winning 5 Ulster Senior Cup medals, in 1922, 1923, 1927, 1928 and 1929), scoring 2 international tries, one on his debut against France. A sportsmaster, he was also a cricket international, playing 13 internationals for Ireland as a right hand batsman and bowler between 1925 and 1933, taking 17 wickets and scoring 343 international runs in all.

DOUGLAS, DAN.
G.A.A. footballer, Laois. He was a member of the Laois side which reached the All-Ireland Senior Football Chamapionship final in 1936, when beaten by Mayo, and he also won Leinster S.F.C. medals in each of the following years, 1937 and 1938. He won 4 Railway Cup medals with Leinster, in 1930, 1932, 1933 and in 1935.

DOUGLAS, PAUL.
Amateur heavyweight boxer. Club: Holy Family, Belfast. He won the Irish National Senior Championship at super-heavyweight in 1989 and 1990, and the heavyweight in 1992 and 1993. He reached the last eight in the Barcelona Olympics tournament, being beaten for the bronze medal by a Dutchman, Arnold van der Lijde.

DOWD, TOMMY.
G.A.A. footballing left half-forward, Meath. Club: Dunderry. A member of the Meath team which lost the 1991 All-Ireland Senior Championship final to Down, he was a member of the panel for the years proceeding to this appearence. He won his first All-Star in 1991, at left half-forward.

DOWDALL, CHARLIE.
Soccer international player. Clubs: St James Gate (winning an F.A.I. Cup medal and an Irish Free State League winner's medal with them in the inaugural year of the competition, 1922), Forsdon, Barnsely, Cork. He won 3 international caps for the Irish Free State between 1928 and 1931.

DOWDALL, PADDY.
Amateur featherweight boxer. Clubs: Myra B.C., and Army. As a corporal in the army, having won 2 Army featherweight titles in 1938 and 1939, he won a European Championship Featherweight gold medal at Dublin in 1939, beating the Pole Anto Czortek in the final. In the same year he went on to win the Golden Gloves in the U.S.A., becoming the only Army man to gain these 2 prestigious titles. He won 3 Irish National Senior Championship titles at 2 weights, in 1940 at featherweight, and in 1942 and 1943 as a lightweight. He later became Professional Light-Weight Champion of Ireland. He died in the early 1960's.

DOWIE, IAIN.
Soccer international forward. Born in Hatfield, 9th January 1965. Club: Luton Town (scoring 16 goals in 66 league games), Fulham (on loan), West Ham, Sunderland (for whom, up to mid 1993, he had scored 20 goals in 66 league matches). He was first capped up front for Northern Ireland in 1990, and has accumulated 17 international caps up to mid 1993.

DOWLING, JOHN.
G.A.A. footballer, Kerry. He captained Kerry from the midfield to win the 1955 Sam Maguire Cup, when they beat Dublin by 0-12 to 1-6 (having captained the losing final side the previous year), and won a 2nd Sam Maguire Cup medal at full-forward in 1959. His daughter was an Irish international basketball player.

DOWLING, MICHAEL.
Handballer. Born in 1914, his club was Ballymore-Eustace. He won the Irish title under Handball union rules in 1935, and again in 1943 under the auspices of the I.A.H.A., beating Austin Clarke (cv) in the final. This places in the unique position of being the only player to win Irish titles under the 2 different unions. He died in 1980.

DOWLING, MICK.
Amateur boxer, bantamweight. Born in Castlecomer, Co Kilkenny. Clubs;

Arbour Hill, British Rail, Castlecomer, and Drimnagh. He has the unique record in Irish amateur boxing of winning the Irish National Senior Championship title at the same weight for 8 successive years, in 1968, 1969, 1970, 1971, 1972, 1973, 1974, and 1975, all at bantamweight. In 1972 he reached the last eight in the Olympic bantamweight event in the Munich, thereby being placed in joint 5th in that weight division; he had previously represented Ireland at the Mexico Olympic Games in 1968. In a distinguished career during which he became the great Irish boxing hope, he was selected as Texaco's Boxing Sportstar of the year for 3 years in succession, in 1968, 1969, and 1970, the only amateur boxer to win such acclaim. He is a sportsshop owner and has been a prominent figure in Irish amateur boxing since his retirement. His wife Emily Dowling, a long-distance runner (born in Rathfarnham in 1950), whose clubs include Avondale and Dublin City Harriers, has represented Ireland 6 times in the World Cross Country Championships, and won the National 5,000 metres title in 1986. She won the 1981 Dublin City Marathon in a time of 2:48:22. As a veteran runner she achieved fine results: in the world championship Veterans in Oregon in 1989 she won silvers medals in both the 10,000 metres and the cross country; while the following year she won both the 5,000 and 10,000 metres titles in Budapest.

DOWLING, RAMIE

G.A.A. hurling goalkeeper, Kilkenny. Club: Eire Og (with whom he won Kilkenny county championship titles in 1944, 1945, and 1947). Although he made only one appearence in an All-Ireland Senior Hurling Championship final (the 1950 final, losing to arch-rivals Tipperary), he was rated as one of the great goalkeepers, winning 3 Leinster S.H.C. provincial titles in all, 1947, 1950, and 1953, and won an Oireachtais medal in 1948. A hurley manufacturer.

DOWNEY, ANGELA.

G.A.A. camogie full-forward, Kilkenny. A native of Ballyragget, she was born in 1957. Club: St Pauls (winning All-Ireland Club Championship medals with them in 1976, 1977, and 1988). A prolific scorer, she has fine individual ball skills, and is regarded as the modern game's top player. She shares with her sister Ann (cv), the distinction of being the only 2 Kilkenny players to feature in all 11 of their O'Duffy Cup wins in the All-Ireland Senior Championship. Having made her senior debut for the county at the age of 15 in 1972, her wins came in 1974, 1976, 1977 (as captain in the 3-4 to 1-3 win over Wexford), 1981, 1985, 1986, in 1987 and 1988 both as captain, and in 1989, 1990 and 1991 (again as captain). She also has won 8 National League Senior titles with Kilkenny, in 1978, 1980, 1982, 1985, 1987, 1988, 1989 and 1990, and has shared in many of Leinster's dominating wins in the Gael Linn championhip since 1978. She in 1985 became the first to win the Gradam Tailte, camogie's Super Star title, on more than one occasion. She is the daughter of Shem Downey, who won an All-Ireland Senior Hurling Championship medal for Kilkenny in 1947 (and 2 other Leinster S.H.C. medals, losing All-Ireland finals both years, 1946 and 1950), and a Junior All-Ireland medal in 1946.

DOWNEY, ANNE.

G.A.A. camogie midfielder, Kilkenny. Club: St Paul's. A sister of Angela Downey (cv), she has won a joint-record 11 All-Ireland Senior Championship (O'Duffy Cup) medals with Kilkenny, in 1974, 1976, 1977, 1981, 1985, 1986, 1987, 1988, 1989 (when captain of the 5-in-arow side which beat Cork in the final), 1990 and 1991. She has also shared in many of Kilkenny's National League wins in the 1980's, and has won some Gael Linn titles with Leinster. She was also a squash player of some substance, reaching international status.

DOWNEY, HENRY.

G.A.A. football centre half-back, Derry. Born in 1967. Club: Lavey (assisting them to win the All-Ireland Club Championship title in 1991). A product of St Patrick's College in Maghera, he won many under-age honours. Captain of the Derry senior inter-county team from 1991, he helped them to win the 1991-92 National Football League. In 1993 he led by example when the county side took their first ever All-Ireland Senior Football Championship, beating Cork by 1-14 to 2-8 in the final to take the Sam Maguire Cup. His younger brother Seamus (a Lavey full-forward) also has played for Derry, and scored the all-important goal in that 1993 win for the Oak Leaf County.

DOYLE, AIDAN.

G.A.A. football forward, Wexford. He was a star member of the Wexford side which won 4 successive All-Ireland Senior Football Championship titles in a row, 1915, 1916, 1917 and 1918. One of Wexford's greatest footballers, he was also on the Wexford side which was beaten in the 2 All-Ireland S.F.C. finals running up to that, in 1913 and 1914 (which was drawn), thus playing in 7 successive finals.

DOYLE, BOBBY.

G.A.A. football half-forward and right full-forward, Dublin. Club: St Vincent's (winning an All-Ireland Club Championship winner's medal in 1976, having been on the losing final side in 1974). A product of St Joseph's CBS, he won 3 All-Ireland Senior Football Championship medals as an important member of the great 'Dubs' side of 1974, 1976 and 1977, playing also on the side which lost 3 All-Ireland S.F.C. finals to their great rivals Kerry, in 1975 (as a sub), 1977 and 1978. He won 2 All-Star awards, in 1976 and 1977 at right full-forward.

DOYLE, BRIDGET.

G.A.A. camogie centre-back, Wexford. Clubs: Cloughbawn, and Adamstown. She was a member of each Wexford side which won the Senior All-Ireland Championship, in 1968, 1969 (when she captained the side which beat Antrin by 4-4 to 4-2), and again in 1975. A member of a famous camogie family from Clonleigh in Wexford, she is one of seven sisters to play for her county. She also won Gael Linn medals, National League medal in 1978, and won a B & I award.

DOYLE, DENIS (DINNY, 'NETTLER').

Soccer international player. Club: Shamrock Rovers (winning an F.A.I. Cup medal in 1925 and Irish Free State League Chammpionship medals in the 1924-25 and 1926-27 seasons). A member of Rovers since their re-formation in 1919, he was on the first Irish international team picked by the F.A.I., in the 1926 match against Italy. He is the uncle of Jackie Mooney (cv).

DOYLE, EDDIE.

G.A.A. hurler, Kilkenny. He won 6 All-Ireland Senior Hurling Championship winner's medals with the 'Black and Amber', in 1904 with Tullaroan, in 1905 with Erin's Own, in 1907 with Mooncoin, in 1909 with Mooncoin, in 1911 in the disputed championship, and in 1912 with Tullaroan. He played in 4 of these All-Ireland Senior Hurling Championship hurling finals alongside 2 brothers, Dick and Mick (ccvv), in 1907, 1909, 1911 and 1912.

DOYLE, JACK ('THE GORGEOUS GAEL').

Heavyweight professional boxer. Born in Cobh, Co Cork, 31st August 1903, he became a 6'5" giant with remarkable good looks. In a checkered career lasting from 1932 to 1942, he won his first 10 professional bouts all inside 2 rounds, making him a sensation in the boxing world. He then lost the British heavyweight crown bout by disqualification to Jack Pedtersen in July 1933. His celebrity status, movie career and singing were then put ahead of his boxing, and his tally of 23 pro fights included 17 wins (13 by a clear knockout, 3 inside the distance), and 6 losses (2 by disqualification).

DOYLE, JACK T.

Rugby international wing-threequarter. Born in 1914. Club: Bective Rangers. He captained the Pres' Bray sides to win the Leinster Junior Cup (in 1929) and Senior Cup (1932). A Champion sprinter, he won one rugby cap for Ireland, when scoring a try against Wales in 1935. He was also a jockey, horse trainer, and a successful racehorse buyer and bloodstock agent (with good horses like Another Flash, Gale Bridge, Mill House, Giacometti and Bruni among those to pass through his hands). A famed raconteur and gambler.

DOYLE, JAMES PATRICK (J.P. or 'CHICK').

Badminton international player. Capped 4 times before he was 21, he represented Ireland 35 times in all between 1950 and 1965. Coached by Frank Peard (cv), he briefly emigrated to Australia. He was an all round player, and won many singles titles (including the Irish National Singles title 8 years-in-a-row from 1954 to 1961, and was runner-up in the Australian Championship); he also formed a formidable doubles partnership with Desmond Lacey. He later became President of the Leinster Branch of the B.U.I. (the Badminton Union of Ireland). His nickname derived from his profession, that of a chicken sexer.

DOYLE, JIMMY.

G.A.A. hurling right-half forward, Tipperary. Born in 1939. Club: Thurles Sarsfields (winning 11 county hurling championship medals including the 5-in-a-row sides of 1961, 1962, 1963, 1964 and 1965; he also won one Tipp county footballl championship medal). He captained the Tipperary side which won the All-Ireland M.H.C. final of 1957, having also played on the winning sides in the 2 previous years. In a senior career extending from 1957 to 1973, he was to captain 2 winning Tipperary All-Ireland Senior Hurling Championship sides, in both 1962 (when they beat Wexford by 3-10 to 2-11) and in 1965 (when Wexford again were the defeated side, this time by 2-16 to 0-10). He also won 4 other Liam McCarthy Cup medals with Tipperary, in 1958, 1961 (scoring 0-9), 1964 (scoring 0-10), and 1971, bringing him a tally of 6, making him joint-second Tipperary player in All-Ireland winning medals tally (he also played for Tipperary in 3 losing finals, in 1960, 1967, and 1968, making in all 9 appearences in the final, 5 of these in the No 10 jersey, and scoring 46 points in these 9 finals). In 1969, he was the country's top scorer, scoring 124 points (from 11 goals and 91 points), a Tipperary record. He holds the Tipperary record of most Railway Cup medals, winning 8, in 1958, 1959, 1960, 1961, 1963, 1966, 1969 and 1970, captaining the side in 1963 and 1966. He also won 6 National Hurling League medals with Tipp, in 1959, 1960, 1961, 1964, 1965 and 1968, and 5 Oireachtas medals. In 1965 he was nominated as Texaco Hurler of the Year, becoming the 5th Tipperaryman to be so honoured in the first 8 years of the awards. His brother Paddy also played hurling for Tipperary.

DOYLE, JOE

Pitch and putt player. Club: Carrigaline P.P.C. One of pitch and Putt's finest men players of the early 1970's, he is the only player to win 3 National Strokeplay Championship titles in the short space of 4 years, achieving the wins in 1969, 1971 and in 1972 (to win back-to-back titles).

DOYLE, JOHN.

G.A.A. hurling right and left full-back and left half-back, Tipperary. Born in 1930. Club: Hollycross (winning 3 county championship medals, including 1948). As a minor with Tipperary, he was on the side defeated in the 1949 All-Ireland M.H.C. final, and was at right full back on the winning side in 1947. During his playing era for Tipperary, which stretched from 1949 to 1967, he was on the winning All-Ireland side 8 times (thus sharing with Christy Ring the record of 8 All-Ireland Senior Hurling Championship winner's medals achieved on the field of play), gaining these medals over a 16 year period: in 1949, 1950, 1951 (at left-corner back in this 3-in-a-row), 1958 and 1961 both as left half-back, and his last 3 titles at right corner back, in 1962, 1964 and 1965. He also shares with Ring in the record of All-Ireland final appearences, with ten (being on the losing side in the All-Ireland finals of 1960 and 1967). He has also won an all-time record number of National League Hurling medals with Tipperary, winning 11 over a 16 year period, in 1949, 1950, 1952, 1954, 1955, 1957, 1959, 1960, 1961, 1964, and in 1965. A winner of 6 Oireachtas medals, he also won 5 Railway Cup medals with Munster, in 1952, 1953, 1955, 1960, 1963, In 1964 he was awarded as Texaco Hurler of the Year.

DOYLE, JOHN and sons, JOHN (JNR), JANES AND JOSEPH.

Jockeys. John Doyle (born in 1876, he died in 1942), rode his first winner on the flat at the age of 12 in 1888, and later rode the winner of England's Cesarawitch in 1892. He was joint winner of the jockey's championship in Ireland in 1911, and was twice second behind John Thompson (cv). He rode the winner of the Irish Derby two years in succession, in 1910 on Aviator and the following year on Shanballymore. His total tally of Irish Classic race winners was 5, having also won 3 Irish Oaks (in 1896 on Kosmos, 1909 on Fredith, and in 1914 on May Edgar). Retiring from the saddle in 1916, he had 4 sons who became jockeys, 3 winning big races: John Jnr (who won the Irish 1,000 Guineas in twice, in 1928 on Moucheron and in 1932 on Petoni); James won the Irish 1,000 Guineas in 1924 on Volti; and James who rode the winner of the Irish Grand National in 1925, Dog Fox.

DOYLE, JOHN JOE (J.J. or 'GOGGLES').

G.A.A. hurling half-back, Clare. Born in 1906. Club: Newmarket-on-Fergus (winning Clare county championship titles in 1925, 1926, 1927, 1930, 1931 and in 1936). First playing for Clare seniors in 1927, he was captain of the Clare side which won the Munster S.H.C. in 1932, the last time the county won this title (they lost the All-Ireland final to Kilkenny). He won Railway Cup medals with Munster in 4 successive years, 1928, 1929, 1930 and 1931. One of the great hurling half-backs of his era, he played on the Ireland side against America in the Tailteann Games of 1932. Getting his nick-name from the self-made protection for the glasses he needed to play his sport, he was selected at left corner-back on the 'Team of the Century' in 1984 for players who never won an All-Ireland medal, and in 1990 he entered the All-Stars Hall of Fame.

DOYLE, JUDY.

G.A.A. camogie player, Dublin. Clubs: C.I.E., and Naomh Aoife. A fine, elusive player, she won 6 All-Ireland Senior Championship medals in the 1950's and 1960's with Dublin, playing many in a lethal partnership with Una O'Connor (cv), with whom she had an uncanny relationship on the field of play. A fine all-round athlete who was a fine hand-passer, she also won 5 Gael Linn medals.

DOYLE, MATT.

International tennis player. Born in Redwood City, California, 13th January 1955. A fine basketball player and golfer as a youth, he is a Yale economics graduate. Introduced to Irish tennis in 1980, he was, along with Sean Sorensen, largely responsible for Ireland getting promotion to division one of the Davis Cup in 1983 (and he played in this event up to 1988). Highlight of his career with Ireland was his win over Eliot Teltscher in the 1983 defeat by the U.S.A. in the Davis Cup, while also in 1983 he won a

Grand Prix tournaament in Cologne, against opposition that included Stan Smith, Brian Gottfried, Sandy Mayer, Tomas Smid and a youthful Boris Becker. He attained a world ranking in the 70's in 1984. He won 6 Irish Open titles, the last being in 1986. He was nominated as Texaco's Tennis Sportstar of the Year three times, in 1982, 1983, and 1985. He was President of the world players body, the A.T.P., from 1985-86, was coach to Mats Wilander for a 1 period in the late 1980's , and in 1989 he was appointed as a professional National Coach for Irish tennis.

DOYLE, MICK.

G.A.A. hurler, Kilkenny. He won a total of 5 All-Ireland Senior Hurling Championship winner's medals with Kilkenny, in 1907 and 1909 with Mooncoin, in 1911 in the awarded final, in 1912 with Tullaroan, and again with Mooncoin in 1913. He was the youngest of three brothers who between them won 18 All-Ireland Senior Hurling Championship winner's medals, Eddie (cv) winning 6, and Dick (cv) winning 7 (the 3 brothers appeared together in a record 4 All-Ireland winning sides together, 1907, 1909, 1911 and 1912).

DOYLE, MICHAEL Gerard Martin (MICK, 'DOYLER').

Rugby international wing-forward. Born in Castleisland, Co Kerry, 13th October 1940. Clubs: Garryowen, Blackrock College (leading them to a Leinster Senior League success in 1974-75), U.C.D. (captaining them to win the Leinster Senior Cup in 1963), Cambridge University (for whom he won a blue in 1965), and Edinburgh Wanderers (making him the only Irish international rugby player to win caps playing for 4 different clubs). He was capped for Ireland 20 times between 1965 and 1968, scoring 2 international tries (including one on his debut), and toured Australia with Ireland in 1967. He toured South Africa with the 1968 British and Irish Lions, winning one Test cap. His younger brother Tommy, a Wanderers flanker who played interprovincial rugby for Leinster twice, won 3 international caps in 1968, all won with Mick on the other flank (they are still the most recent set of brothers to play together for Ireland). Mick was later a successful Leinster coach, leading them to the interprovincial title in 1979, 1980, 1981, 1982 (shared) and 1983. Then as Irish coach in 1985-1987 he was influential in the winning of the Triple Crown and Home International Championship in 1985. He also coached the Irish team for the inaugural World Cup in 1987, and later became a forthright sports writer, releasing a successful autobiography, 'Doyler' in 1991. A veterinary surgeon and companies director, his son Andrew played rugby for Leinster in 1993.

DOYLE, MIKO.

G.A.A. footballer, Kerry. Club: Rock Street. Best known as captain of the Kerry S.F.C side which beat Cavan by 4-4 to 1-7 in the replayed final of 1937 All-Ireland Senior Football Championship final, he had previously won (all before the age of 21) 4 All-Ireland Senior Football Championship winner's medals with Kerry in the famous 4-in-a-row side of 1929, 1930, 1931, and 1932. Also on the losing Kerry All-Ireland S.F.C. side in 1938, he won a Railway Cup medal with Munster in 1931.

DOYLE, PAUL.

G.A.A. football left half-forward, Kildare. Clubs: Caragh, and McKee Barracks. Regarded as one of the finest exponents of the left half-forward position, he made his debut for Kildare at midfield in the 1919 All-Ireland Senior Football Championship-winning final, at the age of 19. He went on to win 2 other All-Ireland S.F.C. medals with Kildare (making him, along with Mick Buckley (cv), one of only 2 Kildare men to win 3 All-Ireland senior medals), in 1927 and 1928, also playing on Kildare sides beaten in 3 All-Ireland S.F.C. finals, in 1926, 1929, and 1931. He won 3 successive Railway Cup medals with Leinster, in the province's first 3 wins, in 1928, 1929, and 1930.

DOYLE, PETER.

Amateur international cyclist. Born in 1946. Club: Bray Wheelers. He won a stage race in the Tour of Ireland in 1967, having won the 50 miles (in record time) and 100 miles TT championships in 1966. In probably his most successful year, 1968, he competed for Ireland in the Olympic Games in Mexico, finished 3rd in the Tour of Britain (winning 2 stages, and winning the points and mountains classifications), won the Tour of Ireland and Tour of Scotland, and also won the Irish Road Championship at Rathfriland. In 1969 having won 6 races on the continent (and deciding not to go professional), he went on to win a stage in the Tour of Britain, finishing 6th. He won stages in the Tour of Britain again in 1970 and 1972 (when he also competed again in the Olympics for Ireland). He won the 25 miles TT chaampionship in both 1970 and 1976. In 1974 he won the Ras Tailteann, leading for all but one day.

DOYLE, RICHARD (DICK).

G.A.A. hurler, Kilkenny. He won 7 All-Ireland Senior Hurling Championship winner's medals, sharing with 3 other countymen all the wins in 1904 with the Tullaroan selection, 1905 with Erin's Own, in 1907 and 1909 both with Mooncoin, in the awarded final of 1911, in 1912 with Tullaroan, and with the Mooncoin Selection again in 1913. He shared 4 of these wins (1907, 1909, 1911 and 1912) with his 2 brothers (ccvv), Eddie and Mick, and the family between them won a total of 18 All-Ireland S.H.C. winners' medals.

DOYLE, TOMMY.

G.A.A. hurling half-forward and half-back, Tipperary. Born in 1918. Club: Thurles Sarsfields (winning 7 county championship titles). Over a senior inter-county career that stretched 17 years from 1937 to 1953, he became the first Tipperary-man to win 5 All-Ireland Senior Hurling Championship medals in 50 years, gaining them in 1937 (at right half-forward), 1945 (at centre half-forward), and as a constant member of the famous 3-in-a-row of 1949, 1950, and in 1951 (all as a half-back). His other Munster S.H.C. success came in 1941. He won 3 National Hurling League medals, in 1949, 1950 and 1952. He won 3 Railway Cup medals with Munster, in 1943, 1946, and 1948. In 1986 he was nominated to join distinguished company as an All-Time All-Star, the first Tipperary-man to be so honoured.

DOYLE, TOMMY ('PRIVATE').

G.A.A. football right half-back, Kerry. Club: Annascaul. Born in New York, 3rd March 1956. He won 3 successive All-Ireland Under 21 Champiponship medals with the Kingdom in 1975, 1976, and 1977. Having been sent off in the Munster S.F.C. final of 1978, he played on Kerry sides to win 6 All-Ireland Senior Football Championship winner's medals, 3-in-a-row in 1979 (as a right half-forward), 1980 and 1981, and the a further 3-in-a-row in 1984, 1985 and 1986 (in which year he captained the side which beat Tyrone by 2-15 to 1-10). He was on the Kerry side beaten by Offaly in the 1982 final, when Seamus Derby eluded his marking to score a famous late goal. He won 3 successive All-Star awards in the right half-back position, in 1984, 1985 and 1986.

DREA, SEAN.

Sculler. Club; Neptune R.C. He graduated from being a Dublin head sculler to become an Irish Champion and an Irish international. When winning a silver medal at the World Sculling Championships in Nottingham in 1975, he became the first rower to put Ireland onto the international rowing map. He won the Henley Royal Regatta's famous Diamond Sculls event in 3 successive years, 1973, 1974 and in 1975 (and also won many international regattas in both

Europe and North America). On 5th July 1975, he set a record of 7 minutes 40 seconds for the one mile course at Henley, the best time for a single scull event there since its inception in 1844. He represented Ireland in 2 Olympic Games, finishing 7th in 1972 at Munich (winning the little final), and being placed 4th in the final of 1976 at Montreal (4 seconds behind the bronze medal), the winner each time being his great rival, Pertti Karppinan. He also went to a total of 4 World Championships and 2 European Championships. He was nominated as Texaco's Rowing Sportstar of the Year 5 years in succession, the first sportsman to accomplish this feat, the years being 1972, 1973, 1974, 1975 and 1976. In 1990 he coached Niall O'Toole (cv). He now runs a construction firm in Philadelphia.

DREAPER, JAMES

Thomas Russell (JIM). National Hunt horse trainer, and former jockey. Born 30th January 1951. As a amateur jockey, he finished 2nd behind Specify in the 1971 Aintree Grand National on Black Secret, and also won the Troytown Chase, the Navan Cup and the Conyngham Cup. His best horses to train include Ten Up (winner of 1975 Cheltenham Gold Cup), Brown Lad (winner of Irish Grand National in 1975, 1976, and 1978, and who finished 2nd in both 1976 and 1978 Cheltenham Gold Cup), Straight Fort, Lough Inagh, Kilkilowen, and the enigmatic but brilliant Carvill's Hill. He also won the Irish Grand National in 1974 with Coleridge. He was leading National Hunt trainer in Ireland many times, including 1972, 1973, 1974, 1975 and 1976. A son of Tom Dreaper (cv), he trains at Greenogue, Kilsallaghan, Co Dublin.

DREAPER, THOMAS William (TOM).

Horse trainer. Born in Donaghmore, Ashbourne, Co Meath, 23rd September 1898, he died in 1975. From his farm stable at Greenogue, Kilsallaghan, he trained an all-time record 5 Cheltenham Gold Cup-winning horses (in 1946 with the classy Prince Regent, a 3-in-a-row in 1964, 1965 and 1966 with the brilliant Arkle, and in 1968 with Fort Leney). He has had more Cheltenham Festival winners than any other Irish trainer, including 6 Champion Two Mile Chases (1960, 1961, 1964, 1966, 1969 and 1970), 4 Arkle Challenge Trophy's, 3 Sun Alliance Chases (which Arkle won in 1963), 3 National Hunt Handicap Chase's, 3 Cathcart Cup's, and one Gloucestershire Hurdle (with the brilliant Flyingbolt in 1964), which brings his tally to 25 winners. Arkle also won the Hennessy Gold Cup in 1964 and 1965 and the Whitread Gold Cup in 1965. His other classy horses include Flyingbolt (who won the Two Mile Champion Chase in 1966), Fortria (who won the Two Mile Champion Chase twice, in 1960 and 1961, 2 Mackeson Gold Cup's in 1960 and 1962, as well as the 1958 Arkle Challenge Trophy), Arkloin, Proud Tarquin, Sentina. He has trained a record 10 winners of the Irish Grand National: Prince Regent in 1942, Shagreen in 1949, Royal Approach in 1954, and then an amazing 7-in-a-row: Olympia in 1960, Fortria in 1961, Ker Foro in 1962, Last Link in 1963, Arkle in 1964, Splash in 1966 and finally in 1967 with Flyingbolt. He was nominated as Texaco's Horse Racing Sportstar of the Year for 1965. He is the father of Jim Dreaper (cv).

DRENNAN, PADDY.

G.A.A. hurling right half-forward, Laois. Clubs: Kilcotton (winning Laois SHC medals in 1920, 1923, 1924 and 1929), and Erill (winning a county championship in 1938). He played in 3 Laois teams who played in 3 Leinster Senior Football Championship finals in succession, getting winner's medals in both 1932 and 1933 (as a sub). In 1932 he became the first player to score a point directly from a sideline puck, in the Railway Cup final win (his only medal) with Leinster.

DREW, NORMAN Vico.

Golfer, amateur and professional. Born in Belfast 25th May 1932. He, as a member of Bangor G.C. and Clandeboye G.C. (winning a Barton Shield medal in 1952), had a spectacularly successful short amateur career, when, after being runner-up in the British Boy's in 1949, he went on to win the East of Ireland in 1952, the Irish Amateur Open in 1952 and 1953, and the North of Ireland twice, in 1950 and in 1952 (when he was also runner-up in the West and South, at the age of only 20). He also represented Ireland in 12 Home international matches in 1952-53, winning 8. These achievemants gained him a Walker Cup place in 1953 (losing his only match, a singles). He then turned professional, representing Ireland in the Canada Cup in 1960 (when Ireland finished 4th) and 1961. In 1959, his wins in the Yorkshire Evening News Tournament, the Irish Professional Championship and the Irish National Matchplay title, helped him to gain a Ryder Cup place, becoming the first man ever to gain both Walker and Ryder Cup honours (he halved his only match). He is also the first of only 2 Irishmen (see Ronan Rafferty) to win Walker, Ryder, and World Cup honours.

DREW, OLIVER.

Handballer. Born in Cork in 1883. At the age of 19 he went to America to challenge for the title of champion of the world, but his match with Mike Egan was not finished in a row over his expenses. He later went back to America, and won the titles of 'International Champion', and the 'Championship of America'. He died in 1938.

DRUMGOOLE, NOEL.

G.A.A. hurling full-back, Dublin. In 1961 he was the captain of the Dublin side which were beaten in the All-Ireland Senior Hurling Championship final by Tipperary. In 1962 he became the only Dublin-man to captain a winning Leinster hurling Railway Cup side. He represented Ireland in 1958, 1959 and in 1961. A quality player, in 1984 he was selected in the full-back position on the 'Team of the Century' for those players who have never won an All-Ireland medal.

DRUMM, TOMMY.

G.A.A. football half-back, Dublin. Born 22nd March 1955. Club: Whitehall Colmcille. He has won 3 All-Ireland Senior Football Championship winner's medals with Dublin, in 1976, 1977, and in 1983 when he captained the side which beat Galway by 1-10 to 1-8. He also played on 3 losing S.F.C. final Dublin teams in both 1978, 1979 and in 1984, all against Kerry. He has won 4 All-Star awards, in 1977, 1978, and 1979 at right half-back, and in 1983 at centre half-back (joining the select few to be the only nomination for his position). In 1983 he became the 4th, and most recent, Dublinman to be honoured as Texaco Footballer of the Year.

DUFF, CIARAN or KIERAN ('DULLY').

G.A.A. football half-forward, Dublin. Born on 14th February 1961. Club: Fingallians. A member of the Dublin minors side which captured the All-Ireland M.F.C. in 1979, he was also brought on a soccer trial to Manchester United. First playing senior championship football in 1980 at the age of 18, he has won one All-Ireland Senior Football Championship medal with Dublin, in 1983 when he was one of 3 Dublin players to be sent off in that torrid final, and was on the losing All-Ireland S.F.C. final sides in both 1984 and 1985. He won another Leinster S.F.C. medal at centre half-forward in 1989 (and was on 5 Dublin sides that lost Leinster finals). He won National Football League medals with the Dubs in 1987 and 1990 (as a sub in the final), and was also on the losing side in 2 N.F.L. finals. He has won 2 All-Star awards, in 1987 and 1988, both at left half-forward. He retired in 1992 after 12 years in and out of the Dublin team.

DUFFY, EILEEN.

Camogie goalkeeper, Dublin. Club: Celtic (with whom she won many county champinship medals). She was an almost permanent figure in goals for Dublin from 1947, winning All-Ireland medals in the 8-in-a-row period of 1948, 1949, 1950, 1951, 1952, 1953, 1954 and 1955. She also won 9 Leinster championship medals.

DUFFY, GERARD Andrew Anthony.

Cricket international right hand batsman and leg break bowler. Born in Dublin, 4th November 1930. Club: Leinster. A product of St Mary's College, he played 16 first class matches for Ireland over the 19 year period from 1955 to 1973, his record being: 16-27-6-317-55(v Scotland in 1966)-15.10-426-15-28.40. He played 55 international matches for Ireland in all between 1953 and 1974, taking 82 wickets for an average of 19.23, and scoring 1,123 runs with an average-per-inning of 18.11 rins. Playing senior league cricket with Leinster spanning 6 decades from 1948 to 1990, he later was a coach with Merrion.

DUFFY, PATRICK J (PADDY).

Fencing champion. Born in Dublin in 1921, he died in 1987. He had a meteoric rise to the top of Irish fencing, and in a short amateur career, he won the National Sabre, Epee and All Weapons titles each year from 1947 to 1952. He represented Ireland in fencing at 2 successive Olympic Games, in London in 1948 and in Helsinki in 1952. Turning professional soon afterwards, he won many Open Championships, and took part in many Masters World Championships. He became the outstanding Irish fencing coach of his time, training many of Ireland's best. He trained the Irish squad to 4 Olympic Games (1960, 1964, 1968 and 1972), and squads of all ages to many World Championships. He was invited by Finland to train their national squads in 1959-60. He was a founder member of the International Academy of Fencing Masters in 1958. He was also a county hurler and footballer with Dublin, being a founder member of the St Vincent's club. His brother Vincent won the Irish foil crown in 1961 and also became a fine sabre exponent in the 1960's. His wife Shirley Armstrong-Duffy was 9 times Irish Ladies Fencing Champion in the 60's and 70's, fenced successfully on the Continent, and represented Ireland at the Olympic Games in Rome in 1960.

DUGGAN, ALAN Thomas Anthony ('DIXIE').

Rugby international wing three-quarter. Born in Dublin, 11th June 1942. Club: Lansdowne (winning 2 Leinster Senior Cup medals in 1965 and 1972). A Castleknock College product, he played 23 senior interprovincial matches for Leinster between 1963 and 1973. In winning 25 international caps for his country over a 10 year period between 1963 and 1972 (when Ireland lost only 8 matches while he was playing), he was for a period Ireland's most capped winger. His 11 tries for his country makes him Ireland's 3rd highest try scorer (he twice had 2 tries in a game, both against Scotland, in 1969 and 1972). He went on 2 tours with Ireland, to Australia in 1967 (his 3 tries in a tour match versus Victoria in Melbourne in 1967 is a shared Irish tour record), and to Argentina in 1970.

DUGGAN, HARRY A.

Soccer international outside-right. Born in Dublin, 8th June 1903. Clubs: Richmond United (scoring 49 goals in 1924-25), Leeds United (signing as a 19-year-old in 1925, scoring 49 goals in almost 200 first class matches with them up to 1936), Newport County (captaining them to the Third Division South title in 1938-39). He was capped 12 times, 8 for the Irish Football Association, and 4 for the Irish Free State, all between 1926 and 1935. He died in Leeds in 1968.

DUGGAN, HUGO.

Athletics long jumper. He is the Irish first male athlete to win 7 B.L.E. National

Champinships, gaining his titles in the long jump discipline over a 17 year period from 1967 to 1983, the wins coming in 1967, 1970, 1971, 1972, 1974, 1980, and 1983.

DUGGAN, JIMMY.

G.A.A. hurling centre-forward and centre-back, Galway. Club: Liam Mellows. Born in 1930. A Galway minor hurler and footballer in 1947, he played hurling up to 1979, when he was 49. He played in 3 Galway sides who were beaten in the All-Ireland Senior Hurling Championship final, in 1953 (the county's first final appearance since 1929), 1955 (when captain of the side beaten by Wexford) and in 1958. He played in 3 losing Railway Cup final sides, and won a National Hurling League medal with Galway in New York 1951, and Oireachtais medals in 1950, 1952 and 1958. A brother of Seanie Duggan (cv), his other brother Paddy played alongside him for Galway many times, including playing in the losing All-Ireland S.H.C. final sides of 1953 (as a sub) and 1955.

DUGGAN, SEANIE.

G.A.A. hurling goalkeeper, Galway. Born in 1922. Club: Liam Mellows (winning 5 county championship medals). In 1947 he captained the first Connacht side to win a hurling Railway Cup, also playing on 4 all-Galway sides beaten in the final (in 1944, 1946, 1949, and 1952). He also played on the Galway side beaten in the 1953 All-Ireland Senior Hurling Championship final, their first final appearence since 1929. He also won 2 Oireachtas medals with Galway in 1950 and 1952, and a National Hurling League medal in New York in 1951. A quality goal-minder, he was selected on the 1984 'Team of the Century' for hurlers who never won an All-Ireland medal. A brother of Jimmy Duggan (cv).

DUGGAN, WILLIAM Patrick (WILLIE).

Rugby international No 8, wing forward. Born in Kilkenny, 12th March 1950. Clubs: Sunday's Well, St Mary's, Blackrock College (winning a Leinster Senior Cup medal in 1983, and 3 Leinster Senior League medals, in 1975, 1982 and 1983). A product of Rockwell College (winning a Munster Senior Schools winner's medal in 1967), he was capped at full international level 41 times between 1975 and 1984, 39 of these caps were as a No 8 (an Irish record for the position), and 2 on the flank. He captained the side twice in 1984, and scored one international try. In the Wales game of 1977 he became, along with Geoff Wheel, the first player to be sent off in the International Championship. He won 4 British and Irish Lion's test caps as an automatic choice on the 1977 tour of New Zealand. An outstanding, tough No 8 forward, his record 19 partnerships with Fergus Slattery and John O'Driscoll in the Irish back row was for many seasons feared by many opponents. He was a leading light in Ireland's 1982 Triple Crown and Championship triumphs, also playing in all of the International Championship winning matches of 1983. He toured with Ireland to New Zealand in 1976, to Australia in 1979, and to South Africa in 1981. In 1977 he was selected as Texaco's Rugby Sportstar of the Year. An electrical supplier.

DUGGAN, WILLIE.

Amateur international boxer. Club: Crumlin. He won 3 Irish National Senior Championship titles, at middleweight in 1952, and then by dropping weights (against the normal trend of boxers), to win 2 at light-heavyweight in 1950 and 1951. He was one of a group of Crumlin boxers to represent Ireland at the Helsinki Olympics in 1952, being KO'd in his first bout.

DUIGNAN, MICHAEL.

G.A.A. dual hurler and footballer, Offaly. Club: St Rynagh's. A product of St Joseph's Garbally (winning a number of Connacht schools championships), he was at full-forward on the Offaly side which won the All-Irelnd M.H.C. in 1986.

He has won 3 Leinster Senior Hurling Championship medals with Offaly in 1988, 1989 and 1990. He has also played for Offaly in Leinster Senior Championship football. Also a rugby player, he played on the Ballinasloe side which won the 1992 Connacht Senior Cup final.

DUKE, P.J.

G.A.A. football mid-fielder and right half-back, Cavan. Clubs: Stradone, and U.C.D. (with whom he won 3 Sigerson Cup medals, in 1947 as captain, and also in 1945 and 1949). A member of the Cavan senior championship side from 1945, he appeared in the losing All-Ireland final S.F.C. team of 1945, then won 2 All-Ireland Senior Championship medals with Cavan, in the Polo Ground of 1947, and again in 1948, before being on the side which lost the final of 1949. A brilliant defender, he won a Railway Cup medal on Patrick's Day 1950 for Ulster, before dying, at the age of 25, on May 1st 1950.

DUNLOP, JOEY ('KING OF THE MOUNTAIN').

Motorcycling road racer. Born in Ballymoney, Co Antrim, 25th February 1952. Machines: Suzuki, Yamaha and (chiefly) Honda. He won the Classic 1,000cc Series in 1980 and 1981, and won the Senior T.T. race in 1985 and 1987. One of the great T.T. riders of all time, from 1977 and through the 1980's he won a remarkable 13 T.T. victories; won a 14th in 1992 (at 125 cc), when equalling the all-time record held by Mike Hailwood, and finally became the most successful T.T. rider in history when winning the 1993 125 cc T.T. (in a record speed pf 107.26 m.p.h.), for his 15th triumph. He has also won a record-equalling 2 'double-trebles', ie 3 T.T. races in the same week (in both 1985 and 1988); his other wins apart from the above coming in 1977, 1980, 1983, 1984, 1986 and twice in 1987, in classes varying from Jubilee, Classic, Formula One, Junior and Senior. Having finished third in the World T.T. Formula One Championship in both 1980 and 1981, he went on to win that coveted title a record 5 years in succession, in 1982 (gaining 36 points), in 1983 (42 points), in 1984 (66 points), in 1985 (90 points), and in 1986 (93 points). He was also to finish 2nd in this championship in 1987, 1988 and 1990. A winner of countless Irish road and short-circuit races (including a record 13 Ulster Grand Prix wins), he has raced in South Africa, the U.S., Macau, and most European countries. Ireland's most successful motorcycle road racer in recent years, he was selected as Texaco's Motor Sport Sportstar of the Year for 3 years in succession, 1984 (when he also became the first Irishman to win the prestigious British 'Motor Cycling News' Man of the Year award), 1985, and 1986. He was awarded the M.B.E. in 1986. He is an older brother of Robert Dunlop (cv).

DUNLOP, ROBERT.

Motorcycle road racer. Born in Ballymoney, 25th November 1960. Having his first racing success in the 1983 Manx G.P. Newcomers race, he won that year's John Players 125cc championship. He won the 1989 Isle of Man T.T. race at 125cc (with an average speed of over 102 m.p.h), repeating the feat in 1990 and 1991, and also won at 250cc in 1991. In 1989 and 1990 he finished 3rd in the World T.T. Formula One Championship. He has won 4 North-West 200 races, in 1986, two in 1990, and in 1991. He won the Macau (China) Grand Prix in 1980. He also has the distinction of having won both the Ulster and the Irish Championships in every class (i.e. 125, 250, 350 and 1,000ccs). He is the younger brother of Joey Dunlop.

DUNLOP, ROBERT.

Rugby international centre and wing-threequarter. Club: Dublin University (winning Leinster Senior Cup medals in 1890 and 1893). Twice playing interprovincial rugby for Leinster, he won

11 caps for Ireland between 1889 and 1894, including playing in the Welsh game in the 1894 Triple Crown success (one of only 2 of his matches that Ireland won), and scored one international try, against Wales in 1890, and thus becoming the first Irish player in international rugby to score a one-point try. He was awarded a C.B.E., and died in 1935.

DUNNE, ANTHONY P (TONY).

Soccer international left or right full-back. Born in Dublin, 24th July 1941. He joined Manchester United from Shelbourne (with whom he won an F.A.I. Cup medal in 1960) for a fee of £5,000, and in 13 seasons he proved to be one of the club's best full-backs from 1960 to 1972; he played in 529 matches for them, winning 2 League Championship medals (in 1964/65 and 1966/67), an F.A. Cup medal in 1963, a European Cup Winner's Cup medal in 1964, and a European Cup medal in the fine victory of 1968. He then played for Bolton Wanderers for 5 seasons (playing 170 league games) in 1973-1978. Regarded as the best left-back in Europe at his peak, he played 32 international matches for the Republic of Ireland between 1962 and 1976, scoring 4 international goals. He was selected as Texaco's Soccer Sportstar of the Year in 1966. His younger brother Pat (born in Dublin, 9th February 1943), a goalkeeper, played for Shamrock Rovers (winning the 'Grand Slam' with the Hoops in 1963/64), Everton, Manchester United (winning a League Championship winners medal in 1964/65) and Plymouth Argyle (playing 152 games for them 1967-71), and won 5 international caps for the Republic of Ireland between 1965 and 1967, 4 times playing in the national side together with Tony.

DUNNE, CYRIL.

G.A.A. football right half-forward, Galway. Having been a member of the Galway side beaten in the All-Ireland Senior Football Championsahip final in 1963, he was a constant member of the famous 3-in-a-row side which captured the Sam Maguire Cup in 1964, 1965, and 1966. The ace free-kick specialist of that Galway side, he was also on county sides beaten in National Football League finals in 1965 and 1967. He won a Railway Cup medal with Connacht in 1967. A son of John 'Tull' Dunne (cv).

DUNNE, DAN.

G.A.A. hurling right full-forward, Kilkenny. Born in 1908. Club: Young Ireland (Dublin, winning one county championship). A talented schoolboy, he was out of the game for 8 years, and then due to injury, his senior inter-county career finished after only 3 seasons, at the age of 25. In 1932 he won a fine haul of 7 gold medals; an All-Ireland Senior Hurling Championhip medal, a National League medal, a Railway Cup medal, a Leinster title, a Tailteann Games medal, and a league and championship medal with Young Ireland. He won his first provincial medal with Kilkenny in 1931, and later won a 2nd Railway Cup medal in 1933. A case of what might have been.

DUNNE, GERRY.

Paralympic swimmer. From Dublin, he has been Ireland's outstanding Paralympic swimmer, competing in 2 celebrations, in Los Angeles in 1984, where he won a gold in the 100m Backstroke (setting a world record), a gold in the 100m Butterfly (also setting a world record), a silver in the 400m Freestyle, and a bronze in the 100m Freesyyle; while in 1988 Games in Seoul, he won gold medals in the 100m Backstroke and the 100m Butterfly (again breaking the world record), and won bronze in the 100m Freestyle, the 400m freestyle, and the 200m Individual Medley. He is also a waterpolo player of note.

DUNNE, JAMES ('FAIRY').

Horse trainer, flat. Born in 1840, he died, aged 87 in 1927. Based at the Curragh, he won 12 Irish Classic races, placing him joint 3rd in all-time achievers in this field. The winners were: 5 Irish Derby's (in 1883 with Sylph, 1885 with St Kevin, Flex Park in 1904, and in 1909 with Wild Bouquet), 5 Irish Oaks (the inaugural running in 1895 with Sapling, in 1904 with Copestone Filly, in 1907 with Rheina, in 1914 with May Edgar, and in 1916 with Captive Princess) and 3 Irish St Leger's (winning in each of the first 3 years the race was run, in 1915 with La Paloma, 1916 with Captive Princess, and in 1917 with Double Scotch).

DUNNE, JAMES (JIMMY, 'JEMMERS' or 'SNOWY').

Soccer international centre-forward. Born in Ringsend, Dublin on 3rd September 1905, he died at the age of 44. He joined Sheffield United from New Brighton in 1926 for £700, and became a scoring machine. In 1929-30, he scored 36 goals in 39 games, and the following season scored 41 goals in 41 games, finishing top scorer in the First Division, this still being a club record. Regarded as one of Ireland's best ever centre-forwards, he later played for Arsenal (winning a First Division medal in 1933-34) and Southhampton, and scored a total of 170 English League goals. He rejoined Shamrock Rovers as captain-coach in 1937 (winning League of Ireland Champinship medals in 1937-38 and 1938-39, and an F.A.I. Cup medal in 1940, scoring a goal in the final). He later coached both Bohs and the Hoops. His League of Ireland goal tally was 52. He played 6 Inter-League matches, and was capped 15 times for Ireland between 1930 and 1939, scoring 12 international goals, one of a select number to score more than 10 goals for the Republic of Ireland; he also scored 4 international goals in 7 matches for the I.F.A. between 1928 and 1933. His son Tommy, an ex-Jacobs, Shamrock Rovers (winning an F.A.I. Cup medal in 1948), Leicester, Exeter, Shrewsbury and Southport half-back, who won 2 successive League of Ireland Championship medals in 1955-56 and 1956-57 with St Patrick's Athletic (and 2 F.A.I. Cup medals in 1959 and 1961), won 3 international caps for the Republic of Irleand in 1956 and 1957. This makes them one of only 6 sets of fathers and sons to play soccer for the Republic of Ireland.

DUNNE, JIM.

Heavyweight bare-knuckle boxer. Born in Co Kildare on 4th October 1842, he died in Elizabeth, New Jersey on 26 June 1906. He claimed the American Heavyweight title in 1863; in New Jersey on 13th May of that year, he defeated fellow-Irishman Jim Elliot for the American title. Dunne won on a disqualification for repeated fouling, but both men were jailed for 2 years after the fight.

DUNNE, JOHN ('TULL').

G.A.A. football midfielder and centre half-forward, Galway. Born in 1911. Having won an All-Ireland junior medal in 1930, he went on to captain the Galway side which won the 1938 All-Ireland Senior Football Championship, when they beat Kerry in a replay by 2-4 to 0-7 (achieving this while county secretary), having already won a Sam Maguire Cup medal in 1934, the county's first title. He was on losing Galway sides in the All-Ireland S.F.C. finals of 1933, 1940 (again as captain), and in 1941. He won 3 Railway Cup medals for Connacht, in 1934, 1937, and 1938. In 1984 he was nominated to join the select few on the All-Time All-Stars roster. A father of Cyril Dunne (cv), he was also a trainer of note, handling the Galway minors to 3 All-Ireland titles (1952, 1960 and 1970), a junior All-Ireland winning side in 1958, and most notably the famous Galway S.F.C. 3-in-a-row side of 1964, 1965 and 1966. He was Galway's Secrtetary of the County Board for 43 years, 1937 to 1980, and was the county's Central County delegate from 1980 to 1988. He died in 1990.

DUNNE, LIAM.

G.A.A. hurling left half-back and centre-back, Wexford. Born in 1968. Club: Oulart-the-Ballagh. Making his inter-county senior debut in 1986, he won his first Leinster S.H.C. medal in the same year. He was the county's only All-Star in the 1990 selection, being picked at left half-back. He was on losing Wexford sides in the county's 3 National Hurling League final appearances of 1990, 1991 and 1993. His brother Thomas played alongside Liam in the National League final and two replays of 1993, while he is a sister of Siobhan Dunne (cv).

DUNNE, MICHAEL J.

Rugby international 2nd Row forward. Club: Lansdowne (winning Leinster Senior Cup medals in 1927, 1928, 1929, 1930, 1931, and as as captain in 1933). Playing 13 times at interprovincial level for Leinster, he was capped 16 times for Ireland between 1929 and 1934, and was a constant member of the International Championship-winning side of 1932. He toured Australia and New Zealand with the 1930 British and Irish Lion's, although not gaining a Test place.

DUNNE, PADDY.

G.A.A. football centre half back, Laois. Club: Park (whom he captained to their first ever county S.F.C. title in 1952). He won 3 Railway Cup medals in succession with Leinster in 1952, 1953, and 1954. One of the best defenders of his day, he was a star member of the Laois sides which were beaten in 2 Leinster S.F.C. finals, by Meath in 1952, and by Dublin in 1959.

DUNNE, PADRAIG.

G.A.A. football midfielder, Offaly. He has won one All-Ireland Senior Football Championship medal in the famous 1982 win over Kerry, having also played in the losing All-Ireland S.F.C. final side of 1981. He was selected at centrefield alongside Jack O'Shea (cv) for the 1982 All-Stars. He won a Railway Cup medal with Leinster in 1985.

DUNNE, SEAMUS.

Soccer international full back. Born in Wicklow, 13th April 1930. Clubs: Shelbourne, and Luton Town. He joined Luton in 1950, at the age of 20, and in 9 years there he played 300 league matches, and helped them to gain promotion from Division Two in 1955. He won 15 international soccer caps for the Republic of Ireland between 1953 and 1960.

DUNNE, SIOBHAN.

G.A.A. ladies gaelic football left full-forward, Wexford. Club: Shemaliers. A member of the Wexford team beaten in the All-Ireland Senior finals of both 1986 and 1989, she had previously won All-Ireland Under 16 winners medals (1981 and 1982), and Under 18 medals (in 1982, 1983 and 1984). A fine all-round sports person, she played on the Wexford camogie team in the All-Ireland semi-final in 1989, and has also played soccer for the Irish ladies team. A sister of Liam Dunne (cv).

DUNNE-FITZPATRICK, CATHY.

Wheelchair athlete. From Cork. She has competed successfully in 3 Paralympics, in 1980, 1984, and 1988. In the 1980 games she won two bronze medals, in the Discus and in the Pentathlon; in the 1984 games she won a gold medal in the Discus, and finished 4th in the Pentathlon; and in the Seoul Games of 1988 she won a silver medal in the Discus and a bronze in the Pentathlon. Also an active coach in the Cork area.

DUNNY, PAT.

G.A.A. hurling left full-back and centre half-back, and footballer, Kildare. Club: Raheens (with whom in 1976 he won, in the same week, the county championship and the Kilmacud-Crokes 7-a-side). After winning (at age 17) an All-Ireland Junior hurling medal in 1963, he went on in 1965, the 2nd year of the competition, to captain the Kildare football Under 21 side to victory in the All-Ireland Championship over Cork (he also played in the Under 21 football side beaten the following year's All-Ireland final). He starred for Kildare in the 1969 All-Ireland intermediate hurling championship. He was the first Kildare hurler (and the only to date) to win Railway Cup medals with Leinster. His tally of Railway Cup hurling medals is 4, winning in 1971, 1972, 1974 and in 1975. He also won a football Railway Cup medal as a sub in the 1974, thus joined the rare band to win interprovincial medals in both codes.

DUNPHY, EAMON M.

Soccer international midfielder. Born in Dublin, 3rd August 1943. Apprrenticed to Manchester United in 1962, he played English League football with York City, Millwall (playing 267 league matches for them 1965-1973, scoring 24 goals), Charlton, Reading, and Shamrock Rovers (winning an F.A.I. Cup medal in 1978). He was capped 23 times for the Republic of Ireland between 1966 and 1977. The 22 caps gained while at Millwall made him that club's most capped player. Later he became a sports journalist and writer, penning the well-regarded 'Only A Game' (about the professional footballers lot), and also writing a biography of Matt Busby. His son is a professional snooker player.

DUNWOODY, Thomas RICHARD.

Jump jockey. Born in Comber, Co Down, 18th January 1964. Moving to England in 1972, he rode his first winner at Cheltenham in 1983, and was later retained by David Nicholson, and from 1993, by Martin Pipe. One of the most accomplished jockeys in Britain, his major race wins have included West Tip in the 1986 Grand National, the 1986 Mackeson Gold Cup on Very Promising, the 1988 Cheltenham Gold Cup on Charter Party, and the 1990 Champion Hurdle on Kribensis. His other wins have included the Whitbread Trophy, the Ritz Club Handicap Chase, the Mecca Hurdle at Sandown, and he won the Ritz Club trophy for most successful jockey at the Cheltenham Festival in 1990. He won 2 King George's on the great Desert Orchid, and was on him when third in the 1991 Cheltenham Gold Cup. Riding over a hundred winners in a season for 4 successive years up to the 1992-93 season, he had strongly challenged Peter Scudamore for the jockey's title of 1990-1991 and had 136 winners in 1991-92. In 1992-93 he become champion jump jockey in Britain for the first time.

DURACK, SEAMUS.

G.A.A. hurling goalkeeper, Clare. Born in 1952. Club: Feakle. A regular in the Clare senior inter-county side from 1970, he was in goals when Clare won the National Hurling League title in successive years of 1977 (their first such award in 31 years) and 1978, having also played on the sides beaten in the 2 previous years' finals. He won a Railway Cup medal in 1978 with Munster. Although he never won a coveted Munster S.H.C. medal, he won All-Star awards on 3 occasions, in 1977 (becoming the first native Munster-man to win a hurling goalkeeper award), 1978, and in 1981.

DURKIN, NOEL.

G.A.A. football left half-forward, Mayo. Club: Ballaghadereen. He won an All-Ireland Under 21 medal with Mayo in 1983, also playing on the side beaten in the final of 1984. He was a member of the Mayo side which reached the county's first All-Ireland Senior Football Championship final in 38 years in 1989, when they lost to Cork. Winning another Connacht S.F.C. medal in 1993, he won an All-Star award in 1989 at right half forward.

DWYER, NOEL M.

Soccer international goalkeeper. Born in Dublin 30th October 1934. He left Ormeau to join Wolves in 1953, later playing for West Ham, Swansea City,

Plymouth and Charlton. He was capped at senior soccer international level in goals for the Republic of Ireland 14 times between 1960 and 1965.

DWYER, PAT.

G.A.A. hurling full-back, Kilkenny. Club: Carrickshock. Born in 1966. A member of the Kilkenny side beaten in the All-Ireland Senior Hurling Championship final of 1991, he went on win 2 successive Liam McCarthy Cup medals with the 'Black and Ambers' in both 1992 and 1993. He was made an All-Star in 1992 in the full-back position.

DWYER, Sgt PATRICK (PADDY).

Amateur international welterweight boxer. Club: Army. In 1924, after winning his only National Irish Senior Championship title in the welterweight division, he reached the semi-final of the Olympic Games in this weight in Paris, but as there was a box-off for the bronze medal in those days, he did not get a medal, losing to the Argentinian, Hector Mendez.

E

EAKIN, PAT and TRACY.

Amateur ladies international golfers, mother and daughter. Pat, a member of Co Louth G.C., was a Leinster player in the mid-60's, and played in the Home international side for Ireland in 1967. Her daughter Tracy, also a Co Louth player (and later Abbotsley GC), has played for the Ireland team in the Home international matches from 1990, thereby completing a mother and daughter representation for Ireland 25 years apart. Tracy reached the semi-final of the British Women's Championship at Saunton in 1992, and in 1993 won the inaugural Irish Women's Open Strokeplay event.

EARLEY, MARTIN.

Cyclist. From Hartstown, Clonsilla, Co Dublin, he represented Ireland in the 1984 Olympic Games Individual Time Trial at Los Angeles, finishing 19th. Turning professional, mainly as a domestique in Sean Kelly's teams, he won a stage in the Tour of Italy in 1986, and has also won 2 stages in the Tour of the Basque Country. In 1989, after winning the Tour of Vacluse and the Tommy Simpson Memorial, he became the fourth Irishman to win a stage in the Tour de France, winning the stage from La Bastide d'Armagnac to Pau. He has also led the tour of Britain, and has finished 7th in the World Championship. Based in Stoke, he is married to British international cyclist Catherine Swinnerton.

EARLY, DERMOT.

G.A.A. footballing midfielder, Roscommon. Born in Castlebar Co Mayo, 24th February 1948. Club: Michael Glavey. In 1966 he was a member of the first Roscommon side to capture the All-Ireland Under 21 title, also winning a provincial Under 21 medal in 1969. In the 1966-67 season he played in Roscommon county minor, junior, under-21, and senior levels, as well as Railway Cup and National League football, thus becoming the first player to play in every grade in the same season. In a career extending from 1965 to 1988 when he was undoubtedly Roscommon's best player, he helped the county to win 5 Connacht Senior Football Championship titles, in 1972 and the 4-in-a-row 1977-1980, and was a member of the last Roscommon side to reach an All-Ireland final, when they gave Kerry a mighty scare in 1980. He also won a National Football League winner's medal with the county in 1979. He won Railway Cup medals in both 1967 (as a sub) and 1969. In 1974 he was the games leading marksman, scoring 126 points from 10 goals and 96 points in 25 matches, with an average of 5.04 per game (a record for a Roscommon player). He won 2 All-Star awards, in 1974 and 1979, both at centrefield. An older brother of Paul Early (cv).

EARLY, PAUL.

G.A.A. football full-forward, Roscommon. Born in 1964. Club: Hyde's. Making his senior debut with Roscommon at the age of 17 in 1981, he has won two Connacht S.F.C. winner's medals with the county, in 1990 and 1991. He won an All-Star award in 1985 in the full-forward position, the only Roscommon player selected that year. A younger brother of Dermot Early (cv), he went abroad for 2 years to Melbourne, playing 'Footie' under Australian Rules.

EDDERY, JIMMY.

Flat jockey. One of many brothers from Doneraile who became jockeys, he was Irish Champion Jockey several times, having success in 4 Irish Classic races: winning the Irish 2,000 Guineas in 1944 with Good Morning (in a dead heat) and in 1945 with Stalino; the Irish Derby in 1955 with Panslipper (on whom he finished 2nd in the Epsom equivalent the same year, and was 3rd in the Epsom Derby again in 1956 on Roistar), and the Irish Oaks in 1957 with Silken Glider (on whom he was just beaten in the Epsom Oaks). He is the father of Pat Eddery (cv), and his wife is the daughter of steeplechase jockey, Jack Moylan (cv).

EDDERY, PATRICK James (PAT).

Jockey, flat racing. Born Blackrock, Co Dublin, 18th March 1952. Riding his first winner in 1969, his retainers have been Frenchie Nicholson, Peter Walwyn, Vincent O'Brien, and Prince Khalid Abdullah. Among his English Classic winners include 3 Epsom Derbys (with Grundy in 1975, in 1982 with his own personal favourite horse Golden Fleece, and in 1990 with Quest for Fame), two 2,000 Guineas (Lomond in 1983 and El Grand Senor in 1984), two Epsom Oaks (Polygamy in 1974, and Scintillate in 1979), the 1,000 Guineas in 1993 on Zaphonic, and 2 St Leger's, in 1986 with Moon Madness, and 1991. His Irish Classic wins include 4 Irish Derby's (1975 on Grundy, 1984 on El Gran Senor, 1985 on Law Society and 1993 on Commander-in-Chief), two 2,000 Guineas (1975 on Grundy and 1981 on King's Lake), 2 Oaks (1986 on Colorspin and 1993 on Weymyss Bight), and the 1985 St Leger on Leading Counsel. He has won 4 Prix de L'Arc de Triomphes (1980 on Detroit, 1985 on Rainbow Quest, 1986 on Dancing Brave, and 1987 on Trempolino), 3 French Derbys (Caerleon in 1983, in 1988 on Hours After, and in 1990 with Sanglamore), and won the French Oaks in 1992 on Jolphya. He has been champion jockey in Britain 9 times, in 1974 (when he became the first ever Irish-born jockey to hold the title over the flat) with 148 winners, 1975 with 164 winners, 1976 with 162 winners, 1977 with 176 wins, 1986 with 176, 1988 with 183 winners (in 1987 he had a seasons best of 195 winners, only to finish 2 behind Steve Cauthen), in 1990 (when he became the first jockey since Gordon Richards in 1952 to top 200 wins in a season, with a final tally of 209), and in 1991. He has ridden over 100 winners in 16 seasons, and his career tally of winners is over 3,200 (he was Irish Champion Jockey in 1982 with 66 winners). He has been Texaco's Horse Racing Sportstar of the Year a joint record number of 5 times, winning in 1971, 1974, 1982, 1986, and 1988. His father is Jimmy Eddery (cv), and his brother Paul (born 14th July 1963), is also a successful flat jockey who has placed 2nd in both the 1986 Epsom Oaks on Bourbon Girl, and in the 1987 Epsom Derby on Most Welcome.

EDWARDS, BRENDAN and MICHAEL.

Amateur international golfers, brothers. Club: Shandon Park (for whom Michael won 5 Irish Senior Cup medals, and Brendan won a record 10 Irish Senior Cup medals out of 10 finals, in 1960, 1961, 1962, 1964, 1966, 1968, 1971, 1972, 1973 and 1978). Michael, the older brother (born in Belfast, 3rd September 1931), won the Irish Close

Championship twice, in 1960 and 1962 (beating Jackie Harrington cv in a record 42 hole final); and the 'North' in 1955 and 1956 (and was runner-up in 1960). In 40 interprovincial matches for Ulster 1956-1963, he won 20; in 7 Home international series for Ireland 1956-63, he won 21 of his 40 matches. He was later an Irish selector and non-playing captain. Brendan won the North of Ireland title in 1966 and 1973. In 54 interprovincial matches for Ulster 1961-73, he won 26; in 49 Home international matches in 9 series for Ireland between 1961 (as a junior golfer) and 1973, he won 18. The brothers played in the same Home International squad in both 1961 and 1962. Brendan became a Walker Cup selector, and captained the Irish team which won the European Amateur Team Championship in Chantilly in 1983.

EDWARDS, R W.

Rugby international forward. Club: Malone. He played only once for Ireland, in their 14-12 win over Wales in 1904. As a result of this unlikely win he became the only Irish international selected on the 1904 Lions tour of Australia and New Zealand, and played in 3 Test matches, 2 winning matches in Australia and one losing test match in New Zealand.

EDWARDS, WILLIAM VICTOR.

Rugby international, swimmer, and water polo player. Born in Strandtown, 16th October 1887, he was killed in action at Jerusalem just after his 30th birthday in 1917. In rugby, as a Malone forward, he won 2 international rugby caps for Ireland in 1912. He was also an Irish water polo champion. In swimming he was Irish 200 yard champion, and has the distinction of being the first man to swim Belfast Lough.

EGAN, JOE.

Amateur and professional boxer. Born in Dublin 1965. Club: Donore. He was Irish National Senior Champion at super-heavyweight for 3 years in succession, in 1987, 1988 and 1989, having also won the event in 1984, and also won a New York Golden Globe award. His total amateur career was 87 wins out of 105 fights (including a win over Stephen Collins cv), and he represented Ireland 11 times in international boxing. He turned pro in early 1990.

EGAN, JOHN.

G.A.A. football left full-forward, Kerry. Born in Tahilla, 13th June 1952. Club: Sneem (winning a Towns Cup medal in 1972). A member of the beaten Kerry side in the 1970 All-Ireland M.F.C. final, he won an All-Ireland Under 21 Championship winner's medal in 1973. Playing senior county football from 1972, he was a star member of the great Kerry side of the 70's and early 80's, winning All-Ireland Senior Football Championship medals at right full forward in 1975, and at left corner forward in each of the 4-in-a-row victories form 1978 to 1981. He captained Kerry in 1982 when Seamus Darby spoiled the county's glorious bid for 5 successive titles, and was also on a losing All-Ireland final side in 1976. One of the modern game's most effective left corner forwards, he won his 6th All-Ireland Senior Football Championship medal with Kerry in the Centenary year of 1984. He has won 4 Railway Cup medals with Munster, in 1975, 1976, 1977, and 1981. He won All-Star recognition 4 times, in 1975 at right corner forward, and 3 times at left full-forward, in 1978, 1980, and 1982. A garda.

EGAN, JOHNNY.

G.A.A. footballing left full-back, Offaly. He was a member of the Offaly side which was beaten in the 1961 All-Ireland Senior Football Championship final by Down, and was captain of the Offaly side which was beaten in the 1969 final by Kerry, both in the left corner back position. He won a Railway Cup winner's medal with Leinster in 1961.

EGAN, MIKE.

Handballer. Born in Galway in 1880, although he was brought up in Pittsburgh, U.S.A. He won the inaugural Amateur American Union Handball championship in 1897. In 1902 he challenged Oliver Drew for the title of world champion (and a purse of 250 dollars), but the match was not completed. He beat James Fitzgerald of Tralee in 1904 in the U.S.A. to win the world title. Based in Jersey City, he died in 1954.

EGAN, THOMAS William (TOM).

Amateur international golfer. Clubs: Monkstown and Cork. Born in Cork, 18th August 1930. He won the Irish Close Championship in 1952, the 'East' in 1962 (and in doing so had an astonishing 8 consecutive birdies in the third round), and was runner-up in the 'South' in 1951. In 72 interprovincial matches for Munster (joint 2nd in most games for his province behind Tramore's Mike Burns) between 1956 and 1969, he won 36 matches; in 7 Home international series for Ireland between 1952 and 1969, he won 22 of his 44 matches. He was a member of the winning Irish side in the European Team championship win of 1967, also playing in 1969, winning 4 of his 10 matches in those years.

EGLINGTON, TOMMY.

Soccer international outside-left. Born in Dublin, 15th January 1923. After a time with Munster Victoria and Distillery (winning an F.A.I. Junior Cup medal in 1942), and a successful period at Shamrock Rovers (winning F.A.I. Cup medals in 1944 and 1945), he joined Everton in July 1946. During his eleven sparkling years at Goodison, he played in 394 league matches, scoring 76 league goals (once scoring 5 goals against Doncaster in 1952), and helping them to promotion from Division 2 in 1953-54. He then spent 3 seasons at Tranmere Rovers, scoring 36 goals. The Donnycarney-man played at international level 6 times for Northern Ireland 1947-1949, and was capped 24 times for Eire between 1946 and 1956.

ELDER, ALEX.

Soccer international full-back. Born in Glentoran, 25th April 1945. After a sparkling Irish league start, he transferred from the Glens to Burnley at the age of 18, winning a Championship medal in his first season with them, while altogether in his 8 seasons with them, scored 13 goals in 271 league appearances. He also got a runners-up medal in the 1962 F.A. Cup final against Spurs. He later played for Stoke. He was capped 40 times for Northern Ireland between 1960 and 1970, scoring one international goal. Injury prone, he was a great tackler, and had great powers of recovery.

ELLIOT, IAN A.

Amateur international golfer. Club: Royal Belfast, Belvoir Park. He won the North of Ireland title in 1986, having won the 'West' in 1975. He has played 83 interprovincial matches for his 2 provinces, Leinster and Ulster between 1969 and 1986, winning 40 and halving 5 of these; in 18 Home international matches 1975-78, he won 8. He also played in the European Team championship in 1975, winning 2 of his 6 matches.

ELLIOT, JIM.

Heavyweight boxer. Born in Athlone, Co Westmeath, 1838, he was killed in a gambling row in a bar in 1883. He claimed the American bare-knuckle heavyweight title in 1867-68. Having been jailed for his role in a championship fight against fellow-Irishman Jim Dunne (cv) in 1863, he won the title in 1867 by defeating Bill Davis of U.S.A. over 9 rounds in Canada in 1867, going on to beat Charlie Gallagher. After a period as a highwayman, and 8 years in jail, he fought for his title again in 1879, losing in another shady fight to Johnny Dwyer. A notoriously dirty boxer, his last fight, at the age of 44, was against the emerging 24-year-old John L Sullivan, who beat him easily in 3 rounds.

ELLIOT, SEAMUS (SHAY).

Cyclist, amateur and professional. Born in Dublin in 1934, he died of gunshot wounds in 1971, aged 36. In 1954, after a bright amateur career with the Southern Road and Dublin Wheelers clubs (which included winning the 50km Grand Prix of Ireland at the age of 17), he, by winning a prize in the An Tostal Race, was sent to a training camp in France. He then went on the professional road circuit on the continent in 1955. Although cast in the role of 'domestique' for the St Raphael-Gitane team, he won 3 Grand Prixs in 1956, 4 races in 1957, 2 in 1958, 6 in 1959 (including the minor classic, the Het Volk), 4 in 1960 (and the 18th Stage of the Giro d'Italia), and 2 wins in 1961. In 1962 he won the 4th stage of the Vuelta d'Espana (Tour of Spain), and led the race for 9 days, before finishing 3rd. In the same year he also won 6 races on the continent including 2 criteriums. In 1962 he also won a silver medal as runner-up in the world professional road championship. He was the first Irishman to wear the coveted yellow jersey (maillot jaune) in the Tour de France, leading the race for a period of 3 stages in 1963 (when he also won the 3rd and 13th stages), before eventually finishing 61st. Winning 2 races in 1964, he went on to win 6 in 1965 and won 7 criteriums in 1967. His career was full of 2nd place finishes, and hard luck stories, but he undoubtably was Ireland's best professional cyclist before the Kelly-Roche era. He was Texaco's Cycling Sportstar of the Year in 1962.

ELWOOD, ERIC Paul.

Rugby international out-half. Born in Galway, 26th February 1969. Clubs: Galwegians and Lansdowne (helping them as their leading points scorer to win Division Two of the All-Ireland League in 1993). A Connacht interprovincial player who came to prominence in the 1993 season, he scored 11 points of the Irish tally in his first cap, against Wales in 1993, when the team won it's first International Championship match in 11 outings, and scored 12 points (including 2 drop goals) in a brilliant display in the historic 17-3 win over England in his next match, only to be left out of the Lion's selection the following day. Also influential in Ireland's semi-final placing in the inaugural World Seven's in 1993, he was named as the R.W.I. Player of the Year for that year.

EMERSON, BILLY.

Soccer international No 6. Playing with Glentoran and Burnley, he was capped 11 times for Northern Ireland between 1920 and 1924, scoring one international goal. While with Glentoran, he won 3 Irish Cup medals, in 1914, 1917, and 1921, and also won 3 Irish League medals, in 1912, 1913 and 1921.

ENGLISH, JIM.

G.A.A. hurling right half-back, Wexford. He captained the Liam McCarthy Cup-winning Wexford side in the 1956 final, when the county beat Cork by 2-14 to 2-8. He was also in the 1955 and 1960 winning sides (making him one of only 6 players to play in a record 3 All-Ireland Senior Hurling Champinship-winning sides for Wexford). A quality half-back, he also played on the Wexford sides which lost the All-Ireland S.H.C. finals of 1954 and 1962, and won National Hurling League medals with the county in 1956 and 1958. He won a Railway Cup medal with Leinster in 1956.

ENGLISH, JOE.

Yachtsman. From Cobh, Co Cork, his clubs have included North Sails (in Kinsale) and McWilliams (in Crosshaven). Emigrating to Australia in 1979, he has helped Harold Cudmore win the World One Ton Cup, and worked for Hughie Treharne (who was tactitian for the famous Australian win in the America's Cup in 1983), Joe supervising the manufacturing of the ground-breaking spinnaker. He was later sail co-ordinator for the 'South Australia' attempt at the America's Cup. In 1989-1990 he was skipper on the N.C.B. Ireland boat which took part in the Whitbread Round-the-World race.

ENGLISH, MICHAEL Anthony Francis (MICK).

Rugby international outside-half. Born in Limerick, 2nd March 1933. Clubs: Lansdowne (winning a Leinster Senior Cup medal in 1965), and Limerick Bohemians. He was capped 16 times for Ireland between 1958 and 1963 as a successor to the great Jackie Kyle (and unusually, although capped in each of the six seasons, 7 others played at out-half for Ireland during that period). He toured New Zealand with the 1959 British and Irish Lion's side, having to come home early due to injury. His scoring total for Ireland was 3 drop goals. He helped Bohemians to 3 Munster Senior Cup wins, in 1958, 1959, and in 1962 when his brother Christy captained this side, sharing in all 3 wins.

ENGLISH, NICHOLAS (NICKY).

G.A.A. hurling left half-forward, and left corner-forward, Tipperary. Club: Lattin-Cullen. He won an All-Ireland M.H.C. medal with the Tipperary side in 1980, and won an All-Ireland Under 21 Championship medal in the following year (also being on the side which lost the 1983 final). He captained the Tipperary side which lost the 1988 All-Ireland S.H.C. final, before winning an All-Ireland Senior Hurling Championshp medal in 1989 (scoring a modern-day record tally of 2 goals and 12 points), and gaining a 2nd All-Ireland S.H.C. medal in 1991. Winning another Munster S.H.C. medal in 1993, he had won a National Hurling League medal with Tipperary in 1988. He has won Railway Cup medals with Munster in 1984 and 1985. He was selected as Ballygowan National Sports Person of the Year for both 1988 and 1989. He won Railway Cup medals with Munster in 1984 and 1985. One of the modern games finest exponents, he has won 6 All-Star awards, three in succession at left half-forward (in 1983, 1984, and 1985), two at full-forward, in 1987 and 1988, and in 1989 at left corner-forward. In 1989 he was selected as Texaco Sports Star of the Year in hurling.

ENGLISH, THEO.

G.A.A. hurling midfielder, Tipperary. He won 5 All-Ireland Senior Hurling Championship winner's medals with Tipperary, in 1958, 1961, 1962, 1964, and in 1965, and was on losing All-Ireland S.H.C. final sides in 1960 and 1967. He won 3 Railway Cup medals with Munster, in 1959, 1961, and in 1963 (as a sub). He was a member of the selection commitee for the Tipp side which won 3 successive Munster Championship titles in 1987, 1988, and in 1989 (when they also won the Liam McCarthy Cup).

ENRIGHT, LEONARD.

G.A.A. hurling full-back, Limerick. Born in 1953. Club: Patrickswell (winning many county championships, and being a member of the side beaten in the All-Ireland Championship Club final in 1991). He was a star Limerick performer in their Munster S.H.C. wins in 1980 (when they were beaten in the All-Ireland final by Galway) and 1981. He has won 2 Railway Cup medals with Munster, in 1984 and 1985, also winning National Hurling League medals with Limerick in the same years. He has been awarded 3 All-Star awards, all at full back, in 1980, 1981, and 1983.

ENSOR, ANTHONY Howard (TONY).

Rugby international full-back. Born in Dublin, 17th August 1949. Club: Wanderers (winning Leinster Senior Cup medals in 1973 and 1978, and Senior League medals in 1973, 1976 and 1979). A product of Gonzaga College, and a Leinster interprovincial over 20 times, he won 22 international rugby caps for Ireland between 1973 and 1978 (including all of the matches in the 1974 International Championship-winning season), as successor to Tommy Kiernan, and scored 28 international points, from one try and 8 penalties. A talented runner with the ball, he toured with Ireland to New Zealand and Fiji in 1976. His brother David B Ensor played one international cricket match for Ireland in 1969.

EVANS, JOHN.

G.A.A. football left full-back, Cork. Club: Skibereen. He was a member of the Cork side which beat Kerry for the first time in 9 years in the 1983 Munster S.F.C. final, and came on as a sub in Cork's All-Ireland Senior Football Championship final loss to Meath in 1987. He was selected as an All-Star at left corner back in 1983.

EWING, Reginald CECIL.

Amateur international golfer. Born in Rosses Point in July 1910, he died in 1973. Club: Co Sligo (Rosses Point), and Portmarnock (helping them to win 5 Senior Cups and 3 Barton Shields). He won the Irish Close Championship twice, in 1948 and 1958, being runner-up in 1946. He was also Irish Open Amateur Champion twice, in 1948 (when completing a rare double with the Close) and 1951, being runner-up in 1950 and 1954. He won the West of Ireland title 10 times on his home course, a record tally he shares with Joe Carr (cv), achieving his wins in 1930, 1932, 1935, 1939, 1941, 1942, 1943, 1945 (when he was also runner-up in the 'South'), 1949, and 1950, and was beaten finalist in this event 8 times (in 1928 when only 17, 1934, 1937, 1944, 1947, 1948, 1956 and 1958). His tally of 14 major Irish championship wins places him 3rd in such all-time wins. He was runner-up in the 1938 British Amateur Championship, losing at Troon in the final to the American Charlie Yates. A member of the first G.B.&I. Walker Cup winning side of 1938 at St Andrew's, he was a selector for Britain and Ireland's second victory in the series in 1971. He played on a total of 6 Walker Cup sides, the others being 1936, 1947, 1949 (when there was a record 4 Irishmen in the team), 1951, and 1953 (his record was 1 win, 7 losses, and 2 halves in the 10 matches he played in). He played in a total of 92 Home International matches for Ireland in 15 series over a 25 year period between 1934 and 1958 (placing him 2nd only in appearances to Joe Carr and he was the first to win 50 'caps'), winning 44 matches. He was one of only 5 players to play interprovincial golf in 1938-39, and again after the 17 gap in the competition, lining out for Connacht from 1957 up to 1963. He was Texaco's Golf Sportstar of the Year in 1967. He was non-playing captain when Ireland captured the European Team Championship in both Sandwich in 1965 and in Turin in 1967, and was President of the G.U.I. in 1970 (when he won the Irish Senior's title).

F

FAGAN, FIONAN.

Soccer international winger. Born in Dublin, 7th June 1930. He joined Hull City from Transport in 1951, for 2 seasons. In 6 seasons and 153 league appearances with Manchester City between 1953 and 1960, he scored 34 goals, winning a runners-up F.A. Cup medal in 1955. He then spent a season with Derby County, scoring 6 goals. He was capped 8 times by the Republic of Ireland between 1955 and 1961, scoring 5 international goals. In 1960 he was selected as Texaco Soccer Sportstar of the Year.

FAGAN, GEORGE ST LEGER.

Rugby international half-back. While attending Kingstown School in 1878, George Fagan won one international rugby cap for Ireland, against England (he also played twice for Leinster in the same season). His younger brother, Arthur, was capped for England once in 1887, giving them a unique place in rugby international history, as the first 2 brothers to play for different countries.

FAGAN, JOHN (JACK, 'KRUGER').

Soccer international forward. Club: Shamrock Rovers (being one of the famous 'Four F's' whose dynamic forward line which brought League of Ireland Championships in 1924-25 and 1926-27, and an F.A.I. Cup win in 1924). He won one international cap for Ireland, in the F.A.I.'s inaugural fixture after the split with the North, in a 3-0 defeat in Italy in 1926.

FAGAN, PATSY.

Snooker professional. Born 15th January 1951. He turned professional in 1976, and reached his career peak in 1977 when he won the prestigious U.K. Championship, beating Doug Mountjoy 12-9 in the final. A journey-man pro for many seasons, he has fought the dreaded yips, particularily with rest-shots.

FAGAN-FRENCH, KATHLEEN.

Wheelchair athlete. From Dublin. She competed in 2 Paralympics, in 1972 and 1976. In 1972 she won a silver medal in the 60m Track race, and a bronze in the Discus. In 1976 she won a silver in the 100m Track, and a silver medal for the Discus.

FAHY, SHAY.

G.A.A. footballing centre-fielder, Cork. Club: Nemo Rangers. Up to 1987 he was a Kildare footballer, and from then till the 1990 All-Ireland S.F.C. final, he did not fail to gain selection for Cork in a championship game. He was a member of the Cork side which was defeated in 2 successive All-Ireland S.F.C. finals by Meath in 1987 and 1988. He won All-Ireland Senior Football Championship winner's medals in both 1989 and in 1990 when selected as Man-of-the-Match in the win over Meath, also being selected that year as Texaco Gaelic Football Sportstar of the Year. He was selected as an All-Star midfielder in both 1988 and 1990. An army-man, he is also a No 8 rugby player, winning a Munster Senior League medal with Highfield, and played in the Munster Senior Cup final of 1987. He was on the Cork team which reached the 1993 All-Ireland S.F.C. final, when they lost to Derry.

FAIRCLOUGH, MICK.

Soccer international centre-forward. Born in Drogheda, 21st October 1952. Clubs: Drogheda, Huddersfield (playing 25 games for them 1971-1974), Dundalk (being the club's top scorer in 1980-81 season when they captured the F.A.I. Cup, and in 1981-82 when they won the League of Ireland Championship). He was capped twice for Republic of Ireland, both as a sub in 1982, while playing for Dundalk (and is the last player from the club to be capped).

FAIRWEATHER, S .

Professional golfer. He won the Irish Professional Championship twice, in 1926 at Malone, and in 1935 at Belvoir. He was the first man to win the Ulster Profesional Championship 5 times, winning 3-in-a-row in 1937, 1938 and 1939, and again in both 1945 and 1948 (he was runner-up in 1946).

FALLON, SEAN.

Soccer international player. Clubs: Glasgow Celtic (winning a Scottish League medal in 1953-54, and 2 Scottish Cup medals, in 1951 and 1954). He was capped 8 times at senior interntional soccer for the Republic of Irleand between 1951 and 1955, scoring 2 international goals.

FALLON, WILLIAM J (WILLIE).

Soccer international outside-left. Born in Dublin, 14th January 1912. Clubs: Brideville, Dolphin, Notts County, Sheffield Wednsday, Exeter City, and Shamrock Rovers (winning an F.A.I. Cup medal in 1940). He was capped 9 times for the Irish Free State between 1935 and 1939, scoring 2 international goals. His younger brother Peter D (born in Dublin 19th October 1922), an inside-right, joined Exeter with him in 1947 and played 110 league matches for them.

FARNAN, PADDY.

G.A.A football and hurling forward, Dublin. He has the distinction of winning All-Ireland minor medals in both codes in the same year, in 1954, when the Dublin hurlers beat Tipperary and the footballers beat Kerry. He went on to score the winning goal in the famous Dublin All-Ireland Senior Football Championship title win of 1958 against Derry (and won a 2nd Leinster S.F.C. medal in 1959). He also won a Railway Cup medal with Leinster in their 1959 win over Munsteer. He died in 1991.

FARQUHARSON, TOM G ('THE PENALTY KING').

Soccer international goalkeeper. Clubs: Anally, Cardiff City (for whom he made 445 1st team appearences between 1922 and 1935). He was on the Cardiff side which lost the F.A. Cup final in 1925, but 2 years later he was on the famous Cardiff City side which caused a major shock when beating Arsenal 1-0 in the F.A. Cup final, the only occasion the Cup has been won by a club outside England. He was capped 4 times for the Irish Free State, and 7 times in all by the I.F.A. (Northern Ireland), and in 1925 became the first player to refuse to play for the I.F.A. His tactic of rushing penalty-takers from the net as they approached the ball led the law to be changed in 1929. Retiring to Canada, he died in 1970.

FARRELL, BILLY ('JUICY').

Soccer centre-forward. Born in Bray, Co Wicklow in 1902. Clubs: Swifts, Bray Unknowns, Shamrocks. The main striker of the famous "Four F's" of Shamrock Rovers of the 1920's, he scored 58 league goals in less than 3 seasons (being League of Ireland's leading goalscorer in both 1924-25 and 1925-26), during which Rovers won the Grand Slam in 1924-25. His career was prematurely ended by a broken thigh in a motorcycle accident, at the age of only 26, not before winning 4 Inter-League caps, but controversially being omitted in the F.A.I.'s first full international in 1926. A brilliant player, he also excelled at cricket, being a Leinster interprovincial, and was a Co Wicklow billiards champion.

FARRELL, GUS.

Amateur boxer light-middleweight. Club: St Saviour's. He won the Irish National Senior Championship at light-middleweieght in 1965. Making a fine impression, later in the same year he was chosen as Texaco's Boxing Sportstar of the Year. He later boxed professionally.

FARRELL, JAMES Leo (JIMMY).

Rugby international 2nd and back row forward. (1903-1979). Club: Bective Rangers (winning Leinster Senior Cup medals in 1925 and 1932, and becoming the club's most capped player for a period). Fifteen times a Leinster interprovincial between 1925 and 1932, he was capped 29 times in the pack for Ireland between 1926 and the International Championship-winning year of 1932, 17 of these games on the winning side. A talented player noted for his high level of fitness, he won 5 Lion's test caps on the 1930 British and Irish tour of Australia and New Zealand. In 1927 he was one of only 3 Irishmen to be selected on a R.F.U. tour of Argentina. A farmer.

FARRELL, PATRICK A (PADDY).

National Hunt jockey. Born in 1930. He went to ride in England, and had 3 high finishes in the English jockey's championship: 5th in 1958-59 with 39 winners, 6th in 1959-60 with 39 winners, and 6th again in 1960-61 with 45 winners. He won the Queen Elizabeth Chase in 1956 on State Secret, and the 1959 Mildmay Chase on Liquidator. Having finished 3rd in the Aintree Grand National in 1961 on O'Malley Point, his career was ended with a broken back which he suffered in the 1964 race. His injury was responsible in a large way to the setting up of the Injured Jockeys Fund in Britain.

FARRELL, PETER B ('THE BOY FROM THE BORO').

Soccer international wing-half. Born in Dublin 16th February 1922. From Dalkey, his early club was Cabinteely United. He joined Everton from Shamrock Rovers (with whom he won an F.A.I. Cup medal in 1944, a shield medal, an inter-city medal, and 5 Inter-League caps) at the age of 24, in August 1946. In eleven fine years at Goodison Park (9 years of which he was captain of the side), he scored 14 goals in 421 league appearences. A tireless worker, he was capped 28 times for Eire between 1946 and 1957, and it was he who scored the famous winning goal (a lob over the head of the goalie, Bert Williams), while playing at inside-right, that beat England in the memorable match at Goodison Park in September 1949, the first time England had been defeated on home soil. He also won 7 caps for the I.F.A. 1947-1949. He later joined Tranmere Rovers, playing 100 games for them as player/manager, and retired in 1959, at the age of 37. He later managed Drogheda, St Patrick's Athletic and T.E.K.

FEARNS, DUGGAN ("THE IRISH BOATSWAIN").

Bare-knuckle prize fighter. He was the 2nd of only 3 Irish-born fighters to win the Bare-knuckle Championship, which he did in a so-called 'cross' (a fix), when, on September 25th 1779, at Slough, he defeated the then champion, Englishman Harry Sellars) in 90 seconds. After that fight Fearns was never heard of again.

FEE, F.

Cricket international bowler. A classy bowler, who although playing only 13 cricket matches for Ireland (between 1956 and 1959), his average of 12.56 runs per wicket is the best post-War average figure for any Irish bowler (he took 58 wickets in his 19 innings). In the 1957 match against Scotland he had the best ever inning's figures of any Irish bowler, with 9 for 26 (and remains as one of only 4 Irish internationals to take 9 wickets in an innings). He also scored a total of 132 runs for Ireland in his 13 matches.

FEENEY, JIMMY M and WARREN.

Father and son soccer internationals. Jimmy, a full-back, was born in Belfast, 23rd June 1921. Clubs: Linfield, Swansea City, and Ipswich. Playing 10 years in English League football, he was capped twice for Northern Ireland, once in 1947 against Scotland, and again in 1950 against England. His son Warren (Glentoran and Linfield), was capped once in 1976 agaist Israel in the No 11 jersey, and played many times for the Irish League, scoring 5 goals for this side.

FEHERTY, DAVID.

Professional golfer. Born in Bangor, Co Down, 13th August 1958. A product of Bangor G.S., he turned pro in 1976, and won the Irish Profesional titles in 1980 and 1982. His European victories include the 1983 Tournament Player's Championship and Bob Hope Classic (in the same month), and the 1989 BMW International (which gave him an Order of Merit placing of 10th; he later finished 8th in 1990 and 14th in 1991), the 1991 Cannes Open and the 1992 Madrid Open. In 1991 he went on to win a Ryder Cup place for the first time, gaining 1 out of a possible 3 points in the losing series at Kiawah Island, U.S.A. (including a win over U.S. Open champion Payne Stewart in the singles). Victories outside Europe include the 1984 ICL Tournament and the 1988 Lexington P.G.A. Championship, both in South Africa. In 1986 he won both the Scottish Open and the Italian Open, and represented Ireland in the Dunhill Cup. He was captain of the Irish side which won the 1990 Dunhill Cup, playing the king-pin role in the final with a brilliant tie-hole win over Howard Clarke at the infamous 17th hole in St Andrew's, and also helped Ireland to finish joint 2nd in the 1990 World Cup, with a final round of 63. He was a member of the European side which won the Four Tours title in Australia in 1991. In the British Open of 1989 he was the highest finishing European challenger. He was selected as golf's Texaco Sportstar of the Year in both 1990 and 1991.

FEIGHERY, CON and TOM.

Rugby international playing brothers. Con (born in Dublin, 16th January 1945), a U.C.D. and Lansdowne 2nd row forward (winning a Leinster Senior Cup medal in 1972), won 3 international caps for Ireland in 1972 (all on winning teams). His older brother Tom, a U.C.D. and St Mary's prop forward (born 15th June 1946), won 2 international caps 5 years later in 1977 (both on losing sides), and also toured New Zealand and Fiji with Irealnd in 1976 (he won Leinster Senior Cup medals with both clubs he played for). Both played senior interprovinsial rugby for Leinster, Con 12 times, and Tom 10 times, being in the side twice together. Con is a brother-in-law of Barry Bresnihan (cv). Both are doctors.

FENLON, PAT.

Soccer midfielder. Born in Dublin in 1969. Clubs: Rivermount (Finglas), Chelsea (for 18 months), St Patrick's Athletic (winning a League of Ireland Championship medal in 1989-90) and Bohemians (winning an F.A.I. Cup medal in 1992). An Under 21 and 'B' international with the Republic of Ireland, he was nominated for the P.F.A.I. player of the year award in 1992.

FENNELLY, GER.

G.A.A. hurling half-forward, Kilkenny. Born 22nd January 1854. Club: Ballyhale Shamrocks. He was on the winning Kilkenny side in the 1972 All-Ireland M.H.C., and 2 years later was captain of the winning Kilkenny Under 21 All-Ireland side in 1974, gaining a second medal in 1975. He was captain, at right half-forward, of the winning Kilkenny side in the 1979 Liam McCarthy Cup, who beat Galway by 2-12 to 1-8 (and when brother Liam was captain of the 1983 side, they became the first brothers to captain All-Ireland S.H.C. sides). He won 2 other All-Ireland S.H.C. medals with Kilkenny, in 1982 and 1983, and was a losing finalist in 1978 and 1987. He was a member of the Ballyhale Shamrocks which won the All-Ireland Club Hurling titles in 1981, 1984 and 1990, and was one of 7 brothers on the side which won the Leinster club Championship in 1989. He won an All-Star award in 1983 at centre half-forward. He is the older brother of both Kevin (cv) and Liam (cv), while another brother, Sean, was captain of the All-Ireland M.H.C. winning side of 1977. A first cousin, Mary Fennelly, captained Kilkenny to win the All-Ireland Camogie Championship title in 1976 against Dublin.

FENNELLY, KEVIN.

G.A.A. hurling goalkeeper, Kilkenny. Club: Ballyhale Shamrocks. He was a member of the winning Kilkenny side in the 1972 All-Ireland M.H.C. title. He was captain of the Kilkenny side which won the 1975 All-Ireland Under 21 Championship title, having played on the victorious side also in 1974. He has won 3 All-Ireland Senior Club Championship medals with Ballyhale Shamrock's in 1981, 1984 (as captain), and 1990. He has won one All-Ireland S.H.C. medal, coming on as a sub in the 1979 Kilkenny win, and played on the losing side in the 1987 All-Ireland final, when four Fennelly brothers played in a final (Kevin, Sean, Ger and Liam), thus emulating the 1970 feat of the Quigleys (cv).

FENNELLY, LIAM.

G.A.A. hurling forward, Kilkenny. Born on 1st January 1958. Club: Ballyhale Shamrocks. A member of the Kilkenny minors beaten in the All-Ireland M.H.C. final in 1976, he has won 3 All-Ireland Senior Hurling Championship medals with Kilkenny; in 1982 at left corner forward, and twice as captain: in 1983 when he led his side from left half-forward to defeat Cork by 2-14 to 2-12, and in 1992 when Cork were again beaten, this time by the score of 3-10 to 1-12, so becaming the first captain to recieve the newly commisioned Liam McCarthy Cup (and therefore the first captain to hold both new and old cups aloft). He was on losing Kilkenny sides in the All-Ireland S.H.C. finals of 1987 and 1991. He has won 4 All-Star awards, in 1983, 1985, 1987 (these 3 at left full-forward), and in 1992 at full-forward. He was a member of the Ballyhale Shamrocks side which won the 1981, 1984 and 1990 All-Ireland club titles. A brother of Ger (cv) and Kevin (cv), his 4 other brothers shared in the All-Ireland Club successes.

FENNIG, SEAMUS.

Amateur snooker and billiards player. A Dublinman, in 1935 he set a world record snooker score for an amateur. Dominating the early Irish championships at both snooker and billiards, he won more than 20 major titles at these sports, ranking him as probably Ireland's finest ever amateur on the 'green baize'. He captured the Irish snooker championship 5 times between 1933 and 1955, and also won the National billiards championships 4 times. He won the All-Ireland snooker title (fought out between the winner of the south and north championships) 4 times. In a famous exhibition match in 1955 against the great Australian player Horace Lindrum, Fenning won by 2-1. In 1974 he was elected into the Texaco Hall of Fame.

FENTON, JOHN.

G.A.A. hurler, midfielder, Cork. Born in December 1954. Club: Midleton (captaining the side to win their first Cork S.H.C. title for 67 years in 1983, winning an All-Ireland Club title with them in 1988, and again winning a county championship in 1991). A product of Midleton C.B.S., he won an All-Ireland Under 21 medal with Cork in 1976 while at right half back, and was on the bench in Cork's 1978 All-Ireland S.H.C. win. Having been on the Cork side which lost the 1983 final, in 1984 he captained the Cork hurling side which won both the Centenary Cup and the All-Ireland Senior Hurling Championship (played at Semple Stadium, thus becoming only the 2nd captain to receive the trophy outside 'Croker'); he also captained the Munster side which retained the Railway Cup (thus becoming the 15th Corkman to do so). He was also, with 96 points, Cork's leading scorer in competitions that season. He won his 2nd Liam McCarthy medal in 1986. He also won 2 other Railway Cup medals, in 1981 and 1985, and won 2 National Hurling League medals in 1980 and 1981. He was made Texaco Hurler of the Year of 1984, and won 5 successive All-Star awards, in 1983, 1984, 1985, 1986, and 1987, all in the midfield.

FERGUSON, DES ('SNITCHIE').

G.A.A. footballing forward, and hurling right corner back, Dublin. Born in Co Down in 1931. Clubs: St Vincent's of Dublin (winning Dublin SFC and SHC medals) and Gael Colmcille (winning 2 Meath SFC medals, including the club's first ever, and one IHC medal). Playing minor at both grades in 1948, his senior inter-county career in both grades spanned from 1949 to 1964. He won 2 All-Ireland Senior Football Championship medals with Dublin, in 1958 and 1963, also playing on the losing side in the All-Ireland S.F.C. final of 1955 (he won 2 further Leinster S.F.C. medals, in 1959 and 1962). In hurling he played with 2 Dublin sides which were beaten in All-Ireland S.H.C. finals (in 1952 and 1961), and won 2 Railway Cup medals with Leinster at right full-back. His son, Terry, was left full-back on the Meath side which won the 1988 All-Ireland S.F.C. winning side, and also played on the losing final sides in 1990 and 1991 (when he won an All-Star award at left half-back), also playing for the Gael Colmcille's club.

FERGUSON, Miss DAISY.

Ladies amateur international golfer. She won the Irish Ladies Close Championship in 1935, having been runner-up in 1932. She won the Ulster Ladies Senior Championship twice, in 1931 and 1933, and was runner-up in both 1930 and 1934. She represented Ireland in 12 Home International series between 1927 and 1938, and was non-playing captain in 1961. In 1958 she was non-playing captain of the British and Irish Curtis Cup side.

FERGUSON, WILLIAM J J.

Amateur international golfer. Club: Malone (winning Senior Cup medals in 1951, 1954 and 1955). He was runner-up in the North of Ireland Championship in both 1973 and 1975. He played in 32 Home International matches in 6 series for Ireland between 1952 and 1961, gaining 32 points from 14 wins and 4 halves. He also played 40 Interprovincial matches for Ulster between 1956 and 1964, winning 24. He was President of the G.U.I. in 1984.

FERRIS, ANN (nee ROONEY).

Jump jockey. From Glengormley, near Belfast, her big wins include the 1976 Ulster Grand National, and the 1979 Sweeps Hurdle at Leopardstown on Irian. In the Irish Grand National of 1984, she rode Bentom Boy, trained by her father Willie Rooney (a Welsh-born jockey who finished 2nd in the same race in 1952 on Barney's Link, and who won a world record 401 point-to-points), to become the first woman jockey to win this prestigious race, while in 3rd place, riding Dawson Prince (also trained by Willie Rooney), was her younger sister, Rosemary Stewart (who married Irish international show jumper George Stewart). Ann and Rosemary have each won a number of awards for leading lady amateur rider of the season, Ann in 1980 (having been leading point-to-point rider in 1976), and Rosemary in 1981, 1982, 1983 and 1984 (having been leading point-to-point rider in 1977). Ann's sister Eyssen Ross took over her father's stables in 1985, and daughter Gay has also ridden winners.

FERRIS, GORDON.

Heavyweight boxer, amateur and professional. Born in Enniskillen, Co Fermanagh, 21st November 1952. Amateur club: Enniskilen. He won 4 Irish National Senior Championship titles as an amateur, 3 at light-heavyweight (1973, 1975, and 1976), and one at heavyweight, in 1977. Turning pro, he won the British Heavyweight title in 1981, beating Englishman Billy Aird for the vacany title. He lost his title 7 months later to Neville Meade of Wales, in a first round knock out. His 26 professional bouts in a 5 year career resulted in a 20-6 win-lose ratio.

FERRIS, J HUGH.

Rugby international scrum-half. Born in 1876. Clubs: Queen's University, Belfast (winning an Ulster Senior Cup medal in 1900). He is one of only 3 Irish internationals to susequently play for another major rugby nation. He was capped 4 times for Ireland in 1900 and 1901, never being on a winning international side. In 1903 he was capped for South Africa against the British Lions, and in his last representative match, at last won an international game.

FERRIS, RAY,

Soccer international wing-half. Born in Newry, 22nd September 1920. Clubs: Brentford, Crewe Alexander, Birmingham City. He won 3 international soccer caps for Northern Ireland while playing at Birmingham, in 1950-1952, scoring one international goal. His father, Jimmy (of Belfast Celtic and Chelsea), won 5 soccer caps as an inside forward for Northern Ireland between 1920 and 1928, also scoring one international goal, although injury cut short his career.

FERRIS, SAMUEL (SAM).

Long-distance athlete. Born in Dromore, Co Down, 29th August 1900.

Club: R.A.F. He won the first 3 runnings of the British A.A.A. marathon titles, in 1925 (in 2 hours, 35 minutes and 58.2 seconds), 1926 (2 hours, 42 minutes and 40.2 seconds), and 1927 (2 hours, 40 minutes and 32.2 seconds), and finished 2nd to the record breaking Harry Payne in 1929. He won the London Polytechnic Marathon 8 times, in 1925, 1926, 1927, 1928, 1929, 1931, 1932 and in 1933. Competing in 3 successive Olympic Games, and having finished 5th in the Olympic marathon in Paris in 1924, and 8th in that race in Amsterdam in 1928, he went on in 1932 while representing Great Britain, at the age of 32, to win a silver medal over the distance at the Olympic Games in Los Angeles, as a fast-finishing 2nd place (18 seconds in arrears) behind the Argentine Juan Zabala (so strong was his finishing burst that it is acknowledged that with different tactics, he won have won easliy), who won in a time of 2 hours 31 minutes and 36 seconds. He also won the Windsor to London marathon many times. He died in 1980.

FETHERSTONHAUGH, ROBERT (BOB or 'OLD BOB').

Horse trainer, flat and National Hunt. Born in Co Westmeath in 1873, he was a trainer for Major D.H.B. McCalmont. His Ballybogan won the Irish Grand National in 1925, also winning the Leopardstown Chase and finishing 2nd in the Aintree Grand National behind Poethlyn. He also won the Irish Grand National in 1925 with Dog Fox. His tally of Irish Classics wins over the flat is 9: one dead-heated Irish 2,000 Guinesa in 1944 with Slide on; 2 Irish 1,000 Guineas (Spy Ann in 1933 and Sunlit Ride in 1949); 2 Irish Derby's (Slide On in 1944 and in 1945 with Piccadilly); 2 Irish Oaks winners (1944 with Avoca and 1949 with Circus Lady); and 2 Irish St Leger winners (1939 with Skoiter and in 1946 with Cassock). His son, Robert N 'Brud' Fethersonhaugh, was a leading amateur jockey, who along with his sister Connie trained the winner of the 1955 Irish Oaks, Agar's Plough, and the 1962 Irish 1,000 Guineas, Shandon Bells.

FILGAS, SIMON.

Hockey international forward. Club: Avoca. First capped for Ireland in 1982, he won 68 international caps up until his retirement, at the age of 29, in 1990, and scored 11 goals for his country. From 1979 up to 1988 he had also won 46 indoor caps. One of Leinster's most gifted players of the 1980's, he won Mills Cup medals with Avoca (1982 and 1985), and Leinster Senior League medals in 1983, 1984, and 1985. He toured with Ireland to 2 Intercontinental Cups (Barcelona in 1985, and New Jersey in 1989), two European Championships (Amsterdam and Moscow), and to the World Cup in Lahore in 1990. His father, Frank M Filgas (born in Carlow, 3rd November 1926), a Clontarf and Leinster right-hand batsman and wicketkeeper, was capped at cricket for Ireland once (against Scotland in 1948).

FINLAY, J and TOM.

G.A.A. hurling brothers, Laois. J captained Laois's only All-Ireland Senior Hurling Championship title-winning side in 1915, when the Ballygeehan team beat the Cork team, Redmonds by 5-4 to 3-2. His brother Tom Finlay was on that team, having also played on the side which were beaten in the final the previous year. Tom also won an All-Ireland S.H.C. medal with Dublin in 1924, and won Laois County Championship medals with the Ballygeehan club in 1914, 1915, 1916, 1917, and 1918.

FINN, JIMMY.

G.A.A. hurling right-half forward and right full-back, Tipperary. Club: Borrisoleigh. A farmer, he was at centre half-back on the Tippearary minor side which won the 1949 All-Ireland M.H.C. He was captain of the Tipperary 1951 Senior Hurling Championship side which beat Wexford by 7-7 to 3-9 in the

All-Ireland final, thus completing the Liam McCarthy Cup 3-in-a-row for the county, he himself having also played in the triumph of the previous year. He won a third All-Ireland Senior Hurling Championship medal in 1958. He won 2 Railway Cup medals with Munster, in 1957 and 1958. He was voted into the right half-back spot on the Sunday Independent's 'Team of the Century' in the 1984 Centenary Year. His son, P J Finn, was a talented national hunt jockey, and later trainer.

FINN, JOHN.

G.A.A. football left half-back, Mayo. Club: Mayo Gaels. He was at left half-back on the Mayo side which won the All-Ireland Under 21 Champinship in 1983, also playing on the side beaten in the final of 1984. A winner of Connacht S.F.C. medals in 1985, 1988, 1989 and 1993, he was on the Mayo Senior Football Championship side which won its way into the All-Ireland final for the first time in 38 years in 1989.

FINN, MAURICE Cornelius ('MOSS').

Rugby wing and centre threequarter. Born in Cork, 29th March 1957. Clubs: U.C.C. and Cork Constitution. A product of P.B.C., Cork, he won a schools international cap in 1975, followed by a 'B' international cap in 1977. He was capped 14 times for Ireland between 1979 and 1986, waiting 15 games for his 2nd cap after his debut in 1979, and was a member of the victorious Irish Triple Crown-winning side of 1982, scoring 2 tries against Wales in that famous year. His total tally of tries for Ireland is four. One of a select few who have represented Ireland at all four levels, School's, Under-23, 'B' level, and Full, he was a member of the famous Munster team which beat the All-Blacks 12-0 in Thomond Park in 1978.

FINNERTY. PETER.

G.A.A. hurling right half-back, Galway. Born on 4th March 1967. Club: Mullagh. A member of the winning Galway minor team in the 1983 All-Ireland Championship, he has won 2 All-Ireland Senior Hurling Championship medals as a powerful wing-back with Galway, in 1987 and 1988. He was also on Galway sides beaten in 4 All-Ireland S.H.C. finals, in 1985, 1986, 1990 and 1993 (as a sub). A fine wing half back, and twice named man-of-the-match for All-Ireland semi-final displays (in 1987 and 1990), he won 4 successive All-Star awards, in 1985, 1986, 1987 and 1988. Being the country's most accomplished right half-back in the late 1980's, he gained a fifth All-Star in that position in 1990.

FINNEY, TOM.

Soccer international forward. Born in Belfast, 6th November 1952. He left Crusaders at the age of 21 to join Luton, later playing for Sunderland and Cambridge, with whom he scored 53 league goals in 181 matches, 1976-1980. He played 14 times for Northern Ireland between 1975 and 1980, 7 of these caps while based at Abbey Stadium, Cambridge, making him that club's most capped player.

FINNUCANE, AL.

Soccer international wing-half. From Quinn's Cottages, Rossbrien, Co Limerick, he was born in 1944. Clubs: Reds United, Limerick (getting 2 F.A.I. Cup runners-up medals in 1965 and 1966 before captaining the winning side in 1971 F.A.I. Cup), Waterford (for 9 seasons, becoming, with the F.A.I. Cup win of 1980, only the 2nd player to captain 2 different clubs to Cup success), and Limerick again (capturing another F.A.I. Cup medal in 1982). Selected to play for the League of Ireland XI 16 times in a League career that stretched for an amazing 28 years, in 1988 he became the oldest player ever to play a European Cup tie, when aged 44 years old. One of the League's great stalwarts, he also won 11 senior international caps for the Republic of Ireland (all while at Limerick), between 1967 and 1972. In 1967 he was voted as the S.W.A.I. 'Player of the Year'.

His brother Anthony was capped at Under 21 level for Ireland as a goalkeeper.

FISHER, BERTIE.

Car rally driver. From Ballinamallard, Co Fermanagh, he was born c 1950. He has won the Irish Tarmac Driver's Championship 3 times, in 1990, 1992 and 1993 (and was unlucky not to win in 1991). His international rally wins have included 2 Ulster Rallys (in 1982 and 1991), a record-equalling 3 Donegal Rallys (1985, 1992 and 1993), the Cork Rally in 1992, and a record 4 Killarney Rally wins (in 4 successive years 1990, 1991, 1992 and 1993). Ulster's best rally driver in recent times, he has won many national rallies on the Isle of Man (he almost won the Manx International rally in 1991), he has yet to win the Circuit of Ireland Rally.

FISHER, CHRISTY.

G.A.A. full-forward, Monaghan. Born in Drogheda, Co Louth. The most celebrated Monaghan player of his day, he played senior inter-county football for the county from 1924 to 1938. He helped the county to win Ulster Senior Football Championship titles in 1927, 1929 (when he scored 5 points in the final replay) and 1930 (when they lost to Kerry in Monaghan's first appearence in the All-Ireland final). Picked to play for Ulster many times, he was a sub on the Ireland team who played America in 1928.

FITZGERALD, CIARAN Fintan ('FITZY').

Rugby international hooker. Born in Galway, 4th June 1952. He was educated at St Joseph's Ballinasloe, Garbally College (in 1970 he was at full forward on the Galway minor hurling side beaten in the All-Ireland M.H.C. final), and at U.C.G. Club: St Mary's College. Capped at B level in 1976, he was capped for Ireland 26 times between 1979 and 1986 (making him the country's 3rd most capped hooker), scoring one try (against Wales in 1980). He captained Ireland 20 times (9 of them wins), his tally of leaderships placing him 2nd for Ireland behind Tom Kiernan (cv). His captaincy of both of Ireland's Triple Crown-winning sides of 1982 and 1985 (he is one of only 6 players to appear in all 6 of the 2 Triple Crown season matches), and of the International Championship in 1983 (a feat on a par with that of Karl Mullen's), ranks him among the great Irish captains at any sport. He was the captain of the British and Irish Lion's that suffered the 4-0 Test series defeat against New Zealand in 1983, the tour record being 18 played, 12 won, 6 lost, scoring 478 points for, and against 276. In 1983, as recognition for his leadership of Ireland's glories of 1982 and 1983, he was selected as Texaco's Rugby Sportstar of the Year. He became the national team's 9th coach in 1990, leading them on tour to Namibia in 1991, and to their successful run to the side's unlucky quarter-final defeat to Australia in the World Cup in 1991. An ex-Army officer, now in business.

FITZGERALD, DESMOND Christopher ('DESSIE FITZ').

Rugby international tight-head prop. Born in Dublin 20th December 1957. Clubs: Dublin University, Lansdowne and De La Salle Palmerston. As a youth he won Dublin and Leinster weight-lifting titles, and was 3rd in the Irish Championship. Having gone on the Irish tour to South Africa in 1981 (playing first for Leinster in 1980), he was capped at Ireland 'B' level in 1983, and since the following year has won 33 (up to June 1992) full international caps for Ireland, playing once on the loose head. He played on the British and Irish Lion's side versus the Rest of the World in 1986 (thus being accorded full Lions honours), and was a World Cup tourist with Ireland in 1987. He toured Namibia with Ireland in 1991, and was a member of the fine Irish side which just lost out to eventual winners Australia in the the quarter-final of the 1991 World Cup.

FITZGERALD, DICK ('DICKEEN').

G.A.A. footballing forward, Kerry. Born in 1884 in College Street Killarney. He is a winner of 5 All-Ireland Senior Football Championship medals with Kerry (the county's first five titles), in 1903 (scoring, at the age of 17, the vital winning goal for the Tralee Mitchells side), then in 1904 and 1909 again for Tralee Mitchells, and finally as captain for the last 2 wins by the Killarney Dr Crokes team, of 1913 (beating Wexford's Raparees by 2-2 to 0-3), and 1914 when the margin over the Blues and Whites team from Wexford was 2-3 to 0-6 after a replay. He thus became, along with Maurice McCarthy (cv), the first Kerryman to win 5 All-Ireland senior medals. He won a total of 10 Munster S.F.C. medals with Kerry, having also appeared in 3 other losing All-Ireland finals, in 1905, 1908, and in 1915 as captain. He died in 1930, aged 46. He wrote the highly acclaimed book, 'How to Play Gaelic Football', a best-seller. Fitzgerald Stadium Stadium in Killarney is named in his honour.

FITZGERALD, EAMONN.

G.A.A. footballer, Kerry, and athlete. He was a member of the Kerry side which won the All-Ireland Senior Football Championship in both 1930 and 1931. In 1932, representing Ireland, he finished 4th in the Olympic Games Hop, Step and Jump (the fore-runner to the Triple Jump), when his leap of 49' 3' was only 4 inches behind the bronze medal position of a Japanese, although 2' 4" behind the world-record-breaking winner, Chuhei Nambu (also of Japan).

FITZGERALD, GER.

G.A.A. hurling corner-forward, Cork. Club: Midleton (winning an All-Ireland Club Championship medal in 1988). He won All-Ireland Senior Hurling Championship medals with Cork in both 1986 and in 1990, and was captain of the Cork side defeated in the 1991 All-Ireland S.H.C. final. His father, Paddy Fitzgerald, had earlier won an All-Ireland S.H.C. medal with Cork in the half-back line of 1966.

FITZGERALD, F JACK and PETER J.

Soccer international brothers. Jack (born in Waterford, 3rd April 1930), scored 130 League of Ireland goals in the period 1951 and 1965, placing him 9th in the all-time list, and he scored 6 goals for the League of Ireland XI in that time. While at Waterford he won 2 international caps for the Republic of Irland, both against Holland, in 1955 (when he scored the only goal) and 1956. His younger brother Peter (born in Waterford, 17th June 1937), was a winger and centre-forward with Sparta Rotterdam, Waterford (winning a runners-up medal in the F.A.I. Cup in 1959), Leeds United, St Patrick's Athletic and Chester, and scored 2 international goals in the 5 Republic of Ireland matches he played in 1961 and 1962 (he also played 4 times for the League of Ireland). Four other brothers also played top level soccer: Denny won inter-League and amateur caps as a winger; Tom was capped as an amateur at right-back; Ned was a Waterford and Dundalk centre-half who was once a reserve for Ireland; and Paul played on the right wing for Waterford. On many occasions in the 1950's 3 or more of the brothers lined out for Waterford F.C.

FITZGERALD, JAMES.

Handballer. Born in Tralee, Co Kerry in 1870, he died of T.B. at the age of 39 in 1909. He was Irish Professional Champion from 1890 to 1898. Emigrating to the U.S.A., he challenged Michael Egan in 1904 for the tilte of World Champion, but lost heavily.

FITZGERALD, JOE.

Pitch and putt player. Clubs: N.B.P.M. and Ferrybank. He won 3 Irish pitch and putt national championship titles in the space of six years, with 2 National Matchplay Championship wins in 1977 and 1981, both played at the Rocklodge Co Cork course (he was also runner-up in 1975), followed in 1982 by his only win in the National Strokeplay Championship. A keen soccer player in his youth, he died in 1986.

FITZGERALD, JOHN Joseph ('PACO').

Rugby international loose head prop forward. Club: Young Munster (winning a Munster Senior Cup medal in 1984 and helping the club to it's historic All-Ireland League success in 1993; his brother Michael was on the Shannon side which beat the Munsters in the 1991 Munster Senior Cup final). Winning his first cap in 1988 on the open side of the scrum in place of the retiring Phip Orr (cv), his international cap tally reached 10 by the end of the 1992 international campaign, during which he scored an international try. He gained his first Munster cap in 1985. He toured Namibia with Ireland in 1989.

FITZGERALD, MAURICE.

G.A.A. football right half-forward, Kerry. Born in 1970. From Cahirciveen. In 1988 (at the tender age of 18 and only recently playing senior inter-county football) he became the only Kerry player to be nominated in the All-Star team, when being placed at right half-forward after only one championship season. In 1989 he won the World long-kicking championship in Melbourne. A brilliant place-kicker, he won his first Munster S.F.C. medal in 1991 (kicking 11 points in the final). His father Ned played inter-county football for Kerry.

FITZGERALD, MICK.

G.A.A. football right full-back, Offaly. Club: Gracefield. A member of the Offaly side beaten by Kerry in the 1981 All-Ireland S.F.C. final, he exacted sweet revenge when he was a star player in the side which won the famous 'Seamus Darby' final for 1982. He was selected at right back on the 1982 All-Star side. His brother, Pat Fitzgerald, played as an attacking wing-back in those All-Ireland final games of 1981 and 1982 with Mick.

FITZGERALD, PAUL.

Amateur international boxer. Club: Arklow. He won six Irish National Senior Championship titles: at bantamweight in 1982 and 1983, while he captured the featherweight title in 1984, 1986, 1987, and 1988. He represented Ireland at 2 Olympic Games, at the Los Angeles Games of 1984 (when winning 2 bouts) and in the Seoul Games of 1988. Latterly based in the U.S.A., he has won the Golden Gloves of both Pennsylvania and Philadelphia.

FITZGIBBON, EDWARD.

Angler. Born in Limerick in 1803. Regarded as one of the world's finest all-time fisherman. Once, on the River Shin in Scotland, in a bout of 55 hours continuous fishing, he caught a total of 55 grilse and salmon. He wrote extensively on fishing, mainly in the 'Observer' newspaper, and his classic books on fishing include 'Handbook of Angling' and 'The Book of Salmon'. A heavy drinker, he died in 1857.

FITZGIBBON, JAMES J.

International badminton and tennis player. From Waterford. He was ranked, along with Frank Peard (cv), as one of the game of badminton's most deadly doubles combination (winning many champinships), and was capped 37 times for his country between 1946 and 1962. In tennis, he played Davis Cup tennis for Ireland in an away match in Monaco in 1952. He twice won the Fitzwilliam L.T.C. club championship (in 1953 and 1954), and with his wife won the Irish mixed doubles title in 1951 (when she also won the Ladies Doubles). He also played inter-county hurling. He had a successful sports shop in Dublin.

FITZGIGGON, JOHN ('SCHILLACHI').

G.A.A. hurling full forward, Cork. Born in 1967. Club: Glen Rovers. He won an All-Ireland M.H.C. winner's medal in 1985, going on to capture an Under 21 All-Ireland Championship medal with Cork in 1988. Winning a Munster S.H.C. medal in 1986, he scored 2 goals (one of which was selected as goal-of-the year) which helped Cork to win the 1990 All-Ireland Senior Hurling Championship final against Galway, and was a member of the side beaten in the All-Ireland final in 1992. Winning a National Hurling League medal in 1992-93, he was selected in the left full-forward berth on both the 1990 and 1991 All Stars. A cousin of Seanie Leary (cv), his great-grandfather Tom O'Mahony won an All-Ireland S.H.C. medal with the Dungourney side in 1902. The Fitzgibbon Cup, for third level colleges, is named after a grand-uncle.

FITZGIBBON, MICHAEL Joseph (MICK).

Rugby international wing-forward. Born in Limerick, 2nd April 1964. Clubs: Trinity College and Shannon (winning Munster Senior Cup medals in 1986, 1991 and 1992). A Connacht inter-pro, he won Irish Universities, Under 25 and Ireland 'B' caps. A product of St Enda's Limerick and Rockwell College (from where he won 5 schools caps), he was first capped for Ireland at senior level iin 1992, playing in all 4 International Championship matches before touring New Zealand with Ireland in 1992. He played minor and under 21 G.A.A. football with Limerick, and his father Noel was a former Leinster junior rugby player.

FITZGIBBON, SANDRA ('SANDIE').

International basketball player, and camogie player, Cork. Born in Cork, 16th March 1964. Basketball clubs: Neptune Pandas, Blarney (winning 13 Cork titles, 3 National League medals, 3 National Cup medals, and in 1990-91 winning the 'Grand Slam' of titles), Tralee. A product of North Presentation school, she played for Ireland at under 15 and under 17 level. Debuting for the Irish senior team in 1986, she has played 51 full and representative matches (up to May 1992). As a camogie player with the Glen Rovers club she has won 6 Cork championship medals and 2 All-Ireland club titles. Winning All-Ireland minor medals in 3 successive years (1977, 1978 and 1979), she has won 4 All-Ireland senior medals with Cork, in 1982 and 1983, 1993 and in 1992 as captain of the Cork side which beat Wexford in the final by by 1-20 to 2-6, also playing in 5 losing All-Ireland sides.

FITZMAURICE, PADRAIG.

G.A.A. hurling right full-back, Limerick. A half-forward on the Limerick side beaten in the 1980 All-Ireland Senior Hurling Championship final, he was a member of the Limerick side which again won the Munster S.H.C. title in 1981. Also helping Limerick to National Hurling League wins in 1984 and 1985, he was selected at right corner back on the All-Stars team of 1984.

FITZPATRICK, BILLY.

G.A.A. hurling forward, Kilkenny. Born in 1953. Club: St Fenian's of Johnstown (winning 4 Kilkenny SHC medals, and a Leinster Club SHC medal). A member of the winning Kilkenny side in the 1972 M.H.C. side, he won 2 All-Ireland Under 21 medals with the 'Cats' in 1974 and 1975. A product of St Kieran's College (winning an All-Ireland Colleges medal in 1972), he has won five All-Ireland Senior Hurling Championship medals with Kilkenny; in 1974; as a 21-year-old captain while playing also at left half-forward in 1975 when Galway were beaten by 2-22 to 2-10 in the first 70 minute final; again in 1979 at centre half-forward; and at right corner forward in both 1982 and 1983 (when he scored 0-10 and was 'man-of-the-match' in the final). He also won Leinster a S.H.C. medal in 1978, when Kilkenny were beaten in the All-Ireland final. He won 2 National League medals, in 1976 and 1982, and a Railway Cup medal with Leinster in 1979. In the 1983 season he was the country's leading marksman, his 116 points from 19 games coming from 6 goals and 98 points, for an average of 6.10 points per game. He has won 2 All-Star awards, in 1982 and 1983, both at right full-forward. His brother Martin, later a Carlow manager, played for Kilkenny in the 1974 All-Ireland S.H.C. semi-final alongside Billy.

FITZPATRICK, MICHAEL P (MICK).

Rugby international prop-forward. Born in Dublin, 25th November 1950. Clubs: Dublin University and Wanderers. Playing in a 'B' international in 1977, he won 10 full international caps for Ireland between 1978 and 1985, one as a reserve. He won Leinster Senior Cup medals, with Trinity in 1976, and with Wanderers in 1978, 1982 and 1984.

FITZSIMMONS, ARTHUR G.

Soccer international inside-forward. Born in Dublin 16th December 1929. He joined Middlesborough from Shelbourne at the age of 19, and in ten years there, he scored 54 goals in 223 league appearences. Later he played of Lincoln, and for a successful two years at Mansfield, scoring 23 goals in only 61 league appearences. He was capped 26 times at senior international soccer for Eire between 1950 and 1959, scoring 7 international goals.

FITZSIMMONS, J

Amateur international golfer. Clubs: Bushfoot and Royal Portrush. He won the Irish Amateur Open title in 1937, and was runner-up in the Irish Close Champinship in 1947. He also won the first 2 stagings of the North of Ireland Championship, in 1947 and 1948. Between 1938 and 1948 he played 3 Home International series for Ireland, gaining 15 out of a possible 32 points.

FIVES, JAMES (JIM).

G.A.A. hurling right full-back, Galway. A fine full-back line player, in lean times for his county side he was twice on Galway sides beaten in All-Ireland Senior Hurling Championship finals, in 1955 when beaten by Wexford, and in 1958 in the loss to Tipp. Also a Railway Cup player, he won an Oireachtas medal in 1958. In 1984 he was selected in the right corner-back position on the 'Team of the Century' for hurlers who never won an All-Ireland medal. '

FLAHERTY, JAMES A and PETER D.

Amateur international golfing father and son. James, born 29th January 1900, and Peter, born 29th May 1939, have the rare distinction of father and son representing Ireland in the home international championships. James, a member of Langley Park, played 24 Home international matches for Ireland between 1934 and 1937, although only winning 8 of his matches. His son Peter, a member of Addington, was runner-up in the Irish Close Championship in 1967. He played 10 Home International matches for Ireland between 1965 and 1967, winning 5 and halving 2 matches: he also played 30 interprovincial matches for Connacht between 1964 and 1969, winning 12 games; he also played for Ireland in the European Team Championship winning sides of 1965 and 1967.

FLAHERTY, JOHNNY.

G.A.A. hurling forward, Offaly. Born 6th February 1946. Club: Kinnity (winning 5 county championship hurling medals; his 4 brothers, Brendan, Eamonn, Joe and Michael also played for the club). He played Offaly minors 1964-65, Under 21 1965-67, and for the senior team from 1966 until 1983. At the age of 35 he was the elder statesman of the Offaly side which won the county's first ever All-Ireland Senior Hurling Championship title of 1981, in the final moments of the final scoring a famous palmed goal to secure victory. He had won a Leinster S.H.C. medal with Offaly in 1980. He won one All-Star award, in 1981 at left corner forward. A hurley maker.

FLAHERTY, M J ('INKY').

G.A.A. hurler and footballer, Galway. As a footballer, he won a National Football League medal as a member of the Galway panel in 1940. It was as a hurling half back between 1936 and 1953 that he was in his best code. He won a Railway Cup medal in 1947 with Connacht (their only hurling success until the 1980's), and in 1951 he captained the Galway side which won the National Hurling League in the Polo Grounds of New York. In 1953 he retired after Galway were beaten in the final of the All-Ireland Senior Hurling Championship by Cork. He refereed the 1949 All-Ireland S.H.C. final between Tipperary and Laois, and he was manager of the Galway team which won the National Hurling League in 1975. In 1989 he was made an All-Time All-Star as a hurler. He was also a boxer of note.

FLANAGAN, DERMOT.

G.A.A. football half-back, Mayo. From Ballaghadereen. Clubs: U.C.D. (winning a Sigerson Cup with them in 1983), and Dublin Civil Service. A member of the Mayo side which won the Connacht S.F.C. title in 1985 (having played championship football first in 1983), he won 4 more provincial medals, in 1988, 1989 (when the county retained the Connacht title and reached the All-Ireland final for the first time in 38 years), 1991 and 1993. He was one of 2 Mayomen winning selection onto the 1985 All-Stars football side, winning his 2nd All-Star award in 1989. A son of Sean Flanagan (cv).

FLANAGAN, JOHN J. ('THE FATHER OF MODERN HAMMER THROWING')

Athlete, hammer and 56lb weight thrower. Born Kilbreedy, Co Limerick, 9th January 1873, he died in 1938. Emigrating to the U.S.A. in 1896 (after playing for Munster hurlers in the first ever inter-provincial match against Leinster earlier in the year), he became a New York policeman. He won three Olympic gold medals at successive Olympic Games (the first athlete to do so, and a feat not equalled until the great Al Oerter did so), all in the hammer event: in 1900 in Paris (throwing 163' 1"), 1904 at St Louis (with 168' 1", an Olympic record), and in 1908 in London (when, in a very strong field, he beat 2 other Irish-born athletes, Matt McGrath and Con Walsh, into the minor medals), with a new Olympic record of 170' 4" (only 3 other track and field athletes have equalled this feat of 3 successive titles). So dominant was he is the hammer discipline that he led the world rankings every year bar three (1902, 1902 and 1907) in the 16 year period between 1985 and 1910, winning the British A.A.A. title in 1896 and 1900, and winning 7 successive A.A.U. hammer titles. He had set the world record in Clonmel in 1895 at 44.27 metres (145' 102), broke it again 16 times (he was the first to throw it 150' and 180'), his last effort of 56.17 metres coming at the age of 41 years and 196 days in 1909 (13 years and 318 days after his first record), making him the world record holder as the oldest athlete to set a world record, when throwing 184' 4" at New Haven, Connecticutt. Also a fine 56lb weight thrower, he won 5 A.A.U. titles at this discipline, and won an Olympic silver medal at the 1904 games; he was also placed fourth in the 1904 Olympic discus. Back in Ireland after many years in the New York Police Department, he won the hammer event in an Ireland v Scotland match in 1911.

FLANAGAN, MATT.

Amateur international light-heavyweight and heavyweight boxer. Club: Garda. He won 6 Irish National Senior Championship titles over a 7 year span from 1925 to 1931. He won 2 at light-heavyweight, in 1925 and 1926, and 4 at heavyweight, in 1927, 1928, 1929, and 1931. He boxed at heavyweight in the 1928 Olympic Games at Amsterdam., being knocked out in his first bout.

FLANAGAN, PAT.

Tug-of War competitor. Although born in Ireland, the place and date are not certain. He was a member of the Milwaukee Police Athletic Club which was one of 4 teams which represented the U.S.A. in the six-team tug-of-war event at the 1904 Olympic Games in St

Louis, Missouri. His team went on to win the gold medal.

FLANAGAN, SEAN.

Amateur interprovincial golfer. Club: Co Sligo (Rosses Point), and Malahide. Reaching the semi-finals of 3 of the Irish 'majors', twice in the West and once in the South, he represented his province Connacht in 78 interprovincial matches in 13 successive series between 1966 and 1978, winning 27, halving 9, and losing 42 (his total of 63 points for his province makes him the 2nd most successful Connacht player in the interprovincial series in terms of points gained). Dying of leukaemia at the age of 50 in 1992, he was enormously popular in the Irish game. His son, also a Co Sligo player, played interprovincial golf for Connacht in 1988.

FLANAGAN, SEAN.

G.A.A. football left full-back, Mayo. Born in Ballyhaunis, Co Mayo, on 26th January 1922. Club: Ballaghaderreen. Educated in St Jarlath's of Tuam, he later won a Sigerson Cup with a highly rated U.C.D. outfit in 1943, also reaching a Dublin senior championship final with them. Having been at left full-back in the Mayo side beaten by Cavan in the 1948 All-Ireland S.F.C. final, and having won a National League medal in 1949, he went on to captain of the fine Mayo side which won 2 successive All-Ireland Senior Football Championships, in 1950 (when Louth were beaten by 2-5 to 1-6) and 1951 (when Meath were beaten by 2-8 to 0-9), these being Mayo's most recent triumphs in the Sam Maguire Cup. Playing 14 successive seasons for the Mayo side, he won one Railway Cup medal with Connacht, as captain, in 1951, and won a 2nd National League medal in 1954. His only Mayo senior championship medal came in the year he retired, 1957, with East Mayo. He was voted to fill the left full-back position in the Sunday Independent 'Team of the Century', in 1984. He was a Dail Deputy in Mayo from 1951 to 1977, a Minister for Health, and for Lands, between 1966 and 1973, and from 1979 to 1984 was an M.E.P. for Connacht-Ulster. He was made a G.A.A. All-Time All-Star shortly before he died in 1993 aged 71. His son Dermot, is an All-Star footballer (cv).

FLANNELLY, MICK.

G.A.A. hurling half-forward and footballer, Waterford. Club: Mount Sion. At the age of 18, he played in 5 county finals in Waterford, in the same year. They were at minor, junior and senior in hurling; and in football, at booth minor and junior. He was on the winning side in 3 contests, the senior and minor hurling, and the minor in football. His tally of senior hurling county championship winners medals with Mount Sion came to 15, all gained between 1948 and 1965. He won Munster S.H.C. medals with Waterford in 1957, 1959 and 1963, winning an All-Ireland Senior Hurling Championship medal in 1959, and appearing in beaten All-Ireland S.H.C. finals in both of the other years.

FLANNELLY, PATSY.

G.A.A. football midfielder, Mayo. A member of the Mayo side beaten in the All-Ireland Senior Football Championship final in 1932, he went on to win a Sam Maguire Cup medal in the 1936 win over Laois. He also won some National Football League medals in the mid-thirties. One of the county's greatest players of that era, he won 3 Railway Cup medals with Connacht, in 1934, 1936, and 1937.

FLAVIN, JOHNNY (JACK).

G.A.A. footballing right half-forward, Kerry and Galway. Born in Moyvane. He holds the unique distinction of winning 2 successive Sam Maguire Cup medals while playing for different counties. In 1937 he helped Kerry in their replay All-Ireland Senior Football Championship win against Cavan. The following year he was on the Galway side which defeated Kerry, ironically also in a replay. He went on to appear in 2 more All-Ireland S.F.C.

finals with Galway, when they lost to Kerry in 1941, and to Roscommon in 1943.

FLEMING, ANDY.

G.A.A. hurling right corner-back, Waterford. Born in 1916. Club: Mount Sion (winning 6 county championship medals). A member of the county panel from 1938 to 1951, he was at right full back on the occasion of Waterford's first ever win in the All-Ireland Senior Hurling Championship final in 1948, which was also his only provincial medal. He has won 7 Railway Cup medals with Munster (a record for a Waterford player), in 1943, 1944, 1945, 1946, 1949, 1950, and in 1951.

FLEMING, CURTIS.

Soccer B international full-back. Born in Dublin, 8th October 1968. Clubs: Belvedere, St Patricks Athletic (winning a League of Ireland medal in 1989-90), Middlesborough (playing in 40 of their games when they secured promotion from Division Two into the newly formed Premier League in the 1991-92 season). He won a place on the All-Star Leage of Ireland XI in 1991.

FLEMING, James GARY.

Soccer international defender. Born in Londonderry, 17th February 1967. Clubs: Nottingham Forest (to whom he was apprenticed, playing 74 league games for them), Manchester City, Notts County (on loan), Barnsley (playing 144 league matches up to mid 1993). He was first capped for Northern Ireland against England in 1987, and up to mid 1993 had played 21 international matches for his country.

FLEURY, PAT.

G.A.A. hurling left corner-back, Offaly. A member of the Offaly side which won the 1981 All-Ireland Senior Hurling Championship final, he was captain of the side which again captured the Liam McCarthy Cup again 4 years later, when Galway were beaten by 2-11 to 1-12 (he had also captained the losing All-Ireland side the previous year of 1984). He has won 2 All-Star awards, in 1982 and in 1984, both at left corner back.

FLOOD, JOHN JOE.

Soccer international forward. Clubs: Shamrock Rovers (being one of the famous 'Four F's' who haunted many defences in the 1920's) and Leeds United. He won 4 League of Irleand Championship winner's medals with Rovers, in 1922-23, 1924-25, 1926-27 and 1930-1931; and won 6 F.A.I. Cup medals with the Hoops also; in 1924, and then in the famous 5-in-a-row of 1929 (when he scored 2 goals in the final), 1930, 1931 (scoring one of the 3 goals in the final), 1932 and 1933. He was capped 5 times for the Republic of Ireland between 1926 (playing on the first F.A.I. Ireland team in their inaugural international match) and 1934, scoring 4 international goals (against Belgium in 1929 he became the first Irish international to score a hatrick). His inter-League exploits included 3 goals.

FLOOD, SEAN OG.

G.A.A. footballing goalkeeper, Louth and Cavan. He won an All-Ireland Senior Football Championship medal playing with Louth in their 1957 win over Cork. Five years later, in 1962, while playing for Cavan, he won an Ulster S.F.C. medal. He also won a Railway Cup medal with Leinster, in 1959.

FLOOD, TIM.

G.A.A. hurling left half-forward and centre-forward, Wexford. Born in 1927. Club: Cloghbaun (winning 2 county championship medals). In a 13 year senior intercounty career from 1949 to 1962, he won 3 All-Irleand Senior Hurling Championship medals with Wexford, in 1955 (scoring the vital last goal in the final), 1956 and 1960. He also won 2 other provincial titles, in 1951 and 1954, when on both occasions the county were beaten in the All-Ireland S.H.C. final. He also won 2 National Hurling League medals with Wexford in

1956 and 1958, and 4 Oireachtas medals, and won 2 Railway Cup medals with Leinster, in 1954 and 1956.

FLYNN, BERNARD.

G.A.A. football right-full forward, Meath. Club: St Colmcille's, and St Joseph's (Laois). He has won 2 All-Ireland Senior Football Championship winner's medals with Meath, in their successive wins of 1987 and 1988, both at right corner forward, and was on the side beaten in both the 1990 final by Cork, and scored 6 points in the defeat by Down in the All-Ireland final of 1991. A winner of National League medals with the Royal County in both 1988 and 1990, he was honoured as an All-Star in the left full-forward position in both 1987 and 1991.

FLYNN, CATHAL.

G.A.A. football left corner forward, Leitrim. Born in 1936. Clubs: Gorvagh and Fenagh (in Leitrim); College of Pharmacy and Sean McDermott's (Dublin, winning 3 Dublin S.F.C. medals in all); Ballinasloe (Galway) and Castlerahan (Cavan). In a senior inter-county career which stretched from 1952 to 1966, he was the starring member of the Leitrim side which were foiled by Galway in 4 successive Connacht S.F.C. finals, 1957, 1958, 1959, and 1960 (he appeared in a 5th final in 1963). Also playing on the Leitrim side beaten in the National Football League semi-final of 1959, in 1958 he became only the 3rd Leitrim footballer to win a Railway Cup medal with Connacht, playing at left corner forward. A consistently top scorer for Leitrim from 1956 to 1963, and again in 1964 and 1965 (his best tally, a county record still, being 81 points in 1959), a total of 10 times on top.

FLYNN, Michael KEVIN ('FLYNNER').

Rugby international centre-threequarter. Born in Dublin, 20th March 1939. Club: Wanderers (winning Leinster Senior Cup medals in 1959 and in 1973 when the club became the first to win the League/Cup double). A product of Terenure College, he was capped 18 times in the centre for Ireland, initially between 1959 and 1966, and after a gap of 6 years, was capped a further 4 times in 1971-73, making him one of only 3 Irish players to play in 3 different decades, having an international career span of 15 years. He scored 4 international tries for Ireland, the most memorable being against England in 1972. He also played 24 interprovincial matches for Leinster between 1958 and 1972. He was an Irish selector 1979-82, and again from 1990. He is the father-in-law of Philip Matthews (cv). His brother Jim, a Wanderers flanker, played interprovincial rugby for Leinster against Connacht in 1973, having previously toured Argentina with Ireland in 1967, but was not capped.

FLYNN, PATRICK J (PAT).

3,000 metre steeplechase athlete. Born in Bandon, Co Cork in 1895. A member of the Paulist A.C. in the U.S.A., he was favourite to win the 1920 Olympic 3,000m steeplechase title for the United States after winning the A.A.U. title of that year in the U.S. record time of 9:58.2. However in the Olympic final in Antwerp, he fell at the water jump, and finished 100 yards behind the winner Percy Hodge (G.B.), whose time was 10:00.4, to win the silver medal.

FLYNN, RAY.

Middle distance international athlete. Born in Longford town, 22nd November 1957. Clubs: Longford, Team KangaRoos. Taking up a scholarship at East Tennessee Stae University, he has held the Irish 1,500m record 3 times, the Irish mile and 2,000m records twice each, and also held the Irish 1,000m record. In 1982 he became the first Irishman to break the 3 minute-50 second barrier for the mile. His major race record at 1,500m is: reached the Olympic semi-final in Moscow in 1980; he reached the World Championship semi-final in 1983 (and heats in 1987); in the European

Championships, he was knocked out in the heats in 1978, and finished 8th in the 1988 final; he finished 2nd in the European Indoors in 1980; he was Irish Champion at 1,500m in 1977 and 1985. At 5,000m, he finished 11th in the Olympic final of 1984 at Los Angeles, having won the AAA title that year, and he also was Irish Champion for 5,000m in 1982. A world traveller for his sport, he now lives in Johnson City, Tennessee.

FOGARTY, AMBY.

Soccer international winger. Born in Dublin, 11th September 1933. Clubs: Glentoran, Sunderland (scoring 37 goals in 152 league matches for them 1957-63), and Hartlepool (scoring 22 league goals for them 1963-66). He was capped at senior international level 11 times for Eire from 1960 to 1964, scoring 3 international goals. His last cap was gained while at the Victoria Ground, which makes him Hartlepool United's only capped player.

FOGARTY, G NOEL.

Amateur international golfer. Club: Royal Dublin (winning a Barton Shield medal in 1968 and a Senior Cup medal in 1969). Runner-up in the Irish Close in 1960, he won the 'East' in 1963 and 1967, and won the 'South' in 1967 (being runner-up in 1969). In 65 matches for Leinster in the Interprovincial series between 1956 and 1970 he secured 65 points, a 50% record. In 26 Home international matches for Ireland between 1956 and 1967 he won 10 and halved 5. He won the Irish Seniors Amateur title in both 1980 and 1981.

FOLEY, BRENDAN Oliver.

Rugby international 2nd-row forward. Born in Limerick, 6th August 1950. Club: Shannon (winning Munster Senior Cup medals in 1977 and 1978 as captain, and in 1982). A product of St Mary's C.B.S. Limerick, he was capped 11 times in the second row for Ireland between 1976 and 1981; he also toured with Ireland to New Zealand and Fiji in 1976, to Australia in 1979, and to South Africa in 1981. A typical Munster forward stalwart, he was a member of the provincial side on 'The Day Munster Beat the All Blacks', 31st October 1978.

FOLEY, DES.

G.A.A. football and hurling midfielder, Dublin. Born in 1940. Club: St Vincent's (winning 4 senior county hurling championships). He captained the Dublin minors who won the All-Ireland M.F.C. in 1958, having been on the winning side also 2 years previously. He was captain of the historic St Joseph's school side which brought the All-Ireland Colleges title to the capital for the first time in 1959. In 1962 he became the only person to play in Railway Cup finals in both codes on the same day, playing against Munster to win the hurling title, and against Ulster to capture the football crown. He also won hurling Railway Cup medals with Leinster in 1964 and 1965. A member of the Dublin inter-county hurling side from 1958 to 1969, he was playing when the county lost the All-Ireland Senior Hurling Championship final of 1961. He went on two year's later to captain Dublin to their All-Ireland Senior Football Championship win over Galway by 1-9 to 0-10. He is a younger brother to Lar Foley (cv).

FOLEY, LIAM (LAR).

G.A.A. hurling and football dual player, Dublin. Club: St Vincent's. He captained the Dublin minors which won the All-Irleand M.F.C. in 1956 (having been a member also of the winning side the previous year). Making his senior inter-county debut for Dublin in 1957, he was, at 19, the youngest member of the Dublin side which won the All-Ireland Senior Football Championship final in 1958, and won his 2nd Sam Maguire Cup medal at full-back in 1963. He was at left back on the Dublin side beaten in the All-Ireland Senior Hurling Championship final in 1961 by Tipperary. He won Railway Cup medals with Leinster hurlers in 1962 and 1964. An older brother of Des Foley (cv), they shared many of their medal successes. He was for many years a successful trainer of St Vincent's hurling side, and later trained the Dublin S.H.C. side in the late 80's and early 1990's, gaining them promotion into Division 1 of the N.H.L., and winning 2 Leinster S.H.C. titles.

FOLEY, SEAN.

G.A.A. hurling half-back, Limerick. Born in London in 1949. Club: Patrickswell (being a member of the successful club side which won 12 county championships from 1966 to 1991, and of the side beaten in the All-Ireland Club final of 1991, at the age of 42). A member of the winning Limerick C.B.S. side which won the All-Ireland Colleges, he was a county minor in 1966 and 1967. A member of the historic Limerick side which won the All-Ireland Senior Hurling Championsjip title in 1973, he was captain of the side beaten in the return final against Kilkenny the following year. He won a National Hurling League winner's medal with Limerick in 1971. He won one All-Star award, in 1973 at left half-back.

FOLEY, THEO C.

Soccer international right-back. Born in Dublin, 2nd April 1937. Clubs: Home Farm, Exeter City (1955-60), Northampton (in his 6 years as captain the club won promotion to Division Two in 1963 and to Division One in 1965), Charlton Athletic. He was capped 9 times in soccer for the Republic of Ireland between 1964 and 1967. He was later assistant manager at Q.P.R., Millwall (helping them to win the League Trophy in 1983, and to promotion to the 2nd Division in 1985) and Arsenal 1986-1990 (helping them to a League Cup win in 1988 and a League Championship in 1990), and in 1990 became manager at Northampton Town.

FORDE, CAROLINE.

Basketball international player. Born in Cork, 26th April 1967. Clubs: Blarney (winning 8 Cork Senior league medals, 3 Natinal League medals, 3 National Cup medals, 2 Top Four competitions, and in 1990-91 was a member of the 'Grand Slam' winning side), and Tralee. Capped at under 15 and under 17 levels, she debuted for the Irish senior team in 1985, and has played for Ireland 68 times (up to May 1992) in full and representitive matches, touring America twice. She was selected as national senior player of the year in 1986, and has twice been chosen for a Cork Jury's Sportstar award.

FORREST, A.J., EDWARD G, and H.

Rugby international brothers. Club: Wanderers. A.J., the oldest brother, a Wanderers forward (1859-1936), played 7 rugby internationals for Ireland between 1880 and 1883, scoring his only international try in his last cap. He captained Ireland in the 1881 sason, when they achieved their first ever win against international opposition, beating Scotland by 4-3. His younger brother, H Forrest, born in 1864, also a forward with Wanderers, won just 2 caps with Ireland in 1893, one with Edward. The youngest of the 3 brothers, Edward G (born in Dublin in 1870), played 13 times for Ireland between 1888 and 1897, scoring a drop goal against England in 1894 when he captained the Ireland side which won the Triple Crown for the first time. All 3 brothers also played for Leinster.

FORREST, MICK.

Pitch and Putt player. Clubs: Rocklodge and Carrigaline. A vastly experienced inter-county player for Cork, he is the only men's pitch and putt player to win the sports 2 prestigious titles in the same year, acheiving the feat in 1976 when winning both the National Strokesplay and Matchplay Championship titles. He was also runner-up in the National Matchplay Championship twice, in 1983 and 1987, and in 1983 he was runner-up in the strokeplay championship.

FORSYTHE, MARK Cliford.

Long jump athlete. Born in Belfast, 10th August 1965. Club: Ballymena and Antrim. He captured the Northern Ireland Championship in the long jump discipline 4 years in succession, 1985, 1986, 1987 and 1988, and won the U.K. Championship in 1989. He did very well to reach the Olympic final in the long jump in the Seoul Games of 1988, finishing 12th (and in the 1992 games in Barcelona he finished 22nd, with a distance of 7.71). He has passed the magical '8 metre' barrier in this event at least 3 times in competition.

FOSTER, ALEXANDER Roulston (ALEX).

Rugby international wing/centre three-quarter. 1890-1972. A Derryman, he was capped 17 times for Ireland between 1910 and 1921 (only 7 of these matches were lost, and Ireland shared the International Championship in 1912), his caps spanning World War One, and he scored 4 international tries for his country. He played for the British and Irish Lions side which toured South Africa in 1910, winning 2 test places (scoring a try on his test debut). A schoolmaster, he captained Ireland 3 times, including during the championship-winning season of 1912.

FOSTER, RICHIE.

Amateur and professional boxer. Born in 1961. As an amateur member of the Phoenix boxing club, he won 2 Irish National Senior Championship titles at bantamweight in 1979 and 1980, and was twice voted best boxer at the national championships. Failing to be selected for the Moscow Olympics in 1980, he turned pro, and boxing in a career based in both Oklahoma and Britain, he eventually got a crack at the W.A.A. world featherweight crown in 1983, losing on points over 15 rounds to Earvin Mitchell. His professional career involved 46 fights, winning 32 and losing 14.

FOUHY, MATTIE.

G.A.A. hurling half-back, Cork. Club: Carrigtwohill. Winning a medal as a non-playing sub for Cork in All-Ireland S.H.C. winning final of 1944, he missed the 1946 final through suspension, and finally won his first Liam McCarthy Cup medal when Cork captured the All-Irleand Senior Hurling Championship in 1952. Winning 2 other All-Ireland S.H.C. medals in the following years, 1953 and 1954, he was also on the Cork side beaten in the final of 1956. He won 3 Railway Cup medals for Munster, in 1950, 1951 and 1952.

FOWLER, Brigadier BRYAN John (B. J.).

Polo international player. Born in Co Meath, 18th August 1898. In the 1936 Olympic Games in Berlin, as he was then a captain in the British Army, he was a member of the Great British team which won the silver medal in polo (the last time this sport was competed for in the Olympics), when they lost in the final by 11-0 to Argentina in front of a crowd of 45,000 people. He was thus he only Irish-born person to win a medal at 'Hitlers Games'. He later achieved some success in Irish horse racing.

FOX, PAT.

G.A.A. hurling right full-forward, Tipperary. Born in 1961. Club: Eire Og-Annacarthy. He won 3 successive All-Irleand Under 21 Championship medals with Tipperary in 1979, 1980 and 1981 (the last 2 at corner-back, winning the Tipperary 'hurler of the year' award in 1981). After serious knee injuries, he has won 2 All-Ireland Senior Hurling Championship winner's medals with the Premier County, in 1989 (the county's first success for 18 years) and 1991 (scoring 5 points from play and being nominated man-of-the-match), and was also a member of the side defeated in the final of 1988 (he won his first Munster S.H.C. medal in 1987). A opportunistic and lethal scoring forward, he has won 3 All-Star awards, in 1987, 1989 and 1991, all at right corner forward. In 1991 he was also selected as both the Texaco Sportsar of the Year in Hurling and also as Ballygowan National Sportstar of the year. He missed (through injury) Tipperary's Munster S.H.C. final success of 1993.

FRANCIS, NEIL Patrick John.

Rugby international 2nd row forward. Born in Dublin, St Patrick's Day 1964. Clubs: Blackrock College (winning a Leinster Senior Cup medal in 1983 aged 19, and again in both 1988 and 1992), and Belvedere College. A product of Blackrock College (winning Leinster Senior Schools Cup medals in 1981 and 1982), he won 5 schools international caps, 2 in 1981 and 3 in 1982. He was a member of the Irish rugby side which participated in the inaugural World Cup competition in Australia and New Zealand in 1987 (winning his first 2 caps on that tour). He came of age in the World Cup of 1991, dominating line-outs in the group games, and has been capped 21 times up to May 1993. He toured New Zealand with Ireland in 1992.

FRANKLIN, CHARLES B.

Motorcycle racer. Born in Drumcondra, Co Dublin, 1st October 1880. A pioneer of motorcycling, he competed in the first speed trials to be held in Ireland, at Portmarnock in August 1904. In the same year he set an end-to-end record for the journey from Mizen Head in Cork to Fair Head in Co Antrim, in 31 hours and 30 minutes. He was the first Irishman to compete in the Isle of Man TT races in 1908, his best placing being 2nd in the 1911 Senior race. Emigrating to the U.S.A. in 1916, he worked as a design engineer with the Indian works, and designed the famous 'Indian Scout' machine. He died in the U.S. in 1932.

FRANKS, JAMES GORDON.

Rugby international forward. 1878-1941. Club: Dublin University (winning 6 Leinster Senior Cup winner's medal, in 1893, 1895, 1896, 1897, 1898 and 1900). He was capped 3 times for Ireland in the 1898 season, and played 8 times for Leinster from 1894 to 1898. In 1899 he captained Ireland's first ever international rugby tour, an 8 venue trip to Canada, when Ireland won 10 out of it's 11 matches (losing only to a side selected from the combination of talents from the province of Nova Scotia and the crews of 7 cruisers of the Atlantic Fleet. It was to be Ireland's only rugby tour for the next 53 years.

FREANEY, OLIVER (OLLIE).

G.A.A. footballing centre half-forward, Dublin. Born in 1929. Club: St Vincent's (helping the Marino club to no fewer than 13 Dublin county championship titles). He was a member of the Dublin minors of 1945 which captured the All-Ireland M.F.C. (also being in the side the following year which lost in the final). Playing senior inter-county football from 1949 to 1960, he won one All-Ireland Senior Football Championship winner's medal, with the Kevin Heffernan-captained Dublin side of 1958, having also been in the side beaten in the decider of 1955, when he scored a unique goal from a 14-yard free (he also won Leinster S.F.C. medals in 1953 and 1954). He won 5 Railway Cup medals with Leinster, in 1952, 1953, 1954 and 1955 (when he was one of only 2 players to play in all 8 games of this first ever 4-in-a-row in this competition), and again in 1959. He also assisted Dublin to 3 National Football League wins, in 1953, 1955 and 1958. He was the country's leading marksman twice, in 1955 (scoring 90 points in 21 games), and in 1959, when his 5 goals and 86 points over 17 games gained him entry into the 'ton up' club, with 101 points, and an average of 5.94 points per game. A skillful player, he also played for Ireland in many matches in the 1950's against the 'Rest'. He later headed up an accountancy firm, and died in 1992, aged 62. His brother Cyril, a left corner forward, played on the Dublin side which lost the 1955 All-Ireland S.F.C. final, alongside Ollie, having also won a minor All-Ireland medal in 1945.

FREEMAN-JACKSON, Capt HENRY (HARRY).

Equestrian rider. Born in Pakistan, he spent 4 years in a German concentration camp, and later settled in Mallow. He was the master of the famous Duhallow Hunt in Mallow for 20 years. He won the 1963 Burghley Horse Trial event, being the most recent person representing Ireland to do so. He represented Ireland in the 3-day event at 4 successive Olympic Games (being the first Irish sportsperson to go to 3 Olympic Games, and being first of only 3 from Ireland to compete in 4 different Olympic celebrations, although his were uniquely in succession): in 1952 in Helsinki on Cuchulainn (when the Irish team finished 6th and himself placed 27th); in 1956 in Stockholm on Cellarstown (finishing 17th in the individual); in 1960 in Rome on St Finbarr and Sonnet (when the team finished 6th), and in 1964 in Tokyo on St Finbarr (when he was 28th but the team achieved a best-ever 4th place). He was later a chef d'equpe for an Irish Olympic team. Also a fine race jockey, he won the Foxhunter's Chase at Cheltenham, and finished 2nd in an Irish Grand National. In 1964 his daughter, Valerie Freeman-Jackson represented Ireland in Tokyo (along with her father), on the horse Sam Weller, having the previous year won the three-day event world championship at Burghley as a member of the Irish team. In 1966 Harry was selected as Texaco's Equestrian Sports Sportstar of the Year. He died, aged 82, in 1993.

FREYNE, MICK.

G.A.A. football right full-forward, Roscommon. Born in 1951. Club: Castlerea St Kevin's. Playing in all grades for the county before making his senior inter-county debut in 1968, he won a Connacht Under 21 medal that year (and was on the side beaten in the All-Ireland final at Under 21 in 1969). He won Connacht Senior Football Championship medals with Roscommon in both 1972 and 1977. He won an All-Star award in 1972 at right full-forward.

FROGGATT, PETER.

Amateur international golfer. Clubs: Malone (winning a Barto Shield medadl in 1961), Royal Portrush, and Belvoir Park (winning a Senior Cup medal in 1957). An Ulster interporvincial in 3 series in the mid-fifties, 1956, 1957 and 1958, he represented Ireland in the Home International Champoinships in 1956. Two of his sons hold the unique distinction of each having captained opposing 'Blues' univerity sides: Mark, who was Ulster Youths Champion in 1983, and who played for Ulster in 1985, captained Cambridge in the 1982-3 'Blues' match (and in 6 matches over 3 contests achieved a record 5 out of 6 points); while Keith was captain of Oxford in 1990-91.

FULLAM, CHRISTY ('BUNNY').

Soccer full-back. Clubs: Bohemians (with whom he won amateur international caps), Shelbourne (winning a League of Ireland winner's medal in 1952-53), Holyhead Town, Drumcondra (with whom he won an F.A.I. Cup medal in 1957, scoring one of the 2 goals in the final, and won a runner-up medal in 1961). Uncapped, he was a League of Ireland favourite for many years.

FULLAM, JOHNNY.

Soccer international wing-half. Born in Dublin, 22nd March 1940. He left Home Farm at the age of 18 to play for a period with Preston, with whom he scored 6 goals in 49 league appearences. He shares with 'Sacky' Glen (cv) the record tally of winning 8 F.A.I. Cup medals in all: firstly with the 5-in-a-row achieved by Shamrock Rovers, in 1964 (when Rovers won the Grand Slam, including the League of Ireland), 1965 (when he scored the only goal in the final), 1966, 1967 and 1968; he then went on to win 2 with Bohemians (in 1970 when he scored one of the 2 goals in the final, and 1976); and won his final medal in 1978 again with Rovers (he is one of only 2 players to captain winning F.A.I. Cup sides with different clubs). He won a second League of Ireland Championship medal, with Bohemians in 1975. Capped for the Republic of Ireland 11 times between 1961 and 1970, he was the first soccer player to win the Irish Soccer Writers Association annual award twice (in 1968 when with Rovers, and in 1975 while at Boh's).

FULLAM, ROBERT (BOB).

Soccer international inside-left forward. Born in Ringsend, Dublin in 1897. Clubs: St Brendan's, North End, Shelbourne (winning an I.F.A. Irish Cup medal in 1920), Shamrock Rovers, Leeds United, and Holly Carburetors in Detroit. A docker with a fine left boot, it is as a Shamrock Rovers player and captain, and 'Free State' goal-scorer that he is best remembered, as one of the prominent players in the early League of Ireland. He was capped twice for the Irish Free State, against Italy in both 1926 and 1927. He scored the Irish Free State's first ever international goal, and scored twice in 6 inter-League appearences. He scored over 90 League of Ireland goals for Rovers, with whom he won many honours, including: 4 Irish Free State League (L of I) winner's medals, in 1923-24 (when he was the league's leading scorer with 27 goals, a Rovers record for one league season), 1924-25 (with 20 goals), 1926-27, and 1931-32; and won 4 F.A.I. Cup medals, in 1924, 1929, 1930, 1931, and in 1932 (when Rovers achieved their 2nd Grand Slam in 8 years). Also playing in England and America, he retired at the top, in 1932, and later coached the Shamrock Rovers side to win 2 successive F.A.I. Cups, in 1944 and 1945.

FULTON, JOHN.

Rugby international full-back. 1871-1948. Club: N.I.F.C. (winning 9 Ulster Senior Cup medals, in 1893, 1894, 1895, 1896, 1897, 1898, 1899, 1901 and 1902, and a similar number of Ulster Senior League medals). In the 10 year period between 1895 and 1904, he won 17 international caps at full-back for Ireland, including playing in one match of Ireland's 1899 Triple Crown success, and also being a member of the Championship-winning side of 1896.

FULTON, ROBERT Patrick (BERTIE).

Soccer international full-back. Born in Larne, 6th November 1906. Clubs: Larne, London Caledonians, and chiefly Belfast Celtic. A great reader of the game's intricacies, he won 10 Irish League winners medals with Belfast Celtic (the 4-in-a-row of 1925-26, 1926-27, 1927-28 and 1928-29; in 1932-33; and the 5-in-a-row of 1935-36, 1936-37, 1937-38, 1938-39 and 1939-40); and also won 4 Irish Cup medals, in 1925, 1937, 1938 and 1941. Guiding the club through its heyday, he also won 6 City Cup medals, 4 Gold Cup medals, 4 Co Antrim Shield medals, and many other trophies at the 'Paradise'. Having won 21 amateur international caps, he was also capped 20 times for Northern Ireland between 1930 and 1938, all while with Belfast Celtic, making him that club's most capped player. He was also a member of the Great Britain team which finished beaten quarter-finalists in the Olympic Games soccer tournament of 1936 in Berlin.

FULTON, ROBERT.

Bowls player. Born in Glasgow, 14th June 1916. Club: Coleraine. He won a Bronze medal at the inaugural World Championship in 1966 at Kyeemagh, and at the Commonwealth Games of 1970 in Edinburgh. He won the British Isles Championship singles title in 1967, and the pairs in both 1966 and 1967. He won 7 I.B.A. singles titles, and 5 pairs titles. He won the Northern Ireland Singles titles in 1956, 1957, 1962, 1964, 1966 and 1967. Playing at interantional level for Ireland over 35 times, he was also capped at the indoor game.

FURLONG, MARTIN.

G.A.A. football goalkeeper, Offaly. Born in 1948. Club: Tullamore (winning county championship medals). Having won an All-Ireland M.F.C. medal with Offaly (the county's first) in 1964, he first played senior inter-county football in 1965. He has the distinction of being the only player to share in all 3 of Offaly's All-Ireland Senior Football Championship-winning sides, being a vital cog in the wins of 1971, 1972, and again in 1982, also winning Leinster titles in 1973, 1980 and 1981 (being on the losing All-Ireland S.F.C. side this year). He won a Railway Cup medal as captain in 1974 with Leinster (the province's first win in 12 years), and played without interruption for Leinster in goals from 1968 to 1975. He won 4 All-Star awards (sharing the record for a football goalkeeper with Dublin's Paddy Cullen cv), in 1972, 1981, 1982 and 1983, and in 1982 he was selected as Texaco's Gaelic Football Sportstar of the Year.

FURLONG, NOEL and FRANK.

National Hunt trainer and jockey, father and son. Noel (who died in 1963), was from Fermoy in Co Cork, but moved to England to train. He trained Reynoldstown to win 2 successive Aintree Grand Nationals, in 1935 and 1936, each time being ridden by his son Frank. He also trained the winners of 2 National Hunt Chases, Robi-a-Tiptoe in 1932 (also ridden by Frank), and Litigant in 1939. Frank, who had previously come third in the 1933 Aintree Grand National on Really True, was killed in action in World War II at the age of 34 in 1944.

G

GAFFIKIN, J.

Soccer international player. He played 15 international games for Northern Ireland while at Linfield Athletic between 1890 and 1895, scoring 5 international goals.

GAGE, JOHN H (JACK).

Rugby international wing threequarter. Born in the Cape Town province of South Africa, 2nd July 1907. Club: Queen's University Belfast. He won 4 rugby caps for Ireland in 1926 and 1927, scoring Ireland's first ever try in Murrayfield in Ireland's 3-0 win over Scotland in his debut 1926. He later emigrated to South Africa, playing for the Orange Free State. In 1933, on South Africa's first tour of Australia, he played in the first Test. He therefore joins a select group of players in Irish rugby history to subsequently play for another major country as well. He won Military Cross in World War Two.

GALBRAITH, EDWARD and RICHARD.

Rugby international brothers. Club: Dublin University. They both played in Ireland's first ever international rugby game, against England in 1875 at the Kennsington Oval. This makes them the first of over 35 sets of brothers to play rugby for Ireland since that date. Only Richard played again for Ireland, gaining 3 caps in all up to 1877, captaining the side in his last match. Both were involved in organising that famous first international match.

GALLAGHER, CHARLIE.

G.A.A. football right and left half-forward, Cavan. He won Ulster Senior Football Championship medals with Cavan in 1964, 1967 and in 1969 when he captained the side. He won 4 Railway Cup medals with Ulster, in 1964 (as a sub), 1965, 1966 (becoming the 4th Cavanman to captain a winning side), and 1968. He is the only Cavanman to score the 'ton up' in one season, his best tally being in 1964 when he scored 6-107, or 125 points, in 20 competitive games. He was also the country's leading football marksman in both 1965 (with 123 points) and in 1967 (with 109) points. In 1984 he was selected on the 'Team of the Century' side for football players who never won an All-Ireland medal. A dentist, he drowned in 1989.

GALLAGHER, JOSIE.

G.A.A. hurling half-forward, Galway. Born in 1922. Club: Gort. In a famous inter-county career which lasted 13 years from 1942 to 1954, during which Galway lost 10 All-Ireland semi-finals, his tally of major honours include only: 1 winner's medal for the National Hurling League in 1951, 2 Oireachtas medals in 1950 and 1952, a Fitzgibbon Cup medal with U.C.C., and a solitary Railway Cup medal with the all-Galway Connacht side in 1947. He was selected on the 1984 'Team of the Century' for hurlers who never won an All-Ireland medal.

GALLAGHER, MATT.

G.A.A. left full-back, Donegal. From Ballintra. Along with his brother Pauric, he won an All-Ireland Under 21 Championship medal in 1982. Having joined the senior squad in 1981, Matt won an Ulster S.F.C. medal in 1990, and in 1992 helped his county to their first ever All-Ireland Senior Football Championship in the final win over Dublin. He won an All-Star award in 1992 in the left corner-back position.

GALLAGHER, PATRICK (PATSY or 'THE MIGHTY ATOM').

Soccer international inside-right forward and midfielder. Born in Milford Co Donegal in 1894, he died in 1954. Joining Glasgow Celtic at the age of 17, he won 4 Scottish Cup medals (in 1914, 1923, then when scoring a great goal in the 1925 final win, and in 1927) and 6 Scottish League Championship medals with Celtic (in 1914, 1915, 1916, 1917, 1919 and 1922). A great goal-scorer and creator, he put the ball in the net 184 times for Celtic in 436 matches from 1911 to 1926. He later played for Falkirk, and scored 19 goals for them in 129 league matches from 1926 to 1932. In a league career from 1911 to 1932 he scored a total of 201 goals in 564 matches. Playing 4 Inter-League matches, he won 11 caps for Northern Ireland between 1920 and 1927, while playing for Glasgow Celtic and Falkirk. While at Falkirk he also won one cap for the Irish Free State.

GALLAGHER, ROSALEEN.

Wheelchair athlete. From Co Mayo. Ireland's most outstanding wheelchair sportsperson, she has competed in 6 Paralympic Games. In Tel Aviv in 1966 she won 2 bronze medals, in the 25m Backstroke, and in the 25m Breaststroke. In the 1972 games, she won a gold medal in the 60m Track, and silver in the Javelin. In 1976 she won gold in both the Pentathlon and in the team Table Tennis; silver in the Shot Putt and Javelin; and bronze medals in the 100m Track, the Slalom, and the Discus. In 1980 she won gold again in the Pentathlon; and bronze medals in the Discus, the Club Throw, and the 60m Track. In 1984 she won a gold in the Shot Putt, a silver in the Javelin, and bronze in the Discus and the Slalom. Also competing (without winning a medal) in the Seoul Paralympics of 1988, her total tally of Paralympic medals is 5 gold medals, 4 silver medals, and 10 bronze medals.

GALLAHER, DAVE.

Rugby international flanker, New Zealand. Born in Ramelton. Co Donegal, 30th October, 1873, he emigrated at an early age to Auckland, New Zealand. He was the All-Black's first ever captain, in their inaugural international against Australia in 1903. He was appointed captain of the first touring All-Blacks side to the British Isles in 1905-1906, missing the games in his native Irelnad through injury. He was killed in W.W.I., at Passchendale, in 1917.

GALVIN, BARRY Jnr.

Water skiing champion. Club: Cork Power Boat and Water Ski Club. From Glanmire, Co Cork, he is Ireland's modern giant of water skiing, and has represented this country at 2 European Championships (1988 and 1990), and 3 World Championships (1987, 1988 and 1991). He broke Irish Dauphin (under 15) records 12 times at the 3 disciplines (slalom, tricks and jumping) from 1982 to 1986. He later broke 5 Junior (under 17) records in the 3 disciplines, and went on to break, after 1988 (and still holds) all the records for the senior (Open) Class, these currently (June 1992) standing at Slalom (1.25. buoys @ 58 Kph, with a 12 metre rope), Tricks (3,700 points), and Jumping (52.3 metres). The only one of the 9 possible Irish records for men (3 age groups, 3 disciplines) he does not hold is the Dauphin Jumping record, which is held by his brother David.

GALVIN, JOHN.

G.A.A. hurling midfielder and defender, Waterford. Born in 1955. Club: Portlaw (winning county championship medals). He was a member of the first Waterford side to win the Munster Under 21 side in 1974. He became the first Waterford player to win an All-Star award in either code when he was selected in the midfield in 1974. He won a 2nd All-Star award in 1982 (the first time in 16 years Waterford had reached the Munster S.H.C. final), this time as a right corner back. Also a county footballer, his father Billy Galvin (a left corner-forward) won an All-Ireland Senior Hurling Championship medal with Waterford in the county's first success in 1948, scoring 1-1 in the final.

GALVIN, TONY.

Soccer international winger. Born in Huddersfield, 12th July 1956. He joined Tottenham Hotspur in 1978 from Goole Town, and in 10 years he scored 20 league goals in over 200 league appearences, winning F.A. Cup medals in both 1981 and 1982, and a U.E.F.A. Cup medal in 1984. He joined Sheffield Wednsday in 1988, later moving to Swindon Town. First capped for Eire in 1983 against Holland, he won 29 caps in all up to 1990, and he made an invaluable contribution towards Ireland's European Championship run in Germany in June 1988. He has scored 6 goals in European club competitions.

GALWEY, MICHAEL Joseph (MICK).

Rugby international 2nd row, flanker and No 8 forward, and G.A.A. footballer, Kerry. Born in Currow, Co Kerry, on 8th October 1966. Rugby clubs: Castleisland, Shannon (winning Munster Senior Cup medals in 1986, 1987, 1988, 1991 and 1992) and London Irish. In 1986 he was a non-playing sub on the Kerry side which won the All-Ireland Senior Football Championship (and in 1987 he was in the midfield when the Kerry side were beaten in the All-Ireland Under 21 F.C. final). Playing rugby for Munster first in 1988, he later played at Under 25 and 'B' level for Ireland. When winning his first cap against France in 1991, he became the first person ever to hold an All-Ireland Senior Football Championship medal and also play senior rugby for Ireland. A fine forward, his cap tally for Ireland was 13 up to March 1993, when he was selected for the British and Irish Lions to tour New Zealand on the flank, having scored his first international try in the famous 17-3 win over England. He has toured Namibia (in 1991) and New Zealand (in 1992) with Ireland.

GANLY, JAMES BLANDFORD.

Rugby centre wing international three-quarter, tennis player and cricketer. Born in Dublin, 7th March 1904. Rugby club; Monkstown. A pint-sized rugby winger, he was capped 12 times for Ireland between 1927 and 1930 (sharing in the International Championship win for Ireland in 1927), and scored 7 international tries for Ireland. A fine all-round sportsman, he was also capped for Ireland in 2 other sports, cricket and tennis. As a cricketer he played 25 times for Ireland between 1921 and 1937, scoring 833 runs for an average of 19.93 per innings (his best figures being an 83). Among the 8 times he captained his country at cricket was their famous win over the West Indies in 1928 in College Park. A cattle salesman, he was killed in a shooting accident in Galway in 1976. His brother Bobby played to nearly international standard in rugby, and was President of the I.R.F.U. in 1980-1981.

GANNON, EDDIE.

Soccer international half-back and inside-forward. Born in Dublin, 3rd January 1921. Clubs: Distillery, Shelbourne, Notts County, and Sheffield Wednesday. Having scored an own goal in Shel's 3-2 defeat in the 1944 F.A.I. Cup final, he left Shelbourne in 1946 at the age of 25, to join Notts County for 2 years, and then went on to play for Sheffield Wedsnday for 6 seasons in 1948-54, playing in 204 league matches for them. He rejoined Shelbourne in 1955. Scoring twice in Inter-League matches, he was capped for Eire 14 times in a 7 year international career between 1948 and 1955. He died in 1989.

GANNON, MARK Andrew.

Amateur internatioinal golfer. Born in Drogheda, Co Louth, 15th July 1952. Club: Co Louth (Baltray). Winner of the Irish Boys championshiup in 1968 and the Irish Youths title in 1971 and 1972, he won the Irish Close title in 1977 (and was twice runner-up, in 1974 and 1979, also reaching the semi-final in 1990). He has won a tally of 5 Irish championships, the others being the South of Ireland in 1973 and 1988, the 'West' in 1974, and the 'East' in 1978 on his home course, also winning the Mullingar Scratch Cup in 1973. He played 98 interprovincial matches for Leinster 1972-92, winning 54 of these, a success rate of over 60%: he has played 62 Home international matches in 12 different series for Ireland between 1973 and 1990, winning 25 and with a success rate of 50%, being on winning sides in 1983, and in the Triple Crown-winning sides of 1987 and 1990 (when he won 4 out of six matches); has played 17 matches in the European Team championship from 1979 to the winning Irish side of 1985, winning 9 of his matches. His brother Frank, also a member of the Co Louth Club at Baltray, is also a fine amateur, being runner-up in the 1984 'West', and playing 25 interprovincial matches for Leinster between 1980 and 1988, winning 14.

GANNON, WILLIAM (BILL, 'SQUIRES').

G.A.A. footballer, Kildare. From near Kildare Town, he died in 1967. He was the captain of the last Kildare side to win the All-Ireland Senior Football Championship title, when in 1928 they beat Cavan 2-6 to 2-5, so also becoming the first man to recieve the Sam Maguire as captain of a winning All-Ireland S.F.C. side. He also played in the Lillywhites S.F.C. triumph of the previous year, 1927, and in the losing finals of 1925 and 1929.

GARA, A.

Soccer international forward. Club: Preston North End. He played in the No 9 jersey in only 3 international matches for Northern Ireland, all in the 3 Home international Championship games of 1902, but he scored a total of 3 goals, all in his debut against Wales in the 3-0 win. This makes him the first Irishman (north or south) to score a hat-trick in his international debut.

GARDINER, FREDERICK T (FRED).

Rugby international forward. 1874-1921. Club: N.I.F.C. (winning Ulster Senior Cup medals in 1901, 1902 and 1908). He was capped 22 times for Ireland over a 10 year period between 1900 and 1909, captaining the side 3 times in 1909, and playing in all 3 of Ireland's winning Championship matches in 1906. A try-scoring forward (scoring 2 for his country), he was regarded as one of Ireland's great exponents of forward play in his time (and was even twice called on to play at out-half for Ireland). He refereed the Scotalnd v England game in 1912, and is a younger brother of Willie Gardner (cv).

GARDINER, JOHNNY (JAMES ?) B.

Rugby international back. 1902-1960. Club: N.I.F.C. A product of Campbell College, he was capped 13 times for Ireland in the years 1923, 1924 and 1925, firstly at scrum-half, and later in the three-quarter line. He then emigrated to Rhodesia to set up a cattle-ranch, and in 1928 played for Rhodesia against the New Zealand All Blacks.

GARDINER, WILLIE.

Rugby international three-quarter. Club: N.I.F.C. (being a member of the fine 'North' side which won 7 Ulster Senior Cups and 8 Ulster Senior League titles in the 1880's). He was capped 17 times for Ireland between 1892 and 1898, including all 3 matches in the Triple Crown success of 1894, and for the Championship win of 1896. He captained the Irish side for his last cap. He is an older brother of Fred Gardiner (cv).

GARDNER, GEORGE.

Light-heavy weight boxer. Born in Ballinslacken, Lisdoonvarna, Co Clare, 17th March 1877, he died in Chicago in 1954. He was World Light-heavyweight champion in 1903. In 65 contests in his professional career, which lasted from 1897 to 1908, he won 41 (19 inside the distance), drew 10, lost 11 and had other decisions in his other 3 fights. Up to the end of 1901 he had lost only 2 of his first 35 pro fights. He won the world title (being only the 2nd man to take the light-heavyweight title, as it had only been created that year) on 4th July 1903, knocking out the Austrian champion, Jack Root in the 12th round in Fort Erie, Canada. He lost the title after only 4 months reign, to a 40-year-old Bob Fitzsimmons in San Fransisco, on points after 20 rounds. Among those to beat him in his career were Joe Walcott and Jack Johnson (who out-pointed him over 22 rounds in 1922). He is an older brother of Jimmy Gardner (cv).

GARDNER, JIMMY.

Welterweight professional boxer. Born in Lisdoonvarna, Co Clare, 25th December 1885. Starting as a lightweight pro, he fought the first of 5 famous bouts against Mike 'Twin' Sullivan. He claimed the World Welterweight title in 1908 after beating Jimmy Clabby for Sullivan's vacant title at New Orleans, but his claim is hotly disputed. He had earlier that year been beaten for the title by Mike 'Twin' Sullivan, and drew with Clabby 19 days after beating him. He later boxed as a middleweight, retiring after a 3-round k.o. in 1912 by Frank Klaus, who became world champion later that year. In his professional career of 100 contests, he won 51, drew 22, had no decision in 22, and lost only 6 bouts. A younger brother of George Gardner (c.v.).

GARGAN, MATT.

G.A.A. hurling midfielder, Kilkenny. He won 6 All-Ireland Senior Hurling Championship winner's medals with Kilkenny, in 1905 with Tullaroan, in 1907 and 1909 with Mooncoin, in the awarded final of 1911, with Tullaroan again in 1912 (when he scored late on to eclipse Cork in this, the last 70 minute final, held at Jone's Road), and finally again with Mooncoin in 1913. He was a complete player, known for his long pucking, and was at home covering any position on the park.

GARNER, (nee MADILL) MAUREEN.

Amateur and professional golfer. Born in Coleraine, Co Derry, 1st February, 1958. Club: Portstewart. As an outstanding amateur, she won the prestigious British Ladies Amateur title in 1979 (beating Jane Lock by 2 and 1 in the final at Nairn), and also captured the 1980 British Open Strokeplay title. She also was a finalist in the 1982 Irish championship, won the Ulster Ladies in 1980 and the Avia Foursomes in 1980 and 1985, and the Sunningdale Foursomes in 1984. She was an Irish amateur international each year from 1978 until 1983, and played in the European Team championships in 1979 (when Ireland won at Hermitage), 1981 and 1983 (when Ireland won again at Waterloo). She played in the Vagliano Trophy in 1979, 1981 and 1985. She won Curtis Cup honours in 1980, halving only one of her 4 matches played. Later turned professional in 1986, she has had reasonable success in this sphere. Her sister, Patricia played interprovincial golf for Ulster in the 1970's.

GARTH, JONATHAN D.

Cricket international. Born 12 January 1965. Club: Y.M.C.A. He played international cricket for Ireland 26 times between 1986 and 1989, scoring 392 runs and taking 24 wickets for his country. Also a rugby flanker with Wanderers, he was a member of the Irish Seven-a-side team which reached the semi-final of the inaugural World Sevens in Edinburgh in 1993.

GARVAN, LIZ.

G.A.A. camogie forward, Cork. Clubs: Old Aloysians and U.C.C. A quality forward with poise and grace, she scored 3-6 in the 1970 All-Ireland Senior Championship final win over Kilkenny, winning 3 more O'Duffy Cup medals in the 3 following years, 1971, 1972, and 1973. She also reached interprovincial level in tennis for Munster, and won many individual awards in that sport.

GARVEY, PHILOMENA K.

Amateur and professional golfer. Born near the Baltray links, Drogheda, Co Louth, 26th April 1927. Club: Co Louth. She won the Irish Ladies Championship title an unrivalled 14 times in a 25 year spell, in 1946, 1947, 1948, 1950, 1951, 1953, 1955, 1957, 1958, 1959, 1960, 1962, 1963, and in 1970, and never lost any final in this event. She reached the quarter-finals of the U.S. Ladies title in 1950. In 1955 she, with Philip Scrutton, won the Worplesdon Mixed Foursomes. She shares the record of being runner-up most times (4) in the British Amateur Championship, in 1946 at Hunstanton to June Hetherington, in 1953 to Marlene Stewert at Portcrawl, in 1960 to Elizabeth Price at Ascot, and in 1963 in the Open event to Barbara McIntire (U.S.A.). However she reached her peak in 1957, winning the British Amateur title by a margin of 4 and 3 in the final at Gleneagles, over the legendary Jessie Valentine. She won Curtis Cup honours 6 times for Great Britain and Ireland (a record for an Irish woman until surpassed by Mary McKenna cv), in 1948, 1950, 1952, 1954, 1956, and 1960, winning 2, halving 1 and losing 8 of her 11 matches played (she refused to play in the 1958 fixture because no recognition was given to Ireland in the team crest). Playing in the Vagliano Trophy in 1959 and 1963, she turned professional in 1964, but was later reinstated in 1968. She played for Ireland in the Home international series 18 times between 1947 and 1969, captaining the side 5 times. Ranking amongst the greats of Irish ladies golf, in 1963 she was made Texaco's Golf Sportstar of the Year.

GASKINS, PEADAR.

Soccer international defender. Clubs: Shamrock Rovers (winning a League of Ireland winner's medal in 1937-38, and an F.A.I. Cup medal in 1935/36) and St James Gate (winning a League of Ireland Championship medal in 1939/40). He played in 7 pre-War international matches for Ireland between 1934 and 1938.

GAVIGAN, MARTIN.

G.A.A. football centre half-back, Donegal. From Ardara, he was born in 1966. A PE teacher, he made his senior championship debut in 1988. In 1990 he won an Ulster S.F.C. medal with Donegal and went on the 'Compromise Rules' tour to Australia. He was a member of the historic Donegal team which captured the county's first ever All-Ireand Senior Football Championship title in 1992, when Dublin were beaten in the final. He won an All-Star award in 1992 in the centre half-back position. His brother Luke won a vocational schools football title in 1984 and an All-Ireland Under 21 medal in 1987.

GAVIN, ENON.

G.A.A. football right full-back, Roscommon. Born in 1971. Club: Clann na nGael (winning a county championship medal with them in 1991, having been a sub for them when they lost the All-Ireland Club Championship final in 1990). In his first year at senior inter-county level with Roscommon in 1991 he helped his county to win the Connacht Senior Football Championship, and to an All-Ireland semi-final place. He won an All-Star in 1991 as a right corner-back.

GAVIN, JOHN (JOHNNY).

Soccer international outside-right. Born in Limerick, 20th April 1928. He left Limerick City in 1948 (being their leading league scorer in the 1937/38 season) to play 12 years in English League football. His clubs there were: Norwich City (who paid £1,500 for him, and for whom he scored 122 league goals in 8 years, 1948-54 and 1955-58, a club record for most league goals in total aggregate); Tottenham Hotspur; Watford, and Crystal Palace. He was capped 7 times for the Republic of Ireland between 1950 and 1957, scoring 2 international goals.

GAVIN, Father THOMAS J (TOM).

Rugby international centre-threequarter. Clubs: Moseley and London Irish. A product of Cotton College of (Staffordshire) and Cambridge University, he was capped for Ireland only twice, but both of these games, against France and England in 1949, came in the year of Ireland's 2nd successive Triple Crown. A headmaster, he has the unique distinction of being the only practicing Roman Catholic priest ever to be capped for Ireland in rugby.

GAYNOR, LEN.

G.A.A. hurling wing back, Tipperary. Club: Kilrane McDonagh's (whom he coached in 1986 to win the All-Ireland Club Championship). A member of the Tipperary minors beaten in the All-Ireland M.H.C. final in 1962, he won All-Ireland Senior Hurling Championship medals with Tipperary in 1965 and 1971, and was on sides beaten in the Liam McCarthy Cup finals of 1967 and 1968. He won 3 Railway Cup medals with Munster, in 1968, 1969 (when he became the 10th Tipp-man to captain the winning side) and 1970, while he won National League medals in 1965 and 1968. He later coached Tipperary (1983-1984) and Clare hurlers (in the early 1990's).

GAYNOR, Mrs P F (nee ZELLIE FALLON).

Amateur international golfer. Born in Mallow in 1924. Club: Douglas. She won the Irish Ladies Championship in 1964, having been runner-up in 1958. She won the Munster Ladies title 5 times, in 1955, 1956, 1957, 1959 and in 1961. She was almost a constant member of the Irish Ladies Home International team for the 20 years from 1951 to 1970, playing in 17 seasons. She was non-playing captain of that side in 1972, and had been captain of the World Team side in 1965.

GEANY, MARY.

Ladies all-round sportswoman. From Castleisland, Co Kerry, and a product of the Ursuline Convent in Cork, she excelled at 4 sports. She played camogie for Cork, and won 3 All-Ireland Senior Championship medals with the Rebel County. As a hockey goalkeeper, and member of Corks Old Ursaline club, she played schools and senior interprovincial, and was first capped for Ireland in 1973. Winning a total of 60 caps, she played on both the Irish side which won the Intercontinental Cup in Kuala Lumpar in 1983, and on the famous side which beat England 1-0. She also played Gaelic Football with Kerry and represented Munster at badminton. Her father Con, a member of the Firies club, won an All-Ireland Senior Football Championship winner's medal with Kerry in 1932, at right half-back. Her brother Dave, a Castleisland Desmonds player, captained the Kerry minors in 1958, and won an All-Ireland S.F.C. winners medal in the Kerry winning side of 1959, at right corner forward.

GEOGHEGAN, SIMON Patrick.

Rugby international wing-threequarter. Born in Knebworth, Herefordshire, 1st September 1968. Clubs Wasps, London Irish. Playing Irish Students, Under 25 and Ireland 'B' in 1990, and starring for Connacht, he made a spectacular debut in the International Championship season in 1991, scoring 3 international tries, and being voted the R.W.I. 'Player of the Year'. Playing for Ireland on tour in Namibia in 1991, and in their fine World Cup run in 1991, this exciting player's tally of tries for his country has reached 4, gained in 16 interntional caps up to March 1993.

GERAGHTY, JOHNNY.

G.A.A. footballing goalkeeper, Galway. Clubs: U.C.G. (winning a Sigerson Cup medal in 1976), and Mountbellew. He was a member of the St Jarlath's of Tuam team which won the 1960 All-Ireland College's final. He won 3 All-Ireland Senior Football Championship medals with Galway, in 1964, 1965 and 1966, not coceding a goal in any of the 3 finals. He also won a National Football League medal in 1965, a Railway Cup medal with Connacht in 1967, and trained Galway's minors to their All-Ireland title win in 1976.

GERNAN, PATSY.

Amateur international boxer. Club: St Andrew's. He won 5 Irish National Senior championship titles, at 3 different weights. In 1936 and 1937 he captured the featherweight crown; he won at lightweight in 1939; and he won at welterweight in 1940 and 1941.

GIBB, J T.

Soccer international player. Club: Wellington Park. He won 10 caps in the early international history of Northern Ireland history, between 1884 and 1889, and he scored 2 international goals.

GIBBONS, JOHN.

G.A.A. footballer,centre-half forward, Mayo and Meath. Born in 1947. Clubs: Louisburgh, Summerhill (winning 3 Meath SFC medals, and one Leinster Club medal in 1975). He played on all grades for Mayo in 1965, also playing at minor and junior hurling. A member of Mayo's National Football League winning side of 1970, he also won a Connacht S.F.C. medal in 1967 (when also on Mayo's All-Ireland Under 21 title-winning side). A replacement All-Star in 1973, he also played senior football for Meath for 3 years between 1975 to 1978. A teacher.

GIBBONS, A (SHAY).

Soccer international forward. Born in Dublin, 19th May 1929. Club's: Whitehead Rangers, St Patrick's Athletic, Holyhead Town, Dundalk. Between 1951 and 1959, he scored 120 (with a club record of 108 with Pat's) League of Ireland goals, making him the League's most prolific goalscorer of the 1950's, and 12th on the all-time list of goalscorers in the league. With St Patrick's Athletic he was 3 times leading goalscorer in the League of Ireland; in 1951/52 with 26 goals in 22 games for the club's first success in the League of Ireland; again in 1952/53 with 22 goals; and finally in 1955/56 with 21 goals, when Pat's had won the 2nd of successive League of Ireland's (in the win of 1954/55 he scored a club record 28 league goals for St Pat's, but was not the League's top goalscorer). Scoring 2 Inter-League goals for the League of Ireland, he won 4 international caps for the Republic of Ireland between 1952 and 1956 (all while at St Pats, making him that club's first and most often capped player). Also a talented Gaelic football midfielder, he subbed for Dublin, and was on the Parnell's side beaten in the Dublin club championship final of 1950. His brother Johnny Gibbons played G.A.A. for Dublin.

GIBSON, Cameron MICHAEL Henderson (MIKE).

Rugby international out-half, centre three-quarter and winger. Born 3rd

December 1942. Educated at Campbell College, Trinity, and Cambridge (for whom he won 3 Blues, 1963, 1964, and 1965), he is a solicitor. Clubs: Cambridge University and N.I.F.C (winning Ulster Senior Cup medals in 1969 and 1973). Probably Ireland's most complete backline player of all-time, his 69 caps for this country over a record 16 seasons, February 1964 to June 1979 (4 months longer than Tony O'Reilly), along with 12 Test caps for the British and Irish Lion's, made him for 13 years from 1978 to 1991, with 81 international caps, the most capped player in the game of rugby. For Ireland, he won 25 caps at out-half, 40 as centre, and 4 on the wing, and scored 9 tries, 7 conversions, 6 drop goals, and 17 penalties, for a total of 115 points (making him Ireland's 5th most prolific scorer of all-time). He was 36 years and 6 months old when he was last capped for Ireland, on the Australian tour of 1979, making him the oldest player to play for Ireland. His other tours with Ireland were to Australia in 1967 and to New Zealand and Fiji in 1976. He travelled on 5 British and Irish Lion's tours, a record, 3 times to New Zealand, in 1966, 1971 (according to many experts this was the peak of his considerable playing abilities), and 1977; and twice to South Africa (1968 and 1974), making a total of 12 consecutive Test appearences (2nd in most consecutive tests behind Willie John McBride, and third in all-time test tally behind Willie John and Dickie Jeeps) in 69 games for touring Lion's sides. His tally of 155 1st class matches for Irish and the Lions' sides is a still a world record. He also has the distinction of being the world's first ever international replacement, when he came on as a sub for Barry John in the 1st Test in South Africa in 1968. In 1973 he was chosen as Texaco's Rugby Sportstar of the Year.

GIBSON, JIMMY.

Wheelchair athlete. From Belfast. A fine all-round sportsman, his fortes were table-tennis, basketball, snooker and lawn bowls. In the 1968 Paralympic Games in Tel Aviv, he won a silver medal in snooker. In the 1972 Games he again took silver in Snooker, and won a much-prized gold medal in Bowls Pairs. He competed again in the 1976 Games, without collecting a medal. His cousin, also from Northern Ireland, Mark Gibson, became a wheelchair sportsman also, and won a Gold Medal in the 1984 Paralympics in the U.S.

GIBSON, MICHAEL Edward ('GIBO').

Rugby international No 8 and 2nd row forward. Born in Dublin, 3rd March 1954. Clubs: Dublin University, Cork Constitution, Lansdowne, and London Irish. Capped four times for Ireland in 1979, when he was voted Player of the Year by Rugby World magazine, he went on later to win 6 other caps for Ireland up to 1988, thus winning 10 international caps over a 10 year period.

GIBSON, W K.

Soccer international. Club: Cliftonville. He was capped 13 times for Northern Ireland between 1894 (in his first international against Wales in 1894 he was only 16 years and 240 days old, making him the youngest player ever to play for Northern Ireland) and 1902, scoring one international goal.

GIFFORD, WILLIE ('BLINKY').

Amateur featherweight boxer. Club: Army. A Dublin army private from 1940, he won the Army Senior Featherweight Championship 5 times, in 1940, 1941, 1942, 1943 and in 1947. He won the Irish National Senior Championship title at featherweight in 3 successive years, 1943, 1944 and 1945. A product of inner Dublin, the war scuppered his chance for international competition. He died in 1978.

GILBERT, ROBERT (BOBBY).

Soccer international forward. Clubs: Shamrock Rovers (winning 3 F.A.I. Cup winner's medals with the Hoops in 1966, 1967 and 1968), Drumcondra and

Dundalk. He won one international cap for the Republic of Ireland, in the 1966 game against West Germany.

GILES, Michael JOHN (JOHNNY or 'GILESEY').

Soccer international midfielder. Born in Dublin on 6th November 1940. Early clubs: St Columbas, Dublin City, Munster Victoria, the Leprechauns and Stella Maris. At 17 he moved from Home Farm to Manchester United as a right winger, scoring 13 goals for them in 114 appearances (and winning an F.A. Cup medal in 1963), until joining Leeds United later in 1963. At Elland Road, he played 380 league matches in 12 great years as the supremo of the Don Revie team, scored 115 goals in all for the club (joint 5th in their all-time list), and won 2 League Championship medals in 1965-66 and 1973-74 (also being on runners-up squads 4 times). He also won an F.A. Cup medal with Leeds in 1972 (and played in 3 losing finals, in 1965, 1970 and 1973), to add to the one he won with United in 1963 (this gave him the joint record of 5 appearances in F.A. Cup finals). A passer of the ball without equal with either foot, with Leeds he also won a League Cup medal in 1967-68. He later played as a player-manager for both W.B.A. (steering them to Division One football) and for Shamrock Rovers (winning an F.A.I. Cup medal in 1978). He also played for Philadelphia Fury and successfully coached the Vancouver Whitecaps. His tally of 99 English league goals was a commendable achievement for any midfielder. He won a then record 60 caps for the Republic of Ireland over a 21 year illustrious span, between 1959 and 1979, scoring 5 international goals (at the time of his first cap he was the then youngest player ever to play for the Republic, 18 years and 361 days. His 13 goals (5 as penalties) in European club competitions is a record for an Irishman, winning a Fairs Cup medal with Leeds in 1967-68 and 1970-71 (and being on 3 Leeds teams beaten in European club finals). Moving into club and international management, he guided Ireland into a new era of international soccer. He was chosen as Texaco's Soccer Sportstar of the Year 3 times, in 1968, 1972 (when he was also chosen as Texaco's Supreme Sportstar of the Year), and 1974. His uncle Matt managed Transport to win the 1950 F.A.I. Cup, and Drumcondra to capture the same trophy in 1950 and 1954.

GILL, JAMES RUPERT.

Cricket international right hand batsman. Born in Dublin, 24th September 1911. Clubs: Civil Service and Leinster. In his only first class match, he attained the unique distinction in world cricket of scoring a century and a duck in the 2 innings of his first 1st class match. He was President of the Irish Cricket Union in 1964.

GILL, MICK.

G.A.A. hurling midfielder, Galway and Dublin. Born in Ballindereen, Co Galway in September 1899, he died in 1980. In 1925 he became the only player in G.A.A. history to win two All-Ireland Senior Hurling Championship medals in the same calendar year. On 14th September 1924 he was on the winning Galway team in the delayed All-Ireland S.H.C. 1923 final victory over Limerick.Then on 14th December of the same year, playing now for Dublin, he won a championship medal again, this time helping to defeat none other than his native county, Galway. A quality player, he went on the win a third All-Ireland S.H.C. winner's medal with the Dublin side of 1927 (when he played an outstanding captain's part, scoring 0-4 in the final), and also played on the losing Dublin side in the 1930 All-Ireland final. He won a Railway Cup medal with Leinster in the inaugural year of 1927. A Garda.

GILL, WILLIAM J (WILLIE).

Amateur international golfer. Club: Sutton (winning a Barton Cup medal in

1928) and Portmarnock (winning 5 Barton Shield and 6 Senior Cup medals). He was leading amateur in the 1931 Irish Open, and was runner-up in the West of Ireland in 1940. Having played for Ireland against Wales in 1931, he went on to play in the first 6 Home international series between 1932 and 1937, winning 13 of his 24 matches. He was Honorary Secretary of the G.U.I. for over 20 years, 1949-67 and 1970-74. He was President of the G.U.I. in 1969, and in 1955 he was the first captain of an Irish side which won the Home international series. The Willie Gill Award, given annually to the amateur golfer who performs most consistently in Irish amateur golf's 5 'majors' (the West, East, North, South and Close), is named in his honour,

GILLESPIE, BILLY.

Soccer international inside-forward. Born in Londonderry 1891, he died in 1981, aged 90. Clubs: Derry City, Leeds United (scoring 10 goals in 24 games), Sheffield (whom he helped to win the F.A. Cup in 1925). He was joint holder, with Joe Bambrick, Gerry Armstrong and Colin Clarke, of the record number of goals scored for his country, Northern Ireland, with 12 goals (until Clarke scored his 13th goal in 1992), which he scored in 25 international games between 1913 and 1931, in an international career span of 18 years. In 1932 he joined Derry City as manager for 9 years, during which period they finished runners-up in 3 Irish Leagues and one I.F.A. Cup final. He is still the most capped Sheffield United player, winning all of his 25 caps while at the club.

GILLESPIE, DECLAN.

Flat jockey. Born into a farming background in Sligo, 28th March 1954. Champion apprentice in 1973 under Kevin Prendergast, he has ridden the winners of 4 Irish classic races: the Irish 2,000 Guineas of 1988 with Prince of Birds; the 1983 Irish Oaks with Give Thanks; and 2 winners of the Irish St Leger (Mountain Lodge in 1983 and Dark Lomond in 1988). He includes many Group winners in his tally of over 750 winners as a jockey. He retired at the age of 36 to train horses.

GILLIC, P J .

G.A.A. football left half-forward, Meath. Club: Carnaross. Born in May 1967. He is the only Meath player to win Leinster Football Championship titles at all 4 grades, minor (1965), junior, Under 21 (1985) and senior. He has won 2 All-Ireland Senior Football Championship medals with the successful Meath side of 1987 and 1988, and was on the losing side in the All-Ireland S.F.C. finals of both 1990 and 1991.

GILMARTIN, JOHN JOE.

Handballer, hardball and softball. Born in 1916 in Kilkenny (or in Boyle, Co Roscommon). Regarded by many as the greatest Irish handballer of all time, he dominated the Irish scene over a 12 year period from 1936 to 1947, winning a record 24 All-Ireland Senior medals in that time (and would have won more but for a 2 year period spent in England), including all 4 titles in 1939. This tally of 24 Irish senior titles was a record until surpassed by Michael 'Ducksie' Walshe in 1993. He won the Dr Harty Cup for the Senior Hardball Singles 10 times in that period (1936-42 and 1945-47). He also won the Irish Senior Hardball Doubles 8 times, 1937-1941 and 1945-1947. He won six Irish Softball titles, 3 at Senior Singles (in 1938, 1939 and 1946) and 3 at Senior Doubles, 1940, 1941 and 1942. His supremacy was such that he never lost a singles hardball match in the 11 years up until he retired in 1947. He died in 1980. His brother Jimmy won the All Ireland Junior Singles and Doubles in 1943, and in the same year won a Leinster S.H.C. medal with Kilkenny in goals.

GILMORE, TOMMIE JOE (T.J.).

G.A.A. football centre-half, Galway, Born in 1951. Club: Cortoon. Making his senior inter-county debut in 1970, he played on 3 Galway sides which were beaten in All-Ireland Senior Football Championship finals in the early seventies, in the 1971 loss to Offaly, in 1973 to Cork and in 1974 to Dublin. He was the only Galway player to be selected as a football All-Star in 1972 being picked at centre half-back, and he gained a 2nd award in the same position the following year.

GILROY, FREDDIE.

Bantamweight boxer. Club:St John Bosco (Belfast). Born in Belfast, 7th March 1936. He won the Irish National Senior Championship title at bantamweight in 1956. He then won a bronze medal at bantamweight for Ireland at the Olympic Games in Melbourne in 1956, defeating the favourite for gold (a Russian, Boris Stepanov) en route to losing to the German Wolfgang Behrent in the semi-final. Turning pro in 1957, he became European Bantamweight champion in 1959-69, was British Empire champion 1959-62 and was British champion in 1959-63. In his 5 year pro career he won 28 (18 inside the distance) and lost only 3 of his 31 contests. A very hard hitter, he won his European title at the Empire Pool in London in November 1958, beating Italian Piero Rollo on points, having earlier in the year beaten the Scot Peter Keenan to win the British Empire and British titles. He defended his Commonwealth title successfully against Bernie Taylor of South Africa, and his 3 titles against the Scot Billy Rafftery. His world title stint against Frenchman Alphonse Halimi in October 1960 was mysteriously given on points against him. He lost to Belgian Pierre Cossemyms for his old Euro crown, and later beat Rafftery again. He beat Johnny Caldwell (cv) in a classic fight in 1962 for his British and Commonwealth crowns in what was to be his last fight. In 1959 he won the prestigious Geoffrey Simpson Award for the best young boxer of the year. A winner of a Lonsdale belt, he was Texaco's Boxing Sportstar of the Year in the inaugural year of 1958, winning again in both 1959 and 1962 (only Barry McGuigan has won more Texaco awards for boxing).

GILROY, MAEVE.

G.A.A. camogie player, Antrim. Club: St Malachy's. An all-action player, she won 2 All-Ireland Senior Championship medals with Antrim, in 1956 and in 1967 in a replay win over Dublin, these 2 victories for Antrim stopping Dublin winning every title from 1948 up to 1967. She was a member of the only Ulster side to win a Gael Linn Senior Interprovincial Championship in 1967. She later became an All-Ireland referee, and was Lady Captain of Balmoral Golf Club.

GILSENAN, MATTY.

G.A.A. footballer, Meath. He captained the Meath Senior Football Championship side which was beaten in the All-Ireland final by Kerry in 1939 by 2-5 to 2-3, and also won a Leinster S.F.C. medal in 1940. He won a Railway Cup medal with Leinster in 1940, when he became the first Meathman to captain a winning side.

GILVARRY, JOE, JOHN and PADDY.

G.A.A. footballing brothers, Mayo. Joe and John were on the Mayo team which were beaten by a point by Cavan in the 1948 All-Ireland Senior Football Championship final, and Paddy was a substitute in that game. Joe went onto win a Sam Maguire Cup medal in Mayo's All-Ireland S.F.C. win of 1950, and also won a Railway Cup medal with Connacht in 1951.

GIVENS, DON.

Soccer international striker. Born in Castleconnell, Co Limerick, 9th August 1949. Clubs: Manchester United (playing only 5 games for them), Luton Town (scoring 19 times in 83 games 1970-72), Queen's Park Rangers (scoring 76 league goals in 242 matches between 1972 and 1977, helping them to promotion from Division 2 in 1973, and to finish 2nd in Division One in 1975-76), Birmingham City, Bournemouth, Sheffield United. He has scored 113 English League goals, and has also scored 9 goals in European club competitions. He spent his last 6 seasons in Switzerland with Neuchatel Xamax, scoring 34 Swiss League goals, and captaining the club to it's first ever Swiss League title. In his 56 international caps for the Republic of Ireland over a 13 year period between 1969 and 1982, he scored a then record 19 international goals (since surpassed by Frank Stapleton cv), the highlights being his 3 against U.S.S.R. in October 1974, and his 4 against Turkey in October 1975 (only the 2nd Irish player to accomplish this feat in an international match). The 26 caps gained while at Q.P.R. from 1973 to 1978 made him that club's most capped player. He was selected in 1975 as Texaco's Soccer Sportstar of the Year.

GLEESON, JACK.

G.A.A. hurler, Tipperary. He won 4 All-Ireland Senior Hurling Championship medals with Tipperary sides at the turn of the century: in 1895 with Tubberadora, in 1899 with Moycarkey, in 1900 with Two-Mile-Borris, and in 1906 with Thurles.

GLEESON, WILLIE.

G.A.A. hurling forward, Limerick. He won 2 All-Ireland Senior Hurling Championship winner's medals with Limerick, in 1918 and 1921 (scoring 2-2 in the first Liam MCarthy Cup final), being also on the team beaten in the All-Ireland S.H.C. final of 1923 (when scoring 1-2). One of Limerick's finest hurlers in the 20's, he was a member of the Munster side beaten in the final of the inaugural Railway Cup series in 1927, which took place in Portlaoise on St Patrick's Day at Croke Park.

GLEN, WILLIAM ('SACKY').

Soccer international right wing-half. His main club was Shamrock Rovers, with whom he won a joint club-record number of 7 F.A.I. Cup medals; in 1925, then in the 5-in-a-row years of 1929, 1930, 1931, 1932, 1933, and lastly in 1936; he was also on 2 losing F.A.I. Cup final sides with the Hoops, in 1922 and 1926. A permanent Rovers fixture from 1922 to 1936, he also won 4 Football League of the Irish Free State winner's medals with Rovers in 1922-23, 1924-25, 1926-27, 1931-32 (when the 'double' was achieved). Later he joined Shelbourne, with whom he won an 8th F.A.I. Cup medal in 1939, scoring the only goal in the final, thereby becoming the first of only 2 players to win a record 8 tally of F.A.I. Cup winner's medals. He was capped for the Irish Free State side 8 times in a 9 year period between 1927 and 1936.

GLENNON, JAMES Joseph (JIM).

Rugby international 2nd row forward. Club: Skerries (the club's first and only capped player). A fine scrummager, he won a 'B' international cap against Scotland in 1979. He was capped 4 times for Ireland between 1980 and 1987, his last cap gained while coming on as a replacememt in the 1987 World Cup in Australia and New Zealand, having previously won 2 caps in 1980. His Leinster career took a similar path, being out of contention for years, after playing for the province for over 5 years in the early 1980's.

GLENNON, JOSEPHINE.

Ladies G.A.A. centre-half back, Westmeath. Club: Rochfortbridge (with whom she has won 11 county championship medals, and 2 Leinster club and 2 All-Ireland club runners-up medals). An All-star in 1985 and 1986, she captained Westmeath for many years, and did so on in their only All-Ireland Senior Championship final appearence in 1987 when they lost 2

Kerry. She has also won 3 All-Ireland titles in athletics.

GLENNON, PETER ('IRELAND'S FIGHTING NEWSBOY' and 'THE WAIF WITH THE WICKED PUNCH').

Amateur featherweight boxer. Club: Unity B.C. Born in Rutland Place in Dublin, he won titles which included juvenile featherweight, Leinster senior bantamweight, and in 1939 he won his only Irish National Senior Championship title at featherweight. In the same year he won the Golden Gloves in the U.S.A., and boxed for Ireland all over the world. After retiring he took up coaching, as is responsible for producing more senior boxing champions than anyone else in Ireland.

GLOVER, JOHN.

Amateur international golfer and administrator. Born in Belfast, 3rd March 1933. Clubs: Queen's University and Knock. Having been runner-up in the inaugural Ulster Boys in 1949, he was the winner of the British Boys title in 1950 (the 2nd of only 4 Irish golfers to do so), and he was runner-up in the 'North' in 1951. He won the British Universities title in 1954 and 1955. He later won the Formby Hare in 1963 and the Lancashire Amateur in 1970. He played 40 Home international matches for Ireland over a 20 year period between 1951 and 1970, securing 42 points, and being a member of the winning side in 1955. He also played 22 interprovincial matches for Ulster, securing 25 points. In 1981 he became Secretary of the Royal and Ancient Rules of Golf Committee.

GLYNN, DESSIE.

Soccer international centre-forward and utility player. Born in Dublin, 7th June 1928. Clubs: Johnville (winning an F.A.I. Junior Cup medal in 1946), Clifton United, Drumcondra (winning a League of Irleand medal in 1948-49, and an F.A.I. Cup medal in 1954, also being on the losing side in the 1955 final), and Shelbourne. He is Drumcondra's highest League of Ireland aggregate goalscorer, with 96 goals, and with 15 more for Shelbourne, his total of 111 League goals places him in top 20 of all-time goal scorers in the League of Ireland. He was the League's leading goal-scorer in 1950/51 season with 20 goals. He was capped twice for the Republic of Ireland, in 1952 against West Germany (against whom he scored the winner in a famous 3-2 win), and in 1955 against Norway. He also scored 3 goals in Inter-League fixtures.

GOLDING, JOHN ('LYE').

Soccer international. Club: Shamrock Rovers (with whom he won F.A.I. Cup medals in 1928, 1929, 1930 and 1931). He was capped for the Irish Free State twice against Belgium, in 1928 and in 1930.

GODWIN, TOMMY, F.

Soccer international goalkeeper. Born in Dublin 20th August 1927. He left Shamrock Rovers (after winning an F.A.I. Cup winner's medal in 1948) at 22 to join Leicester. But it was at Bournemouth that he made his name, playing 357 league matches in the years between 1952 and 1961. He was capped 13 times for Ireland between 1949 and 1958, and the 4 caps he gained while at Bournemouth and Boscomme Athletic made him that club's most capped player, until surpassed by Colin Clarke (cv).

GOOD, Mr T.D. and Mrs T.D.

Badminton players. This husband and wife pair won 21 caps for Ireland between them, T.D. winning 5 caps betwen 1902 and 1913, and his wife (nee Carroll), winning 16 caps betwen 1902 and 1929. Their daughter Barbara won 12 caps for Ireland between 1946 and 1954, usually in doubles partnership with either Nora Conway or Jim Fitzgobbon. Barbara's brother and sister, Norman and Doreen, also played badminton to international standard for Ireland.

GOODALL, ARCHIE L.

Soccer international defender. Clubs: Derby County and Glossop. He was capped 10 times for Northern Ireland between 1899 and 1904, scoring 2 international goals (the only goal in a 9-1 defeat by Scotland in 1899, and one more in the 2-0 win over Wales in 1903). His brother John, a Huddersfield and Derby County striker, played 14 times for England between 1888 and 1898, and scored 12 international goals. This is the only time an Irish international soccer player's brother has played soccer for England.

GOODALL, KENNETH George (KEN).

Rugby international No 8 forward. Born in Leeds, 23rd February 1947. Clubs: City of Derry and Newcastle University. Between 1967 and 1970 he was capped 19 times for Ireland (only 5 of these games were lost), and scored 3 international tries. An outstanding No 8 forward, he scored a memorable try in Landsdowne road against the Triple Crown-seeking Welsh in a famous 14-0 Irish win in 1970. He toured South Africa in 1968 with the British and Irish Lion's, but was injured in his first match. A teacher, he turned to rugby League later that year, joining the Workington club.

GOODWIN, DOUGLAS E.

Cricket international right forearm medium bowler. Born in Dublin 2nd May 1938. Club: Malahide. A product of King's Hospital, he played 11 first class games for Ireland between 1965 and 1973, his record in those matches being 11-16-2-188-39(against Scotland in 1972)-13.43-583-20-29. 15 (his best bowling being 5 for 46 against the M.C.C. in 1968). His total cap tally for Ireland in all matches came to 43 (1965-1975), taking 115 wickets for an average of 22.18 per wicket, while he also scored 494 runs for Ireland, and took 26 catches. His most remarkable bowling performance was as captain of the famous Irish side which beat the West Indies at Sion Hill in 1969 (in a non-first class game), when he bowled 5 out for only 6 runs.

GORDON, EDWARD J (EDDIE or NED).

Bowls skip, outdoor and indoor. Born in Belfast. Club: Falls Bowling Club. He won 21 caps for Ireland outdoors, and 21 further caps in the indoor game (and won about 20 Inter Association caps), injury cutting short his career. He won 7 Irish Senior Cup medals, 8 Private Green Cup medals, and 7 Private Green League medals. He was twice winner of a gold medal in the British Isles Championships (Pairs in 1970, and Fours in 1974), won the Championship of Champions Tournament in 1970, and won a Commonwealth Games Bronze medal in 1970. He later became an international captain, selector, President of the I.B.A., and became a popular B.B.C. commentaor on bowls from 1972 to 1987.

GORDON, H.

Soccer international defender. Club: Linfield (winning Irish Cup medals with them in 1891, 1892, 1893, and 1895). He was capped 11 times for Northern Ireland in the No 2 jersey between 1891 and 1896. A relation, T Gordon, a member of the same dominant Linfield side, won 2 international caps as a goalkeeper in 1894 and 1895.

GORDON, THOMAS GISBORNE.

Rugby international three-quarter. 1852-1935. Educated at Rugby. Club: N.I.F.C. A product of Rugby School, he was capped for Ireland 3 times in international rugby, in 1877 and 1878, and is remarkable in that he played all his international rugby with no right hand, which he lost in a shooting accident.

GORE, ROBERT George.

National Hunt trainer. Born in Ireland in 1859, he moved to England in the 1880's to train at Findon, and died in 1941. He trained the winners of 2 Aintree Grand Nationals, Jerry M in 1912, and Covert Coat the following year. He had previously (in 1910) won the Grand

Steeplechase de Paris on Jerry M. His other fine horse was Cackler, who won the 1908 Champion Chase, and the Grand Sefton in both 1909 and in 1910.

GORMAN, WILLIAM C (BILL).

Soccer international full-back. Born in Sligo 13th August 1911. Clubs: Bury, and Brentford. He was capped for the All-Ireland team 4 times, and the Irish Free State side 13 times between 1936 and 1947, with a gap for World War II. Eleven of his caps came while he was based at Gigg Lane, Bury, making him that club's most capped player.

GORMLEY, ENDA.

G.A.A. football left full-forward, Derry. He was a member of the Derry side which impressively won the National Football League in the 1991-92 season (the county's first win in this competition in 45 years), and who reached the Ulster Senior Football Championship final in the same year. He won an Ulster S.F.C. medal in 1993, having been awarded a 1992 All-Star award in the left corner-forward position, and played on the Derry side which captured the All-Ireland Senior Football Championship for the first time that year.

GORRY, MARY Philomena.

Amateur international golfer. Born in Baltinglass, 11th June 1952. Clubs: Baltinglass and The Grange. She was Irish Ladies Champion in 1975 and 1978. Other wins include the Hermitage Scratch Cup (1978), the South of Ireland Scratch Cup (1975, 1978, 1980), the Midland Ladies (1974 and 1978), the Leinster Ladies in 1977 and 1979, while she was voted Irish Lady Golfer of the Year in 1978 and 1979. She played Home international golf each year from 1971 to 1980 (when Ireland won the title at Cruden Bay), and was non-playing captain in 1988. She was on the Irish Ladies European Team each occasion in the 1970's, 1971, 1973, 1975 and 1979 (when the title was won at Hermitage). She played Vagliano Trophy in 1977.

GOTTO, DAVID.

Squash international player. Born in Belfast, 25th December 1948. Club: Windsor (helping them to win the All-Ireland Club Championship in 1975). He was Irish National (Close) Champion 4 times, in 1976, 1977, 1978, and in 1982 (and was runner-up in 1979 and 1981). He at one time held the world record for most international caps in squash, winning 122 caps for Ireland over a 15 year period. His first cap was against England in the Home internationals at Stirling in 1976, and he won his last cap in April 1989 in the European Championships against Sweeden. In 1977 he became only the third Irishman to win an international match against English opposition, in Cork.

GOUGH, KEITH.

Judo competitor. Born in Coolock in Dublin in 1970. Club: Dublin University JC. A winner, in the same year, of Irish Under 18, Under 21 and Senior All-Ireland judo titles, up to 1992 he had won every national competition he had entered, and was National Under 60kg champion in 1989, 1990, 1991 and 1992. Moving to train in England, he progressed steadily through Welsh, Scottish and British tournaments, and won a bronze medal at the Swiss Open in 1991. Then in 1992 he became the first Irish judoist to be placed in the first six in a major championship when he won a coveted bronze medal at the European Championships in Paris. Based in Cumbria, he represented Ireland in the Under 60kg event at the Olympic Games in Barcelona 1992.

GOUGH, OLIVER.

G.A.A. hurler, Wexford and Kilkenny. One of the small band of G.A.A. players to have won All-Ireland Senior Hurling Championship medals with 2 different counties, he came on as a sub for Ned Wheeler in Wexford's Liam McCarthy Cup triumph in 1955. Eight years later he again came on as a sub (this time for Johnny McGovern) in the Kilkenny win over Waterford in the All-Ireland S.H.C. final. This gives him the unique distinction of having won Liam McCarthy Cup medals for 2 different counties, but without having being in the starting line-up for either.

GOULDING, SIR BASIL.

Squash, cricket and soccer player. Born on 4th November 1904, He captained the Oxford soccer team. In 1940 he won the Irish Squash title, also being capped once in 1949. He also was capped at international level for Ireland at cricket. A successful businessman, he was Chairman of W&HM Goulding.

GOULDING, EAMONN.

G.A.A. hurler and footballer, Cork. He won an Liam McCarthy Cup medal for All-Ireland Senior Hurling Championship in 1954 with Cork at full-forward. Then in 1956 he played on both Cork Senior Hurling and Football sides beaten in All-Ireland Senior Championship finals, coming on as a sub in the football final after playing on the losing side in the hurling final. He also played again on a losing Sam Maguire Cup final All-Ireland S.F.C. side in 1957.

GOULDING, NIALL.

Amateur international golfer. Club: Portmarknock. A Corkman, he was twice runner-up in the Irish Close Championship, in 1989 at Rosses Point and in 1991 at Ballybunion. At Rosses Point he also won the 'West' in both 1990 and 1991 (becoming the first man since Joe Carr in 1962 to retain this title). In 1991 he was also joint runner-up in the 'East'. Winning his first Irish senior spurs in 1989, he was a member of the Irish side which captured the Triple Crown of wins in their first ever win on away soil in Conway, Wales in 1990, and was also on the side which won the Home International Championship in both 1991 and 1992.

GRACE, DICK.

G.A.A. hurler, Kilkenny. He won 4 All-Ireland Senior Hurling Championship winner's medals with Kilkenny sides, in the awarded final of 1911, in 1912 with Tullaroan, with Mooncoin in 1913, and in 1922 (scoring 2 goals in an outstanding display in the final) in the county's win over Tipperary, and their first win in the Liam McCarthy Cup.

GRACE, JACK.

G.A.A. footballer and hurler, Dublin. From Tullaroan, Co Kilkenny., he captained the Dublin sides, represented by Kickhams, which won both the 1906 and 1907 All-Ireland Senior Football Championship titles (both over Cork sides, by scorelines of 0-5 to 0-4 and 0-6 to 0-2 respectively). He also won a further 3 All-Ireland S.F.C. medals, in 1901, 1902, and 1909, bringing his tally to 5 (he was on the losing Dublin side in 1904). Also a useful hurler, he is unique in that he captained All-Ireland senior final sides in both codes, his hurling captaincy came in the losing final of 1908. In the period of July 3rd to 24th 1909, he played for Dublin in 3 All-Ireland senior finals over the space of 4 Sundays. A brother of Pierce Grace (cv).

GRACE, JOE.

Soccer international player. A Bohemians and Drumcondra player, he won one cap for the Irish Free State, in 1926 in the Irish Free State first venturing into international football, against Italy. This cap was gained while at Drumcondra (helping them to the Intermediate Cup and F.A.I. Cup in 1927), and makes him the only current Leinster League player ever to play for the what is now the Republic of Ireland.

GRACE, PADDY.

G.A.A. hurling right full-back, Kilkenny. Clubs: Carrickshock and Dicksboro (winning a tally of 5 county championship medals in all). He won an All-Ireland M.H.C. medal as captain in 1935. In a senior inter-county career for Kilkenny which stretched from 1939 to 1950, he won 2 All-Ireland Senior Hurling Championship medals, in 1939 and 1947, and won 4 other Leinster S.H.C. medals, including All-Ireland final defeats in 1940, 1945 and 1946. He won a solitary Railway Cup medal with Leinster in 1941. He became Kilkenny county board secretary for over 40 years from 1948.

GRACE, PIERCE.

G.A.A. footballer and hurler, Dublin. Although (like his brother Jack Grace cv) he was from Tullaroan in Co Kilkenny, he succeeded with Dublin to win All-Ireland Senior Football Championship medals in 1906 and 1907, on both occasions accompanied by Jack. He went on to win 3 All-Ireland Senior Hurling Championship medals with his native county, Kilkenny in 1911, 1912, and 1913, to become the first of only two players to win more than one All-Ireland title in both codes.

GRACE, THOMAS Oliver (TOM).

Rugby international right wing three-quarter. Born in Dublin, 24th October 1948. Clubs: U.C.D. (winning a Leinster Senior Cup medal in 1970) and St Mary's College (winning Leinster Senior Cup medals in 1971, 1974, and 1975, and Leinster Senior League medals in 1972 and 1978). Between 1972 and 1978, this product of Newbridge College won a then record 25 caps on the wing for Ireland (a tally only recently surpassed by Trevor Ringland and Keith Crossan), 7 of them as captain (in the 1976 and 1977 seasons), and scored 5 international tries. His first cap was in the famous, and most recent, Irish victory on French soil. He toured South Africa with the famous undefeated 1974 British and Irish Lion's (scoring 4 tries versus Grigualand West in one tour match). He captained the Ireland party on their first ever tour of New Zealand and Fiji in 1976, winning 5 out of 8 matches (his own 4 tries made him leading try scorer on the tour). Capped at interprovincial level for Leinster 21 times from 1968 to 1978, he also toured Argentina with Ireland in 1970. He was selected as Texaco's Rugby Sportstar of the Year in 1975.

GRAHAM, DEREK Austin.

International long-distance athlete. Born 22nd September 1944. Club: 9th Old Boys. Competing in the International Cross Country championship for Ireland from 1962 to 1970, he finished 5th in the race in 1965 and a highly creditable 2nd in 1966 at Rabat Racecourse behind Morroccan runner El Ghazi (he also finished 10th in 1967 and 11th in 1968). He was 4th, while representing Great Britain, in the European Championship 5,000 metres at Budapest in 1966, having also represented Britain in the 5,000 metres in the Olympic Games in Tokyo in 1964. He was selected as the Texaco Sportstar of the Year in Athletics in 1965.

GRAHAM, NOEL.

International rowing cox. One of Ireland's most outstanding rowing cox's, he is the only one to steer an Irish coxed boat to reach a World Championship Grand final in either heavyweight or open class, achieving this feat when the coxed pair of Davey Gray (cv) and Iain Kennedy (cv) finished 6th in the Grand Final of the World Championships on Lake Karapiro, New Zealand in 1978.

GRAHAM, WILLIAM Ernest.

Hockey international half-back. Born in 1874. Clubs: Palmerston, Monkstown. Noted as a vigorous tackler, he was capped 10 times for Ireland between 1907 and 1909, and won an Olympic silver medal in 1908 when the Ireland side lost the final to England, having beaten Wales in the semi-final. He was President of the I.H.U. in 1933-1934, the third former international to gain this honour, and spent some time as an Irish selector.

GRAHAM, WILLIAM G L (LEN).

Soccer international full-back. Born in Belfast, 17th October 1925. He played 303 league matches for Doncaster Rovers between 1950 and 1958, scoring 3 league goals, during which time the 2nd Division side reached the 5th round of the F.A. Cup 4 times. His other English

League clubs were Brantwood and Torquay. He was capped 14 times for Northern Ireland between 1952 and 1959, all gained while he was at the Belle Vue Ground, making him Doncaster Rovers most capped player.

GRANT, EDWIN Leslie (EDDIE).

Rugby international wing threequarter. Born in Belfast, 13th April 1946. Club: C.I.Y.M.S. (winning Ulster Senior Cup medals in 1972 and 1974, and Ulster Senior League medals in 1971, 1972, 1973 and 1974). Although he won only 4 senior international caps for Ireland, all in the 1971 season, he scored 3 tries, one in each of his first 3 games, 2 of them from interceptions, making him the first Irish player since Michael Mortell in 1933 scored a try in each of his first 3 internationals.

GRAVES, Charles ROBERT Arthur (BOB).

Rugby international hooker. Born on Valentia Island, off Co Kerry in 1909, he died at age 81 in 1990. Club: Wanderers. A product of Bishop Foy School in Waterford, he played 19 interprovincial matches for Leinster from 1930 to 1938, and was capped 15 times for Ireland between 1934 and 1938, playing in all matches in the 1935 success in the International Championship, the first win for Ireland since 1899. A versatile player, he played 13 matches and won 2 test caps (one as a prop) on the British and Irish Lion's tour of South Africa in 1938, playing in the famous 21-16 final Test victory. An able administrator and a noted after-dinner speaker, he was president of the Leinster Branch of the I.R.F.U. in 1959-60, and was an Irish selector in 1959-61.

GRAY, DAVEY.

International oarsman. Along with Iain Kennedy (cv) and cox Noel Graham (cv), he was 8th in the World Championships in the Coxed pair in 1977, and the following year he won a place in the Grand Final of the World Championships in Lake Karapiro in New Zealand, finishing 6th overall. In the 1980 Olympic Games in Moscow he was the cox in the Irish Coxed 4 boat which finished in 11th place.

GRAY, Robert DISNEY.

Rugby international flanker and No 8. Born in Ballybay, Co Monaghan, 2nd January 1896, he died in 1980. Clubs: Old Wesley and Barbarians. Playing 7 times in the Interprovincial series for Leinster between 1922 and 1925, he won 4 international caps for Ireland in the 1920's, two in 1923, and one each in 1925 and 1926. He also rowed with the Dolphin club, and his son Peter (later to become Treasurer of the Olympic Coucil of Ireland from 1973), competed in the Flying Dutchman class for Ireland at the 1960 Olympic Games in Rome.

GREALISH, ANTHONY P (TONY).

Soccer international midfielder. Born in Paddington, 21st September 1956. Clubs: Orient, Luton Town, Brighton and Hove Albion, and West Bromwich. A classy midfielder, he was capped 44 times for the Republic of Ireland between 1976 and 1986, scoring 8 international goals. In 1982 he was captain of the Brighton side which drew in the Wembley final of the F.A. Cup against Manchester United, but was injured for the 3-0 defeat in the replay. His first cap came while he was at Orient (where he was apprenticed), and he is that club's most capped player, with 7 while based there.

GREEN, W STANLEY.

Hockey international forward. Club: Royal Air Force. He won 22 hockey international caps for Ireland between 1948 and 1955, and scored a goal in the deciding match against England when Ireland won it's most recent Triple Crown in 1949.

GREEN PEREIRA, HAZEL.

Archer. One of Ireland's finest archers, she is one of a select band of Irish sportspersons (and the only archer) to represent Ireland in 3 different Olympic Games, hers being in succession; in Moscow in 1988 when her 2229 pts placed her 19th; in 1984 in Los Angeles when her 2440 pts placed her in 20th place; and in Seoul in 1988 when her 1208 points placed her in 38th place.

GREENE, CHRISTY.

Professional golfer. Born 13th November 1926. Attached to Milltown GC. He represented Ireland in the 1965 Canada (World) Cup in Madrid. He won the 1956 and 1968 Irish National Professional Championship title, and won the Irish Dunlop title in 1964. He won the Southern Irish Professional title in 1965 and in 1974.

GREENE, ERNEST H ('THE SWALLOW').

Rugby international and athlete. Clubs: Dublin University, Kingstown School, Wanderers. Blessed with a magnificent swerve, he played 9 times for Leinster at interprovincial level, and won 5 international rugby caps for Ireland as a wing three-quarter between 1882 and 1886 (although Ireland lost all 5 games), scoring one international try. He was Irish sprint champion over 100 yards in 1885.

GREENE, STEPHEN.

G.A.A. hurling left-corner forward, Waterford. He was a member of the Wateford side which reached the Munster S.H.C. final for the first time in 16 years in 1982, also playing when they reached the 'Munster final' again in 1983. He won one All-Star award in 1982 at left full-forward.

GREENE, TOMMY.

Motorcycle racer. Born in Nottingham, England in August 1886, he was raised and educated in Ireland. He won th 500cc class of the 1913 French G.P., thus becoming the first Irishman to win a Grand Prix. In the 1913 Irish End-to-End Trial, he set a record time of 10 hours, 38 minutes, and also finished 3rd in Bilbao to San Sebastian race in Spain. In 1914 he was 2nd in the Motorcycle circuit of Italy, and in 1921 he won the distinction of capturing the first ever Portland Cup trial. He rode in the Isle of Man T.T. races without success in 1913, 1914 and 1921. He died in Sydney Australia in 1975, aged 89.

GREEVES, THOMAS JACKSON.

Rugby international centre three-quarter. Club: N.I.F.C. (winning an Ulster Senor Cup medal in 1908). He won 5 international rugby caps for Ireland between 1907 and 1909, and later, in 1929-30, became President of the I.R.F.U. He died in 1974, at the age of 88.

GREGG, EAMONN.

Soccer international player. Clubs: Bohemians (winning 2 League of Ireland winner's medals, in 1974-75 and 1977-78, and an F.A.I. Cup medal in 1976), Shamrock Rovers, Dundalk (winning a League of Ireland medal in 1981-82), St Patrick's Athletic, Kilkenny City (as player manager). He was capped at senior level 9 times for the Republic of Ireland in the Johnny Giles era, between 1978 and 1980, all while a League of Ireland player (the 8 caps he won while with Boh's make him the club's most capped Republic of Ireland player). He managed Kilkenny City when the club won the First Division title in 1989-1990, and later managed Bohemians to win the F.A.I. Cup in 1992 (thus winning this trophy both as a player and manager, both with the Gypsies). His family have had a long association with Shamrock Rovers, his brother Jimmy playing regularly for them, winning an F.A.I. Cup medal in 1968.

GREGG, HARRY.

Soccer international goalkeeper. Born in Derry, 25th October 1932. His earlier clubs included Dundalk, Linfield Rangers and the Swifts, and he left Coleraine (for £1,200) at the age of 20 to spend 14 successful years in English league football. He played 93 matches for Doncaster between 1952 and 1957, before signing for Manchester United (for a then world record fee for a goalkeeper of £24,000) for nine years up to 1966, playing in 247 matches for the 'United', being regarded as the club's best ever goalkeeper, although his only honour was an F.A. Cup runner-up medal in 1958). Missing many games through injury, he later played with Stoke. He played in 24 international matches for Northern Ireland between 1954 and 1964, and was a hero for his country in the 1958 World Cup in Sweden, being voted the oustanding goalkeeper of the finals competition (with a brilliant display against West Germany). A brave survivor of the Manchester United Munich air crash, he was crucial in Northern Ireland's defeat of England at Wembley in 1957. He later managed Shrewsbury Town, Swansea City, Crewe Alexander and Carlisle.

GREGG, RICHARD GEORGE STANLEY.

Hockey international. Clubs: Dublin University and Three Rock Rovers. Although only capped 4 times for Ireland at hockey, he was a member of the Irish side which won the silver medal in the 1908 Olympic Games in London, when they were beaten 8-1 in the final by the England.

GREGG, ROBIN JOHNSTON.

Rugby international full-back. Club: Queen's University Belfast. He won 7 international caps for Ireland between 1953 and 1954. He jointly holds the Irish record (with Paul Murray cv) of most conversions in an international, as he kicked 4 in the 1955 International Championship match against Scotland at Murrayfield. His total points tally for Ireland in his 7 appearences was 12 points, all from conversions.

GREGG, TERENCE Adrian (TERRY).

Hockey international forward. Born 23rd November 1950. Clubs: Queens Universtiy Belfast, and Belfast Y.M.C.A. He held until 1988 the record as the most capped home countries hockey player in history, being capped 103 times for Ireland (being only the 2nd Irishman to pass the hundred mark), and 42 times for Great Britain, a total of 145 caps (and would have gained more but for injury cutting short his career). A brilliant goalscorer, he scored the classy solo goal that beat Great Britain in the final of the 8 nation event at Santander in 1972, and once scored 5 goals against Poland. He also played for Great Britain in the Munich Olympic Games of 1972 (when they finished in 6th place), and scored 19 goals for them in his tally of 42 caps from 1972 to 1980. In 1977, with his brilliant captaincy of Ireland's performance in finishing as runners-up in the Intercontinental Cup in Rome, he was the tournament's highest scorer (with 9 goals), was voted 'best player of the tounament', and he was chosen as only the 2nd hockey player to be voted Texaco Sportstar of the Year for this sport.

GREGORY, JOHN Arthur (JACK).

Athletics sprinter, Ireland, and rugby international, England. Born 22nd of June 1923, he was a product of St Andrew's College in Dublin. While he lived in Ireland for the years after World War Two, he captured 6 Irish sprint titles, over 100 and 200 yards, in 1947, 1948 and 1949. He competed for Ireland in athletics in the Triangular international matches in Edinburgh 1947 and Manchester 1948 (against England and Scotland), and competed for G.B. in the Olympics of both 1948 (when he won a silver medal in the 4x100 relay) and 1952 (also in the 4x100 relay). In 1949, while a member of the Bristol club, he was capped for England on the wing in their match at Cardiff against Wales, thereby representing two different countries at 2 different sports. He also played Rugby League (for Huddersfield) in 1947.

GRIBBEN, HUGH FRANCIS, OWEN, and RODY.

G.A.A. footballing brothers, Derry. All three played (Rody as a sub) in the losing Derry side in the All-Ireland Senior Football Championship final against Dublin in 1958. Hugh Francis (in 1960) and Rody (in 1956) were to win Railway

Cups medals with Ulster. Two other brothers, Mickey and Henry, also played for Derry.

GRIFFIN, JOHN.

Long distance runner. Club: Tralee. Born in Co Kerry in 1959. Up to May 1992 he had run 17 marathons (with a best time of 2:14.42), and won 2 successive Dublin City Marathons, in 1988 and in 1989 (when his time was 2.16.45), and finished 3rd in this race in 1991.

GRIFFIN, LESLIE John (LES).

Rugby international lock forward. Born in Arklow, 14th September 1922. Clubs: Wanderers (winning Leinster Senior Cup medals in 1947 and 1954) and Barbarians. A product of St Andrew's College in Dublin, he played in 15 interprovincial series matches for Leinster between 1945 and 1951. His only 2 international caps for Ireland came in winning matches against Wales and Scotland in the Triple Crown-winning year of 1949.

GRIFFIN, KATHLEEN.

G.A.A. camogie player, Tipperary. Clubs: St Patricks (with whom she shared in the clubs only 2 All-Ireland Club Championship titles, in 1965 and 1966), and Roscrea. She played on 4 losing Tipperary side in the All-Ireland Senior Championship finals, in 1953, 1958, 1961, and 1965. She also won Gael Linn medals, and was later secretary of the Munster Council. Also an accomplished badminton player.

GRIFFIN, PAUL.

Amateur international featherweight boxer. Club: Drimnagh BC. Born in 1972. He won 6 Irish titles in the junior ranks, and also won Irish titles at under 18 and intermediate levels. In 1991 he won the Irish Senior National Championship title at featherweight, beating his conquerer of the previous year Roy Nash, and won again in both 1992 and 1993. In 1991 he became the first Irish boxer since Maxie McCullough (cv) in 1949 to take a European Championship title when beating Russian Tatin in the featherweight final, having earlier beaten the world junior champion, Alan Vaughan of England in the semi-final. In 1993 he won a bronze medal (retiring injured) while attempting to defend his European title in Bursa, Turkey. He represented Ireland at the Olympic Games in 1992 at Barcelona at featherweight.

GRIFFIN, PEG.

G.A.A. camogie centre half-back, Dublin. Club: Col San Dominic. One of the game's most accomplished centre backs, she had brilliant ease of movement, and fine positioning sense. She won 4 All-Ireland Senior Camogie Championship medals with Dublin, in 1937, 1938, 1942, and 1943.

GRIMES, ASHLEY.

Soccer international left-back and midfielder. Born in Dublin, 2nd August 1957. Clubs: Villa United, Bohemians (winning an F.A.I. Cup medal in 1976), Manchester United (scoring 11 goals in 77 appearences, helping them to 2nd place in Divison One in 1979-80), Coventry City, Luton Town (helping them to win the Littlewoods Cup in 1987-88 and to their highest ever placing in Division One, 7th in 1985-86). Capped twice at Under 21 level, he was also capped at senior level 17 times for the Republic of Ireland between 1978 and 1988.

GRIMES, EAMONN.

G.A.A. hurling midfielder, Limerick. Born in 1949. Club: South Liberties. From Ballysheedy, he is a product of Limerick C.B.S. (Sexton Street); he won 3 Dr Harty Cup medals in 1964, 1965 and 1966, and won 2 All-Ireland Colleges medals with them in 1964 and 1966. Making his senior inter-county debut in 1966 before he did his Leaving Certificate (he was on the Limerick minors beaten in the All-Ireland M.H.C. final in 1965), he won his first major medal in 1971 when Limerick captured the National League.

He captained the most recent Limerick side to win an All-Ireland Senior Hurling Champinship, in 1973, which they won after a gap of 33 years, by beating Kilkenny by 1-21 to 1-14, scoring 0-4 in a fine game himself. He also played on losing Limerick sides in 2 All-Ireland S.H.C. finals of both 1974 and 1980. He has won 2 All-Star awards, in 1973 and in 1975, both at right half-forward. In 1973 he was chosen as Texaco's Hurling Sportstar of the Year. His father, Ned Cregan, won an All-Ireland S.H.C. medal with Limerick in Jubilee year of 1934 as a full-back, having played on the Limerick side which was beaten in the All-Ireland final of the previous year.

GRIMES, PHIL (PHILLY).

G.A.A. hurling midfielder, Waterford. Born in May 1929, he died on his 60th birthday in 1989. Club: Mount Sion (winning no less than 12 senior county championship medals with his club, 9 of these in succession, 1953 to 1961). In an inter-county career which lasted 19 years from 1947 to 1965, he won only 3 'playing' Leinster S.H.C. medals (he emigrated briefly to America after a first round match in 1948, but got both his provincial and All-Ireland medals as a non-player that year), the wins coming in: 1957 (when captain of the side, and the All-Ireland final's top scorer with 1-6), 1959 when he was on the famous Waterford side which won the All-Ireland Senior Hurling Championshiip (and thus became the first Waterford-man to hold 2 All-Ireland S.H.C. medals), and 1963 (when again they were beaten in the All-Ireland final). In 1948 he won an American S.H.C. winner's medal with Tipperary. He won 2 Railway Cup medals with Munster in 1958 and 1960. He also won a National Hurling League medal with Waterford in 1963, and an Oireachtas medal in 1962. His brother-in-law, Frankie Walsh, was captain of the 1959 Waterford All-Ireland S.H.C. winning side, scoring 14 points between the 2 finals (0-6 in the draw, and 0-8 in the replay).

GRIMSHAW, COLIN.

Rugby international scrum-half. Born 20th March 1947. Club: Queen's University, Belfast (winning an Ulster Senior League medal in 1967). In 1969, in a winning international against England, Roger Young (cv) was injured, and when replaced by Grimshaw, it was the first time in international rugby history that a clubmate substituted for another in the scrum-half position. Grimshaw also became the first Irishman to win his only international cap as a replacement (he came on in the 33rd minute).

GUERIN, MICHAEL.

Amateur international golfer. Club: Killarney (winning a Barton Shield medal in 1980). He won the South of Ireland title 3 years in a row at Lahinch, in 1961, 1962, and 1963, and was runner-up in 1978. He played 48 interprovoncial matches for Munster over a 23 year period from 1960 to 1982, winning 24; he also played Home international golf in 1961 (while still a junior) and 1963, winning 5 of his 8 matches.

GUINAN, LARRY.

G.A.A. hurling right full-forward and right half-back, Waterford. Club: Mount Sion (winning county championship medals). He was one of 6 Mount Sion clubmen to help win Waterford's last Liam McCarthy Cup, in the 1959 win over Kilkenny, and was also in the side beaten in the 1963 All-Ireland final by Kilkenny. He won a National Hurling league medal with Waterford in 1963 also. He won a Railway Cup medal with Munster in 1959.

GUINEY, DAVID (DAVE).

Shot Putt athlete. From a sporting family in Duhallow in Co Cork, he was born in Kanturk. He won 7 All-Ireland junior championships in the shot putt, and first came into senior athletics in 1939. He took his first National Senior title in the shot putt event in 1941, and for a period of 13 years from 1944 to 1956 he was unbeaten in All-Ireland shot putt championships. In 1950 set an Irish record that lasted for 10 years. He won 2 British A.A.A. Shot Putt titles, in 1947 (throwing 14.48 metres) and 1948 (when he threw 14.41 metres). He represented Ireland in European Championships, and in the Olympic Games in London in 1948 (his putt of 45'7" failing to make progress beyond the preliminaries). His international career involved matches against 7 other countries, and he also won an Irish Championship in the long jump discipline. He later became a highly respected sports journalist and sports writer (being behind the enormously successful 'Dunlop Book of ..' series).

GUINNANE, ANN.

Pitch and Putt player. Club: St Anne's (Cork). In the early 1980's she won 4 Irish national titles in succession, the 1980 and 1981 National Strokeplay title, the 1982 National Matchplay title, and then in 1983 she regained her Irish Strokeplay title.

GUINNESS, SIR ALGERNON LEE ('ALGY') and KENHELM LEE ('BILL').

Car racing pioneer brothers. Algy (born in c 1884) bought an 18 litre V8 Darracq car in 1906, and in it September 1907 he became the first person to drive a motor car under official observation to exceed 100 m.p.h., when at Brooklands he went off at 115.75 m.p.h. In 1907 he finished 3rd in the Isle of Man Tourist trophy in the same car, and he finished 2nd in 1908. He also was 2nd in the Circuit of Ardennes in 1907. In 1922 he won the Isle of Man T.T. for 1 litre cars (Voiturettes). His brother Kenneth (known to most as Bill) was 3rd in a works Sunbeam in the 1913 Coupe de L'Auto at Boulogne, and the following year won the Isle of Man T.T over 600 miles in a 2 day race, averaging 56.44 m.p.h. He also won the 1922 Voiturette G.P of the A.C.F. at Le Mans, having been 2nd in 1921. In the 1923 French Grand Prix, along with Henry Segrave (cv) and Albert Divo, he was an Irishman in a winning British car (Sunbeam) in a winning British team, so becoming the first of either category to win a full Continental Grand Prix.

GUIRY, WILLIAM.

G.A.A. footballer, Limerick and Dublin. He is the first player in either code of G.A.A. history to win successive All-Ireland senior titles for different counties. In 1896 he was in the Limerick selection from Commercials that triumphed over Dublin, and the following year won a 2nd All-Ireland Senior Football Championship medal, this time with the Young Ireland selection, representing Dublin.

GWYNN, LUCIUS Henry.

Rugby and cricket international. Born in Ramelton, Co Donegal, 1874, he died in Switzerland at the age of 29, in 1902. In rugby, while playing for Dublin University, he won 7 caps for Ireland on the wing between 1893 and 1898, including being ever-present in the three-quarter line when Ireland won it's first ever Triple Crown in 1894. His brother Arthur P Gwynn, was capped at half-back for Ireland once, against Wales in 1895. Both men also were Irish cricket internationals, Lucius being regarded as Ireland's finest batsman in his day (he also played for Lancashire and the Gentlemen of England, for whom he scored an 80). His playing record for Ireland in 11 international cricket matches gives him the best average runs-per-innings of any pre-W.W.II cricketer (and 2nd of all time), with figures of 38.38, from 499 runs in 15 innings (he also took 14 wickets for Ireland). Arthur played 4 first class matches for Dublin University in 1895, while a third younger brother, Robert M (one of the founder members of D.U.C.A.C.), played in these same games. All 3 brothers played rugby for Leinster. Another brother, Edward J, became Provost of Trinity College from 1927.

H

HACKETT, JOSEPH D (JOE).

Tennis player. He won the Irish junior tennis title in 1942 and 1943, and the Fitzwilliam L.T.C. club championship in 1957 and 1966 (having been a beaten finalist in 1942, at the age of 16). He won Irish Men's Doubles titles in 1950 and 1953, and, with Guy Jackson (cv) he reached the last 16 of the Wimbledon men's doubles in 1953. Regarded as one of this country's best ever tennis players, he represented Ireland in 10 Davis Cup matches between 1950 and 1961 (including taking part in the longest ever Davis Cup match, a doubles in 1950 with 88 games, and being on Irish sides which won matches in 1950 and 1958). Also a noted rugby player with Leinster Senior Cup medals with both U.C.D. (in 1948) and Old Belvedere (in 1951 and 1952), he played interprvincial rugby 5 times for his province Leinster between 1949 and 1952.

HACKETT, MARTIN and STEPHEN.

G.A.A. hurling brothers. In the 1917 All-Ireland Senior Hurling Championship final, Martin played on the winning Collegian's side representing Dublin, while his brother Stephen was on the losing Tipperary side (represented by Boherlahan), the final score being 5-4 to 4-2.

HALE, ALFIE.

Soccer international inside-forward. Born in Waterford, 28th August 1939. In 3 periods in the League of Ireland, 1956-60, 1966-77, and 1981-82, he scored a total of 153 league goals. placing him 5th on the all-time goalscorers list in the League of Ireland, and he was the league's joint top scorer in 2 seasons, 1971/72 with 22 goals and in 1972/73 with 20 goals, both with Waterford. At 21 went to play in English League football, playing with Aston Villa, Doncaster Rovers (for whom, in 119 league matches, he scored 42 goals), while in 34 league matches for Newport County he scored 21 goals. Back with Waterford he won 5 League of Ireland Championship winner's medals in 1967-68, 1968-69, 1969-70, 1971-72 and 1972-73, being the club's leading league scorer in each of these 5 winning campaigns (he was also on 3 Waterford sides beaten in F.A.I. Cup finals, in 1959, 1968 and 1972). He won a 6th League of Ireland Championship medal with Cork Celtic in 1973-74, before finishing his playing career with spells at St Pat's and Limerick. His Inter-League highlights included 6 goals, including a hat-trick. He was capped for the Republic of Ireland 13 times over an 11 year period between 1962 and 1972 (3 times as a sub), scoring 2 international goals. He was the S.W.A.I.'s Player of the Year in 1973. He has the distinction of scoring League of Ireland goals in 4 different decades, the 50's, 60's, 70's and 80's. He later went into football management with Thurles. His father and 2 uncles played in the same half-back line for Waterford in the 1930's, and his three brothers all won honours at soccer; Richard 'Dixie' (a wing half, born 29th May 1935), played over 350 English League games 1959-1969, also gaining youth caps and Inter-League representation; George, a wing-half, won amateur caps; and Harry won schoolboy caps.

HALLARAN, CHARLIE Francis George Thomas.

Rugby international back-row, 2nd row and prop forward. Clubs: Royal Navy, United Services and Wanderers. Killed in action in W.W.II, 1941, at age 44. He was capped 15 times for Ireland in the 2nd row and as a prop forward between 1921 and 1926, sharing in Ireland's joint International Championship success in his final year. Also a Barbarian, he played 6 times at interprovincial level for Leinster.

HALLIDAY, MICHAEL

Cricket international right hand batsman and off-break bowler. Born in

Dublin, 20th August 1948. Clubs: Dublin University and Phoenix. A product of Wesley College, he first played for Ireland in 1970, and before retiring in 1989 he went on to become Ireland's most capped cricketer, with 93 international appearences. Chiefly known a bowler, his figures of 192 wickets off 5819 runs (the most runs ever scored against an Irish bowler) in 129 innings (with an average of 30.30 runs per wicket), make him 5th in the all-time list of most wickets taken for Ireland. His best 1st class bowling figures were 5 for 39 against Scotland in 1979. He also scored 724 runs for Ireland in 81 innings, averaging 15.08, and took 25 catches.

HALLIGAN, BILLY.

Soccer international centre-forward. Born in Athlone c 1888. Clubs: Distillery, Leeds City (playing 24 league games, scoring 12 times for them), Derby County, Wolverhampton Wanderers, Hull City, Manchester United, Rochdale, Preston North End, Oldham Athletic and Nelson. A fine goal-getter, he played one representative Irish League match and 2 Victory internationals, and was capped twice for Ireland in 1911 and 1912.

HALPIN, GARRETT F (GARY).

Rugby international prop-forward, and athletics hammer thrower. Born in Dublin 14th February 1966. Rugby clubs: Wanderers and London Irish. A Kilkennyman, educated in Rockwell College (from where he won 4 Irish schools caps in rugby in 1983 and 1984), he pursued his career in athletics. In a 4 year scholarship in Manhattan College in the U.S.A., he represented Ireland in the World Championships, broke the Irish hammer record, and was 1988 A.I.C.C. Indoor Hammer Champion in America. Returning to rugby with Wanderers in 1989, he toured North America, and before playing for Leinster, gained a cap against New Zealand later in the same year. He later toured with Ireland to Namibia in 1991, and to New Zealand in 1992, his cap tally up to June 1992 reached 5.

HALPIN, THOMAS.

Rugby international forward. Club: Garryowen (winning many Munster Senior League titles, and winning Munster Senior Cup medals in 1904, 1908, 1909 as captain, and in 1911). He won 13 international caps for Ireland between 1909 and 1912, 6 of these on winning sides, and he helped Ireland to share the International Championship in 1912. He died in 1954, aged 66.

HAMILL, GERRY.

Amateur lightweight boxer. Club: Holy Family. He won 2 Irish Senior National Championship titles in the lightweight division, in 1976 and 1977. He represented Ireland in the Olympic Games in Montreal in 1976, losing his first round bout. He went on to win a gold medal for Northern Ireland in the 1978 British Commonwealth Games which were held in Canada, being therefore one of only 6 Northern Ireland boxers to win Commonwealth gold.

HAMILL, MICKEY.

Soccer international centre-half. Born off the Falls Road in Belfast in 1889. Clubs: St Paul's Swifts, Belfast Rangers, Belfast Celtic (with whom in a 20 year career from 1909 to 1929 he won an I.F.A. Cup medal in 1918, and 5 Irish League championships, in 1913-1914, 1920-21, 1926-27, 1927-28 and 1928-29), Manchester United, Manchester City, Glasgow Celtic, and the Forth River team in Boston. One of Irish soccer's greatest centre-halves, he played 1st class football for over 20 years. He was capped 7 times for Northern Ireland between 1912 and 1921 (scoring one international goal), and was captain of the historic Home International Championship winning side of 1913-1914 (when he led the side to only their 2nd win over England in 33 matches). He later managed Distillery.

HAMILTON, BRYAN.

Soccer international midfielder. Born in Belfast, 21st December 1946. Clubs: Linfield (winning an I.F.A. Cup medal with them in 1970), Ipswich (for whom he scored 43 league goals in 142 appearances 1971-75), Everton. Millwall, Swindon, and Tranmere Rovers. Winner of 2 Under 23 caps, he was capped 50 times over a 10 year period for Northern Ireland between 1971 and 1980, scoring 4 international goals. His 7 goals in European competitions places him joint third in the list of Northern Ireland players for this feat.

HAMILTON, BUD H.

All-round sportsman. One of very few Irish sportsmen to play at international level in 4 different sports, he must therefore rank as one of the country's best ever all-rounders. As a cricketer, he played 19 international matches for Ireland between 1891 and 1907, scoring 490 runs for his country in 28 innings, for an average of 18.84. He was also an outstanding bowler, his 95 wickets off 1,436 runs in 34 innings giving him an excellent average of 15.11 runs per wicket. As a badminton player he was was Ireland's first ever champion at both singles and doubles, and had the distinction of becoming Ireland's first ever international badminton player. As a hockey player he won one international cap in 1896, while a member of the Dundrum club. Also an tennis international, he is the brother of Willoughby Hamilton (cv). His son, Arthur, won the first Irish squash title in 1932, and was capped for a total of 15 Irish caps in badminton between 1927 and 1933 (winning the Irish title in 1932 and 1933), often being capped with another son of Bud's, 'Rat' Hamilton.

HAMILTON, GORDON Frederick.

Rugby interantional flanker. Born in Belfast 13th May 1964. Club: Ballymena (winning Ulster Senior Cup medals in 1989, 1990 and 1991). First playing for Ulster and Ireland 'B' in 1991, he played for Ireland throughout the international championship in 1992, toured Namibia, and played in the Irleand's World Cup challenge in late 1991, when he scored 'the try of the championship', which briefly gave Ireland the prospect of beating the eventual winners Australia in the quarter-final. Injury spoiled his 1993 international season and his participation on Ireland's tour of New Zealand in the same season.

HAMILTON, TOMMY.

Soccer international forward. Clubs: Cualann Rovers, Johnville (winning an F.A.I. minor medal), Manchester United (for only a brief spell), Shamrock Rovers (winning 2 F.A.I. Cup medals in 1956 and in 1962 when scoring 2 goals in the final, and also winning 2 League of Ireland Championship winner's medals, in 1956-57, when he was joint leading goalscorer in the league with 15 goals, and 1958-59) and Cork Hibernians. He was capped twice for the Republic of Ireland in 1959, both times against Czechoslovakia. He won the S.W.A.I. Player of the Year award in 1961.

HAMILTON, WILLIAM A (BILLY).

Soccer international forward. Born in Belfast, 9th May 1957. A winner of an I.F.A. Cup medal with Linfield in 1978, he moved to Q.P.R. the same year, before a successful 6-year spell at Burnley, later playing for Oxford United and Limerick City (scoring a club record 21 gaols for them in the Premier League season of 1988-89). He was capped 41 times for Northern Ireland between 1978 and 1986, scoring 5 international goals. He was a star member of the famous Northern Ireland squad which performed with distinction in the 1982 World Cup in Spain, scoring the 2 goals in the 2-2 draw with Austria at Madrid, and was also in the Northern Ireland squad for the 1986 World Cup in Mexico.

HAMILTON, WILLOUGHBY JAMES ('THE GHOST').

Tennis and badminton player. Born in Monasterevin, Co Kildare 1864, he died in Dublin 1943. He won the Irish tennis singles and mixed doubles titles in 1889, having previously won the men's doubles in 1886, 1887 and 1888. He won the Wimbledon Singles Championship in 1890, beating Willie Renshaw 6-8, 6-2, 3-6, 6-1, 6-1, becoming the first winner of 7 Wimbledon titles for Irishmen in the 1890's. He was also an amateur soccer international, playing for Ireland in 1885. A brother, W D ('Drum'), played cricket 14 times for Ireland between 1883 and 1896 (with a fine batting average of 28.05 per innings), also playing cricket for Oxford, and won amateur international soccer caps. 'The Ghost's' niece Mavis MacNaughton, won 20 caps for Ireland in badminton between 1930 and 1939 (and won the Irish title 5 years in succession from 1932 to 1936).

HAMLET, GEORGE THOMAS.

Rugby international forward. Born in Balbriggan in 1881, he died in 1959. Club: Old Wesley (being the club's most capped player until surpassed by Philip Orr in the 1980's). He won 30 international caps for Ireland in a ten year period between 1902 and 1911 (being on the joint-Championship winning side in 1906), making him the most capped pre-Second World War Irish forward, and Ireland's most capped player from 1911 until surpassed by George Stephenson in 1927. He captained the Irish side 8 times from 1908 to 1911. He played interprovincial rugby for Leinster 14 times from 1900 to 1910. He was President of the I.R.F.U. in the 1926/1927 season.

HAMPTON, HARRY.

Soccer international forward. Clubs: Bradford City and Aston Villa (between 1904 and 1920 he scored 213 league goals for the club, a joint record). He won 9 international matches for the Ireland team, all in the Home international series between 1911 and 1914, with his last match being in the famous win over England in the country's first outright win in this championship (and only win until 1979), in 1914. He is Bradford City's most capped player, all of his caps being won while at the Valley Parade Ground.

HANAHOE, TONY.

G.A.A. football centre-half forward, Dublin. Club: St Vincent's (captaining the club to it's solitary All-Ireland Club Championship win of 1976, having also played in the All-Ireland club final with them in 1973). A product of St Joseph's CBS, he was a major force in the revival of the Dubs in their 1974 All-Ireland S.F.C. win over Galway, and then captained the winning Dublin side in the great wins in the 1976 and 1977 All-Ireland Senior Football Championship finals, over Kerry (by a score of 3-8 to 0-10) and Armagh (by 5-12 to 3-6) respectively. He played on 3 All-Ireland S.F.C. final losing sides, firstly in 1975, and then twice more as captain (in both 1978 and 1979 when he became only the 2nd man ever to captain 4 successive senior All-Ireland final sides). He also captained Dublin to a National League victories in 1976 and 1978, and won his only All-Star award in 1976 at right half-forwrd. He later coached the Dublin S.F.C. side.

HANAMY, MARTIN.

G.A.A. hurling left full-back, Offaly. He was the only Offaly player of the side which captured the 1988 Leinster S.H.C. to win an All-Star award that year, winning his place at left corner back. It was his first All-Star award. He also won a Leinster S.H.C. medal in 1989, and was a member of the Offaly side which won it's first National Hurling League title in 1990-91.

HAND, EOIN K.

Soccer international defender, and manager. Born in Dublin, 30th March 1946. Clubs: Swindon (from 1964), Dundalk, Shelbourne, Drumcondra (13 goals scored), Portsmouth (playing 259 league matches for them 1968-1975, scoring 12 league goals), Arcadia

Shepherds of South Africa (14 goals), Shamrock Rovers, Portsmouth again, and Limerick (24 goals). He won 20 international caps for the Republic of Ireland between 1969 and 1976 (all while playing at Fratton Park), scoring 2 international goals, against Chile in 1974, and U.S.S.R. in 1975. He managed Limerick City 1979-1983 (helping them to win the 1979-80 League of Ireland Championship, and the 1982 F.A.I. Cup), and St Patrick's Athletic in 1984-85. He also managed the Republic of Ireland national team from 1980 to 1985.

HANNIFY, JIMMY.

G.A.A. footballer, Longford. Born in 1945. Clubs: Drumlish (Longford) and Civil Service (Dublin), with whom he won a senior county championship medal in 1980). Winning 2 All-Ireland Colleges medals with St Mel's in 1962 and 1963, he was a Longford minor in 1962-64, and an Under 21 player in 1964-67. A senior inter-county player from 1965 to 1976, he was a member of the only Longford side ever to capture the Leinster Senior Football Championship in 1968. He had also been a member of the Longford side which captured the county's only national senior honour, the National Football League in 1966. He also played Railway Cup for Leinster.

HANNON, DESSIE J (DINNY).

Soccer international forward. Club: Bohemians (winning an I.F.A. Irish Cup medal with them in 1908), Athlone Town (winning an Irish Free State Cup, or F.A.I. Cup, medal by scoring the winning goal in 1924, thereby becoming the first player to win medals in both of the premier soccer Cups in Ireland). He played 6 international matches for the I.F.A. side from 1908 to 1913, scoring one goal, and also won 5 amateur international caps up to 1920.

HANRAHAN, CHARLES J (CHARLIE).

Rugby international prop forward. Club: Dolphin. A product of Castleknock College, between 1926 and 1932 he won 20 international caps for Ireland (twice being on sides that shared international Championship titles, in 1926 and 1927), scoring one international try. He played on the second Dolphin side to win a Munster Senior Cup, in 1931. A president of the I.R.F.U. in 1954-55, he died in 1969.

HARBISON, HARRY Thomas.

Rugby international hooker. Born in Dublin,19th August 1957. Clubs: U.C.D. and Lansdowne (winning Leinster Senior Cup medals in 1986 and 1987). A product of Blackrock College (winning Leinster Senior Schools medals in 1974 and 1975), he is one of only a small number of Irishmen to be capped at 4 international levels, School's (1975 against England), Under 23 (1979 v Holland), 'B' (twice, in 1980 and in 1983), and Full. First capped for the senior side in 1984, he previously toured South Africa with Ireland in 1981. He toured Japan with Ireland in 1985. After winning 8 international caps, he injured himself during the World Cup of 1987, and was forced to retire.

HARDY, PHILIP H.

Hockey international defender and midfielder. Clubs: Dublin Y.M.C.A., Hounslow, Cork Harlequins. He was capped 67 times for Ireland between 1973 and 1983, playing in 2 European Cups (Madrid 1974 and Hanover 1982), a World Cup in Buenos Aires in 1978, and the Intercontinental Cup in Kuala Lumpur, playing a few matches as captain. He also won 8 indoor caps for Ireland in 1977/1978.

HARGAN, GERRY ('HARGO').

G.A.A. football full-back, Dublin. Club: Ballymun Kickhams. Born in 1961. In his first senior championship year, this product of St Kevin's CBS was a member of the Dublin side which won the 1983 All-Ireland Senior Football Championship. He was also on the Dublin sides beaten in the All-Ireland S.F.C final by Kerry on both succeeding years (1984 and 1985), playing at full-back in all 3 finals. He was captain of the Dublin side which won the

Leinster S.F.C. in 1989, and was again on a Dublin side beaten in the All-Ireland S.F.C. final in 1992. He won Railway Cup medals with Leinster in 1986 and 1987, won National Football League medals as captain in 1987 and 1989, and toured Australia with Ireland's compromise rules side in 1986. He has won 2 All-Star awards as a full-back, in 1985 and 1989.

HARKIN, TERRY.

Soccer international centre-forward. Born in Londonderry, 14th September 1941. He left Coleraine at the age of 21 to spend 8 years in English league football. In short periods for Port Vale, Crewe Alexander (for whom he scored a club record season's tally of 35 goals in the 4th Division of 1964-65), Cardiff City, Notts County, Southport, and Shrewsbury, he scored 126 goals in 257 English League appearances. He then spent some time in the League of Ireland, being the league's joint leading scorer in 1972-73 with 20 goals, and winning an F.A.I. Cup medal with Finn Harps in 1974. A Northern Ireland Under 23 player, he was capped 5 times at senior level for Northern Ireland between 1968 and 1971, scoring 2 international goals.

HARKINS, SEAN.

Pitch and putt player. Born in Co Cork. Club: Shandon P.P.C. (Dublin). He has won 2 Irish national titles in pitch and putt, the National Matchplay Championship in both 1986 and in 1991.

HARNAN, LIAM.

G.A.A. football centre half-back, Meath. Born in Chicago in 1960. A member of the Meath minors beaten in the All-Ireland M.F.C. final of 1977. He has won 2 All-Ireland Senior Football Championship medals with Meath, playing at centre half-back on both the 1987 and 1988 winning sides, and was on the losing All-Ireland S.F.C. side in the 1991 final. He has also won 2 National Football League medals with the county, in 1988 and 1990.

HARMAN, Dr GEORGE Richard Aniacke.

Rugby international centre three-quarter. Club: Dublin University (winning Leinster Senior Cup medals with them in 1895, 1896, 1897, 1898 and 1890). Born in Crosshaven, Co Cork, 6th June 1874. In 1975, when he died at the age of 101 years and 191 days, he became the longest lived rugby international ever. He played for Ireland only twice, both on winning sides in the centre, therefore helping to capture the 1899 Triple Crown. He played for Leinster 3 times in 1898 and 1899. He also played 1st class cricket with Dublin University, and his brother William R, a middle order batsman, played once for Ireland in first class cricket, in 1907.

HARRINGTON, JACKIE A.

Amateur international golfer. Club: Adare Manor. He won the Irish Close Championship title in 1979, having been runner-up in 1962 (losing only on the 42nd hole in the final). He played 72 interprovincial matches for Munster (placing him joint 2nd in number of appearences for his province) over a 24 year period betwen 1958 and 1981, winning 37 and halving 9, giving him an average of 57.6%: he played 35 Home international matches in 5 series for Ireland between 1960 and 1976, winning 14: and played 6 European Team matches in 1975, winning twice.

HARRINGTON, PADRAIG.

Amateur international golfer. Club: Stackstown. Born in Dublin, 31st August 1971. He was runner-up in the Irish Close Championship in 1990 at the age of 19, and was also runner-up in the 1993 'North'. In 1990 also he was runner-up in both the Scottish and Irish Youth titles, having won the Leinster Boys in 1988. In 1991 he won the inaugural Sherry Cup in Spain, a prestigious event. Winning his first Irish Youth cap in 1990, he also made a sensational debut in the Home international series for Ireland, when winning all 6 of his matches in Ireland's first ever Triple Crown win on away soil, in Conway in Wales (he scored 4 out of 6 when Ireland retained the Home International Championship the following year, and was again on the side which won a hat-trick of victories in 1992). In 1991 he gained selection for the Walker Cup at Portmarnock (losing both of his matches). In 1993 he reached the quarter-final of the Britsh Amateur Championship, which was held in Portrush, and after gaining 5 out of a possible 6 points in the European Team Championship, secured his 2nd Walker Cup place for the match in America (gaining one draw in 3 matches).

HARRINGTON, WILLIAM (BILL).

Cricket international right hand off break bowler. Born in Tempelogue, Co Dublin, 27th December 1869. In the 20 year period between 1902 and 1921, his record in 13 first class matches for Ireland was: 13-21-4-115-28-6.7-0-848-49-17.30. In 1902 he became the first bowler ever in Irish first class cricket to take at least 10 wickets in a match (7 for 76 and 4 for 42). His total international appearences between 1894 and 1921 for Ireland numbered 28, and for 44 innings he took 112 wickets for only 1862 runs (for a fine average of 16.62). He also scored 270 runs with the bat in 42 innings (averaging 8.43), and took 10 catches.

HARRIS, VAL.

Soccer international defender, and G.A.A. footballer, Dublin. Soccer clubs: Pembroke (playing in the Leinster Junior Cup final in 1898); Shelbourne (winning 2 I.F.A. Irish Cup medals, in 1906 and 1920, and getting a runner-up F.A.I. Cup medal in 1923) and Everton. He won 20 caps for Northern Ireland between 1906 and 1914 (being the first Shels player to be capped), including a role in the winning of Northern Ireland's first (and only until 1979) outright Home international Championship of 1913-1914, playing in the No 4 jersey in 2 of the 3 matches (side-lined through injury for the great 3-0 win over England). Previously in 1901 he had been a member of the Dublin side Isles of the Sea which won the All-Ireland Senior Football Championship title, thereby being the first person to win an Irish Cup medal and also the premium award in the traditional football code.

HARRISON, GARFIELD Donald.

Cricket international right hand batsman and right fast/medium bowler. Born in Lurgan, 8th May 1962. Club: Waringstown. In his first cap, and his first class debut, against Scotland in 1983, he scored 83 runs, and took 2 wickets for 30. In 1990 he became the first Irishman in 37 years to take 9 wickets in one innings, doing so against Scotland. He has been capped 71 times for Ireland up to the end of the 1993 season, scoring 1,971 runs (placing him 9th on the all-time list) with an average of 26.28, and he has also taken 103 wickets for an average of 29.73 per wicket. Three of his brothers, all members of Waringstown, were capped for Ireland in first-class cricket: James (born 3rd May 1941), a right hand batsman, played 8 first class matches (and 32 matches in all) for his country from 1969 to 1977, scoring a century against Scotland in 1978; Derek William (born 3rd November 1943), a right hand batsman, played twice in 1st class matches for Ireland in 1978-79 (and 11 times in all); and Roy, a left hand bowler, played one first class match for Ireland, against the M.C.C. in 1968 (and won 3 caps in all). A brother-in-law, Edwin Alexander Bushe (born 11th April 1951, a right hand batsman and wicket-keeper, also of Waringstown), played 7 times for Ireland in 1979-80.

HARRISON, M (Mrs CASEMENT).

Ladies amateur international golfer. Club: The Island. She won the Irish Ladies title 3 years in succession, in 1910, 1911 and in 1912 (being runner-up in 1913). She also played international golf for Ireland in the Home international series in 1909, 1910, 1911, 1912, 1913 and in 1914.

HARTIGAN, BERNIE.

G.A.A. hurler and footballer, Limerick, and field athlete. Born in 1943. Club: Old Christians (winning one Limerick S.F.C. medal). A dual player at county lelvel for a decade, he played both codes for Limerick at minor level in 1959-61 (winning a Munster College's football medal in 1960), at Under 21 in 1964, and at senior level from 1962 to 1974. Along with his brother Pat (cv), he played in the All-Ireland Senior Hurling Championship Limerick winning side in 1973 at left-half forward, and was at centre-field in the 1974 final defeat. Winning a National Hurling League medal in 1971, he also won 3 Railway Cup medals in hurling, in 1966, 1968 and 1970 (and is the only Limerickman to play Railway Cup for Munster at both hurling and football). Also in football he won Divisional honours in the National Football League, and played on the Limerick side beaten in the Munster S.F.C. final in 1965. He was also a field athlete of note, winning county, Munster and Irish titles at the shot, the discus and the hammer. He also represented Ireland at international level at the shot putt, in 1966, 1967 and 1969.

HARTIGAN, FRANK.

National Hunt and flat horse trainer. Born in Ireland in 1880, he went to England to train at Weyhill, and died in 1952. A prolific trainer of winners (his tally over the 2 codes being over 2,000 successes), he won 2 English 1,000 Guineas, with Vaclause in 1915 and with Rose Way in 1919. Training the 2nd placed horse twice in the Aintree Grand National (in 1925 and 1926, both with the same horse, Old Tay Bridge), he finally won the race in 1930 on Shaun Goilin. Another of his quality horses was Wrack, which won 10 times on the flat, and 6 times over hurdles. A nephew of Willie Moore (cv).

HARTIGAN, HUBERT M.

Flat trainer. Champion trainer for 3 years in succession, he is joint 3rd on the all-time list of Irish trainers of Irish Classic races (although he never won an Irish Derby), his winners being: One Irish 2,000 winner, in 1946 with Claro; 6 Irish 1,000 Guineas winners, a joint record tally for this race (in 1942 with Majideh, 1944 witn Annetta, 1946 with Ella Retford, 1947 with Sea Symphony, 1951 with Queen of Sheeba, and in 1954 with Pantomime Queen); 3 Irish Oaks winners (1942 with Majideh, 1948 with Masaka and in 1954 with Pantomime Queen) ; and 2 Irish St Leger winners's (with his own horse Etoile de Lyons in 1941, and with Espirit de France in 1947). Six of these winners were ridden by Joe Canty (cv).

HARTIGAN, PAT.

G.A.A. hurling full-back, Limerick, and shot putt athlete. G.A.A. club: South Liberties. A product of Limerick C.B.S. (Sexton Street), he won Dr Harty Cup medals in 1966 and 1967, and an All-Ireland Colleges medal in 1966. Making his senior inter-county hurling debut (as a forward) in 1968, he represented his county at all grades in both hurling and football. He was a valuable member of the Limerick side which won its long-awaited All-Ireland Senior Hurling Championship title in 1973, (also playing in the 1974 final, when they county lost to Kilkenny). He won one Railway Cup medal with Munster in 1976, and he won a National Hurling League medal with Limerick in 1971. He was a winner of 5 All-Stars in the first 5 years of the scheme, all for the same position, at full back, winning in 1971, 1972, 1973, 1974, and 1975 (thus becoming the first of either code to win 5 awards). In the case of 1973, he was the only nomination for his position. He won the Poc Fada contest on many occasions, including 1961 and 1963. He was also an international athlete, representing Ireland many times at the shot putt. He is a brother Bertie Hartigan (cv).

HARTMAN, GERARD.

Triathlon athlete. Born in February 1962, a former athletic scholarship to the University of Arkansas, has dominated

Irish Triathlon running in the 1980's. National champion 7 times, he has also finished in respectable placings in the famous, gruelling 'Hawaii Ironman' (14th and 24th), which consists of a 2.4 mile swim, followed by a 112 mile cycle, finished off by a full marathon run 26.2 miles).

HARTY, EDWARD PATRICK (EDDIE) and JOHN P (J.P.).

National Hunt jockeys and 3-Day Eventers. Eddie, born 10th June 1937, was an amateur National Hunt jockey (1951-60) who became a professional in 1961, and reached his career highlight by winning the 1969 Grand National on Highland Wedding. A point-to-point specialist (winning over 50 races), his many other big race wins included; the 1968 Mackeson Gold Cup on Jupiter Boy; the 1968 Welsh Grand National on Glenn; 2 Topham Trophy's in 1965 and 1969, and a Conyngham Cup. He later trained in the Curragh. Both he and his brother John represented Ireland in Olympic 3-Day eventing, Eddie being a member of the Irish side which finished 6th in the Team event of 1960, and John a member of the side which came in 4th in the Olympics of Tokyo in 1964. This makes Eddie the only Aintree Grand National-winning jockey to compete in the Olympic Games. John, born in March 1941, rode the winner of the 1976 Sweeps Hurdle, and the Irish Grand National on Daletta. Also a rugby player os some ability (being on a losing Old Belvedere side in the 1958 Leinster Senior Cup final), he also trained horses at Dunboyne. He died in 1990 of Motor Neuron Disease. Along with their brother Christy, the 3 Hartys became the only set of 3 brothers in the 20th century to ride in the Aintree Grand National. Their father, Captain Cyril (C.B.) Harty, was a showjumper for Ireland in the 1930's, and trained the winner of the 1944 Irish Grand National, Kinghis Crest.

HARVEY, MARTIN.

Soccer international wing-half. Born in Belfast, 19th September 1941. He joined Sunderland as a junior in 1958, and in 12 years with them, played 310 league matches, scoring 6 goals, and helping them to get promotion to Division One in 1964. A Northern Ireland Schoolboys, 'B', and Under 23 international wing-half, he played 34 senior international matches (all while at Roker Park, making him Sunderland's most capped player) over an 11 year period for Northern Ireland between 1961 and 1971 (scoring 3 international goals), taking over the berth of Danny Blanchflower. A stylish wing-half, he was a great all-round player.

HARVEY, THOMAS ARNOLD.

Rugby and cricket international. In rugby, having played for Leinster 6 times while playing for Dublin University, he won 8 international rugby caps in the pack for Ireland between 1900 and 1903, and was on Ireland's first ever foreign touring side to Canada in 1899. He also was a cricket international, playing 2 first class matches for Ireland in 1902, scoring 113 runs and taking 2 runs. Two of his brothers, both Wanderers players, were also capped for Leinster and Ireland in rugby, George winning 5 international caps in 1903-1905, and Frederick, who won 2 international caps in 1907 and 1911 (and who also won a Victoria Cross in W.W.I.), making them one of 10 sets of 3 brothers to play for Ireland, winning a total of 15 caps. Thomas later became a Bishop of Cashel.

HASLAM, EDWARD H (TED).

Bowls, snooker and billiard player. Born in Belfast, 10th May 1915. As a bowler he played over 60 games for Ireland from 1951, and won 3 Irish Private Greens pairs titles, 1959, 1961 and 1965. He was also capped over 15 times for Indoor bowls. Also a dab hand on the 'green baize', he was Irish Open snooker champion in 1944, and was Irish Billiards Champion 1939-45 and 1951-52.

HASSETT, MATT.

G.A.A. hurling full-back, Tipperary. From Toomevara. He was a member of the Tipperary side which was beaten in the final of the 1960 All-Ireland Senior Hurling Championship of 1960, and the following year, as captain from right corner-forward in 1961, he became the first Toomevara man to bring home the Liam McCarthy Cup, when Dublin were beaten by 0-16 to 1-12.

HAUGH, DENNIS.

Light-heavyweight boxer. Born in Tipperary. He claimed the British Light-heavy title in 1913-14. In his 7 year pro career, he won 21 of his 45 contests, losing 17, with 6 other decisions. He won the British crown by defeating the Englishman Sid Ellis for the vacant title in 1913, and after 2 successful defences, lost it to Dick Smith of England in 1914.

HAUGHTON, WILLIAM E (BILL).

Hockey international inside forward, and cricket international. Hockey club: Three Rock Rovers. He was capped 29 times for Ireland in hockey between 1952 and 1962, 15 of these as captain. A prolific goalscorer for Ireland (including on his debut against Belgium in 1952), he was an expert exponent of penalty corners. He was also a cricket international (playing 5 times for Ireland between 1947 and 1953), he scored many runs for Trinity. His brother Ken, also a Three Rock Rovers player, played in the same 10 international hockey matches at the start of Bill's career, and they forged an outstanding inside forward combination.

HAVERTY, JOE.

Soccer international outside-left. Born in Dublin, 17th February, 1936. A youth international, he moved from St Patrick's Athletic (where he was on the side beaten in the F.A.I. Cup in 1954, having earlier played with Home Farm) to Arsenal at the age of 18, scoring 33 goals for the Gunners in 165 matches up to 1960. He later played for Blackburn Rovers, Millwall (helping them to win the Fourth Division in 1963), Glasgow Celtic, Bristol Rovers, Shelbourne, and later the Chicago Spurs club. He was capped 32 times for the Republic of Ireland over an 11 year period between 1956 and 1967 (being the first Irish player to be capped from 6 different clubs, 15 at Arsenal, 2 at Blackburn, 6 at Millwall, 1 at Celtic, 1 at Bristol Rovers, and 7 at Shelbourne), scoring 3 international goals. The 7 caps he won while at Shelbourne make him the club's most capped player.

HAWKINS, GERRY.

Amateur international boxer. Club: Holy Trinity. He won 3 National Senior Championships at light-flyweight, in 1980, 1983 and 1984. He represented Ireland twice at Olympic Games, at Moscow in 1980 and at Los Angeles in 1984, being beaten in the first bout on both occasions, both by a margin of 5-0.

HAYDEN, BRENDAN.

G.A.A. footballer and hurler, Carlow. Born in 1935. Clubs: Tinryland and Eire Og in football, winning 4 Carlow SFC medals in all; and, in hurling, Palatine, St Fintan's and Carlow Town (winning 5 Carlow SHC medals in all). He played Carlow minor football in 1953-54 and senior football from 1955 to 1970, and senior hurling for the 'Wee' county from 1962 to 1966. In football he was on the county side beaten in the National League semi-final in 1962. He won 2 Railway Cup medals in football with Leinster. In hurling he won both an All-Ireland junior and intermediate medal. He became an inter-county referee.

HAYDEN, DAVID.

Pitch and putt player. Club: Old County Club. A youthful Dublin player of potential, he has already won 2 National Matchplay Championship titles in succession, in 1988 and 1989.

HAYDEN, TOMMY.

Weightlifter. A Dubliner, he was at the pinnacle of Irish weightlifting for almost 20 years, winning more than 10 All-Ireland titles, and numerous county and provincial events, and set many Irish records. In May 1949 he placed himself among the world's top lifters when, with a bodyweight of under 10 stone weight, he dead lifted 500 lbs (35 stone 10 lbs), a feat very close to a world record. When matched against the Scottish lightweigtht holder, John Kerr, and the British Strandpulling champion, he won Ireland's first ever International Amateur Weightlifting title. In 1960, he was one of the first 2 Irishmen to represent this country at weightlifting in the Olympic Games, doing so at Rome, finishing in 22nd place with a lift of 677.5 lbs.

HAYES, CONOR.

G.A.A. hurling full-back, Galway. Born 11th May 1958. Clubs: Glen Rovers and Kiltomer (whom he helped to win the All-Ireland Club Championship final in 1992). A member of the Galway side which captured the All-Ireland Under 21 Championship in 1978, he won his first All-Ireland S.H.C. medal with Galway in 1980 at right half-back. He then went on to captain Galway to 2 successive All-Ireland Senior Hurling Championship title wins, in 1987 when they beat Kilkenny by 1-12 to 0-9, and again the following year in the win over Tipperary by the score of 1-15 to 1-14, having been on the losing All-Ireland final sides of the 2 previous years, 1985 and 1986. He captained Connacht to win the Railway Cup in 1987, having previously won medals in 1980, 1983, and 1986. He also won National Hurling League and Oireachtas medals in both 1981 and 1988. He has won 3 successive All-Star awards, in 1986, 1987, and 1988, all at full-back. An engineer.

HAYES, JOHNNY.

Long-distance athlete. Born in Nenagh, Co Tipperary in 1886. Having emigrated to New York to work as a clerk in Bloomingdales store, he took up marathon running. Having finished 5th in the 1906 Boston Marathon (and 3rd in 1907), and having won the Yonkers Marathon in 1907, he went on to win a gold medal in the 1908 Olympic Marathon in London (a race infamous for the disqualification, for being aided by track officials, of the 'real' winner Dorando Pietri of Italy). Hayes actually finished 32 seconds behind Pietri, but was still accredited with the Olympic record with a time of 2 hours 55 minutes and 18.4 seconds). He later turned pro, and in 2 famous matches against the Olympic hero Pietri, lost both.

HAYES, LIAM.

G.A.A. football midfielder, Meath. Club: Skryne. Born 27th January 1962. First playing senior inter-county football in 1981, he was a member of the Meath side which won 3 Leinster S.F.C. titles in-a-row from 1986, and an influential member of the side which captured the All-Ireland Senior Football Championship titles in 1987 and 1988 (he was on the losing All-Ireland side of 1990). He then captained the Meath side in their 10-match (including 4 famous matches against Dublin in the first round of the Leinster Championship) run to the All-Ireland final of 1991, before losing gallantly to Down (this brought his tally of Leinster S.F.C. medals to 5, and he played in over 50 championship matches). With the Royal County he has also won 2 National Football League medals, in 1988 and 1990. He has won 2 Railway Cup medals with Leinster, in 1986 and 1986. Retiring from inter-county football in 1992, he was awarded one All-Star award in midfield in 1988. A sports journalist, in 1992 he published a fine account of his life in football, 'Out of Our Skins'. His father, Jimmy, was on the Carlow team beaten in the final of the National Football League in 1954.

HAYES, SEAMUS.

Show jumper. Born in Cork, 5th November 1924. A product of Castleknock College, he grew up in the environs of McKee Barracks. He was the winner of the B.S.T.A. National Jumping Championship of Great Britain 3 years in succession, in 1948, 1949, and 1950, and was leading showjumper of the year

MEDAL PRIDE

Michael Carruth, the winner of an Olympic gold medal for welterweight boxing in Barcelona in 1992, shows off his prize.

Gary O'Toole, the only Irish swimmer ever to win a medal at a major championship, poses with his piece of silver.

HURLING HEROES

Jimmy Barry Murphy, one of Cork's greatest ever hurlers, he was also a football player of great skill.

Nicky English, many peoples idea of hurling's finest modern-day exponent, in determined pose.

THE GOLDEN OLDIES

1

2

3

4

5

6

1 Bertie Donnelly (Cycling)
2 George McVeagh (All-rounder)
3 Paddy Perry (Handball)
4 Stanley Woods (Motor-Cycling)
5 J.J. Parkinson (Horse-Racing)
6 Seamus Fenning (Snooker and Billiards)

GREAT LADIES

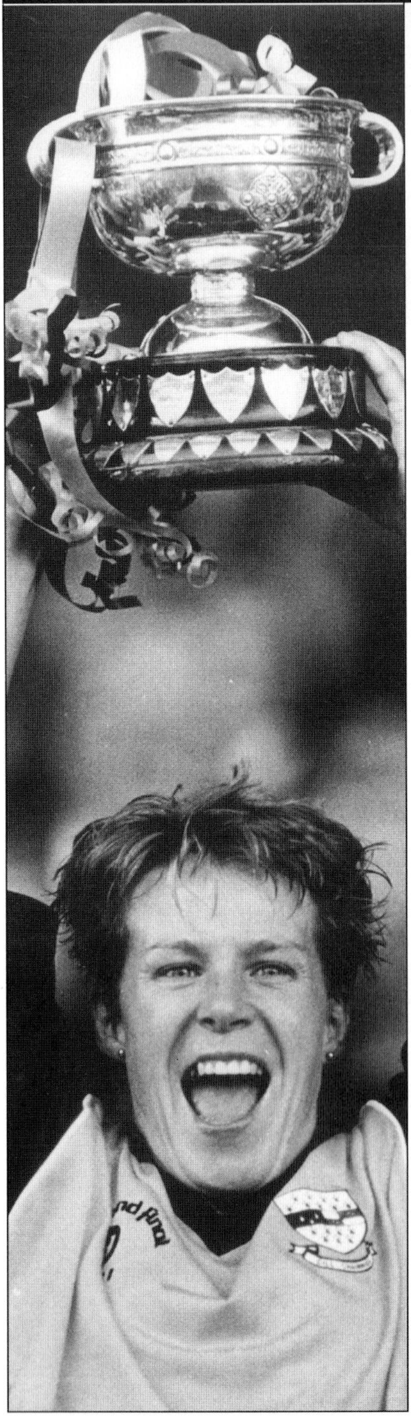

Philomena Garvey, above, undoubtedly among the very best of Irish Lady Golfers.

Angela Downey, the outstanding camogie player of the modern generation.

FOOTBALL GENIUS

Colm O'Rourke: a Meath player of real class, he is regarded as many as one of the modern game's best.

Dinny Allen, a Cork footballer who toiled for many years before attaining his goal – getting a hold of 'Sam'.

RUGBY GREATS

Ciaran Fitzgerald, Ireland's best modern-day captain, leading the country to two Triple Crown wins in 1982 and 1985.

Ollie Campbell, Philip Orr and Willie Duggan, three modern day greats in international rugby, all of them Lions players.

THE FIGHTING IRISH

Wayne McCullagh, the 'Pocket Rocket', who won a silver medal in Barcelona, and is now a budding professional champion.

Barry McGuigan, the enormously popular 'Clones Cyclone', who became world featherweight champion.

SOCCER GIANTS

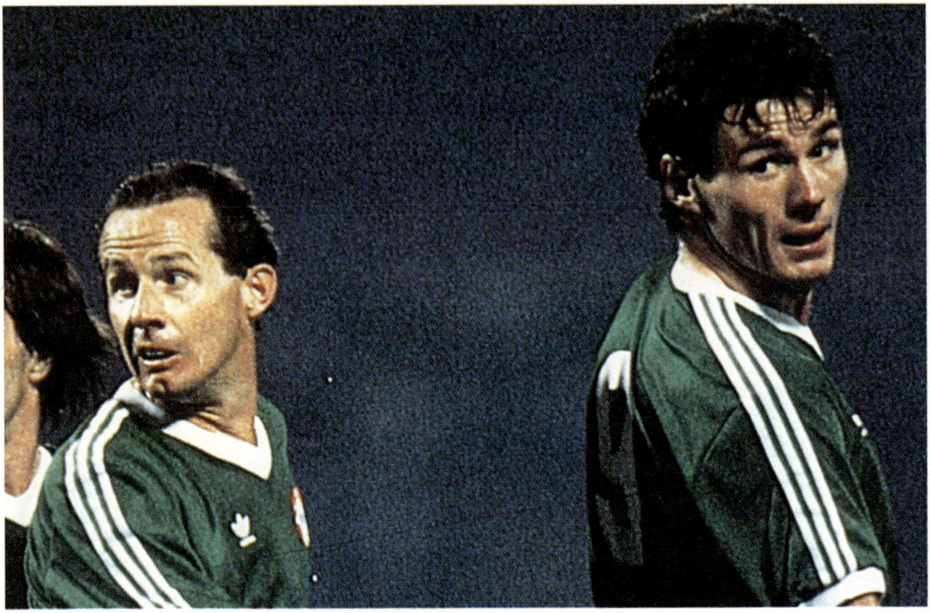

Liam Brady and Frank Stapleton, former greats in the game, seen here playing for the Republic of Ireland.

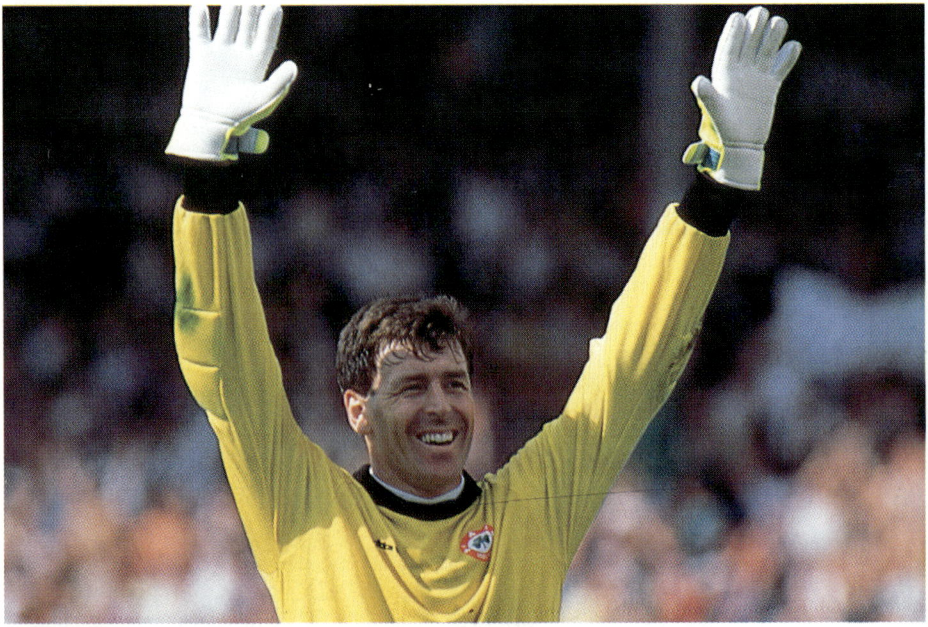

Packie Bonner, who will forever be remembered for his penalty shoot-out save against Romania in Italia 90.

Christy O'Connor, regarded by many as Ireland's finest ever professional golfer.
Mick Dowling, one of many great Irish Amateur Boxers who shone in the ring.
Pat Taaffe, one of Ireland's outstanding jockeys; associated with the great Arkle.
David Wilkins, the only Irishman to participate in five different Olympic Games. He won silver in 1980.

HURLING CLASS

Christy Ring, top left, many people's idea of the greatest who has playedhurling.
Mick Mackey, centre, the Limerick maestro, another hurler thought of as "simply the best".
"Babs" Keating, right, one of many great Tipperary men who have graced hurling.

Noel Skehan, the holder of most All-Ireland senior medals in either code.

SNOOKER CHAMPIONS

Alex Higgins: twice a World Snooker Champion, in 1972 and 1982, he became acclaimed as the 'People's Champion', such was his popularity.

Dennis Taylor, the winner of the closest fought and most exciting World Snooker Championship final in 1985.

SOCCER GIANTS

George Best, the former Manchester United great, who is surely Ireland's most talented ever soccer player.

Paul McGrath, the brilliant midfielder and central defender, who is a kernal to the Republic's recent world ranking status.

at the Horse of the Year Show in 1949, 1950, and 1952. He won the prestigious Daily Mail Cup twice, in 1961 and 1963, and won the British Show Jumping Derby at Hickstead in both 1961 (the inaugural year) and 1964. He was Irish National Champion Show Jump rider in 1950, 1951, and 1952. He was a member of the Irish squad which won the Aga Khan Cup in 1961, 1963 and 1967. He shares the distinction of riding Sheila to two B.S.J.A. championships, a feat not supassed by any other horse. On his horse Goodbye he cleared 7'2" on no less than 6 occasions. He died in 1989.

HEALEY, PATRICK.

Rugby international forward. 1878-1948. Club: Garryowen (winning 7 Munster Senior Cup medals in 1898, 1899, 1902, 1903, 1904, 1908 and 1909). He was capped 10 times in the pack for Ireland between 1901 and 1904, being on the losing side in 7 of these matches.

HEALION, BERT.

Athlete, hammer thrower. Born 17th May 1919. Club: Erris. He won 2 British A.A.A. titles at this event, in 1938 (with a throw of 52.46 metres) and in 1939 (with a throw of 49.28 metres). He returned, in a comeback, to the A.A.A. Championships in 1955 (16 years after his last title), at the age of 46, and although he threw 5 feet longer than his 1939 winning throw, could finish only in 6th place. Starved of competition due to World War Two, in 1943 he, in a handicap event, set a World Best throw of 192'11' at Milltown, Dublin, beating the 13-year-old world record of Pat Ryan cv, by 3 feet. He also played minor hurling for Dublin in his teens, being possessed, not surprisingly, with an enormously long puck-out.

HEALEY, RON.

Soccer international goalkeeper. Born in Manchester, 30th August 1952. Apprenticed with Manchester City and playing with them till 1973, his other clubs have included Coventry City, Preston North End and Cardiff City, playing in 184 league matches for them from 1974 to 1980, winning 4 Welsh Cup medals. He was capped twice for the Republic of Irleand, once in 1977 and again as a sub in 1980.

HEALY, PADDY ('HITLER').

G.A.A. hurling and footballing dual player, Cork. He won 2 All-Ireland Senior Hurling Championship winner's medals with Cork, in 1944 (when coming on as a sub in the final) and 1946. He sandwiched then with a Sam Maguire Cup medal for Cork in the 1945 All-Ireland S.F.C. final, although he was only a non-playing substitute in this game, thus becoming one of a select group of less than 20 men who have won All-Ireland senior medals in both codes.

HEALY, PAT J ('FELIX').

Soccer international midfielder. Born in Londonderry, 27th September 1955. Clubs: Preston, Sligo Rovers, Finn Harps, Port Vale, Coleraine (with the 4 caps he gained while at the Showgrounds, he is the club's joint most capped player), Glentoran (winning 4 Irish Cup medals in succession, in 1985, 1986, 1987 and 1988), Derry City (winning the F.A.I Cup/League of Ireland double in 1989, scoring the winning goal in the replayed F.A.I. Cup final). He has been capped 4 times for Northern Irleand between 1983 and 1984, 2 of these as a substitute. In 1982 he was Ulster Footballer of the Year, N.I.P.F.A. Player of the Year, and N.I.F.W. Player of the Year.

HEALY, TADHG.

G.A.A. football left corner-back, Kerry. A member of the Kerry minors beaten in the All-Ireland M.F.C. final in 1936, he won 4 All-Ireland Senior Football Championship medals, in 1937 at left half back, and at left full-back in the 3-in-a-row team of 1939, 1940, and 1941. He also played for Kerry in the losing All-Ireland final of 1944. He won his only Railway Cup winner's medal with Munster in 1941.

HEARNE, ANGIE.

Ladies G.A.A. football forward, Wexford. Club: Shemaliers. She was at right-half forward in the All-Ireland finals of 1983 and 1988, and at full-forward in the final of 1989, all of these finals being lost to Kerry. An All-Star player, she has also played camogie for Wexford, and has played international soccer for Ireland. Her father, Oliver Hearne, played hurling for the county in the 1960's.

HEARNS, DICK.

Amateur boxer, and Gaelic footballer. Boxing club: Garda. He won 5 Irish National titles, all at light-heavyweight. His wins came in 1933, 1934, 1936, 1937, and 1938. He shares the record for most Irish titles at this weight with fellow club-man, W J Murphy (cv), whom he succeeded. He won 173 of his 198 amateur bouts. As a gaelic player, he played for Roscommon, Longford, Donegal, Cork, Dublin, and was a sub on the Mayo team which played in the 1932 All-Ireland S.F.C. final.

HEERY, EAMONN.

G.A.A. football half-back, Dublin. Born in 1966. Club: St Vincent's. A product of a successful St Joseph's Fairview side, he won an All-Ireland M.F.C. medal with Dublin in 1982, and made his inter-county senior debut in 1986. He has won 3 Leinster S.F.C. medals, in 1989, 1992 (when the Dubs were beaten in the All-Ireland Senior Football Championship final), and 1993. He has won 2 National Football League medals, in 1991 and 1993. Winning an All Star in 1992 at left half-back, he is a draughtsman.

HEFFERNAN, CHRISTY.

G.A.A. hurling full-forward, Kilkenny. Club: Glenmore (winning an All-Ireland Club Championship medal in 1991, and Kilkenny senior championship wins also in 1987 and 1992). Making his senior county debut in 1980, he won a National Hurling League medal in 1982 at the age of 24. He was a star full forward in Kilkenny's 2 successive All-Ireland Senior Hurling Championship title wins of 1982 (scoring 2-3 in the final) and 1983, and played on the losing final sides in the 1987 and in 1991. He won a third Liam McCarthy Cup medal in 1992 as a playing sub, and was a non-paying sub on the Kilkenny side which won another All-Ireland in 1993, retiring after the game. He won one Railway Cup medal with Leinster in 1988. He has won one All-Star award, at full forward in the 1982 selection. He has been President of Glenmore Handball Club. His brother Ray Heffernan also played alongside him in senior Kilkenny sides, and in the Glemore sides which won the clubs first 3 senior county championship medals. In 1990 Christy coached the Waterford side of Ballydurn to the county's Junior Hurling Championship.

HEFFERNAN, KEVIN ('HEFFO').

G.A.A. football left-full forward, Dublin. Club: St Vincent's (helping them to win Dublin county championships in both football and hurling). He was a member of the Dublin minors which were beaten by Kerry in the 1946 All-Ireland M.F.C. decider. He later captained Dublin to win the 1958 All-Ireland Senior Championship final when they defeated Derry by 2-12 to 1-9, having also been at full-forward when Dublin were beaten in the 1955 decider by Kerry. He also helped Dublin to success in 3 National Football League titles, in 1953, 1955 and 1958. He won 7 Railway Cup medals with Leinster (a record for a Dublin player in either code), in an eleven year span, in 1952, 1953, 1954, 1955, 1959 (when he became the 2nd Dublinman to captain the winning side), 1961, and 1962. He has the distinction of playing for Dublin at minor, junior, and senior levels in both football and hurling. A free-scoring roving football full-forward, he scored 52 goals and 172 points in 119 games for the Dubs in the 7 year period from 1955 to 1962. He later went on to train the great Dublin side of the 1970's, when they won All-Ireland S.F.C. titles in 1974, 1976 and 1977, and in 1974 became the first non-player ever to be voted as Texaco Footballer of the Year. He was voted into the left-full forward slot in the Sunday Independent's 'Team of the Century' of 1984, during the Centenery Year.

HEGAN, DANNY.

Soccer international inside forward. Born in Coaltbridge, 14th June 1943. His clubs included Albion Rovers, Sunderland, Ipswich (for whom, in 6 seasons, he scored 34 league goals in 207 matches), West Bromwich Albion, Wolves, and Sunderland. He was capped 7 times for Northern Ireland between 1970 and 1973.

HEGARTY, GER.

G.A.A. hurling midfielder, Limerick. Born in 1967. Club: Old Christian's. A member of the Limerick minors who won the All-Ireland M.H.C. Championship in 1984, he was also a star on the side which won the All-Ireland Under 21 Championship in 1987. First playing senior hurling for Limerick at age 19, he was a member of the side which captured the National Hurling League title in 1992.

HEIGHWAY, STEVE ('BIG BAMBER').

Soccer international winger. Born in Dublin, 25th November 1947, to English parents, he moved to England at the age of 10. He played soccer for English Universities while at Warwick University. He joined Liverpool in 1970 from Skemersdale United, and in 11 years at Anfield shared in all of the club's triumphs in that period, scoring 50 goals in 312 appearences (mainly in the No 9 shirt). He helped them win 5 English League titles (1972-73, 1975-76, 1976-77, 1978-79, and 1979-80), and scored a goal in their 1974 F.A. Cup final 3-0 win over Newcastle (also winning runner-up medals in 1971 and 1977). He also shared in triumphs in 3 European Cup wins, 1976-77 (setting up 2 goals in the final), 1977-78, and 1980-81, and 2 U.E.F.A. Cup wins in 1972-73 and 1975-76, his 11 goals in European club competitions over 64 matches places him 2nd behind Johnny Giles as top Irishmen in this endeavour. Later joining the Minnesota Kickers, he also played indoor football in Philadelphia. A brilliant winger at his peak, he was capped in all 34 times for the Republic of Ireland between 1971 and 1982, winning his first cap before making his league debut with Liverpool. He was selected in 1970 as soccer's Texaco Sportstar of the Year. In 1989 he re-joined Liverpool in a back-room capacity.

HENDERSON, BERNARD (BENNY, 'ROSIE').

Soccer international outside-right. Born in Sandymount, Co Dublin. Clubs: Transport, Ierne, Bohemians, Drumcondra (winning 2 League of Ireland Championship medals in 1947-48 and 1948-49, and 2 F.A.I. Cup winner's medal, in 1946 when he scored the winning goal in the final in his first year in senior football, and in 1954, both in famous wins over cup specialist's Shamrock Rovers), and Dundalk. A Tolka Park favourite nicknamed 'Rosie', equally adept off both feet, he won 4 Leinster Senior Cup medals (in 1944, 1945, 1950 and 1954), was capped twice for the Republic of Ireland in 1948, and scored one goal in Inter-League matches for the League of Ireland, in the famous 1-0 win of the German Hessen League in 1955 (also playing in 1949 and 1954).

HENDERSON, GER

G.A.A. hurling centre half-back, Kilkenny. Club: Johnstown Fenians (with whom he won 4 Kilkenny S.H.C. medals, in 1972, 1973, 1974, and 1977). Born in 1954. He was at right half-back on the Kilkenny side which won the All-Ireland Under 21 title in both 1974 and 1975, having already won an All-Ireland minor medal in 1972, although he did not play in the final. Taking over at centre-half back from his older brother Pat (cv) in 1976, he has won 3 All-Ireland Senior Hurling Championship winner's medal with Kilkenny, in 1979, 1982, and 1983, also being on the losing side in All-Ireland S.H.C. finals twice, as captain in 1978 against Cork, and again in 1987 (he had also won medals as a non-playing substitute in 1974 and 1975). He also won 4 National League medals with Kilkenny, in 1976, 1982, 1983, and 1986, and won Railway Cup medals with Leinster in 1975 and 1979. He has won 5 All-Star awards, in 1978, 1979 (when he was also selected as the 7th Kilkennyman to be named as Texaco's Hurling Sportstar of the Year), 1982, 1983, and 1987, all at centre half-back. He retired in May 1989, aged 35. He is a brother of both Pat and John Henderson (ccvv).

HENDERSON, JOHN.

G.A.A. hurling full-back, Kilkenny. Born in 1957. Club: Johnstown Fenians. A member of the winning Kilkenny All-Ireland Under 21 side of 1977, he has won 3 All-Ireland Senior Hurling Championship medals with Kilkenny, in 1979 at left full-back, and in 1982 and 1983 at right full-back, also playing on a losing final side in both 1987 and 1991. He won National League medals in 1982, 1983, 1986 and 1990. A constant member of the Kilkenny senior team for 12 years from 1979 to 1991, he won one All-Star award, in 1983 at right corner back. He is the younger brother of Pat and Ger Henderson (cv), all three of them being in the losing squad of the All-Ireland S.H.C. final of 1978.

HENDERSON, NOEL Joseph.

Rugby international centre and full-back. Born in Drumahoe, Co Derry, 10th August 1928. Clubs: Queen's University Belfast (winning an Ulster Senior Cup medal in 1951) and N.I.F.C. (winning an Ulster Senior Cup medal in 1955), and Barbarians. A product of Foyle College, he was capped 40 times for Ireland over an eleven year period between 1949 and 1959, 35 of these as centre and his last 5 as full-back, and captained Ireland 11 times in succession from 1956 to 1958 (including captaining the first Irish team to beat a touring side, Australia in 1958, in which he scored a famous try). He scored 54 international points for Ireland, consisting of 4 tries, one drop goal, and 13 penalties. He was part of the Irish side which retained the Triple Crown at Swansea in his first international season of 1949, and of the side which won the International Championship in 1951. He went on to play 2 Lion's Test matches on their 1950 tour of Australia and New Zealand. He became an Ulster and Irish (1969 to 1972) selector, and was President of the I.R.F.U. in 1989-90. He was also capped for Ireland at badminton. He married the sister of Jackie Kyle (cv), Betty, herself captaining Ireland 25 times in hockey. His brother George was President of the Badminton Union of Ireland in the 1980's, and George's son Graham played international badminton.

HENDERSON, PAT.

G.A.A. hurling centre half-back, Kilkenny. Born in 1944. Club: Johnstown Fenians (with whom he won many Kilkenny S.H.C. titles, and reached the All-Ireland Club final in 1975). Winning a minor All-Ireland medal in 1961, he made his senior inter-county debut for Kilkenny in 1964. Playing for his county in 8 All-Ireland S.H.C. deciders over the 10 year period from 1966 to 1975, he was a winner of 5 All-Ireland Senior Hurling Championship medals with Kilkenny, in 1967, 1969, 1972, 1974 and 1975, and was 3 times on losing sides (in 1966, 1971 as captain against Tipperary, and in 1973). He won National Hurling League medals in both 1966 and 1976. He has won 6 Railway Cup medals with Leinster, in 1967, 1971 (as a sub), 1973, 1974 (as captain), 1975, and in 1977. He was chosen as Texaco Hurler of the Year in 1974 (the 5th Kilkennyman to be so honoured), winning All-Star awards in 1973 and 1974, both at centre half-back. He also trained Kilkenny to win 3 All-Ireland S.H.C. finals. He is an older brother of both Ger and John Henderson (ccv).

HENEGHAN, TOM.

G.A.A. football left corner back, Roscommon. A member of the Roscommon squad which won 4 Connacht Senior Football Championship titles on the trot, 1977, 1978, 1979, and 1980, he was not in their side which were beaten in the 1980 All-Ireland S.F.C. final. He was awarded an All-Star place in 1979 at left full-back, when the county won the National League in football.

HENNESSY, D B (DEREK).

Hockey international forward. Clubs: Dublin Y.M.C.A., and Three Rock Rovers (whom he helped to dominate the Dublin hockey scene of the 1950's, winning 10 Leinster Senior League medals, 9 Mills Cup medals, and 3 Irish Cup medals ending in the 1974 success). A fine Leinster player, he was capped 35 times for Ireland between 1957 and 1969, and was a prolific goalscorer, scoring the winner against Scotland at Shotton in Wales which enabled Ireland to win the Home Countries title for the first time in 20 years, in 1968. He was capped 5 times for Great Britain in 1963. In the 1970's he became an Irish hockey selector. He died in 1990.

HENNESSY, JACKIE.

Soccer international player. Clubs: Shelbourne (winning a League of Ireland Championship medal in 1961-62, and two F.A.I. Cup winners' medals, in 1960 and 1963) and St Patricks Athletic. He was capped only 5 times for the Republic of Ireland, but these were obtained over a span on 13 years, being first capped against Poland in 1956, and gaining his last cap against Austria in 1969.

HENNESSY, JOE.

G.A.A. hurling right half back, right full back and midfielder, Kilkenny. Club: James Stephen's (with whom he won 3 Kilkenny county hurling and 2 All-Ireland Club medals, in 1976 and 1982, and 2 county football championship titles). He also won an All-Ireland M.H.C. medal in 1973, and 2 Under 21 medals (in 1975 and 1977). He has won 3 All-Ireland Senior Hurling Championship winners medals with Kilkenny, in 1979 in the midfield position, in 1982 (also at centre-field), and in 1983 at right half-back, being on losing sides in 1978, 1986 and 1987. He won a Railway Cup medal with Leinster in 1979, and 4 National League winner's medals, in 1976, 1982, 1983 and 1986. He has won 5 All-Star awards, in 1978 at right half-back, in 1979 at midfield, in 1983 and 1984 at again at right half-back, and in 1987 at right full-back.

HENNESSY, KEVIN.

G.A.A. hurling left cornerforward. Cork. Born 8th March 1961. Club: Midleton (winning an All-Ireland Club Championship winner's medal in 1988). Winning an All-Ireland M.H.C. medal in 1979 and an All-Ireland Under 21 title in 1982, he has won 3 All-Ireland Senior Hurling Championship titles with Cork, in 1984 while playing at right half-forward, in 1986 at top of the right (scoring 2-1 in the final against Galway), and in 1990 again at right full-forward, scoring 1-4. He also played on losing All-Ireland S.H.C sides 3 times, in 1982 (as a sub), 1983 and in 1992. He has won one All-Star award, in 1986 at left full-forward.

HENRY, CONOR.

Amateur cyclist. Born in Belfast in 1971. Moving to France in 1989 for more experience, he was originally left out of the Irish Olympic squad for the Games in Barcelona in 1992. However, in June of that year he became the first Irishman to win the prestigious 35-year-old British Milk Race, winning by a margin of 19 seconds from Willy Willems of Belgium in 42 hours, 19 minutes and 40 seconds for the 1,000 mile race (a record speed for the race, averaging 27.16 m.p.h.), having held on to the lead he gained after the 8th stage. He then went on to be a member of the Irish team which finished 35th in the Road Race. In 1993 he finished 6th in his defence of the

British Milk Race, 41 seconds behind the winner. He was nominated as the Texaco Sportstar of the Year for cycling in 1992.

HERBERT, ANTHONY (TONY).

G.A.A. hurling half-back and left corner-forward, Limerick and Dublin. Born in Castleconnell, Co Limerick in August 1921. Clubs: Ahane (winning 5 county championship medals) and Faughs (winning 6 Dublin senior county Championship medals). He was a playing sub on the Limerick side which captured the All-Ireland Senior Hurling Championship in 1940. He later played with Dublin, being on 2 sides beaten in the All-Ireland S.H.C. final, in 1948 and 1952. He was a Senator in the late 1970's. His brother Michael also hurled for Limerick county teams for a number of years, and was a Fianna Fail T.D. 1969-1982.

HERBERT, SEAN.

G.A.A. hurling half-back, Limerick. Born in 1923. Club: Ahane (winning 8 county championships). In a senior inter-county career from 1942 to 1953 he failed to win even a Munster S.F.C. medal (playing in 5 unsuccessful finals). He did however win a National Hurling League medal with Limerick in 1947, and won 5 Railway Cup medals with Munster in 3 different positions (half-back, midfielder and half-forward), in 1946, 1948, 1949, 1952 and 1953. In 1984 he was selected in the right half-back position on the 'Team of the Century' for players who had never won an All-Ireland senior championship medal.

HERLIHY, BRENDAN and DERMOT.

Amateur international golfing brothers. Brendan, a member of Portmarnock (with whom he won Barton Shield medals in 1954 and 1956), won the Irish Close title in 1950, played for Ireland in the 1950 Home international series, and played interprovincial golf for Leinster in 1957. Dermot, a member of Royal Dublin GC (winning a Barton Shield medal in 1968), played interprovincial golf for Leinster in 1961, and was selected for the Home International series the same year, although he did not get a match. As a selector for the Irish panel, he died on the Royal County Down course in 1980.

HERON, J EDDIE.

High diving and Springboard diver. Born in 1911. Club: Half Moon S.C. Regarded as Ireland's greatest ever diver, at the age of 13 he won the first of an amazing 25 Leinster high diving championships. He won the Tailteann Games High Diving event in both 1928 and 1930. In 1933 he became the only Irishman to win the British Open title (he was runner-up in both 1932 and 1934). When he retired in 1950 (he had taken part in the Olympic Games of 1948 in London) he had won 18 Irish High Diving Championships and 16 Irish Springboard titles. A useful G.A.A. footballer, playing for the O'Tooles and Kickham's clubs, he played for Dublin in the Leinster Championships. He was installed into the Texaco Hall of Fame in 1966, the only watersportsman to be so far included.

HERRICK, JOHN.

Soccer international player. Clubs: Glasheen, Cork Hibernians (winning a League of Ireland medal in 1971 and 2 successive F.A.I. Cup medals with them the following years, 1972 and 1973), Shamrock Rovers. A fine League of Ireland player, he was capped 3 times in all for the Republic of Ireland, in 1972 and 1973, twice as a substitute.

HERON, JAMES and W T.

Rugby international brothers. Both from N.I.F.C., James, a half-back, was capped twice, against Scotland in 1877 and against England in 1879. W T , also a half-back, was capped twice also, both in 1880. All these games were lost. James became the first President of the Northern Football Union of Ireland in 1875.

HERRON, TOMMY.

Motorcycle racer. Born in Newcastle, Co Down in 1949. At the age of 21 he won the North-West 200 at 350cc class against top opposition. He then went on to race for most of the 1970's on the continent in Grand Prix and international events, reaching the top of the tree with 3 Isle of Man T.T. wins, the 1976 Senior and 250cc races, and the 1978 Senior T.T. race. In 1978 he set the then fastest ever lap of a road race circuit in either Britain or Ireland, with 127.63 m.p.h. in the North-West 200 on a Yamaha 750cc. Joining the Suzuki team of Barry Sheene in 1979, world championship honours seemed imminent, but he was killed, at the age of 30, in an accident in the North-West 200 in that year.

HESKIN, Catherine ANNE and OONAGH.

Amateur international golfing sisters. Club: Douglas. Anne, a dominant figure in ladies golf in Munster in the 70's, was Munster champion 5 times, 1970, 1971, 1974, 1975 and 1978. A Munster senior interprovincial from 1964, she played international golf for Ireland in 1969, 1970, 1972, 1975, and 1977. She was third on 3 occasions in the Irish Strokeplay championship, and in 1990 she became the third Irish Senior Ladies Champion. Oonagh Fitzpatrick (nee Heskin), her sister, won the Midland Ladies in 1962, and played Home international golf for Irleand in both 1967 and 1969, in the latter of these years in the same team as Anne.

HEWITT, DAVID.

Rugby international centre and wing threequarter. Born in Belfast, 9th September 1939. Clubs: Queen's University Belfast and Instonians. A Barbarian and Ulster interprovincial (playing first for the province while still a schoolboy), he was capped 18 times for Ireland between 1958 and 1965, scoring one try, 2 conversions and 3 penalties for his country. An enormously talented straight-running centre, he played in 6 Lion's Test matches on 2 different tours, 5 on the 1959 Australia and New Zealand tour (his best rugby, which included scoring 112 points in New Zealand, including the tour best tally of 13 tries, contributing also 20 conversions, 10 penalties and one drop goal), and one on the 1962 South Africa tour. His cousin, John Hewitt, was an outstanding Instonians out-half, but as understudy to Jack Kyle, won only international 4 caps from 1954 to 1961 (once with David), and was an Irish selector 1971-74 (he was also the first Irish backline player to go on 2 tours with Ireland, in 1952 to Argentina and Chile, and in 1961 to South Africa). Another cousin, William John Hewitt, an Instonians fly-half and winger, won 3 caps for Ireland from 1954 to 1961. And yet another cousin, Francis Gerald Gilpin, won 3 caps in the Irish backline in 1962 while at Queen's University. David is the son of Tom R Hewitt (c.v).

HEWITT, FRANCIS Seymour (FRANK).

Rugby international out-half and centre. Born 3rd October 1906. Club: Instonians (winning Ulster Senior Cup medal in 1927). He was capped 9 times for Ireland between 1924 and 1927, scoring 2 tries before retiring at the age of 21 for religious reasons. He is the youngest player ever to represent Ireland in international rugby, being only 17 years 5 months and 5 days old when he played in his first cap against Wales on 8th March 1924 (he scored a try on his debut, and is therefore Ireland's youngest ever try-scorer). He is the brother of Tom Hewitt (cv), who also scored a try on Frank's debut, and both of them were placed in the Rugby Writers Hall of Fame in 1990.

HEWITT, IRENE.

Squash international player. Born in Belfast, 11th August 1945. Clubs: Bloomfield (Bangor), and Queen's University Belfast. She won the Irish National (Close) Squash Ladies title 5 times, in 1973, 1975, 1976, 1979, and in 1980. Other titles she won in the 1970's and 1980's were the Scottish, Middlesex, Leinster, Ulster, Transvaal, Northern Transvaal, and she twice won the R.T.E. Television tournament, in 1980 and 1981. In 1976 she was a was runner-up in the women's world championship plate in Brisbane, and was she went on to win the plate at the 2nd world women's championship in Sheffield. Her total tally of caps for Ireland came to approximately 39. She played junior and under 21 tennis for Ulster in her early days.

HEWITT, THOMAS R (TOM).

Rugby international wing and centre three-quarter. Club: Queen's University Belfast (winning Ulster Senior Cup medals in 1925 and 1926). He was capped 9 times between 1924 and 1926, scoring 2 tries and 1 conversion. He is the father of David Hewitt (cv), and a brother of Frank Hewitt (cv), with whom he played with 6 times in the international side. Another brother, Victor, won 6 international caps at fly-half in 1935 and 1936, being on the winning side in 4 matches. Tom scored a try on his international debut, when aged 19, on the same day as Frank's debut, making it the first time 2 Irish brothers had scored in the same international. They are one of 10 sets of three brothers to play for Ireland, and are the only one of the 10 to all play against the All Blacks.

HEZLET, MARY LINZEE (MAY), and her sisters FLORENCE and VIOLET.

Amateur international golfers. Club: Royal Portrush. May was born in Gibraltar in 1882, and died in 1969. Having first entered the event at the age of 13, she won an outstanding 3 British Ladies' Open Amateur Championships, in 1899, 1902, and 1907, the first victory coming just after her 17th birthday (making her until 1981 the youngest winner of a major British title). She was runner-up in 1904. She won the Irish Championship 5 times, in 1899 (achieved on her 17th birthday), 1904, while her beaten opponent on the other three of those occasions (1905, 1906, 1908), and in her last British title, was each time her sister Florence, who was runner-up in the British title also in 1909, and twice more in the Irish title, in 1912 and 1920. In the 1905 Irish Ladies' team, the two sisters were placed one and two on the team, with a third sister, Violet, at No 3. Violet was runner in the British title in 1911, 3 times runner-up in the Irish title (1900, 1903, and 1909), and was later Secretary of the I.L.G.U. They are sisters of Charles Hezlett (cv).

HEZLET, Major CHARLES Owen (C.O.H.).

Amateur international golfer. He lived May 1891 to 1965. Club: Poyal Portrush (winning many club championships, including the Adair Cup 10 times 1908-36). He won the Irish Open Amateur title in 1926 and 1929, being runner-up in 1923 and 1925. Having been runner-up in the British Amateur title in 1914, he went on the win the Irish Close title in 1920. Having played for Wales while working there (and being runner-up in the Welsh Amateur Open in 1923), he went on to play for Ireland in 13 International matches against Wales (5 times), Scotland (5 times) and England (3 times), between 1923 and 1931, all before the Home International series started (in 1932). He was Ireland's first player to win Walker Cup honours, in 1924 in Garden City U.S.A., and he went on to be a member of the side again in both 1926 and 1928, losing 5 and halving one of his 6 matches played. He also played for Ireland against South Africa in 1927, and captained a British team to Africa in 1952. He was Irish team captain 10 times before 1932, and 6 times after 1948. He was an Irish selector 1947-53, and is a brother of the Hezlet sisters (c.v.).

HICKEY, Dr DAVID.

G.A.A. football half-forward, Dublin. Club: Raheny Gaels. A product of St Fintan's HS, he has won 3 All-Ireland Senior Football Championship winner's medals at left half-forward with the famous 'Heffo's Army' Dublin side of the 1970's, in 1974, 1976, and 1977, being also twice on the losing side in the All-Ireland S.F.C. decider, in 1978, and in 1979 when his brother Mick was at right corner forward (Mick had won a Leinster Schools Rugby Senior Cup winner's medal with Belvedere College in 1972). David, also a useful rugby player, won 2 National League winner's medals with Dublin in 1976 and 1978, and won 2 All-Star awards, in 1974 and 1976, both at left-half forward.

HICKEY, MICHAEL P.

Tennis and squash international player. He represented Ireland in at least 18 Davis Cup matches between 1962 and 1978, and played on sides which won matches in 1964, 1969, 1971 and 1976. He won the Fitzwilliam Club singles title in 1962, 1964, and 1965. In squash, he played 15 times for Ireland between 1965 and 1972. A useful rugby player with Blackrock, he played senior interprovincial level for Leinster against Connacht in 1965. He later coached Ireland's tennis team in the heady King's Cup days of Sean Sorenson and Matt Doyle (cv).

HICKIE, DENIS J.

Rugby international No 8 forward. Club: St Mary's (winning Leinster Senior Cup medals in 1969, 1971, 1974, and 1975, and a Leinster Senior League medal in the competition's inaugural year of 1972). He played in 20 Senior Interprovincial matches for Leinster over a 13 year period from 1963 to 1975. He was capped 6 times for Ireland, being ever-present in the 1971 season, and playing against France and England in 1972, having toured Australia with Ireland in 1967. His brother Tony, a useful full-back with St Mary's, played 3 times for Leinster.

HIGGINS, ALEXANDER Gordon (ALEX, 'HURRICANE').

Snooker professional. Born in Belfast on 18th March 1949. Having moved to England in 1964 to become an apprentice jockey, he won the Northern Ireland Amateur Snooker championship in 1967 at the age of 18, and turned pro in 1971. He has won the Irish National title 4 times, in 1972, 1978, 1978, and 1983. In 1972 he became the then youngest ever World Professional Champion (at 23 years and 1 month old), beating John Spencer 37-32 in the final in the British Legion club at Selly Park, Birmingham (winning a purse of £480). He won the Embassy World Championship title again in 1982, beating Jimmy White 16-15 in a classic semi-final, and going on to defeat Ray Reardon 18-15 in the final. He was also twice runner-up for the World title, in 1976 to Ray Reardon, and in 1980 to Cliff Thorburn. His other major victories have included the 1983 UK Championship (in a classic win over arch-enemy Steve Davis), the Benson & Hedges Masters in 1978 and 1981, the 1975 Canadian Open, and the 1980 British Gold Cup. He was part of the successful Irish team to win the 1985, 1986, and 1987 World Cup titles. In 1989 he became the first Irishman to win the Benson & Hedges Irish Masters title. A controversial player, dubbed as 'The People's Champion' because of his enormous crowd-pleasing appeal, in 1972 he was selected as Texaco's Snooker Sportstar of the Year.

HIGGINS, EAVAN.

Ladies amateur international golfer. Born on 11th September 1956. Club: Douglas. A fine Munster interprovincial golfer, she was runner-up twice in the Irish Ladies Championship, in 1986 and 1988, before capturing it finally in 1993 at Royal Belfast (also winning the Leitrim Cup in the same year). She was a constant Irish player in the Home International series from 1981 to 1988 (being on the triumphant side in Whittington Barracks in 1986), and regained her place again in 1991.

HIGGINS, JACK.

G.A.A. football centre-back, Kildare. Club: McKee Barracks. Regarded as one of the game's greatest centre half-backs, he was a star member of the great Kildare side which won 2 successive All-Ireland Senior Football Championship titles in 1927 and 1928. He also played on losing 4 All-Ireland final S.F.C. sides, in 1926, 1929 (when he captained the side beaten by Kerry), 1931, and 1935. He holds jointly the record of most Railway Cup medals (five) for a Kildareman, winning in 1928, 1929, 1930, 1932, and 1933 (captaining the winners twice, in 1930 and 1932, the first player to accomplish this feat).

HIGGINS, LIAM.

Golfer, amateur and professional. As an amateur, as a member of Cork Golf Club, he played 24 interprovincial matches for Munster in 1968-1971 (winning 13) and he played 9 Home interprovincial matches. In 1984, as a professional at Waterville, he drove a golf ball, at Baldonnel airport, a distance of 634.1 yards down a runway, making it the longest drive ever then recorded in golf. A successful club pro, he won the Kerrygold Invitational at Waterville in 1974 and 1977. His son David played senior interprovincial golf for Munster in 1992, was runner-up in the Irish Close in 1993, also becoming an amateur international golfer. Liam's brother Ted Higgins was runner-up in the 1970 East of Ireland, played international golf for Ireland as an amateur between 1966 and 1970, and interprovincial golf for Munster (with a points gain of 60% in his 48 matches for Munster between 1965 and 1973), later becoming the club professional at the famous Ballybunion G.C.

HIGGINS, MICK.

G.A.A. footballer, Galway. He captained the Galway side to win the county's 2nd All-Ireland Senior Football Championship in 1934, when they beat Dublin by 3-5 to 1-9. He later won another Sam Maguire Cup medal with the Galway S.F.C. in 1938, while he was on the losing side in the All-Ireland S.F.C. final of 1933. He won 3 Railway Cup medals with Connacht, in 1934, 1936 and 1938.

HIGGINS, MICK.

G.A.A. football centre-half forward, Cavan. Born in New York, June 1922. Clubs: Crosserlough (winning a county championship medal with them in 1958), and Mountnugent (he also won county championship medals in Meath and Louth, and played minor football for Kildare). A product of St Mary's, Dundalk (winning an Ulster College's medal with them), he played senior football for Cavan from 1942 to 1953, winning 7 Ulster S.F.C. medals in the No 11 jersey. He scored 1-2 in Cavan's great All-Ireland Senior Football Championship victory in the 1947 Polo Ground win over Kerry, and the following year won a National Football League medal and another Sam Maguire Cup medal with Cavan. He captained his county to victory in the 1952 All-Ireland S.F.C. final, the last Cavan-man to do so, and scored 7 of Cavan's points in their 0-9 to 0-5 replay win over Meath (having scored 5 of the teams 8 points in the final 10 minutes of the semi-final game against Cork, turning a 2-3 deficit into a famous win). He was also on the Cavan side beaten in All-Ireland S.F.C. decider of 1949. One of the game's finest centre half-forwards, and a fine scheming captain, he won Railway Cup medals with Ulster in 1947 and 1950. A garda, he retired after Cavan were beaten in the Ulster S.F.C. final of 1953. He coached the Longford side which won its first ever Leinster S.F.C. title in 1968. In 1976 he coached Donegal to their first ever Ulster S.F.C. win. In 1987 he became the first Cavanman to be nominated as an All-Time All-Star winner, and in 1989 became only the 3rd footballer to join the Texaco Hall of Fame.

HILL, CHARMIAN D.

Horse trainer, owner and jockey. Born in 1911, one of the Orpen family of Co Waterford. At the age of 63, in 1974, she made history by becoming the first woman to ride against men under rules in Ireland and in Great Britain. She trained Yer Man, winning a chase on him. Buying Dawn Run at Ballsbridge for 5,800 guineas in 1980, she rode the mare to her first win, in a flat race in Tralee on 23rd May 1982, when she was the ripe young age of 71. This was to be her last race as a competitive jockey. She then placed Dawn Run with Paddy Mullins (cv), and the rest (Dawn Run became the first horse ever to win both the Champion Hurdle and the Cheltenham Gold Cup, the 2 premier National Hunt races in this part of the world) is history.

HILL, M JAMES.

Soccer international inside forward. Born in Carrigfergus on 31st October 1935. Clubs: Linfield (winning Irish League titles in 1955 and 1956), Norwich City (for whom he scored 55 league goals in 161 matches in 1958-62, helping them to promotion from Division 2 in 1960), Everton, and Port Vale. He won amateur and 'B' caps for Northern Ireland, and also won 7 senior international caps between 1959 and 1964.

HINGERTY, DANIEL Joseph (DAN).

Rugby international wing-forward. Clubs: Lansdowne and U.C.D. Born in Dublin, 11th January 1920. A product of O'Connell C.B.S. and a Leinster interprovincial, he played in 3 victory internationals in 1946 and was capped for Ireland 4 times in 1947 as a flanker, before getting a job in Ottawa, thus possibly depriving him of a place in Ireland's 'Golden Era' of 1948 and 1949. A professor of clinical biochemistry at U.C.D., he founded the Firbolgs rugby side (a kind of Irish Barbarians side), and continued to play tip rugby into his seventies.

HINTON, EDWARD (TED).

Soccer international goalkeeper. Born in Belfast, 20th May 1922. Clubs: Glentoran, Distillery, Fulham, Millwall, Bangor and Ballymena United. He played 7 international games for Northern Ireland between 1947 and 1951, a highlight being his great save from Wilf Mannion in the famous 2-2 draw with England at Goodison in November 1947.

HINTON, WILLIAM PEART.

Rugby international full-back. 1882-1953. Club: Old Wesley. He played for Leinster 13 times in the interprovincial between 1904 and 1911, and played for Ireland 16 times between 1907 and 1912, scoring 2 conversions for his country. In his last year on the side, he played 3 of the 4 matches which ensured Ireland a share in the International Championship with England. He later became an international referee, and was President of the I.R.F.U. 1920/1921.

HIPWELL, MICHAEL Louis (MICK).

Rugby international wing-forward. Born in Bagnelstown, Co Carlow, 15th July 1940. Club: Terenure College (winning Leinster Senior Cup medals in 1966 and 1967). He played 23 senior Interprovincial matches for Leinster from 1961 to 1970, and was capped 12 times for Ireland in an 11 year period between 1962 and 1972. He has the distinction of being Ireland's first ever international rugby union substitute, coming on for Noel Murphy (cv) in the 1969 match against France. Also a Barbarian, he became a British and Irish Lion in 1971, on the tour of Australia and New Zealand, although not gaining a test place. A pilot.

HOARE, SEAMUS.

G.A.A. football goalkeeper, Donegal. In a barren period for the senior county team (the 1960's) when Donegal reached only 2 Ulster Senior Football Championship finals (both lost), he became the only Donegal player to win 4 Railway Cup medals with Ulster, keeping goal in the successive wins of 1964, 1965 and 1966, and again in 1968.

HOEY, BRIAN and MICK.

Amateur international golfing brothers. Brian, a member of the Shandon Park club (winning Senior Cup medals in 1966, 1968, 1971, 1972, 1973 and 1978, and winning Barton Shield medals in 1970, 1975, 1979 and 1985), won the Irish Close Championship in 1984 at Malone, at the age of 50. He had been runner-up in the German Open Amateur in 1970, and had won the 'North' in 1979 (also being runner-up in 1971). He played 77 interprovincial matches for Ulster between 1958 and 1985, winning 38. He played 28 Home international matches in 6 series from 1970 to 1984, winning 14 (and was a member of the winning Quadrangular side in 1972); he also won 4 of the European Team matches he played in 1971 and 1977. His brother Mick, also a Shandon Park golfer (who won 3 Barton Shield and 5 Irish Senior Cup medals), won 2 successive North of Ireland titles in 1968 and 1969, was runner-up in the 'West' in 1969, and played 22 interprovincial matches for Ulster between 1967 and 1973.

HOGAN, G P SARSFIELD.

Rugby interprovincial player. Clubs: U.C.D. (helping them to win the Leinster Senior Cup for the first time in 1924) and Lansdowne (winning Leinster Senior Cup medals in 1927 and in 1928 as captain). Four times a Leinster interprovincial player in the mid 1920's, and a final Irish trialist, he was unlucky not to be capped. A fine administrator, he represented Ireland on the International Board from 1946 to 1971, and was president of the I.R.F.U. in 1948-49. He was an Irish selector and was also the manager of the Irish tour of Argentina and Chile in 1952.

HOGAN, (ne GREGAN), James Joseph (JIM).

Long distance athlete. Born on 28th May 1933. Club: Polytechnic. He ran for Ireland in the 1962 European Championships in Belgrade at both 5,000 metres and at 10,000 metres (dropping out of both races). In the 1964 Olympic Games he ran the marathon for Ireland, failing to finish. He also ran for Ireland in the International Cross Country Championship in 1963, 1964 and 1965. He changed his allegiance to Great Britain in 1966 and won that year's European Championship marathon event in Budapest with a time of 2 hours, 20 minutes and 4.6 seconds. He later ran in the 1968 Olympic Games 10,000 metres final for Great Britain, finishing 26th.

HOGAN, KEN.

G.A.A. hurling goalkeeper, Tipperary. Born in 1963. Club: Lorrha. He was a member of the Tipperary side which were beaten in the final of the All-Ireland Under 21 Championship. He was in goals for Tipperary in their All-Ireland final defeat in 1988, having also been on the Munster S.H.C. winning side in 1987, when he became only the 2nd Tipperary goalkeeper to be awarded an All-Star award. He went on to win 2 Liam McCarthy Cup medals with Tipp for the All-Ireland Senior Hurling Championship in both 1989 and 1991, while in 1993 he won another Munster S.H.C. medal. A garda.

HORAN, MARGARET.

Pitch and Putt player. Clubs: Clara and Tullamore. Certainly one of Ireland's best lady pitch and putt players, she has won 5 Irish national titles in her sport. As a Clara member she won 3 successive Irish National Strokeplay titles in the late 1970's, in 1977, 1978 and 1979 (and was runner-up, in both 1978 and 1979, of the Irish National Matchplay Championships). She made it 4 nationals in 4 years when she captured her first National Matchplay title in 1980 (she then went on to win this title again in 1989, while playing out of Tullamore). She was also runner-up in the National Matchplay title 4 more times, in 1982, 1983, 1984 and 1987, making it a tally of 6 runners-up spots in this discipline.

HOGAN, PADRAIG F.

Amateur international golfer. Club: Elm Park. He won the East of Ireland

Championship title twice, in 1988 and 1991. In 49 interprovincial matches for Leinster in 1982-88, he won 31; in 21 Home international matches for Ireland 1985-88, he won 13; he was a member of the successful side in the European Team Championship in Austria in 1987 (and also in the Triple Crown-winning side in the Home internationals in Lahinch in the same year), and of the Cartier Trophy in 1988. He is a former Dublin senior gaelic footballer.

HOGAN, WILLIE.

G.A.A. hurling full-forward, Carlow. Regarded as one of the greatest players never to win an All-Ireland Senior Hurling Championship medal, the closest he came to national honours was when he played in the full-forward line on the Leinster Railway Cup hurling side beaten in the final of 1963 by Munster.

HOLMES, E P C.

Hockey international goalkeeper. Club: Cliftonville. Capped 19 times for Ireland at hockey between 1901 and 1908, he was regarded as one of the better keepers of his time. He was a member of the Ireland team which won an Olympic silver medal in the games of 1908 held in London, when beaten 8-1 by England in the final.

HOLMES, PAT.

International canoeist. Born in 1966. Clubs: Salmon Leap and Richmond CC. He has been Irish champion at 500 metres in the K1 discipline for 7 years in succession, 1985, 1986, 1987, 1988, 1989, 1990, 1991 and 1992, and has held the British and Irish records over that distance. In 1992 he won the British Championships at 4 events, the K1 500m, the K1 1,000m, the K2 1,000m and the K4 500ms. He has competed for Ireland at 2 Olympic Games, in Seoul in 1988 and in Barcelona in 1992. His brother Conor (born in 1967), a 1992 K4 British champion, also represented Ireland in the Barcelona Olympics, in the K2 500m and 1,000ms.

HONAN, COLM.

G.A.A. hurling left half-forward, Clare. He was a star member of the Clare side which won successive National Hurling League titles in 1977 and 1978, also being on the Clare side beaten in the Munster Hurling Championship final by Cork in both of these years. He won one All-Star award, in 1976 at left half-forward.

HOOKS, KENNY John.

Rugby international wing-threequarter. Born in Markethill on New Years Day in 1961. Clubs: Bangor and Ards. Winning 4 schools international caps in 1976 and 1977, he won 2 'B' caps in 1979. He initially won one cap for Ireland in 1980, and then after a wait of almost 10 years he was capped a further 7 times for Ireland in 1989-90 and the 1990-91 seasons.

HOOPER, DICK.

Long distance athlete. Club: Raheny Shamrocks. Born in 1957, he made his international debut in 1975 in the world junior cross country in Rabat. In 1978 he won the National marathon title at the first attempt, and went on to win it again in 1980, 1981 and 1982. He won the Dublin City marathon a record 3 times, in 1980, 1985 and 1988 (he was 2nd in 1984, 3rd in 1987, 4th in 1992 and 5th in both 1982 and 1991). One of a select bunch of Irish sportspersons to participate in 3 different Olympic Games, his 3 Olympic marathon runs were in Moscow in 1980 (when he finished 38th), in Los Angeles in 1984 (when he finished in 51st place), and in Seoul in 1988, when he finished in a creditable 24th place. He has also ran at 2 European Championships. In 1990 he won his first marathon in 25 starts, the Pittsburgh Marathon, in 2.15.49, for his most prestigious win. His brother Pat Hooper won a B.L.E. National marathon title, and also competed in the 1980 Olympic marathon in Moscow, finishing 42nd.

HOPKINS, THELMA (later Mrs McLERNON).

High jump athlete and sports all-rounder. Born in Hull, England on 16th March 1936, she spent most of her youth in Northern Ireland. Having finished 4th at the high jump (at the age of 16) in the Olympic Games in Helsinki in 1952 (2 inches behind the bronze medal position), she won a silver medal for Great Britain in the 1956 Olympic Games in Melbourne, finishing 10cm behind the world record-breaking winner, Mildred McDaniel of U.S.A., but being placed 2nd on countback ahead of 5 other athletes who all finished on the same height as her, 1.67m (in this games she also competed in the long jump, without success). She won the Vancouver Commonwealth Games high jump title in 1954, and won silver in the long-jump at the same games. She also won a European Championships high jump gold medal in the Berne Games of 1954, and won the European Cup the same year. She won a total of 33 Northern Ireland athletics titles from 1951 onwards in various disciplines. Her British record height of 1.74 metres (which was a world record when it was set) lasted until 1964, and she held the British record for the pentathlon. Not only versatile at athletics, she also reached international level in 2 other sports. She won 45 caps for Ireland at hockey as a forward (scoring a goal on her debut), being a member of the first British Isles team to make a visit to the United States in 1965. She was also chosen to play for Ireland at squash. She was elected to the Texaco Hall of Fame in 1965, the 2nd athlete to be so honoured. Her sister Moira was also capped for Ireland at hockey.

HOPKIRK, PADDY.

International rally driver. Born 4th April 1933. Teams: Rootes and B.M.C. Having won the Hewison Trophy for the Irish Championship in 1955, he went on to win the Circuit of Ireland 5 times: in 1958 in a Triumph TR3, in 1961 and 1962 in a Sunbeam Rover, and in both 1965 and 1967 in a Mini Cooper S. In 1964, accompanied by Henry Liddon, he won the prestigious Monte Carlo Rally (becoming the 2nd of only 2 Irishmen to do so) in a Mini Cooper S (the first time this car won the race). He won the Austrian Alpine rally in 1964 in a Healey 3,000, and won the race again in 1966. He won the 1967 Acropolis Rally (and would have won this race the previous year but for a penalty for servicing inside a control area). He also won the Coupes des Alpine, having previously won the Silver Coupe in the 1965 race. He finished 2nd in the marathon 1969 London to Sydney rally. During this period he became the best-known rally driver in the world. A popular figure when at his peak, in 1964 he was selected as Texaco's Motor Sports Sportstar of the Year, and in 1988 was elevated into the Texaco Hall of Fame.

HORAN, PADRAIG.

G.A.A. hurling full-back and full-forward, Offaly. Born on 21st April 1950. Club: St Rynagh's (winning county and provincial championship medals, and being on the side defeated in the All-Ireland Club Championship final in 1973). As a forward he was on the Offaly side which captured the Leinster S.H.C. in 1980, and in 1981 he captained Offaly to the county's first ever All-Ireland Senior Hurling Championship success (he is also still the last captain to lead a county to it's initial success in the All-Ireland S.H.C.), when they defeated Galway in the final by 2-12 to 0-15 points; he was also a member of the side which won the Liam McCarthy Cup again in 1985 (when he played a brilliant game), being on the side beaten in the 1984 final. He won 3 successive Railway Cup medals with Leinster at full-back in 1973, 1974 and 1975. He won one All-Star award, in 1985 at full-forward. He later trained the Offaly side which won the county's first ever National Hurling League title in 1990-91.

HORAN, THOMAS P (TOM).

Australian test cricketer. Born in Midleton, Co Cork, 8th March 1854, he died in Australia in 1916. Perhaps the greatest of the many top-class early Australian cricketers to be born in Ireland, Horan toured England with Australia in 1878, 1882, and toured North America in 1878. A right hand batsman and fast/medium bowler, he played test cricket for Australia 15 times between 1876 and 1876. His first class cricket batting career spanned 106 matches, scoring 4027 runs with an average of 23 runs per innings.

HORGAN, DENIS.

Shot putt thlete. Born in Banteer, Co Cork on 18th May 1871. In 1904, from a 7 foot square, he threw a world record 14.32 metres in the shot putt. He won 13 British A.A.A shot putt titles over a 20 year period, a then record for one event in these prestigious championships, and still the joint record (but his are uniquely all outdoors); the years of his triumphs were: seven-in-a-row from 1893 to 1899, twice in succession in 1904 and 1905; 3-in-a-row in 1908, 1909 and 1910; and finally at the age of 41 in 1912. In 1909 he won an American A.A.U. shot putt title. A pioneer figure in world shot-putting, breaking World, British, English, Scottish and Irish records, he was so dominant that if he had entered any of the first 4 Olympic events (1896, 1900, 1904 and 1906), his current form at the time of each games would have made him an overwhelming favourite in each contest (in 1896 he had won 3 titles at over 43', but the gold was won at 36'; in 1900 he broke a world record; in 1904 he threw 3 inches longer that the gold medallist, in the same month;, and in 1906 he threw 6 feet longer than the winner). However, when way past his best, he, representing Great Britain, won only a silver medal in the event at the age of 37 in the Olympic Games at London in 1908, having recovered from a savage attack in 1907 while on the beat as a New York cop, when he was beaten over the head with a shovel. Said to warm up for his events with a dozen eggs added to a pint of sherry, he retired on a pension to Ireland, where he died in 1922, aged 51.

HORGAN, JOHN.

G.A.A. hurling left full-back, Cork. Club: Blackrock (with whom he won 3 All-Ireland Club Championship hurling medals, in 1972, 1974 and 1979, all as captain, being the only man to captain more than one winning side). As a minor he won an All-Ireland M.H.C. medal with Cork in 1967, followed on by 2 All-Ireland Under 21 Championship medals, in 1970 and 1971. He also won 4 All-Ireland Senior Hurling Championship winner's medals with Cork in the 70's, in 1970, in 1976 (as a sub), 1977, and 1978, all at left corner back. He also won 4 National League medals with the county, in 1970, 1974, 1980 and 1981, and won a Railway Cup medal in 1978 with Munster. He has been awarded 3 All-Star places, in 1974, 1977, and 1978 (when he was also selected as Texaco's Hurling Sportstar of the Year), all at left corner back.

HORGAN, PAT.

G.A.A. hurling centre half-forward, Cork. Born 9th February 1958. He was a sub for the winning All-Ireland Cork minors side of 1974, and was on the 1976 Cork All-Ireland Under 21 Championship triumphant side. He was a member of 2 Cork sides which lost in successive All-Ireland S.H.C. finals to Kilkenny, in 1982 at centre half-forward, and in 1983 at right half-back. A member of the Glen Rovers side which won the All-Ireland Club hurling title in 1977, he won a Railway Cup medal with Munster in 1981. He has won 2 All-Star awards, in 1980 and in 1982, both at centre half-forward.

HORLACHER, ALFRED F (FRED).

Soccer international forward and utility player. Born in Blackrock, Co Dublin, 23rd March 1910, he died at the age of 33. Club: Bohemians (winning 4 League of Ireland medals in 1927-28, 1929-30, 1933-34 and 1935-36, and an F.A.I. Cup medal in 1935, when he scored in the final). He scored 85 league goals for the 'Gypsies' between 1927 and 1943, a club record until surapassed by Turlough O'Connor (cv). He was capped for Ireland 6 times between 1930 and 1936. An Olympic reserve water polo player (winning 5 Leinster League medals and one Irish Cup medal with his club Sandycove) and near-Olympic standard swimmer, he once finishing 3rd in the Liffey Swim.

HOSEY, WILLIE.

Squash international player. Born in Carlow 30th April 1960. Club: Fitzwilliam. First capped at international level for Ireland in 1982, he has been capped 52 times up to 1993. He has won a record 9 Irish Close national titles, in 1983, 1984, 1985, 1987, 1988, 1989, 1990, 1991 and 1992. A professional player based in Toronto (he was ranked No 6 in Canada in August 1993) who spends much of his time on a North American circuit, he has won many provincial Opens in Ireland, and won the Irish Open Championship in 1983. His father, Willie Hosey, was a fine Carlow footballer, winning 13 county championship medals, playing at left corner back on the Carlow side which won the Leinster S.F.C. in 1944 (the last time the county reached that stage in the championship).

HOSTY, SEAN F.

Amateur interprovincial golfer. Club: Galway. He was joint runner-up in the 1965 East of Ireland. He played 85 interprovincial matches in 16 series for Connacht in the 24 years between 1957 and 1978 (including being on the winning side of 1965), winning 19, halving 10, and losing 56 matches. This mumber of matches played places him 4th in Connachts all-time list, although his success rate was a poor 28%. He was later Secretary of the Connacht Council of the G.U.I.

HOUGH, W.

G.A.A. hurler, Limerick. He, as captain of the Newcastle West side, led Limerick to win the 1918 All-Ireland Senior Hurling Championship final, when they beat the Wexford selection by 9-5 to 1-3. He was also on the Limerick side which won the All-Ireland S.H.C. again in 1921, only to be on the losing side in the final of 1923.

HOUGHTON, RAYMOND J (RAY).

Soccer international midfielder. Born in Glasgow, 9th January 1962. Clubs: West Ham, Fulham (joining them on a free transfer, and scoring 16 goals in 129 league appearences), Oxford (joining in 1985 for £100,000, scoring 10 goals in 83 league appearences, and scoring a goal in the sides 3-0 Milk Cup final defeat of Q.P.R. in 1986), and Liverpool (joining for a fee of £600,000, helping them to 2 English First Division League titles, in 1988 and 1990, and F.A.I. Cup in both 1989 and 1992, also gaining runners-up medals in First Division in 1989 and F.A. Cup in 1988), Aston Villa (helping the club to finish in runners-up spot in the new Premier Division in 1992-93). First capped for Ireland while at Oxford in 1986 against Wales, his winning goal (while gaining his 16th cap) against England in the 1988 European Championship in Stuttgart assures him a place in Irish soccer folklore. Also playing a fine role in Ireland's World Cup run of 1990, his cap tally up to June 1993 reached 53. The 12 caps he gained while based at Oxford in 1986-87 made him then that club's jointly most capped player.

HOURIHANE, CLAIRE.

Amateur international golfer. Born 18th February 1958. Club: Woodbrook. She has won the Irish Ladies Championship 5 times, 4 times in 5 years in 1983, 1984, 1985, 1987, and again in 1991 at Ballybunion, being a beaten finalist in both 1980 and 1992 (she won the qualifying Leitrim Cup 7 times). She won the prestigious British Strokeplay Championship title at Blairgowrie in 1986, and was third in this event 3 times, and 2nd in 1990. She has won Curtis Cup honours 4 times, in 1984 at Muirfield (winning 2 of her 4 matches), in the victorious GB&I 1986 side at Prairie Dunes in the U.S.A. (playing alongside fellow Irishwomen Mary McKenna and Lilian Behan), in 1988 (when although not playing any matches she was also in the victorious side at Sandwich), and in 1992, gaining 1 points in the fine 10-8 win at Hoylake. She has played in the Vagliano Trophy many times, including 1981, 1983, 1985 and 1987. Favouring strokeplay events, she has won many titles, including the South Atlantic in Florida in 1983 (against top American opposition), the Spanish Championship at Las Brisas in 1987, the Irish Womens Foursomes title 4 times, and many other home titles. A constant member of the Irish side in the Home internationals from 1979 to 1991 (and a member of the winning sides of 1980 and 1986), she played in the European Ladies Team side in 1981, 1983, 1985 and 1987. In 1986 she was selected as Texaco's Golf Sportstar of the Year.

HOWARD, GARRETT.

G.A.A. hurling left half-back, Limerick, Dublin and Tipperary. Born in 1899, he is from Croom, Co Limerick. Clubs: Croom in Limerick, Garda in Dublin, and Toomyvara in Tipperary (winning a total tally of 8 county championship medals). His senior inter-county career for the 3 counties he played for spanned the years 1921 to 1936. He won 5 All-Ireland Senior Hurling Championship medals, 3 with his native Limerick (1921, 1934, and 1936), and 2 in between for Dublin (1924, and 1927), therefore winning more All-Ireland medals than any other Limerick-born player. He was on losing All-Ireland S.H.C. final Limerick sides in 1933 and 1935. He also won 5 National League medals, and won 2 Railway Cup medals, one for each of 2 provinces, with Leinster in the inaugural event of 1927, and with Munster 4 years later, in 1931. In 1982 he joined Mick Mackey as the first two Limerickmen to be selected as an All-Time All-Star award winner.

HOWLETT, GARY.

Soccer international midfielder. Clubs: Brighton and Hove Albion (reaching an F.A. Cup final with them in 1983, when only beaten in a replay by Manchester United), Shelbourne (winning a Premier Division medal with the League of Ireland in 1991-92, and an F.A.I. Cup medal in 1993). Nominated for the shortlist for the P.F.A.I. Player of the Year in 1993, he was capped once for the Republic of Ireland (as a sub against China in 1984).

HOWLETT, MARTIN.

G.A.A. footballer, Wexford. He was a constant member of the great Wexford Blues and Whites 4-in-a-row side which captured the All-Ireland Senior Football Championship in the successive years of 1915, 1916, 1917 and 1918, thus becoming the first county to achieve this unlikely feat.

HUEY, S SCOTT J

Cricket and badminton international. Born in Co Donegal, 21st December 1923. In cricket, as a slow left arm bowler for the Eglington and City of Derry clubs, he played 20 first class matches for Ireland between 1951 and 1966, his record being 20-30-4-135-23-5.19-1203-66-18.23, his best bowling coming in a 1954 match versus the M.C.C., taking 8 wickets for 48 runs (and a combined 14 wickets for 97 runs in the match). He has the distinction of being the last player to dismiss the great English cricketer Sir Len Hutton in a first-class match (in the M.C.C. match in 1960). In all he was capped 36 times for Ireland between 1951 and 1966, and is among the top 10 Irish wicket takers in cricket, taking 112 wickets from 2314 runs in 54 overs, for an average of 20.66 (and he once bowled 6 for 13 against Scotland in 1963). His right hand batting was average, scoring 218 runs in 23 innings for an international average of 5.58 runs per innings. He was also a badminton international.

HUGHES, DESMOND T (DESSIE).

National Hunt jockey and trainer. Born 10th October 1943. As a successful National Hunt jockey, he rode hundreds of winners in Ireland, and won both of Cheltenham's great races, the 1979 Champion Hurdle (on Monksfield), and the 1977 Cheltenham Gold Cup (on Davy Lad). He brought his Cheltenham Festival tally as a jockey to 10 with two Sun Alliance Hurdles', 3 Templegate Hurdles, and 3 Arkle Chases. Taking up training in Kildare in 1979, he has been leading jump trainer in Ireland twice, in 1981 (with 38 winners) and 1983 (with 48 winners).

HUGHES, EUGENE ('NUDIE').

G.A.A. football corner back and left full-forward, Monaghan. A Castleblaneyman, he was a star right full-back on the Monaghan side which won the Ulster Senior Football Championship for the first time in 41 years in 1979, also playing on the Monaghan side which recaptured the title in 1985 and 1988, then playing as left corner forward. He was a member of the Monaghan senior side which won the National Football League in 1985. The only Monaghanman to win 3 All-Stars, he is one of only 5 footballers to win All Star awards both as a forward and as a back, winning as a right full back in 1979, and as a left corner forward in both 1985 and 1988.

HUGHES, EUGENE.

Snooker professional. From Dun Laoghaire, he was born on 4th November 1955. Winning the Irish Amateur Championship in 1976 and 1978, he turned professional in 1981, and has peaked at a World ranking of 17 (the highest ever by a Republic of Ireland snooker player until surpassed by Ken Doherty cv). He has reached the semi-final of both the 1984 Jameson International and the 1986 BCE international. He was a vital cog in Ireland's 3 successive victories in the prestigious World Cup team event in 1985, 1986, and 1987, along with Denis Taylor and Alex Higgins (cccv).

HUGHES, GERRY.

G.A.A. camogie full-back, Dublin. Clubs: C.I.E., and Celtic (with whom she won an All-Ireland Club Championship medal in its inaugural year of 1964). She is joint third in all-time All-Ireland Senior medal holders, winning 9 times, missing only one final of Dublin's 10 in succession in 1954, 1955, 1956, 1957, 1958, 1959, 1960, 1961, 1962, and 1963. She also won 4 Gael-Linn medals with Leinster.

HUGHES, GREG.

G.A.A. football full-back, Offaly. He won 3 Leinster Senior Football Championship medals in his county's first ever wins at that level, in 1960, 1961 and 1969 (reaching the All-Ireland final in the 2 later years). He shares the record of being the first Offaly player to win 3 Railway Cup medals in football, playing in the full back line in the wins of 1959, 1961 and 1962 (when he became the 2nd Offalyman to captain a winning side).

HUGHES, JOHNNY.

G.A.A. football half-back, Galway. Born in 1951. Club: Mountbellew. Attaining senior inter-county status in 1970 for the first time, he was a member of the Galway side which won the Connacht S.F.C. title 3 times, in 1973 and 1974 (when they were beaten All-Ireland S.F.C. finalists on both occasions), and again in 1976. He also won a National Football League medal with Galway in 1980. Known for doing running commentaries on matches he was actually playing in, he received 2 All-Star accolades, in 1974 at left half-back, and in 1976 at centre half-back.

HUGHES, MICHAEL.

Soccer international player. Born in Larne, 2nd August 1971. Clubs: Carrick Rangers, Manchester City (playing 26 league matches for them) and Strassbourg. An Under 23 interntional player, he has also been capped 11 times for the full Northern Ireland soccer side up to June 1993

HUGHES, PATRICK (PADDY).

Amateur international boxer. Clubs: St Tarsicius, and Corinthian's. He won 6 Irish National Senior Championships over a period of 7 years, 2 at each of 3 different weights: in 1929 and 1930 he won flyweight titles; in 1931 and 1932 he captured the bantamweight titles, while in 1933 and 1935 the featherweight championships were added. He boxed for Ireland at bantamweight in the 1932 Olympic Games in Los Angeles.

HUGHES, ROBERT WOOD ('BARNEY').

Rugby international forward. Club: N.I.F.C. (winning a medal in the inaugural year of the Ulster Senior Cup in 1885). He won 12 caps during the formative days of Irish international rugby, between 1878 and 1886, including Ireland's first match in the International Championship, against England in 1883, under the captaincy of George Scriven (cv).

HUGHTON, CHRIS W G.

Soccer international defender. Born in West Ham, 11th December 1958. He joined Tottenham Hotspur as a junior in 1977, and from 1979 to date has played over 270 league matches for them, scoring over 12 league goals, and with whom he has won 2 F.A. Cup medals (1981 and 1982), and an UEFA Cup winners medal in 1984. He joined Newcastle United in 1990. First capped for Ireland in 1980 (when he became the first ever black man to be capped for the Republic), he became a regular in the side, and was ever present in the Irish side which performed so heroicly in the European Championships in West Germany in 1988. He gained his 50th cap for Ireland against Malta in the build up to the World Cup in 1990, and brought his final tally of caps to 53.

HULME, J WILLIE.

Amateur international golfer. Club: Warrenpoint. He won the 'East' in 1944 (and lost 3 in play-offs in 1947, 1949 and 1958), and was runner-up in the Irish Amateur Open in 1955. He played 28 Home international matches for Ireland between 1955 and 1959; having first played for Ulster in 1939, he went on to be one of only 5 players from the old series to take part in the new interprovincial series set up in 1956, playing in 4 series on the trot. He later won the Irish Senior Amateur's Open Championship in 1973. His daughter Dorothy, also a member of Warrenpoint, played interprovincial golf for Ulster.

HUME-DUDGEON, IAN.

Equestrian 3-day eventer. He competed for Ireland in 3 successive Olympic Games (sharing with a team-mate of each year, Harry Freeman-Jackson, the honour of being the first Irish sportsperson to participate in 3 Olympic celebrations for their country). The years were: 1952 in Helsinki on the horse Hope (when the team finished in 6th place and he himself was 28th); in 1956 in Stockholm on Copper Coin (when he was eliminated in the showjumping having completed a clear round to put Ireland in the run for a medal, and when the team did not finish); and in Rome on Corrigneagh in 1960 when the team was again in 6th place, he himself finishing 30th in the individual. His father John Hume-Dudgeon, who had ridden in his younger days for Great Britain in eventing, managed some of the Irish sides in which Ian competed.

HUMPHRIES, WILLIE (or BILLY).

Soccer international outside-right. Born in Belfast, 8th June 1936. Clubs: Glentoran, Ards (for three periods, helping them to their first ever Irish League title in 1958), Leeds United (playing only 25 league games for them), Coventry City (scoring 25 goals in 109 league matches in 1961-64, helping them to win Division 3 in 1963-64), Swansea City (scoring 22 league goals for them in 141 league matches in 1964-67). Representing the Irish League side 12 times, he was capped also 14 times for Northern Ireland between 1962 and 1966, scoring one international goal. He was later manager of Bangor in the years 1983-1985.

HUNTER, ALAN.

Soccer international defender. Born in Sion Mills, 30th June 1946. Clubs: Coleraine, Oldham (playing 83 league games for them 1966-68), Blackburn (playing 84 league games for them 1968-71), Ipswich (playing in over 280 league matches in a fruitful time for them over a 10 year period from 1971 to 1980, and playing on the club's only success in the F.A. Cup, in 1978). Capped for Northern Ireland at both amateur and Under 23 levels, his dependability amassed him 53 caps for Northern Ireland (most often in the No 5 jersey) over an 11 year period between 1970 and 1980, 47 of these while based at Portman Road, making him Ipswich Town's most capped player.

HUNTER, WILLIAM RAYMOND.

Rugby and cricket international. Born in Belfast, 3rd April 1938. Rugby club: C.I.Y.M.S. A dual international from Wallace H.S. in Lisburn, he won a total of 10 international rugby caps for Ireland as a winger and centre between 1962 and 1966, scoring one international try, and one penalty. Also a Barbarian, he was selected for the British and Irish Lions for the 1962 tour to South Africa, but did not play in a test. He also played cricket for Ireland 28 times between 1957 and 1967. He took 33 wickets for 989 runs off 35 innings, for an average of 29.96 (twice taking 5 wickets in an innings). His younger brother Laurence Mervyn Hunter (born in Dunmurry, Co Antrim, 10th October 1943), and also a product of Wallace H.S. in Lisburn, also played international rugby for Ireland, gaining 2 caps, both on winning sides in the 1968 season.

HURLEY, CHARLIE.

Soccer international centre-half. Born in Cork, 4th October 1936. He joined the junior ranks of Millwall in 1953, playing 105 league matches for them before joining Sunderland for £20,000 in 1957. At Roker Park, in 12 seasons from 1957 to 1968, he played in a large tally of 355 league matches, scoring 23 goals for the club, and helping them to promotion into the First Division in 1964. He finished his playing days at Bolton Wanderers with one season, 1969-70. Playing his first match for his country in the World Cup qualifiers of 1957, he went on to be capped 40 times for the Republic of Ireland up until 1969, a span of 13 years in the national side. At the height of his career, in the early 1960's, he was regarded as the finest centre-half in the British game. He was selected as Texaco's Soccer Sportstar of the Year in 1959, and in 1989 he beacame the first person to be installed into the F.A.I. Hall of Fame. His younger brother Chris played soccer briefly for Millwall in 1963-64.

HURLEY, JIM.

G.A.A. hurling midfielder, Cork. Known as one of Cork hurling's greatest midfielders, he won 4 All-Ireland Senior Hurling Championship winner's medals with Cork over a 6 year span, exerting enormous influence in the victories in 1926, 1928, 1929 and 1931, also playing on the losing Leesider's team in the 1927 decider. He also won 3 Railway Cup medals with Munster, in 1928 (the province's first win in this sphere), 1930 and in 1931.

HUSSEY, ALLY.

G.A.A. camogie centre-back, Dublin. Club: Celtic (being a member of the team which won the inaugural All-Ireland Club Championship title in 1964). She accumulated a total of 6 All-Ireland Senior Camogie Championship winner's medals with Dublin, also winning 2 Gael-Linn awards. She won an All-Star award in 1965.

HUTCHING, SHARON (nee McPEAKE).

High jump athlete. Born in Ballymena, 22th June 1962. Club: Ballymena and Antrim. The wife of the British athlete Tim Hutchings, she was 6 times a U.K. international athlete from 1981 to 1989. She won W.A.A.A. Indoor title in 1989. Having finished 9th in the 1982 Commonwealth Games, she reached her career peak in the Edinburgh Commonwealth Games of 1986, when she broke the Northern Ireland record 3 times (with jumps of l.88, 1.89 and 1.90 metres), to capture the silver medal (and just narrowly failed to clear 1.92 metres).

HYDE, TIMOTHY Joseph (TIM).

National Hunt Jockey. He died in 1961. From Cashel, Co Tipperary, he won 2 Irish Grand Nationals, in 1938 with Clare County, and in 1942 with Prince Regent. He is one of the select few jockeys to win both the Aintree Grand National and the Cheltenham Gold Cup, being successful in the Liverpool race in 1939 on the 100-8 shot Workman, while winning the Prestbury Park classic in 1946 on the brilliant Prince Regent (whom he also rode in the Aintree Grand National to finish 3rd in 1946 and 4th in 1947). As a result of a fall, he was partially paralysed in 1956.

HYNES, MATHIAS (MATT).

Tug-of-War competitor. Born in Gortmore, Killanin, Co Galway on 21st January 1883, he died in 26. He was a member of the Great Britain side (represented by the London Police Force) which won the silver medal at the Olympic Games in Stockholm, Sweden in 1908. He had replaced Edmund Barrett (cv) in this side, which had captured the gold medal in 1908. His brother Tom was an Irish champion athlete over 4 miles who was also a professional long-distance runner, and won the first ever marathon race to be held in Ireland over the official distance of 26 miles 385 yards. This took place at Jone's Road football, ground on May 16th 1909, and the Galwayman's winning time was 2 hours, 51 minutes and 51 seconds.

HYLAND, BERT.

Middleweigtht professional boxer. In 1947 he was knocked out by the great Randolph Turpin in the first round of their bout. He beat Jimmy Ingle in an eliminator for the Irish middleweight title in 1949. Also during his speckled boxing career he beat 2 former British Champions, Ernie Roderick and Albert Finch.

I

INGLE, JIMMY.

Flyweight and welterweight boxer. Born in Ringsend, Dublin, 21st July 1921. A product of the St Joseph's B.C., he won the Irish National Senior Championship title at flyweight (while a member of the St Andrew's B.C.) in 1939, and also won the lightweight title in 1941. In 1939 he became, at the age of only 17, the first Irish amateur boxer to win a European title, when he won the flyweight at the European Championships which were held at Dublin. Turning pro as a welterweight, he fought a draw with the reigning British welterweight and middleweight champion, Ernie Roderick, in Dublin's Theatre Royal in 1946. He also had some close decisions against other title-holders, including Spike McCormack, Vince Hawkins, Randolph Turpin and Alex Burton. He was one of a family of 9 brothers, all boxers, from Ringsend.

INGRAM, EDWARD (EDDIE).

Cricket international right hand batsman and leg-break and right hand medium bowler. Born in Dublin 14th August 1910, he died in 1973. Clubs: Leinster and Ealing (for whom he scored over 3,000 runs). He played 19 first class games for Ireland between 1928 and 1953, and for 48 times in total, 8 times as captain. A classy all-rounder, his figures for Ireland in all internationals included 151 wickets (7th on the all-time list) from 73 innings and an average of 20.11; his batting figures included 1,636 runs (14th on the all-time list) from 84 innings for an average of 20.09. A peer of Jimmy Boucher, and a fellow Belvederian, he played 12 first class matches for Middlesex, captaining them in 1948. His overall first class record is : 31-55-4-766-64(v Scotland 1937)-15.02-1896-79-24.00, his best bowling being 5 for 48 against Scotland in 1936.

IRVINE, ROBERT W (BOBBY).

Soccer international player. Clubs: Everton, Portsmouth, Connah's Quay, and Derry City. He was capped 15 times for Northern Ireland between 1922 and 1932, and scored 3 international goals.

IRVINE, WILLIE J.

Soccer international centre forward. Born in Carrickfergus, 18th June 1943. Joining Burnley in the junior ranks in 1960, he played 123 league matches for them 1962-67, scoring 78 goals. He then played 2 seasons at each of Preston North End and Brighton, scoring 27 league goals for each club. Winning 3 Under 23 caps, he later played 23 full international matches for Northern Ireland between 1963 and 1972, scoring 8 international goals. His older brother, Bobby (born in Carrickfergus, 17th January 1942), a goalkeeper who won 3 I.F.A. Cup medals with Linfield in 1960, 1962 and 1963, was capped 8 times for Northern Ireland, three times alongside Willie.

IRVING, SAMUEL Johnstone.

Soccer international. Born in Belfast, 28th August 1894, he died in 1969. Clubs: Newcastle United, Galashiels United, Bristol Shields, Shildon, Dundee, Cardiff City (being a member of the famous F.A. Cup-winning side of 1927, the only time a team from outside England took this competition; and also helping them back to the Division One in 1930), Chelsea and Bristol Rovers. He was capped 18 times for Northern Ireland between 1923 and 1931, all in the Home international series.

IRWIN, Dr DAVID George.

Rugby international centre threequarter. Born in Belfast, 1st February, 1959. Clubs: Queen's University Belfast, and Instonians. A product of R.B.A.I., he won Under 23 and 'B' honours with Ireland in 1979. He became the 800th person to be capped for Ireland when making his international debut in 1980, and and he has been capped 25 times over an 11 year period from 1980 to 1990, scoring 2 international tries. He broke his leg against Wales in the Triple Crown year of 1982, but was ever-present in the Irish side which shared the International Championship in 1983. He toured with Ireland to Australia in 1979. He won a place on the British and Irish Lion's tour of New Zealand in 1983, playing in 3 Test matches. A fine captain of the all-conquering Ulster interprovincial side of the late 1980's, he was twice selected as captain of Irish touring sides (France in 1988, and U.S.A. and Canada in 1989) but was injured out on both occasions. A doctor.

IRWIN, DENIS J.

Soccer international right full-back. Born in Cork, 31st October 1965. Clubs: Everton (of Cork), Leeds United (playing over 80 matches with them), Oldham Athletic (reaching an F.A. Cup semi-final in 1989, and a League Cup final in 1990) and Manchester United. Tranferring for to Old Trafford a fee of £650,000 in June

1990, he was a member of the side which won the European Cup Winner's Cup in 1991 (the club's first success in Europe for 23 years), and also being on the side when the club captured their first ever League Cup trophy in 1992. With 'United' he was also on the side which were runners-up in the 1992 Football League, and which won the inaugural Premier Division Championship in 1992-93. Capped for the Republic of Ireland at schoolboy, youth, under 21, under 23 and 'B' level, he went on to win his first senior cap in 1990 against Morrocco, thereby becoming the first player to win caps for Ireland at 6 levels. A full-back with ability to move forward, his cap tally reached 21 by mid-1993.

IRWIN, GABRIEL.

G.A.A. football goalkeeper. Club: Glenamoy. He was in goals for Mayo's win in the All-Ireland Under 21 Championship of 1983, being also in the nets in their losing in the final of 1984. He was a star in Mayo's feat in reaching their first All-Ireland Senior Football Championship final in 38 years, in 1989, being awarded an All-Star that year for his feats. He won another Connacht S.F.C. medal in 1993.

IRWIN, LIAM.

G.A.A. football centre-field, Laois. He was a member of the Laois side which were beaten by Dublin in the final of the Leinster S.F.C. in 1985. He won a National Football League medal in 1986 (the first time the county had won this trophy since the year of it's inauguration in 1926-27). In 1986, along with Colm Browne (cv), he became one of the only 2 Laoismen to win All-Star awards, being selected in the midfield with Plunkett Donaghy of Tyrone.

IRWIN, Sir SAMUEL Thompson (SAM).

Rugby international forward. Club: Queen's University Belfast (winning Ulster Senior Cup medals in 1900 and 1903). Between 1900 and 1903 he won 9 international caps for Ireland. He became President of the I.R.F.U. for 1935-36, and was an Ulster Member of Parliament. His son, J W Sinclair Irwin, was capped in the back-row for Ireland 5 times before World War 2 in 1938-39, and he also went on to become President of the I.R.F.U., in 1969-70 (thus accomplishing the unique feat of a father and son who both played for Ireland and then both of whom went on to become President of the I.R.F.U.). Sam also served briefly on the International Board.

J

JACK, HARRY W.

Rugby international out-half. A product of Christian Brothers College (winning a Munster Senior Schools medal in 1909), and a member of U.C.C. (winning Munster Senior Cup medals in 1912 and 1913), he is one of 8 Irish players to be capped before and after the First World War, playing twice in the 1914 season, and against Scotland in 1921, for a total of 3 international caps. His friend Vincent ('Macky') McNamara (who died in the war in 1915), won Munster Senior Schools Cup, Munster Senior Cup, and played international rugby with him, in forming a famous half-back pairing.

JACKSON, A R V.

Rugby international centre and wing threequarter. Club: Wanderers (winning the Leinster Senior Cup medal in 1911). Four times a Leinster player between 1910 and 1913, he won 10 international caps for Ireland between 1911 and 1914, scoring 3 tries in his appearences for his country.

JACKSON, GUY P.

International player at tennis, squash, and hockey. A product of Oxford University. He achieved the rare feat of playing for Ireland at senior international level in 3 different sports. As a member of Fitzwilliam L.T.C., he represemted Ireland in 11 Davis Cup matches between 1948 and 1960 (being on sides that won matches in 1948, 1950 and 1956), and won an Irish men's doubles title in both 1952 and 1953 (when he also reached the last 16 in the Wimbledon Men's Doubles with Joe Hackett cv). He won the Fitzwilliams club single twice, in 1951 and in 1958. In squash he won 5 international Irish caps between 1953 and 1955, and became the first Irishmen to beat an English player in an international match, when in 1953 he beat the English No 5, Neville Hooper. In hockey, as a member of Three Rock Rovers, he was capped only once for Ireland, but in that game in Belfast in 1952 against Scotland, he scored 2 goals in the 3-3 draw. He was killed tragically in the 1972 air crash at Staines.

JACKSON, HUGH.

Professional golfer. Born in Newtonards, 28th February 1928. Attached to Knockbracken GC. He won the 1968 Piccadilly tournament, the 1970 Irish National Professional Championship title at Massarene, and the Irish Dunlop tournament in 1968. He won the Ulster Professional title 6 times, in 1963, 1965, 1968, 1969, 1970, and in 1971, and was runner-up in 1966. He represented Ireland in 2 World Cups, in 1970 at Buenos Aires, and in 1971 at Palm Beach.

JACKSON, JANET.

Ladies amateur international golfer. Club: The Island. She won the Irish Ladies Close Amateur Championship title 6 times in all (becoming the first person to win more than 4 titles, and now third in the all-time list of winners of this title), achieving two successive wins before World War 1 (1913 and 1914), and four after the war, in 1919, 1920, 1923 and 1925, and was never beaten in the final. She played in the Home international series 13 times between 1912 and 1930. She later lived in England, and lived to an age of over 95.

JACKSON, PAUL BRIAN.

Cricket international wicket-keeper and right-hand batsman. Born in Belfast, 9th December 1959. Clubs: N.I.C.C. and Ulster. An international from schools, Under 19 and 23 levels, up to the end of the summer of 1993 he had been capped 81 times for the full Ireland side (making him the 5th most capped Irish cricketer), and had taken 130 dismissals (from 102 catches and 28 stumpings), placing him as the 2nd most effective wicketkeeper in Irish international cricket history behind Ossie Calhoun (cv). He has also accumulated 931 runs for Ireland in 80 innings, averaging 14.32 per innings, his best score being 89 runs.

JACKSON, TOMMY.

Soccer international midfielder. Born in Belfast, 3rd November 1946. Club: Glentoran (helping them to an Irish Cup win in 1966, and to 2 successive Irish League wins in 1967 and 1968), Everton (1967-70), Nottingham Forest (1970-74, scoring 6 goals in 73 games), Manchester United (playing 22 games in the 1975-76 season). He played over 120 English League matches in his 9 year stint there. An Under 23 cap, he was capped 35 times for Northern Ireland between 1969 and 1976. He was manager of Glentoran from 1987 to 1993, bringing the club three Irish Cup successes and 3 Irish League titles along with ten other trophies.

JACOB, MICK.

G.A.A. hurling centre half-back, Wexford. Born in 1947. Club: Oulart-the-Ballagh (playing on 3 sides beaten in county championship finals). A member, as a goalkeeper, of the fine Wexford All-Ireland Under 21 H.C. winning side of 1965 (they were beaten in the finals of 1964 and 1966), he then won his senior inter-county debut in goals in 1967. He played in the half-back line on 3 Wexford sides which, having won the Leinster S.H.C., went on to lose the All-Ireland Senior Hurling Championship finals in the same years, in 1970, 1976, and 1977. Winning a National League medal in 1973, he won 3 Railway Cup medals with Leinster, in

1973, 1975 and 1977. He won 3 All-Star awards, all at centre half-back, in 1972 (the first Wexford-man to win this accolade), 1976, and 1977.

JAMESON, THOMAS O (TOMMY).

Squash international player. He lived 1892-1965. He won the first British Amateur Championship which was held in 1922 in London, repeating his success in the event in 1923 also. He was also a first class cricket player, and a rackets player of outstanding ability. His son, W Shane M Jameson, a member of Fitzwilliam, was capped 6 times for Ireland in squash between 1946 and 1950, and was twice winner of the Irish Open Championship title, in 1946 and 1947.

JAMISON, JACKIE.

Soccer international forward. Clubs: Crusaders (winning an I.F.A. Cup medal in 1968), Glentoran (winning an I.F.A. Cup medal in 1973, scoring a goal in the final; he is also the clubs leading goalscorer in European competitions, with 6). He was capped once for Northern Ireland, against Noreway in 1976.

JEFFREY, SAM C ('SHEM').

Horse Trainer. Based at Maryborough (Port Laoise). He trained 10 winners of Irish Classic races, consisting of: 3 Irish Derby's (Portmarnock in 1895, Gulsalberk in 1896 and Oppressor in 1899), One Irish 1,000 Guineas (the inaugural race in 1922, with Lady Violette), 2 Irish 2,000 Guineas (also the inaugural race, a year earlier in 1921 with Soldennis, and again 2 years later in 1923 with Soldumeno); 3 Irish Oaks (the 1897 race with Dabchick, again in 1903 with Mary Lester, and yet again in 1920 with Place Royale); and one Irish St Leger, with O'Dempsey in 1923.

JENNINGS, PAT.

Soccer international goalkeeper. Born in Newry, 12th June 1945. His clubs include Newry Town, Watford, Tottenham Hotspur and Arsenal. First capped (while playing at Watford) in 1964 against Wales, he then spent 12 years at Spurs during which time he played in a club record then of 472 league matches, and won medals for the 1967 F.A. Cup, 2 League Cups (1971 and 1973), a European Cup-Winners Cup in 1968, and a UEFA Cup winners medal in 1972 (and runner-up in 1974). Joining Arsenal after Spurs were relagated in 1977, he won with them an F.A. Cup medal in 1979 (and runners-up medals in 1978 and 1980), and a European Cup-Winners Cup runners-up medal in 1980. Having been capped at Youth and Under 23 level, he went on to break Terry Neill's (cv) record caps for Northern Ireland in 1976-77, and on further to make his own world record amount of full international caps against other national sides, when, on his 41st birthday against Brazil in the 1986 World Cup in Mexico, he won his 119th cap (this record was surpassed in 1990 by Peter Shilton). Having being first capped at the age of 18 in 1963, he spanned a remarkable 24 years in international football. Rated for many years as among the best goalkeepers in the world, the 75 international caps gained while with Tottenham 1965-77 and 1986 make him that club's most capped player. His total of 758 English League appearances places him (as well as the leading Irishman) 8th in the all-time listing, behind leader Peter Shilton. He was voted by the Football Writers' Association as Footballer of the Year in 1972-73, and as the Professional Footballers Association Player of the Year in 1976, the only Irishman to recieve both these prestigious honours. He was made an M.B.E. in 1976, and was awarded an O.B.E. in 1987, the first Northern Ireland Soccer player to recieve both honours. He was twice selected as Texaco's Soccer Sportstar of the Year, in 1973 and again in 1983.

JOHNSON, STEPHEN (STEVIE).

Hockey international defender. Club: Lisnagarvey. He was capped 20 times for

Ireland between 1952 and 1957, playing many fine defensive matches during lean times for Ireland. He was also one of a select band of Irish hockey players who have competed in Olympic Games, having been a member of the Great British side (being the first Irish player to attain this honour at a Games) which finished in 4th place in the 1956 games in Melbourne.

JOHNSTON, CHARLES J (PADDY).

Motorcycle racer. Born in Dublin 1900. His long career involved a record span of 28 years racing at the T.T. races in the Isle of Man, winning one race (the 1926 250cc race on a Cotton machine), and finishing 2nd three times in that period (in 1925 in both 125cc and 250cc, and in 1930 in the 250cc race). He was 2nd in the 1931 European 250cc Championship, and also scored many wins on the famous Brooklands speed track in Surrey. He later ran a horse racing stables in Aldershot, and died in 1970.

JOHNSTON, IRENE.

Hockey international. Club: Pembroke Wanderers (winning 5 Irish Senior Cup medals with them). Winning her first international cap in 1959, she went on to win 24 in all, and captained Ireland in both the 1969-70 and 1973-74 seasons. She toured with Ireland on the 1963 I.F.W.H.A. tournament in Baltimore, and as captain to the I.F.W.H.A. tournament in Cologne in 1967. Later she became an umpire at international level, and in 1993 she became president of the I.L.H.U. during it's centenary year, She is a sister of Harry Cahill (cv), and another brother of her's, Cecil, was capped at amateur international level in soccer many times, while her son Andrew (a member of Old Wesley) has played on the wing for Leinster in rugby.

JOHNSTON, JACK.

Rugby international forward. Club: N.I.F.C. (helping them to win the inaugural Ulster Senior Cup in 1885). A product of both Armagh RS and Belfast Academy, he was capped 8 times for Ireland between 1881 and 1887, being on the winning side only for his first cap. He later went on to be President of the I.R.F.U. in 1902-03, and died in 1911.

JOHNSTON, MARGARET (MAGGIE).

Bowls player. Born 2nd May 1943. From Bellaghy, Co Derry. Club: Ballymoney BC. Participating seriously after 1979, she won Irish and British Isles Singles titles in 1985 and 1986. In 1986 she won a Commomwealth Games gold medal in the pairs event at Edinburgh, and won a bronze in the Singles at Auckland in 1990. She reached the final of the 1988 Super Bowl indoor tournament, becoming the first lady bowls player to reach a major bowls final (she lost, in a classic final to fellow-Northern Irishman David Corkhill, 7-6,6-7,6-7,7-6,7-6). Later in 1988 she won the Women's World Bowls Pairs Championship, when in partnership with Phyllis Nolan (cv), beating Botswana in the final in Auckland, New Zealand. She went on to win the silver medal in the singles title the same year. She won her 2nd Women's World Pairs title (again with Phyllis Nolan) in Ayr in 1992, and also won the World Ladies Singles that year, defeating A Rutherford in the final. In 1992 she also skipped the Irish Triples to win the British Isles title. She has been twice selected, in 1988 and 1992, as Texaco's Bowls Sportstar of the Year.

JOHNSTON, WILLIAM C.

Soccer international forward. Born in Tyrone, 21st May 1942. Clubs: Glenavon, Oldham Athletic. He was capped only twice by Northern Ireland, once against Wales in 1962, and against Mexico in 1966, when he scored a goal after coming on as a substitute. He won an Irish Cup medal with Glenavon in their 5-1 final win over Linfield in 1961.

JOHNSTON, WILLIAM R.

Rugby international full-back, England. Club: Bristol. Born in Dublin in

1887, he won 16 caps for England at full-back between 1910 and 1914, being on the Championship winning side in 1910, 1912 (shared), 1913 and 1914. As an Irish-born player, he was England's most-capped full-back for 57 years, until Bob Hiller won his 17th cap in 1971.

JOHNSTONE, W E, RALPH W, and ROBERT.

Rugby international brothers. These 3 Donegal-born brothers won six Irish rugby caps between them from 1884 to 1892 (although none together), representing Dublin University and Wanderers. Robert, twice capped for Ireland in 1893, was a member of the British and Irish Lion's tour of South Africa in 1896 (and played in 3 Test matces); he was awarded a Victoria Cross for his bravery in the Boer War in South Africa in October 1899. Ralph, who also played cricket for Ireland, was capped 3 times at rugby in the centre in 1890. The third brother, W E, was capped at rugby in the pack once in 1884.

JOHNSTONE, W M.

Hockey international right-wing. Clubs: Dublin University, Three Rock Rovers. He was capped 20 times for Ireland in the 11 year period, 1898 to 1909, 16 of these as captain. He captained the first Irish side to beat England, thus winning Ireland's first ever Triple Crown success in 1904. He served as Secretary to the Leinster Hockey Umpires Association, and wrote invaluable memoirs of the game.

JONES, DAVID.

Professional golfer. Club: Bangor, Co Down. Not a regular tour player, he won the Irish Professional Masters at Hermitage in 1976, and the 1981 Irish National Professional title. He won the Irish Dunlop tournament in 1978 and 1979, and the Ulster P.G.A. title in 1993. In 1978 he was a member of the P.G.A. team that beat their American counterparts for the first time in 21 years, and captained that side in 1982. He won his first international professional tournament in 1989 (at the age of 41) when he became the 4th Irishman to win the Kenyan Open (his previous best finish in an important tournament was 3rd in the 1981 Carroll's Irish Open). He won the individual prize in 1988 Nations Cup tournament. Has latterly moved into course design.

JONES, ERNIE.

Professional golfer. Born at the Curragh Camp, 22nd September 1932. Turning pro in 1951, he has been attached to Carlow and Bangor GCs. He represented Ireland in the 1965 Canada (World) Cup at Madrid. A winner of the Cox-Moore tournament in 1961, he won the Kenyan Open in 1971, and won the Irish National Professional title in 1955 and again in 1964. He won the Ulster Professional title in both 1964 and 1974.

JONES, JIMMY.

Soccer international forward. Born in Keady. Clubs: Shankhill Young Men, Belfast Celtic (winning an Irish Cup medal in 1947 and an Irish League medal in 1948, scoring 63 goals in his first full season of 1947-48 and 33 up to Boxing day of 1948-49), Larne, Fulham (with whom he was not allowed play) and Glenavon (with whom he won 3 I.F.A. Cup medals in 1957, 1959, and 1961, scoring 3 goals in these finals, and Irish League medals in 1956-57 and 1959-60, scoring an average of 50 goals per season). In a 20 year career he scored a massive 750 goals, with a year's best of 74 goals (when with Glenavon). He was capped 3 times for Northern Ireland between 1956 and 1957, scoring a goal on his international debut against Wales, and his tally of 8 inter-league goals for the Irish League places him only one behind the record holder.

JONES, JOHN (JACK, or 'SOLDIER').

Soccer international half-back. Clubs: Linfield (with whom he won 3 I.F.A. Cup medals in 1930, 1931, and 1934), Hibernian, Glenavon. He was capped 23 times for Northern Ireland between 1930 and 1938. Jack's father also won international honours, as did his brother

Sam (a Distillery and Blackpool player), who played 2 internatonal matches in 1934, both with Jack in the side, and scored in one game. His brother-in-law Billy Mitchell (cv) also played for Northern Ireland (and in one game versus Wales in 1933 the 2 brothers and their brother-in-law Mitchell made up the entire half-back line). Two uncles, Joe and Sam Burnison also played soccer for Northern Ireland.

JONES, TOM.

Handballer. Born in Tralee in 1868. He won the professional championship of Ireland before his 20th birthday, and won many handsome purses. He held on to the title for 2 more years. However, with his skill almost legendary, he went into the priesthood at the age of 22, and never played serious handball again. He died at the age of 85 in 1951.

JORDAN, EDDIE.

Motor-racing driver. Born in Dublin, 30th March 1948, he moved from kart-racing (in which he was Irish champion in 1973) to car-racing. Winning 11 races, he won 2 Formula Atlantic championships in 1978 (the Ulster and Irish titles) with Marlboro Team Ireland, and then drove Formula 3 cars until 1981, when he retired to take up team ownership and management. As a manager of drivers like Martin Brundle, Jean Alesi, Johnny Herbert, and Martin Donnelly, he graduated into a Formula One expert. In 1991 he set up a Jordan team in the World Formula One Championships, achieving great results in his first year, with his team amassed 13 world championships points and finished 5th in the constructors contest. Both 1992 and 1993 were less successful.

JORDAN, HENRY Martyn.

Rugby international back, Ireland and Wales. Born in Clifton, Wales in 1865. Club: Newport. One of the smallest ever internationals, in 1884 he is reputed to be one of 2 Welsh players to make the Irish team up to quota in the International Championship fixture in Cardiff versus Wales. As he later played international rugby for Wales in 3 matches, he therefore becomes the only player in Irish rugby history to play for Ireland and another of the 5 nations in the International Championship, and one of only 5 players to represent Ireland and any other country.

JORDAN, WILLIAM (BILLY).

Soccer international forward. Club: Bohemians (winning an F.A.I. Cup winners medal in 1935, scoring 2 of the club's 4 goals in the final; and 2 League of Ireland winners medals, in 1933-34 and in 1935-36). He was capped twice for the Irish Free State, in 1934 against Holland, and in 1938 against Norway.

JOYCE, KIERAN.

Amateur international boxer. Club: Sunnyside. This Corkman, born in 1965, has won 6 Irish Senior National titles, 2 at welterweight, in 1982 and 1983, and 4 at light-middleweight, 1985, 1986, 1987, and 1988. Having represented Ireland in 2 Olympic Games, at welterweight in 1984 in Los Angeles (when he was edged out on points in the quarter-final) and 1988 in Seoul at middleweight, he retired after the latter.

JOYCE, REGINA and MONICA.

Long-distance athletes, sisters. Both girls won national titles at long-distance events in the 1980's. Regina, born 7th February 1957, ran in the 1983 World Championship marathon race in Helsinki, when she flattered to decieve after leading the race by 30 seconds at 25 kms. She later finished 23rd in the Olympic Games Marathon in 1984, in a time of 2:37.57. Her sister Monica also was an international class runner, and represented Ireland at the Olympic Games in Los Angeles in 1984, in the 3,000 metres heats.

JUDGE, H DAVID.

Hockey international full-back. Clubs: Dublin University, and Three Rock Rovers. Born 19th January 1936. He was for a period up to 1991 (when passed out by Billy McConnell cv), the most capped Irish hockey player of all-time. He made a then record all-time 124 appearences for Ireland in a 21 year international career extending between 1957 and 1978, during which period he also represented Great Britain on 15 occasions, making a total of 139 international appearences (making him for a period the most capped home international player). Captaining Ireland 31 times, he also competed in the Olympic Games for Great Britain Tokyo in 1964. He played on Ireland's first Home international-winning side for 19 years in 1968, also playing in the European Championships in Brussels in 1970, the winning Santander 8-Nation tournament of 1972, the South Africa tour of 1973, another European Championship in 1974, the first Intercontinental Cup in Rome in 1976, and he won his last cap in the World Cup in Buenos Aires in 1978. He also played 3 matches for Ireland at the indoor game in 1976. In 1970 he became the first hockey to be honoured in his sport as a Texaco Hockey Sportstar of the Year. His brother Norman Judge was Treasurer of the Leinster H.U. in 1960-1963.

K

KANE, D.J.

G.A.A. football left wing-back, Down. Born in 1966. Club: Newry Shamrocks. A member of Abbey C.B.S. (Newry) side which lost a McRory Cup final, he also assisted in both of the wins in the Sigerson Cup achieved by the University of Ulster, Jordanstown. Making his senior inter-county debut in 1986, he was a member of the Down side which, after a gap of 23 years, won the All-Ireland Senior Football Championship in 1991. His older brother Val also played for Down at senior inter-county level.

KANE, RAYMOND M.

Amateur international golfer. Clubs: Malahide (winning a Barton Shield medal in 1971), and The Island (winning Senior Cup medals in 1967 and 1983). He twice won the Irish Close Championship, in 1971 and 1974. In 1979 he won the West of England championship, having won the Middlesex Amateur title in both 1973 and 1974. He played 78 interprovincial matches in 14 series for Leinster between 1964 and 1982 (placing 3rd only to Brian Malone and Tom Craddock in number of appearences for that province), winning 45, and his tally of 95 points is joint 2nd for that province (his success rate was over 60%); he played 44 Home international matches in series between 1967 and 1978, winning 16 (and helped Ireland to win the Quadrangular match in 1972); and played 10 European Team championship matches 1971-79, winning 4. His father Peter, a member of the Island, won interprovincial honours for Leinster in 1963.

KAVANAGH, J RONNIE ('KAV').

Rugby No 8 international, boxer, water polo player, and high diver. born in Dublin, 21st January 1931. Clubs: U.C.D. and Wanderers (winning Leinster Senior Cup medals in 1954 and 1959). A Blackrock College product, he was capped 35 times for Ireland (then a record for a No 8 player) over a 10 year period, between 1953 and 1962, scoring 4 international tries. This great Irish back-row player was never selected for the British and Irish touring side. His 28 appearences for Leinster in the Interprovincial series from 1951 and 1962 was a record until surpassed by 'Wigs' Mulcahy in 1966, and he was the first Irish forward to go on 2 tours with his country, in 1952 to Argentina and Chile, and in 1961 to South Africa. An older brother, Paddy J Kavanagh of U.C.D. and Wanderers, was capped twice on the flank for Ireland, once in 1952 and again in 1955 (and played 3 times for Leinster), and another brother Gene, also of Wanderers, won a final trial place and played for Leinster 11 times in the interprovincial arena from 1954 to 1960 (ten of them with Ronnie in the side). Both Ronnie and Patrick also represented Ireland at international water-polo. Ronnie also became Irish High Diving champion, and also won an Irish boxing title.

KEADY, TONY.

G.A.A. hurling centre-half back, Galway. Born 5th December 1963. Club: Killimordaly. Having played on a Galway minor team beaten in a M.H.C. All-Ireland final in 1981, he was a winner of an All-Ireland Under 21 title medal with Galway in 1983 (having come on as a sub in their final defeat the previous year). He was a member of the Galway senior side beaten in the All-Ireland S.H.C. finals of 1985 and 1986 (when scoring 5 long-range points), before being a star member at centre half-back of the Galway side which won the title in both 1987 and 1988 (in which he was selected as the man-of-the-match). He was also on the Galway side beaten in the All-Ireland S.H.C. final in 1990. In 1988 he became the 3rd Galwayman to be selected as Texaco's Hurling Sportstar of the Year. He won an All-Star award in 1986 at centre half-back, and again in 1988 in the same position. He hit national headlines in 1989 after the 'Keady Affair', in which he was suspended for 12 months for playing a match in New York without proper clearence.

KEANE, J.J.

G.A.A. footballer for Dublin, athlete, and sports adminstrator. Born at Anglesboro, on the Cork and Limerick borders. He won 2 successive All-Ireland Senior Football Championship medals with Dublin (the Geraldines Selection), in both 1898 and 1899. He also won the 1900 Irish championship at 120 yards Hurdles. A dominant sports administrator, he was secretary (and for a time President) of the Athletic Council within the G.A.A. from 1905 to 1922. He was the first president of the N.A.C.A., and was a prime mover of the Tailteann Games. He was the first President of the Irish Olympic Council and the first Irishman to be elected to the International Olympic Committee, in 1922 (remaining in that post for almost 30 years). He died in 1956.

KEANE, JOHN (JACK).

G.A.A. hurling centre half-back and full-back, Waterford. Born in 1916, he died in 1975. Club: Sion Hill (with whom he won 10 county championship medals from 1938 to 1951, eight as captain). Helping Waterford to win the All-Ireland junior final in 1934 while still a minor, he became a senior inter-county hurler for 19 years from 1935 to 1951, and was a dominant figure on the first Waterford side to win an All-Ireland Senior Hurling Championship title in 1948 (in which he changed roles to play at centre half-forward) having 10 years previously been on the Waterford side that won it's first ever Munster S.H.C. title. Without doubt the greatest Waterford player of his era, he captained his county in 7 Munster Championships. One of the most accomplished of full backs, he (in 9 years in the team) won 7 Railway Cup winner's medals with Munster, 1937, 1938, 1939 (when he was the first Waterfordman to captain a winning side), 1940, 1942, 1943 and 1949. He was voted as the centre half-back on the Sunday Independent's 'Tean of the Century' of 1984. He trained the 1957 Waterford side which were beaten in the All-Ireland S.H.C. final.

KEANE, MAURICE Ignatius ('MOSS').

Rugby international 2nd Row forward. Born in Currow, Co Kerry, on 27th July 1948. Club: Lansdowne (winning Leinster Senior Cup medals in 1979, 1980, 1981 and 1986, and Leinster Senior League medals in 1974, 1977, 1981 and 1986). He was educated at St Brendan's Killarney and at U.C.C.

With 51 international caps gained in the engine room for his country over the eleven year period between 1974 and 1984, he is ranked as Ireland's sixth most capped player. He toured with the British and Irish Lion's to Australia as a replacement to Geoff Wheel in 1977, winning one test cap. He was an integral part of Ireland's 1974 International Championship win (their first in 23 years), the historic Triple Crown victory in 1982, and the Championship success again in 1983, his massive 6'4" frame marking him as one of Ireland's greatest and most liked international rugby players. He went on 2 foreign tours with Ireland, to New Zealand and Fiji in 1976 and to Australia in 1979. Also a member of the famous Munster team that beat the touring All-Blacks in 1978, he is an Agricultural Inspector.

KEANE, ROY.

Soccer international midfielder. Born in Cork to a soccer-playing family on 10th August 1971. Clubs: Rockmount, Cobh Ramblers and Nottingham Forest (playing on the side beaten in the final of the F.A. Cup in 1991, being the youngest player on the field, and winning a Zenith Cup medal in 1992, while gaining a runner-up medal in the 1992 League Cup). A classy exponent of the midfield art, he played for Ireland at Under 15, Under 16, Youths and Under 21 up to 1990, and gained his first full international cap in 1991 against Chile. Twice a runner-up in the Young Player of the Year in Britain, he has won 16 caps up to mid 1993. After Notts Forest were relegated in 1993 he transferred to Manchester United for a record domestic English transfer fee of £3,750,000.

KEARINS, MICHAEL (MICKEY).

G.A.A. football forward, Sligo. Born in 1943, Club: St Patrick's, Dromard (winning 7 Sligo SFC medals with them). He first played minor football for Sligo in 1960, and in 1961 played for the county at all 3 levels. In 17 successive championship seasons with Sligo from 1962 to 1978 (he once scored 0-14 against Mayo in a championship match in 1972), he played in 3 Connacht Senior Football Championship finals, losing in 1965 and 1971 to Galway, before the county's sole success in this title in 1975. One of the games greatest marksman, he was the country's leading scorer in competitive games in 4 different years, in 1966 (scoring 99 points in 17 games), in 1968 scoring 141 points, in 1972, scoring his personal best of 4-130 or 142 points in only 19 games (placing him third behind Matt Connor and Mick O'Dwyer in the best tally in one season's charts), and in 1973, scoring 124 points in 25 games. He won 2 Railway Cup medals in a 13 year career with Connacht, in 1967 and 1969 (and scored 0-12 in the losing 1973 final); he also played in 3 National Football League losing semi-finals with Sligo. He won an All-Star award in the inaugural year of 1971 at left half-forward, the first of only 2 Sligomen to be so honoured (he was also a replacement All-Star in 1972), and in 1984 was selected in the left half-forward position on the 'Team of the Century' for players who never won an All-Ireland senior medal.

KEARNS, TERRY.

G.A.A. football centrefielder, Meath. Winning Leinster Senior Football Championship medals with Meath in 1964, 1966, 1967, 1969 and 1970, he was a star of the Meath side which won the Sam Maguire Cup in 1967 in the All-Ireland Senior Football Championship. In 1970 he was a member of the Meath side beaten in the All-Ireland S.F.C. final, this time at the hands of Kerry.

KEARNS, THOMAS JAMES (T.J.).

High hurdle international athlete. Born in Rathvilly, Co Carlow, 2nd June 1966. Club: Dublin City Harriers. Having won the All-Ireland School championship 110 mtres hurdle title in 1986, he went on to win the National B.L.E. Championship in the 110 metres hurdles in 8 years in succession, 1986, 1987,

1988, 1989, 1990, 1991 (in which year he also broke the Irish record at 13.75 seconds), 1992 (when he extended his Irish record to 13.64 seconds), and 1993 (when he ran his fastest ever time, wind-assisted), and won the Irish indoor title in 1989 and 1990. A winner of the Europa Cup in his event in 1988, 1989 and 1991, he has won the West-Athletic Championship twice (in 1988 and 1990), was 1991 British Indoor 60 metres hurdles champion, and reached the semi-finals of both indoor and outdoor European Championships in 1990. He has run three times in the World Athletics Championships, in 1987, in Tokyo in 1991 (when he broke the Irish record in the heats, before failing in the semi-final) and 1993. He has also competed in 2 Olympic Games, in Seoul in 1988 (reaching the quarter-final) and in Barcelona in 1992. A surveyor.

KEARNEY, JIM.

G.A.A. footballer, Meath. He played at midfield on the Meath side which won their county's first ever All-Ireland Senior Football Championship in 1949, being the only Royal County man from that side who 10 years previously had been on the losing Meath S.F.C. side in their All-Ireland defeat by Kerry. He also won Leinster S.F.C. medals in 1940 and in 1947. He won a Railway Cup medal with Leinster in 1940.

KEARNEY, KENNETH (KEN).

Amateur international golfer. Clubs: Roscommon, Limerick and Portmarnock. He won an All-Ireland County championship medal with Roscommon in 1989. Ireland's most capped boy player in the European Boy's team event (16 matches played 1984-86), he became the first Connacht-born player since 1950 to win the West of Ireland Championship in 1992 (having been runner-up in 1989), and was also runner-up in the 1992 'South', winning the Willie Gill award for that season. He helped Ireland to win the Home International Championship in 1992. For Connacht, he has played 30 interprovincial matches from 1984 to 1992, winning 14. He turned pro in late 1992, only to apply for re-instatement soon afterwards.

KEARNS, MIKE.

Soccer international goalkeeper. Born in Banbury, 26th November, 1950. Clubs: Oxford (as an apprentice), Plymouth, Charlton, Walsall (playing 249 league matches in the period 1973-1978), and Wolves. He was capped 18 times for the Republic of Ireland between 1970 and 1980, the 15 caps he gained at Walsall making him that club's most capped player. His younger brother Oliver played 3 seasons of English League football for Reading as a forward.

KEATING, CLARE (nee Foley).

Pitch and putt player. Club: Woodvale P.P.C. Ireland's most prolific winner of pitch and putt national titles, male or female, she has won a record total of 13 national titles. She won the National Strokeplay Championship a record 5 times, in 1963, 1964, 1965 (when completing a hat-trick), 1973 and 1975 (she was runner-up in both 1968 and 1970). She also won the National Matchplay Championship a record 8 times, in 1963, 1964, 1970, 1972, 1973, 1975, 1976 and 1977 (completing a hat-trick), and was runner-up in both 1971 and 1974. She completed the coveted 'double' of both matchplay and strokeplay titles 4 times, in 1963, 1964, 1973 and in 1975. She later played golf out of the Douglas club, and represented Munster on many occasions.

KEATING, MICHAEL ('BABS').

G.A.A. hurling centre half-forward, and footballer, Tipperary. Born on 17th April 1944, he hails from Ardfinnan, Co Tipperary. Club: Ballybacon Grange (with them he played in 10 successive football county championship finals, winning 5). A product of Grange N.S. and C.B.S. Clonmel, he was at half-forward on the Tipperary minors beaten in 3 consecutive All-Ireland M.H.C. finals of 1960, 1961 and 1962. In 1963 he won an All-Ireland IHC medal at the age of 19, and was a member of the Tipp side which captured the inaugural All-Ireland Under 21 Championship in 1964. Playing senior inter-county hurling from 1963 to 1973 (and football from 1962 to 1975), he went on to win 3 All-Ireland Senior Hurling Championship medals with Tipperary, in 1964, 1965 (as a playing sub) and in 1971, being on losing All-Ireland S.H.C. final sides in both 1967 and 1968, thus bringing his Munster S.H.C. tally to 5. He won 2 Railway Cup hurling medals with Munster, in 1968 and 1970, and won a football Railway Cup medal at right full-forward in 1972 (playing for the province over a ten year period at left corner forward). He was a member of the inaugural All-Stars hurling side in 1971, and the same year became the 6th Tipperaryman to be selected as Texaco's Hurling Sportstar of the Year. He later trained the Tipperary S.H.C. county side to win the All-Ireland S.H.C. finals of 1989 and 1991, also to win 5 Munster titles and a National Hurling League title.

KEAVENEY, JIMMY.

G.A.A. footballing full-forward, Dublin. Born in Dublin, 12th February 1945. Club: St Vincent's (winning many Dublin SFC medals, being also on the side which won 2 Leinster Club titles, and one All-Ireland Club Championship in 1976: he also won 3 Dublin SHC medals with the club). Attending St Joseph's CBS, he played for Dublin minors and Under 21's in both football and hurling from 1962 to 1966, and also played hurling for Dublin seniors from 1964 to 1970. He made his senior football debut with Dublin in 1964, and won his first Leinster S.F.C. medal in 1965, at the age of 20. Having prematurely retired in 1972, he later became a star member of the great Dublin side which won 3 All-Ireland Senior titles in 1974, 1976 and 1977, also playing on the losing side in the 1975 and 1978 finals against arch-rivals Kerry. The 6 Leinster S.F.C. medals he won in the 1970's from 1974 to 1979, added to the win of 1965 make him (joint with Johnny McDonnell cv), the record tally medal winner for a Dublin footballer. He led the country's scoring lists in 1967, and later for 3 successive years, in 1975 (with 8 goals and 95 points, for a tally of 119 points from 20 games, a Dublin record), 1976 (with 101 points from 17 games), and in 1977 (scoring 100 points from 19 games). He holds, jointly with Mickey Sheehy of Kerry, the record individual score in an All-Ireland final, when in the 1977 match against Armagh, he scored 2 goals and 6 points, beating the old record of Frank Stockwell's cv). He also won 2 National Football League medals with Dublin in 1976 and 1978. One of the game's finest full forwards and a folk-hero in his native county, he was only the second player to win 2 Texaco Gaelic Football Sportstar of the Year awards, winning in 1976 and 1977. He also won 3 All-Star awards, in 1974, 1977 and 1978, all at full-forward.

KEEFFE, ERNIE.

Rugby international 2nd row forward. Born in Cork, 16th March 1919. Club: Sunday's Well (winning a Munster Senior Cup medal in 1949, the club's first success in this competition). A product of St Nicholas College in Cork, he was the first Sunday's Well player to be capped for Ireland, gaining 6 in all just after World War 2 (being one of 24 Irishmen to play some part in Ireland's only Grand Slam in 1948, when he won his last cap against France). He may have won more caps if not for that lay-off, having also played in 3 unofficial matches in 1946. A Munster player for 10 years, he was also a Barbarian. He also has the unique distinction of being the only Irishman to represent his country at both rugby and boxing. He died in 1991, aged 72.

KEEGAN, HARRY.

G.A.A. football right full-back, Roscommon. Born in 1952. Clubs:

Castlerea St Kevin's (winning 3 Roscommon SFC medals), and Fingallians (winning one Dublin SFC medal). A Roscommon minor (1969-70) and Under 21 player (1970-72), he won 5 Connacht Senior Football Championship winner's medals, in 1972 (as the youngest player on the team), 1977, 1978, 1979, and in 1980 (when Roscommon reached the All-Ireland S.F.C. final, only to be foiled by Kerry). Although he missed the final, he played a major role in Roscommon's 1979 National League victory. An accomplished defender, he has won 3 All-Star football awards, in 1978, 1980 and again in 1986, all at right corner-back. Also playing Railway Cup, he retired in 1988 after a 17 year career.

KEENAN, DONAL.

G.A.A. football left half forward, Roscommon. Born in 1920. With U.C.D. he won Sigerson Cup medals and captained them to the 1943 Dublin county championship). A product of the rugby playing Clongowes Wood College, he was said to have been promising enough at rugby at U.C.D. to perhaps play for Connacht or Ireland. He was a member of the historic Roscommon side which won the county's only 2 All-Ireland Senior Football Championship titles, in the 1943 replay 2-7 to 2-2 win over Cavan, and in the 1944 victory over Kerry by a score of 1-9 to 2-4. He was also on the side beaten in the 1946 All-Ireland S.F.C final (and had won another Connacht S.F.C. medal the previous year, in 1945). One of his era's finest left half-forwards, he was President of the G.A.A. from 1974 to 1977. A noted G.A.A. administrator, he had served as Roscommon County Board chairman for many years from 1958, and was President of the Connacht Council from 1970 to 1973. His son Donal is a Gaelic Games correspondent with the Irish Independent newspaper. He died in 1990.

KEHER, EDWARD Peter (EDDIE).

G.A.A. hurling left-half and left-full forward, Kilkenny. Born in Inistioge, Co Kilkenny, 14th October 1941. Educated at St Kieran's College, Kilkenny. Club: The Rower Inistioge (winning a solitary county champinship medal in 1968). His Kilkenny senior career stretched from 1959 to 1977. He won 6 All-Ireland Senior Hurling Championship winning medals with the 'Black and Ambers', in 1963 (scoring 14 points in the final), 1967, 1969 (captaining the side in 1969 when Cork were defeated by 2-15 bto 2-9), 1972, 1974 and 1975, and he has scored a record tally of 93 points in All-Ireland S.H.C. finals (7 goals and 72 points). In the 1971 All-Ireland S.H.C. final, when Kilkenny lost to Tipperary by 5-17 to 5-14, Eddie scored a record 2-11 (he was also on Kilkenny sides beaten in All-Ireland S.H.C. finals in 1966 and 1973). A winner of a total of 10 Leinster S.H.C. winners medals, he was hurling's leading marksman countrywide for an incredible 11 years, 1963, 1965, 1966, 1968, 1970, 1971, 1972 (his best year, with 194 points from 20 goals and 134 points in 21 games, with an average of 9.23 points per game), 1973, 1974, 1975, and 1976 (the last seven years being on the trot). He has won a Leinster hurler's record of 9 Railway Cup medals, 1964, 1965, 1967, 1971, 1972, 1973, 1974, 1975 and 1977. He also assisted Kilkenny to win 3 National Hurling titles, in 1962, 1966 and in 1976. He won 5 All-Star awards in succession, the first two, 1971 and 1972, at left-half forward, and the next three, in 1973, 1974 and 1975, all in the left-full forward. One of the game's greatest exponents, he was voted as Texaco's Hurling Sportstar of the Year in 1972, and was voted at left full-forward on the Sunday Independent 'Team of the Century' in 1984. 'Eddie Keher's Hurling Life', by Ultan Macken, was published in 1978. He is a Bank Manager with the A.I.B.

KEHILY, KEVIN.

G.A.A. football full-back Cork. He was a stalwart member of the Cork side which failed to beat Kerry on many occasions during their rampant period of Munster S.F.C. wins 1975-1982, when Cork were regarded by many as the 2nd best side in the country. Helping Cork to win the 1980 National Football League, he won 2 All-Star awards, in 1980 at full-back (one of only 2 Corkmen selected that year), and in 1982 at left corner back, when he was the sole Cork player selected.

KEHOE, PADGE.

G.A.A. hurling half-forward, Wexford. Born in 1925. Club: St Aidan's (he is unique by being on each of the now disbanded club's winning 9 county championship sides). His senior inter-county career stretched from 1946 to 1962. He won 3 All-Ireland Senior Hurling Championship winner's medals with Wexford, in 1955, 1956, and in 1960. His 3 other Leinster S.H.C. winner's medals came when the county lost in All-Ireland S.H.C. finals in 1951 (their first appearence at this stage since 1918), 1954 (when he captained the side), and 1962. A winner also of 4 Oireachtas medals (1951, 1953, 1955 and 1956), he also won Railway Cup medals with Leinster. He was the game's leading marksman in the 1958 competitive season, scoring 20 goals and 26 points, for a total of 86 points in 15 games, with an average of 5.73 per game.

KEITH, ROBERT M (DICK).

Soccer international full-back. Born in Belfast, 15th May 1933. Clubs: Linfield (winning 3 successive Irish League medals, 1954, 1955 and 1956, and an Irish Cup medal in 1953), Newcastle (playing over 200 league matches for the St James Park side in 7 seasons), Bournemouth. He was capped 23 times for Northern Ireland between 1958 and 1962, many times in partnership in the full-back line with Alfie McMichael, and played in all 5 games in the No 2 jersey in Northern Ireland's fine run in the 1958 World Cup in Sweden. He was killed in a freak accident in 1977 at the age of 43.

KELLEHER, HUMPHREY.

G.A.A. football full-back, Cork. Born in 1946. Club: Millstreet (winning one Cork SFC medal with the club). He played for Cork juniors from 1968 to 1970, winning a Munster J.F.C. medal. He played senior inter-county football for Cork from 1970 to 1976, winning 3 Munster S.F.C. medals (in 1971, 1973 and 1974), and reaching a climax in 1973 when Cork went on to win the All-Ireland Senior Football Championship. He also won a Railway Cup medal with Munster in 1975.

KELLEHER, JAMESEY.

G.A.A. hurling full-back, Cork. He captained the winning All-Ireland Senior Hurling Championship side, Dungourney of Cork, in the 1902 final, when they beat the Brian Boru Club of London by 3-13 to nil. He was on 2 other All-Ireland S.H.C. winning sides, in 1894 and 1903, and was on losing sides in the S.H.C. deciders of 1901, 1904, 1907 (as captain of another Dungourney side) and 1912. Renowned as a thinking back with enormous strength (he once scored a point from a puck-out, the ball bouncing over the bar), he is rated as one of the game's greatest exponents. He was also an accomplished cross-country rider.

KELLEHER, ROBBIE.

G.A.A. football left-full back, Dublin. Club: St Margarets and O'Connell's. A product of Colaiste Muire, he won 3 All-Ireland Senior Football Championship medals with the great Dublin side of the 1970's, in 1974, 1976, and 1977, forming a formidable full-back line with Sean Doherty (cv) and Gay O'Driscoll (cv). He also played on the losing All-Ireland S.F.C. final sides in 1975, and in 1978. He won 2 National League medals with Dublin, in 1976 and 1978. A fine corner back exponent, he was a stalwart of 'Heffo's Arny', and won 4

All-Star awards during Dublin's fine run, all at left-corner back, 1974, 1975, 1977, and 1978. An economist.

KELLETT, IRIS Patricia.

International show-jumper. Born in Mespil Road, Dublin, 8th January 1926. The daughter of a Dublin vet, she shot to instant fame when she won the Queen Elizabeth Cup in 1949 on Rusty, and regained this prestigious title (the premier event for ladies at the time) in 1951, again on Rusty, having finished 2nd in 1950. She won the Grand Prix in Dublin, the first woman to do so, in 1948. In 1951, her peak year, she won 4 major victories in the 3 premier shows. An injury in 1952 left her out of the sport until the 1960's. In 1969, twenty years after her initial success, she became Ladies European Champion in Dublin (at the age of 43), defeating Ann Drummond-Hay. She later started a highly successful riding school, her many famous pupils having included Eddie Macken and Paul Darragh. She was selected as Texaco's Equestrian Sports Sportstar of the Year in 1969.

KELLY, ALAN J.

Soccer international goalkeeper. Born in Sallynoggin, Co Dublin, 5th July 1936. After periods with Bray and Drumcondra (with whom he won an F.A.I. Cup medal in 1957 and a League of Ireland Championship medal in 1957-58) he joined Preston North End in 1958, and from 1960 up to 1973, he played in a record (still standing) 447 league matches for this club, winning a runner's up medal in the F.A.I. Cup final of 1964, and winning a Division 3 winner's medal in 1970-1971. He was capped 47 times for the Republic of Ireland over a 16 year period form 1957 to 1973, the first 2 caps being gained while he was at Drumcondra. This made him at the time Irleand's most capped international soccer player. He also won 6 Inter-League caps. Both his sons Gary and Alan played under age soccer in goals for the Republic of Ireland, with Alan (born 11th August 1960), a Sheffield United keeper, gaining his first senior cap in 1993.

KELLY, BILLY ('SPIDER').

Featherweight boxer. Born in Derry, 21st April 1932, the son of Jim 'Spider' Kelly. In his professional career (which started in 1951) he won 56, drew 4, and lost 23 of his 83 contests. He won the British Empire featherweight title in 1954 by beating Roy Ankrah of Ghana, and the British title in January 1955 at the age of 22 by beating England's Sammy McCarthy. He fought for the European title (in Donnybrook bus garage in Dublin) against Ray Famechon, but lost in a controversial decision which led to a 'Donnybrook' riot. He lost his Empire title to Hogan 'Kid' Basey of Nigeria in November 1955, and lost his British title in February 1956 to Scotland's Charlie Hill. He never found the same championship-winning form again, changed to a lightweight without success, and retired in 1961. He is the son of Jim 'Spider' Kelly (cv).

KELLY, DAMAEN.

Amateur flyweight boxer. Born in Belfast in 1973. Club: Holy Trinity. In 1993 he won his first Irish National Senior Championship title at the flyweight division. He went on that year to become only the third Irish amateur boxer to win a medal at the World Championships, when winning a bronze medal at the games at Tampera, Finland, losing in his semi-final bout by a first round knock-out to the Cuban Waldemar Font.

KELLY, DAVID.

Soccer international striker. Born in Birmingham, 25th November 1965. He joined Alvechurch in 1981, and Walsall in 1983, where he was leading scorer in 1986/87 with 25 goals, and in 1987/1988 with 30 goals. He later played for West Ham and Newcastle United (helping them to win the new First Division title, and promotion, in 1992-93). He scored a hat-trick on his international debut for the Republic of Ireland in 1987 against Israel, and was a non-playing member of the squad which performed admirably in the 1990 World Cup finals in Italy. As an able 2nd string international striker, he has scored 7 international goals in his first 15 international matches up to mid 1993.

KELLY, GABRIEL.

G.A.A. football right full-back, Cavan. Club: Cavan Slashers. He played in all but one of Ulster's 18 Railway Cup matches in the 1960's decade, collecting 5 winner's medals, in 1960, 1963, 1964, 1965, and 1968, also winning a medal as a sub in the 1966 win. He also won 4 Ulster Senior Football Championship titles with Cavan in the 60's, in 1962, 1964, 1966, and 1969, and was on the losing Cavan side in the 1960 National League final against Down. One of Ulster's greatest right full-back's, he later managed the Cavan county football team.

KELLY, HUGH R.

Soccer international goalkeeper. Born in Belfast, 17th August 1919. Clubs: Glenavon, Belfast Celtic (winning Irish Cup medals in 1943 and 1944), Fulham, Southampton, and Exeter City. He played for the Irish League side, and was capped 4 times for Northern Ireland, in 1950 and 1951.

KELLY, J .

G.A.A. hurler, Kilkenny. He collected 6 All-Ireland Senior Hurling Championship winner's medals with Kilkenny sides at the beginning of th century, in 1905 with Erin's Owen, in 1907 and 1909 with Mooncoin, in the disputed year of 1911, in 1912 with Tullaroan, and in 1913 again with the Mooncoin side.

KELLY, J PHIL V.

Soccer international full-back. Born in Dalkey, Co Dublin, 10th July 1939. Clubs: Sheldon Town, Wolverhampton Wanderers, and Norwich City (playing 115 league games 1962-66, and helping the club to it's first ever success in the Football League Cup in 1962). A cousin of Peter Farrell (cv), he played international soccer 5 times for the Republic of Ireland in 1961 and 1962.

KELLY, JIM ('SPIDER').

Professional featherweight boxer. Born in Derry, 25th February 1912. He was British Empire and British Champion 1938-39. He won the Irish title in 1935 by stopping Frank M'Alorum, and the Northern Ireland crown in 1937 by beating Dan M'Allister. By outpointing Billy Caplan for the vacant British and Empire featherweight crowns in 1938, he became the first part of a remarkable father-son combination, as 16 years later, in the same King's Hall Belfast, his son would perform the same feat. Jim lost his titles 7 months later to the Englishman Johnny Cusick in June 1939. In his professional career, which stretched over a 21 year period from 1928 to 1948, he fought 150 times, winning 105, drawing 12 and losing 33 contests. He then retired to teach his son Billy (cv).

KELLY, JAMES Charles (JIMMY).

Rugby international scrum-half. Born in Dublin, 8th April 1940. Clubs: St Mary's College, U.C.D. (winning Leinster Senior Cup medals in 1963 and 1964), and Garryowen. He played 14 times for Leinster between 1959 and 1967, and he was capped 11 times at the base of the scrum for Ireland between 1962 and 1964, captaining the side once (in the 1963 match against the All-Blacks). A vet.

KELLY, JIMMY.

Soccer international left winger. Born in Ballybofey, Co Donegal in 1912, he died in 1970. Clubs: Coleraine, Liverpool, and Derry City. In a 20 year career with Derry City, he scored 363 goals for the club, his best season being 1938-39, when he scored 49 goals. He represented the Irish League 16 times (including all 3 goals in their famous win over the English League side at Windsor Park in 1936; his tally of 9 goals is a joint record for the 'League' with Joe Bambrick cv), and played for the the League of Ireland 3 times. He was capped 11 times for Northern Ireland 1932-37 (scoring 4 international goals), and was also capped 4 times for the Irish Free State, 1932-36 (these 15 international caps, all gained while at Derry City, make him the club's first, and most, capped player). A brilliant left foot shot, he scored many sensational goals from long range.

KELLY, JOACHIM.

G.A.A. hurling centrefield, Offaly. Club: Lusmagh. Born 1st December 1956. Beginning his inter-county career in 1977, he was at midfield when Offaly won it's only 2 All-Ireland Senior Hurling Championship titles, in 1981 and 1985 (both in wins over Galway), playing there also in their defeat in the 1984 by Cork, and was one of 5 players to play on all 11 successive Offaly sides which contested the Leinster S.H.C. final from 1980 to 1990, winning the title 7 times (1980, 1981, 1984, 1985, 1988, 1989, and 1990). He was also a member of the first Offaly side to win the National Hurling League, in 1990-91. He was picked for 2 All-Star awards, in 1980 and 1984, both at centrefield. A P.E. instructor at Templemore Garda training centre, he managed Westmeath hurlers in the 1990-1991 season.

KELLY, JOE.

G.A.A. hurling left corner-forward, Cork. Club: Glen Rovers. He won an All-Ireland M.H.C. medal with Cork minor's in 1941. Introduced into the Cork senior side in the Munster final of 1944, he was the hero of the hour when Cork that year completed their 4-in-a-row Liam McCarthy Cup wins (the only one ever achieved in hurling), thus winning his first All-Ireland Senior Hurling Championship winner's medal, and scoring 2-3 of the 2-13 total. He won a 2nd medal in 1946, and was also on the Cork side beaten in the All-Ireland S.H.C. decider in 1947. Noted for his speedy solo runs, he had been runner-up in the Irish sprints championship in 1944. A priest, he went on a mission to New Zealand.

KELLY, JOHN.

Bantanweight boxer. Born in Belfast, 17th January 1932. As an amateur he won a European Championship silver medal. He was European Bantamweight Professional Champion 1953-54. His professional career of 31 contests included only 3 losses, and 28 wins. He won the prestigious Geoffrey Simpson Award for the best young fighter of the year in 1953. He won the European title on 3rd October 1953 when beating the Scot, Peter Keenan on points at the King's Hall, Belfast. While lining up for a match with the Australian world champ, Jimmy Carruthers, he lost in the following February to Robert Cohen of French Algeria, knocked out in the 3rd round, signalling the sad end to a most promising career.

KELLY, L .

G.A.A. footballer, Dublin. He won 4 All-Ireland Senior Football Championship winner's medals with Dublin sides in the late 19th century; with the Young Irelander's Selection in both 1892 and 1894, with the Kickhams side in 1897, and lastly with Geraldines team which captured the title in 1898.

KELLY, MURT.

G.A.A. footballer, Kerry and Dublin. Clubs: Laune Rangers (Killorglin), Erin's Hope (winning a Dublin county championship winner's medal in 1932), Geraldines (winning 3 Dublin county championship medals, in 1940, 1941 and 1943). From Beaufort in Co Kerry, he won 3 Leinster S.F. Championship winner's medals with Dublin (in 1932, 1933 and in 1934 when they lost the All-Ireland S.F.C. final). Then changing allegience to the 'Kingdom', he later won 7 Munster S.F.C. winner's medals with Kerry, and captured 4 All-Ireland Senior Football Championship winner's medals with his native county: in 1937, and in the 3-in-a-row of 1939, 1940 and

1941. He won Railway Cup football medals with 2 provinces, Leinster in 1935 and Munster in 1941.

KELLY, NOEL.

Soccer international inside forward. Born in Dublin, 28th April 1921. Clubs: Bohemians (winning a runner's-up F.A.I. Cup medal in 1945), Shamrock Rovers, Glentoran, Arsenal, Crystal Palace (scoring 6 league goals in 42 matches 1949-50), Nottingham Forest (scoring 11 league goals in 48 league games 1951-54) and Tranmere Rovers. He played Inter-League soccer and was capped once by the Republic of Ireland, in 1954 against Luxembourg. He was later manager at Birkenhead, Ellesmere Port Town and Holyhead Town.

KELLY, PADDY.

G.A.A. hurling left-half forward, Limerick. Club: Kilmallock. He was a member of the Limerick side which captured 2 successive National Hurling League titles in 1984 and 1985. In 1984 he was selected as one of only 2 Limerick players on the All-Star side, at left half-forward.

KELLY, PADRAIG.

G.A.A. hurling left half-back, Galway. Born in 1969. Club: Sarsfield's (starring for them when they won the All-Ireland Club Championship title in 1993). A product of New Inn school, in his first year in senior inter-county hurling, he was a member of the Galway side which were beaten in the All-Ireland Senior Hurling Championship final of 1993 by Kilkenny, his fine performance that day ensuring him the man-of-the-match award for that decider.

KELLY, PAT M.

Soccer international goalkeeper. Born in South Africa, 9th April 1918. Clubs: Aberdeen, Barnsley (playing 145 league games for them 1946 to 1950), and Crewe Alexander. He was capped for Northern Ireland only once, against Scotland in 1950, but was one of 5 Barnsley players to play international football that season, a record for a second division side.

KELLY, SEAMUS.

Rugby international out-half, and G.A.A. footballer. Born in Wexford, 15th March, 1931. Club: Lansdowne (winning a Leinster Senior Cup medal in 1953). A product of Clongowes Wood, he played 18 interprovincial matches for Leinster between 1953 and 1959, and he won 5 international caps at out-half for Ireland between 1954 and 1960, kicking 4 penalty goals in that period. He had previously played senior county football for Wexford in the 1949 and 1950 seasons.

KELLY, SEAN.

Cyclist. Born in Carrick-on-Suir, Co Tipperary, 24th May 1956. He won the Irish Junior Championship in 1972, was Irish Champion over a 50 mile Time Trial in 1975. He won his first professional victories in 1977, at Lugano and Circuit D'Indre. He has won the Nissan Classic on 4 occasions, in it's first 3 years of running (1985, 1986, and 1987), and again in 1991. He has won many classic races, including 3 Giro de Lombardias (1983, 1987 and 1991) and two 'Hell of the Norths' (Paris-Roubaixs), 1984 and 1986. He got his first big break in 1982 when he won the highly prestigious Paris-Nice, and went on to win that race on 7 successive years until 1988 (once regaining the lead after being placed last after an incident), an achievement unprecedented in the cycling world. In 1988, after many years of effort, he finally won his first major, the Vuelta d'Espana (Tour of Spain), in which race in 1980 he won 5 stages and finished 4th overall (his only previous national tour win was the 1983 Tour of Switzerland, which he won again in 1990). His Tour de France accolades in 14 starts up to 1992 include 5 stage wins (one in 1978, 2 in 1980, one in 1981, and one in 1982), and he has had 16 2nd place finishes and many 3rd's: he won a record 4 maillot verde (green jerseys, in 1982, 1983, 1985, and

1989), and finished overall 15th in 1982, 7th in 1983, 5th in 1984, 4th in 1985, and 9th in 1989. He earned the title of FICP/Velo World No 1 for 5 years in succession, 1984, 1985, 1986, 1987, and 1988, and was 4 times Super Prestige Points winner (having 16 wins in 1983, 33 wins in 1984, 19 wins in 1985, 21 wins in 1986). He won the inaugural World Cup event in 1989. He finished 3rd in the World Championship in 1982 at Goodwood and in 1989 at Chambery (and was 5th in 1986 and again behind Stephen Roche in 1987), and won the 1989 Liege-Bastogne-Liege. His tally of 11 classic wins include 2 Milan-San Remo victories in 1986 and 1992. He has been selected as Texaco's Cycling Sportstar of the Year on 10 different occasions, a record for any Irish sportsperson, the years being 1980, 1982, 1983, 1984 (when also chosen as Texaco's Supreme Sportstar), 1985, 1986, 1988, 1989, 1990 and 1991.

KELLY, TOMMY.

Lightweight bareknuckle boxer. Born in Ireland 2nd January 1839, he died in Cresent Beach, Massachussetts in 1887. His reign as American lightweight champion lasted from 1869, when he beat Ted Timmoney of U.S.A. over 10 rounds at Campobello Island, Canada, through until the late 1870's.

KELLY, YVONNE.

Badminton player. Over a 17 year period between 1955 and 1972 she and her doubles partner Mary Bryan (cv) won 16 of the Irish National Singles titles, with Yvonne winning a total of 24 Irish National titles, including 6 singles wins, in 1956, 1957, 1958, 1971, 1975 and 1977. She held the record for the most international appearences of any Irish ladies badminton player, with 57 caps won between 1955 and 1976, a period of 21 years, until surpassed by Barbara Beckett. A very athletic player, she won 10 Open titles and several International Tournaments in singles and doubles. She once reached the semi-final of the All-England Ladies Doubles Championships with Mary Bryan (cv).

KEMP, CYRIL A.

Tennis, squash and table-tennis player. He was a true all-rounder in the racquet sports, playing at international level in 3 sports. In tennis, he won Davis Cup honours for Ireland in 9 successive matches between 1946 and 1952 (two of which were won, in 1948 and 1950). He won the Irish Mens Singles Championship in tennis 3 times in all, in 1941, 1942 and 1950. He also won the Irish Men's Doubles title in 1948 and won the Mixed title 4 times, in 1940, 1941, 1947 and 1950. He won the Fitzwilliam L.T.C. mens singles title an unprecedented record 12 successive years, from 1938 to 1949. In squash he won 12 caps for Ireland between 1938 and 1951, and won the Irish International (Open) Singles title in 1943, being runner-up in 1945 (and won the inaugural Ulster Open in 1954). As a table-tennis player, he won the Irish title no less than 7 times.

KENNEDY, ANDY.

Soccer international left-back. Born in Belfast, 1st September 1897. Clubs: Belfast Celtic, Glentoran, Crystal Palace (helping them to win the 3rd Division South title in 1920-21), Arsenal (playing 142 games for them, helping them to the runner-up spot in the First Division in 1926, and playing in the losing 1927 F.A. Cup final), Everton and Tranmere. He was capped twice for Northern Ireland, in 1923 and 1925. He died in 1963.

KENNEDY, D.

G.A.A. hurler, Kilkenny. He won 6 All-Ireland Senior Hurling Championship winner's medals with Kilkenny sides in the early part of the century, in 1905 with Erin's Own, in 1907 and 1909 with Mooncoin, in the awarded 1911 game, with Tullaroan in 1912, and again with Mooncoin in 1913.

KENNEDY, DAN.

G.A.A. hurling midfielder, Kilkenny. He captained the winning Kilkenny side which won the 1947 All-Ireland Senior Hurling Championship, when they beat Cork by 0-14 to 2-7. He was also on 3 losing Kilkenny sides in the All-Ireland S.H.C. final, in 1945, 1946 and 1950.

KENNEDY, DES.

Soccer forward. Born in Limerick, July 1955. Clubs: Jonesboro (winning 2 schoolboys caps for Ireland), Limerick City (winning a League of Ireland Championship medal in 1978-80 and an F.A.I. Cup medal in 1982), Sligo, Galway United and Newcastle West. Up to the end of the 1986-87 League of Ireland season he had scored 113 League of Ireland goals (103 of these were for Limerick City, a club record) in the period 1972-86. Also a youth international, he played Inter-League level for the F.A.I.

KENNEDY, F and JOHN M P.

Rugby international brothers. Club: Wanderers. F , 6 times a Leinster player from 1878 to 1881, won 3 international caps in the Irish pack, one in each year of 1880, 1881, and 1882. John M P, also a forward, who played twice for Leinster in 1884, won 2 caps for Ireland, in 1882 and 1884, both against Wales, joining his brother for his first appearence.

KENNEDY, GUS.

G.A.A. footballer, Wexford. He was one of a select few Wexfordmen who played in all four of the famous Blues and Whites 4-in-a-row wins in the All-Ireland Senior Football Championship in 1915, 1916, 1917, and 1918. He had also played on the Wexford teams which were beaten in the All-Ireland final S.F.C. in the 2 years running up to 1915.

KENNEDY, IAIN.

International oarsman. Rowing at Coleraine Academy and Queen's University, he came through the National Squad system of the I.A.R.U. (Irish Amateur Rowing Union), to win selection in the Irish World Championship and Olympic Games crews on 5 different occasions. Of these events, his best finishes were 8th in the coxed pair in the World Championships in Amsterdam in 1977, and finishing 6th in the Grand Final of the World's again the following year, on Lake Karapiro in New Zealand. He represented Ireland in 2 Olympic Games, in Montreal in 1976 at coxless 4's, and at coxed 4's in Moscow in 1980.

KENNEDY, JOHN.

G.A.A. football, Dublin. He captained the Young Ireland side which collected Dublin's first 3 All-Ireland Senior Football Championship titles, in 1891 (when they beat Clondrohid of Cork by 2-1 to 1-9, when a goal outweighed any number of points), 1892 (beating Laune Rangers of Kerry by 1-4 to 0-3) and 1894 (winning an unfinished replay over the Nils side from Cork), thus becoming the first player in either code to captain both 2 and 3 All-Ireland senior winning sides.

KENNEDY, JIMMY.

G.A.A. hurling right full-forward, Tipperary. From Puckane, Nenagh. He won 2 All-Ireland Senior Hurling Championship medals with Tipperary, in 1949 (when in 4 Munster S.H.C. matches he scored 2 goals and 27 points, including 2-4 in the final against Laois, thus scoring more than 3 times the opposition's tally of 0-3) and 1950. Also winning National Hurling League medals in 1949 and 1950, he won one Railway Cup medal, in 1950.

KENNEDY, Dr KENNETH William (KEN).

Rugby international hooker. Born in Rochester, Kent, 10th May 1941. Clubs: Queen's University Belfast (winning an Ulster Senior League medal in 1964), C.I.Y.M.S. (winning an Ulster Senior Cup medal in 1967), and London Irish (he is that club's most capped player). Over an eleven year period between 1965 and 1975, this product of Campbell College won 45 international caps for Ireland to become the then world's most capped hooker, although he never scored a try for his country. A lightning striker for the ball, he was one of the game's greatest hookers, and won his only International Championship success with Ireland in

1974, at the age of 32 (being also on the side which were part of a unique 5-way tie in the Championship in 1973). Known for his zest and his loose play, he went on 2 British and Irish Lion's tours, in 1966 to Australia and New Zealand, winning 4 Test caps (2 in each country), and to South Africa in 1974, when he did not make the test side. He also toured Australia with Ireland in 1967. A doctor.

KENNEDY, MARTIN.

G.A.A. hurling full-forward, Tipperary. Born in 1899. Club: Toomyvara (winning 3 county championship winners medals). In a senior inter-county career which stretched 14 years from 1922 to 1935, he won 2 All-Ireland Senior Hurling Championship winner's medals with Tipp, in 1925 and 1930 (having won his first of 3 Munster S.H.C. medals in 1922, when the All-Ireland final was lost). Rated as one of hurling's finest ever score-takers, he set a record of appearing in each of the first 9 Railway Cup hurling finals, and won a then record 6 Railway Cup hurling medals with Munster, in 1928, 1929, 1930, 1931, 1934, and 1935. He also won a National Hurling League medal in 1928.

KENNEDY, MICK.

G.A.A. football right full-back, Dublin. Born in 1959. Club: St Margaret's. In his first year in senior championship football, he was at right full-back in the Dublin side beaten by Kerry in the 1979 All-Ireland S.F.C. final, playing in the same position in the 1984 defeat, and at left corner back in the 1985 defeat, both also by Kerry. He actually won an All-Ireland S.F.C. medal in 1983, but it was as a non-playing substitute in the Dublin win over Galway. He won a 5th Leinster S.F.C. medal in 1989. Playing in each championship season from 1979 to 1991 for Dublin, he won National Football League medals in both 1987 and 1991. He won his only All-Star award in 1988, at right corner back.

KENNEDY, PADDY.

G.A.A. football centre-fielder, Kerry. An Annascaul man, he captained the Kerry side which won the 1946 All-Ireland Senior Football Championship final, beating Roscommon in the replay by 2-8 to 1-10. He had previously won 3 All-Ireland S.F.C. medals, being a constant member of the Kerry 3-in-a-row of 1939, 1940, and 1941 (and was on 3 losing Kerry All-Ireland S.F.C. final sides in 1938, 1944 and the 'Polo Grounds' game of 1947). Regarded as one of the game's greatest midfielders, he won 2 Railway Cup medals with Munster, in 1941 and 1946.

KENNEDY, PADDY ('BEEFY').

G.A.A. football and hurling dual player, Dublin. Clubs: Hurling (Young Ireland's, winning Dublin county championship titles), and Football: Peader Mackens (playing on 2 losing sides in Dublin county finals). Early on he won both hurling and football medals in provincial colleges level. An exciting player, he, in 1942 at the age of 42, became the only Dublin-born player to play in both the hurling and football All-Irleand Senior Championship finals in the same year, when he played at full forward on the S.H.C. side which lost to Cork, and at full-back on the senior football side which beat Galway.

KENNEDY, PADDY.

G.A.A. football full-back, Down. He was the solitary Ulsterman selected on the 1981 All-Star side, at full-back, being a member of the Down side which won the Ulster Senior Football Championship title that year. He won Railway Cup medals with Ulster in 1983 and 1984.

KENNEDY, SEAN.

G.A.A. footballer, Wexford. Club: Blues and Whites. He is the only player to captain 3 successive winning All-Ireland Senior Football Championship sides, when captaining the first three of the Blues and Whites of Wexford's 4-in-a-row. The wins came in 1915 (over the Kerry Selection by 2-4 to 2-1), in the

1916 victory by 2-4 to 1-2 over the Mayo representatives (Ballina Stephenites), and the 1917 success over the Selection from Co Clare by the margin of 0-9 to 0-5. He missed the 1918 game. Having previously captaining the Wexford side which lost to Kerry in the final of 1914, he became the first of only 2 players to captain All-Ireland S.F.C. final sides for 4 years in succession (see Tony Hanahoe cv).

KENNEDY, ROBERT L.

Hockey international player. Club: Banbridge. He was a member of the Irish XI which were beaten 8-1 by England in the final of the inaugural Olympic hockey tounament, which took place at the London Games in 1908, thus securing the silver medal position. His total tally of caps for Ireland was 11, won between the years 1908 and 1911.

KENNEDY, TERRENCE Joseph (TERRY).

Rugby international wing-threequarter. Born in Dublin, 19th October, 1954. Club: St Mary's (winning Leinster Senior League medals in 1978 and 1980). A nippy winger, he was capped on 13 occasions between 1978 and 1981, and scored one international try for Ireland. He also played cricket for Leinster, and played soccer for University College Dublin. His brother Frank, a centre three-quarter for St Mary's College R.F.C., played senior interprovincial rugby for Leinster, against Munster in 1977.

KENNEFICK, MICK.

G.A.A. hurling left-half forward, Cork. Club; St Finbarr's. Born in 1924. He won an All-Ireland M.H.C. medal with Cork minors in 1941. He then won his first All-Ireland Senior Hurling Championship winner's medal the following year, 1942. The following year he went on to captain the winning Cork side of the 1943 All-Ireland S.H.C. hurling title, the third in the Leesider's four-in-a-row, at the age of just 19 (thereby becoming the youngest Corkman to captain a S.H.C. side), by beating Antrim by 5-16 to 0-4, the biggest winning margin in a Liam McCarthy Cup final (27 points).

KENNELLY, COLM.

G.A.A. football left-half back, Kerry. He won an All-Ireland M.F.C. medal with Kerry in 1950. He then went on to win 2 All-Ireland Senior Football Championship winner's medals with the Kingdom in 1953 and 1955, also playing in the losing final in the intervening year of 1954. He shares the distinction (with Kevin Heffernan cv) of being the first to win a Trinity 'Pink' in Gaelic Football. He later played international rugby at full-back for British Guyana seven times between 1957 and 1960, all against Trinidad. He is a brother of the poet Brendan Kennelly, and was captain of Killarney Golf Club when the new Killeen course was opened in 1971.

KENNELLY, TIM ('HORSE').

G.A.A. football centre-half back, Kerry. Born 6th July 1954. Club: Listowel Emmets and Feale Rangers (winning a Kerry county championship with them in 1978). Coming up through the Kerry minor and Under 21 sides (he won an All-Ireland Under 21 winner's medal in 1973), he first played Kerry senior football in 1974. He won 5 All-Ireland Senior Football Championship winner's medal with the Kingdom, in 1975 and then with the famous 4-in-a-row side of 1978, 1979 (when he captained the side which beat Dublin by 3-13 to 1-8), 1980 (when he was named man-of-the-match) and 1981 (when he again won the man-of-the match award). He was also on the Kerry sides which were beaten in the All-Ireland S.F.C. finals of 1976 and 1982. When dropped after the Munster final of 1983, he later turned to Kerry selection. He won 2 successive All-Star awards, in 1979 and 1980, both as a centre half-back. He captained the winning Munster Railway Cup side (the 10th Kerryman to do so) in 1982, winning 3 other medals, in 1977, 1978 and 1981. A farmer and publican.

KENNY, HENRY.

G.A.A. football half-back, Mayo. Club: Castlebar Mitchells. He won an All-Ireland Senior Football Championship medal when Mayo won the title in 1936. He won 3 succesive Railway Cup medals with Connacht, in 1936, 1937, and 1938, and won 7 National Fotball League medals with Mayo in the six-in-a-row from 1934 to 1939, and as captain in the win of 1941. In the 1970's he became a parliamentary secretary, being a Fine Gael T.D. for Mayo South 1954-1969, and Mayo West 1969-75. His death in 1975 led to the election of his son, Enda, still sitting in Dail Eireann.

KENNY, MICHAEL (MICK).

G.A.A. hurling centre half-forward, Kilkenny. From Callan. He won one All-Ireland Senior Hurling Championship medal with Kilkenny in 1957, the county's first win for 10 years. That year he was the game's sharpest marksman, scoring 12-47 or 83 points, for an average of 5.53 for each of the 15 games. In 1950 he had captained the Kilkenny side which was beaten by Tipperary in the All-Ireland S.H.C. final. In between these 2 years, while living in Clonmel, he captained the Tipperary team which won the 1953 All-Ireland junior hurling championship.

KENNY, PADDY.

G.A.A. hurling right full-forward, Tipperary. Clubs: Borrisoleigh and Thurles Sarsfields. He played in 3 successive All-Ireland M.H.C. finals, being on the losing 'Tipp' side in 1945 and 1946, and was captain of the victorious team of 1947. He later won 3 successive All-Ireland Senior Hurling Championship winner's medals with Tipperary, in 1949 (as a playing sub), 1950 (scoring 1-2), and 1951 (when he was the county's star player in the final, scoring 0-7). He also helped Tipperary to win 6 National Hurling League titles, in 1949, 1950, 1952, 1954, 1955 and 1957. One of the most talented 'top of the right' forwards the game has known, he also won 4 Railway Cup medals with Munster, in 1951, 1952, 1953, and 1957.

KENNY, SEAN.

G.A.A. hurling left half-forward, Tipperary. Club: Borrisoleigh. He captained the winning All-Ireland Senior Hurling Championship Tipperary team of 1950 with a fine personal display when they beat Kilkenny by 1-9 to 1-8, a victory which was the middle of a 3-in-a-row, also winning All-Ireland S.H.C. medals in 1949 and 1951. Also winning a number of National League medals, he won 2 Railway Cup medals with Munster, in 1950 and in 1951 (as the 4th Tipperaryman to captain a winning Munster hurling side).

KEOGH, CHRISTY.

G.A.A. hurling right half-forward, Wexford. A member of the Wexford side beaten in the final of the 1973 All-Ireland Under 21 championship, he played at left corner forward in the Wexford side beaten in the 1976 All-Ireland Senior Hurling Championship final, and at right half-forward in the 1977 final defeat, also by Cork. He won Railway Cup honours with Leinster in 1974, and a National Hurling League medal with Wexford in 1973. He won his only All-Star award at right half-forward in the 1977 team.

KEOGH, JOHN.

Soccer international right full-back. He won 5 F.A.I. Cup medals with Shamrock Rovers in 1962, 1964 (when the League of Ireland was also won), 1965, 1966 and 1967. He was capped once for the Republic of Ireland, as a sub against West Germany in 1966, and was also a member of the famous League of Ireland side which defeated the English League for the first time in 1963.

KEOGH, TOM.

G.A.A. footballer, Kildare and Laois. He was a member of the Kildare side which won 2 All-Ireland Senior Football Championship titles in successive years, in 1927 and 1928. In the 1936 All-Ireland S.F.C. final, he was on the

Laois team which lost to Mayo. In the 1932 Tailteann Games, he lined out for America.

KEOHANE, J .

G.A.A. hurler, Kilkenny. He won 5 All-Ireland Senior Hurling Championship winners medals with Kilkenny sides, with Mooncoin in 1907 and 1909, in the awarded final of 1911, with Tullaroan in 1912, and again with Mooncoin in 1913.

KEOHANE, JOE.

G.A.A. football full-back. Kerry. He was a member of the Kerry minors beaten in the 1936 All-Ireland M.F.C. final by Louth. One of the game's great No 3's, he won 5 All-Ireland Senior Football Championship medals with Kerry, in 1937 (when still classified as a minor), then in the famous 3-in-a-row of 1939, 1940, 1941, and finally again in 1946. He also played on 3 Kerry teams beaten in All-Ireland S.F.C. finals, in 1944, 1947 and in 1948, thus playing in 8 All-Ireland final Sundays in the 12 year period from 1937 to 1948 (winning 2 other Munster S.F.C. medals in 1938 and 1942, a tally of 10). He also won 2 Railway Cup medals with Munster, in 1941 and 1948. He later became a Kerry S.F.C. selector, in the great era of the 70's and 80's.

KERINS, JOHN.

G.A.A. football goalkeeper, Cork. Club: St Finbarr's (winning an All-Ireland Club Championship medal with them in 1987). After being on the subs bench in Cork's Munster S.F.C. win of 1983, he was in goals for Cork's 4 successive appearences in the All-Ireland Senior Football Championship finals of 1987, 1988, 1989 and 1990, gaining winner's medals in the last 2 of these years. He has won 2 All-Star awards in goals, in both 1987 and 1990. Winning another Munster S.F.C. medal in 1993, when Cork went on to lose the final to Derry.

KERNOGHAN, NORMAN ('SHIRLEY TEMPLE').

Soccer international winger, No 7. Clubs: Cliftonville, Belfast Celtic (being a member of the famous 5-in-a-row Irish League winning side of 1936, 1937, 1938, 1939 and 1940, and winning four I.F.A. Cup medals with the club in 1937, 1938, 1941 and 1943). In September 1935 he became the youngest player to play in the Home International championship, when he lined out for his first cap against Wales, at the age of 16 years and 9 months, scoring a goal in the 3-2 win. He won 2 further international caps, against Scotland in the same season when he also scored a goal, and against England in 1938.

KERNAN, JAMES.

Show jumper. Born 9th April 1958. From Crossmaglen, Newry, Co Down. He was a member of the successful 3-in-a-row Irish winning team which won the Aga Khan Trophy at the Dublin Horse Show in 1977, 1978, and 1979. He rode Condy on each occasion. He has ridden over 15 Nations' Cup competitions, and has won many domestic competitions. He represented Ireland in the 1992 Olympic Games in Barcelona.

KERNAN, JOE.

G.A.A. football midfielder, half-forward, Armagh. Club: Crossmaglen Rangers (winning senior county championship medals in 1975, 1977 and 1983). A member of the Armagh side which were beaten in the 1977 All-Ireland Senior Football Championship final by Dublin, he later won 2 further Ulster S.F.C. medals with Armagh, in 1980, and 1982. He has won a joint county record of 4 Railway Cup medals with Ulster, including 1979, 1980, and 1984, and was on 2 Armagh sides beaten in National Football League finals, in 1983, and in 1985 (as a substitute in the final), winning a Division 2 winners medal in 1977-1978. He received 2 All-Star awards, in 1977 at midfield, and in 1982 at centre half-forward.

KERR, FRANK.

Amateur international boxer. Club: Arbour Hill. He won 6 Irish National Senior Championship titles, one at flyweight (in 1932), and the other 5 at bantamweight (in 1933, 1934, 1935, 1936, and 1938). He later became a well-known coach at Trinity. His son Brian Kerr became a respected soccer coach, managing St Patrick's Athletic in their League of Ireland title bid in 1989-1990.

KERR, ROBERT (BOBBIE).

Athlete, sprinter. Born in Enniskillen, Co Fermanagh in 1882. He emigrated with his family to Hamilton, Ontario, Canada when he was 7. Having represented Canada in the 1904 Olympic Games at St Loius in 3 sprint events (60m, 100m and 200m) without success, he went on to win a gold medal in the 1908 London Games over 200 metres in a time of 20.6 seconds, beating the American Robert Cloughen by only a foot in the same time; he had earlier won a dissapointing bronze in the 100 meters. He was favourite for both events, having carried off the sprint double in the 1908 British A.A.A. Games a few weeks before, having also set new Canadian records that summer. In 1909 he represented Ireland for the first time as an international, winning both 100 and 200 yards events. He went on to be captain of the Canadian team in the 1928 Olympic Games in Amsterdam, and was later manager of their track and field division.

KERRIGAN, JIMMY.

G.A.A. football left half-forward, Cork. Born 8th March 1959. Club: Nemo Rangers (with whom he has gained 3 All-Ireland Club Championship winner's medals, in 1979, 1982, and in 1984 as captain). He was on the winning Cork side in the 1980 All-Ireland Under 21 championship, won a Munster S.F.C. medal in 1983, and was at left half-forward on the Cork side beaten in the All-Ireland Senior Football Championship final by Meath in 1987. Winning a Railway Cup medal (as a sub) in 1982, he won an All-Star award in 1983 at left half-forward.

KERRIGAN, MATT.

G.A.A. football half-forward and full-forward, Meath. He was a member of the Meath side which won the All-Ireland Senior Football Championship in 1967, playing at centre half-forward, and was on the losing side in the final defeat by Kerry in 1970, winning a third Leinster S.F.C. medal in 1969. He won an All-Star award in 1975, at full-forward, when Meath captured the National Football League.

KEYES, CLEM.

International basketball player. Born in 1942. Clubs: Naomh Joseph, Corinthians, St Vincent's (winning 5 Roy Curtis medals with the club). A product of St Vincent's CBS Glasnevin, he played youth international level for Ireland in 1961 and later played for the senior Irish senior side from 1966 to 1973. An able G.A.A. footballer (winning a Dublin county championship medal with Na Fianna in 1969), he also played senior club rugby for Clontarf as a prop forward to almost Leinster inter-provincial level. He is regarded as the founder of ladies basketball in Ireland, coaching the Fry Cadbury's team, which pointed the way in the ladies game.

KEYES, RALPH P (RALPHIE).

Rugby international outside-half. Born in Blackrock, Cork in on August 1st 1961. Club: Cork Constition (winning 2 Munster Senior Cup and 3 Munster Senior League medals with them; and being a major force when the club captured the inaugural All-Ireland League in the 1990-91 season). A product of Presentation Brothers Cork, he played first for Munster in 1983, and played for Ireland 'B' intially in 1984. He was capped for Ireland initially only once, against England in 1986, having been a substitute as many as 19 times for Ireland in the 1980's. Then in his 2nd cap, in the World Cup of 1991, he broke Ollie Campbell's record points scored in an international for Ireland, when he kicked 5 penalties and 4 conversions against

Zimbabwe for a tally of 23 points. His tally of 68 points in 4 games of Ireland's valiant World Cup 1991 run earned him the 'top scorer of the tournament' accolade, and he was for many observers Ireland's most influential player in that series. In 1991 he won the Texaco Rugby Sportstar of the Year award, along with the Ballygowan International Sportman of the Year award. He retired in 1992 with only 9 caps to his credit. His father Michael Keyes won a Munster Senior Cup medal with 'Cork Con' (in 1957), and played for Munster.

KIELY, Dr M DAVID (DAVE).

Rugby international back-row forward, and amateur golfer. A Munsterman, in rugby, as a Lansdowne wing-forward (winning a Leinster Senior Cup medals in 1965; he had previously won a Munster Senior Cup medal with U.C.C. in 1955), he played 5 international matches for Ireland, against Wales in 1962, and in all four of the International Championship matches of 1963. He was also, as a member of Cork G C, an interprovincial golfer, playing 2 matches for Munster in the 1974 series, winning both (making him one of only 7 players to be unbeaten as an interprovincial). A doctor.

KIELY, LARRY.

G.A.A. hurler, Tipperary, and showjumper. Winning an All-Ireland M.H.C. medal with the 'Premier County' in 1959, he went on to win 2 All-Ireland Senior Hurling Championship winner's medals with Tipperary in succession, in 1964 and 1965, both as a stylish centre-half forward. Also winning National Hurling League medals in both those years (1964 and 1965), he won a Railway Cup medal with Munster in 1966. He was also a showjumper of international class, winning many events inside and outside Ireland.

KIELY, OLIVER ('SONNY').

Rugby interprovincial scrum-half. Club: Shannon (from 1981 to 1992 he played on 10 Shannon sides which reached the Munster Senior Cup final, never missing a cup match, and winning 6 winners' medals, in 1982, 1986, 1987, 1988, 1991 and 1992). He has played for Munster, but his international ambitions reached only as a replacement in an Ireland 'B' side in 1989.

KIELY, THOMAS Francis (TOM).

All-round athlete. Born 25th August 1869 at Ballyneale, Carrick-On-Suir, Co Tipperary, he died in Dublin in 1951. He was a neighbour of the Davin brothers (cv), who also coached him. One of the great early Irish athletes, he won a total of 53 Irish athletics titles, 18 of them in the hammer, and on one day, 10th September 1892, he won seven G.A.A. titles. He also won 16 British Crown gold medals, including 7 in succession, 1890, 1891, 1892, 1893, 1894, 1895 and 1896. He won the British A.A.A. hammer title 5 times, in 1897, 1898, 1899, 1901 and 1902. He set a world record in the hammer of 162 feet in 1899, which although it lasted only 46 days, it made him the first person to throw more than 160 feet. Told he would get a free trip to the 1904 Olympic games at St Louis if he represented Great Britain, he declared for Ireland, and thus had to pay his own way to America; he won the gold medal (at the age of 35) in the All-Round Championship, the only time this event was competed for (it was to become the forerunner of the Decathlon). Competing in 10 events all in one day, he won 4 events and triumphed by a margin of 119 points, with a tally of 6036 points. The events were: 100 yards, Shot Putt, High Jump., 880 yards walk, Hammer, Pole Vault, 120 Yards Hurdles, 56-lb Weight Throw, Long Jump and the Mile. In 1906 he won the All-Round Championship Trophy of America at the age of 37. As a younger man he played in the first ever hurling inter-provincial for Munster against Leinster in 1896.

KIERNAN, FRED W.

Soccer international goalkeeper. Born in Dublin, 7th July 1919. Clubs: Shamrock

Rovers and Southampton. He was capped 5 times for Ireland between 1951 and 1952. He joined Southampton at the age of 32 and played 132 league games for them in 4 seasons, 1951-55.

KIERNAN, JERRY.

Long-distance runner. Born in Co Kerry, 31st May 1953. He won the 3rd Dublin City Marathon in 1982 in a record (still standing) time of 2:13:45, and won the race again in 1992 in a time of 2:17:19 (when it also counted as the National Championship). In 1984 he set a personal best Marathon time of 2:12:20 when finishing a highly creditable 9th place in the Los Angeles Olympic marathon (7 places behind John Treacy cv, who took all the glory). In 1986 he ran a marathon in 2:12:44. He also won two Belfast marathon's, in 1990 and in 1992.

KIERNAN, MICHAEL Joseph.

Rugby international centre and wing three-quarter. Born in Cork, 17th January 1961. Clubs: Dolphin and Lansdowne. A product of P.B.C., Cork, he played school international level twice in 1979. First capped in 1982, he was a member of the Triple Crown-winning side that season. Taking over Ireland's kicking duties, he surpassed Ollie Campbell (cv) as Ireland's top international points scorer (and became the then third highest of all-time international rugby), reaching 308 points (from 6 tries, 62 penalties, 40 conversions and 6 drop goals) in his 43rd international in the French game of 1991. His drop goal in the closing moments of Ireland's Triple Crown match v England in 1985, to secure a 13-10 Irish victory, is etched in Irish rugby lore, and he is one of only 6 players to play in all six matches in the 1982 and 1985 Triple Crown matches. In 1986 he kicked 7 conversions in Ireland's win over Romania, a record. He toured with the British and Irish Lion's to New Zealand in 1983, winning 3 Test caps. He toured with Ireland to South Africa in 1981, Japan in 1985, and Canada and the U.S.A. in 1989 (when his 61 points made him the leading scorer on tour), and was also on the World Cup side in 1987 (again being leading scorer on tour, with 36 points). Nine of his caps have been won as a winger, and his 23 caps earned alongside Brendan Mullin cv in the centre, made them the world's most capped centre combination. He also played over 50 times for Munster. He has also been Irish 200 metre sprint champion. He is the nephew of Tom Kiernan (cv), and Mick Lane (cv), and his father Jim was an Irish selector 1984-87.

KIERNAN, THOMAS Joseph (TOM or TOMMY, 'T.J.' or 'THE GREY FOX').

Rugby international full-back. Born in Cork, 7th January 1939. Clubs: U.C.C. and Cork Constitution. A product of Presentation Brothers Cork, he is Ireland's most capped full-back, winning 54 caps in the 14 years from 1960 to 1973, taking over from Jackie Kyle in 1971 as the then world's most capped player, until surpassed by Willie John McBride in 1974. One of the country's truly great players, he captained Ireland on a record 24 occasions (14 were victories), also scoring 158 points for his country, a then Irish record (and still in third place on the all-time list behind his nephew Michael cv, and Ollie Campbell), including a then Irish record 26 conversions. Actually selected 3 times in the centre for Ireland (although failing to play in any of these games), in 3 matches against the visiting Springboks of 1961, he scored a record 5 tries against them, one in the international. He went on 2 British and Irish Lion's tours, firstly to South Africa in 1962 (winning one Test cap), and then as captain of the 1966 British and Irish touring squad to South Africa, scoring 35 of the Lions's 38 points in the 4 Test matches, a Test record which lasted until 1993 (and a then record 17 points in the first Test). He is also the only Lions player to score all his side's points in 3 tests (the tour statistics were 15 wins, 4 losses, 377 points for and 181 against).

He won 7 Munster Senior Cup winner's medals, one with U.C.C. (in 1963), and 6 with Cork Con (1964, 1965,1967, 1970 as captain, 1972, and 1973). He toured South Africa with Ireland in 1961 (being the tour's leading scorer), and captained 2 Irish tours (to Australia in 1967 and Argentina in 1970), becoming the first player to make 3 tours for Ireland. He coached the Munster side that beat the All-Blacks in 1978, and the Irish side to the great Triple Crown triumph of 1982, and the International Championship of 1983. He was Assistant Manager of the Lions tour to South Africa in 1981, and was President of the I.R.F.U. 1988-89. His father was President of Cork Constitution in 1955-56.

KILCOYNE, BARTON.

Squash international player. Club: Fitzwilliam. In 1951 he was Irish Junior Tennis Champion. In squash, he won 36 caps for Ireland at international level over a period of 14 years between 1956 and 1969, and in a period in which Donald Pratt (cv) was supreme in Irish squash, he lost narrowly to him in many Irish Squash finals, and won his sole title in 1961.

KILCOYNE, DAVID.

G.A.A. hurling forward, Westmeath. A skilful player in one of the 'weak' county's, he was the game's leading scorer in the 1984 season, his 16 goals and 97 points from 20 competitive games, with an average of 7.25 per game, leaving his tally of 145 points to place him third (behind Eddie Keher and Nicky Rackard), in the list of most-points-per-season. He was made an All-Star in 1986 at right full-forward.

KILCOYNE, MICK.

G.A.A. dual footballer and hurler, Westmeath. Born in 1956. Clubs: Thomond College Limerick (assisting them, at right full-forward, to win the 1978 All-Ireland Club Football Championship), Ringtown (hurling) and Castletown-Finea (football). Debuting for his county's S.H.C. side in 1974, he helped them to win the All-Ireland 'B' final in 1975. He first played inter-county football for Westmeath in 1976. He went on the All-Stars trip to the U.S.A. in 1978 as a dual player.

KILGALLON, T.J.

G.A.A. football midfielder and centre half-back, Mayo. Born in 1961. A member of the Mayo minors which won the All-Ireland M.F.C. title in 1977, he then played for Mayo in 14 straight championship seasons from 1980 to 1993, and won 6 Connacht Senior Football Championship medals, in 1981, 1985 (when Dublin beat them in a replay in the All-Ireland semi-final), 1988, 1989 (when they were beaten by Cork in the All-Ireland final), 1992 and 1993 (as a sub). A schoolteacher, he won an All-Star award in midfield in 1992.

KILKENNY, OLLIE.

G.A.A. hurling left full-back, Galway. A member of the Galway side which won the All-Ireland Under 21 Championship in 1982, he had been on the side beaten in the decider of the previous year. He was at left full-back on the Galway side which won the 1987 and 1988 All-Ireland Senior Hurling Championship titles, also playing on the losing county side in the Liam McCarthy Cup finals of 1985 and 1986. He was selected at left corner back in the 1987 All-Star side. He won Railway Cup medals with Connacht in 1986 and 1987.

KILLEEN, GEORGE VALENTINE.

Rugby international forward. Club: Garryowen (winning Munster Senior Cup medals in 1908, 1909, 1911 and 1914). Born in Kilrush, Co Clare in 1884, he died in Tipperary in 1933. He was capped 10 times for Ireland between 1912 (when Ireland shared the International Championship with England) and 1914, being on the winning side on 4 occasions.

KILMURRAY, KEVIN.

G.A.A. football centre half-forward, Offaly. Clubs: Civil Service (Dublin, being a member of the side which captured the Dublin county championship in 1980). He was a member of the Offaly side which won 3 successive Leinster S.F.C. medals in 1971, 1972 and 1973, winning 2 All-Ireland Senior Football Championship winner's medals, in the county's first ever success in 1971, and also in 1972. He had come on as a sub in the All-Ireland final S.F.C. defeat at the hands of Kerry in 1969. A member of the Combined University team which won a historic Railway Cup in 1973, he won his only All-Star award in that year, at centre half-forward.

KIMMAGE, PAUL.

Amateur and professional cyclist. Born in Dublin. He was National Champion in the amateur ranks in 1981 and 1984, and was on the Irish team which was placed 16th in the Team Event in the 1984 Los Angeles Olympic Games, and 27th in the individual road race. In 1983 he was leader in the prestigious Tour of Britain, when a puncture and fall resulted in him falling back to 83rd place. Following his 6th place in the World Amateur Championship in Giavera in 1985 he turned professional and was for 4 years a fine domestique on the European tour. His father Christy, and his brothers Raphael (3rd in the Ras in 1984) and Christopher are all cyclists of some ability. Another brother Kevin (a member of Navan RC) represented Ireland at the Barcelona Olympics in 1992 (finishing 32rd in the individual road race and 17th in the Team Trial), and was a winner of the F.B.D. Milk Ras in 1991, and a stage in the British Milk Race in the same year, the first Irishman to do so since 1984. Paul turned to full-time journalism in 1989, and in 1990 wrote a fine expose book, 'A Rough Ride'.

KINANE, MICHAEL.

Flat jockey. Born Killenaule, in Co Tipperary on 22nd June 1959. After his first winner in Leopardstown in 1975, he became champion apprentice in 1978. Retained in 1984 by Dermot Weld, his Irish Classic race wins include: two Irish 2,000 Guineas (1982 on Dara Monarch, and 1987 on Flash of Steel); the Irish 1,000 Guineas in 1988 on Trusted Performer, and the 1989 Irish St Leger on Alydaress. Other big race successes include the 1985 Prix l'Abbaye on Committed, the 1983 Heinz '57' Phoenix Stakes on King Persian, the 1985 Premio Paroli on Again Tomorrow, the 1990 King George VI on Belmez, and in the same weekend in 1989, the Cartier Million on The Caretaker and the Prix de l'Arc de Trioumphe on Carroll House. He won his first English Classic race, the 2,000 Guineas, in 1990, on Tirol, when he also won one of the U.S. classic's, the Belmont Stakes, on Go and Go. In 1992 he won the Italian Derby on In A Tiff, and in 1993 won the Epsom Derby on Commander-in-Chief. In 1985 he rode 105 winners to become Irish champion jockey, and has ridden 100 winners also in 1988 (with a flat season record of 113 winners), 1989 (with 112 winners), and 1992 (with 100 winners). He has been Irish champion jockey eight times in all, in 6 years in succession, 1984 (88 winners), 1985, 1986 (80 winners), 1987 (66 winners), 1988, 1989, and also in 1991 and 1992. A big race specialist, he was selected as Texaco's Horse Racing Sportstar of the Year in both 1988 and 1989. His father, Tommy Kinane (one of 7 brother's in the horsing game), rode Monksfield to win the Champion Hurdle at Cheltenham in 1978. Tommy's brother Christy (born 18th December 1934), won a Galway Hurdle as a jockey.

KING, MICK.

G.A.A. hurling centre-half forward, Galway. Although he won only one All-Ireland Senior Hurling Championship winner's medal with Galway (in 1923, the county's first title victory), he is regarded as one of the games' greatest centre-half forwards. He later played in 3 other All-Ireland losing S.H.C. finals with Galway, in 1924, 1925 and 1928.

KINGSTON, TERENCE John (TERRY).

Rugby international hooker. Born in Cork, 19th September 1963. Clubs: Lansdowne and Dolphin. A product of Christian Brother College, Cork, he won 3 schools caps in 1982. He was first capped for Ireland during the World Cup tour of 1987. On the Irish tour of Namibia in 1991 he captained Ireland in a non-Test match, and also captained Ireland to a 32-16 win over Japan in a group match in the 1991 World Cup. His tally of international caps for Ireland reached 13 up to March 1993, and he has scored 2 international tries. A fine Munster-type forward, he captained the provincial side to their fine win over the visiting Australians in 1992.

KINLOUGH, FRANKIE.

G.A.A. football forward, Roscommon. He was a star member of the Roscommon team which won the county's only 2 All-Ireland Senior Football Championship titles, playing at left corner forward in 1943, and at right half forward in the successive 1944 win. A great goal-getter, he was also on the Roscommon team which won the Connacht title again in 1946 when they reached the All-Ireland final, only to lose to Kerry.

KINNEAR, JOE.

Soccer international full-back. Born in Dublin, 27th December 1946. He joined his major club, Tottenham Hotspur, from St Alban's in 1965, and in an injury-hit ten seasons with the Spurs, played 189 league matches with them (winning an F.A. Cup medal in 1967 and a U.E.F.A. Cup winners medal in 1972). He then spent a brief spell with Brighton. He was capped 25 times at senior international for the Republic of Ireland between 1967 and 1976. Managing the Shajsh side for 7 years in Dubai, his other management jobs have included Doncaster and (currently) Wimbledon.

KINSELLA, AUSTIN.

Long distance motorcycle racer. Born in Dublin, 8th March 1941. Probably Ireland's best long distance road racer on motorcycle, he won many races at Mondello Park, and won the premier solo road racing championship for southern Ireland in 1977. He won endurance races at Thruxton in England, Brands Hatch, and was twice 2nd overall in the world famous Barcelona 24-hours race, in 1968 and in 1970. He also set records in the Cruagh hill-climb and the Turvey sprint, and was also a scrambler and grasstrack rider. Also a competent car racer, he won races in Formula Ford, Mini-Coopers, Sports Cars and Formula Atlantic.

KINSELLA, EAMONN.

High hurdling athlete. Born on South Circular Road, Rialto, Dublin on the 8th October 1931, he died in 1991. Club: Guinness. One of this country's finest ever high hurdlers, under the tuition of Jack Sweeney he won the Irish N.A.C.A. 120 yards title 3 times from 1950, and other A.A.U. titles. He finished 5th in the British A.A.A. 120 yards in 1954, 2nd in 1956 to his great rival Peter Hildreth, and won the title in 1957 in 14.3 seconds in his greatest achievement, beating Hildreth from the last hurdle in. Having caught the imagination of the Irish public in 1954 by reaching the final of the European Championships at Berne, in 1956 he was the first Irish athlete to compete in Eastern Europe, setting an Irish record for 110 metres hurdles in Dresden. He then represented Ireland at 110m hurdles in the 1956 Melbourne Olympics, and in September 1958 at College Park Dublin, set an Irish record at 120 yards hurdles of 14.2 (when he first set the record it stood at 15.2 seconds), a record which still stands. Arthritis set in in 1959 and he retired.

KINSELLA, JIMMY.

Professional golfer. Born in Skerrries, 25th May 1939. Attached to the Castle GC, he represented Ireland 4 times in the World Cup, 1968, 1969, 1972, and 1973. A winner of the Madrid Open in 1972, he won the Irish National

Professional title twice, 1972, and 1973. He won the Carrolls No 1 tournament in 1967, the South of Ireland Professional title in 1970, and won the Irish Dunlop tournament in 1971. In 1972 he was selected as Texaco's Golf Sportstar of the Year. His father, Billy Kinsella, played 3 international professional matches for Ireland, and was professional at Skerries for many years after 1930. His brother Willie, a member of Skerries, played 6 amateur interprovincial matches for Leinster in 1960. Two younger Kinsellas played international Boy's golf for Ireland in the late 1980's.

KIRBY, GARY.

G.A.A. hurling centre half-forward, Limerick. A member of the Limerick minors which won the All-Ireland Championship M.H.C. in 1984, he was also on the Under 21 side which won the All-Ireland Championship in 1987. He won a National Hurling League medal with the county in 1992. In 1991 he was the only Limerick player to win an All-Star award, getting the centre-forward position.

KIRBY, LIL.

G.A.A. camogie player, Cork. Clubs: Old Aloysians, and U.C.C. She shared in Cork's first 6 All-Ireland Senior Champinship wins, in 1934, 1935, 1936, 1939, 1940, and 1941. She became the first lady to chair the Cork Camogie Board, and in 1940 became President of the Camogie Association.

KIRBY, PAT.

Handballer. Born at Tuamgraney, Co Clare, 12th April, 1936. He won the All-Ireland Junior Softball Singles in 1957. He won 10 Irish Senior Softball Singles titles (in 1974, 1975, 1976 and 1977 on 60x30 courts, and in 1975, 1976, 1977, 1978, 1979 and 1980 on 40x20 courts), and 5 Doubles titles. He won R.T.E.'s Top Ace tournament in 1974 and 1975. Having lived in America from 1959 to 1972, he also won Army titles, 3 American senior titles (1965, 1969, and 1972), 3 Canadian titles, in 1965, 1967, and 1972 (making him the first handballer to win the National titles of 3 different countries), and reached the pinnacle of his long career in 1970 when he became Champion of the World, a title he regained in 1971 and 1972. He was B&I Handballer of the Year in 1975, 1976, and 1977. He won 6 over 40's world titles in the 1980's, and by winning the world over 55 title in 1991, he achieved a record of winning world titles over 3 decades and over a period of 21 years. He played hurling for County Clare at all grades (being a player of the highest class), and also played for the New York Selected side from 1959 to 1972. Four of his 7 handballing brothers also won Irish senior titles: Mick won the Gael Linn Cup in 1961, and won the Munster J.S.S. title along with Danny in 1968; John won junior and intermediate doubles titles in 1972; while in 1978 Pat, Mick, Danny and John all won National titles.

KIRKLAND, ALEC.

Soccer international forward. Clubs: Shelbourne (winning an I.F.A Irish Cup medal with them in 1920), and Shamrock Rovers (winning an F.A.I. Cup winners medal in 1924). he was capped once for the Irish Free State, in 1927 against Italy.

KIRKWOOD, JAMES W (JIMMY).

Hockey international player. Clubs: Queen's University, Belfast, Belfast Y.M.C.A., and Lisnagarvey (winning 6 successive Irish Cup titles with them, in 1988, 1989, 1990, 1991, 1992 and 1993). Born in Lisburn, 12th February 1962. He won an Olympic gold medal, representing Great Britain, in the 1988 Games in Seoul, when they beat West Germany 3-1 in the final (although he did not participate in the final game, he came on as a sub in the matches against South Korea and India). Since the age of 18 in 1981 he has been capped 104 times for Ireland (up to July 1993), and many times in the indoor code. First capped for Great Britain in 1987, he reached 40 caps in 1991 (he has also won over 15 indoor caps). He helped Ireland to 7th place in the European Championships in Paris in 1991.

KIRWAN, JOHN H ('JOCK').

Soccer international outside-left winger, and G.A.A. player, Dublin. Born in Wicklow in 1878. Soccer clubs: Southport, Everton, Tottenham Hotspur (with whom he scored 97 goals in 343 matches from 1899-1905, and won an F.A. Cup medal in their 3-0 triumph over Sheffield in a replay in 1901, and a Southern League medal in 1889-90), Chelsea and Clyde. He was capped 17 times for Ireland, some as captain, between 1900 and 1909, scoring 2 international goals. He also won a gaelic football medal with Dublin in 1904.

KIRWAN, PERCY.

Long Jump athlete. Born in Kilmacthomas Co Waterford, he is a brother of Rody Kirwan (cv), with whom he played G.A.A. football for Waterford. Following on a glorious Irish record in the British A.A.A. long jump championship since it's inception in 1880 (19 of the first 30 titles had already gone to Irishmen), he won the event on 3 successive occasions, in 1910 (at 6.72 metres), 1911 at (7.15 metres), and in 1912 (at 7.07 metres).

KIRWAN, RODDY.

G.A.A. football full-back, Kerry. Clubs: Blackwater Ramblers (Wexford), Castleisland Desmonds (Kerry). Born in Kilmacthomas Co Waterford in 1879, he was picked to play for Waterford in 1903, but moved to Kerry. He was a member of the first two Kerry sides to win the All-Ireland Senior Football Championship title, when Tralee Mitchells won in the successive years of 1903 and 1904. He played opposite his brother Paddy when playing against Waterford in the Munster S.F.C. final of 1904. Also a fine athlete in his early career, he died in 1950.

KISSOCK, BRIAN J S.

Amateur international golfer. Club: Bangor (winning Senior Cup medals in 1981 and 1984). He won the North of Ireland championship twice, in 1974 and 1976 (and was runner-up in 1981). He played 60 interprovincial matches for Ulster (placing him 4th in that provinces all-time list) in the 27 year period between 1961 and 1987 (playing for the winning team 8 times), winning 34 and halving 7, giving him a success rate of 62.5%; he played 22 Home international matches for Ireland in 4 series between 1961 (when still a junior) and 1976, winning 10 matches. He turned professional for a while, later to be reinstated to the amateur ranks.

KNOX, Dr HERCULES JOHN.

Rugby international forward. Born in Gortnor Abbey, Crossmolina, Co Mayo, 1880, he died in Liverpool at the age of 94, in 1975. Clubs: Dublin University and Lansdowne. Seven times a Leinster interprovincial player between 1902 and 1905, he was capped in the pack on 10 occasions for Ireland between 1904 and 1908, including the Championship winning side of 1906. A doctor, he changed his surname by deed poll in 1912 to Beresford-Knox.

KYLE, Dr JOHN Wilson (JACKIE, J.W., 'THE GHOST', and 'THE TWINS').

Rugby international out-half. Born in Belfast, 10th January 1926. Clubs: Queen's University Belfast (winning an Ulster Senior Cup medal in 1947) and N.I.F.C. (winning Ulster Senior Cup medals in 1954, 1956, 1957 and 1958). A product of Belfast Royal Academy school, he is Ireland's most capped outhalf, with 46 international caps for Ireland (6 as captain in 1953 and 1954) and 6 for the British and Irish Lion's over a 12 year period between 1947 and 1958, scoring 7 tries and one drop goal for his country. He was the world's most capped player for any position from 1958 to 1971, taking over from Ken Jones of Wales. He also played in 2 Victory matches in 1946. He played in 42 International Championship matches, and was on the winning side 22 times (a better average than any other Irish leading player). On the British and Irish Lion's tour of Australia and New Zealand in 1950, his brilliance was evident, astounding the locals with his class, and he played in all 6 tests. A master of all aspects of the game, his flair, nonchalont skill, outstanding defensive qualities, and great instinct mark him out as arguably the game's greatest ever fly-half. He was the master player behind Ireland's historic (and only) Grand Slam of 1948, the Triple Crown of 1949, and the victory in the International Championship in 1951 (this is now known among rugby followers as the 'Jackie Kyle era'), and people still talk of the day the referee blew for a forward pass, so perfect was his dummy to a player in front of him. A brother-in-law of Noel Henderson (cv), he is a doctor in Zambia. He was elected into Texaco's Hall of Fame in 1977, the first of only 2 rugby players to be thus far honoured, and to the R.W.I. Digital Hall of Fame in 1991.

KYLE, MAEVE E E (nee SHANKEY).

Sprint international athlete, and hockey international. From Kilkenny, she was born on 26th November 1928. Clubs: Dublin University and Ballymena. Initially concentrating on hockey, she won 58 international caps for Ireland from 1948, including being a part of Ireland's famous Triple Crown success in Wembley in 1950. She later competed for Ireland in 3 Olympic Games (the first of only 2 Irish sportswomen to do so); in the 100 and 200 metres in Melbourne in 1956 (failing to get out of her heats, in times of 12.2 and 26.5 respectively); in the same events in Rome in 1960 (5th in 100m heat in 12.5 and 5th in 200m heat in 22.1); and at the age of 35, in the 400 (7th in semi-final with 55.3) and 800 metres (8th in semi-final in 2.12.9) at the 1964 games in Tokyo. In the European Championships in Stockholm in 1962 she finished 6th in the final of the 400 metres, while she was 5th in her heat in the 800 metres. She won the British W.A.A.A. title over 440 yards in 1961, with a time of 56.3 seconds. In 1961 she set world best indoor times for both 440 yards and 400 metres. In 1970 she set a U.K. veterans record over 400 metres at 55.3, and in 1969 she set the U.K. veterans record for the women's long jump, at 5.28 metres. In all, between 1955 and 1975, she won 41 track titles in the Republic and Northern Ireland, at disciplines which included 80 yards, 100 yards, 220 yards, 440 yards, 880 yards, long jump, high jump and pentathlon.

L

LACEY, WILLIAM (BILLY).

Soccer international winger. Born in Wexford, March 2nd 1889. Clubs: Shelbourne, Everton, Liverpool (winning 2 English League Championship medals in 1922 and 1923, and an F.A. Cup runners-up medal in 1914, scoring 5 goals in 8 cup matches), New Brighton, Belfast United, and Linfield (winning an Irish Cup medal in 1919), Cork Bohemians. He was capped 23 times for Northern Ireland between 1909 and 1923 (his last cap when he was aged 40), and scored 3 international goals. He was a member of the first Northern Ireland side to win the Home International Championship, in 1914, playing in the No 10 jersey in all 3 games, and scoring 2 of the goals in the famous 3-0 victory over England at Middlesborough. He died in 1969.

LALOR, PAT.

G.A.A. hurling right half-back, Kilkenny. A member of the Kilkenny side beaten in the final of the 1968 All-Ireland Under 21 Championship, he has won 3 All-Ireland Senior Hurling Championship medals with Kilkenny, in 1972, 1974 and 1975 (playing a stormer in the county's first successful defence of the McCarthy

Cup since 1933). He was also on the losing All-Ireland S.H.C. final teams in both 1971 and 1973, thus playing in 5 successive Liam McCarthy Cup finals. He has won 4 Railway Cup medals with Leinster, in 1973, 1974, 1975, and 1977. He won All-Star recognition in the first 2 years that they were awarded, in 1971 and 1972, both at right half-back.

LAMBERT, NOEL Hamilton ('HAM').

Rugby and cricket international. Born in Dublin, 5th June, 1910. A product of Sandford Park and Rossall Schools, he, while playing rugby for Lansdowne in 1934, won 2 international caps in the Irish three-quarter line, against Scotland and Wales. He also played 6 times for Leinster betwen 1930 and 1933, and later went on to referee 11 international rugby matches between 1947 and 1952. He also won international honours as a right hand bat cricketer, playing 21 matches for Ireland between 1931 and 1947, while a member of the Leinster club, scoring one international century, for a batting average of 18.03 per innings. He is the son of Bob Lambert (cv).

LAMBERT, ROBERT Hamilton (BOB).

International cricketing all-rounder and badminton player. As a cricketer, he played for Ireland 52 times between 1898 and 1930, scoring 1,995 runs for his country (placing him, up to 1992, 7th in all-time runs for his country), and he scored 100 career centuries (scoring 4 for his country). A fine bowler also, he took 179 wickets (at an average run rate of 18.35), placing him 6th on Ireland's all-time list. Captaining Ireland 13 times, he is regarded as one of this country's finest all-rounders in the game (being described by none other that W.G. Grace as 'a perfect cricketer'), having 3 seasons in a row scored 2,000 runs and taken 200 wickets. He was twice President of the I.C.U. A dual international, in badminton he was capped 11 times for Ireland between 1909 and 1926, and won the Irish Championship in 1917. His brother, Septimus Drummond Lambert played 15 international cricket matches for Ireland between 1902 and 1921 (scoring 387 runs for a creditable average of 20.36), and his sister, Mrs Charlie Anderson, was capped for Ireland at badminton. He is the father of 'Ham' Lambert (cv).

LAMONT, RONALD Arthur (RONNIE).

Rugby international No 8 and wing-forward. Born 18th November 1941. Club: Instonians (winning an Ulster Senior Cup medal in 1965). A Belfast schoolteacher, he was capped for Ireland 12 times in an injury-laden career, between 1965 and 1970, scoring one international try. A fine back-row exponent, he was a member of the British and Irish Lion's touring party to Australia and New Zealand in 1966, playing in 4 tests (including scoring a try in the 3rd test, and 7 tries in all on tour), and in 1970 he toured Argentina with Ireland.

LANDERS, JOHN JOE ('J.J.' or 'PURTY'), TIM ('ROUNDY'), and BILL.

Three brothers, G.A.A. football forwards, Kerry. Club: Strand Street. All three were on the Kerry side (Bill came on as a sub), which beat Mayo 2-7 to 2-4, in the 1932 All-Ireland Senior Football Champinship final. John Joe netted a total tally of 5 All-Ireland S.F.C. medals, in 1929, 1930, 1931, 1932 and 1937 (after a draw), scoring 5-8 in these 6 finals. Tim 'Roundy' also won 5 All-Ireland medals, his winning years being 1931, 1932, 1937, 1939, and 1941 (as a sub). Bill won 2 All-Irleand S.F.C. medals, in 1924 and 1932. Tim and John Joe won Railway Cup medals with Munster in 1931, and both were nominated as All-Time All-Star award winners in 1985, the first brothers to be so nominated.

LANE, DAVID J (DAVE).

Rugby international wing threequater. Born in Cork, 30th September 1913. Club: U.C.C. (winning 3 successive Munster Senior Cup medals with them, in 1935, 1936 and 1937). He was capped 4 times on the wing for Ireland, twice in 1934, and twice in the International Championship-winning year of 1935.

LANE, MICHAEL Francis (MICK).

Rugby international wing threequarter. Born 3rd April 1926. Club: U.C.C. He won 17 international caps for Ireland between the years 1947 and 1953, scoring one international try. He was a member of the 1949 Triple Crown winning side, and of the International Champinship winning side of 1951. He toured Australia and New Zealand with the 1950 British and Irish Lion's, under the captaincy of Karl Mullen (cv), gaining one Test cap in each country, while scoring 4 tries on tour. He also toured Argentina and Chile with Ireland in 1952. A former Irish junior sprint champion, he won 2 Munster Senior Cup medals with U.C.C., in 1950 and 1951. An uncle of Michael Kiernan (cv).

LANE, NOEL.

G.A.A. hurling forward, Galway. From Ballindereen. He won an All-Ireland Senior Hurling Championship medal with Galway in 1980 at left corner forward, having been on the losing side in the previous year's final, and was again on the losing side in the S.H.C. finals of 1981, 1985 and 1986 (when he was captain). He came on as a sub in each of Galway's All-Ireland Senior Hurling Championship winning games of 1987 and 1988, both to telling effect (scoring the winning goal both times), thus bringing his Liam McCarthy Cup medal haul to three. Known as a great goal-getter and dubbed as a 'Super-Sub', he won 2 All-Star awards, in 1983 at left half-forward, and in 1984 at full-forward. He captained the Connacht side (the 6th Galway player to do so) which won the 1986 Railway Cup. He also won a National Hurling League medal in 1988.

LANE, PADDY.

Rugby international prop-forward. Born in Parteen, Co Clare, 7th September, 1934. While playing for Old Crescent, he was selected to play for Ireland once, against Wales in 1964 (Ireland lost 15-6). He played senior interprovincial rugby for Munster for 6 years. He later became President of the Irish Farmers' Association.

LANGAN, DANIEL JOSEPH.

Rugby international full-back. Born in Dublin, 19th March 1910. Club: Clontarf (being a member of the only Clontarf side to win the Leinster Senior Cup, in 1936). He was capped once for Ireland, in the 1934 13-0 loss to Wales in Cardiff. He played 2 interprovincial matches for Leinster, in 1931 and 1932 against Munster. He became President of Texaco (Ireland) Oil Co, and was the father of the colourful London restauranteur, Peter Langan, who died in 1988.

LANGAN, DAVID.

Soccer international full-back. Born in Dublin, 15th February 1957. Clubs: Derby County, Birmingham City, Oxford United, Mirrlies Blackstone. Apprenticed to Derby from Cherry Orchard, he played 3 full seasons with them before moving in 1980 to Birmingham. A fearless tackler, he was capped 26 times for the Republic of Ireland over an eleven year period between 1978 and 1988, including the earlier stages of Ireland's qualifying for the European Championship in 1988.

LANGAN, JACK.

Bare-knuckle prize fighter. Born in Clondalkin in 1799. A friend of Dan Donnelly (cv), he won the Irish prize-fight title in the early 1820's. He fought the English bare knuckle champion, Tom Spring for a purse of £300 at Worcester racecourse on Jan 7th 1824, but after a tremendous tussle lasting 2 hours 20 minutes and 77 rounds, Spring was declared the winner. Later in the same year, on the 8th on June, a rematch (this time for a purse of 500 Guineas) was arranged for Birdham Bridge near Chester, but the result was similar, this time Langan lost in 1 hour 49 minutes, after 76 rounds.

LANGAN, JIMMY.

Table-tennis player. Born in Dublin in 1950. At the age of 12 he became the then youngest player to represent Ireland at international senior level. In the 1970's he was an outstanding Irish table-tennis champion, playing in excess of 200 international matches for Ireland. He played in 4 World Championships and 4 European Championships. He was Irish Senior Champion ten times in the 1960's and 1970's. He retired at the age of 31 in 1981.

LANGAN, JOE.

G.A.A. football forward and midfielder, Mayo. Born in 1942. Clubs: Balla (winning a West Mayo SFC medal) and Castlebar Mitchells (winning 2 Mayo SFC medals). He won a Connacht M.F.C. medal with Mayo minors in 1958, when they were beaten in the All-Ireland final. With the Mayo senior inter-county team he won 2 Connacht Senior Football Championship winner's medals, in 1967 and 1969. He was also on the Mayo side which won the county's most recent national senior title, the National League in 1970. He won a Railway Cup medal with Connacht in 1967.

LANGAN, TOM.

G.A.A. footballing centre full-forward, Mayo. Club: Ballycastle. He was a key, free-scoring player on Mayo's 2 successive All-Ireland Senior Football Championship title wins, in 1950 and 1951. He was also a member of the Mayo S.F.C. side beaten in the All-Ireland final S.F.C. of 1948 by Cavan. He won one Railway Cup medal with Connacht, in 1951. He was selected, amongst fierce opposition, as the full forward on the Sunday Independent's 'Team of the Century', voted in the Centenery Year of 1984.

LANGRISHE, MARY ISABELLA (MAY).

Tennis player. When she won the Irish Ladies' Singles title in 1879 at Fitzwiltom in Dublin, she became the world's first ever national women's singles champion, as it was the first to be held. She won the title again in both 1883 and 1886.

LANGTON, JIMMY.

G.A.A. hurling right half-forward, Kilkenny. Born in 1919. Club: Eire Og (assisting them to 4 county championship wins). He was a member of the Kilkenny minors which won the All-Ireland M.H.C. in 1935 and in 1936. Regarded as one of the game's artists, he won 2 All-Ireland Senior Hurling Championship medals with Kilkenny, in 1939 (when still a teenager) and 1947. He captained Kilkenny when they lost the 1940 All-Ireland S.H.C. final to Limerick, and was also on losing sides in the finals of 1945, 1946, and 1950 (his tally of 8 Leinster S.H.C. medals was made up in 1943 and 1953). An accomplished right-half forward, he won 2 Ralilway Cup medals with Leinster 13 years apart, in 1941, and again in 1954. He was selected at left half-forward on the Sunday Independent's 'Team of the Century' in 1984. Also in 1984 he became the first Kilkenny player to be selected as an All-Time All-Star award winner.

LANIGAN, JIM.

G.A.A. hurling back, Tipperary. He was on the Tipperary minors which won the All-Ireland M.H.C. in 1934. He captained the Tipperary side which won the 1937 All-Ireland Senior Hurling Championship, when they beat Kilkenny by 3-11 to 0-3 in Killarney, the first of only 2 times the Liam McCarthy Cup final was played away from Croke Park. He had previously won an All-Ireland S.H.C. medal with Tipperary in 1930. He won a Railway Cup medal with Munster in 1938, becoming the 2nd captain from the 'Premier County' to accept the trophy.

LANIGAN, PADDY ('ICY').

G.A.A. hurler, Kilkenny. He won 7 All-Ireland Senior Hurling Championship winners medals with Kilkenny sides, in 1904 with Tullaroan, in 1905 with Erin's Own, in 1907 and 1909 with Mooncoin, and won his fifth medal in 1911 when

Kilkenny were awarded the final; he was also in the 1912 Tullaroan side and was a non-playing sub in the Mooncoin side in the 1913 decider. He never played on a Kilkenny side beaten in an All-Ireland S.H.C. final.

LARKIN, PADDY.

G.A.A. hurling right half-back, Kilkenny. He won 4 All-Ireland Senior Hurling Championship medals with Kilkenny, in 1932, 1933, 1935, and 1939. He played in 7 All-Ireland finals in the 1930's, being on the losing side 4 times in all, in 1931, in 1936 as captain, 1937 (and again in 1940). A noted right corner back, he won 3 Railway Cup medals with Leinster, in 1932, 1933, and in 1936 when he became the 4th Kilkennyman to captain a winning Leinster hurling Railway Cup side. He is the father of 'Fan' Larkin (cv). His brother Mick, as a non-playing sub, won an All-Ireland S.H.C. medal in 1935.

LARKIN, PHIL ('FAN').

G.A.A. hurling right full-back, Kilkenny. Club: James Stephens (with whom he won 2 All-Ireland Club Championship medals, in 1976 as captain and again in 1982 at the age of 41). A winner of a Leinster M.H.C. medal in 1959, he played on 4 All-Ireland Senior Hurling Championship winning sides for Kilkenny, in 1972, 1974, 1975, and in 1979 at at the age of 38 (he had won a medal as a non-playing sub in 1963), and was a losing S.H.C. finalist in 1964, 1971, 1973, and 1978 (thus playing in 7 All-Ireland finals in the 70's decade, emulating a feat performed in the 30's by his father, Paddy cv). He captained the Kilkenny side to victory in the National Hurling League title in 1975-76. In 1979 he became the 13th Kilkennyman to captain a winning Railway Cup Leinster side, also winning 5 other Railway Cup medals in 1972, 1973, 1974, 1975, and 1977. He won 4 All-Star awards in the 1970's, in 1973, 1974, 1976, and in 1978, all at right corner-back.

LARMOUR, DAVY.

Flyweight and Bantamweight international boxer. Born in Belfast 2nd April 1952. As an amateur member of the Albert Foundry club, he won a British Commonwealth flyweight gold medal in New Zealand in 1974, one of only 6 Northern boxers to do so. He also won 3 Irish National Senior titles at flyweight, in 1973, 1975, and 1976. He reached the last eight in the 1976 Montreal Olympic Games in this weight division, being beaten by an American, Leo Randolph, by 4-1 in the fight for a bronze medal. He turned pro in 1977, and became British Bantamweight boxing champion for a period in 1983, defeating Hughie Russell at the King's Hall Belfast in March, only to lose the title in September to Englishman John Feeney. His professional career, consisting of 11 wins and 7 losses, was from 1977 to 1983.

LAVAN, SEAN, Dr.

G.A.A. footballer, Mayo, and athlete. Winning a number of Connacht S.F.C. medals with Mayo, he was on the side beaten in the All-Ireland Senior Football Championship final in 1921 by Dublin. He is credited to having introduced the solo-run to gaelic football. He was also a track champion, winning many Irish titles. He competed for Ireland in 2 Olympic Games; in the 200 metres (unlucky not to make the final) and 400 metres in the 1924 games at Paris (when he became the first Irish sprinter to compete in the Olympic Games), and in the 200 metres (6th in his heat) and 400 metres (2nd in his heat, 5th in the 2nd round) in Amsterdam in 1928.

LAW, CON.

Motorcycle racer. From Bellaghy, Co Derry, he had a long career in Isle of Man T.T.'s, Manx Grand Prix, World Championships, and Irish road racing up to the mid-Eighties. He won 2 Isle of Man T.T. races, the 1982 Junior, and the same race the following year (in which he became the first rider in T.T. history to lap the 37.73 mile circuit at over 110 m.p.h. in a 25cc machine). He also finished 3rd in the 1983 250cc race at the Daytona 200 International races in Florida. He retired in the mid-1980's.

LAWLER, JOSEPH F ('ROBIN').

Soccer international left-back and wing-half. Born in Dublin, 28th August 1925. Clubs: Transport, Drumcondra (winning an F.A.I. Cup medal in 1949), Belfast Celtic (winning an Irish Cup medal in 1947 and an Irish League medal in 1947-48), Fulham (in a 12 year career with them he played 281 league matches, and helped them gain promotion from Division 2 in 1959). He was capped 8 times for the Republic of Ireland between 1953 and 1956. His older brother Jim, a wing-half for Glentoran, Portsmouth and Southend (scoring 18 goals in 269 league matches for them 1948-56), played against him in the Irish Cup final of 1947, and won an F.A.I. Cup medal with him in 1949 while with Drums.

LAWLER, PATRICK Joseph (PADDY).

Rugby international 2nd Row forward. Club: Clontarf. A product of O'Brien's institution in Artane, he played 13 senior interprovincials for Leinster between 1951 and 1956. He was capped 12 times for Ireland in the pack between 1951 and 1956, scoring one international try, and in 1952 he toured Argentina and Chile with an Irish squad (and emigrated later to Argentina).

LAWLOR, EILEEN.

G.A.A. ladies football right full-forward, Kerry. Club: Abbeydorney. She has won 9 succesive All-Ireland Senior Championship medals with Kerry, 1982, 1983, 1984, 1985, 1986, 1987, 1988, 1989 and 1990. A sister of Margaret Slattery (cv), all of her wins were with Margaret playing in the side with her. A 4-time All-Star winner, she has also won 9 National League and 6 Interprovincial Championship medals. She has held the position of National P.R.O. for her sport.

LAWLOR, JOHN.

Handballer. Born in Pennsylvania in 1860, he was brought up in Co Wicklow. He won the Irish Professional title in 1885, 1886, 1887 and 1888. He also won the 'Handball Championship of the World'. In 1923 he became the first President of the Irish Amateur Handball Association (I.A.H.A.).

LAWLOR, JOHN (or SEAN).

Hammer throwing athlete. He broke onto the scene in 1958 with a new Irish hammer record, set in Dayton, Ohio at 200'3". In 1961 he won his solitary British A.A.A. title in the hammer, with a throw of 64.12 metres. He, with a throw of 64.95 metres (longer than the 1956 Olympic record), finished in a highly creditable 4th place in the Olympic hammer throwing final in Rome in 1960, 7 feet behind the winner and over 2 feet behind the third man. In the 1962 European Championships in Stockholm he finished 7th with a throw of only 201'8". He competed in his 2nd Olympics in 1964 in Tokyo, failing to qualify for the final. Winning many Irish hammer titles, in 1960 he was the athletics choice as Texaco Sportstar of that Year.

LAWLOR, JOHN C ('KIT'), and MICHAEL (MICK).

Soccer international father and son. Kit (born in Dublin, 3rd Decenber 1922), played for Shamrock Rovers, Drumcondra (winning, as the club's leading goalscorer, 2 successive League of Ireland winner's medals in 1947-48 and 1948-49, and scoring the only goal in Drums F.A.I. Cup final win of 1957, having also won a medal in 1946), and Doncaster Rovers (1950-1954, scoring 46 league goals in 128 league games). He was capped 3 times for the Republic of Ireland between 1949 and 1951. His son Mick Lawlor, was a forward player for Shamrock Rovers (winning 2 F.A.I. Cup winner's medals, in 1968 when he scored in the final, and 1969) and Shelbourne. He won 5 caps for the

Republic of Ireland, four in 1971 and one more in 1973, thus making them one of very few sets of fathers and sons to have played international soccer for the Republic of Ireland. Mick later managed Home Farm. Kit's brother Jim played for Drumcondra, Doncaster and Bradford City (playing 155 league matches for them 1955-61). Another son of Kit's, Martin, has won 3 F.A.I. Cup medals with Dundalk (winning in 1982, 1988 and 1990, and a League of Ireland Championship winner's medal in 1988), and won a League Star award in 1993, while yet another son Robbie won an F.A.I. Cup medal in 1984 with U.C.D.

LAWLOR, JOE.

Amateur flyweight and bantamweight boxing international. Club: Darndale, Dublin. Born in Dublin 1964. Boxing from age 11, and winning many junior titles, he has won 4 Irish National Senior Championship titles, 3 at flyweight, in 1986, 1988 and 1989, being beaten in the final in 1987; and although beaten in the bantamweight final in 1990 and 1992, he won it in 1991. Boxing in the Europeans in Gothenburg in 1991, he represented Ireland in the Olympic Games in Seoul at flyweight in 1988, being beaten by a Russian, Skriabin in his 2nd bout.

LAWRENSON, MARK Thomas.

Soccer international left back and central defender. Born in Preston, 2nd June 1957. He joined Preston North End as a junior, and joined Brighton and Hove Albion from there for £100,000 in 1977. He joined Liverpool in 1982 for £900,000 (then a club record), and helped them (with his mastery of the central defending art) to win 4 English League Championships (1982, 1983, 1984 and 1986), an F.A. Cup in 1986, 3 League Cups (1982, 1983 and 1984), and a European Cup in 1984 (and runners-up medal in 1985), playing for them in 332 league matches, scoring 17 goals. At his peak he was regarded as one of the best defenders in British League soccer (his timing of the tackle and his turn of speed being world class). He was capped 38 times for the Republic of Ireland over a 12 year period between 1977 and 1988, scoring 5 international goals in a distinguished career. In 1988, after retiring through injury, he joined Oxford F.C. as a manager, only to lose his job not long after.

LAWTHER, W IAN.

Soccer international centre-forward. Born in Belfast, 20th October, 1939. Clubs: Crusaders, Sunderland (scoring 41 goals in 75 league matches 1959-60), Blackburn Rovers (scoring 21 league goals 1961-62), Scunthorpe (scoring 21 league goals in 1963-64), Brentford (scoring 43 league goals in 138 games 1964-67), Halifax (scoring 23 league goals in 87 games 1968-70), and Stockport County (scoring 29 league goals in 1971-75). In his 16 seasons in English League football he scored 178 league goals in almost 600 league games. Having won one 'B' cap, he went on to win 4 senior caps for Northern Ireland between 1960 and 1962.

LAYCOCK, EDDIE.

Motorcycle racer. Born in Tempelogue, Co Dublin, May 1961. Starting racing in 1979, he won that seasons I.M.C.U. Streetbkie Championship. He went on to win the Hayes Trophy (the premier road racing championship in southern Ireland) 3 times, in 1982, 1983 and 1985. The Republic of Ireland's most successful motorcycle road racer since Reg Armstrong in the 1950's, he was the first from the Republic since 1952 to win an Isle of Man T.T.race, the 1987 Junior T.T. (winning a 2nd T.T. race in 1989, the Supersport 400 on a Suzuki). He has 6 Ulster Grand Prix wins, one in 1985, 2 in 1986, one in 1988, and 2 in 1989. He won his first international event in 1986, the North-West 200 250cc class, and in 1987 finished 4th in the Daytona 200 International 250cc. From 1988 he rode in the World Championship 500cc Grand

Prix: gaining his first point in 15th place in the Spanish G.P. in 1989, finishing in 17th place in 1990 (with 30 points), 12th place in 1991 (with 57 points and a best place finish of 10th), and in 20th place in 1992 (with a best place of 9th, with 4 points gained). He did not race in 1993.

LEAHY, CORNELIUS (CON).

High jump and Triple Jump athlete. Born 27th April 1876 in Cregane, near Charleville, Co Cork. In a top class career ranging from 1899 to 1908, he won 4 successive British A.A.A. titles at the high jump, in 1905, 1906, 1907 and 1908; and also won the American title in 1907. As an Irishman representing Great Britain, he won 3 Olympic medals: 2 of them one day after his 30th birthday, when he won a gold in the high jump at the unofficial Intercalary Games of 1906 in St Louis (clearing 5'10', or 1.75 metres), and silver in the triple jump with 45' 10", finishing 2nd behind Peter O'Connor of Ireland; he also competed in the long jump. Two years later in the high jump at the London Games of 1908 he finished joint 2nd, clearing 6' 2" (this was to be G.B.'s last high jump medal at a major championship until 1993). A month after the games he jumped an unofficial height of 6'4" in Adare. Soon afterwards he emigrated to the U.S.A., where he died in 1921. One of a family of 7 fine athletics brothers, he is an older brother of Pat Leahy (cv), with whom he made up one of the Olympic Games' most successful set of brothers. Another brother Joe was a 23ft long jumper, while another, Tim, led the world ranking in the high jump in 1912.

LEAHY, DONAL.

Soccer centre-forward. Born in Cork, 31st August, 1938. Clubs: Evergreen United (which in 1959 became Cork Celtic). He was leading goal scorer in the League of Ireland for 3 succesive seasons, in 1956-57 (jointly with Tommy Hamilton cv with 15 goals, in 1957-58 with 16 goals, and in 1958-59 with 22 goals). His total of 162 goals in the League of Ireland between 1956 and 1970 (in only one of these seasons did he fail to score) places him third in the all-time ratings, behind Brendan Bradley (cv) and Turlough O'Connor (cv). In his 17 Inter-League appearences, he has scored a joint record (shared with Liam Tuouhy cv) of 7 goals for the League of Ireland. Although in 3 World Cup qulifying round squads, he was never capped for the Republic of Ireland.

LEAHY, JOHN.

G.A.A. hurling half-back and midfielder, Tipperary. Club: Mullinahone Kickham's. From Mullinahone, he was born 16th September 1969. A member of the Tipp minors side which were beaten in the final of the 1987 All-Irleand M.H.C., he won All-Ireland Under 21 medal in 1989. Making his senior inter-county debut in 1988, he matured quickly to become one of the country's best hurlers, and was a member of the Tipperary sides which won the All-Ireland Senior Hurling Championship in both 1989 and 1991, he was also on the side which lost in the final of 1988. A member also of the Tipp side which won the National League in 1988, he won an other Munster S.H.C. medal in 1993. He has won 2 All-Star awards, in 1989 as a wing-forward, and in 1991 at midfield. He was nominated as Tipperary Hurler of the Year in 1991.

LEAHY, JOHNNY ('CAPTAIN').

G.A.A. hurling left half-back, Tipperary. He captained the Tipperary side, Boherlahan, to defeat the Tullaroan side from Kilkenny, in the 1916 All-Ireland Senior Hurling Championship final by 5-4 to 3-2 (the county's last pre-McCarthy Cup win). He later captained the full county Tipperary side to win the 1925 All-Ireland S.H.C. (thus becoming the first Tipp-man to collect the Liam McCarthy Cup), by beating Galway by 5-6 to 1-5. He also captained the Premier County in 2 losing All-Ireland S.H.C. finals, in both 1917 and 1922. He served on the Munster Council of the

G.A.A. from 1925 till his death in 1949. Three of his brothers from Boherlahan won All-Ireland S.H.C. winner's medals; Paddy in 1925 (alongside Johnny), Mick (for Cork) in 1928, and Tommy in 1930 with Tipperary.

LEAHY, MICK.

Middleweight boxer. Born in Cork, 12 March 1935. He became British Middleweight champion in 1963-64. In May 1963 he gained the title in a first round, 105 second win over George Aldridge. He lost on points to the same opponent in 1964. A globe-trotting boxer, among those he fought were a 44-year-old Sugar Ray Robinson (whom Leahy beat on points over 10 rounds), Laszlo Papp (in an unsuccessful bid for the European title), and the Italian Nino Benvenuti, later a world champion. His 9 year pro career, which included 46 wins and 19 losses in 72 bouts, ended when, at age 30, he lost the use of one eye in a car accident. He was the Texaco Boxing Sportstar of the Year for 1963.

LEAHY, MICHAEL William (MICK), and KELVIN Tremaine.

Rugby international father and son. Mick, a 2nd row forward, was born in Woodford, Co Galway on 6th June 1935. A product of Woodford Normal School and a member of U.C.C. (winning a Munster Senior Cup medal in 1963), he was capped for Ireland only once, in a losing match against Wales in 1964. His son Kelvin Tremaine Leahy (born in Cork 1st September 1965), a Wanderers back-row player, was a schoolboy international, and later played for and captained both Leinster and Ireland 'B', and toured New Zealand with Ireland in 1992, where he gained one full cap for Ireland. Kelvin's brother Colin, a Wanderers winger, played for Connacht against the visiting Austalian tourists, and for the Ireland 'A' side, in 1992.

LEAHY, PATRICK J (PAT).

High jump and Long jump athlete. Born 20th May 1877 in Cregane, Charleville, Co Cork, he died in 1926 in the U.S.A. He won 2 British A.A.A. titles in the high jump, in 1898 and 1899, and held Irish, British and European records in this event. As an Irishman representing Great Britain, he won 2 Olympic medals, achieving a silver medal in the high jump in Paris in 1900 (clearing only 5'10", having reportedly broken 6'4" at least 6 times in training in Ireland, and cleared an unofficial 6'5" in 1898), and bronze in the long jump (jumping 22' 9") at the same games (he also finished 4th in the Hop, Step and Jump, clearing 44 feet, whereas he had bettered that by 5 feet the previous year), thus gaining the reputation of rarely being able to show his real talent outside Ireland. He also competed in the High Jump at the 1908 Olympics. He is the younger brother of Con Leahy (cv), and together they made up the set of brothers that won more Olympic athletic medals than any other family.

LEAHY, TERRY.

G.A.A. hurling centre half-forward, Kilkenny. Born in 1918. Clubs: Young Ireland and Faughs (winning a tally of 7 county championship medals). In an inter-county career which lasted 12 years from 1938 to 1949, he appeared in 5 All-Ireland S.H.C. finals; he won 2 All-Ireland Senior Hurling Championship winner's medals with Kilkenny, in 1939 and 1947 (scoring 0-6, including the equaliser and then the winning point in a classic game), also playing on losing All-Ireland S.H.C. final teams in 1937, 1940 and 1946 (scoring 2-0). Emigrating to New York in 1949, where his skill led him to be called 'Mr Hurling', he won their championship with a Kilkenny (New York) side in both 1950 and 1957. A fine exponent of the drop puck, he was vaunted as one of Kilkenny's greatest hurlers.

LEATHEM, JOHNNY ('HACK').

Soccer international centre-half. Clubs: Belfast Celtic (winning 5 successive Irish League medals, in 1935-36, 1936-37, 1937-38, 1938-39 and in 1939-40, also winning Irish Cup medals in 1937, 1938 and 1941), Dundalk. He represented the League of Ireland, and was capped once for Northern Ireland in 1939 against Wales.

LEDBETTER, PETER.G.

Tennis and squash international player. A winner of many Irish tennis tournaments in the 1970's, he played Davis Cup for Ireland in 1973, 1974, and 1975. A dual international racquet player, he won 4 international squash caps for Ireland in 1972-73.

LEDWIDGE, JACK J (JIMMY).

G.A.A. footballer, Dublin, and soccer international player. He was a member of Geraldines Selection which captured 2 successive All-Ireland Senior Football Championships for Dublin in 1898 and 1899, having also played on the losing side in the final of 1896. He later played soccer with Shelbourne, and won 2 international soccer caps for Ireland in 1906.

LEE, SAMUEL (SAMMY).

Rugby international centre three-quarter. 1871-1944. Club: N.I.F.C. (winning 6 consecutive Ulster Senior Cup medals from 1893 to 1899). A product of R.B.A.I., he won 19 international caps for Ireland between 1891 and 1898, scoring one try, and making him the then joint most-capped Irish player with C V Rooke (cv). He captained Ireland in the 1892-1893 season, again in the 1895-1896 season (when Ireland captured the International Championship), and once in the 1897-1898 season. Regarded as Irish rugby's first great backline player, he was a crafty runner and a fine tackler. He was a crucial member of Ireland's first Triple Crown triumph in 1894. He was president of the I.R.F.U. in 1899-1900, and was an Irish selector 1898-1900. He also refereed the Scotland v England match of 1904.

LEECH, EITHNE (EILEEN).

G.A.A. camogie player, Dublin. A member of the great Dublin side of the late 1950's and early 1960's, she won 8 successive All-Ireland Senior Championship winning medals, in 1959, 1960, 1961, 1962, 1963, 1964, 1965, and in 1966.

LEECH, MICK ('MR GOALS').

Soccer international forward. Born in Dublin, 8th August 1948. Clubs: St Brigid's, Ormeau, Northampton Town (to whom he was apprenticed), Shamrock Rovers (winning 3 F.A.I. Cup winner's medals in 1967, 1968 and 1969, scoring 5 goals in these 3 finals), Boston Rovers (U.S.A.), Waterford (helping them to their League of Ireland triumph in 1977-78), Rovers again, Shelbourne, Drogheda and St Patrick's Athletic. In the period 1966 to 1981, he scored 132 League of Ireland goals, placing him 8th on the all-time list of scorers. He was capped for the Republic of Ireland 8 times between 1969 and 1973, scoring 2 international goals, being on the Irish party which went to the mini World Cup in Brazil in 1972. A great poacher of goals, he was the League of Ireland's chief goalscorer in the 1968/69 season, with 19 goals for Shamrock Rovers, and he added another 35 in other competitions, to give his total for that season at 56, a figure unlikely to be beaten. In his first 2 seasons with the Hoops he scored 104 goals. He was the S.W.A.I. Player of the Year in 1969. Retiring in 1981, he was a secretary of the Players Union, was assistant manager of Dundalk for 4 years, and later managed the Garda and Ballyfermot United clubs.

LEEN, BRIDGET.

Ladies G.A.A. football full-back, Kerry. Club: Castleisland (winning All-Ireland Club Championship winner's medals in 1981 and 1984). From Ballymacelligott, she captained Kerry to their All-Ireland Senior Championship triumph over Leitrim in 1984. In 1990 her All-Ireland winner's medals tally came to eight, missing only the 1986 final (through injury) in the county's

9-in-a-row from 1982 up to 1990. A fine tackler, she has also won 9 Munster Championship and 5 Interprovincial Championship medals to add to a Minor All-Ireland medal she gained in 1981.

LE FANU, VICTOR CHARLES.

Rugby international forward. 1865-1939. Clubs: Cambridge University and Lansdowne. The son of the famous Irish novelist, Sheridan Le Fanu, he was capped 11 times for Ireland between 1886 and 1892, and captained the side in the 1891-1892 season. He was a member of the first Ireland team to win the International Championship, in 1888. In 1884, he was the first Irish international rugby player to play in the annual Inter-Varsity match between Oxford and Cambridge (playing again in 1885 and 1886), and in fact played in 2 trial matches for England.

LENIHAN, DONAL Gerald.

Rugby international 2nd row forward. Born in Cork, 12th September 1959. Clubs: U.C.C. (captaining the Munster Senior Cup side in 1981), and Cork Constitution (winning 3 Munster Senior Cup medals, and assisting them to their initial win in the All-Ireland League in 1991). Educated at Christian Brothers College, Cork (captaining them to Munster Junior and Senior Schools victories), and at U.C.C., he has been capped for Ireland at all four levels available to him, Schools (twice capped in 1977), Under 23, 'B', and at Full. Winning his first senior cap against Australia in 1981, he was selected for the Lions tour of New Zealand in 1983 (not joining it until late in the tour due to injury). He is the 3rd Cork Con man to captain Ireland, doing so 17 times in all, 1986-1991, and was captain of the Five Nations versus the Overseas XV at Twickenham in 1986, and of Ireland in the inaugural World Cup in 1987. A great line-out specialist, he was a vital member of both of Ireland's Triple Crown wins of 1982 and 1985 (beng one of only 6 players to play in all six matches), and also the International Championship win of 1983. One of the greats of Irish rugby, his first 44 international caps for his country were consecutive (behind only Willie John McBride ans Philip Orr in such feats in world rugby), and his tally of 52 caps in the 11 seasons up to 1992 make him Ireland's 6th most capped player.

LENIHAN, JOHN.

Champion hill racer. From Castleisland, Co Kerry. Club: An Riocht AC. A former track runner, he switched to hill running in the late eighties, first specializing in the long course. Switching to the shorter event (actually run up and down a mountain), in 1991 he won the Up and Down division at the 7th World Cup Championship in Hill Running, ran over 10,000 metres over a course at Zermatt in Switzerland. In the same race in 1992, held at the Bardonecchia ski resort in Italy, he finished 6th. A farmer.

LENIHAN, WILLIAM (WILLIE).

Amateur international bantamweight boxer. Club: Arbour Hill. He won his only Irish National Senior Championship title at bantamweight in 1941. Seven years later, without having won another national title in the intervening years, he was selected for, and reached the last 8 in, the Olympic Games bantamweight division at the 1948 games in London, thus finishing equal 5th.

LENNON, JOE.

G.A.A. football centre-fielder and left-halfback, Down. Born in Poyntzpass in 1934. Clubs: Aghaderg and John Mitchel's of Birmingham. A product of St Colman's College, Newry, he won Ulster medals in both Colleges and Minor football championship level in 1952. First playing for Down senior's in 1952, he became a winner of 3 All-Ireland Senior Football Championship winner's medals with Down, in 1960, 1961, and in 1968 when he was captain of the side which beat Kerry by 2-12 to 1-13. He won a total of 7 Ulster Senior Football Championship medals, in 1959, 1960,

1961, 1963, 1965, 1966, 1968, and in 1970. He also helped his county to 3 National Football League titles, in 1960, 1962, and as captain in 1968. He won a total 4 Railway Cup medals with Ulster, in 1960 (his first year playing for the province), 1964, 1966, and in 1968 (when he became the 4th Down player to captain a winning Railway Cup side). A physical education teacher, he wrote a popular book about fitness for gaelic football.

LEWIS, D ALAN.

Cricket international batsman. Born 1st June 1964. Club: Dublin Y.M.C.A. First capped for Ireland in 1984, up to the end of the 1993 season he had been capped 70 times, and had scored 2,170 runs (the 6th biggest tally for an Irishman) in 94 innings for an average of 27.12 runs per innings, scoring 2 centuries (with a best innings of 136 runs). He has also taken 45 wickets (off 60 innings bowled) for an average of 39.66 runs per wicket, and has taken 24 catches for Ireland. His father Ian Lewis (born in Dublin 29th September 1935) was capped for Ireland 20 times between 1955 and 1973 (with a batting average of 12.60), and was President of the I.C.U. in 1989.

LEYDEN, P J (PADDY).

Amateur international golfer. Club: Spanish Point. He won the South of Ireland Championship at nearby Lahinch 4 times (the 2nd highest tally after John Burke cv) in 5 years, in 1953, and for three years in succession, 1955, 1956 and 1957 (he had been runner-up in 1950). He was runner-up in the 'West' in 1959. He played 34 interprovincial matches in 6 consecutive series for Munster from 1956 to 1961, wining 14 and halving 6; he also played 20 Home international matches for Ireland in the 1950's, winning 8 and halving 2.

LEYDEN, SEAMUS.

G.A.A. football half and full forward, Galway. He won an All-Ireland M.F.C. winner's medal with Galway minors in 1960. Having played in a losing All-Ireland Senior Football Championship final with Galway in 1966, he was a member of the famous winning 3-in-a-row side of 1964, 1965, and 1966, all at left half-forward. Also winning Connacht S.F.C. medals in 1968, 1970 and 1971, in 1971 he won an All-Star in the inaugural year at left corner forward, a year in which Galway lost in the All-Ireland S.F.C. final to Offaly. He won his solitary Railway Cup medal with Connacht in 1967.

LIGHTFOOT, EDDIE J ('NED').

Rugby international right-winger. Club: Lansdowne (winning Leinster Senior Cup medals in 1930, 1931 and 1933). Eight times a Leinster interprovincial, he was capped 11 times on the wing for Ireland between 1931 and 1933 (including being part of Ireland's shared win of the International Championship in 1932), scoring 3 international tries, and in 1931 was part of the famous all-Lansdowne international three-quarter line, with Eugene Davy, Morgan Crowe and Jack Arigho.

LINDSAY, HARRY A.

Rugby international forward. Clubs: Dublin University and Armagh. Born in Armagh. A product of Santry College, he was capped 13 times for Ireland between 1893 and 1898 (scoring one try), being a member of the Triple Crown-winning Irish side of 1894, and the International Championship-winning side of 1896.

LINDSAY, PAT.

G.A.A. football full-back, Roscommon. Born in 1949. Clubs: St Faithleach's (winning 3 Roscommon S.F.C. medals), Glencar (Leitrim) and Shannon Gaels (Cavan). He won a Connacht M.F.C. medal in 1966 and played Under 21 in 1970-1971. Playing senior inter-county football from 1970 to 1985, he was a member of the Roscommon side which captured 5 Connacht Senior Football Championship titles, in 1973 and then in 4 successive wins; in 1977, 1978, 1979 and in 1980 when they went on to be beaten in the All-Ireland S.F.C. final. Winning a National Football League medal in 1979, he, after being a replacement All-Star in 1975, won his only actual All-Star award in 1977 at full-back (when he was Connacht's only All-Star of that year). He became the Roscommon Under 21 trainer in 1991-93.

LINDE, HENRY EYRE.

National Hunt trainer. A Co Kildare farmer based at Eyrefield, he was probably Ireland's most successful jump trainer of the 19th century and up to World War II. Apart from having a third and a remarkable five 2nd places in the Aintree Grand National, he won the Liverpool race three times: in 1880 with Empress, in 1881 with Woodbrook, and in 1889 with Frigate. He won the Grand Steeplechase de Paris 4 times, in 1882, 1883, 1890 and 1893, and was also successful in 2 Lancashire Chases, in 1880 and in 1883.

LINDEN, PADDY.

G.A.A. football goalkeeper, Monaghan. Born in 1955. Club: Ballybay. Starting his senior inter-county career in 1977, he was goalkeeper on the Monaghan side which won the Ulster Senior Football Championship in both 1985 and 1988. He was in goals for Monaghan's only success in the National Football League, in 1985. In 1988 he became a popular choice as All-Star goalkeeper, in view of his sterling service to the county.

LINNANE, SYLVIE.

G.A.A. hurling corner-back, Galway. Club: Gort (being on the side which lost the All-Ireland Club Championship final of 1984). He has won 3 All-Ireland Senior Hurling Championship medals with Galway, in 1980 at right half-back, and in 1987 and 1988 at right corner-back, also featuring in four losing S.H.C. finals of 1979 (as a sub), 1981, 1985 and 1986. He was captain of the winning Railway Cup Connacht side in 1983, the 4th Galway player to hold this position, winning medals also in 1980, 1982, 1986 and 1987. He has won 3 All-Star awards, in 1985 and 1986 at left full-back, and in 1988 at right corner-back.

LIPTON, SIR THOMAS Johnstone.

Yachtsman. Born in Glasgow, Scotland of Irish parents, 19th May 1850. He died in London on 2nd October 1931. He represented Ireland (under the banner of the Royal Ulster Yacht Club) in the America's Cup run-offs on 5 successive stagings (1899, 1901, 1903, 1920 and 1930), calling his craft 'Shamrock' each time. Although he lost each time to an American yacht, he was so sportsmanlike and gracious in defeat that he was plauded as 'the world's best loser'. For his yachting performances, in 1930 he was awarded a gold cup for sportsmanship by the Americans. He is best known as a highly successful tea merchant.

LISTON, EOIN ('THE BOMBER').

G.A.A. football full-forward, Kerry. Born in Ballybunion, 17th October 1957. Club: Beale. After winning an All-Ireland Under 21 medal with Kerry in 1977, he went on to play an important role in Kerry's successful run, playing on 6 winning All-Ireland Senior Football Championship sides, being an integral cog in the 4-in-a-row of 1978 (scoring 2-3 against Dublin in the final), 1979, 1980 (he did not play in this final due to injury although he did recieve a medal), and 1981; and again for the 3-in-a-row side of 1984, 1985, and 1986, being on the losing side to Offaly in 1982. He won Railway Cup medals with Munster in 1981 and 1982. One of the modern game's best full-forwards, he has won 4 All-Star awards, 3 in succession (in 1980, 1981, and 1982) at full-forward, and in 1984 at centre half forward. He also played international Compromise Rules football against Australia. He came out of retirement briefly in a failed attempt to win another Munster S.F.C. medal.

LLOYD, John HARDRESS.

Polo player. Born 14th August 1874, he died in 1952. As one of the 4-man Ireland team which represented Great Britain in the 1908 Olympic Games in London, he won a bronze medal. However, there were only 3 teams entered, and the Ireland team was beaten by the gold medalists, Roehampton by 5-1.

LLOYD, RICHARD Averil. (DICKIE).

Rugby international outside-half, and scrum-half. Born in Tamnamore, Dungannon, 4th August 1891, died in Belfast 1950. Clubs: Dublin University and Liverpool. He was capped 19 times for Ireland over an 11 year period which spanned World War One, between 1910 and 1920. A brilliant kicker, incomparable for his era, be it place, drop or punt kick, he holds the record for most conversions in an International Championship season by an Irishman (7 in 1912-1913). He captained Ireland 11 times, including leading his country to a share in the International Championship in 1912. He kicked 7 drop goals for Ireland, which stayed as the record until 1982. A brilliant footballer, he was also a talented cricket international, once setting Trinity club's highest ever stand of 323 in a match, along with H M Read (cv).

LOCKHART, NORMAN.

Soccer international outside left. Born in Belfast, 4th March 1924. Clubs: Linfield (with whom he won Irish F.A. Cup medals in both 1945 and 1946), Swansea, Coventry (for whom he scored 41 league matches in 182 games over 5 years), Aston Villa, and Bury. He was capped 8 times for Northern Ireland between 1947 and 1956, scoring 3 international goals.

LOFTUS, MICK.

G.A.A. footballer and administrator. Born in Kiltoom, Co Roscommon, he has lived most of his life in Crossmolina, Co Mayo. He won 2 All-Ireland Junior Football Championships with Mayo, in 1950 and 1957, and was a sub in Mayo's 1950 senior All-Ireland Senior Football Championship victory. He refereed the 1968 All-Ireland S.F.C. final between Kerry and Galway, and was President of the G.A.A. 1985-1987.

LONG, DAVID C.

Amateur international golfer. Born in Belfast, 13th October 1952. Club: Shandon Park (winning 4 Senior Cup medals in 1971, 1972, 1973 and 1978, and 3 Barton Shield medals in 1975, 1979 and 1985). He won the 'South' in 1974 (and was runner-up in 1973), the 'West' in 1979 (beating Walker Cup player Arthur Pierse on the 8th tie hole in the final), and he 'North' in both 1981 and 1982 (being runner-up in 1984). He also won the prestigious British Open Amateur Strokeplay in 1979. He played 78 interprovincial matches for Ulster between 1973 and 1986 (placing him 2nd in caps won for Ulster), winning 36: he played 42 Home international matches in 7 series between 1973 and 1984, winning 23 and halving 6, with a success rate of 61.9%: and he played 6 matches in the European Team championship of 1979, winning 2.

LONG, DENIS.

G.A.A. football midfielder, Cork. Born in 1949. Club: Austin Stacks, Tralee (gaining an All-Ireland Club football winner's medal at centre half-forward in 1977, and 3 Kerry SFC medals) and Millstreet. He won an All-Ireland M.F.C. medal with Cork in 1967, and an All-Ireland Under 21 medal Championship in 1970. Playing senior inter-county football for Cork from 1969 to 1977, he won 3 Munster S.F.C. medals (in 1971, 1973 and 1974), and he was in centrefield when Cork won the All-Ireland Senior Football Championship in 1973. He won 3 succesive Railway Cup medals with Munster, in 1975, 1976, and 1977. He won 2 All-Stars awards, in 1973, and in 1975 when he was the solitary Cork man in the team.

LOTTY, ALAN.
G.A.A. hurling full-back line and half-back player, Cork. Club: Sarfield's. He was at full-back on the Cork minors which won the All-Ireland M.H.C. in 1938. He then went on to win 5 All-Ireland Senior Hurling Championship medals with Cork, in the great 4-in-a-row of 1941, 1942, 1943 and 1944, and again in 1946. He also played on the Cork sides beaten in the All-Ireland S.H.C. finals of both 1939 and 1947. He won National Hurling League medals with Cork in 1940, 1941 and 1948.

LOUGHMAN, EILEEN.
Orienteerer. Club: Curragh-Naas Orienteering Club (being a founder member). Introduced to the sport in 1975, she has had many successes in Ireland (including as a member of Irish Relay Championship sides), England and Scotland. She has represented Ireland at 9 World Championships (a joint-record with a Swedish athlete), in Scotland, Norway, Finland, Switzerland, Hungary, Australia, France, Sweden and Czechoslovakia. She was runner-up to the Irish Champion in 1993. Also a mountain racer, she has run also in the Dublin City Marathon. She is also heavily involved with the administration of orienteering in Ireland.

LOUGHNANE, BILL (WILLIE).
G.A.A. hurling left full-forward, Dublin. Club: U.C.D. Born in Feakle, Co Clare, 5th August 1915. He won an All-Ireland Senior Hurling Championship with Dublin in 1938, scoring a goal in the final. He later became a Senator, and a Fianna Fail T.D. for Clare and Galway West 1968 to 1982. He also won an All-Ireland Championship with the Tulla Ceili Band as a fiddler. He was chairman of the Clare G.A.A. County Board 1958-1962.

LOUGHNANE, FRANCIS.
G.A.A. hurling right half-forward, Tipperary. Born in 1946. Club: Roscrea (helping the club to win 3 Tipperary SHC, including it's first ever in 1968, and also being a member of the side which won the inaugural All-Ireland Club Hurling Championship in 1971). Having been a member of the Tipperary minor's beaten in the All-Ireland M.H.C. final of 1962, he won an All-Ireland Under 21 championship medal as Tipp's captain in its inaugural year of 1964. Debuting in senior inter-county hurling in 1967, he was a member of the only Tipperary side to win an All-Ireland S.H.C. title in the 70's decade, in 1971, being also a sub for their losing S.H.C. final of 1968. Collecting 3 Oireachtas medals, he won a Railway Cup medal in 1976 with Munster. A fine score-getter, he has won 3 All-Star awards in succession, in 1971 (the inaugural year), 1972, and 1973, all at right wing forward.

LOUGHNANE, GER.
G.A.A. hurling right half-back, Clare. Born in 1954. Clubs: St Patrick's T.C. (Dublin), and Feakle. Making his senior inter-county hurling for Clare in 1972, he was a star member of the Clare side which won 2 National League titles in 1977 and 1978 (both against Kilkenny), having lost the 1976 final in a replay against Kilkenny, and who were beaten in 4 Munster S.H.C. finals in the 1970's, in 1972, 1974, 1977, and 1978. He won 3 Railway Cup medals with Munster, as a sub in his debut provincial year in the 1976 final, and again in 1978 and 1981 (at right corner back). At his peak one of the game's best right half-back's, he won 2 All-Star awards, in 1974 (making him the first Clareman to be so honoured) and again in 1977, both at right half-back.

LOUGHRAN, EAMONN.
Amateur and professional boxer. From Ballymena, he was born there on 5th June 1970. As a teenage amateur he won a World Junior Championship silver medal in 1987 in Cuba. Turning into a welterweight professional in 1987, he fulfilled his promise in November 1992 when capturing the British Commonwealth welterweight title when stopping the experienced Jamaican-born Canadian Donovan Boucher in the 3rd round of their bout at Doncaster.

LOWEY, JOHN.

Boxer. Born in Belfast on 6th August 1966. As an amateur, a member of the Ledley Hall club, he fought 140 amateur bouts, 18 for Ireland, and won 2 Irish Senior National titles at bantamweight in 1987 and 1988 (where his rivalry with Roy Nash is notable). He boxed well in the 1988 Olympic Games in Seoul, after which he turned pro, with fine intitial success, winning his first 13 bouts.

LOWRY, BRENDAN.

G.A.A. football left corner-forward, Offaly. Born in 1959. A useful soccer player in his youth (he was voted in 1981 as Offaly's Soccer Player of the Year while with Ferbane Town), he played his first senior G.A.A. game for the county in 1981, and in a career that stretched into the 1990's he has always played in the No 15 jersey. A prolific scorer, he was a member of the Offaly side which achieved the famous victory over Kerry in the 1982 All-Ireland Senior Football Championship final, having also played on the side beaten by the Kingdom in 1981. His older brother Sean (cv) and another brother Mick also played in the 1982 win. Brendan won an All-Star award in the left full-forward position in 1982.

LOWRY, DINNY.

Soccer international goalkeeper. Clubs: St Patricks Athletic (with whom he won F.A.I. Cup medals in 1959 and in 1961), and Bohemians (winning an F.A.I. Cup medal in 1970). He was capped once as a substitute for the Republic of Ireland in 1962 against Austria.

LOWRY, SEAN.

G.A.A. footballing back and forward, Offaly. From Ferbane, he won 2 All-Ireland Senior Football Championship winner's medals with Offaly, being at centre half-back in the 1972 win, and again in that position in the 'Seamus Derby' win over Kerry in 1982. He was at full-forward on the Offaly side beaten in the All-Ireland S.F.C. final of 1981 (having also won Leinster S.F.C. medals in 1973 and 1980). He is one of only 5 footballers to win All Star awards as both a back and as a forward. He won his first award in 1979 at full-forward, while in 1982 he was honoured at centre half-back. An older brother of Brendan Lowry (cv).

LUCEY, JIMMY, NOEL and VINCENT.

G.A.A. football brothers, Kerry. Both Jimmy (a midfielder) and Noel (a centre half-back) were on the Kerry side which won the All-Ireland Senior Football Championship in 1962. Three years later their brother Vincent was at right half-forward on the Kerry side beaten by Galway in the All-Ireland S.F.C. final. Vincent was again in the Kerry side which lost the 1965 All-Ireland final as well, again to Galway.

LYNCH, BRENDAN.

G.A.A. football right half-forward, Kerry. Born 3rd October 1949. Clubs: Mid-Kerry (being a member of the side which won it's first county championship in 50 years in 1967), U.C.D. (winning 2 Sigerson Cup medals), and Beauford. A goalkeeper in the Kerry minors which lost the All-Ireland M.F.C. final in 1965 to Derry, he won a Munster Colleges medal with St Brendan's Killarney. He went on to win 3 All-Ireland Senior Football Championship winner's medals with Kerry, in 1969, 1970, and in their 1975 win over Dublin, all at right half-forward, and played in All-Ireland S.F.C. final losses of 1968 (as the youngest in the side) and 1972, when he had a fine game in the drawn encounter against Offaly, scoring 1-7. He captained the only Combined Universities side ever to win the Railway Cup, in the historic 1973 win over Connacht, winning a medal again in 1975 with Munster. He won 4 National Football League medals with Kerry, in 1969, 1971, 1972 (as a sub), and in 1973.

LYNCH, FRANK.

G.A.A. football left half-forward, Louth. Club: Geraldines, Haggardstown. At the age of 18, he was the youngest member of the Louth side which won the

1957 All-Ireland Senior Football Championship against Cork, the only time Louth won the Sam Maguire Cup. He won a Railway Cup medal with Leinster in 1961, and was a sub in the Leinster win in 1962. He was Louth County Chairman in 1976-80.

LYNCH, GER.

G.A.A. football left half-back, Kerry. Club: Valentia. He has won 3 All-Ireland Senior Football Championship medals with Kerry, playing at left half-forward on each of Kerry's fine 3-in-a-row successes of 1984, 1985, and 1986. He has recieved one All-Star award, in 1987 at left wing-back.

LYNCH, JOHN.

G.A.A. football left full-back, Tyrone. He was a key member of the Tyrone side which reached the final of the 1986 All-Ireland Senior Football Champinship, also playing on the side which won the Ulster S.F.C. title in 1984. He has won one All-Star award, in 1986 at left corner-back.

LYNCH, JACK.

G.A.A. hurling mid-fielder, and footballing forward, Cork. Born in Cork, 15th August 1917. Clubs: Glen Rovers (hurling, winning 10 county championship medals), and St Nicholas (football); also Civil Service (with whom he shared in the club's first ever Dublin SFC in 1944). First playing senior inter-county hurling for Cork in 1935, he was on the famous Cork hurling side which won 4 successive All-Ireland Senior Hurling Championship titles in the early forties, 1941, 1942 (when he captained the side in their 2-14 to 3-4 win over Dublin), 1943, and 1944. In 1945 he played in the victorious Cork side which won their first ever All-Ireland Senior Football Championship title. Then, by helping Cork to win yet another senior hurling title again in 1946, he became the only player to play in 6 successive winning senior All-Ireland sides. He played on 2 losing Cork S.H.C. finals, as captain in 1939, and again in 1947, thus becoming the only player to play in 7 consecutive senior All-Ireland finals. He also featured in the great Munster finals against Tipperary in the years of 1949 and 1950, before retiring in 1951. He won 3 National Hurling League medals, in 1940, 1941 and 1948, and also won 3 Railway Cup hurling medals with Munster, in 1942, 1943 (as Cork's 4th player to captain a winning side), and 1944. In the Sunday Independent hurling 'Team of the Century' picked to celebrate the Centenery Year in 1984, he was placed at centre-field alongside Lory Meagher of Kilkenny (cv). He was elected into the Texaco Hall of Fame in 1983, the 2nd hurler to be so elevated. His sporting feats gave him a national profile, and after entering politics as a T.D. in 1948, he went on to become Fianna Fail Taoiseach for 2 periods, 1966-73 and 1977-79.

LYNCH, MARTIN.

G.A.A. football midfielder, Kildare. Club: Clane. He was one of the key members of the plucky Kildare side which reached the National Football League final in 1991, his high-fielding and point taking ability shining through. He also helped his county to reach the Leinster S.F.C. final against Dublin in both 1992 and 1993. He became only the 2nd Kildareman to win an All-Star award, when in 1991 he won a midfield spot, 13 years after Ollie Crinigan's previous All-Star award.

LYNCH, MICK.

Soccer forward. Clubs: Ards, Shamrock Rovers (playing for them twice, winning a League of Irealnd winners medal in 1958-59), Drumcondra, Ballymena, Ards, Bohemians (twice), Drogheda, Waterford (winning League of Ireland winners medals in both 1965-66 and 1967-68). He was twice leading goalscorer in the League of Ireland season, in 1962-63 with 12 goals and in 1965-66 with 17 goals. He was uncapped.

LYNCH, NOEL.

International archer. From Co Kildare, he was born in 1956. Club: Kildare Archers. He was Irish National champion in 1988 and 1990, and was Irish Open Champion in 1988, 1989 and 1992, and also held the Irish 50 metres record. He has represented Ireland at 2 Olympic Games (Seoul in 1988 and Barcelona in 1992), 2 World Championships (1989 and 1991), and 3 European Championships (in 1986, 1990 and 1992). Archer of the Year in 1990 and 1991, he won an international tournament in Malta in 1992. A fitter, he was named as Delta Airline Sportsperson of the Year in 1991.

LYNCH, PATSY.

G.A.A. footballer, Cavan. He is the youngest player to appear in an All-Ireland Senior Football Championship final, as he was a mere 16 years old when playing on the losing Cavan team in the 1928 decider against Kildare. He later went on to win an All-Ireland Senior Football Championship medal with Cavan, in their triumph of 1933, when he was then aged 22.

LYNCH, PAUDIE.

G.A.A. football midfielder, left half-back and left-corner back, Kerry. Club: Beauford. Born in 1951. A member of the winning Kerry All-Ireland Under 21 Championship final side of 1973, he had been on the losing side in 1972. He later won 5 All-Ireland Senior Football Championship medals with Kerry, in 1975, and as a constant member of the great 4-in-a-row team of 1978, 1979, 1980, and 1981. He also played on 3 losing All-Ireland S.F.C. final Kerry sides, in 1972, 1976 and 1982. He was honoured with 3 All-Star award selections, in 1974 at centrefield, in 1978 at left half-back, and in 1981 at left full-back. A younger brother of Brendan Lynch (cv), he played alongside him in the winning S.F.C. side of 1975. He retired in 1984.

LYNCH, JOHN Francis (SEAN).

Rugby international prop-forward. Born in Dublin, 22nd September, 1942. Club: St Mary's (assisting the club to 4 Leinster Senior Cup wins, in 1969, 1971, 1974 and 1975, and also to win the inaugural Leinster Senior League competition in 1971-72). Capped for Leinster 16 times between 1969 and 1975, he was capped 17 times for Ireland between 1971 and 1974. Having toured Argentina with Ireland in 1970, he went on the British and Irish Lion's tour of Australia and New Zealand in 1971, and played in all four of the historic winning Test series against the All Blacks, which was won by 2-1 with one draw. A publican.

LYNCH, TOM.

Greyhound trainer. From Blanchardstown, Co Dublin, he was born in 1909. He won the Irish Derby 4 times as a trainer (then a record, since equalled by his brother-in-law Gay McKenna cv), 3-in-a-row with the great Spanish Battleship, in 1953, 1954 and 1955, and also in 1967 with Russian Gun (he also trained the 2nd dog in this race 4 times, in 1944, 1951, 1968 and 1969). He also trained the winner of the Irish Oaks 4 times (Lovely Louise in 1948, twice with Peaceful Lady in 1952 and 1953, and in 1957 with Gallant Maid). His total tally of 11 Irish Classic winners was made up by Mark Anthony in the 1970 Irish St Leger, Spanish Battleship in the 1955 Irish Laurels, and the 1960 Produce Stakes with Springvalley Grand. In 1968 he was chosen as Texaco Sportstar of the Year for Greyhound Racing. His son Thomas (born in 1953), trained the winner of the 1988 Irish Grand National, Handball.

LYNE, TADGIE.

G.A.A. football left half-forward, Kerry. Clubs: Dick Fitzgerald's (winning a Kerry county championship medal in 1951), Dr Crokes (winning a Kerry county championship medal in 1956) and Castleisland Desmonds. Having been on the Kerry minors which were beaten in the All-Ireland M.F.C. final in 1938, he later won 3 All-Ireland Senior Football Championship titles with Kerry, in 1953 (scoring 5 points in the final), 1955 (known to this day as 'Tadgie Lyne's All-Ireland', when he scored 5-42 in the championship), and 1959. Kerry's leading scorer in 1955, 1956 and 1959, he was also on losing All-Ireland final sides in both 1954 and 1960. He played Tailteann Games for Ireland in 1953, 1954 and 1955. His older brother Jackie Lyne, a left full-forward, won 2 All-Ireland Senior Football Championship medals with Kerry, in 1946, and alongside Tadgie in 1953, also winning 3 Railway Cup medals with Munster in 1946, 1948 (the 4th Kerryman to captain a winning side), and 1949. Another brother Denny won a Sam Maguire Cup medal in 1946, and was captain of the Kerry side defeated in the Polo Ground All-Ireland final of 1947 (all-three brothers were on the same Kerry side in the Munster final of 1945). Tadgie's son Domo won a 1985 All-Ireland senior club title with Castleisland Desmonds. Jackie is an uncle of Pat Spillane (cv).

LYNG, RICHARD (DICK).

Handballer. A Wexfordman, he won 2 titles in the 1970 World Championship, capturing the doubles event with Seamus Buggy, and also being a member of the winning Irish team. He was B&I Handballer of the Year in 1978 and 1982. Having first come to notice when winning the Irish Minor Softball Singles in 1961, he won the Gael-Linn title in 1970, 1971, 1973, and in 1978. He won the Irish Senior Softball Singles title in 1978, and Doubles in 1977 and 1979.

LYONS, ERNIE.

Motorcycle racer. Born in Co Kildare 1914. An all-round motor cyclist, he competed successfully in road racing, trials, scrambles, grasstrack, sprints and hill-climbs. He won the 1939 North-West 200 in the 500cc class, and at the age of 32 won the Senior Manx Grand Prix in the Isle of Man in 1946. He never won an Isle of Man T.T. race, but had a 2nd and a 3rd in the 1949 season. In October 1946 he astonished the motorsport world when he he set the fastest time in the famous Shelsley-Walsh Hill-Climb in England, scaling the hill on a 500cc Triumph in 39.44 seconds, faster than all other cylces and cars. A farmer in Kill, Co Kildare.

LYONS, KAY.

G.A.A. Camogie player, Dublin. Club:. She has won 8 All-Ireland Senior Camogie Championship winner's medals with Dublin, in the great era for the capital county, when they won 10 successive titles between 1957 and 1966. She is a relation of the great Kilkenny hurler, Jimmy Langton.

LYONS, MICK.

G.A.A. football full-back, Meath. Born in 1958. Club: Summerhill (winning 3 successive county championship medals in 1976, 1977 and 1978). Making his senior inter-county debut for Meath in 1979, he won a Leinster S.F.C. first in 1986. He then captained the Meath side which won it's first All-Ireland Senior Football Championship title for 20 years when they defeated Cork by 1-14 to 0-11 in the 1987 final, and won his 2nd Sam Maguire medal in 1988 against the same opposition after a replay (he was captain for the drawn game). Winning National League winner's medals in both 1986 and 1990, he was on the Meath side defeated in the All-Ireland S.F.C. finals of both 1990 and 1991. He won a Railway Cup medal as a substitute in 1987. He has won 2 All-Star awards, in 1984 and 1986, both at full-back.

LYONS, PADDY.

Amateur light-heavyweight boxer. Club: Arbour Hill. He has won 5 Irish National Senior Championships at 2 different weights in the 1950's, 3 at light-heavyweight (1953, 1954, and 1955), and 2 at heavy-weight (1957 and 1958).

LYTLE, JAMES Hill and JOHN N.

Rugby international brothers. These two forwards, both products of Methodist College and both playing for the 7-in-a-row Ulster Senior Cup winning side from N.I.F.C. 1893-1899, played international rugby 12 and 8 times respectively for Ireland in the 1890's, and they were the first brothers in the history of rugby to play in all three matches of a Triple Crown-wimnning side, achieving this feat in 1894. John, having already scored the first ever 3-point try in international rugby by an Irish player in the the win over England that season, kicked a penalty against Wales to decide the fate of the Crown (it was the only score in the match), at Ballynafeigh, Belfast, and it was the first penalty goal ever to be scored by an Irishman. James's own individual claim to fame is being the first Irishman to share in 2 Triple Crown wins, in both 1894 and 1899.

M

MACARTNEY, A.

Soccer international player. Clubs: Ulster, Linfield (helping them to gain an Irish League Championship winner's medal), Everton, Belfast Celtic, and Glentoran. He was capped at senior level for the I.F.A. (Northern Ireland) 15 times between 1903 and 1909.

MACAULAY, JOHN (JACK).

Rugby international forward and administrator. 1866-1957. Club: Garryowen (captaining the club to their first 3 Munster Senior Cup wins in 1889, 1890 and 1891, while also winning medals in 1892, 1893, 1894, 1895, 1896, 1898 and 1899, a tally of 10, the first eight being successive). Although he was only good enough, at the age of 21, to play twice for Ireland, against England and Scotland in 1887 (he was said to be the first married man to be capped in international rugby, allegedly getting wed just to get leave of absence to play for Ireland), such was his influence in the formative years of Irish rugby, that he was an almost constant member of the Irish selection committee from 1895 to 1930. He was honorary treasurer of the Munster Branch for over 45 years, and was President of the I.R.F.U. in 1894-95. A miller's agent, he died in 1957.

MACK, GORDON S B ('CURLY').

Badminton and tennis international player. In badminton he won 6 Irish titles (including National Singles wins in 1920, 1922 and 1925, and Open Singles wins in 1923 and 1925), and was capped 21 times for Ireland between 1919 and 1932. For a period he was ranked No 2 in the world behind Frank Devlin (cv), with whom he forged the most devastating badminton pairs of the 1920's, winning the prestigious All-England Doubles title 6 times, in 1923, 1926, 1927, 1929, 1930 and 1931. He also won the All-England Singles title in 1924, and the Mixed title in 1923, to claim wins in all three available championships there. He also played Davis Cup tennis for Ireland. A headmaster at Sandford Park School, he later emigrated to the U.S.A..

MACKEN, EDDIE.

International showjumper. Born in Granard, Co Longford, October 20th 1949. Educated at St Mel's College, Longford. He rode internationally for Ireland as early as 1970, in the Nations Cup at Dublin's R.D.S. on Morning Light. In 1974, he was runner-up in the World Championships on Pele, to Hartwig Steeken, again taking the silver medal in 1978 when with Boomerang he lost by the smallest margin in World Championship history (0.25 points). In Vienna in 1977 he was 2nd in the European Championships. He was top showjumper in the computer ratings in Europe in four successive years, 1976, 1977, 1978, and 1979, and finished 3rd in the World Cup Finals in 1979. On the famous Boomerang, he won 4 successive

Hickstead Derbys', 1976, 1977, 1978 and 1979 (he also won the Hamburg Derby 3 times), and was vital part of Irish team which won the Aga Khan Cup for three years on the trot, 1977, 1978, and 1979, and in 3 subsequent years, including 1992. Since 1979 he has had over 15 top 8 placings in World Cup events, winning in Milan in 1984 on Carroll's El Paso. He has represented Ireland in the Olympic Games once, in Barcelona in 1992. He runs his own stud farm at Rafeehan, near Kells, Co Meath. He has been voted as Texaco's Equestrian Sports Sportstar of the Year 5 times, in 1974, 1975, 1977, 1978, and 1979, and is the only sportsperson to win the Texaco Supreme Sportstar award on 2 occasions (winning in 1976 and 1978).

MACKEN, GERRY.

International oarsman and bobsleigh driver. From Athlone. Rowing Clubs: Athlone BC, D.U.B.C., Lady Elizabeth BC and Neptune BC. He won five Irish titles in the Eights discipline, in 1981, 1984, 1985, 1986 and in 1987. He was a member of the eights team which won the Ladies Plate at Henley in 1986, and has also rowed in 4 World Championships, 3 in succession in lightwiight coxless fours, 1981 at Munich, 1982 at Lucerne (finishing in 4th place), and in 1983 at Duisburg; his fourth was in the lightweight eights at Hazewinkel in 1982. In 1992 he was a bobsleigh driver on the Irish team which became the first from the Republic to compete in any Winter Olympics (when they finished 38th), held at Albertville. His brother J.A. Macken was on a side which won the 'Big Pot' (Irish Eights title) in 1976.

MACKEY, JOHN.

G.A.A. hurling right half-forward and full-forward, Limerick. Born in Castleconnell, Co Limerick in 1914. Club: Ahane. Educated at Limerick C.B.S. (with whom he won a Keane Cup medal in 1928). He won, along with his older brother Mick (cv), a record 20 Limerick Senior Championship medals, 15 of them in hurling (including two 7-in-a-rows, in 1933-39, and 1942-48 inclusive), and 5 Limerick SFC medals in a row, 1935-1939. Having first played minor hurling for Limerick in 1929 (he played senior county football first in 1932), he went on to win 3 All-Ireland Senior Hurling Championship winner's medals with Limerick, in 1934, 1936, and 1940, being also a member of 2 losing All-Ireland S.H.C. final sides, in 1933 and 1935. He was on also on six victorious Munster Raliway Cup sides, in 1935, 1937, 1938, 1939, 1940, 1943 (as a sub), and in 1944. His last major win was a National League with Limerick in 1947, having previously been a member of the Limerick side which won the league record 5-in-a-row, 1934, 1935, 1936, 1937, and 1938. He died in Dublin 1989, aged 75. His father, John 'Tyler' Mackey', was captain of the Limerick side of Castleconnell which were beaten in the 1910 All-Ireland senior hurling final by the Castleridge team from Wexford, his famous nickname coming from the name of a shop in which he bought a new pair of boots.

MACKEY, MICK.

G.A.A. hurling centre half-forward, Limerick. Born on 12th July 1912 in Castleconnell, Co Limerick, he died on 13th September 1982. Club: Ahane (with whom he won 20 Limerick Senior Championship medals, 15 in hurling, including two 7-in-a-rows, 1933-39, and 1942-48 inclusive, and 5 SFC medals, also inclusive 1935-1939). One of the true great's of hurling, his first senior game for Limerick was in 1930, against Kilkenny, when he was 18. Among his many great feats was against Tipperary in the 1936 Munster S.H.C. final, when he scored a record Munster final score of 5 goals and 3 points. He captained Limerick to win 2 All-Ireland Senior Hurling Championship titles, the 1936 victory over Kilkenny by 5-6 to 1-5, and in the 1940 win against Kilkenny by a margin of 3-7 to 1-7. He had also won an All-Ireland S.H.C winner's medal in 1934 in the defeat of Dublin, and was in 2 losing finals, in 1933 and 1935. He won 8 Railway Cup medals (a record for a Limerick-man), in 1934, 1935, 1937, 1938, 1939, 1940, 1943, and 1945, and won 5 National Hurling League medals on the trot in Limerick's wins of 1934, 1935, 1936, 1937 and 1938, captaining the side in the last 2 victories. He later trained the Limerick S.H.C. side (known as 'Mick Mackey Greyhounds') which beat the clear favourites, Clare in the 1955 Munster S.H.C. final. He is the son of a noted Limerick hurler, John 'Tyler' Mackey, and is the brother of John Mackey cv, (another brother Paddy appeared occasionaly in the county colours in the same period). He was the player who won more votes than any other hurler in the 1984 'Team of the Century', being placed at centre half-forward on the team by Sunday Independent readers. A biography, 'The Mackey Story' was written by Seamus O'Ceallaigh and Sean Murphy. Parc na nGael in Limerick has named a stand in his honour.

MACKEY, PATRICK J (PADDY or P.J.).

G.A.A. footballer and hurler, Wexford player. A dual All-Ireland senior championship winner, he won a Senior Hurling Championship medal with the Castle bridge side of Wexford in the 1910 final. He went on then to play for Wexford footballers from the Blues and Whites side in each of their 4-in-a-row All-Ireland Senior Football Championship wins in 1915, 1916, 1917, and 1918, one of 10 players to play in all four winning finals (if replays are counted, he appeared in 7 successive All-Ireland S.F.C. finals, as Wexford were beaten in the finals of 1913 and 1914). His tally of 5 All-Ireland senior championship medals was the joint-biggest haul to include both sports by any player until surpassed by Jack Lynch's 6-in-a-row in the 1940's.

MACKIE, John ALEXANDER (ALEX).

Soccer international right-back. Born in Belfast, 23rd February 1904. Clubs: Forth River, Arsenal (playing 119 matches for them 1922-26, helping them to their highest ever finish up to then in Division One, 2nd in 1925-26), Portsmouth (playing 257 matches for then in 8 years, and being on two F.A. Cup final losing sides, in 1924 and 1934), and Northampton. He won 3 caps for Northern Ireland, one in 1923, and two more 12 years later in 1935.

MACONACHIE, IAN C.

Badminton international player. Club: Sandford. A Geordie of Irish descent, he was capped 19 times for Ireland between 1924 and 1938. Although playing most of his badminton in England, he won 19 Irish National titles, and in 1937 won an All-England Mixed title with Thelma Kingsbury. Also a cricketer and golfer of some worth, he was the youngest player ever to captain a minor county (Northumberland), also playing with the M.C.C., and in golf played off a handicap of plus 3 at the Royal St George G.C.

MADDEN, OWEN.

Soccer international forward. Clubs: Cork City, Cork United. He was Cork United's leading scorer when they won the League of Ireland Championship in both 1940-41 and 1941-42, winning a third successive medal in 1943-44. His 4th and 5th League winner's medals followed with Cork United in the successive years of 1944-45 and 1945-46. He also won 2 F.A.I. Cup winner's medals with Cork United, in 1936 and in 1947 (when he was sent off while captaining the side). He was capped once each for the the Irish Free State (in 1936) and the Irish F.A. (in 1938), and also scored a goal in Inter-League matches.

MADELEY, J F DAVID.

Amateur international golfer. Born in Belfast in 1938. Clubs: Royal Belfast (winning their Scratch Cup 6 times) and Royal County Down. Becoming Ulster

Boys Open champion in 1959, he won the North of Ireland Championship in both 1962 and 1963. Selected for the British and Irish side against the Continent of Europe side in 1962, he went on to be selected for the Walker Cup series in 1963 (alongside Joe Carr and David Sheahan), halving one of his 2 matches played. He played 47 interprovincial matches for Ulster between 1959 and 1968, winning 29 and halving 4, a success rate of 66%; he also played 42 Home international matches in 7 successive series for Ireland from 1959 (when he won all 6 of his matches) to 1966, winning 26 and halving one of these in total, giving him a success rate of over 63%. His wife was an Ulster interprovincial golfer from 1965 to 1968, and played Home international golf for Ireland between 1964 and 1969.

MADDEN, PAT.

G.A.A. hurler, Galway. He was captain of the losing Galway side in the first ever All-Ireland Senior Hurling Championship final, held at Birr, when the Meelick club which he founded, were beaten by a Tipperary side from Thurles. In the 21-a-side game, held at Birr on 1st April 1888 (for the 1887 Championship), Tipp won by one goal, one point and a forfeit point. Madden was strongly associated with the Land League.

MAGAN, MARGO.

Champion swimmer. A daughter of Jim Beckett cv, she was born in 1930. At the age of 14 she became Irish Under 16 100 metres freestyle champion in 1944. She went on to win many Irish senior 100 and 200 metres titles. Eventually marrying a Kilashee, Co Longford farmer, she was a leading light (while a member of the Annally S.C.) of the Connacht Branch of the I.A.S.A. for many years. She became a single handicap golfer, and in 1988 became the inaugural Irish Senior Ladies champion.

MAGEE, LOUIS M.

Rugby international half-back. Born in Dublin, 25th March 1874, he died in Dunboyne in 1945. Clubs: Bective Rangers and London Irish. Playing for Leinster 13 times from 1894 to 1902, he was capped 27 times for Ireland between 1895 and 1904 (being the first Irish player to win 20 caps, and making him at the time Ireland's most capped player until 1910). He was honoured as captain of his country 9 times, and scored a total of 9 international points, from 2 tries and one penalty. He was captain of the victorious Triple Crown-winning side of 1899 (Ireland's 2nd of only six Triple Crown's), playing a captain's role by means of a brilliant last-minute tackle in the 3-0 win over Wales. His brother Joseph T (Joe) Magee, a Bective three-quarter, shared his first 2 international caps in 1895, and played 4 times for Leinster; he also won 2 Test places on the Lions tour of South Africa in 1896, and was also capped for Ireland at cricket in 1907. Joe was joined by Louis on that Lion's tour, during which Louis won 4 Test places, and together they were the first brothers to go on a Lion's tour and to play against South Africa in an international game. A third brother Jim played 3 times for Leinster. Louis is a brother-in-law of Tom Little, a Bective Rangers forward who was capped 7 times for Ireland (all with Louis) in the same era, including 2 of the Triple Crown matches of 1899. A relation of the same name, Louis Magee, a Bective Rangers 2nd row forward, played rugby over 10 times for Leinster in the late 1970's.

MAGEE, PAUL.

Ten pin bowling international player. Born in Dublin, he is the son of the R.T.E. sports commentator Jimmy Magee. He won a bronze medal at the European Youths Chamnpionships in the Doubles event in 1973 and went on to represent Ireland in many junior and senior events. In 1973 he also won a silver in the All Events category at the European Youths. He was Irish National Champion in 1990/1 and Irish Masters Champions in 1991. He represented Ireland in the

World Bowling Cup in Beijing in November 1991.

MAGILL, EDWARD (EDDIE).

Soccer international right full-back. Born in Carrickfergus, 17th May 1939. He joined Arsenal from Portadown in 1959, playing 131 first team matches for them 1959-65. He then joined Brighton in 1966, playing 50 league matches there (and helping them to gain promotion to Division Three). An under-23 international, he was capped 26 times for Northern Ireland between 1962 and 1966. He later took up soccer management in Denmark with 2 clubs, B1909 Odense and Frederikshavn.

MAGILTON, JIM.

Soccer international midfielder. Born in Belfast, 6th May 1969. Apprenticed to Liverpool (for whom he did not play a senior game in his time there), he moved to Oxford United, for whom he has scored 29 league goals in 129 appearences up to mid 1993. He was first capped for Northern Ireland in 1991, and up to July 1993 had been capped 15 times in the international side. These 15 caps, all gained while on the staff at the Manor Ground, made him surpass Ray Houghton as Oxford's most capped player.

MAGNIER, COLIN.

National Hunt jockey, and trainer. Born 16 June 1955. Riding 251 winners as an amateur jockey, his biggest successes were on For Auction (1982 Sweeps Handicap Hurdle, and the 1982 Champion Hurdle), and 2nd in the Grand National on Greasepaint in 1983. Other wins include the Galway Hurdle and the Kim Muir Chase. He took up training at Athboy in 1986.

MAGRATH, JOHN.

Squash and tennis international player. A dual international, he was capped 26 times for Ireland in squash between 1974 and 1976. He was the first men's player to win the Irish National (Close) Squash Championship 3 times, doing so in succession, 1973, 1974 and 1975. He also played Davis Cup tennis for Ireland, playing in Ireland's team in both their away win over Luxembourg and the home loss to Yugoslavia in 1970.

MAGUIRE, ADRIAN.

National Hunt jockey. Born in Dublin (but hailing from Kilmessan, Co Meath) on April 29th 1971. Showing great talent at a young age (he had won the 1990-91 Irish point-to-point jockey's championship), when only 19, and while still an amateur, he won the Kim Muir Chase in Cheltenham and the Irish Grand National on Omerta. The following year (1991-92), when not 21 yet and in his first year as a professional, he brought 25/1 shot Cool Ground home to win the Cheltenham Gold Cup. In the 1992-93 season he had 2 further winner's at Cheltenham, and reached a century of winners while finishing 3rd in the jockey's championship in Britain.

MAGUIRE, LIAM, DES, and BRENDAN.

G.A.A. footballing brothers, Cavan and Meath. All three brothers were born at Cornafean (and played for that club in Co Cavan), but lived in Co Meath. In the replayed 1952 All-Ireland Senior Football Championship final, the 3 brothers played with divided loyalties, both Liam and Des playing for the victorious Cavan team at centre half and left full back respectively, and Brendan at midfield for the losing Meath side.

MAGUIRE, PADDY.

Bantanweight boxer. Born in Belfast, 26th September 1948. As an amateur member of the Vauxhall Motors club he won the Irish National Senior Championship at flyweight in 1965, and won the bantamweight title in 1966 out of the South Belfast club. In his professional career as a bantamweight he fought 7 championship fights, losing 5 and drawing one of these, but winning the British Bantamweight crown in 1975 by defeating Dave Needham. In 1976 he fought a draw with Daniel Trioulaire, before losing his title in 1977 to Franco Zurco. In his 8 year professional career from 1969 to 1977, he won 26, drew one, and lost 8 of his 35 bouts. In 1975 he was selected as Texaco's boxing Sportstar of the Year.

MAGUIRE, SAM.

G.A.A. footballer, London. Born in Maulabracka (near Dunmanway), Co Cork, his career brought him to London, whom he played for 3 losing All-Ireland Senior Football Championship finals in 4 years, beaten by Tipperary in 1900, Dublin in 1901 (losing by a margin of 0-12 to 0-2, when he captained the London Hibernians team), and by Kerry in 1903. Later he was installed as President of the London County Board. A Protestant patriot, a member of the I.R.B., and a friend of Michael Collins, he died aged 48 in 1927. The trophy now awarded to the victorious side in each years All-Ireland Senior Football Championship, first presented in 1928 to Bill 'Squires' Gannon of Kildare, is named in his honour.

MAGUIRE, TOM.

G.A.A. football midfielder and centre half-back, Cavan. He was on the Cavan M.F.C. side beaten in the All-Ireland M.F.C. final of 1952. He was a member of the Cavan side which won 3 Ulster Senior Football Championship titles, in 1955, 1962, and 1964. He won Railway Cup medals with Ulster in 1956, 1960, 1963, 1964, and 1965 (his 5 medals placing him only one behind the county's best tally of Ray Carolan).

MAHER, ANTHONY (TONY).

G.A.A. hurling right full-back, Cork. Club: St Finbarr's (being a member of the side which captured the All-Ireland Club Championship in both 1975 and 1979). He won one All-Ireland Senior Hurling Championship medal in 1970 with Cork, being on the losing side in the S.H.C. finals of both 1969 and 1972. He won a Railway Cup medal with Munster in 1970. He was awarded 2 All-Stars, in each of the scheme's first two years (1971 and 1972), being selected at right corner-back both years.

MAHER, JOHN.

G.A.A. hurling centre half-back, Tipperary. From Killinan, he lived 1908 to 1990. Club: Thurles Sarsfields (winning 9 Tipperary county championship medals with them). Over a period of 17 years with the Tiperary senior side from 1929 to 1945, he won 3 All-Ireland Senior Hurling Champinship winner's medals, in 1930, 1937 and in 1945 when he captained the side (at the age of 37) which defeated Kilkenny by 5-6 to 3-6 in the decider. He won his 4th Munster S.H.C. medal in 1941. He won one Railway Cup medal with Munster in 1937, and an Oireachtas medal in 1945.

MAHER, Patrick JOSEPH (JOEY).

Handball player. Born in Drogheda, Co Louth, 30th March 1934. Club: St Mary's. Having won All-Ireland Junior handball titles at both softball and hardball in 1956, he went on to win 6 All-Ireland Senior Hardball Singles titles, in 1961, 1963, 1964, 1968, 1969 and 1970, and 6 All-Ireland Senior Softball Singles titles, in 1963, 1964, 1968, 1969, 1970, and 1973. He also won the Senior Hardball Doubles in 1964. Emigrating to Canada for 3 years in 1965, he won the Canadian Singles title in 1966, 1967, and 1968, having won the Canadian Doubles in 1965, and won the 1967 World Handball title while representing Canada. He was the first man to win the Gael Linn Cup 3 times, in 1960, 1962 and 1964, winning it again after his return from Canada in 1969.

MAHER, MICK ('BIG MIKEY').

G.A.A. hurler, Tipperary, From Tubberadora, he in one of only 3 men (see Christy Ring and 'Drug' Walsh) to captain 3 winning All-Ireland Senior Hurling Championship teams, in his case all in the space of 4 years. The years were when the Tipp side of Tubberadora won in 1895 (with a margin of 6-8 to 1-0 win over Kilkenny's Tullaroan), 1896 (when the Commercials side of Dublin were beaten by 8-14 to 0-4), and in the 7-13 to 3-10 win over Kilkenny's Threecastle Selection in 1898. He also won 3 other All-Ireland S.H.C. winner's medals, in the inaugural year of the competition with Thurles in 1887, in 1899 with Moycarkey, and his final medal in 1900 with Two-Mile-Borris, giving him a tally of 6 winner's medals. Regarded as one of the greats of Tipp hurling, he also had two brothers who each won 4 All-Ireland S.H.C. medals, J.... who won in the 3 years of Mick's captaincy, and again in 1899, and E.... who won also in the years of Mick's captaincy, and 1900. An uncle of Michael Maher (cv).

MAHER, MICHAEL.

G.A.A. hurling full-back, Tipperary. Born in 1930. Club: Holycross (winning 3 county championship medals, and with whom he was also a fine administrator). In a senior inter-county career that stretched from 1956 to 1966, he won 5 All-Ireland Senior Hurling Championship winner's medals with Tipperary, in 1958, 1961, 1962, 1964, and 1965, and was on the Tipperary side beaten in the 1960 All-Ireland final (thus playing in 6 All-Ireland finals in 8 years). With the Premier County he also won 6 National Hurling League medals, in 1957, 1959, 1960, 1961, 1964 and 1965. He won 4 Railway Cup medals with Munster, in 1958 (as a sub), 1959, 1961 and 1963. A nephew of Mick Maher (cv).

MAHER, PAT ('FOX').

G.A.A. hurler, Kilkenny. He was a member of Kilkenny sides which lost the first 5 All-Ireland Senior Hurling Championship finals in which the county competed, in 1893 (with the Confederation Selection), 1895 (with the Tullaroan Selection), 1897 (again with the Tullaroan Selection), 1898 (with the Threecasltes Selection), and the 1903 Home final (with the Threecastles Selection again). Eventually, in the last All-Ireland S.H.C. final in which he competed, he finally won a medal, in the Tullaroan win of the St Finbarr's Selection of Cork in 1904. He is regarded as one of the first great Kilkenny players.

MAHER, PETER.

Heavyweight boxer. Born 16th March 1869 at Gunnode, near Tuam, Co Galway, he died in Baltimore, Maryland, aged 71. He fought in Ireland, England and America. When in 1895 he beat George Godfrey in 6 rounds, and knocked out the New Zealander Steve O'Donnell after 63 seconds at Long Island, the then retiring world heavyweight champion, James J Corbett, 'presented' his title to Maher. However, this claim to the title was not taken seriously in world boxing circles, and was banished totally when in February 1896 Maher was knocked out after only 95 seconds by Bob Fitzsimmons in Langtry, Texas, spoiling the attempts by the organiser, the famous 'Judge' Roy Bean, to make it the first boxing match to be captured by moving picture (as the cameras were not yet ready when the fight ended). Before retiring in 1908 he fought many other contenders, but his chance had gone. He won 47 of his 77 professional fights. He was elected in 1978 to The Ring magazine's Hall of Fame, in the Old Timers Group.

MAHER, SEAN.

G.A.A. football midfielder, Mayo. Club: Dublin Civil Service. A member of the Mayo side which won the All-Ireland Under 21 Championship in 1983, he was again on the losing team in the following year's final. A fine fielder of a ball, he won Connacht S.F.C. medals in 1985, 1988, 1989 amd 1993, having first played championship football in 1984. In 1989 he was a member of the Mayo side which reached the All-Ireland Senior Football Championship final since 1951. His younger brother Greg, a Claremorris club player, also played in that 1989 final, and won an All-Ireland M.F.C. medal with Mayo in 1985.

MAHON, PADDY J.

Professional golfer. He won 3 successive Irish Professional Matchplay

Championship titles in the late 1930's, in 1937 at Portmarnock, in 1938 at Portrush, and in 1939 at Bundoran. He also won the Moran Cup in 1939.

MAHON, STEVE.

G.A.A. hurling midfielder, Galway. A member of the Galway Under 21 side which won the 1978 All-Ireland title, he went on to win All-Ireland Senior Hurling Championship medals with the county in 1980 and 1987, being on the losing All-Ireland S.H.C. final side for Galway 4 times, in 1979, 1981, 1985, and 1986. He has won 6 Railway Cup medals with Connacht, in 1980, 1982, 1983, 1985, and in 1987, and won a National Hurling League medal, in 1987. He has won 2 All-Star awards, in 1981 and 1987, both in the centre of the park.

MAHONY, HAROLD Sigerson.

Tennis player. Born in either Glasgow or Dromore Castle Co Kerry (on 13th February 1867), he always claimed to be an Irishman. He won 2 Singles and 3 Doubles British Covered Court Championship titles in the early 1890's, and also won the All-England Mixed Doubles every year from 1894 to 1898. One of the world's great tennis players around the turn of the century, he won the Wimbledon Men's Singles' championship title in 1896, beating R Doherty in the five set final by 6-2, 6-8, 5-7, 8-6, 6-3. He was also runner-up in this Wimbledon singles title 3 times, in 1893, 1897, and 1898, and was also Wimbledon mens doubles runner-up in both 1892 and 1903. He later won 3 Olympic Games medals, 2 silver (at mens singles when beaten by H Doherty, and with Mde Prevost in the mixed doubles) and a bronze (at mens doubles), all at the 1900 Games in Paris. He played tennis the world over, was a German Open winner in 1899, and was runner-up in the U.S double's title in 1897. He was killed in 1905 when he fell off his bicycle at the base of Caragh Hill in Co Kerry.

MAHONY, NOEL Cameron.

Cricket international right hand opening batsman. Born in Fermoy, Co Cork, 15th January 1913. He played cricket for Ireland 9 times between 1947 and 1953, captaining the side on 6 occasions. His first class career figures are 5-10-0-116-29-11.60-0-ct 3, while his batting figures in all matches for Ireland were: 299 runs, averaging 18.68, with a best of 48 against Yorkshire. He later took up coaching at Trinity College, becoming the first Irishman to gain the M.C.C. advanced coaching award, and was first N.C.A. director of cricket for All-Ireland. He also coached the Irish Ladies Cricket team for the inaugural Ladies Cricket World Cup in Australia in 1988, and was President of the I.C.U. in 1979. A useful rugby player also, he had won a Munster Senior Cup medal as an out-half with the Dolphin club in 1945.

MAHOOD, JACKIE.

Soccer international winger. Clubs: Belfast Celtic (a member of the side which won the 1928/29 Irish League with 48 out of a possible 52 points, while scoring 116 goals and being unbeaten, he also won Irish League medals in 1925-26, 1926-27 and 1927-28: and also won an Irish Cup medal in 1926), and Ballymena. He scored 50 goals from the left wing for Belfast Celtic, playing often alongside his talented brother, Stanley. He was capped 9 times for Ireland (the I.F.A) between 1926 and 1934, scoring 2 international goals, and he scored 6 Inter-League goals for the Irish League side.

MALONE, ANTHONY.

Pitch and putt player. Club: Lucan P.P.C.. Playing on the Dublin inter-county side 6 times, he won 2 Dublin championships, the 1983 strokeplay and the 1984 matchplay titles. He has won 2 Irish National Strokeplay Championships, in both 1988 and 1991 (and was runner-up in the same discipline in 1984), and has the talent to add to that tally.

MALONE, BRYAN P.

Amateur international golfer. Clubs: Sutton and Portmarnock. He won the 'West' in 1964 (and was runner-up in both 1971 and 1972), and the 'South' in 1975. He has played in a record 100 interprovincial matches for for his province Leinster, in 19 different series (during which he gained a record 10 series wins for any interprovincial player) between 1959 and 1981 (only Rupert de Lacy from Connacht has played in more interprovincial matches since 1956), winning 55 and halving 9, his 119 points gained making the most prolific points scorer in Irish interprovincial golf history (his success rate was 60%). He also played 30 Home international matches for Ireland in 5 series between 1959 and 1975, winning 13; he also played 7 European Team matches for Ireland, winning 4. He turned professional late in his career.

MALONE, GERRY.

Soccer international forward. Club: Shelbourne (winning League of Ireland Championship winner's medals in 1946-47 and in 1952-53). A goalscorer for Shels over a 10 year period (he scored 15 goals in 1955-56), he was capped once for the Republic of Ireland, against the Belgium in 1949.

MALONE, MICK.

G.A.A. hurling midfielder and half forward, Cork. Club: Eire Og. Having been on the All-Ireland winning Cork M.H.C. side of 1967, he was later a member of the Cork Under 21 side which won that All-Ireland competition in 1971. He went on to win 2 All-Ireland Senior Hurling Championship medals with Cork in 1976 and 1977 (being previously on the losing final side in 1972). He has won one All-Star award, in 1976 with fellow Corkman Pat Moylan in midfield.

MANCINI, TERRY J ('HENRY').

Soccer international defender and centre-half. Born to an Irish mother in Camden Town, London, 4th October 1942. Clubs: Watford (playing 66 games for them), Port Elizabeth (in South Africa), Orient (scoring 16 goals in 167 league matches from 1967 to 1971, winning a Third Division medal in 1971), Queen's Park Rangers (helping them with promotion to Division One for the first time in the club's history in 1973), Arsenal (playing 62 games for them 1974-76), Orient (again) and Aldershot. A member of a famous London boxing family, he was capped 5 times for the Republic of Ireland in 1974 and 1975. In 1989 he spent a short period as assistant manager at Luton.

MANDERS, CHARLES H W (CHARLIE).

Motorcycling and motor car road racer. Born in Dublin. One of Ireland's great motorcycling road racing stars of the 1930's; in nine years in the Isle of Man races from 1931 to 1939, he rode in 13 T.T. races, finishing in the top 6 places six times. He rode successfully in many pre-War continental Grand Prix, winning the 1933 French G.P at 250cc class. He also won the 1936 North-West 200 at 250cc class, and the 1938 Leinster 200 at 125cc class. A motor-cycling all-rounder, he also was a successful car racing driver, attaining many high places in Phoenix Park races in the 1930's, and finishing 3rd in the Cork O'Boyle Trophy in 1938, and 2nd in the Leinster Trophy at Tallaght in 1938.

MANGAN, JACK.

G.A.A. footballing goalkeeper, Galway. He captained Galway to win their first Sam Maguire Cup in 18 years in 1956, when they beat Cork by 2-13 to 3-7 inthe All-Ireland Senior Football Championship final. He had won a Connacht S.F.C. medal in 1954, and won 3 more when the county won in successive Connacht Senior Football Championships in 1956, 1957 and 1958. He also captained Connacht to their Railway Cup triumph in 1957, being only the 2nd Tribesman to do so, having previously won a medal in 1951.

MANNION, NOEL Patrick.

Rugby international No 8 forward and flanker. Born in Ballinasloe, 12th January 1963. Clubs: Drumgoyne (of Sydney Australia), Corinthians (winning a Connacht Senior Cup medal in 1988), and Lansdowne (winning a Leinster Senior Cup medal in 1991). A product of St Joseph's Ballinasloe, he became the first ever player from the Corinthians Club to play at full international rugby for Ireland when winning his first cap against Western Samoa in 1988. Against Wales, for his fourth cap, on his first ever game in Cardiff Arms Park, he scored a brilliant block down/interception try, ensuring an Irish victory. Up to the end of the 1992 season he had won 15 international caps for Ireland (he has also been replacement 10 times), and has scored 3 international tries. He played once in the World Cup 1991, and has toured with Ireland to North America in 1989, to Namibia in 1991, and to New Zealand in 1992.

MANNION, SEAN.

Light-middle weight boxer. Born 1957 in Rosmuc, Co Galway, he later emigrated to Boston. He became Irish amateur junior champion when a member of the Girley Co Meath club, Oliver Plunkett's. When in the States, he slowly worked his way up to a world title fight, when in 1984, he fought the Jamaican, Mike McCallum, in Madison Square Garden, New York, for the light-middleweight crown left vacant by Roberto Duran. Mannion was clearly outclassed, and lost heavily on points over 15 rounds.

MANOWN, JOANNE.

Ladies Hockey international forward. Club: Ards H.C.. A junior international in 1980, and an Irish schoolgirl international from 1980-1983, she also played Under 21 and Under 23 level, captaining the Irish Under 21 side to a Bronze medal in the European Junior Cup in Dundee in 1984, being joint top scorer with 6 goals. A forward with great skill, winning her first senior cap for Ireland in 1982, she went on to play in 55 successive international matches for Ireland up to 1989, when she retired from the Irish team. From 1989 she became a member of he Great Britain squad. She also played indoor hockey at international level for Ireland.

MARKS, Mrs J .

Ladies amateur international golfer. She won the Ulster Ladies Senior Championship 6 times, in 1930, 1932, 1936, 1938, 1939 and in 1954, and was runner-up in 1947, 1951 and 1955. She played in 4 Home International series for Ireland in the 1930's, in 1930, 1931, 1933 and in 1935.

MARTIN, CORNELIUS J (CON).

Soccer international full-back, centre-half and forward. Born in Dublin, 20th March 1923. Having played in his youth for St Maur's (Rush) and St Mary's (Saggart), he played 4 years with Drumcondra, followed by a spell with Glentoran. Joining Leeds United in 1947, he played there for one year before transferring to Aston Villa, with whom he played almost 200 league matches in 7 years. Capped for the Republic of Ireland 30 times between 1946 and 1956 (in his debut against Portugal in 1946 he became the first substitute ever used by the Republic of Ireland), he had also been capped for Northern Ireland 6 times between 1947 and 1950, and he scored 6 international goals. One of Ireland's most versatile players, he played at centre-half, right-half, in both full-back positions, centre-forward, and even in goals for his country (against Spain in 1949). He was also a useful cricketer and basketball player. A father of Mick Martin (cv).

MARTIN, DAMIEN.

G.A.A. hurling goalkeeper, Offaly. Club: St Rynagh's (with whom he won 12 county championship medals and many provincial titles, and reached the All-Ireland Club Hurling final twice, in 1971 against Roscrea, and in 1973 against Glen Rovers, losing both games).

First playing senior inter-county hurling in 1964, he won a Railway Cup medal with Leinster in 1971 (as a sub in the final), and in 1972. For 17 long years the closest he got to a major championship medal was in playing on the Offaly side beaten in the Leinster Senior Hurling Championship in 1969, until 1981 when he was a member of the first ever Offaly side to capture an All-Ireland Senior Hurling Championship medal in 1981 (making some brilliant saves in the final). He later played on the Offaly side beaten in the 1984 All-Ireland S.H.C. final, he also won 2 other Leinster S.H.C. medals, in 1980 and 1985. He hung up his inter-county boots in 1986, after 23 years at the peak. A fine goalkeeper, he deservedly was the first hurling goalkeeper to win an All-Star award, in the inaugural year of 1971.

MARTIN, DAVID K ('DAVY BOY').

Soccer international centre forward. Clubs: Cliftonville, Belfast Celtic (winning an Irish League medal in 1932-33), Wolverhampton Wanderers (who paid £7,750 for him in 1934), Nottingham Forest, Notts County, and Glentoran. A prolific league goal-scorer, he scored 7 Inter-League goals for the Irish League. He was capped for the I.F.A. (Northern Ireland) 10 times between 1934 and 1939, scoring 3 international goals.

MARTIN, KEVIN.

Amateur international boxer. He holds a unique place in Irish amateur boxing in being the only boxer (of 11 in all) to represent Ireland at 2 Olympic Games who never won any Irish National Senior Championship title. He fought in the 1948 Games in London at featherweight (losing to the eventual gold medalist, the Italian Ernesto Formenti on points in the 2nd round, and at lightweight in the Helsinki Games of 1952 (when he was selected although beaten in the National Championship by Tony 'Socks' Byrne in the final), again being beaten in his 2nd round bout.

MARTIN, Brigadier General G NOEL C.

Amateur international golfer. Born in Portrush in 1891. Club: Royal Portrush. He won the Irish Open Amateur title in 1920 and 1923 (both finals were against his arch rival Charles Hezlet cv), and the British Army Championship in 1928. While on service in India he won the North Indian Championship twice. He played international golf for Ireland 7 times, against Wales in 1923 and 1929, against Scotland in 1928, 1929 and 1930; and against England in 1929 and 1930 (when he captained the side). He won his place of the Walker Cup side in 1928 (becoming Ireland's 2nd representative in these matches), losing the only match he played in. He was awarded both a S.S.O. and a Victoria Cross.

MARTIN, HERBERT.

Cricket international right hand batsman. Born in Lisburn, 4th May 1927. Club: Lisburn. A product of Friends School and Belfast R.A., he played 19 first class cricket matches for Ireland in the 20 year period between 1949 and 1968, his best score being 88 versus Scotland in 1956. He played for Ireland 39 times in all between 1949 and 1968, scoring 1,282 runs for his country at an average run rate of 18.57, and he also took 31 catches.

MARTIN, JIMMY ('THE REVEREND').

Professional golfer. Born 27th July 1924. He represented Ireland 4 times in the Canada Cup, in 1962, 1963, 1964, and 1966, and in the newly-named World Cup in 1970. He won the 1969 Irish Professional title, the 1964 Southern Irish Professional title, and the 1972 Irish Uniroyal. His biggest win was in the 1965 Carroll's International tournament, having also won the 1964 Picadilly Medal Tournament. He was honoured by Ryder Cup selection in 1965, losing his only match. In 1961 he broke the European record for the number of sub-par figures in one competitive round, with 12, by means of an eagle and 11 birdies. He was voted as Texaco's Sportstar of the Year for golf in 1964.

MARTIN, MICK P.

Soccer international midfielder. Born in Dublin, 9th July 1951, the son of Con Martin (cv). Clubs: Home Farm, Bohemians (with whom he won an amateur international cap), Manchester United (playing 33 league games 1972-74), West Bromwich Albion (playing 85 league games 1975-78, helping them win promotion to Division One in 1976), Newcastle United (1978-1984, playing 147 matches), Vancouver Whitecaps, Cardiff City, Peterborough United, Rotherham United and Preston North End. A midfield workhorse, he was capped 52 times for the Republic of Ireland in a sterling service over a 12 year period between 1972 and 1983, scoring 4 international goals. On retiring, he set up as a bookmaker, and worked at St James Park as a coach. A son of Con Martin (cv).

MARTIN, PADDY.

G.A.A. football half-forward, Kildare. He won 6 successive Leinster S.F.C. winner's medals with Kildare, 1926, 1927, 1928, 1929, 1930, and in 1931, and won a 7th medal in 1935. In two of these years he won All-Ireland Senior Football Championship winner's medals with Kildare, in 1927 and 1928, and played in 4 other Kildare sides beaten in the All-Ireland S.F.C. decider, 1926, 1929 (scoring a fine goal in the final), 1931, and 1935. One of the heroes of Kildare's golden era, he is one of only 2 Kildare footballers to win 5 Railway Cup medals with Leinster, his medals being won in 1928, 1929, 1930, 1932 and 1933.

MARTIN, STEPHEN A.

Hockey international defender and sweeper. Born on April 13th 1959 in Bangor, Co Down. Educated in Bangor Grammar School. Clubs: Y.M.C.A., and Hollywood 87. He represented Ireland 105 times in a 12 year career between 1982 and 1993, captaining the side about 15 times. He won an Olympic bronze medal representing Great Britain in Los Angeles games of 1984, and went on to win a gold medal as a member of the G.B. squad that beat West Germany in the 1988 final in Korea (although he did not play in any game). Up to his retirement in 1993 he represented Great Britain 94 times, bring his tally to 199 international caps in all. He also represented Great Britain in the 1992 games in Barcelona, in which they finished 6th. He has also won at least 30 indoor caps for Ireland. A major influence of the Irish squad which finished 5th in the 1989 Intercontinental Cup, thereby qualifying for the 1990 World Cup, in which he was also a star member. He is the only Ulster sportsman to win 2 successive Olympic medals. He took up a job with the Northern Ireland Sports Council in 1993.

MARTINA, GERRY.

Light heavyweight wrestler. He nearly achieved a sportsman's life ambition when in the Olympic Games in Melbourne in 1956, he finished 4th in the Light Heavyweight (87 kilograms or 192 points) discipline of wrestling, being eliminated in the 4th round by the Russian Boris Kulayev, having earlier competed against a Greek and an Australian. He also competed in the 1960 Olympic Games in Rome, this time retiring hurt in the first round against a South African opponent.

MARTINELLI, (or MARTELLI), E.

Rugby international full-back. Club: Dublin University. He shares a record (with B S Massey and W Ashby cv) for being one of only 3 Irishmen who toured with a British and Irish touring side, and who never played for Ireland. He went on the Lion's first ever tour of Australia in 1899, and played in the first Test, the only one lost by the visitors. His feat is all the more remarkable in that he is not recorded as having ever played for the Trinity College first XV.

MASOOD, MOHAMMED AFZAL ('ALF').

Cricket international batsman. Born in Lahore in Pakistan in May 1952. Playing first class cricket for Punjab University before spending a period with Northampton (being the 2nd XI's best average batsman), he declared for Ireland. In a brilliant Irish career (as a member of Phoenix) from 1982 to 1988, he won 40 caps and has made himself the best average runs-per-innings batsman the country has known. In 40 internationals and 55 innings, he scored 1,940 runs (this places him in the top ten of all-time Irish run scorers) for the record average of 38.80 per innings. He scored 4 centuries for Ireland, including a 138 against the M.C.C. at Lord's in 1985.

MASSEY, B F.

Rugby international forward. Clubs: Hull, E R , and Ulster. He is one of only 3 Irish rugby players who, although never capped by Ireland, was selected to go on a British and Irish touring side. He was on the first Lions side to tour New Zealand, in 1904, during which Australia was also toured, where he won a 3rd Test place, on a winning 16-0 side.

MATTHEWS, TOM.

G.A.A. footballer, Louth. One of the great Louth side which won 2 All-Ireland Senior Football Championship titles, in 1910 (a walk-over against the Tralee Mitchels side from Kerry) and the win over the Shauns side from Antrim in 1912, he also won another Leinster S.F.C. medal in 1909, when the 'Wee County' were beaten in the All-Ireland final by Kerry.

MATTHEWS, JOHNNY.

Soccer left-winger. Born in Meriden, England, 27th August, 1946. Clubs: Coventry City, Waterford United and Limerick. As a No 11, he has no peer in League of Ireland goalscoring prowess. His 156 league goals (143 of them for Waterford) in the period 1966-84, place him 4th in the all-time list of the league's goalscorers, although he was never the leading scorer in the League in any one season. He won 7 League of Ireland Championship medals, 6 with the great Waterford side of the late 60's and early 70's (1965-66, 1967-68, 1968-69, 1969-70, 1971-72 and 1972-73, and with whom he was the leading League scorer in 4 seasons), and one with Limerick City in 1979-1980. Also playing for Cork United and Longford Town, he later managed Waterford United.

MATTHEWS, P DUFF ('DUFFER').

Croquet international player. Born 1886. One of the most charismatic of all-time croquet players, his gift for the game helped him to win 4 English Open Championships (the oldest and then most prestigious title in the world), in 1914, 1919, 1920 and in 1927 (only 4 players have won the title more often). He had won his silver medal while still an undergraduate, and made 13 appearences in the Champions Cup from 1910, winning it just the once, in 1912. He won the Irish Championship twice, in 1953, and sharing it in 1956 (at the age of 70 !) with the New Zealander, W.H. Kirk. A farmer, he died in 1958, but his name lives on in croquet lore, as the tantalising opening gambit, the 'Duffer Tice', is named after him.

MATTHEWS, PHILIP Michael.

Rugby international wing-forward. He was born in Gloucester, England, on 24th January 1960. Educated at Regent House, he won 5 school international caps in 1977 and 1978. Clubs: Queen's University Belfast, Ards, and Wanderers. He won his first cap in 1984 against Australia (making him the first Ards player to be capped), and but for injury was omni-present up to 1991, also playing in the 1987 World Cup Down Under. He was part of a strong back-row in Ireland's Triple Crown victory in 1985. He later was appointed as Ireland's captain of the tour of Namibia, and of the World Cup side which in 1991 performed with distinction to be narrowly beaten by eventual winner's Australia in the quarter-finals. He has won 38 international caps for Ireland in an injury/illness-laden career up to 1992, 13 of these as captain, and has scored 4 international tries. He is a son-in-law of Kevin Flynn (cv).

MAY, CAREY.

Long-distance runner. Winning some B.L.E. National titles, she also won the inaugural Dublin City Marathon in 1980, in a time of 2 hours, 16 minutes and 14 seconds. She represented Ireland in the 1984 Olympic Games in Los Angeles, finshing 28th in the marathon in a time of 2:41.27. She had set a record for the Toronto marathon when winning the title in 1983, at 2:36:07.. She also twice won the Ladies Marathon in Osaka, Japan.

MAYNE, Robert BLAIR.

Rugby second-row forward and strong-man. Born in Newtownards, Co Down, 11th January 1915, he was killed in a car accident at the age of 40. Clubs: Queen's University Belfast and Malone. While he won only 6 caps for Ireland between 1937 and 1939, scoring one try, he won 3 Test match places on the British and Irish Lion's side which toured South Africa in 1938, making a huge impression there with his huge strength as a tight forward in his 20 tour matches, gained from years of lifting weights (although he had the unusual record as the only member of the party not to score on the tour). He was also an Irish Universities Boxing Champion. Such was his distinction in North Africa in W.W.II., that he was given three bars on his D.S.O. and was made Legion d'Honneur.

McADAMS, WILLIAM (BILLY) J.

Soccer international centre-forward. Born in Belfast, 20th January 1934. Clubs: Banbridge Town, Glenavon, Distillery, Manchester City (for whom in 127 league matches in 6 years, he scored 61 goals, though he missed an F.A. Cup medal through injury). Then in the 7 year period between 1960 and 1967, he scored 83 league goals in 216 appearences with, for short periods each: Bolton Wanderers, Leeds United, Brentford (winning a 4th Division medal 1962-63), Q.P.R., Barrow, and finally with non-league Netherfield. In a distinguished career, he was capped for Northern Ireland 15 times between 1954 and 1962, scoring 7 international goals (including a hat-trick against West Germany in October 1960, although on the losing side).

McALARNEY, COLM.

G.A.A. football midfielder, Down. Born in Dublin in 1949. Club: Castlewellan. He was a member of the losing Down minor side in the 1966 All-Ireland M.F.C. to Cork (in fact he won Ulster minor and senior championship medals on the same day in 1966, being a sub for the senior match). A product of De La Salle College, Downpatrick, he went on to play inter-county football for 15 years between 1966 and 1981, winning 4 Ulster Senior Football Championship medals on the field off play with Down, in 1968 (when the county went on to beat Kerry in the All-Ireland S.F.C. final), 1971, 1978, and 1981, being also on the losing Ulster final side 4 times, in 1969, 1973, 1974, and 1975. He was on the Down side which captured the 1968 National Football League title (when they won the 'double'), and also won 4 Railway Cup medals with Ulster, in 1968, 1971, 1979, and 1980. A versatile footballer who played in both attack and defence for his county, he won 2 All-Star awards, both in the midfield, in 1975 and in 1978.

McALINDEN, DANNY.

Heavyweight boxer. Born in Newry, Co Down, on June 1st 1947. As an amateur member of the Edgewick club, he won the Irish National Senior Championship title at heavyweight in 1967. Turning pro in 1969, he was British Commonwealth champion 1972-75, and was British champion over the same period. In his 12 year professional career up to 1981, he won 31, drew 2, and lost 12 of his 45 bouts. He won the British and Commonwealth titles (becoming the first Irishman to hold both) by knocking out Jack Bodell in the 2nd round of their fight, in Birmingham in 1972. In 1975, in his first defence of the 2 titles, he was knocked out by the challenger Bunny Johnson in the 9th round, and later that year failed in his attempt to regain the title, when Richard Dunn knocked him out in the 2nd round. In 1975 he again lost to Johnson in 9 rounds. He was selected as Texaco's Boxing Sportstar of the Year in both 1971 and 1972.

McALINDEN, JAMES (JIMMY).

Soccer international centre and inside forward. Born in the Lower Falls, Belfast 31st December 1917. Clubs: Belfast Celtic (with whom he won I.F.A. Cup medals in 1938, 1941, and 1944, and 5 successive Irish League medals from 1935-36 to 1939-40), Portsmouth (who payed a then record £7,500 for him, and where he played on the F.A. Cup winning side of 1939 in the 4-1 defeat of Wolves), Glentoran, Sligo Rovers, Stoke City, and Southend United (scoring 12 goals in 218 league appearences, 1948-1953). A product of Milford Street School, he was capped 4 times for Northern Ireland (one each year of 1938, 1939, 1947 and 1949), and twice for Eire in 1946. He is the only player in history to appear in successful Irish Cup and F.A. Cup teams in successive seasons (Belfast Celtic in 1938 and Portsmouth in 1939). He later managed Glenavon (helping them to win 3 I.F.A. Cups in 1957, 1959 and 1961, and an Irish League in 1960), Distillery (getting them into European competition for the first time in their history) and Drogheda United.

McARTHUR, KENNEDY Kane.

Long-distance athlete. Born in Dervock, Ballymoney, Co Antrim in 1882. A former postman, he emigrated to South Africa in 1905 (becoming a policeman), and won the South African 5 mile and Cross-Country titles in 1907 and 1908. Setting a South African record in 1911 for the 10 mile distance that was to last for 30 years, he became also an accomplished marathon runner, winning their national title in 1908, 1909 and 1912. Picked to represent South Africa in the Stockholm Olympic Games of 1912, he went on, at the age of 30, to become the 2nd Irish-born winner of the marathon in succession (see Johnny Hayes cv). In very hot conditions (only 34 of the 151 starters finished), he beat another athlete representing South Africa, Christain Gitsham, by almost a minute over a 40,000 metre course in a time of 2 hours, 36 minutes and 54.8 seconds, an Olympic record (and at 6'1" and 13 stone he still remains the biggest man ever to win the Olympic marathon). He died in South Africa in 1960.

McATAMNEY, MAIREAD.

G.A.A. camogie midfielder, Antrim. Club: Portglenone (who with her dominating their side, reached 2 All-Ireland Club Championship finals, in 1973 and 1978, losing both, being the first Ulster club to reach this stage). She won 2 O'Duffy Cup medals with Antrim, in 1967, and in 1979 when she captained her county to victory in the All-Ireland final over Tipperary. She won a Gael Linn medal with Ulster in 1967. A polished performer who could dictate a game, she won a Cuchullain Award in 1965, and a B&I award in 1979.

McAULEY, DAVE ('BOY').

Flyweight professional boxer. Born in Larne in Co Antrim on June 15th 1961. He turned profeesional in 1981 after winning the Irish Amateur Senior Champinship title at flyweight in 1980 while a member of the Larne club. He was crowned British Champion in October 1986 when he knocked out Joe Kelly of Scotland in the 9th round of their fight in Glasgow, to get the title vacated by Duke McKenzie. He then lost two gallant tilts at the W.B.A. world title against Fidel Bassa of Columbia, in April 1987 (when stopped in the 13th in a fight regarded by 'The Ring' magazine as the flyweight bout of the decade), and when beaten heavliy on points in March

1988. However it was third time lucky, when in June 1989 he beat the I.B.F. champion Duke McKenzie on points at Wembley Arena, to become the 2nd Antrim-man (after Rinty Monaghan) to capture a world championship. He defended his crown successfully against Dodie Penalosa in November 1989, in March 1990 against Louis Curtis (U.S.), (when he became the first Irish-based boxer to have taken part in 5 world title bouts), in September 1990 against Rodolfo Blanco, in May 1991 by beating Pedro Feliciano of Puerto Rico on points (although knocked down twice), and in September of that year by knocking out Jake Matlala of South Africa. This made him the first home-based boxer (British or Irish) to successfully defend a world title 5 times (and to fight in 8 world title fights), and therefore ranks him as Ireland's most successful professional boxer in history. In his 9th world title fight, in June 1992, he lost his 3 year hold on the crown to the Colombian, Rodolfo Blanco, in a controversial points decision in Bilbao. Previously working as a part-time chef, he was selected 4 times as Texaco's Sportstar of the Year in Boxing, in 1986, 1989, 1990 and 1991. He was awarded the M.B.E. in 1992.

McAULIFFE, JACK.

Light-weight professional boxer. Born at Meelin, near Bantry, Co Cork on March 24th 1866. He died at Forest Hills, New York in 1937. He claimed the world light-weight title between the years 1886 and 1894. Two years after starting fighting in New York at the age of 18, he (while one month short of his 20th birthday) on 27th February 1886, knocked out the American Jack Hooper in the 17th round, to win the U.S title and claim the vacant world crown. Between then and September 1892, he made 6 successful defences of his title: first against Bill Frazier (won in 21 rounds), then against Harry Gilmore in 28 rounds; then in what was considered his real world title bout in 1887 in Revere Massachusetts, and in what was to be the first ever world title fight draw, he only got the draw when his supporters invaded the ring when it became obvious that he would be knocked out in the 74th round by the British champion, Jem Carney; he later defended successfully against Bill Dacey in 1888 to become the undisputed world champion, and lastly in 1892 he defended against Billy Myer of the U.S.A. (whom he knocked out in 15 rounds). He retired in 1894 but came back for 4 more bouts in 1896-1897. His professional record of 77 contests, with 63 wins, 3 draws, 3 no decisions, and no losses, makes him one of the world's outstanding champions, as it places him as one of only 3 world champions to go through his whole career unbeaten. In 1954 he was elected as one of the founder members of The Ring magazine's Hall of Fame.

McBRIDE, William DENIS.

Rugby international wing-forward. Born in Belfast, 9th September 1964. Club: Malone (winning Ulster Senior Cup medals in 1989 and 1992). Captaining Ulster to win the Interprovincial series in 1992, he has been capped 12 times for Ireland up to March 1993, and has also been capped at Under 25 and 'B' level. He toured with Ireland to North America in 1989, to New Zealand in 1992, and captained the Irish side which reached the semi-final of the inaugural World Sevens championship in 1993. His wife Catriona has played volleyball for Northern Ireland.

McBRIDE, VIOLET.

Hockey international player. From Kilkeel, Co Down, she was born in 1954. Club: Portadown (with whom she has won 5 Ulster and 5 All-Ireland titles). Capped at least 38 times for Ireland, and 63 times for Great Britain 1978-88, she was on the British side that finished 4th in the 1988 Olympics Games in Seoul. A P.E teacher, she has also won 2 world drum major titles in a Cumberland pipe band.

McBRIDE, STEPHEN.

Soccer international forward. Club: Glenavon (scoring 25 goals for them in all competitions in 1989-90, and 37 goals in all competitions in 1990-91, when the club finished 4th in the Irish League, and were runners-up in the I.F.A. Cup). In 1991 he was voted Player of the Year by both the N.I.P.F.A. and the Soccer Writers, and won his first 2 international caps for Northern Ireland.

McBRIDE, WILLIAM James ('WILLIE JOHN').

Rugby international 2nd row forward. Born in Toomebridge, Co Antrim, 6th June 1940. Clubs: Ballymena (winning Ulster Senior Cup medals in 1963, 1970, 1975 and 1976), Arbertillery, Barbarians. Arguably Ireland's greatest ever rugby forward, he is a product of the Ballymena Academy. He won 63 international caps for Ireland over a 13 year period from 1962 to 1975, making him the world's most capped player from 1975 until surpassed by Mike Gibson in 1979 (he is still the world's most capped forward). He scored one try for Ireland, and captained the side on 12 occasions in 1973-75, including leading Ireland to their first win in the International Championship in 23 years in 1974. He has gone on a record 5 British and Irish Lions tours (developing as the tours progressed into the most influential ever forward to tour with the side), and has played in an unlikely-to-be-equalled record 17 tests while on those tours (15 of these tests were consecutive, also a record). He travelled to Australia and New Zealand twice, in 1966 (playing in 3 tests) and 1971 (participating in all 4 tests in the historic winning side), and to South Africa three times, 1962 (2 tests played), 1968 (playing in 4 tests, scoring the only Lions test try of the series), and in 1974 (4 tests), when he was captain, inspiring his side to become the most successful Lion's touring side ever, winning the Test series 3-0, with one controversially drawn, and winning all other 18 games. With Ireland he toured Australia in 1967 and Argentina in 1970. He was later manager of the Ciaran Fitzgerald captained-Lion's tour of New Zealand in 1983, and also of the International XV which toured in 1989. He was coach to the Irish team in 1983-84 (when controversially replaced after only one season at the helm), and was a selector 1984-86. He was voted Texaco's Rugby Sportstar of the Year in 1974, and was also voted as Supreme Sportstar of that year (the first rugby player to be so honoured). A bank manager, he has recieved an M.B.E..

McCABE, F F.

Horse trainer, flat. Born in 1868, he served for some of his career as trainer to the 'Boss' Croker, while as an owner he won the 1898 Irish Oaks with Sabine Queen. He went on to be the trainer of the great Orby, who was the first Irish-trained horse to win the Epsom Derby in 1907 (and the only Irish horse to do so up till Hard Ridden in 1958, 51 years later). Orby went on to win the 1907 Irish Derby also. McCabe moved to Newmarket, and the following year trained the winner of the Epsom Derby again, with Signorinetta.

McCABE, JAMES J (JIM).

Soccer international wing half and half-back. Born in Draperstown, Co Derry, 17th September 1918. Clubs: Billingham Synthonia Juniors, South Bank East, Middlesboough, and Leeds United (playing in over 150 league matches 1948-54), Peterborough United. He won 6 international caps for Northern Ireland between 1949 and 1954, all while at Elland Road.

McCAFFREY, NOEL.

G.A.A. football centre half-back, Dublin. He was a member of Dublin sides beaten in 3 successive Leinster Senior Football Championship finals, 1986, 1987, and 1988. Also helping Dublin to win the National League title in 1987-88, he won an All-Star award in 1988 at centre half-back. A Clontarf doctor.

McCAFFREY, JOHN (SEAN).

Amateur international flyweight boxer. Club: St John Bosco. He won 2 Irish National Senior Championship titles at flyweight, in 1963 and 1964. In 1964 he reached the last eight in the Olympic Games in Tokyo in the flyweight division, beating a Cuban and a Ghanain before losing to an Italian on points in the bronze medal bout, and thereby being placed joint 5th.

McCALL, H CONN.

Cricket international batsman. He played in 15 international cricket matches for Ireland between 1964 and 1968, during which, in 28 innings, he scored a total of 541 runs for an average score of 20.03, his highest being 81, making 3 more 50's, and making 6 catches. He was President of the I.C.U. in 1992.

McCALLEN, PHILIP.

Motor cycle road racer. Born in Portadown in 1964. First racing at the Isle of Man in 1988 in the Manx Grand Prix, he won the 250cc Newcomer's race with an average speed of 103.53 m.p.h.. A winner of many Irish and Ulster road races since 1987, he has won 3 Isle of Man T.T. races, the 1992 T.T. Formula One, the 1992 Supersport 600 T.T., and the 1993 Senior T.T., all on Honda machines. In 1992 he became the first rider to win 5 races in one day at the North West 200 international meeting in Portrush. In 1993 he won 3 Ulster G.P. races at Dundonald.

McCALLIN, ANDY.

G.A.A. football right corner forward, Antrim. Club: St John's (captaining the side beaten in the All-Ireland Club Championship final in 1978). He was a member of the first Antrim side which won the All-Ireland Under 21 Championship in 1969. A county minor in both hurling and football, he was a star member of the most recent Antrim to reach the final of the Ulster S.F.C., when they were beaten by Derry in 1970. Winning an Ulster J.F.C. medal in 1970, he won a Railway Cup medal with Ulster in 1971 (he also played Railway Cup hurling for Ulster). In 1971 he was a member of the inaugural All-Star team (being selected at right full-forward), and is still the only player from Antrim to win such an honour in football.

McCALLUM, Major JOHN D M (JOHNNIE, 'WEE MAJOR').

Badminton and cricket player. At badminton he was capped 8 times for Ireland between 1913 and 1926. He introduced the game into Denmark, a move which led to that country to become on of the leading nations in Europe at badminton, and founded the famous Strollers Club, which toured all over Ireland. He was a major in W.W.I., winning a D.S.O., and went on to be awarded the C.B.E.. He was to become President of the I.B.F. (the International Badminton Federation) from 1961 to 1963, and was Secretary of the Northern Branch of the B.U.I. for 52 years. He was also capped for Ireland as a cricket wicket-keeper, and was an Irish trialist in rugby. He was awarded a D.S.O. and a C.B.E..

McCANDLESS, W A C .('CROMIE').

Motorcycling racer. Born in Co Down c 1921. Highly successful for a few short years in the late 40's and early 50's, he won the Junior Race (and was 2nd in the Senior Race) in the Isle of Man Manx Grand Prix in 1949, on Norton machines. He went on to finish in the top 8 in eight Isle of Man T.T. races between 1950 and 1952, winning the 1951 125cc T.T. (and finishing 3rd in the 125cc World Championship that year). Before retiring at the end of the 1952 season, he won the Ulster Grand Prix at 500cc on an Italian Gilera machine. His brother Rex was also a motor-cycling racer of note, and with their business in Belfast together they developed the Featherbed frame which enabled Norton cycles to handle so well.

McCANN, DES.

International oarsman. Clubs: University College Dublin R.C., Old Collegians R.C., and Neptune R.C.. He was the first Irish oarsman to win six Irish Senior Championships at Eights, being in the winning crews over an 11 year period from 1960 to 1970 (with U.C.D. in 1960, 1961 and 1969, with Old Collegians in 1963 and 1964, and with Neptune in 1970). He also rowed for Ireland in the European Championships of 1964.

McCANN, (nee CATHERINE SYME), Mrs P G ('KITTY').

Amateur international golfer. Born in Clonmel Co Tipperary, 1922. Club: Tullamore G.C.. She achieved a career highlight when winning the British Ladies Open Amateur title in 1951, beating Frances Stephens 4 and 3 in the final at Broadstone GC.. She was also Irish Ladies Close Champion twice, in 1949 and 1961, and was runner-up in this championship 4 times (1947, 1952, 1957, and in 1960). She was honoured with Curtis Cup selection in 1952, when she joined Philomena Garvey in the winning side, although she did not actually play. She was a regular member the Irish international side from 1947 to 1964, playing in 14 different seasons. She was also Irish Midland Champion 3 times (1952, 1957 and 1958), Leinster Ladies Champion in 1958, and was Munster Ladies champion in 1958.

McCANN, JAMES (JIMMY, 'MAXIE').

Soccer international forward. Clubs: Shamrock Rovers (winning 3 League of Ireland Championship medals, in 1953-54, 1956-57 and 1958-59, and 3 F.A.I. Cup medals in 1955, 1956 and 1962), Drumcondra. Scoring 3 goals in the Inter-League scene for the League of Ireland XI, he was capped once for the Republic of Ireland, against West Germany in 1957.

McCANN, JOHN.

Polo player. An Irishman, he was on one of the three Great Britain sides which were the only Polo teams to compete in the 1908 Olympic Games in London. McCann, who played for the Ireland team, won a bronze medal, after the side were beaten by 5-1 by the winning Roehampton team.

McCANN, KATHERINE.

Ladies international golfer. Clubs: Headfort and Milltown. Winning the All-Ireland Girl's Under 22 Championship in the early 1980's, she played on the Irish Ladies junior international side for 3 successive years, 1982-1984, later graduating to the senior international side, and was a member of the side which captured the Home International Championship at Whittington Barracks in 1986. A Graduate of U.C.D. and an accountant by training, in 1991 she was appointed as Director of Golf at the Mount Juliet operation in Co Kilkenny.

McCANN, PADDY.

Soccer international full-back, G.A.A. footballer (Dublin), and champion athlete. As a gaelic fooballer he won 2 All-Ireland Senior Football Championship winner's medals with Dublin, in 1899 with the Geraldines selection, and with the Isles of the Sea selection in 1901. As a soccer player, playing with Belfast Celtic and Glentoran (winning Irish League winner's medals in 1912 and 1913), he later won 7 international caps for the I.F.A., between 1910 and 1913. An all-round sportsman, he also became the Irish Sprint Champion over 100 yards.

McCARRON, RAY.

G.A.A. football half-forward, Monaghan. He was a star member of the Monaghan team which won two Ulster Senior Football Championship titles, in both 1985 and 1988. Also a member of the first Monaghan side to capture a National Football League in 1985, he won his solitary All-Star award at right half-forward in 1986.

McCARTAN, JAMES (JIM) and DAN.

G.A.A. footballing brothers, Down. James, a classy centre-half forward, was a valuable player in Down's famous wins in the 1960 and 1961 All-Ireland Senior Football Championship finals. He was the 3rd Down-man to captain a winning Ulster Railway Cup side in 1969, also winning medals in each of 1964 and 1965. His brother Dan was at centre-half back on each of the All-Ireland winning sides of 1960 and 1961, and was at full-back on the Down side which won the Sam Maguire Cup in 1968 (he won 4 Railway Cup medals, in 1964, 1965, 1966, and 1968). Their father Briany played for Down in the 1930's and 40's. Their first cousins, Sean (cv) and Kevin O'Neill, were also in the fine Down team of the 60's. Two further cousins, John and Jim McCartan, were on the Down side which won the Ulster S.F.C. in 1981, John also being on the winning National League team of 1983. Jim is one of only 3 players (along with Jimmy Keaveney and Jack O'Shea) to win 2 successive Texaco Awards in football, winning in both 1960 and 1961. Jim is also the father of James Jnr (cv), and later was team manager of the Down side which won the National Football League in 1983, while Dan became a county selector.

McCARTAN, JAMES JNR ('WEE').

G.A.A. football left full forward, Down. Clubs: Tullylish, and the London club Tirconnell Gaels (winning a county championship medal in 1990). Born 27th October 1970. A product of St Colman's College Newry, he was a winner of 2 All-Ireland Colleges medals in 1986 and 1988, and a member of the Down side which won the All-Ireland M.F.C. in 1987. In 1990 he won a Sigerson Cup medal with Queen's. He was at left full-forward on the Down side beaten in the National League Final of 1989-90. He was a star member of the Down full-forward line which won the All-Ireland Senior Football final in 1991 against Meath, after a gap of 23 years, being nominated 'Man-of-the-Match'. He won an All-Star award in 1990 at left full forward, and is the son of James McCartan (cv).

McCARTHY, CHARLIE.

G.A.A. hurling right full-forward, Cork. Born in 1947. Club: St Finbarr's (winning 2 All-Ireland Club championship medals with them, in 1975 and 1978). He won an All-Ireland M.H.C. medal with Cork minors in 1964, and 2 years later won an All-Ireland Under 21 Championship medal, in 1966. He has won a total of 5 All-Ireland Senior Hurling Championship winner's medals with Cork, in 1966, 1970 (scoring 1-9), and in the 3-in-a-row years of 1976 (scoring 1-3), 1977 (scoring 0-5) and in 1978 (scoring 0-7, when he captained the side in their 1-15 to 2-8 win over Kilkenny). He also played on 2 losing Cork All-Ireland S.H.C. final sides, in 1969 (scoring 1-6) and 1972; in all of these 7 All-Ireland finals he played in the right full-forward position. He was also on winning Cork sides in 4 National Hurling League successes, won in 1970, 1972, 1974 and 1980. A quality player, he won 3 All-Star awards, in 1972, 1977 and 1978, all at right corner-forward.

McCARTHY, DAVE.

G.A.A. football midfielder, Cork. He was a member of the Cork side which won the All-Ireland Senior Football Championship for the first time in 28 years in 1973, playing at left half-forward. Winning another Munster S.F.C. medal in 1974, he won a Railway Cup medal with the Combined Universities in 1973, and won 2 further Railway Cup medals with Munster, in 1975 and 1977. He won his solitary All-Star award in 1976 in the centre-field.

McCARTHY, GERALD.

G.A.A. hurling midfielder and half-forward, Cork. Club: St Finbarr's (winning 4 county championship medals with them, and also 2 All-Ireland Club Championship titles with the 'Barr's', in 1975 and 1978). He won an All-Ireland Under 21 championship medal with Cork in 1966 as captain. In a 15 year career as a senior inter-county hurler with Cork from 1964 (when only 17) to 1979, he captained the Rebel County (from left half-forward) to win the 1966 All-Ireland Senior Hurling Championship when they beat Kilkenny by 3-9 to 1-10, after a 12 year gap. He later also won 4 other All-Ireland S.H.C. medals with Cork: in 1970, 1976 (at midfield), 1977 (playing a fine game) and 1978 (both at centre-half forward), and was on losing All-Ireland sides in 1969 and 1972. He won 2 National Hurling League medals with Cork, in 1969 and 1970. He captained the Munster hurlers to win the Railway Cup in 1970 (the 11th Corkman to do so), and won other medals in 1976 and 1978. Regarded as one of Cork hurling's great midfielders, and a fine half-forward, he was honoured with one All-Star award, in 1975 in centre-field. He was manager and coach to Cork for the All-Ireland final of 1982, and was trainer for the 1992 side.

McCARTHY, JAMES Stephen (JIM).

Rugby international wing-forward. Born in Cork, 30th January 1926. Club: Dolphin (becoming the club's then most capped player and winning 3 Munster Senior Cup medals with them in 1944, 1945 and in 1948). A product of C.B.C. Cork (winning a Munster Senior Schools Cup medal with the school in 1943), he was capped 28 times for Ireland between 1948 and 1955, captaining the side 4 times in 1954 and 1955, and scoring 8 international tries. An outstanding breakaway forward, he played in all 4 matches in the 1948 Grand Slam year, and for the entire Triple Crown season of 1949. His back row combination with Des O'Brien (cv) and Bill McKay (cv) in those years is among the best in rugby history. He also was omnipresent in the Irish side which won the International Championship in 1951, and toured Argentina and Chile in 1952 with Ireland. He was selected to go on the Lion's tour of Australia and New Zealand in 1950, although not gaining a test place. A flying redhead, he proved an invaluable sidekick for Jackie Kyle (cv), combining with him to devastating extent.

McCARTHY, JOHN.

G.A.A. football corner-forward, Dublin. Born in 1953. Clubs: Na Fianna (winning a Dublin S.F.C. medal in 1979) and Ballymun Kickhams. He won a Leinster M.F.C. medal in 1971 and a Leinster Under 21 Championship medal in 1974. He was on the Dublin senior side from 1973 to 1984, during which time he won Leinster Senior Football Championship medals 7 times, 6 in succession (1974 to 1979), and in 1984. He won 3 All-Irleand S.F.C. medals with the 'Dub's', in 1974 at right corner-forward, and in 1976 and 1977 at left-full. He also played in losing All-Ireland S.F.C. finals in 1975, 1978 and 1979. He is the only Dublin player from the 1976 and 1977 finals not to win an All-Star.

McCARTHY, JUSTIN.

G.A.A. hurling midfielder and half-forward, Cork. From Passage West, his club was Passage. He won an All-Ireland Under 21 medal in 1966 with Cork. He played in only one All-Ireland Senior Hurling Championship winning side with Cork, in 1966 (aged only 21), thus becoming the first player from Passage West to win an All-Ireland medal (he missed the 1969 All-Ireland decider due to a car accident). He won 2 Railway Cup medals with Munster, in 1968 and 1969. He won National League medals with Cork in 1969 and 1972. In 1966 he became the 2nd Cork player to be selected as Texaco Sportstar of the Year in hurling.

McCARTHY, MARION.

G.A.A. camogie player, Cork. Clubs: South Presentation, and Eire Og. She is the only Cork player to win 8 All-Ireland Senior Championship winner's medals in camogie, being on the Cork side on each of its 8 most recent winning sides, in 1970, 1971, 1972, 1973, 1978, 1980, 1982, and 1983, 4 of these gained in outfield positions, and the latter 4 as a goalkeeper. Winning a B&I Award in 1980 and winning many Gael Linn medals, she won 2 National League medals in 1984 and 1986. She is also a fine badminton player,

McCARTHY, MAURICE.

G.A.A. footballer, Kerry. He won 5 All-Ireland Senior Football Championship winner's medals with Kerry teams (sharing with Dick Fitzgerald the record of being the first Kerryman to win 5 All-Ireland medals); 3 with Tralee Mitchell's (in 1903, 1904 and 1909), and 2 with Killarney (in 1913 and 1914). He was captain of the Tralee Mitchell's side beaten by Kildare in the All-Ireland S.F.C. final of 1905 (the first Kerry team beaten in an All-Ireland final), and also played in the team which lost to Wexford in 1915.

McCARTHY, MICHAEL (MICK).

G.A.A. football left full-forward, Cork. Club: O'Donovan Rossa (helping the club to win the county championship for the first time in 1992, and was outstanding in the club's subsequent victory in the All-Ireland club championship in 1993). Playing on the Cork minors beaten in the All-Ireland M.F.C. final of 1983, he then won 3 succesive All-Ireland Under 21 Championship medals with Cork in 1984, 1985 and 1986. He was a member of the Cork side which captured the All-Ireland Senior Football Championship in 1990, having previously been a member of the Cork S.F.C. side when beaten in the All-Ireland senior football final by Meath in 1988. He won a Munster S.F.C. medal again in 1993, going on to lose to Derry in the All-Ireland S.F.C. Final.

McCARTHY, MICK ('CAPTAIN FANTASTIC').

Soccer international central defender. Born in Barnsley, 7th February 1959. Clubs: Barnsley (helping them in his 7 years service, to get from the 4th to the 2nd division), Manchester City (4 years), Glasgow Celtic (winning one Scottish Premier League title and 2 Scottish Cup medals), Olympique Lyonnais, Millwall (eventually becoming their player-manager). First capped for the Republic of Ireland in 1984, he gained 56 senior international caps in a distinguished career, playing in the European Championship finals of 1988, in which he played a crucial role in Ireland's 3 games in Germnany. Thought of very highly by the Republic of Ireland manager, Jack Charlton, he also played a central role in Ireland's qualifying for the World Cup finals in 1990, and captained (thus the nickname) the Irish side in all 5 matches in their historic endeavours at Italia 90 in Sardinia, Sicily, Genoa and Rome.

McCARTHY, SEAN.

G.A.A. hurling full-back and midfield, Cork. Born in 1966. Club: Ballinahassig. A panel member for the 1986 final, he was a member of the Cork side which in 1990 won the All-Ireland Senior Hurling Championship, being also in the side beaten by Kilkenny in the 1992 final. He was a member of the Rebel County side which captured the National Hurling League in 1992-93 (in a 3-game final win over Wexford). He was awarded an All-Star award in 1992 in the midfield position.

McCARTHY, SEAN ('THE KING').

Soccer centre-forward. Born in Cork, 22nd January 1922. Clubs: Clifton, Cork United (winning 4 League of Irleand winner's medals, in 1940-41, 1941-42, 1942-43 and 1944-45, and two F.A.I. Cup medals in 1941 and in 1947 when he scored 6 goals in 7 games), Belfast Celtic (scoring 56 goals for them in the 1945-46 season), Dartford, Bristol City. An outstanding goalscorer in the 1940's, he was the leading goalscorer in the League of Ireland for a joint-record 4 times (and was the first to achieve this feat), including 3 seasons in a row, scoring 16 goals for Cork United in both 1942/43 and 1943/44, while scoring 26 goals in only 14 games in the 1944/45 season for a club record for United; he was on top of the goal-scorers table for the 4th time in 1947-48, with 13 goals. His total of 135 league goals between

1940 and 1955 place him 7th in the all-time League of Ireland goalscorers list (105 of these goals were for Cork United, a club record). Uncapped, he did score 3 goals in 3 Inter-League matches for the League of Ireland, and also played for the Irish League side while at Belfast Celtic.

McCARTHY, TEDDY.

G.A.A. football right half-forward and midfielder, and hurling half-forward, Cork. Born in 1965. Clubs: Sarsfields, Imokilly (winning 2 county championship medals) and Glanmire. As a hurler he has won 2 Liam McCarthy Cup medals, when Cork won the All-Ireland Senior Hurling Championship final in both 1986 and 1990, and was on the side which were runners-up in 1992. As a footballer, he was on the Cork minors beaten by Derry in the All-Ireland M.F.C. final of 1983, and was on 3 succesive Cork winning All-Ireland Under 21 Championship sides, in 1984 (as a sub), 1985, and 1986. A member of the Cork senior side which reached 4 successive All-Ireland Senior Football Championship finals, in 1987, 1988, 1989 (when they won the title), and in 1990 when he made history by becoming the first player to win senior All-Ireland hurling and football medals in the same year. Helping the county to capture the 1992-93 National Hurling League title, this added to the National Football League medal he won in the 1989 season makes him a winner, in both codes, of League and Championship medals. He won an All-Star award in 1989 in the midfield position in football, and in the same year he was selected as Texaco's Sportstar of the Year in Gaelic Football. He won a further Munster S.F.C. medal in 1993, when Cork lost the All-Ireland Final to Derry.

McCARTHY, TADHG and his grandson PAT.

G.A.A. hurler and footballer, Kerry. Clubs: Kilmoyley and Ballyduff. Tadhg, along with his brother Phil, was on the Ballyduff side which captured Kerry's only All-Ireland Senior Hurling Championship success, in 1891 against the Wexford side of Crossbeg. In 1975, 84 years later, Tadhg's grandson Pat McCarthy, of the Churchill club, was at midfield on the famous Kerry 'young lions' side which won the All-Ireland Senior Football Championship. Pat also played in the 1976 final loss to Dublin, and won another All-Ireland S.F.C. medal in 1978 as a non-playing sub, also winning a Railway Cup medal with Munster.

McCARTHY, THOMAS ST GEORGE.

Rugby international centre three-quarter, and G.A.A. co-founder. While playing rugby for Trinity College (for whom he had played in the first ever Leinster Senior Cup tie, versus Phoenix, in 1881), he played one international rugby match for Ireland, on a losing side to Wales in 1882 in the first international match between these nations. Two years later, he became a co-founder of the G.A.A., attending the meeting in Hayes Hotel in Thurles on 1st November 1882. He was a District Inspector for the R.I.C. in Tipperary.

McCARTHY, TIM.

Basketball international player. Born in Cork, 9th August 1960. Clubs: Iona Boys (winning many All-Ireland juvenile medals), Blue Demons (winning 6 Cork Senior League medals). In 1982, at the age of 21, he captained the Cork side which won the Federation Cup in Scotland (which is to date Ireland's only club international tournament won abroad). First playing at senior level for Ireland at the age of 20, he was capped 38 times in all, and actually played 103 times for Ireland (if representative matches are included), captaining his country for 2 seasons, 1984/85 and 1988/89 (when Ireland gained a silver medal in the inaugural Promotions Cup in Malta). He also played in 2 European and 2 Olympic qualifying tournaments with Ireland, and toured the U.S.A. 4 times with the national side. He was a member of the Blue Demons club which won 3 National League medals (in 1984-85, 1986-87 and 1988-89), 3 National Cup medals (1978-79, 1980-81 and 1986-87), 2 National Championship medals (1984-85 and 1986-87), and many tournament medals. He retired in 1988-89 at the age of 29.

McCLEERY, WILLIAM (BILL).

Soccer international half-back, and cricket international. Born in Belfast. Clubs: Queen's Island (with whom he won an I.F.A. Cup medal in 1924), Blackburn Rovers, Cliftonville. He won 10 soccer caps for Northern Ireland between 1922 and 1933. He also played cricket for 'The Gentlemen of Ireland'. He later managed Linfield soccer club.

McCLELLAND, JOHN T (JACK).

Soccer international goalkeeper. Born in Lurgan, 19th May 1940. Clubs: Glenavon (winning an Irish League Championship medal in 1960), Arsenal (playing 49 first team games for them 1961-1964), Fulham, Lincoln City, Barnet (winning an F.A. Trophy runner-up medal in 1972). He was capped for Northern Ireland 6 times between 1961 and 1967. He died, aged 35, of a cancer-related illness in 1976.

McCLELLAND, JOHN.

Soccer international centre-half and defender. Born in Belfast, 7th December 1955. Clubs: Portadown, Cardiff City, Bangor City, Mansfield (playing 125 league games, scoring 8 times, 1978-81), Glasgow Rangers (for 2 seasons), Watford (moving there for £225,000, playing in over 150 league games), Leeds United (helping them to win the First Division Championship in 1991-1992). Since his first cap against Mansfield in 1980, he played for Northern Ireland 53 times (scoring one international goal), including all 5 matches in the No 4 jersey in Northern Ireland's successful World Cup run of 1982 (he was also in the World Cup squad in 1986). He played for the Football League against the Rest of the World at Wembley in 1987. The 6 caps he gained while he was at Mansfield make him the Quarry Lane club's most capped player. In 1993 he was appointed manager of the Scottish Premier League side, St Johnstone.

McCLELLAND, Dr THOMAS ALEXANDER.

Rugby international prop, 2nd row, and back row forward. Club: Queen's University Belfast (winning Ulster Senior Cup medals in 1921, 1924 and 1925, and 3 successive Ulster Senior League medals in 1922, 1923 and 1924). He was capped 16 times for Ireland between 1921 and 1924 (11 of these matches being lost), scoring 2 international tries.

McCLINTON, ARTHUR NORMAN.

Rugby international half-back. Club: N.I.F.C. (winning an Ulster Senior Cup medal in 1908). Although he was capped for Ireland on only 2 occasions, against Wales and France in 1910, scoring one conversion, he was however considered a good enough player to be selected on the 1910 Lions tour of South Africa, led by fellow-Irishman Tom Smyth (cv), although he did not gain a Test place.

McCLOUGHLIN, JOHN.

International bowls player, indoor and outdoor. Born in Lisburn on 9th March 1958. Club: Belfast BC. He has represented Northern Ireland at Commonwealth Games level, winning a silver medal at Four's in 1990 at Auckland. Adept at both indoor and outdoor game, he was a member of the Irish side which won the World Championship Four's gold medal in 1988.

McCLUGGAGE, ANDY.

Soccer international full-back. Clubs: Bradford, Burnley. He was capped 12 times for Northern Ireland betwen 1924 and 1931, scoring 2 international goals, one of them on the famous day Joe Bambrick scored Northern Ireland's record 6 goals, in a 7-0 win.

McCOMBE, WILLIAM McMachan (BILLY).

Rugby international out-half. Clubs: Dublin University, and Bangor. Born in Uganda, 6th February 1949. A product of Campbell College, he was capped for Ireland first in 1968, against France, but did not get the next of his 5 caps until 1975, a gap of 32 games, a then record gap between first and second caps until succeeded by Kenny Hooks (cv) in 1989. His tally for Ireland in his 5 international caps was 32 points, consisting of 4 penalties, 2 drop goals, 5 conversions, and 1 try.

McCONKEY, ROBERT (BOB).

G.A.A. hurler, Limerick. Club: Young Ireland. He captained Limerick to success in the 1921 All-Ireland Senior Hurling Championship, when they beat the Faughs side from Dublin by 8-5 to 3-2 in the final (scoring 4 goals himself, to be the side's leading scorer in the decider), thus becoming the first captain to accept the Liam McCarthy Cup, as it was the first year it was competed for. He won 2 other S.H.C. All-Ireland medals, in 1918 and in 1934 (when at the age of 39 he played in the drawn game), and was also on the losing All-Ireland final side of 1923.

McCONNELL, Dr Albert ARTHUR McGown.

Rugby international prop-forward. Born in Belfast, 29th October, 1919. Clubs: Q.U.B., Collegians and Barbarians. Although capped only 7 times for Ireland, he won 4 of them in the greatest year of Irish rugby, the Grand Slam year of 1948, one of only 9 players to play in all of these games for Ireland. He also played against England in the Triple Crown win of 1948.

McCONNELL, ENGLISH.

Soccer international defender. Clubs: Cliftonville, Glentoran, Sunderland, and Sheffield Wednsday. He was capped at international soccer 12 times for Northern Ireland between 1904 and 1909.

McCONNELL, ROY M and FRANK P.

Amateur international golfing brothers. Club: Royal Portrush. Roy McConnell won the Irish Close Championship in 1935, and was runner-up 3 times, in 1934, 1936 and 1939. He won the Irish Amateur Open title in 1927, having been runner-up the previous year. He played 14 International matches for Ireland against the Home countries between 1924 and 1931, 5 against Wales, 5 against England, and 4 against Scotland. He then played in 4 successive Home International series for Ireland, in 1934, 1935, 1936 and 1937, winning 9 of his 19 matches. His brother Frank P McConnell, was runner-up in the Irish Close Championship 3 years in succession, in 1929, 1930 and in 1931, and he played 8 matches for Ireland against the Home countries between 1929 and 1931 (7 alongside Roy), and played once in the Home International series, in 1934.

McCONNELL, WILLIAM D R (BILLY).

Hockey internatioanal defender. Born in Newry, Co Down in 1956. Club: Queen's University and Belfast Y.M.C.A.. Making his international debut in 1979, it took him 10 years, during the Intercontinental Cup in New Jersey in 1989, to become the third Irish player to be capped 100 times, and in 1991 he passed out David Judge to become (at 125 caps) Ireland's most capped hockey player, finishing at 135 caps when retiring from the international scene in 1991 (80 of these caps were consecutive). He won an Olympic bronze medal with the Great Britain side in the Los Angeles games of 1984, and played in 51 tests for them in all between 1982 and 1988. He was one of thé stars in Ireland's World Cup campaign in Pakistan in 1990, and of the side which finished 7th in the European Championships in 1991. A brilliant and rugged defender, he was voted as Texaco's Hockey Sportstar of the Year for 1984, only the 3rd hockey player to achieve this recognition.

McCONNELL, W G .

Soccer international full-back. Club: Bohemians. He was capped 6 times for Northern Ireland between 1912 and 1914, 3 of these being in the No 2 jersey in Northern Ireland's first historic win in the Home International Championship in 1914.

McCONNELL, W G.

Amateur international golfer. Club: Portmarnock. He won the West of Ireland title twice, in 1925 and 1929, and was runner-up in the 'West' in both 1924 and 1926. He was also twice runner-up in the South of Ireland, in 1924 and 1927, and was runner-up in the Irish Close Championship in 1919. He played for Ireland once, against England in 1925.

McCONNELL, WILLIAM R (BILLY).

Soccer international defender. Club: Reading. He won 8 senior international caps for Northern Ireland between 1925 and 1928, all while at Reading, making him that club's most capped player.

McCONVILLE, TOMMY.

Soccer international defender. Clubs: Dundalk (winning 2 League of Ireland Championship medals, in 1975-76 and 1978-79, and two F.A.I. Cup medals, in 1977 and 1979), Shamrock Rovers, Waterford (winning a League of Ireland Championship medal in 1972-73). A strong able defender for many years in the League of Ireland, he was capped 6 times for the Republic of Ireland, once in 1972, and 5 times in 1973.

McCOOLE, MIKE.

Bareknuckle boxer. He was born in Ireland on 12th March 1837, and he died in New Orleans on October 17th 1886. Moving to the U.S.A., he became a well-known fighter. He claimed the American bareknuckle heavyweight title for the years between 1867 and 1873, and was the undisputed bare-knuckle world heavyweight champion in 1869-1870.

McCORMACK, J.J. (JOE, 'HOBBY HORSE').

Cyclist. Born in Birr, Co Offaly in 1926. An almost legendary figure in the cycling game, in a 25 year winning career from 1938 (winning a race in Birr at the age of 12) to 1963, he won 26 Irish Championship titles, starting with the 3,000 metres title in 1948. He won the N.C.A. race in 1951 and 1952. He represented Ireland 21 times internationally, in 6 world championships, in 8 Manx Internationals etc. He later became one of the leading cycling administrators in Ireland. His son Paul was 2nd in the 1988 Archer Grand Prix in England, won F.B.D./Milk Ras in both 1987 and 1988, represented Ireland in the Olympic Games in Seoul in 1988, and was later a pro in the U.S.A.. Another older son Alan was also a representative of Ireland in the Olympics of 1976 in Montreal and later turned professional on the American circuit, with some moderate success.

McCORMACK, Doctor JOHN DILLON ('J.D.').

Amateur international golfer. Clubs: Hermitage (winning a Senior Cup medal in 1926), Portmarnock (winning Senior Cup medals in 1928, 1933, 1934, 1935 and 1937, and Barton Shield medals in 1928, 1929, 1934 and 1935), and the Grange. Born in 1891. An enormous-hitting player prior to W.W.I. (playing for Ireland against Wales in 1913), he was paralysed from the waist down for 6 years due to injury received in the W.W.I. (and suffered shell-shock, being close to death). Learning to walk again in 1922, he made such a recovery that he later won the Irish Close Championship title 3 times, 1923, 1924 (when he also was runner-up in the Irish Open Amateur title), and 1927. He reached the quarter-final of the British Amateur Championshiip in 1924, and the semi-final of the same event in 1931. He won selection for the Walker Cup in 1924, but could not get the neccessary leave to compete. He played international golf for Ireland over a 24 year period from 1913 to 1937, captaining Ireland in his last 3 years on the side, and playing in the first 6 of the Home International series form 1932 to 1937.

McCORMACK, JOHN ('YOUNG').

Light-heavyweight boxer. Born in Dublin on 11th December 1944. In 40 amateur boxing bouts while a member of the Consolata club, he lost just 2 of them. He went on to become British light-heavyweight champion in 1967-69. In 1967 he won the vacant title when the referee stopped his fight with Welshman Eddie Avoth in the 7th round in June 1967. After a successful defence against another Welshman, Derek Richards with a k.o. in round 7, he lost his title after 19 months in 1969, by being defeated by old rival Eddie Avoth, in Nottingham, being disqualified for allegedly butting. He fought 5 championship bouts in total, including losing again to Avoth in 1970. He fought all over the world, and was enormously popular. His professional career record reads as 33 wins, 1 draw, and 8 losses in 42 bouts. He was voted as Texaco's Boxing Sportstar of the year in 1967. An older brother of Pat McCormack (cv).

McCORMACK, PADDY.

G.A.A. football full-back, Offaly. He played at right corner back on the first Offaly team to reach an All-Ireland Senior Football Championship final in 1961. He was the county's outstanding player for the 60's decade, and was a starring full-back on the Offaly side which won its first Sam Maguire Cup in 1971, winning a 2nd championship medal in 1972. He also played on the Offaly side beaten in the 1969 All-Ireland S.F.C. final by Kerry. He also won 2 Railway Cup medals with Leinster, in 1961 and 1962. Known as 'The Iron Man from Rhode', he received one All-Star award, in 1972, at full-back. Injury led to retirement in 1972.

McCORMACK, PAT.

Light-welterweight boxer. He was born in Dublin, April 28th 1946. He held the British light-welterweight title for 8 months in 1974. In March 1974 he became champion by knocking out the Jamaican-born Des Morrison in the 11th round at the Albert Hall, London. In November of that year he was outpointed by Joey Singleton of England, to lose his title. His professional career of 7 years from 1968 to 1975 consisted of 49 bouts, and included 30 wins, 18 losses, and one draw. He is a younger brother of 'Young' John McCormack (cv).

McCORMICK, TOM.

Welterweight professional boxer. Born in Dundalk, Co Louth on August 8th, 1890, he lived to the age of only 26, being killed in action in France in 1916. Having learnt his trade in Britain, he went to Australia, beating Johnny Summers to claim the British and Empire titles in Sydney over 20 rounds in January 1914. Two weeks later he claimed the world welterweight title when, on 24th January 1914, he defeated Waldemer Holdberg of Denmark by disqualification in the 6th round, in their contest at Melbourne, Australia. After defending successfully against Summers a month later by a first round knock-out, he lost his titles in March of the same year in Sydney, when the Englishman Matt Wells beat him on points over 20 rounds. In the 3 years and 10 months (the 3rd shortest ring career of all world boxing champions) and 46 contests of his professional career, he lost only 6 fights.

McCORMICK, W G.

Hockey international player. He was the winner of a silver medal in the 1908 Olympic Games with an Ireland team which, having successfully bypassed Wales by 3-1 in the semi-final, were then beaten by 8 goals to one in the final by England. This final was the only time he represented Ireland.

McCOURT, FRANK J.

Soccer international wing-half. Born in Portadown, 9th December 1925. Clubs: Bristol Rovers, Shamrock Rovers, Manchester City (helping them to gain promotion to Division One in 1951), Colchester. He was capped 6 times at wing-half for Northern Ireland, twice in 1952 and 4 times the following year.

McCOURT, JIM.

Amateur international boxer. Club: Immaculata B.C. (Belfast). He won the first of 7 Irish Senior National titles in 1963 at featherweight (when he was also Irish Junior champion), then winning at lightweight in 1964, and winning 5 subsequent titles at light-welterweight, in 1966, 1967, 1968, 1969, and 1972. In the 1964 Olympic Games in Tokyo, he won a bronze medal (at the age of 19) in the lightweight division (beaten in the semi-final in a controversial decision by the Russian Viktor Barranikov), and from then until 1980, he reigned as the 'last Irishman to win an Olympic medal' (representing Ireland). The following year (1965) he won a European Championship bronze medal in East Berlin. In 1966, he became the second of only 6 Northern Irish boxers to win a Commonwealth Games gold medal, succeeding at the games in Jamaica, at light-welterweight. He competed in his 2nd Olympic Games in 1968 (carrying the Irish flag at the opening ceremony), only to be beaten in his first bout. He was voted as Texaco's Boxing Sportstar of the Year twice, in 1964 and in 1966.

McCOY, JAMES Joseph (JIM).

Rugby international prop-forward. Born in Enniskillen 28th June 1958. Club: Dungannon. A product of Portora R.S., he has been capped at all 4 levels for Ireland, Schools (1975 and 1976), Under 23 (1982), 'B' also in 1982, and Full (one of the first 7 players to do so). Playing in his first Senior cap in 1985, he played in all matches in Ireland's famous Triple Crown win of 1985. He toured with Ireland to Japan in 1985, France in 1988, and played in the World Cup side Down Under in 1987. An Ulster regular (playing in all 18 games in their 6-in-a-row Interprovincial Championship wins in 1983-1989), for several seasons he vied with Des Fitzgerald for the tight-head berth on the Irish team.

McCOY, RAYMOND.

Soccer international forward. Club: Coleraine. He was capped once for Northern Ireland, in 1987 as a sub against Yugoslavia. He is also an Irish League representative, scoring one goal for them. He was both Ulster young Footballer of the Year and Most Promisiung newcomer in 1983, and in 1987 he was both Ulster Footballer of the Year and N.I.P.F.A. Player of the Year. He was again picked in the Northern Ireland squad in 1992.

McCRACKEN, WILLIAM (BILLY).

Soccer international full-back. Born in Belfast, 29th January 1883. Clubs: Distillery (winning an Irish Cup medal in 1903), Newcastle United (joining for a transfer fee of £50, playing 377 league matches for them 1903 to 1924, and winning an F.A. Cup medal with them in 1910, being on the runners-up sides of 1908 and 1911; he also won 3 League Championship medals, in 1905, 1907, and 1909), and Hull City. A noted penalty taker, he is said to be the man responsible for the alteration of the offside trap rule into soccer, due to his tactic with the 'one-back game'. He was capped 15 times for Northern Ireland over an international career spanning an astonishing 22 years, between 1902 and 1923, and scored one international goal. His first ten caps were before 1907, and there was then a 13 year gap before he was next capped in 1920 (he had been exiled for asking 5 times the normal fee for a match). He later managed Hull City, Millwall, and Aldershot. He died at the ripe old age of 96 in 1979.

McCREA, Wing Commander WILLIAM E (BILL).

Amateur international golfer. Clubs: Walton Heath and Royal Portrush. Born in Ramelton, Co Donegal, 3rd April 1921. On the home front he was runner-up in the 'North' in 1964. Travelling a lot for his golf, he was Austrian Amateur

Champion in 1965, Dutch Amateur Champion in 1966, West of England Amateur Champion in 1962, and in 1968 he finished 2nd in the English Open Amateur Stroke Play title. He played for Ulster in the interprovincial series between 1963 and 1967, winning 13 and halving 2 of his 24 matches. He played 17 Home International matches in 3 series for Ireland betwen 1965 and 1967, winning 8 matches. He also played on the winning Irish side in the 1965 European Championship, winning 3 and halving one of his 6 matches in the triumph.

McCREADY, Samuel MAXWELL (MAX).

Amateur international golfer. Born in Belfast, 8th March 1918. Clubs: Dunmurry, Royal Portrush, Portmarnock, etc. He was capped in 5 Home International series for Ireland, in 1947, 1949, 1950, 1952 and 1954, winning 14 and halving 3 of his 28 matches. He won the 54th British Amateur title (the 2nd of only 4 Irishmen to win this 'major') at Portmarnock in 1949 (the first time it was held outside Britain), beating previous winner Willie Turnesa of the U.S.A. in the final by 2 and 1. Leading amateur in the Irish Open in 1947, he was Derbyshire Open champion in 1953 and Kent Amateur champion in both 1955 and 1956. He won places in 2 Walker Cup sides, 1949 and 1951, losing all three matches in which he played (he had been a reserve in 1947). He had the rare distinction of also winning the Jamaican Open in 1948, and won the R.A.F. championship in 1947. A wealthy cigar tycoon, he was an all-round sportsman, excelling also at boxing, badminton, cricket and rugby. He emigrated to South Africa.

McCREERY, DAVID ('SUPERSUB' or 'ROADRUNNER').

Soccer international midfielder. Born in Belfast, 16th September 1957. Clubs: Manchester United (whom he joined as an apprentice in 1974, playing 108 games for them (51 as a sub), and winning an F.A. Cup medal in 1976 as a playing substitute, while gaining a runner-up medal in 1977), Q.P.R. (1979-81), Tulsa Bay Rowdies, Newcastle United (playing over 250 league games for them 1983 to 1989), Hearts. After being capped at schoolboy and Under 21 levels, he was capped 67 times for Northern Ireland over a 13 year period between 1976 and 1988. He was a major influence on Northern Ireland's fine World Cup campaign's of 1982 and 1986, playing in all 5 matches in the historic 1982 campaign in Spain, and in all 3 matches in the less successful venture in Brazil in 1986.

McCRORY, SAM.

Soccer international centre-forward. Born in Belfast, 11th October 1924. Clubs: Linfield, Swansea City (scoring 46 goals in 103 league matches 1946-49), Ipswich Town (scoring 38 goals in 98 league matches 1949-51), Plymouth Argyle (scoring 11 goals in 50 league matches from 1952-54), and Southend (scoring 90 goals in 205 league matches from 1955 to 1959, including a joint club record of 31 league goals in the 1958-59 season, bringing his English League goals tally to 185). He was capped at 'B' international level for Northern Ireland, and gained only one senior cap for his country, scoring a goal in the 3-2 win over England in 1957.

McCULLOUGH, KEILLER.

Soccer international defender. Clubs: Belfast Celtic (winning Irish League Championship winner's medals in 1932-33 and 1935-36) and Manchester City. An attacking defender with a great heading ability, he was capped 5 times for Northern Ireland between 1935 and 1937.

McCULLOUGH, MAXIE

Amateur international lightweight boxer. Club: Corinthians B.C. (Dublin). He won the Irish National Senior championship title twice at lightweight, in 1947 and 1949. In 1948 he reached the last eight of the Olympic Games lightweight division in the London celebrations, thus being placed joint 5th in the event. He won a European Amateur Championship title at lightweight in Oslo in 1949, the most recent Irish boxer to achieve this feat until Paul Griffin (cv) repeated the deed 42 years later at Gothenburg..

McCULLOUGH, RAY.

Motorcycling road racer. From Dromara, Co Down. In a a career that stretched from 1961 to 1984, he was among the most successful of Ireland's road racers, winning at least 107 races, including victories in England (winning the Isle of Man's 'Southern 100' a total of 9 times), and in Holland. In 1971 he won his only Grand Prix race, the Ulster 250cc title at Dundrod, sensationally beating the then multi-world champion Phil Read. He was voted as Texaco's Motor Sport Sportstar of the Year in 1971.

McCULLOUGH, WAYNE ('THE POCKET ROCKET').

Amateur flyweight and bantamweight boxer. Born in Belfast, 7th July 1970. Club: Albert Foundry, Belfast. He won the Irish National Senior Championship title at fly-weight in 1988 (when he also won the Under 18 and Junior titles at this weight) and 1990, and won at bantamweight in 1992. He represented Ireland in the 1988 Olympic Games in Seoul at light-fly, reachimg the 3rd round (and carried the flag at the opening ceremony). In 1990 he became the 6th Northern Ireland boxer (and first since Barry McGuigan in 1978) to win a Commonweaalth Games Gold Medal, when beating Nokuthula Tshabangu of Zimbawbwe in the final of the fly-weight division in Auckland, New Zealand. Later that year he was one of only 3 European boxers to win a medal (bronze) at the World Cup in Bombay, India. Fighting in his 2nd Olympic Games in 1992 at bantamweight in the Barcelona Games, he fought brilliantly to win a silver medal by beating a Ugandan, an Iraqi, a Nigerian (M Sabo) to win bronze, a Korean (G Sik Li) to reach the final, and fought a brave fight in the final before losing by a margin of 14-8 to Joel Casamayor. He turned pro in early 1993, with good initial progress (winning his first 8 fights up to September 1993). Also a keen bowler, his brother, Alan McCullough, is a professional bantamweight boxer.

McCULLOUGH, WILLAIM J (BILLY).

Soccer international full-back and left-half. Born in Woodburn, 27th July 1935. Clubs: Barn United, Y.M.C.A., Ballyclare Comrades, Portadown, Arsenal (with whom he played, mostly at left back, over 350 matches 1958-1965, missing only 5 games from 1960-61 to 1963-64), Bedford Town, Millwall, Cork Celtic (where he was player-manager), and Derry City. An Irish League XI player, he was capped 10 times for Northern Ireland between 1961 and 1967, all in the No 6 jersey. In 1967 he came back to Ireland, and managed Cork Celtic and Derry City.

McCUSKER, EAMONN.

Amateur international light-middleweight boxer. Club: St John Bosco B.C. (Belfast). He won 4 Irish National Senior titles at light-middleweight, in 1965, 1967, 1968, and 1969. He represented Ireland at the Olympic Games of 1968 in Mexico in the light-middle division, losing to a Cuban in his first bout.

McCUTCHEON, RODNEY.

International bowls player. Born in Bangor, 2nd April 1962. He first came to prominance at the age of 20 by winning both the Irish and British Isles Singles. In 1988 he was a member of the Ireland side which captured the World Champinship Fours title in New Zealand. In 1990 he was a member of the Northern Ireland side which won a Commonwealth Games silver medal at the games in Auckland in 1990.

McDAID, DANNY.

Long-distance runner. He was the winner of the Irish National B.L.E. marathon championship 3 times, in 1974, 1976, and 1983. He represented Ireland at 2 Olympic Games in the marathon event, in 1972 when he finished 23rd in Munich when timed at 2:22.25, and again in Montreal in 1976, when he finished in 42nd place in a time of 2:27.075.

McDERMOTT, PETER ('THE MAN IN THE CAP').

G.A.A. footballing left full forward, Meath. Born in 1918, he made his senior inter-county debut in 1940. He was captain of the Meath team that defeated Kerry by 1-13 to 1-7 in the 1954 All-Ireland Senior Football Championship final, retiring that year. He had previously won a Sam Maguire Cup winner's medal with Meath in 1949. He was also on the Meath side which lost 2 All-Ireland S.F.C. finals in succession, in 1951 and 1952. The year before his captaincy of the winning All-Ireland side, 1953, he refereed the final between Kerry and Armagh, and he later refereed the 1956 final betwen Galway and Cork. He also won a Railway Cup medal. One of the game's great left corner-forwards, he won an All-Time All-Star award in 1989. He was known as 'the man in the cap'. A pioneer of the Australian Rules 'connection', he managed the first Ireland team to play in the international series. He was a secretary and vice-chairman of the Meath County Board for many years.

McDONAGH, DESSIE.

Horse Trainer. Formerly a jockey, he trains at Moynalty, Kells, Co Meath. He trained the great Monksfield to win 2 successive Champion Hurdles at the great National Hunt Festival at Cheltenham, in both 1978 and 1979. The horse also won the Templegate Hurdle at Aintree twice. His other good horses have included Stranfield (winner of the 1979 Waterford Crystal Supreme Novices Hurdle at Cheltenham), and Brevet.

McDONAGH, JIM M.

Soccer international goalkeeper. Born in Rotherham on 6th October 1952. Clubs: Rotherham (to whom he was apprenticed, playing 121 league games for them 1970-75), Bolton Wanderers (1976-79 and 1982 to 84), Everton (1980-82), Notts County (1984-88), and Wichita. Although capped for England at youth level in 1971, he declared for the Republic of Ireland, and won 25 international caps from his debut in 1981 until 1988.

McDONAGH, MATTIE.

G.A.A. football midfielder and centre half-forward, Galway. A dual player as a youth, he, in the space of one week in 1953, legally played minor football for Galway against Rosconmmon one Sunday, and 7 days later played minor hurling for Roscommon against Galway. The Ballygar man went on to become the only Galway player to win 4 All-Ireland Senior Championship Football winner's medals, which he achieved in 1956 (in midfield) and in the famous 3-in-a-row side of 1964, 1965, and 1966, all at centre half-forward. He also won 5 other Connacht S.F.C. medals, in 1957, 1958, 1959 (when Down beat them in the All-Ireland final), 1960, and in 1963 (when they were beaten in the All-Ireland final by Dublin), and was on 2 Galway sides beaten in National Football League finals, in 1965 and 1967. He won one Railway Cup medal with Connacht, in 1958. In 1966 he became only the 3rd Galway man to be nominated as Texaco Footballer of the Year.

McDONAGH, PAT.

Rowing international and bobsleigh driver. Rowing clubs: Commercial and Neptune. At rowing, he won 6 Irish Championship titles, at eights in 1978, 1986 and 1987, in coxed fours in 1987 and 1988, and in the coxless pairs in 1988. He won 2 championships at Henley, the 1982 Britannia Cup (in coxed fours), and the 1986 Ladies Plate in eights. He rowed in 2 World

Championships, in 1979 at Bled and in 1987 at Copenhagen. He also represented Ireland at 2 Summer Olympics, Moscow in 1980 in the coxed 4's which finished 11th, and in 1988 in Seoul, being unplaced in the coxed pairs. In 1992 he became one of the first two Irishmen to join the exclusive club of 'Double Olympians' (i.e. Summer and Winter Games) when he was a driver in the bobsleigh event at Albertville (also joining the exclusive band of Olympians to represent Ireland at 3 different Olympic celebrations).

McDONAGH, SEAMUS.

Heavyweight boxer. Born in Co Meath 1963. As an amateur member of the Baconstown club, he won All-Ireland amateur titles. Emigrating the New York in 1983, he turned professional, won the U.S. Golden Gloves tournament, and up to June 1990 had won 19 (with 14 k.o's), lost one and drawn one of his fights, and had reached World ranking of 10. He later (unsuccessfully) fought Evander Holyfield in Atlantic City for a shot at the world title.

McDONAGH, W. PATRICK.

Hockey international outside right. He lived from 1902 to 1961. Clubs: Dublin University, East Antrim, and Cliftonville. He was capped 29 times for Ireland between 1923 and 1934, and played on the Triple Crown winning side of 1933. Also a fine cricketer and tennis player, he was an artist and poet. His younger brother J A McDonagh, a member of Dublin University, played hockey 11 times for Ireland between 1936 and 1939, including 8 of the 9 matches in the 3-in-a-row Triple Crown side of 1937, 1938, and 1939.

McDONALD, ALAN.

Soccer international defender. Born in Belfast, 12th October 1963. Clubs: Queen's Park Rangers (to whom he was appremnticed, playing in over 250 league matches for them up to 1993), Charlton Athletic (on loan). He has been capped 41 times for Northern Ireland from 1986 to mid 1993, and played in the No 5 jersey in all 3 of Northern Ireland's matches in the 1986 World Cup finals in Mexico.

McDONALD, BARRY.

International gymnast. Clubs: Grange G.C. and University of Illinois, Chicago. Born in 1972, and from the South Circular Road in Dublin, he started at the age of 8. In 1990, under the coaching of C.J. Johnson, he reached the rank of No 1 college gymnast in the U.S.A., attaining a score of 56.7 in the National Independent College Championships; in one event in Michigan, he recorded 2 'perfect tens' in a score of 9.95 on the parallel bars, his best event, and the combined demands of the other 5 events (the horse, the floor, the vault, the high bar, and the pommel horse), made him the top performer. His father, Shay McDonald, is a member of the O.C.I..

MacDONALD, JAMES.

Cricket and hockey international player. Born in Comber, Co Down, 17th September 1906. A dual international, as a left hand batsman and a slow left arm bowling cricketer (whose club's included Lincolnshire and Cambridge University), he was one of Ireland's finest in his day. Capped 29 times between 1926 and 1938, his average of 28.47 (from 1196 runs in 48 overs) places him among Ireland's best batsmen. As a bowler he took 82 wickets in 46 overs, for the loss of 1,720 runs, and a respectable average of 20.97 runs per wicket. As a hockey full-back (club: North Down, being by far and away the club's most capped player) he was capped 25 times for Ireland between 1928 and 1936, all in succession (including involvement in Ireland's first ever Triple Crown in the Home International Championship), and captained the side twice. His younger brother Thomas John MacDonald (born in Comber, 27th December 1908), was also a fine international cricket batsman, and is ranked almost identically in the international averages as James (with 28.38 off 738 runs in 27 innings). He was capped in 17 matches for Ireland between 1927 and 1939, and is one of only 7 Irish batsmen to score 3 or more centuries for his country (his best score being a 132 v Scotland in 1928).

MacDONALD, Dr JAMES ALEXANDER.

Rugby international forward. 1849-1928. Clubs: Methodist College, Belfast and Royal University of Ireland. One of the pioneers of international rugby in Ireland (playing in Ireland's first ever international, against England at the Kensington Oval in 1975), he won 13 caps in 10 seasons (only one of these games was won), without missing a season in the Irish side, and when he retired in 1884 after captaining the side for his last 2 matches, he was the only player left who had played in Ireland's first ever international in 1875, and thus he remained Ireland's most capped player for 10 years until passed out by C V Rooke (cv). He was a Chairman of the British Medical Association.

McDONALD, JIMMY.

International athletics walker. A native of New Ross Co Wexford, he was born 11th April, 1964. Club: Dubin City Harriers. He has been Irish champion many times over many of the different distances, including 5 times at 20k (his first being at the age of 18). He has held the Irish record at 3 kilometres and 10 kilometres (track). Finishing 7th in the World Indoors in 1991, in 1989 he became only the 2nd man in history (and the first outdoors) to break 11 minutes for the 3,000 metres. He has represented Ireland at 2 Olympic Games, Seoul in 1988 (when he finished 17th in the 20 kilometres walk, taking 5 minutes off his personal best), and in Barcelona, again in the 20k walk when he finished in a highly creditable 6th place in 85 minutes and 16 seconds (4 minutes behind the winner). A former Christian Brothers novice, he is a teacher in Dublin.

McDONALD, PATRICK J ('BABE').

Field athlete. Born as Pat McDonnell in Co Clare, 26th July 1878, he died 1954 in New York. He won the American A.A.U. shot putt title 6 times, in 1911, 1912, 1914, 1919, 1920, and 1922, also winning 9 indoor A.A.U. titles. One of a group of that time known as the 'Irish Whales', he also won 10 outdoor A.A.U. 56lb shot events (bringing his outdoor tally to 16 A.A.U. wins), the last in 1933 when he was aged 56 years and 339 days, making him the oldest ever winner of an A.A.U. title. A New York policeman by profession, he won a gold medal in the 1912 Stockholm Olympic Games shot-putt event, when throwing an Olympic record (that lasted until 1928) and personal best, at 50' 4", beating the champion and favourite, American Ralph Rose (who had beaten him into the silver medal spot in the now discontinued 'shot putt with both hands' event at the same games). There being no Olympics in 1916 due to war, he went on to, on 21st of August 1920, to became the oldest track and field athlete in Olympic history to win a gold medal, when aged 42 years and 26 days, he won the 56lb weight throw, at Antwerp, with an Olympic record throw of 36' 11", and beating fellow-Irishman Paddy Ryan in to 2nd place, and thus bringing his Olympic medal tally to three in total, 2 gold and one silver. The 56lb-weight event was then discontinued. He finished 4th in the 1920 Olympic shot-putt. He was in the N.Y.P.D. from 1905 until 1946.

McDONNELL, JIM.

G.A.A. footballer, Louth. Having won Leinster S.F.C. medals in both 1950 (when the county were beaten by Mayo in the All-Ireland S.F.C. final) and 1953, he eventually got his just reward, when in 1957 Louth won it's most recent All-Ireland Senior Championship title. One of the best Louth players of his era, he won 3 Railway Cup medals in succession with Leinster, in 1953, 1954, and in 1955.

McDONNELL, JIM.

G.A.A. football left half-back, Cavan. Club: Cavan Gaels (whom he captained to the county championship in 1965). He was a member of the Cavan minors which were beaten by Galway in the All-Ireland M.H.C. final in 1952. He played a memorable game when Cavan were beaten by Kerry in the 1955 All-Ireland Senior Football Championship semi-final replay. In 1960, he was a member of the Cavan side beaten by Down in the first ever all-Ulster National Football League final. He won 4 Railway Cup medals with Ulster, in 1956, 1960, 1963 (when he became the 3rd Cavanman to captain a winning Railway Cup side), and in 1964, all achieved in the No 7 jersey. He also won Ulster Senior Football Championship medals with Cavan in both 1962 and 1964. He was Chairman of the Cavan County Board 1970-74.

McDONNELL, JOHNNY ('THE MAN WITH THE HAT').

G.A.A. football goalkeeper, Dublin. Club: St Laurence O'Tooles. He won 2 All-Ireland Senior Football Championship medals with Dublin, in 1922 and 1923, being on the losing side in All-Ireland S.F.C. finals three times, in 1920, 1924 and in 1934. He played in an astonishing 14 Leinster S.F.C. finals from 1913 to 1934, and was on the winning side 7 times, a record for a Dublin player of either code (later equalled by Jimmy Keaveney cv). He became the first Dublin player to captain a Railway Cup winning side in 1933, and in 1935 became the 2nd player to captain 2 Railway Cup winning sides. His total Railway Cup tally is 5, also gaining honours in 1929, 1930, and 1932. A brother of Paddy McDonnell (cv), he also played for Ireland in 3 Tailteann Games.

McDONNELL, PAT.

G.A.A. hurling full-back, Cork. Club: Iniscarra. A fine rugby player at Pres (Cork) school, he went on to win 2 successive All-Ireland Under 21 Championship hurling medals with Cork, in 1970 and 1971. He also later won 2 All-Ireland Senior Hurling Championship winner's medals with Cork, in 1970 (when aged only 20) and 1976, while he was on the losing side in the All-Ireland S.H.C. decider of 1972. Regarded as one of the Rebel County's most stylish full-backs, in 1970 he became the third Cork hurler to be selected as Texaco Hurler of the Year.

McDONNELL, PADDY.

G.A.A. football full-forward, Dublin. Club: St Laurence O'Tooles. Regarded as one of the game's greatest full-forwards, he won 3 Railway Cup football medals with Leinster, in the province's first 3 victories of 1928, 1929 and 1930. He also won 2 All-Ireland Senior Football Championship titles with Dublin, in 1922 and in 1923 when captaining the side to a 1-5 to 1-3 win over Kerry. He also captained the Dublin side which were beaten by Kerry in the following year's All-Ireland S.F.C. final (having earlier been on the side which also lost the 1920 All-Ireland S.F.C. final). A brother of Johnny McDonnell (cv), sharing his All-Ireland successes with him, he also played for Ireland in the Tailteann Games of 1928.

McELHINNEY, GERRY.

Soccer international defender, G.A.A. right half-forward (Derry), and international boxer. Born in Derry, 19th September 1956. In soccer as a central defender, he has played with Distillery, Bolton Wanderers, Rochdale, Plymouth Argyle, and Peterborough United. He was capped for the Northern Ireland senior international side 6 times, in 1984 and 1985, all while at Bolton Wanderers. He later coached Peterborough United, and became manager of Limerick City in 1991. He has also represented Ireland at international level in 2 other sports. In G.A.A. football he gained international honours by winning an All-Star award in 1975 at right half-forward. He had played in the winning Ulster Senior Football Championship sides with Derry in both 1975 and 1976. He was also capped for Ireland at boxing, thus participating at international level at soccer, gaelic football and boxing.

McENEANEY, EAMONN.

G.A.A. football centre half forward, Monaghan. CLub: Castleblaney. He scored 9 points from frees in Monaghan's Ulster M.F.C. final defeat in 1978. He played a prominent role in Monaghan's fine year of 1985, when they won the Ulster S.F.C., and for the first time won the National Football League, the county's first national title in the senior inter-county grade. McEneaney was the chief scorer for the county in both campaigns, scoring an equalising point in the All-Ireland semi-final draw with Kerry. He also played basketball to Community Games final level, and once scored 2 goals past Packie Bonner (cv) in an F.A.I. youths competition.

McENIFF, BRIAN.

G.A.A. football right half-back, New York and Donegal. Club: St Joseph's of Ballyshannon-Bundoran (with whom he won 6 county championship medals). A minor for Donegal from 1959 to 1961, he later helped New York (as a defender) to win the 1964 National Football League title. A fine defender, he was an influential figure (as player and manager) when Donegal won their first ever Ulster Senior Football Championhsip title in 1972, and was also on the side which regained the title in 1974. He won a Dr McKenna Cup medal in 1974, and won 2 Railway Cup medals with Ulster in 1970 and in 1971, at right half-back. In 1972 he became the first Donegal player, and first Ulster defender, to win an All-Star award, at right half-back. He was manager of the Donegal senior side which gained their Ulster S.F.C. successes in 1983, 1990 and 1992, and led the county to their first ever appearence in an All-Ireland S.F.C. final in 1992, which they won in great style. He has also managed the Ulster Railway Cup team. In 1992 he was voted Manager of the Year.

McENTEE, Dr GERRY.

G.A.A. football midfielder, Meath. Born in the autumn of 1956. Clubs: Nobber and Summerhill. A product of St Finians College, Mullingar, he has won 2 All-Ireland Senior Football Championship winner's medals with Meath, in 1987 and in 1988, both from midfield, and also won 3 other Leinster S.F.C. medals, in 1986, and in 1990 and 1991 (when Meath went on to be beaten in the All-Ireland final). He has won one All-Star award, being honoured at midfield in 1987. In 1987 he became the 4th Meathman to captain a winning Leinster Railway Cup side. A surgeon.

McENTEE, MARJORIE.

Ten pin bowls international player. Club: Stillorgan. Born in Dublin. she won a bronze medal in the European Youth Championship for Ireland in 1975, and has represented Ireland at junior and senior levels many times. She won Irish National titles many times, and 1985 she made the headlines by becoming the first Irish person to win an amateur World Championship title, when in Seoul, Korea, she won the Women's Bowling World Cup, in which after getting to the final after a hard stepladder tournament, she beat the hot favourite for the title, Britain's Judy Howlett, over 2 games by the fine scores of 205 to 177 and by 196 over 167. She was voted as Texaco's Sportstar of the Year in 1985. Soon afterwards she emigrated to the the U.S.A. and married there.

McEVOY, ANDY M.

Soccer international inside forward. Born in Dublin, 15th July 1938. A native of Bray, he (at the age of 18) joined Blackburn Rovers from Bray Wanderers. In the period between 1958 and 1966, he scored 89 league goals in 183 league appearences for Blackburn. His 29 goals for Blackburn in the 1964-65 season placed him as joint top scorer in Division

One football in England, the only Republic of Ireland player since the World War 2 to achieve this feat. Joining Limerick in 1967, he won an F.A.I. Cup winner's medal with them in 1971. He was capped 17 times for the Republic of Ireland, scoring 6 international goals. He was voted as Texaco's Soccer Sportstar of the Year in 1964.

McFAUL, WILLIE.

Soccer international goalkeeper. Born in Coleraine, 1st October 1943. Clubs: Linfield (winning an Irish League winner's medal in 1966) and Newcastle United (playing 290 league matches for them from 1966 to 1974, playing in a losing F.A. Cup final in 1974). A former amateur international, he was capped 6 times for Northern Ireland between 1967 and 1974, and may have won many more but for the presence of Pat Jennings (cv) in the side. After spending 22 years on the books at Newcastle in various capacities, he became manager at Coleraine.

McFETTRIDGE, OLCAN ('CLOOT').

G.A.A. hurling full-forward, Antrim. Born in Ballycastle. Club: Armoy. A county minor in 1980, and senior county player in 1987, in 1989 he was a member of the first Antrim side to qualify for an All-Ireland Senior Hurling Championship final since 1943, scoring two valuable goals in the fine semi-final win against Offaly. He won an All-Star in 1989 in the left half forward position. A plasterer.

McGANN, BARRY J.

Rugby international out-half. Born 28th May 1948. Clubs: Cork Constitution (winning Munster Senior Cup medals in 1970, 1972, and 1973), and Lansdowne. A brilliant schoolboy player with Presentation Brothers, Cork (captaining the winning Munster School's Senior Cup side in 1966), he was capped 25 times for Ireland between 1969 and 1976, and scored a total of 60 points for Ireland, consisting of 11 penalties, 6 drop goals, 3 conversions, and one try. In 1973 he broke George Norton's (cv) seasonal best total score of 25 in the International Championship, when he scored 26 points in four games. A portly but deceptively fleety player, his ability to do magic things with his boot, and his great distribution skills are only part of the reason why he pushed the legendary Mike Gibson (cv) into the centre later in his career. Also a talented soccer player, he played League of Ireland football with Shelbourne, and was a youth international on the Irish XI which beat a Holland side which contained Johan Cruyff in the U.E.F.A. finals, to finish 6th.

McGARRY, BRIDIE.

G.A.A. camogie centre-back, Kilkenny. Club: St Pauls (with whom she has won 7 All-Ireland Club Championship medals, including 1968, 1969, 1971, 1975, 1977, and 1987). She has won 7 All-Ireland Senior Championship medals with Kilkenny, in 1976, 1977, 1981, 1985, 1986, 1987, and 1988, captaining the O'Duffy Cup-winning side in both 1985 and 1987. An attacking player, she has won Gael Linn medals, and has recieved a B&I award.

McGARTY, PADDY (PACKIE).

G.A.A. footballing half-forward, Leitrim. One of Leitrim's greatest players, he was a member of each of the county's sides which were beaten in 4 successive Connacht Senior Football Championship finals by Galway, in 1957, 1958, 1959, and 1960 (and again in another defeat by Galway in 1963). He is the only Leitrim player to win 2 Railway Cup medals with Connacht, playing at left half-forward in the wins of 1957 and 1958. One of the greatest players never to win an All-Ireland S.F.C. medal, in 1984 he was selected at left half-forward on the 'Team of the Century' for those in such predicament.

McGAUGHEY, MARTIN.

Soccer international forward. Clubs; Linfield (winning Irish League Championship winner's medals in the clubs 6-in-a-row of 1981-82, 1982-83, 1983-84, 1984-85, 1985-86 and 1986-87, and again in 1988-89), and also winning an I.F.A. Cup medal in 1982). One of the Irish Leagues finest goal-getters of the 1980's, he scored over 300 goals for the 'Blues' in his first 450 games with the club. He won his only international cap for Northern Ireland in 1985, as a substitute against Israel. His 34 goals in the 1984-85 season make him the first Irish player (North or South) to win any medal in the annual Golden Boot of Europe (taking silver behind Fernando Gomes of Porto). He has also scored a goal for the Irish League representative side. In 1985 he was voted as both N.I.P.F.A. Player of the Year and N.I.F.W.A.A. Player of the Year.

McGEE, PEADAR (PAUDGE).

Handballer. A Mayoman from Newport, he was born in 1943. He won his first Irish title in 1962 when partnering Michael Walsh to the 60x30 Junior Softball Doubles crown. He shares the record (with the great J J Gilmartin) of winning more Irish Senior Hardball Singles titles than any other player, with 10 wins, being champion in 1965 and 1967, then for 6-in-a-row in 1972, 1973, 1974, 1975, 1976 and 1977, winning 2 more titles in 1982 and 1983. He also won 5 Hardball Doubles titles (all with fellow Mayomen), in 1965, 1966, 1967 with P Bolingbrook, in 1974 with B Colleran, and in 1976 with Paddy McCormack. He also won a senior softball doubles title, with W Walsh in 1966. In 1980 he won the All-Ireland 4x20 Senior Doubles Championship with Paddy McCormack. He was voted B&I 'Handballer of the Year' in 1983.

McGEE, PAUL G.

Soccer international forward. Born in Sligo, 19th June 1954. Clubs: Sligo Rovers (playing his League of Ireland debut at just 16 in 1970, spending 8 different terms with them, and being their joint leading goalscorer when they won the League of Ireland Championship in 1976-77), Galway United (2 terms, being the club's career best league goal-scorer with 65 from 1985-89, and also holding the club record season's best goal tally of 20 in the 1987-88 season), Finn Harps (winning an F.A.I. Cup medal with them in 1974), Hereford United, Waterford United, Toronto Mets (being their leading scorer while there), Montreal Castors (being their leading scorer for 3 seasons, and winning a League title), Queen's Park Rangers (they were relegated in 1979), Preston North End (they were relegated to Division 3), Burnley (winning a Third Division winner's medal), Shamrock Rovers (winning a League and Cup double with them in 1984-85), Kidderminster Harriers, Haarlem, Derry City, Athlone Town. A product of Summerhill College in Sligo (helping them to All-Ireland Colleges titles twice), he was capped at youth and Inter-League level for Ireland. He has played for many clubs in many countries (making a phenominal 27 club changes 1969-91), and has scored over 100 league goals in his career. Having twice played for Ireland's Under 21 side, he was capped 16 times for the senior Republic of Ireland side between 1978 and 1981, scoring 4 international goals. He later managed Galway United.

McGEE, WILLIE.

G.A.A. football full-forward, Mayo. Born in 1947. Club: Burrishoole (Mayo, winning a Mayo I.F.C. medal) and Garda (Dublin). A Mayo minor in 1965, he, in the 1967 All-Ireland Under 21 Championship final replay against Dublin, scored 4 goals to give Mayo its first win in this competition (and won a 2nd Connacht Under 21 medal in 1968). In a senior inter-county career from 1967 to 1976, he won a Railway Cup medal and a Connacht S.F.C. medal in 1969, and was on the Mayo side which won it's last national senior title, the 1970 National Football League. He also won a Connacht J.F.C. medal with Mayo and 2 All-Ireland 'Masters' (Over 35) medals with Kildare.

A quality player, in 1984 he was selected in the full-forward slot in the 'Team of the Century' for players who never won an All-Ireland senior championship medal. A Garda superintendent.

McGILLIGAN, BRIAN.

G.A.A. football centre-field, Derry. A member of the Derry side beaten in the 1985 Ulster S.H.C. final, he later played in the county's first title win in 11 years in 1987. In 1992 he was a member of the Derry side which won the National Football League for the 2nd time only (the first being as far back as 1947). Touring Australia with Ireland in the Compromise Rules series in 1986, he has won one All-Star award, in 1987 at centre-field. He won a 2nd Ulster Senior Football Championship medal in 1993, when the county reached it's first All-Ireland final since 1958, and went on to win the Sam Maguire Cup for the first time.

McGIMPSEY, GARTH.

Amateur international golfer. Born Bangor, Co Down, July 1955. Club: Bangor (winning Senior Cup medals in 1981 and 1984, and the club championship 9 times). He has won 10 Irish championship titles (placing him 4th in the all-time list), including: the 'North' 5 times, in 1978, 1984, 1991, 1992 and 1993; the 'West' 3 times, in 1984, 1988 and 1993 (and was runner-up in 1983). one 'East' in 1988 (he was runner-up in 1979, 1980 and 1992), also capturing the Irish Close Championship in 1988. He also won the British Amateur title in 1985 (the most recent of only 4 Irish victors of this 'major') at Royal Dornoch, beating his final opponent by 8 and 7, thus qualifying to play in 2 U.S. Masters tournaments in Augusta, Georgia. He has been a Walker Cup player 3 times, 1985 (winning one and halving 2 of his 4 matches), 1989 (being a member of the first side to capture the trophy on American soil since the competition's inception in 1922, gaining 1 point out of 3 matches), and in the match in Portmarnock in 1991 when he scored 2 wins and 2 losses. Representing Great Britain and Ireland in the St Andrew's Trophy in 1984, 1986, and in 1988, he was on the winning G.B. & Ireland team in the Eisenhower Trophy (the amateur's World Cup) in 1988. Playing for Ulster in interprovincials since 1979, he has a 72% record of success. Playing in well over 100 international matches for his country, he was on winning Irish sides for a record-equalling 5 times in the Home Interantional series, in 1985, 1991 and 1992, and when capturing the Triple Crown wins of 1987 and 1990. In European Team championship matches 1981-1991, out of an Irish record of 33 matches played he has won 21 (being on winning sides in 1983 and 1987). He was also on winning Irish Cartier Trophy winning sides in 1986 and 1988. Probably Ireland's finest modern amateur golfer, he won the Willie Gill Award in both 1984 and 1988, and his handicap has been as low as plus 2.4.

McGINLEY, PAUL.

Amateur and professional golfer. Club: Grange. Born 1967. As a youngster he was a gaelic footballer of some use, winning a Dublin Under 21 Championship medal with Bodenstown St Edna's in 1985. In golf, he has won the European Junior title, the Leinster Youth's title in both 1986 and 1987, and in 1988 he became the Youth's Champion of both Ireland and Scotland. In 1989 he won the Irish Close Champinship at Rosses Point, and was runner-up in the 'North' in both 1990 and 1991. In 1991 he won both the South of Ireland Championship at Lahinch and the Mullingar Scratch Cup. Making his Home International debut in 1989, in 1990 he secured 5 out of a possible 6 points in Ireland's first ever Triple Crown success on foreign soil in this event, at Conway in Wales. He won selection on the Walker Cup side in the match played at Portmarnock in 1991, losing two and winning one of his 3 matches (this victory was in the foursomes against a duo which included the much-vaunted Phil Mickelson of the U.S.). Turning pro soon after the Walker Cup, he then won the 1991 World Under 25 Championship, and went on the win his players card in style, finishing in joint 2nd place in the school, and gaining an exempt card in his first season. His 2nd season as a professional started promisingly, gaining 2nd placings in both the Lyons and French Opens.

McGINNITY, PETER.

G.A.A. football midfielder and right half-forward, Fermanagh. Born in 1953. Clubs: Roslea (winning a county championship medal as a minor), St John's, Belfast (helping them to win the county's first Ulster Club Championship success in 1978, when they were beaten in the All-Ireland final). He played on 2 successive Fermanagh teams beaten in the final of the All-Ireland Under 21 Championship, in 1970 (when only 16) and 1971. A star of the Fermanagh football scene from 1971, although the county has reached only one Ulster S.F.C. final (in 1982, losing to Armagh), in that time. He helped Fermanagh to capture the Dr McKenna Cup for the first time in 44 years in 1977. In 1980 he became the first Fermanaghman to captain a winning Ulster Railway Cup side, also winning medals in 1979, 1983 (again as captain), and in 1984 (making this a record haul for any Fermanaghman), and is the province's leading scorer in this competition. Regarded as one of the finest players who never won an All-Ireland S.F.C. medal, in 1982 he became the only Fermanagh player to date to win an All-Star award, being selected at right half-forward. His brother Gerry played alongside him in the midfield for the county in the Dr McKenna triumph in 1977.

McGLADDERY, F NORMAN.

Hockey international centre-forward. Club: Banbridge (winning Irish Senior Cup medals in 1982 and 1984). He won 50 senior international caps for Ireland between 1977 and 1985 (scoring many international goals), and was a member of the Intercontinental Cup team in 1981, and the World Cup side in 1978 (as a teenager).

McGOLDRICK, EDDIE.

Soccer international midfielder. Born in London, 30th April 1965. Clubs: Nuneaton, Kettering Town, Northampton Town (playing over 100 league matches for them in 1986-1989), Crystal Palace (1989-1993), and moving to Arsenal in 1993 for £1,000,000. Comfortable at sweeper, centre-half, full-back or in the midfield, he has won 8 international caps for the Republic of Ireland (mainly as a 2nd string player) up to mid 1993.

McGOUGH, JOHN.

Middle-distance athlete. A native of Co Monaghan, he was born in 1887, and emigrated to Scotland, gathering a reputation as an 800 yards and 1 mile international runner (mainly running for Scotland against his native Ireland). Competing in the Intercalated Games in Athens in 1906, he failed to qualify for the 800 metres final, but went on to win a silver medal (representing Great Britain) in the 1,500 metres, finishing in 4:12.6, three yards behind the favourite, James Lightbody of the U.S.A.. He also competed unsuccessfully in the 5,000 metres at these Games. Two years later in the Olympic Games of 1908 in London, he failed to qualify for the 1,500 metres semi-final. He died at the age of 80 in 1967.

McGOVERN, JOHNNY.

G.A.A. hurling left half-back and centre half-forward, Kilkenny. Born in 1932. Club: Bennetsbridge (winning 13 county championship medals with them). A member of the Kilkenny minors beaten in the All-Ireland M.H.C. final in 1949, he won 2 Liam McCarthy Cup medals with Kilkenny, in 1957 and again in 1963, also playing on a losing side in the 1959 All-Ireland S.H.C. final. In a senior inter-county career which stretched from 1952 to 1963, he won 2 other Leinster

S.H.C. medals, in 1953 and 1958. He became the 6th Kilkennyman to captain a winning Leinster Railway Cup side in 1954, his only winner's medal in this arena. He also won a National Hurling League medal in 1962, and Oireachtas medals in 1957 and 1959.

McGOWN, THOMAS Melville Whitson (TOM).

Rugby international forward. 1876-1956. Club: N.I.F.C. (winning Ulster Senior Cup and League medals with the club). He won only 3 international caps for Ireland, two of them being in the 1899 Triple Crown side, but proved his ability when he went on the combined British and Irish 'Lion's' tour to Australia of 1899, and played in all 4 Test matches. He won a Blue with Cambridge in 1896.

McGRATH, R CHRIS.

Soccer international midfielder. Born in Belfast 29th November 1954. Clubs: Tottenham Hotspur (to whom he was apprenticed), Millwall (on loan), Manchester United (1976-1980, starting only 15 first team games), Tulsa Roughnecks. He won 21 international caps for Northern Ireland between 1974 and 1979, the last 3 as a substitute, and scored 4 international goals.

McGRATH, GEORGE

Flat racing jockey. Born 28th January 1943. He was Leading Apprentice while attached to Bertie Kerr (having his first winner in 1966), and later, while with Seamus McGrath he was Irish leading Jockey twice, in 1965 and 1970 (with his career highest tally of winner's in a season in Ireland of 54 winners). His 3 Irish Classic wins include the Irish Sweeps Derby in 1973 with Weavers Hall, the Irish 2,000 Guineas in 1974 on Furry Glen, and the Irish St Leger in 1970 on Allangrange. Riding the world over, he also rode winners of all of India's Classic races.

McGRATH, JOE.

G.A.A. football left full-forward, Mayo. He was a member of the Mayo side that won Connacht S.F.C. title in 1981, and was also in the county side beaten in the final of the National Football League in 1978. In 1979, when Mayo were defeated in the Connacht S.F.C. final by Roscommon, he won his only All-Star award, at left corner-forward.

McGRATH, JOHN ('JOBBER').

G.A.A. hurling midfielder, Westmeath. Probably Westmeath's greatest hurler, he was a star for a side which never in his time even reached a Leinster S.H.C. final. He won a solitary Railway Cup medal with Leinster in 1956. One of the greatest hurlers never to win an All-Ireland S.H.C. medal, he was selected in 1984 at midfield on the 'Team of the Century' for those hurlers to fail in this goal.

McGRATH, JOSIE.

G.A.A. camogie player, Cork. Club: Old Aloysians. She won 4 All-Ireland Senior Championship medals, in 1934 (Cork's first win), 1935 (when she was captain of the Cork side which beat Dublin 4-3 to 1-4), 1936, and in 1939. A fine striker of the ball, she later became Lady Mayoress of Cork. Her daughter, Deirdre Young, played camogie for Cork and Munster.

McGRATH, LEONARD.

G.A.A. hurler and footballer, Galway. Born in Leitrim, a parish near Athenry, Co Galway (other sources say he was born in Australia). He was on Galway's first ever All-Ireland Senior Championship-winning sides in both codes, the Hurling Senior Championship win of 1923 (scoring 3 goals in the final), and 2 years later when the county were the winner's of the All-Ireland Senior Football Championship, in 1925. This dual winning of titles in both codes did not happen again until Jack Lynch (cv) won his football title in 1945. McGrath was also on the Galway sides beaten in the finals of the 1924 and 1925 All-Ireland Senior Hurling Championships.

McGRATH, MARY Mrs.

Coursing trainer. A Coalissland, Co Tyrone housewife. She has won the Irish Coursing Derby 6 times, including in 1982 with Martyr Scotch, 1983 with Autumn Crystal, 1986 with Sir Lancelot, 1988 with Pyramid Club, and 1989 with Donovan's Ranger. She also won the 1986 Oaks with Rossa Inn.

McGRATH, MATT.

Field athlete, hammer thrower. Born in Nenagh, 18th December 1879, he died in 1941. He broke the world record for the hammer many times, including October 1911 at 187' 4", or 57.10 metres. He also set world records for the 35lb and the 56 lb weight. He won 7 A.A.U. hammer titles in the 19 year period from 1908 to 1926, and also won seven 56lb weight A.A.U. titles. He then went on to win 3 Olympic hammer medals representing the United States while competing in 4 Olympic Games from 1908 to 1924 (this was then the longest span of track and field events for Olympic medal-winning): he won a silver medal in 1908, 2 feet behind fellow-Irishman John J Flanagan (he also competed in the tug-of-war in this games); a gold medal in Stockholm in 1912 with a distance of 54.84 metres, an Olympic record that lasted 24 years (all of his 6 throws were at least 15 feet longer than any other competitor); and a silver medal again in 1924 at the age of 45 years and 205 days, making him the oldest medalist in the throwing events in Olympic history (in 1920 he was injured, and was placed 5th behind Pat Ryan cv, an Irishman). In 1928 he was controversially left out of the U.S.A. team for the Amsterdam Olympics, thus missing the chance to participate in 5 different Olympic Games. He was a policeman in New York, becoming Chief Inspector of the N.Y.C.P.D.'s Traffic Control in 1936.

McGRATH, MICHAEL ('HOPPER').

G.A.A. hurling right half-forward and right full-forward, Galway. Born in New Inn-Bullaun, Co Galway on 30th June 1963. Club: New Inn-Bullaun (winning the 1989 county championship, and reaching the All-Ireland Club semi-final), and Sarsfields (winning the 1993 All-Ireland Club Championship). Winning 2 All-Ireland Vocational Schools medals with New-Inn, he was on a losing All-Ireland M.H.C. final Galway side in 1981, and won an All-Ireland Under 21 medal at right corner-forward with Galway in 1983. He went on to win 2 All-Ireland Senior Hurling Championship medals with Galway in 1987 and 1988, being also on the losing Liam McCarthy Cup final side 4 times, in 1985, 1986, 1990 and in 1993 when he captained the side which lost to Kilkenny. He won 4 Railway Cup medals with Connacht in 1986 and 1987, and has also won 2 National League medals. He has won 2 All-Star awards, in 1987 at right half-forward, and in 1988 at right full-forward. His younger brother Joe 'Jackson' McGrath (born in 1973), who also won an All-Ireland Club Championship medal in 1993, played in his senior county championship debut in the forward line when 'Hopper' was captain, losing in the final of 1993.

McGRATH, MICK.

Soccer international wing-half. Born in Dublin, 7th April 1936. Clubs: Home Farm, Blackburn Rovers (in an 11 year career there between 1955 and 1965, he appeared in 269 league games, scoring 8 goals, and helped the club to promotion to Division One in 1957-58, and to a losing F.A. Cup final in 1960), Bradford. Having played once for the Ireland B side, he went on to be capped 22 time for the Republic of Ireland between 1958 and 1967, scoring 3 international goals.

McGRATH, OLIVER ('HOPPER').

G.A.A. right full-forward. Wexford. He played on 3 Wexford sides which played in All-Ireland Senior Hurling Champinship finals, in 1960 (when he scored 1-2 in their win over Tipperary to win the Liam McCarthy Cup), and in the losing finals of 1962 and 1965 (as a sub). He won a Railway Cup medal with Leinster in 1962. He gave his nickname, by association, to Michael 'Hopper' McGrath (cv), the Galway hurler.

McGRATH, Dr PATRICK John (PADDY).

Rugby international centre and wing three-quarter. Born in Burma, 20th August 1941. Club: U.C.C. (winning Munster Senior Cup/League/Charity Cup treble in 1963), and the Barbarians. A product of Rockwell College (winning a Munster Schools Senior Cup medal in 1959), he played for Munster many times in the 1960's. He was capped 10 times at international level for Ireland between 1965 and 1967, scoring 3 international tries, including one in his last cap. A doctor, he moved to Canada.

McGRATH, PAUL ('OOH AAH').

Soccer international central defender and midfielder. Born in Ealing, London on the 4th December 1959 (to an Irish mother and a Nigerian father). Clubs: Pearse Rovers, Dalkey, St Patrick's Athletic (sold to Old Trafford for £30,000), Manchester United (playing over 200 league and cup matches for the Reds, establishing himself as one of the best central defenders in Britain, and winning an F.A. Cup medal in 1985) and Aston Villa (playing a major role for them in their failed bid for the inaugural 1992-93 Premier League Championship). First capped for the Republic of Ireland as a substitute in 1985 against Israel, he has been a major presence since (with over 60 appearences in the side), both as a central defender, and in midfield, scoring 6 international goals. He was a vital cog in the famous Republic of Ireland exploits in the European Championships in West Germany in 1988, and in qualifying for the World Cup finals of 1990 in Italy. He was the outstanding Irish player in a fine side which reached the quarter-finals of Italia 90, playing a vital central midfield role in all 5 games in which Ireland excelled. He won the 'Player of the Year' F.A.I. award in both 1990 and 1991, and in 1993 won the prestigious Player's Player of the Year in Britain, only the 2nd ever Republic of Ireland player to be so awarded.

McGRATH, PAUL.

G.A.A. football right full-forward, Cork. Club: Bishopstown. Born in Tralee on May 23rd 1966. A U.C.C. Sigerson Cup player for 4 years, he won All-Ireland Under 21 Championship winner's medals with Cork in both 1985 and 1986 at right full-forward. A member of the Cork Senior Football Championship side which won the All-Ireland S.F.C. finals of 1989 and 1990, he also appeared (at right half-forward) in the losing final of 1988. He also won a National Football League medal with Cork in 1989, a feat his father had previously accomplished. In 1989, in his inaugural year, he was one of 2 players to win All-Star awards by being the only person nominated for his position, in his case right half-forward. He then became the only Kerry-born winner of an All-Star in 1990, when he was selected at right corner-forward.

McGRATH, ROBERT John Murray ('ROBBIE').

Rugby international scrum-half. Born in Dublin, 18th July 1951. He was educated at Newbridge College, where he won a Leinster Senior Schools winner's medal in 1970. Club: Wanderers (winning Leinster Senior Cup medals in 1973, 1978, 1982, and 1984, and Leinster Senior League medals in 1973, 1976, 1979, and 1985). An interprovincial player for Leinster in the early 70's, he later changed allegiance to Connacht, for whom there was fewer better servants. He has won 16 international caps for Ireland between 1977 and 1984, one as a reserve. He was a valuable ever-present member, partnering Ollie Campbell (cv), of the Irish Triple Crown-winning side of 1982, and of the International Championship-winning side in 1983. He toured New Zealand with Ireland as a replacement in 1976, and was on the Ireland tour of South Africa in 1981.

McGRATH, SEAMUS.

Horse trainer. Born on 21st February 19??. A son of the great Irish breeder and owner, Joe McGrath, his stables were at Glencairn. His 6 Irish Classic wins are: an Irish 2,000 Guineas with Furry Glen in 1974; an Irish 1,000 Guineas win with Royal Danseuse in 1964: 2 Irish Derby wins, in 1959 with Panslipper, and in 1973 with Weaver's Hall; an Irish Oaks win in 1957 with Silken Glider; and a Irish St Leger victory in 1970 with Allangrange. He also trained Levmoss to win the 1969 Prix de l'Arc de Trioumphe in Paris. His career tally of winners was about 1,350. He was selected as Texaco's Horse Racing Sportstar of the Year in 1969.

McGRATH, TOM.

G.A.A. football goalkeeper, Wexford. He was a constant member of the famous Wexford side which won 4-in-a-row All-Ireland Senior Football Championships, playing for the Blues and Whites team representing the county in 1915, 1916, 1917 and 1918. He was also on the Wexford side beaten in the 1914 All-Ireland S.F.C. final.

McGRATTAN, GERARD.

G.A.A. hurling right half-forward, Down. Born in 1972, he is from Portaferry. Such was his impression in his first senior year of 1992 (his inter-county debut was in the Ulster S.H.C. semi-final), when he played a starring for his county in the All-Ireland S.F.C. semi-final loss against Cork), that he was selected as an All-Star award winner in 1992 in the right half-forward position, making him his county's first ever hurling All-Star (and Ulster hurling's only 5th winner).

McGUIGAN, FINBAR Patrick (BARRY, 'THE CLONES CYCLONE').

Featherweight boxer. Born in Clones, Co Monaghan, 28th February 1961. As an amateur, boxing from the Wattlebridge and Smithboro clubs, he won a gold medal in the 1978 Commonwealth Games (he is one of only 6 to go on to win a world title) at Toronto, when aged 17, the same year capturing the Irish senior bantamweight title. Having lost a third round bout in the 1980 Olympics at Moscow, he turned pro under the management of Belfast bookmaker Barney Eastwood, and trainer Eddie Shaw, losing only to Peter Eubanks in his run up to the British title, another blow being the death of the Nigerian Alimi Mustafa 5 months after a fiercesome right to the jaw in the 6th round of their bout in October 1982. McGuigan was voted 'Best Prospect of 1982' by Boxing News. In November 1983 he won the vacant British title by stopping Vernon Penprase of England in the 2nd round. In November 1983, by defeating Valerio Nati of Italy by a 6th round knock-out in Belfast, he became European champion, the 5th Ulster pro boxer to win a European title. On June 8th 1985, he became W.B.A. featherweight champion of the world, when in an emotion-packed Queen's Park Rangers football ground in London, he outpointed the classy champion of 7 years, Eusebio Pedroza of Panama, over 15 rounds. After successful defences against American Bernard Taylor (whom he stopped in 8 rounds), and the Dominican Republican, Danielo Cabrera (stopping him in 14 rounds), he lost his title to the American Steve Cruz, in the intense heat of Los Vegas, Nevada, in June 1985. Having then retired, he made a brief 4-fight comeback in 1988, only to lose to Jim McDonnell in a 4th round stoppage in June 1989. He has been selected as Texaco's Sportstar of the Year for boxing 5 times, as an amateur in 1978, and for 4 years in succession as a professional, in 1982, 1983, 1984, and 1985 (when he also became Supreme Sportstar).

McGIUGAN, FRANK.

G.A.A. football full-forward, Tyrone. He was on the Tyrone minors which were beaten in the All-Ireland M.F.C. final in 1972. For many years at the heart of the senior inter-county forward line, he was a member of the first Tyrone side in 11 years to win the Ulster Senior Football Championship title in 1984, and won a 2nd medal in 1986. He also won a Railway Cup medal with Ulster in 1984. He has won one All-Star award, in the 1984 side, at full-forward.

McGUIGAN, TERESA (nee KENNEDY).

Pitch and putt player. Club: Shandon (Dublin). She ranks 2nd only to the great Clare Keating (cv), in number of Irish national titles won in pitch and putt, men or women. She captured 8 titles over a 15 year period from 1962 to 1976. She won 4 National Strokeplay championships, in 1962, 1966, 1968 and in 1976, and also won 4 National Matchplay championships, in 1965, 1966, 1967 (when completting a treble) and in 1974. She won the coveted 'double' in 1966. Over that period she was also runner-up in 9 national championships, 5 in the Matchplay (the inaugural year of 1961, and in 1964, 1969, 1972 and 1977), and 4 in the National Strokeplay Championships (1964, 1972, 1974 and 1975).

McGUIRE, EDWARD A (NED).

Tennis international player. Club: Fitzwilliam. A product of Clongoes Wood, he represented Ireland in 17 Davis Cup matches between 1924 and 1939 (missing only one tie), Ireland winning 4 of these ties, he himself recording some notable victories. A winner of the Irish Men's Championship Singles title in 1931, he also won 3 Irish men's doubles tennis titles, in 1929, 1931 and 1937, and won the Irish Mixed doubles title in 1931. He was President of Fitzwilliam L.T.C. 1951-53, and was club champion in 1922 and from 1926 through to 1931. A founder president of the Federated Union of Employers, he became a Senator, and died in 1992 at the age of 91.

McGUIRK, PADDY.

Professional golfer. Born in Co Louth, 23rd June 1950. Attached to Co Louth GC. Turning professional in 1965, in 1971 he won the Southern Ireland Professional title. In his career peak performance, he won the 1973 Carrolls International tournament at Woodbrook in 1973, with a score of 277, ahead of a field of the best in the British Isles. In 1976, he won the Irish Professional title at Waterville.

McGUIRK, PAT.

Outdoor bowls player. Born in Dublin, 30th July 1910. Club: Leinster. He won the I.B.A fours in 1950, 1953, 1954 and 1960, and the pairs title in 1962. He won 8 county singles titles, 5 in pairs, 3 in triples, and 6 in fours. An Irish international 1954-72, he was captain and skip 1954 to 1972. He was President of the Bowling League of Ireland from 1964.

McGURK, ANTHONY.

G.A.A. football left-full forward and centre half-back, Derry. Clubs: U.C.D., Queen's University (winning a Sigerson Cup medal in 1971), and Erin's Own, Lavey (being 43 years old when one of 7 brothers in the squad who won the All-Ireland Club Championship in 1991, brother John captaining the side; Anthony was assistant manager when Lavey won the Ulster club title in 1993). He was a substitute on the Derry side which captured the All-Ireland Under 21 Championship in 1968, and went on to win 3 Ulster Senior Football Championship winner's medals, in 1970, 1975, and 1976. He was a member of the only Combined Universities side ever to win the Railway Cup, playing at left corner forward in the historic 1973 win over Connacht. He won 2 All-Star awards, in 1973 as a left corner-forward, and as a centre-half back in 1975, making him one of a select bunch to be picked as both a forward and a back. His younger brother John (who captained the Lavey side which won the All-Ireland Club Championship in 1991), helped Derry reach the All-Ireland Senior Football final in 1993 for the first time in

25 years when scoring the winning point against Dublin in the semi-final, before becoming man-of-the match in Derry's triumph in the final.

McHALE, AUSTIN.

Car rally driver. From Rathcoole, Co Dublin. Starting in Irish rallying in 1978-1979, by 1981 he had graduated to contesting British Open Championships, gaining a best of a 3rd overall. By 1984 he had won numerous Group N or Group One class prizes, and went on to win numerous international rally events. Driving rally cars for Opel, Toyota, B.M.W., Ford etc, his many Irish rally wins include those in Cork, Kerry, Galway etc., and the Circuit of Ireland Rally in 1993. He has won 3 Dunlop Tarmac Irish Championship titles, including 1983 and 1985. With 12 international rally wins, he is 2nd behind Billy Coleman's 14 victories in this tally for Irish drivers.

McHALE, LIAM.

G.A.A. football midfielder, Mayo, and international basketball player. In 1984 the Ballina Stephenites player was full forward on the Mayo Under 21 side beaten by Cork in the All-Ireland final (and won 2 other Connacht Under 21 medals, in 1983 and 1985). First playing senior championship football in 1986, he was a member of the Mayo team which won 4 Connacht Senior Football Championship's; in 1988, in 1989 when they reached the All-Ireland S.F.C. final for the first time since 1951, and in both 1992 and 1993. He was voted ACC/Sunday Independent 'Player of the Year' for 1991, although he did not win an All-Star that year. A 6'5" giant, he was also an international basketball player at age 18, as a member of Ballina club, with whom, along with his brothers Sean and Anthony as captain, he won an I.C.S. Cup winners medal in 1991, and a National League medal in 1992, he has represented Ireland at Senior, Under 19 and Under 17 level over 40 times, helping Ireland to win it's first success in international tournament play in Belfast in 1991. His sisters, Jackie and Vanessa, have also played basketball for Ireland.

McHALE, JOHN PATRICK (J.P. or JOE).

Tennis, squash and bridge international player. Born in Dublin, 21st February, 1923. Club: Fitzwilliam. He was Irish Junior Tennis Champion in 1939, and went on to represent Ireland in 4 Davis Cup matches, in 1947, 1948 (twice), and 1949, and was an Irish Hardcourt Champion. He won 24 caps for Ireland in squash between 1948 and 1957, and was twice Irish International Champion, in 1950 and 1951. He was President of Fitzwilliam L.T.C. 1968-1971. A university administrator, he also became an international bridge player, participating in the World Pairs Olympiad in 1962 and being a regular player at the European Bridge Championships from 1952, as well as winning national titles in every discipline.

MacHALE, SEAN.

Rugby international prop-forward. Born in Ballina, Co Mayo, 6th February 1936. Club: Lansdowne (winning a Leinster Senior Cup medal in 1965). A product of Clongowes College, he played in the interprovincial championship for Leinster 5 times in 1964-1966. He was capped in Ireland's international front-row 12 times between 1965 and 1967, and toured Australia with his country in 1967.

McHENRY, JOHN.

Amateur international and professional golfer. Clubs: Douglas and Muskerry. A boys (1980 and 1981) and youths (1980, 1981, 1984) international, he was a member of the winning Irish Youths side in the European Championship in Hermitage in 1984, and won the Irish Youths title a record 3 times, in 1980, 1981 and 1984. He won the Irish Close Championship title in 1986, and the 'South' in the same year, when he also won the Willie Gill award. He also in 1986 won the Virginia Collegiate title and the East Coast (America) Athletic Conference Individual title. In Ireland's great victory in the European Team championships in 1987, he won 5 and halved 1 of his 6 matches (he was also on the winning Quadrangular side in 1986). He was selected for the Walker Cup in 1987, being one of the stars in the losing side, winning 2 and losing 2 of his matches. He turned pro in late 1987, with little initial success, gaining his Tour card eventually in 1992, and having a fine run in the Irish Open in 1993.

McHUGH, MARTIN ('THE WEE MAN' or 'THE LITTLE BIG MAN').

G.A.A. football right corner-forward, Donegal. Born in the Gaeltacht area of Donegal in 1962. Club: Kilcar (whom he helped, by scoring 10 points, to win their first county championship in 55 years in 1980, when he was 18, also winning a medal in 1985). He won an All-Ireland Under 21 Football Championship medal with Donegal in 1982 at right half-foward. Scorer of hundreds of points for Donegal since making his senior county debut in 1980, he was a member of the side which won the Ulster S.F.C. title in 1983, only to be beaten by a point by Galway in the All-Ireland semi-final. He again won Ulster S.F.C. medals in both 1990 and 1992, latterly when the county reached the All-Ireland Senior Football Championship final for the first time, and carried home the Sam Maguire Cup. A prolific scorer from frees, his 1984 tally of 4-95 or 107 points in the season, made him Donegal's first 'Ton-Up' player. He was selected at right full-forward on the All-Star side of 1983, and in the centre half-forward position in 1992, when he was also selected as the Texaco Sportstar of the Year for Football. His younger brother James, also a half-forward, won an Ulster S.F.C. medal in 1990, and an All-Ireland Senior Football Championship medal in 1992 alongside Martin (as well as joining him on the All-Star side that year, as a left half-forward, so becoming the first brothers since 1986 to be in the same All-Star side).

McHUGH, NONO.

G.A.A. camogie player, Galway. Club: Oranmore (with whom she won an All-Ireland Club Championship medal in 1974, the first Connacht side to win). She captained the Galway side which won the All-Ireland Junior Championship in 1973, the only Connacht side to win this competition. She also captained the Connacht sides which won the Gael-Linn Cups in 1973 and 1974, again the province's only success to date in this competition.

McHUGH, SEAMUS.

G.A.A. football left half-back and left corner back, Galway. A member of the Galway S.F.C. side which won 3 successive Connacht titles in 1982, 1983, and 1984, he captained the Galway side which were beaten by Dublin in the bruising 1983 All-Ireland Senior Football Championship final. He was on 4 Connacht sides beaten in Railway Cup finals, in 1977, 1981, 1982, and in 1984. He has twice been selected as an All-Star, in 1981 at left-half back, and in 1984 at left full-back. A national school teacher.

McHUGH, TERRY.

Javelin thrower and bobsleigher. Born in Clonmel (or Nenagh ?)on 22nd August 1963. Club: Dublin City Harriers. Starting the javelin in 1980, he improved steadily until extending the Irish record in Limerick in 1991 to 84.54 metres, 6 metres longer than the previous record (at the time the 5th best in the world that year), placing him in the world's top 50, only the 4th Irish thrower since Pat O'Callaghan to be so ranked. He won the B.L.E. National Championship at the javelin discipline 10 times in succession up to 1993, and has set 15 national records. He competed in the Seoul Olympics in the javelin for Ireland in 1988, finishing 22nd with an Irish record, in the top half of the field, and again in the Barcelona Games of 1992 (finishing

14th in his pool). In 1993, at the World Championships in Stuttgart, he became the first Irish male field event athlete in 30 years to qualify for the final of a 'major' championship, when he went on to finish 10th in the final. Also as a breakman bobsleigher, he also competed in the Winter Olympics in Albertville in France in 1992, thus becoming, along with Pat McDonagh (cv), the first Irishman to compete in these games, and the first Irishman to compete in both Summer and Winter games in the same year (also joining the select band of Irish sportpersons to have competed in 3 Olympic Games celebrations). He has also competed for Ireland at interntional level at Olympic Handball.

McILROY, JIMMY.

Soccer international inside-forward. Born in Lambeg, 25th October 1931. He joined Burnley for £7,000 from Glentoran at the age of 19 in 1950. In 13 years at Turf Moor, he played 437 league matches, scored 114 league goals, helped them win the Division One title in 1960, and was on the side which lost the F.A. Cup final in 1962. He then played 3 seasons at Stoke City, scoring 16 league goals in 98 games and helping them also to a 2nd Division League Championship title in 1962/63; he then played one last season at Oldham. Playing inter-League football twice, he was capped 55 times for Northern Ireland (the 52 of these he played from Burnley making him the Turf Moor club's most capped player), combining with almost telepathic communication with Danny Blanchflower (cv), and scoring 10 international goals. A quality footballer, he wore the No 10 jersey in each of Northern Ireland's 5 games in their commendable display in the 1958 World Cup finals campaign in Sweden. His intelligent, probing ability to open up any defence enabled him to be selected for Great Britain versus the Rest of Europe in 1955. He later managed Oldham Athletic (and was a team manager at Bolton Wanderers for 20 days in 1970), and also was a journalist in Burnley.

McILROY, SAMUEL B (SAMMY).

Soccer international midfielder. Born in Belfast, 2nd May 1954, the son of a Linfield player. Apprenticed to Manchester United in August 1971 at the age of 17, he developed into a fine midfielder, winning an F.A Cup medal in 1977, having been twice on sides beaten in finals, in 1976 and in 1979 when scoring a goal), and winning a 2nd Division Championship medal in 1974-75). He later played with Stoke City (133 games 1981-85), Manchester City (twice), Orgryte (Sweden), Bury (twice, playing almost 100 matches for them), FC Moedling (Austria) and Preston North End. He was capped 88 times for Northern Ireland between 1972 (his first cap was when only 17 years and 198 days old) and 1987, a 16 year career, scoring 5 international goals. His tally total placed him (up to August 1993) 2nd only to Pat Jennings (cv) in international cap tally honours for Northern Ireland. He was an influential member of the Northern Ireland side which performed with gusto in the 1982 World Cup in Spain, playing in all 5 matches. He was also a prominent member of the Northern Ireland side which played in the 1986 World Cup in Mexico, being ever-present in the 3 games played. He was selected as Texaco's Soccer Sportstar of the Year in 1980. In 1986 he became the 4th Northern Ireland soccer player to be awarded the M.B.E..

McILWAINE, E H, and Dr JOHN E.

Rugby international brothers, forwards. Both members of N.I.F.C.. John E won 7 international rugby caps in the pack for Ireland between 1897 and 1899, playing in 2 of Ireland's three Triple Crown-winning matches in 1899. His brother E H was had been capped twice previously, also as a forward, both in the 1895 season.

McINERNEY, GERRY.

G.A.A. hurling half-back, Galway. Club: Kinvara. Born in March 1965. He won an All-Ireland M.H.C. medal with Galway minors in 1983 (having been in losing side in the previous years final). He won 3 successive All-Ireland Vocational Schools titles with Galway in 1981, 1982 and 1983, and he went on to win an All-Ireland Under 21 Championship winner's medal in 1986. A fine half-back, he has been on 2 Galway sides which won All-Ireland Senior Hurling Championship medals, in 1987 (marking Kieran Brennan well) and in 1988 (scoring a decisive point 9 minutes from time), and was on the losing side in the All-Ireland finals of 1986, 1990 and in 1993 (when he made his 5th senior All-Ireland S.H.C. appearence, being man-of-the-match in the semi-final win over Tipperary).

McINERNEY, NIALL.

G.A.A. hurling right full-back, Galway. He was a member of the Galway side beaten in the All-Ireland Senior Hurling Championship finals of 1975 (when he had a fine game), 1979, and 1981, winning his only Liam McCarthy Cup medal in the 1980 Galway side which won the championship for the first time since 1923. He won 3 Railway Cup medals with Connacht, in 1980, 1982 and in 1983. He won 2 All-Star awards, in 1975 and in 1980, both in the right corner-back position.

McINERNEY, PA ('FOWLER').

G.A.A. hurling back, Clare and Dublin. Born in 1893. Clubs. O'Callaghan's Mill (Clare), and Garda (Dublin), winning a tally of 7 county championship medals. He was on the Clare hurling team which won the county's only All-Ireland Senior Hurling Championship, achieved in 1914 when defeating Laois by 5-1 to 1-0. He was on the Clare team which reached the All-Ireland S.H.C. final again 18 years later, in 1932, when the Banner County side were beaten by Kilkenny. In the intervening years while stationed as a Garda in Dublin, he also won an All-Ireland Senior Hurling Championship medal with that county, in 1927, and won 2 other Leinster provincial medals, in 1928 and 1930 (when Dublin were beaten in the All-Ireland S.H.C. final). His senior inter-county career stretched form 1913 to 1933, a 21 year run, in which he also won one Railway Cup medal with Leinster in the inaugural year, and one National Hurling League medal (with Dublin in 1929). In 1983 he was elevated as an All-Time All-Star award winner, the only Clareman thus far honoured.

McINERNEY, PADDY.

G.A.A. hurler, Limerick. Born in Co Clare 1895. Club: Young Ireland (winning 2 county championship medals). Playing senior inter-county hurling for Limerick from 1918 to 1925, he won 2 All-Ireland Senior Hurling Championship winner's medals with them, in 1918 (with the Newcastle West selection) and in 1921, while he also captained the side which lost the 1923 All-Ireland S.H.C. final to Galway. He later emigrated to New Mexico.

MacIVOR, C V.

Rugby international wing three-quarter. Club: Trinity College Dublin. A West Indies-born (in 1891), Portora RS-educated winger, he had played 7 international matches for Ireland between 1912 and 1913 (scoring one international try), when he was killed in training at Trinity by a kick, in October 1913 at the age of only 22.

McKAY, Dr James WILLIAM (BILL).

Rugby international wing-forward and No 8. Born in Waterford, 21st July 1921. Club: Queen's University Belfast. A product of Coleraine A.I., between 1947 and 1952 he won 23 international caps for Ireland (only 7 of these games were lost), scoring 3 international tries. A brilliant and sturdy tackler, he was part of the famous McCarthy-McKay-O'Brien back-row combination of the golden years of 1948 and 1949 when the Grand

Slam and Triple Crown were respectively won (and he was also on the Championship winning side of 1951). He scored a try against England in the Grand Slam year, which was vital to the enormous success Ireland enjoyed in those years. He was selected on the British and Irish Lion's tour of Australia and New Zealand in 1950, played in all 6 Tests, and was the leading forward try-scorer on tour (scoring 10 in his 15 matches). A war-time commando, he emigrated to Gisborne, New Zealand.

McKEE, FRED W ('LIZZIE').

Soccer international goalkeeper. Clubs: Cliftonville (winning Irish Cup medals in 1907 and 1909), Belfast Celtic (winning 3 Irish F.A. Cup medals, in 1915, 1916, and 1919), and Linfield. He was capped 5 times for Northern Ireland, twice in 1906, and three more times eight years later, in the famous 1914 season when he played all 3 games in his country's historic victory in the Home International series (the country's first of only 2 such wins).

McKEE, JOHN.

Hockey international right-back. Club: Belfast YMCA, and Hollywood 87. Having played for the Irish Junior side in the Junior World Cup finals and the European Junior Championships in 1981, he has been capped over 100 times for Ireland at senior level since 1980, and was a member of Irish squads which were placed 4th in the Intercontinental Cup of 1981 in Malaysia, and which finished 5th in the event in 1989 in New Jersey (thus qualifying for the 1990 World Cup). He also played an important role in Ireland's 7th place finishing in the European Championships in Paris in 1991. He has also been capped as an indoor international more than 40 times. He was capped for Great Britain.

McKEE, Wialliam DESMOND (DES).

Rugby international centre three-quarter and winger, and cricket international. Born 27th August 1923, he died in 1982. Rugby club: N.I.F.C.. Between 1947 and 1951, he was capped 12 times for Ireland at rugby, including all matches in both the Grand Slam year of 1948 and the Triple Crown year of 1949, scoring 2 international tries, one against England in the Grand Slam year of 1948, and another (also against England) in the Triple Crown year of 1949. He also played cricket once for Ireland, when as a right hand batsman for the Woodvale club, he played in the international first class game versus Scotland in 1946, scoring 16 runs.

McKEEVER, JIM.

G.A.A. football centre-fielder, Derry. Born in 1931. Clubs: Newbridge (winning 2 Derry SFC medals), Ballymaguigan (winning one Derry SFC medal), Leicester Young Irelands (England) and Downpatrick. Playing for both Antrim and Derry minors, his senior inter-county career for Derry extended from 1948 to 1962. A fine midfielder, he captained the Derry side to their first ever Ulster S.F.C win in 1958, and to their defeat by Dublin in the All-Ireland Senior Football Championship final of the same year (he had previously played when the county was beaten in the Ulster finals in both 1955 and 1957). Also winning one Ulster J.F.C. medal, he was on 2 Derry sides beaten in National League finals (in 1959 and 1961). He won 2 Railway Cup medals with Ulster, in 1956 and 1960. Nominated as the first ever Caltex (later Texaco) Sportstar of the Year for Gaelic Games in 1958, in 1984 he was selected in the midfield on the 'Team of the Century' for footballers who never won an All-Ireland senior championship medal. He also played basketball for Belfast Celtics, Ulster, and Irish sides.

McKELVEY, Dr JAMES Moorehead (JIMMY).

Rugby and cricket international. Born in Belfast, 2nd April 1933. In rugby, while playing for Queen's University, he was capped twice at full-back in 1956 (both on losing teams), against France and England. He was President of the

Ulster Branch of the I.R.F.U. in 1984. A product of Campbell College, he also was capped in cricket, playing in 2 first class international matches for Ireland in 1954 as a left hand batsman.

McKENNA, BEN.

Cyclist, and cycling administrator. A Garda, he died in 1992 aged 54. His cycling career was best over stage events, and included taking part in the Ras Taiteann 21 times, finishing third in 1957, finishing 2nd three times (in 1958, 1961 and 1964), and winning the race for the only time in 1959, when beating off the challanges of Ronnie Williams and Shay Murphy. As an administrator he was an U.C.I. international commissaire, was president of the N.C.A. for 4 years, and was on the Tripartite Committee which healed the split in Irish cycling.

McKENNA, EUGENE.

G.A.A. football midfielder, centre half-forward and full-forward, Tyrone. Born in 1956. Club: Augher (with whom, along with 7 brothers, he won 4 Tyrone county championship medals). A product of Omagh C.B.S. with whom he won a McRory Cup medal, he was a member of the Tyrone All-Ireland M.F.C. winning side of 1973. First playing championship football in 1979, he was captain of the Tyrone side which was beaten 2-15 to 1-10 by Kerry in the All-Ireland Senior Football Championship final of 1986 (the first time the county had reached this stage), and also won Ulster S.F.C. medals in 1984 and 1989. In 1984 he became the only Tyrone man to captain a winning Ulster side in the Railway Cup series, having also won a medal the previous year. He has been selected as an All-Star on 3 occasions, in 1984 at midfield alongside Jack O'Shea (cv), in 1986 at centre half-forward, and at full-forward in 1989. His older brother Dessie was captain of the Tyrone side which captured the All-Ireland M.F.C. in 1973, and played for the county at senior level in midfield and half back.

McKENNA, GAY.

Greyhound trainer. Born in 1924. He has trained the winning dog in a joint record 4 Irish Derbys: in 1965 with Ballyowen Chief, in 1966 with Always Proud, in 1970 with Monalee Pride, and in 1972 with Catsrock Daisy (he also trained the 2nd dog four times, in 1961, 1966, 1971 and 1973). He has also trained the winners of 2 Irish Oaks (1965 with Drumsough Princess, and 1970 with Rosmore Robin), 2 Irish Cesarewitch's (1970 with Postal Vote and 1973 with Rita's Choice), and the winner of one Irish National Sprint (Skip's Choice in 1960), bringing his tally of Irish Classic winners to 9. He was voted Texaco Sportstar of the Year for Greyhound Racing for 2 successive years in 1965 and 1966. His father Joe McKenna (1892-1942), trained the winner of the Irish Grand National of 1935, Druze. His son-in-law, Fraser Black (born in 1952), trained the winner of the 1987 Produce Stakes, Droopy's Jaguar. He is a cousin of Ger McKenna (cv), and a brother-in-law of Tom Lynch (cv).

McKENNA, GER.

Greyhound trainer. From Borrisokane, Co Tipperary, he was born 27th February 1930. He has trained a remarkable 30 Irish Classic race winners including: 3 Irish Derbys (1969 with Own Pride, 1973 with Basher Man, and 1987 with Rathgallen Lady), 6 Irish Laurels (in 1970, 1976, 1980, 1983 with Parkdown Jet, 1984 and 1985); the Irish St Leger 12 times (a record unlikely to be equalled), 1956, 1960, 1962, 1965, 19687, 1969, 1971, 1972, 1975, 1976, 1977, and in 1984; and the Irish Oaks in 1979 with Nameless Pixie; 4 Irish Cesarewitch's (1965, 1967, 1975 and 1987); 2 National Breeder's 2-year-old Produce Stakes (1973 and 1976), and 2 Irish National Sprints (1965 and 1969). Other big race wins include: 3 Guinness 600's, 4 International '525"s at Dundalk, 5 Irish Puppy Derby's, 2 Easter Cups and 2 Tipperary Cups. His dogs have won the Bord na gCon National Greyhound award

6 times, 1967 with Yanka Boy, 1969 with Own Pride, 1975 with Ballybeg Prince, 1979 with Nameless Pixie, 1981 with Parkdown Jet, and 1984 with Moran's Beef. He has also trained 2 winners of the most prestigious race in the British Isles, the English Derby, winning with Parkdown Jet in White City in 1981, and with Lartigue Note in Wembley in 1989. He has won more Texaco Sportstar awards for greyhound racing than any other person, winning 3 times, in 1967, 1973, and 1981. He is a cousin of Gay McKenna (cv), and a brother-in-law of Tom Lynch (cv), both highly successful greyhound trainers.

McKENNA, JOE.

G.A.A. hurling full-forward, Limerick. Born 1952 in Co Offaly, for whom he played minor hurling. Club: South Liberties (winning 4 Limerick county hurling championship medals). He won an All-Ireland Senior Hurling Championship medal in 1973 when playing left-full forward on the winning Limerick side. He helped Limerick to win 3 other Munster S.H.C. titles, in 1974, 1980 (in both these cases to go on to lose in the All-Ireland final), and 1981 (while they were beaten in the Munster final by Cork in 1975, 1976 and in 1979). In 1981 he became the 3rd Limerick hurler to captain a winning Railway Cup Munster side (and the first since Mick Mackey in 1937), also winning medals in 1976, 1978, and 1984; he won a solitary National Hurling League medal with Limerick in 1984. A quality full-forward, it is reflected in the fact that he has won 6 All-Star awards (placing him then in 2nd place in the all-time hurling tally behind Noel Skehan cv); in 1974 at right half-forward, in 1975 at centre half-forward, and for 4 years in a row at full-forward (1978, 1979, 1980 and 1981). He was also selected as Irish Independent Sportstar of the Week 4 times.

McKENNA, JOHN.

Soccer international outside right. Born in Belfast, 6th June 1926. Clubs: Linfield (winning an Irish Cup medal in 1948), Huddersfield Town (scoring 10 goals in 134 league matches in 1948-52), Blackpool and Hartlepool. He was capped 7 times for Northern Ireland between 1950 and 1952, all while at Huddersfield.

McKENNA, LIAM.

Badminton champion. Born in Belfast in 1968, he is based in Guernsey in the Channel Islands. He has won the Irish Men's Singles badminton title 4 times, three in succession (1989, 1990 and 1991), then after not competing in 1992, winning again in 1993. He has the unique distinction of representing Guernsey in one Commonwealth Games, and then to go on to represent Northern Ireland in the following games. He is a grand-son of Jimmy McAlinden (cv), the Northern Irish soccer star.

McKENNA, MARY A.

Amateur international golfer. Born 29th April 1949, in Dublin. Club: Donabate. She has won the Irish Ladies Close Championship 8 times over a 21 year period, in 1969, 1972, 1974, 1977, 1979, 1981, 1982, and 1989, being runner-up in 1968, 1973, 1976, and 1985 (she has also won the pre-qualifying Leitrim Cup 8 times). She won the British Ladies Strokeplay title in 1979 (being voted Daks Woman Golfer of the Year then), having been runner-up in 1976. She has won the Avia Foursomes in 1977, 1984, and 1986. She has won a remarkable record-breaking 9 consecutive Curtis Cup appearances for Great Britain and Ireland, in 1970, 1972, 1974, 1976, 1978, 1980, 1982, 1984 , and on the famous victorious 1986 side at Prairie Dunes U.S.A. (the first time it had been won on American soil), along with Claire Hourihane and Lillian Behan. Her Curtis Cup record was 10 wins, 16 losses and 4 halves in 30 matches, a success rate of 40%. She has played in the Vaglaino Trophy on many successive occasions from 1969. She once reached the semi-final stage of the U.S. Amateur, and reached this stage of the British Amateur twice, including 1991 (this being the one major domestic title she has failed to win). She was often selected for GB&I side in the World Team Championship, captaining the side in 1986 and in 1992 (as a non-player). She was ever-present in the Irish Home international squad for 24 years from 1968 to 1991 (including the winning sides in 1980 at Cruden Bay and in 1986 at Whittingdon Barracks), playing again in 1993, and on all the intervening European Team Championship teams (including the winning sides of 1979 at Hermitage and 1983 at Waterloo in Belgium). She vies with Philomena Garvey (cv) for the crown of Ireland's greatest ever woman golfer.

McKENZIE, GEORGE.

Soccer international player. Club: Southend United. He was capped 9 times for Ireland at soccer over 2 pre-war seasons, in 1938 and 1939, all gained while at Southend, making him that club's most capped player.

McKEON, MICK.

Amateur middleweight boxer. Clubs: St Andrew's (of York Street), St Vincent's, Irish Transport Club, and Crumlin. He won 6 Irish Senior National titles in the middleweight division, in 1945, 1946, 1947, 1949, 1950, and 1951. In the 1948 Olympic Games, he reached the semi-finals in the middleweight division, but had to withdraw from the fight for the bronze medal, which was awarded to the Italian Ivano Fontana (the gold being won by the great Laszlo Papp), with McKeon officially placed 4th. In 1949 he won his bout in a famous 'Golden Gloves' Europe v U.S.A. match in Chicago. He boxed 250 amateur bouts, losing only 6 (and was never knocked down). One of Dublin's finest amateur boxers, he fought for Ireland 33 times. His daughter Clare McKeon is a radio D.J. based in Dublin.

McKERNAN, JAQUELINE.

International athletic discus-thrower. Club: Lisburn. In 1993 she won her fifth successive U.K. Championship Women's discus title (also winning in 1989, 1990, 1991 and 1992), with a throw of 56.72 metres. She won a silver medal in her discipline at the 1990 Commonwealth Games. She represented Great Britain at the Olympic Games in Barcelona in 1992, and also in the Europa Cup and World Championships in 1993.

MacKESSY, WILLIAM.

G.A.A. hurler and footballer, Cork. A dual player from Buttevant, he became the first player to win All-Ireland Senior Championship medals in both the hurling and football codes for his native county, which was Cork (and the 2nd player, after William Spain cv, to complete dual winning's). He won an All-Ireland Hurling Senior Championship medal for Cork in 1903, and eight years later captured an All-Ireland S.F.C. football medal in 1911. Altogether he played in 7 All-Ireland senior finals (3 in hurling, and 4 in football), being on the losing side 5 times (in hurling in 1905 and 1912, and in football in 1901, 1906 and 1907).

McKIBBIN, Dr ALISTAIR Richard.

Rugby international centre threequarter. Born in Belfast, 13th January 1958. Clubs: Instonians (winning an Ulster Senior Cup medal in 1979), St Mary's Hospital and London Irish. A product of R.B.A.I. (winning 3 schools international caps in 1975 and 1976), and winning a 'B' international cap in 1976, he went on to be capped for the full Irish side 14 times between 1977 and 1980 (only 3 of these games were victories). His older brother Harry (born in Belfast, 24th June 1948), a Queen's University full-back, was capped once as a reserve against Scotland in 1976, while another brother Roger played to final Irish trial standard. Their father was Harry McKibbin (cv), and as such they are one of only two sets of 'father and 2 sons' to play rugby for Ireland (see George Collopy cv).

McKIBBIN, HENRY Roger (HARRY).

Rugby international centre three-quarter. Born in Belfast, 13th July 1915. A Queen's University centre, Harry, although winning only 4 international caps for Ireland in 1938-39 (prior to W.W.II.), went on a Lion's tour of South Africa in 1938, winning 3 Test caps while being the star back in the touring party, being used in the latter stages as the chief place-kicker (scoring vital points in the crucial 3rd test win). Harry's younger brother Des, an Instonian's prop forward, was capped 8 times for Ireland a decade after his brother, in 1950 and 1951 (Des's son Brian playing twice for the Irish schoolboys in 1979). Both Harry Snr and Des have been President of the I.R.F.U. (a unique achievement for brothers), Des in 1985-86 (being manager of the Irish touring party to Japan in 1986, and an Irish selector 1964-1968), and Harry in the Centenary year of 1974-75 (he was also Assistant Manager on the Lions tour of South Africa in 1962, and an Irish selector 1961-1963). Harry in the father of Alistair McKibbin (cv) etc.

McKIERNAN, CATHERINA.

Middle distance and cross-country athlete. From Cornafean, Co Cavan, she was born on 30th November 1969. Club: Cornafaen AC. Winning the schools cross-country title in 1988, she finished third in the National senior cross-country title in 1989, and then went on to win it in 3 years in succession, 1990, 1991 and 1992 (also winning the National B.L.E. 3,000 track title in 1989, 1992 and 1993), and she has won the inter-counties cross-country title 4 times, in 1989, 1990, 1991 and 1993. In 1988 she was 73rd in World Cross-Country championship, finished 40th in 1989, and 65th in 1991. Then, in 1992 in Boston at the age of only 22, she won a fine silver medal in these world cross-country championships, only beaten by the 3-times champion Lynn Jennings out of first place by 2 seconds. She gained a silver medal in the same event (held in Spain) again in 1993, 9 seconds behind the winner Albertina Diaz of Portugal. In 1990 she reached had No 3 in the world Grand Prix rankings for cross-county (winning a G.P. in Portugal). In 1991-92 she won 3 successive Grand Prix events at cross-country, in Belgium, France, and Mallusk, to went on to capture the World Cross Country Challenge series in this coveted series, helped by her 2nd place in the Boston race. She again won the World Cross Country Challenge Grand-Prix series in 1993 to place her in the ranks of all-time great Irish athletes. She represented Ireland in the 3,000 metres in the Barcelona Olympics in 1992, and in 1993 broke the Irish record for the 10,000 metres on the track, qualifying her to compete in the World Champoinships at Stuttgart, in which she reached the 10,000 metres final, in which she did not finish. Two of her brothers played inter-county football for Co Cavan.

McKINNEY, STEWART Alexander.

Rugby international wing-forward. Born in Strabane, 20th November 1946. Club: Dungannon (winning an Ulster Senior Cup medal in 1976). A product of R.S. Dungannon, he was capped 25 times for Ireland between 1972 and 1978, being a stalwart in the championship winning side of 1974, and scoring 2 international tries and one penalty goal for his country. His first cap was gained on the famous day Ireland won at Stades Colombes for the first time in 20 years. He went on the victorious British and Irish Lion's tour of South Africa in 1974, led by Willie John McBride, although he did not gain a test place. He also toured New Zealand with Ireland in 1976.

McKINNSTRY, COLM.

G.A.A. football midfielder, Armagh. Born in 1953. Club: Clan Na Gael (winning many county and provincial club champiship medals, and reaching the All-Ireland club final in 1974). Playing senior inter-county football from 1970, he was a member of the Armagh side which won the Ulster Senior Football Championship title 3 times in 6 years, in 1977, 1980, and in 1982, and a star member of the side which reached the All-Ireland Senior Football Championship final in 1977, only to be beaten by Dublin by 5-12 to 2-6. He won one All-Star award, in 1980 at midfield.

McKNIGHT, ALLEN.

Soccer international goalkeeper. Born in Antrim, 27th January 1964. Clubs: Distillery, Glasgow Celtic (playing in 12 matches when the club won the Scottish Premier League in 1987-88), Albion Rovers (on loan), West Ham. Capped for Northern Ireland at Under 23 level, he has also been capped at full international level 10 times from 1988 up to mid 1993.

McKNIGHT, JOHN.

G.A.A. football left full-back, Armagh. A winner of an All-Ireland M.F.C. medal with Armagh minor's in their 1949 win over Kerry, he later won Ulster Senior Football Championship winner's medals with Armagh in 1950 and 1953 (when the team went on to the All-Ireland final, only to be beaten by Kerry by 0-13 to 1-6). One of his county's quality players, he won one Railway Cup medal with Ulster in 1956. He was selected at left corner-back in 1984 on the 'Team of the Century' for players who never won an All-Ireland senior championship medal.

McLARNIN, JIMMY ('BABYFACE').

Welterweight professional boxer. He was born on 19th December, 1906, in Hillsborough, Co Down (some sources say Inchicore, Co Dublin). Emigrating to Canada at age 10, he twice held the world welterweight title, in 1933-34 and again in 1934-35. Having lost a world title lightweight bout to Sammy Mandell in 1928, he first won the welterweight title in 1933 in Los Angeles, when he knocked out the Italian, Young Corbett III, in the first round, in a then record 2 minutes and 37 seconds. He lost it a year later in the first of 3 historic encounters with the American Barney Ross, in New York, beaten on points over 15 rounds. Four months later, however, McLarnin won a rematch at the Polo Grounds in New York, over 15 rounds. But it was Ross again who took his title off him again, in May 1935, also over 15 rounds, and also in New York. In his 13 years of professional boxing, McLarnin won 63 of his 77 contests, drew 3, and lost 11, and an indication of his greatness is that he defeated 13 future, present, or past world champions in 23 bouts against them. Enormously popular, he made a fortune from the sport (estimated to be the largest fortune amassed by any pre-World War 2 fighter), and was left $200,000 by his coach 'Pop' Foster. He was elected in 1956 to The Ring magazine's Hall of Fame, the only Irishman in the Modern Group of this prestigious award.

McLAUGHLIN, CON.

Soccer forward. Born in Milford, Co Donegal, 12th December 1959. Moving from Swilly Rovers to Finn Harps in 1978, he has been a constant goal-getter for Harps, and in the 1991-92 season joined the elite group of players to have scored over 100 goals in the League of Irleand (109 by mid 1992). He was joint League of Ireland leading goalscorer in 1986 (with 11 goals), and has been 3 times leading goalscorer in the First Division (setting a 1st Div record in the 1987-88 with 20 goals), and was joint leader with 12 goals in 1990-91, and joint again in 1992 with 12 more).

McLAUGHLIN, JAMES (JIM) C.

Soccer international winger, and manager. Born in Londonderry, 22nd December 1940. Starting off his playing career with Derry City and with Birmingham City, he spent 13 years in English league football from 1960 to 1973, with Shrewsbury, Swansea City (reaching the F.A. Cup semi-final in 1964), Peterborough, again at

FOOTBALL GENIUS

Pat Spillane: one of the greats in the great Kerry side of the 1970s and 1980s, he has had few equals as a forward.

Brian Mullins, one of the fine Dublin side who had many a fine tussle with Kerry in the late 1970s. A brilliant midfielder.

ATHLETIC GENTS

Eamonn Coghlan in his moment of greatest triumph, the realisation that he was going to win a World Athletics title at 5,000 metres in 1983.

John Treacy, who won two World Cross Country Championships, and later won an Olympic silver medal in the marathon in 1984 at Los Angeles.

OLYMPIAN FEATS

Ronnie Delany winning the 1,500 metres Olympic Gold Medal at the Melbourne Games in 1956.

Mary Peters putting the shot during her exciting win in the Pentathlon at the Munich Olympic Games in 1972.

SOCCER KINGS

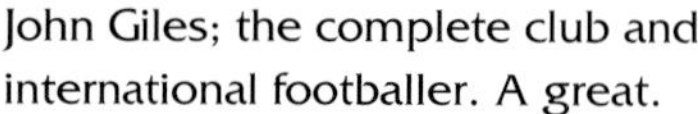

John Giles; the complete club and international footballer. A great.

Johnny Fullam, one of many outstanding soccer players who showed their skills at home.

CYCLING SUPERMEN

Sean Kelly, who in the 1980's became a prolific winner of races on the continent, is living proof that spirit can overcome pain.

Stephen Roche, who in 1987 reached great heights by winning the Tour de France, the Giro d'Italia and the World Championship.

HURLING HEROES

Conor Hayes, the only Galway hurler to captain two county teams to win the All-Ireland Senior Hurling Championships.

Liam Fennelly, one of a great hurling family, holding aloft the 'new' Liam McCarthy Cup after the 1992 final against Cork.

RACING CERTAINTIES

Vincent O'Brien, certainly Ireland's most successful ever horse trainer, both over jumps and latterly on the flat.

Michael Kinane, one of a tradition of brilliant Irish jockeys, he has dominated the domestic flat scene in recent years.

YOUNG BLOOD

Ken Doherty, a former world amateur snooker champion, now a highly ranked professional.

Niall O'Toole, a world lightweight champion with a bright future ahead of him in rowing.

RUGBY GIANTS

Jackie Kyle, top, so good that they called his generation of Rugby "The Kyle Era".

Mike Gibson, above, who would be many persons choice as the most complete Irish back.

Willie John McBride, left, Ireland's most honoured forward, and probably our best.

FOOTBALL SUPREMOS

Kevin Heffernan, left, one of many who was a great player and an equally fine manager.

Mick O'Connell, A footballer without equal; a giant among Kerrymen.

ABOVE PAR

Ronan Rafferty, the former boy-wonder of Irish amateur golf, who has become Ireland's best modern professional golfer.

Christy O'Connor Junior, here in typically determined pose, during his triumph in the 1992 British Masters.

ATHLETIC LADIES

Catherina McKiernan, the Cavan-girl who has twice finished in second place in the World Cross Country Championships.

Sonia O'Sullivan, who has twice finished fourth in major championships, before going on to win a brilliant silver medal in Stuttgart in 1993.

Shrewsbury, and again at Swansea City. He scored 126 league goals (77 at Shrewsbury), and went on to win a player's F.A.I. Cup winner's medal with Dundalk in 1977. Playing 2 Under 23 matches for his country, he was also capped 12 times for Northern Ireland between 1962 and 1966 (the 5 caps he won while playing for Shrewsbury Town made him that club's most capped player), scoring 6 international goals. He was later to become one of the most successful League of Ireland managers in history, achieving the League of Ireland-F.A.I. Cup double 5 times with 3 different clubs, Dundalk (1979), Shamrock Rovers (3 times in succession, in 1985, 1986 and 1987) and Derry City (in 1989). He is the only person the win the Irish Soccer Writer's Association award 3 times, while in 1986 he was selected as Texaco's Soccer Sportstar of the Year.

MacLEAR, BASIL.

Rugby international centre-threequarter. Clubs: Cork County and Monkstown. His qualifications for England were shunned after not getting picked following their trial, and he became an almost legendary player for Munster and Ireland. He won 11 international rugby caps for Ireland between 1905 and 1907, scoring 4 tries and 3 conversions. He scored reputedly one of the greatest tries ever by an Irishman, against South Africa in 1906. In 1905 he played against the visiting All-Blacks 4 times, a record for an Irishman against the same touring side. He was killed in World War One, at the age of 34.

McLENNAN, ALFRED Charles (FREDDIE).

Rugby international wing three-quarter. Born in Dublin, 8th February, 1951. Club: Wanderers (with whom he won Leinster Senior Cups in 1973 and 1978 and Senior League honours in 1973, 1976 and 1979). A product of Newbridge College (winning a Leinster Senior Schools Cup medal in 1970), he was capped 18 times for Ireland between 1977 and 1981, scoring 4 international tries. A talented runner, he later settled in South Africa, after the 1981 Irish tour there, having earlier toured Australia with Ireland in 1979.

McLOUGHLIN, ALAN.

Soccer international midfielder. Born in Manchester, 20th April 1967. Clubs: Manchester United (joining them from local football), Swindon Town, Torquay United (on loan), Swindon Town, Southampton (becoming their first ever 1,000,000 player in 1990), Aston Villa (although not playing a league match), Portsmouth (helping them in their losing promotion challenge for the Premier Division in 1993). First capped for the Republic of Ireland in 1990, he played a minor role in Ireland's great run in the World Cup of 1990 in Italy, and up to June 1993 has gained 12 international caps under the managership of Jack Chalrton.

McLOUGHLIN, GERARD Anthony Joseph (GERRY or 'GINGER').

Rugby international prop-forward. Born in Limerick, 11th June 1952. Club: Shannon. Having won a 'B' cap in 1977 he went on to capped 18 times for Ireland between 1979 and 1984. He played in all matches in Ireland's Triple Crown triumph of 1982, scoring the famous vital try against England, in which he claims he took the whole opposing pack over the line with him. Having been also omnipresent in the Irish side which shared the International Championship in 1983, he went with the British and Irish Lion's touring side to New Zealand in 1983, although not gaining a test place. He was in the side 'the day Munster beat the All-Blacks' in 1978 (also being on the Munster side which beat the Australian tourists in 1981). He also toured twice with Ireland, to Australia in 1979, and to South Africa in 1981. He helped Shannon to win 3 Munster Senior Cup medals, in 1977, 1978, and 1982. A publican and former schoolmaster, now in Wales.

McLOUGHLIN, NEIL.

Amateur international flyweight boxer. Club: St Eugene's (Derry). He won 3 Irish National Senior Championship titles in the flyweight division, in 1971, 1972 and in 1974. In 1972 he reached the last eight in the flyweight division of the Munich Olympic Games, thereby being placed in joint 5th in the event.

McLOUGHLIN, RAYMOND John (RAY, 'WILDER').

Rugby international tight-head prop-forward. Born in Ballinasloe, August 2th 1939. Clubs: Ballinasloe, U.C.D., Athlone, London Irish, Gosforth (being that club's most capped player) and Blackrock College. A product of Garbally College (playing at No 8 for Connacht schools), he represented Ireland at schools level in the shot putt, and also got minor trials for both hurling and gaelic football for Galway. The most capped Connacht player in Irish rugby history, he played 40 times (then a record for an Irish prop forward) for Ireland over a 14 year period between 1962 and 1975, with a 5 year gap between 1966 and 1971, and scored one famous try for his country. His first 18 caps were at tight head prop (1962-66), and the last 22 were at loose head (1970-75). He was a member of the side which won the International Championship for the first time outright in 23 years in 1974. He captained the Ireland side on 8 consecutive occasions from 1965, bringing for the first time a new and innovative scientific approach to Irish international rugby preperations. He captained the first Irish XV to defeat the Springboks in 1965. His captaincies extended to Connacht, Northumberland, British Universities etc.. He went on 2 British and Irish Lion's tours of Australia and New Zealand: in 1966, winning 3 Test caps, and in 1971, where injury deprived him of most of the tour. One of the world's greatest prop forward's, he played on the Barbarians side which defeated the All-Blacks in the famous 1973 match in Cardiff. His younger brother Phelim (born in Ballinasloe 8th August 1941), a member of Northern, won one cap against Australia in 1976, at prop forward, when he was 34 years, 5 months and 9 days old, making him the oldest person in Irish rugby history to win a first cap. Ray was later a successful businessman, heading up James Crean, a dynamic investment company.

McLOUGHLIN, SEAN (JOHN).

G.A.A. hurling left corner forward, Tipperary. He was a member of 2 successive Tipperary minor sides which won the All-Ireland M.H.C., in 1952 and 1953. He later won 4 All-Ireland Senior Hurling Championship winner's medals with Tipperary, in 1961 (coming on as a sub), 1962 (being the sidesw leading scorer in the final with 1-2), 1964, and 1965 (scoring 2-1, again to be the finals leading marksman), and was on 3 losing All-Ireland S.H.C. final sides, in 1960, 1967, 1968, thus appearing in 7 All-Ireland senior hurling finals in the 9 years between 1960 and 1968. He also played Railway Cup with Munster, and won National League medals with Tipp in the 1960's.

McLOUGHNEY, P.

G.A.A. hurling goalkeeper, Tipperary. He was a quality goalkeeper in when times were tough for Tipperary inter-county hurling, but helped them to win the National Hurling League in 1978-1979. He won a Railway Cup award in 1981 with Munster. Although never playing on a winning Munster S.H.C. winning side, he has won 2 successive All-Star awards, in 1979 after the league success, and 1980 when he was the only Tipp player to win the accolade.

McMAHON, BRIAN.

G.A.A. hurling full-forward, Dublin. Born in 1966. He was a member of the Dublin team which made it to the 1st division of the National League in 1987, scoring many goals on route. In 1990 he became only the 2nd Dublin hurler since the scheme's inception in 1971 to win an All-Star award, being picked in the full-forward slot. His grandfather was a member of the only Clare side to win an All-Ireland Senior Hurling Championship, in 1914.

McMAHON, CHARLIE.

G.A.A. hurling left half-back, Dublin. A quality hurler for Dublin in the 30's and 40's, he won one All-Ireland Senior Hurling Championship winner's medal, in 1938 (the county's most recent McCarthy Cup) when the Dubs beat Waterford (he was on Dublin sides beaten in the All-Ireland deciders of both 1935, as a sub, and 1941). In a time the Railway Cup was dominated by Munster, he was on losing final Leinster sides in 1930, 1931, 1934, 1935 and 1938, but won medals in 1932, 1933 and 1936.

McMAHON, JOHNNY.

Soccer international forward. Born in Belfast. Club: Bohemians (he was a member of the Bohs side which won the Grand Slam of Irish Free State titles in the 1928 season: the League, the Cup, the Leinster Shield, and the Leinster; he won another Irish Free State League medal in 1929-30). By winning one cap for the I.F.A. side against Scotland in 1934, he became the only League of Ireland player ever to be capped for the North of Ireland.

McMAHON, JOHNNY.

G.A.A. hurling left full-back, Clare. Born in 1953. Club; Newmarket-on-Fergus (winning Munster club championship medals). Starting his senior inter-county in 1971, he was on Clare teams beaten in 4 Munster S.H.C. finals in the 1970's, in 1972, 1974, 1977 and 1978. He won 2 National Hurling League Championship winner's medals with Clare in successive years, in 1977 and in 1978, having been on the losing final side in 1976. A Newmarket-on-Fergus man, he has won 2 All-Star awards, in 1976 at left corner-back (becoming then only the 2nd Clareman to win an All-Star), and in 1977 at right corner-back.

McMAHON, LAWRENCE B (LARRY).

Rugby international centre-threequarter. Born in London, 4th December 1911. Clubs: Blackrock College, and U.C.D.. He played 18 times for Leinster in the senior Interprovincial series beteen 1930 and 1937. Between 1931 and 1938, he was capped 12 times for Ireland, often in a fine partnership with Aiden Bailey (cv), and he scored 3 international tries. A classy player, with a great pass, his total of 12 caps is less than his ability warranted. An Irish selector for four years between 1942 and 1948, he was President of the I.R.F.U. in 1961-62.

McMAHON, PADDY.

G.A.A. hurling full-forward, Limerick. Born in 1911. Clubs: Kildimo and Ahane (winning 2 county championship medals with them). In a senior inter-county career which lasted only 6 years (it was cut short through injury), he won 2 All-Ireland Senior Hurling Championship medals with Limerick, in 1936 (when he scored 2 gaols in the final) and 1940, having been on the side beaten in the 1935 All-Ireland S.H.C. final (when he also scored 2 goals in the final). He also won 4 successive National Hurling League medals with Limerick, in 1935, 1936, 1937 and 1938. He won an Oireachtas medal in the inaugural year of the competition in 1939, and won 2 Railway Cup medals with Munster, in 1937 and 1940.

McMAHON, PAT.

Long-distance runner. Born 1st February 194?. In 1968, he became the first Irishman to break the 2 hour 20 minute barrier for the marathon, when in Artesia, New Mexico, he clocked 2:19:49.8. His 12th place in the 1968 Mexico Olympic marathon, in a time of 2:29:21 was, until John Tracey's medal in Los Angeles in 1984, Ireland's best performance in this Olympic event.

McMANUS, TONY.

G.A.A. football left full-forward, Roscommon. Born in 1957. Club: Clan na nGael (with whom he won, along with 6 members of his family, including Andrew, Eoin, and Eamonn jnr, 8 successive Connacht Club Championship medals from 1984 to 1990, beaten in the All-Ireland finals 5 times, 1983, 1987, 1988, 1989 and 1990). He won an All-Ireland Under 21 Champinship medal in 1978. A member of the Roscommon S.F.C. team from 1977, he won 4 Connacht Senior Football Championship medals in succession in 1977, 1978, 1979 and 1980 (when he starred in Roscommon's somewhat unlucky defeat in the All-Ireland S.F.C. final by Kerry), being also on the side which won the title in 1990 (the county's first senior provincial title in 10 years). He won 3 Sigerson Cup medals, and with Roscommon he also won a National Football League winners medal in 1979. His brother Eamonn won a Connacht S.F.C. medal with Tony in 1990. A vet, he was one of Connacht's great forwards of the 1980's. He won one All-Star award, in 1989 at centre half-forward.

McMASTER, Arthur WALLACE.

Rugby international wing three-quarter. Born 2nd December 1945 in Ballymena. Club: Ballymena (winning Ulster Senior Cup medals in 1970, 1975 and 1977). A product of Ballymena Academy, he won his first cap in the famous win against France in Stade Colombes in 1972. He went on to be capped for a total of 18 times for Ireland between 1972 and 1976, scoring 2 international tries, and toured New Zealand and Fiji with Ireland in 1976. He was part of the International Championship-winning Irish XV of 1974.

McMICHAEL, ALF.

Soccer international left full-back. Born in Belfast, 1st October 1927. He joined Newcastle, after some outstanding performances for Linfield (winning an I.F.A. Cup medal in 1948), signing for a combined fee of £20,000 with George Hannah at the age of 22, and played 403 matches in 13 glorious years of service at St James Park. A red-head, he was a tenacious tackler, and helped Newcastle to their magnificent 1952 F.A. Cup Final win over Arsenal. Having early in his career played for the Irish League, he went on to be capped 40 times for Northern Ireland between 1950 and 1960 (winning all his caps while at Newcastle United, making him the St James Park club's most capped player), including many as captain. He played a major role in Northern Ireland's qualifying for and participation in the 1958 World Cup in Sweden, wearing the No 3 jersey in all of their 5 games at the finals.

McMILLAN, ANTHONY R W (TONY).

Hockey international left-wing. Club: Belfast YMCA, being a member of the side which won it's first Irish Senior Cup title in 1961). Scoring twice on his international debut in 1958, he went on to play 40 times for Ireland in 14 seasons up to 1971, being a member of the side which won the Home International series for the first time in 19 years in 1968 (he was also a member of the first Irish side in the inaugural European Cup in Brussels in 1970).

McMILLAN, SAMMY.

Soccer international wingman or centre-forward. Born in Belfast, 20th September 1941. Clubs: Boyland YC, Manchester United, Wrexham (scoring 52 goals in 149 appearances 1963-68, helping them to promotion to Division 3 in 1964), Southend United, Chester, Stockport County (scoring 29 goals in 74 games 1970-72). He was capped twice for Northern Ireland in 1963.

McMILLEN, WALTER S.

Soccer international wing-half. Born in Belfast, 24th November 1913. Clubs: Cliftonville, Manchester United, Chesterfield, and Millwall. He was capped 7 times for Northern Ireland before World War 2 (4 of these caps being won while playing for Chesterfield, making him the Recreation Ground club's most capped player).

McMORDIE, ERIC.

Soccer international forward. Born in Belfast, 12th August 1946. Clubs: Dundella, Middlesborough (playing 231 league matches for them in the eight years between 1965 and 1973, scoring 23 goals, helping them to gain promotion from Division Three in 1967), Sheffield Wednesday, York City, Hartlepool. Capped once at Under 23 level, he was capped for Northern Ireland 21 times between 1969 and 1973, scoring 3 international goals.

McMORRAN, EDWARD (EDDIE) J.

Soccer international inside and centre-forward. Born in Larne, 2nd September 1923. Clubs: Ballyclare, Larne Olympics, Belfast Celtic (scoring 60 goals in 1945-46, and winning an Irish Cup medal in 1947); he then went to play in English league football for 10 years, playing for Manchester City, Leeds United, then spending 7 years between Barnsley and Doncaster, and Crewe Alexander, scoring 88 league goals in that period. He later played for Frickley Colliery, and coached Dodswoth Miners Welfare from 1960. Having won a schoolboy international cap while at Larne School, he later represented the Irish League (scoring 2 goals for the team), and was also capped 15 times for the Northern Ireland senior side between 1947 and 1957, scoring 4 international goals. The 9 caps he gained while at Barnsley 1950-52 made him the club's most capped player until passed out by Gerry Taggart (cv). He died in 1984 at the age of 60.

McMULLAN, DAVID.

Soccer international right-half. Born in Belfast. Clubs: Distillery (winning an Irish Cup medal in 1925), Liverpool, New York Giants, Belfast Celtic, Exeter City. An Irish League XI player, he won 3 caps for Ireland in 1926 and 1927, and was so versatile that he played in goals, right and left back, and also as an outside left.

McMULLAN, JOYCE.

G.A.A. football left half-forward, Donegal. Born in 1962. In 1982 he won an All-Ireland Under 21 Championship medal with Donegal. He won Ulster Senior Football Championship medals with Donegal in 1990 and in the watershed year of 1992 when the county team also brought home the Sam Maguire Cup to Donegal for the first time in it's history. In 1990 he was the sole Donegal player to win an All-Star award. An insurance agent.

McNALLY, BERNARD.

Soccer international midfielder. Born in Shrewsbury, 17th February 1963. Apprenticed to Shrewsbury, he played over 330 league matches for them before moving to West Ham. He won 5 caps for Northern Ireland between 1986 and 1988, all gained while at Gay Meadow, thus making him jointly (along with Jim McLaughlin cv), Shrewsbury Town's most capped player.

McNALLY, JOE.

G.A.A. football goalkeper and forward, Dublin. Club: St Annes (Tallaght). Having won an All-Ireland M.F.C. medal while playing in goals in 1982 for Dublin, he went on, in his first championship year and at the age of 19, to win an All-Ireland Senior Football Championship medal with Dublin in 1993 at left-full-forward, and was also on the Dublin side beaten by Kerry in the 2 following All-Ireland S.F.C. finals, playing again at left-full forward in 1984, and at full-forward in 1985 (scoring 2 goals). He won his 4th Leinster S.F.C. medal in 1989. He won a Railway Cup medal with Leinster in 1987. He has won a single All-Star award, in 1983 at left-corner forward.

McNALLY, JOHN.

Amateur bantamweight boxer. Club: White City B.C.(Belfast). After a distinguished youth career, in 1952 this

Belfast boxer became Irish National Senior champion at bantamweight. Later that year the became the first Irish boxer to win an Olympic medal, when after beating a Philipino, an Italian and a Korean (to guarantee a bronze medal), he was beaten controversially in the bantamweight final by Pentti Hamalainen of Finland in a 2-1 decision, to take silver in the bantamweight division at the Helsinki Games. It was the Republic of Ireland's first ever silver medal at an Olympic Games, and was also Ireland's only medal at those 1952 games.

McNAMARA, GERRY.

Powerlift world champion. Born in Limerick, 10th July 1963. Club: Abbey. He has won 11 All-Ireland Senior titles; in the 52.0 Kg class in 1980 and 1981, in the 56.0 Kg class in 1982, 1983, 1984, 1985, 1986; and in the 60.0 Kg class in 1989 and 1990. He also won 2 European Junior titles (breaking 8 European Junior records), and won 3 Senior European titles, in 1986 and 1987 in the 56.0 Kg class and in 1988 in the 60.0 Kg class. He reached his peak in 1987 when he won the World Championship title in the 56.0 Kg class (he was 2nd in the world in 1988 and 1990 in the 60.0 kg class). He also won 6 inter-provincial championships and 11 Munster senior titles (1980-1991). He broke 26 Munster senior weightlifting records, 22 All-Ireland senior records, and 8 Celtic Nations records (he won 3 Celtic Nations Championships, in 1987, 1988 and 1990). Up to 1991 he had won 22 international caps for Ireland.

MacNAMARA, LIAM.

Amateur international golfer. Club: Woodbrook. From Co Roscommon, he was born in 1953. He won the South of Ireland title twice (15 years apart, in 1977 and 1992, and was runner-up in 1986), and was runner-up in 3 other championships, the Irish Close (in 1984), the 'West' and the 'East'. He became a stalwart inter-provincial golfer, playing over 100 matches for Connacht. Between 1977 and 1992 (with a success rate of of over 66%), he was on the winning Irish Home International side a record-equalling (for an Irishman) 5 times, in 1985, 1991 and 1992, and in the Triple-Crown-winning sides of 1987 nd 1990 (when he won 5 out of a possible 6 points); and has played 14 European Team championship matches 1977-87, winning 8, being on the winning sides in 1983 and 1987. In all, up to when he retired in September 1992 he had played over 100 matches for Irish amateur sides. His brother, also a Woodbrook player, has played interprovincial matches for Connacht.

McNAUGHTON, PAUL P.

Rugby international centre three-quarter. Clubs: Trinity College and Greystones. Born in Bray, 18th November 1951. A product of Rockwell College (playing at school interprovincial rugby with Munster), he captained Leinster Under 23's and played for Ireland B level. He was capped 15 times in the centre at senior level for Ireland between 1978 and 1981. Also an accomplished soccer player, he scored 21 League of Ireland goals for Shelbourne in the 1970's. He also played senior gaelic football for Wicklow, thus having the distintion of playing at the highest level in each of Dublin's 3 major sporting arenas, rugby at Landsdowne Road, soccer at Dalymount, and gaelic football at Croke Park.

McNAUGHTON, TERENCE ('SAMBO').

G.A.A. hurling left full-forward and midfielder, Antrim. Club: Cushendall Ruari-Og (playing in all 15 positions on the senior team). Born in 1965. An all-rouund player of much ability who has played in many positions since his senior county debut at the age of 16, he played a crucial role in his county's reaching the All-Ireland Senior Huuring Championship decider for the first time in 46 years in 1989, although trounced by Tipperary in the final. He played at midfield in the 1991 All-Ireland semi-final defeat by

Kilkenny, also playing in the penultimate stage of 1993. He won an All-Star award in 1991 at midfield. His brother Shane was a fine Antrim hurling forward also.

McNEILL, GARY.

Amateur international golfer. Club: Warrenpoint. Born in 1960. He won the Irish Close Championship at Ballybunion in 1991. He was a member of the Irish side (on his senior international debut) that won the 'Triple Crown' of the Home International Championships in Wales in 1990, and in 1991 he scored 4 out of 6 points when Ireland won the Home Internationals.

MacNEILL, HUGH Patrick ('HUGO').

Rugby international full-back. Born in Dublin, 16th September 1958. A product of Blackrock College, he captained the Leinster and Irish School's side of 1976 and 1977. Clubs: Dublin University, Oxford University, Blackrock College and London Irish. A regular for Leinster for many years (and an Ireland 'B' player), he has been capped for Ireland over 35 times since 1981, and has scored 8 international tries (a record for the No 15 jersey for Ireland, arguably making him the country's most attacking full-back of all time). He was a constant and influential member of both the 1982 and 1985 Triple Crown-winning Ireland sides (one of only 6 players to play in all six matches), and the 1983 International Championship victorious XV. He won 3 Test caps on the 1983 British and Irish Lion's tour of New Zealand. He toured Japan with Ireland in 1985, and was in the Irish World Cup side of 1987. He won 2 Oxford Blues in 1982 and 1983 (when he captained them in the Varsity match). A business consultant, he was voted as Texaco's Rugby Sportstar of the Year in 1987. In 1979 he was centre-forward on the Trinity soccer team which won the Collingwood Cup (inter-varsity).

McNICHOLL, DERMOT.

G.A.A football left full-forward, Derry. Born in 1966. Club: Glenullin (captaining the side to win the John McLoughlin trophy for the county championship, for the first time in 58 years, in 1985). A member of the Derry side which's won only the county's 2nd All-Ireland Minor Football Championship crown in 1983, he was a member of the Derry side which won the Ulster S.F.C. title in 1987, being also on the side beaten in the Ulster final of 1985 (during which year he was also captain of the Derry side beaten by Cork in the All-Ireland Under 21 final). In 1992 he was member of the Derry side which won the National Football League. A star member of the Irish side in the Compromise Rules series in 1986 and 1987 (he went to live in Australia in 1988 to play Australian Rules for 2 years with St Kilda), he has won one All-Star award, in 1984 at left-corner forward. In 1993 he was a member of the famous Derry side which won the Sam Maguire Cup for the first time.

McNINCH, J .

Soccer international defender. Club: Distillery (helping the club to its first ever major football trophy success, the 1929 I.F.A. Cup, also being on the side beaten in the final of this competition in the 2 succeeding years). He won 3 international caps for Northern Ireland in 1931 and 1932, all being won while at Ballymena, making him the Showgrounds club's most capped international player.

McNULTY, M STEWART.

Hockey international centre-half. Clubs: Dublin University, Three Rock Rovers, and Inverleith. Capped at Under 23 level in 1965, he was later capped 64 times for Ireland between 1966 and 1975, being a key player in Ireland's forays to the First European Cup in 1970, their win in the Santander 8 Nations tournament of 1972, and the 2nd European Cup in 1974. A fine competitive player, he was captain of the side from 1973, leading Ireland in all on 16 occasions. He later coached the Irish indoor side for 2 seasons, being capped 3 times in this code in 1976.

McPARLAND, PETER J.

Soccer international outside-left. Born in Newry, 25th April 1934. He played for Newry Town and Dundalk before joining Aston Villa at the age of eighteen. In 9 seasons at Villa Park between 1952 and 1961, he scored 98 league goals in 293 league appearances. He scored the winning goal for Villa in their 1957 F.A. Cup final against Manchester United, injuring the opposing goalkeeper Roy Wood in the process, and also won a League Cup medal with Villa in 1961. He then spent a season at both Wolves (who paid £30,000 for him), and Plymouth, scoring 10 and 15 league goals respectfully, bringing his league tally of goals to 129. Playing briefly for Worcester City, he then tried his luck in the U.S.A., before becoming manager of Glentoran. Over an eight year period from 1954 to 1962, he won 34 caps for Northern Ireland, his first being gained at the age of 19 (when scoring 2 goals), and in all he scored 10 international goals (including the hero's role of scoring 5 out of 6 of his country's goals in their successful run in the 1958 World Cup finals in Sweden). Of his 34 caps, 33 were gained while he was at Aston Villa, which made him then the club's most capped player. He also played for the English League side.

McQUAID, JIM and family.

Cyclists. Clubs: Dungarvan, Emerald. Jim, born 18th September 1921, won the Grand Prix of Ireland, a 50km race, no fewer than 6 times, in 1949, 1950, 1953, 1954, 1955 and lastly in 1960. He also won the Hercules Cup (over 100km in the Phoenix Park) 3 times, 1948, 1948 and 1949 (therefore keeping the trophy). He participated in 4 World Championships, and was sent to London for the Olympic Games of 1948, but politics ruled the team out of competition. He won the road race championship in 1950 and 1951. His tussles with J J McCormack in the 1950's and 60's in track meetings at College Park, Santry Stadium, and Landsdowne Road, were memorable. He later managed many Irish teams for Olympic Games etc. His son Pat, an amateur and professional cyclist, won the Tour of Ireland twice in succession (the first cyclist to do so), in 1975 and 1976, and also won the Irish Championship; in 1976 Pat won the prestigious Woolbrock Grand Prix in Britain, and in 1977 he won the Tour of the Cotswolds (turning profesional that year, and later became a cycling commentator on R.T.E.). Two other sons, Kieran and Oliver, represented Ireland on Olympic cycling teams (in 1972 and 1976 respectively), and both of whom have also won the Irish Grand Prix. Another relation, John McQuaid, has won 2 National Championship titles, in 1983 and 1985, and also represented Ireland in the Seoul Olympics in 1988.

McQUILLAN, JACK.

G.A.A. football full-forward, Roscommon. A member of the fine Roscommon side which won 2 sucessive All-Ireland Senior Football Championships in 1943 and 1944 (the county's only 2 titles), he also played on the side beaten in the All-Ireland S.F.C. final replay in 1946 against Kerry, winning another Connacht S.F.C. medal in 1947. He was a T.D. for Roscommon from 1948 to 1961 (and was succeeded in the Dail by a fellow team-mate of his from the 1944 winning side, Hugh Gibbons).

McQUILLAN, MICHAEL.

G.A.A. football goalkeeper, Meath. Born in 1960. Club: St Patrick's. In 1977 he was on the Meath minors beaten in the final of the All-Ireland M.F.C.. Making his senior inter-county in 1978, he won 3 successive Leinster S.F.C. medals with Meath from 1986, including 2 All-Ireland Senior Football Championship medals in 1987 and 1988, and later was on the side which went through 10 championship matches in 1991 (during which he conceded only 6 goals), only to lose to Down in the All-Ireland final. In 1988 he became the 5th Meathman to captain a winning Leinster Railway Cup player. He won an All-Star award in 1991 as goalkeeper.

McSTAY, KEVIN.

G.A.A. football right full-forward, Mayo. Club: Ballymun Kickhams. He was a substitute in Mayo's 1983 All-Ireland Under 21 Championship replay win, playing his first senior championship game that season. A member of the Mayo side which won Connacht Senior Football Championship medals in 1985, 1988 and in 1989 (when the county qualified for it's first All-Ireland S.F.C. final since 1951). He has won one All-Star award, in the right corner forward position in 1985. Also a basketball player of note, he won an All-Ireland Cup medal in 1990 with Connacht Gold Ballina.

McSWEENEY, BRIAN.

Three Day Eventer. Born in Baldonnell, April 15th 1958. Joining the Army in 1976, and commisioned in 1977, in 1981 he became the first Irish rider to win an individual medal at the European 3 Day Event Championships since Eddie Boylan (cv) in 1967, when he won the bronze medal at Horsens, Denmark while piloting Inis Meain. He had previously won the the Irish National 3-day-event championships at Punchestown with Glenannaar.

McTAIGUE, James ANTHONY (TONY).

G.A.A. football left half-forward, Offaly. Born in Clonakilty, Co Cork, 29th January 1946. Club: Ferbane (winning 3 Offaly SFC medals with the club). He won an All-Ireland Minor Football Championship medal at centre half-forward with Offaly in 1964. Playing Under 21 football in 1964-1967, he went on to play senior inter-county football with Offaly from 1964 to 1975. Having been on the side beaten in the All-Ireland S.F.C. final of 1969 by Kerry, he was Offaly's main scoring machine in their first ever All-Ireland Senior Football Championship victories in both 1971 (by 1-14 to 2-8 over Galway), and as captain in 1972 (when Offaly won by 1-19 to 0-13 in a replay over Kerry). He won a 4th Leinster S.F.C. medal in 1973. He gained 2 All-Star awards, in 1971 at right half-forward and in 1972 at left half-forward.

McTIGUE, MIKE.

Light-heavyweight professional boxer. He was born in Ennis, Co Clare on 26th November 1892, and he died in New York on the 12th August 1966. Having fought for 12 years as a middleweight in America, he went to England, and he became world light-heavyweight champion at the age of 30 on St Patrick's Day 1923, when he beat the Senagalese Battling Siki on points over 20 rounds at the La Scala Opera House in Dublin (this was the last world title fight at any weight to go more than 15 rounds). In a 2 year reign, he defended against Young Stribling in Georgia, a match in which he got a controversial draw. However, on May 31st 1925, he was beaten on points over 15 rounds by Paul Berlenbach of U.S.A., at Yankee Stadium, New York. He later lost another title fight, being outpointed against Tommy Laughran in 1927. In his 21 year professional career (his licence to box had to be withdrawn at the age of 38 after he suffered 4 first round k.o.'s), he won 104 (53 inside the distance), drew 6, and lost 45 of his 166 contests.

McVEAGH, Trevor GEORGE Brooke ('T.G.').

International squash, tennis, hockey and cricket player. Born in Drewstown, near Athboy Co Meath on 14th September 1906. A candidate for Ireland's greatest ever all-round sportsman, he played for Ireland at senior international level at 4 different sports. He won the Irish squash title three years in succession in the 1930's, in 1935, 1936, and 1937, and was capped once for Ireland in 1937. In tennis, he represented Ireland in 17 Davis Cup matches between the years

1924 and 1937, won an Irish title at men's doubles (twice beating the great Bill Tilden), and won the Fitzwilliam L.T.C. singles in 1935 and 1950. In hockey, as outside-left and inside-left winger (playing for both Dublin University and Three Rock Rovers clubs), he was captain of arguably Ireland's greatest ever hockey side, which won the Grand Slam 3 years in a row, 1937, 1938, and 1939, being capped for a total of 24 successive times between 1932 and 1939 (his career being curtailed by the War). As a cricketer, he was capped 21 times as a sound left hand batsman between 1926 to 1938, and was one the Irish XI in the famous win over the West Indies in 1928 (himself scoring a century and taking 5 catches). His batting average for Ireland is an outstanding 35.74 runs per innings (placing him 3rd in the all-time Irish figures), made up by 1,108 runs in 36 innings, scoring a best of 109. His versatility is shown in that in 1938 he played international standard in all 4 sports, and that his total number of sports caps in his chosen 4 sports was greater than 70. Also a fine billiards player, he was very skilled as well at shooting game. A lawyer by profession, he died suddenly in 1968, at the age of 60. He is an uncle of Donald Pratt (cv).

McVICKER,, Dr JAMES M (JIM).

Rugby international second-row forward. Club: Collegians (winning an Ulster Senior Cup medal in 1926). Born in Ballymoney in 1896, he was capped 20 times for Ireland between 1924 to 1930, being prominent in helping his country to share the International Championship in both 1926 and 1927. He was the tallest, heaviest and most valuable forward on the 1924 British and Irish Lion's touring side to South Africa, winning 3 Test caps and improving as the tour went on. He was later awarded the O.B.E.. His 2 brothers, Sam (Q.U.B., who had also played hockey once for Ireland in 1914) and Hugh (Army, Richmond), were both capped at rugby as locks for Ireland, 4 and 5 times respectively, in the 1920's. Their combined total of 29 caps makes them the set of three brothers to win most caps for Ireland. Jim and Hugh played together in the Irish side on 4 different occasions.

MacWEENEY, PAUL Denis.

Squash and table-tennis international player. Born in Dublin, 29th June 1909. He won the Irish Squash Rackets Champioships Men's Singles title in 1941 and 1942, and was a squash international. He was also an international player at table-tennis. He reached senior interprovincial level at 2 other sports, lawn tennis and hockey. He later became a respected sports journalist with the Irish Times, being noted for his rugby coverage.

McWILLIAMS, JACKIE.

Ladies hockey international. Born in Ballymoney, Co Antrim, 18th February 1964. Club: Randalstown (whom she has played for since the age of 13, and for whom she has become the club's Senior Player of the Year twice). Up to August 1993 she has been capped 64 times for the Irish ladies hockey side, playing for her country in the World Cup in 1986, in the Interncontinentel Cup in 1989, and in 2 European Cups. She has also won 34 caps for Great Britain at hockey up to August 1993, and in 1992 in the Olympic Games in Barcelona she was a member of the G.B. side which finished in 3rd place, thus gaining a bronze medal (ands becoming the first Irish-born lady hockey player to win any Olympic colour medal). In 1992 she received the Templeton award for Ulster hockey.

MEAGAN, MICK K.

Soccer international wing-half. Born in Dublin, 29th May 1934. He joined Everton from Johnville at the age of 18, having gained schoolboy international honours at St Joseph's, Terenure. Playing in 165 league games for the Toffeemen from 1957 to 1963, he then spent four seasons at Huddersfield, playing 118 league games, followed by a short spell at Halifax, and later for Drogheda and Bray Wanderers. He was capped 17 times for the Republic of Ireland between 1961 and 1970 (in 1969 he became the first Drogheda Utd player to be capped). He was voted Player of the Year in 1971 by the S.W.A.I.. He later managed Shamrock Rovers and the Republic of Irleand team for periods. He once played in the same Rovers team with his son Mark, who later played for Waterford and Athlone Town (winning a League of Irleand Championship medal in 1982-83).

MEAGHER, LORY.

G.A.A. hurling centre-field, Kilkenny. He lived from 1899 to 1973. Club: Tullaroan (winning 6 county championship titles, from his first at 16 in 1916 to his last, aged 35 in 1934). First playing senior inter-county hurling in 1926, he was a winner of 3 All-Ireland Senior Hurling Championship medals in the 1930's with Kilkenny: in 1932, 1933, and in 1935 when as captain he helped Kilkenny to defeat Mick Mackey's Limerick by 2-5 to 2-4. In 1931 he was also captain of Kilkenny, when his absence through injury, in the 3rd of 3 classic encounters with Cork, largely led to Cork winning in an epic series of games. He also played on Kilkenny sides beaten in the All-Ireland S.H.C. finals of 1926 and 1936. He won 2 Railway Cup medals with Leinster, in 1927 and 1933, and won his only National Hurling League medal with the 'Black and Ambers' in 1933. Long before he retired in 1937 he was hailed as a brilliantly stylish hurling midfielder (regarded by many as the finest the game has known), and he was selected (alongside Cork's Jack Lynch cv) to fill the midfield spot on the Sunday Independent's 'Team of the Century' in 1984. Three brothers, Willie, Henry (who both played in Lory's senior debut for his county in 1926, and in the All-Ireland final of that year), and Francis, also played senior county hurling for Kilkenny.

MEARES, ARTHUR WILLIAM DEVENISH ('NEWRY').

Rugby international forward. 1874-1935. Club: Dublin University. He was capped 4 times for Ireland in 1899 and 1900, playing in 2 of the 1899 Championship winning matches. He was selected, three years before he was capped for Ireland, to travel with the first ever British and Irish (Lion's) side, which visited South Africa in 1896.

MECREDY, RALPH J.R.

International cyclist. Club: Trinity College. Born c 1862. Despite nearly having a leg amputated in 1885, he won the 25-mile English tricycle championship in 1886, and in 1887 he won the English 5-mile championship. In 1890 he won all four English championships (using the newly invented Dunlop pneumatic tyres). He subsequently won 7 more Irish cycling titles, and won only the 2nd 100 mile race to be staged in Ireland. He later edited 'Irish Cyclist', and wrote books on motoring and cycling. He was a strong campaigner against the formation of the G.A.A. in 1884.

MEEGAN, PADDY.

G.A.A. football right half-forward, Meath. He won Leinster S.F.C. medals in 1947, 1949, 1951, 1952 and in 1954. In two of these years (1949 and 1954) the county went on to win the Sam Maguire Cup. He captained the Meath side beaten by Cavan in the All-Ireland Senior Football Championship final of 1952, also playing in the side beaten in the 1951 final. He is one of only 2 Meath players to win 4 Railway Cup medals with Leinster, his wins coming in 1945, in 1952 and 1953 (captaining the side in these 2 years), and in 1955.

MEHAFFY, BERTIE.

Soccer international goalkeeper. Clubs: Belfast Celtic, Chelsea, and Belfast Celtic again. He was capped for Northern Ireland first in 1922, and represented his country 4 other occasions. His three brothers, Davy, John ('Finogue') and Sam, were all first-class goalkeepers in senior football. A cousin of Elisha Scott (cv).

MELDON, LOUIS A.

Tennis and cricket player. In tennis, he was a member of the Irish tennis team in 6 Davis Cup matches between 1923 (Ireland's inaugural year in the competition, when India were beaten in the first match) and 1927. Becoming Irish Lawn Tennis Champion in 1924, he also won 4 Irish men's doubles titles in succession (all with different partners, in 1923, 1924, 1925 and 1926, and one Irish mixed doubles title (in 1929). He won the Fitzwilliam Club championship in 1924. He was also a useful cricketer.

MERCER, J T.

Soccer international player. Clubs: Distillery, Linfield, and Derby County. He was capped at senior international level in soccer 11 times for Northern Ireland (the I.F.A.) between 1898 and 1905.

MESITT, BERTIE.

Long-distance athlete. He ran in the Olympic marathon in 1960 in Rome (retiring after 15 miles), the European Championship 10,000 metres in 1958 (finishing 13th), and the European Championship marathon in Belgrade in 1962 (finishing 13th). He also ran for Ireland in the International Cross Country many times, finishing at best 19th in 1958. In 1958 he set an Irish record for the 3 miles, at 13' 44". He was selected, in the inaugural year of 1958, as Texaco's Athletics Sportstar of the Year.

MILLAR, SYDNEY (SYD).

Rugby international tight-head prop-forward. Born in Ballymena, 23rd May 1934. Club: Ballymena (winning Ulster Senior Cup medals in 1963 and 1970). A product of Ballymena Acadeny and Belfast Nautical College, he was capped for Ireland 37 times over a 13 year period between 1958 and 1970, an Irish record then for a prop forward, being the first Irish player to play international rugby in 3 different decades. He went on 2 foreign tours with Ireland, in 1961 to South Africa, and in 1970 to Argentina. He was also the first Irish player to go on 3 different British and Irish Lion's tours, winning 9 Test appearences (the 4th most for an Irishman) out of a total of 44 Lion's appearences: 3 test places on the 1959 tour of Australia and New Zealand, all four on the South Africa Tour of 1962 (as a loose-head prop), and 2 more on the 1968 tour, again to South Africa. He was manager of the 1980 British and Irish Lion's tour of South Africa, having previously been Assistant Manager on the highly successful 1974 tour to the same country (thus touring, in one capacity or another, with the Lions on 4 successive tours of South Africa). He was the coach to the Irish rugby XV between 1972 and 1975, and was a 'Big 5' selector in those years. His son Peter, a Ballymena prop forward, played for Ireland 'B' in 1993.

MILLAR, BILLY.

Soccer international inside-right and centre forward. Born in Ballymena, 22nd March 190?. Clubs: Lochgelly United, Linfield, Liverpool, Barrow (scoring 30 goals in 30 games in the 1931-32 League, then a club record), Newport County, Carlisle. Capped twice for Northern Ireland in 1932 and 1933 while playing with Barrow, he is still that club's only capped player for any country.

MILLER, DICK.

G.A.A. footballer, Laois. Club: Annanough (captaining his club to win the Laois County Championship 3 years in succession, 1924, 1925, and 1926). He captained the famous Laois team which won the inaugural National Football League title in 1926. Other members of the Miller family to play on that occasion included Chris, John, Jim and Bill (nicknamed 'Skinner', who went on to win Railway Cup medals with Leinster in 1927 and 1928).

MILLER, SAMUEL Hamilton (SAMMY).

Motor cycle trialist. Born in Belfast, 11th November 1933. Noted as the world's most successful and accomplished ever trials rider, he started competing at road racing in 1954, riding N.S.U., Ducati, Mondial and C.Z. machines, and finished 3rd in the 1957 World Championship at 250cc (having been 6th in 1955). In 1956 only a gear-box seizure on the last bend on his Mondial prevented him winning the Isle of Man T.T. at 125 c.c. (he had 4 top 6 places in T.T.'s, and was 4th in the 125cc World Championship in 1957). He then took up trial riding and became British champion 11 years in a row (the first six years, 1959 to 1964 on an Ariel 497 c.c., making that bike the most famous in the sport, and the last 5 years, 1965 to 1969, on a 244 c.c. Bultaco), and was European Champion twice (in 1967 and 1969). In a 20-year career, he won 900 victories in trial events, including 5 British Experts, many Irish Experts, 6 Scottish, 7 Scott, 13 Hurst, and 16 consecutive Walter Rusk trials up to his retirement in 1970. He also won 5 gold medals with British teams in 6-Day International Trials. A true vituoso in motorcycling history, in any kind of motor-cycle race, he also won on grass-track, sand racing etc. In 1968 he was selected as the Texaco Sportstar of the Year in motor sport. He also helped Honda to develop its trial machines, and latterly ran a motorcycle museum in New Milton, Hampshire.

MILLIGAN, TERRY.

Amateur international boxer. Club: Shortt and Harland. He won 6 Irish Senior National Championship titles at 4 different weights, featherweight in 1950, light-welterweight in 1951, 1952, and 1953, welterweight in 1954, and light-middleweight in 1955. He represented Ireland at the 1952 Olympic Games in Helsinki, losing the fight for a bronze medal with the Italian Bruno Visintin, thereby finishing equal 5th. He was the first (of only 6) Northern Irish boxers to a win Commonwealth gold medal, achieving this at middleweight in the 1958 Games held in Wales.

MILLIKEN, RICHARD Alexander (DICK).

Rugby international centre-threequarter. Born 2nd September 1950. Clubs: Queen's University Belfast and Bangor (becoming the club's first capped player in 1973). A product of Bangor GS, he was capped 14 times for Ireland between 1973 and 1975, scoring 2 international tries, one of these coming in the 1974 season in which Ireland won the International Championship for the first time in 23 years. He would have won many more caps but for a nasty ankle injury. Also a Barbarian, he played a vital role in all four Test matches when the British and Irish Lion's toured South Africa with great success in 1974, under club-mate Willie John McBride's captaincy, and scored 6 tries in his 13 tour appearances.

MILLNER, Colonel JOSHUA KEARNEY ('JERRY').

Shooting competitor. Born in Irleand c 1849. Taking up the sport in 1871, he toured the U.S.A. with an Irish team in 1874. He went on to shoot for Ireland for 30 years in the Elcho Match, and was non-shooting captain in the 1919 event. He visited America again with a British team in 1887, when they lost the Palma Match. In 1908, at the age of at least 58 (some say he was well over 60), he won a gold medal in the Free Rifle 1,000 yards event (scoring 98 out of a possible 100 points) at the Olympic Games in London (actually held at Bisley), thus making him the oldest person to ever win a gold medal in the Olympics while representing Great Britain. In the same Games he also competed in the Running Deer single shot and the Running Deer double shot events. A Colonel of the Regiment with the famed Carlow Militia, he was the unit's last Commanding Officer. He died in Dublin in 1931.

MILLS, KATHLEEN ('THE CHRISTY RING OF CAMOGIE').

G.A.A. camogie left-wing forward, Dublin. Clubs: Great Southern Railways (later C.I.E.). The game of camogie's best-known player, she has won an astonishing 15 All-Ireland Senior Championship medals, which she won in 18 final games, making her by far and away the highest tally winner of Championship medals. A skilful player with a strong wrist, and a fine point-taker, her O'Duffy Cup successes with the Dubs came in 1942 (a replay win against Cork), 1943, 1944, followed by 8-in-a-row, 1948, 1949, 1950, 1951, 1952, 1953, 1954 and 1955, and another 5-in-a-row, 1957, 1958, 1959, 1960, and 1961 (against Tipperary). Her only 2 losing final appearences were in 1941 and 1947. She retired in 1963.

MILNE, ROBERT G (BOB).

Soccer international midfielder. Clubs: Linfield (with whom he won 7 Irish Cup medals, in 1891, 1892, 1893, 1895, 1898, 1899, 1902 and 1904, also winning Irish League medals in 1894-95, 1897-98, 1901-02 and 1903-04). A Scot by birth, he was capped 27 times for Northern Ireland between 1894 and 1906, all gained while at the Windsor Park club (making him the 'Blues' most capped player), and he scored 2 international goals.

MITCHELL, JAMES Sarsfield.

Hammer thrower, 56lb Weight and Shot putt throwing Athlete. Born in Emly, Co Tipperary, 30th January 1864, he died in New York in 1921. One of the world's finest hammer throwers of his day, he was the predessesor of John Flanagan (cv) in the domination of this event. He won an amazing 76 national championship titles in countries that included Ireland (with 17 titles), England (winning A.A.A. shot titles in 1886 and 1887, and hammer titles in 1886, 1887 and 1888), Canada and the United States (10 of these at the 56lb weight), and broke the world record for the hammer 4 times between 1886 and 1892. In Limerick in 1886 he set the first official British hammer record, with a throw of 119' 5". Later, having won 10 A.A.U. titles, he, at the age of 40, entered for 4 events in the 1904 Olympic Games in St Louis, winning a bronze medal in the 56lb weight throw (finishing one inch behind silver medallist John Flanagan cv, at 33' 4"), also finishing 5th in the hammer, 6th in the Discus throw, and 4th with the New York Police side in the tug-of-war. He was favourite, at the age of 42, for the 1906 Olympic Stone Throw (the only time the event was held at the Games), but dislocated his shoulder when the ship which was carrying the U.S.A. team to Athens was hit by a freak large wave, and had to withdraw (the winner's throw of 66 feet was 9 feet short of Mitchell's current form). He won 60 gold medals for his athletic feats in the U.S.A..

MITCHELL, WILLIAM (BILLY).

Soccer international midfielder and wing-half. Born in Lurgan, 22nd November 1910, he died in 1978. Clubs: Cliftonville, Distillery, Chelsea (playing in over 100 games for them), and Bath City. He was capped 15 times for Northern Ireland between 1932 and 1938.

MOCLAIR, PADDY.

G.A.A. football full-forward, and right full-forward, Mayo. Born in Castlebar, Co Mayo. Clubs: Castlebar Mitchels (winning 5 Mayo county championship medals) and Ballina Stephenites (winning 4 Mayo county champinship medals). Playing football for Clare in 1929, he declared for Mayo in 1930. Said to be the first roving full-forward, and regarded as one of the game's greatest full-forward line players, he shares the record of 4 Railway Cup medals for Connacht for a Mayoman, winning in 1934 (Connacht's first victory), 1936 (as the first winning Mayo captain), 1937, and in 1938 (becoming the first Connachtman to captain 2 winning sides). He was a member of the first Mayo side to win the Sam Maguire Cup in 1936, having previously played in an All-Ireland Senior Football Championship final in 1932 (which the county lost). He also played on winning Connacht S.F.C. medals in 1935, and

1937. A winner of National Football League medals with Mayo in 1939 and 1940, he retired in the latter year. He was a publican.

MOCKLER, ROBERT (BOB).

G.A.A. hurling midfielder, Dublin. Born in Horse and Jockey, Co Tipperary. He captained the Dublin side of Faughs which won the 1920 All-Ireland Senior Hurling Championship final, defeating the Cork Selection by 4-9 to 4-3, also leading the Dublin side beaten in the following year's final (and was on the losing All-Ireland final side in 1919 also). He was on 2 other winning Dublin All-Ireland S.H.C. sides, in both 1917 and 1924. An adept free-taker, punter, and high-ball catcher, he was also a handballer of note.

MOLLOY, ANTHONY.

G.A.A. football midfielder, Donegal. Club: Ardara. He was in midfield when Donegal won the All-Ireland Under 21 championship in 1982, and first played senior inter-county football at 19, in 1981. He has gone on to assist the county to win 3 Ulster Senior Football Championship titles, in 1983, 1990 and in 1992. Playing in over 100 games for the county, in 1992 he achieved the ultimate honour of captaining the Tir Connail side to win the All-Ireland Senior Football Championship for the very first time, when they defeated Dublin by the score of 0-18 to 0-14 in the final. An E.S.B. worker, he won an All-Star award in 1992 at centrefield.

MOLLOY, MICHAEL Gabriel (MICK).

Rugby international 2nd row forward. Born in Cornamona, Co Galway, 27th September, 1944. Clubs: U.C.G., London Irish, The Army, Barbarians and Surrey. This durable and strong Connachtman, a product of Garbally College in Ballinasloe, was capped 27 times for Ireland over an eleven year period between 1966 and 1976 (when Ireland won 14, drew 3 and lost 10 matches), most of them in partnership with Willie John McBride (cv), and scoring 2 international tries. He went on 2 foreign tours with the Irish side, to Australia in 1967 and to Argentina in 1970. A doctor in London, he latterly has been a medical officer for the I.R.F.U.

MOLLOY, PADDY.

G.A.A. hurling midfielder and right full forward, Offaly. Rated as one of the finest hurlers who never won an All-Ireland Senior Hurling Champiobsip medal, he was as his peak when his county enjoyed little fortune, his only appearence in a Leinster Senior Hurling Champonship final being in 1969, when Offaly lost to Kilkenny by 2 points. He did however win 2 successive Railway Cup medals with Leinster, in 1965 and 1967.

MOLLOY, P J .

G.A.A. hurling left-half forward, Galway. Club: Athenry (with whom he reached the 1988 final of the All-Ireland Club Championship). Making his senior debut in 1971, he was a sub on the Galway side which were All-Ireland Under 21 Champions in 1972, and he went on to win 3 All-Ireland Senior Hurling Championship medals with Galway, in 1980, and as a sub in both 1987 and 1988, also appearing in 4 All-Ireland S.H.C. losing finals, in 1979, 1981, 1985 (when he was the leading scorer in the final with 1-6) and 1986 (as a sub). He was the game's leading scorer in 2 seasons, in 1977 (scoring 93 points in 20 competitive games, a record for a Galway hurler, and making him the first Connacht player to top this league) and again in 1982 (scoring 136 points in 20 games, from 15 goals and 91 points). He has won 5 Railway Cup medals with Connacht, in 1980, 1982, 1983, 1986, and 1987 (as a sub). He won his only All-Star award in 1977 at left half-forward.

MOLONEY, JACK.

National Hunt jockey. Born in 1898, he died in 1969. His association with the Aintree Grand National is bitter sweet, as after finishing 2nd three times (1929 on

Easter Hero, 1931 on Gregalach, and 1939 on Delaneige), he was again placed 2nd on Black Hawk only to fall at the last fence. He had more success in the Irish Grand National (winning twice, in 1922 on Halston and in the following year with Be Careful). He also won 2 Grand Seftons (in 1930 and 1936), and won the Welsh Grand National in 1929.

MOLONEY, JOHN Joseph (JOHNNY).

Rugby international scrum-half and wing three-quarter. Born 27th August 1949. Club: St Mary's College (winning Leinster Senior Cup medals in 1969, 1971, 1974 and 1975, and Leinster Senior League medals in 1972, 1978 and 1980). Over 20 times a Leinster interprovincial player, he was capped for Ireland 27 times (23 as a fine scrum-half) between 1972 and 1980, his last four caps being on the wing, and he scored 4 international tries. His try on his debut for Ireland against France in 1972 made him the first scorer of a 4 point try for his country. A talented, running scrum-half, he toured South Africa with the 1974 British and Irish Lion's (not gaining a test place), and toured with Ireland to Argentina in 1970 and to Australia in 1979. He later coached St Mary's, and under-age international sides.

MOLONEY, LAWRERNCE Aanthony (LARRY).

Rugby international full-back. Born 14th June 1951. Club: Garryowen. He was capped 4 times as a rugby full-back for Ireland, twice in both 1976 and 1978, and was a member of the famous Munster team which beat the 1978 All-Blacks touring side. He has won 4 Munster Senior Cup medals with Garryowen, in 1971, 1974, 1975, and 1979.

MOLONEY, PAT.

G.A.A. camogie right below left, Cork. Clubs: Youghal, U.C.C. (with whom she won 4 Ashbourne Cup medals), and Killeagh (winning a medal when they became the only Cork club side to win an All-Ireland Club Championship in 1980). An elusive attacker or midfield player, her style and speed helped her to win 7 All-Ireland Senior Championship titles with Cork, in 1970, 1971, 1972, 1973, 1978, 1980, and 1982 (when she captained the side which beat Dublin by 2-7 to 2-6). She has also won a Gael Linn award.

MOLONY, MARTIN.

National Hunt and flat jockey. His major wins include the fine win in Cheltenham Gold Cup of 1951 on Silver Frame. He rode the winner of 3 Irish Grand Nationals (1944 with Knight's Crest, 1946 on Golden View, and 1950 on Dominic's Bar). He was also an adept flat jockey, being the Irish flat jockey champion in 1948 with 89 winners, having the previous year won the Irish Oaks on Desert Drive (in 1951, on Signal Box, he was 3rd in the Epsom Derby and 2nd in the Irish equivalent). In 1950 he rode 92 jump winners in the calendar year in Ireland, a record he held for 42 years until surpassed in 1992 by Charlie Swan (cv). Regarded as the most gifted post war National Hunt Jockey in Britain (at one stage, on his rare visits there, his winning average was 33%), in 1966 he was selected as Texaco's Sportstar of the Year for horse racing. A younger brother of Tim Molony (cv).

MOLONY, TIM.

National Hunt jockey. Born 14th September 1919. Spending most of his career in England, he was Champion National Hunt Jockey in Britain 5 times, 1948-1949 (60 winners), 1949-1950 (95 winners), 1950-1951 (83 winners), 1951-1952 (99 winners, his best seasonal tally), and in 1954-1955 (67 winners). He is the first National Hunt jockey in Britain to accumulate 500 winners, 600 winners, 700 winners, and 800 winners, his tally when finally retiring in 1958 being 866 winners. He has ridden a record 4 Champion Hurdle-winning horses, achieved 4 years in succession, in 1951 on Hatton's Grace, and then for 3 consecutive years on the great Sir Ken (1952, 1953, and 1954). His other major wins include the 1953 Cheltenham Gold Cup on Knock Hard (having been beaten on Happy Home by the great Cottage Rake in the 1948 race), 3 Seftons, 3 Great Yorkshires, 2 Champion Chases (1948 and 1949) and 2 Stanley Trophys.

MOLONYEUX, T B.

Soccer international player. Clubs: Ligoniel, and Cliftonville. He was capped for Northern Ireland 11 times between 1883 and 1888, scoring one international goal.

MONAGHAN, DONAL.

G.A.A. football right full-back, Donegal. He was a member of the Donegal side which won the Ulster Senior Football Championship title in both 1972 and 1974. Also a Railway Cup player with Ulster, he won his only All-Star award in 1974 in the right corner-back position, only the 2nd Donegal player to be given this honour.

MONAGHAN, JOHN.

Lightweight professional boxer. An Irishman, in 1855 he laid claim to the world professional lightweight boxing title when he knocked out the American Jim Hart in the 45th round at Island Pond, Canada. However, his claim was not universally supported, and he lost in a return fight with Hart a year later, in 1856.

MONAGHAN, JOHN JOSEPH (RINTY, 'THE PRIDE OF BELFAST' and 'THE SINGING IRISHMAN').

Flyweight professional boxer. He was born in Belfast on August 21st 1920, and died in Belfast in 1984. Fighting in the professional game since the age of 14 in 1935, his first reverse was in 1938, losing to Jackie Patterson of Scotland in his 22nd fight. Serving with the British Army in W.W.II., he won the Irish title by k.o. against Bunty Doran in 1945. Knocking out Patterson in a return bout of 6 rounds in a non-title fight in 1946, he won, in October 1947, the NBA(America) and IBBC version of the world crown when he beat the Hawaiian Dado Marino on points over 15 rounds (having 3 months earlier lost on a technicality to the same opponent), doing so in his first fight in London (and after 12 years as a pro). In March 1948 he became undisputed world champion when, in the King's Hall, Belfast, he knocked out Jackie Patterson again, this time in the 7th round, also capturing the British and Empire titles. He thus became Ireland's first world champion since Jimmy McLarnin (cv) in 1934. He made 2 successful defences of his title in Belfast, outpointing Maurice Sandyro of France (which also gave him the European title, adding to his British, Empire and World titles), and in September 1949, drawing with Terry Allen (England). He retired 6 moths later because of a lung complaint, at the age of 30, as an undefeated champion, leaving his title vacant. In his 16 year professional career, he won 51, drew 6 and lost 9 of his 66 contests. In 1969 he was elevated in to the Texaco Hall of Fame, the first Irish boxer to be so honoured.

MONAGHAN, PADDY J ('MONTY').

Soccer international forward. Club: Sligo (being a member of the side which joined the Irish Free State Football League in 1934-35, winning a League Championship winner's medal in 1936-37, while he was in the Sligo side beaten in the F.A.I. Cup final replay of 1939). He was capped twice for the Irish Free State in 1935, both of these caps coming while based at Sligo, thus making him the club's most capped (and only) international player.

MONGEY, EAMONN.

G.A.A. football midfielder, Mayo. Clubs: Civil Service. A member of the Mayo side which won 4 Connacht S.F.C. finals in succession, in 1948, 1949, 1950 and 1951, he played on the side beaten in the All-Ireland S.F.C. final of 1948 before going on to win 2 successive All-Ireland Senior Football Championship medals with Mayo in both 1950 and 1951. He also won a National Football League medal with Mayo in 1948-49, and won a Railway Cup medal Connacht in 1951.

MONTEITH, Jack DERYK Eric.

Rugby international centre three-quarter. Born in Ballymoney, 24th August 1922. Club: Queen's University, Belfast (helping them to Ulster Senior Cup success in 1947). A product of Coleraine AI, he won 3 international caps (2 winning) for Ireland in the 1947 season, and captained the side in each of his last 2 caps. He is an uncle of Keith Crossan (cv).

MONTEITH, J DERMOTT.

Cricket international left arm spinner and right hand batsman. Born in Lisburn, 2nd June 1943. Club: Queen's Lisburn. A product of R.B.A. and Queen's University, he played first class cricket 9 times for Middlesex in 1981-1982. His total haul of 326 international wickets (for an average of 17.37 runs per wicket in 126 innings) for Ireland in all internationals is an Irish record unlikely to be beaten, as is his tally of taking 5 or more wickets in internationals 27 times. His batting tally of 1,712 runs places him 12th in the all-time list, for an average of 20.62 off 99 innings, including seven 50's for his country. Capped 76 times in all for Ireland (making him up to 1992 the 6th most capped Irish cricketer of all-time), in 1984 he, on his 41st birthday, took 4 wickets against the M.C.C. in his 71st international for Ireland, thus bringing his total of 1st class wickets for Ireland to a record 209. Once (in 1973 against the M.C.C.) taking 8 wickets for 44 runs in one innings, he was picked as the cricket Sportstar of the Year by Texaco twice (the only cricketer to win more than once), in 1971 and 1973. He captained his country on a record 37 occasions, and is regarded as Ireland's best post-War bowler.

MONTGOMERY, ROBERT.

Rugby international wing threequarter. Born in 1886. Clubs: N.I.F.C. and Cambridge (winning a Blue in 1891). Although he was capped only 5 times for Ireland (between 1887 and 1892), he became (in a losing match against Wales) the first Irishman to score 3 tries in a rugby international (a feat that was not subsequently passed out until 1991). His younger brother, A Montgomery, a N.I.F.C. centre three-quarter, was capped once for Ireland in the 1895 rugby match against Scotland.

MOONEY, JACKIE.

Soccer international forward. Clubs: Bangor (Wales), Manchester United, Home Farm, Cork Hibernians and Shamrock Rovers. While at Glenmalure Park, he won a League of Ireland Championship winner's medal in 1963-64, when the Hoops also won the F.A.I. Cup, the Shield, the Dublin City Cup and the Leinster Senior Cup, i.e. the 'Grand Slam'; and he won another F.A.I. Cup medal in 1965. He was his club's leading scorer in the League of Ireland in 1961, 1963 and 1966, and was a member of the famous League of Ireland XI which beat the English League XI in 1963 for the first time. He was capped twice for the Republic of Ireland, in 1965. He is a nephew of Denis Doyle cv.

MOONEY, JIMMY.

Yachtsman and sailor. He holds the unique distinction in Irish Olympic history of the biggest gap (12 years) between competing in any 2 different Olympic Games. When first competing in the Firefly class in the 1948 Olympic Games in London, he finished 16th (with a best placing of 4th in the series). When he competed for the 2nd and last time, in the 1960 Olympic Games in Rome, he was in the Dragon class (with Robin Benson and David Ryder), finishing in 12th place (with a best result of 5th in the series).

MOONEY, MAISIE.

Amateur international golfer. Born 11th June 1952. In 1973 she had an amazing year, winning the Irish Ladies Close title, the Dutch Ladies title, and becoming also the Australian champion. She also won Home international and Vagliano Trophy representation. Her performances for that year made her an automatic choice for Texaco's Golf Sportstar of the Year, and she also became the the Supreme Sportstar of the Year for that year. She was also made Daks Woman Golfer of the Year. She then emigrated to Australia in 1974.

MOORE, ARTHUR.

National Hunt jockey and trainer. Born 15th September 1949, son of Dan Moore (cv). As a jump jockey he won over 60 races, including the 1971 Irish Grand National on King's Sprite. Training at Caragh, Naas, Co Kildare, he has won 4 Irish Sweeps Hurdles (Irian 1979, Fredcotteri 1983 and 1984, and Roark in 1988), the Queen Mother Champion Chase (Drumgora, 1981), and 2 Leopardstown Chases. Other top horses under his wing have been Royal Bond, Venture to Cognac, and Bonalma. He had 55 winners in both 1991 and 1992, winning the trainers championship for the first time in the latter year.

MOORE, DANIEL L (DAN).

National Hunt trainer. Born 29th October 1910. A jockey from 1932 to 1948, he was Ireland's leading combined jockey in 1940, and was leading National Hunt jockey in Ireland for 6 years (and once rode 4 winners in one day in Cheltenham). He lost the Aintree Grand National of 1938 by a head on Battleship, and twice rode the winner of the Irish Grand National (on Golden Jack in 1943 and on Revelry in 1947). As a trainer he won 2 successive Cheltenham Gold Cup's with L'Escargot (in 1970 and 1971, and trained the disqualified 1975 winner Tied Cottage), also winning: the 1975 Aintree Grand National (also with L'Escargot), 2 National Hunt 2 Mile Chases (in 1959 with Quita Que and in 1973 with Inkslinger), a Champions Chase, and the Irish Grand National with Tied Cottage in 1979. His Cheltenham National Hunt Festival tally of winners as a trainer is 15, and his good horses include Team Spirit, Hatton's Grace, L'Escargot (who also won the Wills Premier Chase in 1970, having the previous year won the Meadowbank Chase in Belmont Park, U.S.A.) and Tied Cottage. He is the father of Arthur Moore cv.

MOORE, FRANK.

International oarsman. Clubs: Garda Siochana Boat Club and Neptune R.C.. He has won more Irish Senior Championship titles in rowing than any other person in history, with a total of 14. Seven of these came in the 'Eights' (1974, 1975 and 1977 with Garda; and in 1985, 1986, 1987 and 1989 with Neptune), while his others came in three of the only four other classes available to oarsmen, in coxed fours (1987), coxless pairs (in 1980 in a composite team, and with Neptune in 1985, 1986, 1987 and 1988), and double sculls (once with Garda in 1981). He won twice at Henley, in the Thames Cup with Garda and the Ladies Plate with Neptune, while in international class he was a semi-finalist in the Grand Challenge Cup (for eights) and the Prince Philip Cup (for coxed fours), being also a finalist in the Silver Goblets for coxless pairs. He represented Ireland at World Championships four times from 1975 to 1988, his best placing being 8th in the world in the coxed four at Bled in 1979. He represented Ireland in the coxed pairs at the Seoul Olympics of 1988.

MOORE, GARRET and WILLIE.

National hunt jockeys and trainers, brothers. Garrett, the elder of the two (he died in 1908), won the Aintree Grand National as a jockey on Liberator in 1879, while the following year he was 2nd in the same race on Empress. As a trainer he won the 1891 Eclipse Stakes with Surefoot. Willie (an uncle of Frank Hartigan cv), won the 1890 Champion Hurdle at Cheltenham as a jockey, and won the Old Baron Hunt Classic 4 times (in 1883, 1884, 1886 and 1887). As a trainer he sent out the winner of 3 Aintree Grand Nationals in the 1890's: 1894 with Why Not, 1896 with The Soarer, and in 1899 with Manifesto.

MOORE, C MALCOLM, D FRANK, and Sir FREDERICK William.

Three rugby international brothers. From Dublin Universtity and Wanderers, they won respectively two, three and four international caps for Ireland in the years between 1883 and 1888. Frank and Frederick played together in the Welsh match of 1884 (which Frank captained), while Malcolm, 7 times a Leinster player, played in the International Championship winning side of 1888. Frederick Moore went on to become President of the I.R.F.U. in 1889-1890 and was knighted in 1911, while Frank became an international referee.

MOORE, MARY and KATHLEEN.

G.A.A. football twin sisters, Wexford. Club: Adamstown (with whom they won an All-Ireland Club Championship medal in 1988). Mary, a centre half-back, was on the Wexford team beaten in the All-Ireland Senior Championship final by Kerry in both 1986 and 1989 (when she was captain). A winner of 3 All-Star awards, she was on the Wexford side which won the National League in 1986. A winner of 2 All-Ireland M.F.C. medals, she is a versatile player. Her twin-sister Kathleen has been a midfield Adamstown player, her tally of medals matches that of Mary, and she is also an All-Star recipient.

MOORE, PADDY.

Soccer international centre-forward. Born in Dublin in 1910, he died at the age of 41. Clubs: Bendigo, Richmond Rovers, Shamrock Rovers (winning an F.A.I. Cup medal in 1931 by scoring the winning goal, repeating this feat in the win of 1932; in 1936 he again won an F.A.I. Cup medal; he also won an Irish Free State League Championship winner's medal in 1931-32, scoring 48 goals in competitions that year), Cardiff City, Aberdeen (scoring 27 goals in 29 league games), Shelbourne, Brideville. In 6 seasons of league soccer in Ireland (with Shamrock Rovers in 2 periods) and Scotland (with Aberdeen), he scored 79 league goals. He was capped 10 times for the Irish Free State between 1931 and 1937, scoring 7 international goals. On 25th February 1934, he became the first player to score 4 goals in a World Cup match, in the 4-4 drawn qualifying match against Belgium. Also an Inter-League player (scoring 2 goals), he won a cap with the I.F.A. in 1933 while with Aberdeen. A genius on the ball, and compared by many to George Best (cv), he had problems with drink later in life.

MOORE, TERENCE Anthony Patrick (TERRY).

Rugby international No 8 forward. Born in Cork, 29th April 1945. Club: Highfield (winning Munster Senior Cup medals in 1966 and 1968). A product of North Mon school, he won, between 1967 and 1974, 12 senior international rugby caps for Ireland, scoring one try during Ireland's triumphant International Championship year of 1974. He toured with Irish touring sides to Australia in 1967 and to Argentina in 1970.

MORAN, DENIS ('OGGIE').

G.A.A. football centre half-forward, Kerry. Born in Limerick, 16th January 1956. Clubs: Shannon Rangers (winning a county Championship medal at the age of 16), U.C.D. (winning Sigerson Cup laurels) and Beale (winning a county championship medal with them in 1977). Winning 2 All-Ireland College's medals with Gormanston (in 1973 and 1974), and having played Kerry minors for 3 years, he went on to win 3 successive All-Ireland Under 21 Championship medals with Kerry in 1975, 1976, and in 1977 when he captained the winning side. He shares, with 5 other Kerry players from the great side of the 70's and 80's, the distinction of winning a record 8 All-Ireland Senior Football Championship winner's medals, being the only one of them to do so all in the same position, as a centre half-forward. He won Sam Maguire Cup medals in 1975 (when at 19 he was the youngest in a young team), then in all of the four-in-a-row of 1978 (when he captained, at the age of 22, the side which beat Dublin by 5-11 to 0-9), 1979, 1980, 1981, and also for the 3-in-a-row of 1984, 1985, 1986. He also played on losing Kerry side in All-Ireland finals in 1976 and 1982 (and the famous losing semi-final of 1977), all in positions different from centre-forward. He won National Football League medals with the 'Kingdom' in 1977, 1982 and 1984, and won 3 Railway Cup medals with Munster, in centre-field in 1976, in the half-back line of 1977, and at left half-forward in 1982. He won one All-Star award, in 1981 at left half-forward, a poor tally for a man who had achieved so much in the game. He retired from football in 1991 at 35, and took over the managing of the Kerry senior team in 1992.

MORAN, FREDDIE G.

Rugby international wing three-quarter, athlete and clay-pigeon shooter. Club: Clontarf (being a member of the club's only XV to win the Leinster Senior Cup in 1936). He played rugby 9 times for Ireland between 1936 and 1939, scoring 6 international tries. Having been deprived of anything up to 20 caps during W.W.II., he also played in 3 unofficial internationals in 1946, and 3 times versus the British Army in 1943 and 1944. He did play for Leinster both before and after the war, playing a total of 10 times betwen 1935 and 1945. He was also an Irish international sprint champion, winning a 220 yard race in a Triangular match versus England and Scottland in 1938 in 22..6 seconds, and winning N.I.A.A.A. titles at 100 and 200 yards in 1937, as a member of the City and Suburban club. He also represented Ireland at clay pigeon shooting, making him one of the rare breed to represent Ireland at 3 different sports..

MORAN, KEVIN B.

Soccer international central defender and G.A.A. football centre-half back, Dublin. Born in Dublin, 29th April 1954. He is the only man to win both All-Ireland Senior Football Championship winner's medals and English F.A. Cup medals. He won his 2 Sam Maguire Cup medals in the great Dublin side of the mid 70's, in 1976 and 1977, playing a vital role at centre half-back (winning an All-Star award in 1976, and regarded as one of the games finest), also playing on the side beaten in the All-Ireland final of 1978. He won his 2 F.A. Cup medals with Manchester United (whom he joined from Pegasus in 1978, and with whom he played over 250 league matches), in 1983 and 1985 (in this match he became the first player to be sent off in an F.A. Cup final). Also playing for Sporting Gijon in Spain and for Blackburn Rovers (playing a major role in their promotion to the new Premier League in English football in 1992). Since first being capped for the Republic of Ireland in 1980 against Sweden, he has played over 65 matches for his country, playing a pivotal role in Ireland's heroic exploits at the European Championships bid in 1988 and in the Republic's qualification for the World up finals in 1990, and scoring (up to mid 1993) 6 international goals. He was ever-present in the Republic of Ireland's historic exploits in the World Cup finals in Rome in 1990, when they reached the quarter-finals, and continued to perform in his country's quest to qualify for the World Cup in America in 1994 (playing in an Irish record 24 World Cup matches en route). In 1992 he was voted as Texaco's Sportstar of the Year for soccer.

MORAN, MICKEY.

G.A.A. football half-back, Derry. Born in 1952. Clubs: Glen, Maghera (winning 2 Derry IFC medals). A Derry minor in

1968-70 (winning an Ulster medal in 1969) and an Under 21 player in 1971-72, he played senior inter-county between 1972 and 1984 (being player-manager in 1981-84). He won 2 successive Ulster Senior Football Championship medals with Derry in 1975 and 1976, and also won 2 Railway Cup medals with Ulster, in 1979 and 1980 (as a sub). A replacement All-Star in 1977, he became the Derry senior trainer in the early 1990's.

MORAN, MICHAEL ('DYKE').

Professional golfer. Born at Dollymount near the Royal Dublin course in 1886, he died in W.W.I. in 1918 from wounds recieved. Club: Royal Dublin. He finished 3rd in the British Open at Hoylake in 1913, using borrowed clubs and wearing army boots. Known as Ireland's first great professional golfer, he won the Irish Professional Championship 5 years in succession (the only man to do so), in 1909 (when it was matchplay), and in the strokeplay years of 1910, 1911, 1912, and 1913. In 1919 he became the first Irish professional to play in an international series, for the British and Irish professionals against their amateur counterparts. The slang word for a birdie in Irish golf ('dyke') is called after him.

MORAN, PADDY.

G.A.A. hurling midfielder, Kilkenny. Club: Bennetsbridge. A member of the Kilkenny minors beaten in the All-Ireland M.H.C. finals of both 1956 and 1957, he went on to win 4 All-Ireland Senior Hurling Championship winners medal's with Kilkenny, in 1963, 1967, 1969 (coming on as a sub), and in 1972 (also playing as a sub). He was on All-Ireland S.H.C. losing final sides in 1964, 1966, and 1971 (as a playing sub), making in all 7 All-Ireland hurling final appearances. He won 3 Railway Cup winners medals with Leinster, in 1964, 1965 and 1967.

MORE O'FERRALL, RODERIC.

Horse trainer, flat. Based at Kildangan, he has trained the winners of 5 Irish classics, in each classic apart from the Irish Derby. His winners were: two Irish 2,000 Guineas winners (Nearchus in 1938 and Khosro in 1941), one Irish 1,000 Guineas winner with Star of Egypt in 1930, one Irish Oaks winner with Admirable in 1945, and one Irish St Leger winner in 1931 with Beaudelaire. His brother Freddie was a prominent owner and breeder (owning the winner of the 1950 Irish Derby, Dark Warrior), and an older brother Rory owned the winner of the 1961 Irish Oaks winner Ambergris, the 1960 Irish 2,000 Guineas, and the 1971 Irish St Leger Parnell.

MORGAN, BILLY.

G.A.A. football goalkeeper, Cork. Club: Nemo Rangers (captaining the club to their first win in the All-Ireland Club Championship triumph in 1973, and winning another medal in 1979). Playing as a forward as a minor, and having been on the Cork side beaten in the final of the All-Ireland Under 21 Championship in 1965, he later captained Cork to their 1973 All-Ireland Senior Football Championship title, beating Galway by 3-17 to 2-13. He had played on the Cork side which lost the 1967 All-Ireland S.F.C. final to Meath, and also won 3 other Munster S.F.C. medals, in 1966, 1971 and 1974. In 1975 he became only the third Cork footballer to captain a winning Munster Railway Cup side, also winning medals in 1972, 1977 and 1978. He won a solitary All-Star award in 1973 in goals (that year he was the only nominee for that position), and in the same year became the first Cork footballer to be named as Texaco Footballer of the Year. He coached and later managed the Cork S.F.C. team in the 1980's, assisting them to win National Football League titles in 1980 and 1989, and to an All-Ireland S.F.C. wins in 1989 and 1990.

MORGAN, D.J. (DANNY).

National Hunt jockey and trainer. Born in 1912. As a jockey he won two Cheltenham Champion Hurdles (in 1934 on Chenango and in 1947 on National Spirit), and also rode Morse Code to win the 1938 Cheltenham Gold Cup. He rode winners for King Edward VIII and King George VI, and also won 3 Scotish Grand Nationals (1931, 1935, and 1938), the Welsh Grand National of 1936, and 3 Champion Chases at Cheltenham (in 1933, 1936 and 1938). As a trainer he sent out Roddy Owen to win the Cheltenham Gold Cup in 1959. A nephew of Frank Morgan (cv).

MORGAN, FRANK.

Flat jockey and National Hunt trainer. Born in Co Waterford in 1867, he died, aged 103, in 1970. He rode the winner of the 1904 Irish Derby, Royal Arch. As a National Hunt trainer, his best horse was Ballinode, who won the Grand Sefton in 1924 and the Cheltenham Gold Cup in 1925. His sons Dick, Frank, Tommy and Joe followed him into the racing game, and he is the uncle of Danny Morgan (cv).

MORGAN, GEORGE J.

Rugby international scrum-half, and cricketer. Clubs: Clontarf (being a member of the only Clontarf side to capture the Leinster Senior Cup, in 1936) and Old Belvedere. Thirteen times a Leinster player from 1932 to 1937, he was capped 19 times consecutively for Ireland between 1934 and 1939, captaining the side on 8 occasions (1936-1938), and scoring 2 international tries. A lanky but quality player, with a good dummy, he went on the British and Irish Lion's tour to South Africa in 1938, gaining one Test place, in the final, and only winning, test in Cape Town. He also represented Ireland at cricket.

MORGAN, SAMMY J.

Soccer international forward. Born in Belfast, 3rd December 1946. Clubs: Gorleston, Port Vale (playing 109 league matches for them 1969-72, scoring 24 goals), Aston Villa (1973-75), Brighton (1975-76), Cambridge, Sparta Amsterdam. He was capped 18 times for Northern Ireland between 1972 and 1979, scoring 3 international goals. The 7 caps he gained while playing at Vale Park make him Park Vale's most capped player.

MORIARTY, PADDY.

G.A.A. football centre-half back, and left full-forward, Armagh. Club: Derrymacash Wolfe Tones. A member of the Armagh sides which won the Ulster Senior Football Championship 3 times in 6 years, in 1977 (when the side reached the All-Ireland final only to be beaten by a rampant Dublin), 1980 (as captain), and 1982. Debuting at inter-county football in 1970, he won 4 Railway Cup medals, one with the Combined Universities in 1973, and 3 with Ulster, in 1979, 1980, and 1983, all at centre half back. He is one of only 5 footballers to win All-Star awards as a back and in the forward line, winning at centre half-back in 1977, having previously been honoured as the county's initial All-Star in 1972, at left-corner forward (the youngest nominee that year).

MORIARTY, TOM.

G.A.A. footballer, Kerry and Cork. From Castlegregory, Co Kerry. Club: Clonakilty (whom he captained to win the 1952 Cork SFC title). As a minor, in 1946, he won an All-Ireland M.F.C. medal as captain with his native Kerry. He went on, while representing Cork, to win a Junior All-Ireland medal in 1951, also winning both a National Football League medal and a Munster S.F.C. medal with Cork. He later again declared for Kerry, and went on to win an All-Ireland Senior Championship medal at left half back with Kerry in 1955, having also played in the previous year's All-Ireland S.F.C. losing side (against Meath, who had in their side, by coincidence, a Kerry-born full-forward of the same name, Tom Moriarty). He went on to win a further Munster S.F.C. medal with Kerry in 1958.

MORLEY, JOHN.

G.A.A. footballer, centre-half back, Mayo. Born in Faughiff, Knock, Co Mayo,

October 1942. Club: Civil Service. He won All-Ireland College's senior medals with St Jarlath's of Tuam in both 1960 and 1961. He played Mayo minors in 1960, was promoted to a senior player in 1961, and played in a then record 112 senior games for the county up to 1974. In 1967 he captained Mayo to their first Connacht Senior Football Championship victory in 12 years, and also played in the 1969 winning side. He helped Connacht to 2 Railway Cup successes, in 1967 and 1969. He was on the Mayo side that won the 1970 National Football League, the county's last senior title. A Garda, he was killed in the line of duty on 7th July 1980.

MORLEY, PAT ('SKIPPY').

Soccer forward. Born in Cork, 18th May 1965. Clubs: Finn Harps, Glasgow Celtic, Limerick, Waterford, Sunshine George Cross (Australia). Cork City (being a member of the side which lost the F.A.I. Cup final in 1992, and which won the League of Ireland Premier Division in 1993). Debuting in 1984, he has scored over 90 League of Ireland goals up to 1993, all set to join the select group of those who achieved the 'ton-up', and his 20 goals in the 1993 season made him the leading goal-scorer in the Premier Division. He was voted P.F.A.I. 'Player of the Year' in 1991, and was selected on the League Stars team the same year. In 1993 he was named S.W.A.I. Personality of the Year, being also short-listed for the P.F.A.I. award that year. His father, Jack Morley, played for West Ham 1958-61, and later won 4 League of Ireland medals with Waterford, also appearing in 4 losing F.A.I. Cup finals.

MORONEY, Thomas ALOYSIUS (AL).

Rugby international prop forward. Born in Kilmihil, Co Clare, 27th July 1941. Club: U.C.D. (winning Leinster Senior Cup winner's medals in 1963 and 1964), London Irish, Surrey. He played in 17 Senior Interprovincial series matches for Leinster between 1963 and 1969, and 8 other matches for his province. He was capped for Ireland 3 times, against Wales in 1964, and against both Australia and England in 1967. He was also a member of the famous Combined Universities XV which, at Thomond Park in 1965, became the first Irish team to beat the mighty South Africans.

MORONEY, JOHNNY Christopher M.

Rugby international wing three-quarter. Club: Garryowen. Born in Clogheen, Co Tipperary, 28th October, 1945. He won 6 international caps on the wing for Ireland in the years 1968 and 1969 (5 of these matches were won), although he was a club out-half. Against France in 1969 he set a then Irish record for one match which was to last for 10 years, when he scored 14 points, from a try, a conversion and 3 penalties. He won 3 Munster Senior Cup medals with Garryowen, in 1969, 1971, and 1974, and in 1967 he scored a try in Munster's defeat of the Australians, thus becoming the first Irish provincial side to defeat an international touring side.

MORONEY, MICHAEL.

G.A.A. hurling centre-field, Clare. He was a star player on the Clare side which won successive National Hurling League titles, in 1976-77 and 1977-78. He was also a member of Clare sides which contested (but lost) Munster Senior Hurling Championship finals in the 1970's. He won an All-Star award in 1977 in the midfield along with Tom Cashman of Cork.

MORONEY, TOMMY.

Soccer international wing-half. Born in Cork, 10th November 1923, he died in 1981. Clubs Cork United (winning two League of Ireland Championship medals with them in 1944-45 and 1945-46, and an F.A.I. Cup medal in 1947, scoring one of goals in the replayed final) and West Ham. At the age of 23, he left Cork to play for West Ham, and in 5 seasons with them, scored 8 goals in 148 league appearances in 1947-52. An Inter-League representative for the

League of Ireland, he was capped 12 times for the Republic of Ireland between 1946 and 1954. He was also a rugby player of some substance, and may have played international level for Ireland but for his soccer exploits. He played out-half for Munster from 1943, was a magnificent kicker of the ball, and won Munster Senior Cup medals with Cork Constitution in 1943 and 1946. He was also a 'bowles' player of some skill.

MORRIS, CHRIS.

Soccer international right back. Born in Newquay, Christmas Eve 1963. He played Under 19 rugby for Cornwall and the South West, and played cricket for Cornish schools. As a right winger with South West soccer team, he played 4 times for English Schools. Clubs: Sheffield Wednsdsay (5 seasons, some at outside-right), Glasgow Celtic (winning a Scottish Premier Championship and 2 Scottish Cup medals while at Parkhead), Middlesborough. First capped for Ireland in November 1987, he was in the Irish side which performed heroics in the 1988 European Championships in Germany, and in the squad that qualified for, and participated in, the World Cup finals in 1990. His international cap tally up to mid 1993 came to 35.

MORRIS, MICHAEL F ('MOUSE').

National Hunt jockey and trainer. Born 4th April 1951, son of Lord Killanin. As a jockey he won the 1977 Irish Grand National on Billycan, the 1974 National Hunt Chase in Cheltenham with Mr Midland, the Queen Mother Two-Mile Champion Chase on Skymass in 1976 and 1977, and 2 Power Gold Cups (1975 on Golden Lancer and in 1977 on Bunker Hill). Training at Everardsgrange, Fethard, Co Tipperary, he has had 4 Cheltenham winners to add to his 3 wins their as a jockey, the Waterford Supreme Novice Hurdle in 1983 and the Queen Mother Two-Mile Champion Chase of 1986, both with Buck House, Attitude Adjuster in the 1986 Christied Foxhunter, and the Waterford Crystal Stayer's Hurdle in 1990 with Trapper John. He also trained the 2nd placed horse, Cahervillahow, in the 'Grand National that never was' at Aintree in 1993.

MORRIS, MICK F.

G.A.A. footballing centre-half back, Kerry, and amateur international golfer. In football, as a member of the John Mitchell's club, he won an All-Ireland Under 21 Championship medal with Kerry at right full-back in the competition's inaugural year of 1964, and played 3 times on losing All-Ireland S.F.C. final Kerry sides (in 1964, 1965 and 1968) before finally winning an All-Ireland Senior Football Championship winner's medal in 1969 when Kerry beat Offaly 0-10 to 0-07 in the final. As an amateur golfer, and a member of Portmarnock (winning a Senior Cup medal in 1988), he won the Irish Close Championship in 1978 in Carlow (also winning the Willie Gill award that year), and was runner-up in the 'South' in both 1977 and 1980. He played 63 interprovincial matches for Munster 1972-83, winning 32; he played in 5 Home international series for Ireland, 1978, 1980 (when he also helped Ireland to win the Quadrangular Continental match), 1982, in the winning side of 1983, and finally in 1984, winning 16 of his 32 matches played; he played 7 European Team championship matches for Ireland between 1979 and when Ireland won the title in 1983, winning 5 and halving one.

MORRIS, KENNY.

Hockey international forward and right-half. Clubs: Y.M.C.A. (Belfast), and Hollywood 87. He has won over 66 caps since 1983 (when he played in the European Championship squad), and has played in over 35 indoor international matches for Ireland. He won over 40 caps for Great Britain from 1987 to 1988. His brother Ivan (clubs: Belfast Y.M.C.A., and Lisnagarvey, winning 6 successive Irish Senior Cup medals in 1988, 1989, 1990, 1991 as captain, 1992 and 1993), won 39 international caps for Ireland from 1983, and has won at least 35 indoor caps also.

MORRISSEY, EAMONN.

G.A.A. hurling right full-forward, Kilkenny. Club: St Martin's and Muckalee. Born in Radestown, St John's, near Kilkenny in 1966. Playing on a St Kierans College side beaten in the 1984 All-Ireland Colleges final, he won an All-Ireland Club Championship medal with St Martin's in 1985. He was a member of the Kilkenny side beaten in the All-Ireland Under 21 Championship final in 1985. Making his senior inter-county debut in 1989, he was on the Kilkenny side beaten in the All-Ireland Senior Hurling Championship final in 1991, and on the side which won the newly-commisioned Liam McCarthy Cup in 1992, winning his 2nd Liam McCarthy Cup medal in 1993. In 1990 he was the only member of the Kilkenny side which captured the 1989-90 National Hurling League to win an All-Star award, being selected in the right corner-forward position (and he was the county's highest scorer in that League campaign, with 7 goals and 19 points).

MORRISSEY, JOHN.

Bareknuckle boxer. Born in Templemore Co Tipperary, 1831. He died in Saratoga, Florida, on 1st May 1878. He was American heavyweight bareknuckle champion in 1858. In 1954 he one of the founder members of The Ring magazine's Hall of Fame.

MORRISSEY, MICK.

G.A.A. hurling left half-back, Wexford. Born in Co Carlow. Club: Ballygrinnegan. In the 1955 All-Ireland Senior Hurling Championship final, he became the first Carlow-man to win an All-Ireland winner's medal, when playing for Wexford. He won a 2nd Liam McCarthy Cup medal the following year, and played in another final (as a sub) in 1960, when he collected another medal, to bring his tally of All-Ireland S.H.C. medals to three. Emigrating to New York, he later served for many years in the service of the G.A.A. in the U.S.A., and died in 1993.

MORRIS, SEAMUS.

G.A.A. football goalkeeper, Cavan. Club: Cornafean. He was on the Cavan side which were beaten by Meath in the 1949 All-Ireland Senior Football Championship final, but was on the victorious Cavan side which eked revenge on the same opposition in the 1952 All-Ireland S.F.C. final replay. He was captain of the losing Ulster side in the final of the 1956 Railway Cup.

MORROW, ADRIAN C J

Amateur international golfer. Clubs: Hermitage and Portmarnock (winning a Senior Cup medal in 1993). Having won the 'East' in 1975, he went on to win the Willie Gill award in 1983, during which he won the South of Ireland Championship at Lahinch and the East of Ireland for a 2nd time at Baltray. A runner-up in the 'West' in 1992, he played 29 matches for Leinster in the interprovincial series from 1982 to 1989, gaining 27 points from 13 wins and one half. He played in 10 home international matches for Ireland, in 1975 and 1983 (winning only 2), before becoming a member of the winning side in 1992.

MORROW, STEVE.

Soccer international defender/ midfielder. Born in Belfast 2nd May 1970. Clubs: Arsenal (joining as a trainee, playing no matches), Reading (on loan), Arsenal (again). In the 1993 League Cup final he scored the winning goal for Arsenal, but broke his shoulder in the immediate after-match celebrations. He was first capped for Northern Ireland in 1990, he had gained 10 international soccer caps up to mid 1993.

MORTELL, MAURICE P.

Rugby international wing three-quarter. Born in Bandon, Co Cork, 13th March 1930. Clubs: Bective Rangers (winning Leinster Senior Cup medals in 1955 and 1956) and Dolphin. Twelve times a Leinster interprovincial player between 1951 and 1955, he won 9 senior international caps for Ireland between 1953 and 1954, and scored 5 international tries, including one each in his first 3 internationals in 1953, against France, England, and Scotland respectively.

MOULSON, GEORGE B.

Soccer international player. Born in Clogheen, 6th August 1914. His clubs included Grimsby and Lincoln City. Although he was capped only 3 times for the Republic of Ireland, in 1948 and 1949, at the age of 34 and 35, he won all of his caps while at Lincoln City, making him that club's most capped player. A relation, C Moulson (Lincoln City and Notts County), was capped 5 times for Ireland in 1936 and 1937.

MOYLAN, CHRISTY.

G.A.A. hurling centrefield, Waterford. Born in 1916. Club: Dungarvan (winning one county championship medal). A member of the Waterford senior inter-county team for 15 years from 1935 to 1949, he appeared in 2 All-Ireland Senior Hurling Championship finals, in 1935 when losing, and in the famous victorious side of 1948, scoring 1-2 in the final. He won 5 Railway Cup medals with Munster in 1937, 1938, 1939, 1940 and 1942 (he was also picked, but did not play Railway Cup football for Munster).

MOYLAN, JOHN (JACK).

Flat and jump jockey. Born in Churchtown, Co Cork, he finished 2nd in the 1924 Aintree Grand National on Fly Mask. He was leading jockey in Ireland in 1926. He won 7 Irish Classic races: a dead heat for the Irish 2,000 Guineas of 1944 with Slide On; winning the Irish 1,000 Guineas in 1926 on Resplendent; 2 successive Irish Derby's (Slide On in 1944 and Piccadilly in 1945); one Irish Oaks in 1944 on Avoca; and 2 Irish St Leger's (on Skoiter in 1939 and on Cassock in 1946). A grand-father of Pat Eddery (cv), he died in 1949. .

MOYLAN, PAT.

G.A.A.. hurling midfielder, Cork. Club: Blackrock (with whom he won 3 All-Ireland Club Championship medals, in 1972, 1974, and 1979). He won 3 successive All-Ireland Under 21 winner's medals with Cork in 1968, 1969 and 1970, having previously won an All-Ireland M.H.C. medal in 1967, and being on the side beaten in the All-Ireland final of 1966. He later also won 3 successive All-Ireland Senior Hurling Championship medals, in 1976 (when he was a brilliant man-of-the-match), 1977 (coming on as a sub in the final), and 1978, all in the midfield. He won one All-Star award, in 1976, alongside his fellow Corkman, Mick Malone.

MOYLETT, MICK.

Rugby internaional 2nd-row forward. Clubs: Ballina, Shannon (winning 6 Munster Senior Cup medals, in 1982, 1986, 1987, 1988, 1991 and 1992). Capped at both Irish scools level (in 1977 and 1978) and at Ireland 'B' level, in 1982 and 1983, he played for Ireland at full interantional level only once, against England in 1988. His father Brian played interprovincial golf for Connacht in 1956, while a member of Ballina GC.

MUCKIAN, CATHAL.

Soccer interantional forward. Club: Drogheda United (being on the side which lost the F.A.I. Cup final in the club's most recent appearance in 1976, and for whom he scored a club record 21 goals in the 1977-78 League of Ireland season), Dundalk (winning an F.A.I. Cup medal in 1979). He was capped once for the Republic of Ireland, in 1978 against Poland.

MULCAHY, TOMAS.

G.A.A. hurling centre half-forward and right full-forward, Cork. Club: Glen Rovers. He came on as a substitute in the All-Ireland Under 21 Championship title win by Cork in 1982. Playing at right corner-forward in Cork's All-Ireland Senior Hurling Championship win of 1984, he was at right half-forward when winning his 2nd Liam McCarthy medal in 1986 (being on the losing Cork team in the 1983 All-Ireland final). He went on to captain Cork in their win over Galway in the 1990 All-Ireland Senior Hurling Championship final (by a margin of 5-12 to 2-21), and was again on the runner-up side in the 1992 championship. He won a Railway Cup medal in 1984 with Munster at right full-forward, and a National Hurling League medal with Cork in 1992-93. He has won two All-Star awards, in 1986 at right corner-forward, and in 1987 at centre half-forward.

MULCAHY, DENIS.

G.A.A. hurling right full-back, Cork. Born in 1956. Club: Midleton (with whom he has won county championship medals, and an All-Ireland Club Championship medal in 1988, the club's first). Making his senior inter-county debut in 1979, he has won 2 All-Ireland Senior Hurling Championship medals with Cork, in 1984 and 1986, both at right corner back. Called back from retirement in 1991, he was at full-back on the Cork side beaten in the All-Ireland S.H.C. final in 1992. He has also won 2 National Hurling League medals (in 1981 and 1991) and one Railway Cup medal. He has won one All-Star award, at right corner-back in the 1986 selection. Also an able footballer, he won a county championship medal in 1984 and an All-Ireland J.F.C. medal in the same year.

MULCAHY, Dr WILLIAM Albert (BILL, or 'WIGS').

Rugby international 2nd row forward. Born in Rathkeale, Co Limerick, 7th January 1935. Clubs: U.C.D., Bective Rangers (winning Leinster Senior Cup medals in 1955 and 1956), and Bohemians (winning a Munster Senior Cup medal in 1962). A product of St Munchin's College in Limerick, he was capped 35 times for Ireland (23 of these matches were lost) between 1958 and 1965, captaining the national side 8 times between 1962 and 1964. One of Ireland's finest 2nd row forwards, he was honoured by selection on two British and Irish Lion's tours, to Australia and New Zealand in 1959 (winning 2 Test caps), and to South Africa in 1962 (gaining 4 Test places as first-choice 2nd row) when playing in 17 matches, captaining the side on a few occasions. He also toured South Africa with Ireland in 1961. Between the 14 year period 1955 and 1968 he played for Leinster in the Senior Interprovincial series on a then record of 35 occasions (19 of these being victories), playing for Leinster sides on 9 other occasions also. His son Sean (a Skerries hooker) made the Ireland 'B' panel in rugby, while another son Billy won an Ireland 'A' cap in 1993. A doctor, Bill Mulcahy is the uncle of John O'Leary (cv), the professional golfer.

MULCARE, PAT.

Amateur international golfer. Born in Ballybunion, Co Kerry in 1945. Clubs: Woodbrook (winning a Barton Shield medal in 1974), Royal Dublin, Ballybunion and Tralee. He won the East of Ireland title at Baltray 3 years in succession, 1971 (setting a then record low winning aggregate of 281), 1972, and 1973, and he won the South of Ireland in 1971 (being runner-up in 1976). He was honoured by Walker Cup selection in 1975, winning 2 of his 3 matches played (including one against the fine American Dick Siderowf). He played in 72 interprovincial matches for Munster 1967-80 (placing him at joint 2nd in most caps for Munster since 1956), winning 38, and being on sides which won 3 times; he played in 44 Home international matches for Ireland in 10 different series (1968, 1969, 1970, 1971, 1972 when he also helped Ireland to win the Quadrangular Continental match, 1974, 1975, 1978 1979 and 1980, when he again was in a winning Quadrangular team), winning 11; he played 10 European Team matches for

Ireland 1975-79, winning 3. He played for the Britain and Ireland team against Europe in 1972, and in 1978 played for the Continent of Europe against South America. He reached plus one handicap.

MULDOON, JIM.

International oarsman. Club: Garda Siochana Boat Club. He was the first Irish oarsman to win 7 Irish Senior Eights Championships (his wins included 6 with Garda, coming in 1968, 1974, 1975, 1977, 1982 and 1983, as well as 1970 with Neptune). He won once at Henley, in the Thames Cup of 1975. He was a member of the Irish coxed fours which won the 'little final' (therefore finishing 7th) in three major events in 3 successive years, the World Championship of 1975, the Olympic Games Regatta at Montreal in 1976, and the World Championshoips again in 1976. He later coached the successful Irish coxless pair which finished 5th in the World Championship in 1978, and the coxed pair who were fancied to do well in the Moscow Olympic Regatta in 1980, only to be eliminated through illness.

MULLAN, BERNARD ('BARNEY').

Rugby international wing-threequarter. Club: Clontarf. A deft place-kicker, he was capped 8 times for Ireland in 1947 and 1948. He was an ever-present member of the great Irish Grand Slam side of 1948, scoring a great try in the deciding Triple Crown match at Ravenhill against Wales (and being the only player of that side, and the 2nd of only 5 in total, to score in all 3 games of an Irish Triple crown win). In 1948 he set an individual Irish record for an Irish player up to that time, by scoring 13 points against France. His total tally of points for Ireland was 36, from 6 tries, 6 conversions, and 2 penalties. Nine times a Leinster interprovincial player, he became a member of the Barbarians committee, and also represented Ireland at clay pigeon shooting.

MULLEN, Dr KARL Daniel.

Rugby international hooker. Born in Courtown Harbour Harbour, Co Wexford, 26th November, 1926. Club: Old Belvedere (winning Leinster Senior Cup medals in 1945, 1946, 1951 and 1952). Having played in all 4 unofficial internationals in 1946 (all were lost), he went on to be capped 25 times for Ireland between 1947 and 1952, gaining the reputation of the best hooker in world rugby in his era. A brilliant tactical captain, he led Ireland through the golden era of Irish rugby, when they won their one and only Grand Slam in 1948, the Triple Crown in the following year of 1949, and later the International Championship again in 1951, stewarding his country to 10 wins in his 16 stewartships in all. His leadership qualities meant that he was selected as automatic choice for captaincy of the British and Irish Lion's tour of Australia and New Zealand in 1950, bringing 8 other Irishmen (Ireland's highest ever representation on tour) with him, and playing himself in 3 Tests. The tour results were: played 29 games, won 22, lost 6, one drawn: 570 points for and 212 against. He played interprovincial rugby for Leinster 16 times between 1945 and 1951. He was an Irish selector from 1961 to 1964. In 1985 he became the 2nd rugby player to be elevated into the Texaco Hall of fame, and in 1991 he joined the R.W.I./Digital Hall of Fame. A consultant gynaecologist.

MULLEN, TERRY.

Special bowls player. Born in 1937. A cancer sufferer, she took up bowls as a novice in 1985, becoming the following year the first person from the Republic of Ireland to win the All-Ireland title, and went on to win bronze medals in both singles and doubles at the Stoke-Mandeville Games. In 1987, despite falling victim again to her life-threatening illness, she went on to retain her All-Ireland bowls title. To complete her treble of such victories in

1988 involved her leaving St Lukes Hospital to compete. Advised by doctors not to attend the Special Olympics in Seoul later in 1988 as her cancer was now terminal, she nonetheless not only competed, but went on the win the gold medal in her bowls event (beating the Kenyan title-holder in the final). One of the country's bravest ever sportspersons, she died soon after competing in Seoul.

MULLIGAN, ANDREW Armstrong (ANDY).
Rugby international scrum-half. Born in Kasauli, India, 4th February 1936. Clubs: Cambridge University, London Irish, Paris University, and Wanderers. A product of Gresham's School, he won 3 successive Blues for Cambridge, in 1955, 1956 and 1957. He was the last of Jack Kyle's 8 different half-back partners in Irish XV's, and was capped 22 times for Ireland between 1956 and 1961. He was selected on the British and Irish Lion's tour of Australia and New Zealand of 1959, playing in the only test match won by those Lions. A professional journalist, his career was responsible for the liberalisation of the strict no-writing-for-reward rule applied by the I.R.F.U.. He was later an E.C. rrepresentative.

MULLIGAN, DES.
G.A.A. football centre half-forward, Monaghan. Club: Castleblaney Faughs (with whom he has won 6 county champinship medals). A Clones man, he won 2 Dr McKenna Cup medals with Monaghan in 1978 and 1979. He was a member of the Monaghan side which won the 1979 Ulster S.H.C. title, the county's first such title in 41 years. He was also the first Monaghan player to win a B+I Player of the Month award.

MULLIGAN, EUGENE.
G.A.A. football right half-back, Offaly. He was at right half-back on the Offaly minors side which won the All-Ireland M.F.C. in 1964. Having played on the Offaly side which were beaten in the 1969 All-Ireland Senior Football Championship final, he went on to share with his fellow countymen in the winning of Offaly's first 2 Sam Maguire Cups, in both 1971 and in 1972 (in a replay). He won another Leinster S.F.C. medal in 1973, and won a Railway Cup medal with Leinster in 1974. In 1971, he became the first of a select few players to be the only nomination for his position for an All-Star award, when he was unanimously selected at right half-back.

MULLIGAN, PADDY M.
Soccer international defender. Born in Dublin, St Patrick's Day 1945. Clubs: Shamrock Rovers (winning F.A.I. Cup winner's medals in 1965, 1966, 1967 and 1969), Chelsea (1969-72), Crystal Palace (1972-74, during which the club were relegated to Division 2), West Bromwich Albion (1975-77, playing 109 league matches for them, helping them to promotion to Division 1 in 1976), and again with Shamrock Rovers. A stalwart defender and a popular sportsman, he was capped at senior international level 51 times for the Republic of Ireland between 1969 and 1980, thereby playing in 3 different decades for his country. The 14 caps he gained while at Crystal Palace made him the joint most capped player from Selhurst Park.

MULLIN, BRENDAN John.
Rugby international centre-threequarter, and athlete. Clubs: Dublin University, Blackrock (winning Leinster Senior Cup and League medals) and Oxford University (winning Blues in 1986 and 1987). He was born in Israel on 31st October 1963. A product of Blackrock College, he in the holder of a record 6 Irish School's caps (in 1981 and 1982), captaining the side 3 times, and he won his first full cap against Australia in 1983. He scored a vital try in Ireland's fine Triple Crown-winning match against England in 1985, and played in all matches that year. In 1989 he was selected for the Lions tour of Australia, winning one Test place, and he was the leading try scorer on the tour, with 6

scored. In a 10 year stint in the Irish side he won 45 caps between 1983 and 1992 (a record number of caps for an Irish centre), and scored a record 15 international tries for his country, breaking a record held for over 60 years. The 23 caps he gained in the centre alongside Michael Kiernan (cv) was then a world record centre partnership. With Ireland he toured Japan in 1985, Namibia in 1991, and played in both of Ireland's first 2 World Cup appearances in 1987 and 1991. He was voted Irish Rugby writers player of the year in 1989. A talented player, he also broke the 30-year-old Irish 110 metres hurdles record in 1986, and represented Ireland in international athletic events. A stockbroker.

MULLINS, BRIAN.

G.A.A. football midfielder, Dublin. Born on 27th September 1954. Club: St Vincent's (with whom he won an All-Ireland Club Championship medal in 1976, and 3 Dublin SFC medals, captaining the winning side in 1977). A product of Colaiste Mhuire, he was a member of the Dublin side beaten in the All-Ireland Under 21 Championsip final of 1975 by Kerry. He was a towering force in Dublin's 3 All-Ireland Senior Football Championship wins in the mid 70's, in 1974, 1976, and 1977. A car accident in the summer of 1980 interrupted his career, but he regained fitness enough to win another All-Ireland S.F.C. medal with Dublin in 1983 (although he was one of 3 Dubs sent off in that game), and he played also in 5 All-Ireland S.F.C. losing final sides (all to arch-rivals Kerry), in 1975, 1978, 1979, 1984 and in 1985 (when he captained the Dublin side). Along with this tally of playing in nine All-Ireland S.F.C. finals, he also shared in Dublin's triumphs in the National Football League of 1976 and 1978. In 1985 he became the 3rd Dublinman to captain a winning Railway Cup Leinster football winning side. One of the game's great midfielders, he actually won only 2 All-Star awards, in 1976 and 1977, both in midfield. A fine rugby player in his youth, he played with distinction with Blackrock College, and again later with Clontarf R.F.C..

MULLINS, GERRY.

International Showjumper. Born in Croom Co Limerick in 1953. He has won more international show jumping events than any other Irish rider in history, on board such fine horses as Mostrim, Glendalough and Rockbarton (on whom he finished 4th in the World Championships in Dublin in 1982). Helping Irish teams to win Aga Khan Cups in Dublin, he has also represented Ireland at Olympic Games, in Los Angeles in 1984 and in Seoul in 1988.

MULLINS, PADDY.

Horse trainer, National Hunt and flat. Born 28th January 1919, at Graignamanagh, Co Kilkenny. Based at Goresbridge since 1953 (early successful horses being Height O'Fashion and Bobby Hall-Dare), he has trained 4 Irish Grand National winners' (Vulpine in 1967, Herring Gull in 1968, Dim Wit in 1972, and Luska in 1981), but it is for the mare, Dawn Run he is best known. She won the Liverpool, French and Irish Champion Hurdles, and Paddy became the first trainer to in history have a horse to win both the Champion Hurdle (1984) and the Gold Cup (1986), which that mare achieved at the Cheltenham Festival meeting. Other races Paddy won include, the Champion Stakes 1973 (on the flat when the 33/1 outsider Hurry Harriet beat the brilliant filly Allez France), the Jameson Gold Cup, 3 Galway Hurdles, and 2 Irish Cambridgeshires. In 1990 his Grabel (winner of over 22 races) won the inaugural running of the world's richest hurdle race, the Dueling Grounds International in Kentucky. A trainer of 6 Cheltenham Festival winners, he has won the Irish leading jump trainer title 9 times, in 1982, then 7 years in succession, 1984 (78 winners), 1985 (71 winners), 1986 (48 winners), 1987 (55 winners), 1988 (62 winners), 1989 (58 winners), 1990 (55 winners), and in 1991. He is the father of Tony Mullins, the leading Irish jump jockey in 1989 (and joint champion in 1984) and also a trainer; and Willie Mullins, who has won the Amateur riders title in 1985, 1988, and 1989 (and who has turned in recent times successfully to training). His other sons, Tom (his assistant trainer) and George are involved in the stable. Paddy won the Texaco Sportstar of the Year award for Horse Racing in 1984.

MUNN, LIONEL O.

Amateur international golfer. Born in 1887. Clubs: Dublin University and North West (being a member of the first ever club to capture the Barton Shield in 1911). He won the Irish Close Championship 4 times, in 1908 (during which he won a match at the 10th tie hole, a then record longest 18-hole-match), 1911, 1913 and 1914, and was runner up in 1910. He won the Irish Amateur Open 3 times in succession, 1909, 1910 and 1911 (becoming the first of only 5 golfers to hold both the Close and Amateur Open in the same year). He was Belgian Amateur Open champion in 2 successive years, 1931 and 1932. He won the 'South' in 1911, bringing his total of Irish championship wins to 8, placing him joint 5th overall in this tally. He represented Ireland in 3 international matches against Wales between 1913 and 1924, and later played in 2 Home International series for Ireland, in 1936 and 1937, winning 4 of this 12 matches. He lost in the semi-final stage of the British Amateur twice, 24 years apart, in 1908 at the 10th tie hole, and in 1932, when he lost at the 26th hole. In 1937, aged 54, at Sandwich, he eventually reached the final, only to lose to Bob Sweeney. Only the failure to get time off work deprived him of taking up a Walker Cup place in 1938. His brother Ector M Munn, also a member of the winning Barton Shield side of North West in 1911, won the Irish Close Championship in 1922, and played in 4 international matches for Ireland between 1913 and 1927, three of these with Lionel.

MUNNELLY, JOSIE.

G.A.A. football right corner-forward, Mayo. From Crossmolina. Club: Castlebar Mitchels (winning a club record 13 Mayo county championships, one in hurling, and 12 in football, in 1941, 1942, 1944, 1945, 1946, 1948, 1950, 1951, 1952, 1953, 1954, and 1956, being captain for 6 of these wins). He won an All-Ireland Senior Football Championship medal with the winning Mayo side of 1936. Then, in 1957, after a remarkable lapse of 21 years he won an All-Ireland J.F.C. medal with Mayo, a unique span of achievement. Winning Railway Cup medals with Connacht in 1937 and 1938, he also won 7 National Football League medals with Mayo, in the 6-in-a-row of 1934, 1935, 1936, 1937, 1938 and 1939, and again in 1941.

MURPHY, P ALOYSIUS ('WEESHIE').

G.A.A. football full-back, Cork. From Bere Island. He won 4 Munster Senior Football Championship medals with Cork in 1943, 1945, 1949 and 1952. By playing on the Cork side which won the Sam Maguire Cup in 1945 he became the first player from Bere Island to win an All-Ireland medal. He also played football for his province Munster for 9 years, and won 3 Railway Cup medals with them, in 1946, 1948 and 1949.

MURPHY, BARNES.

G.A.A. football centre half-back, Sligo. Clubs: Castlecomer, Enniscrone, Craobh Rua and St Mary's (winning 4 county championships and one Connacht club title). He is a product of St Nathy's in Ballaghadereen. A member of the Sligo SFC side from 1967 to 1979, he was captain of the side which won the county's first Connacht Senior Football Championship in 47 years in 1975, having been also a member of the side which was beaten in the provincial final of 1971. A Connacht player in the Railway Cup from 1973 to 1978, he was both team manager and player of the side which won the series in 1975. He was selected at centre half-back on the 1974 All-Star, making him the 2nd of only two Sligo players to win All-Star awards.

MURPHY, BRIAN.

G.A.A. dual hurling left full-back and football right full-back, Cork. Club: Nemo Rangers (with whom he won a record 4 All-Ireland Club football Championship medals, in 1973, 1979 as captain, 1982, and 1984). A member of the Cork Under 21 hurling side which won the All-Ireland title in 1973, he had earlier won an All-Ireland M.H.C. medal in 1970. In football he won an All-Ireland M.F.C. medal in 1969, and an All-Ireland Under 21 medal in 1971. So, by winning a Sam Maguire medal in Cork's fine All-Ireland S.F.C. win of 1973, followed on by a Liam McCarthy Cup medal in 1976, he became the first player to win All-Ireland medals at all levels (except junior) in both codes. He went on to win 2 other All-Ireland Senior Hurling Championship medals, in 1977 and 1978, and was on beaten teams in the S.H.C. All-Ireland finals of 1972, 1982, and 1983. In 1981 he won a hurling Railway Cup medal at full back, to add to his 3 football Railway Cup medals which he won in 1976, 1977 and 1978, all in the full-back line. He has won 4 All-Star awards, being the first player to win 2 at each code. He was honoured in football in 1973 and 1976, both in the left corner-back position, and his hurling awards came in 1979 and 1981, both in the right corner-back position. One of the great dual players.

MURPHY, CORNELIUS Joseph (CON).

Rugby international full-back. Born in Dublin, 19th September, 1914. Club: Lansdowne. A product of C.U.S. Leeson Street, he won only 5 international caps for Ireland, but these were pre and post World War 2, the only player to span those years. In 1939 this small but skilful full-back won three international caps, and won a further two, as captain, in 1947 (the 22-0 win over England is still a record winning margin for Ireland), true evidence that he would have won many more caps if not for the war. He played in all four of Ireland's unofficial internationals in 1946, as well as 4 times against the British Army in 1943-1945. He also played for Leinster before and after World War Two, representing his province 6 times in all between 1937 and 1946. Also a fine soccer player, he played for Bohemians, and was capped on the Irish Junior team. In 1992 he was a Digital R.W.I. Hall of Fame award recipient.

MURPHY, CON.

G.A.A. hurling full-back and half-back, Cork. Born near Innishannin, Co Cork in 1922. Club: Valley Rovers. A senior inter-county player from 1941 to 1951, he won 4 All-Ireland Senior Hurling Championship medals with Cork, in 1942, 1943, 1944, and 1946, and also played in the side in the 1947 final loss. A fine defender, he also won 2 Railway Cup medals with Munster, in 1948 and 1949. He was later Cork County Board Secretary 1956 to 1973, being strongly associated with the Parc Ui Caoimh project. Having refereed the All-Ireland S.H.C. finals of 1948 and 1950, he became the 26th President of the G.A.A. 1976-78, being the first relative of a former holder of that office, as he was a nephew of Sean McCarthy, President of the G.A.A. in 1932-35.

MURPHY, CON.

G.A.A. footballer, Kerry. He won 4 All-Ireland Senior Football Championship winner's medals with Kerry teams, in 1904 and 1909 with Tralee Mitchells, and in 1913 and 1914 with Killarney. He was also on 2 losing All-Ireland S.F.C. sides in both 1905 and 1915.

MURPHY, CONNIE.

G.A.A. footbll right half-back, Kerry. Born in Killarney, 28th March 1965. Club: Dr Crokes of Killarney (being the star player on the side which won the All-Ireland Club Championship title in

1992). He won a Munster Senior Football Championship medal with Kerry in 1991. In 1989 he was the only Kerryman to be nominated as an All-Star winner, being selected in the right half-back position. A Garda.

MURPHY, FRANK.

Middle-distance athlete. Born 21st May 1947. In 1969, he won the first British A.A.A. title to be run over 1,500 metres (replacing the mile), in a time of 3.40.9. Winning many Irish national middle-distance titles, he represented Ireland at 2 Olympic Games, in the 1,500m in 1968 at Mexico, and in both 800m and 1,500m at the 1972 games in Munich. In 1968 and 1969 he was selected as successive Texaco's Athletics Sportstar of the Year. In April 1990 he shared in the then biggest Lotto jackpot in Irish history.

MURPHY, GARY.

Amateur international golfer. Born in 1973. Club: Kilkenny. In an outstanding year of 1992, he won the Irish Close Championship title and went on, in his first senior year at international level, to have a team-best haul of 5 points of 6 (including a win over the British Amateur champion) when Ireland won the Home international championship.

MURPHY, JOHN Joseph (JOHNNY).

Rugby international full-back and centre three-quarter. Born in Bray, 27th August, 1957. Club: Greystones. A product of Presentation College Bray (winning an Irish schoolboys cap in the first year such a team competed in 1975), he won 3 international caps for Ireland from 1981 to 1984, including one, as a reserve centre, against Scotland in the Triple Crown winning year of 1982. He was the leading scorer on the Irish tour of South Africa in 1981, with 36 points. Also a talented soccer player, he had trials with Arsenal as a teenager.

MURPHY, HENRY Lawson.

Hockey international right half back. Born 12 December 1883. Club: Three Rock Rovers. He won a silver medal with an Ireland side in the 1908 London Olympic Games, when Ireland were trounced in the final of the 4 team event, by 8 goals to one. His total cap collection was 5, all in that famous year of 1908. He was a founder member of the famed Buccaneers (Touring) Hockey Club, and was an Irish Hockey Union representative from 1907 through to the 1930's.

MURPHY, JACK.

G.A.A. football left full-back, Kerry. He won an All-Ireland Senior Football Championship winner's medal with Kerry in 1924. In the 1926 All-Ireland S.F.C. final against Kildare, which went to a replay, he was a star player in the drawn game. However, he fell ill before the replay (which Kerry won), and died of pneumomnia, to be buried only 5 days after the replay.

MURPHY, KATHLEEN.

Ladies G.A.A. football midfielder, Laois. Club: The Heath (with whom she has won 7 county championship medals, 4 Leinster Club Championship medals, and 2 All-Ireland Club Championship winner's medal, in 1986 and 1987). She was at centre-half in the 1985 All-Ireland defeat by Kerry, and was at midfield when Laois lost the 1988 All-Ireland final to the same opposition. An All-Star player, she has won 2 Interprovincial Chammpionship winner's medals with Leinster.

MURPHY, KENNETH John (KENNY).

Rugby international full-back. Club: Cork Constitution (assisting them to success in the inaugural All-Ireland League title in the 1990-1991 season). Born in Cork, 21th July 1966. A product of C.B.C. Cork (winning a schools international cap on the wing in 1985), he toured France with Ireland in 1988 and played for the Irish Under 21 side that year. In 1989 he commenced his Munster career, and won a 'B' international cap against Scotland. He first played for Ireland in the 1990 International Championship, and has won

9 international caps until June 1992. A son of Noel F Murphy and a grandson of Noel A Murphy (ccvv), he is the only Irish rugby international whose father and grandfather played also for their country. He toured with Ireland to Namibia in 1991, and to New Zealand in 1992. His brother Charlie, a Cork Con centre-threequarter, has been a Munster interprovincial, and was also on the winning Cork Con side in the 1990-1991 All-Ireland League (Division One). Kenny is a cousin of Michael Kiernan (cv).

MURPHY, NOEL Francis Snr.

Rugby international back-row forward. Born 27th December 1904. Club: Cork Constitution. He won 11 international caps for Ireland between 1930 and 1933, being an ever present member of the side which shared the International Championship in 1932. He won 2 Munster Senior Cup medals with Cork Con, in 1929 and 1933. He was President of the I.R.F.U. 1960-61, and was manager of the Irish touring side to South Africa in 1961. He is the father of Noel Murphy (cv), and the grandfather of Kenny Murphy (cv), and this family run is the only time in Irish rugby history when a grandfather, his son and grandson have all represented Ireland.

MURPHY, NOEL Arthur Augustine, ('NOISY').

Rugby international wing forward. Born in Cork, 22nd February, 1937. Club: Cork Constitution (whom he helped to win 8 Munster Senior Cups, in 1957, 1961, 1964 and 1965 as captain, 1967, 1970, 1972, and 1973). A product of C.B.C. Cork, he was capped for Ireland on 41 occasions over a 12 year period from 1958 to 1969, scoring 5 international tries. A distinguished open or blind-side wing-forward, he was twice dropped for an entire season, and also captained Ireland 4 times (in 1966-67, which included a victory over the touring Australians; he was also captain of the first Munster side to beat the Wallabies). In 1969 at Cardiff Arms Park, when Ireland were chasing the Triple Crown, he was the recipient of the most infamous punch in the history of the game, from Brian Price. He participated on 2 British and Irish Lion's tours, winning a deserved 8 Test caps (a record for a Lion's flanker), 4 in the 1959 visit to Australia and New Zealand when he was the youngest player on tour (and scoring 5 tries in his 18 games and 3 more in a match against Canada on the same tour), and 4 more test places in the 1966 Lion's visit Down Under. He was coach to the Irish side 1978-1980, being a selector 1976-1980. He also was Coach and Assistant Manager on the victorious Irish tour of Australia in 1979, was Assistant Manager on the 1980 Lions tour of South Africa, and was Manager of the Irish touring party to New Zealand in 1992, and of the Irish team 1992-1993. He is the son of Noel F Murphy Snr (cv), while his son Kenny (cv) has also played for Ireland, a unique family record in Irish rugby.

MURPHY, SEAN OG (or JACKIE).

G.A.A. hurling full-back, Cork. Club: Blackrock. First playing for the Rebel County in 1912, he captained Cork to 2 All-Ireland Senior Hurling Championship victories, in 1926 when Kilkenny were beaten by 4-6 to 2-0, and in 1928 when Galway were beaten by 6-12 to 1-0 (he was also captain of the side which lost the 1927 decider, making him the only Corkman to captain three successive sides in All-Ireland S.H.C. finals, and the first man to recieve the Liam McCarthy Cup twice). He had earlier won an All-Ireland S.H.C. medal in the 1919 Cork win, being also on the beaten finalist's side in both 1915 and 1920. In 1926 he led Cork to victory in the inaugural National Hurling League (and thus becoming the first captain of a 'double' side in senior hurling). He also captained Munster to victory in their first 2 wins in the Railway Cup competition, in 1928 and 1929. One of Cork's finest full-backs, he retired from the game through injury in 1929. He was Secretary of the Cork County Board, and from 1924 until his death in 1956 he was on the Munster Council of the G.A.A.,

MURPHY, SEAN.

G.A.A. footballing right half-back, Kerry. Regarded as one of the game's greatest right half-backs, he won 3 All-Ireland Senior Football Championship winner's medals with Kerry, in 1953, 1955, and in 1959 when his display against Galway in the final was masterly (as was his performance in the semi-final against Dublin); he also played on 2 Kerry sides beaten in All-Ireland S.F.C. finals, in 1954 and 1960. Remarkably he won All-Ireland medals at minor (1950), junior (1949), and senior (1953) levels all before his 22nd birthday, actually winning his junior medal before his minor award. He was selected at right half-back on the Sunday Independent's 'Team of the Century' of 1984.

MURPHY, TOM.

G.A.A. footballer, Wexford. He was one of 10 Wexford players, from the Blues and Whites selection, that won 4 successive All-Ireland Senior Football Championship winner's medals, in 1915, 1916, 1917, and in 1918. He had played also on the teams beaten in the 2 previous All-Ireland S.F.C. finals, of 1913 and 1914 (which included a drawn game), so that he played in 7 successive All-Ireland S.F.C. finals, then a record.

MURPHY, TOMMY.

G.A.A. football full-forward, Wicklow. Born in 1957. Clubs: U.C.D. (winning Sigerson Cup medals three years in succession in 1977, 1978 and in 1979) and Baltinglass (winning 8 county championship medals with them from 1976, and being player/coach when the side won the All-Ireland Club Championship for the first time in 1990). He played on the Wicklow senior county team for 10 seasons from 1975 to 1984. His 2 brothers, Pat and Con, shared in the Baltinglass success of 1990, Con scoring 2-3 in the final. Tommy, a vetinary surgeon, was selected B & I Personality of the month for March 1990.

MURPHY, TOMMY ('THE BOY WONDER OF FOOTBALL').

G.A.A. football midfielder, Laois. Club: Annanough (with whom he won 8 Laois County Championship medals, and 3 Leinster Club Championship medals). From Graiguecullen, Co Laois, he was born in 1921. First playing for the Laois senior inter-county team in 1937 at the age of only 16, his superb football craft was obvious from a very early age, and he played in an All-Ireland S.F.C. semi-final the same year. He played at centre half-back on the occasion of Laois's 6th (and most recent) Leinster S.F.C. win of 1946 (to add to the medals he won in 1937 and 1938), scoring 8 of the 11 points for his county in the final. He also won Railway Cup medals for Leinster in 1940 and 1945 (as a sub), and was on the Laois team which visited the U.S.A. in 1938. His genius in the 30's and early 40's was such as to deserve his nickname, and in 1984 he was selected in midfield on the 'Team of the Century' for those who never won an All-Ireland senior championship medal. Regarded, as one of the game's greatest midfielders, he died in May 1985.

MURPHY, VINNIE.

G.A.A. football right half-forward and full-forward, Dublin. Born in Dublin, 2nd December 1969. Club: Trinity Gaels (winning a Dublin Junior Championship medal in 1988). A product of Holy Trinity School, at the age of 17 he was a member of both the hurling and football senior Dublin panels, and won an All-Ireland Under 14 hurling medal. He won 3 Leinster Senior Football Championship medals with Dublin, in 1989 (scoring the winning goal in the final against Meath), as a star member of the Dublin side which were defeated by Donegal in the All-Ireland S.F.C. final of 1992, and in 1993. Winning a Railway Cup medal with Leinster in 1988, he won 2 National League medals with the Dubs, in 1991 (scoring the crucial only goal in the win over Kildare) and 1993. He won an All Star award in 1992 at full-forward. His father, Vincent, won All-Ireland medals with Dublin at both junior and minor (in 1955) level.

MURPHY, WILLIAM JAMES ('BOY').

Amateur international lightheavy boxer. Club: Garda boxing club (which he helped to dominate Irish amateur boxing for 10 years). He won 5 Irish National Senior titles at light-heavyweight, in 1927, 1928, 1929, 1930, and 1932. In 1932 he finished 4th in the Olympic Games light-heavy event at Los Angeles (he did not win a medal as there was a play-off for the bronze in those days).

MURPHY, WILLIE.

G.A.A. hurling full-back, Wexford. He was at full-back on Wexford's last 2 appearences in the All-Ireland Senior Hurling Championship final, when the county lost to Cork in both 1976 and 1977 (these are also Wexford's last Leinster S.H.C. wins). He won Railway Cup medals with Leinster in 1977 and 1978. He won his only All-Star award in 1976 at full-back.

MURPHY, WILLIE or BILLY ('LONG PUCK').

G.A.A. hurling right full-back, Cork. Club: Ballincollig. Noted for his huge long puck, he won 5 All-Ireland Senior Hurling Championship medals with Cork, in the 'Golden Years' period of the 4-in-a-row of 1941, 1942, 1943 and 1944, and again in 1946. He was also on the Cork teams beaten in the All-Ireland S.H.C. finals in both 1939 and 1947. He also assisted Cork to National Hurling League triumphs 3 times (in 1940, 1941 and 1948), and won 7 Railway Cup medals with Munster, in 1940, 1941, 1942, 1943, 1945, 1946, and 1948.

MURRAY, ALF.

G.A.A. football half-back and half-forward, Armagh. Clubs: Wolfe Tones, and Clann na Gael. One of Antrim's stalwarts of the later 30's and early 40's, he never won an Ulster S.F.C. medal. He won 2 Railway Cup medals (from his 9 appearences between 1937 and 1945) with Ulster, in the finals of 1942 and 1943 (when shooting the winning point), while he was on defeated final sides in 1939, 1941 and 1944. He was later to become President of the G.A.A., serving from 1964 to 1967.

MURRAY, ANTHONY (TONY).

Flat jockey. Born 18th February 1940, he was from Tramore, Co Waterford. He spent most of his working life based in Britain, apprenticing with Frenchie Nicholson. In an 18 year career from 1966 to 1983, he won over 1,000 races, including 6 classic wins: Epsom Oaks in 1972 on Ginerva; Doncaster St Leger in 1975 on Bruni; the Irish Derby in 1980 on Tyrnavos; the Irish 2,000 Guineas in 1979 on Dickens Hill; the 1980 Irish 1,000 Guineas on Cairn Rouge. Later working as racing manager with Tony Budge, he died in 1991 aged 41.

MURRAY, CIARAN.

G.A.A. football centre half-back, Monaghan. An influential member of the Monaghan side which won the Ulster Senior Football Championship in 1985 and again in 1988, he was also a member of the winning Monaghan team which in 1985 became the first (and thus far the only) from the county to capture the National Football League (they were beaten by a single point in the final of the 1986 National League). He has won one All-Star award, in 1985 in the centre half-back position.

MURRAY, DANNY.

G.A.A. football left half-back, Roscommon. Club: St Faithleach's. Playing at minor grade for Longford, he went on to play in the Roscommon sides which won the county's only 4-in-a-row sequence of Connacht S.H.C. wins, in 1977, 1978, 1979, and 1980. In 1979 he won a National Football League medal with Roscommon in their great 0-15 to 1-3 win over Cork. He captained Roscommon, at the age of 24, on their most recent All-Ireland Senior Football Championship final appearance in 1980. A fine defender with the ability to charge forward into attack, he has won one All-Star award, in 1979 in the No 7 jersey at left half-back.

MURRAY, JIMMY.

G.A.A. football centre half-forward, Roscommon. Club: St Patrick's of Knockcroghery. He won an All-Ireland junior medal with Roscommon in 1940. He went on to captain Roscommon to their only 2 All-Ireland Senior Football Championship titles (one of only 6 men to captain successive winning sides), when they beat the footballers of Cavan in the 1943 final after a replay by 2-7 to 2-2, and the Kerry side in the 1944 final by 1-9 to 2-4. He also captained Roscommon in their All-Ireland S.F.C. final defeat in the 1946 replay against Kerry. He is a brother of Phelim Murray (cv).

MURRAY, MILDRED (nee DOYLE).

Pitch and putt player. Club: Shandon P.P.C.(Dublin). She has won 3 Irish national pitch and putt championships, in 1978, 1979 and 1981, all in the National Matchplay discipline (having earlier, in 1975, been runner-up in this event). In 1977 she was runner-up in the National Strokeplay Championship.

MURRAY, Dr PAUL Finbarr.

Rugby international scrum-half, out-half and centre. Born 29th June 1905 in Dublin, he died in 1981. Club: Wanderers. Between 1928 and 1933 he played 11 times for Leinster in the interprovincial series. A gifted and versatile back, he was capped 19 times for Ireland between 1927 and 1933, 7 at scrum-half, 6 at out-half, and 6 in the centre (and was once a reserve full-back), and scored a total of 33 points for Ireland (his 4 conversions against South Africa in 1932 sharing an Irish record). He was selected as a centre for the British and Irish Lion's tour of Australia and New Zealand in 1930, winning 4 Test caps actually as a scrum-half. He became President of the I.R.F.U. for 1965/1966. A scratch golfer, he is the father of Dr John Brendan Murray (born in Dublin 3rd April 1942), a U.C.D. out-half (winning Leinster Senior Cup medals in 1963 and 1964), and who was capped once for Ireland, against France in 1963 (playing also in 7 interprovincial matches for Leinster), who also played many times for Ireland in international tennis. Paul Snr's wife Rachel was an international golfer (in 1952), and his daughter Oonagh played international hockey for Ireland in 1965.

MURRAY, PHELIM.

G.A.A. football wing-back and wing-forward, Roscommon. Club: St Patrick's of Knockcroghery. A brother of Jimmy Murray (cv), he was on the Roscommon sides which won All-Ireland winner's medal at both minor (1939) and junior (1940) levels, a rare achievment. Regarded as one of his county's finest wing players, he was a member (under brother Jimmy's captaincy) of the Roscommon team which won the All-Ireland Senior Football Championship for 2 years in a row, 1943 and 1944, and which lost to Kerry in the final of 1946.

MUSSEN, KEVIN.

G.A.A. football left right-back, Down. From Hilltown, Co Down, he was a product of St Colman's of Newry. Club: Clonduff. Playing for Down minors for 2 years, he played senior inter-county football with the county from 1952 to 1962. A member of the Down side which reached only the county's 3rd Ulster final in 1958, he was also a member of the Down side which won their first Ulster S.F.C. in 1959. He captained, at the age of 26, the first Down side to win an All-Ireland Senior Football Championship final, when he led the footballers to win the first of 2 successive titles, in the 1960 2-10 to 0-8 win over Kerry (thus becoming the first Ulsterman to carry the Sam Maguire Cup across the border). He did not play in the final success of 1961. In the same year

(1960) he also won a National Football League medal with Down. He won Railway Cup football medals with Ulster in both 1956 and 1960 (as a sub). .

MYERS, BILL.

G.A.A. football left or right corner back, Kerry. He won 4 All-Ireland Senior Football Championship winner's medals in the space of 5 years with the 'Kingdom', in 1937, 1939, 1940 and in 1941, while he also played on losing the Kerry All-Ireland S.F.C. final team in 1938. He won his only Railway Cup medal in 1941.

N

NAGLE, DEIRDRE.

Middle-distance runner. Clubs: Guinness and (from 1975) Dublin City Harriers. Setting national records at both 1,500 and 3,00 metres, she had many national and international successes at these distances and at 800 metres. She won the Irish National cross country championship 3 times, won a Scottish 1,500 metres title, and competed in the World Cross Country Championships for Ireland on 13 different occasions, her best placing being 14th in 1976. She won the British W.A.A.A. 3,000 metres title in 1979, and the equally prestigious British W.A.A.A. cross-country title in 1975. Twice a member of the D.C.H. team which captured the European Ladies Club title, she was also on 2 Irish sides which won the Home International cross country title, in 1981 and 1985. She is the daughter of the athletics administrator Brendan Foreman.

NALLEN, JOHN.

G.A.A. footballing midfielder. Born in Co Mayo. A much travelled player, he played senior inter-county football at senior level for 3 different counties, his native Mayo, for Galway, and for Meath. He played in the midfield on the Railway Cup-winning Connacht sides of 1957 and 1958, and he also played for Ireland in 1956 and 1959, both against the Combined Universities. He also played junior football for Cavan.

NALLY, PATRICK W.

Athlete. Born in Balla, Co Mayo, 13th March 1856. In June 1876, at the age of 19, he entered 17 different athletic contests, and finished in the first 2 places in 16 of these contests. It was his urging that caused Michael Cusack to start the Gaelic Athletic Association in 1884. He was also avid republican, was imprisoned, and died at the age of only 33, in 1891. The Nally stand in Croke Park, Dublin is named in his honour, and there is also a monument to him in his native Balla.

NASH, CHARLIE.

Light-weight boxer, amateur and professional. Born in Derry, 10th May 1951. Amateur club: St Mary's, Derry. He won 5 Irish Senior National championships at light-weight, in 1970, 1971, 1972, 1973, and 1975, and represented Ireland 29 times. He reached the quarter-final of the 1972 Olympic Games lightweight division, losing out in the bronze medal bout to the Pole Jan Szczepanski. As a professional he was to become both European champion (1979-80) and British champion (1978-79). In his 8 year professional career, he won 25 and lost 5 of his 30 bouts. He won his European title on 27th June 1979 in Derry, when outpointing the Frenchman Andre Holyk for the vacant title. In December of that year he successfully defended his title against Ken Buchanan of Scotland. Relinquishing his title to make an unsuccessful tilt at the world title of Jim Watt (when the referee stopped the fight after 4 rounds), he regained the European crown in December 1980, when outpointing Francisco Leon of Spain. He again lost his title, when knocked out in the 6th round in Dublin 1980, by Joey Gilbilisco of Italy. His nephew, Roy Nash, was a useful bantamweight and featherweight boxer (from the Ring club), winning Irish National Senior Championship titles, and also winning a silver medal at the Commonwealth Games in Edinburgh in 1986.

NATION, TONY.

G.A.A. football right full-back, Cork. Club: Nemo Rangers (winning an All-Ireland Club Championship medal in 1984). He won an All-Ireland Under 21 Championsip winner's medal with Cork in 1984. Having played in 2 successive losing All-Ireland Senior Football finals for Cork in 1987 and 1988 (when he captained the side), he then won 2 successive Sam Maguire medals in 1989 and 1990, thus appearing in 4 successive All-Ireland S.F.C. finals.

NAUGHTON, MARTIN.

G.A.A. hurling left half-forward, Galway. Club: Turloughmore. A member of the Galway side which won 2 successive All-Ireland Senior Hurling Championship titles in 1987 and 1988, he was also on the side beaten by Cork in both the 1986 and 1990 finals. He won 2 National League medals also with Galway (in 1987 and 1989), and won a Railway Cup medal on the all-Galway Connacht side of 1987. He was selected as an All-Star award in 1988 at left half-forward, and retired at 28 though injury in 1992.

NAUGHTON, TOM.

G.A.A. football right half-forward, Galway. He was at centre half-forward on the most recent Galway team to win the All-Ireland Under 21 Football Championship, in 1972. A member of the Galway side which won Connacht Senior Champinship titles in 1973 (at full forward), 1974 (going on in both years to be defeated in the All-Ireland final, by Cork and Dublin successfully), and 1976, he won one All-Star award, in 1974 at right half-forward.

NEALON, DONIE.

G.A.A. hurling right half-forward and right full-forward, Tipperary. Born at Youghacarra, Nenagh, Co Tipperary, 7th December 1935. Educated at St Flannan's, Ennis (with whom he won a Dr Harty Cup medal in 1954), and at U.C.D. (captaining them to a victory in the Fitzgibbon Cup and the Dublin S.H.C.). He played senior hurling for Tipperary from 1958 to 1969, winning 5 Liam McCarthy Cup medals, in 1958, 1961, 1962, 1964, and 1965, playing on the losing side in the All-Ireland Senior Hurling Champinship finals of 1960 and 1967 (scoring 2 goals in the final). He also won 6 National League medals with Tipp, in 1960, 1961, 1963, 1964, 1965, and in 1970. He won 4 Railway Cup medals with Munster, in 1959, 1963, 1966, and in 1968. In 1962 he became the 2nd Tipperary to be voted as Texaco Hurler of the Year. He has trained Tipperary sides which have won the All-Ireland senior and intermediate championships, and later became Secretary of the Munster Council of the G.A.A.. His father, Rody Nealon, won All-Ireland senior and junior hurling titles with Tipperary, and played for Ireland in the 1924 Tailteann Games.

NEARY, LIZ.

G.A.A. camogie versatility player, Kilkenny. Club: St Pauls, Kilkenny (winning All-Ireland Club Championship medals with them in 1976, 1977, and 1987), and Austin Stacks, Dublin (winning All-Ireland Club Championship titles with them in 1972 and 1973). Educated at Presentation College, Kilkenny (with whom she won All-Ireland Colleges medals in 1969 and 1970), she is a winner of 7 All-Ireland (O'Duffy Cup) titles with Kilkenny, in 1974, 1976, 1977, 1981 (as captain in the replay), 1985, 1986, and 1987. She won the 1981 B+I Camogie Star of the Year title. A brilliant defender.

NEILL, HARRY JAMES.

Rugby international forward. 1861-1949. Club: N.I.F.C. (being a member of the North side which won the Ulster Senior Cup in its inaugural year of

1885). Although he was capped only 8 times for Ireland between 1885 and 1888, he captained his country to it's first ever shared win in the International Championship, when Ireland defeated Wales to share the spoils with Scotland in 1888 (England did not compete).

NEILL, TERRY W J.

Soccer international centre-half, wing-half and manager. Born in Belfast, 8th May 1942. He joined Arsenal from Bangor at the age of 17, and in 10 seasons at Highbury he played 275 first team games for them, scoring 8 goals. He joined Hull City in 1970, playing 103 league matches for the Tigers until 1972. For a period in the early seventies he was Chairman of the P.F.A.. He was capped 59 times for Northern Ireland between 1961 and 1973, making him at that time Northern Ireland's most capped player (and the 15 caps gained while at Hull City made him that club's most capped player); he scored 2 international goals. He moved into a successful career in soccer management, at Hull City (when in 1970 he became the youngest manager in the league), Tottenham and Arsenal (in 7 years there the 'Gunners' were never out of the top 10 in the league, with Terry also bringing them to 3 successive F.A. Cup finals, including winning in 1979, and losing also the 1980 European Cup-Winners Cup final). He also managed Northern Ireland briefly in 1973.

NELLIGAN, CHARLIE.

G.A.A. footballing goalkeeper, Kerry. Born 26th February 1957. Club: Castleisland Desmonds (with whom he won an All-Ireland Club Championship medal in 1985, and a runner's-up medal in 1986). Winning an All-Ireland M.F.C. medal with the 'Kingdom' in 1975, he also won 3 All-Ireland Under 21 F.C. medals with Kerry in succession, in 1975, 1976 and in 1977. He then went on to win 7 All-Ireland Senior Football Championship winner's medals with Kerry, being a constant member of the 4-in-a-row side of 1978 (in which he was sent off), 1979, 1980, and 1981, and also of the 3-in-a-row side of 1984, 1985, and 1986. He was on losing All-Ireland S.F.C. sides in 1976 (as a sub) and 1982, and won his last Munster S.F.C. medal in 1991. He was selected as the All-Star goalkeeper twice, in 1980 and 1986. He was scouted by Manchester United as a soccer goalkeeper, and played League of Ireland football with Home Farm.

NELSON, JAMES Edward (JIMMY).

Rugby international second-row forward. Born in Belfast, 16th September 1921. Club: Malone. A product of Armagh Grammar School, he played for an Irish XV against the British Army in 1944 and 1945. He went on to be capped 16 times for Ireland between 1947 and 1954, scoring one international try. He was a staunch member of the 1948 Grand Slam winning XV of 1948, the 1949 Triple Crown winning XV, and the International Championship winning side of 1951. He was honoured with participation in the 1950 British and Irish Lion's tour of Australia and New Zealand, playing in 18 matches and winning 4 Test caps, 2 in each country (in one international in Sydney he became the only Lion's test forward in history to score 2 tries in a test match, and the only Irishman to accomplish this feat). An accountant, he was an Irish selector 1962-1966, became the Union Honorary Treasurer in 1976, and was President of the I.R.F.U. in 1982-83, when Ireland shared the International Championship.

NELSON, SAMMY.

Soccer international left-back. Born in Belfast, 1st April 1949. Clubs: Arsenal (with whom, over an 11 year period, he played in 324 first team matches, winning an F.A. Youth Cup medal in 1967, a full F.A. Cup medal in 1979, being also in the side which lost in the finals of 1978 and 1980; and also capturing a European Cup-Winners Cup runners-up medal in 1980), Brighton and Hove Albion. Capped for Northern

Ireland at both schools and Under 23 level, he won 51 senior soccer caps at full-back for his country betwen 1970 and 1982 (playing in the famous 1-0 over Spain in Northern Ireland's excellent run in the World Cup of 1982), and he scored one international goal.

NESBITT, JAMES.

International discus-thrower. Born on 22nd September 1913, he died in 1992. He dominated discus throwing in Northern Ireland in the late 30's and 40's, winning 12 Northern Ireland titles between 1935 and 1950. Representing Great Britain 6 times in 1937-49, he represented G.B. at the 1948 Olympic Games in London, and in that year also threw his personal best for the discipline, 45.64 metres.

NESTOR, BRENDAN.

G.A.A. football left full-forward, Galway. He won 2 All-Ireland Senior Football Championship winner's medals with Galway, in 1934 and 1938, and also played on losing All-Ireland S.F.C. final teams in both 1933 and 1940. A quality corner forward, he shares the record for a Galway footballer of winning 4 Railway Cup medals with Connacht, in 1934, 1936, 1937 and 1938.

NEVILLE, MICK.

Soccer centre-half. Born in Dublin, 23rd November 1959. Clubs: Home Farm, Drogheda United (helping them to finish 2nd in the League of Ireland in 1982-83), Shamrock Rovers (winning 4 successive League of Ireland Championship winner's medals, in 1984, 1985, 1986 and 1987, and also winning F.A.I. Cup medals in each of the last 3 of these years to win the 'double' 3 times), Derry City (with whom he won League of Irleand/F.A.I. Cup double in 1988-89, thus becoming the first League of Ireland player to win the 'double' 4 times), and Shelbourne (winning a further League of Ireland medal in 1991-92, and another F.A.I. Cup medal as captain in 1993). Uncapped, he has been among the most talented centre-halves in the League of Ireland, gaining his place on the inaugural League Star side in 1992.

NEVILLE, MICK.

G.A.A. hurler, Dublin and Limerick. From Kilfinny, Co Limerick. He won 2 All-Ireland Senior Hurling Championship winner's medals with Dublin in 1917 and 1920. In 1921 he was a member of the Dublin side defeated in the first Liam McCarthy Cup final (played against his home county). Later, in 1923, he switched back to his native county, Limerick, when they were unsuccessful in their bid to win the All-Ireland S.H.C. final against Galway.

NEVILLE, PADDY.

Cricket and hockey international player, and soccer goalkeeper. Born in Donabate, Co Dublin, 22nd June 1922, he died in 1977. As a right-hand batsman in cricketer and member of Malahide, he played 4 first class matches for Ireland (and 7 in all) between 1956 and 1960, his 1st class record being 4-8-0-143-38(versus Scotland in 1960)-17-88. As a hockey playing forward for the Portrane club, he played at international level 7 times for Ireland between 1947 and 1949, including being a member of the Triple Crown winning sides of 1947 and 1949. As a soccer goalkeeper, he played many seasons for Drumcondra in the League of Ireland (winning an F.A.I. Cup medal in 1954, and a runners-up medal the following year), and was selected to play for the League of Ireland.

NEVILLE, Doctor WILLIAM C.

Rugby international forward. Club: Dublin University. He is one of only 5 players to captain Ireland in their debut international, doing so against England in 1879. He was also captain in Ireland's other match that season, both matches ending in losses. A medical doctor, he also refereed 2 internationals. Having been honorary secretary 1878-1879, he went on to become the first President of the I.R.F.U., being elected to the post on

5th February 1880 (the I.R.F.U. prior to that was known as the I.F.U.).

NEVIN, VINCENT.

Amateur international golfer. Clubs: Ennis and Limerick (winning a Senior Cup-Barton Shield double in 1976, having previously won the Barton Shield in 1967). He won the Irish Close Championship title in 1969, the 'West' in 1972 (and was runner-up the following year), and won the South of Ireland in both 1976 and 1978. He played 66 interprovincial matches for Munster from 1960 to 1973, winning 27; he played 41 Home international matches for Ireland from 1960 to 1972 (when he was also a member of the Irish side which won the Quadrangular Continental match), winning 20; he played 14 European Team championship matches in 3 series for Ireland from 1965 to 1973 (being on the famous winning teams in both 1965 and 1967), winning 7 and halving 2. In 1969 he was selected as Texaco's Golf Sportstar of the Year.

NEWETT, F.B..

Amateur international golfer. Clubs: Royal Portrush (winning 2 Senior Cup medals in 1902 and 1903), Malone (winning 4 Senior Cup medals, in 1905, 1908 and 1909, thus becoming the first player to win 5 such medals). He won 2 Irish Amateur Close Championship titles, in 1902 at Dollymount, and in 1905 at Newcastle when he beat fellow-club member B O'Brien in the final. He played in 5 internationals for Ireland between 1900 and 1904. His brother (?) A.C. Newett, also of Malone, was also an international golfer, and was on the first side (Dublin University) ever to win the Senior Cup, in 1900.

NEWTON, ALBERT L.

Long distance athlete and steeplechaser. An Irishman representing the U.S.A., he ran 5th in the Olympic Games marathon at Paris in 1900, and was 4th in the 1500 metre steeplechase. Four years later in the St Louis Games he improved his standing in both events and won 2 Olympic bronze medals: one in the 2,590 metres steeplechase, and one also in the Marathon, finishing 3rd of only 14 finishers, in a time of 3:47:33, 19 seconds behind the winner.

NEWTON, DES and JOHN.

G.A.A. footballing brothers, Roscommon. They are from the village of Croghan, near Carrick-on-Shannon. Des, born August 12th 1960, won an All-Ireland Under 21 medal with Roscommon in 1978. He was sub for the Roscommon side which won the Connacht S.F.C. in 1980, and was at corner-back on the side which captured the title in 1990 and 1991. He also played with Donegal, winning an Ulster S.F.C. medal with them in 1983. John, born in 1962, a mid-fielder with the Garda Club, was also on the side which captured the Connacht S.F.C. in both 1990 and 1991 (when he captained the side to the All-Ireland semi-final defeat). Their father, J.P. Newton, played for Leitrim for 8 years, and helped his club Croghan win their last Roscommon senior county championship.

NIBLOCK, MICKEY.

G.A.A. football half-forward, Derry. He won an All-Ireland M.F.C. medal with Derry minor's in 1965, and went on in 1968 to be a member of the county side which won the All-Ireland Under 21 Football Championship. He was later a winner of 3 Ulster Senior Football Championship medals with Derry in the 1970's, in 1970, 1975 and 1976. He won 3 Railway Cup medals with Ulster, in 1968, 1970 and 1971.

NICHOLL, CHRIS J.

Soccer international defender. Born in Wilmslow, 12th October 1946. Clubs: Burnley (joining them as a junior), Witton Athletic, Halifax, Luton Town, Aston Villa (playing 210 league matches for them from 1971-1976, scoring 11 goals), Southampton (playing over 200 matches for them from 1977 to at least 1984. He was capped 51 times for Northern Ireland between 1975 and 1984, scoring

3 international goals, and playing in 4 of Northern Ireland's games in the excellent 1982 World Cup experience in Spain. His younger brother Terry (born in 1952) has played in over 300 English League matches as a midfielder (the majority for Gillingham).

NICHOLL, JIMMY M.

Soccer international right-back. Born in Hamilton (near Toronto), Canada, 28th February 1956. Clubs: Manchester United (to whom he was apprenticed, playing over 250 matches for them, and winning an F.A. Cup medal in 1977, a runners-up medal in 1979, and being a member of the side which was 2nd in the First Division in 1980), Toronto Blizzard, Toronto Metro Croatia, Sunderland, Glasgow Rangers (for 2 periods, playing over 100 games for them, winning Scottish League Cup honours in 1984, 1987 and 1988, and a League Championship medal in 1986-87), West Bromwich Albion, Dunfirmline Athletic. A fine defender, he was capped 73 times for Northern Ireland over a 11 year period betwen 1976 and 1986 (and scoring 2 international goals), being one of only 3 players to play in all 8 of Northern Ireland's games in it's 2 most recent qualifyings for World Cup finals, in the fine side in Spain in 1982, and then in Mexico in 1986.

NICHOLSON, JAMES (JIMMY) J.

Soccer international wing-half. Born in Belfast, 27th February 1943. He joined Manchester United as a junior when just 17, and played 58 league games for them in 2 seasons, being recognised early for his talent. In his 9 seasons at Huddersfield Town 1964-73, he played 280 league matches, scoring 28 goals, and helped his side back to the First Division in 1970. This was followed by 2 seasons at Bury, playing in 79 league games. He was capped 41 times for Northern Ireland, his first international cap being earned at the tender age of 17 years and 9 months, and he scored 6 international goals. The 31 caps he gained while at Huddersfield 1965-71 make him the Leeds Road club's most capped international.

NICHOLSON, SIOBHAN.

Tennis international player. Born in Wimbledon, 11th June 1966. She has been Ireland's No 1 ladies tennis player every year between 1986 and 1993. She has played Federation Cup for Ireland every year bar 2 between 1983 and 1993. She has won the Irish Ladies Close Championship 5 out of the 6 times she has entered, in 1983, 1985, 1990, 1991 and 1993, and won the Irish Ladies Open Championship in 1987. Ranked, in August 1993 at No 545 in the world, her victims in the past have included Sarah Gomer. In 1989 she was awarded, by 'World Tennis' Magazine, the title of 'best unsung player of the year'. Her father Martin ran the 3-mile event for Connacht and was 2nd in an Irish championship.

NOLAN, JAMES.

Rugby international player. A Dublin-born back who played for Rochdale Hornets, he was the first Irish-born player to go on a British and Irish tour, when he was a member of the 1888 side which toured Australia and New Zealand. One of the top try scorers of the tour, he in fact never played international rugby for either Ireland or England.

NOLAN, (nee MERCER) PHILIS (PHIL).

Lawn bowls player. Born in Bray Co Wicklow, 10th February 1946. Clubs: Bray B.C. (1972-1977), and Blackrock B.C. (1977-date), with whom she has won 6 All-Ireland League titles, being club captain in 1987. A product of Loreto College Bray, she has won 5 Irish titles, one Pairs, one Triples, and 3 Fours, and has won 2 Ulster Games titles. She became the first person to win the British Isles Women's Bowls Singles title twice in succession, in 1992 and 1993. In November 1988, she became the first bowler from the Republic of Ireland to win a gold medal in the World

Championships, when she partnered Maggie Johnston (cv) to capture the Pairs title, in Auckland, New Zealand (she lost in a play off for the bronze medal in the Fours). In 1992 she again won the World Championship Women's Pairs (again with Maggie Johnston cv), in Ayr, competing a fine double in the event. First capped internationally in 1976, she went on to be skip in 1987/88. She is also an umpire and club coach.

NOLAN, PAT.

G.A.A. hurling goalkeeper, Wexford. He won an All-Ireland Senior Hurling Championship medal in 1956 as a non-playing substitute in the Wexford win, first winning a player's medal in their 1960 win over Tipperary. One of the game's finest keepers, he won a second All-Ireland S.H.C. medal in 1968 in another success over Tipperary, and was also in goals when Wexford lost 3 other Liam McCarthy Cup finals, in 1962, 1965 and 1970. He was overlooked in the Railway Cup successes for Leinster during his peak only because of the presence of Ollie Walsh (cv).

NOLAN, RONNIE.

Soccer international defensive wing-half. Clubs: Shamrock Rovers (with whom he won 6 F.A.I. Cup medals: in 1955, 1956 when he scored the winning goal, 1962, 1964, 1965 and 1966; and 4 League of Ireland Championship winner's medals, in 1954, 1957, 1959, and in 1964, when Rovers won the Grand Slam), and Bohemians (winning with them his 7th F.A.I. Cup winners medal in 1970). Scorer of 2 Inter-League goals for the League of Ireland, he was capped 10 times for the Republic of Ireland between 1957 and 1963. Regarded as one of the best League of Ireland players not to go to England, and known as the best defensive wing-half in the League for a period spanning 20 years, he was selected in 1961 as Texaco's Soccer Sportstar of the Year, and in 1993 he was honoured by the S.W.A.I.. He later helped U.C.D. and the Bank of Ireland sides.

NOLAN, WILLIE.

G.A.A. football goalkeeper, Offaly. Born in 1940. Club: Clara (helping them to their first ever Offaly S.F.C. title in 1957), and the Offaly side in New York. Playing Offaly minors in 1957-58, he played senior inter-county football from 1958 to 1963. A member of the first Offaly side to capture the Leinster Senior Football Championship in 1960, the next year he became the first from the county to captain a side in an All-Ireland S.F.C. final (in the defeat by Down). He also won a Railway Cup medal with Leinster in 1961, and won a National Football League medal with New York in 1964.

NOONAN, AUSTIN.

Soccer forward. Born in Cork, 16th July 1933. Clubs: Evergreen United, Cork Celtic, Cork Hibernian. One of the most gifted goalscorers in Cork's proud soccer tradition, in the 1959/60 season he scored 27 League of Ireland goals, a Cork Celtic record, and was the League of Ireland's top scorer. His career League of Ireland goals tally of 129 places him 10th on the all-time list. He later managed Cork Hibernians.

NORTON, GEORGE William.

Rugby international full-back. Born in Dublin, 1st April 1920. Club: Bective Rangers. Seven times a Leinster player, he was one of Ireland's best place-kickers, and was capped 11 times between 1949 and 1951, his scoring tally was 41 points from 7 conversions and 9 penalties. He was ever present in the 1949 Irish Triple Crown XV, scoring in each match for a total of 26 out of Ireland's 41 championship points that season (this tally remained an Irish record for 26 years). He was selected on the 1950 British and Irish Lion's side that travelled to New Zealand, but was injured early in the tour. He was dropped for the Triple Crown tie of 1951 against Wales, and his absence, due to bad place-kicking, led to a drawn match, but he still had helped Ireland in the International Championship win that season.

NOTLEY, JOHN Robert ('JACK').

Rugby and cricket international. Born in Drumsna, Co Roscommon, 25th June 1926. A dual international, as a rugby player, while a member of Wanderers (with whom he won Leinster Senior Cup medals in 1947 and 1954), he played at centre in 2 winning matches for Ireland (thus being one of a select band of Irish rugby players to have a 100% winning record), in the 1952 games against France and Scotland, scoring one conversion. He also played 11 times for Leinster in the Interprovincial Championship betwen 1945 and 1953. He was also capped once at cricket for Ireland in 1956.

NUGENT, NOEL.

International basketball player. Born in Portumna, Co Galway. Clubs: Army (helping the Eastern Command to several all-Army titles), Dublin Celtics, Garda (helping them to win the Dublin championship double in 1964), Chanel College club (playing with them up until 1978). A member of Dublin minor and senior inter-county sides, he was an automatic choice on the Irish senior international team from 1960 to 1973, renowned especially for his set shooting ability. A major contributor to the evolution of amateur basketball in Ireland, he often paid his own way to international matches, and even bought his own vest. A coach to juniors in latter years.

O'BRIEN, ANN.

Middle-distance athlete. Born 9th May 1943. Dominating Irish women's middle-distance running for a period in the late 60's and early 70's, she won a grand total of 13 B.L.E. national titles over varying middle-distances. She also won the prestigious British W.A.A.A. title at 3,000 metres two years in succession, 1969 and 1970.

O'BRIEN, BRENDAN Anthony ('GINGER').

Cricket international right hand batsman. Born in Galway, 2nd September 1942. Club: Railway Union (in a club career stretching over 5 decades from 1959 to the early 1990's, he scored a Leinster League record of over 19,100 runs for them, and captained them to win the Leinster Senior Cup in 1967). A product of Westland Row C.B.S., he played 11 first class matches for Ireland between 1966 and 1981, his record being 11-17-1-319-45-19.94, his best being 94 against Sri Lanka in 1979. Capped in all 52 times for Ireland (and captaining the side on a few occasions in 1981), he scored 1,636 runs for his country in 86 innings, for an average of 21.24, and took 42 catches. He became coach to the Irish ladies side in 1992. An all-round sportsman, he played for Shelbourne for 4 years 1959-63 (winning a League of Irleand Championship medal in 1961-62), and played soccer at international level as a youth and junior. He also played at inter-provincial level in hockey for Leinster, also with Railway Union. His sons Paul (also a hockey inter-pro with Leinster) and Gerard both play Leinster Senior League Cricket.

O'BRIEN, CHRISTY.

G.A.A. hurling centre half-forward and full-forward, Laois. Club: Borris-in-Ossory (captaining their first ever victory in the Laois County Championship in 1956, and winning medals again in 1957, 1960, 1961, and 1972). Regarded as one of the greatest hurlers who never won an All-Ireland S.H.C. medal, he was a member of the Laois team which won Division II of the National Hurling League in both 1959 and 1965, and he won 3 Railway Cup medals with Leinster, in 1962, 1964 and 1965, the most won by a Laois hurler. In 1984 he was selected at full-forward on the hurling 'Team of the Century' for players who never won an All-Ireland senior championship medal.

O'BRIEN, CHRISTY.

International rower. Club: Garda Siochana Boat Club. He won the Irish Senior Eights Championship 6 times (1974, 1975, 1977, 1979, 1982 and 1983), and also won Irish Senior Championships in 3 out of the 4 other disciplines open to him, namely the coxed fours (in 1983), coxless pairs (1978), and in double sculls (in 1982), giving him a total of 9 Irish elite championship wins. He was 3 times on coxed four teams which finished 7th in major championships (in the 'Worlds' of both 1975 and 1976), and in the Olympic Games of Montreal in 1976 (winning the 'little final' for 7th-12th place in each event). In 1978, along with his fellow rower, Willie Ryan, he finally made a grand final (of the World Championship coxless pairs on Lake Karapiro in New Zealand), finishing a highly creditable 5th place, and for this feat they were selected as Texaco's Rowing Sportstar of the Year. In 1980 he was a member of a fine coxed pair (with Willie Ryan cv), winning silver medals twice in the Lucerne International (behind the reigning Olympic gold medalists, who went on to retain their title), but illness ruled them out of the Moscow Olympic Regatta that year.

O'BRIEN, DERMOT.

G.A.A. footballing centre half-forward, Louth. A member of the Louth team soundly beaten in the All-Ireland S.F.C. semi-final of 1953, he later captained the Louth side to win an All-Ireland Senior Football Championship, in the final of 1957, over Cork by a score 1-9 to 1-7 (this was the county's most recent Sam Maguire success, and their third in all, the previous 2 being in the formative day's of the G.A.A., in 1910 and 1912). Later he became a famed accordionist and dance band leader.

O'BRIEN, DESMOND Joseph (DES).

Rugby international No 8 forward, and squash international player. Born in Dublin, 22nd May 1919. Clubs: London Irish, Cardiff and Old Belvedere. Five times a Leinster player, he was capped on 20 occasions for Ireland between 1948 and 1952, scoring one international try, and captaining the side in his last season. He was a member of the highly thought of Irish back row (with Jim McCarthy and Bill McKay), in the great winning sides of the 1948 Grand Slam, the 1949 Triple Crown, and of the 1951 International Championship winners. He captained the Irish 'Shamrocks' touring side to Argentina and Chile in 1952 which lost only one of its matches. He was manager of the 1966 British and Irish Lion's side that visited Australia and New Zealand under captain Mike Campbell-Lamerton. An all-round sportsman, he also played squash for Ireland (as a member of Fitzwilliam), being capped on 10 occasions between 1952 and 1965, and was beaten in the final of the Irish Open Championship of 1949.

O'BRIEN, DAVID.

Horse trainer. In a career that lasted only 8 years as a trainer, he, in 1984, at the age of only 28, became the youngest ever trainer to win the Epsom Derby, when his Christy Roche-mounted Secreto beat El Gran Senor (trained by his father) in an exciting race. His other great horses include Assert (the first horse to win the Irish and French Derby's in the same season in 1982, also winning the Benson and Hedges Stakes at York), the brilliant filly Triptych (the first of her sex to win the Irish 2,000 Guineas), and Authaal. A son of the famous Vincent O'Brien (cv), he retired from training in October 1988, at the age of only 32.

O'BRIEN, EDDIE.

G.A.A. hurling left full-forward, Cork. He won an All-Ireland Under 21 Championship hurling medal with Cork in 1966. In the 1970 All-Ireland Senior Hurling Championship final he scored 3 goals (the highest individual goal tally in any Liam McCarthy Cup final in the 1970's) in his best game for the county, when Cork beat Wexford. The previous year he had played on the Cork side beaten in the All-Ireland S.H.C. final, while he won a National League medal in 1969-70.

O'BRIEN, EDWARD C M.

Yachtsman. Born in Foynes, Co Limerick, 1865. He is the first Irishman to circumnavigate the globe in his own yacht. He set off in 'Saoirse' at 4.30 pm on the 20th June 1923 from Dun Laoghaire, for New Zealand (on an abortive mountaineering trip), and returned to Dun Laoghaire Harbour exactly 2 years later, at 4.30 pm, June 20th 1925. For this feat he was awarded, 3 years in a row, the Royal Cruising Club's challenge cup. He made other outstanding journeys in later years. He was also a writer of boy's books. He died in Foynes in 1952.

O'BRIEN, JIM.

G.A.A. hurling left full-back, Limerick. He was at left half-back on Limerick's historic, and most recent, All-Ireland Senior Hurling Championship victory in 1973, playing also on the side beaten in the All-Ireland S.H.C. final of the following year. Also winning a National Hurling League medal in 1971 with Limerick, he won his only All-Star award in 1973 at left corner-back.

O'BRIEN, JIMMY.

Handballer. From Tralee, he died in 1992. In a career stretching from 1949 to 1972 he won 15 All-Ireland handball titles. His first success was in the inaugural minor softball singles in 1949. He then went on to win 9 All-Ireland Senior Softball Doubles Championship titles, in 1951 and 1952 with Joe Hassett, and then 7 times with Paddy Downey, in 1955, 1956, and then 5 times in succession with Downey from 1960 to 1965. He also won 4 Senior Hardball Doubles titles, in 1951 with Joe Hassett (cv), and with Paddy Downey 3 times, in 1959, 1960 and 1963, bringing his tally of All-Ireland Doubles titles to 13. His last All-Ireland title came in 1972 All-Ireland Masters Doubles with Downey.

O'BRIEN, KEVIN.

G.A.A. football full-forward, Wicklow. Born in 1965. Club: Baltinglass (being a member of the All-Ireland Club championship winning side of 1990, and which won the Wicklow county championship 5 times in succession from 1987 to 1991, Kevin also winning 2 earlier). A winner of a Railway Cup medal with Leinster and an O'Byrne Cup medal with Wicklow, in 1990 he was a member of the successful Irish Compromise Rules side on their tour of Australia, and he achieved 2 records by being selected in that year as an All-Star footballer in the full-forward position, becoming not only the first Wicklowman to achieve this honour, but also to be the first to gain the honour after being suspended in the season in question.

O'BRIEN, LIAM.

3,000 metres steeplechasing athlete. Born in late 1954. Club: East Cork. A fine competitive athlete, he won the B.L.E. National Championship title at his chosen event, the 3,000 metres steeplechase, no less than ten times up to 1992. He represented Ireland in the 3,000m steeplechase at the 1984 Olympic Games in Los Angeles, finishing 11th in his semi-final.

O'BRIEN, LIAM ('CHUNKY').

G.A.A. hurling midfielder and left half-forward, Kilkenny. Club: James Stephens (with whom he won an All-Ireland Hurling Club Championship winner's medal in 1976). Born in 1950. Making his senior inter-county debut in 1969, he is a winner of 4 All-Ireland Senior Hurling Championship medals with the successful Kilkenny side of the 1970's, being at midfield in the wins of 1972, 1974 and 1975, and at left half-forward in the county's win of 1979 (scoring 1-7 in the final), being voted Man-of-the-Match in the finals of both 1975 and 1979 (he was also on 3 losing All-Ireland S.H.C. final sides with

Kilkenny, in 1969, 1973 and 1978), thus playing in 7 All-Ireland senior finals. His Railway Cup medals for Leinster came in 1973 (as a sub), 1975, and 1977. He has won 4 All-Star awards, three in succession (1973, 1974, and 1975) in the middle of the park, and in 1979 at left half-forward. One of the modern game's best score-getter's, in 1975 he became the 6th Kilkenny player to be named as Texaco's Hurler of the Year.

O'BRIEN, LIAM.

Soccer international midfielder. Born in Dublin, 5th September 1964. Clubs: Shamrock Rovers (winning an F.A.I. Cup medal with then in 1985), Manchester United (playing 36 games for them in all), Newcastle United (helping them to win the Division One title in 1993, thus securing promotion to the new Premiership). He has gained 10 international caps for the Republic of Ireland at various intervals since 1986, the most recent of these being in the 1993 season. His grandfather, Tom Caulfield, won an F.A.I. Cup medal with Shamrock Rovers in 1929.

O'BRIEN, MARTIN D.

Amateur international golfer. Born in Graignamanagh, 14th July 1943. Club: New Ross. He won the Irish Close Championship title twice, in 1968 and 1975, and was runner-up also in 1971. In 46 interprovincial matches for Leinster from 1967 to 1978, he won 24; he played in 44 Home international matches between 1968 and 1977, with a success rate of only 25%; in 5 European team matches for Ireland 1971, he won 3.

O'BRIEN, M T.

Soccer international player. Clubs: Q.P.R., Leicester City, Hull City, Derby County, Walsall, Norwich City, and Watford. A dual international (playing for both associations), he was capped for the I.F.A. (Northern Ireland) 10 times between 1921 and 1927. He also has the unique distinction of playing each of his 4 internationals for the Irish Free State with 4 different clubs. In 1927 he was capped against Italy while at Derby County, in 1929 he played against Belgium while at Walsall, in 1930 while at Norwich City he was again capped against Belgium, and his last cap in 1932 against Holland was while a player at Watford.

O'BRIEN, MICK.

G.A.A. football right full back, Meath. Club: Skreen. He was a member of the Meath team which captured the county's first 2 All-Ireland Senior Football Championship titles, in 1949 and 1954, and also was on the Meath sides beaten in the All-Ireland S.F.C. finals of 1951 and 1952 (thus featuring in 4 finals in 6 years). A fine corner-back, he won a National Football League medal with Meath in 1951, and holds jointly the record number of Railway Cup football medals for a Meathman, winning 4 times in succesion, 1952, 1953, 1954, and 1955.

O'BRIEN, MICHAEL J P.

National Hunt jockey and trainer. Born in Newcastle, 13th March 1943. In 1972 he became the only Irishman to win a jump jockey's championship in the United States. As a result of an accident soon afterwards he had to give up riding and took up training with some success. In 1982 he was the leading jumps trainer in Ireland, and he has had winners in the Mackeson Gold Cup, the Hennessy Gold Cup, and in the Triumph Hurdle at Cheltenham (with Shawiya in 1993). He also has trained the winner of 2 Irish Grand Nationals, in 1982 with King Spruce, and in 1992 with Vanton.

O'BRIEN, NORMA.

Pitch and putt player. Club: Douglas P.P.C. (Cork). In 1991 she became only the third Irish ladies pitch and putt player (after Clare Keating and Teresa McGuigan ccvv), to win the coveted 'double' of Irish Ladies National Strokeplay and Matchplay Championships. She finished runner-up in the 1993 Irish Matchplay title. Her parents, also members of the Douglas club, are fine players, her father Liam being an inter-county player for Cork.

O'BRIEN, PADDY.

G.A.A. footballing centre full-back, Meath. He was a star full-back was on the first Meath side to win an All-Ireland Senior Football Championship title in the historic 1949 win over Cavan. He then became one of 8 of those Meath players to also participate in the county's second All-Ireland S.F.C. title in 1954 (when Kerry were beaten in the final), having also been on the side beaten in the final of 1951 (he won other Leinster S.F.C medals in 1947 and 1952). He won 3 successive Railway Cup medals with Leinster, in 1953, 1954, and in 1955 (as the 3rd Meathman to captain a winning interprovincial side). He also won a National League medal with Meath in the 1950/51 season. A master exponent of the No 3 jersey, he was voted into the full-back berth on the Sunday Independent 'Team of the Century' in 1984.

O'BRIEN, Michael VINCENT (M.V. or 'THE MASTER OF BALLYDOYLE').

Horse trainer, National Hunt and flat racing. Born in Churchwild, Co Cork, 9th April 1917. Starting off in the jump game, he was leading trainer in Britain in 1952-53 and 1953-54. He trained 3 successive winners of the Aintree Grand National, Early Mist in 1953, Royal Tan in 1954, and Quare Times in 1955. His Cottage Rake won the Cheltenham Gold Cup 3 times, 1948, 1949 and 1950 (he also won this race with Knock Hard in 1953), and his total Cheltenham festival tally of 23 winners is only 2 behind the Irish record of Tom Dreaper (cv). His charge Hatton's Grace won the Champion Hurdle 3 times, in 1949, 1950, and 1951. He turned to flat racing in 1953 and has trained: a record number of Irish Derby winners, with six (Chanier in 1953, Ballymoss in 1957, Nijinsky in 1970, The Minstrel in 1977, El Gran Senor in 1984, and Law Society in 1985); and a record number of 8 Irish St Leger winners (with Barclay in 1959, White Gloves in 1966, Reindeer in 1969, Caucasus in 1975, Meneval in 1976, Transworld in 1977, Gonzales in 1980 and Leading Counsel in 1985). He has also won 4 Irish Oaks (Ancasta in 1964, Aurabella in 1965, Gaia in 1969 and Godetia in 1979), 3 Irish 1,000 Guineas (Valoris in 1966, Sarah Siddons in 1976 and Godetia in 1979), and 5 Irish 2,000 Guineas (El Toro in 1959, Jaazeiro in 1978, Dara Monarch in 1982 and Sadler's Wells in 1984), his total tally of Irish Classic wins is a record 25. He has trained a total of 16 English Classic winners (a record for an Irish trainer, and 9th in the all-time list), as follows: 6 Epsom Derby winners (Larkspur in 1962, Sir Ivor 1968, Nijinsky in 1970, Roberto in 1972, The Minstrel in 1977, and Golden Fleece in 1982); four 2,000 Guineas winners (Sir Ivor in 1968, Nijinsky in 1970, Lomond in 1983 and El Gran Senor in 1984); One 1,000 Guineas winner, Glad Rags in 1966; 2 Epsom Oaks winners (Petit Etoile in 1959, and Valoris in 1966); and 3 Doncaster St Leger's winners (including Nijinsky in 1970 and Boucher in 1972). Nijinsky was the first horse since 1935 to win the Grand Slam (English 2,000 Guineas, Derby and St Leger). Alleged, another great horse, won the Prix de l'Arc de Triomphe twice, in 1977 and 1978 (a race he also won with Ballymoss in 1958). He also trained the winners of 3 King George VI and Queen Elizabeth Stakes, a Washington International, and many other major races. He was top flat trainer in Britain in 1966. He is the father of David O'Brien (cv). He has gained 5 selections Texaco's Horse Racing Sportstar of the Year, spanning 19 years, winning in 1958, 1966, 1968, 1970, and again in 1977. He recieved an Hon L.L.D. in 1983.

O'BRIEN, RAY.

Soccer international defender. Born in Dublin 21st May 1951. He left Shelbourne to join Manchester United at the age of 22, but did not get a league game with them so joined Notts County in 1974, playing 279 league matches for them up to 1980. He was capped 4 times for the Republic of Ireland in 1976 and 1977.

O'BRIEN, ROBIN.

Cricket international right hand batsman and off break bowler. Born in Shillong, Assam, India, 20th November 1932, he died aged 36 in 1959. He played 35 first class matches for Cambridge between 1954 and 1956, gaining Blues in 1955 and 1956 (scoring his best first class score of 146 against Oxford in at Lord's). He was also a Cambridge Blue at golf. He played 4 first class matches for Ireland (and 9 times in all) between 1954 and 1958, and played once for the M.C.C..

O'BRIEN, STEPHEN.

G.A.A. football full-back and half-back, Cork. Club: Nemo Rangers. A half-back on the Cork minors beaten in the All-Ireland M.F.C. final of 1987, he was a member of the Cork Senior Football Championship side which captured the All-Ireland title in 1990. He was selected in the full-back berth on the All-Stars team of 1990. Winning another Munster S.F.C. medal in 1993, Cork lost to Derry in the All-Ireland Final.

O'BRIEN, SIR TIMOTHY C(arew) (TIM).

Cricket international. Born in Dublin, 5th November 1861, he died in 1948. A Oxford Blue, he played first class cricket for Middlesex from 1881 to 1898, and for Ireland between 1902 to 1907, captaining his country in it's first ever first class match, versus the London Counties in May 1902. In his 3rd innings for Ireland, he scored his country's first ever first class century (a 167, still an Irish 1st class record). He was also played in 8 innings in 5 Tests for England at cricket (scoring a total of only 59 runs), touring Australia (in 1887) and South Africa (1895) with them. His total first class career runs from 1881 to 1914 was 11,397 (averaging 27.01, including 15 centuries). He scored at least 1,000 first class runs in 3 different seasons. His brother John G O'Brien played once for Ireland at cricket in 1910, and also played first class cricket for Herefordshire.

O'CALLAGHAN, Captain C.L. ('C.L.')

Croquet international player. Lived 1875-1942. One of 3 Irish croquet players who dominated British game in the early 20th century, he won 11 British Open titles between 1905 and 1921, 5 of these being at mixed doubles (1909, 1910, 1912, 1914 and 1921), and 3 in the Open singles (in 1910, 1912 and 1921). He also won the Champions Cup (now the President's Cup) 3 times between 1909 and 1920, won the Gold Medal 4 times, and the Gold Cup at Devonshire 5 times, retiring at the age of 42 in 1922, to take up golf. He introduced the 'Irish Grip' to the game, in which the feet are held close together with the fingers of the two hands pointing to the ground, while the mallet swings between the two legs. Also a gifted horseman, he was made Master of the Fingal Harriers in 1904, and won many point-to-point races on his own horses.

O'CALLAGHAN, KEVIN.

Soccer international forward. Born in London, 19th October 1961. He was apprenticed to Millwall at the age of 17, playing 15 league matches with them before joining Ipswich Town in 1979. His other clubs have included Portsmouth, Millwall and Southend. He was capped at international level 20 times for the Republic of Ireland between 1981 and 1987, 10 of these as a substitute.

O'CALLAGHAN, Doctor PAT ('The DOC').

Hammer throwing international athlete. Born in Duhallow, Kanturk, Co Cork on 15th September 1905. First capped for Ireland in athletics in 1921; he won six Irish athletic titles in 1931, in the hammer (which he won another 4 times), 56lb weight distance, 56lb weight over bar, high jump, shot putt, and discus. In Amsterdam in 1928, only

13 months after first taking up the hammer event, he won an Olympic gold medal (the first sportsperson representing the Republic of Ireland to do so), coming from behind to throw 168'7", (he had thrown 171'8" in Kanturk a few weeks before). Four years later, in Los Angeles in 1932, again behind in the Olympic hammer throw final, he threw 176' 11" on his last throw to become the only Irishman, representing Ireland, to win 2 Olympic gold medals, and at 26 years and 186 days old, to become Ireland's oldest gold medal winner (he was not allowed to compete in the 1936 games because he was a member of the N.A.C.A.I.). Having won the A.A.U. title in 1933, he won his only British A.A.A. title in 1934, throwing 168' 6". In 1937, in Fermoy, Co Cork, despite the fact that the hammer was 6 ozs overweight, and that the circle was 6 inches too small, he threw an astonishing 195' 5", breaking the 24-year-old world record of Irish-born Patrick Ryan (cv), by over 6 feet (the record was not ratified by the I.A.A.F. as it did not recognise the N.A.C.A.I.). His best high jump was 1.88 metres, while his best shot putt was 14.75 metres. He was the first person, in 1960, to be placed into the Texaco Hall of Fame. His younger brother Con performed in the decathlon in the 1928 Olympic Games for Ireland, and won the decathlon at the Third Tailteann Games in 1932 with 6317 points. Pat died in 1991 aged 84.

O'CALLAGHAN, PHILIP ('PHILO').

Rugby international prop-forward. Born in Cork, 25th March 1946. Club: Dolphin. A product of Greymouth P.B.S., he was capped 21 times for Ireland (9 games were lost) over a 10 year period between 1967 and 1976, although he was not picked from 1971 through 1975. Playing also for Munster (helping to embelish a fine tradition against touring sides) and the Barbarians, he toured 3 times with Irish parties, to Australia in 1967, to Argentina in 1970 (being sent off in the fiery first Test), and to New Zealand and Fiji in 1976.

O'CALLAGHAN, REBECCA (nee BEST).

Squash interntaional player. Born in Lancashire to Irish parents on 18th January 1964. A professional player, she has won 6 Irish Women's Squash Championship titles in succession, in 1987, 1988, 1989, 1990, 1991 and 1992, and reached a world ranking into the top dozen, getting as high as No 8 in 1989 (being at No 14 in mid-1993). In 1988 she twice beat the then World No 2, Lisa Opie, and in 1989 beat both the World's No 4 and No 5 ranked players. Up to August 1993 she had represented Ireland 108 times since being first capped in 1981, the same number of times as Marjorie Croke (cv). In 1988 she was voted Texaco Squash Sportstar of the Year, the first Squash person to win this title.

O'COLMAIN, GEAROID (GERRY).

Amateur light heavy and heavyweight boxer. Clubs: Myra (Francis St), C.D.T.C., North City. Born in Dublin in 1924. In 1941 he won a national juvenile heavyweight and also a national junior light-heavyweight title. He went on win a then record 9 Irish National Senior Championships (being the first to achieve this feat), later equalled by Harry Perry (cv), and only surpassed by Jim O'Sullivan (cv) in 1990. He won his titles at two different weights and in the space of only 10 years: his 2 wins at light-heavyweight came in 1943 and 1944, and his 7 wins at heavyweight came in succession, 1946, 1947, 1948, 1949, 1950, 1951, and 1952. He won a heavyweight gold medal at the European Championships which were held in Dublin in 1947, and represented Ireland at the 1948 Olympic Games in London. In 1980 he became the first amateur boxer to be elevated into the Texaco Hall of Fame.

O'CONNELL, ANTHONY (TONY).

Soccer international forward. Clubs: Shamrock Rovers (winning F.A.I. Cup winner's medals in 1962, 1965, and in 1966 when he scored one of the goals in the final), Dundalk (winning a League of Ireland Championship winner's medal in 1967), and Bohemians (winning his 4th F.A.I. Cup winner's medal in 1970). He was capped twice for the Republic of Ireland, against Spain in 1969, and as a sub against Poland in 1970.

O'CONNELL, CARLOS.

International athlete, long-jumper and decathlete. Born in 1964. Club: Crusaders. A product of a scholarship at Mount St Mary's of Maryland, he represented Ireland in the decathlon in the European Championships of 1986 and the Olympic Games in Seoul in 1988. Winning a number of National B.L.E. titles, in 1990 he broke the longest held national record in world athletics, when he broke the 89 year long jump record of Peter O'Connor (cv) of 24'11", to become the first Irishman to break 25 feet in the event, with a mark of 7.63 metres.

O'CONNELL, EOIN.

Amateur international and professional golfer. Club: Killarney. From Ballydesmond on Cork-Kerry border, he was born in Cork 27th March 1968. He won the Irish boy's title in 1984, when he also helped the Irish Youths to win the European Championship in Hermitage. A Wake Forest University of North Carolina communications scholarship graduate, he was leading qualifier at the North Berwick course for the 1987 British Open, breaking the course record (and also was leading qualifier in the U.S. Amateur championship in the same year). His 6 wins out of 6 matches was the highlight of Ireland's fine win in the 1987 European Team Championships, and he went on to win 4 out of 6 matches in the 1989 event (he was a member of the winning Irish quadrangular side in 1988). He was leading amateur of both the 1988 and 1990 Carroll's Irish Open. He was a member of the GB&I team which first captured the Eisenhower Trophy in 1988. In 1989, when finishing 2nd in the prestigious North and South Championship and being leading stroke player in the U.S. Amateur Championship, he also became the first Killarney clubman (and 19th Irishman) to be selected for the Walker Cup side, and was one of the stars in the historic win, being unbeaten in his 4 matches (winning 2 and halving 2, making him, along with Roddy Carr cv, one of only two Irishmen to remain unbeaten at Walker Cup level), when the British and Irish team won the Cup for the first time on U.S. spoil in the 67 years since it's inception. After reaching a handicap of plus 3, he turned pro in mid-1990, with little initial progress.

O'CONNELL, JACKIE.

G.A.A. hurling right full-forward, Limerick. From Banogue. A fine player who won only one All-Ireland Senior Hurling Championship medal, with the Limerick team in 1934, he was also on the side beaten in the All-Ireland S.H.C. final of 1935. Later he was to be Limerick county secretary for 27 years, then county chairman, and was later ensconced in the post of President of the Limerick County Board.

O'CONNELL, MARTIN.

G.A.A. football right half-back, Meath. Born in 1963. Club: St Michael's (helping them to win the Meath intermediate county championship in 1990). Playing senior inter-county football first in the 1982-83 season, he played at left wing-half in the Meath All-Ireland Senior Championship victory over Cork in 1987, and at right half-forward in the 1988 win over the same opposition, being regarded as man-of-the-match. He was on the Meath teams beaten in the All-Ireland S.F.C. finals of both 1990 and 1991, and also won 2 National League medals with the Royal County, in 1986 and 1990, and has won 2 Railway Cup medals. Regarded as one of the best wing-backs of the modern era, he has won 3 All-Star awards, in 1988 and 1990 at right half-back, and in 1991 at left half-back. His brother Robert was goalkeeper on the winning Meath side in the 1990 All-Ireland J.F.C..

O'CONNELL, MICK ('MICKO').

G.A.A. football midfielder, Kerry. Born on Beginish Island in Valentia Harbour, Co Kerry, 4th January 1937. Clubs: Valentia Young Islanders (being the first member of this club to win an All-Ireland S.F.C. medal, and helping them to win 7 South Kerry Senior championships), and (briefly) Waterville. He first played for Kerry minors in 1955, and for the seniors in 1956. Playing in a total of 9 All-Ireland Senior Football Championship finals (ten if the replay of 1972 is included), he won 4 All-Ireland Sam Maguire Cup medals with Kerry: as a 22-year-old captain in the 1959 win over Galway by 3-7 to 1-4, in the 1962 win over Roscommon, and in the 2 successive wins of 1969 (over Offaly) and 1970 (over Meath). He played in 5 other teams from the Kingdom beaten in the All-Ireland S.F.C. final, in 1960 (losing to Down), 1964 and 1965 (both to Galway's 3-in-a-row side), 1968 (to Down again), and in the replay loss against Offaly in 1972. He won 6 National Football League winner's medals with Kerry, in 1959 (beating Derry in the final), 1961 (his own personal choice as his finest hour and the best game he has ever played in, the 4-16 to 1-5 final win over Derry), 1963 (against Down), 1969 (over Offaly), and the 2 wins over Mayo in the finals of 1971 and 1972. His solitary Railway Cup medal came at the age of 35 in the 1972 final against Leinster, Munster's first win in 23 years. In 1962 he was named as Kerry's 2nd player to win the Texaco Footballer of the Year. He won his only All-Star award, at midfield, in the inaugural year of 1972. One of the games truly great players, and arguabably the finest fielder of a ball the game has known, he would be many experts choice as the complete midfielder. He won a place in the Sunday Independent's 'Team of the Century' in 1984, in the midfield alongside fellow countyman Jack O'Shea (cv). He wrote an autobiographical book, 'A Kerry Footballer', published in 1974.

O'CONNELL, SEAN.

G.A.A. football left full-forward and full-forward, Derry. He won three Ulster Senior Football Championship medals, in 1970 (the county's first win since 1958), and again in 1975 and 1976. In 1971 he became the only Derryman to date to captain a winning Ulster Railway Cup team. Regarded as one of the greatest players never to win an All-Ireland Senior Football Championship medal (he was selected in the 'Team of the Century' in 1984 at right half-forward, for those who are in that category), he is the only Derryman to win 4 Railway Cup medals, also collecting in 1966 (as a sub), 1968, and 1970.

O'CONNOR, ARNOLD.

Amateur international and professional golfer. Club: Nass. He was runner-up in the 'West' in 1967. For his province, Connacht, he is the only player to play in over 40 interprovincial matches to have a better than 50% match result average, winning 24 and halving 5 of his 42 matches between 1964 and 1972, with a success rate of 63%. He played in 24 Home international matches for Ireland between 1967 and 1972 (and was a member of the Irish side which won the Quadrangular Continental match in 1972), winning 13 matches in all. Later as a professional he won the Irish Matchplay Championship in 1978 at Ballybunion.

O'CONNOR, ANN.

Breast-stroke and free-style swimmer. She represented Ireland at 2 Olympic Games, in 1968 in Mexico in both the 100m and 200m breaststroke, and in the 1972 Games in Munich in four events, the 100m and 200m breaststroke, the 4x100m freestyle relay, and in the 4x100m relay (in which the Irish team broke the national record, and finished in 14th place). A prolific winner of Irish titles at both breaststroke and the free-style, in 1969 she was selected as Texaco's Swimming Sportstar of the Year.

O'CONNOR, CHRISTY ('SENIOR', 'THE MAESTRO' or 'HIMSELF').

Professional golfer. Born in Co Galway, 24th December 1924. His 'attached' clubs include Bundoran and (from 1959) Royal Dublin. He has won the Irish Professional title 10 times (1958, 1960, 1961, 1962, 1963, 1965, 1966, 1971, 1975, and 1977), and the Irish Dunlop 4 times (1962, 1965, 1966, and 1967). Arguably Ireland's finest ever professional golfer, he won the Harry Vardon Trophy for leading the British Isles Order of Merit in both 1961 and 1962, and finished 2nd in the Order of Merit 5 times, in 1964, 1965, 1966, 1969, and 1970. He won the Carroll's International 4 times (1964, 1966, 1967, and 1972). Among his many other titles are 2 Dunlop Masters (1956 and 1959), the Martini twice (1963 and 1964), the P.G.A. Matchplay in 1957, and tieing for the 1968 Alcan International. Competing 26 times in the British Open Championship, he has had many near finishes, ending in a tie for 2nd to Peter Thompson in 1965, and twice in a tie for third (in 1958 and in 1961). He holds the record of 10 successive Ryder Cup appearences, achieved in 1955, 1957 (GB & Ireland's last win, at Lindrick), 1959, 1961, 1963, 1965, 1967, 1969, 1971 and 1973 (just short of his 50th bithday), during which he played in 36 matches (2nd only to Neil Coles in this tally), winning 11 and halving 4 (with success rate of 36.11%). In 1955, by winning the Swallow-Penfold Tournament at Southport and Ainsdale, he became the first home player to win a 4-figure sum. In September 1970 he won the first ever 5-figure cheque in European golf, a prize of £25,000 in the John Player Classic. He won the World Senior's title in 1976 and 1977, and has won the British Senior's P.G.A. title 6 times, 1976, 1977, 1979, 1981, 1982 and 1983. He played for Ireland 15 times from 1956 to 1975 in the Canada/World Cup, and was on the winning side with Harry Bradshaw in 1958 in Mexico; he played in the Double Diamond for Ireland in 7 successive years 1971-77. A brilliant wind player, he had no equal when using a driver off the fairway, and but for a wristy, unpredictable putting stroke, he could have been an even better player. He was selected as Texaco's Golf Sportstar of the Year 5 times (more than any other golfer), in 1959, 1961, 1966, 1970 (when he was also selected as Supreme Sportstar), and 1977, and in 1991 he joined the Texaco Hall of Fame. His sons Peter and Christy became teaching professionals.

O'CONNOR, CHRISTY (JUNIOR).

Professional golfer. Born in Galway, 19th August 1948. Turning pro in 1965, in 1974 he won his first major professional title, the Zambian Open. He won the inaugural Carroll's Irish Open Championship title in 1975 at Woodbrook, with a four round total of 275. In the same season he also won both the Martini International and the Irish Matchplay (winning this again the following year). This ensured him Ryder Cup honours in 1975 (losing both his matches). He won the Sumrie tournament in 1976 and 1978, the Jersey Open in 1979 and the Kenyan Open in 1990. He represented Ireland in the World Cup in 1974, 1975, 1978 and in 1985 (finishing 2nd in the individual title). His then record 64 in the first round of the 1985 British Open at St Georges led him on to finishing in joint 3rd place. Narrowly missing Ryder Cup selection in 1985, he was picked again in 1989 at the age of 40, 14 years after his only other outing, and won his only match, a singles against Fred Couples, with a magical 2 iron shot to the last green. His best Order of Merit placings have been 7th in 1975, 12th in 1985, and 21st in both 1987 and 1989. In 1992 he won the British Masters title (winning £100,000, becoming the first Irishman to win a 6-figure cheque on the European tour), and was the first Irishman to qualify for the World Championship in Jamaica. A nephew of the great Christy O'Connor, he was selected as Texaco's Golf Sportstar of the Year in both 1975 and 1992.

O'CONNOR, DEE.

G.A.A. footballer full-back, Kerry. He was an ever-present member of the full-back line in the Kerry team which achieved the county's first ever 4-in-a-row in the All-Ireland Senior Football Championship, in the 1929 final win over Kildare, the 1930 success over Monaghan, in 1931 when Kildare were the beaten finalists, and finally in 1932 when Mayo lost to them. He won one Railway Cup medal with Munster in their 1931 win.

O'CONNOR, EDDIE and WILLIE.

G.A.A. hurling brothers, Kilkenny. Club: Glenmore (both being on the side which won the All-Ireland Club Championship 1991, also helping the club to it's only 2 other Kilkenny championship wins in 1987 and 1992). Eddie, a right corner-back and half-back, was born in Waterford on 2nd October 1964. Debuting at senior inter-county level in 1990, he had been a sub on the Kilkenny side beaten in the Leinster M.H.C. final in 1982, and went on to win an All-Ireland Under 21 H.C. medal in 1984 at full-back (being on the losing final side in 1985). He was a member of the Kilkenny S.H.C. side which were beaten in the All-Ireland final of 1991, and won a Liam McCarthy Cup medal in 1992. He was then the Kilkenny captain when the side won the All-Ireland S.H.C. final in 1993, beating Galway by 2-17 to 1-15. His younger brother Willie, a left half-back, was also on the 2 sides which captured the All-Ireland Senior Hurling Championship in both 1992 and 1993, and also shared in the Glenmore club successes. Willie won an All-Star award in 1992 in the left half-back slot.

O'CONNOR, EDDIE.

Hockey international goalkeeper. Clubs: Limerick's Catholic Institute and Munster. Although he was capped only 9 times for Ireland as an international hockey goalkeeper, he made a vital save when Ireland beat England to win the country's most recent Triple Crown in 1949. Winning his last hockey cap in 1950, he had also been a fine rugby player, playing inter-provincial rugby for Munster, and winning 3 Munster senior Cup medals with Cork Constitution, in 1942 (as captain), 1943 and 1946. He died in 1991.

O'CONNOR, GEORGE.

G.A.A. hurling midfielder, Wexford. From Piercestown, St Martin's. Making his senior inter-county debut in 1979 (winning an Oireachtas medal that year), he was a member of the Wexford side which reached (without success) 4 Leinster Senior Hurling Championship finals (losing on the first 3 occasions to Offaly), in 1981, 1984, 1988 and 1993. He was also a member of 5 Wexford sides beaten in National Hurling Leage finals, in 1982, 1984, 1990, 1991 and in the twice-replayed final loss to Cork in 1993. He has won 2 All-Star awards, in 1981 at centrefield, and 7 years later, in 1988, also at midfield. Also a handy footballer, in 1979 he played for 11 different teams at the same time, including senior football (with whom he reached 2 Leinster S.F.C. semi-finals). His brother John also played alongside George many times in inter-county hurling for Wexford.

O'CONNOR, JACK, PETER, and TOM.

G.A.A. footballing brothers, Wexford. When they played on the successful Young Ireland side of Wexford which defeated Cork's Drumtariffe selection by

1-1 to 0-1 in the 1893 All-Ireland Senior Football Championship final (which was in fact unfinished), they became the first set of 3 brothers to play on the winning team in a senior All-Ireland final.

O'CONNOR, JACK and JOSEPH J (JOE).

Rugby international brothers. Both men played for Garryowen. Both were capped only once each, Jack on the wing in 1895, and Joe in 1910, also as a winger. It is for their feats in Munster Senior Cup rugby that they are most famous. Jack has won a record 11 winner's medals in that competition with Garryowen, in 1891, 1892, 1893, 1894, 1895 (as captain), 1896, 1898, 1899, 1902, 1903 and 1904, while his son Mick won four. Joe won 3 medals, in 1908, 1909 and 1914. The O'Connor family has won over 50 Munster Senior Cup medals, the other brothers to contribute to this handsome total being Mick, Charlie, Thade, Bryan and Jim.

O'CONOR, JOHN Hamilton.

Rugby international forward. Born in Letterkenny in 1866, he died in 1953. Club: Bective Rangers (helping them to win their first Leinster Senior Cup in 1889, and winning a 2nd medal in 1892). Thirteen times a Leinster international player between 1887 and 1895, he won 17 caps for Ireland between 1888 and 1896, and was a valuable member of the 1894 Triple Crown-winning side, and the International Championship-winning side of 1896. An outstanding forward, he was President of the I.R.F.U. in 1911-1912.

O'CONNOR , JOSEPH.

Rugby international wing-threequarter. Born in Castleisland, Co Kerry, 27th October 1911. Club: U.C.C. (with whom he won a Munster Senior Cup medal in 1936, also winning the Bateman Cup that season). He was capped 11 times for Ireland between 1933 and 1938, scoring 3 international tries, and he helped Ireland to win the International Championship in 1935.

O'CONNOR, PETER J.

Long-jump, high junp and triple jump athlete. Born on 18th October 1874 in Ashtown, Co Wicklow, he died in 1957 in Co Waterford. He won the British A.A.A. long jump title 6 years in succession, 1901, 1902, 1903, 1904, 1905 and 1906, and won the high jump title twice, 1903 and 1904. Having entered (but not competed in) the 1900 Olympic Games in Paris, he broke the world record (the first I.A.A.F. record in the long jump) a month after those Games. He then broke the world record 4 more times before, in Ballsbridge in Dublin on 5th August 1901, extending it finally to 24' 11", or 7.61 metres (this was ratified as the first ever official I.A.A.F. world record). This world record was not beaten for 20 years, when Ed Gourdin of U.S.A. cleared 7.69 metres, and remained the Irish All-Comers record for 67 years (indeed the first Briton to beat it was Lynn Davies 61 years later), finally been surpassed as an Irish record in 1990, 89 years after it was set. At the age of 34 and well past his prime form, he won a gold medal in the Triple Jump in the 1906 unofficial Olympic Games at Athens, clearing 46' 2" on his final attempt to beat the fellow Irishman Con Leahy (cv). Afterwards, during the medal ceremony, he tore down the Union Jack, and replaced it with the Irish flag, therefore denouncing that he represented Great Britain. He also won a silver medal in the 1906 long jump event, finishing 7 inches behind the winning jump of 23'7" of Meyer Prinstein of U.S.A., and also competed in the high jump in those Athens Games. Retiring after the 1906 games, he was later to be a judge at the 1936 Olympic Games in Berlin.

O'CONNOR, STEPHEN.

Snooker player, amateur and professional. Born in October 1972. Club: Hall of Billiard's, Bachelor's Walk. In 1990 he won, along with the Cork, Galway, and Munster Opens, the Irish Championship and the All-Ireland

Championship. Then in November 1990 he became only the 2nd player ever to win the World Amateur Snooker Championship on his first attempt, being also the youngest ever (being days younger at time of victory than the previous youngest, Jimmy White), and the 2nd Irishman in successive years to win the peak of attainment at amateur level, when in Colombo, he defeated the Belgian Steve Lemmons 11-8 in the final. He was selected as the Texaco Sportstar of the Year for Snooker in 1990, and turned professional, with little initial success.

O'CONNOR, T ('GEGA').

G.A.A. footballing half-forward, Kerry. He won 5 All-Ireland Senior Football Championship winner's medals with the Kingdom, in 1937, 1939 (when he captained the side which defeated Meath by 2-5 to 2-3 in the red jerseys of the county champions Dingle, the Kingdom's 13th success), 1940, 1941 (when the county completed 3-in-a-row), and again in 1946, over a span of 10 years. He was on 2 losing All-Ireland S.F.C. final sides, in 1938 and in the Polo Ground game of 1947. He won 2 Railway Cup medals with Munster, in 1941 and 1949. It is said that "he once pointed a kick-out".

O'CONNOR, TADGH.

G.A.A. hurling wing-back and left full-back, Tipperary. He won an All-Ireland Under 21 medal with Tipperary in their win of 1967. He was at right half-back when captaining the Tipperary side which won the Liam McCarthy Cup in 1971 (the first live colour t.v. final transmitted), when Kilkenny were beaten by 5-17 to 5-14. He was a star member of the Tipperary sides which also won 2 Munster S.H.C. titles in 1976 and 1980. He won 3 Railway Cup medals with Munster, in 1976, 1978, and 1981, and won 2 All-Star awards, at right half back in 1975, and at left corner back in 1979.

O'CONNOR, TURLOUGH.

Soccer international forward and manager. Born in Athlone, 22nd July, 1946. Clubs: Limerick, Athlone Town, Bohemians, Fulham (playing only one 1st team game), Dundalk, Bohemians (winning 2 League of Ireland Championship winner's medals in 1974-75 and in 1977-78, and an F.A.I. Cup medal in 1976), and Athlone Town (where as player-manager he helped them to 2 League of Ireland Championships, in 1980-81 and in 1982-83). His 178 League of Ireland goals in the periods 1964-66 and 1968-85, place him 2nd only to Brendan Bradley in the list of all-time top scorers in the League of Ireland, being the League's season's top goalscorer in 1973-74 (with 18 goals) and 1977-78 (with a Gypsies club seasonal record of 24 goals). A total of 120 of these goals were scored for Bohemians (a club record). As a manager from 1979 the honours have still piled up; he has been in charge of a total of 4 League of Ireland Championship winning sides (Athlone in 1981 and 1983, and Dundalk in 1988 and 1991), 5 League Cups and one F.A.I. Cup (Dundalk in 1988, being runners-up in 1993). Scorer of one Inter-League goal for the League of Ireland, he was capped at youth, amateur and 7 times at senior level for the Republic of Ireland between 1968 and 1973, four of these as a substitute, scoring 2 international goals, including the winning goal in his first cap. His father Turlough played to international level at basketball and amateur junior soccer in the 1930's. His brother Pauric, an amateur international, won a League of Ireland medal (1974-75) and a F.A.I. medal (in 1976) with Bohemians, later becoming their player-manager. Another brother, Michael (born in Athlone, 8th October 1960), an under 21 international, was leading goalscorer in the League of Ireland for 2 seasons with Athlone Town

(1981-82 with 22 goals, and in 1984-85 with 17 goals), winning Championship medals alongside his 2 brothers in 1980-81 and 1982-83. All 3 brothers managed Athlone Town at some stage in their career, a rare family feat.

O'CONNOR, UNA.

G.A.A. camogie forward, Dublin. Club: Celtic (whom she helped to win an All-Ireland Club Championship title in 1964). After Kathleen Mills' 15 titles, she is in 2nd place on the 'most medals won' list for All-Ireland Senior Camogie Championship winning medals, which she won in a 3-in-a-row stretch from 1953 (her debut year for the county) to 1955, and on the all-conquering Dublin side which won 10 successive All-Ireland S.C.C. titles in 1957, 1958, 1959, 1960, 1961, 1962, 1963, 1964, 1965 and 1966, therby amassing 13 winner's medals. She also won 13 consecutive Leinster camogie championship medals. A most elusive forward, and a prolific scorer for both county and club, she is regarded as one of the giants of the sport; in 1966 she was selected as Texaco's Camogie Sportstar of the Year, the first to be so honoured since the inception of the Texaco awards in 1958. She won a Cuchulainn Award in 1963, and also won 9 Gael-Linn interprovincial medals.

O'DEA, DONNCHA.

International swimmer. Club: St Colmcille S.C.. A son of actress Siobhan McKenna and singer Denis O'Dea, he dominated Irish men's swinmming in the 1960's. Altogether he won the astonishing tally of almost 100 Irish swimming titles in both free-style and backstroke, starting from 1963, when he won Irish championships at 400, 800 and 1,500 metres. In 1965 in the Grove Baths in Belfast he broke the famous barrier when he became the first Irishman to swim the 100 metres in less than 1 minute. He also won the Dun Laoghaire Swim twice, and swam a record time in the famous Liffey Swim. He represented Ireland in the Olympic Games in 1968 in Mexico. He was selected Texaco's Swimming Sportstar of the Year in both 1964 and 1965, being the first swimmer to be selected twice. He later became a noted jet-setting poker player, participating in world championships.

O'DOHERTY, MARIAN.

G.A.A. ladies gaelic football half-back, Kerry. Club: Castleisland. She won All-Ireland minor medals in 1979 and 1980, and first played for Kerry seniors in 1979. She is the only Kerry player to play in all of the championship games which brought the Kingdom 9 All-Ireland Senior titles in succession, the wins being in 1981, 1982 (as captain), 1983, 1984, 1985, 1986, 1987, 1988, 1989 and 1990. A winner of 2 All-Stars and 10 National League medals, she was also a handballer of note as a youngster, winning 15 All-Ireland titles in both singles and doubles.

O'DOHERTY, MARTIN.

G.A.A. hurling full-back, Cork. Club: Glen Rovers (with whom he won 2 All-Ireland Club Championship medals, in 1973, and as captain in 1977). As a half-back he won 2 All-Ireland Under 21 Championship medals with the 'Rebel County', in 1971 and in 1973 as captain (having previously won an All-Ireland medal with the Cork M.F.C. side in 1969). He went on to win 3 successive All-Ireland Senior Hurling Championship medals in 1976, 1977 (as captain while playing a 'stormer' in Cork's 1-17 to 3-8 final win over Wexford) and 1978 (in a display thought to be one of the best ever by a full-back). He also won Munster S.H.C. medals in 1975, 1979, and in 1982 (when they were beaten All-Ireland finalists). He won his solitary Railway Cup medal in 1978 with Munster, as captain of the side. He won 3 successive All-Star awards, in 1977,

1978 and 1979, each in the full-back position.

O'DONNELL, Mrs B.L. (MAIRE).

Ladies international amateur golfer. Club: Donegal. She won the Connacht Ladies title twice, including 1976 and was runner-up in 1975 and 1978. She was a constant player on the Connacht interprovincial team from 1964 up to 1980. She played in the Home international series for Ireland once, in 1974. It is as a captain that she excelled, being captain of the Irish Home international side in 1977, 1978, 1979 and 1980 (when Ireland won the series outright for the first time), and leading the side which captured the European Ladies Team Championship for the first time in Hermitage in 1979. She went on to act as non-playing captain to the 1982 Curtis Cup side and the 1981 Vagliano Trophy team.

O'DONNELL, NICK.

G.A.A. hurling full-back, Wexford. Born on 3rd September 1925. Club: St Aidan's (winning 7 county championship medals). He won an All-Ireland junior medal with Kilkenny in 1946, and was a sub for the 'Cats' in their 1947 All-Ireland S.H.C. win. Switching allegiance to Wexford, he went on to be one of only 6 Wexfordmen to win 3 All-Ireland Senior Hurling Championship winner's medals, gaining them in 1955 (when he captained the side to its first success for 45 years, by defeating Galway by 3-13 to 2-8), 1956 (the famous 'Art Foley save' final), and 1960 (again captaining the side, playing a fine game on the day after his 35th birthday, this time to a 2-15 to 0-11 success over Tipperary). He was also on 3 losing Wexford All-Ireland S.H.C. final teams, in 1951, 1954, and in 1962. In an inter-county career that lasted 16 years from 1947 to 1962, he won 4 Oireachtas medals, and 2 National Hurling League medals in 1956 and 1958. He won one Railway Cup medal with Leinster, as captain in 1956. In 1960 he became the first Wexfordman to be named as Texaco Hurler of the Year. He was selected for the full-back berth of the Sunday Independent's 'Team of the Centyry' in 1984, with fellow countyman Bobby Rackard and Tipperary's John Doyle on his flanks. He died in 1988.

O'DONNELL, RODNEY Christopher.

Rugby international full-back. Born in Dublin, 16th August 1956. Club: St Mary's. An outstanding school and club player with St Mary's College, he was capped for Ireland 5 times (4 times on winning sides) between 1979 and 1980 before a horrendous neck injury incurred on the British and Irish Lion's tour of South Africa (during which he played in a Test match), cut short a very promising international career at full-back.

O'DONNELL, WILLIE.

G.A.A. hurling forward, Tipperary. He won his only All-Ireland Senior Hurling Championship medal in the 1937 Tipperary side which beat Kilkenny. In 1942 he became the 3rd Tipperaryman to captain Munster to victory in the Railway Cup, also winning medals in 1938, 1940 and 1943.

O'DONOGHUE, LIAM.

G.A.A. hurling forward and right half-back, Limerick. Club: Mungret. A member of the Limerick team which won the Munster Senior Hurling Championship in 1973, 1974, 1980 and 1981, he was at centre half-forward on the famous Limerick side which recaptured the Liam McCarthy Cup after many years in 1973, and played at right full-forward on the side beaten in the All-Ireland S.H.C. final of 1974, being on the losing side again in 1980. He won 3 Railway Cup medals with Munster, in 1976, 1981 and 1984. A versatile player at home in defence and attack, he is one of the modern game's better hurling all-rounders, winning one All-Star award, in 1981, at right wing-back.

O'DONOGHUE, PATRICK Joseph (PADDY).

Rugby international prop-forward. Born in Dun Laoghaire, 22nd November 1931. Club: Bective Rangers (whom he captained, and with whom he won Leinster Senior Cup winner's medals in 1955 and 1956). A product of C.B.C. Monkstown, he captained Leinster on 7 of the 8 times he played for the province, and also played for the Barbarians. He was capped 11 times for Ireland between 1955 and 1958, being a member of the first Irish side to beat a touring side (Australia in 1958). He was Irish Regional Director for the World Cup in rugby for 1991, and in 1992 was appointed the I.R.F.U.'s secretary/treasurer. A single figure golfer, he also coached his former school and club.

O'DONOUGHUE, PAUDIE.

G.A.A. football full-back, Kerry. Club: Ballydonoghue. He was a member of the Kerry side which won the inaugural All-Ireland Under 21 Championship in 1964, having 2 years earlier won an All-Ireland M.F.C. winner's medal with the 'Kingdom'. Playing as a centre half-back on the Kerry side beaten in the All-Ireland S.F.C. final of 1965, he was a star full-back on the side beaten in the final of 1968, and he then won 2 All-Ireland Senior Football Championship winner's medals with Kerry in 1969 and 1970. In 1972 he was again on a Kerry side beaten in an All-Ireland final, this time in a replay to Offaly. His relation Eamonn O'Donoughue, also a Ballydonoghue clubman, also won All-Ireland medals at left half-forward in the wins of 1969 and 1970, and also played in the losing S.F.C. finals of 1968 and 1972.

O'DONOVAN, AMBROSE ('ROSIE').

G.A.A. football midfielder, Kerry. Club: Gneeveguilla. Born in 1961. He won an All-Ireland Vocational Schools medal in 1977 with Kerry, and an All-Ireland M.F.C. medal in 1980. He captained the Kerry side to win the All-Ireland Senior Football Championship in 1984, when they beat Dublin by 0-14 to 1-6. He was also teamed up with Jack O'Shea (cv) in the Kerry midfield for the next 2 All-Ireland successes in the ensuing years, 1985 and 1986. He won another Munster S.F.C. medal in 1991, before retiring in 1993. His brother Nially won an All-Ireland M.F.C. medal with Kerry in 1975, and an All-Ireland Under 21 medal in 1976.

O'DONOVAN, MICHAEL.

Coursing trainer. Tipperary Town trainer. He has capture the sports greatest honour, the Waterloo Cup, twice, in 1985 with Hear and There, and in 1988 with React Fragile (after a disqualification), both owned by the Ryan family of Limerick.

O'DONOVAN, PADDY.

G.A.A. hurling centre half-back, Cork. From Douglas. Club: Glen Rovers and St Nicholas's (also being a footballer of note). Also a right half-back and midfielder, he was one of 9 players who won 5 All-Ireland Senior Hurling Championship titles with Cork in their golden era, the four-in-a-row of 1941 (as a sub), 1942, 1943 and 1944, and again in 1946. He appeared in 6 finals over the space of 7 years, also being in the side beaten by Kilkenny in the 1947 final. He also won 3 Railway Cup medals with Munster, in 1945, 1948 and 1949. He died in 1990.

O'DRISCOLL, ALAN.

Hockey international forward. Club: Cork Harlequins. He was capped 34 times for Ireland between 1978 and 1981, including his participation in European Championship side in Hanover in 1978 and the Intercontinental Cup in Kuala Lumpur in 1981. His elder brother, Dave (Monkstown) played 4 times for Ireland in 1973, and was capped 3 times at the indoor code in 1981.

O'DRISCOLL, GAY.

G.A.A. football right-fullback. Club: St Vincent's (with whom he won an All-Ireland Club Championship medal in

1976, having previously been on the losing final team in 1973). A product of St Joseph's CBS in Fairview, he won National Football League medals with Dublin in 1976 and 1978. He played at right full-back on the famous 'Dubs' side which appeared in 6 All-Ireland Senior Football Championship finals in a row, being on the winning side in 1974, 1976, and 1977, and losing out to Kerry in 1975, 1978, and 1979 (when he came on as a sub). He has won 2 All-Star awards, in 1975 and 1977, both in the right corner-back position.

O'DRISCOLL, JIM.

Amateur international boxer. Club: Garda. He won 6 Irish National Senior boxing championships at heavyweight over a period of 11 years. His wins came in 1924, 1925, 1926, 1930, 1933, and 1934. He was a key personality in the early years of Irish amateur boxing.

O'DRISCOLL, JOHN (JACKIE).

Soccer international forward. Born in Cork, 20th September 1921. Clubs: Cork United (winning League of Ireland medals in 1942-43, 1944-45 and 1945-46), Swansea City (scoring 26 goals for them in 117 league games from 1947 to 1951, helping them to win Division 3 South in 1949). He was capped 3 times each for the I.F.A. (in the 3 Home International fixtres of 1949) and the F.A.I. (all also in 1949).

O'DRISCOLL, JOHN.

G.A.A. football forward, Cork. Club: Ballingeary. In 1986 he won an All-Ireland UNder 21 Championship medal with Cork. Later that year, while still a teenager on the so-called 'wimps' tour by Ireland Down Under in the International Rules Series, he became a national hero for his exploits in the test matches. Making his senior championship debut in 1986, he was on the verges of the Cork side from then up to 1993, when he finally won a Munster S.F.C. medal, and when the county went on to lose the All-Ireland final to Derry.

O'DRISCOLL, Dr JOHN Brian.

Rugby international wing-forward. Born in Dublin, 26th November, 1953. Clubs: London Irish (captaining them to the R.F.U. Cup final in 1981) and Manchester. A product of Stoneyhurst School, and playing representative rugby for both Lancashire and Connacht, he was capped 26 times for Ireland between 1978 and 1984, 19 of them in a then world-record back-row combination with Fergus Slatery and Willie Duggan, including the Triple Crown XV of 1982 and the International Championship-winning side of 1983, while scoring one international try. A highly rated player, his industry earned him 2 British and Irish Lion's tours as a blind-side flanker, one to South Africa in 1980, winning 4 Test caps (scoring 2 tries in the series), and one to New Zealand in 1983, winning a further 2 Test caps. A Connacht interprovincial, he was selected as Texaco's Rugby Sportstar of the Year in 1980, when he also became the 2nd rugby player to receive the Supreme Sportstar award. He is the younger brother of Barry O'Driscoll, a Manchester R.F.C. full-back who won 4 international rugby caps for Ireland in 1971.

O'DRISCOLL, TIMOTHY J (TIM).

Squash international and rugby interprovincial player. Born in Cork, 6th July 1908. In squash, as a member of Fitzwilliam, he won the Irish International Singles Open title in 1942, having been runner-up to Paul McWeeney (cv) in the previous 2 years. He won his only international squash cap in the home internationals of 1939, being deprived of more during the war years. In rugby, as a member of both Trinity College R.F.C. and Lansdowne (both of whom he captained), he played interprovincial rugby for Leinster once (against Connacht in 1932). He later became a respected travel and tourism consultant. His brother Bob played interprovincial rugby for Munster and was medical officer to the Irish national soccer team from 1971 to 1991, including the World Cup in 1990.

O'DWYER, MICK ('MICKO').

G.A.A. football left half-back, midfielder and forward, Kerry, and coach. Born in Waterville, June 1936. Club: Waterville. First playing Kerry senior football in 1952, he gained a regular place in 1958 (when he won a Munster S.F.C. medal), and went on to win 4 All-Ireland Senior Football Championship medals with Kerry, in 1959 and 1962 at left corner-back, and in 1969 and 1970 at left full-forward, with a 2-year retirement between these victories. He was also on 3 losing All-Ireland S.F.C. sides, in 1960, 1968 and 1972, thus playing in 7 All-Irleand finals. He won 8 National League winner's medals with Kerry, in 1959, 1961, 1963, 1969, 1971, 1972, 1972, and 1974, and won a solitary Railway Cup medal with Munster in the 1972 replay. He was the game's leading marksman for three years in succession: in 1969 (scoring 120 points in 22 championship games), in 1970 (when his tally of 13 goals and 122 points for a total of 161 pooints placed him, until surpassed by Matt Connor in 1980, as the top scorer-per-season ever in football), and in 1971, scoring 135 points in 21 games. Retiring from the game in 1974, he took over the coaching of the Kerry side in 1975, and steered them to 8 All-Ireland victories in 15 years at the helm (making him the game's most successful manager/coach), the victories being in 1975, the 4-in-a-row of 1978, 1979, 1980, and 1981, and the 3-in-a-row of 1984, 1985 and 1986, resigning from the post in 1989 (he took up the job as Kildare county manager in 1990). In 1969 he was voted as the Texaco footballer of the year, the 3rd Kerryman to be so named. He is a hotelier in Waterville.

O'DWYER, NOEL.

Hockey international left half-back. Clubs: Catholic Institute (Limerick), and Lansdowne. When he finished his 13 year career for Ireland in internationals in 1963, he was then Ireland's most capped player, with 43 caps (passing out Stan DeLacy's record of 35 caps in 1960). Regarded as Irish hockey's finest left half-back, he is the son of the owner of the famous racehorse, 'Limerick Lace', Major O'Dwyer. He was later an Irish selector.

O'FARRELL, FRANK.

Soccer international wing-half and manager. Born in Cork, 9th October 1927. He joined West Ham from Cork at the age of twenty, and in six seasons with the Hammer's, he played in 197 league games, scoring 6 goals. He then joined Preston North End for 4 seasons, playing 118 league matches for them. He was capped 9 times for the Republic of Ireland between 1952 and 1959, scoring 2 international goals. He later moved into soccer management (with periods in charge of Weymouth, Torquay, Leicester, and also Manchester United for 18 months in 1971-72). He was selected as Texaco's Soccer Sportstar of the Year for 1971, when he was also voted the Supreme Sportstar, the first soccer personality to win this accolade.

O'FLANAGAN, KEVIN P Dr.

Rugby international wing three-quarter, soccer international outside forward and winger, and athletics champion. Born in Dublin, 10th June 1919. Having been capped at soccer as a teenager at amateur level for Northern Ireland, he went on to win 10 caps for the Republic of Ireland between 1938 and 1947 (thus playing before and after W.W.II.), scoring 3 international goals. A centre-forward and outside-right, his clubs included Bohemians (captaining them to their F.A.I. Cup success in 1945), Arsenal, Casuals, Barnet and Brentford. He was also capped on one occasion for Ireland at rugby as a wing three-quarter, against Australia in 1947, when playing with

London Irish. In 1946, in 3 successive Saturdays, he played rugby for Ireland against France (in an unofficial international), then played soccer against Scotland, and was due to play rugby again for Ireland the following week, but had to miss the game. With his brother Michael (cv), they are the only 2 brothers in history to be capped for their countries at both Association Football and Rugby Union. A truly all-round sportsman, he was also a champion athlete (being Irish champion at 100 yards in 1941, and the Irish broad jump champion 4 times, in 1938, 1939 when he cleared 22' 10", 1941 and 1943); and but for cancellations of the Olympics in 1940 and 1944, he would surely have competed in the Games. He was a fine tennis player also, and a single-figure golfer. He was voted into the Texaco Hall of Fame in 1965 for his all-round sporting ability, the only sportsman to be voted into it for more than one sport. He was the Irish Olympic medical officer for 4 Olympic celebrations, 1960, 1964, 1968 and 1972. In 1976 he became only the 3rd Irishman to be elected to the International Olympic Council.

O'FLANAGAN, MICHAEL (MICK).

Soccer and rugby international player. Born in Dublin, 29th February 1922. He was capped once for Ireland as a centre three-quarter in rugby, when while playing for Lansdowne (with whom he won a Leinster Senior Cup medal in 1949), he played against Scotland in 1948, therefore being part of Ireland's 'Golden Era'. One year earlier, while a member of Bohemians he was capped once also for the Republic of Ireland soccer XI. He was the leading scorer in the League of Irleand in the 1940-41 season with Bohs, and won an F.A.I. Cup medal with them in 1945. A brother of Kevin Flanagan (cv), they played together in his capped match versus England in 1947.

O'GORMAN, BERNARD.

Squash international player. Born in Dublin, 14th June 1944. Club: Fitzwilliam. He was beaten finalist in 3 Irish National (Close) Champinships, in 1973, 1974 and in 1976, and was capped at squash 53 times for Ireland in the ten year period between 1971 and 1980. He won the Ulster Open in 1975 and 1976, the Leinster Open in 1974 and 1975, and the Old Belvedere Open in 1972, 1973 and 1976.

O'GORMAN, JIM ('THADY').

G.A.A. football forward, Kerry. He captained the Killarney side which represented Kerry when the county won it's first All-Ireland Senior Football Championship, in 1903 (a title they actually won in 1905, as it took 3 games to sort out the winners), and scored more points in this trinity of games than the legendary Dickeen Fitzgerald, the hero of the hour. They defeated Kildare by 0-8 to 0-2 in the 2nd replay. He won a 2nd All-Ireland S.F.C. medal in 1904.

O'GORMAN, SEAN.

G.A.A. hurling left-full back, Cork. Born in 1960. Club: Milford. He won an All-Ireland M.H.C. medal with Cork minors in 1978 (having been on the side beaten in the previous year's final). He was the 'Man of the Match' in the 1990 All-Ireland Senior Hurling Champinship final in which Cork beat the more favoured Galway side. He also played on the Cork side beaten in the Liam McCarthy Cup final of 1992, and was on the Cork side which won the National Hurling League in 1992-93. He won his first All-Star in 1990, at left-corner back. A school principal.

O'GRADY, EDDIE.

National Hunt horse trainer. Based at Ballynonty, Thurles, Co Tipperary. His big race wins have included: the 1984 Daily Express Triumph Hurdle with Northern Game, 2 Sun Alliance Novice Hurdle's (1980 with Drumlargan, and 1982 with Mister Donovan), the Count Handicap Hurdle with Staplestown in 1981, the National Hunt Chase in 1974 (with Mr Midland) and 1983 (with Bit of a Skite), and the 1977 Champion Hunters Chase.

He was twice the leading jump trainer in Ireland, in both 1979 (with 64 winners) and 1980 (with 46 winners). His tally of 11 Cheltenham Festival winners is the best of any recent Irish trainer.

O'GRADY, GERRY.

Powerlifting world champion. Born in Dublin, 22nd October 1961. Club: Atlas. He has won 4 All-Ireland Senior titles, in 1982 in the 82.5 Kg class, in 1984 in the 90.00 Kg class, and in both 1985 and 1986 in the 100.0 Kg class. In 1989 he won the World Championship title at the 100.0 Kg class. He has won 2 Celtic National titles, in 1987 and 1990, and he has broken 4 Celtic Nations records. He has also won a Leinster Championship title and has won 4 Inter-provincial titles. Capped 7 times for Ireland, he has set 17 All-Ireland senior records in power-lifting.

O'HAGAN, HUGH.

Amateur international light-heavyweight boxer. Clubs: Shortt and Harland, and Corinthians. He won 2 Irish National Senior Championship titles in the lightweight division, in 1945 and in 1948. In 1948 he reached the quarter-final of the light-heavy division in the Olympic Games in London, losing the bronze medal bout to an Australian, Adrian Holmes, thereby finishing joint 5th.

O'HAGAN, DAMIEN.

G.A.A. football full-forward, Tyrone. Club: Coalisland. He was at full-forward on the Tyrone team beaten in the All-Ireland Under 21 Championship final by Kerry in 1975. Playing senior championship football first in 1979, he was a member of the Tyrone side which won the Ulster Senior Football Championship title in 1984, 1986 (when they went on to lose to Kerry in the All-Ireland final), and in 1989. He won an All-Star award in 1986 at full-forward.

O'HANLON, BARTHOLOMEW Reginald ('BERTIE').

Rugby international wing-threequarter. Born in Cork, 23rd October, 1924. Club: Dolphin (with whom he won 2 Munster Senior Cup medals, in 1945 and in 1948 as vice-captain). A product of Rockwell College (winning a Munster Schools Senior Cup medal in 1942), he was capped 12 times for Ireland as a right winger in the great 'Jackie Kyle' era when Ireland won the Grand Slam of 1948 (Bertie being one of nine who played in all 4 matches), and playing also in the side which captured the Triple Crown in 1949, when he scored a try against England, one of 3 international tries he claimed. Also playing Barbarians, his occupation has been insurance.

O'HANLON, JOHN J.

Chess international player. Born in Portadown in 1874, he died in 1960. One of Ireland's finest ever chess players, he won a record 9 Irish Chess Championship titles, in 1912 (the year the title was first contested), 1915, 1925, 1926, 1930, 1932, 1935, 1936, and in 1940, giving a career span of national title wins of 28 years. He also won many minor (by world chess standards) tournaments in England and on the Riviera.

O'HANLON, SHAY.

Cyclist. A Dubliner who was born in 1942, he started competitive cycling at the age of 16, in 1958. He won the Ras Tailteann on no fewer than 4 occasions (a record tally that still holds), in 1962 when he won 4 stages, and in the remarkable 3-in-a-row years of 1965, 1966 and 1967 when no other rider held the race leaders jersey. His total tally of 26 stage wins in the 'Ras' is also a record. He went to the continent in 1963, winning 5 races, but he soon came back to Ireland. He also won the 100 miles road race championship 5 times, and collected a total of 35 championship gold medals. He won the N.C.A. title in 1979, and won his last championship race in 1980, after a 22 year career. He was president of the N.C.A. from 1973 to 1975, and held the office again from

1985. He was selected as Texaco's Cycling Sportstar of the Year twice, for 1960 and 1961.

O'HARA, DICK.

G.A.A. hurling left full-back, Kilkenny. Club: Thomastown. He won 2 All-Ireland Under 21 Championship medals at centre half-back with Kilkenny in 1975 and 1977 (being on the losing final side in 1976), having won an All-Ireland M.H.C. medal with the 'Black and Ambers' in 1973. He the went on to win 3 All-Ireland Senior Hurling Championship medals with Kilkenny, in 1979 (as a playing sub), 1982, and 1983, having played in a losing All-Ireland S.H.C. final in 1978. He won one All-Star award, in 1983 at left corner-back.

O'HARA, GEORGE W.

Hockey international full-back. Clubs: Cliftonville, Southgate, Anglo Irish (Southgate), and Three Rock Rovers. He won 27 international caps for Ireland between 1947 and 1954, being a regular member of the last Irish team to win the Triple Crown in hockey, in 1949.

O'HARA, PATRICK Thomas J (PAT).

Rugby international wing-forward. Club: Sunday's Well, Cork Constitution. Born in Hornchurch, Essex, 4th August 1961. First capped as a substitute against Western Somoa in 1989, he has travelled to France and North America with Irish sides in 1988 and 1989 respectively. He has been capped 14 times up to March 1993. He also toured Namibia with Ireland in 1991. A grafting Munster flanker, he was selected as the Texaco Sportstar of the Year for rugby in 1990.

O'KANE, LIAM J.

Soccer international centre-half. Born in Londonderry, 17th June 1948. He joined Nottingham Forest from Derry City at the age of 20, and played 186 league matches for the City Ground club in the period 1968-1975. He was capped 20 times for Northern Ireland between 1970 and 1975, all gained while at Nottingham Forest. He later coached Nottingham Forest.

O'KEEFFE, BOB.

G.A.A. hurler, Laois. Although born at Glengrant near Mooncoin in Co Kilkenny, he was a member of the Ballygeehan team which won the All-Ireland Senior Hurling Championship title for Laois in 1915, having the previous year been on the Kilcotton side beaten by Clare in the final. A fine exponent of the Puc Fada, he became President of the G.A.A. for the period from 1935 to 1938 (the only Laoisman to be thus far honoured), and died in 1949. The O'Keeffe Cup, presented annually to the winners of the Leinster Senior Hurling Championship, is named in his honour.

O'KEEFFE, DAN ('DANNO').

G.A.A. footballing goalkeeper, Kerry. Born in 1907 in Fermoy, Co Cork. He won an All-Ireland J.F.C. with Kerry in 1930. For many years he held the record for most All-Ireland Senior Football Championship winner's medals, with seven in all (his wins coming in 1931, 1932, 1937, 1939, 1940, 1941, and 1946). He also held for a long period the record for most All-Ireland S.F.C. final appearences, with 10 over a 16-year period (being on the losing sides in 1938, 1944, and in the famous Polo Ground match of 1947), 3 of which went to replays. He won a huge tally of 15 Munster S.F.C. medals between 1931 and 1948. His 3 Railway Cup medals with Munster came over a period of 17 years, 1931, 1941 (when he was the 3rd Kerryman to captain a winning side), and again in 1948. Retiring after the All-Ireland semi-final of 1949, he won only one National Football League medal, in 1932. He won the goalkeeping spot on the 1984 Sunday Independent 'Team of the Century', beating out many great modern players.

O'KEEFFE, GER (GERO or 'GIDACHA').

G.A.A. football right full-back, Kerry. Born 9th September 1952. Club: Austin Stacks (winning an All-Ireland Club

Championship medal with them in 1977). A product of St Brendan's Killarney, he won an All-Ireland Colleges medal in 1969. He won an All-Ireland Under 21 Championship medal in 1973, having been on the losing team in the final of 1972, and being previously on the Kerry minor side which lost the 1970 All-Ireland final. He later won 3 All-Ireland Senior Football Championship winner's medals playing with Kerry, in 1975 at right corner back, in 1980 at left half-back, and coming on as a sub in the 1981 win, having captained Kerry when they lost the 1976 All-Ireland S.F.C. final to Dublin, and the classic semi-final of 1977. He won a fourth medal as a non-playing sub in the 1979 win, and was injured for the 1980 final. He won his only All-Star award in 1976 when he was selected at right corner back. A sprinter as a youth, he won N.A.C.A. championships in 1968, 1969 and 1970. A cousin of John O'Keeffe (cv).

O'KEEFFE, JOHN ('JOHNO' or 'BIG BIRD').

G.A.A. football centre half-back, midfielder and full-back, Kerry. Born 15th April 1951. Club: Austin Stacks (whom he captained in 1977 to their only All-Ireland Club Championship success). He captained, from centre half-back, the St Brendan's of Killarney side which won the Hogan Cup in 1969, making it the first time the All-Ireland Senior Colleges title had been won by a Kerry school (his brother Tony also won a medal). He was a member of the Kerry side beaten by Galway in the final of the 1972 All-Ireland Under 21 championship. His All-Ireland Senior Football Championship winning tally comes to 6 (the first player in the modern era to reach this total), winning in 1970, 1975, and in the 4-in-a-row of 1978, 1979, 1980, and 1981, being on losing All-Ireland final sides in 1972, 1976 (as captain) and 1982 (he actually won another All-Ireland S.F.C. medal as a non-playing sub in the 1969 win). He won 6 National Football League medals with the county, in the 4-in-a-row of 1971, 1972, 1973 and 1974, and again in both 1977 (when captain at full-forward) and 1982. Regarded as among the finest full-back's in modern times, he won 5 All-Star awards, in 1973 at midfield, and 4 times at his most famous position of full-back, in 1975, 1976, 1978, and 1979 (when he became the first footballer to win 5 awards). In 1975 he became the 5th Kerryman to be named as Texaco Footballer of the Year. He was the first Kerryman to win 4 Railway Cup medals when he won in 1972, 1973 (with the Combined Universities), 1975, and 1977, and he then went on to win a total of 7 medals, winning again in 1978, 1981 and 1982, a county and provincial record in football. He later trained the Limerick S.F.C. side in the early 1990's. His father Frank won an All-Ireland S.F.C. medal with Kerry in 1946, and played in the Polo Ground final of 1947.

O'KEEFFE, J.

G.A.A. hurler, Tipperary. He won 4 All-Ireland Senior Hurling Championship winner's medals with Tipperary teams, in 1898 with Tubberadora, 1899 with Moycarkey, in 1900 with Two-Mile-Borris, and in 1906 with Thurles.

O'KEEFFE, PADDY and JOHN.

Father and son. G.A.A. hurlers, Cork. Paddy, from Carrigtwohill, was on the Blackrock side which represented Cork to win the 1893 All-Ireland Senior Hurling Championship, beating the Confederation side of Kilkenny by 6-8 to 0-2. His son John, a member of Carrigtwohill, was at midfield in the Cork Selection side which beat Collegians of Dublin in the 1919 All-Ireland S.H.C. final. This made them the first father and son to win All-Ireland Senior Championship-winning medals. John also played on the Cork side beaten in the All-Ireland S.H.C. decider of 1920.

O'KEEFFE, TIMOTHY Jim (TIM or 'CANNONBALL').

Soccer international left-winger. Born in Cork in 1910, he died of cancer aged only 33, having scored 105 goals in the League of Ireland for Cork F.C. He also scored one of the goals in their F.A.I. Cup final win of 1934, being the club's leading scorer in the same season, and he played also with Waterford (winning another F.A.I. Cup medal in 1937, when he was the club's leading scorer that season, and the following). He was the first League of Ireland winger to reach the ton, also scoring 21 in the 1937-38 season, and scored 8 goals in the Scottish League with Hibernian (to whom he was transfered for a then League of Ireland record fee of £400). Possessed with a bullet of a left foot, he was capped 3 times for the Irish Free State, once in 1934 and twice in 1938.

O'KELLY, George CORNELIUS (CON).

Wrestler. Born in Gloun, Dunmanway, Co Cork on 29th October 1886. Leaving Ireland in 1903, in 1905 he won the British Heavyweight wrestling championship as a member of the Hull Fire Brigade, He won a gold medal in the Heavyweight Wrestling division of the 1908 Olympic Games, held in London, while representing Great Britain, beating fellow Corkman Edmond Barrett (cv) into a bronze medal (Barrett had previously beaten him in the British Heavyweight Championship). His opponent in the final was the Norwegian Jacob Gundersen, whom he beat by 2 falls in 17 minutes and 2 seconds. He remains the only Irish-born person to win an Olympic gold medal at wrestling. He later became a professional boxer, and won the Northern England heavyweight title, before later moving to America, back to Ireland, and off to England again, where he died in 1947. His son Cornelius Jnr (1907-1968) won the heavyweight boxing championship at the 1924 Tailteann Games, represented Britain as a heavyweight at the 1924 Olympics, before becoming a professional, and later a priest.

O'KENNEDY, GUS.

G.A.A. footballer, Wexford. From New Ross. Winning a Leinster J.F.C. medal in 1911, he was one of 10 Wexford players to win 6 successive Leinster S.F.C. in 1913-1918, and also to get 4 All-Ireland Senior Football Championship winner's medals in succession, in 1915, 1916, 1917 and 1918. He had also been on the side beaten in the All-Ireland S.F.C. finals of 1913 and 1914 (a replay), thus playing in seven successive All-Ireland S.F.C finals. He is a brother of Sean O'Kennedy (cv).

O'KENNEDY, SEAN.

G.A.A. hurler and footballer, Wexford. A dual All-Ireland winner. He assisted the Wexford side from Castlebridge in their 1910 Senior Hurling Championship title win, and was captain later of all three of the successive Blues and Whites sides from Wexford which won All-Ireland Senior Football Chmpionship titles in 1915 (when Kerry were beaten by 2-4 to 2-1), 1916 (when Mayo lost by 2-4 to 1-6) and 1917, when the Clare Selection were beaten by 0-9 to 0-5 (he missed the 4-in-a-row season of 1918), making him the first player to captain 3-in-a-row All-Ireland senior title winner's in either code. From New Ross, he is a brother of Gus O'Kennedy (cv).

O'LEARY, CATHAL.

G.A.A. football utility player, Dublin. A member of the Dublin forward line when the county were beaten in the All-Ireland Senior Football Championship final in 1955 by Kerry, he was a tower of strength in the half-back line on the winning Dublin All-Ireland S.F.C. side in 1958. Winning a third Leinster S.F.C. medal in 1959, he also won 3 National Football League medals with Dublin, in 1953, 1955 and 1958. He won 3 Railway Cup winner's medals with Leinster, in 1952 (as a sub), 1954, and 1955.

O'LEARY, DAVID.

Soccer international central defender. Born in Stoke Lewington, London, 2nd May 1958. After finishing 3rd in the Leinster Schools Cross Country Championship, and captaining the Irish soccer schoolboys and Youths sides, he was apprenticed from Shelbourne to Arsenal at the age of 17 in 1975, and has since broken the club's appearence record, playing his 673rd first class game up to the end of the 1990-1991 season, his final figure reaching 723 in his final match (the 1993 F.A.I. Cup replay win) before moving on free transfer to Leeds United. Among his other trophies for the 'Gunners' are: an F.A. Cup medal in 1979 (being on the losing Arsenal final teams in 1978 and 1980), 2 League Cup medals (in 1987 and 1993); a runners-up medal in the European Cup Winners Cup in 1980, and 2 English League First Division medals in 1989 and 1991. First capped for the Republic of Ireland in 1977, he won 39 international caps up to 1986, then being omitted on many occasions for inexplicable reasons, but made a comeback in the qualifying rounds for Ireland's successful run in to the 1990 World Cup finals in Rome. He was brought on as sub to telling effect in the World Cup last-16 match versus Romania in 1990, scoring the winning penalty kick in the shoot-out. His cap tally was up to 68 in August 1993, making him the then third most capped Republic of Ireland soccer international. His younger brother Pierse (who won an F.A.I. Cup medal with Shamrock Rovers in 1978 and a Scottish Cup medal with Glasgow Rangers in 1985), was also capped for the Republic of Ireland, winning his place seven times, playing alongside David on 4 occasions.

O'LEARY, J .

G.A.A. hurler, Cork. He won 4 All-Ireland Senior Hurling Championship winner's medals with different Cork sides, in both 1893 and 1894 with Blackrock, in 1902 with Dungourney, and in 1903 again with Blackrock. In doing so he became the first Corkman to win 4 Senior Hurling Championship winner's medals, a record not equalled by a fellow 'Rebel County' man until 1929.

O'LEARY, JOHN.

G.A.A. football goalkeeper, Dublin. Club: O'Dwyers. A product of Gormanstown College, he was a member of the Dublin side beaten in the All-Ireland Under 21 Championship final in 1980 (the previous year he had been on the successful Dublin side which captured the All-Ireland Minor Football Championship). Playing senior Championship football first in 1981, he won 3 successive Leinster S.F.C. medals with the Dubs in 1983, 1984, and 1985, going on to play in the All-Ireland final each year, being on the winning side in 1983 (defeating Galway), and losing to Kerry in each of the following years, 1984 and 1985. He brought his Leinster S.F.C. tally of medals to 6 in 1993, also having won in both 1989 and 1992 (when he played on another Dublin side beaten in an All-Ireland S.F.C. final). In 1986 he became the 4th Dublinman to captain a winning Railway Cup Leinster side in football, also winning medals in 1985 and 1987. He has won 3 National Football League medals with Dublin, in 1987, 1991 when 'man of the match' in the final, and as captain in 1993. He captained the Irish side in the home Compromise Rules series against the Australians in 1987, also playing in the series of 1984 and 1986, playing in 7 test matches in all. He has won 2 All-Star awards in goals, in 1984 and 1985. A Building Society manager, he played soccer briefly for Shamrock Rovers B team in 1989.

O'LEARY, JOHN.

Golfer, professional and amateur. Starting off at Foxrock GC, he won the 1970 Irish Youths and the South of Ireland championship. Playing 18 times for Leinster in interprovincial matches, he won 12; he played 12 Home international matches for Ireland 1969-70, winning 5; when he played 5 matches in the 1969 European Team championships for Ireland, he lost only one match. Turning professinal in 1970, he won the Carrolls Irish Open in 1982 with a score of 287, in front of a record 103,000 crowd of spectators. His other wins as a pro include the Sumrie tournament in 1975, the 1976 Greater Manchester Open, the 1975 Swaziland Open, and the Holiday Inns Tournament in South Africa (he also twice finished 2nd in the South African Masters, in 1972 and 1974). His best Order of Merit finish was in 1976, at 16th place. He won Ryder Cup honours for Britain and Ireland in 1975, losing all his 4 matches. He played World Cup for Ireland in 1972, 1980, and 1982. A former leader of the European players union, he lives in South Africa.

O'LEARY, PADDY.

Soccer centre-forward. Born in Cork, 15th May 1918. He scored 118 League of Ireland goals for Limerick, St James Gate, Cork United and Cork Athletic, between 1942 and 1965, being leading goalscorer in the League of Ireland in 1945/46 (when his Cork United team won the league) and in 1948/49 (when his club, Cork Athletic, won the league; he helped them to win it again the following year). He also won 2 F.A.I. Cup medals, with Cork United in 1947, and when Cork Athletic won the double in 1951. In a League of Ireland match versus Drumcondra in January 1946, he scored six goals in their 9-1 victory. Uncapped, he played Inter-League football for the League of Ireland, scoring once.

O'LEARY, SEAN (SEANIE).

G.A.A. hurling left-full forward, Cork. Born on 25th February 1952. Club: Youghal. He won an All-Ireland M.F.C. medal in 1969, and then won 3 All-Ireland Under 21 Championship medals with Cork in a four year period, in 1970, 1971 and 1973. A brilliant goal-getter, he is the winner of 4 All-Ireland Senior Hurling Championship medals with Cork, in 1976, 1977, 1978 and 1984 (his 2 goals paving the way to victory in the final), and was on losing All-Ireland S.H.C. final sides in 1972, 1982, and 1983 (as a sub), thus playing in a total of 7 All-Ireland S.F.C. finals between 1972 and 1984. He won 4 National League medals with Cork, in 1972, 1974, 1980, and 1981. He has won 3 All-Star awards, in 1976, 1977 and 1984, all at left-corner forward.

O'LOUGHLIN, DAVID Bonaventure (DAVE).

Rugby international 2nd row forward. Born in Kilmallock, Co Limerick, 13th July 1916, he died in 1971. Clubs: U.C.C. (winning 2 Munster Senior Cup medals with them, in 1936 and 1937) and Dolphin (with whom he also won 2 Munster Senior Cup medals, in 1944 and 1945). One of the great Munster forwards of his day, he won only 6 international caps for Ireland between 1938 and 1939, World War Two depriving him of many more. He played for Ireland 3 times during the war against the British Army (in 1944 and twice in 1945), and in 2 unofficial internationals in 1946. He was an Irish selector in 1949-1951 and 1954-1956.

O'MAHONEY, MATT.

Soccer international centre-half. Born in Mullinavat, 9th January 1913. Clubs: Bristol Rovers, Newport County, Ipswich. He was capped only 6 times for the Irish Free State between 1936 and 1939, but those 6 caps made him Bristol Rovers' most capped international player for almost 50 years, until 1988 when he was passed out by Neil Slatter of Wales. He was also capped once for the I.F.A. in 1939.

O'MAHONY, DAN (DANNO).

Wrestling world champion. From Ballydehob, Co Cork. Based in the Army for one year, he became a champion at heaving events, winning 3 Army titles at Hammer and 56lb Weights. Emigrating to the U.S.A. in 1934, he went on to become the World Heavyweight Wrestling Champion, when he beat the reigning champion Ed Don George at Braves Field in Boston before a crowd of around 50,000. He defended his title in Dalymount Park in 1936 against Rube Wright. He introduced the 'Irish Whip', a type of throw in the sport. Killed in a car crash in Cork, his brother Florrie was also an Army champion weight thrower, and finished 2nd in the N.A.C.A. 56 lb shot in 1956.

O'MAHONY, PAUDIE.

G.A.A. football goalkeeper, Kerry. Club: Spa. He won a runner's-up medal with Kerry minors in the 1970 All-Ireland M.F.C., and a winner's medal in the 1973 All-Ireland Under 21 Championship. He was in goals on the Kerry side which won the All-Ireland Senior Football Champinship title in 1975, and won 4 more S.F.C. medals (all as a non-playing substitute to Charlie Nelligan in 1978, 1979, 1980, and 1981), and was in goals on the losing Kerry All-Ireland final side of 1976. His one Railway Cup medal with Munster came in 1976. He won one All-Star award in 1976.

O'MAILLIE, CIARAN.

Hockey and cricket international. Born in Dublin 14th June 1925, he died there in 1977. A product of Blackrock College, he was capped 16 times for Ireland at hockey while a member of the Railway Union club, between 1950 and 1954, being a nifty goalscorer. In cricket, as a member of Pembroke, he was capped 5 times for Ireland between 1953 and 1960.

O'MALLEY, GERRY.

G.A.A. football centre half-back, Roscommon. Born in 1929. Club: Brideswell. He won four Connacht Senior Football Championship winner's medals, in 1952, 1953, 1961 and in 1962 when he captained (at the age of 33) the Roscommon side in a masterly display in the Connacht final against Galway, before going on to be beaten by Kerry in the All-Ireland S.F.C. final by 1-12 to 1-6. A quality half-back footballer, he is the only Roscommon player to win 3 Railway Cup winner's medals, being on the triumphant Connacht sides in 1951, 1957 and 1958. He is in the Roscommon Hall of Fame, and in 1984 was selected at centre half-back on the football 'Team of the Century' for players who never won an All-Ireland senior championship medal.

O'MALLEY, ROBBIE (BOBBIE).

G.A.A. football right full-back, Meath. Born in Bettystown in 1965. Club: St Colmcille's, Laytown. A product of Drogheda C.B.S., he made his senior debut in 1983 at the age of 18, and was a member of the Centenary Cup-winning Meath side in 1984. He was a member of the victorious Meath All-Ireland Senior Football Championship winning sides of 1987 and 1988, playing a leading role in both triumphs, and was on the side beaten by Cork in the 1990 final (and played in the first 8 of Meath's ten matches in their 1991 losing saga). He was voted as Texaco's Gaelic Football Sportstar of the Year in 1988, a year in which Meath also won the National Football League. One of the modern games best corner-backs, he has won 3 All-Star awards, all at right corner-back, in 1987, 1988 (as the sole nomination for that position, a rare feat), and 1990. He captained the Irish team in the winning Compromise Rules tour of Australia in 1990, having played in all the preceding Test Series up to that, in 1984, 1986 and 1987. His father, Bob, is a scratch golfer. A bank official.

O'MARA, FRANK.

Middle-distance athlete. From Croom in Co Limerick, he was born on 17th July 1960. Clubs: Limerick A.C., Reebok T.C. (U.S.A.), Mazda T.C. A post-graduate from the University of Arkansas, he won the NCAA title at 1,500m in 1983. He was Irish Champion at 1,500m in 1983, 1986 and 1991. In a career impeded by injury, his major race record is as follows: running in the 1,500m Olympic heats in Los Angeles 1984; 8th place in 1986 European Championships also over 1,500 metres; beaten in the heats in the Olympic Games of Seoul in 1988 at

5,000 metres; and (in his 3rd Olympic Games) beaten in the heats again in the 5,000 metres in Barcelona in 1992. A gifted runner outdoors and indoors, he won the inaugural World Indoor Championships 3,000 metres title in Indianapolis in 1987, beating fellow-Irishman Paul O'Donovan into the silver medal; finishing 5th in the final of 1989, two years later again in 1991 he regained that title again in a stylish performance in Seville, in the 4th fastest time of all-time; he thus shared with Marcus O'Sullivan the honour of winning 2 World Indoor Championship titles for Ireland (he was last in the final in Toronto in 1993, when O'Sullivan won a third title). He broke the Irish record for 5,000m in 1987, at 13.13.02. A member of the Irish 4 x 1 mile squad which broke the world record in 1985, he was voted as Texaco's Athletics Sportstar of the Year for 1987.

O'MEARA, JOSEPH Anthony (JOEY).

Hockey international full-back and sweeper, and cricket international. Hockey club: Railawy Union. A dual international, he was capped 52 times in hockey for Ireland between 1970 and 1977. He took part in many famous wins for Ireland, including Ireland's first entry into the Intercontinental Cup, the tour to South Africa in 1973, and was captain of the famous side which won the 8-Nation Santander Trophy in 1972, beating Great Britain in the final. An exciting full-back, he later was appointed as the 4th Irish National Coach in 1978, leading Ireland to qualification for their first World Cup in Buenos Aires by performing with distinction in Rome, and later coached the Irish Ladies squad to similar success. He was also a selector. Also a cricket international right hand bat and off break bowler, again for the Railway Union club, he played twice for Ireland in 1963.

O'MEARA, JOHN Anthony.

Rugby international scrum-half. Born in Cork, 26th June 1929. Clubs: University College Cork, and Dolphin. A product of C.B.C. Cork and Clongowes Wood, he was capped at scrum-half 22 times (20 of them with the great Jack Kyle cv) for Ireland in the fifties, between 1951 and 1958, and scored 2 international tries. A brilliant passer of the ball, he was ever-present in the Ireland side which captured the International Championship in 1951, and was on the Irish team that beat Australia in 1958, the first victory over a touring side. He toured Argentina and Chile with the Irish 'Shamrocks' touring side of 1952. He also won 3 Munster Senior Cup medals, 2 with U.C.C. in 1950 and 1951, and as Dolphin's captain in their 1956 victory.

O'NEILL, BILLY.

G.A.A. footballer and hurler, Galway. Born in Carrigtwohill, Co Cork, he captained his native county to success in the All-Ireland junior hurling title in 1951. In 1953 and 1955 he appeared in the full back line on 2 losing Galway teams in All-Ireland Senior Hurling Championship finals, and in 1956 he helped Galway to beat his native county, Cork, to win the All-Ireland Senior Football Championship final by a score of 2-13 to 3-7. In an All-Army decider in 1955, while playing for the Western Command, he scored a goal from a puck-out.

O'NEILL, BILLY.

G.A.A. hurler, footballer, rugby player and athlete, Cork. He was a member of the O'Brienites Selection which were beaten in the All-Ireland Senior Football Championship final of 1901. He was a founder member of Sarsfields H.C. in Cork, and was a playing sub on the Dungourney Selection which won the All-Ireland Hurling Championship in 1902, and played on the Blackrock selection which won the championship the following year. As a rugby player he helped Cork Constitution to win 2 Munster Senior Cup medals, and turned down a final Irish trial in 1905 because of the introduction of the ban.

He was also a sprinter, middle-distance, cross-country and marathon runner of note.

O'NEILL, FRANK S.

Soccer international right wing-half. Born in Dublin, 13th April 1940. Starting off with Stella Maris, he spent 5 years with Home Farm, and then had a brief flirtation with Arsenal in 1960, playing only 2 league matches for them. Mostly associated with the great Shamrock Rovers side of the sixties, this classy right wing-half won 7 F.A.I. Cup winner's medals with the 'Hoops', in 1962, 1964, 1965, 1966 (scoring one of their 2 goals in the final), 1967 (again scoring in the final), 1968 and in 1969 (thus winning 6-in-a-row). With Rovers he scored 87 league goals in 13 seasons, won his only League Championship medal in the 'Grand Slam' year of 1964, and was appointed player-manager in 1970. He left Rovers in 1974 to join Waterford. He won 20 caps for the Republic of Ireland between 1962 and 1972, all while with Shamrock Rovers, making him that club's most capped international player. He had a short time as a football manager.

O'NEILL, HENRY O'Hara.

Rugby international prop forward. Born in Portstewart on 1st July 1907. Club: Queen's University Belfast and U.C.C. A product of Coleraine AI, he was capped in all only 6 times in the front-row for Ireland, three times each in the 1930 (when a famous 4-3 win over England on his debut set up his reputation) and 1933 seasons. He was selected for the British and Irish Lion's side that toured Austrlia and New Zealand in 1930, his ability shown in that he played in all 5 Tests on that tour, 4 in New Zealand and one in Australia. A civil servant.

O'NEILL, JAMES A.

Soccer international goalkeeper. Born in Dublin, 13th October 1931. He joined Everton from Bulfin United at the age of 18, and played 201 league matches for Everton up to 1959. He then joined Stoke City for 4 seasons, keeping goal 130 times there, and later played for brief periods at both Darlington and Port Vale. He was capped 17 times for the Republic of Ireland between 1952 and 1959.

O'NEILL, 'JODY'.

G.A.A. football centrefield and half-forward, Tyrone. He was a star on the first Tyrone side to capture the Ulster Senior Football Championship in 1956, and was on the side which retained the crown in 1957. He holds more Railway Cup medals than any of his countymen, winning the 4 medals with Ulster in 1960, 1963 (as a sub), 1964 (as a sub), and in 1965.

O'NEILL, JOHN Patrick.

Soccer international defender. Born in Derry, 11th March 1958. Clubs: Derry Athletic, Leicester City (playing in 313 league matches for them, helping them to the Division Two title in 1980, and to re-gain promotion to Division One in 1983), Queen's Park Rangers, Norwich City. An Under 21 international, he was later capped 39 times for Northern Ireland between 1980 and 1986, including playing in both of Northern Ireland's qualifying sides to the World Cup, in Spain in 1982 (playing in the last 2 matches in the finals) and Mexico in 1986 (playing in all 3 matches). He later managed Home Farm.

O'NEILL, JOHN ('SONNY').

Soccer international centre-half. Born in Dublin, 8th September 1935. Clubs: Drumcondra (winning an F.A.I. Cup medal with them in 1957, and a League of Ireland Championship winner's medal the following year), Preston North End (1958-62, playing 50 league games for them) and Barrow. He won one cap for the Republic of Ireland, in 1961 against Wales.

O'NEILL, JOHN JOSEPH ('JONJO').

National Hunt jump jockey and trainer. Born in Castletownroche, Co Cork 13th April 1952. He rode in England from 1972. In the 1977-78 season, he set a then record of 149 winning rides in one British National Hunt season (being placed in 300 out of his 545 mounts, and with 45 of the winners being with Peter Easterby), which included a 5-timer on 19th April at Perth. He was also leading N.H. jockey in Britain 2 years later in 1979-80, with 117 winners, 51 of these being for Peter Easterby. Other seasons in which he rode over 50 winners in Britain were: 1973-74 (51 winners), 1975-76 (64 winners), 1976-1977 (65 winners), 1978-1979 (62 winners), 1982-1983 (74 winners), and in the 1983-84 season when he did-the-ton for the third time, with 103 winners. His major wins include 2 Cheltenham Champion Hurdles (on his favourite horse Sea Pigeon, in 1980, and on Dawn Run in 1984), 2 Cheltenham Gold Cups (Alverton in 1979 and Dawn Run in 1986, making this the first time the great Cheltenham double was completed), and 2 Scottish Champion Hurdles. Other great horses he rode include Ekbalco and Night Nurse. His injury-interrupted career tally of winners was 901. He was voted as Texaco's Horse Racing Sportstar of the Year in 1978. Despite a bout with cancer, since 1986 he has trained at Ivy Stables in Penrith, Cumbria, with the stable's tally of winners being steady.

O'NEILL, LIAM.

G.A.A. football right-half back, Galway. He was a member of the half-back line for 3 unlucky Galway All-Ireland Senior Football Championship final sides which failed to win the Sam Maguire Cup in a 4 year period, in 1971, 1973, and 1974. Also playing Railway Cup football for Connacht, he won one All-Star award at right half-back in 1973. Also a Railway Cup player, he turned to rugby and in 1977 and 1978 he won Connacht Junior Cup and League medals with Ballina Rugby Club. He later coached both Galway and Mayo senior S.F.C. sides. His son Kevin (born 16th August 1973) was on the Mayo minors beaten in the All-Ireland M.F.C. final in 1991, won a Connacht Club championship medal with Knockmore, and played for Mayo in the Connacht S.F.C. success of 1993 (being their best player in their humbling All-Ireland semi-final defeat by Cork).

O'NEILL, MARTIN H.

Soccer international midfielder. Born in Kilrea, 1st March 1953. Clubs: Distillery, Derry City, Notingham Forest (for whom in 9 sesasons from 1971 to 1980, he scored 48 goals in 164 league game, helping them to win promotion the the First Division in 1977, to win that League in 1978, and with whom he won 2 successive European Champion's Cup medals in 1979 and 1980), Norwich City, Manchester City, Notts County. He was capped 64 times for Northern Ireland between 1972 and 1985, scoring 9 internatioanl goals. He captained Northern Ireland with distinction in their enormously successful World Cup-qualifying run in 1982, and when reaching the quarter-finals in Spain that year. He also played in all 3 of his country's matches in the 1986 World Cup finals in Mexico. He has the unique distinction of being the most capped player for 3 different English League clubs, Nottingham Forest (36 caps in 1972-80), Norwich City (18 caps 1982-83), and Notts County (8 caps in 1983-84, a record he shares). In 1983 he became the 3rd Northern Ireland soccer player to be awarded an M.B.E. He played gaelic football with Derry in his youth, his 2 older brothers being in the Derry squad when the county reached the All-Ireland S.F.C. final in 1958.

O'NEILL, MARTIN.

G.A.A. footballer and hurler, Wexford and Wicklow, and handballer. Born in 1904, he died in 1991. He won a Leinster S.F.C. winner's medal with Wexford in 1925, and in hurling the following year won an All-Ireland JHC medal, again with Wexford. He later won an All-Ireland J.F.C. with the neighbouring county, Wicklow in 1936.

He won 3 Railway Cup winner's medals with Leinster, in 1928 and 1929, and in 1930 as a sub, becoming the first Wexford man to win 3 Railway Cup medals in either code. He played Tailteann Games football for Ireland in the U.S.A. in 1928 and 1932. Also a handballer of some note, he twice (with fellow-countyman Luke Sherry), won All-Ireland handball softball doubles titles, in 1930 and 1931. He also refereed 3 All-Ireland S.F.C. finals, in 1932, 1933, and the famous Polo Ground game of 1947. As an administrator, he was the first full-time Leinster provincial secretary of the G.A.A., from 1927 to 1970, and was a founder member of the Leinster Handball Council, and its secretary 1932 to 1947. His son Ciaran succeeded him as Leinster Secretary, and was later commercial manager at Croke Park.

O'NEILL, M.

Professional golfer. He won 3 successive Irish Profesional Championships in the 1920's, in 1923 at Milltown, in 1924 at Malone, and in 1925 at Portmarnock. He won the Moran Cup 3 years in a row also, in 1920, 1921 and 1922.

O'NEILL, MICHAEL.

Soccer international forward. Born in Portadown, 5th July 1969. Clubs: Coleraine, Newcastle (scoring 12 goals in 21 games in 1988), Dundee United (joining them for a club record fee of £350,000 in August 1989, and playing 60 matches for them up to mid 1993). He was first capped for Northern Ireland in 1988 and has won 22 soccer international caps up to mid 1993.

O'NEILL, PAT.

G.A.A. hurling centre half-back, Kilkenny. From Gowran, he was born in 1971. Club: Young Ireland's. A product of St Kieran's College (winning All-Ireland school's medal in 1988), he won an All-Ireland M.H.C. medal with Kilkenny in same year, and in 1990 he won an All-Ireland Under 21 Championship winner's medal. He was voted 'man-of-the-match' when Kilkenny won the All-Ireland Senior Hurling Championship in 1992 after a nine year absence, and won another Liam McCarthy Cup medal in 1993. His older brother Mick, a Blackrock R.F.C. second-row forward, played rugby for the senior Leinster team in 1992.

O'NEILL, Dr PAT.

G.A.A. football left half-back, Dublin. Born in Rhodesia (now Zimbabwe) in 1951. Clubs: U.C.D. (with whom he won 2 Dublin SFC medals, and the 1975 All-Ireland Club Championship), and Civil Service (helping them to their first Dublin County Championship victory in 36 years in 1980). In 1973 he won a Railway Cup medal with the Combined Universities side. Making his senior inter-county debut in 1969, he won 5 Leinster S.F.C. titles with Dublin in the late 1970's, winning All-Ireland Senior Championship medals with 'Heffo's Army' in both 1976 and 1977, being also on the sides beaten in the following 2 finals of 1978 and 1979, both by Kerry. He also won National Football League medals with the Dubs in 1976 and 1978. He won his only All-Star in 1977 at left half-back. A Dublin selector in recent times, he was appointed Dublin football coach in 1992, helping them to win the National Football League in 1992-93, and to win the Leinster S.F.C. the same year.

O'NEILL, SEAN.

G.A.A. football half-forward, and full-forward, Down. Club: Newry Mitchell's. Winning an Ulster M.F.C. medal with Down in 1958, he went on to become one of the game's great forwards, scoring 85 goals and over 500 points for Down up to the mid 70's. He was a brilliant wing forward in Down's Sam Maguire Cup wins of 1960 and 1961. Later in the county's All-Ireland Senior Football Championship victory over Kerry in 1968, he was an outstanding leader at full-forward. He also won 4 other Ulster S.F.C. medals in

1963, 1965, 1966 and 1971, giving him a tally of 7. A constant member of the Ulster football side from 1960 to 1974, he has won a provincial record of eight Railway Cup medals with his province, in 1960 (when he became the first Downman to captain a winning Ulster side), 1963, 1964, 1965, 1966, 1968, 1970, and 1971. He also won 3 National League medals, in 1960, 1962 and 1968. He was selected at right half-forward on the Sunday Independent 'Team of the Century in 1984, alongside Sean Purcell and Pat Spillane. He was the 2nd Downman to be nominated as Texaco Player of the Year in 1968, and won 2 All-Star awards, in the first 2 years of the scheme, in 1971 and 1972, both in the full-forward position. Winning a Sigerson Cup medal with Queen's University (whom he later coached to more titles), he later coached and advised the Ulster team. His brother Kevin played at left half-back on the winning All-Ireland S.F.C. side of 1960, and came on as a sub in the final of 1961.

O'NEILL, WILLIAM (BILLY or WILLIE).

Soccer international defender. Club: Dundalk (winning an F.A.I. Cup winner's medal in 1942). A stalwart in many Dundalk sides which were near the top of the League of Ireland over a 10 year period, he was capped 11 times in defence for the Republic of Ireland between 1936 and 1939, all of these coming while playing for Dundalk, making him the club's most capped player.

O'NEILL, WILLIAM ARTHUR ('BOLDY').

Rugby international prop forward. Born in Dublin, 15th November 1928. Clubs: U.C.D., and Wanderers. Twelve times a Leinster interprovincial player between 1949 and 1953, he won 6 international caps for Ireland between 1952 and 1954. He was a member of the Irish 'Shamrocks' touring party to Argentina and Chile. His brother-in-law, James C Murphy-O'Connor, a No 8 forward with Bective Rangers, won one cap for Ireland, against England in 1954.

O'REGAN, JIM.

G.A.A. hurling centre-back, Cork. Born at Castle Park, near Kinsale, in 1901. Clubs: Kinsale, and Garda (Dublin). Initially he played with Offaly, winning a Leinster J.H.C. in 1924 (scoring the winning goal in the final), in 1925 he was on the Dublin side which lost the Leinster hurling title on an objection by Laois. However, in a senior inter-county career with Cork from 1926 to 1936, he won 4 All-Ireland Senior Hurling Championship medals, in 1926 (when he also played in county championship finals in both codes), 1928, 1929, and 1931, and won a 5th Munster S.H.C. when Cork lost the All-Ireland final in 1927. He helped Cork also to 2 National Hurling League wins, in 1926 and 1930, and he also won 2 Railway Cup medals with Munster, in 1929 and 1930. He won 2 Tailteann Games medals, in 1928 and 1932, a distinction only matched by Garret Howard (cv). He refereed the All-Ireland S.H.C. final of 1936 soon after he retired, and coached the winning Cork sides for the 1966 and 1970 All-Ireland S.H.C. He was later Chairman of the Cork county board.

O'REILLY, ANTHONY John Francis (TONY or 'A J F').

Rugby international wing three-quarter. Born in Dublin, 7th May 1936. Clubs: Old Belvedere (scoring 40 tries as a centre in both the 1956 and 1957 seasons), U.C.D., Dolphin, Leicester, London Irish. A product of Belvedere College, he was a Leinster schools rugby inter-pro for 3 years, was a fine tennis player and was also a schools cricket inter-pro. He won his first rugby cap for Ireland at the age of 18 (when he was 6'3" in height) after playing only 5 senior games of rugby (and was capped for the Lion's before becoming a Leinster senior inter-pro). He went on to win 29 caps for Ireland (the first 22 were consecutive, playing 13 in all as a centre and 16 as a winger) in an injury-interrupted career over a span of 16 seasons (1955 to 1970, a then-world record span, still so for an Irish player), his last cap in 1970 against England (at the age of 33) coming 7 years after his penultimate one. He scored 6 international tries for Ireland. It is as a Lion's player that his rugby reputation mainly rests, touring twice, to South Africa in 1955 (scoring a record 16 tries there, breaking the record by scoring the winning try in the last Test match), and Australia and New Zealand in 1959 (under the captaincy of Ronnie Dawson cv, he scored a record 22 tries for the Lion's on a single overseas tour in 23 appearences, these including 17 tries in 17 appearences in New Zealand). He is the most capped Lion's test winger (and his tally of 38 tour tries will hardly be equalled), playing in 10 Test matches (he also won 1 Test place as a centre), and in these games he has scored a record 6 Lion's tries in internationals. He also toured South Africa with the Irish team in 1961, and was a Wolfhound and a prominent Barbarian. A major Irish businessman, and President of Heinz Corporation, he is known for his sharp after-dinner speeches.

O'REILLY, BRENDAN M P.

Athlete, high jump, javelin and decathlon. Born in Granard Co Longford, 14th May 1931. As the country's most exciting high jump prospect since 1900, he represented Ireland in international athletics for an 11 year period from 1952 until 1962, and won the 1954 British A.A.A. title, when jumping 1.85 metres (6'5"), a then record for that championship. In 1956 he won the U.S. Big Ten Mid-West high jump title with a clearence of 6'7", and in the same year was selected to represent Irleand in the high jump at the Olympic Games in Melbourne, but was subsequently dropped through lack of funds. He was Irish Javelin Champion in 1952 (and held the Irish record in this event), and was also Irish champion at the decathlon, along with many Irish High Jump titles. He later became an R.T.E. sports presenter and commentator (covering 5 Olympic Games in the process).

O'REILLY, BRIAN.

G.A.A. football back, Cavan. Club: Mullaroan (winning Cavan County Champinship medals in 1942, 1944, 1945, 1947, 1948, 1949 and 1950). He is one of only 4 Cavan players to play in each of the county's 3 All-Ireland Senior Football Championship successful finals, in 1947 (the famous 'Polo Ground' final), 1948, and 1952. He played at full-back in the first 2 victories and at left half-back in the 1952 win. He also won a National Football League medal with the Breffini County in 1947-48.

O'REILLY, GERRY.

G.A.A. football right half-back, Wicklow. A quality player on a county side which failed to even reach a Leinster S.F.C. final in his time, he won 3 Railway Cup medals with Leinster in succession, in 1952, 1953, and 1954. Regarded as one of the greatest footballers who never won an All-Ireland S.F.C. medal (he was selected on the football 'Team of the Century' in 1984 at right half-back, for those who have failed to win this accolade).

O'REILLY, JACKIE.

Soccer international forward. Clubs: Cork United (winning 3 successive winner's medals in the League of Ireland Championship in 1940-41 and 1941-42, 1942-43, and an F.A.I. Cup winner's medal in 1940, scoring 2 of their 3 goals in the final). Scoring 3 goals for the League of Ireland in Inter-League matches, he was capped twice for the Republic of Ireland in 1946 and scored one international goal.

O'REILLY, LEO.

Pitch and putt and soccer player. From Rathmines, Dublin. In his youth he was a prominent goal-scoring League of Ireland football forward, winning League Championship winner's medals with 3 different clubs: Shamrock Rovers in 1956-57 (and with whom he also won 2 F.A.I. Cup medals, in 1955 and 1956, and a runners-up medal in 1957), Limerick in 1959-60, and with Dundalk in 1962-63, also playing with Longford Town. He later became a noted pitch and putt player, winning the Irish National Strokeplay Championship in 1979 as a member of the Glenville Club in Dublin (he was a runner-up in this discipline in 1975).

O'REILLY, JOAN.

Ladies Hockey international player. Club: Muckross H.C. Having played at interprovincial level, in 1948 she gained her first taste of international hockey on a tour to Amsterdam with an Irish team. Gaining her first full cap in 1949 she went on to be capped 46 times for her country. She later became a Leinster and Irish selector, and was an 'A' badge umpire (taking charge of Ireland's Triple Crown winning match against Scotland in 1977, the first time this had been achieved since her playing days finished). She has been the Leinster and Irish President of the I.L.H.U., and has also chaired the Womens Hockey Board of G.B. and Ireland.

O'REILLY, JOE.

Soccer international wing-half and defender. Clubs: Brideville (scoring in his debut against Dundalk in 1929), Aberdeen, and St James Gate (captaining them to a winning League of Ireland medal in 1939-40, and an F.A.I. Cup medal in 1938). A regular League of Ireland representative player, he was capped 20 times for the Irish Free State between 1932 and 1939 (thus making him his country's most capped player before W.W.II., which actually deprived him of many more caps), scoring 2 international goals. A great half-back, he played in Ireland's first World Cup game in 1934, a 4-4- draw with Belgium, and captained his country on a few occasions. The 13 caps he gained while at St James Gate make him that club's most capped (and most recently capped) player. From a sporting family, his father Michael trained Kildare to win the first ever Sam Maguire Cup in 1928, and his younger brother Peter was a centre half-back on the Dublin side which won the All-Ireland S.F.C. in 1942 and 2 Railway Cup medals with Leinster in 1944 and 1945. In 1991 Joe became one of the first 3 players to be initiated into the League of Ireland Hall of Fame. He died the following year, 1992, aged 81.

O'REILLY, JOHN JOE.

G.A.A. footballer, centre and left half-back, Cavan. A product of St Patrick's College (with whom he won 3 McRory Cup medals in 1935, 1936 amd 1937), he won county championship medals with his club, Cornafaen in 1936 and 1937. He was the captain of the famous Cavan side which won 2 successive All-Ireland Senior Football Championships, in 1947 (the famous Polo Ground, New York victory over Kerry by 2-11 to 2-7) and 1948 (over Mayo by 4-5 to 4-4); he had previously been on 3 Cavan S.F.C. sides beaten in All-Ireland finals, in 1937, 1943, and 1945. His tally of Ulster S.F.C. medals reaches 11, as Cavan won the title each year bar two from 1937 to 1949. He was also on the only Cavan side ever to win the National League in football, which they did in the 1947/48 season. He won 4 Railway Cup medals with Ulster, in 1942, 1943 (both these first years as captain, the first Cavanman to captain a winning side), 1947, and 1950 (as captain again, becoming the only footballer to date to captain 3 winning Railway Cup sides). A commandant, he died on 21st November 1952. He was selected at centre half-back on the Sunday Independent 'Team of the Century' in the Centenery Year of 1984. His brother 'Big Tom' O'Reilly was at left full-forward on the 1947 winning side, and had been captain of three losing Cavan sides in All-Ireland S.F.C. finals of

1937, 1943 and 1945; Tom also won Railway Cup medals for Ulster at left corner-back in 1943 and 1944.

O'REILLY, PERCY Philip.

Polo player. Born 27th July 1870, he died in 1942. He was a member of the Ireland team which was one of 3 teams from Great Britain and Ireland to make up the only competing sides in the polo discipline in the 1908 Olympic Games in London. By being beaten by the gold medal side, Roehampton, by 5-1, Ireland, and Percy O'Reilly, won a bronze medal.

O'REILLY , (nee MORAN), THERESE.

Amateur international golfer. Born 29th January 1954. Club: The Grange. She was Irish Ladies Champion in 1986, beating Eavan Higgins 4 and 3 in the final at Castlerock. She won the Leinster Ladies title in 1975 and 1978, and the Irish Ladies Midland title in 1974. She has won a number of important scratch cups. An international player.

O'RIORDAN, ALEX John.

Cricket international all-rounder. Born in Dublin, 20th July 1940. A right hand batsman and left hand fast-medium paced bowler, he is a product of Belvedere College. Clubs: Clontarf and Old Belvedere. Between 1958 and 1977 he played 86 times for his country (making him Ireland's 4th most capped cricketer for Ireland up to 1993). As a batsman he played 121 innings for Ireland, scoring 2,018 runs (making him Ireland's 7th best in this figure) for an average of 19.40. He is one of only 7 Irishmen to score 3 or more international centuries, his best being 119. He is also the 4th best wicket-taker in Irish cricket history, taking 206 wickets off 4,503 runs in 123 innings, for an average of 21.85 runs per wicket (his best figures being 8 for 60 against Holland in 1970). In Ireland's famous victory against the West Indies in Sion Hill in 1969, his figures of 4 for 18 contributed to the astonishing 25-all-out suffered by the much-vaunted visitors, when Ireland won by 9 wickets. He has also taken more catches than any other Irish international cricketer, with 57 in all. Regarded by most as Ireland's best post-War all-round cricketer, he was also a useful rugby player (also for Old Belvedere), playing senior interprovincial rugby for Leinster against Ulster in the 1962/1963 season.

O'RIORDAN, GERRY.

G.A.A. hurling full-forward and right corner back, Cork. Club: Blackrock. He won 4 All-Ireland Senior Hurling Championship winner's medals with Cork, in 1946 at full forward, and in 1952, 1953 and 1954 at right full-back. He played also on the Cork team beaten in the All-Ireland S.H.C. final of 1947. He won 2 Railway Cup medals with Munster, in 1950 and 1955. His brother Mossie, also a Blackrock forward, won 2 All-Ireland Senior Hurling Championship winner's medals, playing in the same teams as Gerry in both 1946 (when he scored 2 goals in the final) and in 1952 (as a sub). Mossie won a Railway Cup medal in 1950. Both won National Hurling League medals in 1948.

O'RIORDAN, TOM.

Middle and long-distance athlete. Club: Donore. He ran for Ireland in the World Cross Counrtry Championship from 1963 to 1974, his best finish coming in 1964, when 15th. A winner of many Irish national middle-distance titles, in 1964 he represented Ireland in the Olympic Games 5,000 metres in Tokyo. He was selected as Texaco's Athletics Sportstar of the Year for 1963. A sports journalist.

O'ROURKE, COLM.

G.A.A. football forward, Meath. Born 31st August 1957. Club: Skryne. First playing senior football for Meath in 1976, he missed a penalty in the Leinster final against Dublin that year. He was on the Meath team which won 3 successive Leinster S.F.C. titles in 1986, 1987 and 1988, winning All-Ireland Senior Football Championship winner's medals in both

1987 and 1988 (when he was a dominant force in the replay victory over Cork), and captaining the Meath side which lost to Cork in the 1990 final. He won a 5th Leinster S.F.C. medal in 1991, and played in the Royal County's protracted 10-match championship run (including the 4 matches against Dublin) which ended in a loss to Down in that All-Ireland final, despite his influential subbing-in which boosted his team into a rally. He has won 2 National Football League medals with the Royal County, in 1986 and 1990. One of Meath's greatest and most influential forwards, he has won 2 All-Star awards, in 1983 as full-forward and in 1991 at right corner-forward. In 1991 he was selected as Texaco Sportstar of the Year in Football.

O'ROURKE, GERRY.

Wheelchair international athlete. Born in Inchicore, Dublin, 22nd August 1963. Losing the power of his legs at 16 due to a railway accident, he went on to win the Dublin City Marathon for disabled athletes on 6 successive occasions, in 1982, 1983 and in 1984 (when he was beaten by Ingrid Kristiansen for first home), 1985 (being first across the tape), 1986, and in 1987. Winning a bronze medal in the 1983 world championships at 5,000 metres, he has competed in 2 Special Olympic Games, in 1984 at Los Angeles, and in 1988 in Seoul when he finished 4th in the marathon and reached the final in both the 100 metres and 1,500 metres. At the World Championships for the disabled in Assen in 1990 he won 3 gold medals (at 200, 500 and 800 metres), and 2 silver (at 100 and 10,000 metres).

O'ROURKE, PADDY.

G.A.A. football centre half-back, Down. Born in 1959. Club: Burren (winning 8 county championship medals with them, and winning 2 All-Ireland Club Championships with them, in 1986 and 1988). He won an All-Ireland M.F.C. medal with Down in 1977 and an All-Ireland Under 21 Championship medal in 1979. Making his senior inter-county debut in 1978, he won Ulster S.F.C. medals with the county in 1978, 1981 (losing to Offaly in the All-Ireland semi-final), and again in 1991. He helped the county to National Football League success in 1983, and was on the losing N.F.L. final side in 1990. He won 2 Railway Cup winning Ulster sides, in 1983 and 1984 (both as a playing sub in the finals). He captained Down to their first appearence in an All-Ireland Senior Football Championship final in 23 years in 1991, when they beat off the Meath challenge by 1-16 to 1-14.

O'ROURKE, PADRAIG.

Amateur international golfer. Club: Kilkenny. He won the South of Ireland title at Lahinch 3 times, 1979, 1981, and 1985. In 56 interprovincial matches for Leinster between 1977 and 1987, he won 34 and halved 2 for a success rate of 62.5%. He played in 24 Home international matches for Ireland between 1980 and 1985, winning 9.

ORR, PHILIP Andrew ('PHILLIE').

Rugby international prop-forward. Born in Dublin, 14th December 1950, he was educated at High School and Trinity College Dublin. Clubs: Dublin University (winning a Leinster Senior Cup medal in 1976) and Old Wesley. With 58 caps (including 49 consecutively), he is the world's most capped prop forward, and Ireland's fourth most capped player. He is also Leinster's most capped interprovincial, being first capped at this level in 1974. First capped at rugby for Ireland in 1976, his international career stretched over a 12 year period until Ireland's bid for the inaugural World Cup in 1987, being 36 years and 6 months old when winning his last cap for Ireland versus Australia, making him (by only 20 days) Ireland's 2nd oldest ever rugby international, behind Mike Gibson. He was a staunch member of the successful Irish Triple Crown winning sides of both 1982 and 1985 (one of only 6 players to take part in all six games), and of the International Championship in 1983. He has made 2 British and Irish Lion's tours, to New Zealand in 1977, and to South Africa in 1980 (when he won 1 Test cap). He has toured extensively with Ireland, making a then record 5 Irish tours, including New Zealand in 1976, Australia in 1979, South Africa in 1981, Japan in 1985, and the World Cup in 1987. He captained his club Old Wesley to their first success since 1909 in Leinster Senior Cup, in 1985. A clothing manufacturer.

O'SHEA, CAROLINE.

Middle-distance athlete. Clubs: Kimmage Manor S.C., Crusaders. A sprinter up to 1976 (winning 2 national junior W.A.A.A. medals), she moved up to 400 metres then and broke the Irish record in 1978. In 1982 she moved up to the 800 metres, breaking the Irish record. In the Olympic Games in Los Angeles in 1984 she achieved a rare feat for an Irish woman athlete, by reaching the final of an Olympic athletics event, finishing 8th in the 800 metres final, in a time of 2' 00.77". Later on that year she defeated the Olympic silver medallist Kim Gallagher when finishing 2nd in an international race.

O'SHEA, JACK ('JACKO').

G.A.A. footballing mid-fielder, Kerry. Born in Cahirciveen, 19th November 1957. Clubs: Cahirciveen, St Mary's. He was a member of the Kerry Under 21 team which won 3 successive All-Ireland Under 21 Championships, in 1975 (when he was at full-forward), 1976, and 1977 (he just failed to equal the record of 4 medals in 1978). He has won 7 All-Ireland Senior Football Championship winner's medals in the golden Kerry era of the 70's and 80's, playing starring roles in midfield in the 4-in-a-row side of 1978, 1979, 1980, and 1981, and in the 3-in-a-row side of 1984, 1985, and 1986. He was also on the losing All-Ireland S.F.C. final side in 1982 against Offaly. He won a last Munster S.F.C. medal with the Kingdom in 1991. He has won 2 National League medals with Kerry, in 1982 and 1984, and is a winner of 4 Railway Cup medals with Munster, in 1977 and 1978 as a sub, and in 1981 and 1982. Regarded by most observers as the finest gaelic footballer of his time, he is the only player from either code to win more than 2 Texaco Player of the Year awards, winning a record 4, in 1980, 1981, 1984, and in 1985. He has been awarded a total of 6 All-Star consecutive awards, in 1980, 1981, 1982, 1983, 1984, and 1985 (the last 2 of these as an unanimous choice), all in midfield (being the only person in either code to win 6 successive awards in the same position). He was captain of the Irish side in the Compromise Rules series against Australia in 1984 and 1986, and also played in the 1987 and 1990 series. He was selected, alongside fellow-countyman Mick O'Connell to fill the midfield roles in the Sunday Independent's 1984 'Team of the Century'. A plumber in Leixlip, Co Kildare, he coached Mayo to their 1993 Connacht S.F.C. success.

O'SHEA, JEROME ('THE BOY BAWN').

G.A.A. football right full-back, Kerry. Regarded as one of the game's greatest left corner-backs, he won 2 All-Ireland Senior Football Championship medals with Kerry, in 1955 (when he became the first Caherciveen man to get a medal by playing in a final) and 1959, being on the beaten All-Ireland S.F.C. finalists side in 1960.

O'SHEA, PAT ('SPRINGHEEL' then 'THE CASTLEGREGORY AEROPLANE').

G.A.A. football midfielder, Kerry. Regarded as one of Kerry's greatest ever midfielders, he was on the county side represented by Killarney which won the All-Ireland Senior Football Championship title in successive years, 1913 and 1914, the losing side on both occasions being Wexford (and was on the team over which Wexford got revenge in the 1915 All-Ireland S.F.C. final).

O'SHEA, PAUDIE ('P-O').

G.A.A football right half-back and right full-back, Kerry. Club: Gaeltacht of West Kerry (with whom he won a Kerry county championship in 1984 and 1985). Born in Dingle, Co Kerry on 16th May 1955. Educated at St Brendan's College, Killarney, he was a Kerry minor from 1971 to 1975, and captained St Michael's College of Listowel to their first ever Kerry senior colleges title. Winning a total of 13 Munster S.F.C. titles with Kerry, he won a record-equalling 8 All-Ireland Senior Football Championship medal's with the county, in 1975, the 4-in-a-row of 1978, 1979 (when he was sent off in the final), 1980, and 1981, and in the 3-in-a-row side of 1984, 1985 (when he captained the side which Dublin by 2-12 to 2-8) and 1986. During these and other All-Ireland finals he conceded only one point to his immediate opponents (against David Hickey in 1976). He was on losing All-Ireland S.F.C. final sides in 1976 and 1982. He won 4 Railway Cup medals with Munster, in 1976, 1978, 1981 and 1982, and won 4 National League winner's medals with Kerry, in 1974, 1977, 1982, and 1984. He won 5 successive All-Star awards, in 1981 and 1982 at right half-back, and in 1983, 1984, and 1985 at right full-back. A great defender with a fine ability to go forward, he was sent off 3 times in his career. A garda turned Ventry publican.

O'SULLIVAN, CHARLIE.

G.A.A. football forward, Kerry. In 1931 he was on the first Kerry minors to capture the All-Ireland M.F.C. final. He went on to win 4 All-Ireland Senior Football Championship winner's medals with the 'Kingdom', in 1937, 1939, 1940 (when scoring the winning point), and 1941, being on the losing side in the All-Ireland final in 1938, thus playing in 5 All-Ireland S.F.C. finals in succession.

O'SULLIVAN, DENIS F.

Amateur international golfer. Club: Cork G.C. (winning Senior Cup medals in 1975 and 1989, Barton Shield in 1990, also winning an Inter-County medal in 1988). He won the Irish Close title in 1985, beating Declan Brannigan (he had previously lost in a Close final to Brannigan in 1976), and captured the 'East' in 1990. He has played 77 interprovincial matches for Munster 1971-1990, winning 38; he has played 21 Home international matches for Ireland between 1976 and 1991 (helping Ireland to win the Home International 'triple crown' in 1987, the Home international Championship in 1991, and also to win the Quadrangular Continental matches in 1986 and 1988), winning 8; he has played 4 European Team championship matches in 1977, winning 2.

O'SULLIVAN, DENIS.

G.A.A. football half-back, right half-back and midfielder, Kerry. Club: Kevins O'Rahillys. In 1963, after winning an All-Ireland M.F.C. title in 1962, he again won a minor All-Ireland medal, but also won a junior All-Ireland and a National Football League medal in that year. He was on Kerry sides beaten in 3 All-Ireland Senior Football Championship finals in 1964, 1965, and 1968. In 1969 he won his only All-Ireland senior medal (as a non-playing sub).

O'SULLIVAN, DONIE.

G.A.A. football utility back and midfielder, Kerry. Clubs: Dr Croke's (winning East Kerry Championship medals in 1957, 1962 and 1965), U.C.D., Spa (winning more East Kerry championship medals). He captained, at left-full back, the Kerry team which won the All-Ireland Senior Football Championship final in 1970 when they beat Meath by 2-19 to 2-18 in the first 80 minute final, having been also a member of the panel which beat Offaly in the previous year's final (he also won medals in 1962 and 1975 as a panel member). He was on 4 losing All-Ireland S.F.C. sides, in 1964 (in midfield), 1965 (at right corner-back), 1968 (at right half-back) and in 1972 (again at right-corner back). He won 4 National Football League medals, in 1969, 1971, 1972, and 1973. He won his only Railway Cup medal with Munster in 1977. He gained 2 All-Star awards, in the inaugural years of 1971 and 1972, both as a left-corner back.

O'SULLIVAN, KEVIN JER.

G.A.A. football right half-back, Cork. A member of the Cork side which won 3 Munster Senior Football Championship titles in 4 years, 1971, 1973, and 1974, he won his only All-Ireland Senior Football Championship winner's medal in Cork's famous 1973 win over Galway. He also won 2 Railway Cup medals with Munster, in 1972 and 1975. He received 2 All-Star awards, in 1972 and 1973, both at left half-back.

O'SULLIVAN, JACK.

Amateur interprovincial golfer. Club: Athlone (winning a Barton Shield medal in 1959). He played in 52 interprovincial matches for Connacht between 1956 and 1965, winning only 13 games. He was non-playing captain when Connacht won (for the first of only 2 occasions) the Interprovincial Championships in 1967. He was Honorary Secretary of the Connacht Branch of the G.U.I. for 25 years. He won the Irish Senior's Championship in 1972, and has been regarded as one of the better of Ireland's scratch golfers not to be capped.

O'SULLIVAN, JOE.

G.A.A. football half-back, Kerry. Clubs: Dingle and U.C.D. He won 4 All-Ireland Senior Football Championship winner's medals with Kerry, all in the county's great 4-in-a-row successes of 1929, 1930, 1931, and 1932. He won his solitary Railway Cup medal with Munster in the all-Kerry side which captured the trophy in 1931.

O'SULLIVAN, JIM (JAMES).

Amateur international boxer. Born October 16th 1959. Club: St Patrick's B.C. of Enniscorthy, Co Wexford). Starting to box in 1970 at tha age of 11, in 1989 he became only the 3rd Irish amateur boxer (after Gearoid O Colmain and Harry Perry) to win 9 Irish National Senior Champinship titles, and in 1990 he became the first (and the only) Irish boxer to win 10 national senior titles. His wins came at 4 different weights over a period of 11 years, starting in 1980 at light-middleweight, then in 1981 he won at light-heavyweight, and he has won 8 titles at heavyweight: in 1982, 1984, 1985 and 1986 in the heavyweight class, and in 1987, 1988, 1989 and 1990 in the super-heavyweight division. In an amateur career of 300 fights, he fought 38 times for Ireland, winning 25 of his bouts, although he was never in an Olympic squad.

O'SULLIVAN, MARCUS.

Middle distance athlete. Born in Cork, 22nd November 1961. Clubs: Leevale, and New Balance T.C. (U.S.A.). A scholarship graduate of Villanova University, his major championship record at 1,500 metres is: semi-final of Olympic Games 1984: semi-final of World Championship 1987; 6th in European Championship in 1986; 2nd (silver medallist) in the European Indoor Championship in 1985; Olympic heats at 1,500 metres in 1988; and (in his third Olympic Games in which he gained semi-final placings) in the 1,500 metres in Barcelona in 1992. He was Irish Champion at 1,500m in 1984, and British A.A.A. Champion in 1985. At 800m he broke the Irish record 3 times (bringing the mark down to 1 minute 45.87 seconds in West Berlin in 1989), and was Irish B.L.E. Champion in 1986, 1989 and 1992. Overtaking Eamonn Coghlan as the world's finest indoor miler from the mid-1980's, he won the inaugural World Indoor Championship 1,500 metres title in 1987 in the Hossier Dome Indianapolis, and successfully defended this prestigious title in Budapest in 1989, thus becoming the first Irishman to win 2 World indoor Championship titles. He finished 4th in the 1991 championships in an attempt to win 3 successive 1,500 metres titles, but won again in 1993 in Toronto to make his tally to 3 wins in this highly prestigious event. In the U.S. indoor circuit, he has won the prestigious Wannamaker Mile 5 times, in 1986, 1988, 1989, 1990 and 1991. In Meadowlands in 1988 he set a new world indoor record time in the 1,500 metres, with figures of 3:35:06. A member of the Irish 4 x 1 mile squad which broke the world record in 1985, he was selected as Texaco's Sports Star of the Year in Athletics in 1989.

O'SULLIVAN, MICHAEL ('MICKEY NED').

G.A.A. football half-forward, Kerry. Club: Kenmare (captaining them to win the 1974 Kerry county championship, winning another in 1987). He was a member of the Colaiste Iosagain side beaten in 4 successive Corn Ui Mhuiri. He was on the Kerry team beaten in the All-Ireland M.F.C. final in 1970, and on the Under 21 side beaten in the All-Ireland Under 21 Championship in 1972, before winning a medal as captain at this grade in the 1973 side. He captained, at 23, the famous young Kerry side to their 2-12 to 0-19 defeat of Dublin for the Sam Maguire Cup in 1975 (the first 70 minute final), although he was substituted during the game, being hospitalised through injury, and thus not accepting the cup. He was on the side, at left half-forward, beaten by Dublin in the 1976 final, and won 2 further All-Ireland Senior Football Championship medals (both as a non-playing sub), although playing in the Munster final and All-Ireland semi-final of 1978. He was also a winner of 4 National League medals with Kerry (1972, 1973, 1974 and 1977), and captured his only All-Star award in 1975, at left wing-forward. In 1989-92 he was trainer to the Kerry senior football team, helping them to win the Munster S.F.C. in 1991.

O'SULLIVAN, PAT.

Amateur international golfer. Club: Tramore. She won the Irish Ladies Close Championship in 1956 (winning by a record margin of 14-and-12 in the 36 hole final at Killarney over Mrs J F Hegarty), and was later to be runner-up in this event 4 years in succession, in 1964, 1965, 1966 and 1967. She played in 16 different series of Home Internationals for Ireland from 1950 to 1967, and captained the side in 1969, 1970 and 1971 (when she also captained the Irish side in the European Ladies Tean event). She won the Midland Ladies in 1961.

O'SULLIVAN, Patrick Joseph ANTHONY (TONY).

Rugby international No 8 forward. Born in Galway, 2nd June 1933. Club: Galwegians (winning Connacht Senior Cup medals in the 5-in-a-row side of 1956, 1957, 1958, 1959 and 1960, and again in 1963 and 1965). A product of St Jarlath's College, he was capped 15 times for Ireland between 1957 and 1963, scoring one international try. A victualler.

O'SULLIVAN, PADDY.

Boxer, amateur and professional. Club: Mourne Abbey. A Corkman, he won 3 Irish Senior National titles at heavyweight, in 1939, 1941, and 1941. Turning pro, he became Irish professional heavyweight champion (a title without much credibility), and he twice fought Martin Thornton (cv), losing the first bout in 3 rounds, and lasting only 77 seconds in the rematch.

O'SULLIVAN, SONIA.

International middle-distance runner. Born in Cobh, Co Cork, 28th November 1969. Clubs: Ballymore-Cobh and Villanova. Having broken National Junior records at 800 metres and 3,000 metres in 1987, she became National Junior Champion in 1988 at both 88 and 1,500 metres. In 1990 she became the A.C.A.A. 3,000 metres champion and the Irish Senior 1,500 metres champion. She won the National B.L.E. Championship title at 3,000 metres in 1991, and also won a gold medal in the World Student Games in Sheffield in the same event. Also in 1991 she became the first Irish woman athlete to break a world track record, doing so at 5,000 metres indoors. In 1992 she finished in a highly creditable 7th place in the World Championship Cross-Country in Boston, 5 places behind her compatriot, Catherina McKiernan (cv), in Boston, and later broke the Irish record for 3,000 metres by an astonishing 12 seconds; she also won the B.L.E. 1,500 metres title. She came to prominence when she finished a highly creditable 4th in the Olympic Games women's 3,000 metres final (being only the 2nd Irish woman to appear in an Olympic final) in Barcelona in 1992. In a 11-day period soon after the games, she broke 5 national records from 1,500 to 5,000 metres (in which event she then became the first Irishwoman to break the 15 minutes mank) also winning the Grand Prix event for 5,000 metres (gaining a $10,000 bonus), and in doing so emerged as a world-class athlete. In 1993 she shattered her own Irish record for the 3,000 metres by over 13 seconds in all (and became the first Irishwoman to run the 1,500m in under 4 minutes). After a hugely successful summer was installed as favourite for the World Championship 3,000 metres at Stuttgart, although she in fact finished 4th behind 3 Chinese women. In the 1,500 metres event at the same games she became the first woman athlete from the Republic of Ireland to win a medal at any major championship, when she finished 2nd (in a time of 4:03:48) behind the Chinese girl Dong Liu, to take the silver. Later in the year she shared in a golden bonanza for winning 4 Grand Prix events, and finished second overall in the Grand Prix series, winning $100,000. She was made Texaco Sportstar of the Year in athletics in 1992.

O'SULLIVAN, TONY.

G.A.A. hurling right half-forward and left full-forward, Cork. Club: Na Piarsaigh (helping them to their first ever Cork county championship in 1990). He won an All-Ireland M.H.C. medal with Cork in 1979, and won an All-Ireland Under 21 Championship medal in 1982. A member of the Cork side which lost 2 successive All-Ireland Senior Hurling Championship finals to Galway in 1982 and 1983, he has won 3 Liam McCarthy Cup medals with Cork, in 1984 (at centre half-forward), 1986 (at left half-forward), and in 1990 at centre-forward. He was the county's leading championship scorer (0-31) when they were beaten in the All-Ireland S.H.C. final in 1992. He won a National Hurling League medal with Cork in 1992-93. He has won 5 All-Star awards, in 1982 and 1986 at right half-forward, and in 1988 (when he was the only Corkman in the team) at left full-forward, and in 1990 and 1992 at left-half forward. In 1990 he was also selected as the Texaco Sportstar of the Year in hurling.

O'SULLIVAN, Dr WILLIAM M (BILLY or 'DOCTOR BILLY O').

Amateur international golfer. Born in Killarney, 13th March 1911. Club: Killarney. He won the Irish Open Amateur title in 1949 (when he just missed Walker Cup selection), and was runner-up in this championship twice, in 1936 and 1953. He was runner-up in the Irish Close championship in 1940. The longest hitter in Ireland at his peak, between 1934 and 1954 he played in 68 Home international matches for Ireland over 12 series, making him up to 1989 Ireland's 4th most capped Home international, winning 36 of these matches. He was President of the G.U.I. 1958-60, during which Ireland hosted the Canada (World) Cup. A legend in Killarney, he was also a fine rugby out-half with U.C.C. (winning 3 successive Munster Senior Cup medals with them, in 1935, 1936, and in 1937 when captain), and he won a final trial place for Ireland.

O'TOOLE, ANTON ('THE BLUE PANTHER' or 'JOE NAMATH').

G.A.A. football right-half and left-full forward Dublin. Born on 18th February

1951. Club: Synge Street PP. Having first played inter-county senior football in 1972, he became a member of the successful Dublin side of the 1970's and early 80's, being on the side which won All-Ireland Senior Football Championship titles in 1974 (at left full-forward), 1976 and 1977 (both at right half-forward). He was also on the sides beaten by Kerry in the 1975, 1978 and 1979 finals. He won a 4th Sam Maguire Cup medal with the winning side in 1983, this time at full-forward, and played in his 8th All-Ireland final in 11 years in 1984, again losing at he hands of Kerry). He was a winner of 3 successive All-Star awards (the first forward in Heffo's Army to do so), in 1975 at left full-forward, and in 1976 and 1977 at right half-forward.

O'TOOLE, GARY.

Swimming international breaststroker. Born 6th August 1968. Clubs: Bray Cove and Trojan. A biochemistry graduate, he is from Bray, Co Wicklow (he played Junior Schools rugby for Presentation College Bray). He made his Irish swimming debut at 16, got a world ranking at the age of 17, and qualified for the European Championships in Stasbourg in 1987. In 1989, having reached a world ranking of No 3 at the 200 metres breaststroke, he became, at the European Championships at Bonn, the first Irish swimmer to win a medal at this level, when, although swimming in lane 8, he finished 2nd in the 200m breaststroke final behind Britain's Nick Gillingham, his time at 2 minutes 15.73 seconds breaking the Irish record by over 2 seconds in the process. In 1990 he set 7 Irish records and, in 1991 won Ireland's first ever swimming medal at the World Student Games, when winning the 200 metres breaststroke in Sheffield in 2.16.75. In 1990 he also failed to qualify for the final of the European 200 metres breaststroke. He was selected, for his Olympic performances of 1988 (qualifying for the 'B' final at 200 metres breaststroke, and setting 4 National records at the games), to be Texaco's Swimming Sportstar of the Year for 1988 (winning again in both 1989 and 1990). In the Barcelona Olympics in 1992 he finished 20th fastest in the heats of his speciality event, the 200 metres breaststroke.

O'TOOLE, MAVIS.

Handballer. Club: Na Fianna (Dublin). By far and away Ireland's most successful handballer since the ladies game came into vogue in the early 1960's, she won the Irish Ladies title each year from its inception in 1970 until 1981, and to add to this 12-in-a-row, she also won 8 Irish doubles titles in that period, partnered by Elizabeth Nichol.

O'TOOLE, MICHAEL A (MICK).

Horse trainer, National Hunt and flat. Born 18th September 1931. Trains at Maddenstown, Co Kildare. His big wins include: the Irish 2,000 Guineas and Eclipse Stakes of 1979 with Dickens Hill, 3 Sun Alliance Hurdles (1974 with Brown Lad, 1975 with Davy Lad and 1976 with Parkhill), and the Cheltenham Gold Cup in 1977 with Davy Lad. Other good horses of his have included Faliraki, Hartstown, and Miami Springs, and his total tally in the Cheltenham Festival is 8 winners.

O'TOOLE, NIALL.

Lightweight sculler. Born in Dublin in 1970. Club: Commercial R.C. Having won the Irish junior sculling championship in both 1987 and 1988 (also competing in the world junior championships), he has won many Irish Senior national titles in both singles (4 up to 1993) and doubles sculls, as well as a number of regattas. He has won 2 successive Match des Seniors (World Lightweight Under 23 sculling) gold medals, in 1989 in Amsterdam and in 1990 in Ottensheim. He took part in the World Senior Lightweight Championships in 1989 (finishing 9th), and at Lake Barrington in Tasmania in 1990, qualifying for (and finishing 6th and last) in the final. By a series of impressive 8 gold medal wins in the 1991 regatta circuit (most notably in Duisberg in May, beating both the gold and silver medalists of the 1990 world championships), this brilliant rower became the No 1 ranked sculler in the world. He confirmed this form, when at the 1991 World Lightweight Championships at Vienna, he became the first Irishman to win a gold medal at this level, when winning in 6:49.17 over the 2,000 metres course. Competing in the Barcelona Olympics in the singles sculls (against heavyweight scullers), illness hampering a serious challenge there, or in any defence of the world title. He won a gold medal at the Lausanne regatta in 1993, but only finished 5th in his attempt to regain the world lighthweight singles sculls that year near Prague. His brother Francis has won the Irish Senior Championship double sculls with Niall on a few occasions and also won the coxed pairs in 1990; he rowed for Ireland in the lightweight mens fours in the world championships (finishing 10th) in Vienna in 1991. Niall won the Texaco Sportstar award for Rowing in 1991.

OWENS, Dr GERARD H (GERRY).

Amateur international golfer. Club: Skerries. He won the Irish Close Championship in Rosses Point in 1939, and was runner-up in the 1942 'West'. A Leinster interprovincial in 1938 and 1939, he played 22 Home Internationals for Ireland between 1935 and 1947, winning 13. In 1984 he donated an Over 70's cup for that section of the Irish Senior's Open, promptly winning it in the first year it was played for. He captained the Irish Home International side in 1957-59. A long-time golf administrator, he was President of the G.U.I. in 1971-72.

OXX, JOHN.

Horse trainer. Born in Dunboyne, Co Meath, 16th January 1910, he died 1987. Trained at Currabeg, Co Kildare. He trained 8 Irish classic winners: 3 Irish St Leger's (with Solferino in 1943, Lyncris in 1960 and Biscayne in 1964); the Irish 2,000 Guineas in 1962 with Artic Storm; and the Irish Oaks 4 times (1960 with Lyncris, 1963 with Hibernia III, 1966 with Merry Mate, and 1967 with Pampalina). His Hidalgo was 2nd in the Irish Derby in 1954, and his Arctic Storm finished 2nd also in 1962. He was champion trainer in 1958. Other fine horses he trained included Lady Kells, and Majority Blue. His son John Oxx, also a flat trainer (born 14th July 1950), trains at Currabeg, Co Kildare, and his best horses include Orchestra, Curravilla, and Green Lucia; his most successful seasons have included 1987 with 54 and 1990 with over 55, and the addition of Aga Khan horses has boosted his winners tally.

P

PADDEN, WILLIE JOE.

G.A.A. football midfielder, Mayo. Club: Belmullet. A charismatic member of the Mayo senior inter-county team from 1977 (when he led the county minor's to a Connacht M.F.C. title), he has won 4 Connacht Senior Championship medals, in 1981, 1985, 1988 (as a playing sub), and 1989. A high-fielder of note who has also featured as a forward, he was a star member of the Mayo team which reached the All-Ireland Senior Football Championship final for the first time in 38 years in 1989. He has won 2 All-Star awards, in 1985 and 1989, both in the midfield .

PARKE, JAMES CECIL.

International rugby centre threequarter, tennis player, and golfer. Born in Clones Co Monaghan, 26th July 1881. In rugby, as a centre threequarter with both Monkstown and Dublin University, he played interprovincial rugby for Leinster 10 times from 1901 to 1908, and won 20 international caps for Ireland between 1903 and 1907, three of them as captain. He scored 31 international points for Ireland, through 2 tries, 5 conversions, 1 goal from mark, and 4 penalties, and was a member of the Irish XV which shared the International Championship in 1906. As a tennis player he won the Wimbledon Mixed Doubles title in 1914, was twice a beaten semi-finalist in the Men's Singles (1910 and 1913), and was 4 times a beaten finalist in the Men's Doubles (1911, 1912, 1913, and 1920). He won the Australian Men's singles and doubles tennis titles in 1912. He played for Britain in the Davis Cup in 1908-09, 1912-14, and in 1920, being twice on the winning side, and was Singles Champion of Europe in 1907. He also won an Olympic silver medal in the Men's Doubles (along with Josiah Ritchie of Britain) at the 1908 games in London. He won 8 Irish Lawn Tennis Singles titles, 1904, 1905, 1908, 1909, 1910, 1911, 1912, and 1913, and won 4 doubles titles (1909-12 inclusive) and 2 mixed titles (1908 and 1912). He was ranked at No 6 in the world tennis in 1914 and at No 4 in 1920. One of Ireland's greatest all-round sportsmen, he became a scratch golfer, playing for Ireland in 2 matches in 1906 while a member of Dublin University (thus representing his country in 3 very different sports). He was also a top-class track and field sprinter, a first class standard cricketer, and played chess for the Clones team at the age of 9. He died on 27th February 1946, at the age of 65.

PARKE, JOHN.

Soccer international full-back. Born in Belfast, 6th August 1937. Clubs: Linfield (winning Irish Cup medals in 1962 and 1963), Hibernian, Sunderland. He spent 3 seasons with Sunderland 1964-67, playing 84 league matches. He was capped 14 times for Northern Ireland between 1964 and 1968, mainly in the No 2 jersey.

PARKINSON, Senator J J (JIM).

Horse trainer and breeder, flat. Born in Tramore, Co Waterford in 1870. A vet and breeder of note based at Maddenstown, he exported horses that he bred all over the world, helping in no small way to gain Ireland's repuation as a prime breeding ground for class horses. Since the inception of Irish trainer's records tables in 1905 (based on stakes money won), he won the Irish title 6 times, was 2nd eight times, and was 9 times in third place on these lists. As a trainer of winners per season he has had few peers in Irish racing, and his record number of 134 winners in 1923 was only surpassed by Jim Bolger (cv) in 1990. His tally of Irish Classic wins is 6: two Irish Derby's (his own horse First Flier in 1917 and Loch Lomond in 1919), and 4 Irish Oaks winners (Royal Mantle in 1901, Blakestown in 1905, Shining Way in 1912 and Athgreany in 1913). He saddled 4 winners on Epsom Derby Day in 1909. His son Billy Parkinson was leading Irish amateur in 1915 (an Irish record tally until surpassed in 1923) and 1916. Jim became a Senator, and is the grand-father of the R.T.E. horse racing commentator Tony Sweeney.

PARNELL, R. F. ('BUSTER') and DAVID.

Flat jockey father and son. 'Buster' rode in England for the Willie Stephenson stable in Royston before coming to Ireland. Riding many winners in Ireland, his 3 Irish Classic winners are: 2 Irish 2,000 Guineas winners in succession (Atherstone Wood in 1967 and Mistigo in 1968; and one Irish 1,000 Guineas winner in 1975 with Miralla. He later trained in Denmark. His son David (born in Dublin 28th June 1965), had three good years riding in Ireland (32 winners in 1987, 39 in 1988 and 47 in 1989), and was beaten by a short-head in the 1989 Irish St Leger, before being killed in a car accident in 1990.

PATTERSON, COLIN Stewart.

Rugby international scrum-half. Born in Belfast, 3rd March 1955. Club: Bristol University and Instonians (winning an Ulster Senior Cup medal in 1979). While studying law at Bristol, he played for

English and British Universities XVs. A product of R.B.A.I., he first played for Ulster in 1976. Having played for Ireland 'B' in 1978, he went on to be capped at senior level 11 times for Ireland between 1978 and 1980, scoring 5 international tries, an average of almost a try in every alternate match. He went on the Lion's tour of South Africa in 1980, and played in 3 test matches. In the penultimate match of this tour he recieved an injury which ended his short but exciting career. A fine player with a knack for scoring tries, he is a solicitor.

PATTERSON, C D.

Rugby player. Club: Malone (winning Ulster Senior Cup medals in 1904, 1905 and 1907, the club's first triumphs in that competition). Although he was never capped by Ireland, he was selected for the British and Irish Lions side which toured Australia and New Zealand in 1904. However, he did not play any Test matches.

PATTERSON, NIALL ('FLOYD').

G.A.A. football goalkeeper, Antrim. Club: Loughgiel Shamrocks (whom he captained to win the All-Ireland Club Championshp title in 1983). A portly figure, and a regular senior inter-county player for many years, he was a prominent figure in the Antrim side which reached the All-Ireland Senior Hurling Championship final in 1989 (for the first time since 1943).

PAUL, GWEN.

Ladies hockey international player. Club: Old Ursalines, Cork. From Cork, she played interprovincial hockey while at school in the Ursaline Convent there. Later she played senior interprovincial hockey, and won 31 international caps for Ireland as a forward between 1981 and 1984. Her career highlight was being voted 'Player of the Tournament' when Ireland won the International Cup in Kuala Lumpur in 1983, when her 6 goal tally was the best in the tournament. She was selected as Texaco's Hockey Sportstar of the Year for 1983.

PAYNE, CHARLES TREVOR ('FATS').

Rugby international front row forward. Club: N.I.F.C. (winning an Ulster Senior Cup medal with them in 1930). He was capped for Ireland 16 times between 1926 and 1930, a period in which Ireland threatened Triple Crown status (without success) but lost only 5 matches, although he was on Irish XV's which shared International Championships in both 1926 and 1927. He was a member of the side which won at Twickenham for the first time in 1929, and he was one of 3 Irishmen who toured Argentina with the unbeaten R.F.U. side in 1927.

PEACOCK, ROBERT (BERTIE, 'THE LITTLE ANT').

Soccer international defender. Clubs: Glentoran, Glasgow Celtic (playing 350 games for them from 1949 to 1960, winning a Scottish Cup medal in 1954, a Scottish League medal in 1953, and League Cup medals in 1957 and 1958), Coleraine (winning an Irish Cup medal in 1965). He was capped 31 times for Northern Ireland between 1952 and 1962, and played in the No 6 jersey in 4 out of the 5 matches in his country's glorious run in the 1958 World Cup in Sweden. He scored 2 international goals, and was a member of the Great Britain side which played the Rest of Europe for the I.F.A.'s 75th anniversary game. He was manager of the Northern Ireland soccer team from 1962 to 1967, and managed Coleraine from 1961 to 1974, helping them to win the I.F.A. Cup in 1965 and 1972 and the Irish League in 1974, among many other trophies. Later he was the owner of the Long Bar in Coleraine.

PEARD, FRANK W.

Badminton player. Ireland's most successful male badminton player since W.W.II. (being capped 30 times for Ireland between 1947 and 1957), he won his singles match against England in

8 successive years. With his partner Jim Fitzgibbon, he was rated as the best in Europe for 2 years in doubles competitions, reaching the All-England Doubles semi-final in 1952. He won the Irish Close singles 4 times in succession (1950, 1951, 1952 and 1953), the men's doubles 9 times with Fitzgibbon, and the mixed doubles 5 times with Mrs B.I. Donaldson. He also played tennis at Wimbledon, representing Ireland. He was later a successful badminton coach, writer and administrator. He married Sue Devlin (cv), the daughter of Frank Devlin (cv), herself the winner of 6 All-England Doubles titles along with her sister, the great Judy Hashman. His son Mark 'Chippy' Peard, played international badminton for Ireland, while his daughter Pam played European Junior badminton for Ireland also.

PEDEN, JOHN.

Soccer international forward. Clubs: Linfield and Distillery. He was capped 24 times for Northern Ireland (mainly in the No 11 shirt) in the country's formative years in international soccer, between 1887 and 1899, and was the scorer of 7 international goals for the I.F.A.

PEDLOW, Alexander CECIL.

Rugby international centre and wing threequarter, and squash international. Born in Lurgan, 20th January 1934. Rugby clubs: Queen's University, Belfast and C.I.Y.M.S. (winning an Ulster Senior Cup medal in 1953, and an Ulster Senior League medal in 1962-63). He was capped at rugby for Ireland 30 times in all, between 1953 (when he scored a try on his debut at St Helen's Park, Swansea) and 1963, scoring 31 points, including 2 tries. He was selected on the Lion's tour of South Africa in 1955, winning 2 Test places, and he scored the Lions first test try on that tour. A skilful and determined back, his lack of pace and poor eyesight were the only reasons why he was not an outstanding player. A dentist, he also played international squash for Ireland, winning 6 international caps between 1964 and 1970 (later winning 12 veterans and 3 vintage international caps, the only Irish person to be capped at all these 3 levels).

PEDLOW, JOSEPH, ROBERT, and THOMAS B.

Rugby international brothers. Joseph (a member of the Bessbrook club) played 2 games for Ireland 1882-1884, Robert, also from the Bessbrook club, won 1 international cap in 1891, and Thomas B (Queen's University Belfast) won 2 caps on the Triple Crown winning Irish side of 1899.

PENNEY, STEPHEN.

Soccer international midfielder. Born in Ballymena, 16th January 1964. Joining Brighton and Hove Albion from Ballymena, he played 138 league matches for the Goldstone Ground club, before later joining Hearts and Burnley. First capped for Northern Ireland in 1985 against Israel, he was capped 17 times up to 1989, scoring 2 international goals, and he played twice in the No 7 jersey in the World Cup side in Mexico in 1986. The 17 caps he gained while at the Goldstone Ground made him the most capped Brighton international player.

PERITON, HAROLD GREAVES (JOE).

Rugby international flanker, England. Born in Ireland in 1901, he died in 1980. Club: Waterloo (the 1st player from the club to be capped for England, and the club's most capped player). He is the only Irish-born player ever to captain England; in 1930 in what was to be his final international season, he captained 'the old enemy' 4 times, including against Ireland in Lansdowne Road (this brought his cap tally to 21 since his 1925 debut). He scored 6 international tries in his English career.

PERRY, HARRY.

Amateur international boxer. Clubs: Terenure and British Railways. In 1962 he became only the 2nd amateur boxer to win 9 Irish National Senior Championship titles (equal with Gerry O'Colmain's record, later passed in 1990 by Jim O'Sullivan), and he achieved them at 4 different weights (more than the other 2 record holders). He won 2 titles at featherweight, in 1952 (he had earlier in the year won the Irish junior championship at this weight) and 1953, one at lightweight in 1954, another one at light-welterweight in 1955, while at welterweight he won 5 titles, in 1956, 1958, 1960, 1961, and 1962. Regarded as too young in 1952 to compete in the Helsinki Olympics, he did compete twice at the Olympic Games, in Melbourne in 1956 and in Rome in 1960, beaten in his first bout both times.

PERRY, PADDY.

Handballer. Born in Co Roscommom in 1911. He won the Irish Junior Softball Singles and Doubles title in 1929. His class showed quickly when, for a period of 8 years in the 1930's, he was unbeaten in singles in softball handball, and won the Irish Senior Softball Singles title 8 years in succession, in 1930, 1931, 1932, 1933, 1934, 1935, 1936, and 1937 (a record tally until surpassed by Michael 'Ducksie' Walsh in 1993). He also won 2 Irish Senior Softball Doubles titles. Also an accomplished gaelic footballer and hurler, he won, on the same day, Dublin Senior Championships in handball, hurling and football. Regarded among Ireland's finest handballer's, he died in 1983.

PETERS, MARY Elizabeth ('MARY P').

Athlete in the Pentathlon. Born in Halewood, Lancashire, 6th July 1939. Club: Spartan Ladies. A Belfast secretary, she competed for Northern Ireland in 5 successive Commonwealth Games from 1958, winning the pentathlon in 1970 and 1974. She also won the Commonweatlth gold medal at the shot putt in 1970 (with a Games record), having won the silver in 1966 (and held the British record at 16.31 metres for 12 years from 1966 to 1978). She won the British W.A.A.A. Pentathlon title 8 times, in 1962, 1963, 1964. 1965, 1966, 1968, 1970, and 1973, as well as the British W.A.A.A. shot putt title 5 times (1964, 1965, 1966, 1970, and in 1972), and the 100 metres hurdles in 1970 (she also broke the British record at this event). She was placed 4th in the 1964 Olympic Pentathlon (behind Irina Press, Mary Rand and Galina Bystrova), also competing in the shot putt; in her 2nd Olympic Games in Mexico she finished 9th in the pentathlon in 1968 when hampered by an ankle injury (she also captained the British women's team at these games). On September 2nd and 3rd 1972 in Munich, at the age of 33 and competing in her 45th pentathlon (and in her 3rd Olympic Games), she set a new world record score of 4801 points when winning the Olympic title at the Pentathlon, beating the challenge of Heidi Rosendhal by 10 points, in the process becoming Northern Ireland's first Olympic gold medal winner (and Britain's only 3rd woman to do so at athletics). In this, her crowning hour, she set personal bests in 4 of the 5 events, including the 100 metres hurdles (13.3 seconds), the long jump, high jump (where her 1.82 metres was 4 cms better than her best and 17cm better than that of Rosenthal), and in the final event at 200 metres, when her new personal best of 24.1 seconds enabled her to win the gold (had she been one tenth of a second slower in this discipline, she would have taken silver). She was chosen as Texaco's Athletics Sportstar of the Year for both 1970 and 1972, and in 1972 was also voted as B.B.C.'s Sports Personality of the Year. She was the British women's team manager for 5 years, including at the Moscow Olympic Games in 1980. An inspiration to athletes in Belfast and Northern Ireland, she initiated the now world famous Mary Peters Track near Belfast (opened in 1976), and now runs a fitness club. She was made an M.B.E. in 1973 and a C.B.E. in 1990.

PETERSON, WALTER E

Hockey international full-back. Club: Palmerston. He was capped 23 times for Ireland between 1903 and 1914. He was a member of the Irish side which won a silver medal at the London Olympic Games of 1908, losing out in the 3 team event by 8-1 to England in the final. He is one of 6 brothers from Avoca School and the Palmerston H.C. who represented Ireland in hockey, 5 of them being on the history-making Ireland XI which won it's first Triple Crown in 1904. The other brothers, including their number of caps won, were: Bertie (2 caps at outside-right, 1900-02), Cecil (8 caps at centre-forward, 1901-04), Jack (20 caps at full-back, 1901-14, forming a fine full-back combination with Walter in the Irish side from 1903 to 1914), Nick (5 caps at right half, 1904-06), and William (8 caps at inside left, 1901-1904). With a combined total of 66 caps, this makes them the first family of 6 brothers to ever represent Ireland at the same team sport. All 6 played in the Palmerston club's run (in 1900-1905) of losing only 2 games out of 160 in 6 successive seasons when the club won 4 Irish Senior Cup titles.

PEYTON, GERRY.

Soccer international goalkeeper. Born in Birmingham, 20th May 1958. Clubs: Atherstone Town, Burnley, Fulham (playing 345 league games for them 1976-86), Bournemouth. He has been capped 35 times for the Republic of Ireland between 1977 and 1992 (in the later years as a 2nd string to Packie Bonner), and was substitute goalie in the Irish squad to the World Cup finals in 1990.

PEYTON, NOEL.

Soccer international inside forward. Born in Dublin, 4th December 1935. Clubs: Shamrock Rovers (winning 2 F.A.I. Cup medals in 1955 and 1956, and 2 League of Ireland Championship medals, in 1954 and 1957), Leeds United (he played 105 league matches for them 1957-62, scoring 17 goals), York City, Barnstable Town (as player-manager), Drumcondra (winning an F.A.I. Cup medal in 1965), and St Patrick's Athletic. Scoring one goal for the League of Ireland in 6 Inter-League matches (playing in the famous 3-3 draw with the English League in 1956), he was capped 6 times for the Republic of Ireland between 1956 (playing in the famous win over World Cup Champions West Germany in his debut) and 1963, having also played one 'B' international.

PHELAN, MICHAEL ('TICH').

G.A.A. hurling midfielder, Kilkenny. Born in 1967. Club: Glenmore. A member of the Kilkenny minors which won the All-Ireland M.H.C. in 1988, he has won 2 All-Ireland Senior Hurling Championship medals with the 'Cats' in 1992 and 1993. He won an All-Star award in 1992 in the midfield.

PHELAN, PADDY.

G.A.A. hurling left half-back, Kilkenny. Club: Tullaroan. He played Railway Cup with Leinster in 1930, before playing senior hurling for his county. He went on to win 4 All-Ireland Senior Hurling Championship medals with Kilkenny, in 1932, 1933, 1935, and 1939. He was on losing Kilkenny All-Ireland S.H.C. final sides 3 times, in 1931, 1936 and 1940. His tally of Railway Cup medals also reached 4, winning with Leinster in 1932, 1933, 1936, and 1941. He was selected at left half-back on the Sunday Independent 'Team of the Century' of 1984, alongside Tipperary's Jimmy Finn and Waterford's John Keane. A legend of the 'Black and Amber', he is the grand-uncle of the 1990's Kilkenny hero, D.J. Carey.

PHELAN, TERRY.

Soccer international left-back. Born in Manchester, 16th March 1967. Clubs: Leeds United, Swansea City, Wimbledon (for £100,000, winning an F.A. Cup medal in 1988), Manchester City (becoming Ireland's then most expensive ever player, and British football's most expensive ever defender at the time, when a fee of £2,500,00 was paid for him in 1993). Playing at Under 21 and Youth level, for the Republic of Ireland, he won his first cap in 1991, and reached 15 senior international caps by mid 1993.

PIERSE, ARTHUR D'Arcy.

Amateur international golfer. Born on 30th April 1950. Club: Tipperary. He won 4 Irish titles, the East of Ireland championship in 1979 (being runner-up in 1974), the 'West' title twice, in 1980 and 1982 (he was runner-up in 1979 when losing on the 8th tie hole to David Long cv, and 1993), and won the 'North' in 1987. A semi-finalist in the British Amateur in 1980, he won Walker Cup selection in 1983, halving one of his 3 matches. He has played 69 interprovincial matches for Munster 1974-90, winning 38; has played 63 Home international matches for Ireland 1976-88, winning 26 (including helping Ireland win the 'triple crown' in 1987); his 18 European Team championship matches for Ireland in 1981, 1983 and 1985 include 8 wins, and he was on the winning Irish team in Chantilly in 1983. He also helped Ireland win the Quadrangular Continental match in 1980. He won the Willie Gill award in 1980.

PIGOT, DAVID Richard Jnr.

Cricket international right hand batsman. Born in Dublin, 28th July 1929. Clubs: Dublin University and Phoenix. His senior league cricket career spanned 6 decades, from 1946 to 1990. A product of Blackrock College and Dublin University, he played cricket for Ireland 44 times between 1966 and 1975, winning his first cap at the age of 37. He scored 1,505 runs for Ireland in 79 innings with an average of 19.39 per innings, his highest score being 88. His father, David R Pigot, played 20 matches for Ireland between the 2 World Wars, 1922-1939. An uncle, James Poole Maunsell Pigot, who played first class cricket for Dublin University and the Madras Europeans in the 1920's, scored a record 194 runs for Phoenix in a Leinster Senior League match in 1923.

PIKE, VICTOR and THEODORE (TED).

Rugby international forwards, brothers. From Tipperary, and both playing for Lansdowne and Leinster, they gained 21 Irish rugby caps between them. Victor (whose clubs also included Aldershot Services and Dublin University), and who was 9 times a Leinster player, won 13 international caps between 1931 and 1934 (including the International Championship-winning side of 1932), while Ted (later to win a C.M.G. and a K.C.M.G.) won 8 international caps between 1927 and 1928, and played 4 times for Leinster. Ted was one of 3 Irishmen to tour Argentina with the unbeaten R.F.U. side in 1927. Three other brothers, all huge forwards, also played interprovincial rugby for Leinster (making the family the only one in Irish rugby history to have 5 brothers play for any province); two of them (Andrew and Robert, who each played once for the province) were close to international standard, while W A played 4 times for his province. Three of the 5 brothers, all from a family of 11 born to a Tipperary clergyman, became bishops: Victor (in Salisbury, Rhodesia), Robert, and St John.

PILKER, MARCUS.

Orienteer. Born 24th February 1974 in Bantry, Co Cork. Taking up the sport in 1984 (at the age of 10), he progressed to become the best ever Irish junior orienteer, winning Irish junior titles in 1986, 1987, 1988, 1991 and 1992 (being a member of the Irish junior squad for the maximum 6 years 1987 to 1992). His other wins include the 1991 German 5-Day and the 1992 Welsh 6-Day. In 1993, while still a junior, he was 2nd (to the world class New Zealander, Alistair Landels), in the Shamrock O'Ringen International (a class reserved for Elite runners), finishing well in front of all the members of the Irish senior squad. A champion of the future.

PILKINGTON, JOHN.

G.A.A. hurling midfielder, Offaly. Club: Birr (helping them to reach the

All-Ireland Club Championship final in 1992). He won an All-Ireland M.H.C. winner's medal in 1987 with Offaly minors. In 1990 he was the only Offaly player to win an All-Star award, being selected in the midfield. He won a National Hurling League medal in 1990-91, the first time his county had won this trophy. His brother Declan has played inter-county hurling for Offaly, and was also on the Birr side beaten in the 1992 All-Ireland Club Championship final.

PIM, DR JOSHUA.

Tennis player. Born in Bray, 2nd July 1869, he died in 1942. One of Ireland's greatest early tennis players, he won the prestigious Wimbledon Singles title twice in succession, in 1893 and 1894, on both occasions beating Wilfred Badeley, who in turn had beaten him in the 1891 and 1892 finals. He also won the Wimbledon Doubles title in 1890 with F O Stoker, being runner-up in this event in both 1891 and 1892. He also won the Irish singles title 3 times in succession, in 1893, 1894, and 1895. In 1902 he played for the British Isles Davis Cup team under the name of 'Mr X'.

PIPER, OLIVER JAMES S.

Rugby international forward. Club: Cork Constitution. Born in Aberavon in Wales, he won 8 international caps for Ireland, playing in all matches for 2 seasons, 1909 and 1910. He was selected for the British and Irish Lion's in 1910 to tour South Africa, winning one Test place. He won a Munster Senior rugby medal with Cork Constitution in 1910.

PLATT, JIM A.

Soccer international goalkeeper. Born in Ballymoney, 26th January 1952. Clubs: Ballymena, Middlesborough (playing 336 league matches for them 1971-1980), Hartlepool, Cardiff City, Ballymena (again), and Coleraine. For many years he was understudy to the great Pat Jennings (cv) in the Northern Ireland side, but still managed to be capped 23 times between 1976 and 1986, and was on the squad in the famous World Cup finals series in Spain in 1982, playing against Austria.

POLDEN, STANHOPE E (STAN).

Rugby international half-back. 1885-1958. Club: Clontarf. He is one of 8 Irish rugby players to be capped both before and after World War One, winning 2 caps in 1913, one in 1914, and one more 6 years later against France in 1920. He was linesman in a controversial incident which deprived Ireland of a Triple Crown in 1937 against England. He became an Irish selector for 11 years between 1922 and 1933, and was President of the I.R.F.U. in 1933-1934.

POLLAND, EDDIE.

Professional golfer. Born 10th June 1947 in Newcastle, Co Down. Turning pro in 1967, he won the Irish Dunlop in 1973 and 1975, and in 1974 won both the Irish professional championship and the Irish Matchplay titles. Important tournaments he won included the 1973 Penfold, the 1975 Sun Alliance Match Play, and he also won the coveted Spanish Open 2 years in succession, 1979 and 1980. His best Order of Merit finish was 6th in 1973, and he finished in 13th place in 1974, 1975, and in 1976. He won Ryder Cup honours in 1973, when he joined with Christy O'Connor Snr at Muirfield, losing both his matches. He played World Cup for Ireland 5 times in the 1970's, in 1973, 1974, 1976, 1977, 1978, and 1979. He was selected for G.B versus Europe 4 times, 1974-1980. He later lived in Malaga, Spain.

POLLIN, ROBERT.K.M. (BOB).

Amateur international golfer. Born in Belfast, 18th July 1946. Club: Royal Belfast. He won 4 Irish championships, namely the Irish Close Championship title in 1973, the 'North' in 1971, and the 'West' twice, in 1967 and 1969. He played 46 interprovincial matches for Ulster 1967-76, winning 21, and also played Home international golf in 1971, and in the European Team side of 1973.

POLLOCK, J STUART.

Cricket and squash international player. Born in Belfast, 5th June 1920. A product of Campbell College, he was a right hand batsman of note with N.I.C.C. He played 20 first class matches for Ireland betwen 1939 and 1957, also playing twice for the M.C.C, and once in a 1st class game for the Free Foresters, his record for these games being : 23-43-2-1036-129(v Scotland in 1951)-25.27. He played 41 international matches in all for Ireland between 1939 and 1957, scoring 1,506 runs for an average of 21.51 off 73 innings, his best score being 129 (against Scotland in 1951). He was President of the I.C.U. in 1980. A dual international, he was also capped 7 times for Ireland in squash between 1951 and 1955. His father, W Pollock, played 5 first class cricket matches for Ireland between 1909 and 1923, and was President of the I.C.U. in 1956.

POPPLEWELL, NICHOLAS James (NICK).

Rugby international prop forward. Born in Dublin 6th April 1964, he was educated at Newtown School in Waterford. Clubs: Gorey, Greystones (helping them gain promotion to Division One of the All-Ireland League). A Leinster, Irish 'B' and Under 25 player, he became a first choice prop for Ireland in the World Cup of 1991, scoring 2 tries against Zimbabwe. He toured with Ireland to France in 1988, North America in 1989, Namibia in 1991, and New Zealand in 1992. His international cap tally for Ireland reached 18 by March 1993, scoring 2 international tries. After a fine International Championship, he was selected on the British and Irish Lions tour of New Zealand in 1993, and played well in all three test matches. A warehouse manager, he was 3 times a schools international hockey player.

POTTER, JACQUI.

Ladies hockey international right wing and link player. Born in 1963. Club: Muckross. She played schools interprovincial, senior interprovincial and at Irish Under 21 level. In June 1990 she surpassed the old record of 83 caps to become Ireland's most capped international ladies hockey player, retiring after the European Championship qualifiers, with a tally of 86 caps (making her then the most capped ladies hockey player in the world), mostly as a link player. She also captained Ireland for 2 seasons. A bank official.

POWER, ANDREW (DANNO).

Amateur international boxer. Club: British Airways. He won 4 Irish National Senior Championship titles, all at light-middleweight, winning in 1958, and then in the three successive years of 1960, 1961, and 1962.

POWER, C F.

Hockey international player. Club: Three Rock Rovers. He was on the Irish team which lost 8-1 to England in the final of the 3 team tournament for the inaugural Olympic Games Men's Hockey event, and therefore a winner of a silver medal. He won his only 3 international caps in that Olympic year.

POWER, EDDIE.

Amateur international golfer. Born in Waterford 17th January 1965. Club: Tramore (helping, along with his younger brother Packie, to win the Irish Senior Cup and Barton Shield double in 1992, the first time either competition had been won by the club). A boys international in 1982 and a Youths international in 1984 and 1986, he won the Irish Close Championship title in both 1987 and 1993, having been runner-up in 1983. He won the Mullingar Scratch Cup in 1993. A Munster interprovincial 1986-1990, he has won 12 of his 22 matches. He was unbeaten in 5 matches played (4 wins and one halve) when on the Irish team which won the Home International Championship in 1987. He is the husband of Eileen Rose Power (cv).

POWER, (nee **McDAID**), EILEEN ROSE.

Amateur international golfer. Born in Letterkenny in 1967. Club: Skibereen. She won the Irish Girls Championship in 1983, and in 1985 she won the Munster Ladies title. She has won the Irish Ladies Close Championship twice, in 1990 and 1992 (being runner-up in the intervening year), and has played in the Home International series every year between 1987 and 1993. She was a non-travelling sub for the 1992 Curtis Cup team. Her mother (nee Rose O'Grady) was capped for Ireland at golf in 1959. Her brother Brendan was twice Irish Youths champion, is Ireland's most capped youth international, and is now a professional in Cork. Her brother Paul Is a professional golfer, while another brother, Kevin, was a boys international golfer in 1980. She is the wife of Eddie Power (cv).

POWER, GER.

G.A.A. football left-half back, mid-fielder, right half-forward and left full-forward, Kerry. Born in Annacotty Co Limerick, 27th June 1952 (his family moved to Kerry 6 days later). Club: Austin Stacks (with whom he won a county championship in 1973, the first the club had won for 37 years, and an All-Ireland Club Championship medal in 1977). He won an All-Ireland Under 21 Championship medal in 1973, having been on the Kerry minors side beaten in the All-Ireland M.F.C. final in 1970. He has won 8 All-Ireland Senior Football Championship medals, a record he shares with 4 other Kerrymen, his winning years being in 1975 (when he was voted man-of-the-match), the 4-in-a-row of 1978, 1979 (although missing the final in this year through injury), 1980 (captaining the side which beat Roscommon by 1-9 to 1-6) and 1981, and the 3-in-a-row of 1984, 1985 and 1986. He was on the losing side in the All-Ireland S.F.C. finals of 1976 and 1982. He won National Football League medals with Kerry in 1977, 1977, 1982 and 1983. He won 6 Railway Cup medals with Munster, in 1975, 1976, 1977, 1978, 1981 (when he became the 9th Kerryman to captain a winning Munster side) and 1982. He won 6 All-Star awards, at mid-field in 1975, at left half-back in 1976, at right-half forward in 1978, 1979 and 1980, and at left full-forward in 1986, making him one of only 5 footballers to win All-Star awards as both a forward and a back (and the first person in either code to win All-Star awards in 4 different positions). One of the great forwards in football history, he is the son of the great Limerick hurler, Jackie Power (cv).

POWER, JACKIE.

G.A.A. hurling centre-forward and centre-back, Limerick. Born in Annacotty, Co Limerick, 30th May 1916. Club: Ahane. He shares with the Mackey brothers, Mick and John, the record of 20 Limerick Senior Championship medals (he won 15 in hurling, including two 7-in-a-rows, 1933-1939, and 1942-1948 inclusive; he also won 5 Limerick SFC medals, also with Ahane, and all on the trot, 1935-193). He also played senior inter-county football for Limerick. In a 15 years span inter-county senior hurling career from 1935 to 1949, he won 2 All-Ireland S.H.C. medals with Limerick, in 1936 and 1940 (scoring 1-2 inthe final). He won 7 Railway Cup medals with Munster, in 1940, 1942, 1943, 1944, 1945, 1946, and 1948. He also won 5 National Hurling League medals with Limerick, in the record 5-in-a-row wins from 1934 to 1938. In later years he coached the famous Limerick side which captured the title again in 1973, after a long wait. A master of the ash, and a versatile player, he is the father of the famous Kerry footballer, Ger Power (cv).

POWER, JOHN.

G.A.A. hurling half-forward, Kilkenny. Born in 1966. Club: John Lockes. He was a member of the Kilkenny minors beaten in the All-Ireland M.H.C. final in 1984. A member of the Kilkenny side beaten in the All-Ireland Senior Hurling Championship final in 1991, he has won 2 Liam McCarthy Cup medals, in 1992 (scoring a vital goal in the final) and 1993. Gaining the reputation of being one of the best forwards in the 1990's, he won an All-Star award in 1992 in the centre half-forward position.

POWER, JOHN T.

G.A.A. hurler, Kilkenny. Born in 1883. Clubs: Piltown and Mooncoin (winning 2 county championship medals). In a senior inter-county career lasting from 1907 to 1925, he won 4 All-Ireland Senior Hurling Championship titles with Kilkenny teams, in 1907 with Moomcoin, in the awarded final of 1911, in 1912 with Tullaroan, and in 1913 again with Mooncoin.

POWER, MATTY.

G.A.A. hurler, Kilkenny and Dublin. Appearing in 9 All-Ireland S.H.C. finals over a 16 year period 1922 to 1937, he won 5 Senior Hurling Championship medals, 4 with his native Kilkenny (1922, 1932, 1933, and 1935), and one with Dublin in between these years, in 1927. His 4 losing All-Ireland S.H.C. experiences were with 1930 with Dublin, and 3 more times with Kilkenny, in 1931, 1936 and 1937. He won 4 Railway Cup medals with Leinster, in 1927 with Dublin, and 3 times with Kilkenny (1932, 1933, and 1936).

POWER, MICHAEL (MICK).

Amateur international golfer. Club: Muskerry. He won the Irish Close Championship title in Cork in 1951, and was runner-up again in 1953. He also captured the East of Ireland in 1951, being tied runner-up in 1954. He twice won the South of Ireland, in 1950 and 1952, and was runner-up in this event 3 times, in 1953, 1956 and 1957. He played in 7 series of the Home internationals for Ireland between 1947 and 1954, having a success rate of 50%.

POWER, RITCHIE.

G.A.A. hurling half-forward and midfielder, Kilkenny. Born 8th April 1957. Club: Carrickshock (one of 5 brothers playing for the intermediate South Kilkenny club). A member of the Kilkenny All-Ireland minor-winning panel in 1975, he was on the Under 21 team which became All-Ireland Champions in 1977, and was at right half-forward on the Kilkenny senior side which won the Liam McCarthy Cup in both 1982 and 1983. In 1987 he was at left half-forward in the Kilkenny side beaten in the All-Ireland S.H.C final, and was at midfield in the loss of 1991. A winner of 4 National League medals in 1982, 1983 and 1986, and 1990, he has won 2 All-Star awards, in 1982 at left-half-forward, and in 1986 at midfield. A fine Kilkenny stalwart, he retired from inter-county activity in 1992, aged 35.

POWER, SEAMUS.

G.A.A. hurling midfielder, Waterford. Born in 1929. Club (Mount Sion, winning 12 county hurling championship medals, including 9-in-a-row 1953-1961, and also 5 county football titles). In a senior inter-county career from 1948 to 1964, he won one All-Ireland Senior Hurling Championship winner's medal, in 1959 (scoring a crucial goal in the dying minutes of the drawn game), and also won 2 other Munster S.H.C. medals in 1957 and 1963 (when the county went on to lose both All-Ireland S.H.C. finals). He won 5 Railway Cup medals with Munster, in 1955, 1958, 1959, 1960 and 1961, and won a National Hurling League medal with Waterford in 1963. He played for the Rest of Ireland in 1960 and 1962.

PRATT, DONALD Montague.

Squash international player, and cricketer. Born in Dublin, 9th July 1935. Squash club: Fitzwilton. A product of St Columba's, he won the Squash Rackets Championship of Ireland Men's title on a record 10 occasions, in 1959, 1960, 1962, 1963, 1964, 1965, 1966, 1969, and in 1972, and was beaten in 4 finals (in 1956, 1961, 1967 and 1969). He was capped 52 times at squash for Ireland between 1956 and 1972, then a world record. He was a dual international, his cricket clubs being Dublin University and Phoenix. A left hand batsman, he played 10 international cricket matches for Ireland between 1963 and 1966 (often captaining the side), with his record for those matches being: 282 runs in 20 overs for an average of 16.58 per innings, his best of 58 being scored against the New Zealanders in 1965. He also played hockey for Leinster (captaining Three Rock Rovers for 3 years), and is a nephew of the great all-rounder T.G. McVeagh (cv).

PRENDERGAST, KEVIN.

Flat jockey and horse trainer. Born 5th July 1932. His classic winners include one in England (the 1977 2,000 Guineas with Nebbiolo, beating The Minstrel into third); in Ireland his Classic winners include two Irish 1,000 Guineas (with Pidget in 1972 and Artique Royale in 1981), the 1976 Irish 2,000 Guineas with Northern Treasure, and 2 Irish St Leger's (in 1972 with Pidget, and in 1973 with Connor Pass). His Northern Treasure finished third in the 1976 Irish Derby, having previously had a 2nd in the race in 1973 with Ragapan (which was 5th in the Epsom Derby). A son of Paddy Prendergast (cv).

PRENDERGAST, PADDY (P.J. or 'DARKIE').

Horse trainer, flat racing. Born 19th March 1909. Among his classic wins are 21 Irish Classics (ranking him 2nd only to Vincent O'Brien in total wins): 4 Irish 2,000 Guineas's, (1960 with Kythnos, 1963 with Linacre, 1972 with Ballymore and with Nikoli in 1980), 5 Irish 1,000 Guineas wins, (Sunlit Ride in 1950, Gazpacho in 1963, Wendyune in 1969, Sarah Siddons in 1976 and More So in 1978): Eight Irish Derby winners, including Dark Warrior in 1950, Thirteen of Diamonds in 1952, Ragusa in 1963 and Meadow Court in 1965; One Irish Oaks (Five Spots in 1952), and 3 Irish St Leger's (Artic Vale 1962, and Christmas Island 1963, and Mistigri in 1974). He also won the English 1,000 Guineas in 1964 with Pourparier, the 2,000 Guineas in 1960 with Martial, the Oaks with Noblesse in 1963, the St Leger in 1963 with Ragusa, his one failure in British Isles Classic's being the Epsom Derby. He trained 22 winners at Royal Ascot, including 2 Coronation Stakes, 6 Coventry Stakes, and 2 Queen's Vase's, He was top trainer in Britain in 1963 (when he became the first Irish trainer to do so), 1964 and 1965, and was Leading Trainer in Ireland 7 times starting from 1950. He was voted as Texaco's Horse Racing Sportstar of the Year in both 1960 and 1963.

PRENDERGAST, PADDY.

G.A.A. hurling full-back and left half-back, Kilkenny. A member of the Kilkenny Under 21 team which won that All-Ireland title in 1977, he had been on the losing side in the previous year's All-Ireland M.H.C. final. A winner of 3 All-Ireland Senior Hurling Championship medals, in 1976 at full-back, and at left half-back in the wins of 1982 and 1983, he captained the Kilkenny side beaten in the final of 1987 (being also on the losing final team in 1978). He won a National Hurling League medal in 1981. He won his only All-Star award in 1982 at left half-back.

PRENDERGAST, TOM.

G.A.A. football right half-back, Kerry. Club: Keel. He was at right corner forward on the Kerry side beaten in the All-Ireland S.F.C. final of 1968, and won 2 All-Ireland Senior Football Championship winner's medals, in 1969 and 1970 as a right half-back. In 1972 he was the Kerry captain in the replayed All-Ireland S.F.C. final, which they lost to Offaly. He won a Railway Cup medal with Munster in 1972. In 1970 he became the 4th Kerryman to win the Texaco All-Star Footballer of the Year.

PRIESTMAN, (nee HORNE), JOAN.

Ladies hockey international defender. Club: Muckross. A product of Muckross and Wicklow, she played school interprovincial hockey, and later on became Leinster's most capped senior interprovincial player. She was capped for Ireland 43 times between 1952 and 1965, captaining the side many times, and in 1965 she played with the Great Britain & Ireland side in America. Later she became secretary of the I.L.H.U. 1971-1975, was President of the Leinster Branch of the I.L.H.U. 1987-90, and was Chairperson of the World Cup Steering Committee for the 1994 World Cup in Ireland.

PRINGLE, IAN.

Canoeist. Born in Lucan, Co Dublin in 1953. Club: Salmon Leap (Leixlip). A schools Leinster trialist in rugby, he won under 14, 16 and 18 Irish canoeing titles. From 1972 (at the age of 19) up to 1990 he won the Irish canoeing championship on 16 occasions, also winning the Liffey Descent 12 times. An Irish international at both sprints and long distance from 1968 to 1990, he won the British 10,000m title in 1978, and was 8th in the World 10,000m championship in both 1982 and 1983. In 1986 he won the Sella Descent (the Spanish Open Championship) ahead of 1,000 competitors, and in 1990 he won the K2 class in the Liffey Descent (defeating the current world champions from New Zealand). He is the first Irish canoeist (and one of only a select group) to represent Ireland at 3 different Olympic Games (he only narrowly failed to make the 1972 Games in Munich). These were in 1976 at Montreal in the K2 (finishing 18th overall) and the K4 (finishing 19th overall); at Moscow for the 1980 Olympic Games in the K1 1,000m; and finally in Los Angeles in 1984 in both the K1 500m and the K1 1,000m, reaching the semi-finals in both categories. Twice a competitor in Irish Superstars, finishing 4th in 1979, he retired in 1991 through injury.

PRIOR, J A.

Cricket international batsman. He was capped 37 times for Ireland at cricket, between 1981 and 1986. In 48 innings he scored 1,134 runs for Ireland with an average of 25.77 (making one century, seven 50's and taking 25 catches). He has the distinction of scoring the quickest ever century for Ireland, when reaching the 100 off 51 balls in 51 minutes in an innings of 119 against Warwickshire in 1982.

PURCELL, KIERAN.

G.A.A. hurling full-forward, Kilkenny. He 3 won All-Ireland Senior Hurling Championship medals with Kilkenny, in 1972, 1974, 1975, and was on the losing McCarthy Cup final teams in both 1971 and 1973 (as a sub). He won 4 successive Railway Cup medals with Leinster in 1972, 1973, 1974 and 1975. He received 3 successive All-Star awards, in 1973, 1974, and 1975, all at full-forward.

PURCELL, MARY (nee TRACEY).

Middle and long-distance runner. Clubs: Guinness A.C. and Crusaders A.C. Dominating Irish ladies running from 1971 to 1983, having started at the age of 20, she was the first Irish woman athlete to win 7 B.L.E. National titles, winning the 1,500 metres in 1972, 1973, 1974, 1975, 1976, 1978, and 1980. She won the British W.A.A.A. 800 metres title twice in 1972 and 1973, and won the 1975 and 1976 W.A.A.A. 3,000 metres titles. In a career which ranged from sprints initially to the marathon at the end of her career, she represented Ireland in the 1972 Olympic Games in Munich (at both 800 and 1,500 metres) and at the 1976 games in Montreal (at 1,500 metres). She also had a successful indoor season in th U.S.A. and Canada in the 1979 winter indoor season. She won (on her debut run in the race) the 1982 National Marathon Championship, later won the 1983 Dublin City Marathon in a time of 2:46:09, and in her 2 other runs in this race, she finished 2nd and 5th.

PURCELL, NOEL MARY.

Rugby and waterpolo international. Born 14th December, 1897 (or 14th

November 1891?), he died in 1962. A product of Belvedere College and Trinity College, he played interprovincial rugby for Leinster 8 times over a 12 year period from 1910 to 1921, and played Barbarians rugby before the war. He was capped at rugby for Ireland 4 times in the pack in 1921 while captain of Lansdowne. He also is the only Irish rugby international to win an Olympic gold medal, which he won in Antwerp in 1920 when competing for Great Britain and Ireland in the waterpolo event, beating Belgium (and a hostile local crowd) 3-2 in the final. A member of Dublin University S.C. from 1910 (when he was first capped) until 1928 (his last cap), he captained of the Irish water polo team for much of this time. He won the Irish 880 yards swimming title in 1911. He was captain of Ireland in the waterpolo event at the Paris Olympics of 1924, becoming the first man to represent 2 different countries at the Olympic Games, thus giving him a unique place in Olympic sport. He was also picked for the Olympic Games for Ireland in 1928, but did not travel, preferring to give his place to younger squad members. A solicitor, he later became a rugby international refereee, and later still a rugby international selector (in 1938-41).

PURCELL, PHIL.

G.A.A. hurling left half-back, Tipperary. Although he only won one All-Ireland Senior Hurling Championship medal with Tipperary (in 1930), his ability in the left half-back position enabled him to win 5 Railway Cup medals with Munster, in 1928, 1929, 1930, 1931 (becoming the first Tipperaryman to captain a winning side), and 1934.

PURCELL, SEAN.

G.A.A. football centre half-forward, Galway. Club: Tuam Stars (with whom he won 10 Galway S.F.C. titles). Brought up on Bishop Street in Tuam, he won an All-Ireland Colleges medal with St Jarlath's of Tuam in 1946, and played in his first Connacht S.F.C. final in 1948. He won one All-Ireland Senior football medal, being a vital member of the Galway side which beat Cork by 2-13 to 3-7 in the 1956 final, and later captained the Galway side beaten in the 1959 final by Kerry. He was the game's leading marksman in 1958, his 11 goals and 74 points in 22 games bringing his tally to 107, and an average of 4.86. He is one of 'The Terrible Twins' (along with Frank Stockwell), with whom he created a dynamic partnership, highlighted by one of the game's greatest goals, when Galway beat Kerry by 1-8 to 0-7 in the 1956/57 National League final. He won 3 Railway Cup medals with Connacht, in 1951, 1957, and in 1958 (becoming the 3rd Galwayman to captain a winning side). Although he was adept at any position on the park, he is placed by most experts as the games greatest centre half-forward. In 1984 he was the player who most clearly won his place on the Sunday Independent's 'Team of the Century', being placed at centre half-forward, alongside Down's Sean O'Neill and Kerry's Pat Spillane. A teacher.

PURDON, BILL BROOKE.

Rugby international half-back. Club: Queens University Belfast. He won only 3 international caps for Ireland, but all were in the Triple Crown and International Championship winning side of 1906, and he scored a try in the match against England. In the deciding match against Wales at Belfast, he was taken off injured before half-time.

PYPER, JAMES and JOHN (JACK).

Soccer international brothers. Club: Cliftonville (winning Irish Cup medals together in 1897 and 1900, Jim winning a third in 1901). Both brothers were capped late in the 19th century for Northern Ireland, James 7 times between 1897 and 1900, and John 9 times between 1897 and 1902, three times playing together in the international side, against Scotland and Wales in James's first 2 games, and again in 1900 against England.

QUAID, TOMMY.

G.A.A. hurling goalkeeper, Limerick. Born in 1956, he is from Feoghenagh, near Milford, and plays for the Feoghenagh club. First playing senior inter-county hurling in 1975, he won Munster Senior Hurling Championship medals with the county in 1980 (his only All-Ireland S.F.C. final appearance) and 1981. He has also won 3 National Hurling League medals with Limerick, in 1985, 1986 and 1992. He won his only All-Star award after 18 years of senior hurling, when given the 1992 goalkeeping slot.

QUIGLEY, DAN.

G.A.A. hurling right full-back, Wexford. Born in 1944. Club: Rathnure (winning 9 county championship winner's medals, 4 Leinster Club titles, and losing 3 All-Ireland club finals in 1972, 1974 and 1978). Winning an All-Ireland Colleges medal in 1964 with St Peter's, he played minors for Wexford in 1961-62, and Under 21 in 1964-1965 (winning an All-Ireland medal in 1965). In 1964, before playing any senior championship game for Wexford, he was in the Railway Cup final, playing for the winning Leinster side. He won a total of 3 Railway Cup medals with Leinster, gaining honours again in 1966 and 1971 (when he became the 2nd Wexfordman to captain a winning Railway Cup Leinster team). He was captain of the winning Wexford side in 1968 which beat Tipperary by 5-8 to 3-12 in the All-Ireland Senior Hurling Championship final, and won 2 other Leinster S.H.C. medals, in 1965 and 1970 (both ended in defeat in the All-Ireland final, the 1970 final being notable for 4 Quigley brothers playing; Dan, Pat, Martin and John). Dan and Pat were both on the Wexford side which had won the All-Ireland Under 21 title in 1965, having also been on the side beaten in the final in the inaugural year of the championship in 1964 (Pat had won an All-Ireland M.H.C. medal in 1963). Both were also on the Wexford side beaten in the All-Ireland S.H.C. final of 1965. Dan also won a National Hurling League medal with Wexford in 1967. In 1968 he became the 2nd Wexfordman to become Texaco Hurler of the Year. He retired in 1971.

QUIGLEY, MARTIN.

G.A.A. hurling half-forward, Wexford. Club: Rathnure (winning many county championships, 3 Leinster club titles, and playing, along with brothers Dan and John, in 3 losing All-Ireland Club Championship finals). Martin won an All-Ireland M.H.C. medal with Wexford at right half forward in 1968, having been on the side beaten in the 1967 final (he also won a Colleges medal). He was on 3 successive Wexford sides which were beaten by Cork in the final of the All-Ireland Under 21 championship, in 1968, 1969, and 1970. He also played in 3 Wexford teams which lost All-Ireland Senior Hurling Championship finals, in 1970 (when he played alonside his 3 brothers), 1976 and 1977. He won 4 Railway Cup medals with Leinster, in 1973, 1974, 1975 and 1976. A quality player, he won 4 All-Star awards in succession, in 1973 at right corner forward, in 1974 at centre half-forward, in 1975 at right half forward, and in 1976 again at centre half-forward. In 1984 he was selected at centre half-forward on the 'Team of the Century' for those players who failed to win All-Ireland senior championship medals.

QUIGLEY, JOHN.

G.A.A. hurling right full-forward, Wexford. Club: Rathnure (winning county and Leinster championships, see above). A brother of Martin and Dan Quigley, he came on as a sub to win a medal in the All-Ireland Senior Hurling Championship final of 1968, and all four brothers were on the Wexford side beaten in the All-Ireland final of 1970, John, Martin and Pat making up the entire half forward line, with Dan at centre half back. John won an All-Star place in 1974 at right corner forward, and later played with Martin on 2 further All-Ireland S.H.C. final losing sides, in 1976 and 1977. John was the first player to hurdle in 5 All-Ireland hurling finals in the same year (in 1966 when involved in one replay in the minors and two in the under 21 final). He captained the county to their National Hurling League triumph in 1973.

QUINN, BRENDAN.

G.A.A. football half-back, Dublin. Club: Parnell's (winning a Divison 2 Dublin City League medal in 1938 and 2 Dublin SFC medals, in 1939 and when captain in 1945). After a fine minor career as captain of the Dublin side, he also captained Dublin in 1940 to win the Arus Na Gael Cup tournament. Having won a Leinster S.F.C. medal in 1941, he was in the half-back line when Dublin captured the All-Ireland Senior Football Championship title in 1942. He later was a referee (being an umpire in the All-Ireland final in 1953), and was a selector when Dublin next won the Sam Maguire Cup in 1958; in 1963 he was the coach when the Des Foley-captained Dubs side recaptured the Cup. He has thus, over a period of 22 years, won Sam Maguire medals as player, selector and as a coach. He later trained both Kildare and Westmeath.

QUINN, JACK.

G.A.A. football full back, Meath. Club: Kilbride (winning 5 Meath county championships, including the three-in-a-row of 1969, 1970 and 1971). He won 4 Leinster S.F.C. winner's medals with Meath, in 1964, 1966, 1967 and 1970. He, along with his 2 brothers Gerry (at right corner forward) and Martin (as a playing sub), played for the Meath side which lost the 1966 All-Ireland S.F.C. final to Galway by a margin of 1-10 to 0-7. He won his only All-Ireland Senior Football Championship winners medal in 1967 as a star full-back in the win over Cork, and was later captain of the Meath team which were beaten in the All-Ireland S.F.C. final of 1970 by Kerry.

QUINN, JAMES M (JIMMY).

Soccer international striker. Born in Belfast, 18th November 1959. Clubs: Oswestry Town, Swindon Town, Blackburn Rovers, Swindon Town again (with whom he scored 40 goals in 111 league matches, being also in 1988 the leading scorer in the English League Cup, with 8 goals, the only Irish player, north or south, to gain this distinction), Leicester City (scoring 6 goals in 31 games), Bradford City (scoring 14 goals in 35 games), West Ham (scoring 18 goals in 48 league games, and helping them to promotion to Division One in 1990-91), Bournemouth (scoring 19 goals in 43 league games) and Reading (scoring 17 goals in 42 league games), scoring over 100 league goals for all his clubs. He was capped for Northern Ireland first in 1985, and up to the middle of 1993, he had played in 34 games for his country.

QUINN, JOSEPH PATRICK.

Rugby international wing three-quarter. Born in Dublin, 23rd November 1888, he died in 1955. Club: Dublin University (winning Leinster Senior Cup medals in 1912 and 1913). He won 15 international caps for Ireland between 1910 and 1914. In the 1913 match versus France, he equalled the then record of Robert Montgomery (cv) for most tries in a international for an Irish player, with 3, a record only surpassed in 1991. His nine tries scored in his 15 internationals makes his average of better than one try in every 2 games an average not equalled in Irish rugby, and was an Irish record until surpassed by George Stephenson cv. In his last cap, versus Scotland in 1914, he was captain of Ireland for the only time. He won the Military Cross. His son, also J P Quinn, was capped 5 times as a centre for England in 1954, while playing for New Brighton, and played Test rugby on the British and Irish Lions tour of South Africa in 1955; he was also British national Modern Pentathlon champion, and won a Cup winners Cup with Leeds in the Rugby League Cup; he also coached both tennis and swimming.

QUINN, KEVIN Jospeh.

Rugby international centre threequarter, and cricket international. Born in Gort, Co Galway, 14th March 1923. In rugby, while playing for Old Belvedere, he, despite his enormous talents, won only 5 international caps for Ireland, 2 in 1947 and 3 more in 1953, while he also played in 3 Victory internationals of 1946. He played 15 interprovincial matches for Leinster between 1944 and 1952, and 8 more during W.W.II. His brother Brendan won one international rugby cap of the wing for Ireland in 1947. Another brother Gerry played rugby for Leinster (and both played with Kevin in 2 unofficial internationals in 1946). Both Brendan and Gerry were also members with Kevin of the great Old Belvedere side which won 7 consecutive Leinster Senior Cups from 1940 to 1946. Kevin was also was an Irish cricket international, playing 3 first class games (and 7 in all) for Ireland between 1957 and 1959, as a Phoenix right hand batsman. Another older brother of Kevin's, Frank M (born in Gort, 8th December 1912), a batsman from Phoenix, also played cricket for Ireland, 12 times in all between 1936 and 1948, scoring 140 against Scotland in 1946 and 291 in all for his country: while his brother Gerry also played one first class cricket match for Ireland in 1937.

QUINN, MICHAEL Anthony Mary (MICKY).

Rugby international outhalf. Born in Dublin, 31st May 1952. Club: Lansdowne (winning Leinster Senior Cup medals in 1979, 1980, 1981, 1984, and Leinster Senior League medals in 1974, 1977 and 1981). He played interprovincial rugby for Leinster 17 times between 1972 and 1978. He played 10 international matches at out-half for Ireland between 1973 and 1981, being an ever-present member of the International Championship winning squad of 1974. His last cap was obtained on the Irish tour of South Africa in 1981 (joining it as a late replacement), 4 years after he had previously been capped. A popular international, he had previously toured New Zealand and Fiji with Ireland in 1976, on which he was top scorer, with 5 conversions and 3 penalties for a tally of 19 points. An architect.

QUINN, MICKEY.

G.A.A. football midfielder, Leitrim. Club: Aughanwillan. A quality player whose county side achieved little during his tenure in senior inter-county fare, he has played Railway Cup for Connacht. In 1990 he became the first ever player from Leitrim to win an All-Star award, being selected in the midfield position.

QUINN, MIKE.

Soccer international striker. Born in Liverpool, 2nd May 1962. Clubs: Derby County (apprenticed), Wigan Athletic, Stockport County, Oldham Athletic scoring over 90 goals for these 3 clubs, and Portsmouth. In 1986-87 season he became the only Northern Ireland player since the war to be leading goalscorer in any division of the English Football League, when his 22 goals for Portsmouth was best. He won his first cap for Northern Ireland as a substitute against France in 1988.

QUINN, NIALL J.

Soccer internatioanl striker. Born in Dublin, 6th October 1966. In 1983 he helped Drimnagh Castle become All-Ireland schools soccer champions, and was also on the Dublin minor hurling team beaten in the final of the All-Ireland M.H.C. by Galway. He joined Arsenal from Eire Youth, playing first-team football at 18, and scored over 10 league goals (and more than 100 goals at all levels) for them, winning a Littlewoods Cup medal in 1987, and helping the club to the 1989 League Championship. He joined Manchester City for £750,000 in 1990. First capped for the Republic of Ireland in the run-up to the 1990 World Cup finals, he was a member of the squad which participated in 'Italia 90', the Republic of Ireland's first time to reach the final, and gaining his place in Irish soccer folklore by scoring the equalising goal in the Group 6 match versus Holland, which ensured that Ireland qualified for the last 16. He had a tremendous season for both club and country in 1990-1991, scoring the equaliser in the European Championship qualifier against England at Wembley. He was named as Texaco Soccer Sportstar of the Year in 1991. A powerful and popular player, his cap tally up to mid 1993 had reached 40, scoring 10 goals. His father Billy won an All-Ireland medal at gaelic football.

QUINN, NOEL.

Hockey international player. Clubs: Queen's University Belfast, and Lisnagarvey. He was capped for Ireland 62 times between 1972 and 1978, also winning 3 indoor caps in 1976. A member of the touring side to South Africa in 1973, the first Intercontinental Cup in Rome, the World Cup in Buenos Aires in 1978.

QUINN, REGINALD J (REG).

Hockey international player. Clubs: Queen's University, Belfast, and Lisnagarvey. He was capped 23 times for Ireland between 1966 and 1973, and was on the team which played in Ireland's first entry into the European Championship in Brussels in 1970, and the fine winning side in the 8 Nation tournament in Santander in 1972.

QUINN, SEAN.

G.A.A. football left half-back, Armagh. He won one Railway Cup medal with Ulster, in 1950, and won 2 Ulster Senior Football Championship medals with Armagh, in 1950 and in 1953 (when he captained the side which reached the All-Ireland S.F.C. final, only to lose by 0-13 to 1-6 to Kerry). A great footballer, in 1984 he was voted into the left half-back position on the football 'Team of the Century' for those who did not win All-Ireland medals.

QUIRKE, JOHNNY.

G.A.A. hurling right-full and full forward, Cork. Born in 1911. Club: Blackrock (winning 3 county championship medals). A native of Milltown Co Kerry, he played senior inter-county hurling from 1932 to 1946. He was ever-present on the famous Cork 4-in-a-row All-Ireland Senior Hurling Championship run of 1941 (scoring 2 goals in the final), 1942 (scoring 1-1 in the final), 1943 (scoring 2-2 in the final), and 1944 (he was in a losing final in 1939). He was the first Corkman to win 7 Railway Cup medals for Munster, winning medals in 1937, 1938, 1940, 1942, 1943, 1944, and in 1945 (when becoming the 6th Corkman to captain a victorious Munster team). He won 2 National Hurling League medals with Cork, in 1940 (scoring 2-4 in the final) and 1941.

QUIRKE, JOHNNY M T.

Rugby international scrum-half. Born in Dublin, 26th June 1944. Club: U.C.D. and Blackrock College. He won 3 international caps for Ireland, the first against England in 1962 when he was under 18 years old, making him the second youngest player ever to play for Ireland, and one of only 2 not to have reached their eighteenth birthday on the day of their first cap (see Frank Hewitt cv). His last cap was in 1968 against South Africa (6 years after his initial appearance in the Irish jersey). He also played 4 interprovincial matches for Leinster between 1961 and 1965.

QUIRKE, E MARTIN.

Flat jockey. Born at Lattin, Co Tipperary, 5th November 1898, he died in 1988. Over a 30 year career from

1916 to 1946, he rode 9 Irish Classic winners: Loch Lomond in the 1919 Irish Derby (he was 2nd in the race 22 years later on Khosro); a joint-record 5 Irish 2,000 Guineas winners (Salisbury in 1929, Glannarg in 1930, Museum in 1935, Nearchus in 1938 and Khosro in 1941), 2 Irish Oaks winners (Soloptic in 1929 and Santaria in 1932); and one 1,000 Guineas winner, Soloptic in 1929. In 1929 alone he rode 3 Irish Classic winners. He was champion jockey in 1923, his 86 winners being a record not surpassed until 1972 by Johnny Roe. He later trained at Mountjoy Lodge, and in 1957 won the Irish 2,000 Guineas as a trainer with Jack Ketch. His son Stephen Quirke succeded him as a flat trainer, and has sent out the winner of 3 Irish classics, with two Irish 2,000 Guineas in succession, Atherstone Wood in 1967 and Mistigo in 1968; and the 1971 winner of the Irish St Leger, Parnell.

QUIRKE, PAUL.

Shot putt and discus athlete. From Walkinstwon, Dublin, he was born on 5th August 1963. Club: Crusaders. He has been Irish shot-putt champion 6 times, including 1987 and 1992. By becoming the first Irishman to throw beyond the 20 metre barrier (in July 1992 he threw 20.04 metres), he was selected for the Barcelona Olympics in 1992. He has also been B.L.E. National Champion at the discus 3 times. A journalist (and a graduate from Manhattan College) who has appeared in movies, his wife Laura is a marathon runner.

QUISH, TOM and JOHN.

Handballers. From Hospital, Co Limerick. As individuals, Tom won the 1980 All-Irleland Junior Singles title, and John was runner-up in the All-Ireland Senior Softball Singles in 1982. As a pair, they won the All-Ireland Junior Softball and Hardball Doubles titles in 1980. In 1984 they combined to win the World Championship 60x30 Senior Doubles crown, in Dublin, beating a U.S. pair of Denis Haynes and Jamie Paredes handily (by 21-6 and 21-8) in the final. Undoubtedly one of the games best all-time doubles combinations, they were unbeaten throughout 1983 and 1984, when they won the Senior Softball and Handball Doubles both years; they also won the Centenary and All-Ireland doubles titles in 1984. They retained the Senior Hardball Doubles title in 1985, 1986, and 1987. In 1986 they won the All-Ireland 4x20 Championship Junior Doubles title.

R

RACKARD, NICHOLAS (NICKY).

G.A.A. hurling full forward, Wexford. Club: Rathnure. Born in Killanne, Co Wexford, 28th April 1922. He was the starring light in the great Wexford double-winning All-Ireland Senior Hurling Championship side of 1955 (when they beat Galway) and 1956 (when Cork were the victims, his 2 brothers, Billy and Bobby ccvv, being also on the side for both years). He was the game's top marksman in both 1955 (with 91 points in 18 games) and 1956, when his tally of 35 goals and 50 points in 19 games amounted to a record national tally of 155 points (only Eddie Keher has scored more in one competitive season). He had captained the Wexford side beaten by Tipperary in the final of the 1951 All-Ireland S.H.C. (scoring 3-2 in the final, the highest individual score by any hurler in a McCarthy Cup final inthe 1950's), and was on the side which was defeated by Cork in the 1954 final. He won a solitary Railway Cup medal with Leinster in 1956, being also on five losing final teams. Another brother, Jimmy, played on the losing Wexford side in the 1951 All-Ireland final. Regarded as one of hurling's finest exponents, Nicky was voted at full forward on the Sunday Independent 'Team of the Century' of 1984. Also a fine footballer, he was at full-forward on the Leinster Railway Cup team beaten in the 1950 final, and he headed the national scoring table for football in 1955 and 1956, making him the country's highest scorer for both codes for 2 successive seasons. A veterinary surgeon, his mother was a sister of John Doran, who won an All-Ireland S.F.C. title with Wexford in 1918.

RACKARD, ROBERT (BOBBIE).

G.A.A. hurling right full back and centre-back, Wexford. Born in Killane Co Wexford on 6th January 1927. Club: Rathnure (winning 4 county championship medals). A senior inter-county player for 13 years from 1945 (as a 19-year-old) to 1957 (retiring from an accident), he won All-Ireland Senior Hurling Championship medals with Wexford in 1955 and 1956, in both years playing alongside his brothers, Nicky and Billy (ccvv), having previously been on losing All-Ireland S.H.C. sides in both 1951 and 1954. He won one Railway Cup medal in 1956 with Leinster, and won a National Hurling League medal in 1956. Rated on a par for class with his more illustrious brother Nicky, he was voted at right full-back on the Sunday Independent's 'Team of the Century' in 1984, giving them a unique family double honour. Along with brother Billy cv, he was made an All-Time All-Star in 1992.

RACKARD, WILLIAM (BILLY).

G.A.A. hurling corner-back, wing-back and centre half-back, Wexford. Born in Killane, Co Wexford in 1930. Club: Rathnure (winning 4 county championship medals), and Faugh's (Dublin). After a fine under-age career with Good Counsel College (New Ross) and St Kieran's College, Kilkenny, he played for Wexford at senior inter-county level from 1950 to 1963. After playing minors in both codes for the county in 1947-48, he, along with his brothers, Nicky and Bobby, was on the Wexford side which won the 1955 and 1956 All-Ireland Senior Hurling Championship. He won a third All-Ireland S.H.C. medal in 1960, thus surpassing the tallys of his more illustrious brothers in this field. He captained the Wexford S.H.C. side beaten in the 1962 All-Ireland final, and was on 2 other losing final sides, in 1951 and 1954. He won 4 Railway Cup medals with Leinster, in 1954, 1956, 1962, and 1964. He won 4 Oireachtas medals, and 2 National Hurling League medals, in 1956 and 1958. Also a Wexford footballer (winning both a Wexford JFC and SFC with Rathnure, he was on the Wexford side beaten in the Leinster S.F.C. final in 1953). He shared an All-Time All-Star award in 1992 with his brother Bobby cv. A 4th brother, Jim, shared with Nicky, Bobby and Billy, in the Leinster S.H.C. win of 1951.

RAFFERTY, JOE.

G.A.A. footballer, Kildare. He was a star player on the Kildare side of Roseberry which captured the county's first ever All-Ireland Senior Football Championship title in 1905. He had previously captained the Clane side representing Kildare to their All-Ireland S.F.C. final defeat in 1903.

RAFFERTY, RONAN.

Golfer, amateur and professional. Born in Warrenpoint, Co Down, on 13th January 1964. A sensational golfer as a boy, in 1979 he won the Munster and Ulster Youths, the Irish Youths, and the Britsh Boys titles. In 1980 he won the Irish Close title, tied the British Amateur Strokeplay title, and reached the quarter-final of the British Amateur. He won Walker Cup honours in 1981 (making him at 17 years, 8 months and 15 days, the youngest ever Walker Cup player) at Cypress Point, California, winning 2 great foursomes matches with Philip Walton. Turning pro in late 1981, he won the 1982 Venezualan Open, and showed steady progression up the European Order of Merit. He won 3 titles in the 1987-88 winter tour of Australia. He was a member of the historic Irish trio which captured the 1988 Dunhill Cup at St Andrew's in Scotland, when beating Australia in the final in dramatic style, and in 1990 became the only Irishman to play on 2 winning Dunhill sides. His best Order of Merit placings have been in 1986 (9th), and 1988 (again 9th), and 1st in 1989 (the first Irishman since Christy O'Connor to win the coveted Vardon Trophy) when he won the Italian and Scandinavian Opens and the Volvo Masters, bringing his prize money for that season to over 400,000; he was 5th in 1990. In 1989 he also won Ryder Cup selection as top of the order (making him Ireland's 2nd player to win both Ryder and Walker Cup player), winning a crucial singles in the tied match. In 1990 he won the Melbourne Classic and the PLM Open in Sweden. In 1992 he won 112,000 first prize in the Palm Meadows Golf Cup, Australia's richest tournament, which he immediately followed by three 2nd places and then a win in the Portugese Open. He won the 1993 Austrian Open, and just missed selection for the Ryder Cup that year. He was voted as Texaco's Sportstar of the Year for golf in 1980 as an amateur, and in 1989 as a professional.

RAMBAUT, DAVID FREDERICK.

Rugby international centre-threequarter, and athlete. Club: Dublin University. He won only 4 rugby caps for Ireland in 1887 and 1888, but he scored Ireland's 2 conversions in their first ever Championship win over England in 1887. In 1888, in Ireland's first ever International Championship title victory, he played against the Welsh (also Ireland's first ever victory over that nation). He also was Irish 120 yards champion. He was known as 'the fat little fellow'.

RAMSBOTTOM, SUE. Ladies

G.A.A. football forward, Laois. Club: The Heath. From Timahoe, she was the youngest player on the Laois team beaten by Kerry in the All-Ireland Senior Final in 1988, being again on the losing All-Ireland sides in 1990 and 1991. A classy high-scoring forward, she has won all kinds of medals and honours at junior level, and was a member of the Heath side which captured the All-Ireland Club Championship in 1987.

RAMSEY, PAUL.

Soccer international midfielder. Born in Derry, 3rd September 1962. Club: Leicester (to whom he was apprenticed, and for whom he played 290 league matches, scoring 13 goals), Cardiff (playing 69 games for them up to mid-1993). He was first capped for Northern Ireland in 1984, gaining 14 caps by the end of the 1989-90 season.

RANKIN, JAMES L.

Badminton international player. A world class player, he was capped 32 times for Ireland in a 21 year international career between 1929 and 1949, and won many Irish Championships in Singles and Doubles. He won the All-England Men's Doubles with Thomas Boyle (cv) in 1939. He was Secretary of Londonderry County Council.

RAPHAEL, IAN G.

Hockey international half-back, link man, and inside forward. Clubs: Friend's School Old Boys, Queen's University Belfast, and Lisnagarvey. He was capped 70 times for Ireland between 1969 and 1978, also winning 3 caps for the indoor code in 1977. He was a key member of Irish squads to the Intercontinental Cup in Rome, and later made 6 appearences for Ireland in the World Cup in Buenos Aires in 1978.

REA, DES.

Junior-welterweight boxer. Born in Belfast, January 8th, 1944. A pro boxer from 1964, he was the first ever British Junior-welterweight champion in 1968, beating the Englishman Vic Andretti over 15 rounds in London. In an attempt to add the European crown, he lost to Bruno Arari in San Remo. He lost the British title to Andretti a year later, also on points. In an effort to regain the title yet again from Andretti later that year, he was knocked out in the 4th round. Not retiring until a career tally of 69 professional bouts in 1974, he has the unusual distinction for a boxing champion of having lost more fights (36) than he won (25).

REA, JACKIE.

Snooker professional. Born 6th April 1921, in Dungannon Co Tyrone. He was 1947 Northern Ireland Amateur Champion. Turning pro in 1948, he reached his career peak in 1957, being beaten 39-34 by John Pullman in the final of the World Snooker Championship. He reached the quarter-final stage of the World Championship event twice again in his late 40's, in 1969 and 1970, and competed for the title each year for 31 years. He won the News of the World Championship title in 1955, beating Joe Davis in the final. Winning the Irish title in 1950, he won the Northern Ireland Professional Championship an astonishing record 20 times over a 26 year period between 1947 and 1972. In recent years his highest world ranking was in 1983 when placed at No 48.

REA, JIMMY.

G.A.A. football left full-forward, Carlow. Regarded as one of the finest players never to win an All-Ireland S.F.C. medal, he was a member of the first 2 Carlow sides to play in (and lose) Leinster S.F.C. finals, in 1941 and 1942, and went on to play on the only Carlow side to win the Leinster Senior Football Championship title, 2 years later in 1944 (this was also the last time the county reached the final). He went to to win 2 Railway Cup medals with Leinster, in 1944 and 1945.

REA, MICHAEL P.

Cricket international batsman. Clubs: Bangor and Clontarf. First capped for Ireland in 1984, up to 1993 he has played 38 international matches for his country, scoring 1,531 runs for an average of 29.44 per innings, and scored over 400 runs for Ireland in both 1992 and 1993, the first Irish international batsman to do so in successive seasons. He has made 2 centuries for Ireland (with a best of 119 in 1993), and has had eight 50's.

READ, HENRY Marvelle (HARRY).

Rugby international scrum-half, cricket and tennis international. Born at Dungar, Roscrea, 8th November. One of very few Irishmen to represent his country at 3 different sports, he captained Trinity at rugby, cricket and tennis in 1911. At rugby, while a member of Dublin University, he played senior interprovincial for Leinster 8 times 1909-1912, and won 13 international caps for Ireland between 1910 and 1913, 12 of these in a famous partnership with Dickie Lloyd at out-half (this made them the first pair to specialize in these 2 positions in the International Champoionship). He was later to be President of the I.R.F.U. 1955-1956. He also won his international place for Ireland in tennis. As a cricketer he played at international level for Ireland and once setting a Trinity club record for the highest stand when with Dickie Lloyd (cv) a stand of 323 runs was made.

READE, HAROLD E.

Amateur international golfer. Club: Royal Belfast. He is the first man to win the Irish Close Championship 3 times, being successful in 1897, 1899 and in 1903, and he was runner-up in 1901. He played international golf for Ireland 8 times between in 1900 and 1913. His brother (?), P.E Reade also played for Ireland twice, along with Harold, in 1902.

REDDIN, TONY.

G.A.A. hurling goalkeeper, Galway and Tipperary. Born in 1919, he was a native of Mullagh, Co Galway, and played junior and senior hurling as a full-forward with Galway up to 1946. Moving to Tipp in 1947 to join the Lorrha club, he played senior inter-county with them from 1947 to 1957, and won 3 All-Ireland Senior

Hurling Championship winner's medals with Tipperary, in the great 3-in-a-row side of 1949, 1950, 1951. He also won 6 National League winners medals with Tipperary, in 1949, 1950, 1952, 1954, 1955 and 1957. He totalled 5 Railway Cup winner's medals with Munster over a 6 year period, in 1950, 1951, 1952, 1953, and 1955. He out-voted class opposition to win his place as goalkeepr on the Sunday Independent's 'Team of the Century' in honour of the Centenary Year of 1984.

REDDY, ANDREW (ANDO).

Amateur boxer. Club: Sandymount. He won 6 Irish National Senior Championship titles (2 each at three increasing weight divisions) over an eleven year period between 1951 and 1961. His wins came at flyweight in both 1951 and 1952, two titles at bantamweight in 1953 and 1954, and 2 further titles at the higher weight, featherweight, in 1960 and 1961. His brother Tommy (a member of both the Crumlin and Sandymount club's), who died at age 63 in 1992, won 2 Irish National Senior Championship titles, at bantamweight in 1953, and again at featherweight in 1957. Both brothers, who were from the famous Downpatrick Road in Crumlin which produced many fine boxers, represented Ireland at the Helsinki Olympics in 1952, both being beaten in the first round, while Ando went on to fight at featherweight in the 1960 Games in Rome.

REDMOND, CHARLIE.

G.A.A. football wing-forward, Dublin. A product of Beneavin in Finglas. Club: Erin's Isle. A member of Dublin side beaten in the All-Ireland S.F.C. final of 1985, he missed a penalty against Meath in the 1988 Leinster Championship final. Missing the vital stages in 1989, his place-kicking helped Dublin to reach the 1992 All-Ireland Senior Football Championship, and to win the 1993 Leinster S.F.C. again. He won a National League medal in both 1991 and 1993.

REID, BRIAN.

Motorcycle road racer. Born in Banbridge, Co Down on 3rd September 1966, he started racing in 1976. From 1981 to 1984 he won 8 Ulster and 5 Irish titles at 250 cc, 350cc, and 500cc in the Irish Road Racing Championships, all on Yamaha machines. Having finished 3rd in 1984 with 25 points, he went on twice to win the World Championships at T.T. Formula Two class, in 1985 with 45 points, and in 1986 with 32 points, all on a Yamaha. He was the first rider to lap the Temple circuit in Co Down at 100 m.p.h., and was also the first rider to lap the Castletown circuit in the Isle of Man at 100 m.p.h. In the 1985 T.T. Junior Race he set a class lap record at 112.08 m.p.h., and won the 1986 Formula Two T.T., and the 1990 Supersport 600 T.T., having been 2nd in the Junior T.T. in both 1987 and 1988. In 1990 he won the 600cc Irish Regal Championship.

REID, JOHN.

Flat jockey. Born in Dromore Co Down, 6th August 1955. Riding over 100 winners as an apprentice to Major Verly Bewick, he has ridden more than 50 winners in Britain every year bar 1983 between 1978 and 1989, averaging 64 per season, his best seasons tally being 84 in 1989. In 1992 he rode the winner of the Epsom Derby, Doctor Devious. His other classic race wins include the Irish Derby in 1987 on Sir Harry Lewis and the 1981 1,000 Guineas at Newmarket with On the House. Other big wins include the 1988 Prix de l'Arc de Trioumphe with Tony Bin, and wins with Ile de Bourbon in the Coronation Cup and the King George V1 in 1978.

REID, J CHARLES (CARL).

Rugby international centre three-quarter. Club: N.I.F.C. (winning Ulster Senior Cup medals in 1899, 1901 and 1902). Although he won only 4 international caps for Ireland, the first two of these were in the year in which Ireland won it's 2nd Triple Crown in 1899, when he scored a try in the 9-3 win over Scotland, and also in the deciding match against Wales.

REID, PATRICK Joseph (PADDY).

Rugby international centre three-quarter, and hockey player. Born in Limerick, 17th March, 1924. Rugby club: Garryowen (whom he captained to win their 25th Munster Senior Cup triumph in 1947). Although he was only capped 4 times for Ireland, three of these were gained during Ireland's only Grand Slam Year of 1948, Reid scoring a try in the game against France, and missing only the Scottish match that season. He shares, with these 3 wins in his only 3 International Championship games, the record of the Irish player with the longest 100% record in the championship. He later joined Huddersfield Rugby League club. As a hockey player, he founded and ran the Lansdowne club in Limerick, and was a fine centre-half.

REID, THOMAS Eymard (TOM or 'COLONEL').

Rugby international 2nd row forward. Born 3rd March 1930 in Limerick. Club: Garryowen (winning Munster Senior Cup medals in 1947, 1952, and in 1954 as captain). He won 13 international rugby caps in the pack for Ireland between 1953 and 1957. Also a Barbarian, he was selected on the British and Irish Lions tour of South Africa in 1955, and won 2 Test places (first as a No 8, then as a 2nd row forward). A sales rep, he emigrated to Canada.

REIDY, CHARLES J P.

Rugby international prop forward, and athletics international. Rugby Clubs: London Irish, The Army (and he also played for the London Counties against the All-Blacks). Born in London in 1912, he died in 1992. As a rugby player, he played for Leinster 6 times 1935-1937, and won one international cap for Ireland, on a winning Irish side against Wales in 1937, while playing for London Irish. An Army man and a professor, he was also an Irish international athlete, and was a skilled boxer at Cambridge.

REIDY, GERALD F.

Rugby international wing-forward. Clubs: Dolphin (winning a Munster Senior Cup medal in 1956), and Lansdowne. Born in Cork, 13th 5th 1926. He won 5 rugby international caps on the flank for Ireland between 1953 and 1954. He was President of the I.R.F.U. in 1983/1984, and is Tom Kiernan's brother-in-law.

REIDY, LIAM.

G.A.A. hurling left full-forward, Kilkenny. Club: Erin's Og. He played in 3 All-Ireland Senior Hurling Championship finals for Kilkenny, twice on the losing side (in 1946 and 1950), and on the winning side in the full-forward line in the Liam McCarthy Cup success against Cork in 1947. Also a Railway Cup player with Leinster, he later turned to golf at Kilkenny GC, winning Provincial Towns and Barton Cup medals, and became President of the G.U.I. in 1992.

REILLY, BRIAN PATRICK.

Irish chess master. Altough born in Menton in England on 12th December 1901, his Irish ancestry was such that he opted to represent this country. He took part in 9 Olympic team tournaments for Ireland between 1935 and 1968, 3 times being on the top board (he sensationally beat the grandmaster Rueben Fine in the Warsaw Games of 1935); he also was an Irish representative at 7 F.I.D.E. Congresses. He won the Irish chess championship in both 1959 and 1960, and his tournament wins included Nice in 1931.

REITH, MICHAEL STEVENS.

Cricket international left hand bat and right hand medium paced bowler. Born in Lurgan 2nd May 1948. Clubs: Waringstown and North Down. Between 1969 and 1980 he played 44 international cricket matches for Ireland, his 1,838 runs scored placing him in 11th place on the all-time runs list for Ireland up to 1992. These were achieved in 81 innings to an average rate of 23.26, with one century, a 129 against Holland in

1970 (he also had eleven 50's). He has taken 41 catches for Ireland (i.e. almost one a match), the best percentage per match of all the top Irish cricketers.

RENNICKS, KEN.

G.A.A. football centre half-forward, Meath. Born in 1951. Club: Bohernean-Martyr Harps. He moved from minor in 1968 to senior inter-county football in 1969. He had played at right full-forward in the Meath side beaten in the final of the 1970 All-Ireland Senior Football Championship by Kerry. His fine play at centre half-forward enabled Meath to win the 1975 National Football League title. He won a Railway Cup medal with Leinster in 1974 after a 12 year absence for the province. In a career hit by injuries, he won his only All-Star award in 1975 in the centre half-forward position.

RENTOUL, A L, J L, R W R, and W W.

Hockey international brothers. Club: Queens University Belfast. These 4 brothers won a total of 11 caps for Ireland while they attended Queen's University in Belfast towards the beginning of the century. A T won 3 caps in 1909-1912, J L won 3 caps in 1909-1911, R W R won a single cap in 1911, and W W won 4 international caps for Ireland between 1920 and 1922.

REYNOLDS, HARRY ('THE BALBRIGGAN FLYER').

Cyclist. Born in Balbriggan, Co Dublin. Club: Wanderer C.C. He won many Irish Championships at many different distances, and won many races in England, Australia, New Zealand, Sweden etc. In 1895 he won both the Irish 5 mile and 50 mile championship, as well as the gold medal in the Surrey '100 Guinea' Cup. On 15th August 1896, after being overlooked when the Irish team went to the Olympic Games in Athens, he became the first Irishman to win the World Championship title in cycling (beating the Olympic Champion Paul Masson and a Swede called Schrader by a mere 3 inches), which he achieved in Copenhagen, Denmark (the next Irishman to win was Stephen Roche, who won in Austria in 1987). On his return home he was greeted by an enthusiastic crowd of about 250,000. Soon turning professional, he went on to win many races in Australia, and again back in Ireland from 1906 to 1910 he won many road races here again. Known as the 'Father of Irish Cycling', he was reputed to train by racing the train from Skerries to Balbriggan (the train always lost), and to also cycle up Barnageera hill backwards. He died in Balbriggan in 1940.

REYNOLDS, JOHN.

Soccer international right half. Clubs: Distillery, Ulster, West Bromwich Albion (winning an F.A. Cup winners medal in 1892, scoring a goal in the final), Aston Villa (winning 2 more F.A. Cup winners medals, in 1895 and 1897). He was capped 5 times for the I.F.A. side in 1890 and in 1891, scoring one goal for the Irish side. Then on joining West Bromwich, it was discovered that he was born in England, and so played for England against Scotland in 1892, thus becoming the first player to play for 2 different countries in international soccer. He went on to be capped a further 7 times for England up to 1897 (scoring 3 international goals for them), thus bringing his total tally of caps for the 2 countries to 12.

REYNOLDS, PAT.

G.A.A. football left half-back, Meath. He was a member of the Meath team which won the All-Ireland Senior Football Championship in 1967, being also on losing All-Ireland S.F.C. final teams in 1966 and 1970, each time at left wing-half. He won his only All-Star award in the inaugural year of these awards, in 1971 at left half-back, making him the Royal County's first winner.

REYNOLDS, RICHARD (DICK).

G.A.A. left wing-forward, Wexford. One of 10 Wexford footballers who won 4 successive All-Ireland Senior Football

Championship winner's medals, in 1915, 1916, 1917 and in 1918. He had also been a member of the Blues and Whites side beaten in the All-Ireland finals of the 2 years before the great 4-in-a-row run (i.e. 1913 and 1914, a draw), thus playing in 7 All-Ireland final games in succession.

RICE, Miss HELENA Bertha Grace (LENA).

Ladies tennis player. Born at Marlhill, Newinn, Co Tipperary, 21st June 1866. She is the only Irish woman to win a Wimbledon Ladies Singles title, which she achieved at the age of 24 in 1890, defeating Miss M Jacks by 6-4, 6-0, winning the princely sum of £21 for her efforts (she had been narrowly beaten in the previous year's final by Blanche Hillyard, and also that year became the first ever woman line judge at Wimbledon). Her only other title of note was the Irish Championship mixed doubles of the previous year, 1889 (with Willoughy Hamilton cv). She died in Newinn aged 41, in 1907, coincidently on the same date as her birth, in the same house. Her sister Anne also played at Wimbledon.

RICE, PAT.

Soccer international right-back. Born in Belfast, 17th March (St Patrick's Day) 1949. Moving to London (to a house 200 yards away from Highbury) at the age of 10, he signed junior forms for Arsenal in 1966, and played 397 league games for the club over a 14 year career up to 1980, scoring 11 league goals. With the 'Gunners' he won a F.A.I. Youth Cup medal in 1968; two F.A. Cup medals, in 1971 and in 1979 as captain (and three runners-up medals, in 1972, and as captain for the two losing finals of 1978 and 1980, thus having the club record of 5 F.A. Cup final appearences); a League Championship medal in 1970/71 (the year the club did the 'double'); and a runners-up medal as captain in the 1980 European Cup Winners Cup. He holds 2 other Arsenal club records, the most F.A. Cup games played (67), and the most games in European competitions (27). He later joined Watford, helping them to gain promotion to Division One. Having played two Under 23 international caps, he was also capped 49 times for the Northern Ireland senior team between 1969 and 1980, all of these gained while at Arsenal, making him then (until surpassed by Kenny Sanson in 1985) the club's most capped player. In 1987-88 he coached the Arsenal Youths side which won the F.A. Youth Cup.

RICHARDSON, DAMIEN.

Soccer international forward. Born in Dublin, 2nd August 1947. Clubs: Shamrock Rovers (winning F.A.I. Cup medals in 1968 and in 1969 when he scored one of the 4 goals in the final), Gillingham (helping them to gain promotion from Division 4 in 1974, and scoring over 90 goals in over 310 league matches from 1972 to 1980). He was capped 3 times as a substitute for the Republic of Ireland between 1972 and 1980, the last 2 being while at Priestfield Stadium, making him then (until surpassed in 1986 by Tony Cascarino cv) Gillingham's most capped player. He later went into football management, taking charge of Cork City in 1993.

RIGBY, ALF.

Soccer international forward. Clubs: Bray Unknowns, St James Gate (playing on 2 sides beaten in F.A.I. Cup finals in 1934 and 1937, and being on the side which finished runner-up in the League of Ireland in 1934-35), Dundalk (playing on a 3rd losing side in the F.A.I. Cup final of 1938). In successive years he was leading goalscorer in the League of Ireland, scoring 13 goals in 1933-34 and 17 in 1934-35, both with St James Gate. He was capped 3 times for the Irish Free State in 1935, and scored 2 goals in Inter-League matches.

RIGNEY, BRIAN Joseph.

Rugby international 2nd row forward. Born in Portlaoise, 22nd September 1963. Clubs: Portlaoise, Highfield, Bective Rangers, Greystones. Born in

Portlaoise. Taking up rugby at the late age of 19, he was a 'B' international in 1988, he won his first 5 international caps in 1991, injury depriving him of further representation. He toured with Ireland to New Zealand in 1992. His brother Niall, a talented midfielder, has played inter-county hurling with Laois since 1987 (also winning 3 county championship medals with his club Portlaoise), having also played for Leinster Juniors in rugby (along with another brother Noel), while another brother Des has played senior rugby with Greystones.

RING, CHRISTOPHER Nicholas (CHRISTY, 'RINGY' or 'THE MASTER OF CLOYNE').

G.A.A. hurling half-forward and left full-forward, Cork. Born in the village of Cloyne, Co Cork, on 12th October, 1920, he died on March 2nd 1979. Clubs: Cloyne (winning the county junior final in 1939) and Glen Rovers (winning a record 11 Cork SHC medals, in 1941, 1944, 1945, 1948, 1949, 1950, 1953, 1958, 1959, 1960, 1962, 1964, and 1967; he won a Cork SFC medal with St Nicholas in 1954). He won All-Ireland M.H.C. medals with Cork as a sub in 1937 and at left half-back in 1938. Making his senior inter-county debut in 1939, he shares with John Doyle of Tipperary (cv) the distinction of eight winning appearances in All-Ireland Senior Hurling Championship victorious sides, in 1941, 1942, 1943, 1944, 1946, 1952, 1953, and 1954 (by captaining the sides in 1946, 1953 and 1954 he became the only man to captain 3 winning Liam McCarthy Cup teams). In the 1956 final, only a brilliant save by the Wexford goalkeeper, Art Foley, deprived him of his 9th S.H.C. title (he was also on the losing All-Ireland S.H.C. side in 1947). He has won a record 18 Railway Cup medals with Munster between 1942 and 1963 (failing to win only in 1947, 1954, 1956, and 1962), appearing in an amazing 22 successive finals (also a record). He won 4 National Hurling League medals with Cork, in 1940, 1941, 1948, 1953. He was the game's leading marksman for 3 years, in 1959 (when scoring 22 goals and 35 points, to become the only player in the ratings to average over 10 points per game), in 1961 (with 104 points in 13 games), and in 1962, when sharing the top spot with Jimmy Doyle, with 99 points. Regarded by many as the game's finest exponent, he was selected in the right half-forward position on the Sunday Independent 'Team of the Century' of 1984, and was elected to the Texaco Hall of Fame in 1971, the second of only 2 hurlers to be thus far elected. Val Dorgan wrote his biography in 1981, 'Christy Ring'. Louis Marcus produced a film, launched by Gael Linn in 1964, 'Christy Ring'.

RINGROSE, Colonel WILLIAM A (BILLY).

International show jumper. In 1956 in Stockholm, he was one of the Irish team of three which finished 7th in the Olympic Prix de Nations (Team) event. As a captain in the Irish Army, he was one of the Irish team which won the 1963 Nation's Cup in Dublin (Aga Khan Cup); in 1967, now a commandant, he was again on the winning Irish Aga Khan Cup team, both times riding Loch an Easpaig. He represented Ireland at 2 Olympic Games, in 1956 at Melbourne (when the team finished 7th) and at Rome in 1960. He also won 6 prestigious Grand Prix events on Loch an Easpaig in Harrisburgh, London, Rome, Marseilles, Toronto and Nice, and with the great horse also won Puissance events at Dublin and Barcelona.

RINGLAND, TREVOR.

Rugby international wing three-quarter. Born in Belfast, 13th November 1959. Club: Ballymena. A product of Larne Grammar School, he was first capped against Australia in 1981, and was a valuable member of both of Ireland's Triple Crown victories of 1982 (scoring a try against Wales) and 1985, when he scored 2 tries against Scotland. A resolute and determined attacking player, he accumulated 34 caps up to retiring in June 1989, being briefly Ireland's most capped winger, surpassing the 25 caps of Alan Duggan and Tom Grace, before being surpassed himself in 1991 by Keith Crossan. He scored 7 international tries for Ireland, and on Ireland's tour of Japan in 1985, he scored a record 6 tries for an Irish tourist. He toured Australia and New Zealand with the British and Irish Lions in 1983, gaining one Test cap, and was also selected on the Combined Five Nations XV versus the Overseas side of 1986. He also made many fine contributions to a dominant Ulster XV in the interprovincial series in the late 1980's.

RINGSTEAD, ALF.

Soccer international winger. Born in Dublin, 14th October 1927. Clubs: Northwich, Sheffield United, and Mansfield. In 8 seasons and 247 league matches with Sheffield United between 1950 and 1958, he scored 101 league goals, helping them to gain promotion as champions to Division One in 1953. He won 20 senior international caps for the Republic of Ireland between 1951 and 1959, scoring 7 goals for his country.

RITCHIE, JAMES S (JIM).

Rugby international wing-forward. Club: London Irish. He won 2 caps for Ireland in 1956, and on both of these occasions he was captain of the side, being the 4th of only 5 Irish players to captain the side on their international debut. Against France, Ireland lost 14-8, but against England the losing score was 20-0, England's biggest margin of victory up till that time. Ritchie, along with 4 other Irishmen, never played Championship rugby again. He is the son-in-law of Ernie Crawford (cv).

ROBB, TOMMY H.

Motor cycling road racer. Born in Belfast in 1934. Initially a track rider, he won at the age of 16. Changing to road racing (on Bultaco machines) at the age of 20, he won the Irish 500cc title in 1961, and rode for Honda in 4 classes in 1962 (at 50cc, 125cc, 250cc, and 350cc). He won the 1963 250cc road racing championship. He also won 2 other World Championship Grand Prix victories, the Ulster 1962 250cc and the 350cc Finnish G.P. in the same season. He finished 3rd in the 1962 125cc World Championship, 6th in the 1962 50cc title race, and 4th in the 1963 250cc world championship. In 1973, after a career in which he won 29 TT replicas (and 17 top 10 T.T. places since 1958), he finally won his only T.T. title, the 125cc (on a borrowed Yamaha); he retired in the same year. He was selected as Texaco's Motor Sport Sportstar of the Year in 1962.

ROBBIE, JOHNNY Cameron.

Rugby international scrum-half. Born in Dublin, 17th November, 1955. Clubs: Dublin University, Cambridge University and Greystones. He won 9 rugby caps for Ireland between 1976 and 1981. He has the unenviable record of being on the losing side in each of his international games. He toured with the British and Irish Lions to South Africa in 1981 (winning one test place), and later in the year returned with an Irish touring party. Deciding to emigrate there, he played a record number of matches for Pretoria, and became a reserve for the Springboks in 1984. A captain of note, he led the High School side to win the 1973 Leinster Schools Cup, and the Dublin University XV which won the 1976 Leinster Senior Cup. He won Cambridge Blues in 1977 and 1978. He had earlier captained the Irish schools cricket team. He later became a popular radio journalist in South Africa.

ROBERTS, FRED.

Soccer international centre-forward. Club: Glentoran. In 6 seasons with Glentoran he scored 250 goals, helping them to win 2 Irish Cup medals in 1932 and 1933. In the 1930-31 season he scored the record highest aggregate of goals for a single season in British or Irish football, when he scored an amazing 96 goals (55 in the Irish League which

Glentoran won, 28 in the Belfast City Cup, 4 in the Irish Cup, 7 in the County Antrin Shield and 2 in the Belfast Charity Cup). He won one cap for Northern Ireland, in a 0-0 draw against Scotland in 1931.

ROBERTS, Mrs (nee EITHNE PENTONY).

Ladies amateur international golfer. Born in Dublin in 1909. Clubs: Limerick and Lahinch. She won the Irish Ladies Championship twice, in 1931 at Rosses Point, and at Newcastle in 1933. In 1933 she also captured the Danish Ladies title. She played Home internarional matches for Ireland in 6 diffferent series in the 1930's, and was a member of the L.G.U. team who travelled to South Africa in 1933.

ROBINSON, (nee NESBITT), CLAIRE.

Amateur international golfer. Born 7th March 1953. Clubs: Knock and Royal Portrush. She won the Irish Ladies title twice, in 1976 and 1980, and was runner-up in 1979. She won the Ulster Ladies title in 1976 and 1978. She was on the successful Irish Ladies team which captured the European Team title in 1979 at Hermitage, having also played in 1975 and 1977. She was selected for Curtis Cup honours in 1980, halving 2 of her 3 matches at St Pierre.

ROBINSON, BRIAN Francis.

Rugby international No 8 forward. Born in Belfast, 20th March 1966. Club: Ballymena (winning Ulster Senior League medals in 1990 and 1991 and 3 successive Ulster Senior Cup medals in 1989, 1990 and 1991), and London Irish. First capped for Ulster in 1987 and for Ireland in 1991, he developed quickly into a classy No 8 forward, and in the opening group match of Ireland's World Cup challenge against Zimbabwe, he became the first Irish rugby player ever to score 4 tries in an international game (it also equals the world record for a forward in an international match), 3 of these coming from push-over tries. His international cap tally for Ireland reached 18 by June 1993, with a total of 5 international tries. He toured New Zealand with Ireland in 1992. In 1993 he was appointed as a Rugby Development Officer by the I.R.F.U.

ROBINSON, FRANK L.

Hockey international player. Clubs: Malone, and Staines. He was capped for Ireland 14 times at hockey between 1908 and 1914. He won a silver medal at the 1908 Olympic Games at London in 1908, when he was a member of the Ireland team which lost by 8-1 to England in the final of the event.

ROBINSON, MICHAEL J (MICK).

Soccer international striker. Born in Leicester, 12th July 1958. Clubs: Preston North End (apprenticed in 1975), Manchester City (who paid £750,000 in 1979), Brighton and Hove Albion (who paid £400,000 in 1980, and for whom he scored 37 goals in 113 matches, gaining an F.A. Cup runners-up medal in 1983), Liverpool (who paid £200,000 in 1983, and with whom he won a European Cup medal in 1984, and a League Championship in the same season), Queens Park Rangers (who paid £100,000 in 1984, and with whom he won a League Cup runners-up medal in 1986), and Osasuna FC (in Spain). Through the parentage rule, he was first capped for the Republic of Ireland in 1981, and he went on to be capped 23 times up to 1986, scoring 4 international goals.

ROBINSON, THOMAS TREVOR HULL.

Rugby international half-back. Club: Wanderers (winning Leinster Senior Cup medal in 1906). Five times a Leinster player, he won 10 international rugby caps for Ireland over the 3 year period from 1904 to 1907, scoring one international try. He won a D.S.O. in W.W.II.

ROBINSON, George WILLIAM (WILLIE).

National Hunt Jockey. Born in 1934, he had his first winner in 1955. Having finished 2nd in the Epsom Derby of 1958 on Paddy's Point, he turned to the fences and moved to England in the early 1960's. His major wins include: the Cheltenham Gold Cup of 1963 on Mill House; the Aintree Grand National of 1964 on Team Spirit; and 2 Cheltenham Champion Hurdles (in 1962 on Anzio and in 1965 on Kirriemuir). His other wins on the great Mill House include the 1963 runnings of the King George VI Chase and the Hennessy Gold Cup (which he won on other horses in both 1961 and 1968). He won 2 Grand Seftons, in 1960 on Mildway Memorial and in 1963 on Team Spirit.

ROCHE, CHRISTY ('THE MAN FROM BANSHA').

Flat jockey. Born in Bansha, Co Tipperary in 1950. In his first year as a jockey he won the Autumn double in Ireland, the Cambridgeshire and the Cesarawitch. He has worked for Paddy 'Darkie' Prendergast, Vincent O'Brien, David O'Brien and Jim Bolger. He has been leading Irish flat jockey 6 times, including 1979 (68 winners), 1980 (69 winners), 1981 (66 winners), 1983 (63 winners), and in 1990 (his best ever season, when by his tally of 113 he became only the 3rd Irish based jockey to have century of winners in a season, and equalled the record of Michael Kinane cv). He also was runner-up in the title many times (including 1981 and 1989, when he rode 83 winners each season, and in 1992 with 92 winners). He has won 9 Irish Classic races: two Irish Derby wins (in 1982 on Assert and on the course record and record margin winner St Jovite in 1992), three Irish 2,000 Guineas (1972 on Ballymore, Nikoli in 1979, and Triptych in 1985), 2 Irish 1,000 Guineas (Sarah Siddons in 1976, and More So in 1978); and 2 Irish St Leger's (Mistigri in 1974, and Authaal in 1986). In 1992 he won 2 Italian Classics, the 1,000 Guineas on Treasure Hope, and the Oaks on Ivyanna. His career highlights came when, in the 1984 Epsom Derby he rode the 14/1 shot Secreto to win the Epsom Derby from the hot favourite El Gran Senor, and in the 1990 Epsom Oaks when he won the race by 10 lengths on the 50/1 shot Jet Ski Lady. His other major horse success was Assert, on whom he won in the same year both the 1982 French and Irish Derbies.

ROCHE, CON.

G.A.A. hurling left half-back, Cork. Club: St Finbarr's (with whom he won an All-Ireland Club Championship medal in 1975). A member of the Cork team which won the All-Ireland Under 21 Championship in 1966, he had previously won an All-Ireland M.H.C. medal with Cork in 1964. A winner of an All-Ireland Senior Hurling Championship medal in 1970, he was also on losing Cork final side in 1972. He was a winner of 2 All-Star awards, in 1972 and 1974, both at left half-back.

ROCHE, JIM.

G.A.A. hurling left half-forward, Limerick. He won 3 All-Ireland Senior Hurling Championship medals with Limerick, in 1934, 1936, and again in 1940, thus joining one of a group of only 7 Limerickmen to win a record 3 All-Ireland S.H.C. medals with their county. He was also on the Limerick S.H.C. side which lost the All-Ireland finals of 1933 and 1935, both to Kilkenny.

ROCHE, JEM.

Professional boxer. Born in 1878 at Killurin, near Kilmuckridge, Co Wexford, being a blacksmith by trade, and he died at the age of 56. Having played gaelic football for Wexford in the Leinster S.F.C. in 1905, he turned his hand to boxing. With suspect pedigree, he challenged Tommy Burns of Canada for the World Heavyweight Championship title, which took place on St Patrick's Day 1908 at the Theatre Royal, Dublin. He was knocked out after 88 seconds of the first round, making it the shortest of any world heavyweight title fights, until

1982. He later became the coach of the famous Wexford 4-in-a-row All-Ireland Senior Football Championship winner's, 1915-1918. His grandson is the noted Wexford playwright Billy Roche.

ROCHE, MICK.

G.A.A. hurling midfielder and centre half-back, Tipperary. Born in 1944. A member of the Tipperary minors beaten in the All-Ireland M.H.C. final of 1961, he went on to be a member of the Tipperary side which captured in inaugural All-Ireland Under 21 Championship in 1964. A product of C.B.S. in Carrick-on-Suir, he was born a natural hurler, and came through the minor, Under 21 and intermediate grade before making his senior inter-county debut. He won 3 All-Ireland Senior Hurling Championship winner's medals with Tipperary, in 1964, 1965, and in 1971, and was captain of the losing final sides in both 1967 and 1968 (beaten by Kilkenny and Wexford respectively, and thus becoming the first of only 3 hurlers to captain 2 losing McCarthy Cup finals). In 1964 and 1965 he was also on Tipperary sides which won National hurling Leagues and Oireachtas Tournament, along with the Liam McCarthy Cup successes, thus completing 2 dominant 'trebles'. He captained the 1968 Railway Cup-winning Munster side (becoming the 9th Tipp man to do so), also winning medals in 1966 and 1970. A quality hurler, he retired before his 30th birthday. Both his father and an uncle won All-Ireland J.F.C. medals with Tipperary in the 1930's.

ROCHE, PATRICK J (PADDY).

Soccer international goalkeeper. Born in Dublin, 4th January 1951. Clubs: Shelbourne, Manchester United (playing over 45 league matches with them from 1974 and 1980, as understudy to Alex Stephney and Gary Bailey), Brentford (playing 71 games for them 1982-84), Halifax (playing 184 matches for them between 1984 and 1988). An under-rated 6'1" goalkeeper, he was capped 8 times for the Republic of Ireland between 1972 and 1976.

ROCHE, STEPHEN.

Cyclist, amateur and professional. Born in Ranelagh, Dublin, 28th November 1959. In 1979, at the age of 19, he won the Ras Tailteann, and in 1980 he finished 24th in the Olympic Road Race in Moscow, and also won the prestigious Paris-Roubaix as an amateur. He turned professional in 1981, winning the Paris-Nice that year (and being 2nd in 1984). In his first Tour de France in 1983 he finished as best newcomer, to win the white jersey. He finished 3rd in the 1985 Tour, but was only placed 48th in 1986. In 1987, having early in the season won the Tour of Valencia, he reached the peak of his career, and in an amazing season, he became the first Irish winner of the Giro d'Italia (after a tense battle with local favourite, Roberto Visentini); he then became the first Irish winner of the world's premier stage-race, the Tour de France (defeating the Spaniard Pedro Delgado into 2nd place, at an average speed of 23.173 mph), and to cap it off, he won the World Championship at Villach in Austria. This feat of winning these 3 major events (only the 3rd cyclist ever to achieve it) earned him a huge home-coming to Dublin and the honour of being made the 58th person (and only sportsman) to become Freeman of Dublin, is regarded among the finest by any Irish sportsman at any level. His 1988 season was wiped out by injury, and he withdrew injured from both the 1989 and 1990 Tours de France. He has won 3 stages in all in the Tour de France, one in each of 1985, 1987 and 1992 (when he finished 9th in the race overall). He retired in 1993, after finishing 13rd on the Tour de France. In 1990 he won the Dunkirk 4-day race, the Catalan Tour and the Criterium International (which he had won also in 1985), and in 1993 he finished 9th in the Giro d'Italia. His teams have included Peugeot, La Radoute, Carrera, Fagor, Histor and Ton Ton Tapis.

A winner of a total of 57 professional races, he was voted as Texaco's Cycling Sportstar of the Year for 1987. In 1989 he was voted Sportsman of the Decade in the Ballygowan polls. His younger brother Laurence was a professional cyclist for 3 years 1989-1991, winning a pro-am Criterium in Brittany, and achieving an overall sprints win in the Tour of Limousin in 1991, when he also finished 153rd in the Tour de France (being only the 6th Irishman to compete in the race).

ROCHE, WILLIAM J.

Rugby international forward. Club: U.C.C., Cardiff, Newport. Although he was capped only three times for Ireland, against, England, Scotland and France in 1920, four years later, while playing for Newport in Wales, he was selected to travel on the British and Irish Lions side which toured South Africa, in 1924, although winning no Test places. As a boxer he won an uncontested Welsh A.B.A. title.

ROCHFORD, JACK.

G.A.A. hurling full-back, Kilkenny. Club: Threecastles. He shared the record (with 3 other Kilkennymen) of being the first player to gather 7 All-Ireland Senior Hurling Championship winner's medals, which he achieved in 1904 with the Tullaroan side, in 1905 with Erin's Own, in 1907 and 1909 with Mooncoin, in 1911 in the awarded final, in 1912 with Tullaroan, and in 1913 again with Mooncoin. Their record was not surpassed until 1954, when Christy Ring won his eight medal.

ROCK, BARNEY.

G.A.A. football forward, Dublin. Club: Ballymun Kickhams. Born 10th January 1961. A member of the Dublin minor side which won the 1979 All-Ireland M.F.C. title, he was at right half-forward on the Dublin team which won the Sam Maguire Cup in 1983, also playing on the losing All-Ireland Senior Football Championship final teams in both 1984 and 1985, and winning a 4th Leinster S.F.C. medal in 1989. A winner of a National Football League medal with Dublin in 1987, he won a Railway Cup medal with Leinster in 1985. Last playing for Dublin in 1991, he has won 2 All-Star awards, both at right half-forward, in 1983 and 1984. He stood as a Progressive Democrats candidate in the 1991 local elections.

ROE, JOHNNY.

Jockey, flat racing. He won 2 Irish Classics, the 1964 Irish Oaks with Royal Danseuse and the 1967 Irish Oaks with Pampalina. In 1972 he finished 12th in the Irish Derby on the red hot 15/8 favourite Roberto. A prolific rider of winners for many stables, he was Irish Champion Jockey over the flat 9 times over the twelve year period from 1963 to 1975. In 1972 he broke by one the record of winners per season held by Martin Quirke (cv), but his new record of 87 lasted only 5 years, when it was surpassed by Wally Swinburn (cv). He was selected as Texaco's Horse Racing Sportstar of the Year in both 1967 and 1972.

ROE, ROBIN.

International rugby hooker. Club: Lansdowne (winning Leinster Senior Cup medals with the club in 1949, 1950 and 1953). Born in Ballybrophy, Co Laois, 11th January 1928. A product of the King's Hospital school, he was capped 21 times for Ireland over a 6 year period between 1952 and 1957. He was selected for the British and Irish Lions tour of South Africa of 1955, although winning no Test places. A successor to Karl Mullen, he was a fine hooker, and played in the interprovincial series for Leinster 14 times between 1949 and 1954. He won a Military Cross in Aden in 1967.

ROGAN, ANTON.

Soccer international full-back. Clubs: Glasgow Celtic (playing in 127 league matches for them, winning a Premier League Championship medal in

1987-88, and a Scottish F.A. Cup medal in the same season), Sunderland (playing 46 league matches for them up to mid 1993, being on the side which were beaten finalists in the 1992 F.A. Cup final). First capped for Northern Ireland in 1988, his cap tally up to mid 1993 has reached 17.

ROGERS, CHARLES.

National Hunt trainer. He lived 1899-1977. He won the Cheltenham Gold Cup of 1940 with Roman Hackle, to complete the double as he had earlier won the 1940 Champion Hurdle with Solford. He won a 2nd Champion Hurdle in 1946 with Distell. He also won 3 Irish Grand Nationals, in 1931 with Impudent Barney, in 1932 with Copper Court, and in 1943 with Golden Jack.

ROGERS, EAMON.

Soccer international winger. Born in Dublin, 16th April 1947. He joined Blackburn as an apprentice in 1965, and in 6 seasons, scored 30 league goals in 159 league appearences. He also played for Charlton Athletic and Northampton Town. He won 19 soccer caps for the Republic of Ireland between 1968 and 1973, scoring 5 international goals.

ROGERS, GEORGE LYTTELTON.

Tennis player. Club: Fitzwilliam. He represented Ireland in 17 Davis Cup matches over a period of 11 successive years between 1929 and 1939, winning 18 singles contests in that stretch, during which time Ireland won 5 matches. He won the Irish Singles Lawn Tennis Championship 3 times, 1928, 1936 and 1937, won the Irish Men's Doubles in 1936 and 1938, and won the Irish Mixed Doubles's in 1932 and 1936 (when he completed the slam). At his peak he was one of the finest players in his day, beating every top-class player, including Wimbledon champions. A 6'6" giant, he went to the U.S.A. as a professional coach in 1939, but was later re-instated as an amateur.

ROGERS, Capt DARBY.

Horse trainer, flat. Based at Curraqgh Grange, he trained the winning horse in 8 Irish Classic races: 2 Irish 2,000 Guineas winners (Mighty Ocean in 1950, and in the following year with Signal Box, later to finish 2nd in the Irish Derby), 2 Irish 1,000 Guineas winners (Northern Gleam in 1953 and with the Sir Winston Churchill owned Dark Issue in 1955); One Irish Derby winner in 1946 with Bright News; one Irish Oaks winner in 1947 with Desert Drive; and 2 Irish St Leger winners (1940 with Harvest Feast and in 1945 with Spam). He also won the Champion Curragh Stakes 9 times, including with his favourite horse, Heron's Bridge, who also won the Chester Cup and the Ascot Cup. A son of J T Rogers (cv), he is the father of J M Roger (cv).

ROGERS, KEVIN, LIAM and SEAMUS.

Pitch and putt brothers. Club: Portmanock P.P.C. Between them these three brothers won 6 Irish National pitch and putt titles: Kevin won 3 National Strokeplay Championships, in 1962, 1965 and 1967; Liam won 2 National Strokeplay Championshiip titles, in 1960 and 1961; and Seamus won the National Matchplay title in 1966. Also capable golfers with the Island club, Kevin won an Irish Senior Cup medal with the club in 1983, while another brother Bernard who shared that win with Kevin. Bernard, won an Irish Senior Cup medal in 1967 also, and was a Leinster senior inter-provincial golfer in 1977-1979. Kevin's daughter Aideen has played senior international golf for Ireland.

ROGERS, JIM.

G.A.A. footballer, Wicklow. One of his county's star players of the 1950's, he never played in any Leinster S.F.C. final, as Wicklow's fortunes were not great in those days. He is, however, the only Wicklow player to win 4 Railway Cup medals with Leinster, getting them in succession, in 1952, 1953, 1954 and in 1955.

ROGERS, JOHN T (JACK).

Horse trainer. An English jockey who missed the ride on the Aintree Grand National winner of 1905 due to injury, he moved to Ireland to train in 1915. Based in the Curragh, he was leading trainer in Ireland for 3 seasons in succession, 1935, 1936 and 1937, before dying in 1940. He won 11 Irish Classic races, placing him 6th on the total tally list for these races. He won 3 Irish 2,000 Guineas (in 1931 with his own horse Double Arch, in 1935 with Museum, and in 1937 with Phideas); 2 Irish 1,000 Guineas (in 1935 with Smokeless and the following year with Harvest Star); 2 Irish Derbys (Museum in 1935 and Phideas in 1937); One Irish Oaks, in 1935 with Smokelsss; and he had 3 Irish St Leger winners (1932 with Hill Song, 1935 with Museum, who was completing for the trainer the Irish Triple Crown in the process and a clean sweep in the Irish classics that season for the trainer, and in 1936 with Battle Song). He also trained the winner of the Phoenix Stakes 5 times. He is the father of Captain Darby Rogers (cv) and grandfather of Mickey Rogers (cv).

ROGERS, J MICHAEL (MICKEY).

Horse trainer, flat racing. Based at Stepaside in the Curragh, Co Kildare, his 20 year career stretched from 1950 to 1970 before he retired at the age of only 45. He trained the winning horse in 5 Irish Classic races: the Irish Derby in 1964 with Santa Claus, and 4 winners of the Irish 2,000 Guineas (D.C.M. in 1952, Arctic Wind in 1954, Hard Ridden in 1958, and Santa Claus in 1964). He also trained 2 Epsom Derby winners, Hard Ridden in 1958 (the first Irish-trained winner since Orby in 1907, 51 years before), and Santa Claus in 1964. Other quality horse he trained included Stephanotis, Prince Poppa, Royal Sword, Barrons Court and Candy Cane. He was selected as Texaco's Horse Racing Sportstar of the Year for 1964. He is the son of Capt Darby Rogers (cv) and grandson of Jack Rogers (cv). Between them these three trainers have won 24 Irish Classic flat races.

ROICE, (ROYCE), BARNEY.

G.A.A. footballer, Wexford. One of the great 'Super Subs'. He was awarded winner's medals in 4 All-Ireland Senior Football Champinship finals in a row for the Blues and Whites Wexford side in 1915, 1916, 1917 and 1918, and 6 Leinster S.F.C. titles on the trot (from 1913 to 1918), without ever having to go on to the field of play in any of these 10 finals. He did however play against Laois in the 1913 All-Ireland semi-final.

ROLLO, DAVE.

Soccer international full-back and midfielder. Clubs: Brantwood, Linfield (with whom he won 4 Irish Cup medals, in 1913, 1915, 1916, and 1919), Blackburn Rovers (playing 225 matches for them), and Port Vale. He was capped 16 times for Northern Irealnd between 1912 and 1927, including playing in 2 of the famous Home International Championship winning matches in 1914.

ROOKE, CHARLES VAUGHAN (C.V.).

Rugby international flank forward, Club: Dublin University. He was capped 19 times for Ireland between 1891 and 1897 (captaining the side once, against Scotland in 1895), and surpassed J A McDonald's record as the most capped Irishman in 1895, keeping the record until Louis Magee (cv) won his 20th cap in 1902. He played in all 3 Triple Crown-winning matches of the 1894 season, and in the 3 Championship-winning matches of 1896. A fine dribbler of the ball, he is regarded as one of the initiators of flank forward play. He was Secretary to the Leinster Branch of the I.R.F.U. for a time, later becoming an Anglican Minister in New Zealand, and he died in 1946 in Wellington.

ROSE, A DIXON.

Hockey international left-half. Born in Belfast in 1934. Club: Cliftonville (winning Irish Senior Cup medals in 1975 and 1976). Making 106 appearences for his province Ulster, he was capped 14 times for Ireland between 1957 and 1969 (helping to win the Home International Championships for the first time in 19 years in 1968), and captained the side in 1966. He has been president of both the Irish Hockey Union (1985-1987) and the Irish Cricket Union (1984) and was made chairman of the Centenary committee of the I.H.U. His father Andrew Rose was President of the Irish Hockey Union in 1931-32.

ROSS, J P.

Rugby international forward. Club: Lansdowne. He played 4 times for Ireland at rugby, against England and Scotland in both 1885 and 1886, captaining Ireland for his last cap. Ireland lost all four games in which he played. Two of his brothers also played for Ireland, D J (a member of Belfast Academy) winning 4 caps from 1884 to 1886, and J F (a member of N.I.F.C.) winning one cap in 1886 against Scotland, a match in which all three brothers played together, with J P as captain.

ROSS, T C.

Cricket international bowler. He played 19 international cricket matches for Ireland between 1894 and 1910, and was one of the country's finest early bowlers. His average of 14.62 runs per wicket (which is Ireland's 4th best), stems from 86 wickets taken in 27 innings for the loss of 1,258 runs. He took 10 wickets in one international match twice for Ireland and took 5 or more wickets 9 times; he also once took 9 for 28 against South Africa in 1904 (the 2nd best figure for one innings by any Irish international bowler). Also a competant batsman, in 31 innings for Ireland he scored 491 runs for an average of 16.93, and a best of 89 runs.

ROTHERHAM, AUSTON Morgan.

Polo player. Born 11th June 1876, he died in 1947. He won a bronze medal for Ireland at polo in the 1908 Olumpic Games in London. The Ireland team, one of 3 teams entered by Britain to compete in a 3-team event, finished last (being beaten by the winner's Roehampton by 5-1), but he still goes down as an Olympic bronze medallist.

ROWLANDS, D R .

Hockey international left half. Club: Monkstown (winning Irish Senior Cup medals in 1910 and 1914). Regarded as one of Ireland's finest left halves, he was capped 26 times for Ireland between 1910 and 1923, captaining the Irish team which won their 2nd Triple Crown in 1920.

RUSK, WALTER.

Motorcycling road racer. Born in Belfast in 1910, he died of pneumonia in 1940. He finished 2nd in the 1934 European 350cc Championship, on a Velocette. Although he never won a T.T. race, he had 2 third places, and was 2nd on a Norton in the 1935 Junior T.T. In 1939 he was the first rider to lap the 20 mile Ulster Grand Prix Circuit in Clady, Co Antrim at 100 m.p.h., on a 500cc 4-cylinder AJS. He had some success on the continent, including class wins in the German and Swiss G.P.'s of 1935. He became a pilot at the start of W.W.II.

RUSSELL, HUGHIE.

Flyweight and bantamweight boxer, amateur and professional. Born in Belfast, 15th December 1959. As an amateur, boxing out of Holy Family B.C. (Belfast), he won 2 Irish Senior National titles at flyweight, in 1979 and in 1981. He also won a bronze medal at the Commonwealth Games in Edmonton at flyweight in 1978. In 1980 at the Moscow Olympics, he won an Olympic bronze medal in the flyweight division, being beaten for the silver medal by the eventual winner, Peter Lessov of Buylgaria. Turning pro in 1981, he was British Professional bantamweight champion 1984-85, winning the Lonsdale Belt outright, only the 2nd Irishman to do so. He won the title when

Kelvin Smart retired after the 7th round of their King's Hall Belfast fight in January 1984. He defended the title twice successfully, against the Scots' Danny Flynn and Charlie Brown. His 4 year professional record was 17 wins and 2 losses. He was voted as Texaco's Boxing Sportstar of the Year for 1980. Later he became a professional photographer.

RUSSELL, JOHN (JACK).

Rugby international second row forward. Club: U.C.C. A product of St Colman's College in Cork, he won 19 rugby caps for Ireland between 1931 and 1937, scoring 2 international tries, and played in 3 of the 4 matches in the 1935 Five Nations' Championship-winning side. He won 3 successive Munster Senior Cup medals with U.C.C. in 1935, 1936, and 1937.

RUSSELL, PAUL.

G.A.A. football right half-back, Kerry. Born in Killarney, 2nd July 1906. He won 6 All-Ireland Senior Football Championship winner's medals with Kerry, in 1924 (at the age of 18), 1926, and in the great 4-in-a-row team of 1929, 1930, 1931, and 1932. He was also on 2 Kerry S.F.C. sides beaten in All-Ireland finals, in 1923 and 1927. He won 3 Raliway Cup medals, with Munster in the inaugural year of 1927, with Leinster in 1928, and again with Munster in 1931. He also won 4 National League medals with the 'Kingdom', in 1928, 1929, 1931 and 1932. He played club football for 8 clubs in 8 counties: Kerry (being the only Dr Crokes player to win 6 All-Irleand S.F.C. medals), Dublin (winning a Dublin county championship medal with the Gardai), Waterford, Galway, Monaghan, Cavan, Meath, and Weatmeath.

RUTH, MATT.

G.A.A. hurling half-forward and right full-forward, Kilkenny and Limerick. In his senior inter-county championship debut match, he played for Limerick in their All-Ireland Senior Hurling Championship final defeat at the hand of his native county Kilkenny in 1974. By 1978 he was playing for Kilkenny, and was at right corner-forward on the side beaten in the All-Ireland S.H.C. final. He finally won a Liam McCarthy Cup medal with his native county Kilkenny in 1979, again as a corner forward. He won a Railway Cup medal with Leinster in 1977.

RYAN, AIDAN.

G.A.A. hurling half-forward and full-forward, Tipperary. Club: Borris-Ileigh (with whom he won an All-Ireland Club Championship title in 1987). Having been a substitute on the Tipperary side which won the All-Ireland M.H.C. title in 1982, he became a member of the Tipperary side which broke a 16-year drought by winning the Munster S.H.C in 1987, and who the following year reached the All-Ireland final, only to be foiled by Galway. He came on as a sub in Tipperary's win in the 1989 All-Ireland Senior Football Championship final win, and was at midfield on the winning side of 1991. Winning another Munster S.H.C. medal in 1993, he won an All-Star award in 1987 at left half-forward. A brother of Bobby Ryan (cv) and a nephew of Pat Stakelum.

RYAN, BOBBY.

G.A.A. hurling left half-back, Tipperary. Born in 1962. Club: Borris-Ileigh (with whom he won an All-Ireland Club Championship winner's medal in 1987). In 1978 he won a Dr Harty Cup medal, and an All-Ireland Colleges medal with Templemore C.B.S. He was a member of the winning Tipperary Under 21 team in the 1981 All-Ireland championship. A member of the Tipperary S.H.C. side beaten in the All-Ireland final of 1988, and in the All-Ireland semi-final of 1987, in 1989 he captained the Tipperary side which won its first All-Ireland Senior Hurling Championship title since 1971, when they beat Antrim by 4-24 to 3-9. He won his 2nd Liam McCarthy medal in 1991, and won another Munster S.H.C. medal in 1993. A brother of Aidan Ryan (cv), his father Tim Ryan won 3 All-Ireland S.H.C. medals as a half-forward with Tipperary, in 1949, 1950, and 1951 (scoring 2 goals in this final), and his uncle Mike Ryan also won All-Ireland and Munster S.H.C. medals. Bobby has won 3 All-Star awards, in both 1986 and 1988 at left half-back, and in 1989 as a centre half-back.

RYAN, DEREK.

Squash interntional player. Born in Dublin on December 10th 1969. First capped for Ireland in 1988, his tally of caps up to mid-1993 had reached 50. He reached (and was defeated in) 5 P.S.A. finals up to August 1993, before he finally he won his first world ranking squash tournament, the 1993 Hungarian Open, in Budapest, easily beating the World No 32, John Ransome in the final. His world ranking had reached No 37 in August 1993. His older brother Noel is also a squash international player (playing over 20 times for Ireland), and in 1988 they became the first brothers to play for Ireland in squash.

RYAN, DECLAN.

G.A.A. hurling right half-forward, Tipperary. Born in July 1968. Club: Clonoulty-Rossmore. Having captained Tipperary at Under 21 level, he was a member of the Tipperary side which won its first Munster S.H.C. title in 16 years in 1987, and again a member of the side beaten in the 1988 All-Ireland final. He has won 2 All-Ireland Senior Hurling Championship winner's medals, in the 1989 win over Antrim, and the 1991 win over Kilkenny, and won another Munster S.H.C. medal in 1993. An All-Star hurler, selected at right half-forward in the 1988 team, he was nominated for 3 different positions in 1989 without winning an award. His uncle T.J. Butler won an All-Ireland Under 21 Hurling Championship medal with Tipp in 1964.

RYAN, EANNA.

G.A.A. hurling right half-forward and corner-forward, Galway. Born in Attymon, Athenry in 1963. Club: Killimor-Daly. He was at full-forward on the Galway M.H.C. side beaten by Kilkenny in the All-Ireland final of 1983 (and was a playing sub on the Galway side which won the All-Ireland Under 21 title in the same year). Making his senior inter-county debut in 1984, he was a member of the Galway Senior Hurling Championship side which captured the Liam McCarthy Cup in 1987 and 1988. He was awarded an All-Star award in 1989 in the position of right half-forward. His brothers John and Pascal played senior hurling for Galway, John winning an All-Ireland S.H.C. medal as a playing sub in the final of 1980. His sisters Ann and Dolores were fine camogie players, Ann playing on the Galway side beaten in the All-Ireland final of 1993.

RYAN, GERRY J.

Soccer international forward. Born in Dublin, 4th October 1955. Clubs: Bohemians (winning an F.A.I. Cup medal in 1976, and a League of Irland winners medal in 1977-78), Derby County, Brighton and Hove Albion. He was capped 16 times for the Republic of Ireland betwen 1978 and 1985 (7 as a substitute), the 15 caps he gained while at Brighton made him, until surpassed by John Barnes in 1986, the club's most then capped player.

RYAN, JOHN (JACK).

G.A.A. footballer, Kerry. Club: Boherbee and Rock Street (Tralee). He won 6 All-Ireland Senior Football Championship winner's medals with Kerry, in 1924, 1926, and in the great 4-in-a-row team of 1929, 1930, 1931, and 1932. He was twice on the losing side in the All-Ireland S.F.C. finals of 1923 and 1927, and he also won 2 Railway Cup medals with Munster, in 1927 and 1931.

RYAN, JOHN (JACK).

Rugby international forward. Club: Rockwell College. From Cashel, Co Tipperary, a team-mate of his at full-back and centre at Rockwell, was Eamon de Valera, later to become Taoiseach and

President of Ireland. Along with his brother Mike (cv) he shared in a then record 13 caps together (to last until 1928) out of his total tally of 14 Irish rugby caps between 1897 and 1904. The brothers formed a formidable combination in the pack, and they were the only 2 brothers to play international rugby in both centuries. Ryan and his brother Mike were also among only 5 players to play on all 3 games of Ireland's Triple Crown win of 1899. He was also a well-known athlete.

RYAN, JOHN.

Soccer forward. Born in Dublin, 27th February 1968. Clubs: St Patrick's Athletic, Bray Wanderers (in 1989-90 he scored a club record 16 goals to be leading scorer in the First Division of the League of Ireland), St Pat's (again). In 1990, by scoring 3 goals (including 2 penalties) for Bray Wanderers in the F.A.I. Cup final against the fellow-minnow's, St Francis, he joined a select number of players to score a hat-trick in an F.A.I. Cup final.

RYAN, JOHN.

Handballer. Club: Trinity. This Wexfordman won 4 Irish Senior Hardball Singles titles, in 1952, 1953, 1956, and 1957, but it is as a doubles player that he is most notable. Between 1952 and 1962, he won 7 Senior Irish Senior Hardball Doubles titles, 5 with his fellow-Wexfordman, John Doyle. He also won 4 Senior Softball Singles Irish titles, 1952, 1954, 1955, 1956, and 1957.

RYAN, MIKE.

Rugby international forward. Club: Rockwell College. He was capped 17 times for Ireland, 13 of them alongside his brother Jack (cv), between 1897 and 1904, and both played in both 19th and 20 centuries, a unique record for international rugby brothers. He was a member, with Jack, of the Ireland side which won its second Triple Crown, in 1899, both players being in a group of only 5 players to participate in all 3 deciding games. An athlete and G.A.A. player of note also (both he and Jack played in the Munster S.F.C. for Tipperary), he holds an almost legendary position in Irish rugby, both he and his brother making up an awesome partnership in the Irish international sides at the turn of the century.

RYAN, MICHAEL (MICK).

Rowing stroke. Club: Garda Siochana Boat Club. He was stroke on the outstanding Garda eight when they won the Irish Senior Championship Eights in 1975 and 1977 (and in 1978 he stroked the only composite eight to win the Irish Championship). He was also stroke of the Irish coxed four who finished 7th in both the World Championships of 1975 and 1977, and in the Olympic Regatta at Montreal in 1976 (winning the Little Final for 7th-12th place in each event).

RYAN, MICK.

G.A.A. football right corner-back, Offaly. Having won an All-Ireland M.F.C. medal with Offaly minors in 1964, he went on to be a half-back on the Offaly S.F.C. side beaten in the All-Ireland S.F.C. final in 1969. He was a member of Offaly's first team to win an All-Ireland Senior Football Championship title in 1971, playing also on the team which won the following year, both times playing a right corner-back. He won a Railway Cup medal with Leinster in 1974. He won 2 All-Star awards, in 1972 at right full-back, and in 1973 at full-back.

RYAN, MICK.

G.A.A. hurling centre half-forward, Tipperary. He was a constant member of the famous Tipperary All-Ireland Senior Hurling Championship 3-in-a-row side when in 1949, 1950 and 1951, they won successive 3 Liam McCarthy Cups. A fine centre-half forward, he won 5 Railway Cup medals for Munster, in 1949, 1950, 1951, 1952 and 1957. He also won 6 National Hurling League medals with Tipp, in 1949, 1950, 1952, 1954, 1955 and 1957.

RYAN, NICOLE.

International rower. Clubs: Anna Liffey (up to 1983), Commercial R.C. (1984-88), and Workmen's Club, Killarney (from 1989). In a long career she won an outstanding 13 Irish Senior titles, all in coxless pair and coxed fours (for 3 club sides and some composite teams). Her pair's wins were in 1983, 1984, 1985, 1986, 1987, 1988 and 1989, while her fours wins were in 1982, 1983, 1984, 1985, 1986 and 1989. She represented Ireland in 3 different World Championships, in the women's pairs in Duisburg in 1983, and twice in the coxless fours, in Nottingham in 1986 and in Copenhagen in 1987.

RYAN, PADDY.

Bareknuckle boxer. He was born in Thurles, Co Tipperary on March 15th 1853, and died at the age of 47, in 1901, near New York. Doing all of his prize-fighting in the U.S.A., he became American heavyweight champion (bareknuckle) in 1880, when defeating Joe Goss at Vancouver in 87 rounds (84 minutes). He lost his title to John L Sullivan over 9 rounds in Mississippi City in 1882, when the purse was $5,000. He lost to Sullivan twice again, including 3 years later when he was beaten after only 50 seconds. He was elected in 1973 to The Ring magazine's Hall of Fame, into the Pioneer Group.

RYAN, PATRICK J (PADDY).

Athlete, hammer-thrower. Born in Old Pallas, Co Limerick in 1882. He emigrated to New York in 1910, and won the American (A.A.U.) hammer title 8 times, 1913, 1914, 1915, 1916, 1917, 1919, 1920, and 1921. He set a world record hammer throw (the first I.A.A.F. hammer record in this event) that was to last for 25 years on 17th August 1913, with 189' 6" (it lasted as the U.S. record for 40 years). Representing the U.S., he won the 1920 Olympic hammer gold medal in Antwerp (his throw of 173'5" giving him the event's biggest ever winning margin of 15 feet), helped by the fact that fellow-Irishman Matt McGrath had to retire after only 2 throws. He won a silver medal in the 56 lb weight event also in Antwerp, behind Patrick 'Babe' McDonald, another Irishman. Having won his first Irish championship in 1903 (defeating the then world record holder Tom Kiely cv), he returned to Ireland in 1919, and won it yet again, bringing his tally to 12 Irish titles in total. He became a farmer at Pallasgreen, Co Limerick, and died, aged 82, in 1964.

RYAN, REGGIE A.

Soccer international inside-forward. Born in Dublin, 30th October 1925. He signed for West Bromwich Albion from Nuneaton during World War Two, playing well over 200 league matches up to 1954, scoring at least 28 goals. He then spent three seasons at Derby County, scoring 90 goals in 133 league appearences. From there he transferred to Coventry City, playing there until 1960. He was capped 16 times for Eire between 1950 and 1956, scoring 3 international goals, and was capped once for Northern Ireland in 1950 against Wales.

RYAN, T.

G.A.A. hurler, Tipperary. He won 4 All-Ireland Senior Hurling Championship winner's medals with various Tipperary teams, in 1896 and 1898 with Tubberadora, in 1899 with Moycarkey, and in 1900 with Two-Mile-Borris.

RYAN, TIMMIE.

G.A.A. hurling midfielder, Limerick. Born in 1910. Club: Ahane (winning 15 county championship medals with the Mackeys etc.). He was on the great Limerick team of the 30's, and won 3 All-Ireland Senior Hurling Championship medals, in 1934 (when he captained the side which defeated Dublin in a replay by 5-2 to 2-6), 1936, and 1940. He also won 2 other Munster S.H.C. medals with Limerick, in 1933 and 1935 (on both occasions losing All-Ireland finals). He shared in Limerick's record 5-in-a-row

National Hurling League wins from 1934 to 1938. He also won 5 Railway Cup medals with Munster, in 1934 and 1935 (both as captain, making him the 1st Limerickman to captain a winning side, and only the 2nd hurler to captain 2 victorious teams), 1937, 1938, 1939. One of hurling's finest ever midfielders, his senior inter-county career spanned from 1930 to 1945.

RYAN, WILLIE.

International rower. Born 28th September 1953. Club: Garda Siochana. He won 12 Irish Senior rowing Championships: 6 in the 'eights' (1974, 1975, 1977, 1979, 1982 and 1983), and the other six shared between coxed fours (1982, 1983 and 1984), coxless pair (1978 and 1981), and one in double sculls in 1982. He was in 3 different winning teams at Henley, the Thames Cup in 1975, and twice in the Prince Philip Cup (in 1977 and 1979). In the Moscow Olympic Paired-Oared Shell Without Coxswain event in 1980, he and his partner Pat Gannon finished 7th (he also finished 7th in 3 World Championship coxless pairs, in 1975, 1976 and 1977. In the 1978 World Championships on Lake Karapiro, New Zealand in 1978, he, along with Christy O'Brien cv, qualified for the final, finishing 5th in the world. This feat meant that in 1978 the pair shared the Texaco Rowing Sportstar of the Year award. His brother Ted was also an international rower, capturing 3 Irish Senior Rowing Eights Championships, in 1979, 1982 and 1983, all with Willie, and represented Ireland at the 1980 Olympics in Moscow.

RYDER, KAY.

G.A.A. Camogie player, Dublin. She shares with Gerry Hughes (cv) the third spot in all-time winner's medal tally for All-Ireland Senior Camogie Championship titles, with Dublin. Her 9 medals were won in 1955, and then in 8 of Dublin's great 10-titles-in-a-row from 1957 to 1966.

S

SALMON, JOE (JOEY).

G.A.A. hurling midfielder, Galway. From the Eyrescourt area of Galway, he lived 1930-1991. Clubs: Eyrescourt and Liam Mellows (Galway), and Glen Rovers of Cork (winning 6 county championships with them between 1957 and 1964). A member of the Galway minors beaten in the final of the All-Ireland M.H.C. in 1947, he went on to become one of the greatest players never to win an All-Ireland Senior Hurling Championship medal (being selected in 1984 in the midfield on the 'Team of the Century' for those without Liam McCarthy Cup medals). He was one of the great players of the 1950's, playing senior inter-county hurling from 1949 to 1964. He was 3 times on Galway teams beaten in All-Ireland Senior Hurling Championship finals, in 1953 to Cork, in 1955 to Wexford, and in the 1958 decider to Tipperary. One of the games great stylists, he was also 3 times on losing Connacht sides in the Railway Cup final, in 1949,, 1952 and 1955 (the last 2 of being all Galway sides). A quality player who won many accolades but few major medals, he did win 3 Oireachtas medals, in 1950, 1952 and 1958. He had little part in the county's win in the 1958 National Hurling League. He also won a few Connacht sprint titles.

SAMMOM, LIAM.

G.A.A. football midfielder and half-forward, Galway. He won one All-Ireland Senior Football Championship winner's medal with Galway, in 1966, the last of the 3-in-a-row years. He also won Connacht S.F.C. medals in 1968, 1970, 1971, 1973, and 1974, playing in 3 losing All-Ireland S.F.C. final teams, in 1971 (as captain when Offaly won), 1973 (again as captain when they were defeated by Cork), and in 1974. He won a National League winner's medal in

1967. He won 2 All-Stars, in the inaugural year of 1971 in the midfield position, and in 1973 at left half-forward.

SANCHEZ, LAURIE.

Soccer international midfeielder. Born in Lambeth, 22nd October 1959. Moving from the amateur game to Reading, he scored 28 league goals in 262 games for the club. Moving to another long stint at Wimbledon, his tally of league goals reached 30 while playing in over 212 games for them. He scored the winning goal in Wimbledon's F.A. Cup final success of 1988. He has been capped 3 times for Northern Ireland from 1987 up to mid-1993.

SANDERSON, (nee KNOX), BARBARA.

Squash international player. Born in Armagh, 8th December 1939. Clubs: Queen's University Belfast, and Brenfield, Essex (helping them to many England national titles from 1984 to 1990). An Ulster interprovincial, she was capped 54 times for Ireland over a 17 year period from 1964 to 1980, being captain for several seasons. She was a member of the Irish team at the first Women's World Team Championships in Birmingham in 1979. She won an Irish Open title in 1969, and the Irish Close in 1974. Living in Essex from 1965, she won the Essex Open in 1971, the Essex Closed in both 1968 and 1970, the East of England Open in 1971, and in 1982 won the British Open Veteran's title. She was captain of Essex from 1966 to 1983.

SANDERSON, VINE.

Hockey international left-half. Club: Imperial Tobacco Company. A product of St Patrick's Grammar School in Dublin. Although he was capped only 9 times for Ireland, each of his caps make up the 3 matches in each year of Ireland's famous 3-in-a-row Triple Crown victories in 1937, 1938, and 1939.

SAUNDERS, ROB.

Rugby international scrum-half. Born in 1971 in Nottingham, of Scottish parents. Club: London Irish. A product of B.R.A. and Queen's University, he played for Ulster schools, Irish schools, Irish Universities, and captained Ireland at Under 21 level in a fine win over Scotland in 1989. In 1990, before he ever played for the Ulster senior side, he won his first cap against France, and was also picked as captain (becoming only the 5th, and first in 35 years, to captain the national side on his first cap, and at 22, the 3rd youngest captain in Irish rugby). He played in the Irish team which performed well in the 1991 World Cup, and has brought his cap tally to 11 (up to June 1992). A talented all-round sportsman, he played for Ireland at schools international level in squash, and was also an Ulster shot putt champion. His father was a Sottish rugby trialist.

SAUNDERS, TERENCE Robert Beaumont.

International Rower. Born in Ireland, 2nd June 1901, he died in Surrey in 1985. Educated at Eton and Cambridge, he was stroke on the Cambridge boat in University Boat Race of 1923. Among his successes were 3 successive wins in the Steward's (in 1922, 1923 and 1924), and he was also a member of the Leander eight which were victorious in the Grand in 1929. In 1924, representing Great Britain in the Olympic Games in Paris, he won an Olympic gold medal in the Coxless Fours event, when beating Canada into the silver placing.

SAWARD, PAT.

Soccer international wing-half. Born in Cork, 17th August 1928. Clubs: Crystal Palace (as an amateur), Millwall (scoring 14 league goals in 120 games 1951-54), Aston Villa (playing 152 league games 1955-60, helping them to become Division 2 champions in 1959-60), Huddersfield Town, and Coventry City. He was capped 18 times for the Republic of Ireland between 1954 and 1963.

SAYERS, H J MIKE.

Rugby international No 8. Clubs: Lansdowne and Aldershot Services. He won 10 international caps for Ireland in the pre-war years of 1935 to 1939, in the last of which he was ever-present in the Irish side which were frustrated, for the 7th time, by Wales at the final hurdle of a Triple Crown bid (he had dropped a goal from a mark in the Scottish game). He was killed in an air crash at the age of 32.

SCANLON, PADDY.

G.A.A. hurling goalkeeper, Limerick. He won 2 All-Ireland Senior Hurling Championship medals with Limerick, in 1936 and 1940, having also been in goals when the county were beaten in the All-Ireland S.H.C. final of 1935. Rated as one of hurling's best goalkeepers, he won 5 Railway Cup medals with Munster, in 1934, 1935, 1937, 1938, and 1940.

SCANNELL, BRENDAN J (BRENNIE).

Amateur international golfer. Club: Woodbrook. A winner of the East of Ireland Championship 3 times, in 1947, 1954 and 1955 (and was runner-up in 1953), he was runner-up in the 1946 and 1954 West of Ireland Championships. He was also runner-up in the Irish Close in 1948, and the Irish Amateur Open in 1949. He played 32 Home international matches in 7 series for Ireland between 1947 and 1954, winning 14 and halving 5; between 1956 and 1962 he played 16 interprovincial matches for Leinster, winning 8 and halving 4, having also played for his province in 1938 and 1939, one of only 5 players to survive the 17 year-break. He won the Irish Senior title in 1972 and 1976. He went on to win the Over 60's version of that title in 1977, 1978 and 1979, the over 65's in 1983, and the over 70's in 1988, the only golfer to achieve wins in all categories of the Seniors. An administrator of note, he was an Irish selector in 1968-78, and he was President of the G.U.I. in 1979-80.

SCHUTE, F GEOFFREY, and FREDERICK.

Rugby internationals, father and son. Fred, 4 times a Leinster interprovincial with Wanderers, played 2 matches for Ireland in the late 1870's, against England twice, in 1878 and 1879. His son F Geoffrey (Dublin University), who represented Leinster twice in 1912, played 3 games for Ireland, in 1912 against South Africa, and in 1913 against England and Scotland, scoring one international try.

SCOTT, DENNIS, and ROBERT Desmond.

Rugby international brothers. Donald, a wing-forward with Malone, won 3 international caps for Ireland in 1961-1962, while Robert D, a wing-threequarter with Queen's University Belfast (winning an Ulster Senior League medal in 1967), played rugby 5 times for Ireland in 1967 and 1968.

SCOTT, ELISHA (LEE or 'LI').

Soccer international goalkeeper. Born in Belfast, 24th August 1894. Clubs: Broadway United, Liverpool (playing 429 matches for the first team in 22 years with the club, winning 2 successive First Division Championship medals in 1921-22 and 1922-23), and Belfast Celtic (where he was also manager from 1936 until the club's demise in 1949, helping them to win 31 major trophies, including 6 Irish League titles (5-in-a-row from 1936 to 1940, and again in 1943), 6 I.F.A. Irish Cups (in 1937, 1938, 1941, 1943, 1944 and 1947), 8 Gold Cups, 3 City Cups, 5 County Antrim Shields and 3 Regional Leagues (as a player with the club, while on war-time loan from Liverpool, he won an Irish Cup medal in 1918). Regarded in his day as on of the world's greatest goalkeepers, and renowned for his rivalry with the great Dixie Dean of Everton, he was capped 31 times for Northern Ireland between 1920 and 1936 (when he was 41 years of age), his last 4 caps were while with Belfast Celtic. A brother of Billy and Tom Scott (cv), he is a cousin of Bertie Mehaffy (cv). He died in 1959.

SCOTT, JOHN (JACKIE).

Soccer international outside-left winger. Born in Belfast, 22nd December 1933. Clubs: Ormand Star, Manchester United, Grimsby Town (scoring 51 league goals in 241 matches 1956-62), and York City. Although he won only 2 caps for Northern Ireland, they were in the fine side which performed miracles in the World Cup in Sweden in 1958, Scott playing in the No 9 jersey in the famous 2-1 victory over Czechoslovakia, and in the 4-0 defeat by France.

SCOTT, PETER W.

Soccer international defender. Born in Liverpool, 19th September 1952. Clubs: Everton (apprenticed), York City, and Aldershot. An England Youth international in 1966, he was later capped 10 times for Northern Ireland between 1975 and 1979, and became the most capped player in 2 English League clubs, namely York City (7 caps in 1976-78) and Aldershot (one cap gained in 1979).

SCOTT, TOM.

Soccer international goalkeeper. Club: Cliftonville (with whom he won an Irish Cup in 1897). He was capped at soccer 13 times in goals for Northern Ireland between 1894 and 1900. A brother of Elisha and Billy Scott (cv).

SCOTT, WILLAIM (BILLY).

Soccer international goalkeeper. Clubs: Linfield (winning Irish Cup medals in 1902 and 1904), Everton (winning an F.A. Cup medal in 1906), and Leeds City. He was capped 25 times for Northern Ireland between 1903 and 1913, thus making the tally of 55 caps for 2 brothers in the same position, as his younger brother Elisha won 30 caps (cv). Another brother is Tom Scott (cv).

SCRIVEN, GEORGE.

Rugby international forward. Club: Dublin University (winning a Leinster Senior Cup medal in it's inaugural year of 1882). He won 8 international caps for Ireland between 1879 and 1883 (all were lost), being captain for his last 2 caps, against Scotland and England in 1883. He is the only person to become President of the I.R.F.U. twice, being at the helm in 1882-1883 (during which time he was also captain of the side and chairman of the selection committee), and again in 1885-1886. He also became an international referee, and it was his interpretation of the laws of the game in the 1884 clash between England and Scotland that led to the 2 countries halting matches between each other for a period. A doctor.

SCROOPE, GERVASE, CHARLIE and SIMON.

Tennis international brothers. Club: Fitzwilliam (Simon won the club championship title in 1911 and 1920 and Charlie won it in 1925). Simon played Davis Cup for Ireland in 1923 (the first time the country competed, and they beat India in the first round) and 1925. Charlie (who won the Irish Lawn Tennis Singles title in 1923) played Davis Cup in 1925 (with Simon), 1928, and twice in 1931; he also won the Irish Men's Doubles title in 1908, 1914 (with Charlie), while Charlie also won in 1919 and 1931 (Gervase won this title in 1924). In 1921, in a match against England at Buxton, all three brothers played for Ireland.

SCULLION, TONY.

G.A.A. football left full-back, Derry. Born in 1962. Club: Lavey of Ballinascreen (winning an All-Ireland Club Championship medal with the club in 1991, and an Ulster title again in 1993). From Draperstown, he was a member of the Derry Under 21 side which lost the All-Ireland U-21 final in 1983, also making his senior inter-county debut in the same year. He was in the county side which won the National Football League in 1992, the county's first since 1947. Also a winner of 3 Railway Cup medals, he has won 2 All-Stars, in 1987 and 1992, both in the left corner-forward. He played in the Compromise Rules series against Australia in 1987. He was a star member of the Derry side which won the Ulster Senior Football Championship in 1987 after a 13 year gap, when they beat Armagh by 0-11 to 0-9, he also won an

Ulster S.F.C. medal in 1993, when the county qualified for their first All-Ireland S.F.C. final in 25 years, going on to win the title for the first time.

SEALY, JAMES.

Rugby international forward, and hockey international. Club: Dublin University (winning Leinster Senior Cupmedals in 1895, 1896, 1897, 1898 and 1900). Seven times a Leinster interprovincial, he was capped 9 times for Ireland in rugby between 1896 and 1900, scoring 2 international tries, and was one of only 5 men who played in all 3 of Ireland's Triple Crown winning matches on 1899. He went on the British and Irish Lions tour of South Africa in 1896, and played in all 4 test internationals. In hockey, while playing with the Dundrum club, he was capped once in 1895, the first year in which international hockey was played. A High Court judge, he was an Irish rugby selector, and later became President of the I.R.F.U. in 1927-1928.

SEGRAVE, Major (later Sir) HENRY O'NEAL DE HANE ('THE FASTEST MAN ON EARTH').

Car racing pioneer. Born in Baltimore, Maryland in 1896 to Irish parents, the family moved to Wicklow soon afterwards. Later moving to London, he won the Junior Car Club's 200 race at Brooklands three times, in 1921, 1925 and 1926. He went on to become the leading post-war racing driver, winning 2 Grand Prix, the 1923 French G.P. at Tours (then considered the 'blue riband' of motor car racing) in a Sunbeam (at an average speed of 75.31 m.p.h., thus becoming the first 'British' winner of a G.P.), and the 1924 San Sebastian, also in a Sunbeam. He also had the fastest lap in 2 other Grand Prix (in France in 1926 at 76.7 m.p.h., and in the 1926 British G.P. with 85 m.p.h. in a Talbot). He also won the Boulogne Voiturettes Grand Prix, and the 1927 Grand Prix de Provence. He was however more famous for his exploits in the World Land Speed arena, breaking it 3 times: in 1926 in a 4 litre Sunbeam at Southport Sands, he set a world record of 152.33 m.p.h.; in 1927 when he became the first to pass the 200 m.p.h. barrier when he drove a 1,000 h.p. Sunbeam at 203.79 m.p.h. at Daytona, Florida; and for the final time, again at Daytona, he set it at 231.44 m.p.h. in an Irving-Napier. Knighted for these deeds, he was killed in 1930, aged 33, on Lake Windemere while attempting the World Water Speed record in Miss England II.

SEMPLE, TOM.

G.A.A. hurler and long puck expert, Tipperary. From Thurles. He won 3 All-Ireland Senior Hurling Championship winner's medals with Tipperary, in 1900 with the Two-Mile-Borris Selection, and then twice as captain, in 1906 when the Thurles Selection beat Dublin's Faughs by 3-16 to 3-8, and again in 1908 when the Thurles side this time defeated Kickham's side from Dublin by 3-15 to 1-5 in a replay. He also captained the losing Thurles Selection in the 1909 All-Ireland S.H.C. final defeat by Kilkenny's Mooncoin Selection. He won the 1906 Long Puck Championship of Ireland, when, using a 9 ounce ball, when he 'lift and hit' the ball 96 yards. A legend in his home district, Semple Stadium in Thurles is named in his honour.

SHARKEY, TOM.

Heavyweight boxer. Born in 1883, in Dundalk, Co Louth. On 3rd November 1899, he challenged the world champion, James J Jeffries of U.S.A. for the world heavyweight title (and a winner-take-all stake of $25,000) at Coney Island, New York. He lost on points in a famous struggle over 25 rounds. In an illustrious career, he otherwise claimed victories over Jim Corbett and Bob Fitzsimmons (in a fight which was refereed by the gunslinger Wyatt Earp), both world heavyweight champions in their day. He was elected in 1959 on to The Ring magazine's Hall of Fame, into the Old Timers Group.

SHEAHAN, Dr DAVID B.

Amateur international golfer. Born in Southsea, England, 25th February 1940. Clubs: U.C.D., The Grange. He won the Irish Close Championship title 3 times, in 1961, 1966, and 1970; he was runner-up in the 'North' of 1959 and the 'South' in 1963. In 49 interprovincial matches for Leinster from 1959 to 1976, he won 22; he played 44 Home international matches for Ireland 1961-1970, winning 21; he contributed 4 wins out of his 10 matches in the 2 Irish winning sides in the European Team Championships of 1965 and 1967. In 1962, after winning the Boyd Quaich event, he went on to become the only amateur ever to win a European professional tournament, the Jeyes, held in Royal Dublin (this amazing feat earned him the Texaco Sportstar of the Year award fo golf for 1962). He went on to capture Walker Cup honours in 1963, when in one day, he beat the champions of both America and Britain, the Americans Richard Davies and Labron Harris, each by one hole (he lost his other 2 matches).

SHEARER, E DONALD R.

Cricket international right hand batsman. Born in Harrow, Middlesex, 6th June 1909. Clubs: City of Derry, N.I.C.C., North Down, and Free Foresters. He played once for the M.C.C. in 1947, and in the 20 year period from 1933 to 1952 he played 32 international cricket matches for Ireland. He scored 1,300 runs for Ireland, off 58 innings with an average rate of 23.42 runs per innings, and scored 2 international centuries (one of these, against Cahn's XI in 1937 taking only 80 minutes, then a record quickest 100 for Ireland). He was President of the I.C.U. in 1966. He also played amateur soccer for England, was a Chairman of N.I. Sports Council, and was awarded an O.B.E. for his services to sport.

SHEEDY, KEVIN.

Soccer international midfielder. Born in Builth Wells, Wales, 21st October 1959. Clubs: Hereford United (apprenticed), Liverpool (4 unhappy years), Everton (scoring over 67 goals in 276 league games for them, winning 2 English League Division One Champions medals in 1985 and 1987, while being runners-up in 1986; and an F.A. Cup winner's medal in 1984 and 3 runner-up medals in 1985, 1986 and 1989; and gaining a European Cup Winners Cup medal in 1985), and Newcastle United (helping them to win the Fisrt Division in 1993, and gain promotion to the Premiership). He has been capped 46 times for the Republic of Ireland between 1984 and mid 1993, scoring 9 international goals. Having played in the European Championship successes of 1988, he played an important role in helping Ireland to qualify for the World Cup finals for the first time in 1990, and scored the goal which enabled Ireland to draw against England in their Group 6 match.

SHEEDY, JACK.

G.A.A. football centre forward, Dublin. Born in 1963. Club: Garda. A product of Lucan Sarsfield's GC, he was a county junior player in 1985 and 1986. He was a member of the Dublin side which won the National Football League in both 1991 and 1993, and was a major force in the epic 4-match battle versus Meath in the Leinster S.F.C. game of 1991, his first year in championship football. He was a prominent member of the Dublin side beaten in the All-Ireland S.F.C. final in 1992, and which won the Leinster S.F.C. in 1993.

SHEEHY, JOHN JOE.

G.A.A. footballer, Kerry. Born in Tralee, Co Kerry in 1898, he died in 1980. He won 4 All-Ireland Senior Football Championship winner's medals with Kerry, in 1924, in 1926 (when he captained the side that beat Kildare by 1-4 to 0-4 in a replay), in 1929, and in 1930 (when he again captained the side, this time to defeat Monaghan by 3-11 to 0-2 in the decider). He was on losing Kerry sides in All-Ireland S.F.C. finals twice, in 1923, and in 1927 as captain against Kildare. He played for Munster at Railway Cup level in both football (being captain of the first ever winning Railway Cup side, the all-Kerry team of 1927) and hurling, and played in the 1928 Tailteann Games. Retiring at the age of 33 in 1931, he later represented Kerry on the Munster Council from 1936 to 1973. He was selected as the first Gaelic footballer to join the Texaco Hall of Fame in 1963. His 3 sons, Paudie (3), Niall (2), and Sean Og (1), won 6 All-Ireland S.F.C winning medals between them.

SHEEHY, MICHAEL (MIKEY).

G.A.A. football right full-forward, Kerry. Born July 28th 1954. Club: Austin Stacks (winning an All-Ireland Club Championship medal with them in 1977). He won 2 All-Ireland Under 21 Championship medals with Kerry in 1973 and 1975. He is one of 5 Kerry footballers to share the record of 8 All-Ireland Senior Championship winner's medals, winning in 1975, then in the 4-in-a-row of 1978, 1979 (his tally in this game of 2-6 is a joint record for a final), 1980, and 1981 (his total contribution to the run of 15 games in the 4-in-a-row was 115 points), and winning his last 3 in the 3-in-a-row of 1984 (although not playing in the final), 1985, and 1986. He was also on the beaten All-Ireland S.F.C. final sides of both 1976 and 1982. He won 7 All-Star awards, all at right full-forward, in 1976, 1978, 1979, 1981, 1982, 1984, and in 1986 (placing as the 2nd most honoured footballer in this arena). He was voted Texaco Footballer of the Year in 1979 (the 7th Kerryman to be so honoured), when he was the game's leading marksman, his 19 goals and 77 points in 20 competitive matches making up a tally of 134 points, with an average of 6.70 per game. He has scored more points in All-Ireland S.F.C. finals than any other Kerryman. One of gaelic football's greatest artist's, in 1984 he was voted into the right full-forward spot on the Sunday Independent's 'Team of the Century', alongside Tom Langan of Mayo and Kevin Heffernan of Dublin.

SHEEHY, NOEL.

G.A.A. hurling full-back, Tipperary. Born in 1964. Club: Silvermines. He won an All-Ireland Under 21 Championship winner's medal in 1985 (having been on the side beaten in the final of the previous year). A member of the Tipp side beaten in the All-Ireland Senior Hurling Championship decider in 1988, he went on to win 2 Liam McCarthy Cup medals on the winning sides of 1989 and 1991. He won another Munster S.H.C. medal in 1993. He was the only Tipperary back to win an All-Star in the awards of 1990, gaining the full-back slot, and won his 2nd award in this position in 1991.

SHEEHY, SEAN OG and NIALL.

G.A.A. footballing brothers, Kerry. Sean Og, a right half-back, was captain of the Kerry team which beat Roscommon by 1-12 to 1-6 in the 1962 All-Ireland Senior Football Championship final. That day his 2 brothers, Paudie (cv) and Niall, also played in the side. By captaining the side, Sean Og became the first son of a former winning captain (John Joe Sheehy cv), to repeat this winning feat. His brother Niall, a full-back, had already won an All-Ireland S.F.C. medal in 1959, and was on 3 losing sides in the All-Ireland S.F.C. finals of 1960, 1964 (as captain of the side beaten by Galway), and 1965.

SHEEHY, PAUDIE.

G.A.A. football half-forward and left full-forward, Kerry. A winner of an All-Ireland M.F.C. medal in midfield with Kerry minors in 1950, he was on the team beaten in the previous year's final. He won 3 All-Ireland Football Championship medals with Kerry, in 1955, in 1959 (playing alongside his brother Niall), and in 1962 (with his brother Sean Og as captain, and Niall also in the side). He had captained Kerry in their losing All-Ireland S.F.C. final of 1960, also playing in the final loss of

1954. He is the son of the great John Joe Sheehy (cv).

SHERIDAN, JOHN ('SHEZ').

Soccer international midfielder. Born 1st October 1964 at Stretford in Manchester. Clubs: Manchester City, Leeds United (6 seasons, 230 league games and 49 goals, reaching an F.A. Cup semi-final, but not gaining promotion), Nottingham Forest (who paid £650,000 for him), Sheffield Wedsnsday (his single goal to beat Manchester United in the 1991 English League Cup final gave the club it's first major trophy in 59 years; he also played influential roles in the club's appeerences in 2 losing finals in 1993, the League Cup and the F.A. Cup). A fine passer of the ball, he has been capped for the Republc of Irleand at Youth, Under 21 and Under 23 levels, also gaining 14 senior caps up to mid 1993. He took part in Ireland's run-up to the European Championship in 1988, and was in the squad for the ground-breaking World Cup finals in Italy in 1990. His brother Darren was a junior player with Leeds United in 1984.

SHERIDAN, MARTIN ('MARTY').

Field athlete. Born in Bohola, Co Mayo, 28th March 1881. Emigrating to New York in 1900, he became a New York cop. In his heyday he was universally called 'the world's greatest athlete', having won the A.A.U. all-round championship (then regarded as the world title) 3 times, in 1905, 1907, and 1909; and also won the A.A.U. discus title 4 times between 1903 and 1911. Breaking the world discus record in 1901 at 36.77 metres, in 1902 he became the first man to reach 40 metres in only his third effort at this his speciality event, and held the world record for 10 years (breaking his own world record mark 8 times, finally reaching 43.69 metres). In three successive Olympic Games he excelled for his adapted country, U.S.A., by winning 5 gold, 3 silver and 1 bronze medal, his tally of 9 making him the joint 3rd athletics medal winner in U.S. history. In 1904 St Louis Games he won gold in the discus (in the first ever Olympic throw-off, against team-mate Ralph Rose, winning by 5 feet), and finished 4th in the shot. In the Intercalated Games at Athens in 1906 (in which he competed for the U.S.A. in all the field events, but actually in only 7 of the 14 events that he was entered for!), he won 5 medals, gold at both discus and shot putt, and 3 silver medals, in the 14lb stone throw contest, the standing broad jump and in the standing high jump; he was disqualified in the Greek style discus, and had to withdraw from the pentathlon, while favourite for gold. In 1908 Games in London he again won the discus gold (with an Olympic record of 134' 2" and his third successive Olympic gold medal in this event), adding to it the Greek style discus title, and won a silver in the standing broad jump (he was also placed 9th in the triple jump). Over his career he set an amazing 16 world records. He died in 1918 in New York, of pneumonia, at the age of 37. His brother Richard, who was his inspiration, won the A.A.U. discus in 1898, 1899, 1901 and 1902.

SHERLOCK, VICTOR.

G.A.A. football centre-field, Cavan. Born in Co Meath. Club: Kingscourt. He won 2 All-Ireland Senior Football Championship medals with Cavan, in 1948 over in their win over Mayo and in 1952 against his native Meath (playing a vital role in this replay win), thereby gaining revenge as he was a a member of the Cavan side beaten in the final of the All-Ireland S.F.C. in 1949 by The Royal County. He won a Railway Cup medal in 1950 with Ulster. Also a noted handballer, he won the All-Ireland Junior Softball Singles title in 1949. A father of R.T.E. presenter Linda Sherlock, he won the Lotto in July 1990, with a prize of over £400,000.

SHERRY, BRENDAN Francis.

Rugby international scrum-half. Born in Cork, 7th June 1943. Club: Terenure College (winning Leinster Senior Cup medals on the only 2 occasions the club triumphed in the competition, in 1966 and 1967). A Connacht player, he was capped for Ireland 6 times in all between 1967 and 1968. His relation Mick J A Sherry of Lansdowne was capped twice on the flank for Ireland in 1975.

SHORT, JOHN Francis (JACK).

Cricket international right hand batsman. Born in Cork, 12th April 1951. Clubs: Cork Bohemians and Leinster. A product ot Presentation College Cork, he played 56 international cricket matches for Ireland between 1974 and 1984. He scored 2,515 runs for Ireland in those eleven years (making him 4th in the all-time runs list), scored in 98 innings, for a fine average of 29.24 (eighth on the all-time list of best international averages for Ireland). A quality batsman, he scored 3 centuries for Ireland, his best being 114 (he also scored fifteen 50's for his country).

SIGGINS, JOHN Allen Edgar (JACK).

Rugby international No 8 forward. Born in Belfast, 28th June 1909. Club: Belfast Collegians. A product of Methodist College in Belfast, he was capped 24 times for Ireland between 1931 and 1937, scoring one international try and 3 penalties, and he captained the side for 3 seasons (for a total of 10 matches), 1933-34, 1934-35 (when Ireland won the Five Nations Championship), and 1935-36. Later he managed the Lions tour of South Africa in 1955, became President of the Ulster Branch, and was President of the I.R.F.U. in 1962-63. He was Irish representative on the International board 1957-71, and was an Irish selector during the Triple Crown years of 1947-1949. He was awarded the Irish Rugby Writers Hall of Fame award in 1989.

SILKE, SEAN.

G.A.A. hurling centre half-back, Galway. Born in 1952. Clubs: Maynooth College (helping them to Fitzgibbon Cup wins in 1973 and 1974) and Mellick-Eyrecourt. A county minor who graduated to senior hurling in 1972, he was a member of the Galway side beaten by Kilkenny in the 1975 All-Ireland Senior Hurling Championship final, and by Cork in the 1979 decider. He won a Liam McCarthy Cup medal in 1980 in the win over Kilkenny, only to be captain of the side beaten in the final of 1981 by Offaly. He captained the Connacht team to win the Railway Cup in 1982, the 3rd Galwayman to do so, winning a medal also in 1980. He won National Hurling League medals with Galway in 1976 (playing a leading role), 1977 and 1981. He has won 2 All-Star awards, both at centre half-back, in 1975 and 1980. In 1975 he and his sister became the first brother and sister to play in All-Ireland finals in the same year, as she played on the Galway team which lost the All-Ireland Ladies G.A.A. final to Tipperary.

SIMCOX, REDMOND.

Amateur international golfer. Club: Cork (winning 2 Senior Cup medals in 1931 and 1939, and Barton Shield medals in 1937 and 1938). He won the South of Ireland Championship in both 1926 and 1927, and was runner-up in 1936; he was runner-up in the Irish Close in 1938 to Jimmy Bruen cv. He played 37 Home international matches for Ireland between 1930 and 1938, with a 50% points record. He was President of the G.U.I. in 1950-52.

SIMPSON, LIAM.

G.A.A. hurling corner-back, Kilkenny. Born in 1966. Club: Bennetsbridge. Making his senior debut in 1989, in 1990 he won an All-Ireland J.H.C. medal with the 'Cats'. A star member of the Kilkenny side which lost the All-Ireland Senior Hurling Championship final in 1991, he won Liam McCarthy medals in both 1992 and 1993. A nephew of Seamus Cleere (cv), he won an All-Star award in 1992 in the left full-back position.

SIMPSON, WILLIAM J (BILLY).

Soccer international centre-forward and inside-forward. Clubs: Linfield, Glasgow Rangers (costing a then club record fee of £11,500 in 1950, and playing in a total of 239 games for the club while scoring 165 goals, making him one of only a select few players to score 100 league goals in Scotland since the War, and assisting the club in winning Scottish League Championship medals in 1952-1953, 1955-56 and 1956-1957, and a Scottish Cup medal in 1953), and Stirling Albion. A fine header of the ball, he was capped 12 times for Northern Ireland between 1951 and 1959, scoring 5 international goals for his country, including the winner in the 3-2 win over England in 1957.

SINNAMON, W MARK.

Hockey international left-back or left of midfield. Club: Banbridge. He was capped for Ireland 61 times between 1975 and 1983, captaining the side in his last 2 seasons. He scored 4 goals in Ireland's fine performance in the 1977 Intercontinental Cup, and played also in the World Cup in Buenos Aires.

SKEHAN, NOEL.

G.A.A. hurling goalkeper, Kilkenny. Born in 1946. Club: Bennetsbridge (winning 6 Kilkenny S.H.C. medals). He was a member of the Kilkenny minors which won the All-Ireland M.H.C. in 1962. He has won a record 9 All-Ireland Senior Hurling Championship medals, although 'only' 6 of these from the field of play; in 1972 (when he captained the side which beat Cork by 3-24 to 5-11 in the final), 1974, 1975, 1979, 1982 (when the oldest man on the pitch), and 1983. He had previously won 3 All-Ireland S.H.C. winner's medals as a non-playing substitute to Ollie Walsh (cv) in Kilkenny's Liam McCarthy Cup wins of 1963 (his debut year in the senior squad), 1967 and 1969 (thus winning All-Ireland senior medals 20 years apart, 1963 and 1983). He was also on 2 losing All-Ireland S.H.C. sides, in 1973 and 1978, his Leinster S.H.C. tally of medals being 11. He won 4 Railway Cup medals with Leinster, in 1973, 1974, 1975 and 1979, as well as 3 Oireatchtas medals. He is hurling's most honoured All-Star award winning player, being selected for 7 awards in total in goals over a 12 year period (the longest span of years between first and last All-Stars of any player in either code); he took his first 5 awards in successive years, in 1972, 1973, 1974, 1975, and 1976, winning 2 more in 1982 and 1983. Clearly one of the game's finest ever goal-minders, in 1983 he became the 8th Kilkenny player to be named as Texaco Hurler of the Year. Retiring in 1985, he later became a league standard squash player. In 1993 he was Kilkenny's junior manager.

SKERRITT, PADDY.

Professional golfer. Born in Lahinch in 1930. In 1970, he won the Alcan International Champinship at Portmarnock, and in the same year won the Carrolls Irish Matchplay at Mullingar. Attached to St Annes GC, he won the Irish Professional National title in 1977. He won the British (European) Seniors title twice, in 1978 and 1980. One of 8 brothers; 2 of them, Austin and Mick, both members of Lahinch, played 22 and 18 interprovincial golf matches respectively for Munster between 1958 and 1965, and both became successful club professionals.

SLATTERY, John FERGUS ('SLATS').

Rugby international open-sided wing-forward. Born in Dun Laoghaire on 12th February 1949. Club: Blackrock College (winning a Leinster Senior Cup medal in 1983). A product of Blackrock College (winning a Junior Schools Cup medal in 1964), he was a brilliant open-side wing forward, being capped for Ireland 61 times over a 15 year period between 1970 and 1984, scoring 3 international tries, making him then the world's most capped flanker, and Ireland's third most capped player. He was a member of the Irish side which won the International Championship of 1974, and was a staunch member of the Irish Triple Crown-winning side of 1982 (forming a formidable 19 match record back-row combination with Willie Duggan and John O'Driscoll). He captained Ireland 17 times (ranking him third behind Tom Kiernan and Ciaran Fitzgerald), including for two overseas tours, to Australia in 1979, and to South Africa in 1981. He went on 2 British and Irish Lions tours, to Australia and New Zealand in 1971 (not gaining a test place), and on the great side which were unbeaten in South Africa in 1974 (in which he played a vital role in all 4 tests; his 'good' last minute try in the final Test, to give the Lions a 100% tour record, was disallowed). He was also invited to be considered for 3 other Lions tours (1977, 1980 and 1983), but declined each tour. He played for the Barbarians 20 times, also playing for the French and South African Barbarians. He was voted as Texaco's Rugby Sportstar of the Year in 1979. An auctioneer and estate agent.

SLATTERY, MARGARET (nee LAWLOR).

G.A.A. ladies football full forward, Kerry. Club: Abbeydorney (winning a county championship winner's medal in 1990). Born in 1960. She is the first and only ladies footballer to win 10 All-Ireland Senior Ladies Football Cahmpionship medals, winning in 1976 (Kerry's first win), and in the 9-in-a-row sequennce of 1982, 1983, 1984, 1985, 1986, 1987, 1988, 1989 and 1990. Since playing first for Kerry in 1976 she has played in 41 of the county's 43 championship matches. A leading score getter for the Kingdom, she has been treasurer of the Kerry Ladies County Board, and is the sister of Eileen Lawlor (cv).

SLAVEN, BERNIE.

Soccer international forward. Born in Paisley, 13th November 1960. Clubs: Morton, Airdrie, Queen of the South, Albion Rovers (scoring 27 goals in his 42 games for them), Middlesborough (scoring 114 goals in 289 matches for them up to the end of the 1991-92 season), Port Vale (winning an Autoglass Trophy medal in 1993). Debuting for the Republic of Ireland in 1990 (and scoring on his debut), he has been on the fringes of the Irish XI since then, gaining 6 caps up to 1993.

SLEVIN, COLUM.

Table-tennis international player. Born in Stillorgan, Co Dublin in 1964. At 12 years of age he was an Irish senior international player, and has been capped for Ireland in excess of 135 times since. At 14 he became Ireland's No 1, and was rated No 5 in the world boys listing. Having joined the professional ranks in 1983, he reached a World Ranking of 157th, the only Irish table tennis player to be in these rankings, and has beaten World No 10 and Seoul Olympic bronze medallist Eric Lindh of Sweeden. He has played in 4 World and European Championships. He has won the Irish Close Championships 7 times, on each of the occasions that he has entered. He latterly lived in and played from Hamburg in West Germany.

SLOAN, HAROLD A de B.

Soccer international forward. Clubs: Bohemians. He was capped 8 times for the I.F.A. Ireland international side between 1903 and 1908, and scored 4 international goals. All of his 8 caps came when he was a Bohemians player, making him the club's joint most capped player (see Eamonn Gregg cv), all with the I.F.A.

SLOAN, MARTIN (MARTY).

Hockey international midfielder. Club: Cookstown. First capped in 1982, he was the captain of the Irish squad which finished last in the 1990 World Cup in Lahore, and gained his 100th international cap for Ireland while leading Ireland to 7th place in the European Championship in 1991. Captain of

Ireland from 1987 to 1993, his cap tally came to 123 in mid 1993. An inspirational player, he has also been capped at the indoor code. He won 4 caps for Great Britain between 1978 and 1988.

SLOAN, TOMMY ('STICKEY').

Soccer international midfielder. Clubs: Crusaders, Cardiff City (winning a famous F.A. Cup medal with them in 1927), Linfield (winning an Irish Cup medal in 1934). He was capped 11 times for Northern Ireland between 1926 and 1931.

SLOCUM, MICHAEL.

G.A.A. football right half-back, Cork. Club: St Finbarr's. On the Cork minors beaten in the All-Ireland M.F.C. final in 1983, he went on to win 3 successive All-Ireland Under 21 Championship winners medals, in 1984, 1985 and 1986 (when he captained the victorious side). He has won 2 All-Ireland Senior Football Championship winner's medals with the Rebel County in successive years, 1989 and in the double-winning year of 1990. He won an All-Star award in 1990 in the right half-back position.

SLUDDS, MARTIN.

Amateur and professional golfer. As an amateur member of the Island, he won the prestigious Lytham Trophy in 1982, and won the East of Ireland in the same year. He played 12 interprovincial matches for Leinster, and 6 international matches for Ireland, also being capped for Great Britain and Ireland against Continental Europe. Having failed to make Walker Cup, he immediately turned professional, gaining his players card at first attempt. Success has come slowly, although he has won the Irish National P.G.A. Championship twice, at Skerries in 1984 and at the K Club in 1993. He spent some time as an assistant in England, and won the Assistant's Matchplay Champinship in 1987. He finished 6th in the 1988 Irish Open. Based at Hesketh, near Southport in England.

SMITH, ALEXANDER Victor ('SANDY').

Cricket international batsman, and amateur soccer international. Born on 11th May 1945. He played international cricket 7 times for Ireland, scoring 147 runs, averaging 24.5. He has scored over 7,500 runs for his club, Phoenix (placing him 2nd in their all-time batting tally). As a soccer player, he played 2 seasons of League of Irleand with Shamrock Rovers in the early 1970's, and played in an amateur international match in 1971 against Yugoslavia in the Olympic Games qualifying match.

SMITH, BRIAN Anthony.

Rugby international out-half and scrum-half. Born in St George's, Queensland, Austrlia, 9th Septmber 1966. An Australian Schools player, he later won 7 caps for Australia, including against Ireland in the 1987 World Cup (and in another game against a World XV, he scored a record 26 points), mostly as a scrum-half. Having gained a Blue at Oxford in 1988, he declared for Ireland, having a grandmother from Co Wexford. In 1989, by playing against the All Blacks for Ireland, he became the first player in Irish rugby history to play for Ireland after representing another country. He toured Ireland to North America in 1989. His controversial cap tally for Ireland reached 9 up to the end of the International Championship of 1991, when he suddenly decided to join the Australian Rugby League side, Balmain.

SMITH, ERNEST (ERNIE).

Amateur international featherweight and lightweight boxer. Club: Garda. He won a total of 8 Irish Senior titles, and holds the record of most Irish National Senior lightweight titles, with 7, won with 6-in-a-row 1933, 1934, 1935, 1936, 1937, 1938, and again in 1940. He had won the Irish title at featherweight in 1932, and that year also reached the last eight in the Olympic Games in Los Angeles at featherweight, thereby being placed joint 5th.

SMITH, JIM.

G.A.A. football centre-half back, Cavan. Born in Killinkere, Co Cavan. Club: Bailieboro. Captain of the Cavan side which lost the 1927 All-Ireland S.F.C. final against Kildare (their first appearance in the final), he then captained the side to win the 1933 Sam Maguire Cup, the county's first All-Ireland success, when they beat Galway before a then record attendance of 45,188 at Croke Park. He won another All-Ireland Senior Football Championship medal in 1935. His tally of Ulster S.F.C. medals is 13, achieved in 1920, the 4-in-a-row of 1923, 1924, 1925 and 1926, in 1928, and in the 7-in-a-row years of 1931, 1932, 1933, 1934, 1935, 1936, and 1937. One of the great footballers of the 20's and 30's, and arguably Cavan's greatest footballer, he represented Cavan on the Ireland team in the Tailteann Games in 1924, 1928, and 1932, and was on the first Ulster team to reach the Railway Cup final in 1928. Earlier he won many Dublin S.F. trophies with the renowned Garda team in Dublin.

SMITH, JOHN HARTLEY.

Rugby international prop-forward. Born in Dungannon, 27th July 1926. Clubs: Queen's University Belfast, and London Irish. He was capped 12 times for Ireland between 1951 and 1954, being a constant member of the 1951 International Championship winning side in his first year in the Irish jersey.

SMITH, STEVE.

Rugby international hooker. Born in Belfast, 18th July 1959. Club: Ballymena (winning Ulster Senior League medals in 1990 and 1991, and 3 Ulster Senior Cup medals in succession in 1989, 1990 and in 1991). A product of Belfast Academy, he was first capped in 1988, and in 1989 he went on a British and Irish Lions tour to Australia. One of Ireland's best forwards in the early 1990's, he has been capped 22 times up to June 1993, has scored 2 international tries, and toured New Zealand with Ireland in 1992.

SMYTH, AILISH.

Middle and long distance athlete. Born in 1958. Clubs: Good Counsel Club and Dublin City Harriers. From Walkinstown, she in a product of Our Lady of the Assumption. She won the Dublin City Marathon in 1984, and won the National Marathon Championship title in 1986. She won the B.L.E. National title at 3,000 metres in 1985 and at 5,000 metres in 1987. A competitor at the Seoul Olympics in 1988, she has also ran at Hiroshima (1985), Portugal in 1986 (when D.C.H. won the European Ladies Club Championship), and in London and Berlin in 1987.

SMYTH, JIMMY.

G.A.A. football centre half-forward, Armagh. Born in Donaghcloney, Co Armagh, 1949. Club: Lurgan Clann na Gael (winning a record 9 Senior County Championship medals, in 1968, 1969, 1971, 1972, 1973, 1974, 1976, 1980 and in 1981, also winning with them 3 Ulster Club Championships in succession in 1972, 1973 and 1974). He won McRory Cup medals with St Colman's College in 1966 and 1967. He captained the most recent Armagh team which reached an All-Ireland Senior Football Championship football final (they had already won the 1977 Anglo Celt Cup for the Ulster Senior Championship for the first time in 24 years), when Dublin beat them by 5-12 to 3-6 in 1977, winning a 2nd Ulster S.F.C. medal in 1980. He won a Railway Cup medal with Ulster in 1979, coming on as a sub in the final. Also a holder of Division Two and Division 3 National League medals, he won an All-Star award in 1977 at centre half-forward. A P.E. teacher.

SMYTH, JIMMY.

G.A.A. hurling midfielder right and full-forward, Clare. Born in 1931. Club: Ruan (winning 5 county championship medals). Picked for the Clare minors at only 14, he also won 3 successive All-Ireland College medals with St Flannan's of Ennis, in 1945, 1946 and

1947. After a record 5 years of minor football, his senior inter-county career went from 1948 (when he was 18) up to 1967, during which he only played in one Munster S.H.C. final, a loss in 1955. A member of the Clare side which won the Oireachtas tournament in 1954, he played Railway Cup hurling for Munster for 10 years, winning 6 medals (more than any other Clareman in either code), in 1955, 1958, 1959, 1960, 1961 and 1963. His talent would have brought him All-Ireland medals with any of the powerful hurling counties, and in 1984 he was placed at right corner forward on the 'Team of the Century' for hurlers who never won an All-Ireland medal.

SMITH, ROSEMARY Joy.

International rally driver. Born in Dublin, 7th August 1937. While working as a works driver with the Rootes Group from 1962 to 1967 she was leading woman in all the major rallies at one time in that period. Her Coupes des Dames Award (or ladies prize) rally successes included the London/Sydney, the Monte Carlo once, the Circuit of Ireland Rally 5 times, the Scottish International Rally 6 times, the Shell 4,000 twice, the Canadian Rally twice, the Geneva, the Tour de France twice, the Alpine, the R.A.C. Rally of Great Britain, the London/Mexico, the Total Rally of South Africa, the Safari Rally, the Acropolis, and the East African. She also won the Ladies Award in the London-Mexico World Cup Rally. She did have one important outright rally success, when in her Imp she defeated her team-mate Tiny Lewis in the Tulip Rally in 1965. She was selected as Texaco's Motor Sport Sportstar of the Year for 1965. In 1970 she was voted Woman of the Year in London.

SMYTH, DES.

Professional golfer. Born in Drogheda, 12th February 1953. Turning pro in 1973 after a fine amateur career out of Laytown Bettystown, he won the 1979 PGA Matchplay and Irish Professional titles. He won Ryder Cup honours twice, in 1979 at White Sulphur Springs, and in 1981 at Walton Heath (winning 2 and losing 5 of his 7 matches). In 1980 he won a rarely achieved feat of 3 successive tournaments, the Greater Manchester Open, the Irish Dunlop Masters, and the Newcastle Brown 900. In the 1982 British Open he led the event briefly in the final round. He later won the 1981 Coral Classic and the 1983 Sanyo Open. In 1988 he became the first Irish golfer to win £100,000 in official earnings on the European Tour. He was the hero of the successful Irish trio which captured the $100,000-per-man top prize in the 1988 Dunhill Cup at St Andrew's Scotland. He beat Nick Faldo and Roger Davies in the semi-final and final respectively, in dramatic fashion. A week later he won the £20,000 Jersey Open. He finished in the Top 25 of the European Order of Merit each year from 1979 to 1988, the last year of these being his highest ever finish, at 6th. In 1992 he became the 23rd person to earn 1 million pounds on the European tour. Four times the Irish Professional champion (1980, 1985, 1986 and 1990), he represented Ireland in the World Cup in 1979, 1980, 1982, 1983, and 1988. He has twice been selected as Texaco's Golf Sportstar of the Year, in 1979 and 1988. His brother Val (Laytown and Bettystown), was joint runner-up in the 1991 East of Ireland, played 35 interprovincial matches for Leinster 1970-1984, winning 27 and losing 8 (giving him a success rate of 77%, a record for the competition), and played 12 matches in the Home Internationals for Ireland 1981-82, winning 5.

SMYTH, M .

Ladies international amateur golfer. Club: Royal Co Down. She won the Ulster Ladies Championship 3 times, in 1951, 1958 and 1959 (and was runner-up 6 times, in 1938, 1948, 1950, 1952, 1953 and in 1957). She played in each of

Ireland's 13 Home International series sides from 1947 to 1959, and was non-playing captain in 1962.

SMYTH, MICK.

Soccer international goalkeeper. Born in Dublin, 13th May 1940. Clubs: Drumcondra (playing on a losing F.A.I. Cup final side in 1961, when he also won a League of Ireland Championship medal), Barrow, Shamrock Rovers (winning F.A.I. Cup medals 5 years in succession, in 1965, 1966, 1967, 1968 and in 1969), Bohemians (winning a 6th F.A.I. Cup medal in 1976, having won a League of Ireland Championship winner's medal in the previous year). He was capped once as a sub for the Republic of Ireland, against Poland in 1969.

SMYTH, P J .

G.A.A. football goalkeeper, Galway. He was in goals for the Galway side which was beaten by Offaly by the score of 1-14 to 2-8 in the All-Ireland Senior Football Championship final of 1971, and also won Connacht S.F.C. medals in both 1968 and 1970. He won a single All-Star award, taking up the goalkeeping spot in the inaugural year of 1971.

SMYTH, ROBERTSON STEWART.

Rugby international forward. 1880-1916. Clubs: Dublin University, Wanderers. Although he won only 3 international caps for Ireland in 1903 and 1904, he was selected on the British and Irish Lions Tour of South Africa in 1903, and won 3 Test places while there. Also a Barbarian, he was killed in W.W.I, aged 36.

SMYTH, SAMMY.

Soccer international inside and centre forward. Born in Belfast, 25th February 1925. Clubs: Distillery, Linfield (winning amateur international and Irish League representative honours), Wolverhampton Wanderers (joining in 1947, scoring 33 league goals in 102 appearances, and scoring a fine goal for Wolves in the 1949 F.A. Cup final win over Leicester), Stoke City and Liverpool, scoring 19 league goals for each of the last 2 clubs. He joined Bangor in 1955 for a then record Irish League club signing fee of £2,000. He won 9 caps for Northern Ireland between 1948 and 1952, scoring 5 international goals, including 2 on his debut against Scotland.

SMYTH, Dr THOMAS (TOM).

Rugby international utility forward and prop. Born in Co Antrim in December 1884, he died at the age of 43 in 1928. Clubs: Malone and Newport, Wales. A product of Ballymena Academy, he was capped for Ireland 14 times between 1908 and 1912, scoring one international try. In 1910, having captained Ireland only once (in a losing game against Wales that season, his only time to do so), he was appointed as the first of eight Irishmen to be captain of the British and Irish touring side (later to be nicknamed the Lion's). Bringing 6 other Irish players with him, the side won 13, lost 8, and drew 3 of their 24 match tour of South Africa, Smyth himself playing in only 2 of the Tests, scoring 5 tries in his 18 matches on tour. Two of his brothers, William S and Patrick J , both from the Collegians Club, also played for Ireland: each getting 3 international caps, William S being capped twice in the pack in 1910 (his first while Tom captained the side), and once more ten years later in 1920 (making him one of only 8 players to play for Ireland before and after World War One), while Patrick (also a forward) was capped while still at school in 1911, playing alongside Tom in each of his 3 matches.

SMYTHE, TIM F.

Cross-country athlete. Club: O'Callaghan's Mills A.C., Co Clare. He was born in 1906. He won the Irish Cross-Country Championship title in 1929 and in 1931 (when he won by over 600 metres). He made Irish athletic's history at Baldoyle Racecourse in 1931 when he won the individual title at the World Cross-Country Championships, the first Irishman to do so in the 20th

Century, and the last to do so before John Treacy (cv) repeated the success in 1978 and 1979. He led the race from start to finish in mucky conditions, winning by 100 metres. He had finished 44th in 1929, and was in 42nd place in 1932. His son Tim captained London Irish R.F.C. in their Pilkington Cup final appearence in the early 1970's, while another son Harry played hurling for Clare.

SOLOMONS, Dr BETHEL Albert Herbert.

Rugby international forward. 1885-1965. Clubs: Dublin University (captaining the side in 1907 and 1908 when the Leinster Senior Cup was won), and Wanderers. A product of St Andrew's College, he was capped 10 times for Ireland between 1908 and 1910, only 2 of these matches being victorious. A fine forward. he played interprovincial rugby for Leinster 7 times between 1904 and 1919. A distinguished medical man associated with the Rotunda Hospital, his brother Edwin was a boxer of note.

SOULBY, D E B.

Amateur international golfer. Clubs: Fairhaven, Fortwilliam and Portmarnock (winning a Barton Shield in 1920). He won 2 successive Irish Close Championship titles, in 1927 at Castlerock, and in 1928 at Dollymount (having previously been a beaten finalist in 1924). He was runner-up twice in the Irish Amateur Open Championship, in 1927 and 1931. He played international golf for Ireland 6 times in 1929 and 1930.

SOYE, TOM.

Handball player. A Dublinman, he was the first handballer to win the 6 successive All-Ireland Senior Hardball Singles Championships, achieving this feat in 1926, 1927, 1928, 1929, 1930 and in 1931. He also won the All-Ireland Senior Hardball Doubles title for Dublin 3 times, in 1927 and 1928 with T O'Reilly, and in 1930 with G Brown.

SPAIN, WILLIAM J. (WILLIE).

G.A.A. dual player, hurler with Limerick and footballer with Dublin. Born in Nenagh, Co Tipperary, he was the first man in G.A.A. history to win an All-Ireland Senior Championship winner's medal in each code, achieving them with 2 different counties. With the Commercials side of Limerick he won the first ever playing of the All-Ireland Senior Football Championship in Clonskeagh on 29th April 1888 (for the 1887 championship). Then in 1889 he helped the Kickhams side of Dublin to defeat the Tulla side of Clare in the All-Ireland Senior Hurling Championship final, thus becoming the first dual player of All-Ireland senior title history.

SPEAK, JONATHAN.

Soccer forward. Born in Sion Mills, Northern Ireland. Clubs: Dundalk, Ballymena United, Derry City (helping them to win the First Division of the League of Ireland in 1986-87, and the Premier Division in 1988-89, and an F.A.I. Cup medal in the same season, having won a runner-up medal in 1988). He has scored more League of Irleand goals for Derry City than any other player (over 55), and holds the Premier Division record for one season, with 24 goals in the 1987-88 season.

SPENCE, DEREK W.

Soccer international forward. Born in Belfast, 18th January 1952. Clubs: Crusaders, Oldham, Bury (scoring 44 league goals in 144 league appearences 1972-1976), Blackpool (2 spells, scoring 20 goals in 82 league appearences), Olympiakos, Southend (scoring over 25 league goals). He was capped 29 times for Northern Ireland (16 of these being as a substitute) between 1975 and 1982, scoring 3 international goals.

SPILLANE, Dr BRIAN Jeremiah.

Rugby international No 8 forward. Clubs: U.C.C. and Bohemians. Born in Cork, 26th January 1960. A product of C.B.S. Limerick, he also played for Irish Universities and Munster. He has been capped 9 times for Ireland from 1985 to 1987, and was a prominent member of the exciting 1985 Irish side which won the Triple Crown (of his 9 caps, these 3 games were the only ones Ireland won). A doctor.

SPILLANE, MIKE.

G.A.A. football left full-back, Kerry. Club: Templenoe. He won an All-Ireland M.F.C. medal with Kerry in 1975, and also won 3 successive All-Ireland Under 21 F.C. winner's medals, in 1975, 1976 and in 1977. He has won 7 All-Ireland Senior Football Championship winner's medals, in 1978 and 1979 as a left full-back, in 1980 (as a non-playing sub), in 1981 as a left half-back, and again as a left corner-back for the 3-in-a-row of 1984, 1985 and 1986. A brother of Pat (whom he played with in 6 All-Ireland final wins) and Tom Spillane (with whom he played with in his last 3 All-Ireland finals), the three brothers playing together in the finals of 1984, 1985 and 1986. He won a solitary All-Star award at left full-back in 1985.

SPILLANE, PAT.

G.A.A. footballing left half-forward, Kerry. Born 1st December 1955, he is a product of Templenoe N.S., St Brendan's Killarney and Thomond College (with whom he won an All-Ireland Club Championship winner's medal in 1978). One of the truly great gaelic footballers, he is one of a select band of 6 Kerrymen who share the record for the most All-Ireland Senior Football Championship winner's medals, winning in 1975 (as the 2nd youngest in the young side), in the great 4-in-a-row of 1978, 1979, 1980, and 1981 (playing only the last 10 minutes due to injury); and also in the 3-in-a-row of 1984 (winning the Man-of-the-Match award), 1985 and 1986, thus winning 8 medals. He later won a Munster S.F.C. medal again in 1991, at the age of 35. Playing also in the losing All-Ireland sides of 1976 and 1982 (as a sub), he has also won 4 National Football League medals with Kerry, in 1974, 1977, 1982 and 1984. He won 4 Railway Cup medals with Munster, in 1977, 1978, 1979, and 1981. He has won 9 All-Star awards, making him the most honoured player in either code in this scheme; his wins came in 1976 at left full-forward, and then 8 times at left half-forward, 1977, 1978 (when he was the unanimous selection), 1979, 1980, 1981, 1984, 1985, and in 1986. He was twice selected as Texaco Footballer of the Year, in 1978 and 1986. He won his place on the Sunday Independent 'Team of the Century', selected in 1984, alongside Sean Purcell and Sean O'Neill in the half forward line. In 1979 he won the inaugural Irish Superstars title. A school teacher and publican, he is the older brother of both Tom and Mick Spillane (ccvv). His father won a Railway Cup medal with Munster in midfield in 1948 and a Kerry county Championship medal in 1946 with Killarney Legion.

SPILLANE, TOM.

G.A.A. football centre half-back, Kerry. Born 10th March 1962. Club: Templenoe. He came on as a sub in the All-Ireland M.F.C. win by Kerry in 1980. Making his senior inter-county debut in 1981, he won a Sam Maguire medal as a squad member in 1981, and played in the side beaten by Offaly in the 'Seamus Darby' final of 1982. He was at centre half-back for Kerry's most recent 3-in-a-row success, in the All-Ireland Senior Football Championships of 1984, 1985 and 1986 (switching to full-back in this final). He has won 3 All-Star awards, all at centre-half back, in 1984, 1986 and 1987. Later to be a full-back (playing in the All-Ireland S.F.C. semi-final of 1991), he is the youngest of the 3 Spillane brothers, who together have won 19 All-Ireland S.F.C. medals.

SPRING, RICHARD Martin (DICK), and DONAL Eugene.

Rugby international brothers. Dick, a full-back, was born in Tralee, Co Kerry on 29th August 1950. His clubs included

Dublin University and Lansdowne. A product of Roscrea College, he was capped three times for Ireland in 1979, against France, Wales and England. He also played inter-county football and hurling with Kerry. He became a T.D. for North Kerry in 1981, leader of the Labour Party in 1982, and became Tanaiste in 1982-1987 and 1992-date. His younger brother, Donal (born in Tralee, Co Kerry, 23rd August 1956), a Trinity College and Lansdowne 2nd row and No 8 forward, who captained Ireland's first ever School's side in 1975 (also playing Under 23 and 'B' level for Ireland), was capped at full international level 7 times in an injury-laden career for Ireland 1978-81. Although the brothers never were together in the Irish side, they played alongside each other for 3 seasons with Munster (Donal playing in the famous 1978 win over the touring All Blacks). Another brother Arthur, an amateur golfer attached to the Tralee club, played 19 interprovincial matches for Munster between 1977 and 1984.

STACK, AUSTIN.

G.A.A. footballer, Kerry. Born at Ballymullen, Tralee, 7th December 1879. He captained the Tralee Mitchel's team which beat Kickhams of Dublin by 0-5 to 0-2 in the 1904 All-Ireland Senior Football Championship final, having been on the successful Kerry side the previous year also. He was President of the Kerry County Board from 1918 for 11 years until his death. He became heavily involved in the revolutionary movement (in 1918 becoming the first All-Ireland medal holder to become a Dail deputy), and was sentenced to death (this was later commuted). He died in 1929 after not fully recovering from a 41 day hunger strike. Austin Stack Park G.A.A. grounds in Tralee is named in his honour.

STACK, GEORGE HALL.

Rugby international forward, Club: Dublin University. A product of Raphoe College, he was Ireland's captain in their first ever international rugby match, against England on February 15th 1875, which was lost. He was one of 9 Trinity players on that side, making this the greatest club representation on any Irish side. It was to be his only cap, and he died the following year.

STACK, ROBERT (BOB).

G.A.A. footballer, Kerry. A New York-born Ballybunion man, he won 6 All-Ireland Senior Football Championship medals with Kerry, in 1924, 1926, 1929, 1930, 1931, and 1932 (and also played in the losing All-Ireland S.F.C. final of 1927). He won 2 Railway Cup medals with Munster, in 1927 and 1931, and also won 3 National Football League medals.

STACK, SEAN.

G.A.A. hurling centre-back, Clare. A quality half-back, he played for Clare in 4 losing Munster Senior Hurling Championship finals, in 1977, 1978, 1981 and 1986. He won 2 Railway Cup medals for Munster in 1984 and 1985. He captained Clare to win the county's 2nd National Hurling League title in 1977, winning another medal the following year. In 1984 he was selected at centre-back on the 'Team of the Century' for players who never won an All-Ireland senior championship medal. He won an All-Star award in 1981 in the centre-back position.

STACK, THOMAS Brendan (TOMMY, 'STACKY').

National Hunt jockey. Born in 1946 in County Kerry. His first ride over fences was a winner at Cheltenham, as an amateur, riding And Well Packed. He was Champion jockey over fences twice in England, in 1974/1975 (with 82 winners), and in 1976/1977 (with 97 runners), also riding over 50 winners in 5 other seasons there; in 1970-1971 (50 winners), 1971/1972 (53 winners), 1972/1973 (71 winners), 1973/1974 (76 winners), and 1974/1975 (82 winners). He rode the great Red Rum to victory in the horse's third Aintree Gand National in 1977. Other big wins include the 1977

Scweppes Gold Trophy on True Lad and the 1978 Whitbread Gold Cup on Strombulus. Retiring at the age of 32 in 1978, he is now a trainer at Thomastown Castle Stud in Golden Co Tipperary.

STAKELUM, PAT.

G.A.A. hurling centre back, Tipperary. Born in 1927. Club: Holycross (winning 3 county championship medals). A member of the Tipperary minors beaten in the All-Ireland M.H.C. final of 1946, he went on to have a sparkling 9 years of senior inter-county hurling with Tipperary from 1949 to 1957. He won 3 successive All-Ireland Senior Hurling Championship medals with Tipperary, in 1949, 1950, and 1951, captaining the side in 1949 when they beat Laois by 3-11 to 0-3. A brilliant centre-back, he also won 5 Railway Cup medals, in 1950 (as captain, the 4th Tipperary hurler to lead a winning side in the interprovincial series), 1951, 1952 (again as captain, only the 3rd hurler to lead 2 winning sides), 1953, and 1955. He also won 6 National Hurling League medals with Tipp, in 1949, 1950, 1952, 1954, 1955, and 1957. His nephew Richard Stakelum was Tipperary captain in their 1987 Munster S.H.C. win (the county's first in 16 years), and later won a Liam McCarthy Cup medal (as a non-playing sub in 1989): two other nephews are Aidan and Bobby Ryan (ccvv).

STAFFORD, BRIAN.

G.A.A. football full forward, Meath. Born 4th June 1964. Club: Kilmainhamwood. A member of the Meath side which won 3 successive Leinster S.F.C. titles in the late 1980's, he is a winner of 2 All-Ireland Senior Football Championship medals, in 1987 and 1988, and also played in the losing All-Ireland final sides of 1990 and 1991 (when he scored 4 goals and 62 points in the 10-match run up to the final). A cool, accurate place-kicker and full-forward, he scored 7 of Meath's 13 points in 1988 final replay win over Cork. He has won 3 All-Star awards, in 1987, 1988 and 1991, all as a full-forward.

STANFIELD, OLPHIE M.

Soccer international forward. Club: Distillery (winning 3 Irish Cup medals with them, in 1889, 1894 and 1896). He was capped for Northern Ireland 30 times between 1887 and 1897, missing only 3 of his country's games in that eleven year span, and scoring 9 international goals.

STANLEY, LARRY.

G.A.A. footballer, Kildare and Dublin, and athlete. A high jumper of international standard, he broke the Irish record, and was a member of the 1st Irish side represented at an Olympic Games, in Paris in 1924. In 1924 he also, in the inaugural Tailteann Games at Croke Park, fought a terrific duel with the newly crowned Olympic high jump champion, Harold Osborne of the the U.S.A. A classy footballer also, he won All-Ireland Senior Championship football medals with 2 counties, Kildare in 1919 (captaining the Caragh side to a 2-5 to 0-1 win over the Galway Selection), and Dublin in 1923. He later lost another All-Ireland S.F.C. final with Kildare (with whom he actually only played for on 17 occasions between 1916 and 1932), beaten by Kerry in 1926. In 1970 he became the second Gaelic footballer to join the Texaco Hall of Fame. A great player.

STAPLES, JAMES Edward (JIM).

Rugby international full-back. Born in Bermondsey, 20th October 1965. Clubs: Bromley, Sidcup, London Irish. Winning Ireland 'B' and Under 21 caps in 1991, he was first capped in 1991, played in all 4 of Ireland's World Cup matches that year, and has scored 3 international tries and 2 converts in his 10 caps up to June 1992. He toured Namibia with Ireland in 1991, and went to New Zealand with them in 1992.

STAPLETON, DAN J.

G.A.A. hurler, Kilkenny. Club: Erins Own. At 18 he won an All-Ireland Senior Hurling Championship medal with Kilkenny in 1904. He captained the winning Erin's Hope side again the following year, aged 19, when they defeated Cork's St Finbarr's by 7-7 to 2-9. He won a third All-Ireland S.H.C. medal in 1907.

STAPLETON, FRANK.

Soccer international striker. Born in Dublin, 10th July 1956. Apprenticed to Arsenal in 1973 at the age of 17, he played league football with them the following year. In a 8 year period with the Gunners, he played 223 league matches, scoring 75 goals, and won an F.A. Cup medal in 1979, scoring the 2nd goal in the famous 3-2 victory over Manchester United (he was also on 2 losing F.A. Cup final sides with Arsenal, in 1978 and 1980), and was twice player of the year at Highbury. Joining Manchester United in 1980, he scored 60 league goals in 223 matches up to 1987, and won 2 F.A. Cup medals with them, in 1983 (when he became the only player in F.A. Cup history to score for 2 different winning clubs), and 1985. His other clubs have included Ajax Amsterdam, Derby County, Le Havre, and Blackburn Rovers. First capped for Ireland against Turkey in 1977, he has scored a record 20 international goals for Ireland, breaking Don Given's record while playing against Malta in 1990 (gaining his 71st international cap, placing him 2nd to Liam Brady in all-time Republic of Ireland cap winnings). He captained the Irish team which performed with distinction in the 1988 European Championshps in West Germany in 1988, and was a squad member of the team which qualified for the Republic's first ever jaunt at the World Cup finals, in Rome in 1990. At his peak he was regarded as the best striker in British Football. Retiring in 1991, he became a Football League manager in 1992. In 1991 he published an autobiography, 'Frankly Speaking'.

STAUNTON, RUPERT de LACY.

Amateur international golfer. Club: Castlerea. He was runner-up in the Irish Close Championship in 1973, and won the South of Ireland twice, in 1965, and 1972; he was runner-up in the 'West' in 1966. He played in an Irish record 124 interprovincial matches for Connacht between 1962 and 1985, winning 44, and losing a record 65 matches, with a success rate of 40%, although by gaining 101 points he is placed 2nd in all-time in this feat. He also played 16 Home international matches for Ireland 1964-1972, winning 6, and was a member of the European Team championship winning side of 1965. His brother Hugh, also a member in Castlerea, played interprovincial golf for Connacht in 1970, and won the Hong Kong Championship. Their father, Maurice de Lacy Staunton, was President of the G.U.I. in 1974-75.

STAUNTON, STEVEN ('STAN').

Soccer international defender. Born in Drogheda, 19th January 1969. Clubs: Dundalk (playing only 3 games for them), Liverpool (he went on a brief loan to Bradford City), Aston Villa (helping them to 2nd place in the inaugural Premier League title in 1993). As a youngster he played for Louth Under 16 in gaelic football, and for the Irish Schools in soccer. He won an F.A. Cup medal with Liverpool in 1989, and was on the team 'robbed' of the double that year at Highbury (he did win a League Championship medal with Liverpool in 1990). Capped first at international level for the Republic of Ireland in 1989, he played in 6 of the 8 matches which helped Ireland qualify for their first ever World Cup finals, in Italy in 1990, and played his part in the historic run to the quarter-finals in Rome. His cap tally had reached 41 by mid 1993, scoring 4 international goals, helping Ireland's quest for World Cup qualification again.

STEELE, HAROLD William (HARRY).

Rugby international No 8 and second row forward. Born in Cookstown, 4th September 1948. Clubs: Queen's University Belfast and Ballymena (winning Ulster Senior Cup medals in 1975 and 1977, and Ulster Senior League medals in 1976, 1978 and 1979). He was capped 10 times for Ireland between 1976 and 1979, all in partnership with Moss Keane (cv). He toured with Ireland twice, to New Zealand and Fiji in 1976, and to Australia in 1979.

STEENSON, BRIAN.

Motorcycling road racer. Born in Crossgar, Co Down in 1947. Coming to the fore in 1966, he won many Irish races, and competed in the Isle of Man T.T. (finishing 2nd in the 1969 Junior T.T. on a Aermacchi), the Southern 100, and in English international races. He finished 5 times in the top 5 places in various 250cc, 35cc and 500cc World Championship Grand Prix events from 1967 up to 1970, when he was killed in a crash at the Senior T.T. in the Isle of Man, at the tender, promising age of 23.

STEEPE, IAN S.

Hockey international defender. Clubs: Limerick PYMA, Dublin YMCA, Three Rock Rovers, Instoninans, and Hounslow. He was capped 31 times for Ireland between 1961 and 1972. A member of the first Irish team to compete in the European Championships in Brussels in 1970. He became Irish men's coach from 1975 to 1978, leading them to the Intercontinental Cup in 1977 and the World Cup of 1978 in Buenos Aires. He later coached the international ladies side.

STEPHENSON, Dr GEORGE Vaughan.

Rugby international centre three-quarter. Born 22nd February 1901, he died in 1970. Club: Queen's University Belfast, and London Hospitals. A product of R.B.A.I., he won a then world record of 42 rugby international caps over an 11 year period with Ireland between 1920 and 1930, surpassing the Irish most-capped record shared by G T Hamlet and Ernie Crawford of 30 caps, and his record lasted for 25 years. He scored more international tries than any other Irishman (until surpassed in the 1990's by Brendan Mullin), with 14 (and scored 2 tries in 3 internationals, also an Irish record); his tally of 94 points for Ireland is completed by 14 conversions and 7 penalties. He captained Ireland during his last 3 seasons in the side, for a total of 11 matches, Ireland winning seven of these games. In his long career Ireland did not win any honours, although sharing the Inrternational Championship in 1926 and 1927. A fine defensive player and an adept place kicker, he is regarded as one of the game's greatest ever centre three-quarters. With his older brother Harry (cv) he shared 14 of his caps, a record for Irish brothers.

STEPHENSON, HENRY William Vaughan (HARRY).

Rugby international wing-threequarter. Born in Dromore Co Down, 28th November 1900, he died in 1958. Club: United Services. He won 14 caps for Ireland between 1922 and 1928, all of them in which his better-known younger brother George (cv) played, making a record total in which brothers played together for Ireland. He scored 3 international tries, all in in the 1925 international championship season, including one on the same day as George, against Wales.

STEVENSON, ALEX E ('WEE ALEX').

Soccer international inside-forward. Born in Dublin, 2nd March 1912. Clubs: Dolphin (playing on a losing F.A.I. Cup final side in 1932), Glasgow Rangers, Everton (for whom he played over 400 league matches, winning a First Division Championship medal in 1938-39). A brilliant winger, his partnership with Jackie Coulter (cv) for Everton was much feared. He was capped 7 times for the Irish Free State (over a span of 17 years from 1932 to 1949), and 17 times for Northern Ireland over a 15 year period between 1934 and 1948, scoring 5 international goals for Northern Ireland. The gap of 14 years between his first and 2nd caps for what is now the Republic of Irleand constitutes a record.

STEVENSON, ROBERT ('THE MAJOR').

Rugby international forward. Born in 1866. Club: N.I.F.C. Dungannon and Lisburn. A product ot R S Dungannon, he was capped 14 times for Ireland between 1887 and 1893, being captain for the Welsh match in 1891. He lived till the age of 94, dying in 1960, having been President of the I.R.F.U. 47 years previously, in 1912/1913. His brother, James, a Dungannon three-quarter, won two internatioanal caps for Ireland , in 1888 against the Maoris, and in 1889 against Scotland, on both occasions playing with Robert. Both were linen manufacurers.

STEWART, IAN.

Soccer international midfielder. Born in Belfast, 10th September 1961. Clubs: Q.P.R. and Newcastle United. He was capped 31 times for Northern Ireland between 1982 and 1987. He was a member of the famous Northern Ireland squad which performed heroics in the 1982 World Cup in Spain (gaining his first international cap in the 4-1 loss to France), and played in all 3 matches (the first 2 as a sub) in his country's bid in the World Cup finals in Mexico in 1986.

STEWART, Dr WILLIAM JOSEPH.

Rugby international full-back. 1900-1958. Club: Queen's University Belfast, and N.I.F.C. He was capped for Ireland 10 times between 1924 and 1928, a good period for Ireland in which they lost only 3 games in which Stewart played (and thus sharing the International Championship in both 1926 and 1927).

STOCKWELL, FRANKIE (one of 'THE TERRIBLE TWINS').

G.A.A. football full-forward, Louth and Galway. Playing his earlier career with Louth, he went on to form a highly effective parthership with Sean Purcell (cv) in the maroon colours of Galway, gaining a huge reputation among opponents and fans alike (thus the nickname). In the All-Ireland Senior Football Championship final success of 1956, he scored 2-5, making this the highest tally in gaelic football history in a 60 minute final (and was an all-time final record for 20 years). He was also on the Galway side beaten in the All-Ireland S.F.C. final of 1959, winning 4 other Connacht S.F.C. medals, in 1954, 1957, 1958 and 1960. Winning a National League (football) medal in 1957, he also won 2 Railway Cup medals with Connacht, in 1957 and 1958.

STOKER, FREDERICK Owen (FRANK).

Rugby international forward and tennis player. Born in May 1867 in Dublin, he died in 1939. In rugby, as a Wanderers player, he played interprovincial rugby for Leinster 6 times, and won 5 international caps for Ireland between 1886 and 1891, being part of Ireland's first ever Championship winning side in 1888. In tennis he twice won the Wimbledon mens' doubles title (making him the only rugby international to win a senior Wimbledon title), in 1890 and 1893, both in partnership with Dr Joshua Pim (cv), and was runner-up in 1891. He also won the Irish doubles titles 4 times in the 1890's. His brother Ernest Wilson Stoker of Wanderers and Leinster, was twice capped for Ireland in rugby in the pack in 1888, once alongside Frank. Both brothers were related to the creator of 'Dracula', Bram Stoker.

STOKER, NORMA.

Badminton, tennis, and hockey international player. One of Ireland's best all-round women sports woman, she won international status in 3 sports. In badminton, as a Leinster player, she won many Irish Open titles (including one in singles in 1937), and played 13 times for her country between 1930 and 1949. In tennis, she won the Irish Ladies Doubles

Championship 6 times, with Hilda Wallace in 1930, 1931, 1933 and in 1935, with E Goddard in 1940, and with Mrs P Egan in 1941. She was also a hockey international.

STOKES, Dr DICK.

G.A.A. hurling midfielder and half-forward, Limerick. Born in 1920. Club: U.C.D. (being the only player from that club to win Dublin county championship medals in each code, football in 1943 and hurling in 1947). Winning a Munster and All-Ireland Senior Hurling Championship medal in his first year on the Limerick senior team in 1940, he never again matched that achievement in 13 more years at the top in hurling (in this period Limerick were beaten in 5 Munster S.H.C. finals). He did however win 5 successive Railway Cup medals with Munster (1942, 1943, 1944, 1945 and 1946), and a National League medal in 1947.

STOKES, Dr PADDY.

Rugby international back-row forward. 1890-1970. Clubs: U.C.D. and Garryowen. A Tipperaryman, he was capped 12 times over a 10 year period for Ireland between 1913 and 1922, the World War interupting his service (therefore being one of 8 to play before and after the war). He scored 4 international tries, and won 2 Munster Senior Cup medals with Garryowen, in 1920 and 1924. A doctor.

STOREY, SAM.

Boxing super-middleweight amateur and professional. As an amateur member of the Holy Family club, he won the Irish Senior National Championship at light-middleweight in 1984 and at middleweight in 1985. As a professional, he won the British super-middleweight championship in 1989, successfully defending it once.

STRATHDEE, ERNEST (ERNIE).

Rugby international scrum-half. Club: Queen's University Belfast (winning an Ulster Senior Cup medal in 1947). A product of Belfast High School, he won 9 rugby caps for Ireland during the golden era, and was a member of both the Grand Slam side of 1948 and the Triple Crown sides of 1949, all in partnershup with his clubmate Jack Kyle (cv). He captained Ireland twice, in 1947 against Australia, and in 1948 against France. A strong player with an accurate pass, he also played in 2 post-war Victory internationals, and was a Barbarian. A presbyterian minister and T.V. sports journalist, he died in a hotel fire in Belfast in 1971.

STYNES, JIM.

Australian Rules player and G.A.A. footballer. G.A.A. clubs: St Enda's and Ballyboden. He was a starring midfielder on the Dublin minor side which won the All-Ireland M.F.C. in 1984. Soon after that achievement he emigrated to Australia to play their 'Rules' game for Melbourne. After 3 years in the junior ranks, he became a senior player in 1987, and developed to such an extent as to become their star player (playing an astonishing 107 consecutive matches for them), and in 1991 won 2 awards which put him at the top of the tree in that sport, namely the Players Association Award, and the most prestigious award in the sport, the Brownlow Medal. In the Compromise rules series he played for Australia in 1987 and for Ireland in 1990. His younger brother Brian was on the Dublin minors which lost the All-Ireland M.F.C. final in 1988, before he too tried his hand at 'Aussie Rules' in Melbourne.

SUGDEN, MARK.

Rugby international scrum-half, and cricket international. Rugby club: Wanderers. Born in Leek, Staffordshire, in 1902, he was a product Denstone College and Trinity College (where he played in the centre), he played 10 rugby interprovincial matches for Leinster between 1923 and 1932, and played for the Barbarians. He was capped for Ireland in rugby 28 times at scrum-half between 1925 and 1931, and was the most capped Irishman in this position until surpassed by Michael Bradley (cv) in 1993, having scored 4 international tries. Having played 22 international matches in partnership with Eugene Davy (including the famous 6-5 win over England at Twickenham in 1929, Ireland's first at that venue, when he scored a try), he captained the side 4 times during his last season. A minute player who had a great dummy, he served Ireland with distinction, and was placed in the Digital Hall of Fame in 1987. He died in 1990. He was also a first class cricketer, playing 8 first class matches for Dublin University and Ireland between 1922 and 1930, his record being 8-16-1-263-17-7-6-48-5. He is relation of Danie Craven of South African rugby fame.

SULLIVAN, DAVE.

Featerweight boxer. Born in Cork on 19th May 1877. Died in 1929. Emigtrating as a young boy to America, he started his pro career in 1874 with a k.o., and lost a bout which would have given him partial recognition as world bantamweight champion in 1897. However he became, in only his 5th professional fight, the surprise world featherweight champion for 46 days in 1898, gaining it when he broke the arm of Solly Smith in the 5th round at Coney Island, New York. However, after the shortest reign in world featherweight history, he lost on a disqualification (after a foul in the 10th round) to George Dixon. He tried to regain the title 6 years later against Young Corbett, but was stopped in 11 rounds, and fianly retired in 1905 after a k.o. loss to Kid Herman. His professional career, all fights bar one taking place in the U.S.A., included 28 wins (18 inside the distance), 16 draws, 12 loses, and 2 no decisions in his 58 contests.

SULLIVAN, TED.

G.A.A. hurling forward, Cork. Club: Midleton. He won an All-Ireland M.H.C. medal with Cork minors in 1938. A member of the Cork S.H.C. side defeated in the All-Ireland final of 1939, he went on to win All-Ireland Senior Hurling Championship medals, in 1941 (scoring 2-1 in the final) and 1943 (scoring 1-2 in the final). He won National Hurling League medals with Cork in 1940 and 1941.

SULLY, C, VICTOR, and LES.

Hockey international brothers. C , a fine inside right, was a Railway Union player who won 15 caps for Ireland between 1923 and 1935. His brother Victor (also a Railway Union plyer), won 9 international caps between 1924 and 1932, and Les, the oldest of the 3 brothers who played his hockey for Richmond, won one single international hockey cap in 1910.

SUTCLIFFE, PHIL.

Amateur international light-fly, fly, and bantamweight boxer. Club: Drimnagh. He has been an Irish National Senior Champion 5 times in 3 different increasing weights, in 1977 at light-flyweight, in 1978 at flyweight, and in 1984, 1985 and 1986 at bantanweight. He won bronze medals at 2 European Championships, 1977 at light-fly and in 1979 at flyweight. He also represented Ireland at 2 Olympic Games at bantamweight, in Moscow in 1980 and in Los Angeles in 1984, being beaten in his first bout on both occasions. A popular, crowd-pleasing boxer, he was voted as Texaco's Sportstar of the Year for 1977.

SWAN, CHARLIE.

National Hunt jockey. Born in Cluoghjordan, Co Tipperary, 20th February 1968. Winning his first race on his debut ride (Final Assault at Naas in 1983 on the flat on a horse trained by his father), he finished 2nd in the apprentices championship in 1986 with 17 wins (and had 57 winners in total over the flat before turning to the fences). In 1988 he had 23 winners over fences, and in 1989-90 was leading Irish

National Hunt jockey with a record equalling 73 winners, at the age of 22. He also won the championship in each of the following 3 seasons (in the 1991-92 season his tally of 79 broke the record). In 1992 he surpassed the 42-year-old record of Martin Molony (cv) of 92 winners in a calendar year, to go on to set a new total of 109, when again becoming champion jockey. His most important wins to date include the 1993 Irish Grand National on Ebony Jane, and at the National Hunt Festival in Cheltenham (winning on Trapper John in 1990, and riding 4 winners at the 1993 Festival; Montelado, Fissure Seal, Shawiya and Shuil Ar Aghaidh, to be the first Irish-based jockey to win the Ritz Club Trophy for most wins at the meeting). He won the Texaco Sportstar of the Year award in 1992 for horse racing.

SWEENEY, NICKY.

Discus international athlete. Born on 26th March 1968. Club: D.S.D. A product of Wesley College, he won 4 Irish Schools rugby international caps in 1986. A scholarship graduate of Harvard University, he set the Irish national discus record 4 times in 1991, the 3rd being in his win of the National B.L.E. Championship (which he had earlier won in 1987), at 58.46 metres. In 1992 he became the first Irish discus thrower to throw over 60 metre (throwing 62.45 metres at a meet in the U.S.A), and represented Ireland at the Olympic Games in Barcelona (the first Irish discus thrower to do so since 1948). He won the B.L.E. Championship again in both 1992 and 1993. In the World Championships at Stuttgart in 1993 he became the highest placed Irishman in a field event of a major championship in 30 years, when he finished 6th in the discus event with a throw of 61.66 metres (being at 25, by far the youngest in the final). His father Niall was a fine triple-jumper with Dundrum.

SWINBURN, WALLY.

Flat jockey. Born 11th January 1937. Having his first winner in 1953, he went on, at the age of 40, to become the first jockey to pass the 100 mark in a flat season in Ireland in 1977 (his tally being 101, beating Johnny Roe's record of 87 of 1972), being also champion jockey in 1976. His major Irish wins include 3 Classic races: Pidget in the 1,000 Guineas of 1972, the Irish Oaks of 1981 with Blue Wind, and Prince's Polly in the 1982 Irish 2,000 Guineas. Other wins include 2 National Stakes, 3 Tetrarch Stakes, 2 Phoenix Stakes wins, and 3 Derby Trial Stakes. A traveller of note, he won 17 Indian Classic races including 5 Indian Derbies. He is the father of Walter Swinburn (cv).

SWINBURN, WALTER ('THE CHOIRBOY').

Flat jockey. Born in Ireland on 7th August 1961. Riding his first winner in 1978, he was stable jockey to the Michael Stoute stable during the 1980's, and later retained by Sheikh Maktoum Al Maktoum. His major race wins include 8 English Classics: 2 Epsom Derby wins (1981 at the age of 19 on Shergar, and 1986 on Shahrastani), 2 Epsom Oaks (on Unite in 1986 and in 1989 on Alysa), the 1988 2,000 Guineas on Doyoun, and three 1,000 Guineas (in 1989 on Musical Bliss, in 1992 with Hatoof, and in 1993 with Sayyedati, thereby winning all the English Classics except the St Leger). Other big wins include 2 Coronation Stakes (1986 on Sonic Lady and 1987 on Milligaram), 2 King George VI and Queen Elizabeth Stakes, and the 1983 Prix De L'Arc De Trioumphe on All Along. He has also won, to date, 7 Irish Classics winners: two Irish 1,000 Guineas (1986 on Sonic Lady and 1992 on Marling); One Irish 2,000 Guineas on Shaadi in 1989; 2 Irish Derbys (1983 on Shareef Dancer and in 1986 on Shahrastani); and 2 Irish Oaks (on Unite in 1987 and on Melodist, in a dead heat, in 1989). A jockey who is at his best in important races, his best season's tally in

Britain was 111 winners in 1990, and he has averaged over 80 winners a season in Britain from 1981 to 1993. He is the son of Wally Swinburn (cv).

SYNNOTT, JOHN and JOE.

G.A.A. footballing brothers. Dublin. John won 3 All-Ireland Senior Football Championship winners medal's with Dublin, in their 3-in-a-row side of 1921 (with the St Mary's selection), 1922 (on the O'Tooles side), and in 1923. Joe played in both the 1922 and 1923 victories. Two other brothers, Stephen (who played along with Joe in the All-Ireland S.F.C. loss in 1924, while Stephen, John and Joe all played in the losing final of 1920) and Pat, also played for Dublin.

T

TAAFFE, PAT.

National Hunt jockey and trainer. Born in Rathcoole, Co Dublin, 9th March 1930, he died in 1992. Ranked as one of this country's greatest National Hunt jockeys, he rode his first winner in a point-to-point in 1946. He was Irish National Hunt champion jockey six times, including both 1952 and 1953 when he was also the combined flat-steeplechasing champion. Chiefly associated with trainer Tom Dreaper (cv), he rode 4 Cheltenham Gold Cup-winning horses, with 3-in-a-row on the brilliant Arkle in 1964, 1965 and 1966, and again with Fort Leney in 1968, a record for any jockey in this great race. His other wins on Arkle include the Hennessy Gold Cup twice, the Leopardstown Chase twice, and the Whitbread Gold Cup. He also rode 2 Aintree Grand National winners, in 1955 on Quare Times, and in 1970 on Gay Trip. He rode the Irish Grand National winning horse on 6 occasions (with Royal Approach in 1954, Umm in 1955, Zonda in 1959, Fortria in 1961, Arkle in 1964, and in 1966 with Flyingbolt). He rode the winner of 5 National Hunt Two-Mile Champion Chase's (in 1960, 1961, 1964, 1966 and 1970), and rode 28 Cheltenham Festival winners in all, a record for an Irish jockey. Among the great steeplechasers he also rode were Flyingbolt (on whom he finished 3rd in a Champion Hurdle), Royal Approach (also winning the 1945 Cathcart Cup) and Fortria (riding him also to win a Two Mile Champion Chase, and to 2nd in the 1962 Cheltenham Gold Cup). A brilliant horseman, he was selected as Texaco's Horse Racing Sportstar of the Year for 1962. He later turned trainer, his peak coming in 1974 when his Captain Christy won the Cheltenham Gold Cup (this horse also won a Sweeps Hurdle, 2 Scottish Champion hurdles and 2 King George Chases). His father, Tom Taaffe of Rathcoole, trained the winner of the 1953 Irish Grand National, Mr What. Pat's younger brother Thomas 'Toss' Taffe (born 11th August 1933), was an amateur and professional jockey for a period of 15 years from 1949 to 1964, and as a trainer of horses such as Golden Vulcan he has prospered. Another brother Willie was an amateur jockey. Pat is the father of the jockey, Tom Taffe (cv).

TAAFFE, TOM.

National Hunt jockey. Born Straffan, Co Kildare, 16th January 1963. He has won the Leopardstown Handicap Hurdle 4 times (in 1983 and 1984 on Fredcoteri, and in 1986 on Bonalma, and in 1988 with Roark); he has also won the Leopardstown Chase in 1987 on the Ellier, and has won the 1987 Irish Grand National on Brittany Boy. A son of Pat Taaffe (cv). He was runner-up in the jockey's championship in 1991-92 with 58 winners.

TAGGART, GERRY.

Soccer international player. Born in Belfast 18th November 1970. Clubs: Manchester City and Barnsley (scoring 11 goals in 133 league matches for them). He has been capped 21 times for Northern Ireland up to mid 1993, scoring

5 international goals, and all of these caps have come while based at the Oakley Ground, thus making him Barnsley's most capped player, taking over from Eric McMorran (cv) in that role.

TATE, W S (BILLY).

Outdoor bowls player. Born in Belfast, 7th January 1918. Club: Shaftesbury. His big win was in the British Isles singles in 1963, while has also won 4 I.B.A. titles. He won a bronze medal at the 1970 Commonwealth Games for Northern Ireland in the fours event, and was an Irish international over 50 times.

TAYLOR, DENNIS.

Snooker professional. Born in Coalisland Co Tyrone, 19th January 1949. Turning professional in 1971, he has won the Irish Snooker Championship title 6 times, in 1980, 1981, 1982, 1985, 1986 and 1987. Having been runner-up in the 1979 World Championship final to Terry Griffiths, he later won the 1984 Rothmans Grand Prix at Reading, beating Cliff Thorburn 10-2 in the final. His career reached a great peak in 1985 when he became Embassy World Champion, by defeating Steve Davis 18-17 in the closest and most memorable final in snooker history, winning on the famous black ball final frame which lasted a record 68 minutes. He became Benson & Hedges Masters Champion in 1987, defeating Alex Higgins in a memorable final, 9-8. In 1990 he reached the final of the Asian Open. He has shared the Irish victories with Alex Higgins and Eugene Hughes in the 1985, 1986, and 1987 World Cup titles. He was selected as Texaco's Snooker Sportstar of the Year in both 1985 and 1987.

TAYLOR, JOHN WILGAR.

Rugby international forward. 1859-1924. Clubs: Queen's University Belfast and N.I.F.C. He played 8 rugby international matches for Ireland between 1879 and 1883, including 2 as captain, in 1882 and 1883. He was a member of the first Irish rugby team ever to win an international match, in 1881 against Scotland.

TEDFORD, ALFRED.

Rugby international forward. 1877-1942. Club: Malone (winning Ulster Senior Cup medals in 1904, 1905 and 1907). A product of Methodist College, he won 23 international caps for Ireland between 1902 and 1908, being ever-present in the Championship winning side of 1906 (scoring 2 tries in the win over England), while scoring 6 international tries in all, a great feat for a forward in those days. He captained Ireland once, against England in 1907. He was selected on the British and Irish tour of South Africa in 1903, winning 3 Test places, and was voted as the outstanding forward on the tour. He was an Irish selector in 1923 and 1924, and was President of the I.R.F.U. in 1919/1920.

TEEHAN, CHARLIE.

Rugby international hooker. Born in Buttevant, Co Cork, 3rd May 1919. Clubs: U.C.C. and Cork Constitution. A product of Pres Cork, he won 3 international caps, at the age of only 19, for Ireland just before W.W.II., and may have won many more in other circumstances. He won 3 Munster Senior Cup medals, one with U.C.C. in 1939, and for Cork Constution in 1943 and 1946.

THOMAS, PETER.

Soccer international goalkeeper. Club: Waterford (winning medals in each of the club's only 6 League of Ireland Championship successes, during the glory years of 1966, 1968, 1969, 1970, 1972 and 1973, and being on 2 losing F.A.I. Cup final sides, in 1968 and 1972). He won 2 international caps for the Republic of Ireland in 1974, against Poland and Brazil. In 1970 he won the S.W.A.I. Player of the Year award.

THOMPSON, CHARLES.

Rugby international wing three-quarter. Club: Belfast Collegians (helping them to their first win in the Ulster Senior Cup in 1906). He won 13 rugby international caps for Ireland between 1907 and 1910, scoring 3 valuable tries. In 1909, in Ireland's 19-8 win over France in Dublin, he scored the opening try, thus becoming the first Irish player to score against France.

THOMPSON, FRANK W.

Soccer international No 11. Clubs: Cliftonville (winning an Irish Cup medal in 1909), Bradford City (winning an F.A. Cup medal in 1911, the first year the present trophy was presented), Linfield, and Clyde. He won 12 international caps for Ireland between the years 1910 and 1914, playing in 2 of the matches which gave Northern Ireland their first win in the Home International Championships in 1914. He scored 2 international goals.

THOMPSON, JOHN J.

Flat jockey. Born in Bunclody, Co Wexford. Apprenticed to and attached to the J J Parkinson stable for all of his career, he was the first leading Irish jockey to adapt the American 'seat and crouch' style of riding. Winning the Cambridgeshire on Berrull as an apprentice in 1900, he went on to specialise in sprint races. His Irish Classic winner's included 3 Irish Oaks successes (1901 on Royal Mantle, 1905 on Blakestown and 1912 on Shining Way). The finest stylist of his day, this expert 'stick jockey' won a record (until surpassed by Morney Wing) nine Irish Jockey's Championship titles, in 1901, 1902, 1904, 1905, 1906, 1907 (with 53 winners), 1910, 1911 (when he shared the title with John Doyle cv) and in 1912. He was fatally killed in a fall during schooling in 1913, failing to win his life ambition, the Irish Derby (having finished 2nd in both 1901 and 1905). .

THOMPSON, Dr JOHN KNOX STAFFORD.

Rugby international flanker and No 8 forward. Club: Dublin University (winning Leinster Senior Cup medals in 1920 and 1921). A product of R S Dungannon, he was capped 8 times in the back-row for Ireland between 1921 and 1923, captaining his country 4 times in 1923 (to win the Wooden Spoon).

THOMPSON, ROBIN Henderson.

Rugby international No 8 forward. Club: Instonians (winning 4 Ulster Senior Cup medals, in 1954, 1956, 1957 and 1958). Born in Belfast, 5th May 1931. A product of R.B.A.I., he was capped for Ireland 11 times between 1951 and 1956. He captained Ireland 3 times in 1955, to win the Wooden Spoon. He was then picked as as Ireland's 4th captain of the British and Irish Lions, who travelled to South Africa in that year. Gaining 3 Test places himself, he was one of 5 Irishmen on the tour, during which the Lions won 2 of the 4 Tests, and recorded 18 wins and one draw out of 24 matches played; they scored 418 points, while conceding 271, Thompson being the first skipper this century to share a Test Series with South Africa. He later joined Warrington Rugby League Club and became a journalist and t.v. reporter.

THOMPSON, SYDNEY James (SYD, 'BIG SYD').

Bowls player. Born in Belfast, 29th August 1912. Club: Willowfield (playing for them since 1940, being many times singles and pairs champion, and being President of the club in 1958). He broke the then world record of the greatest number of international appearances in the outdoor game by any bowler, representing Ireland 78 times, achieved over the span of 26 years, between 1947 to 1973. He was captain of the Irish team that won the British Championship of 1951 (their first title since 1905), and kept that role until 1966. He was a bronze medal winner in the 1970 Commonwealth Games pairs event. He won 10 Northern Ireland Private Greens championships, 3 at singles, 2 in pairs, and 5 at fours. He has also won a further 50 indoor caps. He was President of the Irish Bowling Association in 1964, when he was also President of the British Isles

Council. He becane an international selector for both oudoor and indoor bowls. He also played billiards and cricket to a high standard. A company director, he was awarded the O.B.E. in 1970.

THORNHILL, BATT.

G.A.A. hurling full-back, Cork. Club: Buttevant. He won Munster J.H.C. medals with Cork in 1937 and 1938. A member of the Cork team beaten in the All-Ireland Senior Hurling Championship final in 1939, he was ever-present in the Cork hurling side which won the Liam McCarthy Cup for four years in succession, in 1941, 1942, 1943, and 1944. He won National Hurling League medals with Cork in 1940 and 1941, and he also won 3 Railway Cup medals with Munster, in 1942, 1943, and 1944.

THORNHILL, THOMAS.

Rugby international half-back. Club: Wanderers. Five times a Leinster interprovincial, he played at half-back for Ireland on 4 occasions between 1892 and 1893, being on the winning side only once. A barrister, he was later to become President of the I.R.F.U., in 1901-1902. He died in 1939.

THORNTON, MARTIN ('THE CONNEMARA CRUSHER').

Heavyweight boxer. Born in Spiddal, Connemara, Co Galway. A feared opponent at his prime, his fight against the British Champion Bruce Woodcock, in 1945 at the Theatre Royal Dublin, in which his seconds threw in the towel in the 4th round, is marred by the claim (exacerbated by Thornton's yarns) by a bribe scandal. He was the winner of 25 of his 36 professional fights.

THORPE, MARIA.

Ladies G.A.A. football full-back, Wexford. Club: Shemalier (winning 4 county championship winner's medals). A member of the Wexford side beaten by Kerry in the All-Ireland final of 1983, she was captain of the county side three years later when Wexford yet again succumbed to Kerry in the All-Ireland final.

THRIFT, HARRY.

Rugby international wing three-quarter. 1882-1958. Club: Dublin University (winning Leinster Senior Cup medals in 1904, 1907 and 1908). A product of High School in Dublin, he was seven times a Leinster interprovincial, and was capped for Ireland 18 times between 1904 to 1909, scoring 5 international tries, including one on his debut. He captained Ireland once, in 1908 against England, and it is no wonder, because that day Ireland had 7 players from Trinity in the side, the greatest 20th century club representation in the international side. He was also a sprinter of international class, winning the 100 yards at Trinity's College Races 7 years insuccession, and he won the Irish 440 yards championship in 1906. He was Chairman of the International Board in rugby from 1933 to 1956, and was one of the greats of world rugby administration. An Irish selector in 1921-1922, he was President of the I.R.F.U. in 1923-24. A professor at Trinity College, his brother W.E. Thrift was a fine cyclist, was a Provost at Trinity College, and was the fist chairman of the D.U.C.A.C., followed by Harry in this post.

THUILLIER, HARRY.

Fencing champion. He won the Irish Foil Championship first in 1952 and held onto the title every year until 1960. He represented Ireland at 2 Olympic Games at fencing, in 1952 at Helsinki in the foil, and again in Rome in 1960 in the foil, winning one bout in all, and being eliminated in the 1st round pool both times. His older brother, Nick Thuillier, had previously won the Irish Foil Championship, and also represented Ireland at the Olympic Games, taking part in the foil (individual and team) discipline at the 1948 Games in London. Harry later became a radio personalituy.

TIEDT, FREDDIE.

Amateur welterweight boxer. Born in 1939. Club: South City and St Andrews (Dublin). He won a silver medal at welterweight at the 1956 Melbourne Olympic Games in Moscow, when, although he recieved more points than his opponent (the Romanian Nicolae Linca) in the controversial final, he lost the vote by 3 to 2 (2 judges went for him, one against, 2 marked it a draw, but each of these gave Linca the nod), a result that astonished nearly everybody present in the arena. The following year he won his only Irish National Senior Title, at welterweight. He later became a coach and an international referee.

TIERNAN, CLARRIE (later Mrs VAL REDDAN).

Amateur international golfer. Born in Drogheda, Co Louth, 3rd July 1916. Club: Co Louth. She won the Irish Ladies Close Championship in 1936 and was runner-up in both 1946 and 1948. She was runner-up in the British Ladies in 1949, beaten 3 and 2 in the final at Newcastle by Frances Stephens. A much-travelled golfer, she won the New Jersey State Ladies title in 1937, and was runner-up in the 1938 Canadian Ladies Championship. She played Home International golf for Ireland between 1935 and 1949. She first won Curtis Cup honours in 1938, and again won selection ten years later in 1948, and has the distinction of being one of the few G.B.& Ireland players in this contest to maintain an unbeaten record for her matches played (winning 2 and halving one of her 3 matches). Her son Barry Reddan, also of the Co Louth club, won the Irish Close Championship title in 1984, and played Home international golf for Ireland in the series of 1985 (he played interprovincial golf for Leinster from 1978 to 1988).

TIGHE, TONY.

G.A.A. football right half-forward and full forward, Cavan. Born in 1927. He played in the midfield in Cavan's losing All-Ireland Senior Football Championship final against Cork in 1945, at the age of 18. In the great 1947 and 1948 sides, he was at right half-forward, winning 2 All-Ireland S.F.C. medals, and also won a National Football League medal. When he won his third Sam Maguire Cup medal, in 1952, he was playing at full-forward, and this made one of only 4 players to play in each of Cavan's victories in All-Ireland S.F.C. finals. He won one Railway Cup medal with Ulster, in 1950.

TISDALL, ROBERT Morton Newburgh (BOB).

400 metres hurdles athlete. Born 16th May 1907, at Nuwara Eliya in the then Ceylon, to a Nenagh, Co Tipperary family. He won 4 events for Cambridge in the Inter-Varsity match of 1932 (shot putt, 120 yards hurdles, 440 yards and long jump). In 1929 he set South African and Canadian records in the 220 yards low hurdles, and in 1930 set Greek records in the same event, along with the shot and 120 yards hurdles. While still a student in Cambridge, he decided, in March 1932, to try for a place in the Irish Olympic squad at the 400 metres hurdles. Having won the Irish Championship in only his third race over the distance in June 1932 in a time of 54.2 seconds, he qualified for the team to go to L.A. As a virtual novice therefore, he won, at the age of 25, the 1932 Olympic 400 metres hurdles title in Los Angeles (in only his 7th race at the event). In doing so he bettered the world record of 52.0 held by F Morgan Taylor, with a time of 51.7 seconds, but was not credited with the record (as he had knocked down the final hurdle, and stumbled for a few scary moments), and even the Olympic record was not given to him, but instead to Glenn Hardin, the American who finished in 2nd place, 2 tenths of a second behind Tisdall (and also inside the old world mark). He won his gold medal in the same hour that Dr Pat O'Callaghan won his 2nd hammer

gold medal, thereby being part of Ireland's greatest athletic day. Four days later he finished 8th in the decathlon, winning 3 disciplines, the 110 metres hurdles, the 400 metres (in record time) and the final event, the 1,500 metres, for a points total of 7,327. His later career was an ant-climax, and he moved from country to country trying to settle.

TOBIN, JOHNNY.
G.A.A. football left full-forward, Galway. Born in 1953. Club: Tuam Stars (coaching them in 1984 to their first county championship win in 22 years). A member of the victorious Galway side in the final of the 1970 All-Ireland M.F.C., he was also at left corner-forward on the 1972 All-Ireland Under 21 winning side. He was at at left full-forward on the Galway team beaten in the All-Ireland Senior Football Championship final of 1974 by Cork (having missed the 1973 final with a broken jaw), and came on as a sub in the All-Ireland S.F.C. defeat of 1983. He won his only All-Star award in 1974 at the left corner-forward position. He coached Galway minors to All-Ireland success in 1986, and later trained the seniors in 1989 and 1990.

TODD, ANDREW W P.
Rugby international rugby full-back. 1892-1942. Club: Dublin University. He won 3 consecutive international caps for Ireland in the 1913 and 1914 international seasons, all played on different days of the week. A Major in the R.A.M.C. who won a Military Cross in W.W.I., he is the father of the Dublin-born Oscar-nominated actor, Richard Todd.

TODD, SAM.
Soccer international wing-half. Born in Belfast, 22nd September 1945. He joined Burnley from Glentoran at 18, and played in 108 league matches for them 1963-69. He then spent 2 seasons at Sheffield Wednesday, and a short period at Mansfield. He won 11 full soccer caps for Northern Ireland betwen 1966 and 1971, and also won 4 under 23 caps.

TOMPKINS, LARRY.
G.A.A. football centre half-forward, Kildare and Cork. Born in Co Kildare, 13th June 1963. Clubs: Eadestown (winning Kildare junior and intermediate championship medals) and Castlehaven (winning a Cork county and Munster championship in 1989). He first played senior championship football in 1979 at age 16 for Kildare (also playing at minor and Under 21 for the Lillywhites) he then played for New York in 1985-1987, before declaring for Cork in 1987. A fine place-kicker, he was a member of the Cork side beaten in 2 successive All-Ireland Senior Football Championship finals by Meath in 1987 and 1988. He won his first Sam Maguire Cup medal in the 1989 All-Ireland S.F.C. final against Mayo, and was captain of the winning Cork side again in 1990 which, by beating Meath by 0-11 to 0-9, brought off the 2nd part of a historic double, the senior All-Ireland wins in both hurling and football, and thus bringing his tally of Munster S.F.C. medals to 4-in-a-row. A highly rated player, he also won a National League medal in 1989 with the Rebel County. Injured for the Munster S.H.C. final success of 1993, he won 3 successive All-Star awards in 1987, 1988 and 1989, all at centre half-forward. A publican, he has had an injury-laden career.

TOOHILL, ANTHONY.
G.A.A. football right half-forward and midfielder, Derry. He was a member of the Derry football side who had an outstanding year in 1992, winning the National Football League and reaching the Ulster S.F.C. final. He won an All-Star award in 1992 in the left half-forward position. He won an Ulster Senior Football Championship winner's medal in 1993, helping Derry to reach their first All-Ireland final in 25 years, when they beat Cork to win the Sam Maguire Cup.

TORRANS, SAM.
Soccer international defender. Club: Linfield (winning 6 Irish Cup medals in

1891, 1892, 1893, 1895, 1898, and 1899). He was capped 26 times for Northern Ireland in the 12 year period between 1889 and 1901. His relation R Torrens, also a Linfield player, played with him in one international, against Scotland in 1893.

TOWEY, JANETTE.

Singles sculler. Clubs: Fermoy R.C. and Garda Siochana Boat Club. She was Irish junior sculling Champion 3 years in succession, 1985, 1986 and 1987, and was then Irish senior sculling champion for 3 consecutive years, 1988, 1989 and 1990. In the Match des Seniors, the world Under-23 Championships of 1990, she won a silver medal in the Lightweight singles sculls.

TOWNSEND, ANDY.

Soccer international striker. Born in Maidstone, 23rd July 1963. Clubs: Welling, Weymouth (joining them for £13,000), Southampton (joining fee: £35,000), Norwich City (whom he joined in 1988 for £300,000), Chelsea (joining them in 1990 for £1,150,000), and Aston Villa (from 1993 for a fee of £2.1 million). With Norwich he helped them to lead the First Division in 1989 before finishing third, for which he was nominated in the shortlist for P.F.A. Player of the Year. Making his Republic of Ireland debut against France in 1989, he went on to play in 6 of Ireland 8 matches in their run to qualify for the World Cup finals in Italy in 1990 for the first time, and playing a pivotal role in their successful 5 match run. A quality mid-fielder, his cap tally up to mid 1993 was 37, scoring 4 international goals. His father, Don (born in Swindon, 17th September 1930), played as a full back for 8 years for Charlton 1954-61, and for Crystal Palace.

TRACEY, EDDIE.

Amateur international boxer. Club: Arbour Hill. He won 4 Irish National Senior Championship titles at 3 different weights: at bantamweight in 1961, at featherweight in 1965 and 1968, and at lightweight in 1969. Fighting in 25 international matches for Ireland, including at the Golden Gloves in the U.S.A., he also represented Ireland at the 1968 Olympic Games in Mexico, losing in his 2nd bout at featherweight on points to the eventual gold medallist, Antonio Rolden of Mexico.

TRACEY, JOE.

Motor car racing pioneer. Born in Co Waterford in 1883, he emigrated to the U.S.A. in 1902, at 19. He won national headlines in the U.S. in 1905 when he finished 2nd in the Havana 100 miles race, and 2nd also in the Vanderbilt Cup Eliminating race. By finishing 3rd in the actual Vanderbilt Cup in 1905 (watched by 100,000 people in New York), he became the first American driver (and car, a Locomobile, nicknamed 'Old Vic' and now one of America's most revered historic cars) to show any class against the then dominent European cars and drivers. In 1906 he set a lap record in the Vanderbilt Eliminating race, and having set a fastest lap in the Cup proper, he retired from the race and from racing entirely after injuring 2 people.

TRAYNOR, FRANK.

Bantamweight amateur boxer. Club: St Paul's. One of Ireland's best amateur boxers of the 1920's, he won 3 successive Irish National Senior Championships at bantamweight, in 1926, 1927 and 1928. In the 1928 Olympic Games in Amsterdam he finished 4th, being beaten for the bronze medal by the South African, Henry Isaacs (he had earlier lost on points to the gold medal winner, Vittorio Tamagnini). He went on to win a Tailteann Games title. When he died at the age of 86 in 1991 he was the oldest surviving Irish Olympian.

TRAYNOR, TOMMY J.

Soccer international full-back. Born in Dundalk, 22nd July 1933. Clubs: Dundalk and Southampton (for whom he played 434 league matches over a period of 14 years from 1952 to 1965, and scored 7 league goals, and helping them to win the English 3rd Division in the 1959-1960 season). He was capped 8 times for the Republic of Irleand over an 11 year period from (with an 8 year gap between his first and 2nd cap) 1954 to 1964, all while with the Saints.

TREACY, JIM.

G.A.A. hurling left full-back, Kilkenny. Born in 1943. Club: Bennetsbridge (winning 6 county championship medals). His senior inter-county career with the county lasted from 1966 to 1975. He captained Kilkenny to beat Tipperary by 3-8 to 2-7 in the All-Ireland Senior Hurling Championship final of 1967 (the first time they had defeated the 'auld enemy' in an All-Ireland final for 45 years), and went on to win 3 further Liam McCarthy Cup medals, in 1969, 1972 and 1974, playing also in the losing All-Ireland S.H.C. finals in 1966 and 1971 (he won a 7th Leinster S.H.C. medal in 1973). He won 3 Railway Cup medals, in 1971, 1972 (when he became the 10th Kilkennyman to captain the winning Leinster side) and 1973, also winning a National League medal in 1966, and 3 Oireachtas medals. He won All-Star awards in both the inaugural two years of the scheme, 1971 and 1972, both at left corner-back.

TREACY, JOHN.

Middle and long distance athlete. Born 5th June 1957 at Villierstown, West Waterford. Club: Deise. Having finished 3rd in the World Junior Cross Country in 1975, he went on to win the World international cross-country title 2 years in succession, in 1978 at Bellahuston Park in Glasgow, and in 1979 at Limerick. A product of Providence University, his major championship performances include, at 5,000m: 7th in 1980 Olympic Games in Moscow, 18th in 1987 World Championship, 4th in European Championship in 1978. At 10,000m he finished 9th in the 1984 Olympic Games, having passed out in the heats in 1980. He has been Irish Champion at 5,000m 5 times (in 1978, 1980, 1981, 1983, and 1984), and has been 10,000m champion in 1978, 1985, and 1987, being A.A.A. 10,000 metres champion in 1979. He has 3 times held the Irish record at 5,000m, twice at 10,000m, and once each at 3,000m, the marathon, and the 1 hour run. His career highlight was in the 1984 Olympic Games in Los Angeles, when he finished 2nd to Carlos Lopez of Portugal in the marathon, beating Charlie Spedding of G.B. in a battle for the silver medal. In 1988, although pulling out during the Olympic marathon in Seoul, he finished 3rd in the New York marathon (he was also 3rd in the Boston Marathons of both 1988 and 1989). He won the Los Angeles marathon in 1992 in a time of 2 hrs 12 mins 28 seconds, later that year becoming one of only 3 Irish sportspersons to represent the country at 4 different Olympic Games, finishing 51st in the marathon at Barcelona. He was selected as Texaco's Sportstar of the Year for Athletics 3 times, in 1978, 1979 (when he also won the Supreme Sportstar award), and again in 1984. The first sportsman to be given the Freedom of the City of Waterford, his twin sister Elizabeth Bullen ran in the European Championship martahon for Ireland in 1990.

TREACY, P T.

G.A.A. football full forward and right full-forward, Fermanagh. In 1963, he became the first Fermanagh player to win a Railway Cup medal, when he played on the winning Ulster side at full-forward. He was at full forward again on the winning side of 1964, and he brought his total of Railway Cup medals to 4 (all gained in succession), when fielding at right full-forward in 1965 and 1966. He never played in an Ulster S.F.C. final for his county.

TREACY, RAYMOND C T (RAY, 'TRACER').

Soccer international forward. Born in Dublin, 18th June 1946. Clubs: West Bromwich Albion (to whom he was apprenticed), Charlton Athletic (scoring

43 goals in 144 league appearences 1967-1971), Swindon Town (scoring 16 goals in the 1972-73 league season), Preston North End, Oldham Athletic (on loan), West Bromwich Albion (again), Shamrock Rovers (winning an F.A.I. Cup medal in 1978, when he scored the only goal in the final, a penalty). He holds the League of Ireland record for the most penalty kicks converted. Over a 15 year period between 1966 and 1980 he was capped for the Republic of Ireland 43 times (7 times as a sub), scoring 5 international goals. He later managed Home Farm and Shamrock Rovers, and is a travel agent.

TREACY, SEAN.

G.A.A. hurling left half-back, Galway. Born in March 1965. Club: Portumna. He helped the Galway minors to capture the county's first ever All-Ireland M.H.C. title in 1983. Later becoming a Galway senior player in 1989, when they won the National Hurling League and the Railway Cup, and although his county were beaten by Tipperary in the All-Ireland S.H.C. semi-final, his form was such that he won an All-Star that year in the left half-back spot. He was on the Galway side beaten in the All-Ireland Senior Hurling Championship final by Cork in 1990. In 1991 he helped Galway win the Oireachtas Cup, and won a 2nd All-Star. In 1993 he was at full-back on the Galway side which were beaten in another All-Ireland S.H.C. final.

TREACY, TOMMY.

G.A.A. hurling centre half-forward, Tipperary and Dublin. Born in 1904. Club: Young Ireland (winning 4 county championship medals). In an inter-county career which stretched from 1926 to 1942, he won 2 All-Ireland Senior Hurling Championship winner's medals with Tipperary, in 1930 and 1937, and also won another Munster S.H.C. medal in 1941. In the intervening years he also won a Leinster S.H.C. medal with Dublin in 1934, when they went on to lose the All-Ireland final. He won 3 Railway Cup medals, in 1930, 1931 and 1934, and won a National League medal in 1928.

TREACY, REGINALD C R (REG).

Hockey international left wing. Club: Cork Church of Ireland (winning 3 successive Irish Senior Cup medals in 1967, 1968 and 1969). He was capped for Ireland 53 times between 1960 and 1974, a record for a forward at that time. A forward of fine skill known for his weaving runs, he was on the European Cup squad to Brussels in 1970, the famous Santander victory, and was also on the European Cup team of 1974, his last year. He was also capped 4 times for Great Britain between 1963 and 1968. He is from a famous Munster family of hockey players; his brother George, also a left winger, won 2 international caps in 1968 (playing alongside Reg on the team which won the Home International series for the first time in 19 years), and later became the Chairman of the National Coaching and Developement Committee, while another, Fred, was capped at Under 22 level (both also being on the famous C C of I team in the 1960's).

TUBRIDY, MICK.

G.A.A. football right half-forward, Cork, and showjumper. Born in Kilrush, Co Clare. He was a member of the first Cork All-Ireland Senior Football Championship side which won the Sam Maguire Cup in 1945, when he played in the half-forward line in the famous victory. He later became a renowned showjumper for Ireland, but in 1954, at the age of only 32, he died from a fall from a horse.

TUCKER, COLM Christopher.

Rugby international wing-forward. Born in Limerick, 22nd September, 1952. Club: Shannon (being the first player from that club to play for the Lion's). A product of St Munchin's College, Limerick, he played only 3 international matches for Ireland, and one of these was as a reserve (Fergus Slattery cv was around in his time), but he was good enough to warrant selection for the 1980 Lions tour of South Africa, on which he played in 2 Test matches. In an injury prone career, he gave great service to Shannon, winning 3 Munster Senior Cup medals, in 1977, 1978, and 1982, and to Munster (playing on the famous side which beat the All Blacks in 1978). He is a cousin of soccer international Tony Galvin (cv).

TUKE, BENJAMIN Burland (BEN).

Rugby international half-back. 1870-1936. Club: Bective Rangers (playing for the club when it won the Leinster Senior Cup on the first 2 occasions, in 1899 and 1892). Twice a Leinster player, he won 9 international caps for Ireland between 1890 and 1895, and was ever-present in Ireland's first ever Triple Crown-winning side of 1894.

TULLY, CHARLES Patrick (CHARLIE) ('THE CLOWN PRINCE OF FOOTBALL').

Soccer international No 11. Born in the Falls Road of Belfast in 1924. Clubs: Whiterock, Forth River, Ballyclare Comrades, Cliftonville, Belfast Celtic (for whom he played a senior game at the age of 14, as well as scoring the winning goal in the 1947 Irish Cup final), Glasgow Celtic (transfered for £10,000, and winning Scottish League and Cup medals in 1954, being a favourite at Parkhead throughout the 1950's, reaching a peak in the famous 7-1 defeat of Rangers in 1957 League Cup final), Cork Hibernians. One of the games great characters, he was capped only 10 times for Northern Ireland between 1949 and 1959, scoring 3 international goals (including 2 in a 2-2 draw with England in 1952). He later managed Bangor and Portadown, and died in 1973.

TUOHY, LIAM W ('RASHER').

Soccer international winger, outside-left, and manager. Born in West Wall, Dublin, 27th April 1933. A fast player with a good eye for the ball, he joined Shamrock Rovers at 18 from St Mary's, East Wall, and played over 700 matches in all for the club, winning: 2 F.A.I. Cup medals in 1955 when he scored the winning goal in the final, and 1956, and 3 League of Ireland medals, in 1953-54, 1956-57, and 1958-59. He played with the 'Hoops' until the age of 27, when he joined Newcastle United for 3 seasons, scoring 9 league goals in 38 league appearences. He returned to Rovers in 1963, playing a vital role in the further F.A.I. Cup successes of 1964 and 1965. He became a successful player-manager at Milltown from 1964 (when the club won the domestic Grand Slam), which coincided with his best League of Ireland goal-scoring season, with 15 out of his total of 96 league goals. He shares with Donal Leahy (cv), the record of 7 goals scored for League of Ireland Selections, which he scored in 25 league caps. He also managed Shelbourne (for 7 weeks), the Republic of Ireland national squad (1971-73, with some success), and the Irish youths team (helping them to qualify for 3 European Championships, reaching one semi-final, and one World Cup). Has capped 8 times over a 9 year period for the Republic of Ireland between 1956 and 1965, scoring 4 international goals. In 1966 he was voted as the S.W.A.I. personality of the year.

TURLEY, Patrick NOEL.

Rugby international flanker, and Laois G.A.A. footballer. Born in Co Laois, 13th December, 1936. He won one international cap for Ireland at rugby, on a losing side against England in 1962, while playing for Blackrock College. He played 3 times for Leinster in the 1965/66 interprovincial season. He has coached the Irish schools rugby side, and has also played inter-county football for Laois.

TURNER, C J .

Soccer international player. Clubs: Southend United and West Ham United. He was capped 10 times at international soccer for the Irish Free State side between 1936 and 1939, scoring 4 international goals.

TWOHILL, TIM.

Handballer and G.A.A. footballer, Cork. Born in Cork in 1872. He became Irish Professional Champion in 1898, and held on to the title until 1905. He previously played for the Dunmanway side which represented Cork in the 1897 All-Ireland Senior Football Championship final, being beaten by the Dublin team from Kickhams.

TWOMEY, JIM F.

Soccer international goalkeeper. Born in Newry, 13th April 1914. Clubs: Newry Town, Leeds United (playing 109 league matches for them 1937-39), Newry (during the war), Halifax Town (later being a trainer-coach there). Capped first for Northern Ireland while still a resesrve player at Elland Road in March 1938, his only other cap came in a 7-0 drubbing by England. He died in 1984.

TYRRELL, SIR WILLIAM.

Rugby international forward. Club: Queen's University Belfast. He was capped 9 times for Ireland between 1910 and 1914, scoring 2 international tries. He was selected on the British and Irish tour of South Africa (captained by fellow-Ulsterman Tom Smyth) in 1910, although not winning a Test place. Becoming an Air Vice-Marshall with the R.A.F., in W.W.I. he won a D.S.O. with a bar, a Belgian Crois de Guerre, and was made a K.B.E. in 1947. He was President of the I.R.F.U. during the Championship winning season of 1950/1951.

TYRELL-SMITH, HENRY GEORGE (HARRY).

Motorcycling road racer. Born in Blackrock, Co Dublin, 3rd May 1907. An engineering graduate from T.C.D., he was one of Ireland's best ever motorcyclists. He was European Champion twice, in the 500cc class in 1931, and the 250cc class in 1936. He had 15 top ten finishes in the Isle of Man T.T. races over a 13 year period between 1927 and 1939, and won one T.T. race, the 1930 Junior on a Rudge. Living in England from the early 1930's, he later helped to design the famous D-type Jaguar Le Mans Car. He died in Birmingham in 1982.

U

UPRICHARD, W NORMAN M.

Soccer international goalkeeper. Clubs: Distillery, Swindon Town and Portsmouth. He was capped 18 times in goals for Northern Ireland between 1952 and 1959, including playing in his country's famous 2-1 victory over Czechoslovakia in the World Cup finals match in Malmo in 1958, when as understudy to Harry Gregg (cv), he was one of the heroes of this great venture.

V

VARD, JACK.

Amateur wrestler. As a youngster he was a fine chess player, and hit the headlines by being the only Irishman to obtain 2 draws against the 2 chess masters, Alexhine and Kilkonoski, in simulataneous matches. Later joining the Apollo Wrestling club, he soon won club and Irish championships, and went on to win 2 British Lightweight titles, in 1949 and 1952 (losing by default at the weigh-in in 1950). In a career spanning over 20 years in the amateur game, he beat many world renowned wrestlers, and represented Ireland in the Olympic Games in 1952 in Helsinki. A furrier.

VERNON, JACKIE.

Soccer international centre-half. Born in Belfast, 26th September 1918. Clubs: Spearmint, Dundela, Belfast Celtic, W.B.A., and Crusaders. He played 190 league matches for West Bromwich Albion (who paid £10,500 for him) between 1946 and 1951. He won 17 international caps for Northern Ireland between 1947 and 1952, having won 2 caps for Eire in 1946. He also played centre-half on the Great Britain team in

1947 at Hampden Park, and captained the Rest of Britain team at Cardiff in the Welsh 75th anniversary celebrations. A former gaelic player, his brother Harry Vernon, an Antrim goalkeeper, played in a Railway Cup final in gaelic football for Ulster in 1944, on the same day that Jackie captained the North Regional League side to a win over the League of Ireland in Dublin.

WALSH, ANNETTE.

G.A.A. ladies football midfielder, Kerry. Club: Castleisland (with whom she won All-Ireland Club Championship medals in 1981 and 1984). She has won 7 All-Ireland Senior Championship winner's medals with the Kingdon, in 1983, 1984, 1985, 1986 (captaining the side from left full forward to beat Wexford in the final), 1987, 1988, and 1989. One of the games finest exponents, she has won 3 All-Star awards, and has won 9 National League medals, 2 Minor All-Ireland medals (in 1980 and 1981), and 3 Interprovincial Championships.

WALSH, BILLY.

Amateur international boxer. Club: St Joseph's and St Ita's, Wexford. From Enniscorthy, he has won 7 Irish Senior National titles, two at light-welterweight (1983 and 1984), and five at welterweight (1986, 1987, 1988, 1989 and 1991). He won 24 of his first 36 international bouts for Ireland up to 1988, and over 250 of his 300 amateur bouts. He represented Ireland in the Seoul Olympic games of 1988. In 1991 he became the first Irish boxer to win an E.C.C. title, winning it in the welterweight division in Belgium.

WALSH, CON.

Hammer throwing athlete, and G.A.A. footballer, Cork. Born in Carriganimma, Co Cork. He played on the losing Cork selection in the 1901 All-Ireland Senior Football Championship, and won the Irish championship for the place kick in 1901 (at 69 yards), 1905 (195') and 1906 (224'4"). Later he was to become British A.A.A. hammer champion in 1908, and was also Canadian Champion in this discipline each year from 1907 to 1912. He won the A.A.U. hammer title in 1911 with 179' having the previous year won the 56lb shot event. Representing Canada, he won a bronze medal in the hammer throw at the 1908 Olympic Games in London. His throw of just over 159 feet was more than 11 feet behind the winner John Flanagan (cv). As a third Irish-born athlete finished in 2nd place (Matt McGrath cv), this is the only occasion in Olympic history in which 3 Irish-born sportsmen swept the board in any Olympic competition, by winning gold, silver and bronze medals.

WALSH, DAVID J. (DAVY)

Soccer international centre-forward. Born in Waterford, 28th April 1923. He transferred from Linfield to W.B.A. in 1946, scoring 94 goals in 165 league appearances for them in four seasons. He then spent four seasons with Aston Villa, scoring 37 goals for them in 108 league appearances. He played briefly for Newport County in 1955. He was capped 20 times for the Republic of Ireland between 1946 and 1954, and 9 times for Northern Ireland from 1947-50, scoring 5 international goals.

WALSH, DENIS.

G.A.A. dual hurling and football player, Cork. From Ballynoe, 13 miles from Midleton, he was born in 1965. Club: St Catherine's and Imokilly. He won 3 successive All-Ireland Under 21 football champioship medals with Cork in 1984, 1985 and 1986. He played at left half-back on the Cork Senior Hurling Championship winning side of 1986, and at full-back in the winning side of 1990 (also playing on the losing side in the 1992 final). He also won a National Hurling League medal with Cork in

1992-93. In 1987 he played at left corner-back on the Cork side beaten in the All-Ireland Senior Football Championship final by Meath, and again played in the drawn game of the All-Ireland S.F.C. final of 1988. He was a non-playing substitute in Cork's All-Ireland S.F.C. winning side of 1989, and was a panel member for the All-Ireland S.F.C. win of 1990 (thus winning Senior All-Ireland medals in both codes in that year, although only playing in the hurling final).

WALSH, DICK ('DRUG').

G.A.A. hurler, Kilkenny. Club: Mooncoin. He is one of only 3 hurlers to captain 3 All-Ireland Senior Hurling Championship winning teams, doing so with the Mooncoin selection in 1907 (when they beat Cork's Dungourney by 3-12 to 4-8), 1909 (when the Thurles side from Tipp were beaten by 4-6 to 0-12), and 1913 (the first 15-a-side final, when Toomevara of Tipperary were beaten by 2-4 to 1-2). He also won 4 other All-Ireland S.H.C. winners medals: in 1904 with Tullaroan, 1905 with Erin's Own, in the walk-over final of 1911, and in 1912 again with Tullaroan, making his 7 winner's medals over a 10 year period a joint record (with 3 team-mates) not beaten until Christy Ring did so many years later.

WALSH, DENIS.

G.A.A. hurler, Tipperary. He won 4 All-Ireland Senior Hurling Championship winners medals with Tipperary sides in the late 19th century, playing for the Tubberadora team in the 3 years of 1895, 1896 and 1898, and for the winning Moycarkey side in 1899. A brother of Johnny Walsh (cv).

WALSH, EDDIE.

G.A.A. footballing half-back, Kerry. He has won 4 All-Ireland Senior Football Championship winner's medals with Kerry, in 1939, 1940, 1941, and 1946. He was also on losing All-Ireland S.F.C. final sides in 1944 and in the Polo Ground in 1947. He also won 2 Railway Cup medals with Munster, in 1941 and 1946.

WALSH, EDWARD J (NED).

Rugby international forward and athlete. (1868-1939). As an athlete, he won the Irish 120 yards hurdles championships twice (in 1884 and 1885), and in 1885 he became world champion in that event, when he challenged the American Malcolm Ford, and beat him decisively. In rugby, while playing for Lansdowne (being a member of the side which won the club's first Leinster Senior Cup in 1891) and Leinster, he won 7 international caps for Ireland between 1887 and 1893, scoring 2 international tries against Wales in 1892, and playing on the first Irish side that beat England in 1887. An entertaining sportsman, he was later to become the Accountant-General of the Supreme Court of Ireland.

WALSH, GARY.

G.A.A. football goalkeeper, Donegal. He played a major role in helping his county to reach the All-Ireland Senior Football Championship final for the first time in 1992, when they went on to defeat the favourites Dublin and take the Sam Maguire Cup in style. He won an All-Star award in 1992 in the goalkeeper's spot.

WALSH, JACK.

G.A.A. football corner full-back, Kerry. From Asdee. He won 6 All-Ireland Senior Football Championship winner's medals with Kerry, in 1924, 1926, 1929, 1930, 1931, and 1932, and was on the losing All-Ireland side in 1927. He also won 4 Railway Cup medals with Munster, in 1927, 1929, 1930, and 1932.

WALSH, JIMMY.

G.A.A. hurling right half forward and midfielder, Kilkenny. Club: Carrickshock. From the Ballyhale area of the county, he won 4 All-Ireland Senior Hurling Championship winner's medals with Kilkenny in the 1930's. He was twice the winning captain (being the first

Kilkennyman to captain 2 Liam McCarthy Cup wins), in 1932 (when at the age of just 21 he led the side that beat Clare by 3-3 to 2-3) and in 1939 (this time to a 2-7 to 3-3 win over Cork, scoring the winning point in this, the famous 'Thunder and Lightning' final), also winning medals in 1933 and 1935. He was on the Kilkenny sides which lost the All-Ireland S.H.C. finals of 1936 and 1940 (both to their great rivals, Limerick). He won Railway Cup medals with Leinster in 1932, 1933 and 1936.

WALSH, Dr JEREMIAH Charles (JERRY).

Rugby international centre three-quarter. Born 3rd November 1938. Clubs: U.C.C., and Sunday's Well. A product of Presentation Brothers College, he was capped 26 times in the centre for Ireland between 1960 and 1967, many of them in an effective partnership with Kevin Flynn (cv). His only international try came in his last match, against Australia, on the Irish tour Down Under in 1967. He toured Australia and New Zealand with the Lions in 1966, although not getting a Test place. He captained the Combined Universities side which beat the touring South Africans in 1965, and also played for the Barbarians. One of the game's finest crash tacklers, he won a Munster Senior Cup medal with U.C.C. in 1963. A medical doctor, he died suddenly in 1992, at the age of 53.

WALSH, JOHNNY.

G.A.A. hurler, Tipperary. Born in 1877, in Tubberdora, Co Tipperary. He won a total of 5 All-Ireland Senior Hurling Championship winner's medals, and all before the age of 23. His first 3 wins came in 1895, 1896 and 1898 with Tubberdora, he won in 1899 with Moycarkey , and 1900 he was on the winning Two-Mile-Borris selection. His brother Dick (cv) also won 4 medals.

WALSH, MICHAEL A (MICK).

Soccer international forward. Born in Chorley, 13th August 1954. Clubs: Chorley, Blackpool (scoring 72 league goals for them in 172 league matches between 1973 and 1977, being the English 2nd Division's leading goalscorer in the 1976-1977 season with 26 goals), Everton, Q.P.R., Porto. He was capped 22 times for the Republic of Ireland between 1976 and 1985 (10 of these as a substitute), scoring 3 international goals.

WALSH, MICHAEL ('DUCKSIE').

Handballer. From Butt's Green, Co Kilkenny. He won progressive U.S.A. titles at Under 15, Under 17, Under 19 and Under 23, in 1982, 1984, 1986 and in 1989. He won All-Ireland minor softball singles titles in 1982, 1983 and 1984, minor hardball singles in 1984, minor softball doubles in 1982, 1983 and 1984, and minor hardball doubles in 1984 (he also won an All-Ireland Junior softball doubles in 1983). He won a record 9 All-Ireland Senior Softball Singles Championships in succession (the first person to match the record of successive titles since the 8-in-a-row of Paddy Perry in the 1930's), in 1985, 1986, 1987, 1988, 1989, 1990, 1991, 1992 and 1993 (he won the Hardball Singles in 1987). He also won the Softball Doubles titles, including 1985, 1987, 1988 and 1991. Up to 1993 he has won 47 national titles of various levels, and holds the record of 25 senior national titles. He has been beaten at semi-final and final stage of World Championships.

WALSH, MICHAEL.

G.A.A. goalkeeper, Kilkenny. Club: Dicksboro. Born in 1962. Playing junior level soccer for Ireland 4 times, once as captain, with Evergreen he lost a Junior F.A.I. Cup final (he also played League of Ireland for a season with EMFA). He played hurling in 3 (losing) All-Ireland minor and Under 21 finals, and played in goals for Kilkenny seniors from 1990 (he had won an Oireachtais medal with them in an outfield position in 1984, and 2 All-Ireland J.H.C medals in 1988 and 1990). He was in the losing All-Ireland Senior Football Championship team of 1991, before winning 2 successive Liam

McCarthy medals in 1992 and in 1993. He also won a National Hurling League with Kilkenny in 1993. A son of the great Ollie Walsh (cv), he won an All-Star award in 1991.

WALSH, OLLIE.

G.A.A. hurling goalkeeper, Kilkenny. Club: Thomastown (with them he played in, but failed to win, 2 senior county championship finals). He was born on 13th July 1937. Hunted as a soccer goalkeeper in his youth, he stuck with the hurling game. Playing in 8 All-Ireland Senior Hurling Championship finals for Kilkenny spanning 3 decades between 1956 and 1971, he won 4 All-Ireland S.H.C. medals, in the 1957 and 1963 wins over Waterford, in the 1967 final against Tipperary (one of his finest performances), and in 1969 against Cork. He was on the losing All-Ireland S.H.C. side in the 1959 replayed final (to Waterford), in 1964 when beaten by Tipperary, and in 1966 and 1971. His Leinster S.H.C. medal haul came to 9 with a win in 1958. Twice Puc Fada champion, he also won 2 National Hurling League medals with the 'Black and Amber', in 1962 and 1966, and won 4 Oireachtas medals. He won 4 Railway Cup medals with Leinster, 1962, 1964, 1965, and in 1967 when he became the 9th Kilkennyman to captain the winning side. In 1967 he became the 2nd Kilkenny hurler to be nominated as Texaco Hurler of the Year. Having coached the Kilkenny Junior's to All-Ireland success in 1984, 1986, 1988 and 1990, he took over as Kilkenny senior manager in 1990, guiding them to 3 successive All-Ireland S.H.C. finals in 1991 (when losing), and winning in both 1992 and 1993. His 3 sons are prominent sportsmen, Michael (cv); Billy was goalkeeper on the only Kilkenny C.B.S. team to win the All-Ireland Colleges Championship, and played soccer with the Kilkenny City side which won the First Division title in the 1989-1990 League of Ireland soccer season; and Ollie Jnr has played League of Ireland soccer for Bohemians.

WALSH, PATRICIA.

Field Athlete, discus. From Co Waterford, she has emigrated to the U.S.A. Dominating Irish ladies discus for a decade, she won a record 9 successive B.L.E. Irish National titles in the discus, in 1978, 1979, 1980, 1981, 1982, 1983, 1984 and in 1985. She represented Ireland at the Olympic Games in Los Angeles in 1984, throwing 55.38 metres in the final to finish in a highly creditable 9th place.

WALSH, SEAN (SEANIE, 'SUPERSUB').

G.A.A. football midfielder and full-back, Kerry. Born 6th April 1957. Club: Kerins O'Rahilly's, Tralee. He won an All-Ireland M.F.C. medal with Kerry in 1975, and 3 successive All-Ireland Under 21 winner's medals with the county in 1975, 1976 and 1977. A sub in the All-Ireland S.F.C. final of 1976, he went on to win 7 All-Ireland Senior Championship medals with Kerry, firstly as a midfield partner to Jack O'Shea in the famous 4-in-a-row side of 1978, 1979, 1980, 1981 and later as a full-back in the 3-in-a-row of 1984, 1985, and 1986. He was also at midfield for the 'Seamas Darby final' of 1982. He won Railway Cup medals with Munster 4 times, in 1978, 1978, 1981 and 1982, and he won 2 All-Star awards, in 1979 at centre half-forward and 1981 at centre-field.

WALSH, Mr T M (TED).

Amateur jump jockey. Born in 1950. Reared on his father's stables in Kill, Co Kildare, he started in point-to-points, and rode his first winner in 1969. Since his first Irish amateur jockey's championship title in 1972, he went gone on the win that crown an astonishing eleven times, including 1980 (35 winners), 1981 (30 winners), 1982 (41 winners), 1983 (33 winners), and 1984 (31 winners), a record. His regular trainers have been

Peter McCreery, Mick O'Toole and Ted Curtin, and he won over 550 races. His career highlights were his four winners at the Cheltenham Festival, on Castleruddery and Prolan in 2 successive Kim Muir Chases in 1974 and 1975, on Hilly Way in the 1979 Queen Mother 2-Mile Champion Chase, and on Attitude Adjuster in 1986. In 1984 he took up T.V. commenating on jump racing, with success. In 1991 he took over the yard of his deceased trainer father, Ruby Walsh.

WALSH, WILLIAM.

Soccer international defender. Born in Dublin, 31st May 1921. After World War 2 he spent 3 seasons with Manchester City, playing over 100 league games for them. He won 9 international caps for the Irish Free State between 1947 and 1950, and 9 for Northern Ireland in 1948 and 1949 in the No 4 jersey.

WALSHE, CLAIRE.

Track athlete. Born 22nd July 1942. Between 1968 and 1973 she won a total of 16 Irish National titles, 6 at 200 metres, 4 at 100 metres, 4 at 400 metres, one at 800 metres, and one at the pentathlon. She represented Ireland at 800m at the Olympic Games in Munich in 1972. She was selected as Texaco's Athletics Sportstar of the Year for 1971. Her daughter Patricia (a member of the Dundrum South Dublin club) won 2 B.L.E. Irish National Championships at 400 metres, and represented Ireland at the 1986 European Champinships.

WALTON, MARITA

Field Athlete, shot putt. She was the first Irish athlete to win 8 B.L.E. National Championship titles in the same event, winning the shot putt in 1976, 1977, 1978, 1980, 1981, 1982, 1983, and in 1984.

WALTON, PHILIP.

Golfer, amateur and professional. Born in Malahide, Co Dublin, 28th March 1962. Club: Malahide. He twice won the Leinster Boys (1978 and in 1979 when he also won the Leinster Youths), and tied for 1st in the British Youths in 1979 (being beaten in a play-off). He helped the Irish Youths team to win the European Championship in 1979. A student at Oklahoma State University (whom he helped win the prestigious N.C.C. title), he won the Scottish Strokeplay Open and the Spanish Amateur in 1981. He won the Irish Amateur Close title in 1982 (also winning the Willie Gill award). His European Team record for Ireland is 10 wins out of 12 matches in 1981 and 1983, helping Ireland to their triumph in the latter year, also helping Ireland to win the Quadrangular Continental match in 1980. He won Walker Cup selection in 1981 (winning a singles and 2 great foursomes with Ronan Rafferty), and in 1983, also winning 3 out of 4 matches (his total of 6 wins and of 12 points gained make him Ireland's most successful Walker Cup player ever). He was selected as Texaco's Golf Sportstar of the Year in 1981 and 1983. He turned pro in 1983, and won the Irish National Professional title in 1987, and the Irish Professional Championship in 1989 (by 9 strokes) and 1991. He finished 2nd in the 1989 Irish Open title, and although finishing 11th in the Ryder Cup points table, he was pipped on to the team by Christy O'Connor Junior (cv). He won his first European Tour event in 1990, the French Open at Chantilly, and apart from being a member of the successful Irish side which won the Dunhill Cup in great style at St Androw's, finished 20th in the Order of Merit for that year.

WALTON, SAM ('SLIM').

G.A.A. hurler, Kilkenny. Club: Tullaroan. He shares with 3 other Kilkenny-men the distinction of being the first players to win 7 All-Ireland Senior Hurling Championship winner's medals. His victories with Kilkenny came in 1904, 1905, 1907, 1909, 1911, 1912, and 1913, with selections from Tullaroan, Erin's Own and Mooncoin. One of the game's greats in his time, he captained the winning All-Ireland S.H.C. side twice, in 1911 (in an awarded final), and in the 1912 game in the 2-1 to 1-3 win of the Mooncoin side over the Toomevara team of Tipperary.

WARD, ANTHONY Joseph Patrick (TONY).

Rugby international out-half. Born in Dublin, 8th October 1954. Clubs: Garryowen, St Mary's and Greystones. A product of St Mary's College, he played rugby for Munster, and for Ireland B in 1976 and 1977. He was capped 19 times for Ireland between 1978 (during this his first year in the International Championship, he scored a then record of 38 championship points) and 1987, scoring 113 points in all for Ireland, from 27 penalties, 4 conversions, and 3 drop goals, placing him 4th in Ireland's all-times scorers list. A hugely talented out-half, he suffered from selectorial indifference for much of his career. He toured South Africa with the Lions of 1980, winning one test place, on that day setting a then Lion's test match scoring record of 18 points (and also equalled the most test penalties in a match with 5). He starred on 'the Day Munster beat the All Blacks' in 1978, scoring 8 of their 12 points. On the 1979 Irish tour of Australia he suffered the biggest setback of his long career, forfeiting his place to the abundantly talented Ollie Campbell, with whom he shares the Irish touring record of 19 points in one match. He won 2 Munster Senior Cup medals with Garryowen, in 1975 and 1979. He was selected as Texaco's Sportstar of the Year for rugby in 1978, and won the Golden Boot as European Player of the Year in 1979. He was also a talented soccer player, being capped at schoolboys level, and won an F.A.I. Cup medal with Limerick City in 1980. A P.E. teacher and journalist.

WARD, GERALDINE (nee McLERNON).

Pitch and put player. Club: Portmarnock P.P.C. A matchplay specialist, she has won 5 Irish National Matchplay Championship titles from 1984, including a 3-in-a-row in 1984, 1985 and 1986, also winning the title in both 1990 and 1993. In 1993 she was runner-up in the Irish National Stroke-play Championship.

WARD, LIAM.

Jockey, flat racing. Born in Rathkeale, Co Limerich, 18th May 1930. Accumulating a huge number of winning rides, he was Irish flat jockey's champion 6 times in all, including 1959 and 1961. He has won 11 classic races, 10 of them Irish: one Irish 2,000 Guineas on D.C.M. in 1952; one Irish 1,000 Guineas on Zenobia in 1960, 2 Irish Derbys (Sindon in 1958, and the great 1970 victory on Nijinsky, whom he rode more often than Lester Piggott); 3 Irish Oaks winners (Amante in 1958, Aurabella in 1965 and Gaia in 1969), and 3 Irish St Leger winners (Do Well in 1951, White Gloves in 1966 and Reindeer in 1969); he also won the 1962 French St Leger (Prix Royal Oak) on the Irish-trained Sicilian Prince, the first overseas success in a French classic in years. He was 2nd on the great Sir Ivor in the 1968 Irish Derby. Later a manager of Ashleigh Stud, he was selected as Texaco's Horse Racing Sportstar of the Year for both 1959 and 1961.

WARE, CHRISTIE and JIM.

G.A.A. hurling brothers, Waterford. Club: Erin's Own (winning 10 and 11 senior county championship winners medals respectively, between 1927 and 1947). Christie (born in 1903), an older brother and a fine full-back, won 3 Railway Cup medals with Munster in 1930, 1931 and 1935, and was a member of the Waterford side beaten in the All-Ireland S.H.C. final of 1938, his only Munster title in a fine career stretching from 1923 to 1938. Jim (born in 1908), a quality goalkeeper whose inter-county career continued on and off from 1926 to 1949, a period of 24 years, was captain of the Waterford side which captured the county's first All-Ireland

Senior Hurling Championship in 1948, when they beat Dublin by 6-7 to 4-2 (Christie was a selector for this famous win). He also won 3 Railway Cup medals, in 1944, 1945 and 1949 (when he was the 2nd Waterford-man to captain the winning side).

WARKE, LAWRENCE (LARRY).

Cricket international right hand batsman and medium paced bowler. Born in Belfast, 6th May 1927. Club: Woodvale (winning many league and cup medals), Leinster and Trinity. He was capped 34 times for Ireland between 1950 and 1950, scoring 786 runs in 57 innings for an average of 14.29, his best batting being a 120 against Scotland in 1954 (and in 1957 he scored a century at Lords, against the M.C.C.). Also a rugby player of note, he was many times a sub on the Irish team, although never winning a cap. Later he became an international hockey selector. His son is Stephen J S Warke (cv).

WARKE, STEPHEN J S.

Cricket international right hand batsman. Born in Belfast, 11th July 1959. Clubs: Woodvale and Ulster clubs. From 1981 to the end of the 1993 international season, he had played 92 times for Ireland in cricket (placing him then 2nd on the all-time caps list, one behind Michael Halliday cv). He has scored 3,524 runs (the 2nd most by an Irish interntional batsman) in 127 innings for an excellent average of 30.16 (the 5th best of all time). Captaining the Irish side many times, in 1992 he helped set a new record wicket stand for Ireland with 224 against Wales, and in the same innings became only the 2nd Irish batsman ever to score 3,000 runs for his country. Undoubtedly one of Ireland's best modern batsmen, he has scored 4 centuries for Ireland, has made 21 other 50's and has taken over 51 catches. He is the son of Larry Warke (cv).

WARNOCK, JIMMY.

Flyweight boxer. Born in Belfast in 1913. He was known in Belfast as 'the uncrowned champion of the world'. Twice, in non-title fights, he beat the reigning world champion, Benny Lynch. Despite this accomplishment, he never held any worthwhile boxing title, and he was beaten in his 1937 eliminator for the world title by Peter Kane. He had 3 brothers also in professional boxing.

WARREN, ROBERT GIBSON.

Rugby international half-back. Club: Lansdowne. A product of Rathmines College, he played 12 times for Leinster, and was capped 15 times for Ireland between 1884 and 1890, scoring one international try. He had 2 terms as Irish captain, in the 1886-1887 season, and the period between 1889 and 1890, a total of 8 times in charge. He later became one of Ireland's, and rugby's, leading administrators. He was an Irish representative on the International Board for 51 years, 1887-1938, and during that time was one of the leading lights in the developement of the game. He was also an Irish selector, and was President of the I.R.F.U. in 1895-96.

WATSON, JOHN.

Formula One Grand Prix motor racing driver. Born in Belfast, 4th May 1946. The son of a motor trader and amateur racer, he began racing in an Austin-Healey Sprint, and scored his earliest success at Kirkistown. He graduated from Irish sports car racing to Formula 2 with Chevron in 1969. Racing his first Formula 1 race in a Brabham in 1972, in 1976 he became the first Irishman to win a Formula One Grand Prix when he won the Austrian Grand Prix for the Penske team. His 2nd Grand Prix win did not come until the British G.P. in 1981. He won his 3rd and 4th Formula One races in the 1982 season, the Belgian G.P. and the Detroit G.P. (which he won from 17th place on the grid), giving him joint most wins of that season, and with 39 points he finished joint 2nd in the World Championship Formula One Driver's Championship, only 5 points behind winner Keke

Rosberg. In the last of his 5 wins, the 1983 Long Beach Grand Prix, he came from 22nd place on the grid in his McLaren-Ford right through the field to win the event, making this the biggest place catch up victory in Formula One history. He finished 6th in the World Driver's Championship race 3 times, in 1978, 1980 and 1983. His total of 152 Grand Prix starts (from which he scored an average of more than a point per race competed, with a tally of 173 points) from 1972 to 1983 places him 3rd behind Graham Hill and Nigel Mansell in the all-time British and Irish list of race starters. In that time he had 5 fastest laps, and started in pole position twice. He finished 2nd in the 1987 World Endurance Championship. He was selected as Texaco's Motor Sport Sportstar of the Year for 1976.

WADDOCK, GARY P.

Soccer international midfielder. Born in Kingsbury, 17th March 1962. Clubs: Q.P.R. (to whom he was apprenticed, and with whom he played over 200 league matches), Charleoi, Q.P.R., Swindon and Bristol Rovers. An Under 21 international, he played 20 times for the senior Republic of Ireland side from 1980 to 1990, scoring 3 international goals. A major injury in 1986 curtailed his career for some years, but a remarkable comeback enabled him to play again at international level, only to be left out, at a very late stage, of the Republic's World Cup squad in the summer of 1990.

WADE, THOMAS Joseph (TOMMY).

International showjumper. Born June 1st 1937. With his horse Dundrum (which a diminutive size of only 15 hands and 1 inches in height) he was many times victorious in the 1960's, including: the Victor Ludanum at Wembley of 1961; leading international rider at Dublin in 1961; the Prix du President at Ostend in 1962 (when Dundrum cleared 7'2"), and the King George V Cup in 1963. He was National Champion at Dublin's Spring Show at least 6 times, and was a member of 2 Aga Khan Cup-winning Irish shjowjumping teams, in 1963 and 1967, both times riding Dundrum. He was twice selected as Texaco's (then Caltex) Equestrian Spoorts Sportstar of the Year for both 1961 and 1963.

WALKER, Mrs J B (PAT).

Amateur international ladies golfer. Club: Gosford. She was born in Ireland, 21st June 1896. She won the Irish Ladies Championship in 1930, and was runner-up in 1934. She won the Australian Ladies Championship in 1935, and was runner-up in the New Zealand Championship the same year. A winner of the Ayrshire Ladies 3 times (1934, 1937 and 1938), she was in the Irish Home International side each year from 1928 to 1939, and again in 1948. She played Walker Cup 3 times for Great Britain and Ireland, in 1934, 1936, and 1938, winning 2 and halving one of her 6 matches. She was made an M.B.E, and once had 2 holes in one in the same week.

WALKER, SAMUEL (SAM or SAMMY).

Rugby international prop forward and hooker. Born in Belfast, 21st April, 1912. Club: Instonians (winning Ulster Senior Cup medals in 1934 and 1938). A product of the R.B.A.I., he won 15 rugby caps for Ireland between 1934 and 1938, scoring one international try and 2 conversions. Having captained Ireland for the only time against Wales in his last cap (Ireland lost 11-5), he was then selected as Ireland's 2nd captain of the British and Irish touring side (called 'Lions' for the first time), on their 1938 summer tour of South Africa, bringing 7 other Irishmen with him. He himself won 3 Test places and in all played 20 matches on that tour. The official tour record was: played 23; won 17; lost 6; points for 407, against 272. In the last match of the test series, all 8 Irishmen in the panel (a record) played in the winning game. Later a B.B.C. commentator, he died suddenly in 1972, aged 59.

WALKER, RALPH and STEWART I.

Hockey international father and son . Ralph, an outstanding forward with Leinster Y.M.C.A. and Dublin Y.M.C.A., was capped 17 times between 1947 (when Ireland achieved a famous Triple Crown) and 1952 (when injury forced his retirememt). He was a member of another Triple Crown side in 1949 and was captain of his country four times in 1951. His son Stewart, a goalscoring winger, and a member of Dublin Y.M.C.A. (winning an Irish Senior Cup medal in 1979), was capped 33 times for Ireland between 1975 and 1979, being a member of the away squads in Rome and for the World Cup in Argentina in 1978.

WALKINGTON, R B and DOLWAY B.

International rugby full-backs, brothers. R B , while playing for N.I.F.C., won 10 international rugby caps between Ireland's first international match (against England in 1875) and 1882 (when he became Ireland's most capped player), captaining the side in 1878. He became President of the I.R.F.U. in 1881/1882. His younger brother Dolway B, a full-back from Dublin University and N.I.F.C., dropped Ireland's first ever drop goal (against Wales in 1891); famous for wearing a monacle on the field of play, he won international caps for Ireland 8 times between 1887 and 1891.

WALL, ANTHONY (TONY).

G.A.A. hurling half-back, Tipperary. After winning an All-Ireland M.H.C. medal with the county in 1952, he went on to captain the Tipperary side which captured the 1958 All-Ireland Senior Hurling Championship when they beat Galway in the final by 4-9 to 2-5. He later brought his All-Ireland S.H.C. medal-winning tally to 5, winning again in 1961, 1962, 1964 and 1965, and was on the losing final sides of both 1960 (when he again captained the side) and 1967. He also captained 2 Railway Cup-winning Munster sides, in 1959 and 1961, as well as winning 3 other medals, in 1958, 1963 and 1966. He won a total of 5 National Hurling League medals with Tipperary, in 1959, 1960, 1961, 1964 and 1965.

WALLACE, (WALLIS), HILDA.

Ladies tennis international player. She won the Irish Ladies Lawn Tennis Championship 4 times, in 1924, 1926, 1930 (when she beat one of the leading English internationals, Mrs Hill), and in 1933. With her regular partner, Norma Stoker (cv), she won 4 Irish Ladies Doubles titles, in 1930, 1931, 1933 and 1935. One of the great Irish ladies tennis players of the 1920's and 1930's, she also won 3 Irish Mixed Doubles titles, in 1924, 1930 and 1933, all with different partners. She is a sister of Joe and James Wallace (ccvv).

WALLACE, (WALLIS), JOSEPH (Joe) and JAMES.

Rugby international brothers. Both Wanderers men, Joseph, 7 times a Leinster interprovincial, won 10 international caps for Ireland between 1903 and 1906 (playing on the Triple Crown-clinching side of 1906) and played 3 Test matches on the British and Irish Lions tour of South Africa in 1903. James played for Ireland only twice, against Wales and Scotland (alongside Joseph) in 1904, and played 5 times for Leinster. He also went on the tour of South Africa with the Lions, making them the 2nd set of Irish brothers to tour with the British and Irish side. Their sister Hilda (cv) won the Irish Ladies Singles Tennis Championship 4 times.

WALLACE, RICHARD Michael.

Rugby international wing three-quarter. Clubs: Cork Constitution and Garryowen (winning a Munster Senior Cup medal in 1993, and being a valuable member of the side which captured the All-Ireland League in 1991-92). Born in Cork, 16th January 1968. Making his Munster and Ireland B debuts in 1991, he was first capped at senior level later that year as a sub in Namibia. A talented winger, he has won 10 international caps up to May 1993, scoring 3 international tries. He played on the Munster side which beat the much-vaunted touring Australians in 1992, and his try against Australia in the same year was the first 5-point try scored by an Irish player in interntional rugby. He went on the British and Irish Lions tour of New Zealand in 1993 as a replacement, although he did not play in any test matches. A dual international, he has represented Ireland at Sailing (in the Laser class in the 1990 European Championships), and is also the holder of a private pilot's licence.

WALLACE, (WALLIS), Dr THOMAS.

Rugby international centre three-quarter. Born in Ballymayo, 1892, he died in 1954. Clubs: Queen's University, Cardiff, Barbarians. While working in Wales, he won 3 caps for Ireland in 3 losing matches in 1920, captaining the side in his last match. Three years later, after many years of great service to the Cardiff club (playing 155 matches for them), he captained a Wales XV in an unofficial match against the English Civil Service, so therefore achieving a unique distinction of captaining 2 different countries at rugby.

WALLIS, ARTHUR Knight and WILLIAM Armstrong.

Rugby international forwards, brothers. Club: Wanderers. Arthur won 5 rugby caps for Ireland in 1892 and 1893. William also played in 5 matches for his country, between 1880 and 1883. Two of their nephews, Thomas G Wallis (who scored 14 points for Ireland in his 5 caps in 1921-22), and Clive Wallis, (one international cap in 1935), also represented Ireland. All four played for Leinster.

WEIR, IKE O'NEILL ('THE BELFAST SPIDER').

Featherweight professional boxer. He was born in Lurgan, Co Armagh on 5th February 1867. He died, aged 41, in Charlestown, Mass, U.S.A. in 1908. Emigrating to the U.S.A. in 1886 after a year in Manchester, he lost only one of his first 28 pro fights up to 1881. He claimed (although not universally accepted) the world featherweight title in 1889, when he drew with the Englishman, Frank Murphy, after the police stopped the fight in the 80th round in Kouts, Indiana (this is the longest world champinship bout ever fought). He then lost his bid for the vacant title in San Francisco in January 1890, when knocked out in the 14th round by 'Torpedo' Billy Murphy of New Zealand. Unbeaten for the next 4 years (including a win over former champion Murphy), he lost his only other fight in 3 rounds to ex-world champ Young Griffo in March 1894, and promptly retired. Weir's nine year professional record included 29 wins, 8 draws, 3 losses, and one no decision in 41 contests.

WELD, DERMOT K.

Horse trainer, flat and National Hunt. Based at Rosewell House stables, he has become Ireland's most prolific modern trainer of winners on the flat. He has been leading flat trainer in Ireland in terms of numbers 15 times (and in prize money terms 5 times), including 1977 (when becoming the first Irish trainer to have 100 winners in a year), 1979 (55 winners), 1981 (77 winners), 1982 (56 winners), 1983 (71 winners), 1984 with 88 winners, 1985 (120 winners, a then personal best), 1986 (95 winners), 1987 (74 winners), 1988 (103 winners), 1989, and in 1991 (when he broke the year old record of winners in a calendar year, to train 150 winners). He trained 106 runners in 1992 to be runner-up in the trainer's table. He trained the winner of the American Classic race, the Belmont Stakes, in 1990, Go and Go, and in 1992 won the Italian Derby with In a Tiff. His total tally of 8 classic winners include the Irish and Epsom Oaks in 1981 with Blue Wind. Also a trainer of National Hunt horses, his Perris Valley won the Irish Grand National in 1988. His tally of winners sent out reached 1,800 in 1992, and his charges have won major stake races on 3 continents. He was selected as Texaco's Horse Racing Sportstar of the Year in both 1981 and 1985.

WELLS, H G.

Rugby international wing three-quarter. Club: Bective Rangers. He played rugby for Ireland 4 times, twice each in 1891 and 1894. In the Triple Crown year of 1894, he scored the winning try (the games only score) against Scotland to set up the final deciding match against Wales. He was injured for that vital game, and was never to be capped again.

WELSH, ERIC.

Soccer international outside right. Born in Belfast, 1st May 1942. Clubs: Distillery, Exeter City (scoring 18 goals in 105 league matches, 1959-1965), Carlisle United (scoring 17 league goals in 72 games), Torquay United and Hartlepool. An Under 23 cap, he was capped 4 times for Northern Ireland, 3 times in 1966 and once again in 1967 (this tally making him Carlisle Uniteds most capped player), scoring one international goal.

WHEELER, NED.

G.A.A. hurling centre half-forward, midfielder and centre half-back, Wexford. Born in 1932, he was a native of Co Laois. Club: Faythe Harriers (winning 3 county championship medals). His senior inter-county career with Wexford spanned from 1949 to 1965, winning 3 All-Ireland Senior Hurling Championship winner's medals, in 1955, 1956 and 1960, while he won 4 more Leinster S.H.C. medals with the Model County, in 1951, 1954, 1962 and 1965, when on each occasion they were defeated in the All-Ireland S.H.C. final. He won 2 National Hurling League medals with Wexford in 1956 and 1958, and also won 4 Oireachtas medals. He also won 3 Railway Cup medals with Leinster, including 1954 and 1956.

WHELAN, LIAM.

Soccer international inside-forward. Born in Dublin 1st April 1935. Clubs: Home Farm, Manchester United (winning 2 League Championship winners medals, in 1955-56, and in 1956-57 when he scored 30 goals in 45 matches, from the inside-forward position). A brilliant dribbler, he was capped 4 times for the Republic of Ireland, once in 1956 and 3 times in 1957, and scored 2 international goals. He was developing into a world-class player (scoring 52 goals in 96 games for Man United) before being the only Irishman killed in the Munich Air Crash in February 1958, at the tender age of just 22.

WHELAN, PATRICK Charles ('PA').

Rugby international hooker. Born in Limerick, 2nd May 1950. Club: Garryowen. A product of Crescent College, he won 19 international caps for Ireland between 1975 and 1981, having been for many years understudy to Ken Kennedy (cv). He won 3 Munster Senior Cup medals with Garryowen, in 1974, 1975, and as captain in 1979, before injury cut his career short. He was on the famous Munster team that beat the All Blacks in 1978. He is a son-in-law of Paddy Reid (cv), and trained Munster in the late 1980's.

WHELAN, RONNIE Snr.

Soccer international forward. Born in Dublin, 17th November 1936, he died in 1993. Clubs: Home Farm, St Patrick's Athletic, Drogheda (winning a runners-up medal in the F.A.I. Cup in 1971), Aer Lingus. With St Pat's he scored over 60 goals in a Leinster Senior League season early on, and later scored the 5th goal in their win over Shamrock Rovers in the F.A.I. Cup final of 1961, having also won a medal in 1959 (he won a League of Ireland Championship winner's medal with Pats in 1955-56). In his League of Ireland career, which extended from 1956 to 1973, he scored 109 league goals (in 3 different decades), the majority for St Patrick's Athletic, placing him in the League's top 20 all-time scorers. Scoring 2 Inter-League goals for the League of Ireland (including the famous winner against the English League in 1963), he was capped twice for the Republic of Ireland while playing part-time League of Ireland football. Along with his son Ronnie (cv), he forms one of only 6 father-and-son pairing to be capped for the Republic of Ireland in soccer. Another son Paul (born Dublin 10th May 1965), captained Bohemians to win the F.A.I. Cup in 1992, on his 27th birthday.

WHELAN, RONNIE.

Soccer international defender and midfielder. Born in Dublin, 25th September 1961. Clubs: Home Farm (playing a League of Ireland match for them on his 16th birthday), Liverpool, winning the Football League's 'Young Player of the Year' in his first season in the first team (and with whom he has won every major award: 6 League Championships (1981-82, 1982-83, 1983-84, 1985-86. 1987-88 and 1989-90), 2 F.A. Cup medals (in 1986, and while captaining them to a 3-2 win in the 1989 F.A. Cup final over Everton, missing the 1992 final through injury), a European Cup medal in 1983-84 (and runner-up medal the following year at the Heysel stadium), 5 Charity Shields, and 3 League Cups. An Irish Youths and Irish Under 21 player, up to mid 1993 he has been capped at international level for the Republic of Ireland 44 times, captaining the side for the first time in the match which ensured Ireland's qualification for the World Cup finals for the first time, against Malta in the 2-0 win in November 1989 (earlier he became the first Republic player to score against Northern Ireland in the 3-0 win), but injury kept him out of an important role in the finals themselves. He was a member of the glorious Irish team which performed with distinction in the European Championship finals in Germany in 1988, scoring the brilliant goal against the Russians. A son of Ronnie Whelan (cv).

WHELEHAN, BRIAN.

G.A.A. hurling half-back, Offaly. He won an All-Ireland minor medal with Offaly in 1987. A star young hurler in the ageing Offaly side of the late 1980's and early 1990's, he was made an All-Star at right half-back in 1992, the only Offaly player that year to gain this distinction.

WHITE, Francis ('CHALKIE').

Swimming champion. Born in Dublin, 26th April 1965. Clubs: Guinness and Kings Hospital. Starting swimming at the age of 9, he was an international swimmer from 1968 to 1980. Winning a scholarship to Villanova University (1972-76), in 1975 he won 2 Eastern Collegiate titles, at 200m butterfly and at 400m I.M., and held 5 Villanova school records. In 1969 he was 6th in the European Junior 1,500m freestyle, and later finished 10th in the Senior European 100m butterfly. He won the 1975 European Cup at 1,500 metres freestyle in Athens. He is a winner of over 40 Irish national senior titles at freestyle, backstroke, butterfly and individual medley. Turning to masters swimming in 1992, he was inside the World Masters times at 400m, 800m and 1,500m freestyle in August 1993, and a month later won the 4 European Masters titles in Germany at 200m, 400m and 800m freestyle as well as the 200m backstroke. He has coached 2 swimmers to Olympic Games, in 1988 in Seoul, and in Barcelona in 1992, and he himself was picked as Texaco's Swimming Sportstar of the Year in 1971.

WHITE, STEPHEN.

G.A.A. footballing left half-back, Louth. He won one All-Ireland Senior Football Championship winner's medal when Louth captured the title for the third time in 1957, by beating Cork by 1-9 to 1-7. He also won Leinster S.F.C. medals in both 1948 and 1950 (when they were beaten by Mayo in the All-Ireland final). He won 4 successive Railway Cup medals with Leinster, in 1952, 1953, 1954 (as captain, the 2nd and most recent Louthman to captain a winning side), and 1955 (being one of only 2 players to play in all 8 games of this famous run). He was selected at left half-back on the Sunday Independent's 1984 'Team of the Century', in honour of the centenary of the G.A.A. His son Stefan, a free-scoring forward for Castlebellingham O'Connells and Castleblnay Faughs, won 2 Colleges medals with Dundalk C.B.S., and played inter-county football for Louth and Monaghan. Stefan's uncle Jim McDonnell was also won a Sam Maguire medal in 1957.

WHITESIDE, NORMAN ('RAMBO').

Soccer international striker and midfielder. Born in Belfast, 6th May 1965. Clubs: Manchester United (playing in 206 league matches for them, winning 2 F.A. Cup medals, in 1983, and in 1985 when he scored the cheeky winning goal) and Everton. A youthful prodigy, on 17 June 1982 he became the youngest player to play in a World Cup finals match, when he was 17 years and 42 days old, having only played only 102 minutes of football with Manchester United before it. Known for his toughness and his unflinching tackles, he played in 4 of his country's 5 matches in their famous run in that World Cup, and was ever present in the side which played 3 matches in the World Cup in Mexico in 1986. On 26 May 1983, he became the youngest player to score a goal in an F.A. Cup Final, at the age of 18 years, and 19 days (weeks earlier he became the youngest player to score in any Wembley final, the Milk Cup). Up to Oct 1987 he scored 8 international goals in 36 international appearances, and had captained his country. Serious injury led to early retirement in 1990 and he turned to physiotherapy as a career.

WHYTE, DELL.

G.A.A. ladies football full-back, Kerry. Club: Austin Stacks. She won her first All-Ireland Senior title in Kerry's first win in 1976. She has added a further 5 title-winning medals to her tally, up to 1989. A 4 time All-Star and prolific scorer (her tally of 8-30 has been a county record for championship games), she has also won 6 National League and 2 Interprovincial Championship medals.

WICKHAM, PHILOMENA and CAROL.

Amateur international golfers, sisters. Club: Laytown and Bettystown. Philomena (born 16th December 1957) has won 4 Irish Foursome's titles with Claire Hourihane, 3 Connacht Ladies titles (1982, 85 and 87), and was on the successful Irish side in the 1983 European Team title win. Carol (born 23rd December 1960) was Irish Girls champion in 1978, and is also an international player.

WILEY, IAN.

K1 slalom canoeist. Born in Dublin, 5th May 1968, he lives in Chapelizod. Club: Wild Water Kayak Club. An Irish youth international in 1981, he won Irish Open Canoe Slalom Championship in the K1 discipline at either junior or senior level each year from 1983 to 1993 (winning the senior event 8 years out of ten up to 1993). Finishing 2nd in the World Juniors in 1986, he was 13th in the World Seniors in 1987, being placed 14th in 1989. Having finished 2nd in the Europa Cup in 1990, he went on to win the Pre-World Championships in the Canoe Slalom in Tacen, Yugoslavia in the same year. In 1991 he was ranked as the World's No 2 canoeist, winning the pre-Olympic International Slalom over the games course at La Sea d'Urgel in Pain in 123.93 seconds, and finishing 2nd in the World Cup to the Briton Richard Fox. Holding the World No 2 rank into 1992, he finished in 8th place in the Olympic Games in Barcelona, while one of the favourites to win the event.

WILKINS, DAVID.

Yachtsman, Flying Dutchman class. Born in Dublin, 30th April 1950. Clubs: Malahide Y.C., and Rutland S.C. He started sailing at age 16, and was Irish Finn Champion in 1971. In 1974 he was British Tempest Champion, and finished 9th in the World Championships: in 1975 he was 5th in European Tempest and 2nd in British, and 1976 he was 12th in World and 3rd in British Tempests. He has also won many British Open sailing events and international competitions. In the 1980 Moscow Olympics yachting events, which took place at Tallinn, he and James Wilkinson (c.v.) took the silver medal in the Flying Dutchman class (at 30 years and 91 days he became Ireland's oldest Olympic medallist), with 30.0 points, behind the Spanish pair of Alesandro Abascal and Miguel Noguer, who were clear winners. In 1988 he became the 2nd person (of only 3 in total) to represent Ireland in four Olympic Games. His other representations were: in Tempest class in 1972 when he became the first Irishman to win a series race in yachting, finishing 8th at Kiel; 1976 again in a Tempest, finishing 10th at Kingston; in glorious Moscow in 1980; and again in the Flying Dutchman Class at Pusan in 1988 (finishing 10th), when he again won a series race). In 1992 he became the first Irishman to compete in 5 different Olympic Games celebrations, when competing in the Flying Dutchman class in Barcelona. In 1989 he won his first British Open Championship in the Flying Dutchman class. He shared with Wilkinson the Texaco Yachting Sportstar of the Year for 1980. He now lives in Leicestershire.

WILKINSON, JAMES (JAIMIE).

Yachtsman, Flying Dutchman class. Having being placed 19th in his first Olympic Games appearence in Montreal in 1976 in the Flying Dutchman class (with Barry O'Neill), he joined up with David Wilkins (cv), winning a silver medal in the Moscow Olympic Games of 1980. Sailing in the Flying Dutchman class at Pirita, 6 miles from Tallinn, they finished well behind the winning combination from Spain (who had 3 firsts, 1 second and 2 4th places). For being part of Ireland's first ever Olympic medal haul in yachting, he shared with Wilkins Texaco's Yachting Sportstar of the Year award for 1980.

WILKINSON, THOMAS F.

Basketball international player. Born in Cork, 3rd February 1955. Clubs: Killester, Neptune (winning 7 National League titles, 3 National Cup titles, 2 National Top Four titles, and 1 Roy Curtis title), Blue Demons (winning 1 National League title and 2 National Top Four honours, captaining the side to a clean sweep of 6 competitions in 1980-81). The 8 National League titles he has won (7 with Neptune and one with Blue Demons) is a record for Ireland's premier competition. He represented Ireland in over 100 international matches from 1976 to 1988 (captaining the side in 1985-88), touring the U.S.A. 5 times. He is also a winner of many M.V.P. and other basketball awards.

WILLIAMS, JOE.

Soccer international full-back and centre-half. Clubs: Bray, Shelbourne, Shamrock Rovers (winning League of Ireland Championship winner's medals in 1937-38 and in 1938-39, and F.A.I. Cup medal in 1936 and 1940). He was capped once for the Irish Free State, in the 1938 match versus Norway.

WILLIAMSON, KEVIN.

Swimmer. Among other Irish national swimming titles he won, he won a remarkable 10 consecutive National titles at the 1,500 metres freestyle, in 1977, 1978, 1979, 1980, 1981, 1982, 1983, 1984, 1985, and in 1986. He represented Ireland at 2 Olympic Games, in both 1976 at Montreal and in1980 at Moscow, on each occasion at 3 diffferent disciplines (200m, 400m and 1,500m freestyle).

WILSON, DANNY J.

Soccer international midfielder. Born in Wigan, 1st January 1960. Clubs: Wigan Athletic, Bury (scoring 8 goals in 90 league appearences), Chesterfield (scoring 13 goals in 100 league appearences), Nottingham Forest, Scunthorpe (on loan), Brighton and Hove Albion (scoring 33 league goals in 135 league games) and Luton Town (scoring 24 goals in 110 league matches, helping them to the League Cup win of 1988), Sheffield Wedesnday (winning a League Cup medal with the Owls in 1991, and being in the squad which lost 2 big finals in 1993, the League Cup and the F.A. Cup). He has played 24 international matches for Northern Ireland up to mid 1993, scoring one interantional goal.

WILSON, Dr HUGH GILMER.

Rugby international forward. 1879-1941. Clubs: Glasgow University, and Malone. A product of Coleraine A.I. and R.B.A.I., he was capped at rugby in the pack 18 times for Ireland (only 6 of these being on winning sides) between 1905 and 1910, and played in all of Ireland's Championship-winning matches in 1906.

WILSON, KEVIN J.

Soccer international forward. Born in Banbury, 18th April 1961. Clubs: Ruscotte Sports, Banbury United, Derby County (scoring 30 goals in 120 league appearences), Ipswich Town (scoring 34 goals in 98 league appearences), Chelsea (scoring 43 league goals for them, helping them to win the 2nd Division in 1989), Notts County. He has played 33 international games for Northern Ireland since debuting in 1987 (up to mid 1993), scoring 4 international goals.

WILSON, JOHN.

G.A.A. footballing half-back, Cavan. Born at Callanagh, Kilcogy, Co Cavan, 8th July 1923. A product of Mel's College in Longford, he won 4 Leinster Colleges medals with them. With Cavan he won five Ulster S.F.C. medals (in 1944, 1945, 1947, 1948 and 1949), two All-Ireland Senior Football Championship winner's medals (one as a non-playing sub, and the other in the famous Polo Ground win over Kerry in 1947), and one National League medal in 1948. A classics teacher by profession, he became a T.D. for Fianna Fail in 1973; his Ministerial posts have included Education (1977-81), Posts and Telegraphs (1982), Minister of Communications (1987-89), and Marine (1990-92). He was a candidate for the Fianna Fail nomination for the Presidency of Ireland in 1990.

WILSON, SAMMY J.

Soccer international forward. Clubs: Glenavon (winning Irish Cup medals in 1957, 1959 and 1961, and an Irish League Championship winner's medal in 1960-61), Falkirk, Dundee. He was capped 12 times in the front-line for Northern Ireland at soccer between 1962 and 1968, scoring 7 international goals, including 2 against England in the 8-3 defeat of 1963.

WING, MORNINGTON (MORNY).

Flat jockey. Born in and apprenticed in England, he came to Ireland in 1917, and stayed here. He holds the record for the most wins in Irish classic races by a jockey, with 23 successes, including a record number of 6 Irish Derby wins (with Ballyheron in 1921, Waygood in 1923, Rock Star in 1930, Rosewell in 1933, and Windsor Slipper in 1942): a record number of Irish 1,000 Guineas winners, with seven (in 1922 with Lady Violette, 1923 with Glenshesk, 1931 with Spiral, 1937 with Sol Speranza, 1940 with Gainsworth, 1945 with Panastrid, and in 1947 with Sea Symphony); and a record number of Irish St Leger winners (7), with Kirk Alloway in 1920, O'Dempsey in 1923, Sol de Terre in 1930, Ochiltree in 1938, Windsor Slipper in 1942, Spam in 1945, and with Espirit De France in 1947). He also won two

Irish 2,000 Guineas (in 1932 with Lindley and in 1942 with Windsor Slipper in 1942), and one Irish Oaks (with Sol Speranza in 1937). He broke the then record of J.J. Thompson for most Irish Jockey Championship successes, winning it 8 times. As a trainer he won the 1951 Irish St Leger with Do Well.

WOOD, Benjamin GORDON Malison.

Rugby international loose-head prop forward. Born in Limerick, 20th Jume 1931, he died in 1982. Clubs: Garryowen and Lansdowne. A product of Crescent College, he was capped 29 times for Ireland between 1954 and 1961, scoring one international try. He was selected for the British and Irish Lions tour of Australia and New Zealand in 1959, winning 2 Test places. He formed a formidable front row in the late 50's and early 60's with Sid Millar and Ronnie Dawson. He won 2 Munster Senior Cup medals with Garryowen in 1952 and 1954.

WOODS, STANLEY.

All-round motor-cyclist. Born in Dublin in November 1903, he died in 1993. As a road racer (starting with his first win in Bangor in 1921), he won 40 international events in the years from 1923 up to the start of World War Two. He competed in his first TT in 1922 at the age of 17, gaining his first win at the age of 23. He raced in 18 successive Isle of Man TT seasons, a record, and his 10 victories was a record until surpassed by the greats like Joey Dunlop (cv) and Mike Hailwood. He won five Senior 500cc T.T. titles, in 1927 (on a Norton, averaging a speed of 70.90 m.p.h.), in 1933 (Norton), 1934 (Husqvarna), 1935 (on a Moto Guzzi), and 1936 (on a Velocette, averaging a speed of 86.98 m.p.h.), and was placed in 8 Senior T.T. races in all, a record that still stands. He also won 5 Junior Race T.T.'s, in 1923, 1932, 1933, 1938 and 1939. In 33 T.T. race starts, he finished 21 races and had 11 fastest laps. He also won an astonishing 22 continental Grand Prix races, 3 in 1927, 2 in 1928, one in 1930, 4 in 1931, 5 in 1932, 3 in 1933, 2 in 1934 and one win each in 1935 and 1936, all in 350cc or 500cc class races, and all on Norton machines. He won 7 Ulster Grand Prix races from 1924 to 1939, two at 600cc, 4 at 500cc and one at 350cc. He also excelled at speedway, hill climbs, trials (winning the Portland Cup Motorcycle Trial 5 times, 1926, 1929, 1931, 1932 and 1938), sand racing, scrambles, grass-track, and even long-distance record events. In 1957, 18 years after retiring, he set a T.T. course record speed of 86 m.p.h. during a Jubilee celebration, while 30 years later again (at the age of 87) he lapped the Isle of Man course at over 80 m.p.h. One of the great all-round motor-cyclists of all time, he was the first motor-sportsman to be elevated into the Texaco Hall of Fame, in 1967. He ran a motor business in Pearse Street Dublin, and retired to Tyrella, Downpatrick.

WORTHINGTON, NIGEL.

Soccer international defender. Born in Ballymena, 4th November 1961. Clubs: Ballymena United, Notts County (playing 67 league matches for them), Sheffield Wednesday (playing in over 233 league matches for them, helping them to win the League Cup in 1991, and to gain promotion to Division One in the same year, while in 1993 being in the side which lost both the F.A. Cup final and the League Cup final). First capped for Northern Ireland in 1984, he played in the World Cup matches in Mexico in 1986, and has 44 caps up to mid 1993.

WRIGHT, TOMMY J.

Soccer international goalkeeper. Born in Belfast, 29th August 1963. Clubs: Linfield, Newcastle United (helping them to a fine year in 1992-93, when they won the First Division, and were promoted to the Premiership Division), Hull City (on loan). First capped in goals for Northern Ireland in 1989, his tally had reached 15 in mid 1993.

WRIGHT, WILLIAM (BILLY).

Amateur boxer. Club: Phoenix. He won 2 Irish National Senior Championship titles, one at lightweight in 1927, and another at welterweight in 1929. His son Sean won an Irish Senior Lightweight title in 1954, and another son, Billy, boxed internationally for Ireland.

WYNNE, FRANK.

Flat jockey. Born in 1857. He was champion jockey in Ireland more than once. He was the first jockey to ride the winner of 3 Irish Derby's, winning the race 3 times in 4 years, with Redskin in 1877, Madame Dubarry in 1878, and (having finished 5th in 1879) with King of the Bees in 1880 (he went on to be 2nd in both 1881 and 1882). His father, Denny Wynne, was the rider of only the 2nd Irish-trained horse to win the Aintree Grand National, in 1847 on Mathew. Both Denny Wynne and another son Joe were also Irish champion jockey at least once each.

Y

YOUNG, EAMONN.

G.A.A. football half-forward, Cork. Born in Dunmanway, Co Cork. Winning a Munster S.F.C. medal in 1943, he was a member of the Cork side which captured the county's 3rd All-Ireland Senior Football Championship in the 1945 Sam Maguire Cup by beating Cavan in the final. He won 2 Railway Cup medals with Munster, in 1941 (the only Corkman playing with 14 Kerrymen in the side) and 1946. A brother of Jim Young's (cv), his father Jack (a Nils player) had won an All-Ireland S.F.C. medal in 1911 with Cork. Also a Munster squash champion, his son John Young was an international squash player for Ireland.

YOUNG, JIM.

G.A.A. hurling left half-back and wing-forward, Cork. A native of Dunmanway, he was born in 1915. Clubs: U.C.C. (winning 2 Fitzgibbon Cup medals in hurling in 1939 and 1942, and 2 Sigerson Cup medals in football in 1943 and 1946), and Glen Rovers (winning 8 county championship medals). Having won a Munster S.H.C. medal in 1939, he was a constant force in all of Cork's famous 4-in-a-row All-Ireland Senior Hurling Championship winning side of 1941, 1942, 1943, and 1944. He won his 5th Liam McCarthy Cup medal when Cork regained the title in 1946. In a senior inter-county career (which also included football) lasting from 1935 to 1949, he won 3 National Hurling League medals with Cork in 1940, 1941 and 1948. He also won 4 Railway Cup hurling medals with Munster, in 1943, 1944, 1945, and 1946. He died in 1992, at the age of 77. A brother of Eamonn Young (cv), both were Munster squash champions in the 1950's; Jim reached a golf handicap of 4 also, and was also a useful tennis player (being non-playing captain of the Irish Davis Cup team in Monaco in 1967).

YOUNG, ROGER Michael ('KOO-KOO').

Rugby international scrum-half. Born in Belfast, 29th June 1943. Clubs: Queen's University Belfast and Collegians. A product of Methodist College, he played rugby for Ireland in 26 internationals between 1965 and 1971, most of them in half-back partnership with Mike Gibson (cv), and scored one international try. Noted for initiating scissors movements with his backlines, he was selected for 2 British and Irish Lions tours, to Australia and New Zealand in 1966 (winning 3 Test places), and to South Africa in 1968 (gaining one Test place). A dentist, he later emigrated to South Africa.

YOUNG, SAM.

Soccer international No 8. Clubs: Linfield (winning an Irish Cup medal in 1915) and Airdrieonians. He was capped 9 times for Ireland between 1907 and

1914, playing in all three matches of Northern Ireland's historic Home International Championship triumph of 1913-1914 (the first of only 2 such successes in that series), and scoring 2 goals in the process, against Wales in the 2-1 win, and in the draw against Scotland in that season.

YOUNG, WALLY.

Orienteer. He was a national junior and colleges wrestling champion in 1968, and also played Under 21 G.A.A. football for Roscommon. His major sport has been orienteering, becoming the National Orienteering Champion 3 times in all. He also represented Ireland in a total of 7 World Orienteering Championships, finishing 4th on the first leg of the relay race in Finland in 1979, and having a best overall placing of 27th in the 1981 championships in Switzerland. He has also attended 14 C.I.S.M. Military World Orienteering Championships (his best finish was 25th in 1976). He was a member of the Irish Hill Running team in Snowdon in 1986, and has a marathon best of 2 hours 35 minutes (in London in 1980).

Selected Bibliography

The Encyclopaedia of Badminton, by Pat Davis.

The Aga Khan Trophy, 50 years on, by M E Tinsley. Published by Pontoon Press.

The Sunday Indepenent's Complete Handbook of Gaelic Games, by Raymond Smith. Published by Sporting Books Publications, Dublin.

The Football Immortals, by Raymond Smith. Published by Aherlow Publishers.

Giants of the Ash, by Brendan Fullam. Published by Wolfhound..

Irish Olympians, by Lindie Naughton and Johnny Watterson. Published by Blackwater Press.

The Story of the G.A.A., by Seamus O'Ceallaigh. Published by the G.A.A.

Munster G.A.A. Story, by Jim Cronin. Published by the G.A.A..

The Guinness Book of Car facts and feats, edited by Anthony Harding. Published by Guinness Superlatives.

The Story of the G.A.A.. by Seamus O Ceallaigh. Published by the Gaelic Athletic Association.

The Guinness Book of Records, edited and compiled by Ross and Norris McWhirter, many editions. Published by Guinness Superlatives.

The Guinness Book of the Marathon, by Roger Gynn. Published by Guinness Superlatives.

Encyclipaedia of Track and Fields Athletics, by Mel Watman. Published by Robert Hale Ltd.

The Guinness Book of Darts, by Derek Brown. Published by Guinness Superlatives.

The Guinness book of Golf facts and feats, by Donald Steel. Published by Guinness Superlatives.

The Guinness Book of Motorcycling Facts and Feats, by l j k Setright. Published by Guinness Superlatives.

The Guinness Guide to Steeplechasing, by Gerry Cranham and Richard Pitman. Published by Guinness Superlatives.

Rothmans Football League Players Records (the complete A-Z 1946-1981), compiled by Barry J Hugman. Published by Rothman's Publications.

Rothmans Snooker Yearbook, editor Janice Hale. Published by Rothmans Publications

Rothmans Rugby Yearbook (various editions). Published by Rothmans Publications.

The Story of Irish Rugby, by Edmund Van Esbeck. Published by Stanley Paul.

The Men in Green, The Story of Irish Rugby, by Sean Difflay. Published by Pelham Books.

The Complete Who's Who of International Rugby, by Terry Godwin. Published by Blandford Press.

90 Years of the Irish Hockey Union, compiled by T A Wynne, and edited by Chris Glennon. Published by the Leinster Leader Ltd.

The Book of Irish Goalscorers, by Sean Ryan and Stephen Burke. Published by Irish Soccer Co-Op.

100 Years of Irish Football, by Malcolm Brodie. Published by Blackstaff Press.

Brendan Foster's Olympic Heroes 1896-1964, by Brendan Foster, published by Harrap.

Track and Field, the Great Ones, by Cordner Nelson. Published by Pelham Books.

A Dictionary of Irish History, by D J Hickey and J E Doherty. Published by Gill & McMillan.

Greats of Gaelic Games, Volume 3, by O McCann. Published by Gaelic Publications.

Irish Horse-racing; an illustrated history, by John Welcome. Published by Gill and MacMillan.

The Irish Derby (1866-1979), by Guy StJohn Williams and Francis P M Hyland. Published by J.A. Allen.

Encyclopaedia of Bowls, by Ken Hawkes & Gerard Lindley. Published by Robert Hale Ltd.

The Concise Dictionary of Tennis, by Martin Hedges. Published by Bison Books.

The Fighting Irish, by Patrick Myler. Published by Brandon Press.

Sport in Ireland, by Noel Carroll. Published by the Department of Foreign Affairs.

Kingdom Come, by Eoghan Corry. Published by Poolbeg Press.

Cork's Hurling Story, by Tim Horgan. Published by Anvil Books.

The Fitzwilliam Story, by Ulick O'Connor. Published by Browne and Nolan.

Who's Who, by Avia Watches, 1988.

Benson an Hedges Golfer's handbook, 1987 (and other years).

The Complete Book of the Olympics, by David Wallechinsky. Published by Viking Press.

The Irish Racing Manual, (various years). Published by Aherlow Pres.

Directory of the Turf 1988 (and other years). Published by Pacemaker.

The Book of Irish Lists and Trivia, by John Gleeson. Published by Gill and Macmillan.

Many other reference books, newspapers, magazines were consulted, too numerous to mention.